Advances in Consumer Research

Volume
XXIV

Editors: Merrie Brucks & Deborah J. MacInnis

International Standard Book Number (ISBN): 0-915552-37-X

International Standard Serial Number (ISSN): 0098-9258

Merrie Brucks and Debbie MacInnis, Editors

Advances in Consumer Research, Volume 24

(Provo, UT: Association for Consumer Research, 1997)

Preface

The twenty-fourth Annual Conference of the Association for Consumer Research (ACR) was held at the Loews Ventana Canyon Resort in Tucson, Arizona on October 10-13, 1996. This volume is comprised of the papers presented at that meeting.

In our role as conference co-chairs, we were afforded the opportunity to determine a conference theme. The theme we selected was "Breaking Out of the Box". The Call for Papers encouraged the submission of individual papers and special sessions that break out of the box by (1) developing innovative ways of thinking— such as new paradigms, new linkages between theories, new phenomena, or new methods; and/or (2) reflecting a diversity of methodological and/or theoretical perspectives. Such developments should create synergy by solidifying our appreciation of core research disciplines in consumer behavior. Many of the papers in this volume reflect this orientation. Our "Breaking out of the Box" theme does not imply that fruitful research "boxes" should be abandoned, however. Thus, this volume also contains interesting advances in traditional research streams in consumer behavior.

This year the conference had three types of papers. As is the tradition in ACR, one form is completed papers submitted for competitive review. These are referred to as Competitive Papers and all accepted papers are published in this volume. Another traditional form is the Special Topic Session. These are reviewed as proposals containing abstracts of 3-4 related papers. Summaries of each of the Special Topic Sessions are also included in this volume. The third type of paper presented at the 1996 conference is the Working Paper. Working papers are reviewed as complete papers, but are not published in their entirety at the author's request. Instead, an abstract of each paper appears. You may contact the author to obtain a complete copy of the paper. In addition to these papers, the conference was kicked off with ACR's first-ever Plenary session, with talks from four leading scholars addressing issues related to Breaking Out of the Box. Three of these talks appear in this volume.

Fifty ACR members served on this year's Program Committee. These individuals both reviewed proposals for special topic sessions, and provided valuable insight to the actual planning of the program. Another 248 ACR members served as reviewers for competitive and working papers. Some of these ACR members were also involved as session chairs or synthesizers. We are grateful to all these scholars for the diligence, commitment, and creativity they brought to this year's conference.

Members of the Association submitted 191 competitive and working papers, and 90 special session proposals to the conference. Of these, 64 competitive papers, 41 working papers and 43 special sessions were accepted for presentation at the ACR conference. The extent to which the papers fit with the conference theme was regarded as an important criterion for acceptance.

Many people were involved in making this year's conference a success. Keith Hunt was (and continues to be) a great source of knowledge regarding all aspects of ACR. His upbeat character, knowledge, and general confidence were invaluable resources during the planning of the conference. The past ACR co-chairs have done an excellent job of documenting the conference planning process. Their accumulated wisdom provided us with the background necessary to make the planning process and the conference itself run smoothly. Jeff Inman once again served ACR by running his computer program that helps match reviewers with authors. Wanda Wallace served as Poster Session Arrangements Chair, and Eric Arnould served as the Coordinator for the Round Table Discussions. Rajiv Vaidyanathan developed ACR's first website. For the tenth consecutive year, Jim Muncy managed the task of converting individual papers submitted on diskettes into the form you see now. Gerry Gorn first suggested and then executed the conference's Plenary Session. Melanie Wallendorf, Brian Sternthal, and Jerry Zaltman worked with Gerry as speakers. The cover art for this volume was designed by Ron Pimentel. Our colleagues and the PhD students at the University of Arizona and the University of Southern California (especially Samar Das and Jeanie Han) provided a great deal of support. We are deeply appreciative to all those who contributed their time and talents to the success of this conference.

Finally, we want to thank ACR president Debbie Roedder John for the confidence she showed in us as ACR Co-Chairs. We have found our involvement in this conference to be a personally and professionally rewarding experience. Over the past years, the ACR conference and proceedings have had a profound influence on our development as scholars. We are pleased to have the opportunity to partially repay our debt to ACR.

Merrie Brucks, University of Arizona
Debbie MacInnis, University of Southern California
1996 ACR Conference Co-Chairs/1997 Proceedings Editors

Julia Bristor
Susan Broniarczyk
Christina Brown
Steve Brown
Anne Brumbaugh
Carol Bruneau
Lauranne Buchanan
Sandra Burke
Jim Burroughs
Margaret Campbell
Goutam Chakraborty
Subimal Chatterjee
Joel Cohen
Cathy Cole
Leslie Cole
Larry Compeau
Janeen Costa
Carolyn Costley
Joe Cote
Robin Higie Coulter
Eloise Coupey
Ayn Crowley
Mary Curren
David Curry
Kalpesh Desai
Rohit Deshpande
Ravi Dhar
Cornelia Droge
Laurette Dube
Pam Ellen
Basil Englis
Jennifer Escalas
Corinne Faure
Ed Fern
Leslie Fine
Adam Finn
Eileen Fisher
Gavan Fitzsimmons
Susan Fournier
Jonathan Frenzen
Marian Friestad
Hubert Gatignon
Jim Gentry
Guliz Ger
Mary Gilly
Elizabeth Gilster
Linda Golden
Cathy Goodwin
Steve Gould
Don Granbois
Kent Grayson
Eric Greenleaf
Jennifer Gregan-Paxton
Dhruv Grewal

Michael Guiry
Flemming Hansen
William Harris
Manoj Hastak
Curt Haugtvedt
Bill Havlena
Scott Hawkins
Tim Heath
Deb Heisley
Geraldine Henderson
Beth Hirschman
Susan Holak
Michael Houston
Wes Hutchinson
Easwar Iyer
Shailendra Jain
Gita Johar
Richard Johnson
Christopher Joiner
Joseph Jones
Annamma Joy
Lynn Kahle
Mike Kamins
James Kellaris
Kevin Keller
Punam Anand-Keller
Rob Kleine
Susan Kleine
Amna Kirmani
Parthasarathy Krishnamurthy
Shanker Krishnan
Hannu Kuusela
John Lastovicka
Angela Lee
Moonkyu Lee
Roxanne Lefkoff-Hagius
Katherine N. Lemon
Wai-Kwan Li
Donnie Lichtenstein
Barbara Loken
Kenneth Lord
Therese Louie
Karen Machleit
Carole Macklin
Tom Madden
Jayashree Mahajan
Durairaj Maheswaran
Katryna Malafarina-Johnson
Ken Manning
Susan Mantel
Howard Marmorstein
Ingrid Martin
Charlotte Mason
Michael Mazis

Jim McAlexander
Ann McGill
Mary Ann McGrath
Geta Menon
Satya Menon
Joan Meyers-Levy
Mimi Morrin
Paul Miniard
Sanjay Mishra
Anusree Mitra
John Mittlestaedt
Anthony Miyazaki
Kent Monroe
David Moore
Elizabeth Moore-Shay
Vicki Morwitz
David Mothersbaugh
John Mowen
Jim Muncy
Amitabh Mungale
Michael Munson
A.V. Muthukrishnan
Kim Nelson
Rick Netemeyer
Steve Nowlis
Peter Nye
Sue O'Curry
Kathleen O'Donnell
Cele Otnes
Julie Ozanne
Kay Palan
Pallab Paul
Mark Pavelchak
Cornelia Pechmann
James Peltier
Greta Pennell
Laura Peracchio
Al Petrosky
Michael Pham
Carol Pluzinski
Lydia Price
Bill Qualls
S.P. Raj
Brian Ratchford
S. Ratneshwar
Aric Rindfleisch
Debra Ringold
Mark Ritson
Scott Roberts
Dennis Rook
Bill Ross
Marty Roth
Michael Rothschild
Jay Russo

Gad Saad
Jaideep Sangupta
Alan Sawyer
Robert Schindler
John Schouten
Jonathan Schroeder
Drue Schuler
David Schumann
Rich Semenik
Shahana Sen
Venkatesh Shankar
Stewart Shapiro
Terry Shimp
Baba Shiv
Carolyn Simmons
Itamar Simonson
Surendra Singh
Dan Smith
Ruth Smith
Michael Solomon
Mark Spence
Susan Spiggle
Rich Spreng
Joydeep Srivastava
Barbara Stern
Pat Stout
Elnora Stuart
Harish Sujan
Charles Taylor
Kimberly Taylor
Craig Thompson
Rao Unnava
Joe Urbany
Stijn Van Osselaer
Mark Vanhuele
Meera Venkatraman
Robert Veryzer
Beth Walker
Wanda Wallace
Brian Wansink
Jim Ward
Marc Weinberger
William Wells
Pat West
Jackie Williams
Russ Winer
Bob Woodruff
David Wooten
Peter Wright
Manjit Yadav
Richard Yalch
Carolyn Yoon
Judy Zaichkowsky
George Zinkhan

Table of Contents and Conference Program

ASSOCIATION FOR CONSUMER RESEARCH
ANNUAL CONFERENCE

OCTOBER 10-13, 1996
TUCSON, ARIZONA

THURSDAY, OCTOBER 10

ACR BOARD OF DIRECTORS MEETING
10:00 a.m. - 5:00 p.m.

REGISTRATION
4:00 p.m. - 9:00 p.m.

EARLY BIRD RECEPTION
5:30 p.m. - 7:30 p.m.

FRIDAY, OCTOBER 11

REGISTRATION
7:00 a.m. - 6:00 p.m.

PLENARY SESSION
Perspectives on Breaking Out of the Box
8:00 - 8:55 a.m.

Plenary Session: **Perspectives on Breaking Out of the Box**

Session Chair: Gerry Gorn, The Hong Kong University of Science and Technology

---

FRIDAY, OCTOBER 11

SESSION 1
9:00 - 10:30 a.m.

1.1   *Special Session*: **New Approaches to the Role of Similarity in Consumer Research**

Co-Chairs: Shi Zhang, Columbia University
                Kathryn Fitzgerald, UCLA
Synthesizer: Joan Meyers-Levy, University of Chicago

1.2   *Special Session*: **Cognitive Appraisals, Consumer Emotions, and Consumer Response**

Co-Chairs: Anand Kumar, Vanderbilt University
                Richard L. Oliver, Vanderbilt University
Synthesizer: Mark Peterson, SDR Incorporated

Appraisals, Emotions, and Coping Responses in Customer Service Encounters
    Richard P. Bagozzi, University of Michigan
    Mahesh Gopinath, University of Michigan

Distinguishing Satisfaction from Delight: An Appraisals Approach
    Anand Kumar, Vanderbilt University
    Richard Olshavshy, Indiana University

1.3 *Special Session*: All in the Family: Intergenerational Influences on Consumer

Chair: Elizabeth S. Moore-Shay, University of Illinois
Synthesizer: Les Carlson, Clemson University

Intergenerational Product Transfer: The Advertising Factor
    Barbara Olsen, SUNY-Old Westbury

Investigating the Process of Intergenerational Transfer: A Coorientational Approach
    Elizabeth S. Moore-Shay, University of Illinois
    Richard J. Lutz, University of Florida

Women as Generational Spanners: A Longitudinal Study of Giving to Parents and Grandparents, and Giving as Parents
    Cele Otnes, University of Illinois
    Tina M. Lowrey, Rider University
    Mary Ann McGrath, Loyola University of Chicago

1.4 *Special Session*: Consuming Desire and Desirous Consumption: Toward a Deeper Understanding of the Social Construction of Consumer Wants and the Nature of Consumption Symbolism

Co-Chairs: Craig Thompson, University of Wisconsin, Madison
                  Douglas B. Holt, Pennsylvania State University
Synthesizer: Tom O'Guinn, University of Illinois

The Discourse of Advertising and the Construction of Consumer Desire
    Richard Elliott, University of Oxford

Utopian Consumer Desires and the New Traditionalist Lifestyle
    Douglas B. Holt, Penn State University
    Craig J. Thompson, University of Wisconsin, Madison

Transaction Decoupling: The Effect of Temporally Separating Payments from Benefits of Consumption
   John Gourville, Harvard University
   Dilip Soman, University of Colorado

The Effects of Promotion on Consumption: Buying More and Consuming it Faster
   Kusum Ailawadi, Dartmouth College
   Scott Neslin, Dartmouth College

FRIDAY, OCTOBER 11

SESSION 2
10:45 a.m. - 12:15 p.m.

2.1   *Special Session*: Consumer Behavior, Avoidance, and Coping with Negative Emotion

Co-Chairs: Mary Frances Luce, University of Pennsylvania
                  Julie Irwin, New York University
Synthesizer: Don Lehmann, Columbia University

Anomalies in Weighing Environmental Against Other Product Attributes
   Julie Irwin, New York University
   Joan Scattone, New York University

Choice/Matching Preference Reversals and Coping with Tradeoff Difficulty
   Mary Frances Luce, University of Pennsylvania
   Marlene D. Morris, Duke University
   James R. Bettman, Duke University
   John W. Payne, Duke University

Coping with Stress
   Harish Sujan, Penn State University
   Mita Sujan, Penn State University
   James R. Bettman, Duke University

2.2   *Special Session*: Embodied Cognition: Towards a More Realistic and Productive Model of Mental Representation

Co-Chairs: George S. Babbes, University of California, Berkeley
                  Alan Malter, University of Wisconsin, Madison
Synthesizer: Dipankar Chakravarti, University of Colorado, Boulder

Embodied Cognition: Theory, Evidence and Directions for Research
   Alan Malter, University of Wisconsin, Madison

Metaphor and Embodied Cognition: A Content Analysis
George S. Babbes, University of California, Berkeley
Pamela Morgan, University of California, Berkeley

Eliciting Consumer Representations Through Embodiment Basics
Gerald Zaltman, Harvard University

2.3 *Competitive Session*: Consumer Behavior Within the Household

Chair: Peter Reingen, Arizona State University
Synthesizer/Prospector: Elizabeth Moore-Shay, University of Illinois

2.4 *Special Session*: I Am Not....Therefore, I Am: The Role of Avoidance Products in Shaping Consumer Behavior

Co-Chairs: Basil G. Englis, Berry College
                    Michael R. Solomon, Auburn University
Co-Synthesizers: Michael R. Solomon, Auburn University
                    Basil G. Englis, Berry College

SPECIAL SESSION SUMMARY

Learning Not to Want Things
Richard Wilk, University of Indiana

Exploring Anti-Constellations: Content and Consensus
Margaret K. Hogg, University of Manchester
Paul C. N. Mitchell, University of Manchester

Reference Group Influence on Teen Smoking: The Effects of Smoking in Movies and Anti-Smoking Ads Before Movies
Cornelia Pechmann, University of California, Irvine
Eric Shih, University of California, Irvine

2.5 *Special Session*: Affecting Consumers Through Identity and Design

Chair: Alex Simonson, Georgetown University
Synthesizer: Peter Bloch, University of Missouri

SPECIAL SESSION SUMMARY

2.6   *Special Session*: Narrative Theory and Consumer Research: Theoretical and Methodological Perspectives

Chair: Kent Grayson, London Business School
Synthesizer: Susan Spiggle, University of Connecticut

2.7   *Special Session*: Cross-Category Interactions in Product Perceptions and Choice

Chair: Amitabh Mungalé, Rutgers University
Synthesizer: Wes Hutchinson, University of Pennsylvania

FRIDAY, OCTOBER 11

LUNCHEON
12:20 - 2:20 p.m.

FERBER AWARD
(given by the *Journal of Consumer Research*)

Winner:
Microcultural Analysis of Variation in Sharing of Causal Reasoning About Behavior
Ajay Sirsi

Honorable Mentions:
How Consumers Consume: A Taxonomy of Consumption Practices
Douglas B. Holt

Decision Ambiguity and Incumbent Brand Advantage
A.V. Muthukrishnan

Caring Consumers: Gendered Consumption Meanings and the Juggling Lifestyle
Craig Thompson

JCR BEST PAPER AWARD
(given by the ACR Policy Board)

Winners:
Structure, Cooperation, and the Flow of Market Information
Jonathan Frenzen, University of Chicago
Kent Nakamoto, University of Colorado
(December, 1993)

BUSINESS MEETING

PRESIDENTIAL ADDRESS
Deborah Roedder John, President
Out of the Mouths of Babes: Lessons from Child Psychology

FRIDAY, OCTOBER 11

SESSION 3
2:30 - 4:00 p.m.

3.1 *Special Session*: **How Do I Prefer Thee? Let the Way Decide for Me: An Examination of Task Effects and Consumer Preference Formation**

Co-Chairs: Ziv Carmon, Duke University
               Steve Nowlis, Arizona State University
Synthesizer: Don Lehmann, Columbia University

3.2   *Special Session*: New Directions in Research on Self-Referencing

Co-Chairs: Douglas M. Stayman, Cornell University
                  H. Rao Unnava, Ohio State University
Synthesizer: Richard Yalch, University of Washington

3.3   *Competitive Session*: Children, Family, and Consumer Behavior

Chair: Peter Nye, University of Washington, Bothell
Synthesizer/Prospector: Janeen Costa, University of Utah

3.4 *Special Session*: **How Do Ads Mean: New Directions in Cultural Advertising Research**

Chair: Douglas B. Holt, Penn State University
Synthesizer: John Sherry, Northwestern University

3.5 *Special Session*: **Ferber Awards**

Chair: Robert Burnkrant, Ohio State University

3.6 *Special Session*: **Understanding Altruism: Stories, Experiments, and Cross-Cultural Comparisons**

Chair: Michal Strahilevitz, University of Miami
Synthesizer: Bill Wells, University of Minnesota

3.7   *Special Session*: Extending Measures of Advertising Effectiveness: Ads' Effects on Price Sensitivity

Chair: Ronald C. Goodstein, Indiana University
Synthesizer: Stephen J. Hoch, University of Pennsylvania

FRIDAY, OCTOBER 11

1997 ACR Program Committee Meeting
4:00 - 5:30

Co-Chairs
Joe Alba, University of Florida
Wes Hutchinson, University of Pennsylvania

FRIDAY, OCTOBER 11

SESSION 4
Working Paper Session
4:30 - 6:00 p.m.

Session 4:   **Working Paper Session**

Abstracts for each presentation will appear in the text from pages 112 - 120.

The Impact of Contextuality on Experimental Research in Consumer Behavior
    Jean Perrien, University of Québec at Montréal
    Sylvie Paradis, University of Québec at Montréal

Stimulus Generalization in Classical Conditioning: An Initial Investigation
    Brian D. Till, Saint Louis University
    Randi Prilvek Grossman, Yeshiva University

Towards an Understanding of Homosexual Consumers
    James Marshall, Arizona State University
    Renee D. Shaw, Arizona State University

Probing Exchange Theory: A Comparison of Consumers in Three Rural Communities
    Nancy J. Miller, Iowa State University

Public Perceptions of Consumption by Low Income Households
    Linda F. Alwitt, DePaul University

Towards a Portrait of Arts Consumption in Postmodernity
    Laurie A. Meamber, University of California, Irvine

Variables that Influence Consumers' Inferences About Physician Ability and Physician Accountability for Adverse Health Outcomes
    Manuel C. Pontes, Fairleigh Dickinson University
    Nancy Pontes, New York University

Mood Effects Upon Customers' Responses to Service Organizations and Service Encounters: An Experimental Analysis
    Patricia A. Knowles, Clemson University
    Gregory M. Pickett, Clemson University
    Stephen J. Grove, Clemson University

A Theoretical Basis for a Latitude Conceptualization of Service-Encounter Evaluation: Directions for Future Research
    Stephen L. Vargo, University of Oklahoma

FRIDAY, OCTOBER 11

RECEPTION
5:00 - 7:00 p.m.

JCR EDITORIAL REVIEW BOARD MEETING
5:30 - 7:00 p.m.

Co-Chairs:
Brian Sternthal, Northwestern University
Bob Burnkrant, Ohio State University

SATURDAY OCTOBER 12

JCP REVIEW BOARD MEETING
7:00 a.m. - 8:15 a.m.

REGISTRATION
7:30 a.m. - 5:00 p.m.

NEWCOMER'S BREAKFAST
7:30 a.m. - 8:30 a.m.

5.1   *Special Session*: *Really*-Low Involvement Consumer Learning

Chair: Michael Tuan Pham, Columbia University
Synthesizer: Terry Shimp, University of South Carolina

5.2   *Special Session*: Hide or Seek: Factors Influencing Ambiguity Aversion versus Preference

Co-Chairs: Patricia West, University of Texas, Austin
                       Susan M. Broniarczyk, University of Texas, Austin
Synthesizer: Colin Camerer, California Institute of Technology

5.3   *Special Session*: Children and Decision Making

Chair: Kim Corfman, New York University
Synthesizer: Carole Macklin, University of Cincinnati

5.4 *Competitive Session*: The Symbolic Meaning of Things and Spaces: Cultural and Cross-Cultural Perspectives

5.5 *Special Session*: The Target and Its "Other": Exploring the Social Context and Interaction of Consumer Segments

5.6 *Special Session*: **Puzzles, Choirs and Archives: Perspectives on Crossing the Quantitative-Qualitative Methodological Divide**

Chair: James C. Ward, Arizona State University
Synthesizer: John Sherry, Northwestern University

5.7 *Special Session*: **New Directions in Price Signaling Theory and Research**

Chair: Joydeep Srivastava, University of California, Berkeley
Synthesizer: Russell Winer, University of California, Berkeley

SATURDAY, OCTOBER 12

SESSION 6
10:15 - 11:45 a.m.

6.1 *Competitive Session*: **The Relationships Among and Effects of Knowledge, Involvement, and Perceived Risk**

Chair: Curt Haugtvedt, Ohio State University
Synthesizer/Prospector: Ratti Ratneshwar, University of Connecticut

6.2   *Special Session*: Decision Biases in Evaluating Ambiguous Information

Co-Chairs: Christina L. Brown, New York University
                    Alex Chernev, Duke University
Synthesizer: Steven J. Hoch, University of Pennsylvania

6.3   *Competitive Session*: Attitudes Toward People, New Products, and New Behaviors

Chair: Mike Kamins, University of Southern California
Synthesizer/Prospector: Therese A. Louie, University of Washington

Narrative Frames and Consumer Representations of Experience
> Daniel Padgett, University of New Orleans
> Jerry C. Olson, Penn State University

6.7 *Special Session*: Monetary Promotions vs. Non-Monetary Promotions: Which is More Effective?

Chair: France Leclerc, University of Chicago
Synthesizer: Linda Schneider Stone, University of Minnesota

The Effects of Price vs. Sampling Promotions on Short Term Sales and Brand Loyalty
> Karen Gedenk, Dartmouth College
> Scott Neslin, Dartmouth College

A Penny Saved is Not a Penny Earned: Responses to Different Types of Promotions
> Sue O'Curry, DePaul University

Price Promotions: Providing Reasons to Reject the Brand
> France Leclerc, University of Chicago
> John Little, Massachusetts Institute of Technology

SATURDAY, OCTOBER 12

SESSION 7
1:30 p.m. - 3:00 p.m.

7.1 *Special Session*: The Effects of Negative Information in the Political and Marketing Arenas: Exceptions to the Negativity Effect

Co-Chairs: Baba Shiv, University of Iowa
                 Rohini Ahluwalia, University of Kansas
Synthesizer: Dipankar Chakravarti, University of Colorado

Limits to the Effectiveness of Negative Advertising: An Accessibility-Diagnosticity Perspective
> Baba Shiv, University of Iowa
> Julie Edell, Duke University

Cross-National Differences in Negativity Judgments of Presidential Candidates: The United States, Poland, and Hungary
> Jill Klein, Northwestern University
> Grzegorz Sedek, Warsaw University
> Agnes Toth, Budapest University

The Perceived Diagnosticity of Negative Information: Is Negative Information Always More Diagnostic in the Product Context?
> Rohini Ahluwalia, University of Kansas
> Robert E. Burnkrant, Ohio State University
> Rao Unnava, Ohio State University

7.2 *Competitive Session*: Understanding Attitudes: What Are They and What Affects Them?

Co-Chairs: Rajeev Batra, University of Michigan
                     Laura Peracchio, University of Wisconsin, Milwaukee
Synthesizer: Laura Peracchio, University of Wisconsin, Milawukee

7.3 *Special Session*: The Intergenerational Flow of Wealth in the Family

Co-Chair: Deborah D. Heisley, UCLA
Synthesizer: Dennis Rook, University of Southern California

7.4 *Special Session*: New Directions in Cultural Psychology: The Effects of Cultural Orientation on Affect and Cognition

Co-Chairs: Jennifer Aaker, UCLA
                     Durairaj Maheswaran, New York University
Synthesizer: Bernd Schmitt, Columbia University

7.5   *Special Session*: Beyond Brand Equity: Managing Mature Brands

Chair: Cynthia Huffman, University of Pennsylvania
Synthesizers: Brian Wansink, University of Pennsylvania
                    Cynthia Huffman, University of Pennsylvania

7.6   *Competitive Session*: Philosophical and Methodological Issues in the Study of Consumer Research

Chair: Karen A. Machleit, University of Cincinnati
Synthesizer/Prospector: Carol Pluzinski, Yale University

7.7 *Special Session*: **Psychological Correlates of Deal Proneness and Deal Responsiveness Behavior**

Co-Chairs: Donald R. Lichtenstein, University of Colorado
                    J. Jeffrey Inman, University of Wisconsin, Madison
Synthesizer: Terry Shimp, University of South Carolina

SATURDAY, OCTOBER 12

SESSION 8
3:15 p.m. - 4:45 p.m.

8.1 *Competitive Session*: **Exploring the Relationships Between Attention, Memory and Choice**

Chair: Stewart Shapiro, University of Baltimore
Synthesizer: Angela Lee, Northwestern University

8.2 *Special Session*: Music, Meaning, and Magic: Revisiting Music Research

Chair: Wanda Wallace, Duke University
Synthesizers: Morris Holbrook, Columbia University
                Linda Scott, University of Illinois

8.3 *Special Session*: Consumer Behavior and Public Health

Co-Chairs: Anthony Cox, Indiana University
                Dena Cox, Indiana University
Synthesizer: Anthony Cox, Indiana University

8.4 *Special Session*: Consumers and Brand Meaning: Brands, the Self, and Others

Co-Chairs: Albert M. Muniz, Jr., University of Illinois
                Jennifer E. Chang, Northwestern University
Synthesizer: John Sherry, Northwestern University

What a Brand Means: A Symbolic Interactionist Perspective
Jennifer E. Chang, Northwestern University

Brand Community and the Negotiation of Brand Meaning
Albert M. Muniz, Jr., University of Illinois

Meaningful Self-Brand Connections and Consumer Product Experience Stories
Jennifer Escalas, University of Arizona

8.5   *Special Session*: MEET THE EDITORS

8.6   *Competitive Session*: New Issues and Insights in Qualitative Research

Chair: Gary Bamossy, Vrije Universiteit
Synthesizer/Prospector: Elizabeth Hirschman, Rutgers University

8.7   *Special Session*: Understanding Reference Prices: New Directions in Reference Price Research

Chair: Ziv Carmon, Duke University
Synthesizer: Russell S. Winer, University of California, Berkeley

A Comparative Analysis of Internal Reference Price Models
Richard A. Briesch, New York University
Laksman Krishnamurthi, Northwestern University
Tridib Mazumdar, Syracuse University
S. P. Raj, Syracuse University

Do Past Prices Really Matter? The Formation of Reference Prices in the Grocery Shopping Environment
Eyal Biyalogorsky, Duke University
Ziv Carmon, Duke University

Investigating the 'Incidence' of Reference Effects: A Nested Logit Approach with Latent Segments
David R. Bell, UCLA
Randolph Bucklin, UCLA

8.8 *Special Session*: **Measuring Consumption and Consuming Measurement: The Challenge of Studying Consumers from a Federal Perspective**

Chair: Frederick Conrad, Bureau of Labor Statistics
Synthesizer: Norbert Schwarz, University of Michigan

Food Labeling Research at the FDA
            Alan Levy, Food and Drug Administration

Scripted Versus Conversational Survey Interviewing: A Cost-Benefit Analysis
            Frederick Conrad, Bureau of Labor Statistics
            Michael Schober, New School for Social Research

A Federal Government Perspective on Customer Satisfaction Measurement
            Tracy Wellens, US Bureau of the Census
            Elizabeth Martin, US Bureau of the Census
            Frank Vitrano, US Bureau of the Census

SUNDAY, OCTOBER 13

SESSION 9
8:30 a.m. - 10:00 a.m.

9.1 *Special Session*: **On the Elusive Value of Value: Determinants of Consumers' Value Perceptions**

Co-Chairs: Dan Ariely, Duke University
                 Ziv Carmon, Duke University
Synthesizer: Drazen Prelec, MIT

Insights Into the Willingness-to-Pay Willingness-to-Accept Discrepancy: The Multifaceted Value of Attending a College Basketball Game
            Ziv Carmon, Duke University
            Dan Ariely, Duke University

Possessive Females and Detached Men: Gender Differences in the Effects of Ownership on Object Valuation
            George Lowenstein, Carnegie Mellon University
            Michal Strahilevitz, University of Miami
            Catherine Shatto, Carnegie Mellon University

Predicting Preferences for a Future State of Affairs
            Daniel Kahneman, Princeton University
            David Schkade, University of Texas, Austin

9.2   *Special Session*: Influence Professionals: Their Ethics, Persuasion Theories, and Abilities to Circumvent Negative Stereotypes

Chair: Harish Sujan, Penn State University

9.3   *Competitive Session*: Consumer and Marketer Misbehavior

Chair: David Wooten, University of Florida
Synthesizer/Prospector: Debra Ringold, Willamette University

9.4   *Special Session*: Meanings and Methods: International Perspectives on the Use of Information Communication Technologies

Chair: Mara Alexander, Bilkent University
Synthesizer: Alladi Venkatesh, University of California, Irvine

Information and Communications Technology Usage and Culture: Barriers and Motivators in Turkey
Güliz Ger, Bilkent University
Mara Alexander, Bilkent University

9.5   *Competitive Session*: Are Marketers' Behaviors Fair to Consumers?

Chair: Anthony Miyazaki, University of Miami
Synthesizer/Prospector: Chris Moorman, University of Wisconsin

9.6   *Competitive Session*: Exploring the Determinants of Brand Switching vs. Brand Commitment

Chair: John Barnes, University of Texas, El Paso
Synthesizer/Prospector: Eugene Anderson, University of Michigan

9.7   *Competitive Session*: Consumer Motivations, Perceptions, and Reactions to Price

Chair: Kapil Jain, University of Arizona
Synthesizer/Prospector: Dhruv Grewal, University of Miami

SUNDAY, OCTOBER 13

SESSION 10
10:15 a.m. - 11:45 a.m.

10.1 *Competitive Session*: How Does What We Say in Ads Affect Consumers' Interpretations?

Chair: Carolyn Yoon, University of Toronto
Synthesizer/Prospector: Manjit Yadav, Texas A & M University

10.2 *Competitive Session*: Emotions, Individual Differences and Consumer Information Processing

Chair: Kim Nelson, University of Arizona
Synthesizer/Prospector: Mike Rothschild, University of Wisconsin

10.6 *Competitive Session*: Using Information Technology Within the Home

Chair: Michael Guiry, Fairleigh Dickinson University
Synthesizer/Prospector: Ruth Bolton, University of Maryland

10.7 *Competitive Session*: Exploring Temporal Issues in Consumer Behavior

Chair: Eric Johnson, University of Pennsylvania
Synthesizer/Prospector: Joe Cote, Washington State University

1996 ACR Proceedings Contribution

Errata

An error was made in last year's *Advances in Consumer Research: Research Frame Synergies*, Volume 23 in which a co-author's name was omitted. The paper was titled "The Relationship Between Environmental Issue Involvement and Environmentally-Conscious Behavior: An Exploratory Study" by Linda R. Stanley, Karen M. Lasonde and John Weiss. The name of Dr. John Weiss, Colorado State University, was inadvertently omitted from the paper.

In addition, due to a clerical error, a paper was omitted from last year's volume entitled "Constellations, Configurations and Consumption: Exploring Patterns of Consumer Behaviour Amongst U.K. Shoppers" by Margaret K. Hogg, Manchester School of Management, UMIST, UK and Paul C.N. Michell, Manchester Business School, UK. The complete paper appears in this year's Volume 24 at the end of the regular volume. We apologize for these errors and any inconveniences they may have caused.

Out of the Mouths of Babes: What Children Can Tell Us

Deborah Roedder John, University of Minnesota

The theme of this year's conference is "Breaking Out of the Box." This morning, in the plenary session, we heard several viewpoints about the boxes we find ourselves in as consumer researchers. Though boxes have their advantages and disadvantages, the theme of the conference certainly suggests that breaking out of boxes is a worthwhile endeavor.

Extending this theme, I would like to take this opportunity to talk about a box that I have spent an entire career trying to stay out of–and encouraging others to do so as well.

The box I'm talking about is the "adult" box. Most consumer research is about adults, those famous 18-54 year-olds revered by practitioners and academics alike. Added to this, almost all of our research is guided by theories developed by scholars in other fields that also focus most of their attention on adults. Though we have enthusiastically adopted ideas from diverse areas–such as cognitive psychology, sociology, and anthropology–we have yet to fully appreciate what areas such as child psychology and developmental psychology have to offer.

I found my way out of the adult box quite by accident. As a first year student in the doctoral program at Northwestern, I had to take the traditional consumer behavior seminar from Sid Levy. Of course, since Sid Levy was giving the seminar, it was anything but traditional! As part of this seminar, we were required to write a literature review on a topic of our choice. Not knowing much about consumer behavior, I picked a topic that I found interesting from a public policy angle, namely television violence and its effects on children.

I spent the next two months stationed at the copy machines in the library. I found out that the topic of media violence and children had spawned an enormous literature, which contained the most amazing set of theories from areas such as psychology, sociology, and child psychology. Of these, the ones I found most interesting came from child development, as researchers studied the issue from the vantage point of how children processed and interpreted violent behaviors found in television programs. Here, I found discussions about children's memory, selective attention, moral judgments, and such. What I found interesting, and still find interesting, was how cognitive and social development provided a frame for understanding the world around us.

As time has gone by, I have often wondered why more of my colleagues haven't been drawn into the study of children's consumer behavior. But, more importantly, I've often wondered why more researchers haven't seen child psychology as offering ideas and insights that might shed light on research related to adults. I've come to the conclusion that a lot of us are imprisoned in an adult box. Once we define our subjects as adults, we believe that there's little to be gained from looking at similar issues in literature concerned with children and their development. With so many possible literature bases to look at, it's probably a survival instinct that keeps us from churning through every conceivable area of scholarly research for insights. Yet, the adult box is still a box, with all the attendant disadvantages of ignoring potentially fruitful areas such as cognitive development.

My talk today has one main purpose. It is to convince you to get out of the adult box and take a look at what child psychology has to offer, whether you are interested in children or adults as consumers. Realistically, this is a task that should take longer than the 25 minutes I have left with you. But, what I will try to accomplish is to simply point out a few areas of research that could and should shed light on how we think about adult consumer behavior. To do so, I am going to focus on the topic of knowledge and knowledge development, which is a key area of intersection between consumer research and cognitive development. Children, and the research about them, have something to say to us... *if* we are willing to listen.

DESCRIBING KNOWLEDGE DEVELOPMENT

What We Know

Over the last decade, consumer researchers have been increasingly interested in understanding how different levels of knowledge impact consumer behavior. Examinations of this variety have featured comparisons between experts and novices *or* between consumers who have low, medium, or high degrees of knowledge in an area. These studies have provided insights into how different levels of knowledge affect everything from information gathering to product evaluation to product choice.

Much less is known, however, about the nature of the knowledge itself and how it develops. That is, though we presume there are interesting differences in the knowledge possessed by an expert versus a novice consumer, we have not focused much effort on finding out what those differences might be and how they arise (see Sujan, Sujan, and Bettman 1988 for a notable exception).

What Children Can Tell Us

What can children tell us about the way knowledge changes as it develops? Can research with children give us some hints about the types of changes we should expect? What really changes with change?

Though this is a complex question, and one whose answer might be different from domain to domain, there are a number of generalizations that *do* emerge in the vast literature on knowledge acquisition and development in children. To provide a concrete base of reference, let me begin by giving an example of how researchers have described knowledge development in one specific domain, specifically economic exchange.

The most inclusive description in this area is provided by two Italian psychologists, Anna Berti and Anna Bombi, in a 1988 book, *The Child's Construction of Economics*. They gave children a number of questions and tasks designed to tap their knowledge of the role of money in buying and selling objects. Children's responses were reflective of several levels of understanding, as follows:[1]

Level 0: No Understanding of Money. Children do not have a clear idea that money is necessary for the exchange of goods. Coins and bills are simply objects.

Level 1: Money is Used to Buy Something. Children understand that money is a necessary part of buying and selling, but do not understand why. They do not understand why people get "change" as part of the buying process and believe that

---

[1]The description of Berti and Bombi's levels is based on material from Karsten (1996).

change is given out indiscriminately, regardless of how much money is offered in exchange.

Level 2: Not Every Kind of Money Buys Everything. Children begin to understand the value of money at this point. They know that some coins are worth more than others, though the exact relationship is unclear and sometimes intransitive. A child may say a dime is worth more than a penny, but may reverse the ordering just a short time later.

Level 3: Some Money Buys More than Others. Children recognize that certain types of money are worth more than others, and that these higher valuations allow one to buy more-costly goods. However, the criteria used to decide the value of money is usually tied to its physical size. For example, children at this level usually believe that a nickel is worth more than a dime because it's larger.

Level 4: Strict Money-Object Correspondence. Children at this level understand money values and prices. Their ideas of exchange are still developing, though. For example, children will say that it is necessary to pay for goods with the exact amount of money, no more and no less. They might deny the possibility that a $2 item could be purchased with a $5 dollar bill. The concept of change is still not well understood, even though children have the basic math skills to calculate change amounts.

Level 5: "Correct" Ideas. Children finally understand money valuation, the relation of money values to prices, and how change works to balance the transaction. They understand, for the first time, that one can pay more than an item costs and receive the difference in change.

What do we learn by looking at knowledge development in this domain? Well, practically speaking, those of us with children probably understand, maybe for the first time, why our children do not understand the value of money and why they continually ask us for expensive toys and clothes. It should be obvious why all of our admonitions, such as "Money doesn't grow on trees," fall on deaf ears.

Beyond this, our picture of children's growing knowledge base illustrates several characteristics of knowledge development found across domains. First, the changes that occur are both *qualitative as well as quantitative* in nature. In our example, one sees changes of a quantitative nature as children learn to recognize more coin values over time (e.g., a nickel, dime, and quarter). One also sees changes that are more qualitative in nature. For example, the transition from viewing money as simply another object to viewing it as having economic value represents a qualitative shift in the child's way of thinking.

Second, the changes that occur in knowledge development are both *abrupt as well as gradual.* Though we tend to think of development as a gradual accretion, many knowledge bases emerge as a function of very abrupt changes in thinking as well as gradual ones. In our example, we see gradual developments in children's understanding of "change" as a mechanism for balancing transactions. In fact, a true understanding of this concept does not emerge until the last level. But, we also see abrupt development, as illustrated by the transition from viewing money as an object to viewing it as having economic value.

Third, knowledge development consists of changes that are both *modular as well as systemic* in nature. By modular, I am referring to the fact that some changes seem to occur in isolation and

have little influence on other changes that are occurring. In our example, a change in the ability to recognize coin values is more modular in its effect. It takes quite a while for children to sort out the fact that dimes are worth more than nickels, but this lag in understanding does not necessarily inhibit the child's ability to develop a more advanced notion of buying transactions. In contrast, changes in children's thinking that allow them to understand that some coins are worth more than others, whatever the value, are more systemic in nature. That is, these changes are necessary for other changes in children's thinking to occur, such as the concept of giving change as a way to balance the amount of money tendered with the cost of the item.

Fourth, and perhaps most interesting, is the notion that knowledge development is often accompanied by changes that are both *regressive as well as progressive.* Usually, we think of knowledge development as a process that results in progressively more advanced ways of thinking. In our example, there are a number of components related to children's knowledge of economic exchange that conform to this view. However, we also see evidence of developmental changes of a regressive nature. Consider how children's understanding of "change" comes about. At lower levels, children erroneously believe that change is given out as part of every transaction, and that the amount is given out indiscriminately. One might expect that children would start out from this base and develop more advanced notions that sometimes change is given and sometimes it is not. But, this is not what happens. Before they reach this more advanced notion of change, they go through a stage where they often insist that items can only be purchased if the exact amount of money is tendered, actually denying that change plays a role in transactions. Children actually regress, in a sense, before they advance toward a more mature understanding.[2]

What We Can Learn

What can we learn from this picture of knowledge development? As a beginning, these characteristics of development can serve as guideposts for the types of changes we may find in consumers as they become more knowledgeable and develop more expertise. There is every reason to suspect, as some recent research in problem solving suggests, that the pattern of development in adults has many parallels with that of children (Kuhn 1995). We can take advantage of these parallels as we attempt to describe consumer knowledge development in more detail.

EXPLAINING KNOWLEDGE DEVELOPMENT

What We Know

If we admit to knowing very little about the nature of consumer knowledge development, we also have to own up to the fact that we know even *less* about the process that drives such development. Clearly, understanding the process is as important as understanding the types of changes that occur as consumers become more knowledgeable and more expert.

What Can Children Tell Us

What can children tell us about the way knowledge develops as one becomes more advanced or more expert? Can research with children give us some hints about the type of process we should expect?

---

[2]An interesting example of regressive and progressive change can be found in a recent conceptualization of change in the context of addictive behavior (Prochaska, DiClemente, and Norcross 1992).

Once again, I am compelled to say that this is a complex topic with relatively few simple answers. If there is any question that dominates research with children, this is it. There simply isn't a more compelling question than how knowledge is acquired, transformed, and structured. Instead of providing an overview of the long and lengthy history of process explanations in the literature, I would like to focus on relatively new ways of thinking about the process of knowledge development, contrasting these approaches with the more traditional view.

The Staircase Metaphor. The most traditional view of knowledge development is that children progress through a series of stages in acquiring new skills and concepts. Think of it as a staircase, with children climbing up a series of steps, each representing more advanced thinking. Once a child has climbed up to a particular step, they never climb back down to less advanced ones.

This traditional view is most closely associated with Jean Piaget's theory of cognitive development, which views development as a series of dramatic qualitative shifts that occur in children's thinking. The most well-known feature of his theory is the depiction of four qualitatively different stages (or steps) of development: sensorimotor, preoperational, concrete operational, and formal operational. These stages are characterized by different underlying mental structures, which drive the way children think and reason across domains. A child in the preoperational stage, for example, is very egocentric in viewing the world, whereas a child in the concrete operational stage can represent other people's points of view (for a full description, see Ginsburg and Opper 1988).

Stage theories, such as Piaget's, do quite a remarkable job of explaining why there are regularities in the way children of a particular age think and reason across domains. Consider, for example, the development of number conservation in children. One test of this concept involves showing children a row of buttons spaced evenly apart. The experimenter then removes one button, and spreads out the remaining ones so that the length of the row is the same as before. Young children, under the age of 8, will typically say that the new arrangement has the same number of buttons as the old arrangement, even though one button has been removed. They judge number by using "length" as cue, rather than encoding other features of the display that would point to the correct answer.

We see this same pattern repeated in other domains. Moral judgments are a good example. In testing children's concepts in this domain, researchers present several scenarios to the child, each describing an unfortunate incident that has occurred, such as a child breaking a teacup. In one scenario, the child has broken the cup entirely by accident, shattering it into a million pieces. In a second scenario, the child has only chipped the cup, which can be repaired easily, but did so because he was trying to steal cookies from a plate sitting nearby. When asked which of these children is the most "naughty," young children say it is the child who totally shattered the teacup, even though this was a "true" accident. This outcome obtains because, once again, the child is encoding and using a single cue, the consequences of the behavior, rather than other, more important, cues such as the individual's motives.

As important as these regularities are, both across children and across domains, researchers have managed to find a host of situations that defy description in terms of the staircase metaphor. Though these are too numerous to survey, let me point out two of the most important anomalies. First, there are instances where children show different levels of understanding in very similar domains. Second, there are instances where children show different levels of understanding on the very same task from day to day.

Of course, this type of behavior drives every parent crazy! Your child acts mature and responsible one day, and turns into a "terrible-two" the next day. You can take heart in the fact that it not only drives us crazy, but it also drives researchers in cognitive development crazy, too. Crazy enough, in fact, to develop new theories and new metaphors for knowledge development. I would like to share the ideas behind two of these new theories, both quite new and provocative.

The Workshop Metaphor. The workshop metaphor illustrates the basic tenets of dynamic systems theory. Dynamic systems theory suggests that knowledge develops as the result of an interaction between independently developing subsystems. Each subsystem, or component, has its own unique course of development. Subsystems develop at different rates, at different times, in different children. For example, applying these notions to children's knowledge of economic exchange, we would say that progress from one level to the next is a function of developing and interacting subsystems. These subsystems might be related to children's understanding of coin values, trading, and concepts such as "more" and "less" (see Karsten 1996).

Dynamic systems theory offers the idea that children construct solutions and knowledge based on the subsystems of knowledge they have, in whatever form they have them. In other words, using a workshop metaphor, children pull tools from their mental toolkit to solve a problem or construct an interpretation of their environment.[3] The combined condition of the tools they use influences the result of their efforts, which may be inhibited by the existence of an immature or poorly-developed tool.

These ideas are nicely captured in a passage from a recent book, *How Children Discover New Strategies* (Siegler and Jenkins 1989, p. 1):

"A child's mind is like a workshop. This workshop contains a remarkable collection of materials (knowledge) and tools (learning processes) that can be used to make new products (rules, strategies, hypotheses, schema, causal networks, etc). Some of the tools and materials are useful for a great many tasks. Many others are specialized for a particular purpose, but are invaluable when they are needed.

Orders constantly arrive at the workshop for products that need to be made. Most of the requested products are familiar, and the child already knows how to make them. Others are new, though. Choosing the tools and materials for building these new products can be frustrating, but it also challenges the workshop to produce its finest wares.

Many products that are fabricated in the process of meeting one order themselves become materials and tools for making additional products. For this reason, the broader the range of products the workshop has produced in the past, the greater its potential for meeting future demands."

As this passage suggests, the workshop metaphor differs from the traditional staircase view in several important respects. First, it allows for variance across children at a particular age by proposing that not all children at that age will possess the same subsystems at the same level of maturity. Though there may be strong age-related trends in the nature of the subsystems, one seven-year-old may differ from another because one of the important subsystems is a bit more mature or more accessible for one of the children. Second, it

---

[3]The emphasis on construction is similar to recent views of constructed preferences (e.g., Slovic 1995) and decision-making strategies (e.g., Payne, Bettman, and Johnson 1993).

allows for variance in children across settings by proposing that not all subsystems will be recruited in the same manner on every task. Though certain tasks may suggest the need to recruit some tools more than others, the possibility exists that a particular tool may be missing as children attempt to complete a particular task. Thus, the difference in one component or subsystem can totally change the type of knowledge or understanding exhibited by a child from one task to another.

The Wave Metaphor. The notion that a child's knowledge can look so very different on different occasions is at the center of the newest metaphor, the wave metaphor, recently advanced by Robert Siegler in a new book, *Beyond the Immaculate Transition: Change Processes in Children's Thinking.* Siegler argues that the traditional stage or staircase model is too rigid and fails to account for much of the complexity we see in cognitive development. Instead of viewing development as a progression of steps or stairs, Siegler proposes that we think about development as a series of overlapping waves, where each "wave" represents the ebb and flow of ideas and strategies. Instead of viewing development as new material replacing the old, the notion of a wave suggests that the replacement is more gradual, as the use of old concepts or strategies fades and the use of new concepts and strategies gradually builds to a crest and overtakes the old ones.

This metaphor is a particularly apt one for procedural knowledge development in problem-solving or decision making. Consider, for example, research on the development of arithmetic skills in children. Much of this literature addresses the strategies that children use for solving single-digit addition problems, such as "1 + 2," "4 + 5," and "6 + 8." Though you may not remember from your childhood, there are a number of ways to add single-digit numbers. A favorite one of preschoolers is to count out the first addend on the fingers of the left hand, count out the second addend on the fingers of the right hand, and then count all the fingers on both hands. For example, to add "5 + 2," one would count 5 fingers on the left hand, 2 fingers on the right hand, and then count the fingers on both hands to arrive at the number "7." This is referred to as a "sum" strategy in the literature.

While this works well for many basic problems, there are shortcuts that children learn by kindergarten or first grade for solving these problems. Referred to as the "min" strategy, children select the largest addend and then count upwards by the number of times indicated by the smaller addend. For example, to add "5 + 2," a child would start at 5 and count upward 2 counts ("5, 6, 7"). The min strategy produces faster response times, as well as being very useful when the addends are larger than the number of digits on one's hands or toes!

Until recently, researchers viewed the development of strategies for single-digit addition as a sequential process, with children progressing from the use of a relatively simple "sum" strategy as a preschooler to the use of the more advanced "min" strategy as a kindergartner or first grader. That is, children were viewed as progressing from strategy A to Strategy B to Strategy C, giving up the use of an old "inferior" strategy as soon as they discovered a better one. Thus, development was characterized as a series of stages, consistent with the staircase metaphor.

Current developments have uncovered a more complex picture of how arithmetic skills develop in children. Specifically, studies in this area (e.g., Siegler 1987; Siegler and Shrager 1984), have revealed that children simultaneously use a variety of strategies to solve single-digit addition problems, including a mix of rather primitive and advanced strategies. On a single day, a child might use a "sum" strategy on one problem and a "min" strategy on another. Or, he might use these two strategies to solve the same problem on different days. What changes over time, as children

become more knowledgeable, is the relative *frequency* of using different strategies. As children move from preschool to first grade, use of the sum strategy declines, while use of the min strategy increases. That is, knowledge development is not an abrupt shift from one type of strategy to another, but a gradual shift from a reliance on less-sophisticated strategies to more advanced ones over time. Development is really more wave-like than step-like.

The wave metaphor differs from the traditional staircase view in several important respects. First, it allows for variance across children at a particular age by proposing that not all children will be riding the same wave, or that the wave may be at different levels of cresting or falling. Though there may be strong age-related trends in the existence of particular waves (strategies), one seven-year-old may differ from another because the wave is just cresting for one, but is falling for the other. Second, it allows for variance in children across different settings by proposing that children do not ride only one wave, but have several in motion at any one time. Though certain waves (strategies) may be more favored, the possibility exists that a child may choose to ride quite a different wave at any one point in time.

What We Can Learn

Taken together, what can we learn from these metaphors? How can we apply the workshop and wave metaphors to deepen our understanding of consumer knowledge development and inform our research?

As a beginning, let me suggest two very concrete ways that we can use the ideas behind these metaphors in our research. First, if knowledge does not develop in invariant stages, but develops in a more constructive and wave-like manner, we need to employ different data collection methods. Specifically, instead of measuring consumer knowledge or strategies at one point in time, we will need to assess them at multiple points in time. Using such approaches, called microgenetic methods (cf., Kuhn 1995), is one of the few ways of capturing anything other than a strict stage-like progression of knowledge development.

Second, continuing with this theme, we need to employ different data analysis methods. Our current methods, based upon analyses of group means, hide much of the variance that is the very focus of the workshop and wave metaphors. If the process of development is not stage-like, it will be hard to detect if we do not search for the possibility that differences exist among groups of consumers we wish to label "experts" or "novices." The metaphors I have described encourage us to look beyond what is happening at a group level and consider what the within-group variance can tell us about how consumer knowledge or strategies are developing.

CONCLUDING COMMENTS

Whether you realize it or not, you have broken out of the adult box for the last 30 minutes. I have not discussed even one adult study, based on one adult theory, about one adult consumer. Hopefully, you've found some of the ideas and concepts interesting.

My objective today has been to convince you to break out of the adult box to see what child development research has to offer. By necessity, I narrowed the discussion of relevant research to one topic, knowledge development, but be assured that others could be equally interesting. For example, if you are interested in consumption symbolism, you might find studies of adolescent gang behavior to offer some very important insights. If you are interested in ethics or consumer misbehavior, you might find the literature on children's moral judgments to offer some interesting direction.

Children do have something to tell us...if only we are willing to listen. Follow the example of scholars who have used research in child development to enrich their thinking, regardless of whether they are studying adults or children. Consider Greg Murphy and Doug Medin, two prominent cognitive psychologists. In their frequently-cited 1985 article titled "The Role of Theories in Conceptual Coherence," Murphy and Medin argue that individuals have "theories" about how objects "hang together" (Murphy and Medin 1985). If you read this article carefully, you will note that much of the empirical support they marshal for their ideas comes from the concept development literature in child psychology.

This is, by no means, an isolated example. In their 1993 book titled *The Adaptive Decision Maker,* John Payne, Jim Bettman, and Eric Johnson reference work on children's problem-solving abilities in their discussion of why individuals sometimes fail to adapt. In their recent article titled "The Persuasion Knowledge Model: How People Cope with Persuasion Attempts," Marian Friestad and Peter Wright incorporate ideas pertaining to children's developing cognitive and social abilities in their discussion of how persuasion knowledge develops (Friestad and Wright 1994). As a final example, Joe Alba and Wes Hutchinson incorporate literature on analytic and holistic classification in children in their well-known 1987 article titled "Dimensions of Consumer Expertise" (Alba and Hutchinson 1987).

Let me suggest that you can go even further than this if you are willing to spend more time out of the adult box. Even if your research agenda finds you squarely in the adult domain, you may find interesting extensions of your research by studying similar phenomena with children. Some of your colleagues have done so, such as Russ Belk, Merrie Brucks, Kim Corfman, Terry Shimp, Mita Sujan, and more. You need not spend most of your time outside the adult box, though you are also welcome to do so. Some of us–such as Marv Goldberg, Gerry Gorn, Carole Macklin, Laura Perrachio and myself–go back and forth between boxes quite happily.

Whatever your course, I hope you'll remember the notion of the adult box and will think about breaking it out of it, at least every now and then. Children do have something to tell us...I hope you'll keep listening!

ACKNOWLEDGEMENTS

I would like to thank Sara John and Tessa Druley for providing the illustrations that accompanied my address. I would also like to acknowledge the many helpful comments received on a previous version of the address from Jim Bettman, Marv Goldberg, Jennifer Gregan-Paxton, Carole Macklin, Laura Peracchio, Terry Shimp, and Alice Tybout.

REFERENCES

Alba, Joseph W. and J. Wesley Hutchinson (1987), "Dimensions of Consumer Expertise," *Journal of Consumer Research,* 13 (March), 411-454.

Berti, Anna and Anna Bombi (1988), *The Child's Construction of Economics,* New York: Cambridge University Press.

Friestad, Marian and Peter Wright (1994), "The Persuasion Knowledge Model: How People Cope with Persuasion Attempts," *Journal of Consumer Research,* 21 (June), 1-31.

Ginsburg, Herbert P. and Sylvia Opper (1988), *Piaget's Theory of Intellectual Development,* Third Edition, Englewood Cliffs, New Jersey: Prentice-Hall.

Karsten, Yvonne Cariveau (1996), "A Dynamic Systems Approach to the Development of Consumer Knowledge: Children's Understanding of Monetary Exchange," Unpublished Doctoral Dissertation, University of Minnesota.

Kuhn, Deanna (1995), "Microgenetic Study of Change: What Has It Told Us?" *Psychological Science,* 6 (May), 133-139.

Murphy, Gregory L. and Douglas L. Medin (1985), "The Role of Theories in Conceptual Coherence," *Psychological Review,* 92 (July), 289-316.

Payne, John W., James R. Bettman, and Eric J. Johnson (1993), *The Adaptive Decision Maker,* Cambridge: Cambridge University Press.

Prochaska, James O., Carlo C. DiClemente, and John C. Norcross (1992), "In Search of How People Change: Applications to Addictive Behaviors," *American Psychologist,* 47 (September), 1102-1114.

Siegler, Robert S. (1996), *Beyond the Immaculate Transition: Change Processes in Children's Thinking,* NY: Oxford University Press.

_____ and Eric Jenkins (1989), *How Children Discover New Strategies,* Hillsdale, New Jersey: Lawrence Erlbaum Associates.

_____ and J. Shrager (1984), "A Model of Strategy Choice," in *Origins of Cognitive Skills,* C. Sophian (Ed.), Hillsdale, New Jersey: Lawrence Erlbaum Associates, 229-293.

Slovic, Paul (1995), "The Construction of Preference," *American Psychologist,* 50 (May), 364-371.

Sujan, Harish, Mita Sujan, and James R. Bettman (1988), "Knowledge Structure Differences Between More Effective and Less Effective Salespeople," *Journal of Marketing Research,* 25 (February), 81-86.

Breaking Out of the North American Box

Gerald J. Gorn, The Hong Kong University of Science and Technology

Did you ever wonder why the "Middle East" is called the "*Middle* East" and the "Far East" the "*Far* East"? What is *Middle* and *Far* about them? These labels reflect a Western European view of the world. From Vancouver where I have lived, you would head straight west, not east, to get to Asia. Most maps we see have North America and Europe in the top portions with Australia "down under." There are Australian "south-up" maps with Australia in the north and centre, and North America on the bottom left and also "upside down". We may know in our heads that it is arbitrary which pole goes on top and that these Australian maps are as accurate as any "north-up" map, but it still looks strange to anyone from the northern hemisphere. As a North American, it looks strange to me to see the U.S. where it is, with Canada below the U.S. The whole map looks upside down.

As an example of North American dominance, on the Internet, firms registered outside the U.S. have been required to identify their country of origin with a two letter extension —e.g. for Australia it is 'com.au', for Canada, it is 'com.ca'—whereas firms registered in the U.S. are exempted from this requirement. As an article in the Economist put it, "because the United States dreamt up the Internet, most of its users grandly carry no country code" (The Economist, June 8, 1996, p. 71). The situation is, of course, changing, as the proportion of non-Americans to Americans using the Internet increases.

My remarks here concern breaking out of an ethnocentric North American box in our field, something which is already happening, and which I would like to reinforce here. Perhaps one of the few universal truths is that, oddly enough, we are all, at least to some extent, ethnocentric (c.f. LeVine and Campbell 1972, and Triandis 1994, 1996 for a discussion of ethnocentrism); even scientists. This is one of the points the philosopher of science Thomas Kuhn made when he described scientists from competing paradigms as seeing the world differently, leading them to live in different worlds (Kuhn 1970). Where you stand depends on where you sit!

Sumner, back in 1906, defined ethnocentrism as "the technical name for this view of things in which one's own group is the center of everything, and all others are scaled and with reference to it" (Sumner, 1906, p. 12). It is the latter part of this definition that I find most intriguing. The constructs, relationships, samples and measures we use as researchers undoubtedly bear our cultural stamp, and therefore testing for their generalizability to other cultures may be biased and insufficient. It may not do justice to the cultures to which we are trying to generalize, cultures which may be better captured by more indigenous as opposed to "imported" constructs. Hofstede (1980, 1983) in his well-known research on cultural values, uncovered four dimensions of culture, namely individualism-collectivism (focus in the society on the development and welfare of the individual versus the collective), power distance (attitude towards unequal power in organizations and in society in general), uncertainty avoidance (tolerance of ambiguous situations and the desire to avoid them), and masculinity-femininity (the extent to which the society favors assertiveness or nurturance). These four dimensions emerged from a questionnaire developed by researchers from six Western countries. In subsequent research, Chinese scholars were asked to develop a similar questionnaire, and like with Hofstede's original research, the questionnaire was then administered to respondents in different countries. Four dimensions emerged in the Chinese study as well, but only three were the

same. In the Chinese study, uncertainty avoidance did not emerge, whereas a new dimension called Confucian dynamism emerged. Confucian dynamism contains such values as thrift, perseverance and respect for tradition (see Chinese Cultural Connection 1987, and Hofstede 1994 for a more detailed discussion). As another example of constructs important in other cultures, but less so in North America, there are emotions that have special significance in the Japanese culture but not in the North American culture (e.g. *"ki ga sumanai"*, an ongoing dissatisfaction with oneself, *"amae"*, indulging one's sense of dependency on others).

Japanese constructs like *"ki ga sumanai"* and *"amae"* were brought into the literature by a Japanese psychiatrist, Takeo Doi (see Heine and Lehman 1996a, and Heine, Lehman, Kitayama, and Markus 1996). In the field of consumer behavior as well, it may be non-North American researchers who have a special role to play in bringing into our field constructs from other cultures, constructs that they have a feel for first hand. As gatekeepers of new knowledge, they also have a special role to play as reviewers and editorial board members. There are, by my rough count, about 15% on the editorial board of both the *Journal of Consumer Research* and the *Journal of Consumer Psychology*, who from what I can gather are non-North American. Perhaps they have this special role of bringing new knowledge from other cultures into our field. North American scholars interested in breaking out of the geography box, are likely to benefit greatly from interacting with, and doing research with, those from other cultures, and this cross-cultural research collaboration would seem to be increasing. Those from another culture can serve as guides to that culture, which may help those viewing it with foreign eyes to see something new. It should also help them reflect back on their own culture and take a fresh look at it.

I would like to digress a little here to say that powerful economies like Japan and Germany have taken their place alongside the U.S. The U.S. dollar is no longer the only powerful currency, and the only currency against which all others are measured. This change should lessen the feeling that the U.S. is the centre of the world, which in turn should help stimulate an interest in at least the cultures or countries that are becoming more powerful. Perhaps it has been in part the growing economic power of other countries that has spurred interest in their culture. Economic success may be the validation that is needed to really spur interest. For example, the interest in Japanese management theories and the Japanese in general was probably stimulated, at least in part, by their economic success. "How do they do it, those Japanese?" And what we are finding out is that, not surprisingly, they are very different from North Americans. If the 21st century is in fact "the Asian century", the 20th century being perhaps the American one (Dale, 1996) then there is much more learning on the part of North Americans to come, because Asian cultures are so different from the cultural environment those of us from North America have grown up in.

Research in Japan has already challenged some psychological truths from North American research findings, that I have always felt were so basic and universal. Research in North America has shown that people like to think well of themselves. We like to think of ourselves as competent, independent and confident (e.g. Sampson 1977, Markus and Kitayama 1991, and Heine and Lehman 1996a). We strive to do better, and be successful. It is also well-documented in this research that we even make use of self-serving biases to

Advances in Consumer Research
Volume 24, © 1997

bolster an unrealistically positive view of ourselves (e.g. Taylor and Brown 1988) and of our future (Heine and Lehman 1995a); and there is the well-known attribution finding in North American research that we tend to take credit for our successes but blame our failures on external factors (see Zuckerman, 1979 for a review of this literature).

Are these fundamental human tendencies? Would people from cultures which do not place so much of a premium on individual success, and reward it so much, think and act the same way? From what I can tell, the answer at this point seems to be "no". Many of our robust findings in North America simply do not hold up in cultures which value interdependence. One example is the one I just mentioned of the tendency for people to take credit for successes while blaming failure on others.[1] It has been shown to be less pronounced in cultures that emphasize integration with the group as opposed to self-enhancement (Kashima and Triandis 1986). In fact, at least when it comes to the Japanese, they do not appear to view themselves as better than others in the society around them (Markus and Kitayama 1991, Heine and Lehman 1996c), and they do not seem to want to stand out from the crowd; whereas we say "the squeaky wheel gets the grease", the Japanese have a saying "the nail that stands out gets pounded down" (Markus and Kitayama 1991). As another example of a difference between Americans and Japanese and of the previously mentioned Japanese construct *"ki ga sumanai"*, a study done by the Prime Minister's office in Japan found that while 93% of North American students felt they were doing well in school, only 37% of Japanese students felt this way. If anything, research shows that the Japanese tend to be unnecessarily pessimistic (Heine et al. 1996). As Heine et al. (1996) note, the North American slogan "where there's a will, there's a way" can be contrasted with the Japanese saying "there is no way".[2] This ongoing sense of dissatisfaction about oneself serves an important function in the interdependent Japanese culture. Focusing on their negative characteristics in their interactions with others is a way the Japanese use to find out what has to be done to enable them to integrate better with, and obtain the approval of, the group (Heine and Lehman 1996a).

If we accept that cultures are different, and also that our culture shapes us in profound ways, then we should be able to accept that there are going to be major cultural differences in the way people think, feel, and act, including the ways they behave vis a vis both advertising and products.[3] Furthermore, the more we appreciate how deep-seated these cultural differences often are, the more likely we are to realize that there are limits to the notion of a "global person" or "global consumer" (c.f., Levitt 1981, and Segal-Horn 1992); the more likely to be challenged are some of the truths that we believe to be universal.

It will be interesting to see what important differences emerge as more consumer behavior studies are conducted in other cultures, particularly in cultures very different from our own, namely non-western cultures. About 70% of humans live in non-western cultures (Triandis 1996); and learning about cultural differences

should be, clearly, all the more relevant today with the recent emergence of consumer markets in Asia, and parts of Latin America as well.

As a final comment I would have you consider the following. When going through the consumer behavior journals, we all realize how much of our knowledge comes from studying college students. We often joke about this and the limitations and biases involved in having such a restricted sample base. What we joke about less is that the sample is typically one of *North American* college students. If as a field we are trying to do more than simply understand the American consumer, perhaps we should be as sensitive to any shortcomings of a sample being North American as we are to it being one of college students.

REFERENCES

Anonymous (1996), "The Internet: Names Writ in Water," *The Economist*, June 8, 71-2.

Chinese Cultural Connection (a team of 24 researchers), "Chinese Values and the Search for Culture- free Dimensions of Culture," *Journal of Cross-Cultural Psychology*, 18 (2), 1987, 143-164.

Dale, Reginald (1996), "U.S. Needs a Plan to Prolong 'American Century'," *International Herald Tribune*, November 29, p. 15.

Diener, E., E. M. Suh, H. Smith, and L. Shao (1995), "National Differences in Reported Subjective Well-Being: Why Do They Occur?" *Social Indicators Research*, 34, 7-32.

Heine, S. J. and D. R. Lehman (1995a), "Cultural Variation in Unrealistic Optimism: Does the West Feel More Invulnerable Than the East?" *Journal of Personality and Social Psychology*, 68 (4), 595-607.

Heine, S.J. and D. R. Lehman (1995b), "Social Desirability Among Canadian and Japanese Students," *Journal of Social Psychology*, 135, 777-779.

Heine, S. J. and D. R. Lehman (1996a), "Culture, Self Discrepancies, and Self-Satisfaction," working paper.

Heine, S. J. and D. R. Lehman (1996b), "Culture, Dissonance, and Self-Affirmation," *Personality and Social Psychology Bulletin*, in press.

Heine, S. J. and D. R. Lehman (1996c), "Culture and Group-Serving Biases," working paper.

Heine, S. J., D. R. Lehman, S. Kitayama, H. R. Markus (1996), "Culture and the Need for Positive Self-Regard," working paper.

Hofstede, G. (1980), "Motivation, Leadership and Organization: Do American Theories Apply Abroad?" *Organizational Dynamics*, Summer, 42-63.

Hofstede, G. (1983), "National Cultures in Four Dimensions: A Research-based Theory of Cultural Differences Among Nations," *International Studies of Management and Organization*, vol. XII, nos. 1-2, 46-74.

Hofstede, G. (1994), "Management Scientists are Human," *Management Science*, 40 (1), 4-13.

Kashima, Y. and H. C. Triandis (1986), "The Self-Serving Bias in Attributions as a Coping Strategy: A Cross-Cultural Study," *Journal of Cross-Cultural Psychology*, 17, 83-97.

Kuhn, T. S. (1970), *The Structure of Scientific Revolutions*. Second Edition, Chicago: University of Chicago Press.

LeVine, R. A. and D. T. Campbell (1972), *Ethnocentrism: Theories of Conflict, Ethnic Attitudes, and Group Behavior*. New York: John Wiley and Sons.

Levitt, T. (1981), "The Globalization of Markets," *Harvard Business Review*, May-June, 92-102.

---

[1]Another example of a North American finding that does not seem to hold as strongly in other cultures is the tendency to reduce dissonance between attitudes and behavior (see Heine and Lehman 1996b).

[2]And the evidence shows that it is more than a matter of modesty (Diener, Suh, Smith, and Shoa, 1995, Heine and Lehman 1995b).

[3]As but one recent example of this, see Schmitt, Pan and Tavasolli's (1994) research for how language, an aspect of culture, shapes consumer information processing.

Markus, H. R. and S. Kitayama (1991), "Culture and The Self: Implications for Cognition, Emotion, and Motivation," *Psychological Review*, 98, 224-53.

Sampson, E. E. (1977), "Psychology and the American Ideal," *Journal of Personality and Social Psychology*, 35, 767-82.

Schmitt, B. H., Pan Y., and N. Tavassoli (1994), "Language and Consumer Memory: The Impact of Linguistic Differences Between Chinese and English," *Journal of Consumer Research*, 21 (3), 419-31.

Segal-Horn, Susan (1992), "Global Marketing, the Global Consumer, and International Retailing," *Journal of Global Marketing*, 5 (3), 31-61.

Sumner, W. G. (1906), *Folkways*. New York: Finn.

Taylor, S. E. and J. D. Brown (1988), "Illusion and Well Being: A Social Psychological Perspective on Mental Health," *Psychological Bulletin*, 103, 193-210.

Triandis, H. C. (1994), *Culture and Social Behavior*. New York: McGraw-Hill.

Triandis, H. C. (1996), "The Psychological Measurement of Cultural Syndromes," *American Psychologist*, 51, 407-15.

Zuckerman, M. (1979), "Attribution of Success and Failure Revisited: The Motivational Bias is Alive and Well in Attribution Theory," *Journal of Personality*, 47, 245-287.

Breaking Out of Boxes: Creativity, Community, and Culture

Melanie Wallendorf, University of Arizona

At the beginning of my Marketing Theory seminar, I use a role-playing exercise. I am a movie casting director and the students are consultants regarding what to look for in casting the role of a scientist. Their advice is always the same: get a 50-60 year old white male with unkempt hair, out-of-fashion clothing, and glasses to correct myopia. When I probe what this person is like at a party, they chuckle: he is socially inept and shrinks to the side of the room until asked about the only thing he can talk about—his work.

What I then attempt to do in class is uncover the assumptions about scientific creativity that underlie this distinct image.

In preparing this speech, I read widely on the topic of creativity—scientific and otherwise. I am happy to report that the literature does not support my students' image of creative scientists. I will be describing what I have learned about the links between "Creativity, Community, and Culture," drawing most heavily from these two books:

Mihaly Csikszentmihalyi (1995), *Creativity: Flow and the Psychology of Discovery and Invention*, New York: Harper Collins.

Howard Gardner (1993), *Frames of Mind: The Theory of Multiple Intelligences*, tenth anniversary edition, New York: Basic Books.

I'll focus on the sociocultural context, that is, the community and culture, that facilitate creativity.

I will not focus on the psychological characteristics common among people who produce creative work, because I agree with Csikszentmihalyi that creativity is not a characteristic of a person. Instead, creativity emerges from the interaction between a person's thoughts and the sociocultural context. I'll reserve the term originality for novel and unusual ideas. I'll use the term creativity for people having novel and unusual ideas (that's the psychological part), AND having those positively evaluated within a field (that's the sociocultural part). To be specific: your work is original when none of the content or methodological codes for a conference fits your paper. It is creative when the paper is accepted and goes on to be heavily cited and/or win an award.

I have 9 suggestions for our collective nurturance of creativity. For people to be creative, rather than just original, they have to be in a sociocultural context that accepts good new ideas; they have to be in the right place at the right time. In this respect, creativity is like automobile accidents: there are characteristics of people that make them more prone to the event, but both automobile accidents and creativity arise through complex properties of systems rather than through characteristics of individuals.

I: Accept the Relativity of the Concept of Creativity.

Creativity is a relative concept: if some ideas are creative, then others are less so. We can't all be the highly creative ones, or as my Aunt Deanne used to say when she tried to manage six young cousins: "we can't all be chiefs; what we need here are a few good Indians." [In the late 1950's, even she did not have the political sensitivity to use the term "native Americans."]

Not everyone in a field breaks out of boxes. Recognizing that allows us to be less fearful of the novel ideas of those few individuals who are enormously creative. Allowing them to push the edge doesn't lead to anarchy or the demise of the field. Despite the predictions of some, Phil Kotler and Sid Levy's notion about broadening the concept of marketing did not bring about the demise of the field of marketing. Instead, it broadened its impact and its audience.

We must encourage those few individuals who profoundly expand our range of knowledge.

II: Be on the Lookout for Creative Students.

Those of us who are college professors play an important role. Csikszentmihalyi found that his sample of eminent creative people weren't popular as adolescents and lacked nostalgia for their teenage years.

However, college and graduate school were high points. Specific college professors provided intellectual challenges that aroused their interest. This isn't always an easy task since these students often ask "difficult" questions about taken-for-granted assumptions.

Today's undergraduates include people who could make creative contributions to consumer research in the future. If it weren't for my undergraduate professors at SMU, especially Mike Harvey and Roger Kerin, I might have taken a job in bank marketing. Instead, in 1974, they suggested I enter a Ph.D. program. I thought being paid $3000 a year to read books and write papers sounded good, so I went.

We must watch for and mentor students who might make creative contributions.

III: Recruit and Nurture Multiple Intelligences.

But we must look beyond students already in our courses to find talented people. To optimize its creativity, a field needs people with diverse strengths and predispositions that make them sensitive to the multiple dimensions of human experience.

It is in this suggestion that the work of Gardner becomes useful. He identifies six relatively autonomous types of intelligence:

1. Linguistic
2. Musical
3. Logical-mathematical
4. Spatial
5. Bodily-Kinesthetic
6. Personal

Our field is set up to select people with high logical-mathematical intelligence, who confront the world and attempt to find patterns that can be represented in abstract propositions expressed through the symbols of mathematics. These are important abilities, and we continue to need their contributions. But in requiring that everyone have high logical-mathematical intelligence, our field has overlooked the potential contributions of people with other types of intelligence, especially linguistic and personal.

Those with high linguistic intelligence are keenly attuned to the shades of meaning of words. For most consumer researchers, language is a communication tool, rather than the substantive focus of their scholarship. However, our field also needs scholars who study topics such as how the persuasive language of advertising carries meaning. Because our field has recently incorporated some scholars trained in the analysis of language and its use, namely literary critics such as Linda Scott and Barbara Stern, we are now understanding much more about topics requiring linguistic intelligence. Yet the road must be made more inviting for others who might contribute in this way.

Similarly, consumer research has not maximized what could be contributed by scholars with high personal intelligence. Personal intelligence has two aspects: The first is access to one's own feeling life, which then is the basis for the second: the ability to notice and distinguish among other people's moods, temperaments, motivations, and intentions. Typically, these abilities are overlooked in fields focusing on cognition as the basis for action. The recent inclusion of ethnography and phenomenology in consumer research has opened a pathway for the entry of a few scholars with this capacity.

Broadening our field's range of intelligences may require changes in entry and training requirements. But ultimately, it would contribute to the production of creative insights.

IV: Be Open and Critical Simultaneously.

Creativity requires the flexibility to move between being open and critical. Openness encourages people to be sufficiently playful and imaginative to have original ideas.

But openness to carefully considering new ideas is different from uncritically accepting all new ideas. A field must rigorously determine whether original work makes a creative contribution and meets the high standards appropriate to that type of work.

Our challenge is to help new people internalize rigorous evaluative criteria without stifling their abilities to form novel connections. Internalized standards allow people to focus on their original ideas that have the greatest creative potential. To achieve this dualism of being open and critical, evaluative criteria must be clear at a fairly high level of abstraction, so they are applicable to a wide range of original ideas. Focusing attention on our highest scholarly values as criteria prevents us from mistaking frequently-used indicators of high quality with high quality itself.

This is the delicate balance between being open and critical that creativity requires.

V: Fight Bureaucratically-Induced Boredom.

We must protect our scholarly environment from a form of pollution that limits its ability to bear creative fruit. That pollution is what I call bureaucratically-induced boredom. Its the exhausted feeling we have at the end of a day of being busy, but creating nothing. Creative ideas come in quiet reflective time, and tend not to come to overburdened, exhausted people. Creative ideas come to intrinsically motivated people with the time to pursue their interests.

The Nobel Prize winners in Csikszentmihalyi's sample were proud of their work not for the awards it received, but for its intrinsic satisfactions. Interestingly, it was the women in the sample who sometimes pointed to extrinsic satisfactions such as awards as a major source of pride. In large measure this was because they were keenly aware of the difficulties women have in getting institutional recognition for their scholarly work.

We must let our colleagues know that we value their creative contributions. And we must permit them to erect barriers against distractions, even when our own requests turn out to be one of those distractions.

VI: Model Intellectual Enthusiasm.

Rather than being a solitary enterprise, creativity is heightened by being around those who express intellectual enthusiasm for their own ideas and the ideas of others. There are three phrases that anyone who has had the good fortune to be around Jerry Zaltman hears him use frequently. They are: "I had an idea the other day." and "Yesterday I was reading a fascinating article." And, in response to the ideas of others, "That's interesting." And somehow those magical incantations produce more ideas, more fascination, and more interest.

This is the kind of stimulation and encouragement we can provide to our colleagues, especially those who are junior.

VII: Garner Resources.

To permit people to address important problems creatively, a field should be well connected to the rest of the social system in ways that bring in resources for doing excellent work.

As Alan Andreasen indicated in his 1992 ACR Presidential Address, there are many vitally-important, well-funded consumption arenas that are not being used by consumer researchers as the contexts for their theory-driven studies. Vast amounts of money are available to study attitudes, memory, persuasive communication, and social influence in contexts such as adolescent cigarette smoking, recycling behavior, the use of condoms to prevent HIV, and the household food insecurity of impoverished Third World consumers emulating Western food consumption patterns. In the next fiscal year, the State of Arizona alone will spend $15 million on tobacco prevention and education, much of it for research set in the context of this lethal form of consumption. Yet, oddly, many consumer researchers persist in studying small samples of undergraduates responding to fictitious brands, but, of course, noting this limitation. Our society is not ignoring its many consumption problems; it is paying economists, nutritionists, physicians, psychiatrists, and agricultural economists to do consumer research While several in our field have received research funding from breaking out of this box, many more could strengthen the creativity of their empirical work by garnering resources.

VIII: Facilitate Cross-Disciplinary Contact.

Because most scientific breakthroughs involve linking previously-unrelated information, creative people are gregarious in crossing disciplinary boundaries. Our field needs revitalization of its diversity of disciplinary perspectives to fuel our creative potential. While psychology offers a valuable approach to studying consumer behavior, so could other social science, biological science, and humanities disciplines that are annually scarce or absent at ACR. Scholars in those fields have not come knocking on our door in response to our annual laments to each other. We must be proactive in cultivating their participation and contributions.

We can do this when we send doctoral students across campus to take courses. We can read current material in other fields that has been assigned to our students, and then contact faculty across our campuses to discuss the relevance of their perspectives to consumer research. In so doing, we forge connections that enhance creative possibilities.

IX: Accommodate Personal Lives.

I would be remiss if I only addressed professional aspects of the sociocultural context that facilitate creativity. There is ample evidence of the inaccuracy of the image that links creativity with social isolation. Csikszentmihalyi found that his sample of eminent creative people, all over age 60, mostly enjoyed stable, committed marital relationships that contributed to the peace of mind needed for creative work.

The men in the sample thanked their wives for buffering them from many daily life distractions. In contrast, the women in the sample did not feel the need to express such thanks; in fact, they sometimes mentioned wishing they had a wife who would do such things for them.

Perhaps most interesting were the results of asking this sample, "Of the things you have done in life, of what are you most proud?" Given their biographies, it is not surprising that 70% mentioned professional accomplishments. What is somewhat surprising is that 30% mentioned their families as their greatest source of pride: this was 40% of the women and 25% of the men.

I am pleased that the University of Arizona Marketing Department has been the scholarly home for the production of 3/10 papers named as *JCR* Best Articles. Yet as proud as the faculty members who did their award-winning work in my department have been in receiving that award, they also each hold dearly to the vital importance of their familial relationships.

What that means is that our profession must make it possible for people to live full lives that include reciprocal, close relationships with others outside of work. Regardless of the professional awards or recognition someone attains for their creativity, we must recognize that they may not regard consumer research as their defining achievement as life draws to a close.

As this speech draws to a close, I hope my comments result in collective efforts to insure that our field provides a fertile context for nurturing creativity. We do not have to don out-of-fashion clothing or engage in erratic behavior, as imagined by my students. Instead, we only need to become active agents in constructing the community and culture that allow us to attain our collective creative goals.

Breaking Out of the Box: Meaning and Means

Gerald Zaltman, Harvard University

INTRODUCTION

As a field like ours matures, there is increased specialization. As a consequence, the field as a whole becomes more eclectic and richer while the viewpoints of individual researchers become more bounded. This paradox is compounded by exciting developments in the social and biological sciences and in the humanities, which themselves are increasingly fragmented. But, when these developments are considered they can broaden widely a researcher's perspective.

The fragmentation and narrowing of perspective produced by specialization would not be a problem except for two things. First, the consumer world isn't organized along disciplinary and subdisciplinary lines. People's lives don't follow the social organization of research. Second, the frontiers of knowledge are found disproportionately at the boundaries or intersections between fields rather than at the respective centers. If increased specialization causes us to look inward, it also creates great learning opportunities to look outward; we benefit from specialties that might intersect with our own, even if not in obvious ways.

One way to enjoy the upside of specialization (deeper insight) and limit its downside (overly narrow focus) is to develop switching rules. These are rules that enable us, on an *ad hoc* basis, to temporarily alter our frames of reference, to cross boundaries. Put differently, we need periodic sojourns to foreign intellectual lands. However, to change (and mix) metaphors, this does not mean licking the frosting on someone else's cake; it requires sufficient indentured servitude to see how the entire cake is baked. One needs to look deeply no matter where understanding is sought.

In the time available, I'd like to do two things. First, I'd like to comment briefly on the expression, "breaking out-of-the-box." Second, I'd like to reflect on commonalities among some rules-of-thumb for breaking out-of-the-box. These commonalities provide design criteria for developing ways of expanding our thinking.

Stressing individual rules-of-thumb is appropriate to the conference organizers' desire to use this plenary session as a launching pad for the sessions to follow. However, I would like to note that as important as individual rules-of-thumb are cultural forces have an even greater impact on individual creativity. These forces operate at the level of society, the discipline, and in our immediate places of work.

BREAKING OUT-OF-THE-BOX: THE MEANING

Metaphors are powerful because they simultaneously reveal and hide ideas. The breaking out-of-the-box metaphor highlights a need to escape the prison-like confines of customary thinking but hides the nature of the force required for a jailbreak. It conveys the freedom and refreshment of escape but hides the fact that breaking out of one box entails breaking into another. It even implies a limited number of directions in which to go. For me, breaking out-of-the-box brings forth the sharp sound and bright light of public commitment, followed by a torn and uninviting surface. Both make reentry unpleasant. This image hides the fact that our customary boxes generally serve us well: even when we "break out," we generally return. Recidivism isn't entirely bad. In my judgment, the problem is not in returning, but in the failure to leave frequently enough and long enough to collect worthwhile ideas for redecorating our primary lodging.

BREAKING OUT-OF-THE-BOX: THE MEANS

There are many guidelines for breaking out-of-the-box that appear to work well. I don't claim to practice many of them. It would drive me crazy. Also, it's a bit like typing. The skill works best when used tacitly. Once you start thinking about it, you start making errors and slow down. More importantly, thinking is a highly personal process. Thinking about thinking is even more so. Telling people how to think is even more of an affront than telling them what to think. It is unlikely that what works (sometimes) for me or someone else would work for you. However, there do seem to be some common, underlying reasons *why* various rules-of-thumb seem to work. Our task is to use these reasons as design criteria when developing our personal rules-of-thumb for thinking differently.

As a way of surfacing some design criteria, I will share a few guidelines I find helpful. Again, what is of interest are the processes they activate, not the guidelines themselves. So, as you listen, focus on what the underlying dynamic might be and how you do or could integrate it into your unique system of thought.

A preview of some of the implied design criteria as I "hear" them may be helpful. First, capitalize on what makes you restless. Second, develop an eye for and appreciation of the irregular. Third, be stubborn, but also be honest with others and above all with yourself. Fourth, develop wide cognitive peripheral vision. Fifth, be mischievous. Direct mischief mostly at yourself. Finally, follow your own counsel. If you are going to get in trouble, you might as well have the satisfaction of being the primary cause.

Commit a Crime: View Conclusions as Commencements.

It may have been Roger Schank who described researchers as detectives solving crimes. What are the crimes they solve? Tough research questions. But someone has to commit the crime—create the mischief—which may be difficult for detectives to do. Yet research findings—solved crimes —are great starting points for formulating new questions. Embedded in every conclusion is a commencement. Some simple questions to ask are, "What would I need to know that would make me uncomfortable with a conclusion (finding, etc.)?" "Do I know that this isn't so?" "What question would cause the most mischief with these results?" "What are the data mum or silent about?"

Get Out-of-Date.

Children automatically practice an important rule: "If it ain't broke, break it." This is consistent with my behavior as a child, my children's behavior, and the behavior of children visiting our home. I am convinced there is a gene for this. However, tremendous socialization processes eventually convert that rule to, "If it ain't broke, don't fix it."

My compromise in the tug of war between biology and society has produced the following valuable question: "How can I make what I do or know now, no matter how adequate it seems, look outdated or old fashioned as soon as possible?" Just having the question in mind serves as a filter for tying all kinds of seemingly irrelevant reading to my current research in a way that forces me to look at that research differently. The question helps focus attention on going somewhere else rather than being content where you are now.

Commitment to a Process Rather than an Outcome.

It is important to maintain a stronger commitment to the process of developing good ideas than to the outcomes or ideas themselves. Ideas aren't like diamonds—they don't last forever—although a good one can last a long time. The real value added is not so much in wearing a diamond but in mining in the right place, having the motivation to dig, recognizing an uncut diamond, and skillfully cutting it. I think a greater commitment to mining than to wearing good ideas keeps us from the trap of being enamored with our own thoughts and having someone else make us look out-of-date.

Cool Passion

One needs cool passion. Passion is necessary to fuel thinking, cool is required to harness the energy. Thinking must be acknowledged as the product of emotion and reason. Reliance on either alone is only half right and hence also half wrong. Reason and emotion need to co-mingle without censuring. One acquires new insights by allowing them to bump into one another and then adjudicating the conflict, if there is one.

The Courage of Your Convictions

When I was a graduate student seeking a faculty position where I could roam across fields comfortably, Everett Rogers offered me the following caution: if you plan to bridge fields, expect to be walked on. Breaking out-of-the-box is not for the faint of heart. You need to be willing to stand alone or, again switching metaphors, to be willing to wade into the mainstream before others even know where the mainstream is. This requires particularly careful preparation for one's position since it will be examined more closely than normal, as should be the case, by people in the domains being bridged. They don't like people just licking the frosting off their cake.

Think Generically.

It is important to formulate the generic question in any research effort. Put differently, why would someone in a different discipline or concerned with a different audience want to read my research results? The value of identifying the generic issue is twofold. First, it identifies literatures one may have missed that may contain useful ideas. For example, if I am interested in computer mediated communication as a marketing tool, I am also exploring the generic issue of how a sense of community and association is created, maintained, and lost. For this reason the literatures on community development and volunteerism, for example, might be very helpful. Second, identifying the generic issue helps broaden applications within marketing.

Wonder about the Crumpled Horn.

Remember the cow with the crumpled horn (that tossed the dog, that worried the cat, that ate the rat, and so on, in *This is the House that Jack Built*)? Weren't you curious about, "Who crumpled the cow's horn?" "Why did they do it?" "How did it happen?" "Has the cow discovered it yet?" And I must admit to wondering, "How would I crumple a cow's horn?" The basic rule-of-thumb here is, what irregularity might I create that would add life to an issue? Remember that we are wired to think causally when we perceive irregularities: we see something unexpected (asymmetric) and wonder what caused it. A crushed can or a crumpled horn, for instance, engages our attention more than an undamaged one standing next to it. The crushed can or horn is more interesting: it has a past.

Remove the Shin Guards On Your Research.

I get physically fidgety when people present research in which they have not allowed for surprises. They know what the results will be well in advance of their data collection and these certainly don't include crumpled horns. The research process was too careful and protective. When I ask why a particular result wouldn't be obtained I usually receive a puzzled look. Their research is wearing shin guards. This lessens the likelihood of having conclusions which contain interesting commencements.

Avoid Premature Dismissal.

One cause of narrow cognitive peripheral vision is the tendency to dismiss ideas without first asking about the importance of their consequences *if* they were true. That is, we should ask first, "Would there be significant consequences if this idea or theory had substantial support?" If the answer is yes, then it pays to proceed and assess its conceptual and/or technical validity. I think we assess validity differently (maybe more leniently) when we think something is of greater rather than lesser consequence. We tend to too easily dismiss ideas because they don't appear on the surface or on initial inspection to have validity or merit. Hence, we never get to assess their utility. When I read something speculative in neuroscience, for instance, I find I understand it better and appreciate it more if I begin by saying, "Let's suppose this was correct, what does it imply or say about surfacing mental models or designing advertising?" Pragmatic validity becomes a useful truth test to help avoid premature dismissal.

UNDERLYING PROCESSES

What do rules-of-thumb such as these have in common? What are the implied design criteria that might help you create rules-of-thumb more compatible with your own habits of mind? Some criteria will be suggested by describing certain design questions. First, there is a kind of *restlessness* implied, especially in trying to make your own work out-of-date as soon as possible or in viewing conclusions as commencements. The design question to answer is: what makes you restless? Whatever that is, maintain a big dose of it.

Wondering about the crumpled horn, being as committed to the research process as you are to an outcome, taking the shin guards off, and getting out-of-date share an *appreciation of the irregular*; a welcoming attitude toward the unexpected. The design question here is: "How do I increase the chances of encountering anomalies and improve my skills in detecting them?" Relatedly, "How do I create anomalies?"

The matters of cool passion, being committed to the process of generating quality ideas more than to the ideas themselves and maintaining the courage of your convictions, share the notion of reasoned but visceral stubbornness. When you think and feel you are right, *be stubborn* and strong enough to support those who are walking on you. Stubbornness is made easier by having deep knowledge of the fields you are bridging, i.e., by demonstrating that you know how their respective cakes are baked and by seeing convergence on an idea from different fields. The design question to be answered here is: "What 'foreign' fields are most fun and most important to visit?" Whatever these are, go often and stay a while.

Thinking generically and avoiding premature dismissal also helps you get out-of-date and perceive the new questions in your findings. This brings the quality of *wide cognitive peripheral vision* to your research. This, in turn, requires curiosity about crumpled horns and an inclination to cause one or two. The design questions to answer here are: "What makes you curious and nosy to the point of being mischievous?" "What tempts you to break things that appear fixed?"

CONCLUSION

In all of this you need *honesty* with yourself. You've got to be as able and willing to say you are wrong as you are that you are right and to do so publicly as well as privately. You've also got to *honor someone else's ideas* no matter how ordinary they may seem. There is always a good chance that you just don't know enough to see the crumpled horn or the courage in their work.

New Approaches to The Role of Similarity in Consumer Research

Shi Zhang, Columbia University
Kathryn A. Fitzgerald, University of California-Los Angeles

Similarity is a central component of many cognitive processes and theories of categorization and concept learning, both in psychology and in applied field such as consumer behavior. It is also an elusive concept resistant to comprehensive yet precise definition. Recent advances in theories of similarity have opened new avenues for consumer researchers to examine a range of empirical problems. The objectives of this special session are twofold: (1) to generate an appreciation of the important role that can be played by the new approaches to similarity in consumer behavior research, and (2) to advance recently developed theories of similarity by providing empirical evidence from the field of marketing and consumer research, thus establishing a direction for coordinated future research in the field of consumer behavior.

Consumer research has been influenced by the contrast model (Tversky, 1977), and has utilized it as the basis for constructing theories of brand-extension, consumer learning and product categorization (Block and Johnson 1995, Dhar and Sherman 1996, Loken and Ward 1989, Park et al 1990, among others). This model represents a significant advance over the mental distance model (e.g. Shepard 1974, Rips, Shoben and Smith 1973). Recent theoretical advances have extended the contrast model by identifying and addressing some incompleteness of the model (e.g. Medin, Goldstone and Gentner 1990). In particular, researchers have questioned the assumption that similarity between two items can be represented by lists of features alone and that judgement of similarity simply requires direct feature mapping between the lists (aside from differential weights given to the features). It is proposed that similarity is best characterized as a comparison of structured representations (e.g. Falkenhainer, Forbus and Gentner 1989, Gentner and Markman 1994, Markman and Gentner 1993). The representations are composed of features (i.e. attributes) of objects, objects, and functions, and more importantly, the relations between these representational elements. In other words, similarity is a function of both attributes and the relations of the attributes between a pair of items.

The papers in this session each explored the use of the above views or closely-related views of similarity in different areas of application: product concept learning, consideration set formation, and cross-cultural variation in similarity-directed conceptual organization. Taken together, the papers suggest the inappropriateness of feature-bundle views of products.

Kathryn Fitzgerald presented a paper that uses theory concerning analogical reasoning, the theoretical underpinning of the structured view of similarity, to examine consumers' learning about novel products and products with complex feature structures. Learning about new offerings stimulates comparison to familiar products, which in turn involves similarity judgment. As the novelty of a new product introduction increases, detecting similarity becomes less routine and must be created. This is accomplished by constructing a mapping that aligns systems of elements. Such a mapping provides a basis for creating inferences about attribute-consequence linkages (likely price changes over time, and other attitudinal and purchase-relevant issues). The paper showed that the use of analogy was distinguishable from a previously studied form of advertising rhetoric, resonance. Both analogy and resonance were found to have a substantial presence in advertising of products in complex and very new categories.

The second paper by Felcher, Malaviya and McGill draws upon recent research that examines the type of features that objects are perceived to share. One notion of similarity is that judgments are influenced by whether the feature structure consists of attributional or relational features. Other research suggests that objects could also share features that are context-independent or context-dependent. This paper builds on these two observations and examines their implications for various choice processes, including the formation of consideration sets. Similarity is construed on both these distinctions, and it yields distinct results in the formation of consideration sets (via categorization). When taxonomic categories are the basis for the consideration set formation, attributional features and context-independent features are invoked, but when goal-derived categories drive consideration of alternatives, relational aspects and context-dependent features become focal. These differences, as shown by the results, influence consumer learning, memory, and generation of additional alternatives when making within and across-category product comparisons. Results also show that subjects who are more familiar with a consumption situation are likely to construct more narrowly defined, within category choice sets, whereas less familiar consumers construct broader, across-category choice sets.

Finally, the paper by Schmitt and Zhang focused on the process of categorization and similarity judgment, and its impact on judgment and choice. It proposes that cognitive systems of different language-based segments of consumers influence their mental representation of objects, recall of the objects, and judgment of products (attitude towards the product). In this approach to studying consumer categorization, similarity is no longer manipulated, but rather is assumed to be part of the cognitive system of groups of consumers (Chinese vs. Japanese vs. English). One of the paper's foci centers on the automatic aspect of information processing embodied in language classifiers. We conceptualize classifiers as possessing both attributional and conceptual similarities of objects. For example, the classifier "ba" for items that are graspable or have handles (e.g. knife, umbrella, comb, paper fan) can be said to relate items with a perceptual property, a handle, or with a conceptual property, graspability. Classifiers represent a general classification category that takes as members many diverse objects. These objects fall naturally into the traditional characterization of non-comparable. Experiments 1-3 show how the presence of classifiers in Chinese and their absence in English affect the perceived similarity between objects, attribute accessibility and concept organization. Experiment 4 demonstrates the differential effect of classifier structures in Chinese and Japanese on perceived similarity. Experiments 5-7 demonstrate the role that classifiers play in inference-making, judgments and choice. These results not only provide support for the linguistic relativity hypothesis but also suggest new ways of segmenting consumers on the basis of language-influenced cognition.

Joan Meyers-Levy, as synthesizer, provided directions for future studies by raising a series of questions regarding inference-making in a featural context. Some of these questions are: How do people resolve incompatibilities in inferences suggested by difference factors? Do inferences suggested by visual factors dominate those implied by verbal factors (e.g. analogy-driven advertisements)? What factors qualify when these (inference) effects emerge? She also encouraged future research on the role of common features and their associated inferences, the development sequence of sensitivity to such factors in conjunction with difference features.

Cognitive Appraisals, Consumer Emotions, and Consumer Response

Anand Kumar, Vanderbilt University

Richard L. Oliver, Vanderbilt University

In the past few years marketing practitioners have increasingly turned their attention to understanding consumer emotions. These practitioners believe that the best way to gain customer loyalty is to ensure that customers have an "emotional" experience with products or services. However, there is a big gap in management's understanding of what constitutes an emotional experience for a consumer. This issue, until recently, was a black box to academic scholars as well. The situation is now changing with the growing acceptance by cognitive psychologists of an appraisal theory of emotions. This theory has been widely tested recently and so far has stood up well to empirical analysis. The theory proposes that emotions are formed as a result of a process of appraisals of what an event/stimulus can do for one's well-being. Further, the pattern of evaluations made by an individual on a small set of appraisals determines what emotions are felt by the person. Cognitive psychologists are now trying to understand the appraisals associated with different emotions, and also the antecedents of these appraisals.

Current appraisal theory of emotion has potential for application in different areas of consumer behavior research. Research based on this theory can help us understand what appraisals would constitute a particular "emotional experience" for consumers. This has implications for design of service environments, product features, etc. Yet, in spite of its potential wide ranging application to consumer behavior research, there has been very little work in marketing based on appraisal theory. This session tried to stimulate consumer researchers' interest in applying recent advances in appraisal theory and in the study of emotions to improve our understanding of consumer emotions. The session included a theoretical presentation, which introduced the appraisal approach to studying emotions and its relationship to current postpurchase response frameworks, and two presentations which showed the application of appraisal theory in two different consumer behavior contexts.

The first presentation by Craig A. Smith and Richard L. Oliver consisted of two parts. In the first part, Smith provided a theoretical overview of the appraisal approach to emotion. This approach posits that one's emotional state is a product of how one appraises, or evaluates, the implications of one's circumstances for personal well-being. Different evaluations are hypothesized to result in the experience of different emotions. For instance, fear results from appraisals of danger or threat, sadness from the appraisal of an irreparable harm or loss, anger from blaming someone else for an undesirable situation, and so on. A specific model detailing both the key issues, or questions, evaluated in appraisal, and the specific appraisal outcomes, or cognitions, that were associated with specific emotions (e.g., anger) was described. At a global level, the two main appraisal issues that are addressed are–"What's at stake?" and "What resources and options do I have to cope with what's happening?" Empirical evidence supporting the model was reviewed, and the conceptual relations between the appraisals associated with specific emotions and the adaptational functions proposed to be served by those emotions were also discussed. It was emphasized that the appraisal approach also enabled researchers to make inferences about the kind of cognitions or evaluations made by consumers based on a knowledge of their emotional experience.

In the second part, Oliver discussed appraisal theory in the context of current frameworks of postpurchase response. Beginning with the expectancy disconfirmation model, he suggested how disconfirmation may be evocative of various consumption-specific appraisals consistent with those in appraisal theory. Using an approach similar to that of Ortony, Clore, and Collins (1988), disconfirmation was viewed as priming an appraisal structure consisting of three branches, namely the favorable outcome sequence, the unfavorable outcome sequence, and the surprising outcome sequence. Each sequence was further evaluated in terms of whether the outcome was yet to happen, has happened, or has not yet happened and is unlikely to do so. The specific emotions resulting from these appraisal sequences were shown to describe the affective content of the satisfaction response as currently interpreted and as reported in Oliver (1997).

The second paper, by Baggozi and Gopinath, showed the results of three studies designed to test the effects of particular combinations of appraisals in service settings upon discrete emotions and coping responses. The studies used a framework built on Roseman's (1991) structural theory of the determination of emotions by cognitive appraisals, which was similar in form and content to that proposed by Lazarus (1991), Smith and Ellsworth (1985, 1987), and others.

Study 1 was a 2 (low/high motive inconsistency) x 2 (low/high power) x 3 (agency: self, other, circumstances) experiment. Subjects (N=200) read a brief scenario about a protagonist (self) experiencing a breakdown with the transmission in their car and subsequent encounter with a repair person. The appraisals were manipulated so as to produce one or more of nine emotions (e.g., disgust, frustration, anger) and one or more of twenty action tendencies or coping responses (e.g., want to seek comfort or advice). High and low motive inconsistency were manipulated by the cost to the consumer ($360 vs. $36). High and low power were manipulated by giving the person relevant foreknowledge or not with respect to actions taken. Agency was manipulated by having the self, another person, or an accident produce the failure.

The expected three-way interaction was found, but only for the self and not the protagonists. Main effects were found for disgust, frustration, anger, dislike, regret, shame, and guilt, but not distress or sadness. Moreover, each emotion was related to action tendencies, according to predictions (e.g.,disgust or boil inside, want to hurt or lash out). Gender differences were found as well.

Studies 2 and 3 manipulated appraisal conditions in a 2 (motive consistent/inconsistent) x 2 (pleasant/unpleasant) x 3 (agency: self, other, circumstances) design. Study 2 (N=202) was conducted in Kerala, India; Study 3 was conducted in Ann Arbor, Michigan (N=220). The setting in both was decision making with friends in a movie going context. A scenario approach was again used with both a protagonist and the self as the focal person. Motive consistency/inconsistency was manipulated with either a good or bad movie outcome. Pleasantness and unpleasantness were manipulated through different process oriented experiences related to comfort of seats, air conditioning, noise level, ambiance, etc. Agency was manipulated by protagonist (self) convincing others to see a particular movie, a friend convincing all, or the circumstances leading to the choice.

Combinations of appraisals were found to predict intensity of experienced emotions, specific action tendencies and coping responses to the positive and negative emotions. Moreover, based on work done by Frijda et al (1989), action tendencies and emotions were correlated with each other according to theories of coping. Example action tendencies and coping responses were wanting to patronize the theater again, positive or negative word of mouth, complaint behaviors, asking for refund, wanting to lash out, seek comfort, or hide feelings. Gender and cross-cultural differences in the pattern and intensity of emotional experience and in coping were found.

The third paper by Kumar and Olshavsky presented the results of a study which used appraisal theory as the basis for distinguishing between satisfaction and delight. The results of two studies were presented as evidence of the distinction between delight and satisfaction. The first study was done in three phases. In the first phase, subjects defined what they thought was meant by satisfaction and delight in a consumption context. In the second phase, a different set of subjects described recent personal experiences where they felt satisfied or delighted (between subjects design was used in this phase) as consumers. The responses from these two phases were coded by independent judges and then analyzed to identify differences between satisfaction and delight. The results indicated that satisfaction was associated with subjects' expectations being met, subjects feeling they got "fair" value, and subjects feeling contented, while delight was associated with subjects feeling surprised, their expectations being exceeded, and feelings of elation. In the third phase, subjects were prompted with a long list of phrases and emotion adjectives and asked whether each phrase/ emotion was characteristic of consumption situations where they experienced satisfaction or delight. They also had the options of saying that the phrases or emotions were equally characteristic of both satisfaction and delight or neither characteristic of satisfaction or delight. The results indicated that satisfaction and delight clearly differed in many more respects than what was revealed in the first two phases of this study.

In the second study, the authors first identified a set of appraisals which may be relevant in a consumption context. This was done on the basis of a review of the emotions literature and the marketing literature. The literature review identified appraisals that were likely to be made in consumption contexts. Next, an air travel scenario was used to systematically manipulate the appraisal of volition (i.e., extent to which customer perceives firm's actions as being done volitionally by the firm and not under pressure) and the extent of surprise. A 2 (volition: high/low) x 2 (surprise: high/low) between subjects design was used. Scales were developed and validated to measure other appraisal dimensions that were considered relevant in consumption situations. The emotions of satisfaction and delight were also measured. It was found that, as hypothesized, there were differences in the set of appraisals that predicted the emotions of satisfaction and delight. Specifically, the perceptions of volition was found to be a significant predictor of delight and not a significant predictor of satisfaction.

The session ended with Mark Peterson, the session synthesizer, emphasizing the significance of the real world applications of the research presented in the session. Mark encouraged questions from the audience and this led to a lively discussion on appraisal theory and consumer emotions.

REFERENCES

Frijda, N.H., Kuipers, P., & ter Schure, E. (1989), "Relations among emotion, appraisal, and emotional action readiness," *Journal of Personality and Social Psychology*, 57, 212-228.

Lazarus, R.S. (1991), *Emotion and adaptation*. New York: Oxford University Press.

Oliver, R.L. (1997), *Satisfaction: A Behavioral Perspective on the Consumer*, New York: McGraw Hill.

Ortony, A., Clore, G.L., and Collins, A. (1988), *The Cognitive Structure of Emotions*, Cambridge, England: Cambridge University Press.

Roseman, I.J. (1991), "Appraisal determinants of discrete emotions," *Cognition and Emotion*, 5, 161-200.

Smith, C.A., & Ellsworth, P.C. (1985), "Patterns of cognitive appraisal in emotion," *Journal of Personality and Social Psychology*, 48, 813-838.

Smith, C.A., & Ellsworth, P.C. (1987), "Patterns of appraisal and emotion related to taking an exam," *Journal of Personality and Social Psychology*, 52, 475-488.

All in the Family: Intergenerational Influences on Consumer Behavior
Elizabeth S. Moore-Shay, University of Illinois

SESSION OVERVIEW

The generational transmission of knowledge, resources and orientations within the family is a fundamental mechanism through which a culture both maintains and reproduces itself. Through communication, both explicit and unspoken, cultural precepts and understandings are made available to, and internalized by, the individual. Questions that focus on how this process occurs and what aspects are reproduced are central to intergenerational inquiry. The objectives of this special session were to: (1) examine how intergenerational influence is manifested at various stages of the life course, (2) explore the processes of intergenerational transmission, and (3) highlight the synergies obtained through the use of multiple perspectives and methods in intergenerational study. The session addressed these issues both conceptually and on the basis of empirical evidence drawn from textual analysis, life-histories, depth interviews and survey methods.

Derived from traditional socialization theory, intergenerational research has emphasized childhood learning in recognition of the significant impact these early experiences may have in shaping patterns of thought and behavior later in life. As an emerging research area, empirical efforts have tended to focus on the documentation of the phenomenon rather than its explanation. Although there is evidence suggesting that intergenerational patterns may take a variety of forms ranging from the sharing of specific preferences to more overarching attitudes about the marketplace (e.g., Arndt 1972; Carlson et al. 1994; Childers and Rao 1992; Moore-Shay and Lutz 1988), relatively little is known about the processes by which influence occurs or the forces that generate solidarity beyond childhood.

To understand the role of heritage in the acquisition and maintenance of consumer preferences and decision making requires a broader perspective than has typified research in this area. Intergenerational processes are at work across the life course, taking on new forms as a function of the developmental or ontogenetic status of each generation. Relationships are renegotiated as parents, children and grandparents take on new roles and relinquish others. Attention to the evolutionary dimensions of family influence, how generational processes are influenced by the historical context in which family members are embedded, as well as the fundamental processes by which intergenerational influence occurs are significant issues, and the collective focus of the three papers that were presented in this session.

SUMMARY OF INDIVIDUAL PAPERS

Intergenerational Product Transfer: The Advertising Factor
Barbara Olsen, SUNY Old Westbury

Over the course of the last 60 to 100 years, certain product categories and brands have become firmly woven into our family histories and the tapestry of everyday life. In this paper, Olsen brings a broader perspective to the investigation of intergenerational transfer of favored brands through the inclusion of grandparent, as well as parent and child generations (Olsen 1993; 1995). Interviews with three generations of family members were conducted, revealing a lasting relationship with product categories and brands (76 families). Great grandparent and grandparent generations figured significantly in the initial product adoption within these families.

According to Olsen, ancestral generations established family patterns for product preference; and advertising archival data resonate with the promotional logic that helped to forge bonds between brands and consumers. However, potential customers had to be convinced initially of the need for a new product, and persuaded to buy a particular brand. When interviewed, grandparents reported seemingly adequate solutions to daily needs without resorting to store-bought commodities. New products were often perceived as superfluous.

Drawing upon advertising archival data, Olsen suggests that early advertising strategies for seminal brands reveal the nuances of persuasion that turned earlier generations into consumers. Early promotional approaches are illustrated in advertising copy appeals that sold then revolutionary product ideas such as deodorant, rubber heels, nail polish, laundry soap, baby powder, new food forms and cosmetic preparations. Her analysis suggests that the persuasive appeals for these brands were variously based on intimidation, social ostracism and fear, as well as information for keeping up with "modern" times. Olsen suggests that many of the themes established in the early twentieth century resonate today in contemporary family values and consumption aesthetics.

Investigating the Processes of Intergenerational Transfer: A Coorientational Approach
Elizabeth S. Moore-Shay, University of Illinois
Richard J. Lutz, University of Florida

Reflecting the inherent difficulties involved in studying socialization, little is known about the processes by which parents influence the development of their children's brand preferences, decision strategies and marketplace beliefs. Researchers have identified three primary learning processes: (1) observation or modeling, (2) direct communication, and (3) experiential learning (Ward, Wackman and Wartella 1977). Though researchers have identified these processes in conceptual terms, appropriate methodologies have not yet been applied to examine these learning processes empirically. Drawing upon a coorientational model of interpersonal communications, Moore-Shay and Lutz examined the relative contribution of these learning processes within mother-daughter dyads.

The coorientational model is predicated on the assumption that the influence an individual has on someone else's point of view cannot be adequately understood through simple measures of consensus (MacLeod and Chaffee 1972). While measures of agreement provide an index of intergenerational convergence, such measures indicate little about the transmission process when considered in isolation. The measurement models posits two additional structural relations. One of these, accuracy, was incorporated in the empirical research presented. Defined as the individual's ability to state correctly the cognitions of the other person in the dyad, accuracy is viewed as an essential indicant of communication effectiveness. From the levels of agreement and accuracy observed in mother-daughter dyads, the relative contribution of each of the primary learning processes to intergenerational transfer may be inferred.

Female college students and their mothers (n=103 dyads) completed questionnaires independently, which asked them to report their own preferences and beliefs as well as predict those of their partner. Survey findings revealed significant intergenerational agreement across brand and product preferences, shopping rules and marketplace beliefs. The level of brand preference similarity increased substantially when brands were visible within the home, thus providing opportunities for observational learning. When coupled with low levels of accuracy, learning might be attributed to modeling influences. Effective intra familial communication, on the other hand, was reflected through moderate to high levels of accuracy irrespective of the level of agreement evident within the dyad. Experiential learning, operationalized as a daughter's involvement in household shopping had little incremental impact on the transmission of beliefs and preferences when mother-daughter communication was substantial. The bidirectionality of intergenerational influences was apparent in the relative insight or accuracy mothers and daughters had into one another's preferences. Illustrated by this study is the potential value the coorientational approach offers in extending understanding of intergenerational phenomena beyond a straightforward description of the presence or absence of carryover effects.

Women as Generation-Spanners: A Longitudinal Study of Giving to Parents and Grandparents, and Giving as Parents
Cele Otnes, University of Illinois
Tina M. Lowrey, Rider University
Mary Ann McGrath, Loyola University, Chicago

While the topic of gift giving has been vigorously investigated in consumer behavior, the way in which recipient characteristics influence the selection of gifts has not been fully explored. In this paper, Otnes, Lowery and McGrath examine this issue through the analysis of longitudinal data collected during the 1990, 1992 and 1994 Christmas seasons. They studied the ways in which five key informants shopped for their children, parents and grandparents, incorporating a total of 25 recipients. Each year, two long interviews and two shopping trips were conducted with these informants, yielding over 500 pages of text. Through use of the analytical method of pattern recognition (Lincoln and Guba 1985), themes that emerged when shopping for children, parents and grandparents were explored.

By interacting with the informants over a span of five years, the authors were able to trace the ways that gift exchange changed for the different generations of recipients, to compare the constraints that existed in giving to each generation, and subsequently to articulate the strategies used for these recipients. For example, it became apparent that givers expressed similar roles to recipients during Christmas gift giving (Otnes, Lowrey and Kim 1993). However, this study revealed that motivations for expressing these roles might differ greatly, depending upon the generation of the recipient. For example, the authors observed that when givers expressed the role of Compensator to their children, they were typically "making up" for the loss of a material good, and often merely replaced that object through their gift selection. However, when expressing the role of Compensator to a parent or grandparent, the informants apparently were attempting to make up for a more permanent loss (such as the loss of a loved one or the loss of one's health). As such, the gifts they gave could not be direct replacements, and the giver felt compelled to explain how the products or services they selected could serve as compensatory items at all.

Moreover, the informants described different constraints when shopping for recipients at different stages of the life cycle. For example, children were often categorized as being too young to "need anything," parents were often so financially well off that they "had everything," and grandparents were often in ill health or had other physical restraints that made gift selection challenging. The paper lends insight into how roles expressed through gift exchange are influenced by such developments as entry into school, puberty and, on the other end of the spectrum, illness, widowhood and retirement.

Synthesis of Session
Les Carlson, Clemson University

In his synthesis of the three papers, Les Carlson raised a number of important theoretical and methodological issues. Recognizing the challenges inherent in intergenerational research, he argued that interpretive approaches used in conjunction with more traditional methods, offer great opportunity to further understanding in this area. Disentangling the influence of one family member on another, from other outside influences, is a formidable task both conceptually and empirically. Use of interpretive approaches may be particularly useful in clarifying complexities introduced by other socialization agents, as well as in deepening understanding of the nature and structure of family communications. He also suggested that perspectives on intergenerational influence might be enriched through a merging of existing theoretical paradigms with the interpretations and coorientational findings represented in the three papers. In particular, he noted that consideration of the theoretical frameworks that have proved useful in the classification of parent-child interaction patterns as well as parents' consumer socialization tendencies might serve to strengthen and extend conceptualization in this area. Through an illustration drawn from each of the three papers, he showed how consideration of parental communication styles might lend additional insight into the empirical findings presented, as well as frame research questions for the future.

REFERENCES

Arndt, Johan (1972), Intrafamilial Homogeneity for Perceived Risk and Opinion Leadership, *Journal of Advertising*, 1 (1), 40-47.

Carlson, Les, Ann Walsh, Russell N. Laczniak and Sanford Grossbart (1994), Family Communication Patterns and Marketplace Motivations, Attitudes, and Behaviors of Children and Mothers, *Journal of Consumer Affairs*, 28 (1), 25-53.

Childers, Terry L. and Akshay R. Rao (1992), The Influence of Familial and Peer-based Reference Groups on Consumer Decisions, *Journal of Consumer Research*, 19 (2), 198-211.

Lincoln, Yvonna and Egon G. Guba (1985), *Naturalistic Inquiry*, Beverly Hills, CA: Sage.

McLeod, Jack M. and Steven H. Chaffee (1972), "The Construction of Social Reality," in *The Social Influence Process*, ed. J. T. Tedeschi, Chicago: Aldine-Altherton, 50-99.

Moore-Shay, Elizabeth S. and Richard J. Lutz (1988), Intergenerational Influences in the Formation of Consumer Attitudes and Beliefs About the Marketplace: Mothers and Daughters, in *Advances in Consumer Research*, Vol. 15, M.J. Houston (ed.), Provo, UT: Association for Consumer Research, 461-467.

Olsen, Barbara (1993), "Brand Loyalty and Lineage: Exploring New Dimensions for Research, in *Advances in Consumer Research*, Vol. 20, L. McAllister and M. L. Rothschild (eds.), Provo, UT: Association for Consumer Research, 575-579.

Olsen, Barbara (1995), "Brand Loyalty and Consumption Patterns: The Lineage Factor," in *Contemporary Marketing and Consumer Behavior: An Autobiographical Sourcebook*, J.F. Sherry, Jr. (ed.), Sage, Newbury Park, CA: 245-281.

Otnes, Cele, Tina M. Lowrey and Young Chan Kim (1993), "Gift Selection for Easy and Difficult Recipients: A Social Roles Interpretation," *Journal of Consumer Research*, 20 (September), 229-244.

Ward, Scott, Daniel B. Wackman, and Ellen Wartella (1977), *How Children Learn to Buy: The Development of Consumer Information Processing Skills*, Beverly Hills, CA: Sage.

Consuming Desire and Desirous Consumption: Toward a Deeper Understanding of the Social Construction of Consumer Wants and the Nature of Consumption Symbolism

Craig J. Thompson, University of Wisconsin at Madison
Douglas B. Holt, Penn State University

The social construction of *consumer desire* has played a pivotal role in the emergence of the modern consumer economy (Campbell 1987; Falk 1994; Forty 1984; Leach 1993). However, the consumer research literature has scarcely addressed this construct in any systematic way. The three studies presented in this special session sought to bridge this gap by drawing from historical research, cultural analyses, and poststructural theories to analyze the construct of desire. The three presentations respectively addressed cross-cultural differences in consumer desire, the symbolic expression of desire through sexually evocative advertising, and the role of desire in forming and maintaining consumer lifestyles.

BACKGROUND

An important historical work that provided a conceptual linkage across the three presentations was Campbell's (1987) *The Romantic Ethic and the Spirit of Modern Consumerism*. While Campbell does address institutional factors—such as mass production and transformations in the socio-economic order—his analysis of consumer desire has a decided experiential focus. In brief, Campbell contends that consumer culture has emerged from a Romantic orientation that he describes as modern hedonism. Whereas the traditional hedonist sought immediate gratification, Campbell argues that the modern hedonist revels in an imaginative longing for consumption experiences that are not readily attainable. Rather than affording experiences of frustration, however, the delay of gratification heightens desire and provides a context for pleasurable states of reverie. Campbell further argues that these rich consumptive fantasies have the paradoxical outcome of "rendering real consumption as a disillusioning experience" (Campbell 1987, p.89). From this perspective, the modern phenomenon of seemingly inexhaustible consumer "wants" is portrayed as a cycle of anticipatory desire and experienced disappointment in which consumers constantly desire yet-to-be possessed products toward which they can direct new dreams and fantasies.

Campbell's historical analysis of consumer desire offers an intriguing thesis by positing a triadic linkage between consumer fantasy and dreams, the self-generation of desire, and the symbolic manifestations of these desires in coveted material goods. The papers in this session developed this implication by investigating the manifestation of consumer desire across a number of different consumption contexts and by bringing to bear three distinct research perspectives.

SUMMARY OF THE PRESENTATIONS

Belk, Ger, and Askegaard investigated whether the nature and focus of consumer desires differs across cultures. Projective fantasy measures were used to the tap the deep psychological dimensions of the construct. Using collages, story-telling, sentence completion, and word associations, they found that, while desire is similarly regarded as an intense emotional state in the United States, Turkey, and Denmark, its expression and focus differ across these cultures and by gender. Across cultures, however, the urgency and intense emotional nature of consumer desire were found to be remarkably similar. They contrasted this finding to more typical and prosaic depictions of consumers' demand for goods and ser-

vices. By utilizing projective measures, a rich fantasy laden realm of consumption aspirations was revealed that had gone largely undetected in the majority of consumer research. They discussed cultural and gender differences that harbor social and political issues about how and what people want. These issues were outlined and an agenda for further research was described.

Elliott employed a poststructuralist perspective to analyze the relationship between advertising imagery, language, and the construction of consumer desire. Drawing from the work of Lacan (1977), he argued that desire emerges in the void between that which can be expressed in language and the flux of bodily emotions and unconscious impulses. From this perspective, consumption practices may function as a language of desire by symbolically representing unconscious wishes that may be expressed more easily once they have been portrayed. Elliott proposed that this symbolic function is particularly relevant to the psychological effects generated by the sexualization of many consumer goods through advertising. He further suggested that the symbolic function of advertising is particularly important to younger consumers (i.e., adolescents and young adults) who are in the process of negotiating psychological conflicts related to identity and sexuality. To highlight some of these discourses of desire, a number of advertisements targeted at younger consumers were deconstructed using a Lacanian framework. The analysis revealed several standard image formats used to evoke a sexualized reading of the advertisement and to ascribe the advertised product in a nexus of desirous, sexualized meanings.

Holt and Thompson analyzed the relationship between desire, lifestyle, and community. They first discussed a genre of social theory contending that the traditional bonds of community have been eroded by the conditions of modernity and, hence, individuals face increasing difficulty in forging and sustaining a viable sense of collective identity (Bellah et al 1985; Gergen 1991; Morris 1996). Holt and Thompson contended that the very notion of a traditional, socially integrated, and emotionally bound community is a mythical construct. They proposed that this mythic ideal generates consumer desires that can only be realized symbolically and that require consumers to engage in complex interpretive activities to insulate their symbolically constructed lifestyle enclaves from the challenges wrought by everyday experience. Their analysis showed that consumers' appropriation of this Utopian image of the close-knit traditional community, and its corresponding desires, provided a potent principle of social affiliation and a foundation for the consumption meanings that characterize the "new traditionalist" lifestyle.

Tom O'Guinn served as the session synthesizer. He drew from his own research on symbolic consumption and the effects of mass media on consumer perceptions to synthesize the various perspectives offered on consumer desire and to moderate the ensuing discussion of the presentations.

In sum, a good time was had by all.

REFERENCES

Bellah, Robert, Richard Madsen, William Sullivan, Ann Swindler, and Steven Tipton (1985), *Habits of the Heart*, New York: Harper & Row.

Campbell, Colin (1987) *The Romantic Ethic and the Spirit of Romantic Consumerism*, Oxford, UK: Blackwell.

Falk, Pasi (1994), *The Consuming Body*, London: Sage.

Forty, Adrian (1986), *Objects of Desire*,

Gergen, Kenneth J. (1991), *The Saturated Self: Dilemmas of Identity in Contemporary Life*, New York, NY: Basic Books.

Lacan, Jacques (1977), *Ecrits: A Selection*, London; Tavistock.

Leach, William (1993), *Land of Desire*, New York: Pantheon.

McCracken, Grant (1988), *Culture and Consumption*, Bloomington, IN: Indiana University Press.

Morris, Paul (1996), "Community Beyond Tradition," in *Detraditionalization*, eds. Paul Heelas, Scott Lash, and Paul Morris, London: Blackwell, 223-249.

Consumer Desire in Three Cultures: Results from Projective Research

Russell W. Belk, University of Utah
Güliz Ger, Bilkent University
Søren Askegaard, Odense University

ABSTRACT

Using collages, story-telling, sentence completion, word associations, and other projective techniques, we investigated the nature of consumer desire among students in the United States, Turkey, and Denmark. While we detected some cultural differences, gender differences were generally stronger and tended to be similar across the three cultures. Desire is primarily interpersonal, but it's interpersonal nature differs between men and women. For both men and women however, consumer desire is an intensely passionate positive emotional experience steeped in fantasies and dreams rather than an experience involving reasoned judgments. Desires are also dangerous, both because they are often transgressive and because they threaten a loss of control. We further found a cycle of desire in which, either because desire has been rationalized or realized, it is tamed and must be revitalized through developing new foci.

CONSUMER DESIRE

This paper is part of an on-going multi-method multi-cultural study by the authors into the nature of consumer desire. As discussed in an earlier paper exploring metaphors of consumer desire in English, Turkish, Danish, and French (Belk, Ger, and Askegaard 1996), desires are seldom mentioned in the consumer behavior literature, and are generally either trivialized as wants or naturalized as needs. But we contend that desires are instead belief-based passions that involve longing, yearning, and fervently wishing for something. In our earlier work we found that three of the most widely used metaphors for characterizing consumer desire are hunger (or thirst), sexual lust, and addiction. We may speak of hungering for, lusting after, or craving certain consumer goods as if they were delicious foods, alluring sexual mates, or addictive drugs. It is this intensity of feeling toward objects of our desire that we wish to better understand.

We believe that current approaches to human motivation in general and consumer motivation in particular are limited through their instrumental and utilitarian use of ubiquitous need satisfaction models. Such perspectives not only miss much of the rich symbolic meanings of consumer goods, but also neglect the essentially emotional manner in which consumers may well relate to these goods. By focusing on consumer motivation as a mental process, we as consumer researchers have studied what may often be verbal rationalizations of behaviors that derive from a more emotional and corporeal basis. This is the message of a great deal recent theorizing about consumption (e.g., Coward 1984; Falk 1994; Featherstone 1991; Firat and Venkatesh 19995; Joy and Venkatesh 1994; Lupton 1996). Whereas a view of consumers as information processors implies that mass media and advertising provide information about products and that consumers transform this information into implicit calculations of the need satisfying abilities of certain bundles of attributes, a focus on desire and the body opens other possibilities. By viewing consumers as having desiring bodies and minds, we may be able to better appreciate the largely neglected role of myth, fantasy, and imagination in consumption (e.g., Berger 1991; Budd, Craig, and Steinman 1983; Crisp 1987; Levy 1986; Rook 1988).

In order to achieve this potential and to begin to learn about the nature of consumer desire, traditional methods of both qualitative and quantitative research may be limited. They are simply not well suited to eliciting consumer fantasies or forthright and revealing characterizations of consumer desire. Since we are interested in better understanding the nature of consumer desire, we turned to a number of projective methods in this phase of our research. Such methods have recently proven useful in a variety of consumer research contexts in which more direct questioning methods fail to capture an adequate understanding of consumer behavior processes and consumption symbolism (e.g., Branthwaite and Lunn 1985; Gordon and Langmaid 1988; McGrath, Sherry, and Levy 1993; McWilliam and Dumas 1985; Sherry, McGrath, and Levy 1992, 1993, 1995; Zaltman 1995; Zaltman and Coulter 1995; Zaltman and Higie 1993; Zaltman and Schuck 1995; Zaltman, Zaltman, Crameri, Finkle, and Randel 1995).

METHODS

Informants were graduate and undergraduate students at the three universities of the authors. The American students in Salt Lake City consisted of 16 women and 22 men. The Turkish students in Ankara were 13 women and 16 men. And the Danish students in Odense were 9 women and 8 men. The exercise was completed in class as part of a demonstration of projective methods. There were 10 parts to the exercise, completed in the following order:

1. *Collage*: Using a variety of popular magazines from the country of the study (some supplied by the students and others brought by the researchers) students cut out any material they wished and constructed a collage expressing the concept of desire. They were encouraged to let themselves go and express their feelings, intuitions, imaginings, fantasies, and associations. Following their completion of their collage they wrote down interpretations, logical or not, of what it represents.

2. *Associations*: Informants were asked to imagine swimming in a sea of things (objects, experiences, people) that bring them the greatest pleasure. They identified these things and described the sensations they imagined having in this context.

3. *Fairy tale*: Everyone wrote a fairy tale in which someone experiences great suffering, but in the end finds great happiness. They were asked to describe the setting, the central character, the source of their suffering, and the source of their final happiness.

4. *Antonyms*: Informants listed states that they regarded to be the opposite of desire.

5. *Antonym Objects*: Students named things toward which they feel the opposite of desire and described their feelings about these things.

Advances in Consumer Research
Volume 24, © 1997

6. *Metaphoric Portraits*: Informants were asked to name or describe anything that came to mind when trying to imagine 1) desire and 2) the opposite of desire, as:
   a. *a taste*
   b. *a smell*
   c. *a color*
   d. *a shape*
   e. *a texture/feel/touch*
   f. *a sound*
   g. *an emotion.*

7. *Sketches*: People were told to imagine that they were artists who had been given commissions to create two artworks to be called "Desire" and "Not Desire." They were told to sketch the works they envisioned and to add any interpretation that might be useful in understanding these sketches.

8. *Desires versus Wants*: Students were asked to give an example of an object, experience, or person X that Person A desires and Person B wants. They were then asked to describe how each of these two people feels about X and how their behaviors might differ as a result.

9. *Synonyms*: Informants were asked to name an object, experience, or person X that they desire and to list as many words or phrases as they can that might be used in the blank in the sentence "I _____ X."

10. *Synonym Examples and Feelings*: People were asked to name some things a person might strongly desire and for each one to describe the feelings a person might have about it 1) before they get it, 2) at the moment they get it, and 3) after they get it.

Questions and responses were in English, Turkish, and Danish, as appropriate to each country. They were analyzed independently by the author for whom this was a native language. In addition, a multinational group of students completed the exercise in English at INSEAD in Fontainebleu, France, where English is the lingua franca. These responses are not analyzed here, but were examined by all three authors in an effort to detect our own analytical differences. In addition, we reconsidered our interpretations of the informants from our own countries after seeing the interpretations of the other authors in their countries. We were attentive to differences that emerged by country, by gender of the informant, and by type of projective measure. The following results are a summary of the findings that evolved from this iterative process.

RESULTS

In general there were stronger gender differences than cultural differences, with a high degree of convergence across cultures and type of projective exercise. Therefore, for the sake of clarity and brevity, we present the results by topic, noting differences by gender, culture, and exercise type where there are systematic differences.

Desire is a Positive Emotional State

While there are some states of desire that are negative in character, desire is depicted overwhelmingly as a positive emotion. This is seen in collages that show exotic, luxurious, and desirable persons, places, and things as well as associations of desire in these collages with sexual longing, hunger for delicious foods and beverages, and as dreams, fantasies, and intriguing departures from the ordinary and everyday. In collages and synonyms, desire is depicted as fun, exhilarating, passionate, imaginative, romantic, hopeful, and empowering. It is seen in the antonyms which characterize non-desire in either negative terms (hatred, loathing, disgust, fear) or in terms of apathy, indifference, laziness, lacking in motivation, and being without future goals to strive for. As one American man put it, "Apathy destroys the core of the individual, while controlled desire guides us to success." However for some, especially Danish, informants, the notion of controlling desire was itself oxymoronic, for desire was seen as wild, impassioned, and incapable of total control. When it was controlled in the sense of being tamed or civilized, some suggested that a surrogate or alternate source of less controlled desire was substituted as a new object for desire. This is examined more completely in a theme discussed below.

The metaphors and sketches of desire and its opposite also emphasize the positive emotional character of desire. It is depicted as sweet, fragrant, red (passionate, hot), round, smooth, soft, silky, gentle sounding (e.g., surf), loving and peaceful, whereas its opposite is depicted as sour, rotten, or bland, black or gray, angular, coarse, loud and harsh, and hateful, angry, or sad. Compared to wanting, desire was consistently characterized as more intense, profound, and powerfully motivating. Because it has to do with fantasies and the imaginary it takes on a somewhat mystical, childish, and surprising quality that appears quite antithetical to reasoned calculation. The synonym of worship may come closest to capturing this aspect of desire. The highly positive characterizations of desire are consistent with contentions of Campbell (1987, p. 86) that desire is a state of enjoyable frustration and longing, and of Lefebvre (1991, p. 394) that we have a "desire for desire." Thus perhaps it is not surprising that Santa Claus and Christmas showed up in several of the American desire collages.

Desire is Interpersonal

The interpersonal character of desire was especially emphasized in the sea of things associations and the fairy tales, and was present in collages as well. The things depicted in the sea of desire were overwhelmingly people—family, friends, loved ones—in all three countries. For males these people were sometimes nude females. These people or inanimate (generally luxury) objects in the sea of desire were described as providing feelings of being supported, soothed, loved, excited, and sexually aroused. Sometimes they also resulted in feelings of beauty, joy, freedom, peace, comfort, relaxation, harmony, warmth, and fond memories. The womb-like quality of some of these feeling states may however be related to the sea context as well as the desire context. In fairy tales both the sources of problems and the basis for their resolution were more often people than material conditions.

Often in the fairy tales there was a transformation of the central character and his or her conditions resulting in gaining greater acceptance, success, recognition, or control of his or her future. These are stories of a desire realized, either through personal action or the action of other people. In either case, the results (and implicitly what is beneath specific focal desires) involve an improved interpersonal situation. There is some tendency in the U.S. for men to frame interpersonal issues of desire more in terms of competition, power, and mastery, and for women to frame these issues more in terms of love, comfort, and relationships. That desire should be largely interpersonal is consistent with Lacan's (1977) contention that the fundamental human desire underlying all other desires is to fill a lack or an incompleteness that we feel in our selves by turning to an other. That is, the Lacanian formula specifies that desire is always desire for the Other (Leather 1983).

Desire and Desired Objects Differ Between Men and Women

In collages as well as illustrations of things wanted in response to questions 8 and 10, men and women tended to focus on differing objects of desire. While both sexes focused desires on luxury cars, trucks, and motorcycles, males were more likely to do so. Both sexes also focused on other people as objects of desire, but in quite distinct ways. Men were more likely to use attractive, nude, or scantily clad women in their collages and examples. Women were more likely to depict man-woman couples and specify relationships as the interpersonal objects of their desire. That is, men tended to desire women as objects, whereas women were more likely to desire on-going relationships. This objectification versus personalization was also evident in specifications and depictions of non-desire where men cited types of people they hate (e.g., lazy or dishonest people, fat women) whereas women cited problematic interpersonal relationships more often (e.g., being lonely, being treated badly). For women, these and other instances of non-desire were often internalized (e.g., being fat, being mean, being cold and dirty), whereas for men sources of non-desire were more often external in origin (e.g., listening to opera, Mormon church meetings, bills).

Other objects of desire that emerged with greater frequency for women were homes, furnishings, and food—especially chocolates. Sweets in general (Coward 1984; Mintz 1986; Willis 1991) and chocolates in particular (Barthel 1989, Lupton 1996) have long been associated with women, romance, luxury, reward, indulgence, decadence, and sensuality. Recognizing this temptation, men have traditionally used gifts of chocolate as part of the courtship ritual. And Otnes and McGrath (1994) found in studying three- to five-year-old children's birthday rituals that girls were especially enamored of being able to eat anything they wanted on their birthdays; something the authors attributed to the stronger normal taboo against girls eating and gaining weight. At the same time, we also find that both men and women expressed desires to appear attractive—women through slender bodies, new clothes, and perfumes, and men through muscular bodies, cars, and other symbols of status.

Desire Can Be Dangerous

In interpreting their collages, American women sometimes described certain desires for such things as dessert foods, chocolates, sex, and alcohol as being not only decadent and indulgent, but sinful. This is closer to Bataille's (1991) notions of desire as transgression and as potentially involving guilty pleasures. Notions of transgression were evident in Turkey as well, but framed as matters of imbalance and a lack of control rather than sin and guilt. We see here the dangerous nature of desires and the tensions between control and non-control, pleasure and victimization, and rationality and animality (id drives). Desire is seen by many as something that must be controlled, but ironically this very control tames the desire and robs it of its power and passion; the thrill is gone. This may in turn lead to a new, reintensified desire (see the following section). Desire is thus potentially a Damocles' sword. It can lead us to great pleasure, but we are inevitably balancing on the edge of falling victim to the uncontrollable character of our transgressive desires.

For one Turkish man this transgressive character was expressed by the dirty smells inhaled by a cartoon rat in a toilet. Another man's collage showed the police photos of Hugh Grant and Divine Brown after they were picked up for an act of public fellatio. And another showed the actor John Malkovich from the film version of "Liason Dangereux" and explained it as "passion running after pleasure." Desires derive their power through their affiliation with our "animal" self—our id or unconscious drives. Some described this is childish in the sense of not having inhibi-

tions. Desire was also often seen to come about by surprise rather than through conscious planning. Because of their transgressive animal character we must rationalize and socialize these desires in order to find socially acceptable expressions of this power. But doing so diminishes the basic power of the desire and a search for new thrills ensues that may well lead to new revitalized desires.

The fear of loss of control is also evident in some expressions of the addictive potential of compulsive desire. One Turkish drawing of desire represented this by showing a person caught in the middle of a large spider web. Part of the interpretation offered was that "People want lots of things, as if our lives are based on these desires. Some of these desires we can reach, others we cannot. Our lives go by in efforts to reach them. As we reach them, we fall prey to new desires. Our desires sometimes enslave us." Or as a Danish informant put it, "It is an obsession, you don't control it."

There is a Cycle of Desire

The final projective question asked informants to describe a person's feelings before, during, and after getting something that is strongly desired. The feelings described for the before state were predominantly positive, although they were more mixed (positive and negative) where the desired object was another person. At the moment of acquisition, feelings were almost uniformly positive (either active emotions such as excited, joyful, and thrilled or more passive positive emotions such as relaxed, content, and relieved). In addition, the emotions during acquisition were sometimes indicated victory, as if a battle had been waged and won (success, triumph, arrogance, accomplishment, pride). These victorious reactions were more common for women upon acquiring a desired lover, and were more common for men upon acquiring possessions (e.g., a car), states of being (e.g., fitness), or goals for which the person had worked long and hard (e.g., an MBA degree).

Perhaps most interesting of the three focal points is the "after" state. Here the most common description of feelings was negative: worry, burdened, sad, scared, let down, disrespectful, unappreciative, discouraged, frustrated, unsure, bored, exhausted, disappointed, jealous, broke, anxious, fearing loss, confused, lazy, empty, without goals, remorseful, having lost interest, regret, or needing something more. More positive (and often passive) emotions were associated with experiences like travel and sex and after realizing desires to have a child or a lover (e.g., reflective, content, calm). With boyfriends and girlfriends there were still some negative reactions however. A number of informants described being briefly happy with the newly acquired and formerly desired object, and then becoming bored, indifferent, and anxious to turn to a new source of desire. This cycle of desire accords well with Colin Campbell's (1987) description of contemporary hedonism. A similar cycle of desire has been used to explain high divorce rates today (Barnett and Magdoff 1986). And this cycle suggests again that the thrill lies more in the desire than it does in its realization.

CONCLUSION

Using a variety of projective methods we find similar notions of desire across three cultures that are distant from one another. We find that desire is a positive emotional state and that non-desire is an empty or negative state of being. We passionately desire the luxurious, the exotic, the Other. We desire something thought to be capable of totally transforming us and our lives through magic. Perhaps this was best depicted in an American woman's collage that highlighted Cinderella's glass slipper. At the same time, desire is interpersonal. Whether in a competitive invidious sense of desiring more and better things than others or in the sense of wanting approval and love from others, our desires are not simply person-thing relationships; they inevitably involve other people.

We also find that men and women differ in the nature and focus of their desires. The men studied are more likely to desire cars and women as sex objects. The women studied are more likely to desire homes, food, and relationships with men. These women see sweet foods in general and chocolates in particular as being indulgent, decadent, and sometimes sinful. This also exemplifies the transgressive and dangerous nature of desire. Desires are dangerous because they transgress the ordinary and verge on the socially outrageous. A part of the allure is this transgressive character. Because of the danger of losing control to desire and of appearing obsessed, we may try to civilize and rationalize these desires so that they appear more socially acceptable. But ironically, doing so robs the desire of its mystical power and leads us to new desires. A similar sequence of rising, waning, and renewing desire was found in the cycle that is involved in desiring, obtaining, and becoming bored with objects, leading to revitalizing desire through new focal objects.

In a word, what we have learned is that the passionate and positive emotional basis for desire is hope. Crawford (1994, pp. 112-113) tells the ancient Jewish tale of a rich man who, knowing his riches will be of no value to him when he dies, seeks to give his fortune to someone who has abandoned all hope. He finds a man in rags and bestows the riches upon him. But rather than gratitude, the man replies that the gift is the opposite of kindness and is more like death. For "only the dead are without hope." Rather than paraphrase this tale and suggest that only the dead are without desire, we prefer to turn it around: to desire is to hope, to hope is to live.

REFERENCES

Barnett, Steve and JoAnn Magdoff (1986), "Beyond Narcissism in American Culture of the 1980s," *Cultural Anthropology*, 1 (November), 413-424.

Barthel, Diane (1989), "Modernism and Marketing: the Chocolate Box Revisited," *Theory, Culture and Society*, 6, 429-438.

Belk, Russell W. Belk, Güliz Ger, and Søren Askegaard (1996), "Metaphors of Consumer Desire," *Advances in Consumer Research*, Vol. 23, Kim P. Korfman and John G. Lynch eds., Provo, UT: Association for Consumer Research, 368-373.

Berger, Arthur Asa (1991), "The Manufacture of Desire: Alcohol Commercials and Society," in *Media USA: Process and Effect*, 2nd ed., New York: Longman, 324-333.

Branthwaite, Alan and Tony Lunn (1985), "Projective Techniques in Social and Market Research," in Robert Walker, ed., *Applied Qualitative Research*, Aldershot, England: Gower, 101-121.

Budd, Mike, Steve Craig, and Clay Steinman (1983), "'Fantasy Island': Marketplace of Desire," *Journal of Communication*, 33 (Winter), 67-77.

Campbell, Colin (1987), *The Romantic Ethic and the Spirit of Modern Consumerism*, Oxford: Basil Blackwell.

Coward, Rosalind (1984), *Female Desire*, London: Paladin.

Crawford, Tad (1994), *The Secret Life of Money: Teaching Tales of Spending, Receiving, Saving, and Owing*, New York: George P. Putnam's Sons.

Crisp, Roger (1987), "Persuasive Advertising, Autonomy, and the Creation of Desire," *Journal of Business Ethics*, 6, 413-418.

Falk, Pasi (1994), *The Consuming Body*, London: Sage.

Featherstone, Mike (1991), "The Body in Consumer Culture," in Mike Featherstone, Mike Hepworth, and Bryan S. Turner, eds., *The Body: Social Process and Cultural Theory*, London: Sage, 170-196.

Firat, A. Fuat and Alladi Venkatesh (1995), "Liberatory Postmodernism and the Reenchantment of Consumption," *Journal of Consumer Research*, 22 (December), 239-267.

Gordon, Wendy and Roy Langmaid (1988), *Qualitative Marketing Research: A Practitioner's and Buyer's Guide*, Brookfield, VT: Gower.

Joy, Annamma and Alladi Venkatesh (1994), "Postmodernism, Feminism, and the Body: The Visible and the Invisible in Consumer Research," *International Journal of Research in Marketing*, 11 (September), 333-357.

Lacan, Jacques (1977), *Ecrits: A Selection*, Alan Sheridan, trans., New York: Norton.

Leather, Phil (1983), "Desire:; A Structural Model of Motivation," *Human Relations*, 36 (2), 109-122.

Lefebvre, Henri (1991), *Critique of Everyday Life*, Vol. 1, London: Verso (original *Critique de la Vie Quotidienne I: Introduction*, Paris: L'Arche, 1958).

Levy, Sidney J. (1986), "Dreams, Fairy Tales, Animals and Cars," *Psychology and Marketing*, 2 (2), 67-81.

Lupton, Deborah (1996), *Food, the Body and the Self*, London: Sage.

McGrath, Mary Ann, John F. Sherry, Jr., and Sidney J. Levy (1993), "Giving Voice to the Gift: The Use of Projective Techniques to Recover Lost Meanings," *Journal of Consumer Psychology*, 2 (2), 171-191.

McWilliam, Gil and Angela Dumas (1995), "Using Metaphors in New Brand Research," London: London Business School Centre for Marketing Working Paper No. 95-401.

Mintz, Sidney (1986), *Sweetness and Power: The Place of Sugar in Modern History*, New York: Penguin.

Otnes, Cele and Mary Ann McGrath (1994), "Ritual Socialization and the Children's Birthday Party: The Early Emergence of Gender Differences," *Journal of Ritual Studies*, 8 (Winter), 73-93.

Rook, Dennis W. (1988), "Researching Consumer Fantasy," in Elizabeth Hirschman and Jagdish N. Sheth, eds., *Research in Consumer Behavior*, Vol. 3, Greenwich, CT: JAI Press, 247-270.

Sherry, John F., Jr., Mary Ann McGrath, and Sidney J. Levy (1992), "The Disposition of the Gift and Many Unhappy Returns," *Journal of Retailing*, 68 (1), 40-65.

Sherry, John F., Jr., Mary Ann McGrath, and Sidney J. Levy (1993), "The Dark Side of the Gift," *Journal of Business Research*, 28 (3), 225-244.

Sherry, John F., Jr., Mary Ann McGrath, and Sidney J. Levy (1995), "Monadic Giving: Anatomy of Gifts Given to the Self," in John F. Sherry, Jr., *Contemporary Marketing and Consumer Behavior: An Anthropological Sourcebook*, Thousand Oaks, CA: Sage, 399-432.

Willis, Susan (1991), *A Primer for Daily Life*, London: Routledge.

Zaltman, Gerald (1995), "Amidword: Anthropology, Metaphors, and Cognitive Peripheral Vision," in John F. Sherry, Jr., *Contemporary Marketing and Consumer Behavior: An Anthropological Sourcebook*, Thousand Oaks, CA: Sage, 282-304.

Zaltman, Gerald and Robin A. Coulter (1995), "Seeing the Voice of the Customer: Metaphor-Based Advertising Research," *Journal of Advertising Research*, 35 (July-August), 35-51.

Zaltman, Gerald and Robin A. Higie (1993), "Seeing the Voice of the Customer: The Zaltman Metaphor Elicitation Technique" Marketing Science Institute Report Number 93-114, September.

Zaltman, Gerald and Linda J. Schuck (1995), "Sensing the Voice of the Customer," paper presented at the Harvard Business School Colloquium, "Multimedia and the Boundaryless World," November 16-17.

Zaltman, Gerald, Ann Zaltman, Nicole Crameri, Marion Finkle, and Kathy Randel (1995), "The Dimension of Brand Equity for Nestle Crunch Bar," report for QUEST and Associates.

Life-Event Transitions and Consumer Vulnerability
James W. Gentry, University of Nebraska

OVERVIEW

Much attention has been given in recent literature to vulnerable segments of the US consumer market (i.e., the special issues of the *Journal of Public Policy and Marketing* and the *American Behavioral Scientist* edited by Ron Hill). Membership in vulnerable segments may be a relatively steady state phenomenon in many cases, but it can also be due primarily to life-event transitions. The focus of our session was on transition-induced vulnerability, incorporating three phenomenological studies of different life-event transitions. The three studies all involve unsought (though possibly inevitable) transitions: the death of a loved one, the awareness that one is losing one's sight, and the many transitions associated with aging.

While transitions may take on many different forms, the three studied here share the common preference for the exit role (Ebaugh 1988) being given up as opposed to the entry role that one must face. The dominant future-oriented time orientation found in North America tends to emphasize the expectation of concern with entry roles and to discount the prominence of exit roles. While recent marketing literature has dealt with exit roles (McAlexander, Schouten, and Roberts 1993; Patterson, Hill, and Maloy 1995; Schouten 1991), we expect that the norm in our society is to expect people to adjust quickly to transitions. The three studies provide insight into the nature of painful transition periods.

The Grieving Process: The Most Unpleasant Transition
James W. Gentry and Cathy Goodwin

The presentation began with justification for a concern with life-event transitions. The steady-state mentality prevalent in Marketing has led to a focus on trajectories, and not on transitions. Even our best known stage models, such as the family life cycle, are models of trajectories and ignore the often painful interface between stages. All consumers will face many life-event transitions, all of which are associated with increased stress due to the disruption aroused by the breaking of familiar routines. The discontinuities associated with life-event transitions often mean that past behavior can no longer be used as the best predictor of future behavior. Frequently, consumption patterns change, not due to changes in the marketing mix initiated by marketers, but due to the changed nature of the individual's life.

A brief summary of models of Life-Event Transitions was given as well as a summary of the many underlying theoretical bases in an attempt to demonstrate the depth and breadth of the area. Many models focus on particular stages of the life course and are therefore limited in scope. For example, Ruble's (1994) Phase Model of Transition evolved from her excellent work covering transitions faced relatively early in life (adolescent females' transition to junior high, marriage, the college transition), and has a strong focus on social learning. This social learning emphasis is not consistent with the passivity/ withdrawal noted among those in grief after the loss of a love one (Gentry et al. 1995).

Most efforts to develop general models of life-event transitions have been based on study of normative, positive transitions. A perspective more inclusive of more negative transitions and more typical of those occurring later in the life course would consider the following adjustments:

- more emphasis is needed on exit roles and less emphasis on entry roles;
- more emphasis is needed on secondary control processes (Heckhausen and Schulz 1995) such as denial, reduction in aspiration level, downward social comparison, and pre-decisional self-handicapping by avoiding effort;
- more acknowledgment of the social context is needed, including the rather obvious observation that many life-event transitions relate to changes in the number of strong-tie contacts;
- less emphasis may be perceived for increased "independence" occurring as a result of the transition;
- the meanings of possessions labelled by Silver (1996) as anchors (ties to the past) and markers (indicants of the new role) need to be broadened to range from "charms" (sacred reminders of a loved one) to "taboos" (items so emotionally charged that they must be destroyed or eliminated quickly); and
- the emphasis placed on new peer relationships may not be dominant as suggested by Silver (1996); more attention may need to be paid to lost relationships.

A broadened perspective of transitions may help guide marketing action involving those undergoing transitions. The "Welcome Wagon" approach is appropriate for those transitions in which social learning is indeed dominant. However, when the consumer is focusing on the exit role rather than on the entry role, such an approach may well alienate the consumer.

The Meaning of Stress for Visually Impaired Service Consumers: the Transition into Blindness
Stacey Menzel Baker and Cathy Goodwin

This paper explores how the meaning of service encounters changes as one moves from being a "visually impaired" consumer to being "blind." More specifically, we investigated how the transition into blindness affects the consumer's experience of stress in service encounters. Informants provided the definitions that "blind" individuals are those who have accepted that they have lost their sight and have decided that "life must go on," while "visually impaired" individuals have not accepted that they are losing their sight and they are "impaired" by their visual disability such that they are almost totally dependent on others.

Consistent with phenomenological methods described by Thompson, Locander, and Pollio (1989) and Weiss (1994), we explored the experiential aspects of service experiences by conducting in-depth interviews. Eight 60-90 minute interviews were conducted with 11 individuals considered to be legally blind (three blind married couples and six blind individuals were interviewed). In at least two of the cases, the individuals have been considered legally blind for less than six months. In fact, one of the informants still wore her glasses everywhere she went, although she admitted that she does not see anything except in brightly lit areas.

Blind consumers discussed service encounters in terms of psychological stress (threats to independence and difficulties dealing with ambiguity), social stress (treated badly by others and awareness of other's anxiety when dealing with the individual), and service-related stress (dealing with the service environment, assessing service quality, and issues of accessibility). Visually impaired consumers also experienced the three types of stress, but the stress took on different forms. The psychological stress was due more to the emotional distress caused by the loss of sight in general and to trying to adjust to the loss of visual information. Social stressors deal with low social self-confidence and in feeling stigmatized in social interactions, while virtually all aspects of the service encounter were found to be stressful.

"Blind" consumers coped differently than "visually impaired" consumers. Their acceptance of their blindness and of themselves as independent and worthy people led them to seek information about the service environment, to establish relationships with specific service providers, and to be assertive in terms of what they do and do NOT need. On the other hand, "visually impaired" consumers coped by relying on others for transportation, for making decisions, and for emotional support or by avoiding situations entirely.

Service providers need to differentiate between blind and visually impaired consumers. The latter need higher service levels, while the former want to be more independent and may well resent intrusions on their ability to make their own choices. The best way for service providers to determine the appropriate level of service is to ask.

"If One Thing Doesn't Get You, Another Will:" Old Age Transitions and Market Vulnerabilities
Linda L. Price and Carolyn F. Curasi

A particularly significant aspect of aging is adapting to the common losses of later life. These losses include dispersion of children, loss of social roles, decline in income, death of spouse and loved ones, decline in sensory acuity, and restricted mobility due to failing health. The specific purpose of the research is to *begin* to understand the relationships between life transitions and the market vulnerability of older consumers.

The inquiry is based on three data sets: (1) in-depth interviews and focus groups with over 40 residents of retirement communities about later life transitions (especially losses, but also remarriages and personal growth programs); (2) observations of the daily life of over 20 older consumers; and (3) a telephone survey of 347 older consumers about their marketplace attitudes, behaviors, life satisfaction, and recent life transitions.

The complexity of understanding the combined effect of a series of life transitions on personal functioning is addressed explicitly, illustrating the need for a more dynamic, multi-causal theory of the relationship between life transitions and individual response. For example, the move to a "support" community is commonly triggered by not one but by a series of life transitions (often losses). Thirty-seven percent of the sample have experienced three or more life transitions in the past two years. Our results support that older consumers experience many difficult life transitions that have a *cumulative* significant negative effect on their life energy and cognitive age, but not their life satisfaction. The experience of difficult life transitions does not differ significantly by gender, income, or (within this age group) by age.

The environment significantly affects the experience of life transitions and attitudes and approaches to coping with these life transitions. Both the experience of life transitions and perceptions of vulnerability are socially constructed and must be understood in the context of a physical and social system. Several examples from our data are noteworthy, but one outstanding illustration is how older consumers in retirement communities respond to the death of a spouse or close friend. Because of their location within age-restricted communities, their response is often quite different from that reported in the Gentry and Goodwin paper (this session).

We explicitly examine older consumers' perceptions of their market vulnerability and link this to the number and types of life transitions experienced within the last two years. Recent consumer behavior studies have tended to *infer* vulnerabilities based on life transitions rather than exploring perceptions of vulnerability more directly. The observational data in this investigation provide an interesting point of comparison with the perceptions of the older consumers themselves. Although older consumers typically report that they are not vulnerable or disadvantaged in the marketplace, observations of their daily lives, at times, offers a different picture. We found a complex and subtle relationship between difficult life transitions and marketplace vulnerabilities. We measured two aspects of older consumers' feelings of power in the marketplace: ability to deal with aggressive salespeople and willingness to complain and return products. There is no strong evidence of a relationship between difficult life transitions and these specific vulnerabilities. However, the experience of difficult life transitions is significantly related to more negative attitudes toward business ($r=.35$, $p<.001$). Negative attitudes are, in turn, related negatively to retail satisfaction ($r=-.26$, $p<.001$). A major implication of our research is that defining marketplace vulnerability for this group of consumers is extremely problematic. Vulnerability may be reflected in subtle relationships between older consumer' experience of life transitions and their marketplace beliefs and activities.

Discussion
Ronald Paul Hill

Ron discussed "vulnerable," "vulnerabilities," and the role of the marketplace. Specifically, the unique contribution of consumer researchers to this vital area of research is our concern for and knowledge of the marketplace's role; at the same time, Ron argues that the marketplace should not have to be central in the written work of social marketers.

The consideration of transitions adds much to the concept of vulnerability, as he noted that the movement from vulnerability may also make consumers more vulnerable. Finally, Ron encouraged more advocacy efforts by those doing social marketing research. As associate editor of the *Journal of Public Policy and Marketing*, he will actively try to promote the research included in the journal to the press and to government sources.

REFERENCES
Ebaugh, H. R. F. (1988), *Becoming an Ex: The Process of Role Exit*, Chicago: University of Chicago Press.

Gentry, James W., Patricia F. Kennedy, Catherine Paul, and Ronald Paul Hill (1995), "The Vulnerability of Those Grieving the Death of a Loved One: Implications for Public Policy," *Journal of Public Policy and Marketing*, 14 (Spring), 128-142.

Heckhausen, Jutta and Richard Schulz (1995), "A Life-Span Theory of Control," *Psychological Review*, 102, 284-304.

Hill, Ronald Paul (1995), *Marketing and Consumer Research in the Public Interest*, Thousand Oaks, CA: Sage.

McAlexander, James H., John W. Schouten, and Scott D. Roberts (1993), "Consumer Behavior and Divorce," in Russell W. Belk (Ed.), *Research in Consumer Behavior*, Vol. 6, 231-260.

Patterson, Maggie Jones, Ronald Paul Hill, and Kate Maloy (1995), "Abortion in America: A Consumer-Behavior Perspective," *Journal of Consumer Research*, 21 (March), 677-694.

Ruble, Diane N. (1994), "A Phase Model of Transition: Cognitive and Motivational Consequences," *Advances in Experimental Social Psychology*, Mark I. Zanna (Ed.), Vol. 26, New York: Academic Press, 163-214.

Schouten, John W. (1991), "Personal Rites of Passage and the Reconstruction of Self," *Advances in Consumer Research*, Vol. 18, 49-51.

Silver, Ira (1996), "Role Transitions, Objects, and Identity," *Symbolic Interaction*, 19 (No. 1), 1-20.

Thompson, Craig J., William B. Locander, and Howard R. Pollio (1989), "Putting Consumer Experience Back into Consumer Research: The Philosophy and Method of Existential-Phenomenology," *Journal of Consumer Research*, 16 (September), 133-146.

Weiss, Robert S. (1994), *Learning from Strangers: The Art and Methods of Qualitative Interview Studies*, New York: The Free Press.

The Socio-Cognitive Development of Market Realities: Three Perspectives

José Antonio Rosa, University of Illinois at Urbana Champaign

Consistent with the conference theme "breaking out of the box," this session cut across consumer research paradigms to yield new perspectives on consumer markets. Three papers were presented on the topic of shared conceptual structures and their socio-cognitive origins, coming at the phenomenon from demographic, cognitivist, and symbolic interaction perspectives. Each of the presentations enhanced our understanding of 1) shared conceptual systems among consumers, 2) shared conceptual systems between consumers and producers, and 3) the implications of shared conceptual systems for consumer behavior. The fact that consumers and producers bring intricate and multi-dimensional conceptual systems to the market place is well documented in the consumer research literature. This session focused attention on how these conceptual systems can be identified in unique ways, how they are shaped, reconciled and expanded through consumer and producer interactions in the marketplace, and how they influence highly significant purchase decisions.

In the first presentation, Frenzen combined Simmel's theory of social circles with Blau's data visualization methodology (Blau space) to offer a means of exploring consumer interaction and behavior patterns, and the shared conceptual structures such interactions and behaviors imply, in large arrays of data. Simmel observed that people's demographic characteristics were strong determinants of their activities and associations in society, and that in turn these shared patterns of interaction had a strong influence on people's attitudes and behaviors, but he found it difficult to test such observations empirically. Recently, it has become possible through the Blau space data visualization technique to have graphical representations of large customer groups (e.g., all consumers in one or more SMSA) by demographic, behavioral, and attitudinal criteria, and to use such representations to identify the equivalent of Simmel's social circles; groups of people or consumers in close demographic proximity who are tightly linked by patterns of interaction and known to share many consumption attitudes and practices. Frenzen argues that the use of Blau space techniques allows marketers to identify clusters of consumers with similar conceptual systems without having to identify the social networks that link those customers. He argues further that similar conceptual systems are the likely cause of many of the consumption behavior similarities also observed through the Blau space technique. Visualizing customer behavioral and attitudes clusters through Blau space techniques has implications for various areas of marketing, such as product market management and media purchases.

Rosa and Porac followed Frenzen, but focused attention instead on the development of conceptual systems for a new product across the consumer-producer divide. They argued for a social-constructionist view of markets, in which market realities are enacted by consumers and producers, and are captured by both consumer and producers in complex hierarchical representations used to navigate future market encounters. In stable markets, consumer and producer mental representations have been reinforced by repeated encounters and should be stable and partially shared between them. When new product concepts are introduced into established markets, however, existing representations are upset and enactments become less predictable and coherent as a result. Markets, therefore, become conceptually unstable, and regain coherence and stability only after multiple cycles of market exchange between consumers and producers result in a new set of shared mental representations. In a study of the minivan market, Rosa and Porac argue that the current mental representation of the minivan, with core attributes such as front wheel drive, V-6 engine, room for seven, and car-like ride, was not always an accepted category prototype. They suggest, based on analyses of market publications, that there was considerable competition between widely diverse conceptual representations of the minivan in the early stages, and that the currently accepted prototype emerged from iterative enactment cycles to which both consumers and producers contributed. Rosa and Porac combined data from archival and content analysis research to argue that 1) minivans destabilized a shared conceptual system for motor vehicles in the US which clearly separated cars and trucks, 2) that there was considerable market confusion over the prototypical usages and attributes of minivans in the early years of the product market, 3) that both producers and consumers contributed to the early conceptual confusion and later to the restoration of market coherence, and 4) that the market's move from confusion to coherence was shaped by both behavior (the sale of different artifacts) and the public discourse around the product.

In the third presentation, Wright-Isak also focused on shared conceptual systems, directing attention to the mental associations between residential community images and community ethos that are held by many people, and to the implications of these associations for purchase and satisfaction with real estate purchases. She argued that in the purchase of residential real estate, most people make intricate connections between physical characteristics (e.g., picket fences, tree-lined streets, cul-de-sacs) and the community's ethos; the emotionally toned set of beliefs, values, presuppositions, rules, and prescriptions that organize day-to-day life. The imagery evoked by the community ethos, in turn, leads consumers to hold expectations and enact behaviors that give meaning to their experiences of community life and in most cases affirm the community ethos. In the absence of community ethos imagery, however, it is possible that consumer interpretations of ambiguous community experiences will cause alarm and dissatisfaction, and lead to movement away from the purchase decision. Wright-Isak supported her arguments with data from in-depth interviews of recent purchasers of homes in "small town" communities. She found satisfaction and dissatisfaction were related to whether or not the consumers had physical exposure to the "small town" before the purchase decision, and had relied on the community ethos imagery to anticipate community life and make a decision.

At a broad level, the session argued that consumer mental representations of product markets and their responses are strongly shaped by social interactions in the marketplace. Zaltman, as synthesizer, captured the theme well when he concluded that "consumer minds are not the possession of individual consumers." He argued further that the meanings of products (and behaviors towards them) are co-produced *with* people we don't know and *by* people we don't know, and that in the aggregation of consumer minds much can be learned of benefit to consumer research. In a sense it can be argued that shared conceptual systems make possible the mutual understanding and collaborative behavior of exchange.

Does Holding On To A Product Result In Increased Consumption Rates?
Dilip Soman, University of Colorado at Boulder

Consumer behavior research has focused largely on the act of choosing between products or on events that are antecedent to the purchase occasion. The actual product usage occasion has received relatively little attention (but see Folkes, Martin and Gupta 1993, Wansink 1996). One fundamental question relates to how consumers evaluate products at the time of consumption and consequently how willing they are to consume them. An examination of this evaluation process is important at two levels. At the theoretical level, it provides an understanding of how consumers evaluate transactions and consumption experiences in general, and the role of time on these evaluations in particular. At a practical level, this translates into an understanding of how delayed consumption and bulk buying might increase consumption rates, category sales and profits. The three papers in this special session focused on the effect of the temporal delay between purchase and consumption and the supply quantity on consumption rates. The papers address different aspects, use different kinds of data and methods of analysis and use diverse paradigms in studying these issues.

Consider a consumer making a routine cash and carry purchase where she gives up a quantity of money in exchange for goods or services. Research on Prospect Theory and Mental Accounting (Thaler 1985) and the principles of hedonic editing (Thaler and Johnson 1990) would suggest that consumers will attempt to integrate the costs and benefits of the transaction and hence will not experience a separate "loss" at the time of payment and a "gain" on receipt of the product benefit.

However, as the costs and benefits associated with a transaction become separated in time, Gourville and Soman (1996) argue that the hedonic impact of the upstream cost diminishes. Consequently, the payment is "depreciated" and it results in the reduced valuation of the downstream benefits. Since the impact of the cost decreases over time, the benefits take on the nature of "pure" or "windfall" gains. If this happens, it would result in increased consumption rates and greater willingness to forego the benefits. Papers presented in this session examined different aspects of this process.

Mental Accounting of Past Purchases: Invest Now, Consume Later, Spend Never
Eldar Shafir, Princeton University
Richard Thaler, University of Chicago

In this paper presented by Richard Thaler, the authors explored situations in which consumers had to buy objects that could only be consumed properly at a later date (e.g. wine, concert tickets). Their presentation attempted to investigate the mental accounting processes that occur in such circumstances and asked the following specific questions: First, when the consumer buys the good in advance, is this act considered "spending" or "investing"? Then, when the consumption takes place, does the consumer feel as if she is spending or simply drawing down some asset? Does the accounting in the latter case depend on the market value of the good in question, or whether the item is consumed or simply lost?

Thaler presented results of the following questions posed to the subscribers of a wine auction newsletter:

1. Suppose you bought a case of a good 1982 Bordeaux in the futures market for $20 a bottle. The wine now sells at auction for about $75 a bottle. You have decided to give one bottle of this wine to a friend as a gift. Which of the following best captures your feeling of the cost to you of giving away this bottle? (Check one).

   a) Giving away the bottle does not feel like it costs me anything. I paid for the bottle already, many years ago, and probably don't remember exactly what I paid for it anyway. _____

   b) Giving away the bottle fees like it costs me $20, the amount I roughly remember paying for it. _____

   c) Giving away the bottle feels like it costs me $20, the amount I originally paid for it, plus whatever the interest would have been on the money I paid. _____

   d) Giving away the bottle feels like it costs me $75, the amount it would take to replace it. _____

   e) Giving away the bottle feels like I am saving $55, because I am able to give a $75 gift for which I only paid $20. _____

2. Which answer would you choose if instead of giving the bottle away, you dropped the bottle and broke it? How much would it feel like you had lost in this case?

   (a) $0 _____
   (b) $20 _____
   (c) $20 plus interest _____
   (d) $75 _____
   (e) a $55 saving (relative to a bottle bought recently) _____

Responses to these questions revealed that consumers, even sophisticated wine collectors, adopt the convenient mental accounting fiction that they are investing when they make their initial purchase but that they are not spending money when they eventually drink the bottle. Few respondents, other than economists, paid much attention to the market value of the good in question.

Payment Depreciation: The Effects of Temporally Separating Payments from Benefits on Consumption
John Gourville, Harvard University
Dilip Soman, University of Colorado at Boulder

In the second presentation John Gourville and Dilip Soman presented their theory of payment depreciation and transaction decoupling. Under the label "Transaction Depreciation", they proposed that as the time between cost incursion and benefit consumption increases for any given transaction, the downstream benefit will increasingly take on the look and feel of a "windfall" gain. As a result, they predicted that individuals will be willing to consume such a product more readily, lend such a product more freely, or forego its benefits more willingly.

This presentation built on the sunk cost research of Thaler (1985) and others (Arkes & Blumer 1985). To highlight the sunk cost effect, Thaler argues that a family will be more willing to drive thorough a snowstorm to attend a basketball game had they purchased tickets to that game than had they been given (free) tickets. He attributes this difference in behavior to the desire to psychologically integrate the costs and benefits of a consumer transaction, resulting in the unused tickets being perceived as a "pure loss" when paid for but as a "foregone gain" when free. Gourville and Soman proposed that this sunk cost effect is moderated by time, with upstream costs becoming less salient and increasingly "depreciated" at the consumption occasion as the time between costs and benefits increases. As a result, the downstream benefits increasingly take on the characteristics of a pure or "windfall" gain. Gourville presented the results of several of their studies to support this argument.

In one study, they showed that individuals were significantly more likely to use their car under adverse conditions when they had fully paid for that car three years prior than when they had financed that car over the past three years with payments only recently completed. In a second study, they found theater-goers to be significantly more likely to miss a show due to illness if tickets for that show had been purchased six-months in advance as opposed to one-day in advance. Further, they found that the likelihood of missing the theater event due to illness was the highest when the tickets were free, and that the passage of time did not significantly affect the likelihood in the free ticket scenarios.

Consumers may also undervalue the benefit if they are not able to correctly assign a cost to each unit of consumption. This is referred to as "Transaction Decoupling", and can happen through packaging (large multiple unit pack sizes vs. small unit pack sizes), physical format of the transaction (2 liter bottles of soda vs. six packs, season ticket in the form of a pass vs. a booklet of tickets) or bundled pricing. They showed that ski vacationers are more likely to forego a day of skiing (and demanded lesser compensation if the weather was bad) if their season ticket was in the form of a pass as compared to when it is in the form of a booklet of tickets. In the case of bulk purchasing, both "Payment Depreciation" and "Transaction Decoupling" would act to reduce valuation of the product leading to the prediction that it would be consumed more readily.

The Effect of Promotion on Consumption: Buying More and Consuming It Faster

Kusum Ailawadi, Dartmouth College
Scott Neslin, Dartmouth College

Ailawadi and Neslin's presentation used scanner data to provide empirical evidence for the increased consumption rates that arise from promotion-induced stockpiling of certain product categories. This paper identified two mechanisms–fewer stockouts and faster usage–by which promotion can increase category demand. Both stem from the power of promotions to induce consumers to buy more of the product category either by increasing the number of purchase occasions or by encouraging larger purchase quantities per purchase occasion. The use-faster mechanism is examined by modeling weekly consumption as a function of inventory levels and incorporating this into a purchase incidence model. The usage rate model requires only one parameter to be estimated. This parameter measures the degree to which consumers are willing to change their usage rate depending on their inventory levels. Ailawadi discussed two product categories, yogurt and ketchup, across which the authors expected the consumption effect of promotion to differ substantially.

The model was estimated via maximum likelihood procedures. An iterative grid search was used to obtain the usage rate parameter that maximizes the log-likelihood of the purchase incidence model. Results showed that the fit of the Ailawadi and Neslin

model was significantly better than a status quo model using a constant usage rate. Further, the estimates of the usage rate parameter for very different for the two product categories, thus providing strong discriminant validity for the model. As hypothesized, usage rate for yogurt was much more flexible than that for ketchup.

A Monte Carlo simulation of the model was used to quantify the total consumption effect. The simulation provided both face and discriminant validity for the results. In the yogurt category, the simulation illustrated how promotion can increase consumption by loading consumers up with product that they consume quickly. In the ketchup category, a smaller increase in consumption was shown to be distributed over a much longer period of time. In addition, the simulation showed how the model can be used to decompose the long-run effects of promotion into brand switching versus increased consumption.

DISCUSSION
Synthesizer
Richard Thaler, University of Chicago

This session dealt with the general issue of the evaluation of the product at the time of consumption and the resultant "flexibility" in the consumption rate. The first two papers raised the notion that the consumption rate of a product may be related to the "price tag" (or value) that the consumer attaches to a unit of consumption *at the time of consumption*. This value is a function of how salient the cost is at the time of consumption. The third paper used real world data to show that usage rates vary with inventory holding, at least for some product categories, therefore promotion can expand category demand by inducing consumers to stockpile the product. The three papers in this session examine different aspects of this underlying phenomenon.

Richard Thaler, the synthesizer for the session, stressed the importance of consumption research in marketing. He pointed out the similarities among the three papers and called for further research that provided more "real world" evidence of increased consumption rate. Thaler spoke about the sales of ski passes and how it affected consumption rates. Consistent with some results presented earlier in the session, he proposed that if ski passes were sold in advance as a package, consumers were likely to purchase more tickets than they would use and eventually not feel bad about the unused (and hence wasted) tickets. He also gave the example of vacation homes as a purchase where some of the phenomena raised in the session were particularly applicable. Finally he engaged the audience in a discussion with the authors. Issues that came up in the audience discussion included comments about the importance of consumption research, specific comments on the research reported in the three papers and other areas of application.

REFERENCES

Arkes, Hal and Catherine Blumer (1985), "The Psychology of Sunk Cost," *Organizational Behavior & Human Decision Processes,* 35(1), 124-140.

Folkes, Valerie S., Ingrid M. Martin and Kamal Gupta (1993), "When to Say When: Effects of Supply on Usage," *Journal of Consumer Research,* 20 (3), 467-477.

Gourville, John and Dilip Soman (1996), "Payment Depreciation: The Effects of Temporally Separating Payments from Consumption," Working Paper, University of Chicago, Graduate School of Business.

Thaler, Richard H. (1985), "Mental Accounting and Consumer Choice," *Marketing Science,* 4, 199-214.

Thaler, Richard H. and Eric J. Johnson (1990), "Gambling with the House Money and Trying to Break Even: The Effect of Prior Outcomes on Risky Choice," *Management Science*, 36, 643-660.

Wansink, Brian (1996), "Can Package Size Accelerate Usage Volume?," *Journal of Marketing*, 60(3), 1-14.

SPECIAL SESSION SUMMARY
Consumer Behavior, Avoidance, and Coping with Negative Emotion

Mary Frances Luce, University of Pennsylvania
Julie R. Irwin, New York University

BACKGROUND

The discipline of cognitive psychology has undergone a resurgence of interest in emotion and coping, after many years of focusing primarily on cognition (e.g., Lazarus 1991). This paradigm shift is consistent with calls in consumer research for more focus on hedonic and experiential aspects of consumer behavior (e.g., Holbrook & Hirschman 1982). Considering the emotional side of behavior makes it clear that individuals may undertake action in order to cope with or minimize negative emotion. These coping behaviors are extremely diverse, but can be classified into two main categories: 1) problem-focused coping involves direct, planful action designed to solve environmental problems leading to negative emotion, while 2) emotion-focused coping, including avoidance and denial, involves actions that mitigate negative emotion but that are not directed towards the source of that emotion. For instance, a consumer may deal with a stressful consumer choice by avoiding difficult tradeoffs involving morally-charged attributes (engaging in emotion-focused coping), or by carefully completing these tradeoffs in order to ensure that moral concerns are resolved in a manner that accurately reflects her goals (engaging in problem-focused coping). The objective of this session was to consider the implications of this new coping framework for consumer behavior. All three presentations addressed how consumers cope with difficult or stressful situations. Further, the three presentations took a contingent view of coping, noting that individuals will exploit aspects of their environments in order to cope with difficult tasks, leading to varied coping behaviors.

OVERVIEW

The first presentation, by Irwin & Scattone, addressed anomalies in the weighting of environmental attributes during consumer choice. Consistent with research on anomalies in the valuation of environmental goods, the authors recognized the moral, and therefore potentially emotion-laden, component of these attributes. By demonstrating increased anomalies for environmental (versus other) attributes, this paper illustrates some of the common ways that consumers may choose to cope with environmental concerns in everyday purchases. Further, in contrast to some research on environmental concerns, Irwin & Scattone demonstrated that consumers are to some degree willing to confront potentially emotion-laden tradeoffs between environmental and other attributes in consumer choice, and that this willingness to confront environmental tradeoffs seems to vary with the task. The second presentation, by Luce, et al., addressed tradeoffs that are emotion-laden because the relevant attributes involve highly-valued concerns, including environmental and other issues (e.g., pollution caused or personal safety in a car purchase). They demonstrated that decision makers will sometimes avoid trading off emotion-laden attributes in choice tasks, where it is possible to simply choose the alternative with the best value on the problematic attribute, leading to choice/judgment preference reversals. Thus, the Irwin & Scattone and the Luce, et al. presentations both reported increased decision bias with more morally charged attributes; their findings are attributable, at least in part, to consumers' desires to cope with the emotion elicited by these attributes. Finally, the Sujan, Sujan & Bettman presentation was centrally focused on coping, and reported a descriptive study

investigating how individuals intuitively express the stress they feel as consumers. They presented a broad taxonomy of coping behaviors, and linked these behaviors with a wide variety of aspects of the consumer decision environment. Finally, they linked the variety and nature of reported coping behaviors to consumers' feelings of overall stress and of self-efficacy, noting that perceived self-efficacy is related to the types of coping strategies reported. This presentation therefore provided a framework for understanding the behaviors discussed in the first two papers. Sujan et al.'s general hypothesis that effective coping may involve varied forms of both problem-focused coping and emotion-focused coping helps explain the earlier papers' findings that people will make difficult tradeoffs in some situations, but avoid these same tradeoffs in other situations, leading to apparently biased (e.g., logically inconsistent) response patterns. Sujan et al.'s conceptual framework explains these results in terms of decision makers exploiting their environments in order to engage in both problem-focused and emotion-focused coping, depending on the situation. The overall goal of the special session was to encourage members of the audience to think broadly about avoiding negative emotion in particular, and coping in general, as potential motivators behind the consumer behaviors that they study.

Holbrook, Morris B. & Elizabeth C. Hirschman (1982) The experiential aspects of consumption: Consumer fantasies, feelings, and fun, *Journal of Consumer Research*, 9 (September), 132-140.

Lazarus, Richard S. (1991). Progress on a cognitive-motivational-relational theory of emotion. *American Psychologist*, 46 (8), 819-834.

Anomalies in Weighing Environmental Against other Product Attributes

Julie R. Irwin & Joan Scattone

Many consumer goods today are expressed in terms of environmental attributes such as recycled content and biodegradability. These environmental attributes are assumed to add value to a brand, to distinguish it from brands without such descriptions and/or to communicate that this particular brand has superior levels of the attribute. When adding an attractive attribute, regardless of whether it is environmental or not, it would be especially useful to be able to assume that this addition increases overall attractiveness in certain reasonable ways; we would usually expect that adding the attractive attribute would increase purchase likelihood, and that higher levels of the new attribute would result in greater attractiveness (all other things being equal). However, in studies of environmental values for policies such as a change in air quality, researchers have uncovered anomalous valuation tendencies that make it difficult even to make the simple assumptions outlined above. It is possible that these anomalies likewise might affect environmental attributes of everyday products. The studies presented here tested, using two value measurement techniques (willingness to pay and conjoint measurement), whether, in fact, such anomalies were obtained for environmental attributes of ordinary consumer goods. Environmental policies (such as an increase in air quality, or cleaning up a landfill) can be especially complex, unfamiliar, and morally charged, and the valuation of these special goods has become an intensely researched area. Because the tradeoff between the environment and more mundane and less emotionally charged attributes (such as money) can be difficult, studies of environmental preferences have shown that values for environmental policies are often anomalous (e.g., Irwin, Slovic, Lichtenstein, and McClelland 1993, Kahneman and Knetsch 1993, Schkade and Payne, 1993). For instance, respondents often refuse to make any tradeoffs at all, or their values are systematically and consistently context dependent in ways that violate normative and commonsense expectations. In three studies, one using willingness-to-pay, and two using conjoint measurement, we tested whether environmental attributes show these same sorts of anomalies. We also measured familiarity, morality, and experience, all of which could play mediating factors in the tradeoff difficulty which underlies the anomalies. We found that one anomalie, unwillingness to trade off environmental attributes, was much more prevalent in willingness-to-pay modes than in conjoint modes. Conjoint presumably provides a natural format for reasoning about difficult, emotional tradeoffs, while keeping the explicit nature of the tradeoff (i.e., giving up environmental quality for money or some other attribute) relatively hidden. We also found that context effects (e.g. valuing an environmental attribute less in the presence of another, uncorrelated, environmental attribute) were prevalent in both value measurement conditions, and that moral content mediated this effect. We concluded that environmental attributes of everyday products can present difficult, emotional tradeoffs, but that consumers are able to make these tradeoffs to a large degree, especially when they are presented in a way that both is evocative of everyday purchasing and makes the explicit nature of the tradeoff less obvious. Thus, consumers may be more willing to make difficult tradeoffs in order to gain decision accuracy when the psychic costs of those tradeoffs are mitigated by the decision environment.

Irwin, Julie R., Paul Slovic, Sarah Lichtenstein, and Gary H.McClelland (1993), "Preference reversals and the measurement of environmental values," *Journal of Risk and Uncertainty*, 6, 5-18.

Kahneman, Daniel and Jack Knetsch (1992), "Valuing public goods: the purchase of moral satisfaction," *Journal of Environmental Economics and Management*, 22, 55-70.

Schkade, David A. and John W. Payne (1993). "Where do the numbers come from?: How people respond to contingent valuation questions," in *Contingent Valuation: A Critical Assessment*, (Jerry A. Hausman, Ed.) Elsevier: Amsterdam.

Choice / Matching Preference Reversals and Coping with Tradeoff Difficulty
Mary Frances Luce, Marlene D. Morris, James R. Bettman & John W. Payne

Important consumer decisions can be distressing or emotion-laden when they require difficult tradeoffs such as between automobile safety and price. Our research explores how decision makers cope with this source of decision stress, focusing on the degree to which decision makers cope by avoiding problematic tradeoffs. Thus, we investigate whether decision makers engage in emotion-focused coping (e.g., avoiding distressing attribute tradeoffs) at the expense of problem-focused coping (e.g., making tradeoffs in the service of decision accuracy; see Lazarus 1991 on coping and Luce, Bettman & Payne Forthcoming on coping with decision tasks).

We address tradeoff avoidance using a well-established paradigm for eliciting preference reversals: the choice-matching phenomenon (e.g., Lichtenstein & Slovic 1971; Fischer & Hawkins 1993). Many studies demonstrate that choice is more lexicographic

(i.e., more strongly influenced by prominent attributes) than judgment. This behavior is easily explained in terms of lexicographic strategies preserving cognitive economy in choice. However, we explore a complementary reason for this effect: in some cases, making a lexicographic choice shields the decision maker from emotionally taxing between-attribute tradeoffs.

In experiment one, we presented subjects with pairs of automobiles described in terms of both price and a second (low or high emotion) non-price attribute (e.g., price / styling versus price / safety). Responses to matching questions eliciting a price that makes two alternatives equally-valued are inconsistent with the choices subjects make when presented with pairs of alternatives constructed based on their own prior matching values. Further, we find that choice-matching preference reversals where choices favor the alternative with the higher value on the non-price attribute are reliably more prevalent as that attribute is more emotion-laden. This pattern of results holds even when price is more important. Our findings therefore extend the usual finding that choices favor the alternative that is best on the most important attribute. Thus, there may be multiple explanations for the choice-matching preference reversal phenomenon, involving both cognitive economy and motivations to cope with negative emotion. Overall, therefore, decision makers appear willing to sacrifice some consistency or accuracy in their decision behavior in the interest of avoiding processing operations that elicit negative emotion, particularly when the environment facilitates avoidance (e.g., one may easily avoid tradeoffs by using a lexicographic choice rule).

A replication study involved a differing operationalization of emotion. A pretest indicated that subjects find alternative pairs with relatively low (e.g., low versus average safety) versus relatively high (e.g., average versus high safety) values to be more emotion-laden. As expected, the replication demonstrated an increased incidence of choice / matching preference reversals for alternative pairs involving poorer attribute values.

A final study broadened both the type of avoidance behavior addressed and the environmental source of emotion. Instead of directly considering the tendency to avoid between-attribute tradeoffs, we considered tendencies to avoid a choice altogether (e.g., procrastinating). Further, we operationalized tradeoff difficulty within a high velocity consumer decision context; such a context may itself introduce conflict and uncertainty into the decision situation, eliciting negative emotion.

Fischer, G.W. & Hawkins, S.A. (1993). Strategy compatibility, scale compatibility, and the prominence effect. *Journal of Experimental Psychology: Human Perception and Performance*, 19, 580-597

Lazarus, R.S. (1991). Progress on a cognitive-motivational-relational theory of emotion. *American Psychologist*, 46 (8), 819-834.

Lichtenstein, S. & Slovic, P. (1971). Reversals of preference between bids and choices in gambling decisions. *Journal of Experimental Psychology*, 89, 46-55.

Luce, M.F., Bettman, J.R., & Payne, J.W. (Forthcoming). Choice processing in emotionally difficult decisions. *Journal of Experimental Psychology: Learning, Memory, and Cognition.*

Coping With Stress
Harish Sujan, Mita Sujan & James R. Bettman

Considerable research in psychology has focused on how individuals deal with stress, the responses they use, and their success in coping. Much of this research has supported the notion that some particular coping strategies are more effective than others. It has been found that problem-focused coping and active coping contribute positively to well-being, while emotion focused coping and coping through avoidance are detrimental to health and well-being .(Carver, Scheier & Weintraub 1989; Aspinwall & Taylor 1992).

A critical evaluation of this research raises the possibility that the general support for some types of strategies (problem focused) over others (emotion focused) might be methodological, because much of the work on coping has adopted a trait approach in which general coping styles are seen as operating across many situations. Thus, a situational analysis might produce more contingent results; it may be that problem-focused coping is predominant when individuals believe something can be done whereas emotion-focused coping predominates when the stressor has to be endured (Rothbaum, Weisz & Snyder 1982; Parkes 1984).

An exploratory study investigated how 60 individuals describe the stresses and stressors associated with consumption episodes. These subjects reported an extremely wide variety of purchase-related stressors and coping strategies.

Based on self-reported scales, respondents were classified into four groups reporting: 1) high perceived coping self-efficacy and low experienced stress, 2) high perceived coping self-efficacy and high experienced stress, 3) low perceived coping self-efficacy and low experienced stress, and 4) low perceived coping self-efficacy and high experienced stress. The number of self-reported stressors is higher in the high perceived stress groups, as one would expect. When coping behaviors are analyzed by group, one finds that a wider repertoire of coping strategies is associated with feelings of high coping self-efficacy coupled with high experienced stress. Further analyses described the composition of preferred coping behaviors by stressor and by efficacy / stress group. Future work will address whether better copers are more flexible, showing greater variability in choice of coping strategies across stressors. Similarly, better copers may buffer themselves against stress more successfully by using both a wider range of coping strategies per se and a wider range of coping strategies for any given stressor.

Aspinwall, Lisa G. and Shelley E. Taylor (1992), "Modeling Cognitive Adaptation: A Longitudinal Investigation of the Impact of Individual Differences & Coping on College Adjustment & Performance," *Journal of Personality and Social Psychology*. 63(6), 989-1003.

Carver, Charles S., Michael F. Scheier and Jagdish Kumani Weintraub (1989), "Assessing Coping Strategies," *Journal of Personality and Social Psychology*, 56(2), 267-283.

Parkes, Katharine R. (1984), "Focus of Control, Cognitive Appraisal & Coping in Stressful Episodes," *Journal of Personality and Social Psychology*, 46(3), 655-668.

Rothbaum, Fred, John R. Weisz and Samuel S. Snyder (1982), "Changing the World and Changing the Self: A Two-Process Model of Perceived Control," *Journal of Personality and Social Psychology*, Vol. 42 (No. 1), 5-37.

Embodied Cognition: Towards a More Realistic and Productive Model of Mental Representation

George S. Babbes, University of California, Berkeley
Alan J. Malter, University of Wisconsin, Madison

The objective of this session was to present and discuss embodied cognition as an alternative approach to conceptualizing the mind in consumer research. The embodied view of cognition was proposed as a more realistic and productive model of mental representation than traditional models of mind, such as the dominant mind-as-computer approach (e.g., information processing). More specifically, this session aimed to: (1) argue that cognitive structure and processes are based on embodied mental representations; (2) present empirical evidence from marketing and other disciplines in support of the principal tenets of embodied cognition; and (3) consider implications of adopting an embodied perspective for theory and method in consumer research.

This session was motivated by the growing sense that the traditional structuralist models of memory and cognition, which are so widely used in consumer research, cannot adequately account for consumer experience in a dynamic and interactive world. Embodied cognition offers a promising alternative approach that: (1) is well-grounded in the cognitive science literature (e.g., philosophy, Johnson 1987; cognitive linguistics, Lakoff 1987; Lakoff and Johnson 1980; cognitive psychology, Barsalou 1993; Glenberg, in press; neurobiology, Damasio 1994; Edelman 1992; and anthropology, Stoller 1995); (2) is an actively researched topic across a number of cognitive science disciplines; and (3) has important implications for consumer research. Though a few researchers have recently discussed the notion of embodied cognition in the marketing literature (e.g., Malter 1996; Rosa 1995; Zaltman and Coulter 1995), this view has not been thoroughly addressed in the major marketing journals, nor has it been the focus of a special session. This session was designed to fill this gap and to stimulate consumer research from an embodied perspective.

In brief, the papers in this session presented: (1) an overview of the basic theory of embodied cognition, initial empirical support from cognitive and developmental psychology, and directions for future consumer research; (2) a pioneering empirical study of the pervasive use of embodied metaphors in print advertisements; and (3) the neurobiological aspects of an embodied cognitive system and the significance of embodied cognition for human understanding. These presentations are summarized below.

Embodied Cognition: Theory, Evidence, and Directions for Research

Alan J. Malter, University of Wisconsin, Madison

In his overview paper, Malter noted that consumer research has been dominated by traditional structuralist models of memory and cognition, exemplified by the mind-as-computer approach of information processing (Hirschman 1993). These "disembodied" models are generally characterized by mind-body dualism, in which the human mind is viewed as operating completely independently of the body. In this approach, mental representations involve the manipulation of meaningless abstract symbols, linked by propositions, and governed by a set of extrinsic constraints (i.e., a set of rules which are external to the system of mental representations). Concepts are represented by lists of features, or attributes. This artificial intelligence view of the mind-as-computer breaks down

when trying to account for everyday memory in a dynamic world (e.g., Neisser 1982).

Malter proposed the emerging theory of embodied cognition as a more realistic and productive view of the human mind than traditional approaches. For example, in contrast to the information processing approach (e.g., Bettman 1979) based on Cartesian dualism and its separation of mind from body, embodied cognition views the mind as a dynamic and flexible meaning system serving a fully integrated human organism. The body is not considered to be merely a support structure for the mind, but an integral part of an indissociable mind-body whole. The "embodied" aspect of embodied cognition refers to the view that human knowledge uses a person's own body as the basic frame of reference and is encoded in memory in terms of multisensory, perceptual, image-schematic elements (not inherently meaningless, abstract symbols). In the embodied view, a process of conceptual metaphor extends basic embodied mental representations to account for abstract concepts.

Malter described and synthesized two types of embodied cognition theories which have been proposed recently by cognitive and developmental psychologists: (1) theories based on continuous and mutually constraining physical interaction between an individual and the environment (e.g., Glenberg in press; Thelen and Smith 1994); and (2) theories focusing more on the perceptual properties of mental representations and the dynamic process of conceptual combination (e.g., Barsalou 1993; Mandler 1992). The growing body of empirical evidence from the cognitive psychology literature was also reviewed, including findings that a physical manipulation (e.g., making various hand shapes) could affect performance on a cognitive task (e.g., sensibility judgments, Klatzky et al. 1989), that body positioning enhances spatial orientation (Rieser et al. 1994), and that embodied physical experience (e.g., professional typing skills) influences categorization and preferences (Van den Bergh et al. 1990). Finally, implications were discussed of adopting an embodied view of cognition in consumer research, including placing greater emphasis on process and change, and focusing more on physical, sensory, and other experiential aspects of consumption.

Metaphor and Embodied Cognition: A Content Analysis

George S. Babbes, University of California, Berkeley
Pamela Morgan, University of California, Berkeley

In an empirical study of conceptual metaphor in print advertisements, Babbes and Morgan found support for the view that cognition is embodied. In his presentation, Babbes first explained how conceptual metaphor differs from the traditional Aristotelian view that metaphor is simply a deviant use of language, and the objectivist view that it is irrelevant to meaning. In the cognitive view of conceptual metaphor (e.g., Lakoff 1993), something concrete (and usually embodied) is used to provide a cognitive structure for something which is abstract; this structuring is the result of a cross-domain mapping between a source (concrete) domain and a target (abstract) domain in the conceptual system. For example, in the metaphor, "Life is a journey," the concrete language of a journey (source domain) is used to talk about abstract life events (target domain). In talking about life events we might say things like, "the promotion is around the corner," "I'm at a crossroads," or "it's downhill from here."

The premise is that the human conceptual system is inherently metaphorical, using experiential gestalts to structure unfamiliar and abstract domains. As such, metaphor is expected to be (1) pervasive in ads and (2) often embodied. That is, Babbes and Morgan expected to find pervasive use of both conceptual metaphor (efficient communication) and embodied source domains (effective communication), particularly for more abstract products which would presumably benefit most from adopting the structure of favorable and well-understood conceptual domains.

To test these hypotheses, ads were pulled from *Time, Business Week,* and *Money* (2/95 to 10/95), for four progressively abstract product categories: cars, computers, money management, and insurance. Two trained coders independently coded 70 items with respect to each element of the ad (e.g., headline, picture, logo, tagline). The principal findings (based on a headline analysis) were: (1) conceptual metaphor is used extensively in ads for both concrete products (e.g., automobiles) and abstract products (e.g., insurance), each with about 60% in the headline; (2) the key selling idea of the ad is significantly more likely to be an inference of the metaphor for abstract versus concrete products (.57 versus .13); and (3) while conceptual metaphors in most ads use an embodied source domain, the use of embodied metaphors was significantly greater in insurance ads than in automobile ads (.82 versus .58). This is consistent with the view that abstract products need the most structured source domains. The high baseline use of embodied metaphors in ads is likely due to the fact that concrete products are often communicating abstract consumer benefits, e.g., cars as sources of escape and power. In addition, all of the ads for a given product category could be reduced to a very small set of source domains (almost always embodied). For example, nearly every financial services ad used the source domain of either "physical well-being" (e.g., the Travelers umbrella) or "journey" (e.g., a compass to good retirement).

Babbes and Morgan concluded that conceptual metaphors are pervasive in advertising and are often embodied, particularly for abstract product categories. These findings have implications for communication, learning, inference-making, and public policy. A future extension of this work is to examine metaphor-use cross-culturally.

Eliciting Consumer Representations Through Embodiment Basics
Gerald Zaltman, Harvard University

In his paper, Zaltman explained that though it may be new for consumer researchers to study how the human brain works, more experienced experts in cognitive science are still struggling with understanding basic mental structure and processes. Therefore, consumer researchers should not back away from investigating these issues, even though they are among the most challenging and seem to defy explanation.

Zaltman's work on eliciting consumers' "deep root" metaphors shows that there may be an overall mental architecture for any particular concept. This view is supported by Edelman's (1987, 1992) theory of neuronal group selection, whereby groups of neurons form concepts and networks of concepts on particular themes or topics. Edelman's theory explains the neurobiological basis of self-organizing dynamic systems of the type postulated in psychological theories of embodied cognition (e.g., Thelen and Smith 1994). Neuronal groups share certain common features, which leads to a literal wiring between the groups and a global mapping (i.e., metaphor), such as for a specific category or brand.

In other words, Edelman's work provides the neurological underpinnings of how conceptual metaphors are stored in memory.

Zaltman suggested that this type of process may explain how executives approach ill-structured and messy problems, or how consumers may literally form mental models of product categories, e.g., automobiles. The use of metaphor elicitation techniques (e.g. Zaltman and Coulter 1995) to uncover deep root metaphors can help managers to better understand consumers' core concepts for particular products and find others which are related.

Discussion and Synthesis
Dipanker Chakravarti, University of Colorado, Boulder

Chakravarti's synthesis and discussion of embodied cognition focused on some of the key issues in the 400-year-old mind-body dualism debate. He noted that the view of embodied cognition proposed in the three presentations was not simply a multisensory information processing perspective. Rather, it elaborated on the core image of mind-body dualism in which some mental representations have "gray" material properties, while others contain "colorful" thoughts and feelings. Chakravarti argued that as consumer researchers approach work on embodied cognition, they must be cognizant of the positions they take on the mind-body dualism debate.

Drawing on Chalmers' (1996) book, *The Conscious Mind,* Chakravarti noted that consumer researchers (like other social and natural scientists and philosophers) may adopt one of several alternative positions on the mind-body dualism issue. One position rejects dualism, denying the independent reality of matter. The focus is purely on subjective experience–an extreme interpretivism as in deconstructionist poetry. A second (and dominant) position also rejects dualism, but denies the independent reality of mind. Manifested in "materialism" in its various forms, some researchers even deny the problem, finding resolution in identification (labeling the experience), behaviorism, (e.g., focusing on "purchase behavior" as reflected in scanner data without considering its mental antecedents) or functionalism (treating the mind as merely the processing functions performed by the brain).

Following Chalmers, Chakravarti suggested that perhaps a more tenable position in consumer research is to accept dualism and then try to bridge the gap in the research context. The core problems (and issues) that arise will require that researchers deal with the issues of "intentionality" (control) and "aboutness" (locus) of mental activity concerning the subjective experiences surrounding consumption objects; find targets for words such as "availability" and "accessibility" that populate the psychologists' lexicon; avoid ambiguous metaphors (e.g., the "structure of expertise") that act as if the problem and the problem-solver can be separated; and distinguish evidence of "brain workings" from subjective experience. The problems are challenging, but consumer researchers must deal with them as they try to understand how the mind and the body are implicated in consumption. The three research papers presented in this session are a promising start.

REFERENCES

Barsalou, Lawrence W. (1993), "Flexibility, Structure, and Linguistic Vagary in Concepts: Manifestations of a Compositional System of Perceptual Symbols," in *Theories of Memory,* eds., A.F. Collins, S.E. Gathercole, M.A. Conway, and P.E. Morris, Hillsdale, NJ: Erlbaum, 29-101.

Bettman, James R. (1979), *An Information Processing Theory of Consumer Choice,* Reading, MA: Addison-Wesley.

Chalmers, David J. (1996), *The Conscious Mind: In Search of a Fundamental Theory,* New York: Oxford University Press.

Damasio, Antonio R. (1994), *Descartes' Error: Emotion, Reason, and the Human Brain,* New York: Putnam.

Edelman, Gerald M. (1992), *Bright Air, Brilliant Fire: On the Matter of the Mind,* New York: Basic Books.

———— (1987), *Neural Darwinism: The Theory of Neuronal Group Selection,* New York: Basic Books.

Glenberg, Arthur M. (in press), "What is Memory For," *Behavioral and Brain Sciences.*

Hirschman, Elizabeth C. (1993), "Ideology in Consumer Research, 1980 and 1990: A Marxist and Feminist Critique," *Journal of Consumer Research, 19* (4), 537-555.

Johnson, Mark (1987), *The Body in the Mind: The Bodily Basis of Meaning, Imagination, and Reason,* Chicago: University of Chicago Press.

Klatzky, Roberta L., James W. Pellegrino, Brian P. McCloskey and Sally Doherty (1989), "Can You Squeeze a Tomato? The Role of Motor Representations in Semantic Sensibility Judgments," *Journal of Memory and Language, 28,* 56-77.

Lakoff, George (1993), "The Contemporary Theory of Metaphor," in *Metaphor and Thought,* second edition, ed. Andrew Ortony, New York: Cambridge University Press, 202-251.

———— (1987), *Women, Fire, and Dangerous Things: What Categories Reveal About the Mind,* Chicago: University of Chicago Press.

———— and Mark Johnson (1980), *Metaphors We Live By,* Chicago: University of Chicago Press.

Malter, Alan J. (1996), "An Introduction to Embodied Cognition: Implications for Consumer Research," in *Advances in Consumer Research,* Vol. 23, eds. Kim P. Corfman and John Lynch, Provo, UT: Association for Consumer Research, 272-276.

Mandler, Jean M. (1992), "How to Build a Baby: II. Conceptual Primitives," *Psychological Review, 99* (4), 587-604.

Neisser, Ulric (1982), *Memory Observed: Remembering in Natural Contexts,* New York: Freeman.

Rieser, John J., Anne E. Garing and Michael F. Young (1994), "Imagery, Action, and Young Children's Spatial Orientation: It's Not Being There That Counts, It's What One Has in Mind," *Child Development, 65* (5), 1262-1278.

Rosa, Jose Antonio (1995), "Adaptive Selling Behavior: The Role of the Embodied System," in *Proceedings of the 1995 AMA Summer Educators' Conference,* Vol. 6, eds. Barbara B. Stern and George M. Zinkhan, Chicago: American Marketing Association, 400-410.

Stoller, Paul (1995), *Embodying Colonial Memories: Spirit Possession, Power, and the Hauka in West Africa,* New York: Routledge.

Thelen, Esther and Linda B. Smith (1994), *A Dynamic Systems Approach to the Development of Cognition and Action,* Cambridge, MA: MIT Press.

Van den Bergh, Omer, Scott Vrana and Paul Eelen (1990), "Letters From the Heart: Affective Categorization of Letter Combinations in Typists and Nontypists," *Journal of Experimental Psychology: Learning, Memory, and Cognition, 16* (6), 1153-1161.

Zaltman, Gerald and Robin Higie Coulter (1995), "Seeing the Voice of the Customer: Metaphor-Based Advertising Research," *Journal of Advertising Research, 35* (4), 35-51.

Relative Influence In Purchase Decision Making: Married, Cohabitating, and Homosexual Couples

Michelle C. Reiss, Mississippi State University
Cynthia Webster, Mississippi State University

ABSTRACT

The purpose of this paper is to develop the conceptual foundation for investigating the extent to which established relative influence concepts—resource theory, least-interested partner hypothesis, ideology theory, and involvement—explain relative influence of partners in married, cohabitating, lesbian and gay dyads in purchase decisions. Based on the established theories and a review of the consumer behavior, sociological, and psychological literatures, we introduce several propositions regarding relative influence in decision making for both the traditional and less traditional couples. Emphasis is placed on laying the foundation for future research in the relative influence area.

For several decades spousal roles in purchase decision making have received considerable research attention. On the other hand, very little research attention has been given to the decision-making behavior of nonmarried[1] couples. This paucity of research attention is surprising because nonfamily households are growing at a much faster rate than family households.

The purpose of this research is to provide the conceptual foundation for investigating relative influence in purchase decision making between partners in traditional and nontraditional couples. Specifically, the four primary concepts which have provided the theoretical foundation for explaining relative influence—resource theory, least-interested partner hypothesis, ideology theory, and involvement—will be applied to relative influence patterns between married, cohabiting, lesbian, and gay couples.

The remainder of this paper is organized according to the theoretical underpinnings. A theory is presented first and propositions are then made for the traditional and nontraditional couples. It is important to remember that not all propositions are based on equal evidence—the external validity of certain studies was lessened due to the use of smaller sample sizes in limited geographical areas. The propositions are formulated to guide and stimulate future research endeavors.

Resource Theory

Resource theory holds that the party who possesses the greatest socioeconomic resources is the one who will have more power (Rodman 1967). Resources include socioeconomic factors such as education, occupational status, income and other resources such as community participation and organizational membership (Lee 1987). According to Rodman (1972), the U.S. is considered a transitional egalitarian society, meaning that norms are becoming more egalitarian but are not yet sufficiently certain to guarantee that all marriages will be egalitarian. This normative ambiguity allows resource factors to operate freely. When power is negotiable, resources become relevant in the manner described by resource theory, and they correlate positively with power in marriage (Lee 1987).

Married couples. Research relying on resource theory as an explanation of relative influence has generally focused on married couples and has generally concluded that resources maintained by each spouse provide a degree of leverage in the exchange relationship (Lee 1987). Significant relationships have been found between relative influence in marriage and education (e.g., Rosen and Granbois 1983), job status (e.g., Rosen and Granbois 1983), and income (e.g., Green and Cunningham 1975). Men have traditionally possessed more power because they held more of these resources. However, the relative influence of married females in the U.S. has increased in recent years because more wives are working outside the home and questioning the traditional sex roles. Married couples with a more modern sex-role orientation are more willing to shop jointly for major items that would have been the responsibility of one spouse in more traditionally-oriented families (Lavin 1993).

Cohabiting couples. The institution of marriage supposedly gives the husband more influence over his wife than the male over his partner in cohabitation (Stafford, Backman, and Dibona 1977). The difference in influence is primarily due to the stronger social sanctions associated with the institution of marriage (Nock 1995). More specifically, the more one is committed to a relationship, the greater the likelihood of tolerating an inequitable situation (Blau 1964).

Compared to married partners, partners in cohabiting dyads appear to be more similar with respect to age, income, education and job prestige, and attitudes regarding egalitarianism (Kurdek and Schmitt 1987). Further, cohabitating women, as opposed to married women, are more likely to be employed outside of the home and to consequently have their own income (Blair 1994). Thus, we expect that resource theory will be a better predictor of relative influence among married couples than among cohabiting couples.

Proposition 1: Purchase decision making among cohabitating couples is less likely to be influenced by resource-related characteristics than among married couples.

Lesbian couples. While some studies have implied that resource theory explains relative influence among lesbian couples (Caldwell and Peplau 1984), other studies found no association between resources and power in lesbian dyads (Bell and Weinberg 1978; Blumstein and Schwartz 1983; Reilly and Lynch 1990). Further, lesbian partners tend to be similar to one another with respect to both demographic and socioeconomic characteristics (Kurdek and Schmitt 1987) and tend to agree on the equitable nature of their relationships. Therefore, we propose that resource theory will be less applicable to relative influence among lesbian couples than among married couples.

Proposition 2: Compared to married couples, purchase decision making among lesbian couples is less likely to be influenced by resource-related characteristics.

Gay couples. Decision-making equality is a prerequisite of successful gay relationships (Dines 1990). Perhaps this is due to the fact that—compared to married heterosexuals—gay partners tend to be more similar to each other in the possession of traditional bases of power (Harry 1982). Since both parties in a gay relationship are typically employed and have a relatively high educational attainment, the importance of resources as a basis for power declines.

---

[1]The term "nonmarried" is used here to refer to heterosexual and homosexual couples who reside together and who have not legally married.

Advances in Consumer Research
Volume 24, © 1997

Proposition 3: Compared to married couples, relative influence in decision making among gay male couples is less likely to be affected by resource-related characteristics.

As mentioned previously, lesbian partners tend to share similar socioeconomic characteristics. Comparably, both partners in gay couples tend to be equitable along resource factor lines and in the possession of traditional bases of power (Harry 1982). Therefore,

Proposition 4: No differences in the relation between resources and relative influence will exist between gay male couples and lesbian couples.

However, age was found to be a significant predictor of power in decision making within gay relationships, especially among gay cohabitors (Harry 1983). The older partner frequently provided direction and stability to the younger partner, thus creating a complementary dyad (McWhirter and Mattison 1984). Gays who prefer a dominant role are more likely to prefer younger partners than partners lower in socioeconomic status. Similarly, gays who prefer a subordinate role are likely to be more attracted to older men than to peers.

Proposition 5: Age will be a stronger predictor of relative influence among gays than socioeconomic variables.

Proposition 6: The older partner in a gay dyad will possess greater relative influence in purchase decision making than his younger counterpart.

Ideology Theory

Ideology theory or role theory concentrates on social norms and culturally determined attitudes to predict the role each spouse will perform within the marriage (Qualls 1987). Ideology or gender roles are sets of behavior that society considers appropriate for members of each sex (Marecek, Finn, and Cardell 1982). Traditionally, society considered it appropriate for females to be socialized to perform the nurturing, social-emotional, homemaker role and males to be socialized to perform the competitive, breadwinner role (Thompson and Walker 1989). Past research has found a significant relationship between sex-role orientation and relative influence in decision making (e.g., Green and Cunningham 1975; Qualls 1987; Webster 1994).

Married couples. Research published in the 1970s revealed that sex-role differences in purchase decision making exist among married couples. For instance, decisions regarding some products (i.e., appliances, groceries) tend to be in the domain of the wife who adheres to traditional sex roles, whereas other decisions (i.e, insurance, automobiles) tend to be in the domain of the patriarchal husband. Similarly, the husband had more influence over more important and functional product attributes, whereas the wife had more influence over relatively minor, aesthetic product attributes (e.g., Green and Cunningham 1975; Woodside and Motes 1979). In general, the adherence to more traditional sex roles positively relates to husband dominance where more modern sex roles are associated with greater equality in decision making (Green and Cunningham 1975; Webster 1994).

One study on family gender roles found that while roles (i.e., women working outside the home) and attitudes (i.e., positive feelings toward women's involvement in work) are becoming more egalitarian, behavioral change (i.e., joint decision making) has occurred at a much slower pace (Caycedo, Wang and Bahr 1991;

Bahr 1991). With respect to attitudes, per se, women and relatively young individuals were found to have more egalitarian attitudes than men and older individuals. Another study, focusing on Chinese and American males, found a positive correlation between the perceived number of joint decisions and egalitarianism for the final-decision stage (Ford et al. 1995). Males exhibiting a higher level of egalitarianism tend to be more sensitive toward the inclusion of both husband and wife in the final decision phase and are associated with less patriarchal societies.

Cohabitating couples. The relation between conventional sex roles and marriage has been established within the literature (Kotkin 1985; Stafford et. al. 1977), whereas, the results have been mixed concerning the relation between less conventional sex roles and cohabitation. Some researchers have suggested that both married and cohabitating couples report fairly traditional sex role behavior (Risman et al. 1981; Stafford et al. 1977; Yllo 1978), while others have found that cohabitants display less traditional sex-roles in both their attitudes and behavior (Kotkin 1985; Tanfer 1987; Cunningham and Antill 1994; Huffman et. al. 1994).

Based on the most recent research, the disposition to cohabitate is related to more liberal attitudes toward sexual behavior, less traditional views of marriage, and to less traditional views of sex roles (Huffman et. al. 1994). Intuitively, it follows that if cohabitors have less traditional views of sex roles, they will also portray more egalitarian purchase decision making within their relations. Therefore, we propose that individuals in cohabitating couples who adhere to less traditional sex roles will exhibit more equitable purchase decision making:

Proposition 7: Ideology theory will be a better predictor of relative influence for married couples than for cohabitating couples.

Homosexual couples. Most contemporary homosexual relationships do not conform strictly to traditional "masculine" and "feminine" roles; instead, role flexibility and turn-taking are more common patterns (Dines 1990). Gender role playing is diminished in lesbian and gay couples because of the tendency to endorse feminist values, the efforts to eradicate traditional gender roles and the striving of both lesbians and gays to create new forms of relationships different from those of heterosexual couples (Marecek et al. 1982). Research has revealed that heterosexual couples tend to be more sex-role differentiated than lesbian couples, who, in turn, are more sex-role differentiated than gay males (Cardell et al. 1981). Lesbians tend to have higher masculinity scores than heterosexual women due to higher self-ratings on *independence*. Gay men tend to have lower masculinity scores than heterosexual men due to low *competitiveness* ratings (Finlay and Scheltema 1991). These findings indicate that masculinity and femininity measures are useless and unreliable when studying the traits of homosexuals. Hence, a focus on personality characteristics may be more beneficial in determining purchase decision influence.

Lesbian Couples. Research has shown that less than 20 percent of lesbians actually engage in role playing based on traditional gender roles (Dines, 1990). Therefore, the traditional heterosexual marriage is not the predominant model for lesbian couples (e.g. Blumstein and Schwartz 1983; Caldwell and Peplau 1984; Lynch and Reilly 1985). Lesbian couples have not created their relationships around many of the traditional variables that have accorded one partner greater power over the other, thus indicating that the egalitarian ideal is prevalent in lesbian relationships (Reilly and Lynch 1990). Thus,

Proposition 8: Compared to married couples, purchase decision making among lesbian couples is less likely to be influenced by traditional sex role based differences.

Gay Couples. Early writers on gays suggested that these men modeled their relationships on traditional heterosexual gender roles (Bieber et al. 1962; Socarides 1968; McDonald and Moore 1978; Jones and DeCecco 1982; Storms 1980). However, other works have found little support for this notion (Haist and Hewitt 1974; Harry 1982; Saghir and Robins 1973). Indeed, some gay men have been found to have the ability to be flexible in their sex-typed roles and are able to switch between typically masculine and feminine behaviors (Westmoreland 1975). Thus,

Proposition 9: Compared to married couples, relative influence in decision making among gay couples is less likely to be influenced by traditional sex-role differences.

Since traditional role bases, such as the social construction of masculinity versus femininity, is not considered reliable for describing same-sex couples, how should roles be measured in these relations? Several authors have found that the relations of lesbians and gays involve less gender role playing and that the traditional sex role inventories (i.e., Bem Sex Role Inventory) do not predict sex role differentiated behavior (Cardell et. al. 1981; Finlay and Scheltema 1991).

In an early conceptualization, three hypothetical models were presented describing how roles might be allocated in same-sex couples (Marecek et. al. 1982). The first model posited that realistic factors lead one partner to accept certain responsibilities. Additional behaviors associated with the original behavior will then be assumed by this partner. The second model presumes that the masculine role is valued and rewarded more than the feminine role; therefore, the claim to the masculine role will be made by the partner who is the most powerful in the dyad. The final model is based on gender identities or how "male" or "female" one feels. The authors propose that in homosexual couples, even small differences in gender identities might lead to assuming different gender roles and consequently to a different levels of influence in purchase decision making. The authors point out that this view is speculative and perhaps controversial.

Although the literature reveals several conceptualizations of how roles are played out in same-sex couples, very few, if any, have been empirically tested. Therefore, it can be informally concluded that the question remains unanswered as to how roles are allocated in same-sex couples, as well as how they affect relative influence in purchase decision making.

Least-Interested Partner Hypothesis

The least-interested partner hypothesis states that power can be understood in terms of who is less committed or less involved in the relationship (Waller 1938; Peplau 1984). The least-interested partner will feel that he/she has less to lose, resulting in less willingness to please the other partner. This decrease in dependence results in an increase in power for the less-in-love partner (Sprecher 1985). On the other hand, the more "interested partner" is more anxious to maintain the relationship even if he/she offers more resources and receives fewer in return (Safilios-Rothschild 1976).

Married couples. Applications of the principle of least-interest have revealed that the more wives loved their husbands, the less coercive they were; the more husbands were committed to their wives and the marriage, the less control they possessed; and the greater the husband's income relative to his wife's, the more power

he possessed in decision making (Safilios-Rothschild 1976; Godwin and Scanzoni 1990).

Cohabitating couples. In general, research in the U.S. has found that cohabitating couples report significantly less commitment than married couples (Macklin 1983; Nock 1995). Further, the male in cohabitating couples is particularly less committed (Lyness et. al. 1972). Based on the least-interested partner hypothesis, the individual who has less interest will hold more power in that relationship. If cohabitating males actually are less committed to their partners, they may have more of a power base than that of married males over their partners (Johnson 1972).

Proposition 10: There will be no significant difference between cohabitating and married couples regarding the extent to which the least-interested partner hypothesis explains relative influence.

Proposition 11: The male in cohabitating couples will be more likely to be the least-interested partner than the female in cohabitating couples and, therefore, dominate in purchase decision making.

Since the least-interested partner hypothesis appears to be not affected by sex-role orientation, it can be applied also to homosexual couples. The partner least concerned about preserving the relationship can deter opposition to his or her choices by being more willing than the other partner to leave the relationship. Since these same factors operate in marriage, it is proposed that the least-interested partner hypothesis will affect relative influence of married and homosexual couples in the same manner.

Proposition 12: There will be no significant difference between married and homosexual couples regarding the extent to which the least-interested partner hypothesis explains relative influence.

With respect to lesbian relationships, two distinct value orientations have been presented in the literature–dyadic attachment and personal autonomy (Peplau et al. 1978). First, dyadic attachment emphasizes emotionally close love relationships and is characterized by wanting to spend more time with the partner and worrying less that personal independence will create difficulties for the relation (Peplau et al. 1978). Second, personal autonomy emphasizes independence and self-actualization that may lead to questioning the traditional patterns of love relationships. Autonomy is characterized by wanting to spend less time with the partner, being less willing to maintain the relation at the expense of work or education, and worrying about having an overly dependent partner (Peplau et al. 1978). Hence, it seems likely that these value orientations will affect which individual is the least-interested partner in a lesbian relationship. Lesbians who endorse the value orientation of personal autonomy are likely to have less interest in the relationship and maintain more power in purchase decision making. Thus,

Proposition 13: In a lesbian couple, the partner who endorses personal autonomy orientations to a greater degree than dyadic attachment orientations will maintain greater relative influence in purchase decision making.

Involvement Theory

Involvement theory posits that the individual in a relationship that is more highly involved with a product will have more decision-making power regarding that product (Qualls 1987). Within the marital dyad, one study found that involvement—the relative importance of the task goal to an individual—is the most important predictor of decision making influence (Corfmann and Lehmann 1987). Dated studies found that men have more power in purchase decisions regarding products in which men have traditionally been interested (i.e., insurance and automobiles) (Bonfield 1978; Davis and Rigaux 1974; Green et al. 1983; Sharp and Mott 1956; Wolgast 1958; Woodside and Motes 1979). Similarly, women have been found to have more power regarding products in which women were traditionally interested (i.e., groceries and appliances) (Bonfield 1978; Davis and Rigaux 1976; Green et al. 1983; Sharp and Mott 1956; Wolgast 1958; Woodside and Motes 1979).

To date, empirical research has not been published on relative influence of nonmarried couples that uses the involvement concept as a theoretical base. With respect to cohabitants, it seems reasonable to expect that no significant difference in the way involvement affects relative influence in purchase decision making will exist when compared to married couples. With respect to homosexual couples, research has shown that lesbian couples tend to characterize their relationships as relatively egalitarian in decision making for household task assignments, leisure activity choices, residence location, finances, and selection of friends (Bell and Weinberg 1978; Brooks 1981; Blumstein and Schwartz 1983; Schneider 1986; Brooks 1981; Caldwell and Peplau 1984; Tanner 1978). Further, equality in decision making was found to occur across several product categories (e.g., cars, insurance, money for food, vacations, restaurants, leisure, and house or apartment) (Lynch and Reilly (1985/86). Therefore,

Proposition 14: No differences will exist among married, cohabitating, or homosexual couples concerning involvement theory. The partner most interested and involved in the purchase of a particular product will have more relative influence concerning that product.

Interaction Between Involvement and the Least Interested Partner Hypothesis

A possible link or interaction effect may exist between involvement theory and the least-interested partner hypothesis. The partner in a relationship (whether it be a married or nonmarried couple) who is less in love will maintain the greatest power in purchase decision making due to his or her emotional independence from the other partner. Intuitively, one instance in which this power may be lessened is when the "more in love" partner is more involved with a specific purchase. In this case, the importance of the task goal (purchase of the product) will override feelings of strictly wanting to please the dominant partner and will result in an increase in power. Based on this line of thinking, we speculate that:

Proposition 15: Involvement will override the least-interested partner hypothesis in decision making. Specifically, the "more interested," more highly involved partner will have more influence in decision making than the "less interested" (i.e., the partner less in love), less involved partner.

DISCUSSION

The premise of the current research is to broaden our understanding of relative influence in purchase decision making by propositioning the extent to which established concepts explain relative influence of partners in four different types of couples: the traditional married couple and three more contemporary types of couples—cohabitating heterosexual, lesbian, and gay. Our inclusion of less traditional couples is deemed important because of the

drastic increase in the number of households comprised of nonmarried individuals.

Four main theories were used as the theoretical orientation for the proposed research—resource theory, ideology theory, the least-interested partner hypothesis, and the involvement concept. The proposed research provides a preliminary step toward determining the extent to which established theory applies to more contemporary households.

Research on power and purchase decision making of married couples was used as the reference point to which nonmarried households were compared. No differences between the married, cohabitating, lesbian, and gay couples were proposed to exist with respect to the least-interested partner hypothesis and the involvement concept.

On the other hand, the parameters of the relationships between the two other theories, resource and ideology, and relative influence in purchase decision making are expected to differ across couple type. Based on previous research, cohabitating couples are expected to be influenced less by resource-related characteristics and sex-role orientation behaviors due to their demographic and socioeconomic similarities and their display of more non-traditional sex-role related behaviors when compared to married couples.

Homosexual couples are proposed to be less influenced by resource-related factors and sex-role orientation behaviors. With respect to lesbian couples, the distribution of power appears to be not dependent upon age, income, education, or asset differences (Reilly and Lynch 1990). Resource factors have also not been found to be significant determinants of power in gay relationships; however, age appears to be an influential factor. Furthermore, the traditional role variables that have accorded one partner greater power over the other in marital dyads seem to be not applicable to both lesbian and gay couples. Therefore, this research proposes that predicting relative influence among homosexual couples strictly by the roles associated with sexual orientation may be misleading. Future research should examine how personality traits and value orientations create differences in influence in purchase decisions within the homosexual couple. For instance, male homosexuals have been found to be less masculine, more tender-minded, less dominate, more unconventional, and less submissive to authority than heterosexual males (c.f. Delozier and Rodrique 1996). Conversely, lesbians have been found to be more dominant, independent and tough-minded than heterosexual females. These traits and values may lead to differences in the allocation of power in purchase decision making.

The preceding conceptualization also provides further direction for future research. For example, a variable possibly affecting each of the discussed theories—commitment—will be investigated by the authors. For cohabitors, both men and women have been found to display significantly less commitment than other couples (Macklin 1983). This could lead to an imbalance of power (Huffman et. al. 1994). It has been found that the major motivation of men and women in cohabitating relations is substantially different—men are likely to perceive cohabitation as a convenience, where women are likely to perceive cohabitation as a path to marriage (Huffman et al. 1994). These differences in perception could lead to an imbalance in power favoring the male. For homosexuals, the lowest levels of commitment have been reported by gay males (Duffy and Rusbult 1985/86).

Second, the role of time allocation patterns in household consumption is another area of interest that will be extended to nontraditional families. In married households, the most important factors influencing a household's choice of purchase decision maker are hours of market labor supplied by the male and female

(Blaylock and Smallwood 1987). This research could easily be extended to determine if any differences exist between married and nonmarried households.

Third, the application of human capital theory (Becker 1975) to both traditional and non-traditional families may add to our understanding of relative influence. The primary basis of human capital theory relies on the concept of return on investment. When individuals invest such resources as time, money and energy toward education, training, etc., they are likely to expect some return on their investment. This return on investment could be expected in the form of monetary returns or even social recognition. In regard to relationship dyads, they may also expect to have a certain degree of influence in purchase decision making relative to their investment. This influence may be heightened if inequality exists between the partners' "resources". Thus, research effort should be expended on determining the extent to which human capital theory explains relative influence across different types of couples.

Finally, lifestyle characteristics of non-traditional families, such as social class, earnings, occupation, and family structure could contribute to different consumption processes. We intend to ascertain if demographic and socioeconomic differences between married and homosexual couples contribute to distinct allocations of power in purchase decision making. Further, research might focus on determining the psychographic differences and similarities between married and nonmarried couples and whether psychographic factors moderate the extent to which a particular theory (i.e., resource) predicts relative influence.

REFERENCES

Allen, Katherine R. and David H. Demo (1995), "The Families of Lesbians and Gay Men: A New Frontier in Family Research", *Journal of Marriage and the Family*, 57 (1), 111-127.

Bahr, Stephan (1972), "Comment on the study of family power structures: A Review 1960-1969", *Journal of Marriage and the Family*, 34 (August), 239-241.

Becker, Gary (1975), *Human Capital*, New York: National Bureau of Economic Research.

Bell, A.P and M.S. Weinberg (1978). Homosexualities: *A study of Diversity Among Men and Women.* New York: Simon and Schuster.

Bieber, I., H.J. Dain, P.R. Dince, M.G. Drellich, H.G. Grand, R.H. Gundlach, M.W. Kremer, A.H. Rifkin, C.B. Wilber and T.B. Bieber (1962), *Homosexuality: A Psychoanalytic Study.* New York: Basic Books, Inc.

Blair, Sampson Lee (1994), "Marriage and Cohabitation: Distinctions and Similarities Across the Division of Household Labor", *Family Perspective*, 28 (1), 31-52.

Blaylock, James R. and David M. Smallwood (1987), "Intra Household Time Allocation The Case of Grocery Shopping", *The Journal of Consumer Affairs*, 21 (2), 183-200.

Blau, Peter (1964), *Exchange and Power in Social Life*, New York: John Wiley and Sons.

Blumstein, P. and Schwartz, P. (1983). *American Couples.* New York: William Morrow.

Brooks, V.R. (1981), *Minority Stress and Lesbian Women.* Lexington, MA:D.C. Heath.

Caldwell, M. and L.A.Peplau (1984), "The Balance of Power in Lesbian Relationships", *Sex Roles*, 10, 587-599.

Cardell, Mona, Stephen Finn and Jeanne Marecek (1981), "Sex-Role Identity, Sex-Role Behavior, and Satisfaction in Heterosexual, Lesbian and Gay Male Couples", *Psychology of Women Quarterly*, 5 (3), 488-494.

Caycedo, Julio C., Gabe Wang, and Stephen J. Bahr (1991), "Gender Roles in the Family", in Stephen J. Bahr (eds.), *Family Research: A 60 Year Review, 1930-1990, Volume 1*, New York, NY: Lexington Books.

Corfman, Kim P. and Donald R. Lehmann (1987), "Models of Cooperative Group Decision-Making and Relative Influence: An Experimental Investigation of Family Purchase Decisions", *Journal of Consumer Research*, 14 (June), 1 13.

Cunningham, John D. and John K. Antill (1994), "Cohabitation and Marriage: Retrospective and Predictive Comparisons", *Journal of Social and Personal Relationships*, 11 (1), 77-93.

Davis, Harry L. and Benny P. Rigaux (1974), "Perception of Marital Roles in Decision Processes", *Journal of Consumer Research*, 1 (June), 51-62.

_____ (1970), "Dimensions of Marital Roles in Consumer Decision-Making", *Journal of Marketing Research*, 7 (May), 168-177.

Delozier, M Wayne and Jason Rodrique (1996), "Marketing to the Homosexual (Gay) Market: A Profile and Strategy Implications", *Journal of Homosexuality*, 31 (1/2), 203-211.

Dines, Wayne K. (1990), *Encyclopedia of Homosexuality*, New York: Garland Publishing, Inc.

Duffy, Sally M. and Caryl E. Rusbult (1985/86), "Satisfaction and Commitment in Homosexual and Heterosexual Relationships", *Journal of Homosexuality*, 12 (2), 1–23.

Finlay, Barbara and Karen E. Scheltema (1991), "The Relation of Gender and Sexual Orientation to Measures of Masculinity, Femininity, and Androgyny: A Further Analysis", *Journal of Homosexuality*, 21 (3), 71-85.

Ford, John B., Michael S. LaTour and Tony L. Henthorne (1995), "Perception of Marital Roles in Purchase Decision Processes: A Cross-Cultural Study", *Journal of the Academy of Marketing Science*, 23 (2), 120-131.

Green, Robert T. and Isabella C. M. Cunningham (1975), "Feminine Role Perception and Family Purchasing Decisions", *Journal of Marketing Research*, 12 (August), 325-332.

_____, Jean-Paul Leonardi, Jean-Louis Chandon, Isabella C.M. Cunningham, Bronis Verhage, and Alain Strazzieri (1983), "Societal Development and Family Purchasing Roles: A Cross-National Study", *Journal of Consumer Research*, 9 (March), 436-442.

Godwin, Deborah D. and John Scanzoni (1989), "Couple Consensus During Marital Joint Decision-Making: A Context,Process, Outcome Model", *Journal of Marriage and the Family*, 943-956.

Haist, M. and J. Hewitt (1974), "The butch-fem dichotomy in male homosexual behavior", *Journal of Sex Research*, 10, 68-75.

Harry, Joseph (1982), "Decision Making and Age Differences among Gay Male Couples", *Journal of Homosexuality*, 8 (2), 9–21.

Huffman, Terry, Karen Chang, Pat Rausch, and Nora Schaffer (1994), "Gender Differences and Factors Related to the Disposition Toward Cohabitation", *Family Therapy*, 21 (3), 171-184.

Johnson, M.P. (1973), "Commitment: A Conceptual Structure and Empirical Application", *Sociological Quarterly*, 14, 395-406.

Jones, R.W. and J.P. DeCecco (1982), "The Femininity and Masculinity of Partners of Heterosexual and Homosexual Relationships", *Journal of Homosexuality*, 8 (2), 37-44.

Kahan, Hazel and David Mulryan (1995), "Out of the Closet", *American Demographics*, 17 (5), 40-47.

Kotkin, Mark (1985), "Sex Roles Among Married & Unmarried Couples",*Sex Roles*, 9 (9), 975-985.

Kurdek, Lawrence A. and J. Patrick Schmitt (1987), "Partner Homogamy in Married, Heterosexual Cohabitating, Gay, and Lesbian Couples", *The Journal of Sex Research*, 23 (2), 212-232.

Lavin, Marilyn (1993), "Husband-Dominant, Wife-Dominant, Joint: A Shopping Typology for Baby Boom Couples?", *Journal of Consumer Marketing*, 10, 33-42.

Lee, Gary R. (1987), "Comparative Perspectives", in Marvin B. Sussman and Suzanne K. Steinmetz (Eds.), *Handbook of Marriage and the Family*, New York, NY: Plenum Press.

Lynch, Jean M. and Mary Ellen Reilly (1985/86), "Role Relationships: Lesbian Perspective", *Journal of Homosexuality*, 12 (2), 53-69.

Lyness, Judith L., Milton Lipetz and Keith Davis (1972), "Living Together: An alternative to Marriage", *Journal of Marriage and the Family*, 34 (May), 305-311.

Macklin, Eleanor D. (1983), "Nonmarital Heterosexual Cohabitation: An Overview", 49-75.

Marecek, Jeanne, Stephen E. Finn and Mona Cardell (1982), "Gender Roles in the Relationships of Lesbians and Gay Men", *Journal of Homosexuality*, 8 (2), 45-49.

McDonald, G.J. and R.J. Moore (1978), "Sex-role Self-Concepts of Homosexual Men and Their Attitudes Toward Women and Male Homosexuality", *Journal of Homosexuality*, 4 (1), 3-14.

McWhirter, D.P. and A.M. Mattison (1984), *The Male Couple: How Relationships Develop*. Englewoods Cliffs, NJ: Prentice-Hall.

Nock, Steven L. (1995), "A Comparison of Marriages and Cohabitating Relationships", *Journal of Family Issues*, 16 (1), 53-76.

Peplau, L., S. Cochran, K. Rook and C. Padesky (1978), "Loving Women: Attachment and Autonomy in Lesbian Relationships", *Journal of Social Issues*, 34 (3), 7-27.

_____ (1984), "Power in Dating Relationships", in J. Freeman (Ed.), *Women: A Feminist Perspective*, Palo Alto, CA: Mayfield.

_____ (1996b), "We're Here, We're Queer, and We're Going Shopping! A Critical Perspective on the Accommodation of Gays and Lesbians in the U.S. Marketplace", *Journal of Homosexuality*, 31 (1/2), 9-41.

Qualls, William J. (1987), "Household Decision Behavior: The Impact of Husbands and Wives Sex Role Orientation", *Journal of Consumer Research*, 14 (September), 264-279.

Reilly, Mary Ellen and Jean M. Lynch (1990), "Power-Sharing in Lesbian Relationships", *Journal of Homosexuality*, 19 (3), 1-29.

Risman, B.J., C. T. Hill, Z. Rubin, and L.A. Peplau (1981), "Living Together in College: Implications for Courtship", *Journal of Marriage and the Family*", 43 (1), 77-83.

Rodman, (1972), "Marital Power and the Theory of Resources in Cultural Context", *Journal of Comparative Family Studies*, 3, 50-69.

Rosen, Dennis L. and Donald H. Granbois (1983), "Determinants of Role Structure in Family Financial Management", *Journal of Consumer Research*, 10 (September), 253-258.

Saghir, M., and E. Robins (1973), *Male and Female Homosexuality*, Baltimore: Williams and Wilkins.

Safilios-Rothschild, Constantina (1976), "A Macro- and Micro-Examination of Family Power and Love: An Exchange Model", (May), 355-361.

Schneider, M.S. (1986), "The Relationships of Cohabitating Lesbian and Heterosexual Couples: A Comparison", *Psychology of Women Quarterly*, 10, 234-239.

Sharp, Harry and Paul Mott (1956), "Consumer Decisions in the Metropolitan Family", *Journal of Marketing*, 21 (October), 149-156.

Socarides, C. (1968), *The Overt Homosexual*. New York: Grune and Stratton.

Sprecher, S. (1985), "Sex Differences in Bases of Power in Dating Relationships", *Sex roles*, 12, 449-462.

Stafford, Rebecca, Elaine Backman and Pamela Dibona (1977), "The Division of Labor Among Cohabitating and Married Couples", *Journal of Marriage and the Family*, (February), 43-57.

Storms, M.O. (1980), "Theories of Sexual Orientation', *Journal of Personality and Social Psychology*, 38 (5), 763-792.

Tanfer, D.M. (1978), *The Lesbian Couple*. Lexington, MA: D.C. Heath.

Thompson, L. and Walker, A.J. (1989), "Gender in Families; Women and Men in Marriage, work, and parenthood", *Journal of Marriage and the Family*, 51, 845-871.

U.S. Bureau of the Census (1994), *Marital Status and Living Arrangements: 1993* (Series P-20 No. 484). Washington, DC: U.S. Government Printing Office.

Waller, Willard (1938), *The Family: A Dynamic Interpretation*, New York, NY: Dryden Press.

Webster, Cynthia (1994), "Effects of Hispanic Ethnic Identification on Marital Roles in the Purchase Decision Process", *Journal of Consumer Research*, 21 (September), 319-331.

Westmoreland, C. (1975), "A Study of Long-Term Relationships Among Male Homosexuals", Unpublished Doctoral Dissertation, United States International University, San Diego, California.

Wilkes, Robert E. (1975), "Husband-Wife Influence in Purchase Decisions: A Confirmation and Extension," *Journal of Marketing Research*, 12 (May), 224-227.

Woodside, Arch G. and William H. Motes (1979), "Perceptions of Marital Roles in Consumer Decision Processes for Six Products", in *American Marketing Association Proceedings*, Neil Beckwith et al. (eds.), Chicago, IL: American Marketing Association, 214-219.

Yllo, K.A. (1978), "Non-Marital Cohabitation: Beyond the College Campus", *Alternative Lifestyles*, 1 (1), 37-54.

Family Type Effects on Household Members' Decision Making

Fréderique Holdert, Erasmus University, the Netherlands
Gerrit Antonides, Erasmus University, the Netherlands

ABSTRACT

This study investigates the influence of the long-term properties of a family, the so-called 'family-structure', on family buying decision processes. The results of an empirical survey involving 74 Dutch families showed that on average the children's influence was relatively high in the later stages of the decision process at the expense of the wife's influence. However, children in modern families had more influence than those in traditional families in the problem recognition stage. Cohesive families relatively often evaluated alternatives jointly and took into account another's desires. Non-cohesive families relatively often had conflicts and formed coalitions to solve conflicts.

INTRODUCTION

Research on family decision making has developed in several ways. To assess the role of the family members in the decision process, many studies have focused on the (relative) influence of the family members and how the influence varied with the type of decision, decision stage or subdecision (Davis, 1970; Davis and Rigaux, 1974; Wilkes, 1975; Davis, 1976). Furthermore, research has dealt with the factors determining the relative influence of family members, such as the importance of the outcome of the decision, the knowledge of the product and the fact whether the product is for one's own use (Corfman and Lehmann, 1987; Mittal and Lee, 1989; Foxman, Tansuhaj and Ekstrom, 1989b).

Another development is the acknowledgement of children's influence in family decision making, whereas in earlier research a dyadic representation of the family was studied (including spouses only). At first, only the husband and the wife were described as the family (Davis, 1970; Davis, 1976) and thus either husband or wife or both were interviewed. With the growing influence of children and adolescents in family decision making, they were gradually taken into account in assessing the different roles and influences within families (Szybillo, Sosanie and Tenenbein, 1977; Belch, Belch and Ceresino, 1985; Foxman, Tansuhaj and Ekstrom, 1989a, 1989b; Mangleburg, 1990; Beatty and Talpade, 1994).

Several factors influencing the family decision making process have been proposed, such as power, parental style and communication patterns. Moreover, the influence of a person on the decision process depends on the importance *to that person* of the good involved (personal relevance; Mangleburg, 1990; Corfman and Lehmann, 1987; Beatty and Talpade, 1994). In general, research did not go further than describing factors and describing the situation in which family decision making took place. However, as Johnson, McPhail and Yau (1994) state, it is not enough for marketeers only to know how much influence children have on family decisions. Marketeers should understand the *behavioral interaction* between mother, father and children. Only when these interactions are known, are attempts at influencing the decision making process realistic. In our study, we use information from both children and their parents to investigate their influence in various stages of family buying processes.

The structure of the family, its long-term properties, determines the behavioral interactions (the dynamics) between family members in the decision process. In our study, two structural dimensions, power and cohesion are used to describe the type of family. The effects of these dimensions on four stages of family purchase processes are investigated. Four different purchases are studied: holidays, adult and child clothing and sandwich filling. We assume that if behavioral interactions differ across family types, the buying process also differs across these family types. Indeed, we find that modern and traditional families differ with respect to the influence of family members in the problem recognition stage. Also, we find differences regarding strategies used in decision making.

Next, the two dimensions determining the family type will be considered and several hypotheses regarding the family purchase process will be formulated. The methodology of the study will then be dealt with and the results of an empirical survey will be shown. Finally, conclusions for the study of consumer behavior and marketing will be drawn.

TWO STRUCTURAL DIMENSIONS

The structure of the family consists of the long-term properties of the relationship between family members. Family dynamics consist of the interactions between family members.[1] Several authors have attempted to describe families by means of specific variables. For instance, Olson and McCubbin (1989) distinguished cohesion, the ability to adapt and communication style. Fitzpatrick (1984) described autonomy versus interdependance, conflict-involvement versus conflict-avoidance and convention versus tradition. Kirchler (1989) argued that in order to comprise all these factors, two underlying structural dimensions can be distinguished: power and cohesion.

Power

In the literature, there is no single definition of power. However, there is agreement about the difference between potential power and power actually exerted, called influence (Corfman and Lehmann, 1987). Potential power is the ability of a person to change the attitudes, opinions or behavior of other people. Influence is the consequence of the active or passive exercise of power. In a relationship, the division of power has been described as traditional versus modern, considered to be a continuum. The distribution of power in the relationship affects the way decisions are made.

Traditional distribution of power. According to Ferber (1973), the responsibility of the husband in a traditional relationship is earning the money whereas the wife is responsible for housekeeping and child care. Davis (1976) claims the existence of large authority differences in traditional relationships. This may frequently take the form of a hierarchical structure. According to Hagenaars and Wunderink-Van Veen (1990) a strictly hierarchical family has a patriarchal structure where the husband and father is considered the head of the family. Kirchler (1989) states that many decisions in a traditional relationship are taken autonomously by

---

[1]Kirchler (1989) states that the current structure forms the starting point of the interaction; it influences the way in which the interaction proceeds. On the other hand, the current structure is the result of interactions in the past. So, in order to avoid drawing tautological conclusions it is important to restrict consequent interactions to *one specific area of interaction*, namely the family buying decision process.

TABLE 1
Classification of Family Types

Traditional type	Strong, traditional role-differentiation Autonomic decision making Coalition formation
Modern type	Equal division of power between partners Short power distance between parents and children Joint decision making
Weakly cohesive type	Low interdependance Disharmony Egoistic, individually driven
Strongly cohesive type	Strong interdependance Harmony Altruistic, consideration for others

one of the spouses. Also, in traditional families coalition formation is likely, as the 'weak' partner will try to find support from other family members.

Modern distribution of power. Modern relationships are characterized by a high degree of joint participation in carrying out tasks and taking decisions (Davis, 1976). Hagenaars and Wunderink-Van Veen (1990) state that husband and wife have equal influence in a modern relationship. Also, the power distance between parents and children is shorter in modern than in traditional families. Kirchler (1989) states that in egalitarian relationships, spouses decide much less by role-segregation than in traditional relationships. However, both spouses wish to fulfill their individual desires. As a consequence, many decisions are made together but conflicts arise due to different opinions. Summarizing, these descriptions lead to the classification shown in table 1.

The family type is a structural dimension and has been defined generally. As a hypothesis regarding the family purchase process, we expect the influence on decision making to show a relatively large variation in traditional family types and a relatively small variation in modern family types.

Cohesion

The second underlying structural dimension is cohesion, which is considered a continuous dimension. Cohesion is indicated by the degree of harmony in a family, the degree of interest in each other and the coalition dynamics. In general, cohesion includes the (degree of) emotional bonds between family members. Research has shown that a higher degree of cohesion is associated with a more harmonious family life and less egoistic decision making by the family members (Kirchler, 1989). See table 1.

As a hypothesis relating the structural dimension to family purchases, cohesive families are expected to evaluate alternatives jointly, to take into account another's desires and to be involved in conflicts less often than non-cohesive families. Coalition formation is expected less often in cohesive families than in non-cohesive families, since the former are more likely to form the 'grand coalition' involving all family members. (See Murnighan, 1978 for an overview of coalition formation models.) Regarding the type of conflict resolution strategies used in different family types, we have no a priori expectations.

METHODOLOGY

A survey was carried out among 103 families, June 8-29, 1995. In each family, one child and its parents were questioned, to obtain a clear picture of the family as a whole. Children aged 8-12 years were selected since they are able to think conceptually and they can finish concrete tasks by themselves (Ginsberg and Opper, 1969). Beyond the age of 12 years, children are in their puberty, leaving primary school, etcetera. The children were approached at three different schools. They completed the questionnaires in each of their classes in order to avoid problems with the younger children. Each child was asked to take home two parents' questionnaires with an accompanying letter including a request to complete them separately and independently. No other children or family members were questioned.

The parents' questionnaires were divided in two parts. In the first part, the family buying decision process was dealt with stage by stage: the problem recognition stage, information search, evaluation of alternatives and decision/purchase. In the second part, questions were asked to determine the family type, following methods used by, for instance, Moschis and Moore (1979) and Carlson, Grossbart and Tripp (1990). To categorize families into these types, statements referring to both dimensions were included. Agreement with the statements was assessed by means of 4-point Likert scales. For example, division of power was measured by questions such as: "Within our family, the parents have the final word, whereas the children have no say" and "I believe that my child should treat me with respect." Cohesion was measured by questions such as: "The relationships within our family can be described as very strong" and "I see my family functioning as a team rather than as a group of independent individuals." Then, following Moschis and Moore (1979) the scales were summed and families were classified as 'high' or 'low' on each dimension by splitting up at the median.

Davis (1976) concluded that the influence of the family members varies across product categories. We selected four different goods to represent four different buying processes: family vacation (specialty good), adult clothes and children's clothes (shopping goods) and sandwich filling (convenience good). The goods selected differ with respect to the length of the decision process and their importance to the family. The goods have been

TABLE 2

Influences of Family Members on the Decision Process Regarding Four Commodities, Averaged Over Four Decision Stages

(Standard Errors Between Parentheses)

	Husband	Wife	Child
Holiday	2.80 (0.05)	3.08 (0.05)	1.62 (0.04)[a]
Sandwich filling	2.13 (0.09)	3.22 (0.07)	1.84 (0.06)[b]
Adult clothing	2.32 (0.09)	3.17 (0.07)	1.51 (0.07)[c]
Child clothing	2.01 (0.08)	3.41 (0.08)	2.29 (0.09)[d]

[a] $F=416$, $df(2,53)$, [b] $F=136$, $df(2,53)$, [c] $F=290$, $df(2,52)$, [d] $F=117$, $df(2,53)$
All effects are statistically significant at the 0.001 level.

used in earlier research and typically are *family goods*, frequently requiring joint decision making, not particularly wife-dominated.

Three versions of the questionnaire were constructed. Each version included questions about the decision process regarding three of the four goods, for example: "Are you allowed to take part in a conversation about the shop to buy your clothes?" (children's questionnaire) and "Please indicate how much influence different family members have on the joint evaluation of child clothing" (parents' questionnaires). The children's influence on the buying process was measured by asking how much influence they thought they had themselves. The parents were asked to report both their own influence and the perceived influence of their spouses and the children concerned.

RESULTS

The response rate to the questionnaire was 74.7%, involving 77 families. Due to partial non-response and incomplete families, observations included 71 males, 74 females and 77 children. On average, the husband's age was 41 years, the wife's age was 39 years and the child's age was 10 years. The average number of children in the families was 2. Regarding schooling, 47.8% of the husbands and 26.4% of the wives had completed higher vocational education or university.

The unit of observation was the family and responses given by the members were considered as family variables. The type of family with respect to tradition and cohesion was classified on the basis of the average score of the spouses on the questions concerned. For incomplete families, the score was based on the score of one parent only. The correlations between spouses' scores were 0.62 and 0.45 for tradition and cohesion, respectively.

The influence of the family members on the decision process regarding the four commodities was measured by averaging the influence reported by the focal individual, and the influence of the focal individual as perceived by the second and third members of the family, each measured by means of 4-point scales. In the case of missing information, the average was computed using information from the remaining individuals. The correlations of measures from the spouses were generally in the 0.20 - 0.60 range. Those between spouses' and children's opinions were generally in the 0.00 - 0.20 range. Table 2 shows the influence of family members, aggregated over the four stages of the decision process.

Since each family answered questions concerning three issues only, a full factorial analysis would have resulted in substantial missing information. For this reason, four MANOVA's with repeated measures designs were run to test the significance of the family member effects for each issue separately. In each MANOVA, the families were considered as the observation units. Children clearly exerted the least influence in decision making and the wife had the most influence for all four issues. It appeared that children's influence was the strongest for child clothing, followed by sandwich filling. Apparently, the wife's influence on child clothing was much stronger than the child's own influence. The husband's influence on holiday decision making was relatively high as compared with his influence on other decisions. Negotiation theory predicts more influence if the importance of the issue is high (e.g. Belch, Belch and Ceresino, 1985; Foxman, Tansuhaj and Ekstrom, 1989; Corfman and Lehmann, 1987; Beatty and Talpade, 1994). In our survey, we asked each family member how important the issues were to themselves by means of 4-point Likert-type scales. Although the average influences varied considerably, we found little variation in average importance of the issues:

-   for holidays, the average importances reported by the family members individually were in the 3.20-3.22 range;
-   for sandwich filling, the average importances were in the 2.63-2.92 range;
-   for adult clothing, the average importance range was 2.49-2.55;
-   for child clothing, the range was 3.06-3.27.

It appeared that the variation in influence was virtually unrelated to the variation in issue importance, contrary to the prediction from negotiation theory (Corfman and Lehmann, 1987; Beatty and Talpade, 1994).

The influence of the family members may vary across the different stages of the decision making process. Table 3 shows the average influence of the family members across the four issues.

A full factorial MANOVA with a repeated measures design was run to test the significance of the effects. Both the main effects and the interaction effect were statistically significant. In general, the husband had less influence in the problem recognition stage than in the other stages. The wife had the most influence in general and particularly in the first two stages of the decision making process. Children had more influence in the stages of alternative evaluation, choice and purchase than in problem recognition and information search. These results also hold for the relative influence of the

TABLE 3

Influences of Family Members on the Stages of the Decision Process, Averaged Over Four Commodities

(Standard Errors Between Parentheses)

	Husband	Wife	Child
Problem recognition	2.06 (0.06)	3.35 (0.05)	1.56 (0.04)
Information search	2.35 (0.10)	3.35 (0.12)	1.52 (0.14)
Alternative evaluation	2.58 (0.06)	3.05 (0.05)	2.26 (0.06)
Choice and purchase	2.35 (0.06)	3.06 (0.09)	1.84 (0.03)

Stage effect: $F=29$, $df(3,67)$, Member effect: $F=510$, $df(2,68)$,
Stage by member effect: $F=36$, $df(6,64)$
All effects are statistically significant at the 0.001 level.

TABLE 4

Influence of Members of Traditional and Modern Families in the First Stage of Decision Making, Aggregated Over Issues

(Standard Errors Between Parentheses)

Problem recognition	Husband	Wife	Child
Traditional type	2.01 (0.09)	3.44 (0.07)	1.45 (0.06)
Modern type	2.11 (0.07)	3.26 (0.06)	1.63 (0.06)
Correlation between family type and influence	0.28[a]	-0.28[a]	0.21[b]

[a] $p<0.05$, [b] $p<0.10$

family members, i.e. as percentages of total influence perceived. In general, the alternative evaluation stage yielded the highest overall perceived influence, possibly due to its impact on the final outcome of decision making.

Tables 2 and 3 showed the influence of family members regardless of family type. To study the effect of family type on decision making, traditional and modern families were distinguished such that modern families scored above the median of the distribution (24, summed over 9 items) and the remaining families were considered traditional. The analyses above were repeated with the modern versus traditional distinction added as a between-subjects factor in the MANOVA's.[2] Family type was not found to be a significant factor in the influence of family members on the aggregated decision process per issue (see table 4). With the influence aggregated over issues, the interaction of family type, family member and decision stage yielded an F-ratio of 1.94, $df(6,63)$ which was significant at the 10% level. The interaction effect was evident mainly in the first decision stage (problem recognition). The influence of family members in the problem recognition stage (aggregated over issues) is shown in table 4. In addition, we computed correlations between the influence of each member and the 'score' on the traditional versus the modern scale, which are reported in table 4. It appeared that, on average, the husband's and the child's influence in problem recognition were stronger in modern than in traditional families, whereas the influence of the wife was less strong. So, in modern families the power was distributed more equally than in traditional families in the problem recognition stage. In the other stages, no significant differences were found. Our hypothesis regarding the effect of family type on decision making has only partially been confirmed.

Next we considered the strategies of decision making used in weakly and strongly cohesive families. Cohesion was correlated with the following variables: individual versus joint evaluation of alternatives, taking another's desires into account to a large or small extent, whether or not conflicts arise sometimes, how often coalitions are formed (i.e. including the opinion of a third member of the family in the conflict) and the use of other problem solving strategies. These variables were constructed at the family level using the information from both spouses as follows: for 2-point scales (whether or not conflicts arise), disagreement between spouses was scored in between the values of the two points;[3] for 3-point

---

[2] A MANOVA including both the traditional versus modern and the cohesion dimensions resulted in non-significant cohesion effects, which are not reported here.

[3] The 2-point scale served as a selection device for further questions regarding conflicts.

TABLE 5
Rank Correlations Between Cohesion and Strategies Used in Decision Making, Regarding Four Issues

	Joint evaluation of alternatives	Taking another's desires into account	Conflicts	Coalition formation
Holiday	0.24[b]	-0.12	-0.03	0.06
Sandwich filling	0.21[c]	0.23	-0.24[c]	-0.20[b]
Adult clothing	-0.06	0.00	-0.15	0.03
Child clothing	0.40[a]	0.33[b]	-0.03	0.04

[a] $p<0.01$, [b] $p<0.05$, [c] $p<0.10$

TABLE 6
Conflict Resolution Tactics Used by Weakly and Strongly Cohesive Families

	Discussion and Gathering information	Persuasion	Negotiating	Other
Weakly cohesive type	59%	9%	25%	7%
Strongly cohesive type	54%	5%	21%	20%

$\chi^2 = 4.49$ df(3), not significant

scales (the other variables, except coalition formation), extreme disagreement was scored at the middle of the scale and disgreement by one point was scored in between the values of the two points concerned. The 4-point coalition formation scale was simply averaged over the spouses. For each consumption issue, Spearman rank correlations between cohesion and the type of strategy are shown in table 5.

It appeared that strongly cohesive families evaluated alternatives jointly more often than weakly cohesive families, except for adult clothing which is after all a personal consumption item. Furthermore, it appeared that strongly cohesive families took into account another's desires relatively often, had fewer conflicts and less often formed coalitions regarding sandwich filling. This is in agreement with our expectations.

Finally, spouses were asked which tactics were used in case of conflict: discussion and gathering more information, persuasion, negotiating (trading off issues) and other tactics (see table 6). It appeared that discussion and gathering information was used most, followed by negotiation. Other techniques were used relatively often in strongly cohesive families. The latter result was not statistically significant, however.

CONCLUSIONS

The wife's influence on household decision making appeared to be considerably stronger than the husband's and the latter's influence appeared to be stronger than the children's. This could hardly be explained by product type since typical family products were selected, the choice of which is not necessarily wife-dominated. In the problem recognition stage, the wife's influence in modern-type families turned out to be slightly less than her influence in traditional types, although it remained considerably stronger than the husband's. This suggests that the modernization of the Dutch family is only beginning.

The influence of children appeared to be higher in the evaluation and decision stages than in problem recognition and information search, contrary to findings by Belch, Belch and Ceresino (1985). We cannot rule out the possibility that the type of product has mediated this effect. In general, for low interest products and in democratic families, we assume that parents would allow their children to influence the decision. Although advertising may influence children's knowledge and preferences regarding alternatives in unrestricted choice (Gorn and Goldberg, 1982; Goldberg, Gorn and Gibson, 1978), its effect on family decision making seems limited, given the children's low influence in the first stages of decision making.

Cohesion was associated with decision making strategies in several instances. Cohesive families relatively often evaluated alternatives jointly, frequently took into consideration another's desires and ran into conflicts less often. Problem solving tactics were used relatively often in our sample, confirming Johnson's suggestion (1995) that this strategy will be used frequently in triadic relationships. This finding is in contrast with Belch, Belch and Schiglimpaglia (1980) who found bargaining and persuasion strategies in triads relatively often. A future research question may include the agreement of family members' perceived influences in relation to cohesion.

The children's influence on child clothing was stronger than on the other issues, suggesting some association between issue importance and influence. Importance of clothing might be partly due to its symbolic value (Solomon, 1983). However, the low variation in issue importance was inconsistent with the high variation in influence of the members on the decision process. This may be due to a discrepancy between individually perceived influence and aggregate influence as indicated by the average perceptions of the family members.

Since we have considered family type and the influence of family members as family characteristics, the unit of observation was the family and the variables were aggregates constructed from individual information. Although our research was limited by the number of families in the sample, we are convinced that our approach is to be preferred because the variables are less affected by subjective distortions than by using the individual as the unit of observation.

Although children's information processing may differ across different ages (Roedder-John and Whitney, 1986; Gregan-Paxton and Roedder-John, 1995), parental style may be roughly constant and children's relative influence in family decision making may not change much across different family types. The investigation of different age groups should be left for future research, however. Future research may also be aimed at generalizing our results with respect to different age classes, family composition (e.g. single parent families, small and large families), children's gender, different products and cultures.

Because of the different roles of the family members in the decision making process, marketeers should not consider the family as a whole. Rather, they should make use of the role specializations within the family and of the knowledge that the structure and the dynamics of the family are determining factors in the family buying decision process.

REFERENCES

Beatty, Sharon E. and Salil Talpade (1994), "Adolescent Influence in Family Decision Making: A Replication with Extension," *Journal of Consumer Research*, 21 (September), 332-341.

Belch, Michael A., George E. Belch and D. Schiglimpaglia (1985), "Conflict in Family Decision Making: An Exploratory Investigation," *Advances in Consumer Research* 7, 477-478.

Belch, George E., Michael A. Belch and Gayle Ceresino (1985), "Parental and Teenage Child Influences in Family Decision Making," *Journal of Business Research*, 13, 163-176.

Carlson, Les, Sanford Grossbart and Carolyn Tripp (1990), "An Investigation of Mothers' Communication Orientations and Patterns," *Advances in Consumer Research*, 17, 804-812.

Corfman Kim P. and Donald R. Lehmann (1987), "Models of Cooperative Group Decision-Making and Relative Influence: An Experimental Investigation of Family Purchase Decisions," *Journal of Consumer Research*, 13 (June), 1-13.

Davis, Harry L. (1970), "Dimensions of Marital Roles in Consumer Decision Making," *Journal of Marketing Research*, 7 (May), 168-177.

Davis, Harry L. (1976), "Decision Making within the Household," *Journal of Consumer Research*, 2 (March), 241-260.

Davis, Harry L. and B.P. Rigaux (1974), "Perception of Marital Roles in Decision Processes," *Journal of Consumer Research*, 1 (January), 51-62.

Ferber, Robert (1973), "Family Decision Making and Economic Behavior," in: *Family Economic Behavior, Problems and Prospects*, ed. E.B. Sheldon, Philadelphia: J.B. Lipindt Co.

Fitzpatrick, Mary A. (1984), "A Typological Approach to Marital Interaction: Recent Theory and Research," in: *Advances in Experimental Social Psychology*, 18, ed. Leonard Berkowitz, New York: Academic Press, 2-47.

Foxman, Ellen R., Patriya S. Tansuhaj and Karin M. Ekstrom (1989a), "Adolescents' Influence in Family Purchase Decisions: A Socialization Perspective," *Journal of Business Research*, 18, 159-172.

Foxman, Ellen R., Patriya S. Tansuhaj and Karin M. Ekstrom (1989b), "Family Members' Perceptions of Adolescents' Influence in Family Decision Making," *Journal of Consumer Research*, 15 (March), 482-491.

Ginsburg, Herbert and Sylvia Opper (1969), *Piaget's Theory of Intellectual Development*, Englewood Cliffs, NJ: Prentice Hall.

Goldberg, Marvin E., Gerald J. Gorn and Wendy Gibson (1978), "TV Messages for Snack and Breakfast Foods: Do They Influence Children's Preferences?" *Journal of Consumer Research*, 5 (September), 73-81.

Gorn, Gerald J. And Marvin E. Goldberg (1982), "Behavioral Evidence of the Effects of Televised Food Messages on Children," *Journal of Consumer Research*, 9 (September), 200-205.

Gregan-Paxton, Jennifer and Deborah Roedder John (1995), "Are Young Children Adaptive Decision Makers? A Study of Age Differences in Information Search Behavior," *Journal of Consumer Research*, 21 (March), 567-580.

Hagenaars, Aldi J.M. and Sophia R. Wunderink-Van Veen (1990), *Soo Gewonne Soo Verteert. Economics of the Household Sector*, (in Dutch) Leyden: Stenfert Kroese.

Johnson, Melissa, Janelle McPhail and Oliver H.M. Yau (1994), "Conflict in Family Purchase Decision Making: A Proposal for an Investigation of the Factors Influencing the Choice of Conflict Resolution Strategies by Children," *Asia Pacific Advances in Consumer Research*, 1, 229-236.

Johnson, Melissa (1995), "The Impact of Product and Situational Factors on the Choice of Conflict Resolution Strategies by Children in Family Purchase Decision Making," *European Advances in Consumer Research*, 2, 61-68.

Kirchler, Erich (1989), *Buying Decisions in the Private Household*, (in German) Göttingen: Hubert & Co.

Mangleburg, Tamara F. (1990), "Children's Influence in Purchase Decisions: A Review and Critique," *Advances in Consumer Research*, 17, 813-825.

Mittal, Banwary and Myung-Soo Lee (1989), "A Causal Model of Consumer Involvement," *Journal of Economic Psychology*, 10, 363-389.

Moschis, George P. and Roy L. Moore (1979), "Family Communication and Consumer Socialization," *Advances in Consumer Research*, 6, 359-363.

Murnighan, J. Keith (1978), "Models of Coalition Behavior: Game Theoretic, Social Psychological and Political Perspectives," *Psychological Bulletin* 85(5), 1130-1153.

Olson, David H., Hamilton McCubbin, Howard L. Barnes, Andrea S. Larsen, Marla J. Muxen and Marc A. Wilson (1989), *Families. What Makes Them Work?*, Beverly Hill, CA: Sage.

Roedder John, Deborah and John C. Whitney, Jr. (1986), "The Development of Consumer Knowledge in Children: A Cognitive Structure Approach," *Journal of Consumer Research*, 12 (March), 406-417.

Solomon, Michael R. (1983), "The Role of Products as Social Stimuli: A Symbolic Interactionism Perspective," *Journal of Consumer Research*, 10 (December), 319-329.

Szybillo, George J., Arlene K. Sosanie and Aaron Tenenbein (1977), "Should Children Be Seen But Not Heard?" *Journal of Advertising Research*, 17 (6) (December), 7-13.

Wilkes, Robert E. (1975), "Husband-Wife Influence in Purchase Decisions - A Confirmation and Extension," *Journal of Marketing Research*, 12 (May), 224- 227.

Toward a Theory of Intergenerational Influence in Consumer Behavior: An Exploratory Essay

Reshma H. Shah, University of Pittsburgh
Banwari Mittal, Northern Kentucky University

ABSTRACT

Intergenerational Influence (IGI)— the influence of one generation on another— is at work whenever adult consumers seek advice from their parents, or vice versa. Despite its occurrence in everyday observations and its impact on consumer behaviors, research on IGI in marketing has been sparse. We examine this topic here, pondering such issues as what it is, and why and how it occurs. Building on current literature, we conceptualize its domain, identify some of its determinants, and speculate on their interplay. Our essay is without closure yet, and at this time, is forwarded to motivate a momentum of new theorizing on this important and under-researched topic.

I. INTRODUCTION

Do *adult* consumers look to their parents for information and advice about what to buy? Or, for that matter, to their grand parents? Do they look to them the same way they did when they were young and helpless children, wholly dependent on their parents for day-to-day living? Does the parental influence on the now grown-up children depend on the kind of product under consideration? Is such parental influence, as may be found, universal and uniform across families or do different family members exert different types of influence? And finally, when, if at all, is such influence sought and/or accepted? These are important questions to answer to better understand consumer decision making for a range of products and services. However, these questions have been addressed in the literature at best only tangentially (Moschis 1985; Moore-Shay and Lutz 1988; Heckler, Childers and Arunachalam 1989; Childers and Rao 1992).

We subsume these questions, as have other researchers, under the rubric of "Intergenerational Influence" (IGI). Our purpose in this paper is to review and reflect on the extant literature on IGI, and extend that literature toward a more cohesive set of concepts and interrelationships among diverse variables that constitute and determine IGI. Our task and this essay proceed as follows: (i) we first define and delimit the domain and scope of IGI; (ii) next we identify a set of concepts and variables that play a role in the study of IGI; and, finally, (iii) we build relationships among these concepts, explaining when, why, and how IGI occurs. Our effort is an exercise in theory generation— anchored in and building upon previous similar works by others, but also expanded by projecting on intuition and informed speculation. We particularly view the utility (to ourselves and to others) of sharing such an "embryonic," essay in the discussion that the ACR forum affords. While our efforts here are exploratory, our goal for this paper is to provide additional insight to the foundation literature on the topic which, in our view, is insightful but remains somewhat equivocal.

II. DEFINING IGI AND ITS DOMAIN

IGI can be defined as the influence of one generation on another in terms of the transfer of skills, attitudes, preferences, values, and behaviors. The IGI in *consumer behavior* can be defined as the influence of one family generation on another in terms of acquiring skills, attitudes, preferences, values, and behaviors related to the *marketplace* (Heckler et. al 1989; Childers and Rao 1992). Given this, IGI can involve the within-family intergenerational transfer of knowledge with regard to a range of

consumer behaviors such as information search, brand, product and store selection, use of evaluative criteria, and receptivity to marketing mix variables. Examples of IGI can include parents influencing their adult children in their life insurance choices, and adult children influencing their parents' choice in music. IGI, which involves intrafamily interaction and communication, is likely to influence a host of decisions including product class preference, brand loyalty, and deal proneness.

While IGI can span multiple generations and can involve numerous members of a family, in our essay, we are concerned only with *dyadic* IGI, or the influence between two members of a given family. Specifying the particular unit of analysis under consideration improves the validity of our contructs. Although differences between different types of dyads (e.g., mother-daughter; father-son, etc.) may result in some variability regarding the strength of our proposed relationships (see Moore-Shay and Lutz 1988 for a discussion), we do not consider them here, but rather pose them as questions for future research. Similarly, we acknowledge that in addition to these structural differences, varying individual differences, such as gender, age, eduction and income, can have a differential impact on IGI. Our essay is, therefore, limited by a lack of theorizing the impact of these individual differences on IGI.

IGI and Consumer Socialization

It is useful to compare and contrast the concept of IGI with the concept of consumer socialization. Consumer socialization has been defined as "processes by which young people acquire skills, knowledge, and attitudes relevant to their functioning as consumers in the marketplace" (Ward 1974). While similarities exist between consumer socialization and IGI, researchers have expounded on the value of making distinctions between them. Moschis (1988) has drawn attention to the limitations of viewing socialization and IGI interchangeably. Based on his and others' views, we propose the following distinctions between socialization and IGI (see Figure 1):

(i) Consumer socialization can occur from various agents of which parents are only one. Other agents include peers, institutions other than the family (e.g., schools), the media and other marketing sources. IGI is expressly limited to parental influence, or more broadly, influence within the family.

(ii) Consumer socialization within the family is limited, at least in the extant studies in consumer behavior (see Moschis 1985), to the influence of parents on children. IGI can occur in either direction, forward or reverse. Forward IGI involves the influence of parents (or grand parents) on adult children; and reverse IGI involves the influence of adult children on parents (or on grand parents).

(iii) Consumer socialization begins with early childhood. Its onset is marked by the child's first learning of any consumption related skill, attitude, or preference, when the child has a "blank slate" so to speak, and has little independence of thought and faculty of reasoning. IGI begins much later, in the adult years of children, when children acquire the resources for independent decision making.

FIGURE 1
Consumer Socialization versus IGI

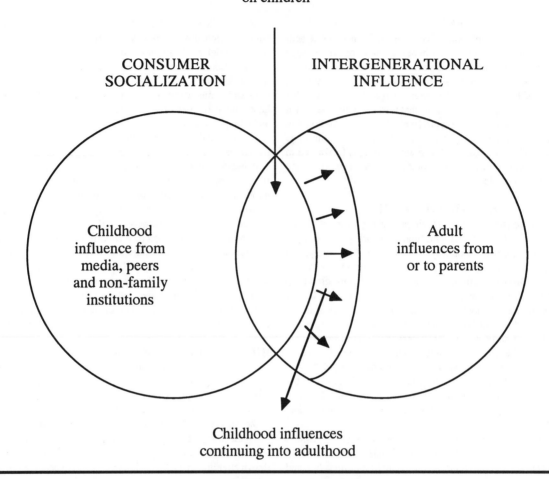

This last point is controversial, in two respects. First, when does childhood end and adulthood begin? Any such division is bound to be arbitrary. And second, why should childhood learning not be studied under IGI? Influences acquired during childhood are often the most enduring ones (see Sujan, Bettman and Baumgartner 1993). Our rationale is as follows. Adulthood begins when: (i) children begin to make independent decisions; (ii) when they acquire, at least partially, independent income and resources; (iii) when they are no longer the "wards" of their parents; and definitely, (iv) when they form a separate household, such as when they live in a college dorm, or take up a separate apartment, or get married, etc.

We further distinguish childhood socialization from influence during adult years based on the financial and psychological independence acquired by adult children. By no stretch of the imagination, can the giving and/or the acceptance of parental influence on adult children be of the same genre as that on small children. By merely viewing parental influence on adult children as an extension of influence during childhood years, we forego the opportunity to identify any fundamental differences in influence mechanisms and moderators.

The demarcation of the precise beginning of adult years is also a question of perspective rather than precision. For contrast, one might examine the two extreme cases of the influence continuum: very early childhood socialization at the one end, and IGI when adult children no longer live with their parents, at the other. If we find differences in these two "ideal types," both in degree and in kind, with respect to influence mechanisms, processes, and outcomes, then we would have established a case for studying IGI and socialization separately. In this initial conceptualization, limiting IGI only to adult children living in households *separate* from their parents affords us the opportunity to explore the IGI process in a more focused manner. Therefore, the present essay is concerned with intergenerational family influences across households.

Also inherent to the general mechanisms of IGI are its *associative* and *dissassociative* properties. By this we mean that influence can be both positive and negative, and that this can result in either approach or avoidance behavior. In other words, the same antecedents of IGI may make it entirely likely that adult children (or parents) may consciously avoid, rather than emulate those preferences, attitudes and consumption behaviors of their parents (or children). For example, when disharmony and dysfuntion exist between family member, IGI may not only be low, it may be negative. For the purpose of this essay, we focus only on associative or positive IGI and its main determinants.

III. DETERMINANTS OF IGI

Family Relationship

The primary determinant of IGI is proposed to be a concept we term the *perceived strength of the family relationship* (SFR) (see Figure 2). [Insert Figure 2 about here] This refers to the degree of mutual respect and trust between parents and adult children. It also refers to the harmony of relations and communication between them in all areas of life, and not just in the marketplace context (Spiro 1983; Moschis 1988). The strength of the family relationship is impacted by a number of factors including the family environment, family cohesion, structural effects such as proximity, and communications orientations (Heckler et al 1989; Hogan, Eggebeen and Clogg 1993). With the multiplicity of factors, in this essay, we propose the *perceived* strength of family relationship since relationship strength can be construed differently by different family members. As such, in this construct, we also define relationship strength as how well parents and children want to get along with each other and their *mutual* desire for a lasting relationship. If IGI is to occur at all (in either direction), the existence of a harmonious and mutually respectful relationship in the family across generations must be a prerequisite. Therefore,

P1: IGI will be positively related to the perceived strength of family relationship (SFR).[1]

Bases of Influence

Three processes of interpersonal influence have been identified in the literature: informational, instrumental, and identificational (Deutsch and Gerard 1955; Kelman 1961; Park and Lessig 1977; Bearden, Netemeyer and Teel 1989). Informational influence occurs when the influencing agent provides useful information that guides, facilitates, or alters the choices the influence recipient makes. Instrumental influence occurs due to the ability of influence agents to reward or punish the influence target. This subsumes what some have called the "normative" influence— the expectations of significant others. Finally, identificational influence occurs when the influenced identifies with the influencer, viewing the latter as a role model, and emulating his or her behavior. Park and Lessig (1977) have referred to these respectively as informational, utilitarian, and value-expressive influence.

Corresponding to these three general influence processes, we propose three *sources* of influence—i.e., the characteristics that the influence agents must possess to effect these influence processes. These are: (i) expertise; (ii) resource control; and, (iii) perceived similarity.

Expertise Expertise refers to product information and knowledge about the appropriate evaluation criteria, and about specific brands. Expertise works through the informational influence mechanism where the perception of possessing accurate, up-to-date and reliable information about specific products and brands or stores, etc., helps to offset purchase risk. Researchers have shown that the level of product or brand expertise an individual possesses is related to his or her experience, knowledge and familiarity that individual has about and with a particular item (Bettman and Park 1980; Brucks 1985). Therefore, whichever generation perceives the other

to possess expertise on the product category, a specific brand or other marketplace phenomena, that generation will seek and receive IGI from the other. Thus, adult children might perceive parents to be experts on home buying, and would seek their advice. Alternatively, parents might perceive adult children to be experts on new technological products (e.g., computers) and might seek advice from them. Thus,

P2a: IGI will be stronger the more one generation perceives the other as possessing expertise on the product under consideration.

Resource Control Resource control refers to who (either parents or children) finances the expense for the purchase under control. When parents finance the purchase, they would exercise IGI. In essence, they are exerting utilitarian, or instrumental, control over their children (Park and Lessig 1977). If adult children finance the purchase, even if partially, to that extent, IGI is reduced. This can be seen for adult children living at home. If they pay rent, for example, they are less likely to accept unbridled influence from parents. Likewise, if they want to buy something for their own room (e.g., a stereo system) with their own money (e.g., earned from a part time job), they will have a lot more freedom on the purchase decision. If adult children move back with parents, parents may again be in a position to exercise influence on their grown-up children. On the other hand, if retired parents depend on their grown up children financially, then reverse IGI may be more prominent. In each of these cases, the influence mechanism is some form of reward or punishment. At the very least, the generation with the resource control can simply refuse to finance the purchase. Therefore,

P2b: IGI will be stronger the more one generation controls more of the resources necessary for a purchase to be made by the other.

Perceived Similarity Perceived similarity refers to the lifestyle similarity between generations. Lifestyle similarity can be reflected in actual or perceived attitude, preference and/or behavior congruence or in desired attitude, preference and/or behavior congruence. Thus, a mother might perceive the daughter to be an expert on new fashions, but if she perceives her daughter's lifestyle to be different from hers (she considers herself to be a conservative professional, and wears formal, conservative styles while her daughter sports the "grunge look"), then she (the mother) is not going to seek or accept her daughter's influence for clothing. Perceived similarity of lifestyle drives the influence via the identificational mechanism resulting in a form of value-expressive influence (Park and Lessig 1977). In essence, one generation aspires to be like the other (e.g., the mother wants to be as trendy as she perceives her daughter to be), and values IGI. Therefore,

P2c: IGI will be stronger the more one generation perceives the other as being similar in product-relevent lifestyle.

Product and Brand Types

One distinction that has been made in the literature concerns the product type. Products can be functional or expressive. Functional products are those which are bought primarily for their physical performance. Expressive products are those that are consumed to fit one's personality and lifestyle, for making favorable social impressions, for communicating to the world the type of person one is, and for living and fulfilling one's own self-concept (Mittal 1988). Other related distinctions are those classifying

---

[1] As an illustration of how IGI differs from consumer socialization in the case of family relationship strength, it might be argued that since young children have no independence or may even perceive no need for independence, early socialization will occur even when SRF is low or absent.

products as being hedonic, symbolic or functional (Woods 1960) and those distinguishing products in terms of the type of need they fulfill: functional, symbolic or experiential (Park, Jaworski and MacInnis 1986). Finally, some researchers have distinguished public or conspicuous products such as sneakers or watches, from private or inconspicuous products such as underwear and birth control (Bearden and Etzel 1982; Childers and Rao 1992). In all these distinctions, both functional and expressive underpinnings are evident and these product differences result in different forms of influence being operational.

Since functional products are appraised by a consideration and weighing of product's inherent features, product expertise becomes more relevant in interpersonal influence. Therefore, expertise based influence will be more pertinent to functional products. On the other hand, since expressive products are appraised for their fit with the desired personality, self-concept, and life-style, such appraisal benefits from the observation of role models and aspirational referents (Midgely 1983; Richins 1991). As such, life-style similarity as a source of influence will be more relevant for expressive products. Finally, for either type of product, if the item entails a major expense, resource control will be the relevant source for influence. It follows then, that

P3a: The basis of IGI is more likely to be expertise when the product is functional rather than expressive.

P3b: The basis of IGI is more likely to be perceived lifestyle similarity when the product is expressive rather than functional.

P3c: The basis of IGI is more likely to be resource control when the product entails significant financial outlay rather than when it does not.

Perceived Risk

A related variable is the degree of purchase risk. Purchase risk captures the degree or likelihood that a wrong or substantially suboptimal choice could be made. In part, it depends on financial outlay, and in part, on the lack of parity or differentiation between alternatives (Cox 1967). Products vary in the risk they entail. The risk can itself be broadly divided into performance, financial, and social-psychological (Bettman 1973). Consumers will tend to seek advice more for products that entail some risk than for low perceived risk products. If the risk is performance related, IGI will occur if one generation perceives the other to possess expertise. If the risk is psycho-social, then IGI will occur only if the two generations perceive lifestyle similarity. When the risk is financial, resource control will enable the IGI. Accordingly,

P3d: IGI will be greater for high risk than for low risk purchases.

P3e: The basis of IGI is more likely to be expertise when the product entails performance risk rather than social/psychological or financial risk

P3f: The basis of IGI is more likely to be the perceived lifestyle similarity when the product entails social/psychological risk rather than performance or financial risk.

P3g: The basis for IGI is more likely to be resource control when the product entails financial risk rather than performance or social/psychological risk.

Products as Shopping, Convenience, and Specialty Goods

Another typology of products is that of shopping, convenience, and specialty goods (Witt and Bruce 1972; Heckler et. al 1989). Convenience goods are purchased by habit and past experience (including childhood socialization). Shopping and specialty goods are both perceived to be risk entailing, either due to more substantial financial outlays, or due to the inherent value-expressive and identification needs they often possess. Therefore, advice and support is likely to be sought more for these purchases. Since each type can entail all three types of risk (performance, social/psychological and financial), it is not productive to limit the influence to one rather than another type of source (expertise, lifestyle similarity, or resource control). However, one characteristic of products is whether or not they have changed over a decade or two, and whether or not they entail high technology. Generally, adult children will be perceived as possessing more expertise for technologically complex products, and likewise for products which have changed considerably over time. In contrast, there are some products, whose principal value lies in preserving tradition (e.g., cedar chests, porcelein and china, authentic jewelry) or those which have not changed substantially over time (e.g., Morton Salt, Heinz Catsup). We call these products "old world" products. Therefore,

P4a: IGI will be greater for shopping and specialty goods than for convenience goods.

P4b: IGI will be greater from adult children to their parents for (i) high tech products than for low tech products; and (ii) for products considerably changed over time than for products staying unchanged.

P4c: IGI will be greater from parents to their children for "old world" products than from children to their parents.

Product Evaluation Mode

Products have also been classified in terms of the type of attributes used to evaluate them. This classification suggests the existence of search, experience and credence goods based on their mode of evaluation (Nelson 1970; Darby and Karni 1973). Search goods largely contain attributes that can be evaluated prior to purchase (e.g., a computer or laundry detergent), whereas experience goods generally must be tried or used before they can be evaluated (e.g., restaurant service or a car). Finally, credence goods are those that often cannot be sufficiently evaluated even after trial or use (e.g., appendectomies or religious objects). Search quality products require and allow pre-trial product appraisal based on the product's inherent features. Consequently, the propensity to seek marketer provided information regarding product performance would be the highest for search goods. Evaluations made about experience and credence quality goods tend to be based more on summative judgments about overall satisfaction, and not as much on reasoning based assessments stemming from domains of knowledge. Therefore, expertise-based influence is most likely to occur for search quality products.

Experience and credence goods require trial for an adequate evaluation of their appraisal. And, particularly in the case of credence goods, even after product trial, consumers may not know enough about the product to make an adequate assessment or evaluation of its benefits. Influence for these types of products is more likely to be based on others' gestalt experiences and/or summative judgments. Moreover, this form of influence becomes more likely if perceived lifestyle similarity exists between the influencer and the influenced. Consequently, the propensity to rely on brand name and equity and other symbolic cues would be the highest for credence goods, followed by experience goods. Therefore, perceived similarity based influence is most likely to occur for experience and credence quality products. Thus,

> P5a: The basis of IGI is more likely to be expertise in the case of search goods than experience or credence goods
>
> P5b: The basis of IGI is more likely to be perceived similarity in the case of experience and credence goods than search goods.

IV. MODERATING VERSUS MAIN EFFECTS

While the foregoing hypotheses are stated as main effects, the interactive role among these determinants is important to explore, and we outline this here briefly. We propose that the strength of family relationship (SFR) is the principal determinant. Without family relationship strength, IGI will be mimimal, at best.[2] Thus, SFR is the necessary facilitator of IGI. Other factors moderate this key direct relationship. Illustratively, if the product does not entail some sort of risk, then IGI is unlikely to be sought. Thus, IGI may not occur even in high SFR generations. At the same time, if the resource dependence of one generation on the other is absent, then the instrumental basis would be absent even for expensive purchases.

In the same vein, if lifestyles are perceived to be dissimilar, then for expressive products, IGI may not occur. Moreover, if one generation does not perceive the other to possess expertise, then informational IGI will not be sought, and, if given, it will not be accepted, even in the case of high SFR. Under high SFR, influence attempts will be politely declined or dismissed when these other moderating conditions are absent. Finally, if the products of interest are typically considered to be search goods, rather than experience or credence goods, even under high SFR, IGI may be low. The rationale is as follows. By definition, search goods largely possess attributes which can be objectively evaluated prior to trial and as elucidated earlier, are the least likely to be influenced by interpersonal sources. Therefore,

> P6a: Under high SFR, IGI will occur only if one or more bases/sources of influence exist. One generation must view the other as possessing expertise, similarity, or resource control.
>
> P6b: The positive association between SFR and IGI will be stronger for expressive than for functional products.
>
> P6c: The positive association between SFR and IGI will be stronger for shopping and specialty goods than for convenience goods.
>
> P6d: The positive association between SFR and IGI will be stronger for high risk than low risk products.
>
> P6e: The positive association between SFR and IGI will be stronger for experience and credence products than for search products.

Figure 2 depicts the relationships among all the variables discussed above.

V. CONCLUSION

We have proposed that Intergenerational Influence (IGI) be construed as the influence of *adult* members of one generation over the *adult* members of another generation, both *within* the family. In so defining it, we separate the concept, by design, from the *childhood* socialization of young consumers. This allows us to focus on a special case where the targets of IGI have a separate and independent living from the influence agents. We believe that the *processes* and *outcomes* of early childhood family socialization are fundamentally different from the IGI during the adult years. We have not yet articulated these differences. Illustratively, however, these are: (i) Childhood socialization will be based much more on simple imitation; (ii) In terms of each of the three sources of influence–expertise, resource control and perceived similarity, parents will almost exclusively be the influence agents in infancy and childhood; and (iii) Influence will occur in infancy and early childhood, despite low SFR. We leave an explication of these for future research.

The IGI studies are sparse in the literature. And, in most cases, they are simply a replication of the childhood socialization perspective with the exception that respondents are chosen to be adult children rather than young children. We believe that an *ab initio* conceptualization of IGI can yield fresh insights. Such is the perspective we have adopted. An effort such as ours is necessarily based as much on intuition as on prior theory. Their interplay, made more poignant by the exchange of views among researchers in a discussion forum, can advance our understanding in this important, and under examined area of consumer behavior.

REFERENCES

Bearden, W.O. and M.J. Etzel (1982), "Reference Group Influence on Product and Brand Decisions," *Journal of Consumer Research*, 9, (September): 183-194.

_____, R.G. Netemeyer, and J.E. Teel (1989), "Measurement of Consumer Susceptibility to Interpersonal Influence," *Journal of Consumer Research*, 15, (March): 473-481.

Bettman, J.R. (1973), "Perceived Risk and its Components: A model and Empirical Test," *Journal of Marketing Research*, 10, (May): 184-190.

_____, and Park, C.W. (1980), "Effects of Prior Knowledge and Experience and Phase of the Choice Process on Consumer Decision Processes: A Protocol Analysis," *Journal of Consumer Research*," 7, (December): 234-248.

Brucks, M. (1985), "The Effects of Product Class Knowledge on Information Search Behavior," *Journal of Consumer Research*, 12, (June): 1-16.

Cox, D.F. (1967), ed., *Risk Taking and Information Handling in Consumer Behavior*, Boston, MA: Graduate School of Business Administration, Harvard University

Childers, T.L. and A.R. Rao (1992), "The Influence of Familial and Peer-Based Reference Groups on Consumer Decisions," *Journal of Consumer Research*, 19, (September): 198-211.

Darby, M.R. and E. Karni (1973), "Informational Social Influence and Product Evaluation," *Journal of Law and Economics*, 16, (April): 67-88.

Deutch, M. and H.B. Gerard (1955), "A Study of Normative and Informational Social Influences Upon Individual Judgment," *Journal of Abnormal and Social Psychology*, 51, 624-636.

---

[2]Considering dysfunctional families or acrimonious relationships and the possibility of dissassociative or negative IGI, while entirely plausible, is beyond the scope of this paper.

FIGURE 2
A Conceptual Model of Intergenerational Influence

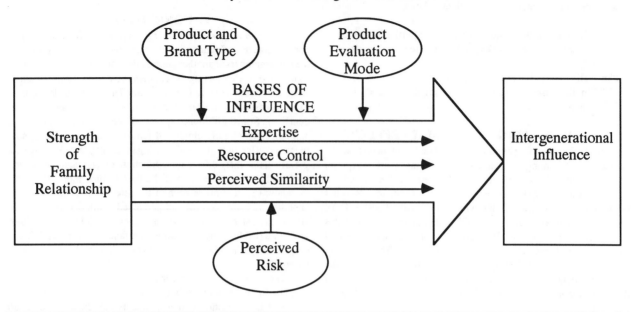

Heckler, S.E., T.E. Childers and R. Arunachalam (1989), "Intergenerational Influences in Adult Buying Behaviors: An Examination of Moderating Factors," *Advances in Consumer Research*, 16, ed. Thomas Srull, Provo UT: Association for Consumer Research, 276-284.

Hogan, D.P., D.J. Eggebeen, and C.C. Clogg (1993), "The Structure of Intergenerational Exchange in American Families," *American Journal of Sociology*, 98, (May), 1428-1458.

Kelman, H.C. (1961), "Processes of Opinion Change," *Public Opinion Quarterly*, 25, 57-78.

Midgely, D.F. (1983), "Patterns of Interpersonal Information Seeking for the Purchase of a Symbolic Product," *Journal of Marketing Research*, 20, (February): 74-83

Mittal, B. (1988), "The Role of Affective Choice Mode in Consumer Purchase of Expressive Products, *Journal of Economic Psychology*, 9, 499-524.

Moschis, G.P. (1985), "The Role of Family Communication in Consumer Socialization of Children and Adolescents," *Journal of Consumer Research*, 11, (March): 898-913.

_____, (1988), "Methodological Issues in Studying Intergenerational Influences on Consumer Behavior," in *Advances in Consumer Research*, ed. M. Houston, 15, Ann Arbor, MI: Association for Consumer Research, 569-573.

Moore-Shay, E.S. and R.J. Lutz (1988), "Intergenerational Influences in the FormationConsumer Attitudes and Beliefs About the Marketplace: Mother and Daughters," in *Advances in Consumer Research*, ed. M. Houston, 15, Ann Arbor, MI: Association for Consumer Research, 461-467.

Nelson, P. (1970), "Information and Consumer Behavior," *Journal of Political Economy*, 78, (March/April): 311-329.

Park, C.W. and P. Lessig (1977), "Students and Housewives: Differences in Susceptibility to Reference Group Influence," *Journal of Consumer Research*, 4, (September): 102-110.

_____, B.J. Jaworski and D.J. MacInnis (1986), "Strategic Brand Concept/Image Management," *Journal of Marketing*, 50, (October): 135-145.

Richins, M.L. (1991), "Social Comparison and the Idealized Images of Advertising," *Journal of Consumer Research*, 18, (June): 71-83.

Spiro, R.L. (1983), "Persuasion in Family Decision Making," *Journal of Consumer Research*, 9, (March): 393-402.

Sujan, M., J.R Bettman, and H. Baumgartner (1993), "Influencing Consumer Judgments Using Autobiographical Memories," *Journal of Marketing Research*, 30 (2), (November): 422-436.

Ward, S. (1974), "Consumer Socialization," *Journal of Consumer Research*, 1, (September): 1-16.

Witt, R.E. and G.D. Bruce (1972), "Group Influence and Brand Choice Congruence," *Journal of Marketing Research*, 9, (November): 440-443.

Woods, W.A. (1960), "Psychological Dimensions of Consumer Decision," *Journal of Marketing*, 24, (January): 15-19.

I Am Not ... Therefore, I Am: The Role of Avoidance Products in Shaping Consumer Behavior

Basil G. Englis, Berry College

Michael R. Solomon, Auburn University

SESSION INTRODUCTION

Consumption preferences represent important data employed both by the self and by others to signify a person's social identity (see, e.g., recent reviews in Englis and Solomon 1995; 1997). Choices of products, services, and activities tell us what "social type" a person is and what "type(s)" he or she is not. Consumption choices also act as social signals that can identify reference groups the individual is motivated to emulate or avoid. Although the impact of reference group influences in identifying "approach products," or other positively valued consumption cues, is well-acknowledged in the literature (e.g., Bearden and Etzell 1982), scant attention has been paid to the role that avoidance groups and their associated patterns of consumption play in the formation of the extended self. This may be a crucial oversight, insofar as we cannot ignore the possibility that consumers may be as motivated to avoid associations with negatively-valued others as they are to express the desire to approach positively-valued others by emulating their (assumed) consumption choices. The goal of the session was to redress the imbalance by presenting a range of perspectives on avoidance consumption.

We take a symbolic perspective on consumer behavior, which has as its central tenet the notion that many products are consumed because of their symbolic value to the individual and his or her social setting. The use of consumption activities as a form of self-expression is often related to strong associations between products and social roles. Whether YUPPIES, sports teams, or motorcycle gangs, group identities often coalesce around forms of expressive symbolism. The self-definitions of group members are derived from the common symbol system to which the group is dedicated; these symbols define the group's "personality." As a result, each social category has its associated collection of products and activities which are taken by society to define that category (e.g., Englis and Solomon 1995; McCall and Simmons 1982; Solomon 1983).

Such groupings of consumption activities and/or products may hold little or no inherent relationship to each other, but may instead be related through a socio-cultural process of association and ascription of meaning (see, e.g., Englis and Solomon 1996; Solomon and Assael 1987). A particular product grouping, then, is valued for its ability to communicate social messages within a particular culture at a particular historic moment. Thus, for example, tie-died t-shirts, patched blue jeans, and Army fatigue jackets identified a member of the "counter-culture" of the 1960s and, more currently, a member of the 1990s' "Generation X." Because of its cultural basis, this form of self-expression is predicated on the consumer's ability to decode a culture's Zeitgeist correctly (to know which product groupings connote which identities) and to encode the "appropriate" identity (to enact the desired role).

Though one would seem to be on safe ground in hypothesizing that consumers are likely to skew their purchase decisions toward those products that bring them closer to an "ideal self," the less apparent role of products that are *to be avoided* may be equally important. Although perceived correspondence to the ideal self is surely an important force in self assessment, appraisals may also be framed in terms of perceived distance away from an undesired self-image – what one *does not* want to be (Ogilvie 1987). For example, in the 1990s a consumer may wish to dissociate from the somewhat tarnished YUPPIE ideal of the 1980s and, therefore, avoid such products as Brie cheese, white-wine spritzers, Rolex watches, and BMWs. This panel explores the role of negatively-valued consumption choices in consumers' formulations of their self-concepts and in their definition of social reference groups.

Learning to Not-Want Things
Richard Wilk, University of Indiana

What we do not want to consume is often as personally and socially important as what we desire. The question posed by the present research is, how do we learn not just to want things, but to not want things? Are these really two separate bodies of knowledge; do we keep separate conceptual categories of good and bad, of things to be sought out and things to be avoided? Or, are the positive and negative aspects of goods always intimately related to each other, so that we learn a series of relationships between desire and disgust, or desired and detested objects? This inquiry was prompted by a long-term study of consumption in the Central American country of Belize. As part of this work a survey of 389 adult consumers was conducted. With several exceptions, the survey protocol was modeled on Bourdieu's research instrument (1984, also Wilk 1995). However, it became clear during pretest interviews that respondents had a great deal more to say about their distastes and dislikes than about their desires. Because of this response in the pretest, a few distaste questions were added to the survey, specifically concerning music and food tastes.

It is notable that none of the preferences for particular items (consumption activities) correlated strongly ($r^2 > .45$) with any measured social, ethnic, or personal variables. In sharp contrast, distastes were much more powerful social predictors than preferences. For example, the "loving food" index correlated significantly (1-tailed, $p < .01$) with only one variable, education level. More highly educated people tended to love fewer foods. On the other hand, the index of "food hatred" correlated significantly with eight out of ten social variables. Urban people tended to hate more things, and members of the Creole ethnic group had significantly more hates than members of other ethnic categories. People who were richer, had higher household incomes, were better educated and in higher status occupations all tended to have fewer hates. The fraction of the population that would in Belize be considered the urban poor, were much more likely to dislike a broad range of foods, though the number of things they liked was almost the same as the best educated and richest Belizeans. This suggests that rising in class is more a matter of learning to stop hating things, learning tolerance, rather than the conventional account of class mobility, which stresses the acquisition of new tastes.

These results are based on only a few survey items, added as almost an afterthought to a more conventional study of likes and preferences. The original intent was to develop contrasts with work on consumers in developed countries. This has not proven possible, because there has been almost no systematic empirical work on distastes and dislikes in developed countries, with the exception of a relatively narrow body of work on consumer dissatisfaction with items that have already been purchased.

Exploring Anti-Constellations: Content and Consensus
Margaret K. Hogg, University of Manchester
Paul C. N. Michell, University of Manchester

The creation of meaning via consumption involves both positive and negative choices. Consumers use product, brand, and activity choices to mark inclusion and exclusion. Consumption constellations have been used to model the complementarity of positive choices among multi-category products (e.g., Solomon and Assael 1987). Consumption anti-constellations have been proposed to represent the complementarity of negative choices across multi-category products (Hogg 1995). Anti-constellations involve two aspects of consumers' negative choices: non choice and anti choice. Non choice includes products and services which are simply not bought, often because they are not within the means of the consumer. Anti choices, which are more important and relevant here, include products and services which are positively not chosen because they are seen as incompatible and inconsistent with the consumer's other consumption choices and preferences.

The experiment described here is modeled on an earlier study of constellations (Solomon and Assael 1987), which examined consumers' understanding of the groups of products associated with different occupations. The present study extends this earlier work by examining anti-constellations: the inventories of products and services which would specifically *not* be associated with prototypical social role occupants. Sixty Management Science students from a British university were asked to generate anti-constellations for three occupations. The first occupation, that of "student," was chosen because all the respondents would have a high degree of familiarity with this reference group. The second occupation was chosen to represent the students' "aspirational occupation" – students were asked to imagine themselves in their career in five years' time. The third occupation was that of each respondent's father (familial). For each occupational category, respondents were asked to generate a list of products which they would not associate with that occupation.

A number of findings emerge clearly from the experiment. First, consumers can generate anti-constellations in response to occupational cues. Second, consumers can provide information about anti-constellations at product and brand level; but there is more detailed brand knowledge of anti-constellations related to occupations with consumers are in close proximity. Consumers provide less detailed information about anti-constellations associated with occupations with which they have less affinity. Third, respondents generated fifteen product categories for the anti-constellations associated with the cue "student," and eleven each for the other two occupational cues: aspirational and familial (father's occupation). The major product categories which appeared across all the anti-constellations were clothing/footwear, cars, and food. Public transport and fast food/takeaways appeared only in the aspirational and familial anti-constellations. Consistent with the findings of Solomon and Assael (1987), knowledge and understanding of product-to-role associations are linked to respondents degree of familiarity with the occupational cue.

Studies of symbolic consumption have concentrated largely on individual products and positive choices. This study has extended an earlier American study of consumption constellations, which represent positive choice, to anti-constellations, which represent the complementarity of negative choices across multi-category products.

Reference Group Influences On Teen Smoking: The Effects Of Smoking In Movies And Anti-Smoking Ads Before Movies
Cornelia Pechmann, University of California, Irvine
Chuan-Fong (Eric) Shih, University of California, Irvine

In many movies, even PG-rated movies, young, sexy, glamorous stars are cast as smokers. Smoking by these stars (e.g., Winona Ryder and Ethan Hawke in Reality Bites; Demi Moore and Rob Lowe in St. Elmo's Fire) may suggest to vast teen audiences that by smoking they can present themselves more favorably to their reference groups and, thereby, enhance their self esteem. Most teens are very concerned about reference group approval because they need such approval to feel good about themselves (Schlenker 1980). Running anti-smoking ads before movies, specifically ads that portray smoking as socially unacceptable, could potentially offset the effects of smoking by glamorous movie stars.

We conducted an experiment to examine whether smoking by the lead characters in a youth-oriented movie might enhance teens' perceptions of smokers, and whether running an anti-smoking ad before the movie might negate such effects. We professionally edited a recent PG-rated movie that cast popular young movie stars as smokers (Reality Bites – MCA Universal Studio) to remove the smoking while preserving the quality and content, i.e., dialog, music, and length. We also showed either a anti-smoking or control ad before each movie, to examine whether a single 30 second anti-smoking ad would neutralize the effects of the movie's large number of smoking scenes. The anti-smoking ad was produced in California and tested very well with teens, but had not run for several months and thus was unlikely to manifest wear out. The ad used humor to portray reference group disapproval of smoking, suggesting that teens who smoke are ostracized by peers. The control ad warned teens that alcohol abuse can lead to promiscuity and AIDS. We asked teens to record their affective responses to the movie, scene by scene, to examine if smoking influenced affect, particularly arousal. The other dependent variables included smokers' self presentation and self esteem, and intent to smoke (see Pechmann and Knight 1996). Subjects were 130 ninth-graders (nonsmokers) from three high schools in Southern California who volunteered, with parental and teacher permission, to participate during school hours. None of the subjects had seen the movie.

We found that teens who saw the control ad and the smoking (vs. non-smoking) movie rated teen smokers more favorably on self presentation and self esteem. These same subjects also reported being more aroused during the movie. Showing the anti-smoking ad before the movie nullified these effects. The same pattern of results obtained regardless of whether subjects had a prior interest in smoking. These findings imply that to combat underage smoking it might be beneficial to run anti-smoking ads before youth-oriented movies that contain heavy amounts of smoking. In our study the anti-smoking ads did not alter overall liking of the movie so there may be little downside risk. If anti-smoking ads are not run, movies may inadvertently promote underage smoking by suggesting that it leads to peer approval and enhanced self esteem.

DISCUSSION

Several important themes run through this group of papers: One is the notion that symbolic aspects of consuming (or of not consuming) certain products may have as much to do with positioning the self in closer proximity to an aspirational, ideal self as in opposition to an avoidance, anti-ideal self. In contrast with consumer tastes, which may be closer reflections of the behavior of aspirational groups, distastes may be more "socially constructed" in that they may be more reflective of in-group perceptions than of marketplace realities (e.g., Englis and Solomon 1995). As indicated by the analysis of Hogg and Michell, there exists an important, yet under-studied, distinction between consumers' non-choice and their active avoidance of certain products. And, this may relate to important social-developmental life transitions during the course of which consumers abandon some tastes in preference for others: thus, a taste for Twinkies and milk may give way to a penchant for biscotti and lattè. Such transitions may involve an active "refusal" of old tastes. This is in sharp contrast to the "fixation" of taste represented by nostalgic attachment to certain consumption objects.

REFERENCES

Bourdieu, Pierre (1984), *Distinction: A Social Critique of the Judgment of Taste*, Cambridge, MA: Harvard University Press.

Bearden, William O. and Michael J. Etzel (1982), "Reference Group Influence on Product and Brand Purchase Decisions," *Journal of Consumer Research*, 9 (2), 183-194.

Englis, Basil G. and Michael R. Solomon(1995), "To Be *and* Not to Be: Lifestyle Imagery, Reference Groups, and *The Clustering of America*," *Journal of Advertising*, 24(Spring), 13-28.

Englis, Basil G. and Michael R. Solomon (1996), "Using Consumption Constellations to Develop Integrated Marketing Communications," *Journal of Business Research, 37* (3), 183–191.

Englis, Basil G. and Michael R. Solomon (1997), "Where Perception Meets Reality: The Social Construction of Lifestyles," in *Values, Lifestyles, and Psychographics*, ed. Lynn Kahle and Larry Chiagurus, Hillsdale, NJ: Lawrence Erlbaum, pp. 25–44.

Hogg, Margaret K. (1995), "Conceptualizing and Investigating patterns of Consumer Behaviour Towards In-Home Shopping," Doctoral Thesis, University of Manchester, UK

McCall, George J. and J.C. Simmons (1982), *Social Psychology: A Sociological Approach*, New York: The Free Press.

Ogilvie, Daniel M. (1987), "The Undesired Self: A Neglected Variable in Personality Research," *Journal of Personality and Social Psychology*, 53, 693-702.

Pechmann, Cornelia and Susan J. Knight (1996), "Cigarette Ads, Anti-smoking Ads and Peers: Why do Underage Youth Start Smoking Cigarettes?" forthcoming in *Advances in Consumer Research*, Volume 23, Kim P. Corfman and John Lynch, eds., Provo, Utah: Association for Consumer Research.

Schlenker, Barry R. (1980), *Impression Management: The Self-Concept, Social Identity, and Interpersonal Relations*, Monterey, California: Brooks/Cole.

Solomon, Michael R. (1983), "The Role of Products as Social Stimuli: A Symbolic Interactionism Perspective," *Journal of Consumer Research* 10 (December), 319-329.

Solomon, Michael R. and Henry Assael (1987), "The Forest or the Trees?: A Gestalt Approach to Symbolic Consumption," in ed. Jean Umiker-Sebeok, *Marketing and Semiotics: New Directions in the Study of Signs for Sale*, Berlin: Mouton de Gruyter, 189-218.

Wells, William D. and Douglas J. Tigert (1971), "Activities, Interests, and Opinions," *Journal of Advertising Research*, 11 (August), 27-35.

Wilk, Richard (1995), *Economies and Cultures: Foundations of Economic Anthropology*, Boulder, CO: Westview Press.

Affecting Consumers Through Identity and Design
Alex Simonson, Georgetown University

SESSION OVERVIEW

In the move from brands to design, there are numerous CB issues that arise. We might be interested in the effects of color or shape in packaging; in isolating various elements of typefaces or logos affecting perceptions; in determining how consumer tastes for product appearances shift or why certain designs appear "outdated" while others remain "classical."

We might see a need for a framework to understand people's reactions to design or to "trade dress," that entire bundle of non-functional stimuli, like the shape of the Coca-Cola bottle, the look of the Nike logo, the motif of the Starbuck's coffee shops, the scent and sounds in the Crabtree and Evelyn stores.

This session comes on the heals of a long line of work on the experiential aspects of consumption pioneered in major part by Morris Holbrook. But, two major differences distinguish this session. Here, the focus is on all kinds of products and services rather than on inherently aesthetic products like fashion and music. And, here, we move towards bridging the gap between a field of academic inquiry and a field of business practice–corporate identity and design–one that is crying out for academic insights.

Design firms from the largest like Landor Associates, Siegel & Gale and Chermayeff and Geismar, to the smallest one-person graphic design shops, strive for insights in understanding consumer reactions to design, in devising methodologies to explore possible effects, and in using conceptualizations to help bridge the consumer behavior concerning design and the management of design processes.

We're now sitting five years after what we can call the great fall-out of the early 1990's, when identity and design in the industrial world went through turmoil—companies no longer wanted to spend seven-figure pay-outs for corporate identity projects, identity departments were disbanded, and many designers left the field. But what has evolved is more interesting, a world where ad agencies have acquired design firms, so design is viewed as part of an overall communications program, where designers must not only be concerned with art but also with consumer behavior and communications strategies. In this new environment, academic research can no doubt provide theoretical, empirical and strategic insights.

Those interested in this area will note that design or trade dress is a system of interrelated stimuli, like corporate buildings and lobbies, retail spaces, web sites, product and service offerings, packaging and promotional materials. Research streams have sprung up to study certain aspects of the system. The papers that will be presented here draw from a variety of research streams mixing empirical and conceptual approaches.

We begin (in the context of logos) exploring "style," the basic element of design, and how it impacts reactions to design. We then move (in the context of packaging) to empirical studies on how design affects choice. Finally, we conclude with an overall strategic conceptualization of consumer perceptions of trade dress.

SUMMARY OF EACH PRESENTATION

Designing Better Logos: The Influence of Aesthetics (empirical paper)
Pamela Henderson, Washington State University
Joseph Cote, Washington State University

Background

Virtually every company uses a logo as part of its corporate aesthetics. Currently, logo selection is frequently based on a CEO's preference from a small set of options presented by a design company. A major problem is the lack of empirical research on the determinants of reactions to logos. The recommendations about logos in the marketing and graphic design literatures are usually based on the expertise of professionals. This paper examines the experimental aesthetics, gestalt psychology, graphic design, and marketing literature to develop an empirical study to test which aesthetic characteristics influence evaluations of a logo's recognition, liking and meaningfulness. Our goal is to identify the underlying design dimensions (factors) that capture a variety of aesthetic characteristics. We then use the underlying design dimensions to explain reactions to logos and suggest general guidelines for logo design.

The major problem has been that each literature discusses only one or two design characteristics at a time (e.g., complexity and meaningfulness), ignoring the complex relationships among all the characteristics. As such, there has been no development of an integrated theory. But, taken together (we will discuss the literature), the different research streams reveal that there are 9 aesthetic characteristics that should influence reactions to logos: complexity, symmetry, durability, representativeness, cohesiveness, activeness, flatness, roundness, and organicness.

Study

Values for all 9 aesthetic characteristics and three types of reactions were collected for 195 foreign logos from Kuwayama (1973). Following Berlyne's (1974) guidelines, an average rating of large numbers of subjects or ratings by trained experts were used as measures (Berlyne 1974). Confirmatory factor analysis (CFA) was used to construct factor scores for the 9 aesthetic characteristics and 3 types of responses. The factor scores for each aesthetic characteristic was included in an exploratory factor analysis (i.e., a second order factor analysis). Factor scoring coefficients were estimated and used to calculate factor scores for the design dimensions. These design dimensions were then used as independent variables into three regression analyses to predict recognition, affective reactions, and meaningfulness. Both main effect and all interactions were included in the regression model. To avoid problems associated with multicollinearity, hierarchical regression was used. The main effects model was fit first, and the interactions were regressed against the residual of the main effects model.

Results

Preliminary results indicated that durability and cohesiveness could not be adequately measured. The remaining 7 aesthetic characteristics were captured by three factors. Elaborateness combines complexity, activeness, and depth and appears to capture richness of design. (It should be noted that elaborateness is not the same as intricacy or detailed. Rather it suggests the use of simple lines to capture the essence and meaning of something.) Naturalness combines representativeness, organicness, and roundness to reflect the degree to which the design reflect something common to everyday experience. Lastly, symmetry is retained as a "factor" of it's own. The three aesthetic factors explain a significant amount of recognition, affect and meaning. Examples of logos were presented to highlight the design guidelines suggested by our results.

References

Berlyne, Daniel E. (1974), *Studies in the New Experimental Aesthetics: Steps Toward An Objective Psychology of Aesthetic Appreciation*, Washington, D.C.: Hemisphere Publishing Corporation.

Kuwayama, Yasamura (1973), *Trademark and Symbols Vol. 1: Alphabetical Designs* and *Vol. 2: Symbolic Designs*, New York NY: Van Nostrand Reinhold Co.

The Effects of Very Similar Package Appearance on Purchase Consideration and Choice
(empirical paper)

Lawrence L. Garber Jr., Appalachian State University
Raymond R. Burke, Harvard Business School

Background

With the ongoing fragmentation of mass media, point of purchase promotion plays an increasingly important role in the promotional mix. Managers have two major options. One approach is to copy the look of other brands in the category, including the elements such as color, package shape and graphics. Another is to design packaging that intentionally looks different from other brands. The former approach, an "imitation" strategy, has the virtue of reassuring the shopper by fulfilling the expectations of what a brand in the category should look like (Dichter 1965, Loken and Ward 1990). This provides a measure of legitimacy and credibility, which essentially borrows from the visual conventions established and made meaningful by one's competitors. The latter approach, looking different, offers the virtue of noticeability through surprising contrast (Dichter 1965). This approach, however, is also risky, because novel appearance, though visually striking, may also convey an image or a meaning to the consumer that is deemed unfavorable or inappropriate, which would disqualify it as a credible candidate for purchase consideration.

Study 1

In empirical research using a computerized grocery store simulation, the authors have demonstrated that novel package appearance may effectively evoke purchase consideration if it is also appropriate to its category. In so doing, they have devised a means by which novelty and appropriateness can be measured independently. In this research, the identity and recognizability of individual brands were carefully maintained across changes to existing packaging, to reveal the relationship between novelty and appropriateness and purchase consideration.

Study 2

Conversely, in ongoing research, the authors explore the effects of very similar packaging on purchase consideration and choice. We attempt to answer the following questions. What is the reaction of the shopper when confronted with a package so similar to a competitor's package that one may be mistaken for the other? Will the shopper be put off, or does this confusion of identities allow for one brand to trade profitably on the image and equity of another? Does it matter if the shopper recognizes the intentions of the mimicking brand?

Methodology for Both Papers

In these studies, subjects are recruited by newspaper to shop using a computerized grocery simulation (Burke et al. 1992) designed to mimic the original market environment. Shoppers may manipulate the display to browse the facings, touch the screen to pick and turn a package, or put a package into their shopping cart. The subjects go on a series of shopping trips instructed to shop as they normally would in their own grocery stores. In the course of their shopping, the packages of some brands are exchanged for packages systematically altered to represent certain visual types. Exposure to these new visual stimuli are hypothesized to evoke certain behaviors at several stages in the choice process (Shocker et al. 1991).

References

Burke, Raymond R., Bari A. Harlam, Barbara E. Kahn and Leonard Lodish (1992), "Comparing Dynamic Consumer Choice in Real and Computer-Simulated Environments," *Journal of Consumer Research*, 19 (June), 71-82.

Dichter, Ernest (1965), *Packaging: The Sixth Sense? A Guide to Identifying Consumer Motivation*, Boston: Cahners Books.

Loken, Barbara and James Ward (1990), "Alternative Approaches to Understanding the Determinants of Typicality," *Journal of Consumer Research*, 17 (September), 111-126.

Shocker, Allan D., Moshe Ben-Akiva, Bruno Boccara, and Prakash Nedungadi (1991), "Consideration Set Influences on Consumer Choice: Issues, Models and Suggestions," *Marketing Letters*, 1:3, 181-197.

Consumer Perceptions of Trade "Dress"
(conceptual paper)

Alex Simonson, Georgetown University
Bernd H. Schmitt, Columbia University

Background

The "visual style of an organization" is seen as a critical means for differentiating products, securing customer loyalty, and creating positive impressions among the public at large (Olins 1990). Indeed, since the rise of a modern consumer society in America in the 1920s and 1930s, styling and aesthetics have been part of all consumer products and services. Styling and aesthetics are intentional or unintentional 'add-ons' to the physical/utilitarian features of tangible consumer products and the tangible aspects of services. Yet, to date, despite several programmatic attempts (e.g., Hirschman and Holbrook 1981), consumer researchers have not presented a systematic, strategically useful, conceptualization or empirical research programs to address styling and aesthetics without regard to "aesthetic" products pre-se.

Conceptual Framework

Based on prior research (e.g., Schmitt, Simonson and Marcus 1995), we present a conceptual framework that constitutes a systematic categorization of relevant concepts. We distinguish three relevant concepts: aesthetic styles, aesthetic themes and overall impressions. Analogous to the concept of a mental representation (prevalent in the information-processing paradigm of consumer research), aesthetic styles refer to the form (or format) of consumers' perceptions of styling. Aesthetic themes refer to their content. Overall impressions are consumer perceptions created out of combinations of styles and themes.

As defined in Webster's dictionary, the concept of "Style" refers to a distinctive quality or form, a "a manner of expression." We draw from literature in the arts where, according to the art historian Meyer Shapiro, style is "the constant form—and sometimes the constant elements and expression—in the art of an individual or a group. Style, is above all, a *system of forms*." We discuss how *styles* and their various underlying aesthetic elements can affect consumers, marketers and society, identifying various aesthetic styles (e.g., complexity, representational, and perceived movement dimensions) and the perceptions of their underlying components (e.g., colors, shapes, materials). Aesthetic *themes* originate in various ways and language acts as a filter for creating themes. We discuss themes in the form of labels, slogans, and narratives. Finally, *overall impressions* result from bridging styles and themes. The dimensions (e.g., time and space dimensions) result in various overall cognitive and affective responses.

References

Hirschman, E. and M. B. Holbrook (1981), *Symbolic Consumer Behavior*. Ann Arbor, MI: Association for Consumer Research.

Olins, W. (1990), *Corporate Identity*, Cambridge, MA: Harvard Business School Press.

Schmitt, B. H., A. Simonson and J. Marcus (1995), "Corporate Aesthetics: Managing Your Company's Image and Identity," *Long Range Planning*, 28 (5), 82-92.

DISCUSSION

The discussant focused on the relation of design in various aspects of our experiences and consumption activities. He showed how design can become part of buildings, part of advertisements, etc. He then led a discussion of the papers.

Narrative Theory and Consumer Research: Theoretical and Methodological Perspectives

Kent Grayson, London Business School

Narrative theory seeks to account for the integral role that stories play in our psychological and social lives. The theory has been applied and developed in a number of disciplines, including anthropology (e.g., Rayfield 1972), linguistics (e.g., Gee 1985), psychoanalysis (e.g., Cohler 1982), social psychology (e.g., Sarbin 1986), literary criticism (e.g., Jameson 1981), cognitive psychology (Black and Wilensky 1979), and philosophy (e.g., Ellos 1994). Narrative theory's application in such diverse disciplines suggests that it offers a potentially useful perspective for consumer researchers of all types. Yet, it has been applied in only a small number of consumer-behavior studies, and has been used for the development of rather divergent theories and conclusions:

- Deighton (1992) and Arnould and Price (1993) lend support to the idea that the appreciation of consumption experiences depends on how well the experience can be captured and remembered as a story.
- Hirschman (1988) and Stern (1995) use structural analysis to show how stories told in commercials and television shows can provide models or templates for consumers' lives.
- Deighton, Romer, and McQueen (1989) and Peracchio (1993) have given credence to the proposition that consumers process and store narratives differently than other kinds of information.

This list of research projects suggests that narrative theory's potential contribution to consumer research is both promising and problematic. On one hand, narrative theory is rich enough to be applied in so many disciplines that the opportunity for interdisciplinary inquiry is high. To fully appreciate narrative theory, one must think beyond traditional academic boundaries, because it is applied in remarkably different literatures and disciplines. Thus, narrative theory offers a fertile research perspective that prompts both divergent and convergent thinking about dynamic social events.

On the other hand, the multi-disciplinary development of narrative theory has led to confusion and disagreement about the theory's domain, concepts, and constructs. As Chase (1995, p. 1) writes, scholars "disagree about what constitutes narrative and develop divergent approaches to the relations between narrative and life, narrative and subjectivity, narrative and culture, and narrative and fiction or truth . . . ." The result is a fragmented research perspective that sometimes seems too diffuse to support cohesive programmatic inquiry.

The purpose of this session is to explore the value of narrative theory in understanding, describing, explaining and predicting consumer behavior. In pursuit of this purpose, the session reflects both the multi-vocality and the unified focus of narrative research. Each session presenter builds from a distinct background in the narrative literature, examines a unique consumer-research activity, and emphasizes a different methodology. Yet, the participants also share a common background in narrative theory, and a common interest in understanding the impact of narratives on consumer behavior.

The Positive Effects of Narrative Thought in Response to Advertising
Jennifer Edson Escalas, University of Arizona

Consumer research has documented that brands and possessions have meaning for consumers (e.g., Belk, Wallendorf, and Sherry 1989; McCracken, 1986; Richins, 1994). However, little is known about the process by which objects become meaningful. On a broader scale, people make sense of their lives via narrative thought (e.g., Bruner 1986, 1990; Gergen and Gergen 1988; Polkinghorne 1991). Through the structure of narrative thinking, specifically spacio-temporal dimensionality and causal inferences, people organize their experiences, create order out of what might otherwise be random incidents, and explain unusual events. Furthermore, people naturally construct these stories or narratives to give their lives coherence and to create their identities.

Consumers can construct narratives involving brands, and as a result of this meaning-making process, some brands become more important than others to consumers. Some brands take on symbolic meaning, represent who one is or wants to be, perhaps communicate some aspect of self to others, and become significantly related to consumers' mental representations of self. It is these types of connections that marketers wish to build between their brands and targeted consumers. Meaningful self-brand connections will lead to strong, favorable brand attitudes, and brand loyal behavior.

I hypothesize that one way marketers can build these connections is by evoking favorable narrative thought about their brand. Consumer stories linking themselves to the brand can form meaningful self-brand connections. To test this, I manipulated the text in a print ad for running shoes. The three conditions resulted in three distinct levels of narratively structured thought in response to the ad. Text inviting subjects to imagine themselves running in the shoe evoked the most narrative thought, followed by a third person story about the shoe, followed by an analytical, feature-focused text.

The results of the study show that the more narratively structured consumers' thoughts were in response to the running shoe ad, the stronger their meaningful self-brand connections to the fictitious shoe brand. As narrative thought increased, so did attitude towards the ad, attitude towards the brand, and a combined measure of behavioral intentions (willingness to try on the shoe, willingness to pay for the shoe, and purchase intentions). Meaningful self-brand connections mediated the effect of narrative thought on brand attitudes and intentions.

Meaningful self-brand connections are built by linking the brand to the self. Thus I hypothesize that for subjects with a relevant, well-developed aspect of self (in this case a "runner" aspect of self), narratively structured thought will enhance meaningful connections more than for subjects who are not runners. The study results support this assertion. Finally, narrative thought has been linked to our experiences of emotion. Therefore, as narrative thought increases, emotional responses to the print ad should also be enhanced. Again, the study results support this hypothesis: narrative thought positively affected upbeat and warm feelings, and negatively affected disinterested feelings.

In conclusion, it appears that marketers may be able to enhance the formation of meaningful connections between their brands and targeted consumers through the use of advertising that encourages narratively structured thought. Meaningful connections are in turn related to many favorable outcome measures of interest to marketers.

Stories and Selling: The Narrative Strategies of Direct Sales Agents

Kent Grayson, London Business School

From Aesop's fables to Sesame Street; from the Bible's allegories to modern cinema, stories have long been tools of persuasion. Kenneth Burke (1945, 1966) has written extensively in support of this proposition, and some consumer researchers (Deighton, Romer, and McQueen 1989; Stern 1995; Wells 1988) have begun to examine the strategies and mechanisms of narrative persuasion. To further enhance our understanding of narratives and consumer behavior, this presentation examines the stories used by direct sales agents as part of their sales repertoire. In particular, this research focuses on the strategies used to achieve verisimilitude in narratives. Previous research (Deighton, Romer and McQueen 1989) has suggested that verisimilitude is essential in narrative-oriented (as opposed to argument-oriented) persuasion. Network marketing (a type of direct selling – see Grayson 1996) is a particularly appropriate arena for studying commercial narratives because it often involves high-energy recruitment meetings, where top salespeople literally go on stage to tell their success stories. Sales agents are also encouraged to "tell your story" as part of their one-on-one sales presentations (Clothier 1994).

The research project is divided into two parts. First, a number of sales narratives were transcribed and examined using a combination of functional and structural narrative analysis (e.g., Labov and Waletzky 1967, Propp 1928). Coders were asked to examine the stories and to categorize them on a variety of dimensions. The coding resulted in low agreement among coders on many of these dimensions, but had high reliability in their assessment that the stories tended to follow the structure of a "transformation narrative." In the Labov and Waletzky (1967) terminology, a complicating action is brought to resolution by a company product—or by involvement as a company sales agent—and as a result, the narrator's life or identity is changed.

In the second part of the research, direct sales agents were asked to comment on the persuasive (in)efficacy of transformation narratives, paying particular focus to why transformation narratives might be useful in achieving verisimilitude in persuasion. The goal was to develop a narrative "persuasion knowledge model" (Freistadt and Wright 1995) that helps to account for the potential persuasive impact of commercial narratives. To the distributors interviewed, narratives achieve verisimilitude because they are a true reflection of what "really happened."

This view of narratives is a simplified version of that presented by Ricoeur (1983), whereby narratives are the most appropriate way in which human beings can describe and understand the passage of events. By this persuasion knowledge model, network marketing narratives achieve verisimilitude because they are a reflection of actual happenings in distributors' lives. However, this model does not recognize – as Ricoeur's (1983) does, along with Scholes (1980), Schechner (1985), Bauman (1986) and others – that the "causality" may go in the other direction: The structure of narratives may help us to organize our understanding of events, rather than the events structuring the narratives.

The findings from this research prompt the need for further research of a longitudinal nature. If events structure narratives, then it is likely that narratives should be relatively invariant over a the career of a network marketing distributor. However, if narratives structure one's understanding of events, then the narratives (and the distributor's memory of the events) may change over time.

Postmodern Consumer Research Narratives: Problems in Construct Definition, Structure, and Classification

Barbara Stern, Rutgers University

This presentation aims at breaking the narrative box altogether by attacking the notion that a consumer research story is unitary and integrated. A consumer narrative is not a monolothic box into which prose is stuffed, but is instead multi-level and fragmented. This complexity is especially acute in postmodern research, which seeks to represent consumers' voices directly by means of verbatims drawn from focus groups or individual interviews and observations. Thus, at least two different sets of narrative accounts co-exist: one produced by the consumer informant and another by the researcher. Fusing the layers into one obscures "relationships between author, narrator(s), characters, and audience" (Lanser 1981, p. 26).

This presentation uses narrative data in published consumer interviews to illustrate the unique difficulties that these complex data present to researchers, and suggests potential approaches for handling these difficulties. Three challenges are highlighted and illustrated: defining the construct of consumer narratives, handling what is not said, and addressing the truth value of narratives.

Construct Definition. Because we are all familiar with stories and story-telling, the term "narrative" appears to be "so natural, so universal, and so easily mastered as hardly to seem a problematic region" (Miller 1990, p. 66). Nonetheless, the conflict-ridden body of literary theory indicates that no definition can be taken for granted. Further, none fits consumer research accounts with double narration (researcher/author and consumer/character). The challenge in consumer research is to develop a coherent narratology capable of increasing our understanding of both the what and the way of research stories.

Handling Silence. Narratives represent presence—what the narrator says to the narratee about the narrated events—as distinct from absence—"what is not said, what is not shown, what points of view or narrative possibilities are not present, who does not speak or see" (Lanser 1981, p. 341). This raises the dynamic of dominance/subordination, for those who do not speak are as relevant to the story as those who do speak (Lanser 1981). Feminist, Marxist, and minority theory deals with the political implications of marginalization—muting or disappearing some voices at the expense of others—that permeate consumer research as well as other disciplines.

Addressing Narrative Truth. The third problem is one of "truth" versus "fiction." Narrative describes the recounting of events that really happened (history, biography, social science) as well as those that are invented. Despite the fact that all stories are "made" or crafted in the sense that they impose order on a welter of experiences, research accounts are assumed to be representations of "things that really happened exactly as they really happened" (Miller 1990, p. 68) rather than crafted objects. Thus, the construct of narrative is problematized by multidimensionality, patterns of exclusion, and permeable borders between stories that are true fictions and/or fictionalized truths.

The imperfect fit between narratological theory and consumer research data does not imply that literary theory is inapplicable to non-literary material. Rather, storytelling is considered a cultural staple, universally engaged in by all known communities, including the scholarly one. What the gap between data and theory suggests is that we need to break out of unitary thinking and define narrative in context-specific terms, such that commonalities among research stories and typological differences between them come clear. A relevant classification system can contribute to clarification of postmodern research modes by specifying attributes and combinations characteristic of one type or another. The narratological lens can be used to pull what is now blurry into clearer focus, enabling better criteria for research representations.

Narrative Strategies, Persuasion, and Textual Transformations
Susan Spiggle (Session Synthesizer), The University of Connecticut

Narrative theory provides us with a framework for enhancing interpretation and re-presenting our interpretations to others. The three papers in this session link persuasion processes with narrative constructions. They do so in three different ways. Escalas' model of the persuasion process presents narratives as consumer cognitive and affective representations in response to marketing stimuli (ads). The narrative intervenes between the marketing stimuli and behavioral and purchase intentions. Here the narrative serves as a structure for connections between the advertised brand and the self. This representation of mental structure is an alternative to the semantic networks model where nodes form connections with others in a reticular structure. As Escalas implies, narratives impose or permit a particular way of organizing meanings—story-like, situated in time and space, with characters, motives, and other narrative elements. Escalas' insight is to suggest the role of narrative thought in shaping receiver effects through brand-self linkages.

Grayson proposes narrative—story-telling as a persuasive communication device in network marketing. He notes that these commercial narratives attempt to persuade through verisimilitude, as opposed to argument, and operate by structuring sequences of events. Grayson's insight is his recognition of the potential persuasive power of narrative as a marketing stimulus. Stern addresses the issue of transforming consumer narratives—consumer voices—into research narratives—journal articles. We encounter, even here, how narrative operates in persuasion. Stern's insight is her use of narrative to address the problem of re-presentation—how the consumer's voice is re-presented through the author's voice—how researchers persuade readers of their point of view. Grayson and Stern both focus upon how narrators invoke "truth" through narrative structure.

The juxtaposition of these authors' works raises an interesting issue. In each proposed persuasive chain—marketing stimulus, narrative response, intentions, outcomes (Escalas); narrative (as marketing stimulus), potential recruit response (Grayson), and consumer narrative, consumer researcher narrative, reader (Stern)—the narrative plays a different, but persuasive role and requires us to understand narrative or textual transformations. An important question arises: can we identify rules whereby narrative transformations occur? How does advertising text transform consumer mental responses into brand connections? How do network marketers transform their personal experiences into a shared text? How do consumer researchers transform consumer narratives into a coherent research narrative?

Ruling out alternative explanations remains a challenge to interpretive consumer research. The prevailing interpretive view holds that multiple (valid) interpretations of a text can and do exist. One might argue that some interpretations are more valid, or better than others. The specification of rules of textual transformation from narrative theory might provide guidance for this issue.

REFERENCES

Arnould, Eric and Linda Price (1993), "River Magic: Extraordinary Experience and the Extended Service Encounter," *Journal of Consumer Research*, (June), 24-45.

Bauman, Richard (1986), *Story, Performance and Event*, Bloomington, IN: Unversity of Indiana Press.

Belk, Russell W., Melanie Wallendorf and John F. Sherry, Jr. (1989), "The Sacred and the Profane in Consumer Behavior: Theodicy on the Odyssey," *Journal of Consumer Research*, 16 (June), 1-38.

Black, J. G. and R. Wilensky (1979), "An Evaluation of Story Grammars," *Cognitive Science*, 3, 213–230.

Bruner, Jerome (1986), *Actual Minds, Possible Worlds*, Cambridge, MA: Harvard University Press.

_____ (1990), *Acts of Meaning*, Cambridge, MA: Harvard University Press.

Burke, Kenneth (1945), *A Grammar of Motives*, London: Advent.

_____ (1966), *Language as Symbolic Action*, New York, NY: Palace.

Chase, Susan E. (1995), "Taking Narrative Seriously: Consequences for Method and Theory in Interview Studies," in *Interpreting Experience: The Narrative Study of Lives*, eds. Ruthellen Josselson and Amia Lieblich, Thousand Oaks, CA: Sage, pp. 1-26.

Clothier, Peter (1994), *Multi-Level Marketing: A Practical Guide to Successful Network Selling*, London: Coogan Page

Cohler, Bertram J. (1982), "Personal Narrative and Life Course," *Life Span Development and Behavior*, vol. 4, Paul B. Baltes and Orille G. Brim, Jr. eds., New York, NY: Academic Press.

Deighton, John (1992), "The Consumption of Performance," *Journal of Consumer Research*, 19 (December), 362-372.

_____; Daniel Romer and Josh McQueen (1989), "Using Drama to Persuade," Journal of Consumer Research (December), 335-343.

Ellos, William J. (1994), *Narrative Ethics* (Sydney: Avebury).

Freistadt, Marian and Peter Wright (1995), "Persuasion Knowledge: Lay People's and Researchers' Beliefs about the Psychology of Advertising," *Journal of Consumer Research*, (June), 62-74.

Gee, James P. (1985), "The Narrativization of Experience in the Oral Style," *Journal of Education*, 167, 9–35.

Gergen, Kenneth J. and Mary M. Gergen (1988), "Narrative and the Self as Relationship," *Advances in Experimental Social Psychology*, 21, 17-56.

Grayson, Kent (1996), "Examining the Embedded Markets of Network Marketing Organizations," in *Networks in Marketing*, ed. Dawn Iacobucci, Thousand Oaks, CA: Sage, 325–341.

Hirschman, Elizabeth (1988), "The Ideology of Consumption: A Structural-Syntactical Analysis of 'Dallas' and 'Dynasty,'" *Journal of Consumer Research*, 15 (December), 344-359.

Jameson, Fredric (1981), *The Political Unconscious: Narrative as a Socially Symbolic Act*, Ithaca, NY: Cornell University Press.

Labov, William and Joshua Waletzky (1967), "Narrative Analysis: Oral Versions of Personal Experience," *Essays on the Verbal and Visual Arts*, June Helms, ed., Seattle, WA: University of Washington Press.

Lanser, Susan Sniader (1981), *The Narrative Act: Point of View in Prose Fiction*, Princeton: Princeton University Press.

McCracken, Grant (1986), "Culture and Consumption: A Theoretical Account of the Structure and Movement of the Cultural Meaning of Consumer Goods," *Journal of Consumer Research*, 13 (June), 71-84.

Miller, J. Hillis (1990), "Narrative," in *Critical Terms for Literary Study*, eds., Frank Lentricchia and Thomas McLaughlin, Chicago: The Univeristy of Chicago Press, 66-79.

Peracchio, Laura (1993), "Young Children's Processing of a Televised Narrative: Is A Picture Really Worth a Thousand Words?" *Journal of Consumer Research*, (September), 281-293.

Polkinghorne, Donald E. (1991), "Narrative as Self-Concept," *Journal of Narrative and Life History*, 1, 135-153.

Propp, Victor (1928/1968), *Morphology of the Folktale*, 2nd ed., Austin, TX: University of Texas Press.

Rayfield, J. R. (1972), "What is a Story?" *American Anthropologist*, 74, 1084–1106.

Richins, Marsha L. (1994), "Valuing Things: The Public and Private Meaning of Possessions," *Journal of Consumer Research*, 21 (December), 504-521.

Ricoeur, Paul (1991), "Life in Quest of Narrative," *On Paul Ricoeur: Narrative and Interpretation*, David Wood, ed., New York, NY: Routledge, 20-33.

Sarbin, Theodore R. ed. (1986), *Narrative Psychology: The Storied Nature of Human Conduct*, New York, NY: Praeger.

Schechner, Richard (1985), *Between Theater and Anthropology*, Philadelphia, PA: University of Pennsylvania Press.

Scholes, Robert (1980), "Language, Narrative and Anti-Narrative," *On Narrative*, ed. W. J. T. Mitchell, Chicago, IL: University of Chicago Press, 200–208.

Stern, Barbara (1995), "Consumer Myths: Frye's Taxonomy and the Structural Analysis of a Consumption Text, *Journal of Consumer Research*, 22 (September), 165-185.

Wells, William (1988), "Lectures and Dramas," *Cognitive and Affective Responses to Advertising*, Pat Cafferata and Alice Tybout eds., Lexington, MA: D.C. Heath.

Cross-Category Interactions in Product Perceptions and Choice

Amitabh Mungalé, Rutgers University

Most studies of product perception, preference, and promotion have tended to focus on single product categories in the past. This has led to the neglect of a study of cross-category effects which might not be gleaned at all if researchers were to restrict themselves to one product category at a time. This special session focused on multi-category situations instead of a single-product or a single-product category. The papers in this session looked at issues in variety-seeking, cross-promotions, and perceptions of inter-product relationships, using a mix of experimentation and game-theoretic models.

The first paper, "The Impact of Cross-Category Stimulation on Shopping Behavior," by Satya Menon and Barbara Kahn looked at the process mechanism that leads to differences in choice of novelty in products as a function of initial availability of novelty when contextual stimulation was high or low. Basing their work on theories of exploratory behavior, the authors suggest that consumers seek to maintain an optimal level of stimulation in their shopping environment and that the amount of stimulation provided by the initial products in a shopping trip may affect shopping behavior for products encountered later in the same trip. The authors argue that exposure to novel, unfamiliar products initially in a shopping trip decreases the amount of stimulation sought in the rest of the shopping trip by affecting the nature of information search, choice of novel products, willingness to spend money, unplanned purchases, and extent of browsing behavior. They presented the results of a laboratory experiment supporting this hypothesis. Specifically, the experiment found that when contextual stimulation was lower, subjects tended to search for more novel features and/or more novel items in the product category, and to choose a more novel item from the choice set, as compared to subjects in the higher contextual stimulation condition. In addition, a second, planned study was described, designed as an internet shopping task which aims to show that contextual stimulation via initial products may also affect other characteristics of the shopping trip such as browsing time, willingness to pay, and willingness to engage in unplanned purchases in addition to the nature of product sites chosen for browsing. The paper suggested managerial implications for design of store lay-outs, web-sites and promotions.

The second paper, "Assessing the Impact of Cross-Category Promotion: The Case of Cross-Promotion," by Suman Basuroy and Mendel Fygenson, studied the phenomenon of cross-promotion wherein a firm promotes a particular brand through a different brand. The presenter explained the concept of cross-promotions in some detail, providing "real-world" examples such as cents-off manufacturers' coupons redeemable upon the joint purchase of Dannon Yogurt and Post Grapenut Cereals, and coupons for Diet Pepsi in packages of No-Nonsense Pantyhose. The paper stated that the two main features of cross-promotion important for a manufacturer to consider are the choice of the outside product category and the process of implementation. It further focused on questions such as why a firm (or brand) should cross-promote as opposed to self-promoting itself, and discussed methods of implementation. Using game-theory principles, the authors developed a model showing a way in which firms can utilize outside products (not provided by the firm) to segment the firm's customers. The model captures segmentation due to partnerships with the outside product category as well as the effect of possible cross-price sensitivities between the segments. The paper showed that the strategy of cross-promotions works if customers who buy both products are more price-sensitive than those who only buy one of the products. Also, contrary to extant research, the authors contend that cross-promotions need not be done with complementary products to be successful. The authors showed that in some situations, profitable cross-promotions occur when the products are either independent or negatively complementary.

The third paper, "A Cognitive Method for Determining Cross-Category and Within-Category Relationships," by Amitabh Mungalé and J. Wesley Hutchinson, examined the connection between consumers' cognitive structures and the economic relationships between products, which may be complements/independent (cross-category relationships) or substitutes (a within-category relationship). Drawing on psychological theory, the paper introduced a memory-based definition of "cognitive" ("c-") -substitutes, "c-complements" and "c-independents". Free recall tasks were used to identify 18 different schema structures, and inter-product relationships between resulting stimuli were classified as c-substitutes, c-complements and c-independents. The resulting classifications were then experimentally verified for each of the schemas using two dependent measures: a semantic rating measure and a derived-utility measure for each item. It was hypothesized that the joint utility for two items would be super-additive for complements, sub-additive for independents, and additive for independent products. The results supported the schema-based method of identifying inter-product relations. An implication of this approach (demonstrated by a second set of experiments) is that the same two items may be complements in one situation but may be substitutes in another situation–aggregate measures such as traditional cross-price elasticity measures may mask such relationships. The paper noted that this cognitive method of determining inter-product relationships could provide insight into product purchase, consumption, and usage which should aid managerial decisions in product development, positioning, communications and promotions strategies.

The synthesizer, Wes Hutchinson, integrated the findings of the papers presented in the session, pointing out their novel aspects as well as the way in which they complemented each other. In particular, he emphasized how the work presented constituted research that typified "breaking-out-of-the-box" thinking.

How Do I Prefer Thee? Let the Task Decide for Me: Examining Task Effects and Consumer Preference Formation

Ziv Carmon, Duke University
Stephen M. Nowlis, Arizona State University

Previous research has shown that the task, or the manner in which consumer preferences are elicited, can significantly affect these preferences (e.g., Payne, Bettman, and Johnson 1992). Examples of task effects that have been documented over the years include effects of time pressure, of the response mode, and of scaling. Different theoretical perspectives have attempted to explain these results, with varying degrees of success. The major objective of this session was to improve our understanding of why, how and when task characteristics influence consumer preferences by examining some of the central task effects. To accomplish this, each of the papers in the session focused on a different aspect of task effects. One focused on the way in which preferences are measured, another on the perceived goal of elicitation tasks, and the third on the effect of justification and anticipated evaluations. Each aimed to improve our understanding of how and why these factors affect the resulting preferences.

The first paper, by Alan Cooke and Barbara Mellers, examined how the response mode and the context jointly affect elicited preferences. Respondents evaluated apartments described by monthly rent and distance to campus. Both response tasks and contexts varied, and preferences for the same pairs of apartments reversed in different contexts (holding the task constant) and in different tasks (holding the context constant). The authors found support for their suggestion that context appears to influence attribute perceptions, whereas the response task appears to impact the weights of the attributes. The paper provided a better understanding of the differential impact of the task and the context, which are typically studied separately.

The second paper, by Greg Fischer, Ziv Carmon, Dan Ariely, and Gal Zauberman investigated the effect of the perceived goal of the response task on differences in the preferences that it elicits. Focusing on the Prominence Effect (greater weighting of the prominent attribute in choice versus in matching), they compared preferences elicited by several variants of choice and of matching tasks. They found strong support for their hypothesis that equivalent tasks that have different underlying task-goals result in significantly different preferences. In fact, when they directly manipulated the perceived goal of two tasks the preferences were significantly altered. They concluded with a brief review of other task effects that can be better understood in light of respondents' underlying task-goals.

The third paper, by Itamar Simonson and Stephen M. Nowlis, looked at how aspects of the social situation can impact consumer preferences. Specifically, social interactions following a purchase decision have two key components: the buyer explains the choice made to some audience (e.g., superior, spouse) and the audience forms an evaluation of the decision. This paper proposed that, although these task components have often been studied simultaneously (often referred to as accountability), they have independent and often conflicting effects on buyer behavior. Specifically, a need to provide reasons was hypothesized to promote behavior that is designed to appear rational and unique, whereas anticipation of evaluations by others encourages conformity to norms. Consistent with the analysis, the results of the studies demonstrated a wide range of choice phenomena for which providing reasons and being evaluated by others lead to systematically different purchase behaviors. The studies also provided insights into the mechanisms underlying these effects.

The discussion leader, Donald Lehmann, suggested that research on task effects was initially mostly concerned with documenting their existence. At the current stage the focus has turned more to a deeper understanding of when and why these effects occur. He suggested that future research investigate how substantial these effects are (e.g., in terms of market inefficiencies). Another direction would be to study how to control for these effects either in terms of "inoculating" decision makers or countering these biases with the use of decision aids.

REFERENCE

Payne, J. W., J. R. Bettman, and E. J. Johnson (1992), "Behavioral Decision Research: A Constructive Processing Perspective," *Annual Review of Psychology* 43, 87-131.

New Directions in Research on Self-Referencing

Douglas M. Stayman, Cornell University
H. Rao Unnava, Ohio State University

Research has suggested that the extent of self-referencing done by viewers of persuasive messages can influence the persuasion process and thus the impact of messages. However, different explanations have been proposed and different persuasion results found. According to the elaboration explanation, self-referencing affects the elaboration of message information which causes messages with strong arguments to be more persuasive. The affect transfer explanation, on the other hand, argues that when subjects access positive experiences from memory, the affect that is linked to them is transferred to the product whose ad is being processed. Positive attitudes resulting from self-referencing are attributed to this affect transfer mechanism. The purpose of this special session was to bring together self-referencing researchers working from different perspectives to gain insight on how to reconcile and expand on the varying explanations and results in the literature.

In the first paper, "Self-referencing, Persuasion and the Role of Affect," Lien and Stayman used affect as a moderator to explore the influence of self-referencing on message elaboration and the role of affect in influencing persuasion outcomes. Since positive affect, like self-referencing, has been found to induce a large positive set of associations, Lien and Stayman argued that the effects of affect and self-referencing may be interdependent. They proposed that the interdependence may account for effects in which self-referencing could lead to increased or decreased elaboration, since the influence of self-referencing may depend on the level of affect.

Lien and Stayman discussed five studies. The first three studies demonstrated that affect and self-referencing could be manipulated and measured independently and thus their interdependence could be studied experimentally. The fourth and fifth studies manipulated both affect and self-referencing to assess their interdependence as well as manipulating argument strength to assess the influence of the self-referencing/affect interdependence on message elaboration and persuasion. The results presented suggest that affect and self-referencing do interact in their influence on persuasion as expected from an elaboration framework, with increased elaboration due to self-referencing in neutral, but not positive affect conditions.

The second paper, "How Self-Referencing Affects Information Processing: Attention vs., Elaboration," by Unnava, Burnkrant and Jewell contrasted the elaboration explanation and the affect transfer explanations of the self-referencing effect. The authors argued that if elaboration is NOT the cause of the self-referencing effect, then affecting the extent of elaboration that a subject can perform on an advertising message should not have any effect on the self-referencing effect on attitudes. Subjects were assigned to one of three conditions of elaboration: a) high elaboration condition in which they had as much time as they needed to read the target ad, b) medium elaboration condition in which exposure to ads was limited at 75 seconds each, and, c) low elaboration condition in which subjects were limited to 75 seconds of reading per ad and were also required to do a concurrent task of writing an unrelated digit sequence on a separate sheet of paper. These three conditions were crossed with self-referencing such that half the subjects in each elaboration condition received either the high or the low self-referencing copy. Self-referencing was manipulated in the tradi-

tional way by reminding subjects of their experiences with their calculator and how the target product, another brand of calculator, could solve their problems.

The results were supportive of the elaboration explanation of self-referencing effects. When elaboration was high, the classic self-referencing effect emerged on recall and attitude with high self-referencing subjects showing greater recall and more positive attitudes than low self-referencing subjects. As the elaboration was reduced, the advantage of self-referencing disappeared. Under low levels of elaboration, the self-referencing effect actually reversed with the low self-referencing subjects recalling more than the high self-referencing subjects. This was attributed due to the fact that the high self-referencing copy could not be processed in its entirety due to competing demands of the concurrent task as well as the elaboration demanded by the ad copy.

The third paper, "Variations in Self-Referencing: An Empirical Investigation," by Krishnamurthy and Sujan, investigated self-referencing as a mode of ad processing using the current advances in understanding the self as a complex multi-dimensional knowledge structure. Krishnamurthy and Sujan presented a framework for systematically organizing the variations in self-referencing that may be relevant in a consumer behavior context. More specifically, they investigated whether referencing past versus future selves related to outcome variables like attitude toward the ad and brand, and behavioral intention. Krishnamurthy and Sujan presented results from an initial study in which they found that when consumers describe what makes advertisements personally relevant, thoughts relating the ad to their past are more likely to be about specific episodes and contain contextual detail about the episode, whereas thoughts relating the ad to their future are likely to be more general and lack detail. In their second study Krishnamurthy and Sujan built on this and manipulated the temporal orientation of self-referencing and the amount of contextual information in the ad. They found that, when consumers engage in retrospective (past-based) self-referencing, providing more contextual information in the ad reduces ad effectiveness because consumers tend to contrast the information in the ad with the detail associated with their experiences, whereas providing minimal contextual information encourages consumers to assimilate the ad into their own experiences and thus enhances ad effectiveness. On the other hand, when consumers engage in anticipatory (future-based) self-referencing, Krishnamurthy and Sujan find that contextual information in the ad provides the resources for generating episodes of the future, thus, contrary to the retrospective self-referencing condition, a contextually detailed ad enhances ad effectiveness whereas a contextually impoverished ad reduces ad effectiveness. Their mediation tests indicate that the effects of temporal orientation in self-referencing and contextual detail in the ad on ad effectiveness may be mediated by the extent to which consumers could form brand-related consumption visions.

The discussion leader, Rich Yalch, did triple duty during the session. Due to extenuating circumstances the authors of the second paper could not present. Therefore, Rich ended the session by presenting a distillation of the second paper, providing integrative insights and then leading a wide ranging discussion on self-referencing. Several points in the discussion indicated the need for continuing work on how self-referencing influences persuasion, particularly using process measures or other methods to examine more closely the process(es) underlying the varying effects reported in the session and the literature.

Consumption of Child Care: A Social Construction Perspective

Jyotsna Mukherji, University of Memphis

ABSTRACT

This paper examines the issue of child care from the mother's perspective. Using Ritzer's (1992) framework of levels of social analysis, I have studied the phenomenon of child care through actors, actions and interactions. The epistemological basis of this research is that there are multiple and coexisting realities. Through in-depth interviews I have examined the reality of child care as constructed by mothers and discovered four major themes. These themes are: process of finding and maintaining child care, differences between family care and day care, conceptualizing and maintaining trust, social and market relationship, and information systems.

INTRODUCTION

The decision, for parents, especially mothers, to find child care is an important one. For most families this decision is difficult and involves significant emotional and financial stress. These stresses are compounded by reports in the media of cruel treatment of children in some day care centers, and inability of public officials to track and control these violators. How do parents go about finding child care? What are the characteristics they look for in care providers which makes them entrust their children to strangers?

The issue of child care has attracted an increasing amount of attention from a number of different groups, including the disciplines of sociology, economics, psychology, and public policy. As mothers of small children have entered the work force in large numbers in the last two decades, child development experts, sociologists, policy makers, and advocacy groups have placed child care high on the research agenda (Blau 1991). However, the consumption of child care is a phenomenon which has not been addressed adequately in the field of consumer behavior.

I was interested in understanding the social reality of mothers who sought child care. Figure 1 outlines the major levels of social analysis that can be applied to the study of child care (Ritzer 1992). At the macro level this phenomenon looks at the influence of the economy, World War II, and the feminist movement. At the micro level would be stress and emotional related issues like guilt, regret, and fear (these issues were pointed out to me by a very insightful reviewer). Using Ritzer's framework of social analysis, (given in figure 1) I realized that the phenomenon I was studying was between the objective and the subjective continuum. The phenomenon was in the middle, in that it had both the objective and the subjective elements. I saw objective aspects through actors, actions, interactions and subjective aspects through the construction of reality, norms, and values. This research adopts the phenomenological approach and uncovers the phenomenon of the consumption of child care from the consumer's experiences, and the meanings they ascribe to these experiences.

CONTEXTUAL FORCES

The phenomenon of child care has been shaped by changes in society over the past many years. In the following sections I review the major forces that have influenced the consumption of child care.

Women's Participation in the Work Force

Women's participation in the work force has been on the rise during this century. At present, more than 19 million women are in the labor force, which is six out of every ten American women (Moen 1992; Davidson and Gordon 1979). Even more striking has been the growth in employment of mothers of preschool children.

In 1950 only 12 percent of mothers of preschoolers were in employment, but by 1990 this had grown to 59.4 percent (U.S. Bureau of Census 1990b).

Several reasons can be ascribed to the increase in women's employment (Moen 1992). Chief among them is the decline in importance of physical strength in most jobs, which have made them open to women. In addition, two sectors of the economy which have traditionally employed women have grown, these are clerical and administrative work, and sales and service jobs. World War II provided a major impetus to women's employment. Both the proportion (from 27 percent in 1940 to 35 percent in 1944) and composition of the female segment of the labor force changed significantly. Prior to World War II, the female labor force was composed of single women often from minority and low income strata of society, but during the war married women with children joined the labor force. In fact, war became synonymous with patriotism, and woman power became crucial to winning the war (Moen 1992).

The Feminist Movement

The 1970s saw the flowering of the feminist movement which not only inspired legislation, but also gave legitimacy to women's quest for equality. That decade was marked by a transformation in the attitude toward women's roles, specifically, an increasing acceptance of women's participation in paid work outside the home (Davidson and Gordon 1979). The cultural impact of the feminist movement has altered the life expectations of married American women. Married women with children looked for growth opportunities outside the traditional maternal role (Csikszentmihalyi and Rochberg-Halston 1981). There were other forces which shaped women's lives and in many ways contributed to their participation in the labor force; these include reduction in fertility, delays in marriage, delays in having children, rise in educational attainment for women, increased incidences of single parenthood, decline in real wages, and the threat of poverty.

Dominant Ideologies

One predominant ideology that affects the consumption of child care is the doctrine of two spheres (Moen 1992). According to this doctrine, the home and family are held as private arenas, where children are raised and family values are taught. The sanctity of the family means that government has very little to do with matters pertaining to the family, including child care. On the other hand, the spirit of free enterprise and individualism has prevented the government from adopting family goals on its political agenda. The implication for child care is that this continues to be a private concern with parents making their own arrangements with little help from government, unlike in countries like Sweden (Davidson and Gordon 1979). In Sweden 73 percent of the preschool children are cared for in publicly funded institutions (Ferber, O'Farrell, and Allen 1991).

Another factor is the cultural dilemma that takes place with the employment of mothers, especially mothers of young children, being at cross purposes with family values. In our society, mothers still have the primary responsibility of raising children (Uttal 1993). The messages society sends are mixed. On the one hand, society sends a message which reinforces the primacy of domesticity in women's lives, and on the other hand, it also stresses the importance of women's employment, as it did during World War II.

FIGURE 1
Levels of Social Analysis in Child Care
(adapted from Ritzer, 1992)

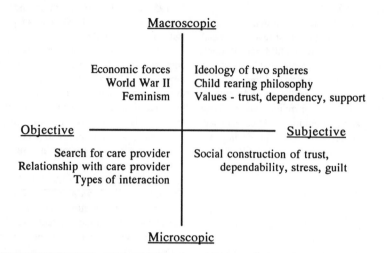

Macroscopic

Economic forces World War II Feminism	Ideology of two spheres Child rearing philosophy Values - trust, dependency, support

Objective ——————————————————— Subjective

Search for care provider Relationship with care provider Types of interaction	Social construction of trust, dependability, stress, guilt

Microscopic

Expenditures on Child Care Arrangements

Parental expenditures for child care are substantial. The National Child Care Survey (Hofferth, Brayfield, Deich, and Holcomb 1990) found that employed mothers with a preschool child spent an average of $63 (10% of family income) per week and unemployed mothers spent $35 (6% of family income) a week. For those with school age children, the costs were $30 (5% of family income) and $20 (4% of family income) per week respectively.

METHODOLOGY

In identifying a methodology to study the phenomenon of child care I was guided by the axioms of the naturalistic paradigm (Lincoln and Guba 1985, p.37). I quote the axioms because they are useful in understanding how I chose the methodology for this research:

Realities are multiple, constructed, and holistic.
Knower and known are interactive, inseparable.
Only time and context–bound hypotheses are possible.
All entities are in a state of mutual simultaneous shaping, so that it is impossible to
distinguish
causes from effects.
Inquiry is value bound. . .

According to Sandra Harding (1987, as cited in Uttal 1993), it is important to understand the differences between methods, methodology, and epistemology. Methods are tools used to collect and analyze information, methodology is the researcher's logic for the choice and use of particular methods, and epistemology considers the assumptions and/or world view that guides the researcher in the questions asked and how the analyses are done.

Epistemology, Methodology, and Methods

The epistemological basis of this research is the view that there are multiple coexisting realities. I have used the realities Uttal identifies for her research. They are material and historical reality, ideological reality, and constructed meaning. Uttal defines material and historical reality as the most common and predictable patterns of social practices of societies which can vary from society to

society. For example, division of labor by gender and capitalism as the basis of the economy are two representations of material and historical reality. Ideological reality is the partial vision of the material and historical reality. For example, if one's material reality is that there is a division of labor on the basis of gender, this sexual division of labor will be perceived as "the natural order," "sexism," or "skill-based segregation" depending on one's particular social location in relation to society as a whole. Constructed reality is the reality that each individual constructs on the basis of highly particular meanings from both the material and ideological realities. I have concentrated my research on the reality as constructed by mothers. The constructed meanings of the consumption of child care have been collected and understood by in-depth interviews.

IN-DEPTH INTERVIEWS

The interview structure followed in this method of data collection is the unstructured format, which is non-standardized and the interviewer does not seek any normative responses, but rather a reaction to the issues raised by the interviewer. According to Dexter (as quoted by Lincoln and Guba 1985, p. 268), this form of interviewing involves stressing the interviewee's definition of the situation, encouraging the interviewee to structure his or her account of the situation, and letting the interviewee introduce to a great extent his or her ideas of what are relevant.

Choice of Interviewees

There are two concerns that are dominant in the criticisms of qualitative research, and these pertain to the choice of a sample. The first is the non-random sampling method, and the second is the small sample size. These criticisms arise from the concerns of representativeness and generalizability, namely who do the findings represent, and does the sample reproduce the researchers' social world or is it generalizable to the larger world?

I addressed this problem by increasing the diversity of my sample so that I would have the opportunity of getting many perspectives. To maximize my sample I did not choose a single organizational site from which to locate interviewees. Secondly, I used a number of dimensions to choose my interviewees, these included ethnicity, type of child care chosen, and occupation of the mother (Uttal 1993). I interviewed eleven mothers, of whom two were undergraduate students, one was a doctoral student, two were computer analysts, four were clerical and secretarial workers, one was a marketing manager and one was a university professor. The ethnicity of the respondents was also different, five were Caucasians, three were African-American, two were Asian-Indian and one was Japanese-American. The child care facilities used included family care and day care centers. Maximizing the diversity of my sample allowed me to get the fullest picture of the meaning of "consumption of child care" with variety and contrast used as criteria.

Interview Process

Respondents were informed of the purpose of the research, and they were assured that confidentiality would be maintained. Interview sessions ranged from an hour to an hour and a half in duration, during which I asked the mothers about their child care experiences. Questions included: how they located their care arrangements, any stories they had to tell me about their children, and feelings in general about the relationship with their care providers. Follow up and probing questions were built into the format of the interview (Tepper 1994).

"Human as Instrument"

I used myself as "human as instrument" (Lincoln and Guba 1985), because of the appropriateness of this method for naturalistic inquiry. By using this method I could be responsive to all the personal and environmental cues, adapt to different situations and collect information from different perspectives, summarize data during the interview and get feedback from the respondent, and lastly capture the holistic nature or gestalt of the phenomena (Folkes and Kiesler 1991; Lincoln and Guba 1985). I used three styles of interviewing: active listening, interactional interviewing, and analytic interviewing (Reinharz and Davidman 1992).

Coding and Analysis

In keeping with the naturalistic paradigm, I did not work with any a priori theory or variables rather I hoped that these would emerge from the inquiry. Therefore, the interviews were analyzed inductively. The coding of the transcripts was done by identifying all the themes, problems, and opportunities. Analysis of the data was done through two iterations. In the first iteration all the themes were identified, and in the second iteration the themes were grouped into mutually exclusive categories. The process of iteration helps in induction by developing concepts and constructs from data. Further, by utilizing the "back and forth and part and whole" process (Spiggle 1994; Tepper 1994), a more unified interpretation was obtained. In order to bring in some level of objectivity, a second researcher who was not involved in the study was asked to study the transcripts and identify the themes, problems, and opportunities (Eisenhardt 1989). Thus, specific raw units of information were analyzed and interpreted to arrive at categories of information that reflected the issues and themes in the consumption of child care. Finally, I used the technique of triangulation for improving the probability that the findings and interpretations will be found more credible by using a second investigator to verify the contents of the transcriptions of the interviews.

EXPERIENCES OF MOTHERS

In my interviews I found that the overarching concern of mothers was with the continuity between the child's home and the environment at the care facility. I found mothers looking for themselves in care providers and for features of their homes in the care settings. In the minds of the mothers, the ideal care centers are

their homes and the ideal care givers themselves. In my analysis and interpretation of data I found the following themes: process of finding and maintaining child care, differences between family care and day care, conceptualizing and identifying trust, reasons for finding child care, social and market relationships, and information systems.

Finding and Maintaining Care Arrangement

Caring for young children continues to be women's work. All the women I interviewed were the ones who had found child care for their children. Besides the gendered division of responsibility, reasons cited for this include lack of expertise in men, and lack of confidence that the men will have the skills required to locate and assess child care facilities. However, after the choice was narrowed down, the fathers were consulted.

Search for facilities is hampered by the lack of knowledge of the range of options available. Most often the women depended on their network of friends, work colleagues, and relatives. One respondent consulted her mother from whom she got the name of the center. Referrals are taken very seriously. Some of the comments made by respondents included:

My care giver goes to the same church I do . . .
My best friend has her two children at this center, so it was natural for me to send mine to the same. . . .

However, one respondent went about the search process in a professional manner. She called all the child care centers in her geographical area. This is what she said:

I had figured out how much I could afford, so the choice was narrowed down. I went to all the centers in my list and talked to the care givers. In most cases I would observe how the person behaved. How she would settle disputes between children, find distractions for them, attend to their needs. One time a toddler was hanging onto her legs and fussing. I liked what the care giver did, she picked up the toddler and rubbed her back. Of course I considered their schedules, meal plans, you know what they served for lunch and snacks, their policy on sick children. I left nothing to chance.

Mothers search for themselves in their care givers and want to replicate their home environment for their children. One mother visited the care giver on a Saturday so that she could observe how the care giver dealt with her own children. Another mother was very particular to send her child to a clean and tidy place. This is what she said:

I wanted a woman who was soft spoken and had a gentle nature, after all I was entrusting my four-month-old child to a woman who would be the mother for those hours.

(While she was talking to me, I realized why she was so insistent on these qualities, this mother had the softest voice and the gentlest manner of speaking).

One mother had a very realistic attitude toward her care arrangement. This is what she said:

Sure, like everyone I wanted a place that was reasonable, convenient, stimulating, full of warmth and caring, and also safe. I wanted care provided by trained, competent, and loving care givers, just like I would, but finding such care is impossible. So what do I do, I get realistic, have fewer expectations and become extra vigilant. I know I can't have it all. . . .

Differences Between Family Care and Day Care Centers

Mothers choose family care for their infants and younger children. Of the four mothers I spoke to, two of them chose family care for their child when he or she was an infant and when the child was older (could eat by herself, was potty trained, and could speak) they opted for day care. Mothers in articulating their reasons for family care selection spoke of the importance of a "homelike" environment for their infants and younger children. They looked for a provider who would keep their children safe and tend to their everyday needs. Mothers spoke of the need for the children to play by themselves, learn to be left alone for periods of time, to be able to amuse themselves, and above all for the need for "warmth, love and intimacy." One mother describes her child's family care arrangements as follows:

My child gets a family like atmosphere. She plays for a while, draws, reads. Then they have lunch and after lunch it is quiet time. At 3:00 in the afternoon the provider's children return from school and then Megan gets to play with older children—much like her own family, I mean brothers and sisters, when she has one (laughs).

In inquiring about the reasons for finding day care, I was told by mothers that they wanted to have some structure in their children's lives. They wanted their children to be able to play with other children, share toys, and be socialized. One mother emphasized learning the alphabets and development of social skills. Mothers also stressed the importance of discipline in their young children. They gave importance to the following: not hitting other children, table manners, eating on their own, playing in a group, respecting others' property, and asking for some thing when they need it, rather than grabbing.

Conceptualizing and Identifying Trust

Trust, the ability to use the services of day care with feelings of satisfaction and peace of mind, seems to be an overarching concern with the mothers I interviewed. Many economists, psychologists, sociologists, and management theorists appear united on the importance of trust in the conduct of human affairs (Hosmer 1995). Trust is "vital for maintenance of cooperation in society and necessary as grounds for even the most routine, everyday transactions" (Zuker, as cited in Hosmer 1995, p. 389). According to Butler and Cantrell (1984), there are five specific components of trust, or characteristics of people. These dimensions are (1) integrity— the reputation for honesty and truthfulness on the part of the trusted individual; (2) competence— the technical knowledge and the interpersonal skill needed to perform the job; (3) consistency— the reliability, predictability, and good judgement in handling situations; (4) loyalty— benevolence or the willingness to protect, support, and encourage others; and (5) openness— mental accessibility, or the willingness to share ideas and information freely with others.

In my interviews I observed the display of some of the dimensions of trust. One respondent told me the following:

Initially I would leave Anna, who was four months old at that time, with my sitter. I started using the services of a sitter in the fall. However as the days began to get cold, I found it very difficult and heart breaking to take a sleeping Anna all covered in blankets to her house. One day I was shocked when my sitter told me that she would come over to my house and be there till Anna got up. After Anna got up, the sitter would change her

and take her to the sitter's own house. From that day onwards my discomfort and feelings of guilt decreased. In fact, we became friends. My sitter would often come over to my house to pick up milk or juice for Anna.

In the above case I found shades of all dimensions of trust were manifested in the relationship. Specifically, the care giver established trust by being competent in the interpersonal skill needed to perform the job, in her good judgment in handling situations, and in her openness to be willing to be creative in solving problems. To me her ability to be flexible and offer to watch Anna at her client's home was an act of creativity and openness and an important basis for trust.

In some cases mothers viewed things like regulation, licensing, and professionalism as symbols of trust. One mother said this:

Most of my friends get their mothers and mothers-in-law to baby sit. They feel they can trust them. I don't think blood relationship is enough or the only criterion for trust. I mean a regulated place is more likely to be inspected for safety. I know these providers are professional, I mean they attend classes. I look at their schedules and know what activities my Katie had done. . . . Clearly for this mother trust is a function of being sure she gets what she wants and regulation is viewed as a reason to trust the center. Professionalism, training and regulation are viewed as symbols of trust, in that they convey attributes of competence, reliability and consistency to the mother.

Social and Market Relationships

I found that one of the areas of conflict between the mother and the care provider was in the nebulous realm of child care relationship. According to Nelson (1992), both mothers and providers would prefer a market relationship with clearly defined obligations, rules, and social distance. One mother described her choice of a center because of the following:

I checked out places that had a professional accreditation. You know I wanted to be certain, professionalism meant the staff would be trained, follow good business practices, insist on children being immunized, have a schedule for payment. I did not want to mess with getting friendly and all that.

In the description of the care arrangements I found that mothers negotiated with the providers. They agreed about hourly or weekly fees, supply of snacks and hot meals, supply of diapers, and extra fees for late pick-ups. In many ways both parties mimic the form of a contractual relationship. Child care providers see themselves as professionals who provide a service. However, both mothers and providers realize that a full description of their relationship is rarely so simple. I found that mothers expect and hope for a relationship that goes beyond a market exchange. Mothers spoke of diffused obligations, the role of trust and emotional attachment care givers and children felt for each other. One respondent spoke of problems and confusion of expectations in the following manner:

. . . I was surprised when after a few weeks, my care giver told me not to bring food, juice and milk for Uma. When I offered to pay instead, she was offended and said "How much does Uma eat anyway?" You know I should have been happy that I had found a care giver who was so generous and loving, but I was uncomfortable. I hoped she was more professional; I was worried when she would tire of this decision of hers.

Another mother expressed her confusion in her expectations from her care provider in the following manner:

I was very upset when I realized that I had been charged for the five minutes I was late in picking up my child from day care. She was so good to my child and Ryan loved her very much, so I imagined that she would not be so business like!

Thus, these two sets of norms and expectations generate significant ambiguity and conflict in the mothers' relationship with their care providers.

Communication and Information Systems

Mothers who sent their children to day care centers emphasized the importance of information systems maintained by the centers. One mother told me how detailed the daily information sheet was. She told me that, by looking through the sheet, she was able to get a very clear idea of her child's day. She got information like nap times, quantity of milk consumed, food eaten, mood disposition, and any non normal changes in the child's health. Mothers feel that by looking at these reports, they are sharing in the daily routine of their children. Further, they attached values of professionalism to centers who had a detailed reporting system.

Communicating with the care givers is viewed as important by some respondents, while some feel they need to be professional, and so maintain minimum level of communication. Being able to talk to the care providers made the mothers feel they were not missing out in the daily life of their children. Some mothers became friends and learned many things from their care givers. One mother described it very well:

I would be very tired by the time I went to pick up Sam, so it was very natural for me to flop down on the floor and breast feed my son. Soon I began talking to the care giver and she would fill me up with the little details of Sam's day. What he did, how much he ate, slept. If I remember right, I learnt most of my mothering from those ladies. You know when to see a doctor, what to do when Sam had a cold. One time I remember I was frustrated because Sam was unable to sleep through the night. I talked to my care giver and followed her suggestions, they helped. I felt very comfortable with this center.

DISCUSSION

Overall I found that mothers' satisfaction was associated with (1) their child's experience with the care arrangement, namely the provider's warmth, daily activities, attention the child receives, discipline, and opportunities for learning; (2) the features of the center, namely amount of space, security, safety, cleanliness, and atmosphere; (3) communications, verbal, written and informal; and (4) quality of interactions with providers. I found it surprising that the mothers I interviewed did not find important, and therefore did not mention (very often), concerns such as cost, location of facility, and flexibility of hours and rules. My understanding is that these issues are important and do influence the choice of a care arrangement, but once an arrangement has been made, the mothers are more concerned with factors that influence the happiness and well being of the child. To summarize, the phenomenon of consumption of child care can be understood from two perspectives: one is the structural perspective and two is the process perspective (see figure 2).

Structural Perspective

Family-based care was normally chosen for infants and toddlers. Mothers chose this type of arrangement because they wanted to replicate the atmosphere of a home. The qualities desired included: warmth, caring and flexible schedules. In short family-based care can be viewed as extension of the child's family, with the care provider often extending her mothering role to the children.

Center based care on the other hand is chosen when the child is older and has developed some social and motor skills. Mothers chose centers because they viewed them as professional. Being professional meant that the centers would be regulated, therefore checked by a licensing authority. The staff would be trained in child care philosophies and in child rearing techniques. Mothers valued the educational and leisure activities and a sense of structure, these activities lent to their child's lives.

Process Perspective

From a process point of view, child care can be viewed as a social or an economic exchange. Mothers who spoke of these phenomena as a social exchange valued features like the nature, personality, and manners of the care giver. They placed emphases on the relationship they developed with the care giver. For these mothers' trust was implicit in the social relationship with the care arrangement and the provider.

Mothers who viewed this phenomenon as a market exchange emphasized the professional and structural characteristics of the centers: the schedules, educational programs, play and leisure activities, philosophy of child care and equipment. For these mothers the contract they had with the center and the explicit characteristics were important to establish trust.

Clearly, choice of and satisfaction with a care arrangement is dependent on the mother's philosophy and what she thinks is important for her children. A successful relationship between a provider and a mother will depend on a match between a mother's expectation, whether it is a market or a social relationship and the structural and process or explicit and implicit characteristics the arrangement provides.

IMPLICATIONS FOR CONSUMER BEHAVIOR

The findings from this research have implications for consumer behavior, specifically in the service industry. According to Arnould and Price (1993), the model of choice and satisfaction in consumer behavior is based on defined expectations and choice of an alternative in terms of its ability to satisfy expectations. Two assumptions are implied in this model: one is that consumers have expectations and second is that satisfaction is a function of deviations from the expected. My research in the consumption of child care shows that consumers are not so clear about the expectations they have from this service. Expectations are confusing, contradictory and unclear. This is seen in the conflict between the norms of social exchange and market exchange that are evident in the mother/provider relationship most commonly seen in family based care. However, this conflict is reduced in day care settings where the relationship is formal and expectations between the parties is contractual.

Trust

Experiences of mothers enable both users and providers of child care to understand what the dimensions of trust are, and the many ways in which trust can be displayed, established, broken, and reinforced. This research shows that trust is developed when expectations of a consumer are met. In some instances, acts of ingenuity, intelligence, or critical thinking seem to have been the points where a mother decides that the evidence of those unique behaviors is enough for her to trust the care giver. Finally trust building issues of consistency, dependability, and competence are emphasized.

FIGURE 2a
Model of Structural Perspective

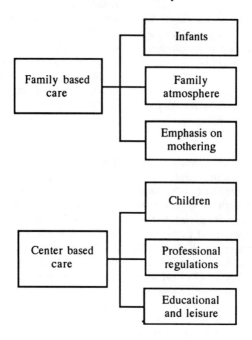

FIGURE 2b
Model of Process Perspective

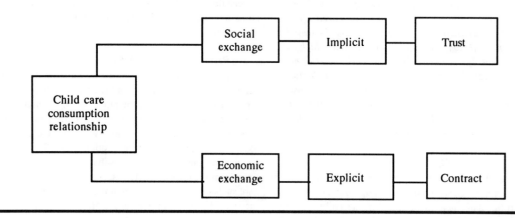

Affect

The research shows the importance of features such as setting, process, and the mother/provider relationship in determining consumer satisfaction. Arnould and Price (1993) write that service quality literature has primarily focused on the technical and functional aspects of a service. But in order to be effective, service deliverers must concentrate on process elements along with structural elements. This research shows that in order to be effective, a service encounter that is dependent on affect must transcend the purposive, task oriented and commercial nature of the ordinary service encounters (Arnould and Price 1993).

In summary, this research throws light on boundary open, temporally extended service encounters where expectations are vague and satisfaction is complex (Arnould and Price 1993). It emphasizes the importance of relationships between client and provider, and shows the dependency element in the relationship. It also shows that this relationship is characterized by the active participation of the consumer. Finally, it shows how consumption of some services is highly subjective, interpretive, vague, complex, and affective (Parsuraman, Ziethaml, and Berry 1985).

CONCLUSION

The number of women in the work force has tripled over the last forty years and the proportion of working mothers of young children has grown four times (Moen 1992).This significant social transformation has had an impact on a number of our institutions including the need for child care services. It was for this reason I thought it would be important to understand the characteristics of child care services. I choose to construct the meaning of this consumption from the mother's point of view.

The phenomenon of child care needs to be addressed from many perspectives, the macro, and the micro. I have concentrated on the meso perspective. One limitation of this research is that it has focussed on satisfaction issues and neglected issues of dissatisfaction. I recognize that micro-subjective issues of feelings, emotions, and stress are an important part of the constructed reality and should be addressed in subsequent research as should the historical construction of the child care phenomenon.

Despite the dominant ideology of domesticated motherhood, the reality is that most families require two incomes. The employment of women reflects, in part declining wages and a desire for a higher standard of living. In my research, I went to the mothers and asked them what their experiences with child care had been. I listened to their stories and tried to understand the reality and the meanings they ascribed to the different aspects with the intention of getting a first hand experience of the phenomenon. I thought a phenomenological approach was essential because volumes have been written about the economics of child care, but very few studies actually attempted to construct and describe the phenomenon from the mother's perspective.

Findings from this research will help the consumers, and providers, to understand the concerns and issues that are critical to this phenomenon. An alternate view point of the care providers is needed to understand their point of view and the issues they think are important. This way one can develop a complete picture and understand the relationship in its totality.

REFERENCES

Arnould E. J. and Linda Price (1993), "Extraordinary Experience and the Extended Service Encounter," *Journal of Consumer Research*, 20, 24-45.

Beau, David M. (1991), *The Economics Of Child Care.* New York, NY: Russel Sage Foundation.

Butler, J. K. and R. S. Cantrell (1984), "A Behavioral Decision Theory Approach to Modeling Dyadic Trust in Superiors and Subordinates, *Psychological Reports*, 55: 19-28.

Csikszentmihalyi, M. and Eugene Rochberg-Halston (1981), *The Meaning of Things: Domestic Symbols and the Self,* Cambridge: Cambridge University Press.

Davidson, L. and L K. Gordon (1979) *The Sociology of Gender,* USA, Rand McNally Publishing Company.

Dexter, Lewis. A. (1970). *Elite and specialized interviewing,* Evanston, IL: Northwestern University Press.

Eisenhardt, Kathleen M. (1989), "Building Theories from Case Study Research," *Academy of Management Review*, 14 (October), 532-550.

Ferber, M. A., B. O'Ferrell, and L. R. Allen (1991), Work and Family: Policies for a Changing Work Force. Washington, D.C. National Academy Press.

Folkes, Valerie S. and Tina Kiesler (1991), "Social Cognition: Consumers' Inferences about the Self and Others," in *Handbook of Consumer Behavior,* eds. Thomas Robertson and Harold Kassarjian, Englewood Cliffs, NJ: Prentice Hall, 281-315.

Harding, Sandra (1987), "Is There a Feminist Methodology?" in *Feminism and Methodology: Social Science Issues,* Bloomington, IN, Indiana University Press.

Hofferth, S. L., A. Brayfield, S. Deich, and P. Holcomb (1991), *National Child Care Survey, 1990,* Urban Institute Report 91-5. Washington, D.C.: The Urban Institute Press.

Hosmer, L. T. (1995), "Trust: The Connecting Link Between Organizational Theory and Philosophical Links," *Academy of Management Review*, 20 (April), 379-403.

Lawrence, Barbara (1984), "Historical Perspective: Using the Past to Study the Present," *Academy of Management Review*, 9 (April), 305-312.

Lincoln, S. Yvonne and Egon G. Guba (1985), *Naturalistic Enquiry*, Sage Publications, Newbury Park, CA 91320.

Moen, P. (1992) *Women's Two Roles. A Contemporary Dilemma,* Westport, CT 06881 Auburn House

Nelson Margaret, M. (1990), *Negotiated Care, The Experience of Family Day Care Providers,* Temple University Press, Philadelphia 19122.

Parsuraman, A., Valerie A. Ziethaml, and Leonard L. Berry (1985), "A Conceptual Model of Service Quality and its Implications for Future Research," *Journal of Marketing*, 49(Fall), 41-50.

Reinharz, Shulamit and Lynn Davidman (1992), *Feminist Methods in Social Research*, New York, NY: Oxford University Press.

Ritzier, George (1992), Sociological Theory, 3rd. New York: NY: McGraw-Hill, Inc.

Spiggle, Susan (1994), "Analysis and Interpretation of Qualitative Data in Consumer Research," *Journal of Consumer Research*, 21 (December), 491-503.

Tepper, Kelly (1994), "The Role of Labeling Processes in Elderly Consumers' Responses to Age Segmentation Cues," *Journal of Consumer Research*, 20 (March), 503-519).

U.S. Bureau of the Census (1990 b.). *Statistical Abstract of the United States.* Washington, DC: U.S. Government Printing Office.

Uttal, Lynet (1993), *Shared Mothering: Reproductive Labor, child care and the meaning of Motherhood*, Ph.D. Dissertation, University of California, Santa Cruz.

Zuker, L. G. (1986), "Production of Trust: Institutional Sources of Economic Structure, 1840-1920," in *Research in Organizational Behavior*, eds., B. M. Staw and L. L. Cummings, Greenwich, CT: JAI Press, 8, 53-111.

Materialistic Values and Susceptibility to Influence in Children

Gwen Bachmann Achenreiner, St. John's University

ABSTRACT

Materialistic attitudes of children, ranging in age from 8 to 16, were examined using a multi-item materialism scale for children. The findings indicate that materialism is a relatively stable trait, varying only marginally with age, despite the numerous developmental changes taking place as a child gets older. The study also examined the relationship between materialism and susceptibility to peer influence and found a significant correlation of .44. The findings support the hypothesis that materialism and susceptibility to influence are positively related. This research is critical for better understanding how materialistic attitudes develop and the role peer influence has on these attitudes.

INTRODUCTION

The decade of the '90s has been characterized by a return to basic values. Consumers today are more concerned with quality and value, than prestigious brand names and high prices. Americans are spending less, saving more and borrowing more prudently. While financial security is still important and people are not giving up material goods, there has been a significant increase in the importance placed on core values such as "respect for one another, responsibility for one's actions, and providing a 'loving and caring environment' for one's family," (Schwartz, 1991; p. 14). Seventy-five percent of Americans between the ages of 24 to 49 say they would like "to see our country return to a simpler lifestyle with less emphasis on material success," (Henkoff, 1989; p.41). And, the family is holding more importance and becoming a more central value, with 62 percent of working Americans saying, "a happy family life" is the most important indicator of success (Henkoff, 1989; p.41). However, while the majority of Americans report satisfaction with their own family lives, 57 percent believe family values have declined (Schwartz, 1991; p.14).

Likewise, parents and educators have become increasingly concerned with the commercialization and materialistic attitudes of youth today. Children between the ages of 4 to 12 spend an estimated $8.6 billion per year and influence parent's purchases by $132 billion per year (McNeal, 1992). And, with the increasing number of single-parent families and dual-income families, the roles children play as consumers are becoming more profound, increasing in terms of both responsibility and diversity. Children are often responsible for purchasing and influencing many of the products purchased, not only for themselves, but also for the household, such as grocery products and cleaning supplies.

Along with concern over children's growing consumer responsibilities and promotions directed towards children, are concerns that children are developing materialistic values at a rather young age. In fact, attitudes toward materialism as a life goal have increased dramatically from the early '70s to the late '80s in high-school seniors and entering college freshmen (Easterlin and Crimmins, 1991). It seems having the "in" products such as Nike athletic shoes and Starter jackets is extremely important to children, and has resulted in numerous thefts and even attempted murder (Diaz, 1992). In response, many schools have implemented school uniforms as a means of directly controlling individual differences between students from different financial and ethnic backgrounds and indirectly controlling materialism and crime in the schools. So while materialistic values, in general, have declined, there is still concern regarding materialistic values in children.

Studies of materialism with adults have typically focused on defining and measuring materialism (Belk, 1984; Belk, 1985; Richins and Dawson, 1992), generational differences in possessions valued (Belk, 1985; Csikszentmihalyi and Rochberg-Halton, 1981; Kamptner, 1991), and personality and behavior traits associated with materialism (Fournier and Richins, 1991; Braun and Wicklund, 1989; Hunt, Kernan, Chatterjee and Florsheim, 1990). However, very few studies have examined materialistic values in children. The studies that have been done were limited by small sample sizes and qualitative measures such as content analysis and referencing of consumer products in children's free speech (Dickins and Ferguson, 1957; Lipscomb, 1988). While providing an interesting first look at children's materialistic attitudes, the validity of these measures is questionable. In addition, other studies having adequate sample sizes and more quantitative measures have focused exclusively on children in their teenage years (Moschis and Churchill, 1978; Ward and Wackman,1971). Virtually no research has been done on children's attitudes toward materialism across a wide age span, including children of elementary school age through junior and senior high age. Likewise, personality and behavior traits associated with materialism have not been examined at the children's level. Of particular interest, in this study, is the relationship between materialism in children and susceptibility to peer influence. The issue here is, are children who are more susceptible to influence, also more likely to hold materialistic attitudes? While the adult materialism literature and children's socialization research shed some light on the issue, the relationship between materialism and susceptibility to influence has not been directly examined. Thus, the purpose of this research is twofold:

(1) to examine the materialistic attitudes of children across a wide age span, using a large sample, and a multi-item materialism scale, and

(2) to examine the relationship between materialistic attitudes in children and susceptibility to peer group influence.

This information is critical for better understanding how materialistic attitudes develop and the role peer group influence has on these attitudes.

CONCEPTUAL DEVELOPMENT

The concept of materialism has been defined in a number of ways. Belk (1984, 1985) defines materialism as, "the importance a consumer attaches to worldly possessions. And at the highest levels of materialism, such possessions assume a central place in a person's life and are believed to provide the greatest sources of satisfaction and dissatisfaction," (Belk, 1984, p. 291; Belk, 1985, p.265). Personality traits associated with materialism include envy, nongenerosity and possessiveness (Belk, 1984). Ward and Wackman (1971, p. 422) define materialism as, "an orientation which views material goods and money as important for personal happiness and social progress." Richins and Dawson (1992, p. 307) define materialism as representing "a mind-set or constellation of attitudes regarding the relative importance of acquisition and possession of objects in one's life. For materialists, possessions and their acquisition are at the forefront of personal goals that dictate 'ways of life.'

Advances in Consumer Research
Volume 24, © 1997

They value possessions and their acquisition more highly than most other matters and activities in life."

Materialism as a Value.

Materialism has also been discussed in the literature as being a *value*, and individuals vary in regards to the level at which they subscribe to the value (Richins and Dawson, 1992; Fournier and Richins, 1991). As discussed by Richins and Dawson (1992, p. 307), a value is "an enduring belief . . . having a transcendental quality to it, guiding actions, attitudes, judgements and comparisons across specific objects and situations." Richins and Dawson (1992) conceptualize materialism as a value that guides people's choices and conduct in a variety of situations and consumption experiences. They suggest that materialism influences the type and quantity of goods purchased and the allocation of resources, including time.

If it is true that materialism is a value or an enduring belief that has a "transcendental quality" guiding actions and attitudes across time and situation, it seems plausible, then, that materialistic attitudes should not vary significantly as a function of age. Empirical support for this hypothesis can be drawn from a study by Ward and Wackman (1971) which found no significant differences between junior and senior high respondents regarding attitudes toward materialism. Thus, the first hypothesis of this study is that materialistic attitudes will not vary significantly by age.

Ho. 1a: Materialistic attitudes will not vary significantly by age.

Cognitive and Social Development.

It is important to keep in mind, though, that as children age, fundamental changes are taking place in terms of cognitive development, psycho-social development, and social development. Consumer socialization is the process by which young people develop consumer-related skills, knowledge and attitudes (Moschis and Churchill, 1978). Theories related to consumer learning typically focus on cognitive development and/or social learning. Cognitive development theories tend to suggest that socialization is a function of qualitative changes or stages in cognitive development, whereas social learning theories suggest that socialization agents, such as parents, schools, church, peers and mass media, transmit attitudes, motivations and behaviors to the learner through various interactions (Moschis and Churchill, 1978).

Cognitive Development. In order to associate possessions with satisfaction or to envy others' possessions, a minimal level of development is probably necessary. And, as children age, important changes take place in terms of cognitive development. For example, in order to appreciate the psychological value or status associated with owning a given possession, a person must have the ability to think abstractly. Likewise, in order to understand different people's motivations or reasons for owning certain products and that the public and private meanings associated with products may vary, a person must have the ability to take on another's perspective. These cognitive skills have been theorized to develop around age 8, and are fully developed and equal to that of an adult by age 12 (Selman, 1980; Barenboim, 1981). Given that one's cognitive skills tend to become more advanced with age it seems plausible that materialistic attitudes might also become more developed with age.

PsychoSocial Development. Another theory, Erikson's PsychoSocial theory (1972), is somewhat different from cognitive development theories in that it describes change throughout the life span and is more socially-oriented, suggesting that individuals go through eight social-conflict stages in a life time. Of interest, is that

in previous research, the possessions most valued by subjects at different ages tended to reflect their psychosocial stage (Kamptner, 1991). For example, in the infant and toddler years the psychosocial task is that of developing a sense of trust and children at this age treasured those possessions promoting comfort and security such as a blanket or a teddy bear. Likewise, during the adolescent years Erikson's task is to develop a sense of self-identity and treasured possessions are those facilitating independence and accomplishment (Belk, 1985). Given that possessions serve as symbols and self-affirmation of one's identity (Belk, 1985; Lipscomb, 1988; Fournier and Richins, 1991), and teenagers are struggling with their self-identities, it seems plausible that older children may hold more materialistic attitudes than younger children.

Social Development. While important changes are taking place cognitively and psycho- socially as children age, they are also becoming more adept socially. As children get older, they develop a larger repertoire of consumer experiences, including simply knowledge about the functional and psychological values or meanings associated with possessions, number of shopping experiences and exposure to advertising which could imply that as children develop greater consumer knowledge and have more exposure to shopping experiences and advertising, their attitudes toward materialism may also become more developed or pronounced.

According to Moschis and Churchill (1978), consumer learning should be viewed not only as a cognitive-psychological process of adjustment to one's environment, but also a social process. As children age their cognitive skills become more sophisticated and their consumer experiences become more vast, which suggests that children's understanding and attitudes regarding materialism may also become more advanced with age. Empirical support for this hypothesis can be drawn from a study by Lipscomb (1988), which found that older children were more inclined to mention consumer products or possessions in their free speech than younger children. Likewise, exposure to television appears to facilitate materialistic attitudes and adolescents' social motivations for consumption (i.e., self expression through possessions or conspicuous consumption) (Moschis and Churchill, 1978; Ward and Wackman, 1971; Richins, 1987; Belk, 1985). Thus the second hypothesis, which competes with hypothesis 1a, is that materialistic attitudes will increase with age.

Ho. 1b: Materialistic attitudes will increase with age.

Materialism, Personality and Behavior

As previously mentioned, several adult studies have linked various personality and behavior traits with materialism. For example, Belk (1984, 1985) and associates measure materialism with the personality traits: envy, nongenerosity and possessiveness, with the relationship between materialism and envy being positive (Richins and Dawson, 1992). Materialists have also been characterized as acquisitive, pre-occupied with status, competitive and having a need for superiority (Fournier and Richins, 1991). Thus, they are also more likely to show patterns of conspicuous consumption and compulsive consumption (Fournier and Richins, 1991). However, these traits and behaviors may be based upon underlying feelings of insecurity (Fournier and Richins, 1991), poor self-esteem (Richins and Dawson, 1992), and incompleteness or inadequacy (Braun and Wicklund, 1989), which have also been tied to materialism. In a number of studies, materialists have been found to be less satisfied or happy with their lives (Richins, 1987; Belk, 1984; Belk, 1985; Richins and Dawson, 1992; Fournier and Richins, 1991). Materialists have also been characterized as self-centered, alienated, unconcerned for others and social issues, and having weaker interpersonal relationships (Fournier and Richins,

1991). While materialists tend to be unconcerned with others, it is interesting that their reference system tends to be other-oriented, with attributions being based on external factors or factors outside their control rather than being based on an internal locus of control (Hunt, Kernan, Chatterjee and Florsheim, 1990). Surprisingly, while materialistic values have been associated with characteristics such as envy, competitiveness, status-consciousness and conspicuous consumption, its relationship to susceptibility to reference group influence has not been examined. It is to this topic that I now turn.

Susceptibility to Peer Influence

Consumer susceptibility to influence has been defined as "any tendency of the person to change as a function of social pressures" (McGuire, 1968). Bearden, Netemeyer and Teel define it more specifically as, "the need to identify with or enhance one's image in the opinion of significant others through the acquisition and use of products and brands, the willingness to conform to the expectations of others regarding purchase decisions and/or the tendency to learn about products and services by observing others and/or seeking information from others" (Bearden, Netemeyer and Teel, 1989). Basically the construct being referred to is a multidimensional construct representing how predisposed a person is to being influenced. Studies have found that the degree of consumer susceptibility is related to other factors such a self-confidence and self-esteem (Cox and Bauer, 1964; Locander and Hermann, 1979; Berkowitz and Lundy, 1957; Janis and Field, 1959), inner/other orientation (Kassarjian, 1962; Kassarjian, 1971; Janis and Field, 1959), and self-monitoring (Lennox and Wolfe,1984; Bearden, Netemeyer and Teel, 1990), to list only a few.

Self-Confidence and Self-Esteem. Several studies have found an inverse relationship between self-confidence and susceptibility to influence (Locander and Hermann, 1979; Berkowitz and Lundy, 1957; Janis and Field, 1959). Likewise, people low in self-esteem were more likely to comply with other's suggestions (Cox and Bauer, 1964) and were higher in susceptibility to influence (Bearden, Netemeyer and Teel, 1990). Since materialistic attitudes have been associated with insecurity or low self-esteem, it seem logical, then, that consumers having more materialistic attitudes would also be more susceptible to influence.

Inner/Other Orientation. The inner/other scale, meaning if one relies more on internal values versus external values, was found to correlate positively with susceptibility to influence (Bearden, Netemeyer and Teel, 1990; Janis and Field, 1959). As previously mentioned, materialists were also found to be more externally-oriented in terms of locus of control (Hunt, et.al., 1990.) Again, this suggests that a positive relationship may exist between materialism and susceptibility to influence.

Self-Monitoring. People high in self monitoring are effective at social integration and adjusting to what is situationally appropriate. And, again, a positive relationship tends to exist between self-monitoring and susceptibility to influence (Bearden, Netemeyer and Teel, 1990). Snyder (1987) suggest that when people are in transitional roles, they are more inclined to be high in self-monitoring because they are often uncertain about how they should act and thus, look to others for guidance. This seems to imply that when people have feelings of inadequacy or insecurity, which is characteristic of materialists, they are higher in self-monitoring and are more susceptible to influence. This implies that a positive correlation should exist between materialism and susceptibility to influence. In conclusion, then, a number of personality traits associated with susceptibility to influence also seem to be related to characteristics or traits associated with materialism. While this research provides insight into the possible relationship between materialism

and susceptibility to influence, consumer socialization and materialism research, previously discussed, provides additional evidence.

Consumer Socialization and Materialism Research. Fournier and Richins (1991) describe materialists as "continual information gatherers," who study catalogs and magazines, shop actively and observe what others have. These behaviors seem to imply that consumers high in materialistic values tend to monitor the environment and are influenced by others' behaviors and possessions. Likewise, Moschis and Churchill (1978) found a positive relationship between frequency of adolescent communication with peers regarding consumption matters and materialism and social motivations for consumption. They also found as social utility reasons for viewing television shows and advertisements increased, so did materialism and social motivations for consumption. These findings also support the notion that there is a positive relationship between materialism and susceptibility to influence.

Ho. 2: A positive relationship will exist between materialism and susceptibility to peer group influence.

METHOD

Sample

Three hundred children were recruited from the second, third, sixth, seventh and tenth grades within a midwestern school district. The specific ages targeted were 8, 12 and 16, referred to as young, middle and older children. Of those returning parental consent forms and participating in the study, 76 children were in the youngest age group (36 boys, 40 girls), 118 children were in the middle age group (46 boys, 71 girls, 1 not reported), and 106 were in the oldest age group (51 boys and 55 girls). As an incentive, the school district was given a donation and participants were either given a small prize or entered into a drawing for larger prizes.

Design

The study employed a 3 (age) x 3 (susceptibility to influence), between subject design and analysis of variance (Anova) was used to test the hypotheses.

Independent Variables

The independent variables were age and susceptibility to influence.

Age. Based on theoretical differences in cognitive and social development, and the hypotheses of interest, three age groups were included in the study: second and third graders, sixth and seventh graders, and tenth graders.

Susceptibility to Influence. The measure of peer group influence was developed from similar scales used in previous studies of reference group influence in adults (Bearden and Etzel, 1982; Bearden, Netemeyer and Teel, 1989; Childers and Rao, 1992; Park and Lessig, 1977). In modifying the scale for use with children, the number of items was kept at a reasonable number to avoid fatigue, and the scale points were kept at a minimum to make it easier for younger children to respond. The final scale, adapted from the Bearden, Netemeyer and Teel scale (1989), included seven items that children indicated their agreement or disagreement with on a four-point Yes-No scale ("YES" "yes" "no" "NO"). This modified children's version of the susceptibility to influence scale has been used in previous research (Bachmann, John and Rao, 1993). Children's responses to the items were summed, based on results indicating that the scale was unidimensional. The scale had a coefficient alpha of .85. Subjects were then divided into three susceptibility to influence groups using the 34th and 67th percentiles. The cutoffs used to divide subjects into low, medium and high

TABLE 1
Materialism Means and Standard Deviations by Age

	<u>Yng</u>	<u>Med</u>	<u>Old</u>
Mean	13.59	14.07	13.44
Std Dev	4.14	3.19	2.86
Sample	n=76	n=116	n=104

Note: Higher Scores = greater materialism

susceptibility to influence categories were held constant across age groups.

Dependent Variables

Materialism. The materialism scale used was a 5-item, 4-point YES/NO scale similar to that used by Richins (1987). Children indicated their degree of agreement/disagreement with statements such as, "It is important to me to have really nice things," and "I would like to be rich enough to buy anything I want."[1] Children's responses to the five items were again summed, based on results indicating that the scale was unidimensional. The coefficient alpha for the materialism scale was .66, which is within the recommended range of .6 to .8 for basic research (e.g., Peter, 1979).

Procedure

Questionnaires were administered to younger children in their class rooms and junior and senior high students met in the school cafeteria to participate in the study. After receiving general instructions about the study and specific instructions about the YES/NO scale, subjects answered five demographic questions and two practice questions relating to the YES/NO scale, which would be used to measure susceptibility to influence and materialism. The susceptibility to influence and materialism scales were embedded in filler items in order to disguise the true focus of the study. Older students then proceeded to work through the questionnaire independently. To help control for limited reading skills in the youngest age group, the directions and questions were read aloud as the students read along silently. Students in this age group were also required to stay on the same page until all subjects had finished the page. To conclude, subjects were debriefed, given their prizes and thanked for their participation. The study took approximately 30 minutes to complete, with older children finishing sooner.

RESULTS

Age Hypothesis (Ho: 1a and 1b)

Hypotheses 1a and 1b are competing hypotheses regarding the influence of age on children's development of materialistic attitudes. Hypothesis 1a suggests that materialistic attitudes should not vary as a function of age given that materialism is an enduring belief

---

[1]The five items used in the materialism scale are:

1. It is important to me to have really nice things.
2. I would like to be rich enough to buy anything I want.
3. I'd be happier if I could afford to buy more things.
4. It bothers me when friends have things that I don't have.
5. It's really true that money can buy happiness.

that is held across time and situations. Hypothesis 1b, though, suggests that given the vast changes in cognitive development, psycho-social development and social development that tend to correspond with age, materialistic attitudes may become more developed as a child ages.

The means and standard deviations are shown in Table 1.

By examining the means, it appears that there may be a non-monotonic effect with middle aged children being higher in materialism than the other two groups. However, the results of the statistical analysis in this study do not strongly bare this out. Children's responses to the materialism scale were analyzed using a 3 (age) by 3 (susceptibility to influence) between subject ANOVA design. The ANOVA results are presented in Table 2.

By examining Table 2, it seems that the results of this study are more inclined to support hypothesis 1a, in that, despite the numerous developmental changes taking place as a child gets older, the materialistic attitudes of one age group were not significantly different, at the .05 level, from those of other age groups.[2]

Since the cutoffs used to divide subjects into low, medium, and high susceptibility to influence were held constant across ages, it was possible to further examine these findings by looking at age differences within each level of susceptibility to influence. Again, materialistic attitudes did not vary significantly by age within each level of susceptibility to influence. This finding is also evidenced by the fact that the age by susceptibility to influence interaction effect was not significant. Thus, we can conclude that materialism is a relatively stable trait that does not vary dramatically as a function of age for children between the ages of 8 and 16.

Susceptibility to Influence Hypothesis (Ho: 2)

Hypothesis 2 suggests that the relationship between materialism and susceptibility to influence is positive in nature, meaning children who are more susceptible to influence may also hold more materialistic values. While this study is based on descriptive research, it can not necessarily be inferred that susceptibility to influence *causes* materialistic attitudes or that materialistic attitudes *cause* susceptibility to influence. However, the study found a significant correlation of .44, suggesting that there is a positive relationship between susceptibility to influence and materialism. The materialism means and standard deviations are shown in Table 3.

By examining the means in Table 3, it becomes clear that, regardless of age, children who are higher in susceptibility to influence also tend to be more materialistic. The ANOVA results presented in Table 2, provide similar findings, with the susceptibil-

---

[2]There were also no significant differences in materialism between any two age groups.

TABLE 2

Analysis of Variance for Materialism

	DF	F	P-Val
Age	2	2.70	.07
Influence	2	28.48	.00
Age x Influence	4	.51	.73

TABLE 3

Materialism Means and Standard Deviations by Susceptibility to Influence and Age

		Susceptibility to Influence		
		Low	Med	High
All Ages	Mean	12.31	13.64	15.58
	Std Dev	3.59	2.65	2.86
	Sample	n=107	n=98	n=88
Young	Mean	12.41	14.06	16.71
	Std Dev	4.32	2.98	3.17
	Sample	n=44	n=18	n=14
Medium	Mean	12.44	14.39	15.57
	Std Dev	3.14	2.55	5.87
	Sample	n=41	n=31	n=42
Old	Mean	11.86	13.02	15.09
	Std Dev	2.83	2.48	2.66
	Sample	n=22	n=49	n=32

Note: Higher Scores = greater materialism

ity to influence main effect being significant (p<.01), across all age groups and within each specific age group.[3] The age by susceptibility to influence interaction effect was not significant (p>.20).

Gender Differences

Several studies in the literature report gender differences with males tending to be more materialistic than females (Lipscomb, 1988; Belk, 1984; Moschis and Churchill, 1978). Although there were no hypotheses relating to gender proposed in this study, the data support previous gender research findings in that male respondents, having a mean score of 14.21, were significantly higher in their materialistic values (p<.05), than female respondents, having a mean score of 13.35.

---

[3]All three susceptibility to influence groups (low, medium and high) are significantly different from each other at the .05 level using modified LSD contrasts.

DISCUSSION

The decade of the '90s has been characterized by a return to basic values, with materialistic attitudes and conspicuous consumption being on the decline. However, parents and educators have become increasingly concerned with the commercialization and materialistic attitudes of youth. Children are considered an important and influential target market, whose consumer roles have become more profound, in terms of both responsibility and diversity. While children have become an increasingly attractive market, their attitudes toward materialism have also become more evident. Popular products, such as Nike athletic shoes or Starter jackets, are not only desired, but *demanded* by children. And many schools have implemented school uniform policies in an attempt to curb materialistic attitudes and resulting crime.

While considerable materialism research has been conducted with adults, very few studies have examined the materialistic values of children. Likewise, personality and behavior traits commonly associated with materialism have not been studied at the children's level. More specifically, no research has *directly* examined the relationship between materialism and susceptibility to influence. Thus, the purpose of this study was to examine the materialistic attitudes of children, ranging in age from 8 to 16, and to examine the relationship between materialistic attitudes in children and susceptibility to influence.

Three hundred children, ages 8, 12 and 16, participated in the research study and the data was analyzed using analysis of variance procedures. The results seem to indicate that materialism is a fairly stable trait, varying only marginally with age, despite the numerous developmental changes taking place as a child gets older. A significant, positive correlation of .44 was also found between materialism and susceptibility to influence. Likewise, children who were more susceptible to peer influence, had significantly higher materialism scores across all three age groups studied. These findings appear to support the hypothesis that materialism and susceptibility to peer influence are positively related. Since these findings are based on descriptive research, though, it can not be inferred that susceptibility to influence *causes* materialistic attitudes or that materialistic attitudes *cause* susceptibility to influence.

While this research provides valuable insight regarding the development of materialistic attitudes and the relationship between materialism and susceptibility to influence, additional research is warranted. Given that the relationship between materialism and susceptibility to influence has not been previously studied, it is important to test the validity of this finding with adults. In addition, as previously mentioned, a limitation of the current research is that it is descriptive in nature and thus, can not demonstrate cause and effect. It is necessary to further explore the relationship between materialism and susceptibility to peer influence using an experimental methodological design in order to better understand the *causal* relationship between these two variables. Likewise, given that values are culturally and socially defined, a longitudinal study would provide additional insight into the development of materialistic attitudes. Other factors that may play a role and should be examined include family income, social class, household size, parental age and parental susceptibility to influence. Research in this area should also be extended across geographical and ethnic backgrounds, given that previous adult research suggests that differences in materialistic values exist based on ethnic background (Crispell, 1993). This research is valuable to parents and educators responsible for establishing school and social policy. It is imperative that adequate information be available regarding the development of materialism and its relationship to other personality and behavioral traits given the many negative consequences associated with materialism, such as compulsive buying, conspicuous consumption, unhappiness, low self-esteem, greed, and poor interpersonal relationships .

REFERENCES

Bachmann, Gwen, Deborah Roedder John and Akshay R Rao (1993), "Children's Susceptibility to Peer Group Purchase Influence: An Exploratory Investigation," *Advances in Consumer Research*, 20, 463-468.

Barenboim, Carl (1981), "The Development of Person Perception in Childhood and Adolescence: From Behavioral Comparisons to Psychological Constructs to Psychological Comparisons," *Child Development*, 52, 129-244.

Bearden, W. and Etzel, M. (1982), "Reference Group Influence on Product and Brand Purchase Decisions," *Journal of Consumer Research*, 9, 183-194.

Bearden, W., Netemeyer, R., and Teel, J. (1990), "Further Validation of the Consumer Susceptibility to Interpersonal Influence Scale," *Advances in Consumer Research*, 17, 770-776.

Bearden, W., Netemeyer, R., and Teel, J. (1989), "Measurement of Consumer Susceptibility to Interpersonal Influence," *Journal of Consumer Research*, 15, 473-481.

Belk, Russell W. (1985), "Materialism: Trait Aspects of Living in a Material World," *Journal of Consumer Research*, 12, 265-280.

Belk, Russell W. (1984), "Three Scales to Measure Constructs Related to Materialism: Reliability, Validity and Relationships to Measures of Happiness," in T. Kinnear, (ed.), *Advances in Consumer Research*, 11, Provo, UT: Association for Consumer Research, 291-297.

Berkowitz, Leonard and Richard Lundy (1957), "Personality Characteristics Related to Susceptibility to Influence by Peers or Authority Figures, " *Journal of Personality*, 25, 306-316.

Braun, Ottmar and Robert Wicklund (1989), "Psychological Antecedents of Conspicuous Consumption," *Journal of Economic Psychology*, 10, 161-187.

Childers, Terry and Akshay Rao (1992), "The Influence of Internal and External Reference Groups on Consumer Decision Making: A Cross Cultural Study," *Journal of Consumer Research*, 19, 198-211.

Cox, donald and Raymond Bauer (1964), "Self-Confidence and Persuasibility in Women," *Public Opinion Quarterly*, 453-466.

Crispell, Diane (1993), "Materialism among Minorities," *American Demographics*, August, 14-16.

Csikszentmihalyi, Mihaly and Rochberg-Halton, Eugene (1981), *The Meaning of Things: Domestic Symbols and the Self*, Cambridge: Cambridge University Press.

Diaz, Kevin (1992), "Symbol of Status, Target of Violence: Jackets may put Teens in Danger," *Minneapolis Star and Tribune*, April 22, 1992.

Dickens, Dorothy and Virginia Ferguson (1957), *Practices and Attitudes of Rural White Children and Parents concerning Money*, Mississippi Agricultural Experiment Station, Technical Bulletin 43.

Easterlin, Richard and Eileen Crimmins (1991), "Private Materialism, Personal Self-Fulfillment, Family Life, and Public Interest," *Public Opinion Quarterly*, 55, 499-533.

Erikson, Erik H. (1972). "Eight Stages of Man," in *Readings in Child Behavior and Child Development*, C.S. Lavatelli and F. Stendler (eds.), San Diego, CA: Harcourt Brace Jovanovich.

Fournier, Susan and Marsha Richins (1991), "Some Theoretical and Popular Notions Concerning Materialism," *Journal of Social Behavior and Personality*, 6, 403-414.

Henkoff, Ronald (1989), "Is Greed Dead?" *Fortune*, 14, 40-46.

Hunt, James, Jerome Kernan, Anindya Chatterjee and Renee Florsheim (1990), "Locus of Control as a Personality Correlate of Materialism: An Empirical Note," *Psychological Reports*, 67, 1101-1102.

Janis, Irving and Peter Field (1959), "Sex Differences and Personality Factors Related to Persuasibility," in *Personality and Persuasibility*, C. Hovland and I. Janis, eds., New Haven, Conn., Yale University Press, 121-137.

Kamptner, N. Laura (1991), "Personal Possessions and their Meanings: A Life-Span Perspective," *Journal of Social Behavior and Personality*, 6, 209-228.

Kassarjian, Harold (1971), "Personality and Consumer Behavior: A Review," *Journal of Marketing Research*, 8, 409-418.

Kassarjian, Waltraud (1962), "A Study of Riesman's Theory of Social Character," *Sociometry*, 25, 213-230.

Lennox, Richard and Raymond Wolfe (1984), "Revision of the Self-Monitoring Scale," *Journal of Personality and Social Psychology*, 46, 1349-1364.

Locander, William and Peter Hermann (1979), "The Effects of Self-Confidence and Anxiety on Information Seeking in Consumer Risk Reduction," *Journal of Marketing Research*, 16, 268-274.

Lipscomb, Thomas (1988), "Indicators of Materialism in Children's Free Speech: Age and Gender Comparisons," *Journal of Consumer Marketing,* 5, 41-46.

McGuire, William (1968), "Personality and Susceptibility to Social Influence," in *Handbook of Personality Theory and Research,* E.F. Borgatta and W.W. Lambert, eds., Rand McNally, 1130-1187.

McNeal, James (1992), *Kids as Customers*, New York: Lexington Books.

Moschis, George and Gilbert Churchill, Jr. (1978), "Consumer Socialization: A Theoretical and Empirical Analysis," *Journal of Consumer Research*, 15, 599-609.

Park, W. and Lessig, V. (1977), "Students and Housewives: Differences in Susceptibility to Reference Group Influence," *Journal of Consumer Research*, 4, 102-110.

Peter, J. Paul (1979), "Reliability: A Review of Psychometric Basics and Recent Marketing Practices," *Journal of Marketing Research*, 16, 6-17.

Richins, Marsha (1987), "Media, Materialism, and Human Happiness," in M. Wallendorf & P. Anderson (eds.), *Advances in Consumer Research*, 14, Provo, UT:Association for Consumer Research, 352-356.

Richins, Marsha and Scott Dawson (1992), "A Consumer Values Orientation for Materialism and Its Measurement: Scale Development and Validation," *Journal of Consumer Research*, 19, 303-316.

Schwartz, Matthew (1991), "Materialism Declining in U.S.: Survey," *National Underwriter*, December 23, 14.

Selman, Robert L. (1980), *The Growth of Interpersonal Understanding*, New York: Academic Press.

Snyder, M. (1987), *Public Appearances/Private Realities: The Psychology of Self Monitoring*, New York: Freeman.

Ward, Scott and Daniel Wackman (1971), "Family and Media Influences on Adolescent Consumer Learning," *American Behavioral Scientist*, 14, 415-427.

Materialism as a Coping Mechanism: An Inquiry Into Family Disruption

James E. Burroughs, University of Wisconsin
Aric Rindfleisch, University of Wisconsin

Materialism is a popular and important topic in consumer research, with the majority of researchers appearing to focus on the dark-side aspects of this issue. This study, in contrast, posits that in certain instances materialism may play a functional role as a coping mechanism during difficult life transitions. In specific, we suggest that material objects may assist children in reducing the stress associated with parental separation or divorce. To examine this hypothesis, we conducted two empirical studies (one quantitative, one qualitative). The results of these studies suggest that materialism moderates the relationship between family disruption and family stress by helping to restore a sense of identity, permanence, and control in these children's lives. In addition to furthering a broadened conceptualization of materialism by highlighting its instrumental qualities, this paper also contributes to a deeper understanding of the interplay between family structure and consumption.

INTRODUCTION

Over the past decade, materialism has been one of the most complex and elusive concepts in consumer behavior. One of the central issues surrounding materialism is its purported effects on both the individual and society. The predominant perspective appears to largely view materialism as an inescapable and undesirable aspect of our consumer culture. As Pollay (1986) carefully documents, a number of prominent social commentators have decried the growth of our consumer culture and its associated emphasis on material possessions. Moreover, recent consumer research has empirically associated materialism with a variety of negative individual traits and orientations including possessiveness, self-centeredness, greed, and general life dissatisfaction (Belk 1985; Richins and Dawson 1992). Thus, on one hand, materialism appears to be at least partially culpable for a host of modern-day social ills.

On the other hand, researchers have also cautioned that the development of materialistic attitudes may hold some normative value under certain conditions. These researchers remind us that material objects often serve functional roles and are an integral part of our daily lives (Belk 1985; Fournier and Richins 1991). Likewise, Csikszentmihalyi and Rochberg-Halton (1981) provide a conceptual distinction between the detrimental effects of terminal materialism (i.e., the ownership of material objects simply for the sake of possessing them), and the potentially positive impact of instrumental materialism (i.e., using material objects as a means to a higher end). For example, Holt (1995) adopts an instrumental approach to materialism by noting the potentially functional role of material objects and consumption experiences for creating valued interpersonal interactions (e.g., the consumption of a baseball game as a bonding experience between father and son).

Previous research has found that children from disrupted family backgrounds display higher levels of materialism (Rindfleisch, Burroughs, and Denton 1997). However, this research failed to provide a conclusive explanation of the underlying dynamics behind this relationship. This paper provides one possible explanation. Sociologists consistently find that family disruption is a highly stressful life event for many children and is often characterized by dramatic changes (typically negative in nature) in their social and economic well-being (see Wallerstein and Kelly

1980 for a review). We propose that children and young adults may develop an enhanced level of materialism as a way of coping with these stresses. In this sense, we suggest that materialism may play an instrumental role for these affected individuals, specifically helping to restore a sense of stability, permanence, and identity in their lives. We employ both quantitative and qualitative approaches to examine this possibility.

LITERATURE REVIEW AND HYPOTHESIS DEVELOPMENT

Materialism and Consumer Behavior

Materialism has been defined as "the importance a person places on possessions and their acquisition as a necessary or desirable form of conduct to reach desired end states, including happiness" (Richins and Dawson 1992, p. 307). As noted earlier, the bulk of previous research appears to have focused on the dark-side of materialism, emphasizing its negative aspects for both society and the individual (see Belk 1985; Pollay 1986; Richins and Dawson 1992). For example, Richins and Dawson (1992) find that people who highly value material objects tend to be more self-centered and have higher levels of dissatisfaction with their lives. Similarly, Belk (1985) suggests that materialism is associated with possessiveness, nongenerosity, and greed. Belk (1985) also found an inverse relationship between materialism and life happiness. However in explaining these results he notes that:

It should be emphasized that the latter finding does not allow one to infer the direction of causality. While it is plausible that materialistic people pursue false sources of happiness, and that therefore such people must be disappointed, it is also possible that those who have for various reasons experienced dissatisfaction in life turn to materialism in their effort to find happiness. Since arguments for and against materialism as a source of satisfaction have been suggested, any such causal interpretations must await future research (p. 274).

Belk goes on to observe, however, that it is impossible to exist completely absent of material possessions. It has also been suggested that extreme forms of material denial (i.e., asceticism) may be equally undesirable, and may be related to anorexia-nervosa, bulimia, masochism, and other self-destructive tendencies (Belk 1985; D'Arcy 1967; Masson 1976).

The mixed discussion suggests that a more refined approach to materialism is needed. Csikszentmihalyi and Rochberg-Halton (1981) provide such refinement by reconceptualizing materialism as being of two types—instrumental versus terminal (see also Belk and Pollay 1985). Terminal materialism represents a high level of preoccupation with the acquisition and ownership of material objects simply for the sake of possessing them. In this form, materialism is usually considered detrimental in so far as such a preoccupation may reflect a malnourished sense of self and a lack of healthy social relationships. Such a person is, in effect, only a shell of what they own. Conversely, instrumental materialism does not connote such adverse consequences (and may even be necessary) in so far as things are used merely as a means to achieving some higher end(s). For example, unlike terminal materialism, where objects may serve in lieu of meaningful relationships, under

Advances in Consumer Research
Volume 24, © 1997

instrumental materialism the material objects may actually facilitate the development of healthy relationships and a positive self-image.

In sum, while materialism may be detrimental in many respects, it is clearly a complex construct, perhaps even operating on multiple levels—both positive and negative—simultaneously. As outlined in the following sections, material values may serve as an important coping mechanism in helping to reduce or alleviate the stress associated with painful life transitions such as the disruption of one's family through parental divorce or separation.

Family Disruption: Stress and Coping

Family Disruption and Stress. Divorce is widely recognized as a stress-producing event for both parents and children (Amato 1993; Berman and Turk 1981; Wallerstein and Kelly 1980). Family researchers estimate that one out of every two American children will experience the divorce or permanent separation of their parents before reaching the age of eighteen (Cherlin 1992). For most of these children, the disruption of their families is associated with a variety of stressful events including parental conflict, movement to a new place of residence, loss of friends and relatives, and changes in adult caregivers (Amato 1993; Berman and Turk 1981; McLanahan and Booth 1989; Martinson and Wu 1992; Wu and Martinson 1993).

The first two to three years following a family disruption are especially stressful for both parents and children. For example, nearly 40% of divorced mothers change residences within their first year after their divorce (McLanahan and Booth 1989). In general the first couple of years following a family disruption are often emotionally and financially draining, and marked by frequent and often unpredictable change. The children often experience a "chaotic lifestyle" with erratic meals and bedtimes, inconsistent discipline patterns, shifting household routines, and problems with tardiness and truancy at school (Cherlin 1992; McLanahan and Booth 1989; Martinson and Wu 1992). Not surprisingly, parental divorce and separation are generally ranked among the most stressful events in the life of a child, occurring at a time when their self-concept is still formative and vulnerable (Sarason, Johnson, and Siegel 1978; Wallerstein and Kelly 1980).

Developmental psychologists have long stressed the importance of stability in caregivers and resource providers in order to ensure the healthy development of children, who may often lack the emotional or psychological maturity needed to cope with stressful life changes (Craig 1993). The instability and change associated with family disruption frequently results in emotional and behavioral problems that are sometimes severe and long-lasting (see Wallerstein and Kelly 1980 for examples of case histories). Family researchers warn that if the stress associated with family disruption is allowed to build up in an individual and is not vented in a healthy manner it may lead to destructive consequences (Aneshensel 1992; Hodges 1990; Wolchik et al. 1985).

Family Disruption and Coping with Stress. Highly stressful life events, such as the divorce or separation of one's parents, often serve as significant life transitions, where a person is forced to exit a familiar existing role and face the uncertainties associated with a new set of roles. Young (1991) characterizes parental divorce as an "involuntary dispositional experience," which represents an important life transition for many children. Children seek to reduce the distress of divorce or separation by enacting various coping mechanisms in order to minimize the disharmony in their lives (Anthony 1991; Young 1991). Family researchers have found that children of divorce enact a broad array of coping strategies ranging from direct emotional confrontation to a state of repression in which they pretend that the divorce isn't really an issue at all (Wallerstein and

Kelly 1980). One especially prominent coping mechanism is to divert or refocus their pent-up tensions and anxieties into alternative activities such as sports or work.

Although they do not directly address the issue of materialism *per se*, McAlexander, Schouten, and colleagues have systematically examined the relationship between consumption and key life transitions such as divorce (cf. McAlexander 1991; Schouten 1991, McAlexander, Schouten, and Roberts 1993). In this research, they suggest that divorce leads to "acts of consumption which function as mechanisms for coping with stress and other negative emotional states" (McAlexander et al. 1993, p. 177). However, these researchers seem to stop short of exploring the specific underlying mechanisms of how materialism may function in this regard.

Additional support for materialism as a stress coping mechanism for children of divorce comes from discussions by Belk (1988) and Richins (1994), who describe the importance of material possessions in fulfilling the symbolic role of maintaining interpersonal ties. Children of disrupted households may come to rely on certain "special" possessions to reduce stress by bridging the physical gap between themselves and an absentee parent (e.g., a son placing special value on a baseball glove in order to induce a recollection—or perhaps an illusion—of a close relationship with his father). Finally, general evidence of a relationship between material objects and coping with the stresses and difficulties of life comes from related work, including findings of: a reliance on security blankets by infants during times of separation from their mothers (Furby and Wilke 1982); the use of special possessions by the elderly in coming to terms with their advancing years (Sherman and Newman 1977-1978); and a reliance on collections by the mentally retarded to help provide a sense of place and purpose (Carroll 1968).

Based on all of the preceding evidence and discussion, we now formally offer our hypothesis. In conceptual terms, we suggest that *materialism serves as a moderator of the relationship between family disruption and family stress. In specific, we expect that young people who have higher levels of materialism will have lower levels of family stress associated with their family disruption.* Two empirical studies are utilized to investigate this hypothesis.

STUDY I: QUANTITATIVE APPROACH

Method

Measurement. In order to provide a quantitative test of our hypothesis, we developed a survey instrument which contained multi-item measures of family stress and materialism, a single item measure of family structure, and a standard set of demographic variables including gender and race. The materialism measure was Richins and Dawson's (1992) Material Values Scale (with its three dimensions of centrality, happiness, and success). Consistent with Richins and Dawson's results, our application of this scale demonstrated acceptable reliability with an overall coefficient alpha of .86. Family stress was assessed using a Likert-type scale over ten items, which was adapted from an established stress research instrument, the Life Experiences Survey (Sarason, Johnson, and Siegel 1978). Because this scale is new to consumer research we list its items in Appendix A (along with our measure of family structure). The family stress scale also demonstrated adequate reliability with a coefficient alpha of .74. The summary statistics for these measures are provided in Table 1.

Data Collection. The subjects for this study were 200 young adults (aged 20-32) from a medium-sized midwestern metropolitan area of approximately 200,000. These subjects were initially recruited through a mail survey targeted to include people in their twenties, while excluding zip codes with large student populations.

TABLE 1
Key Measure Statistics

	Mean	SD	Family structure	Family stress	Material values
Family structure	na	na	(na)		
Family stress	1.56	.40	.52[a]	(.74)	
Material values	2.86	.62	.22[a]	.11	(.86)

NOTE.— [a]Statistically significant at $p \le .01$. The coefficient alpha for each measure is on the diagonal and the intercorrelations among the measures are on the off-diagonal.

TABLE 2
Test of the Moderating Effects of Material Values on the Relationship Between Family Structure and Stress

Dependent Variable	Independent Variables	Coefficient	p-value
Family Stress	Family structure (FS)	.88	.001
	Material values (MV)	.24	.06
	FS x MV	-.16	.05

NOTE.— $F = 25.35$, $p \le .001$, $R^2 = .28$

Of 557 mailed questionnaires, 23 were returned as undeliverable, leaving an effective sampling frame of 534 potential respondents. Of these, 138 were returned for a 26% response rate. After eliminating questionnaires due to missing or improperly completed data, we were left with a sample size of 135 respondents (31 of whom were from disrupted families).

Because our initial mail survey resulted in an unacceptable number of respondents from disrupted families, we conducted an over-quota sampling of disrupted individuals drawn from the same geographic area through a targeted newspaper advertisement. This ad, in the Sunday edition of the city's major newspaper (circulation 168,000), asked for persons aged 20-30 who came from divorced families to participate in an unspecified university research project. As an incentive, readers were informed they would be paid five dollars for their participation. From this ad, we mailed out an additional 70 questionnaires (after which we closed the survey), out of which 67 were returned for a 96% response rate. Problems with two of the surveys reduced the effective number to 65, bringing the total number of usable surveys of 200 (96 disrupted, 104 intact). In order to guard against the possibility of having introduced a method artifact into the study by using two different data collection techniques, we conducted a t-test comparison of the mean scores on the key variables for our disrupted subjects for both the mailer and the newspaper ad. Finding no significant differences in means, these two sampling frames were combined for analysis. Of our 200 subjects 71 were male, 129 were female, 88% were white, and their mean age was 26.

Analysis

Recall that we predicted that higher levels of materialism would act as a moderator to produce lower levels of stress among children from disrupted family backgrounds. To formally test for this moderating effect, we followed the procedures outlined by Cohen and Cohen (1983). According to Cohen and Cohen, hierarchical regression analysis (HRA) is the most appropriate test for examining moderators which produce differences in the form of the relationship between a predictor and a criterion variable. In HRA, a test of moderation is performed by entering the individual predictor variables first followed by the product term for their interaction. A moderating effect is confirmed by the presence of a statistically significant two-way interaction. The results of this analysis are documented in Table 2. As recommended by Cronbach (1987), the independent variables were mean-centered in order to reduce the collinearity between the predictors and their product terms. These results indicate a significant moderating effect (b=-.16, p≤.05) of material values on the relationship between family structure and stress.

In order to better understand the nature of the moderating influence of material values upon the relationship between family disruption and family stress, we examined the interaction of family structure and material values. In specific, we estimated the mean levels of family stress for respondents with low (one standard deviation *below* the mean materialism score of 2.86) and high (one standard deviation *above* the mean) levels of material values across both intact and disrupted family structures. As displayed in Figure

FIGURE 1
Interaction of Family Structure and Material Values

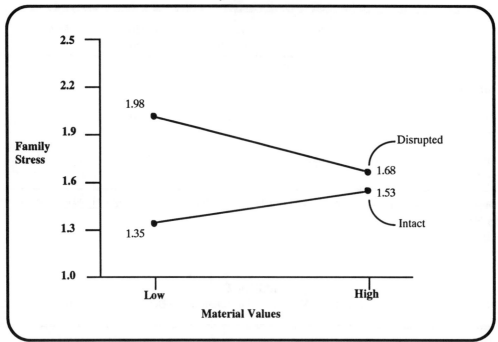

1, while material values is *positively* associated with family stress for subjects from intact families (low material values group mean stress=1.35; high material values group mean stress=1.53), material values and family stress are *negatively* related among subjects from disrupted families (low material values group mean stress=1.98; high material values group mean stress=1.68). In sum, this analysis suggests that young adults with higher levels of material values experience lower levels of stress related to a family disruption compared to young adults with lower levels of material values. Therefore, our hypothesis is supported.

STUDY II: QUALITATIVE APPROACH

Method

In order to enrich our understanding of the relationship between materialism and the stress associated with family disruption, we employed semi-structured depth interviews among a set of six students (three male, three female) at a large midwestern public university. All six students had experienced the divorce or separation of their parents prior to their 18th birthday. These informants were recruited from an introductory marketing class and were offered a nominal amount extra credit for their participation. Each interview was conducted by the lead author, with the second author in the room to take field notes. Each interview lasted approximately 30 minutes, and all six interviews were audiotaped for later transcription.

Each interview commenced with the following "grand tour" questions (see McCracken 1988), "What can you tell me about your parents' divorce/separation?" "How did it come about?" and "How old were you?" These questions were adapted from McAlexander et al.'s (1993) recent study of the relationship between consumer behavior and divorce. After gathering this background data, informants were asked to respond to two additional questions, "How has the divorce/separation changed your life?" and "Are there any special things you did or acquired during your parents'

divorce or separation that you especially remember?" Otherwise, the interview progressed following the guidelines suggested by McCracken (1988) where the questions were for the most part unplanned, the interview iterated between broad and focused issues, and the interviewee was generally allowed to set the direction of the interview. Informants were allowed to decline answering any questions which made them uncomfortable. A summary of informant profiles is provided in Appendix B.

Analysis

Analysis proceeded using the guidelines provided by Spiggle (1994). First, we briefly conferred after each interview to assess how the research was progressing and noted any interesting issues. Once all of the interviews were completed and transcribed, we independently summarized individual and then collective themes as each of us saw them. After completing this task, we met to discuss our findings, and found a considerable degree of convergence in identifying collective themes. Where discrepancies occurred, they were resolved by iterating back and forth on each issue and by continuously referring back to the transcripts for clarification. Outside input was solicited from an external researcher versed in qualitative interviewing techniques as well as from the interviewee's themselves. From these efforts, three principle themes emerged in reflection on the role of materialism as a coping mechanism for the stress associated with family disruption. These themes are: *permanence, control,* and *identity*. As a caveat, we note that these are not necessarily the only possible themes or even that they are mutually exclusive. We do however feel that they capture a broad range of the phenomenon in question.

Permanence. Family sociologists observe that much of the stress associated with family disruption appears to be due to the instability created by divorce and separation (Berman and Turk 1981). Immediately following a family disruption, virtually everything in the child's world is in a state of flux, especially the nature of his relationship with his or her parents. Security and permanence are often replaced by insecurity and transience; within a short span of time (a year or two) children of divorce often experience the removal of one parent from the family household, one or more changes in residence, a severe drop in financial well-being, and changes in adult caregivers. These transitions were also noted by our informants, many of who recollected their experiences of facing a noticeable decrease in financial resources and having to move to a smaller residence (typically an apartment) following their parents' divorce.

In order to compensate for this increased instability and sudden transience, children often seek to establish permanence and stability by forming interpersonal bonds with counselors, teachers, siblings, etc. (Wallerstein and Kelly 1980). Similarly, all of our informants reported a clear desire for permanence, quality, and durability in the material objects they purchased. Several informants explicitly stated that they wanted to purchase items that were going to "last," as they expected to possess the object for a long time. For example, Cindy described her general purchasing orientation in the following manner:

Cindy: I mean I take care of everything I have! You know, its kind of like if you are going to buy something, you should not necessarily buy the best but buy something that is going to you know, last. Like if you are going to buy a stereo you don't just go to Kmart and buy the cheapest one you can. You should get something that is going to last.

Thus, having faced impermanence in their relations with others, children of divorce and separation appear to look toward possessions as sources of a needed element of stability in their lives. This desire for permanence was also evident in our informants' discussions of their interpersonal relations. As all four of the respondents who were either married or involved in long term relationships expressed a intense desire to maintain these relationships and avoid the fate of their parents.

Control. For many children, the stress and unpredictability surrounding family disruption are often exacerbated by the fact that the events of their parent's divorce and separation are largely out of their control (Wallerstein and Kelly 1980). For example, our informants revealed that their parents' divorce had been caused by such events as marital infidelity, spousal incompatibility, and domestic violence (see Appendix B). In addition to the loss of control of their family lives, children of divorce often go through at least a temporary period of financial hardship in which they witness the loss of control of the ability of their single parent (typically their mother) to provide for their tangible resources such as food, shelter, and clothing (McLanahan and Booth 1989). Several of our informants noted that their families had become at least partially reliant on either relatives or governmental assistance for their basic sustenance following the divorce or separation of their parents. For example, Steve recounts how his single mother often had difficulty providing for her family's needs following her divorce:

Steve: Basically my father left and took everything and left us in a house with no money. My mother had three children and at the time my mother was a housewife and my dad was, you know, working and supported the family. When he left he left us with nothing and my mom didn't have a job or any money and so we were pretty much screwed, you know. And it got to the point where our electricity was turned off and we fell on some pretty hard times.

The theme of control was evident in the transcriptions of all six of our informants, several of whom noted that they felt that the disruption of their family left them in a disadvantageous life position compared to their peers from intact families. This theme of control also transcends into their discussions of their buying and consumption habits; as five out of our six informants claimed that they were quite particular and very cautious in terms of buying, owning, and using material objects. Most notably, when asked to describe a recent purchase, these informants recounted several examples of extreme deliberation and extensive cognitive processing in their buying behavior. For example, Vincent recollects the fear of a loss of control which he faced when buying a new motorcycle:

Vincent: For the Harley it was the same thing. [We] drove all the way to Milwaukee and it is a rare deal because you have to wait two-and-a-half years to get a bike. The owner said, 'well here is the bike, do you want to buy it?' And then I said sure and he said fourteen-five. And I looked and I said I came here and this is not what I had...and my wife she loved the bike, and I loved the bike. And she said, well are you ready to buy it, this is your dream bike, here it is. And I completely got scared again, and I said no, I am not going to buy it. And she said, why. And I go, 'what if something happens?' That is my biggest concern...you know, you lose everything. And I went back, drove all the way back to Madison [over 75 miles each way], and then my wife was getting mad already because this was the second time going down there, and the same thing happened again. And I mean it took three days, going back and forth, back and forth, to finally get the bike. And now that I have the bike, now it is the same process again when I am buying these big [gas] tanks, customizing it.

Vincent also revealed that he engaged in extensive deliberation in order to allay similar fears and anxieties when buying both his new car and his television set. Although Vincent's case may be extreme, it is by no means unique. As noted, many of our other informants also reported being very deliberate and cautious in their general approach to purchasing objects (which ranged from watches for Ann to kitchenware for Carl). Thus, the purchase and consumption of material objects appears to provide a venue for the reassertion and reestablishment of control—and thus the alleviation of the stress otherwise associated with their experiences of lack of control—which informants enact through careful and deliberate prepurchase decision making activities. Indeed, a majority of informants seemed to take both pride and comfort in their purchasing prudence.

Identity. In addition to facing instability and a loss of control, the disruption of one's family may often damage a child's self concept and sense of identity (Wallerstein and Kelly 1980). Family sociologists find that children of divorce typically have lower levels of self-esteem compared to children living in intact families (Demo 1993). Much of this decrease in self-esteem and loss of self-identity may be due to the fact that many children feel that they are at least partially to blame for the divorce or separation of their parents (Wallerstein and Kelly 1980).

This theme of self-identity was most clearly manifested by the presence of a strong sense of independence and self-reliance among many of our informants. Having experienced the loss of both tangible resources and intangible parental support, these young adults noted that they felt that they are unable to rely on others and must accept primary responsibility in terms of financing their education, furnishing their residences, and providing for their daily needs. This development of a strong sense of independence is clearly evident in our conversation with Heather:

Interviewer: Is there any other particular ways that this divorce or separation has changed your life?

Heather: I think it made me a lot more independent person. Because I don't really talk to my mom about anything and neither do my other brothers. It keeps me really separated from my sisters too.

Interviewer: Let me ask you this. You say you are more independent. Could you expand on what independence means to you?

Heather: As far as being able to handle things myself. And not needing other people's opinions. You know like help and assistance. Financially I am independent—100%. And as far as what I think, what I buy, who all I go out with and everything along that line. Because I honestly don't communicate with my mom on that level. It is more like, O.K., I am going to do this or I am going to do that. Or she asks me, you know, are you going to be home for Christmas? And I'll say yeah or no. I don't actually have a heart-to-heart conversation with her and I haven't since you know this whole thing started.

Interviewer: When you say that you are more independent and you buy things for yourself, what types of things do you buy?

Heather: Well, everything that I need.

Interviewer: Everything?

Heather: Everything that I need; food, clothes...anything.

Also, in discussing their material objects, four of our six informants reported that they had established collections or prized possessions during or immediately following their family disruption. According to Belk (1988), collections provide a sense of self-definition and often serve a role as "transition objects or security blankets" (p. 154). Likewise, the symbolic self completion thesis of Wicklund and Gollwitzer (1982) suggests that the addition of objects to a collection helps persons with low self-esteem achieve a more complete sense of self-identity. Thus, where a family disruption assaults a child's sense of self, material objects appear to help them restore a sense of their identity.

Finally, on a very pragmatic level, investing one's time, energy, and self into a prized possession or collection might also relieve stress if for no other reason than by serving as a distraction from the realities of the home. Several informants' self-reports were consistent with this notion. For example, Carl noted that his expansive comic book collection helped take his mind off his parent's divorce:

Carl: I collect comic books. A lot of them, like several thousand of them. We would trade and focus a lot on it.

Interviewer: Any reflections on why you think you got so into it?

Carl: Later on I think it helped me out with, um, you know keeping myself busy.

In the aggregate then, material objects appear to serve an important role in restoring a sense of self-identity among our informants by (1) providing an outlet through which these young people assert their independence and self-reliance, and (2) enhanc-

ing their self-esteem by serving as an outlet for the stress associated with the disruption of their family. In summary, these six interviews revealed that material objects appear to contribute to a reduction in the stress associated with family disruption by providing a mechanism for children and young adults to develop permanent relations, reestablish a sense of control, and enhance their self-identity. We turn now to a consideration of the implications of our findings and suggest possible directions for future research.

DISCUSSION AND CONCLUSIONS

In 1985, Russ Belk noted that, "One of the foremost issues involving materialism that needs to be addressed is whether materialism is a positive or a negative trait" (p. 266). Since Belk made this plea, more than a decade has passed and this question remains largely unanswered. Our research effort takes an important step in this direction by combining quantitative and qualitative approaches in exploring the instrumental role that the development of material values may play in helping individuals reduce or alleviate the stress produced by significant life transitions such as family disruption. First, we present quantitative evidence which suggests that materialism acts as moderator of the relationship between family structure and family stress. In specific, while material values is positively related to family stress among children from intact families, material values and family stress are negatively related among children whose parents have divorced or separated. This quantitative evidence is enriched by a set of qualitative depth interviews among young adults who experienced the divorce or separation of their parents while growing up. These interviews suggest that material objects play an important role in providing a sense of permanence, a re-establishment of control, and a bolstering of self-identity among children whose lives have been destabilized by the disruption of their family structure.

Our results present a number of important questions for future research. First of all, although materialism appears to reduce stress in our disrupted group, it is positively related to stress in our intact group. Why this discrepancy? As initial conjecture, what we might be seeing are the differential effects of instrumental versus terminal materialism, as described earlier. Even though researchers have been frustrated in trying to empirically discriminate among these two forms of materialism (Richins and Dawson 1992), this presents an intriguing possibility for future research.

Our results also leave us wondering under what other circumstances might material values similarly play a functional role? Clearly, family disruption is only one of the many stressful life events which confront a person during their life course. In other research, Mehta and Belk (1991), and Hill and Stamey (1990), implicate material objects as important transition mechanisms in helping to alleviate the stress associated with immigration and homelessness respectively. Perhaps materialism might also play an instrumental role in helping people cope with the stress of major life events such as difficulties in school or problems with intimate relationships. Might the death of a family member or close friend produce a similar need for the use of material objects as coping devices? Additionally, to what extent might materialism as a coping mechanism differ across these various life events? As Berman and Turk (1981) note, coping strategies appear to be problem specific. These are important issues, and their assessment stands to enrich the domain of materialism research. It would appear that, at a minimum, we as researchers need a broadened conceptualization of materialism and the role of material objects in people's lives.

As a couple of final caveats, we do not wish to imply that materialism is the only coping mechanism operant in children who experience parental breakup, or even necessarily the most impor-

APPENDIX A
New Measures

Measure	Source
Family Stress: (No Stress to Extreme Stress)	*Adapted from Sarason et al. (1978)*

Considering up through your 18th birthday, please circle the overall extent to which each of the following events impacted your life (positively or negatively) around the time(s) they occurred. Use "No Impact" if the event made no difference or never occurred.

1. Move(s) to a different home or place of residence.
2. Difficulties with school work.
3. A major, abrupt change in your family's financial status.
4. Frequent or lengthy periods in which one or both parents were temporarily absent.
5. Difficulties establishing and/or maintaining social relationships with peers.
6. The loss (other than death) or separation from family members or loved ones.
7. Encounters with juvenile authorities or police.
8. Physical abuse by parents or other family members.
9. Arguments between parents or other family members (including self).
10. Changes in the membership or composition of your family unit other than the divorce of your parents (e.g., remarriage of your parent(s), birth or your own child, etc.).

Family Structure: *New Item*

Up until your 18th birthday, did you live in the same home as both your biological mother and father for your entire life, not counting time spent away at college and other temporary periods in which you were away from home?

What was the initial reason why you didn't live with both of your biological parents through your 18th birthday? (included a "doesn't apply" option).

APPENDIX B
Informant Profiles

Heather: Female; mother filed for divorce in the summer of her sophomore year in high school at age 15; father committed suicide during divorce proceedings; lives at home with her mother and stepfather.

Carl: Male; parents divorced at age 2 due to father's infidelity; father maintained regular contact during childhood but Carl only rarely sees him now; raised by his single mother.

Vincent: Male; parents divorced at age 6 due to father's abuse and questionable business activities; had minimal contact with father during childhood and father never paid any child support; raised by his single mother and experienced multiple changes of residence. Is currently married.

Ann: Female; parents divorced at age 10 due to incompatibility; grew up with her mother, who has remarried; maintained regular contact with father but received only minimal amounts of child support.

Steve: Male; parents divorced at age 9 due to father's infidelity and physical abuse; had very little contact with father following the divorce; regards mother and stepfather as his primary family; is currently married and has a young daughter.

Cindy: Female; mother was twice married and twice divorced; first breakup occurred at age 2 due to father being over-controlling; second breakup occurred at age 11 due to suspected infidelity and a lack financial reliability on the part of her stepfather; felt stepfather was a poor parent and role-model.

tant one. Given how central possessions are to our everyday lives, however, it is not surprising to find material objects in this role. Moreover, our research relies on retrospective accounts in developing its thesis. This, of course, raises the possibility that individuals' experiences could be distorted with time. While always a possibility, a broad reading of the literature suggests that children often have an acute awareness of their experiences during a divorce, and that these memories decay quite slowly (Paykel 1983; Wolchik et al. 1985). In closing, we would like to pose a question which somewhat brings us back full-circle: "Is the role of materialism as a coping mechanism the genuine article or only an ersatz solution?" In other words, are individuals who are affected by family disruption trading off the long-term benefits of directly dealing with their problems and experiences for some shorter term "fix" of material relief? Or does materialism indeed provide an instrumental (if only temporary) mechanism, for dealing with life's traumatic events? We leave the answer to this question to future research.

REFERENCES

Amato, Paul R. (1993), "Children's Adjustment to Divorce: Theories, Hypotheses, and Empirical Support," *Journal of Marriage and the Family*, 55 (February), 23-38.

Aneshensel, Carol S. (1992), "Social Stress: Theory and Research," *Annual Review of Sociology*, 18, 15-38.

Anthony, E. James (1991), "The Response to Overwhelming Stress in Children: Some Introductory Comments," in *Stress and Coping: An Anthology*, Alan Monet and Richard Lazarus, eds. New York: Columbia University Press.

Belk, Russell W. (1985), "Materialism: Trait Aspects of Living in a Material World," *Journal of Consumer Research*, 12 (December), 265-280.

_____ (1988), "Possessions and the Extended Self," *Journal of Consumer Research*, 15 (September), 139-168.

_____ and Richard W. Pollay (1985), "Images of Ourselves: The Good Life in Twentieth Century Advertising," *Journal of Consumer Research*, 11 (March), 887-897.

Berman, William H. and Dennis C. Turk (1981), "Adaptation to Divorce: Problems and Coping Strategies," *Journal of Marriage and the Family*, 43 (February), 179-189.

Carroll, Marilyn N. (1968), "'Junk' Collections Among Mentally Retarded Patients," *American Journal of Mental Deficiency*, 73 (2), 308-314.

Cherlin, Andrew (1992), *Marriage, Divorce, Remarriage*, Revised edition. Cambridge, MA: Harvard University Press.

Csikszentmihalyi, Mihalyi and Eugene Rochberg-Halton (1981), *The Meaning of Things: Domestic Symbols and the Self*, Cambridge: Cambridge University Press.

Cohen, J. and P. Cohen (1983), *Applied Multiple Regression/ Correlation Analysis for the Behavioral Sciences*, 2nd ed. Hillsdale, NJ: Erlbaum.

Craig, Grace J. (1993), *Human Development*, 6th ed. New York: McGraw Hill.

Cronbach, Lee J. (1987), "Statistical Tests for Moderator Variables: Flaws in Analyses Recently Proposed," *Psychological Bulletin*, 102 (3), 414-417.

D'Arcy, P. F. (1967), "Asceticism (Psychology of)," in *New Catholic Encyclopedia*, Vol. 1. New York: McGraw-Hill, 941-942.

Demo, David H. (1993), "The Relentless Search for Effects of Divorce: Forging New Trails or Tumbling Down the Beaten Path?" *Journal of Marriage and the Family*, 55 (February), 42-45.

Fournier, Susan and Marsha L. Richins (1991), "Some Theoretical and Popular Notions Concerning Materialism," *Journal of Social Behavior and Personality*, 6 (6), 403-414.

Furby, Lita, and Mary Wilke (1982), "Some Characteristics of Infants' Preferred Toys," *Journal of Genetic Psychology*, 140 (June), 207-219.

Hill, Ronald Paul and Mark Stamey (1990), "The Homeless in America: An Examination of Possessions and Consumption Behaviors," *Journal of Consumer Research*, 17 (December), 303-321.

Hodges, William F. (1990), "Stress in Parents and Late Elementary Age Children in Divorced and Intact Families and Child Adjustment," *Journal of Divorce and Remarriage*, 14 (1), 63-79.

Holt, Douglas B. (1995), "How Consumers Consume: A Typology of Consumption Practices," *Journal of Consumer Research*, 22 (June), 1-16.

Martinson, Brian C. and Lawrence L. Wu (1992), "Parent Histories: Patterns of Change in Early Life," *Journal of Family Issues*, 13 (September), 351-377.

McAlexander, James H. (1991), "Divorce, the Disposition of the Relationship, and Everything," in *Advances in Consumer Research*, 18, John F. Sherry and Brian Sternthal, eds. Provo, UT: Association for Consumer Research, 43-48.

_____, John W. Schouten, and Scott D. Roberts (1993), "Consumer Behavior and Divorce," in *Research in Consumer Behavior*, 6, Janeen A. Costa and Russell W. Belk, eds. Greenwich, CT: JAI Press, 153-184.

McCracken, Grant (1988), *The Long Interview*. Newbury Park, CA: Sage.

McLanahan, Sara S. and Karen Booth (1989), "Mother-only Families: Problems, Prospects and Politics," *Journal of Marriage and the Family*, 51 (August), 557-580.

Masson, J. Moussaieff (1976), "The Psychology of the Acetic," *Journal of Asian Studies*, 35 (August), 611-625.

Mehta, Raj and Russell W. Belk (1991), "Artifacts, Identity, and Transition: Favorite Possessions of Indians and Indian Immigrants to the United States," *Journal of Consumer Research*, 17 (March), 398-411.

Paykel, E. S. (1983), "Methodological Aspects of Life Events Research," *Journal of Psychosomatic Research*, 27, 341-52.

Pollay, Richard W. (1986), "The Distorted Mirror: Reflections on the Unintended Consequences of Advertising," *Journal of Marketing*, 50 (April), 18-36.

Richins, Marsha L. (1994), "Valuing Things: The Public and Private Meanings of Possessions," *Journal of Consumer Research*, 21 (December), 504-521.

_____ and Scott Dawson (1992), "A Consumer Values Orientation for Materialism and Its Measurement: Scale Development and Validation," *Journal of Consumer Research*, 19 (December), 303-316.

Rindfleisch, Aric, James E. Burroughs, and Frank Denton (1997), "Family Structure, Materialism, and Compulsive Consumption," *Journal of Consumer Research*, 23 (March), forthcoming.

Sarason, Irwin G., James H. Johnson, and Judith M. Siegel (1978), "Assessing the Impact of Life Changes: Development of the Life Experiences Survey," *Journal of Consulting and Clinical Psychology*, 46 (5), 932-946.

Schouten, James W. (1991), "Selves in Transition: Symbolic Consumption in Personal Rites of Passage and Identity Reconstruction," *Journal of Consumer Research*, 17 (March), 412-425.

Sherman, Edmund and Evelyn S. Newman (1977-1978), "The Meaning of Cherished Personal Possessions for the Elderly," *International Journal of Aging and Human Development*, 8 (2), 181-192.

Spiggle, Susan (1994), "Analysis and Interpretation of Qualitative Data in Consumer Research," *Journal of Consumer Research*, 21 (December), 491-503.

Wallerstein, Judith S. and Joan Berlin Kelly (1980), *Surviving the Breakup: How Children and Parents Cope with Divorce*. New York: Basic Books.

Wicklund, Robert A. and Peter M. Gollwitzer (1982), *Symbolic Self Completion*, Hillsdale, NJ: Lawrence Erlbaum.

Wolchik, Sharlene A., Irwin N. Sandler, Sanford L. Braver, and Bruce S. Fogas (1985), "Events of Parental Divorce: Stressfulness Ratings by Children, Parents, and Clinicians," *American Journal of Community Psychology*, 14 (1), 59-74.

Wu, Lawrence L. and Brian C. Martinson (1993), "Family Structure and the Risk of Premarital Births," *American Sociological Review*, 58 (April), 210-232.

Young, Melissa Martin (1991), "Disposition of Possessions During Role Transitions," in *Advances in Consumer Research*, 18, John F. Sherry and Brian Sternthal, eds. Provo, UT: Association for Consumer Research, 33-39.

How Do Ads Mean? New Directions in Cultural Advertising Research

Douglas B. Holt, Penn State University

Understanding how advertising works is necessarily both a multidisciplinary and interdisciplinary enterprise. Ads are at once informational, rhetorical, cultural, artistic, and magical. So comprehensive understanding requires diverse theoretical perspectives and methods to plumb these dimensions. Consumer research has over the past two decades made enormous strides in understanding how ads, as information, are cognitively processed. However, as we have single-mindedly pursued this goal, other important dimensions of advertising have been relatively neglected.

Recently a new research stream of advertising scholarship has emerged—what we will call the cultural paradigm of advertising research—that has begun to build theoretical sophistication in understanding these relatively neglected dimensions of advertising. Cultural advertising research emphasizes understanding how ads mean (McCracken 1987; Sherry 1987; Mick and Buhl 1992). While relatively new in consumer research, this paradigm has generated an extensive literature in mass communications, cultural studies, semiotics, and sociology, often drawing upon textual theories from literature, film, and rhetoric.

In the "first wave" of cultural advertising research, consumer researchers with training outside marketing have offered sophisticated primers on the key conceptual tools necessary for this endeavor: culture/structuralism/post-structuralism (Sherry 1987; McCracken 1987; Scott 1992), rhetoric (McQuarrie 1989; Scott 1990, 1994a, 1994b), and formal analysis from literature and film (Stern 1989, 1993). In particular, Scott's (1990, 1994a, 1994b) programmatic series of *Journal of Consumer Research* articles has outlined an interdisciplinary program of research the goal of which is to integrate key ideas from literary and cultural theory to develop a cultural theory of advertising.

The next step in the evolution of cultural advertising research requires advancing these existing theoretical insights within the context of research questions central to consumer research. And, in particular, since most of these insights emanate from the humanities and so are posed strictly as formal analytic tools, it is necessary to adapt and integrate these ideas into the empirical social science tradition that dominates consumer research. Several studies have begun this process, in particular the work of David Mick (Mick and Politi 1989; Mick and Buhl 1992), Ed McQuarrie (McQuarrie and Mick 1992, 1996), and John Deighton (Deighton, Romer and McQueen 1989; Deighton and Hoch 1993). These three presentations continue the evolution of this second wave trajectory, developing yet new ways to extend and integrate central insights from literary and cultural theory into empirical advertising research. We take a broad view of the cultural advertising paradigm—defining it conceptually in terms of theoretical assumptions and important research questions rather than in terms of methods—which allows for linkages to research streams in advertising that have not historically made use of cultural research, and, also, allows for the application of an wide and eclectic array of methods chosen to fit the research problem.

"The Reading Profile: An Interpretive Framework for Analyzing the Meanings of Ads"

Douglas B. Holt, Penn State University
Michael Mulvey, Rutgers University

The foundational premise of cultural advertising research is to understand "how ads mean." The incorporation of contemporary literary theory into ad research has led to a radical shift in conceptualizing the meanings of ads, moving from an "ad as information" metaphor to understanding the ad as a polysemic cultural text in which meanings are constructed relationally through a variety of intertextual linkages to "cultural codes" that exist outside the ad itself. In this conception, ads are indeterminate semiotic resources that facilitate and constrain but do not actually contain meaning. Thus, ad meanings only become concrete as particular audiences produce them. These powerful ideas have significant consequences for the empirical study of ad meaning, making obsolete common empirical techniques for studying ad meaning such as content analysis. But because these ideas emanate in the humanities, no alternative empirical approach has yet been offered. The vast promise of these theories for opening a new terrain of advertising research remains limited until these theoretical advances can be recast into tools for conducting empirical research.

The primary purpose of this study is to draw upon contemporary literary and cultural theory to develop an interpretive framework and accompanying data elicitation and analytic method for describing the meanings of ads. In this pilot study, we develop the reading profile to describe the meanings of a dramatic, figurative ad for Kellogg's Frosted Flakes) viewed by a group of forty-six demographically diverse adult informants. The goal of the data elicitation process is to generate the richest interpretations possible from a sample large enough to describe patterns of meanings, while minimizing influencing these interpretations. Informants watch the ad three times in a row, and then are asked to write in essay form responses to four open-ended questions that cue well-established aspects of ad interpretations ("What story does the ad tell?" "How does the ad relate to you life?" "What does the ad say about XX brand?" "Do you like the ad? Why or why not?"). They are then given as much time as they need to do so, averaging about twenty minutes.

The analysis of these data begins with a skeletal nomothetic framework based upon the three predominant interpretive stances used to read ads—the textual, referential, and critical perspectives—and then seeks to build idiographic categories of interpretation for each of these dimensions. After a number of iterations required to build comprehensive and reasonably orthogonal categories, the process follows typical content analysis procedures using multiple independent coding.

The result of the elicitation and analysis is what we term the *reading profile*—a graphic depiction of the patterning of ad meaning that an ad evinces from a given audience. The reading profile is intended to assist analysis in three predominant advertising research streams in the cultural advertising paradigm: 1) cultural advertising theory, which seeks to conceptualize the nature of ad meaning, particularly how it is structured by various formal and structural characteristics of the ad-text and cultural characteristics of the audience, 2) sociological research, which seeks to apply cultural advertising theory to describe differences in ad meanings across socially-constructed interpretive communities, and 3) managerial research, which seeks to diagnose how well ads communicate meanings intended by their producers. After we developed the reading profile, we used the Frosted Flakes reading profile to briefly demonstrate that the technique can usefully contribute to each of these research streams.

"Visual Rhetoric in Advertising: An Experimental Inquiry"

Edward McQuarrie, Santa Clara University
David Glen Mick, University of Wisconsin–Madison

The traditional approach to meaning analysis in consumer advertising research has been largely verbal in orientation, and has focused on claims made vis-a-vis product attributes. Even a casual examination of advertising, however, shows ads in most media to be aggressively visual. Moreover, content analyses have shown that over the course of this century magazine ads have steadily increased the relative emphasis placed on visual as opposed to verbal elements.

This research effort will apply rhetorical and semiotic analysis to illuminate the question of precisely how visual images in advertisements convey meaning. In this vein, Scott (1994a) offers a pioneering discussion of how the visual text of an ad could be "read." Her rhetorical approach to visual imagery differs in many respects from earlier conditioning or association models, and also from conventional information processing models. The present study continues Scott's rhetorical emphasis but brings multiple methods to bear, most notably a laboratory experiment, in order to produce a systematic, causal account of how rhetorical structure in advertising visuals can trigger the construction of meaning by consumers. The role model for this effort is McQuarrie and Mick (1992) where semiotic, rhetorical, phenomenological, and experimental approaches were combined to investigate the impact of advertising resonance (visually triggered puns).

By definition, any rhetorical analysis of advertising must be attentive to variations in the form and style of an advertising text; i.e., to rhetorical structure. The premise underlying rhetoric is that specific choices concerning form and style can be expected to bear a lawful and regular relation to specific consumer processing outcomes. For instance, an ad that makes use of visual repetition or echoing will, ceteris paribus, increase the probability that a consumer encountering that ad will respond in a certain way—most likely, by inferring that some substantive similarity exists between the real world referents for the two visually similar elements.

The specific idea to be investigated in this study is that the notion of a rhetorical figure can be fruitfully applied to visual elements of advertisements. In terms of language, a rhetorical figure is an artful deviation from expectations. Familiar examples of figures include metaphor, rhyme, pun and the like (McQuarrie and Mick 1996). It has been argued that a limited number of rhetorical figures exist, constituting templates into which specific instances fall. Transferred into the visual realm, this suggests that a small number of distinctive visual forms may exist, each of which can be shown to have a characteristic effect on consumer processing. The goal of this study is to experimentally manipulate such instances of visual rhetoric in order to provide a causal analysis of their impact on consumer processing. In our presentation we reported preliminary experimental data from several such manipulations, along with a theoretical account of how visual rhetoric achieves its effect.

"The Cognitive Basis of Cultural Differences in Responses to Advertising"

Anne M. Brumbaugh, Case-Western Reserve University

Theoretical explanations of cultural differences in advertising response have relied principally on social psychological theories including identification (Whittler 1989), similarity (Whittler and DiMeo 1991), and felt ethnicity (Stayman and Deshpande 1989). The current research suggests that a cognitive cultural approach—which emphasizes differences in the content of cultural knowledge systems across groups—further enhances our understanding of how advertisements trigger differential reactions across cultural groups.

This cognitive approach to understanding cultural differences in people's reactions to advertising draws on literature from cognitive anthropology (see Holland and Quinn 1987; D'Andrade and Strauss 1992) that suggests that we are socialized into a certain body of knowledge specific to the cultural group in which we are raised. This knowledge, stored in cognitive structures or schemas called *cultural models*, is shaped by social and historical context and, so, varies from cultural group to cultural group. Whenever we view an ad, some of these countless cultural models are activated. This activated knowledge ranges from schemas for how to use the product to schemas for other themes depicted in advertising like success, family, or patriotism. Advertisers count on activating this information to enable us to envision ourselves using their product (i.e., activate an affect-laden schema for weddings in Kodak ads), or to otherwise enhance our interpretation of the ad.

The current research asserts that ethnic minorities in the United States are members of two important cultural groups: the dominant white culture, and their own ethnic subculture. Where knowledge about a topic is the same in the two cultures (e.g., baseball rules), members of the ethnic subculture and members of the dominant culture who are not members of that subculture share the same knowledge about that topic. In this case, we would not expect minority group members' reactions to ads that activate this knowledge to differ from reaction of those in the dominant culture. However, where that knowledge is different, members of the subculture will be familiar with both knowledge of the dominant culture and of their subculture. Effectively, they have available in memory two cultural models for that subject that may be activated depending on other cues in the environment. These cues, including ethnicity of characters depicted in the ad, signal to the cognitive systems of these multicultural viewers which of the two schemas is to be activated. Viewers' reactions to ads may differ by viewer ethnicity based on the knowledge that is activated and used to interpret and respond to the ad.

Several studies that test the existence of multiple cultural models of family for African-American and white populations and the activation of these models is discussed. Focus group results show that the cultural model of the typical American family is white and significantly different from the cultural model of the typical African-American family in terms of the number of family members, relationships amongst family members, living arrangements, socio-economic status, and other factors. Importantly, the two models do not differ significantly between African-American and white respondents, indicating that these models are widely shared among both groups. Results of structural equations modeling of subjects' reactions to ads varying in ethnicity of characters depicted and other cues show that differences in viewers' reactions are attributable to activation of these different cultural models, even after controlling for ethnicity-based identification with characters in the ad.

There are substantive differences in the content of different groups' understanding of the world as contained in cultural models. It is important to understand how this cognitive basis of cultural distinctiveness impacts viewers' interpretations and evaluations of ads in order to create inclusive advertising and to make appropriate segmentation and targeting decisions across culturally diverse populations.

Discussion Leader
John F. Sherry, Jr., Northwestern University
John Sherry initiated discussion by offering interpretations of several recent postmodern print ads, deploying a plethora of cutting edge terms that the panelists now wish they could remember.

REFERENCES

D'Andrade, Roy and Claudia Strauss (1990), *Human Motives and Cultural Models*, New York: Cambridge University Press.

Deighton, John and Stephan Hoch (1993), "Teaching Emotion With Drama Advertising," in *Advertising Exposure, Memory, and Choice*, ed. Andrew Mitchell, Hillsdale, NJ: Lawrence Erlbaum & Associates, 261-281.

Deighton, John, Daniel Romer, Josh McQueen (1989), "Using Drama to Persuade," *Journal of Consumer Research*, 16(December), 335-343.

Holland, Dorothy and Naomi Quinn (1987), *Cultural Models in Language and Thought*, New York: Cambridge University Press.

McCracken, Grant (1987), Advertising: Meaning or Information?" in *Advances in Consumer Research*, Vol. 14, eds. Melanie Wallendorf and Paul Anderson, Provo, UT: Association for Consumer Research, 121-124.

McQuarrie, Edward F. (1989), "Advertising Resonance: A Semiological Perspective," in *Interpretive Consumer Research*, ed. Elizabeth C. Hirschman, Provo, UT: Association for Consumer Research, 97-114.

McQuarrie, Edward F. and David Glen Mick (1992), "On Resonance: A Critical Pluralist Inquiry into Advertising Rhetoric," *Journal of Consumer Research*, 19 (September), 180-197.

_____ and _____ (1996), "Figures of Rhetoric in Advertising Language," *Journal of Consumer Research*, 22 (March), forthcoming.

Mick, David Glen and Laura Politi (1989), "Consumers' Interpretations of Advertising Imagery: A Visit to the Hell of Connotation," in *Interpretive Consumer Research*, ed. Elizabeth Hirschman, Provo UT: Association for Consumer Research, 85-96.

Mick, David Glen and Claus Buhl (1992), "A Meaning-Based Model of Advertising Experiences," *Journal of Consumer Research*, 19 (December), 317-338.

Scott, Linda M. (1990), "Understanding Jingles and Needledrop: A Rhetorical Approach to Music in Advertising," *Journal of Consumer Research*, 17(September), 223-236.

_____ (1992), "Playing With Pictures: Postmodernism, Poststructuralism, and Advertising Visuals," in *Advances in Consumer Research, Vol. XIX*, eds. John F. Sherry Jr. and Brian Sternthal, Provo, UT: Association for Consumer Research, 596-612.

_____ (1994a), "Images in Advertising: The Need for a Theory of Visual Rhetoric," *Journal of Consumer Research*, 21 (September), 252-273.

_____ (1994b), "The Bridge From Text to Mind: Adapting Reader-Response Theory to Consumer Research," *Journal of Consumer Research*, 21(December), 461-480.

Sherry, John F., Jr. (1987), "Advertising As A Cultural System," in *Marketing and Semiotics*, ed. Jean Umiker-Sebok, New York: Mouton de Gruyter, 441-461.

Sherry, John F., Jr. and Eduardo Camargo (1987), "'May Your Life Be Marvelous: English Language Labelling and the Semiotics of Japanese Promotion," *Journal of Consumer Research*, 14(September), 174-188.

Stayman, Douglas and Rohit Deshpande (1989), "Situational Ethnicity and Consumer Behavior," *Journal of Consumer Research*, 16 (December), 361-371.

Stern, Barbara B. (1989), "Literary Criticism and Consumer Research: Overview and Illustrative Analysis," *Journal of Consumer Research*, 16 (December), 322-334.

_____ (1993), "Feminist Literary Criticism and the Deconstruction of Ads: A Postmodern View of Advertising and Consumer Responses," *Journal of Consumer Research*, 19(March), 556-566.

_____ (1994), "Classical and Vignette Television Advertising Dramas: Structural Models, Formal Analysis, and Consumer Effects," *Journal of Consumer Research*, 20(March), 601-615.

Whittler, Tommy E. (1989), "Viewers' Processing of Actor's Race and Message Claims in Advertising Stimuli," *Psychology and Marketing*, 6(4), 287-309.

Whittler, Tommy E. and Joan DiMeo (1991), "Viewers' Reactions to Racial Cues in Advertising Stimuli," *Journal of Advertising Research*, December, 37-46.

Understanding Altruism: Stories, Experiments, and Cross-Cultural Comparisons

Michal Strahilevitz, University of Miami

"How selfish soer man be supposed, there are evidently some principles in his nature, which interest him in the fortune of others, and render their happiness necessary to him, though he derives nothing from it, except the pleasure of seeing it."- *Adam Smith, The Theory of Moral Sentiments (1869), p.47*

"Feel good about yourself. Give blood!"- *Advertisement, The American Red Cross*

"It's a wonderful feeling to know that today many people are alive and some of them married and have their children, and that their children will have children because I did have the courage and the strength."- *Irene- A German gentile woman who was honored by Yad Va Shem for rescuing Jews in Nazi Europe. (Monroe, Barton, and Klingmann 1990).*

OVERVIEW

As the above quotes suggest, altruistic acts make those who perform them feel good. Indeed, altruism has been described as the consumption of "warm glow" (Andreoni 1989, 1990), the purchase of moral satisfaction (Kahneman and Knetsch 1992), and an act motivated by the desire for praise, appreciation and improved self esteem (Becker 1974). One way of thinking of altruism in the context of consumer behavior is to view those engaged in altruistic behavior as consumers of the various psychological benefits derived from "doing the right thing." Clearly, there is some sort of utility associated with acts of altruism. Otherwise, people would not behave altruistically. Regardless of whether altruists pay for this utility by donating cash, contributing their time, or risking their own welfare, something must be motivating them to perform their good deeds.

The papers presented in this special session offered a wide-range of approaches to studying altruism. Indeed, the methods used included cross-cultural comparisons, lab experiments, and qualitative analysis of children's stories. The three papers presented also investigated a diverse range of forms of altruism. The first paper investigated the time consuming, painful, and potentially dangerous act of donating bone marrow. Meanwhile, the second looked at financial contributions to a variety of charitable organizations. Finally, the third paper examined the personal sacrifices involved in the giving of birthday gifts. Surprisingly, many common threads were observed between the three papers— most notably that seemingly "altruistic" behavior appears to be motivated by a combination of both "egoistic" and truly "altruistic" motives.

SUMMARY OF THE PRESENTED PAPERS

The first paper was "Cultural Factors in the Decision to Donate Bone Marrow" by Richard P. Bagozzi, Kam-Hon Lee, and M. Frances Van Loo. This research examines why some people donate bone marrow while others do not. The explanatory framework is based on a theory of ethnicity which attempts to account for decisions as functions of differences in moral, ethical, normative, cognitive, and emotional responses. Data were collected from four cultural groups (Hong Kong Chinese, Chinese Americans, black Americans, and white Americans). All respondents were asked to express their psychological reactions to donating bone marrow for each of four targets: immediate family members, close relatives, ethnic strangers, and total strangers.

Main effects for culture were found such that the strongest psychological reactions in favor of donorship occurred for Hong Kong Chinese and Chinese Americans and the weakest in favor of donorship occurred for black and white Americans. However, as the authors pointed out, these findings must be interpreted in light of the significant interactions, where the largest impact for some reactions (e.g., desires, affective responses) occurred for immediate family members and close relatives while other reactions (e.g., evaluations, normative responses) occurred for strangers. Decisions were found to be functions of unique hedonic and utilitarian components of attitude, as well as emotional implications of normative pressures. Differences in family orientations accounted for the interactions noted above. Rather than being limited to nominal categories based on race, ethnicity was found to be characterized by a pattern of psychological, social, and behavioral responses.

The second paper was "Cause-Based versus Charity-Specific Satiation in Charitable Giving" by Michal Strahilevitz. This work examined the phenomenon of variety seeking both between specific charities (e.g., World Wild Life Fund, Green Peace, American Cancer Society) and between general cause categories (e.g., saving endangered animals, sponsoring needy children, funding medical research). The results suggest that allocation among multiple charities from multiple cause-categories can be affected by budget constraints, time elapsed between solicitations, presentation format, and whether or not subjects are asked to indicate a favorite cause-category before making their allocations decisions.

Specifically, it was demonstrated that both larger budgets and shorter time lapses between contributions increased variety seeking between charities, but only the latter had an effect on variety seeking between causes. As hypothesized, when individual charities were listed in a random order, variety seeking between cause-categories was significantly lower among subjects who had been asked to state their favorite cause. However, in the absence of asking subjects to state a favorite cause, variety seeking between causes was significantly greater when the charities were presented by cause-category rather than in a random order with no indication of cause category. The interaction between whether subjects were prompted to indicate a favorite cause-category and whether they were presented with the list of charities by cause category was significant. The results suggest that both variety seeking and loyalty can be influenced both at a general cause level and at a specific charity level. However, cause-based satiation and charity-specific satiation can respond very differently to the same combinations of external stimuli.

The third paper by Russell Belk and Kimberly Dodson was entitled "Lessons of Altruism and Egoism in Children's Stories." This paper was based on a qualitative analysis of 100+ contemporary children's' stories which involved birthday celebrations. The authors discussed how birthdays have become democratized celebrations of self among literate, urban, calendar-keeping societies. As is typical of this genre, the stories examined by the authors involved not only singular attention to the birthday person, but also occasions of both communal and familial support and the giving and receiving of gifts. It was noted that, for young children especially, birthdays are a time of avid material desire and anticipation. In both giving and receiving birthday gifts, children have a critical opportunity to learn about giving and getting. Like older fairy tales, these stories convey morals and often focus on selfishness and greed versus altruism and generosity. Thus children's birthday stories and the morals contained in them can be viewed as socialization vehicles.

One especially interesting observation in this research was that "bad" egoistic and materialistic behavior are seldom punished in the stories. Instead, happy endings are either created by a transformation of egoism into altruism or by allowing material rewards and self-indulgence to result from ostensibly altruistic acts. In other words, the honest, caring and generous character succeeds and thrives, while the unscrupulous, selfish, greedy character suffers and fails. This "you can have it all" message makes altruism an instrumental act, not its own reward.

In pursuing a deeper understanding of the moral messages in these birthday stories, the authors examined the roles of gender, age, time period (by decade), and the symbolic roles of sacrifice, obedience, greed, sharing, caring, individualism, wealth, surprise, magic, ritual, transformation, and growth. While there were nuances and subthemes detected in this finer analysis, the overall message of these children's books was found to be a conservative one— that altruistic acts are a means to self-gratification via a deus ex machina rewarding individualistic deservingness. The subtheme of altruism as its own reward was feminized by its depiction almost exclusively among females and older persons. The very young, very old, and impoverished are most commonly the recipients of such "true altruism." A second subtheme was that of communalism which involves a support system of family, friends, and community. But their largesse is also largely directed to those who are morally deserving. The authors concluded with an assessment of the implications of such lessons for altruism, egoism, and personal, political, and community relations.

SYNTHESIS

This session concluded with a great deal of graciousness on the part of our discussant, William Wells. Alas, due to there being so much interesting material to present in the three papers, we ran out of time. Wells had suggested right at the start of the session that it would be interesting to attempt to apply some of the lessons learned from the research to the task of raising funds for universities. In addressing this idea, several possibilities come to mind. The work by Bagozzi , Lee and Van Loo suggests that propensity to donate may be influenced by cultural background. Their findings also suggest that the more individuals feel like the university is part of their "family," the more likely they will be to contribute. Their results also indicate that the degree to which a sense of "university=family" influences donation behavior may be influenced by both the psychological make-up and the cultural background of the potential donors. The results of the Strahilevitz paper suggest that universities may be able to increase total donations by offering a variety of sub-causes that donated funds can be earmarked for (e.g., a new gym, student scholarships, medical research, a new building for the business school, etc.). Strahilevitz's research also suggests that the more money a potential donor has budgeted to charitable giving, the greater will be their need for variety. Furthermore, her results suggest that frequent requests for donations may in some cases result in lower total donations than more greatly spaced apart requests. Indeed, as Linville and Fischer's renewable resource theory (1991) suggests, longer time lapses between requests may give donors a chance to renew their ability to derive pleasure from the act of contributing to a specific cause. Finally, the work by Belk and Dodson suggests that many individuals, especially males, may have been socialized from a very early age to believe that giving more eventually leads to receiving more. Therefore, rather than just focusing on the idea of giving for the sake

of giving, universities may want to offer potential donors some sort of extrinsic rewards or "gifts" in exchange for their generous behavior. Indeed, the norm of reciprocity (Walster, Berscheid, and Walster 1973) suggests that those donors who receive a reward will be more likely to give again at a later date. Be it putting the donors' names on a new building, offering free tickets to both cultural and sporting events, or sending out ceramic mugs with the university's logo— it is likely that the money universities put into "reciprocating" may be a wise investment in future fund-raising potential.

REFERENCES

Andreoni, James (1989), "Giving with Impure Altruism– Applications to Charity and Ricardian Equivalence," *Journal of Political Economy*, 97 (December), 1447-1458.

_____ (1990), "Impure Altruism and Donations to Public Goods–A Theory of Warm-Glow Giving," *Economic Journal*, 100 (June), 464-477.

Kahneman, Daniel and Jack L. Knetsch (1992), "Valuing Public Goods: The Purchase of Moral Satisfaction," *Journal of Environmental Economics and Management*, 22, 57-70.

Linville, Patricia and Gregory Fischer (1991), "Preferences for Separating or Combining Events," *Journal of Personality and Social Psychology*, 60 (1), 5-23.

Walster, Elaine, Ellen Berscheid, and William G. Walster (1973), "New Directions in Equity Research," *Journal of Personality and Social Psychology*, 25, 2 (February), 151-76.

Lessons Of Altruism and Egoism in Children's Birthday Stories

Russell Belk, University of Utah
Kimberly Dodson, University of Utah

ABSTRACT

A popular category of American Children's books involves children celebrating their birthdays or the birthdays of friends or family members. Like older fairy tales, these stories convey morals and often focus on selfishness and greed versus altruism and generosity. However, in our analysis of contemporary stories, "bad" egoistic and materialistic behavior is seldom punished. Instead, happy endings are either created by a transformation of egoism into altruism or by allowing material rewards and self-indulgence to result from ostensibly altruistic acts. This "you can have it all" message makes altruism an instrumental act; not its own reward.

Stories, such as those of Aesop's Fables and Grimm's Fairy Tales, have long been used to convey moral lessons to children. Many of these stories attempt to valorize altruism and villainize egoism. It is the honest, caring, and generous character who succeeds and thrives, while the unscrupulous, selfish, and greedy character fails and suffers (e.g., Belk 1995; Gooderham 1993; Tetenbaum and Pearson 1989). At the same time, the successful children's tale relies not on didactic moralizing, but on the emotional power of magically and mysteriously dealing with deep questions such as identity and how life is to be lived (e.g., Bettelheim 1976, Winston 1994). A popular contemporary genre addressing issues of egoism and altruism is the children's birthday story. For young children especially, birthdays have become a time of avid material desire and anticipation. Birthdays provide a significant tableau against which contemporary morality plays may be enacted in both the actual celebration and in children's stories written about these celebrations. In offering and receiving birthday gifts, children have a critical opportunity to learn about giving and getting. Thus we turned to contemporary (largely post-1950) children's birthday stories to see what moral lessons are presented in these socialization vehicles.

CHILDREN'S BIRTHDAYS

Children's birthdays have not always been occasions for parental indulgence or even for celebration. While the ancient Persians, Egyptians, Greeks, and Romans celebrated birthdays, such celebrations were primarily restricted to adult males of high rank (Linton and Linton 1952). The early Christian church found individual birthday celebrations to be too egoistic and materially indulgent; it sought to substitute instead celebrations of the death days of Christian martyrs (Lewis 1976). For the first 1500 years of Christianity, church opposition combined with general illiteracy to eliminate birthday celebrations or even recognition of dates of birth (Lewis 1976). In Medieval Europe, children's birthday celebrations were absent as children were not considered unique people to be attended and indulged. Only in the Sixteenth Century was childhood beginning to be recognized as a formative period deserving special attention (Aries 1962). Still, in Nineteenth Century Great Britain and America, there was concern that excessive attention to children might make them self-indulgent rather than generous and caring people (Lewis 1976). Birthdays were celebrated, but restraint and modesty were considered essential.

In the Twentieth Century however, restraint and modesty seem to have given way to indulgence and celebration of the birthday child as a "king" or "queen" for the day (Dodson and Belk 1996b). Birthday cards directed to children emerged in the early 1900s (Chase 1927), and the first half of the century has been labeled the "Golden Age" of childhood and children's literature (Goldstone 1986). Goldstone's (1986) analysis of children's literature concludes that starting with the baby boom and the 1950s, these stories depict childhood less as a time of hope, innocence, and magic, and more as a training ground for learning about the world and preparing to assume adult responsibilities. While this may be true of children's stories generally, birthday stories continue to depict one of the few occasions where the child's desires are encouraged and indulged. It is therefore worth considering the general meanings that surround the contemporary American child's birthday which is the focus of our analysis.

Birthdays have become democratized celebrations across social classes in literate, urban, calendar-keeping societies. As detailed by Dodson and Belk (1996a, 1996b), contemporary American birthday celebrations appear to serve four important functions for the birthday person. First, they are perhaps the key rite of passage in our society. As Chudacoff (1989) demonstrates, the Twentieth Century in America has been a time of increased attention to age-grading in education, parenting, advertising, medicine, law, and the popular press. This is especially true for the childhood years, and childrens' birthday celebrations help in marking and adapting to biological as well as socially expected age-related changes. In this sense, birthdays are a celebration of life progression (Humphrey 1988). Milestone birthdays in American society include those preceding major life changes such as entering school and entering puberty, and help precipitate and prepare the child for these major changes. Through gifts and other ritual elements, we help convey what is deemed appropriate behavior in each new life cycle stage. Gender roles, play roles, work roles, and family roles are all potentially encoded and shaped for the birthday recipient.

A second function of birthdays in western cultures is individuation. Birthday celebrations are the primary American celebration of the individual and serve to convey and reinforce a sense of uniqueness and personal value. Through the celebration, attention, deference, and license granted to the birthday person (e.g., indulging material and other wishes and lifting food taboos), the birthday person is made to feel special and worthy. Individuation generally seems to correspond more to the male conception of a separate/objective self that relates to others in terms of reciprocity between distinct individuals (Lyons 1983).

In spite of the individuating function of birthday celebrations, a third function of the birthday occasion is to provide a sense of group membership. The attentions of the celebrants helps to assure the birthday person of continuity and support (Rosenthal and Marshall 1988). This is especially the case with children's birthdays, where family and communal support and recognition help children to know they are not alone or unloved, but rather a part of a family and community of friends who demonstrate their connection and care this one time each year. Next to Christmas, birthdays are the most widely celebrated family ritual in the United States. While we and the world around us may change, the yearly birthday ritual provides a stabilizing sense of continuity and support in our lives. The communal function of birthdays seems to correspond more to the female conception of a connected self that relates to others in terms of care and concern for their well-being (Lyons 1983).

A final function of the birthday celebration involves the material and non-material gift transfers made. One of the goals of the perfect gift is to provide pleasure and delight to the birthday person (Belk 1996). Thus, birthday gifts ideally respond to the needs, wants, wishes, and desires of the recipient. Significant for the present analysis, this forum provides a critical arena in which material values and behavior patterns are implicitly taught. This includes patterns and concepts of egoism and altruism, delayed and deferred gratifications, selfishness and generosity, gratitude and ingratitude, earned and unearned reward, expectation and satisfaction, delight and disappointment, and anticipation and surprise. The opportunity for learning material values is critically focused on this one day each year, as birthdays involve the one time when children's wishes and fantasies are encouraged and often fulfilled by well-wishing family members and friends.

It is worth noting that the birthdays of friends and family members provide a different sort of socialization opportunity for children who are called upon to be givers rather than receivers and celebrants rather than celebrities. Just as the birthday person is assured that he or she is a loved and valued family member, others' birthdays provide opportunities for the child to demonstrate his or her care for someone else. Participation in others' birthdays also provide a means of incorporating a child into the community. Children not invited to another child's birthday party are likely to feel left-out rather than a part of a loving community of mutually supportive friends.

An additional function of a child's birthday for the celebrants is that of emersion in a reciprocal birthday celebratory cycle. The child who is invited to another child's birthday party is generally expected to reciprocate when his or her own birthday occurs. Reciprocity in terms of staging a party and providing gifts may be less expected of children toward adults due to age and wealth inequalities, but a part of the socialization process involves gradually accepting this reciprocal obligation toward older family members and friends as well. The notion of reciprocity may, however, operate more within a male conception of self as autonomous individuals rather than as interconnected through an ethos of care (Gilligan 1982, Kohlberg 1981, Lyons 1983).

Just as there are material lessons to be learned and enacted as a recipient of birthday gifts and well wishes, so there are material lessons to be learned and enacted as a giver of gifts to someone on his or her birthday. Participation in birthday rituals provides an opportunity to demonstrate real or feigned altruism, generosity, and sensitivity to the birthday person's wishes and desires. For the child giver, this may require putting aside selfish egoistic interests and learning to be a gracious giver. To do so seems to require taking the perspective of the recipient. Here, too, there are important social values that may be encoded and learned with the aid of reinforcement from the birthday child and from those adults who are present. Otnes and McGrath (1994) found that these lessons are better learned by girls than boys, at least among three- to five-year-old children. This is consistent with findings in other gift-giving contexts that a disproportionate portion of the responsibility for choosing gifts and staging celebrations inevitably falls on women (e.g., Cheal 1988; Fischer and Arnold 1990; Wallendorf and Arnould 1991). In addition to gender, culture, age, and social class may also be important sources of difference in the lessons of material values involving egoism and altruism in the context of children's birthday celebrations.

Thus, whether as giver or receiver of birthday gifts and well wishes, children regularly encounter critical opportunities to learn material values and behavioral patterns in birthday celebrations. Besides the events themselves, children's stories about such events provide important socialization vehicles. We found that there was a rapid growth in children's birthday stories since the 1950s, and these stories form the major text for our analysis.

METHODS

We gathered all American children's birthday stories we could locate, but did not attempt to be exhaustive. We excluded non-fiction, stories intended for adults, and non-American stories. The 99 stories used for our qualitative analysis were distributed as follows by year of publication: 1930s, 2; 1950s, 1; 1960s, 11; 1970s, 8; 1980s, 47; and 1990s, 30. The stories were most commonly targeted to preschool and elementary school aged children. In these stories, 41 of the focal characters were female and 65 were male (in some cases as with animal characters gender was not evident; in other cases both male and female focal characters were highlighted). There were biases in these stories toward depicting white, middle-class, two-parent, suburban families, although each of these biases lessened in more recent materials. Of the 99 stories, 69 were written by women. However, as in a study by Tetenbaum and Pearson (1962), we did not find a systematic pattern of differences based on the gender of the story authors.

The birthday stories vary, but they most often involve a birthday party celebrated in the home of the child having the birthday. Less frequently, a non-focal child or an adult is the birthday person and the focal child or children are gift-givers. The settings and artifacts depicted in the birthday celebrations are highly consistent. There is a birthday cake with candles, ice cream and other treats, wrapped gifts, party hats and decorations, party games, and party favors for guests.

Our analysis was based on a close reading of written material as well as the nearly ubiquitous illustrations in these stories. Each author analyzed a portion of the stories with coordination through a series of discussions and re-examinations of the material. In this collaborative, iterative process, two primary opposing themes emerged: the ideal/altruistic and the pragmatic/egoistic. The tension between these two visions of birthday celebrations runs through the majority of stories, often forming the central motivating drama in the tale. We present results within each of these themes below and discuss their resolution in the tales.

RESULTS

Ideal/Altruistic Elements

Perhaps the ideal story of altruistic giving is the Christmas gift-giving of the young married couple Della and Jim in O. Henry's "The Gift of the Magi" (Porter 1922). The story, in which Della cuts and sells her beautiful hair to buy Jim a platinum watch chain, and Jim sells his treasured watch to buy Della tortoise shell combs for her hair, illustrates each of the six characteristics that Belk (1996a) sees as characteristic of the perfect gift: (1) The giver makes an extraordinary sacrifice; (2) The giver wishes solely to please the recipient; (3) The gift is a luxury; (4) The gift is something uniquely appropriate for the recipient; (5) The recipient is surprised by the gift; and (6) The recipient desires the gift and is delighted by it.

In stories in which children are gift-givers to another child or adult, there are several examples that come close to this ideal. In one such story, after hearing an older woman next door speak wistfully of visiting China, Alexis digs a hole in her backyard and goes there herself. While in China she buys a postcard for the neighbor's birthday and returns with this gift, much to the woman's delight. In another story, seven-year-old Daniel decides to give his sister a "half-birthday party" to celebrate her first six months. He decorates, makes treats, invites guests, and coordinates the party. The guests do everything in halves and Daniel's gift to his sister is the half-moon outside. As these stories illustrate, both boys and girls are shown to exhibit such altruistic and ideal giving, but such stories most often feature girls as the thoughtful, caring, and altruistic givers.

One story clearly offers the lessons of the perfect gift and altruistic giving. After hearing his friends wish for a "magical tool" to do their work for them on their birthday, William (an adult cooper) decides to act as the "magical tool." During the early morning hours of each of his friends' birthdays, he sneaks into their businesses and secretly fulfills their wishes. When each man is surprised by the "magic," William does not claim his part in it, and instead reflects on how happy his friends are and how much pleasure he gets from making them happy. In the end, William himself is visited by a "magical fairy" on his birthday and finds his wishes fulfilled. This story shows the emotional and sometimes tangible rewards for giving a gift solely to please the recipient and not with thought of personal gain. In the various stories, such a gift is never received with ingratitude, so there is a message that altruistic giving brings feelings of self-satisfaction by bringing delight to a loved one.

Given the modest material resources of children, the perfect gift may not be a luxury by the recipient's standards, but it ideally involves a sacrifice that shows loving concern of the child giver. This sacrifice is often depicted financially. Many stories show the child completely emptying his or her piggy bank in order to buy a gift. In one example of this "spare no expense" ethos, Bear dumps all of the money out of his piggy bank in order to buy Moon a new hat. Interestingly, the child's "savings" are often not enough for the gift, which necessitates an additional sacrifice on the part of the child. The child must give of him or herself in some way, supporting Ralph Waldo Emerson's (1983) credo that, "The only gift is a portion of thyself." Thus, 5-year-old John John is unable to afford the Muumuu or lei that his mother would like, so he makes a lei himself by stringing yellow flowers on a vine. Similarly, Snipp, Snapp, and Snurr are unable to find enough money to buy their mother red shoes for her birthday, so they find ways to earn the money. In one story, the sacrifice is intensified when five sheep shop for a gift for their friend and their piggy bank does not provide adequate funds. So they shear themselves and trade their wool (literally a piece of themselves) for the gift. And Little Pig is unable to decide on the perfect gift for his mother, so he ties a ribbon around his head. In response, Little Pig's mother says, "This is the best present you could possibly have given me. There's nothing in the world I'd rather have" (Gray 1990, p. 24).

The maxim that it's the thought that counts is also evident in these stories, such that even when gifts go wrong they still bring delight to the recipient. For instance, when Little Fox mistakenly believes that it is his mother's birthday and attempts to bake her a cake, he makes a mess in the kitchen. But learning what he has tried to do, his mother gives him a loving hug and he earns the respect of his father and siblings. In some instances, the child gives a gift that is a luxurious treat perfectly suited to the birthday recipient, as when young Martha gives his favorite Swedish tobacco and a handmade card with raised letters to her Swedish grandfather who is blind and living in a nursing home. But more often the child giver's sincerity, sacrifice, and limited resources seem to excuse the modesty of their gifts. This is seen, for example, in a story in which a six-year-old black girl goes by bus with her unemployed father to purchase a flat of annual flowers for her working mother. The success of this gift is evident in her mother's delight when she sees the flowers in the planter in the window of their apartment.

If there is little moral conflict in tales such as these, it is because the recipient is made to seem especially deserving, whether it is a hard-working mother, a blind old grandfather who misses his homeland, or a kind neighbor woman. The implicit message is that

we should express love toward those who are themselves good, kind, sympathetic people. Johnson (1996) finds a similar tactic used in certain children's animal stories in order to evoke sympathetic attitudes and actions toward these animals. In stories where children's fervent birthday wishes are gratified by adults who must sacrifice in order to do so, the child generally is also made to appear clearly deserving. For example, when Chris longs for a bike like his friends Miles' for his twelfth birthday, he realizes that his out-of-work-father can ill-afford to give it to him. He nevertheless uses his talent at wood carving to make gifts for others for Kwanzaa. When his relatives all pool their money to get him the longed-for bike, he not only takes a job delivering papers with the bike, but also arranges for his father to take over as newspaper route manager. He mistakenly comes to believe that his father needs to post a $300 bond to get the job, and is willing to give up his loved bicycle to obtain the money. His deservingness of the bicycle under these circumstances is made almost melodramatically evident. Such deservingness bases for acting benevolently toward someone do not convey strong messages of altruism however. They suggest instead a morality based on justice and rights rather than a morality based on care and concern for others (Tetenbaum and Pearson 1989—c.f. Kohlberg 1981 and Gilligan 1982). Ironically it is in some of the stories involving elements of egoism where the stronger moral messages about altruism may be found.

Pragmatic and Egoistic Departures from the Altruistic Ideal

There are several major types of departures from the altruistic ideal of the perfect gift in these stories. One variant, especially common among adult male characters, is an emphasis on pragmatism over what is depicted as sentimental idealism. In one story, a father sends his 14-year-old daughter to learn what his wife really wants for her birthday because his past gifts to her have been failures. He learns that what she truly desires is a magical cake that her mother used to bake for her. After dismissing it as impractical because his wife is always dieting, he suggests that they order it from a bakery. When his daughter explains that a magical cake can't be purchased so easily, he becomes frustrated and gets his wife a bathrobe. The daughter perseveres in baking the cake and succeeds in recreating the magical recipe. Similarly, when Jasper is asked by his father what he wants for his upcoming seventh birthday, his father also admonishes him to be certain it is something practical. He quickly dismisses Jasper's wish that he could drive a horse and buggy around Central Park by the light of the moon and serenade a beautiful princess. The father suggests something more practical like a bicycle or summer camp, and eventually buys Jasper a wooden rocking horse. As in several other of the birthday stories, the horse magically comes alive and helps Jasper fulfill his fantasies. The polarities here are consistent and revealing. Children, and to a lesser degree women, live in a world of fantasy that depends on sustaining magical belief in the face of adult male pressures to "grow up" and become rational and practical. As with Peter Pan who refuses to grow up and Dorothy and her magical shoes, belief in fantastic wishes transcends the pragmatic bounds of rationality that threatens the magical world of children's fantasies as well as the ideal of altruism.

Another threat to the ideal of altruism, also depicted most commonly among males, is a tendency toward egoism, selfishness, and greed. In one alliterative story entitled *The Birthday Burglar*, Bassington has been abandoned by his wealthy parents to the care of Baker the Butler. Feeling he needs a special day and learning that he cannot buy one, the boy proceeds to steal birthdays from others. He is eventually discovered and made to return the birthday trimmings and gifts. A more prosocial message is attempted in a tale in which Peter teaches his younger brother Davy that they must get their mother something she would like for her birthday rather than only things they would like. Nevertheless, Davy spends all of their money on a pinwheel he likes and they are able to salvage a well-received gift only by creatively turning it into part of a "birthday tree" gift for mother. In a similar story, a four-year-old is invited to his friend Maria's birthday party. When shopping with his mother, the boy selects gifts that are all things he likes. In response, his mother helps him select a gift (a blue ball with yellow polka dots) that Maria will like and it turns out to be just what she wanted. In stories such as these, selfish egoism is presented as the natural state that must be overcome by learning proper expected gift-giving behaviors.

A related theme in several stories is the depiction of children at birthday parties (again especially boys) as real or metaphoric "monsters." In one of the literal stories of this sort, Muck the monster goes to a fellow monster child's birthday party only to be disgusted by the other guests' and guest-of-honor's behavior in pouring punch on each other, throwing birthday cake, butting heads, jumping on beds, and throwing dirt. Hiding from the chaos, he meets a lizard and the two of them go to Muck's house where they enjoy peanut butter sandwiches and milk. In stories such as this, selfish egoism is portrayed as the natural state of boys and as something they must learn to overcome. There are exceptions (including some noted above) in which boys are caring and altruistic, but there are few tales in which girls are shown as innately selfish.

An exception, and another type of threat to the ideal of altruism, involves sibling rivalry. Because the birthday of a sibling takes attention away from non-birthday children in the family and gives it, as well as numerous treats and delights, to the sibling, both boys and girls are shown to suffer from envy. In one story, Sister Bear becomes a "green-eyed monster" when she eyes Brother Bear's new bicycle and becomes envious. She is unwilling to repress her envy and accept that the new bike is just too big for her, until she has a nightmare in which she wrecks the new bike. At the end of the story, Father Bear begins to feel envy for his friend's new car, and after a gentle reminder from Sister Bear to watch out for the "green-eyed monster," he congratulates his friend and the story ends happily. In many of the sibling rivalry stories, the sibling relationship is shown to be stronger than the envy, and sometimes the joy of giving is able to overcome the envy. However, in other stories, the tension is eased only by a reciprocal promise that everyone must get their turn at being special on their birthday and that the focal character will have his or her chance as well.

The sibling rivalry theme in birthday stories is also seen in stories of twins or triplets who share the same birthday. A common element in these stories is striving for individual recognition rather than being perceived as part of a set of identical siblings. Besides convincing others to respect them as individuals, these stories also sometimes are about learning to share. Thus, the triplets Cleo, Mirabelle, and Gertrude repeatedly learn that when they all want the same thing, they all lose as a result. But after they learn that they must share in order to have a pet dog, they find that sharing brings the best results. As a negative example, the story of Snyder Spider involves his running away on his birthday only to be captured by one of the twin sister "kangapuses," who sings to her sister:

Oh, I got it [a captured Snyder], you want it, but it belongs to me!; You won't forget it and you won't admit it,; But you're jealous as can be!; You're jealous of my face, you're jealous of my grace,; You're jealous of my smile, you're jealous of my style,; You're jealous of my hospitality!; You're jealous of my feet, you're jealous that I'm sweet,' You're jealous of everything I do!; Well, you fight and fuss, you old kangapus; But I'm not jealous of you! Yeah, I got it, you want it, but it belongs to me!; If you ever get it, you won't regret it,; But you ain't gonna get it from me! (Bach 1986, p. 10).

Here too, Snyder learns from these bad examples. The Kangapuses are two of the many "bad" forest creatures who are not invited to his birthday party. Snyder Spider returns to his surprise birthday party as a more grateful and less jealous spider.

The triplet story also involves a common plot element of wanting a pet for a birthday. Usually these stories provide dramatic tension through some element that seemingly precludes having the pet, only to overcome the obstacle and achieve a happy ending. The common childhood desire for a pet can be read in several very different ways. One reading is that pets provide another being to care for and teach nurturance, responsibility, and care-giving to the child. In a number of the stories involving birthday pets this is made explicit as the child agrees to accept responsibility in exchange for the joys of owning a pet. A very different reading of some of the same pet acquisition stories is that the child seeks and acquires an animal that they will be able to dominate in much the same manner that their parents dominate them. Johnson (1996) describes this as "a dream where prestige and power will accompany the ecstasy of possessing another creature" (p. 7). A third take on the child-pet animal relationship is that the animal provides a mirror through which the child is able to projectively see him or herself. As Fiedler (1978) has observed, children may wonder "whether they are beasts or men: little animals more like their pets than their parents" (p. 28). And Bataille (1993) suggests that children are "animals becoming human" (p. 65). There is also an aspect of extended self in pet ownership, in that many pets extend the range of what the child is able to do, as expressed most dramatically in magical birthday stories in which a toy horse comes alive and takes its owner away to adventures. This is a very different type of egoistic involvement with pets than either the care-giving or possessive interpretations. It appears to us that each of these interpretations of the desire for a birthday pet are plausible for at least some of the stories (see also Belk 1996b). No doubt this multivocality in the meanings of pet ownership extends beyond the birthday context examined here, but in the present context, the focus on desire for a pet draws the greatest attention to the acquisitive and possessive aspects of wishing for pets. Only in two stories concerning pets (of more than a dozen) do we see a primary focus on care-giving.

A final egoistic theme in the children's birthday stories analyzed involves fulfilled and unfulfilled wants, wishes, and desires. In one variant of these stories noted above, the wish is blocked by some impediment that is overcome to result in a happy ending of wish fulfillment. In these stories the intensity and fervency of the wish is often stressed, including the Kwanzaa-related birthday story noted earlier in which Chris prays for the bike he so strongly desires. Often, as in Chris's case, wish fulfillment is accompanied by deservingness. In a second variant, magical surprises fulfill a child's unspoken wishes—another characteristic of the perfect gift (Belk 1996a). Inevitably in such stories, the child reflects that this was the best birthday ever. But a third variant of the wish stories is the unfulfilled wish. Thus Billy, who longs for a bike like his friend Carlos gets for his birthday, learns that his single mother cannot afford it. In this case Billy's brother builds him a soap box racer that he uses to win the non-bike race in the park. In another story, eight-year old Treehorn longs for a television and other fantastic birthday gifts only to have his pragmatic father and shopaholic mother give him a sweater just like the one he has outgrown since his last birthday. When he finds a magic lamp and a genie who grants him three wishes, he wishes only for a birthday cake, candles, and his name on the cake. Still a final undisclosed wish as he blows out the candles leaves open the possibility of a happier future outcome. And when Hannah, who loves gorillas, finds that her father is always too busy to take her to the zoo, the toy gorilla that she gets for her birthday comes alive, dons a hat, coat, and bow tie, and takes her to the zoo as well as dancing on the lawn. When she awakes the next day, the gorilla is a toy again and her father takes her to the zoo. These stories, together with a number of stories in which the child fears that his or her birthday will be forgotten, suggest equating gifts with love. To worry that wishes will be unattended is not simply a matter of egoism, it reveals a deeper anxiety that the child is not loved. Nevertheless, the happy endings of almost all of the stories provide hope that parents love their children altruistically and unconditionally.

CONCLUSION

The resolution of the tension between egoism and altruism in children's birthday stories makes altruism the victor, but less because it is itself more rewarding than because it leads to better material rewards for the altruist. Most often a way is found through which a child can be both altruistic and egoistic. Commonly this is through a test or demonstration of humility, generosity of spirit, or other altruistic acts of deservingness, which culminate in getting what the child wants. That is, unlike many of the older fairy tales, these contemporary tales have happy endings suggesting that the child can have their wishes granted if they are good enough. One way to be "good" is by behaving generously and graciously toward others. In pursuing a deeper understanding of the moral messages in these birthday stories, we found that girls and older children show more sacrifice, sharing, and caring, and less greed, individualism, and egoism to be overcome. The idea that altruism is its own reward is feminized by its depiction almost exclusively among females and older persons. The very young, very old, and impoverished are most commonly the recipients of such "true altruism." A more universal ideal is that of communal support for birthdays involving a system of family, friends, and community. But their largesse is also largely directed to those who are morally deserving. Thus the overall message about altruism these children's books is that altruistic acts are a means to self-gratification via a *deus ex machina* rewarding individualistic deservingness.

REFERENCES

Aries, Phillipe (1962), *Centuries of Childhood*, Robert Baldick, trans., London: Jonathon Cape.

Bach, Othello (1986), *Snyder Spider's Birthday Surprise*, New York: Caedmon.

Bataille, Georges (1993), *The Accursed Share: An Essay on General Economy, Vols. II and III*, New York: Zone Books (Originally *L'Histoire de l'Éroticism et la Souseraineté*, in Georges Bataille, *Oeuvres Complétes*, vol. 8, 1976, Editions Gallimard).

Belk, Russell W. (1995), "Awards, Rewards, Prizes, and Punishments," *Advances in Consumer Research*, vol. 22, Frank Kardes and Mita Sujan, eds., Provo, UT, 9-15.

Belk, Russell W. (1996a), "The Perfect Gift," in *Gift Giving: A Research Anthology*, Cele Otnes and Richard F. Beltramini, eds., Bowling Green, OH: Bowling Green State University Popular Press, 59-84.

Belk, Russell W. (1996b), "Metaphoric Relationships with Pets," *Animals and Society*, 4 (2), 121-145.

Bettelheim, Bruno (1976), *The Users of Enchantment: The Meaning and Importance of Fairy Tales*, New York: Alfred A. Knopf.

Chase, Ernest Dudley (1927), *The Romance of Greeting Cards*, Cambridge, MA: University Press (reprinted 1971, Detroit: Tower Books).

Cheal, David (1988), *The Gift Economy*, London: Routledge.

Chudacoff, Howard P. (1927), *How Old Are You? Age Consciousness in American Culture*, Princeton, NJ: Princeton University Press.

Dodson, Kimberly J. and Russell W. Belk (1996a), "The Birthday Card Minefield," *Advances in Consumer Research*, Vol. 23, Kim P. Korfman and John G. Lynch, eds., Provo, UT: Association for Consumer Research 14-20.

Dodson, Kimberly J. and Russell W. Belk (1996b), "Gender in Children's Birthday Stories," *Gender, Marketing and Consumer Behavior: Third Conference Proceedings*, Janeen Arnold Costa, ed., Salt Lake City, UT: University of Utah Printing Service, 96-108.

Emerson, Ralph Waldo (1983), "Gifts," *The Collected Works of Ralph Waldo Emerson*, Alfred R. Fergusson, ed., Cambridge, MA: Belknap Press, 91-96.

Fiedler, Leslie (1978), *Freaks: Myths and Images of the Secret Self*, New York: Simon and Schuster.

Fischer, Eileen and Stephen J. Arnold (1990), "More than a Labor of Love: Gender Roles and Christmas Gift Shopping," *Journal of Consumer Research*, 17 (December), 333-345.

Gilligan, Carol (1982), *In a Different Voice*, Cambridge, MA: Harvard University Press.

Goldstone, Bette P. (1986), "Views of Childhood in Children's Literature Over Time," *Language Arts*, 63, 791-798.

Gooderham, David (1993), "Still Catching Them Young? The Moral Dimension in Young Children's Books," *Children's Literature in Education*, 24, 115-122.

Gray, Nigel (1990), *Little Pig's Tale*, New York: Macmillan Publishing Company.

Humphrey, Theodore C. (1988), "A Family Celebrates a Birthday: Of Life and Cakes," in Theodore Humphrey and Lin T. Humphrey, eds., *"We Gather Together": Food and Festival in American Life*, Ann Arbor, MI: UMI Research Press, 19-26.

Johnson, Kathleen R. (1996), "The Ambiguous Terrain of Petkeeping in Children's Realistic Animal Stories," *Society and Animals*, 4 (1), 1-17.

Kohlberg, Lawrence (1981), *The Philosophy of Moral Development: Moral Stages and the Idea of Justice*, San Francisco: Harper & Row.

Lewis, Linda Rannells (1976), *Birthdays: Their Delights, Disappointments, Past and Present, Worldly, Astrological, and Infamous*, Boston: Little, Brown.

Linton, Ralph and Adelin Linton (1952), *The Lore of Birthdays*, New York: Henry Schuman.

Lyons, Nona P. (1983), "Two Perspectives: On Self, Relationships, and Morality," *Harvard Educational Review*. 53. 125-145.

Otnes, Cele and Mary Ann McGrath (1994), "Ritual Socialization and the Children's Birthday Party: The Early Emergence of Gender Differences," *Journal of Ritual Studies*, 8 (Winter), 74-93.

Porter, William Sydney (O. Henry) (1922), "The Gift of the Magi," *The Four Million*, New York: Doubleday, 16-25.

Rosenthal, Carolyn and Victor Marshall (1988), "Generational Transmission of Family Ritual," *American Behavioral Scientist*, 31, 669-684.

Tetenbaum, Toby Jane and Judith Pearson (1989), "The Voices in Children's Literature: The Impact of Gender on the Moral Decisions of Storybook Characters," *Sex Roles*, 20, 381-395.

Wallendorf, Melanie and Eric Arnould (1991), "'We Gather Together': Consumption Rituals of Thanksgiving Day," *Journal of Consumer Research*, 18 (March), 13-31.

Winston, Joe (1994), "Revising the Fairy Tale Through Magic: Antonia Barber's *The Enchanter's Daughter*," *Children's Literature in Education*, 25 (June), 101-111.

Extending Measures of Advertising Effectiveness: Ads' Effects on Price Sensitivity

Ronald C. Goodstein, Indiana University

Behavioral research on advertising effectiveness has typically been measured in terms of recall, attitudes, and purchase intentions. While these measures are vital determinants of an ad's effects, they fail to incorporate a key economic measure, namely the influence of advertising on price sensitivity. Economists offer two different arguments on the relationship between advertising and price sensitivity. If ads simply associate brands, then they argue that advertising is simply a form of information about market alternatives (Nelson 1974). As such, it would serve to raise price sensitivity in the marketplace (Mitra and Lynch 1995). Much advertising, however, works to differentiate one product from others in the category. This form of advertising provides market power to the brand and decreases the price elasticity of demand (e.g., Comanor and Wilson 1979). Thus the brand builds equity as evidenced by the ability to demand a premium price in the marketplace (Aaker 1991).

Instead of trying to address whether advertising provides market power or information, the set of papers presented in this session assumes that advertising has the ability to do either depending upon the content of the ad. That is, there are certain types of advertisements that are intended to provide information and others that are meant to differentiate brands and build equity. However, the research presented goes beyond this traditional perspective to investigate the contingencies existing toward these economic predictions.

The paper by Mitra and Lynch, for instance, suggests that the effects of advertising on consumer price elasticity and prices paid depends on the degree to which the choice situation requires brands to be recalled in order to be considered. They find that when the choice context forces consumers to recall ads from memory, then the ads serve to increase price elasticity. However, when brand names are available in the choice context, advertising serves to lower elasticity, indicating that the ads differentiate the brands. Goodstein and Kalra illustrate the classic effects of advertising positioning on price sensitivity. Specifically, holding ad content constant, they find that relative to feature-based positioning (Aaker 1991), value positioning increases both brand and category price sensitivity, while unique attribute positioning decreases both. Minor brand versus premium brand positioning serves to decrease brand price sensitivity, but increase category-level sensitivity. Finally, premium versus premium brand positioning lowers both brand and category sensitivity.

Mela, Gupta, and Lehmann then examine the relative effectiveness of advertising versus promotions on price elasticity depending on the time frame used to investigate these effects. Using data from a proprietary consumer panel incorporating eight years of weekly observations, they show that while promotions increase purchases over the short-run, they negatively affect elasticity over the long haul. This counters earlier predictions (e.g., Davis, Inman, and McAlister 1992) stating that promotions have no "bad" long-term effects. Their data concerning advertising are more encouraging. Advertising may have less of an effect on sales, relative to promotions, in the short-run. However, the long-term effects of advertising are to increase brand equity as evidence by a decrease in price elasticity over this time horizon.

Thus this session serves to take us "beyond the box" of what we currently know about the relationship between advertising and price sensitivity. The session uses both experimental and panel-based methodologies to explore these issues. Further, the session

illuminates several important and rather common contingencies affecting this relationship. Our discussant, Steve Hoch, highlighted the important contributions of this research and suggested other contingencies that should be examined to test the boundaries of the economic models. Further, Steve worked with the authors and audience to develop an agenda for future research in this area, focusing on interesting ways to combine economic and behavioral methodologies to gain additional insights into this stream of research.

On the Connection Between Advertising Effects on Price Elasticity and Consumer Welfare

Anusree Mitra, American University
John G. Lynch, University of Florida

Two competing research streams in economics have postulated divergent theoretical accounts and have made conflicting predictions about the economic and welfare effects of advertising. The first model emphasizes the ability of advertising to "artificially" differentiate products, which lowers the price elasticity and makes consumers unwilling to switch from their favorite brands to cheaper alternatives. The second model stresses that advertising provides information about alternatives and actually increases price elasticity and lowers prices paid. This research contributes to the debate on the economic effects of advertising by identifying the two conflicting perspectives as parts of a generalized theoretical model of advertising effects on price elasticity at the level of the individual consumer. Results of an experiment conducted to test theoretical predictions based on our model showed that the effects of advertising on consumer price elasticity and prices paid depends on the degree to which the choice situation requires brands to be recalled in order to be considered. In accordance with our theoretical predictions, in this study we found support for both the schools of thought (Mitra and Lynch 1995).

In a second study, we focused on the effects of advertising on consumer welfare. In Experiment 1 we had observed that when the effects of advertising on brand name recall for consideration set formation were superfluous, advertising decreased price elasticity and increased purchase prices. The market power view would argue that this occurred because advertising leads consumers to value and therefore pay a premium for differentiating attributes that would otherwise be seen as trivial; therefore, advertising has detrimental effects on consumer welfare. On the other hand, information economists contend that even if advertising and reduces price sensitivity and increases prices paid, consumers may nonetheless be better off. Rosen (1978) argues that advertising helps match brands and consumers in the presence of dispersion of the product attributes among brands and heterogeneity of preferences among consumers. Stated differently, attribute information in advertising allows consumers to concentrate search efforts on their most preferred brands and thereby enables consumers to choose brands that more closely reflect their personal tastes than would be true without advertising.

In Experiment 2, we examined the effect of advertising on consumers' ability to choose in line with their personal tastes by closely replicating two conditions out of the six cells from Experiment 1. Subjects either saw no advertising or differentiating advertising, and then made choices. Our results suggest that advertising need not always have detrimental effects on consumer welfare as predicted by the market power view. In conditions nearly identical to those in Experiment 1 that showed differentiating ads decreased price sensitivity and increased prices paid, we showed that these ads provided useful information that allows consumers to make choices more in line with their personal tastes than would be possible without advertising (Mitra and Lynch 1996). Taken together, these experiments enabled us to develop new insights into the informative versus persuasive roles of advertising that have been central to the debate in the economics literature.

The Impact of Advertising Positioning Strategies on Consumer Price Sensitivity

Ronald C. Goodstein, Indiana University
Ajay Kalra, Carnegie-Mellon University

Recent criticism argues that much of today's advertising fails to differentiate the brands available to the consumer (e.g., Achenbaum 1992). In fact, many ads associate brands as being more alike than distinctive (Pechmann and Ratneshwar 1991). Other advertising, however, works by providing pricing information (e.g., Popkowski Leszczyc and Rao 1990) or by differentiating brands in the market (e.g., Comanor and Wilson 1979). We believe, like others, that these different advertising strategies affect the brand and market in very different ways, even though the ads may contain the same factual information (Kaul and Wittink 1995; Mitra and Lynch 1995). For instance, the predicted effects on price sensitivity are conceptualized to be that price-oriented and non-differentiating advertising increases sensitivity, while differentiating ads reduce sensitivity (e.g., Bolton 1989; Popkowski Leszczyc and Rao 1990). To date, the limited empirical support for this conjecture has been criticized as being open to other interpretations (Mitra and Lynch 1995). While aggregate data have been used to study these effects, little experimental research has examined individual-level reactions to different types of advertising positioning on the price sensitivity of demand. We believe that this type of experimentation provides opportunities for examining micro-level ad differences that may be obscured by aggregate level data collection (i.e., scanners) and analyses.

This research is similar in spirit to others examining the impact of ad strategies on price sensitivity (e.g., Krishnamurthi and Raj 1985; Mitra and Lynch 1995) with several notable exceptions. First, we present a conceptual model that differentiates between information-based and power-based positioning strategies and test their effects on price sensitivity. Specifically, we test how different ad positioning tactics affect price sensitivity using a variety of measurements. The positioning tactics examined differ in terms of their highlighting price versus non-price attributes (though the ad information is constant across conditions), and in terms of how many brands in the competitive set contain the highlighted attribute (one in the case of noncomparative ads and two in the case of comparative ads). The positioning tactics examined include various comparative advertising appeals (e.g., Pechmann and Ratneshwar 1991) and unique attribute advertising (e.g., Nowlis and Simonson 1996). Second, other work in this area typically examines the price elasticity for an advertised brand within a product category. However, the competitive marketplace dictates that advertising affects both the sponsor's brand as well as the competitive offerings in the category (e.g., Unnava and Sirdeshmukh 1994). Thus, our study examines price sensitivity at both the brand and category levels.

To investigate these issues, in Study 1 we test the effects of advertising content on willingness to pay for a *brand* and the relative importance of the price attribute in *category* decisions. More details on both brand and category reactions are provided in

Study 2 by adding choice level measures of price sensitivity to our dependent measures. Our measures extend those traditionally used to test advertising effectiveness by illustrating that advertising's effects on price sensitivity may be a good indicator of effects when ad attitude measures fail to differentiate between ads.

Our two studies reveal that although many ads contain equivalent attribute information, the positioning adopted to present that information will differentially impact price sensitivity. Further, we show that the same ad positioning strategy can affect brand and category price sensitivity in opposite directions, much as end-of-aisle displays lower price sensitivity for the displayed brand and raise it for the product category (Bolton 1989). In Study 1, we found that positioning tactics associating a minor brand to a premium brand, as well as unique attribute positioning, raise consumers' willingness to pay for a brand. Value-oriented positioning, however, lowers their willingness to pay for the advertised product. Additionally, we show that these same strategies have different effects on category sensitivity. While unique attribute advertising lowers the importance of price within the category, both value-oriented and associating positioning increase price sensitivity at the category level.

Study 2 replicated and extended our findings from the first experiment using additional measures, a different product, and different subjects. In particular, we again find that value-oriented ads increase price sensitivity at both the brand and category levels. We also replicate the finding that comparisons positioning the minor brand as more similar to the premium brand decrease price sensitivity at the brand level, while increasing sensitivity at the category level. When the positioning adopted compares two premium brands, however, we find decreased price sensitivity for the brand, but mixed evidence on category sensitivity.

The Long Term Impact of Promotions and Advertising on Consumer Brand Choice

Carl F. Mela, Notre Dame University
Sunil Gupta, Columbia University
Donald R. Lehmann, Columbia University

This paper examines the long term effects of promotion and advertising on consumers' brand choice behavior. Specifically, we use eight years of panel data for a frequently purchased packaged good to address two questions: (1) Do consumers' responses to marketing mix variables, such as price, change over a long period of time? (2) If yes, are these changes associated with changes in manufacturer's advertising and retailer's promotions? Based upon these results, we draw implications for manufacturers pricing, advertising, and promotion policies.

According to Progressive Grocer (1995), almost 70% of firms have increased their trade promotions between 1990 and 1995, mostly at the expense of advertising. Currently, total trade and consumer promotional expenditures represent $70 billion annually. The effect of this reallocation of marketing dollars is much debated in the industry. On the one hand, some believe the shift has made consumers more price sensitive (Brand Week 1993) while others believe the shift has helped brands (Wall Street Journal 1992). Implicit in all the speculation is that there exist short term effects (what is the effect of a price change on choice behavior this week?) and long term effects (how has years of price promotions or advertising affected the response to a price change?).

Academic researchers have achieved somewhat greater consensus regarding the defection of marketers from advertising. The long-term impact of advertising on choice behavior has been summarized by Kaul and Wittink (1995) and Mitra and Lynch (1995). In essence, advertising is hypothesized to reduce price sensitivity (and presumably price promotion sensitivity) to the extent advertising is i) brand rather than price oriented and ii) consideration sets are relatively stable. Both conditions are likely true for mature product categories such as the one we analyze. We therefore hypothesize that advertising leads to a reduction of price and price promotion sensitivity in our data. Additional insights regarding advertising's effects are obtained by considering possible heterogeneity in consumer response to advertising. As loyals are relatively price insensitive, we expect that any effects of advertising will likely be stronger for non-loyals than loyals. Finally, as mass media advertising has been shown to reduce consumer price sensitivity and build loyalty, we expect that advertising will increase the size of any loyal segment that exists.

Somewhat less consensus exists regarding the effect of price promotions on brand choice. Speculation that promotions hurt brands has been advanced by Dodson, Tybout, and Sternthal (1978) who use consumers are likely to attribute their behavior to the presence of promotions rather than brand preferences. Increased promotion in a category is likely to lead to a perception that the key differentiating feature of a brand is its price (Sawyer and Dickson 1983). However, many researchers (Davis, Inman and McAlister 1992, Ehrenberg, Hammond, and Goodhardt 1994, Hariharan 1992, Johnson 1984) have found little evidence of the negative long term effect of promotions. However, consistent with the consumer behavior theories and the converse effects of price promotions to those described in that advertising literature, it is our expectation that price promotions will have many of the opposite effects of advertising.

The effect of display advertising, on the other hand, may depend upon whether consumers perceive displays to function as advertising or as signals of price cuts. According to Inman, McAlister, and Hoyer (1990), promotional signals have a positive impact on the "low need for cognition" individuals. However, high need for cognition individuals react to a *promotion signal only when it is accompanied* by a substantive price cut. Loyals, as habitual buyers, are less motivated to actively process pricing information and may therefore focus less on price in response to display advertising. Non-loyals, as active processors, are likely to become think of displays as price promotions than advertising and therefore become more price sensitive in response to displays.

To capture these advertising and promotion effects, we use a two-stage modeling approach. In stage one, we estimate a segment level logit model for each quarter of the data to capture the effect of short term (weekly) variables on consumers' brand choice. In stage two, we use the partial-adjustment model to see if consumers' responses to short term marketing activity can be explained by medium term advertising and promotion effects (quarterly). We then calculate the long term advertising and promotion effects (e.g., over an infinite horizon).

Our results are consistent with the hypotheses that consumers became more price and promotion sensitive over time and that these changes correlated with reductions in advertising and increases in promotions over the eight year duration of the study. The effects were found to be significantly larger for non-loyal consumers then for loyal consumers. Decreases in advertising also correlated with a reduced number of loyals. In general, compared to the "good" effects of advertising, promotions were found to have significantly larger "bad" long run effects on consumer's price and promotion sensitivities.

The Impact of Contextuality on Experimental Research in Consumer Behavior

Jean Perrien, University of Québec at Montréal
Sylvie Paradis, University of Québec at Montréal

This paper explores a new way of explaining result discrepancies between experiments in consumer and marketing research. Following a framework developed by Cronbach (1986), it is argued that contextuality is probably one explanation to conflicting results observed by experimenters in consumer research. A case study is made with two classic experiments: Gorn (1982) and Kellaris and Cox (1989) replications of it. It is demonstrated that on three dimensions of contextuality, these two experiments are quite different. Implications of this situation on building and consumer research are also discussed.

Stimulus Generalization in Classical Conditioning: An Initial Investigation

Brian D. Till, Saint Louis University
Randi Prilvek Grossman, Yeshiva University

Growing interest in the classical conditioning of attitudes towards brands has led to examination of areas such as second-order conditioning, backward conditioning, and latent inhibition/CS pre-exposure. This study examines stimulus generalization–the extent to which a conditioned response (e.g., a favorably conditioned attitude) transfers to a similar stimulus (e.g., a brand name). Conditioning trials (15 conditioning pairings) generated a favorable attitude toward Garra mouthwash. Subjects in both conditioning and random control groups also evaluated other brands. The results support stimulus generalization. Attitude toward a similar name (Gurra) in the same category (mouthwash) was greater in the conditioning than the control group. The difference between the conditioning and control group was marginally for the same name (Garra) in a different category (soap). No differences were found between conditioning and control groups for a different name (Dutti) in the same category or a different name in a different category.

Perspectivism: A Response to the Philosophy of Science Debate in Consumer Research

Per Ostergaard, Odense University
A. Fuat Firat, Odense University

There has been a heated debate about epistemology in consumer research during the 1980's and the early 1990's that seems to be in a lull. In this debate there were two camps represented by a logical empiricist and a humanistic/ relativistic position. It is shown how both sides omit fundamental epistemological concepts like power and contextualization in their approach. It is the argument that this omission creates the debate and keeping it away from a solution. Perspectivisim as an epistemological concept is introduced. It is argued that this approach can bring the debate further beyond the mere quarrel for or against objectivity/relativism.

The Bogus Advertising Simulator: A New Method of Eliciting Lay Peoples' Implicit Theories of Advertising

Mats Georgson, The University of Connecticut

How do lay people think advertising works? How would lay people design advertising if they had a chance? In this study, an unconventional method, inspired by ethnomethodology, was used to investigate these broad questions. A computer program posing as an advertising simulator was used by the subjects, who could design commercials by selecting features on a plethora of menus. Thereafter, random "measurements of advertising performance" were presented, and the subjects were invited to try to explain why their ads "did like they did". Although the results are still under analysis, the research procedure proved extremely generative.

Thinking Into It: Consumer Interpretation of Complex Advertising Images

Barbara J. Phillips, University of Saskatchewan

This study tests a new conceptualization that characterizes complex advertising images as figures of rhetoric from which consumers infer advertising messages. Results of this qualitative study, where informants drew inferences from six ads containing pictorial metaphors, support the conceptualization of advertising images as sources of information. Informants easily drew both shared, primary inferences and multiple, secondary inferences solely from the images in the ads. Informant responses also provided insight into the inference process, illustrating how cultural, product, and advertising knowledge helps consumers draw inferences and receive pleasure from interpreting images.

Gender Issues in the Language Used in Television Advertising

Nancy Artz, University of Southern Maine
Jeanne Munger, University of Southern Maine

The portrayal of gender in advertising has received considerable attention over the last several decades, although there is a void in the research on issues relating to gender bias in the language of advertising. This investigation is thus designed to explore the incorporation of gender in broadcast advertising language. Although the majority of ads did not exhibit gender bias, gender bias occurs. Bias is more evident in ad pictures than in ad language and is more evident in songs, dialogue or when popular culture is involved than in formal speech.

Effects of Color as an Executional Cue: They're in the Shade

Gerald J. Gorn, Hong Kong University of Science and Technology
Amitava Chattopadhyay, Hong Kong University of Science and Technology
Tracey Yi, University of British Columbia
Darren W. Dahl, University of British Columbia

In designing print ads, one of the decisions the advertiser must make is which color(s) to use as executional cues in the ad. Typically, color decisions are based on intuition and anecdotal evidence. To provide guidelines for these decisions, this research proposes and tests a conceptual framework linking the hue, chroma, and value of the color(s) in an ad to consumers' feelings and attitudes. In an experimental study, the three dimensions of color used in an ad are manipulated using a between subjects design. The results support the hypotheses that ads containing colors with a higher level of value lead to greater liking for the ad, and this effect is mediated by the greater feelings of relaxation elicited by the higher value color. Feelings play an equally important role in the effect of chroma. Consistent with the hypotheses, higher levels of chroma elicit greater feelings of excitement, which in turn increase ad likability.

The Effects of Theme-Based Incongruency on Ad and Brand Attitudes

Yih Hwai Lee, University of North Carolina, Chapel Hill
Charlotte H. Mason, University of North Carolina, Chapel Hill

This study investigated the effects of ad information expectancy and relevancy on ad and brand evaluations. The definitions of expectancy and relevancy follows extant research (Heckler and Childers 1992). More positive ad and brand attitudes were found for ads with unexpected than expected pictorial information. The reverse was found when the pictures were irrelevant in nature. The effects of humor on ad and brand attitudes were also studied within the incongruency framework. The results indicated that the augmenting effect of humor on attitudes was attenuated by the nature of the information incongruency. Implications of the findings are discussed and suggestions for future research furnished.

Attitude Resistance In Low Involvement Advertising Situations

Jaideep Sengupta, University of California, Los Angeles

Advertising researchers often use the initial product attitude evoked by the advertisement as a measure of ad effectiveness. However, in today's marketplace, consumers get exposed to a number of competing ads and brands in every product category. Further, the use of such attack tactics as negative advertising and comparative advertising is on the increase. It is therefore important to study the issued of attitude resistance, which may be defined as the degree to which an initial attitude can resist an attack. Prior research on this outcome suggests that attitude resistance is generally associated with high involvement processing, even though advertising is more often processed as a low involvement communication. We hypothesize that attitude resistance may be obtained in low involvement contexts when the primary cue contained in an ad is relevant to the product category being evaluated. Consistent with this hypothesis, results from two preliminary studies provide some indication that under low involvement, though both relevant and irrelevant cues evoke similar initial attitudes, only when the cue is relevant do attitudes successfully resist negative information about the product.

Cause-Related Marketing: Does the Cause Make a Difference in Consumers' Attitudes and Purchase Intentions Toward the Product?

Barbara A. Lafferty, Florida State University

Cause-related marketing, where a firm contributes a specified amount to a charitable cause when consumers purchase designated products, is becoming a popular strategy in corporate marketing. Using a laboratory experiment, this study examines whether the importance of the cause to consumers will produce a more favorable attitude toward the product and an increase in purchase likelihood. The results indicate that the relative importance of the cause does make a difference in both attitudes and purchase intentions. In fact, using a less important or unfamiliar cause may actually have negative consequences. The findings should provide insight into the usefulness of CRM as s strategic approach for companies considering implementation of this type of program.

Matching Advertisements to Experimentally Induced Needs

Deana L. Julka, University of Notre Dame
Kerry L. Marsh, University of Notre Dame

The functional perspective on persuasion suggests that individuals are more persuaded by appeals that match their needs. The purpose of these studies was to provide a strong test of the functional perspective by utilizing an experimental approach to induce certain attitude functions. Study 1 validated the situational manipulations of value-expressive and knowledge functions. In Study 2, these value-expressive or knowledge functions were aroused or made salient, and participants then read function-relevant or function-irrelevant advertisements. Function-relevant ads were more appealing than function-irrelevant ads, supporting the matching hypothesis.

There are Many Reasons to Drive a BMW—Surely You Know One: Imagined Ease of Argument Retrieval Influences Brand Attitudes

Michaela Wanke, Universitat Heidelberg
Gerd Bohner, Universitat Mannheim
Andreas Jurkowitsch, Universitat Mannheim

Previous research has shown how subjectively experienced ease in argument retrieval moderates the impact of argument content. The present paper investigated the effects of the *imagined* ease or difficulty of retrieving arguments in response to an advertisement that instigates the self-generation of product-related information in response to an advertisement that instigates the self-generation of product-related information. Subjects who were exposed to an ad that asked them to think of *one reason* for driving (against driving) a BMW, which was experienced as easy, reported a more positive (negative) attitude toward BMW than subjects who were asked to generate *ten reasons*, which was imagined as difficult. The opposite attitude pattern emerged for the competitor brand Mercedes-Benz. The results are discussed in terms of the role of subjective experience in attitude formation.

The Dimensionality of Measures of Product Similarity Under Goal-Congruent and Goal-Incongruent Conditions

Ingrid M. Martin, Boston College
David Stewart, University of Southern California

Product similarity or fit is a commonly used yet confusing construct in the brand extension literature. The present study examines the relationships among various measures of product similarity and fit that have been proposed in the marketing literature. It also considers the relationship of these various measure to measures of attitude and purchase intention. These measures are examined in the context of products linked by a common brand name that are congruent and incongruent with respect to common product goals. Factor analyses reveal several dimensions of similarity. These dimensions of similarity are related in the case of goal congruent products, but are relatively independent in the case of goal incongruent products. Brand attitudes and purchase intention exhibit different relationships to the underlying dimensions of similarity depending on whether goals are congruent or incongruent. implications of these finding for research on brand extensions are discussed.

Oh, To See the Abstract Directly in the Sensuous...

Jan P.L. Schoormans, Delft University of Technology
H.M.J.J. (Dirk) Snelders, University of Namur

It is argued that product attributes are abstract because they describe product characteristics that interact with the context in which they are presented - not because they are inclusive of concrete product attributes. This means that abstract attributes need not be conceptually derived from more concrete attributes, and it is best to think of them as being perceptually complex. Research is discussed where abstract attributes are shown to be perceived directly and not derived form concrete attributes in consumer arguments. Instead, they are shown to be understood against more diverse contexts.

The Construction of Preferences Over Time: The Interaction between Preference Elasticity and the Decision Process

Steve Hoeffler, Duke University
Dan Ariely, Duke University

Relying on the notion that preferences are constructed yet have a true base, we introduce the notion of preference elasticity. We put forth a theory of decision-based preference formation over time to explain the mechanisms associated with preference elasticity in the decision process. The key ideas in this theory are: 1) preferences have a true but fuzzy base, 2) the preference construction is driven by the goal of resolving the ambiguity inherent to the task, and 3) constructing preferences in a choice task decreases their elasticity in subsequent tasks. We present an experiment that explores and supports these notions.

Affect Transfer Through Ingredient Branding: An Exploratory Empirical Evaluation

Rajiv Vaidyanathan, University of Minnesota
Mark G. Brown, University of Minnesota

Can using an established national brand ingredient help a private brand without affecting the national brand? Such an alliance could benefit both parties - national brands can reach a value conscious market segment and private brands can gain a competitive advantage by influencing consumer perceptions of quality and value if affect towards the national brand is transferred to the private brand. An experiment showed that a private brand with a name brand ingredient was perceived more positively. At the same time, the national brand was not diminished by the association with the private brand. Implications and future research directions are discussed.

Brand Portfolio Effects in Consumers' Preference for Umbrella Branded Products

V. K. Srinivas, Rutgers University–Newark

This paper proposes a model of preference for umbrella branded products. Intrinsic to the model is a term which accounts for *brand portfolio effects*. Simply stated, *brand portfolio effects* are the effects induced by the other products on consumers' subjective utility for a particular product *j* in the brand portfolio. Based on the notions of *brand portfolio effects* and preference interdependence, this paper raises some research questions. This research is a preliminary step toward building a framework for analyzing consumer choice for umbrella branded products.

The Role of Justification and Stimulus Meaningfulness on the Attraction Effect: An Elaboration-Likelihood Perspective

Prashant Malaviya, University of Illinois at Chicago
K. Sivakumar, University of Illinois at Chicago

The "attraction effect" refers to the phenomena in which the introduction of a new product increases the choice probability of an existing product relative to a competitor. The new alternative is such that it is dominated by the target but not by the competitor. This paper investigates how the magnitude of the attraction effect is moderated by the need for justification of choice and stimulus meaningfulness. Experimental results show that (a) when product information is less meaningful, the need for justification of choice increases the attraction effect; (b) when product information is more meaningful, instructions to justify choice decrease the attraction effect. The study also finds that the justification-stimulus meaningfulness interaction is observed for subjects whose need for cognition is high, for those who find it easier to perform numerical calculations, and for those who perceive the choice task to be relatively easy. These results are explained in terms of the Elaboration -Likelihood Model. Specifically, it is hypothesized that justification increases the motivation of people to process information and stimulus meaningfulness influences the type of choice rule used for decision making and for justifying those decisions. Both these processes together influence the magnitude of attraction effect.

Re-Addressing the Issue of Recall—Information Processing and the Fear of Invalidity

Tiffany Barnett, Duke University

The present experiment offers a re-analysis of the relationship between recall and advertisement judgement previously posited by Lichtenstein and Srull (1985). The re-analysis is in light of a concept called the fear of invalidity posited by Kruglanski (1983). It was predicted that persons who have evaluated a product and are then exposed to outside information or conditions causing the fear of an invalid product judgement would attempt to recall the information that led to the evaluation before recommitting to it. This mental double check has implications for the reaction times found in the aforementioned experiment. Specifically, it was hypothesized that subjects in high fear of invalidity conditions would exhibit slower response latencies than those in no fear conditions. It was expected, moreover, that the correlation between recall and judgement would be higher as a function of fear than the same correlation in no fear conditions. Higher response latencies combined with higher recall/judgement correlations suggest the process of evaluation validation or rejection transpired—as a function of the fear manipulation. This likely to be true because when the fear of being invalid is high, subjects will attempt to recall not only their evaluation, but the message arguments that led to the formation of that evaluation as well. These hypotheses were validated and support a greater emphasis on the value of specific ad recall data as a predictor of persuasion.

Effects of Time Pressure on Information Processing: A Conceptual Framework

Rajiveesh Suri, University of Illinois
Kent B. Monroe, University of Illinois

After reviewing the past empirical research efforts on the effects of time pressure, this research concluded that there is still a research gap in the existing conceptualization on the effects of time pressure on information processing. Specifically, the review suggests that past research efforts have only considered the negative effects of time pressure on information processing and have not considered its positive (or motivating) effects. This research integrates the scattered evidence on the effects of time pressure and presents a new conceptual framework. This framework accommodates both the effect of time pressure into an existing conceptualization provided by the process theories on attitude formation and change.

Preferences for Bundled and Unbundled Options: A Consumer Behavior Perspective

Sujata Ramnarayan, Researcher

Prior research on bundling has primarily taken on a seller orientation from an economic, and more recently, from a marketing perspective. In general, buyers are treated as purely economic individuals. The current study takes a consumer orientation and considers the demand side incentives for offering bundled and unbundled options. This study examines the information processing basis for bundle preferences, including the conditions under which bundled vs. unbundled products are preferred. Two experiments were conducted to understand consumer perceptions of the non-economic benefits associated with bundled and unbundled options and the conditions under which each option is preferred. As hypothesized, consumer knowledge and time pressure were found to influence preferences for, as well as perceptions of non- economic benefits, associated with each option.

Tradeoffs Between Price and Quality: How a Value Index Affects Preference Formation

Elizabeth H. Creyer, University of Arkansas
William T. Ross, Temple University

Our research examined how the availability of information about the value of a product, expressed as a ratio of the quality received per dollar, influences preference formation. This index, similar to unit price, which provides information about how much *quantity* is received per dollar, provides consumers with information regarding the *quality* received per dollar. An experiment is reported which compares consumers' preferences inferred from a choice task, in which the most attractive option is chosen from a set of options, and from a conjoint task, in which the attractiveness of each option is rated. Consumers, presented with an index of quality received per dollar paid, were more likely to choose a lower priced, higher value option than a higher priced higher quality option compared to consumers presented with only price and quality information and compared to their own preferences as measured in the conjoint task. Clearly, how a consumer will choose to "get the best for his or her money" depends on the processability of available information.

A Model of Adoption and Diffusion Incorporating Protection Motivation Theory

Derrick S. Boone, Duke University

Pro-innovation bias, or the tendency to regard an innovation as desirable and investigate primarily successful or success prone innovations, has limited the focus of adoption and diffusion research by de-emphasizing or ignoring products that do not fit into these categories. Accordingly, much of the emphasis of adoption and diffusion research has been on the innovation itself (e.g., perceived innovation characteristics, uncertainty surrounding use of the innovation, effect of marketing efforts, etc.), while surprisingly little research has been devoted to understanding the underlying causes of adoption (or non-adoption) from a behavioral perspective. This paper addresses the relative lack of research investigating individual-level innovation adoption processes by expanding E.G. Rogers' (1983) earlier work on the innovation decision process, and modifying and adapting R.M. Rogers' (1983) model of protection motivation to a consumer adoption context.

Beyond Price-Reduction: The Multiple Functions of Sales Promotions

Pierre Chandon, Groupe HEC and University of Pennsylvania
Gilles Laurent, Groupe HEC

With its emphasis on the sole financial function of sales promotions, the early literature on consumer deal-proneness cannot explain why consumers' response to sales promotions is so high compared to their response to price reductions. Based on a literature review and on in-depth consumer interviews, we show that consumers value sales promotions because they help them save money, upgrade to a new or a better product, express their self-concept, simplify their decision process, suggest new purchases, or remind them of non accessible alternatives. We then develop a scale measuring each function and are currently testing its construct validity and its structure.

Simultaneous Presentation of Savings on the Individual Items in A Bundle: To Tell or not to Tell?

Rajneesh Suri, University of Illinois
Sung Ho Lee, University of Illinois
Kent B. Monroe, University of Illinois

To sellers which use the price bundling strategy, how to present savings information on bundles so as to increase consumers' perception of bundle offers is a very important question. To address this important issue which has not been answered by prior research, we examine how (1) different formats to present savings information in bundles and (2) consumers' purchase intentions interactively affect consumers' perceived value of bundles. Hypotheses proposed on the basis of information integration theory were supported by the results of our experimental study.

Expertise Effects on Prechoice Decision Processes and Final Outcomes: A Protocol Analysis

Antti J. Kanto, Helsinki School of Business Administration
Hannu Kuusela, University of Tampere
Mark T. Spence, Southern Connecticut State University

The purpose of this study was to determine the effect of expertise on prechoice decision processes. By examining the frequency and type of elementary information processes made by 90 individuals, we found that experts, relative to less knowledgeable decision makers, evoked a greater number of problem framing statements; made more references to why an option was being retained for further consideration; and used more compensatory decision rules. In addition, we found that misunderstanding provided information mediates the expertise-choice relationship. Experts and novices were nearly equal in their tendency to eliminate one or more brands based on a misunderstanding. However, novices were more prone to retain an option for further consideration because of a misunderstanding. As a result, there was greater variance in novices' choices than was the case with experts'.

The Effects of Return Policy on the Framing and Evaluation of Remote Purchases

Stacy Wood, University of Florida

Whether through catalogs, direct mail, Internet, or interactive marketing, consumers' use of remote purchases is increasing rapidly. This study looks at the effect of return policy on two topics: consumers' framing of the purchase and consumers' evaluation of the purchase. Prior research on framing, reference points, and the endowment effect, plus the new concept of creeping commitment, are used to support the hypothesis that lenient return policies create a "trial" frame for consumers in ordering products, which reduces the conflict in that decision to order, and that this frame shifts during the delivery time. Research on signaling and confirmation bias and research on self-manipulation tastes and dissonance predict conflicting hypotheses about how return policy can effect a consumers' evaluation of an ordered product. An experiment was designed to test the above hypotheses and preliminary support was found for both reference frame shifting and the influence of signaling and confirmation bias in evaluation.

Do Credit Cards Increase Spending?

Dilip Soman, University of Colorado

Previous research has suggested that the use of credit cards might enhance consumer spending. This paper develops five possible theoretical mechanisms to explain why such an effect might happen. We hypothesize that the use of credit cards might influence either the likelihood of buying an additional product or the amount spent on a purchase. In three laboratory experiments, we demonstrate these effects. Further, our results show that subjects tended to confuse spending power with wealth, and that they tended to use credit limit as an anchor to estimate an individual's wealth. Ongoing research is discussed and directions for future research are suggested.

A Model of the Consumer Evaluation Process of Firm Ethicality

Elizabeth Creyer, University of Arkansas
William T. Ross, Jr., Temple University
Anne M. Velliquette, University of Arkansas

Existing theoretical models of business ethics focus on the process decision-makers within a firm or organization go through when faced with problems containing ethical dimensions. Little or no emphasis has been placed on the decision processes of the individual consumer who is ultimately affected by the firm's actions and/or behaviors. This article (a) proposes a model of the perception and evaluation of the ethicality of an act from a consumer's point of view, (b) examines the relationship between the consumer (perceiver), the firm (actor) and the consequences (object of the act) of the firm's unethical acts or behaviors,(c) offers four research proposals and (d) discusses implications of the model and directions for further research.

AIDS and Me, Never the Twain Shall Meet: Factors Affecting Judgments of Risk

Priya Raghubir, Hong Kong University of Science and Technology
Geeta Menon, New York University

Five studies investigate the effect of the self-positivity bias, similarity of the other person to oneself, order of elicitation of risk estimates, the ease with which related information can be retrieved from memory, the diagnosticity of such accessibility, and the content of the information retrieved from memory, on people's perceptions of risk of AIDS for oneself and other people. Theoretical implications regarding the use of the accessibility of information as a diagnostic cue, and the self-positivity effect are discussed, and practical implications regarding social marketing and commercial advertising are offered.

Effects of Television Viewing on Self-esteem: An Explanation Based on Festinger's Theory of Social Comparisons and the Self–Discrepancy Theory

Raj Raghunathan, New York University
Merrie Brucks, University of Arizona
Helen Anderson, Helen Anderson Consulting

761 subjects responded to a survey questionnaire on their television viewing habits. The participants were asked, among other things, to rate themselves on five dimensions: how confident, secure, sexy, attractive and thin they felt after watching attractive models television. It was hypothesized that subjects' self-esteem (measured by these 5 constructs) would be lowered as a consequence of watching attractive same sex models on television. Based on the self discrepancy theory (Higgins et al., 1986) that self-esteem is affected as a result of a discrepancy between the actual and the ideal self, and the fact that women's ideal self is likely to place greater emphasis on physical attractiveness, it was hypothesized that women' self-esteem would be lower more than that of men as a consequence of watching attractive same sex models on television. Further, based on the self-discrepancy theory in conjunction with Festinger's theory of social comparisons (Festinger, 1954) that comparisons occur with similar others, it was hypothesized that women belonging to the ethnic minority groups (that is , the African American, Asian American, Hispanic and Native American subjects) would be less affected than the Caucasian female subject. Finally, it was hypothesized that the self-esteem levels of older female subjects would be less affected than that of the younger female subjects. Our findings, in general, support all our hypotheses at least directionally if not significantly. In the cases where wo do not find significant support for out hypotheses, we offer alternative explanations for our results. We conclude our paper by examining the implications of our findings for advertisers.

Material Culture and Symbolic Consumption

Søren Askegaard, Odense University
A. Fuat Firat, Odense University

This paper discusses the concepts of material culture, symbolic consumption, and the dichotomy of the functional and the symbolic. This is done first through a discussion of the historical contexts of the development of modernity and the modern market, and the role of material culture herein. After these arguments, it is shown how modernity has an ambivalent relation to the symbolic dimension of its material culture, on the one hand belonging to the realm of the non-functional and non-productive and thus regarded as inferior, but, on the other hand, being the important dimension for distinguishing classes and categories in society. Finally, the false dichotomy of the functional and the symbolic is addressed, and in the conclusion, an alternative metaphor for understanding and organizing the institution of the market is suggested.

Cues that Trigger Compulsive Buying

Ronald J. Faber, University of Minnesota
Stephen L. Ristvedt, Washington University School of Medicine
Thomas B. Mackenzie, University of Minnesota
Gary A. Christenson, University of Minnesota

Research in compulsive buying has tended to focus on the factors that may cause people to develop this problem. What has received much less attention is the catalysts may elicit or exacerbate specific episodes of this behavior among people who are susceptible to it. This paper examines the specific cues that compulsive buyers indicate trigger or worsen their buying problems. Two types of factors are found to be commonly named. One set involves items associated with purchasing such as malls and money. The second factor is comprised of negative affective states. Implications of these findings and their relationship to other disorders is discussed.

The Effects of Consumer Ethnocentrism on Domestic and Foreign Brand Preferences in Poland

Terrence H. Witkowski, California State University, Long Beach
Bohdan Roznowski, Catholic University of Lublin
Andrzej Falkowski, Catholic University of Lublin

This paper applies the consumer ethnocentrism scale (CETSCALE) to the Polish market. Age and income were statistically significant correlates of ethnocentrism, while education and city size tended toward significance. Subjects with high CETSCALE scores exhibited much different preference maps for domestic and foreign detergent brads than did subjects with low scores. In contrast to consumers in the West, the more ethnocentric respondents did not discriminate sharply between Polish and foreign brands and did not form coherent categories of domestic and foreign products. Additional analyses investigate how ethnocentric tendencies shape the perception of and affect toward brands. The findings have practical implications for companies operating in Poland.

Towards an Understanding of Homosexual Consumers

James Marshall, Arizona State University
Renee D. Shaw, Arizona State University

This manuscript reports the first stage of a research project which is aimed at explicating the relation of homosexual identity and consumer behavior. This first phase of this research employs interviews as a means to identify themes which are applicable to gay male consumers, and which may be distinct from the larger population. These themes are categorized within a framework which explains the development of homosexual identity. By first gaining an understanding of the thoughts, activities, and preferences of gay consumers, subsequent research which builds upon the themes uncovered in this first stage of research is suggested.

Probing Exchange Theory: A Comparison of Consumers in Three Rural Communities

Nancy J. Miller, Iowa State University

Increasing economic uncertainty in rural communities warrants greater attention to consumer shopping behavior. The major purpose of this empirical study was to determine whether a community's 'pull factor' score, as one proxy for local market-place exchange, also reflected aspects of social exchange. Adult consumers from three rural communities were examined for differences in levels of reciprocity, community attachment, motivation, satisfaction with local retail facilities, and their intention to shop locally. Lower pull factor scores coincided with lower levels of social and market-place exchange dimensions. Men and women were also found to differ significantly on several aspects of community and exchange.

Public Perceptions of Consumption by Low Income Households

Linda F. Alwitt, DePaul University

The non-poor public has a generally inaccurate perception of expenditures on 17 products and service by poor households, proportionate to expenditures by households with average incomes. This conclusion is based on a comparison of perception by 300 respondents to behavioral data from the Consumer Expenditure Survey. Accuracy of perceptions did not vary by age, education, or sample selection, but 'experts', people who work with the poor, were more accurate than non-expert respondents. Those non-expert respondents who had more accurate perceptions were more likely to favor increasing governmental expenditures to benefit the poor, as were the 'expert' respondents.

Towards a Portrait of Arts Consumption in Postmodernity

Laurie A. Meamber, University of California, Irvine

This study highlights issues related to arts consumption in postmodernity. Grounded theory interpretation and analysis procedures were used to analyze interviews with 15 arts/non-arts consumers. Primary themes which emerged from the data include: interest/investment, social influence, and self-expression. The themes indicate that motivation for arts consumption involves more than instrumental and rational factors. The consumption of the arts can become a symbolically charged experience for consumers, a social statement, and also contribute to a notion of themselves and their view of the world.

Variables that Influence Consumers' Inferences About Physician Ability and Physician Accountability for Adverse Health Outcomes

Manuel C. Pontes, Fairleigh Dickinson University
Nancy Pontes, New York University

Previous research has not provided definitive evidence for the *causal* influence of the interpersonal management of patients on inferences about physician ability of accountability. The present research experimentally manipulates three variables, 1) Patient involvement with treatment decisions, 2) Financial incentives by third-party payers to encourage cost-effective medicine, and 3) Use of new treatment practices that have not been widely adopted by other physicians, in a description of a medical case which resulted in patient death. Results showed that greater patient involvement had a strong positive influence on respondents' inferences about the physician's ability and accountability for the patient's death. Financial incentives had the opposite effects; they had a negative influence on respondents' inferences about the physician's accountability for the patient's death. The use of new treatment practices had no effect on these dependent variables.

Mood Effects Upon Customers' Responses to Service Organizations and Service Encounters: An Experimental Analysis

Patricia A. Knowles, Clemson University
Gregory M. Pickett, Clemson University
Stephen J. Grove, Clemson University

Subjects were induced into positive or relatively negative moods and then confronted with retail banking service encounters involving positive, neutral, negative or mixed cues. Results of our research indicate that mood has no statistically significant effect on memory, yet did indirectly affect subjects' evaluation and behavioral intentions toward banking. We also found that the nature of the service encounter (positive, neutral, negative, and mixed) affected subjects' memory, evaluation, and behavioral intentions toward it. Thus, while our results indicate that one's mood had only limited impact on subject's responses to service encounters, the nature of the encounter had a significant impact across almost every measure.

A Theoretical Basis for a Latitude Conceptualization of Service-Encounter Evaluation: Directions for Future Research

Stephen L. Vargo, University of Oklahoma

How consumers evaluate service-encounters has profound implications for how marketers manage these encounters. However, there is disagreement concerning the appropriate model for understanding consumer evaluations. Recently, models based on ranges of acceptability have been suggested as alternatives to the traditionally accepted disconfirmation of expectations models. This paper explores the similarities and implications of social judgement-involvement theory to these "latitude" models, particularly the "zone of tolerance" model of service quality proposed by Zeithaml, Berry, and Parasuraman (1993).

Really-Low Involvement Consumer Learning

Michel Tuan Pham, Columbia University

Thirty years have passed since Krugman (1965) urged us to study advertising effects from the perspective of low involvement learning. Most promotional messages indeed receive minimal levels of attention, active processing and elaboration. Yet, in the past three decades advertising effects have been examined almost exclusively under conditions of moderate to high involvement. Even in the "low involvement" condition of the typical persuasion experiment (e.g., Petty, Cacioppo and Schumann 1983), the exposure context and instructions call for substantial deliberate processing. Given that consumers generally do not want to process promotional messages, much is left to be learned as to how advertising operates under conditions of *really* low involvement. Obviously, a theoretical understanding of how communication works under such conditions also has important managerial implications.

Two reasons seem to explain the field's lack of attention to really low involvement learning. The first reason lies in the fact that, historically, persuasion research in marketing and consumer behavior has been strongly influenced by work in social psychology. After all, concepts such as source credibility and fear appeal were originally introduced by social psychologists (Hovland, Janis, and Kelley 1953)—the so-called "Yale School" of communication. The notions of cognitive responses (Greenwald 1968) and elaboration likelihood (Petty and Cacioppo 1981) also emanated from social psychology. Given the type of issue that social psychology usually examines (e.g., racial prejudice), it should come as no surprise that consumer persuasion research that was inspired by social psychological theorizing has assumed moderately high audience involvement. The second reason is essentially methodological. It is simply difficult to produce really-low involvement in a lab. For instance, creating such conditions almost always raises issues of demand characteristics; it also requires delicate stimulus calibrations.

Departing from earlier research on consumer persuasion, the three papers presented in the session explore the processes through which consumers learn from exposure to marketing communications under conditions of minimal involvement. The researchers used different methodologies to create *incidental* exposure to various promotional stimuli (advertising claims, brand names, and fragments). A common thread among the papers is that they all involve measures that isolate the subtle memory processes underlying really-low involvement learning. A second commonality is that they all attempt to delineate the conditions under which such learning effects can be observed.

In the first paper, Holden and Vanhuele explored the possibility of dissociations between explicit and direct measures of memory (e.g., recognition) and implicit measures of memory (e.g., response facilitation in a lexical task). They argued that incidentally exposed information may result in learning effects that cannot be detected through direct measures of memory but can be uncovered with indirect measures. They also hypothesized that the sensory modality match between exposure and retrieval (auditory /auditory vs. auditory/visual) would have differential effect on implicit vs. explicit memory measures. These propositions were tested in an experiment that, in combination with an innovative probabilistic modeling approach, decomposes implicit and explicit memory effects (Vanhuele 1995). The findings replicated the "false fame" effect (Jacoby, Kelley, Brown and Jasenchko 1989), in that inciden-

tal exposure to unknown brand names caused these names to be mistaken for well-known brands. The experiment also yielded an intriguing pattern of results about the effect of sensory modality match on implicit vs. explicit memory measures. Contrary to the authors' expectations, sensory modality match influenced the explicit measure without affecting the implicit measure.

In the second paper, Hawkins, Meyers-Levy, and Hoch elaborated on their earlier work on the "truth effect." Hawkins and Hoch (1992) had shown that (1) repetition of a statement increased people's belief in the truth of this statement, (2) this effect was stronger under lower involvement (initial exposure with comprehension v. truth rating task), and (3) memory for the claims mediates the impact of repetition on belief. In the experiment presented at the session, Hawkins, Meyers-Levy, and Hoch examined whether similar effects are observed with exposure to related feature claims all of which suggest a common benefit—an issue that maps onto "variations on a theme" advertising (e.g., Schumann, Petty and Clemons 1990; Unava and Burnkrant 1991). They reported that exact repetition of a single claim does increase belief in that feature claim, but it does not increase belief in the general benefit implied by the feature claim. On the other hand, exposure to more related feature claims does not increase belief in a target feature claim, but it does increase belief in the general benefit. An explicit test of mediation confirms that belief in a general benefit can be increased by exact repetition of a specific feature claim (the truth effect) and related repetition of more feature claims (the inference effect).

In the third paper, Vanhuele and Pham discussed the communication effects of what they call advertising "fragments" (i.e., minimal messages often restricted to a brief mention of the brand name). These types of messages are increasingly pervasive in today's communication landscape (e.g., event sponsorships, product placements in movies, brand logos on the Internet, tv program endorsements; see, e.g., Pham 1992). They presented an experiment which examined whether brief exposures to fragments carrying only brand names (e.g., "Marlboro") can result in instantiation of the brands' core associations (e.g., masculinity). The experiment manipulated the number of exposures to the fragments and whether attention to these fragments was focal or nonfocal. Instantiation of the core brand association was assessed through a reaction-time methodology. The results suggest that even brief exposures to advertising fragments carrying only brand names may increase the accessibility of core brand associations, thereby perhaps sustaining brand equity. The findings also indicate that this "extended reactivation" effect follows a threshold pattern. The effect appears only after a minimum number of repetitions; the required number of repetition being lower under focal attention than under nonfocal attention. Once the threshold has been reached, additional repetition does not appear to further increase the effect.

The discussion was lead by Terence Shimp, who is well known for his research on classical conditioning (e.g., Shimp, Stuart, and Engle 1991)—another paradigm of low involvement learning. He agreed with Holden and Vanhuele's thesis that the "false-fame" effect is an interesting phenomenon to study in order to understand the role of implicit memory in consumer behavior. He pointed out that the stimuli used in the Holden and Vanhuele study—largely meaningless multisyllabic pharmaceutical names—maximized the chances for confusion. One could therefore wonder whether a false-fame effect would also have been uncovered, had simpler and more concrete brand names (e.g., soap names such as Irish Spring) been used. It would therefore be useful to replicate the findings with simpler and more meaningful brand names. He also noted that the Holden and Vanhuele study reinforced the fact that multiple marketing communication methods are mutually reinforcing—a point also raised by Vanhuele and Pham. Regarding Hawkins et al.'s study, Shimp stressed the importance of the finding that beliefs in *general* brand benefits is augmented with multiple repetitions of *related* (rather than exact) feature claims. This results represents an important extension of Unava and Sirdeshmukh's (1994) research on the *encoding variability hypothesis*, which demonstrated that memory for brand messages increases when multiple pathways are created via (1) use of multiple media, or (2) variation of the advertising message. With respect to Vanhuele and Pham's paper, Shimp remarked that the concept of "fragments" fits nicely with the integrated marketing notion of *contacts*. He added that the increasing usage of "blib-type" forms of communication justifies serious academic research on the topic of advertising fragments. Shimp suggested that the Vanhuele and Pham results were interesting, both from a practitioners' viewpoint and for implicit memory theory. However, he stressed that in this study, there was an actual match between the learning context and the testing context (both were conducted using individual computers). Citing the *encoding specificity hypothesis,* he suggested that the match between learning and "retrieval" contexts may have improved subjects' implicit memory performance. Given that in the real world fragments are often processed in rather unique environments, it may be useful to manipulate the match between learning and testing contexts.

The discussion was then opened to the general audience. A lively exchange followed, as numerous questions were asked and very helpful suggestions were offered by the audience. For instance, one person wondered how the Vanhuele and Pham results would vary depending on whether the brand is very well-known or less familiar. Another raised the issue of statistical error in studies of false fame effects, where subjects are tested on dozens of stimuli. Based on the session's attendance and the audience's *high* involvement, there appears to be much interest in the issue of really-low involvement consumer learning. Interested readers are strongly invited to contact the authors directly.

REFERENCES

Greenwald, Anthony G. (1968), "Cognitive Learning, Cognitive Response to Persuasion, and Attitude Change," in *Psychological Foundations of Attitudes*, Greenwald, Anthony G, Timothy C. Brock, and Thomas M. Ostrom (Eds.), San Diego, CA: Academic Press.

Hawkins, Scott A. and Stephen J. Hoch (1992), "Low-Involvement Learning: Memory without Evaluation," *Journal of Consumer Research*, 19 (September), 212-225.

Hovland, Carl I., Irving L. Janis, and Harold H. Kelley (1953), *Communication and Persuasion*. New Haven, CT: Yale University Press.

Jacoby, Larry L, C. Kelley, J. Brown and J. Jasechko (1989) "Becoming famous overnight: Limits on the ability to avoid unconscious influences of the past," *Journal of Personality and Social Psychology*, 56 (3), 326-338.

Krugman, Herbert (1965), "The Impact of Television Advertising: Learning without Involvement," *Public Opinion Quarterly*, 3 (Fall), 349-356.

Petty, Richard and John Cacioppo (1981), *Attitudes and Persuasion: Classic and Contemporary Approaches*, W. C. Brown Company Publishers.

Petty, Richard, John Cacioppo, and David Schumann (1983), "Central and Peripheral Routes to Advertising Effectiveness: The Moderating Role of Involvement," *Journal of Consumer Research*, 10 (September), 135-146.

Pham, Michel Tuan (1992), "Effects of Involvemment Arousal and Pleasure on the Recognition of Sponsorship Stimuli," in *Advances in Consumer Research*, Vol. 19, eds. John F. Sherry and Brian Sternthal, Provo, UT: Association for Consumer Research, 85-93.

Shimp, Terence A, Elnora W. Stuart, and Randall W. Engle (1991), "A Program of Classical Conditioning Experiments Testing Variations in the Conditioned Stimulus and Context," *Journal of Consumer Research*, 18 (June), 1-12.

Schumann, David W., Richard E. Petty, and Scott D. Clemons (1990), "Predicting the Effectiveness of Different Strategies of Advertising Variation: A Test of the Repetition-Variation Hypothesis," *Journal of Consumer Research*, 16, 192-202.

Unava, H. Rao and Robert E. Burnkrant (1991), "Effects of Repeating Varied Ad Executions on Brand Name Memory," *Journal of Consumer Research*, 28, 406-416.

_____ and Deepak Sirdeshmukh (1994), "Reducing Competitive Ad Interference," *Journal of Marketing Research*, 31 (August), 403-411.

Vanhuele, M. (1995) "The cognitive dynamics behind the mere exposure effect," in *Advances in Consumer Research*, Vol. 22, eds., M. Sujan and F. Kardes, 171-175

Hide or Seek: Factors Influencing Ambiguity Aversion versus Ambiguity Preference

Patricia M. West, University of Texas at Austin
Susan M. Broniarczyk, University of Texas at Austin

Ambiguity arises from having scanty, unreliable or conflicting information about the outcome of events, and gives rise to one's expected value of decision alternatives and degree of "confidence" in choice (Ellsberg 1961). Preference for certain probabilities over vague or uncertain probabilities, ambiguity aversion, has been demonstrated in many experiments using variations of Ellsberg's gambling task.

Camerer and Weber (1992) recently reviewed the research on ambiguity across multiple disciplines and conclude "uncertainty about the composition of an urn of balls is just one kind of missing information. Feeling ignorant about football or politics, having doubts about which of several experts is right, wondering whether your child has a predisposition to the side effects of a vaccine, or being unsure about another country's economy are all manifestations of missing information" (p. 360). Recently, there has been a sprinkling of evidence that in some real-world contexts, consumers may in fact seek ambiguity (Kahn and Sarin 1988).

The focus of this session is to examine various factors influencing consumers' attitude toward ambiguity and when they will display ambiguity seeking versus ambiguity aversion. Each of the three papers presented highlight different factors that effect how consumers respond to ambiguity in real-world decisions that step beyond the traditional balls and urn gambling task. Consumer reaction to ambiguity in the form of unfamiliar or new product decision environments, and environments where expert opinions conflict on product quality were examined. The impact of ambiguity on consumer judgment and decision making has important implications for marketers, managers, and public policy makers alike.

Rather than characterizing individuals' as having an inherent "preference" for, or "aversion" to ambiguity a richer understanding is beginning to emerge that isolates a variety of factors that influence consumer response to ambiguity/uncertainty. The papers and panel members have identified several underlying variables related to the decision maker, product category, and situation that inspire either conservatism (ambiguity aversion) or optimism (ambiguity seeking). In particular, consumer knowledge, prior opinions, and the perceived risk associated with the decision are shown to influence consumer response to ambiguous alternatives.

Kimberly A. Taylor and Barbara E. Kahn as well as *Craig R. Fox* follow up on the recent observation of Heath and Tversky (1991) that consumer knowledge is an important factor in determining tolerance for ambiguity. In particular, people are more willing to bet on their uncertain beliefs when they feel particularly knowledgeable about an area, and prefer to bet on known probabilities when they do not. *Kimberly A. Taylor and Barbara E. Kahn* find that domain knowledge interacts with accountability and perceived control of a decision outcome to stimulate ambiguity seeking. *Craig R. Fox* finds that effects associated with domain knowledge disappear when people are asked to evaluate either an ambiguous or an unambiguous alternative in isolation (a noncomparative context) rather both alternatives together (a comparative context). He also finds that willingness to act is influenced by the decision maker's relative knowledge of other items evaluated in the same context and by the order in which items are evaluated.

Kimberly A. Taylor and Barbara E. Kahn argue that ambiguity seeking is more prevalent with high knowledge individuals because they perceive lower risk associated with the ambiguous outcomes, and enjoy the psychological rewards associated with taking credit for successful choices. *Patricia M. West and Susan M. Broniarczyk* carefully examine the interplay between perceived risk associated with a product and conflicting information about product quality. Their results indicate that as the perceived risk associated with a decision outcome increases, consumers respond more favorably to product alternatives where there are differing opinions as opposed to consensus regarding product quality. A reference-dependent model is proposed to explain how and when consumers will exhibit ambiguity seeking versus ambiguity aversion when evaluating product alternatives.

Ambiguity has been characterized in many ways ranging from second order to probability to conflicting or missing information. The collection of papers presented in this session spans this range. *Patricia M. West and Susan M. Broniarczyk* operationalize ambiguity as the variance in response between three critic ratings of a given alternative, *Craig R. Fox* uses the degree of familiarity with the events on which outcomes depend to distinguish an ambiguous from an unambiguous option, and *Kimberly A. Taylor and Barbara E. Kahn* use a new product scenario where ambiguity is manipulated by offering claims and historical data on an existing product versus claims but no historical data for a new product.

Ambiguity Aversion and Context
Craig R. Fox

Willingness to act under uncertainty depends not only on the degree of uncertainty but also on its source, as illustrated by Ellsberg's observation of ambiguity aversion. Specifically, people prefer to bet in areas in which they feel knowledgeable or competent rather than areas in which they feel ignorant or incompetent. A series of studies suggests that this feeling of confidence or vulnerability underlying source preferences depends crucially on the context of a decision. Source preferences seem to disappear in the absence of a direct comparison between items. Moreover, absolute willingness to act can be diminished or enhanced, respectively, by having a person evaluate more or less familiar items in the same context. Putting these effects together, absolute willingness to act is influenced by the order in which items are presented.

Knowledge, Control, Accountability, and Decision Frame as Determinants of Consumer Ambiguity Seeking
Kimberly A. Taylor and Barbara E. Kahn

Many consumer decisions are made in ambiguous contexts, such as when one buys a new product or adopts an innovation. At best, in such situations, consumers may develop subjective probability estimates of the likelihoods of the various outcomes. In this research, we attempt to provide a comprehensive road map exploring under what circumstances ambiguity would be tolerated, or even preferred. In a series of laboratory experiments, the effects of consumer knowledge, perceived control, and accountability on ambiguous decisions are explored. Further, how these factors are affected by whether the decision is framed as a gain or a loss is also examined.

Integrating Multiple Critic Opinions: The Role of Aspiration Level on Consumer Response to Critic Consensus
Patricia M. West and Susan M. Broniarczyk

Two studies examine the process by which consumers integrate critic opinions and attribute information in their product evaluations and how critic consensus affects this process. A reference-dependent model is proposed such that consumer response to critic consensus depends on whether the average critic rating for an alternative is above or below an aspiration level. Critic consensus is shown to be preferred for alternatives above an aspiration level whereas critic disagreement is preferred for alternatives below an aspiration level. Consumers exhibited a tendency to prefer critic disagreement for high priced products or decisions associated with high social risk because most alternatives fell below their high aspiration levels. Additionally, critic opinions appeared to be used as an initial screening mechanism for evaluating product alternatives with attribute information only given serious consideration for alternatives evaluated favorably by the critics.

Discussion
Colin Camerer

Colin Camerer pointed out the importance of understanding the interaction between situational ambiguity (i.e., missing or conflicting information) and personal preference (i.e., the utility derived from a decision outcome). In particular, while ambiguity seeking is expected when the situation allows a decision maker to take credit for good outcomes, ambiguity aversion is expected to prevail when the decision maker is likely to be blamed for bad outcomes. This observation suggests that the impact of credit versus blame on a consumer's decision outcome needs to be directly incorporated into the utility assessment process.

While a number of important variables that affect consumer response to ambiguity were considered in the three talks (e.g. the reference point adopted and knowledge of the decision maker, degree of control or accountability associated with the decision outcome, and the amount of information that is missing), Colin suggested others that should be considered in future research on the topic. These additional variables include: (1) preference for information; (2) time pressure; (3) the stakes associated with the decision; and (4) the effect of dyadic relationships.

REFERENCES

Camerer, Colin and Martin Weber (1992), "Recent Developments in Modeling Preferences: Uncertainty and Ambiguity," *Journal of Risk and Uncertainty*, 5, 325-370.

Ellsberg, Daniel (1961), "Risk, Ambiguity and the Savage Axioms," *Quarterly Journal of Economics*, 75, 643-669.

Heath, Chip and Amos Tversky (1991), "Preference and Belief: Ambiguity and Competence in Choice Under Uncertainty," *Journal of Risk and Uncertainty*, 4, 5-28.

Kahn, Barbara E. and Rakesh K. Sarin (1988), "Modeling Ambiguity in Decisions Under Uncertainty," *Journal of Consumer Research*, 15 (September), 265-272.

Children as Decision Makers

Kim Corfman, New York University

SESSION OVERVIEW

Children have become a major consumer market, with estimated total spending power of around $150 billion in 1993. Not only do they have a large amount of their own discretionary income, they also influence a wide variety of minor and major family purchases, from toys to restaurant meals to cars. As a result of this and the projected growth in the number of children, we are seeing a steadily increasing stream of new child-oriented products and advertising. Despite this boost in child-directed marketing activity, we still know remarkably little about how children make decisions, what determines how much influence they have when parents are involved, and how these vary across different ages. This session succeeded in bringing together researchers interested in children who are exploring various dimensions of children's decision making in different ways, providing some perspective on the processes involved, and identifying remaining gaps in our understanding.

The literature on children's decision making is quite sparse. While we know that children younger than 10 or 11, are far less able to adapt to increasing complexity in decision environments than older children, previous work has not addressed how adaptive decision making develops as children mature. The first presentation, delivered by Jennifer Gregan-Paxton and Deborah Roedder John, explored age differences in children's decision making and how children become adaptive decision makers. Though we know that adaptivity develops during early and middle childhood, we know virtually nothing about the mechanisms responsible for this development. The authors proposed that young children face two general classes of obstacles, called knowledge deficits and utilization deficits, in adapting to complex decision environments. They then reported empirical evidence to support their view that utilization deficits can be the sources of younger children's difficulties in effectively adapting their decision-making strategies to more complex tasks.

When children are not making consumption decisions alone, they are most often making them with a parent. The second and third papers in this session addressed the influence processes surrounding parent/child consumption decisions.

The second presentation, delivered by Kay Palan (co-authored with Robert Wilkes) investigated parent-child interaction in family decision making. In the family purchase decision making process, adolescents often try to sway the purchase decision through a variety of influence strategies. Parents react to adolescent influence attempts with their own inventory of response strategies. This paper examined the interaction process that occurs between parents and adolescents in family purchase decisions. Through the use of discovery-oriented research methods, both adolescent influence strategies and parental response strategies to adolescent influence were identified. In addition, the authors used interpretive analysis to develop underlying motivations that determine strategy choice, which are used to propose a conceptual framework of parent-adolescent interactions.

The third presentation, delivered by Kim Corfman and Bari Harlam (co-authored with Paschalina Ziamou), examined the relative influence of parents and children in the purchase of products for children. The authors proposed and presented preliminary tests of a model of children's influence in the family choice process, which included *a)* the effects of factors relating to the child, the parent, the family structure, and past decisions and *b)* what determines whether

children will be influential in a particular product category. The focus was on the role of the *communal consequence* of the product category represented in the decision—the degree to which other family members are involved or affected when a child consumes a product. Their method allowed objective assessment of relative influence by examining the decision making process through an experiment in which parent-child dyads make a series of joint choices.

While these papers shared the common theme of children as decision makers, the differences among them added to their value as a set. First, the combination of papers permitted comparison across a wide range of ages—from 7 to 17. Studies of children rarely make the explicit comparisons among age groups that were possible with the juxtaposition of the papers in this session. Second, the methodologies used in this session represented a broad range of approaches—from information display boards, to observation of choices in an experimental setting, to discovery-oriented, in-depth interviews. These papers provided encouraging evidence of innovation in our approaches to studying children as consumers and that we have moved far beyond learning about children by simply asking their parents.

PRESENTATION SUMMARIES

"Age Differences in Children's Decision Making: Deciding How to Decide"
Jennifer Gregan-Paxton and Deborah Roedder John

How do children become adaptive decision makers? Though we know that adaptivity develops during early and middle childhood, we know virtually nothing about the mechanisms responsible for this development. In this paper, the authors proposed that young children face two general classes of obstacles, called knowledge deficits and utilization deficits, in adapting to complex decision environments. Knowledge deficits refer to the lack of basic skills and knowledge needed to perform a task. Utilization deficits, on the other hand, refer to difficulties in using whatever knowledge or skills are available in a particular learning or problem-solving situation. When these obstacles are removed, either through experience, maturation, or the task environment itself, more adaptive decision making emerges.

These propositions were tested empirically by focusing on utilization deficits as a source of young children's decision-making difficulties. Specifically, the authors report the results of an experiment with children aged 7 to 11 years, in which children's decision-making strategies were monitored as they made a series of choices from information boards. Second grade and fifth grade children played a game called "treasure hunt," in which they were allowed to pick a "treasure box" from several depicted on information boards. Each child made a choice from four different information boards that varied in complexity, manipulated by the number of treasure boxes (alternatives) they could choose from and the number of individual prizes (dimensions) included in each treasure box. Information about the prizes in each treasure box could be obtained by uncovering "curtains" hiding the information on the display board.

Children's abilities to adapt to increasingly complex information boards were assessed by monitoring the overall amount and proportion of information they gathered prior to choice, the general nature of their search strategy (e.g., exhaustive versus satisficing), and the degree to which they selectively gathered information from some alternatives, but not others. To examine whether young children could be prompted to be more adaptive in these respects, search costs were made salient for half of the subjects by requiring them to pay (i.e., give up a piece of candy) for each peice of information gathered from the board. The introduction of search costs was viewed as providing a cue to young children that exhaustive processing of information had a substantial cost, encouraging them to utilize whatever simplifying strategies they might have available.

Consistent with prior research, results indicate that younger children were often less effective in adapting to complex decision environments than older children. But, when provided with a cue in the form of substantial search costs, younger children used whatever strategies they possessed in a more effective manner, sometimes equaling that of much older children. These findings provide evidence, for the first time, that age differences in decision making are attributable, in part, to utilization deficits and that younger children can be encouraged to be more adaptive with the aid of decision-making cues that facilitate strategy usage.

"Adolescent-Parent Interaction in Family Decision Making"
Kay M. Palan and Robert E. Wilkes

In the family purchase decision making process, adolescents often try to sway purchase decisions through a variety of influence strategies. Parents react to adolescent influence attempts with their own inventory of response strategies. The interaction between adolescent strategy choice and parental strategy choice determines the impact of the adolescent influence attempt on the purchase process. That is, some adolescent-parent interchanges will be more effective than others in affecting the purchase decision outcome. In order to increase our understanding of adolescent-parent interactions in purchase decisions, a discovery-oriented research method–depth interviews with one hundred mothers, fathers, and adolescents-was conducted for two purposes. First, both adolescent influence strategies and parental response strategies to adolescent influence attempts were identified. Seventeen adolescent influence strategies and twelve parental response strategies were identified; based on the understanding of these strategies that emerged from the interviews, the strategies were organized into seven different strategy categories–bargaining, persuasion, emotional, request, expert, legitimate, and directive.

Second, interpretive analysis was used to suggest underlying motivations that determine both adolescent and parental strategy choice. Specifically, the authors proposed that adolescent strategy choice is determined by two factors: (1) adolescent expectations of parental resistance to adolescent influence attempts, and (2) adolescent willingness to engage in resource expenditure. Parental response strategy choice is motivated by the degree of management parents choose to exert in the interaction process. These motivations were combined to propose a conceptual framework of parent-adolescent interactions. It was proposed that parent-leveraged decision making is characterized by high parental resistance, high adolescent resource expenditure, and high parental management; despite adolescent influence attempts, parents will be the primary decision makers in parent-leveraged decisions. Adolescent-leveraged decision making, on the other hand, occurs when there is low parental resistance, low adolescent resource expenditure, and low parental management; for these decisions, adolescents are successful in their influence attempts and may actually make purchase decisions with very little parent interaction.

"Relative Influence of Parent and Child in the Purchase of Products for Children"
Kim Corfman, Bari Harlam, and Paschalina Ziamou

Parents and, increasingly, marketers understand the importance of children's influence in the purchase of a wide variety of products for use by the family and children themselves. We know from past studies that there is substantial variation among families and product categories in the amount of influence children have over purchase decisions and we know a little about reasons for variation *among families*. However, we know much less about reasons for the observed variation *among product categories*. This study looked at the effects of parent preference intensity, the outcomes of past joint choices, child personality, parenting styles, and family structure on children's influence and what determines whether children will be influential in a particular category.

A variety of methods have been used to assess children's involvement in family decision making. Almost all past studies have used parents' perceptions of children's influence. Only a very few studies have used more objective approaches and observed the outcome or the influence process and outcome, permitting accurate inferences about relative influence to be made. These authors observed both the influence process and outcome, and measured a more comprehensive set of predictors than has been possible with other methods.

In this paper the authors described and reported preliminary tests of a model of influence in the family choice process that includes the factors indicated above, which are expected to determine children's influence in the purchase of products and services. Of particular interest were characteristics of the product category in determining how strongly the parent feels (preference intensity) and, thus, how much influence he or she exerts. They examined the parent's perceptions of how good or bad the product is for the child, the product's price, and the *communal consequence* of the product category. Communal consequence is a construct developed for this study, which indicates the degree to which other family members are involved or affected when a child consumes a product or service. A product low in communal consequence might be a book or puzzle. A loud drum set, messy paints, and clothing (to the degree that it reflects on the parents) may have greater communal consequence. Items jointly consumed, such as a family movie or restaurant outing, are high in communal consequence.

The decision making process was examined using an experiment in which parent-child dyads made joint choices from four pairs of products, after rating the items independently. The four choice pairs were designed based on the individual ratings to ensure that the parent and child had conflicting individual preferences. They were from four product categories—two low and two high communal consequence categories. Preliminary results indicate that how good or bad the product is and its degree of communal consequence affect relative influence through the parent's preference intensity. Other factors affecting relative influence include aspects of parenting style (consistency, control, and child's spending power), child personality (cooperativeness and compliance), and family structure (number of parents in household, hours parents spend at work, an income). The outcomes of past decisions did not appear to play a role.

REVIEW OF DISCUSSION

The discussion revolved around two integrative questions. First, what are the key influences on a child's decision making? Second, how does the child influence others' decision making? Answers to both questions were pursued from the perspectives of what we know and what we do not know as children's researchers.

Each paper made a unique contribution to answering these questions. The synthesizer made the following observations. The first paper, by Gregan-Paxton and John, reminded us of the importance of task design when conducting research with children. They devised a clever game called "treasure hunt" that provided us with a view of when and how children of different ages adapt to complex decision environments. The second paper, by Palan and Wilkes, informed us of the complexity of adolescent-parent decision making. Using interpretive analysis, these authors revealed how the adolescent's influence attempts in the purchase process are affected by the interaction between the child's strategy choice and the parent's strategy choice. Third, Corfman, Harlam and Ziamou provided insight into the decision making process by considering factors related to the child, the parent, the family structure, past decisions, and the product category. These authors examined actual parent-child dyads in an experimental setting.

The synthesizer observed that the three papers also shared major themes and invited discussion of them. The following commonalities were discussed: 1) the emphasis shared by the first and second papers on strategic development of competencies, 2) the use by the first and third papers of unique experimental designs with an emphasis on age-appropriateness, and 3) the similarity of the last two presentations in their focus on the family unit, with parent-child dyads included in the data collection process.

Symbolic Consumption in China: The Color Television as a Life Statement

Kathleen Brewer Doran, Babson College[1]

ABSTRACT

The People's Republic of China is just emerging as a consumer market. As consumption opportunities develop for the Chinese, certain products are taking on enormous symbolic meaning within the Chinese culture. Consumer electronics is one of the product categories in which symbolism has become very important, especially color television sets. This research describes and analyzes the decision process used by consumers for buying color TVs, how the product is used within the home and its importance in modern Chinese life as a symbol of economic and political freedom.

INTRODUCTION

The People's Republic of China is just emerging as a consumer market. As consumption opportunities develop for the Chinese, certain products are being imbued with symbolic meaning within the Chinese culture. Consumer electronics is one of the product categories in which symbolism has become very important, especially for color television sets.

The purpose of the study was to develop a deep description and analysis of symbolic consumption of electronics in the People's Republic of China. This research builds on a largely North American-based stream of research into symbolic consumption, symbolic interactionism and semiotics by introducing symbolic consumption in a dramatically different and under-researched culture.

While China's expose to television has been brief by Western standards (about 10 years), penetration rates are very high, with estimates of about 80%. Partly because television introduction came so late, and partly because of the importance attributed to televisions in modern China, most of those sets are color and relatively large (18 inches and up). This phenomenon is more startling when viewed in combination with the generally low income levels in China. Urban income in China in 1993 was still only about 3,150RMB (less than US$400) per year, while rural income averaged only 1,200RMB annually. In Special Economic Zones (SEZ's), developed in 1984 to gradually move from a planned to a market economy, and major coastal municipalities, incomes are much higher. For example, in the Shenzen SEZ, bordering Hong Kong, 1993 household income averaged about 27,900RMB. Guangzhou, also in the south, followed at 17,500RMB. In addition, there appears to be a thriving underground cash economy, which would tend to result in the under-reporting of incomes. Finally, China's rapid growth rate, averaging about 12% annually in GDP over the past few years, is an indicator that consumption of items like televisions will continue to grow.

BACKGROUND

There is a significant body of research into the symbolic meaning of consumption (e.g. Solomon, 1983; Belk, 1985; 1988; McCracken, 1988; Belk, Wallendorf and Sherry, 1989; Hirschman and LaBarbera, 1989; Holbrook and Hirschman, 1993). This stream of research is a major contributor to the holistic understanding of consumer behavior. However, most of this research concentrates on consumption experiences in North America. This study extends the knowledge of symbolic consumption along cross cultural lines, by analyzing symbolic consumption in a group culturally distant from those usually studied. Those studies which have looked at cultures other than North America, such as Arnould's (1989) study of preference formation in Niger and McGuinness, Campbell and Leontiades (1991) study of selling machinery in China do show significant differences in the consumption experience.

Moreover, interpretive studies of consumers and consumption events appear to help form a bridge toward developing better studies of multiple cultures. Only when a deeper understanding of culturally-driven behaviors has been developed can researchers begin to develop appropriate, culturally-sensitive or culture-free instruments. This topic is addressed by Adler, Campbell and Laurent (1989) with particular regard to China and the lack of existing basic information about behavior within China. The interpretive approach employed here is one which has met with some success.

METHOD

The study utilizes interpretive research techniques as outlined in Strauss (1987), Hudson and Ozanne (1988), Belk, Wallendorf and Sherry (1989), Strauss and Corbin (1990) and Arnould and Wallendorf (1994). Data on Chinese consumers and their behavior was developed through a series of focus groups and in-depth interviews. This method for data gathering was chosen because so little information exists on Chinese consumers. Fifteen individuals participated in 3 focus groups, while in-depth interviews were conducted with 30 different individuals. Follow-up interviews were conducted at a later time with an additional 10 participants. Interviews and focus groups were conducted in accordance with the criteria developed by Lincoln and Guba (1985) and Wallendorf and Belk (1989). Focus groups averaged two hours in length, while interviews ran from one hour to two and one half hours. Participants were identified using a snowball sample and covered a broad range of ages (23-81), occupations (doctors, professors, clerks, political workers, factory workers, etc.), income levels ranged from about 500 yuan (about $60) to 10,000 yuan (about $1200) per month. In addition, the sample included an approximately even mix of men and women.

Interview protocols were developed through a series of 25 interviews of Chinese individuals currently living in North America. Where appropriate, data from these preliminary interviews are included here. Interviews were conducted either in English (primarily the North American interviews), or in Mandarin Chinese. Since the researcher was not fluent in Chinese, several interpreters were used. All interviews were either videotaped or audiotaped, and translation was checked by a second set of interpreters for accuracy. Participants were primarily from Beijing, but interviews were also conducted with participants from a total of 13 different municipalities and provinces. Interviews were primarily conducted at the researcher's office, but a few were conducted in participants' homes or workplaces.

Since the consumption environment was so important to the consumption behavior of the participants, a study of that environment was also undertaken, including advertising, store selection, store size, store staffing, and product availability. Visits to individuals' homes were also undertaken to document the use of

---

[1]The author wishes to thank Babson College and the Canadian International Development Agency (CIDA) for their assistance in providing backing for this project.

products within the home, as well as to assess general living circumstances. Data was gathered during four trips to China over a period of about one and a half years.

Since so little is known about the decision processes of Chinese consumers, or even what influences them, this type of descriptive research is important in building a body of research on which to base additional studies of both a qualitative and quantitative nature.

LIVING CONDITIONS IN CHINA

Living conditions in China are a key indicator in understanding the importance that televisions have in modern Chinese life. While living conditions in China vary dramatically from location to location, some observations can be made which help increase understanding of how living conditions may affect consumption behavior. In the People's Republic of China, the communist regime of the last 50 years has created an environment where the work unit is paramount. Not only do individuals work with their colleagues, but the work unit also provides housing and off-duty socialization. Since housing is generally provided by the employer, rent is nearly always a nominal amount (often the equivalent of only US$1-2 per month). By the same token, for most people, housing is provided according to an established set of needs, and not based on what one can afford. As a result, Chinese savings rates can run as high as 60%, with the remainder falling into a monthly budget for food (50%), clothing (30%) and incidentals (20%). Television and other electronics purchases generally come out of savings. For most Chinese owning an automobile is not only impossible financially, but practically due to lack of parking and severe limitations on licenses for private cars. Consumer electronics, particularly television, therefore takes on importance as a way to display one's wealth.

In general, Chinese homes are quite small. The stated goal of the Chinese government is to provide each family unit with 40 square meters (slightly more than 400 square feet) of living space. However, in 1995, average living space in China was 7.9 meters (83 square feet) per capita, or 23.7 meters (about 250 square feet) for a family of three. With such small homes, the television set becomes a focal point of the home.

THE TELEVISION AS A SYMBOL

Certain products have developed a symbolic consumption importance for Chinese consumers. While a number of product categories were accorded importance during the interviews, none achieved the level of significance that electronics did. The television, in particular, has reached even into rural China as a statement of life as it differs from traditional Chinese life. Since ownership of major items such as houses or cars is seldom viable, consumer electronics play an important symbolic role in establishing one's financial image as well as projecting an aura of personal success. "[The television we choose] is how we are evaluated by others." (M,25) One particularly vivid illustration of this symbolic importance was the role the selection and purchase of a television made on a couple's wedding plans and subsequent marital success. All of those questioned indicated that owning a color television was a prerequisite to marriage in urban (and many rural) areas of today's consumption-oriented China. Saving for an appropriate make and model was an ordeal for most that helped set the wedding date. Many couples indicated they were willing to wait two years to be able to afford the best possible TV.

The image of the television selected was extremely important. One participant (M, 46) noted that his wife's younger brother was planning to marry, and the participant had offered to help with the purchase of a television as a wedding present. However, when he suggested to his future brother-in-law that he buy a domestic make, the brother-in-law was scandalized. "Buying a Chinese TV will give my marriage a poor start," he said. "I must wait until I can buy a Japanese TV to project the right image to my friends."

Yet financial and personal success are not the only symbolic meanings for televisions in China today. The television, more than any other consumer item, represents freedom from the past and access to information. It is an educational tool as well as entertainment. It provides news programming to those who otherwise would have little access.

Size of the television selected was also important. While most Chinese live in very cramped surroundings, large television sets (21" and up) are more the norm than the exception. A very common comment was, "I want the largest television that will fit into my room." (F,34) It should be noted, however, that these considerations apply essentially to the primary TV in a given household. Older, smaller televisions were usually kept as a second set for the bedroom, where participants had more than one room.

Another interesting element to the television-as-symbol is the role it plays in gift-giving for overseas Chinese. When an overseas Chinese returns to visit family in the PRC, they are expected to bring a television set as a gift to the family. This often creates consternation on the part of the overseas Chinese, who generally remember a pre-television era China, and are surprised by television's importance and the specificity of the request (which often includes brand and size). Moreover, they are understandably daunted by the prospect of getting a large television to China in their luggage. Importation of consumer electronics has become such a problem that the Chinese government strictly regulates the process through customs inspections and declarations for all overseas Chinese entering the PRC.

Urban versus Rural Consumption

Television has achieved a surprisingly high rate of penetration in China, both in urban and rural areas. Estimates suggest that overall television penetration is upwards of 80%, with urban penetration approaching 98% of homes. Most of this growth has occurred within the last 10 years. This phenomenon was noted by several respondents, "Where once the television was considered a luxury, now it a necessity." (M,57) There are, however, relatively few differences in television consumption between urban and rural individuals. The one strong difference is in brand choice. In both cases, brand selection is usually driven by national origin: urban Chinese prefer Japanese televisions by a wide margin, while rural Chinese prefer to express their patriotism by buying Chinese. "There are more brands now to choose from, but I still prefer Chinese brands because they are easier to repair and it is more patriotic." (F, 28, Shandong Province)

On the other hand, urban Chinese tend to be more concerned with perceived quality than patriotism. "Price is not so important...but it is very important that it comes from Japan...that shows good quality. I have a 25" Toshiba — it has a nice look and my friends are impressed." (F, 31, Beijing)

There is, however, a sense that consumerism may be overtaking patriotism, particularly for those who have migrated to urban areas from the countryside. One man (29), formerly from Jianxi Province, but recently relocated to Beijing, noted that he had an 18" color model which had been made in Shanghai. He went on, though, to note, "I want a new one, because it's a bit old. It won't be the same...it should be a "hot" brand — Japanese — and a nice appearance. It must be bigger and have good functions, like Karaoke."

How Televisions Are Used

Television sets, perhaps because they are a newer addition to every day life in China as compared to the West, are used quite differently than in North America. First, programming is not available all day. Rather, programming is provided by several government-run networks for a few hours in the morning and evening. In some areas of southern China, Hong Kong's StarTV is also available. Cable is not available, although there are plans for the launch of China's first four cable stations in late 1996 (China News Digest,12/95). Commercials are given slots between programming, and many participants tuned in to view commercials (often about 15 in a 5 minute time slot), much like normal programming. Nearly all respondents watched news and cultural or entertainment events. Special serial programs were a favorite: during the interviews, most participants were watching a 100 part series recreating one of the traditional Chinese "great books," *The Romance of the Three Kingdoms*, a favorite for more than 400 years. Alternative programming, such as sports, Chinese soap operas, movies, children's programming and educational programming (the most popular of which was Business English) is also available and watched by somewhat smaller audiences. The television is rarely kept on in the background; rather, shows are chosen from the TV Guide in the paper, and watched by all family members.

A large color television set is usually the focal point of a Chinese family's main room. Often when not in use, the set is protected with a cover and unplugged. Because Chinese homes are so small, and the televisions are relatively large; proportionally, TVs consume a large amount of space. The set is often, though not always, accompanied by a VCR and Karaoke equipment. In fact, these two associated pieces point to three other major uses for televisions: for viewing prerecorded movies (often black market American movies), for viewing home-made videos of the family taken with camcorders, and as an integral component of a Karaoke system. Karaoke is immensely popular throughout China, not only in bars and restaurants, but also at home.

Decision Processes

Both because of the collective nature of Chinese culture, and the symbolic importance of the purchase, participants relied heavily on their reference groups for assistance. Most often, an engaged couple, who were saving for their television, would go around to friends' and family's homes to view the sets for themselves. This tactic seemed to function both on a marketing level and a social one. While the couple was "shopping" they were also creating an image with friends of a serious, dedicated couple.

However, while there was certainly a dependence on personal sources of information, some participants did admit to being influenced by advertising, "My impression of Japanese electronics has been shaped since my childhood by Sony ads...they have been here and very strong since China first opened to outsiders." (M, 25) Electronics producers were, in fact, among the largest advertisers on television or in newspapers during the course of the study.

Most televisions were bought in large department stores. The vast majority of respondents felt that this was too important a purchase to be trusted to street vendors or even specialty stores. Selection in department stores was impressive. A count by the researcher of different models available on the floor of major Beijing department stores averaged about 60. However, discussions with sales people indicated that about 80% of television sales came from only about 5 models. This benchmark was confirmed in the television ownership of participants and in the homes visited. The most popular model was a 21" Sony. The most desirable models were 25" or 29" Sony's or Panasonic's. The evoked set of most buyers appears to be restricted by recommendations from friends and family as well as a strong need to project a particular self-image.

Perhaps consistently with the importance of the television purchase, and the reflection on self-image, price was rarely a factor in choosing a TV. Price is irrelevant compared to quality (Japanese TVs are several times the price of the best Chinese TVs, for example), except within model. But since there are rarely sales, and most department stores are priced similarly, often price is not a part of buying equation.

The Meaning of Television Ownership

Television ownership is a much more meaningful state for the participants in China than for most North Americans. The television one owns is very much a representation of one's own self-worth. For most, the television had become almost as much a part of getting married as saying their vows. One engaged man (24), who was saving for his TV so he could get married, noted that he wanted a 25" or 29" Japanese model. He was willing to save for up to two years (a commonly quoted time frame) before revising his sights downward. Price was not nearly as important as projecting "a good image" to others. He was concerned about getting off to a good start. Several respondents noted that the purchase of the appropriate television set was more important than having furniture when considering marriage.

Yet television is an important social statement for all ages. At one point during the study, the researcher visited the home of an 80 year old widower in Beijing. While he knew of the study, he said since he was such an old man that possessions were not important to him. He asked questions about what the researcher had found thus far. When the researcher mentioned the symbolic nature of televisions, he started to smile. He led the researcher into his home where a large rectangular object was in a prominent position, under a deep red velvet dust cover. "You are right," he said, and unveiled his 29" Sony Trinitron. "I get great enjoyment from this, although otherwise, I live quite simply, but this [the TV] is important."

A television also represents freedom from oppression and the wealth and promise of the "new" China. Throughout China, hanging off small balconies on high-rises, on top of traditional one-floor houses where coal is still burned in braziers for heat, there are personal satellite dishes. While additional sales of these personal dishes were outlawed a few years ago, there are still a significant number. These satellite dishes, combined with their home TV sets, represent the ability to reach the outside world, a significant achievement in a nation which has restricted entry throughout most of its long history. The television, much like the telephone (which unlike television, has only a 3% penetration nationally), represents links with a modern, global economy.

Finally, while the Chinese love to dine out, most entertaining is done at home. Since homes are small, gathering in front of the TV has become a popular form of recreation. In fact, the television is well-suited to entertaining in cramped Chinese apartments, where many other activities would take up too much space. Yet a large part of the television's appeal as an entertainment device stems from two areas: Karaoke and the Chinese fascination with the formerly forbidden west. Karaoke is tremendously popular in China, both in restaurants and at home; the TV is an integral part of the Karaoke system. When friends tire of singing, the television then provides a link to the west. As such, the television represents an escape from the crowding, noise and dirt of everyday life in most of China.

CONCLUSIONS

The television has emerged as perhaps the most symbolic purchase an individual or couple makes in modern China. Part of the reason for this phenomenon lies in the fact that the Chinese public is still restricted in the number of products categories available to them. Purchases which might be considered more symbolic in the West, such as cars or houses, are seldom possibilities in China. Therefore, a television and accompanying purchases, such as a VCR and Karaoke system, are often the most expensive purchase Chinese make. Yet the TV's importance cannot be explained solely with financial logic. The television is also a symbol of economic and political freedom.

Finally, in addition to what the study shows regarding the symbolic importance of televisions in modern China, it is important to note that the findings in this study are consistent with past research in other areas. In particular, many of the activities described here have also been found in research into reference group influence (e.g. Bearden and Etzel, 1982; Brown and Reingen, 1987; Childers and Rao, 1992). In addition, the importance of televisions being of Japanese origin for many Chinese consumers is consistent with other studies of country-of-origin effects (see Erickson, Johansson and Chao, 1984; Johansson, 1989). Moreover, the differences in rural and urban consumption patterns noted here are also consistent with similar existing studies in other cultures (see Bearden and Etzel, 1992; Bearden, Netemeyer and Teel, 1989).

REFERENCES

Adler, Nancy, N. Campbell and A. Laurent. 1989. In Search of Appropriate Methodology: from Outside the People's Republic of China, Looking in. *Journal of International Business Studies*, 20(1): 61-74.

Arnould, Eric, J. 1989. Toward a Broadened Theory of Preference Formation and the Diffusion of Innovations: Cases from the Zinder Province, Niger Republic. *Journal of Consumer Research*, 16(September): 239-267.

Arnould, Eric J. and Melanie Wallendorf. 1994. Market-Oriented Ethnography: Interpretation Building and Marketing Strategy Formulation. *Journal of Marketing Research*, 31(November): 484-504.

Bearden, William O. and M.J. Etzel. 1982. Reference Group Influence on Product and Brand Purchase Decisions. *Journal of Consumer Research*, 9(September): 183-194.

Bearden, William O., Richard G. Netemeyer and Jesse E. Teel. 1989. Measurement of Consumer Susceptibility to Interpersonal Influence. *Journal of Consumer Research*, 15(March): 473-481.

Belk, Russell W. 1988. Possessions and the Extended Self. *Journal of Consumer Research*, 15(September): 139-168.

Belk, Russell W. 1985. Materialism: Trait Aspects of Living in the Material World. *Journal of Consumer Research*, 12(December): 265-280.

Belk, Russell W., Melanie Wallendorf and John F. Sherry. 1989. The Sacred and the Profane in Consumer Behavior: Theodicy on the Odyssey. *Journal of Consumer Research*, 16(June): 1-38.

Belk, Russell W. and Magda Paun. 1995. Ethnicity and Consumption in Romania. In *Marketing in a Multicultural World: Ethnicity, Nationalism, and Cultural Identity*, Janeen Costa and Gary Bamossy, eds. Thousand Oaks, California: Sage Publications.

Brown, J. J. and P. H. Reingen. 1987. Social Ties and Word-of-Mouth Referral Behavior. *Journal of Consumer Research*, 14(December): 206-215.

Childers, Terry L. and Ashkay R. Rao. 1992. The Influence of Familial and Perr-Based Reference Groups on Consumer Decisions. *Journal of Consumer Research*, 19(September): 198-211.

Costa, Janeen and Gary Bamossy. 1995. Perspectives on Ethnicity, Nationalism and Cultural Identity. In *Marketing in a Multicultural World: Ethnicity, Nationalism, and Cultural Identity*, Janeen Costa and Gary Bamossy, eds. Thousand Oaks, California: Sage Publications.

Doran, Kathleen Brewer. 1994. Exploring Cultural Differences in Consumer Decision Making: Chinese Consumers in Montreal. *Advances in Consumer Research*, Volume XXI. Chris T. Allen and Deborah Roedder John, eds. Provo, Utah: Association of Consumer Research.

Erickson, Gary M., Johny K. Johansson, and Paul Chao. 1984. Image Variables in Multi-Attribute Product Evaluations: Country-of-Origin Effects. *Journal of Consumer Research*, 11(September): 694-699.

Ger, Güliz. 1992. The Positive and Negative Effects of Marketing on Socioeconomic Development: The Turkish Case. *Journal of Consumer Policy*, 15: 229-254.

Hirschman, Elizabeth C. and Priscilla A. Labarbera. 1989. The Meaning of Christmas. *Interpretive Consumer Research*, Elizabeth C. Hirschman, ed., Provo, Utah: Association of Consumer Research.

Holbrook, Morris B. and Elizabeth C. Hirschman. 1993. *The Semiotics of Consumption*. New York: Mouton de Gruyter.

Hudson, L. and J. Ozanne. 1988. Alternative Ways of Seeking Knowledge in Consumer Research. *Journal of Consumer Research*, 14(March): 508-521.

Johannson, Johny K. 1989. Determinants and Effects of "Made-In" Labels. *International Marketing Review*, 6(1): 47-58.

Joy, Annamma and Melanie Wallendorf. 1996. The Development of Culture in the Third World: Theories of Globalism and Localism. In *Consumption and Marketing*, Russel Belk, Nikilesh Dholakia and Alladi Venkatesh, eds. Cincinnati, Ohio: Southwestern Publishing.

McCracken, Grant. 1988. *Culture and Consumption: New Approaches to the Symbolic Character of Consumer Goods and Activities*. Bloomington, Indiana: Indiana University Press.

McGuinness, N., N. Campbell and J. Leontiades. 1991. Selling Machinery to China: Chinese Perceptions of Strategies and Relationships. *Journal of International Business Studies*, 22(2): 187-207.

Mick, David Glen. 1986. Consumer Research and Semiotics: Explaining the Morphology of Signs, Symbols and Significance. *Journal of Consumer Research*, 17(December): 322-332.

Solomon, Michael R. 1983. The Role of Products as Social Stimuli: A Symbolic Interactionism Perspective. *Journal of Consumer Research*, 10(December): 319-329.

Strauss, Anselm. 1987. *Qualitative Analysis for Social Scientists*. Cambridge, England: Cambridge University Press.

Strauss Anselm and Juliet Corbin. 1990. *Basics of Qualitative Research: Grounded Theory and Techniques*. Newbury Park, California: Sage Publications.

Venkatesh, Alladi. 1995. Ethnoconsumerism: A New Paradigm to Study Cultural and Cross-Cultural Consumer Behavior. In *Marketing in a Multicultural World: Ethnicity, Nationalism, and Cultural Identity*, Janeen Costa and Gary Bamossy, eds. Thousand Oaks, California: Sage Publications.

Sense vs. Sensibility: An Exploration of the Lived Experience of Camp

Steven M. Kates, University of Northern British Columbia

ABSTRACT

Hedonic and experiential modes of consumption are important, yet relatively unexplored areas of the consumer research discipline. This research uses long, semi-structured interviews and participant observation in order to explore the homosexual subcultural style known as 'camp.' Three themes emerged from the data: camp products, camp celebrities and people, and gender subversion. Camp phenomena are subsequently discussed in the context of meaning transfer between the homosexual subculture and the dominant, mainstream culture. Directions for future research in this topic area are noted.

The purpose of this article is to empirically explore 'camp' sensibility within the contexts of the larger, theoretical question of meaning transfer from culture to product as expounded by mainstream consumer researchers such as McCracken (1986, 1989) and cultural semioticians such as Gottdiener (1995, 1985). Camp is a consumption phenomenon which has been neglected in the consumer research literature. According to Sontag (1964), the camp aesthetic–along with 'Jewish moral seriousness'–are the most importance influences upon our modern culture. Moreover, it is arguable that the empirical study of camp–as a set of meanings tied to gay subculture and as manifested within certain goods and services– has a great potential to enrich the consumer behaviour literature, as consumer researchers have the opportunity to both expand the understanding of this strange, elusive, and somewhat ineffable mode of consumption and expand the knowledge domain of hedonic consumption (Holbrook and Hirschman 1982).

In previous works, consumer researchers have made progress in addressing the conceptual and theoretical aspects of the consumption of experience (e.g. Celsi, Rose, and Leigh 1993; Arnould and Price 1993; Wallendorf and Arnould 1991; Holbrook and Hirschman 1982) and considerable progress in understanding the deeper meanings of possessions (Richins 1994, 1994a; Belk, Wallendorf, and Sherry 1989; Belk, Sherry, and Wallendorf 1988). These and other works illuminate a host of social occasions in our society during which people gather and obtain social benefit by the public use or sharing of goods or consumer experience. This branch of the discipline is of great imporance, as broad yet intangible cultural forces shape consumption practices and meanings, and in turn, people's consumption shapes culture (Wallendorf and Arnould 1991).

THE ABSOLUTELY *FABULOUS WORLD* OF CAMP MEANING

Camp may be considered the product of a sensibility–a mode of feeling– and an aethetic–a form of artistic expression. Since Sontag's (1964) now famous essay, little has been written about it within the social sciences literature, but it has been discussed in the gay and lesbian studies work (eg. Sullivan 1995; Newton 1993; Bergman 1993). Camp is manifested in goods or practices which are highly stylish but not substantial. According to Sontag's essay, it is the 'homosexual aesthetic' which is 'off,' exaggerated, or gently comical. Kleinberg (1992) notes that camp is an ironic sensibility as related to a product (or often, a work of art) because the physical object itself conceals a deeper, hidden meaning beneath a facade of absurdity.

Camp is the aesthetic taste which might prompt someone to exclaim, 'it's so dreadful! It's wonderful!' The juxtaposition of the two opposite sentiments in this statement should be noted carefully. The apparent contradiction therein summarily enforces the notion that camp art or products contain within themselves important paradoxes, inversions, and contradictions which may help to subvert conventional order, tradition, or orthodoxy (Bergman 1993; Newton 1993; Babcock 1978). Camp is a *style* found in things or experiences which may be described as artifice or extremity. There is a significantly subjective aspect to camp, and it is worthwhile to list some examples of things which are widely considered 'campy': John Waters' films, Andy Warhol's art, plastic pink flamingoes, feather boas, Steve Reeves movies, drag queens and female impersonators, and a host of female entertainers such as Bette Midler, Marilyn Monroe, and of course, Judy Garland. More precisely, it has been asserted that camp is not a thing itself, but rather, it is a relationship *between things* (Newton 1993) or *between people and things*: "...camp inheres not in the person or thing itself but in the tension between that person or thing and the context or association..." (Newton 1993; p. 47). Thus, camp refers to a person-object relationship and as such, may constitute a rich, sophisticated, and complex set of cultural meanings which lend themselves to empirical enquiry by consumer researchers.

Bergman (1993) asserts that there are four important areas of agreement about camp, and in order to provide a foundation for empirical, critical enquiry, these separate but related points must be noted. First, camp is a style which emphasizes exaggeration, extremity, and artifice. Second, 'camp exists in tension with popular culture...' (p. 5). Third, camp is generally only recognized, understood, or appreciated by someone outside the cultural mainstream. And finally, camp is associated with gay subculture. This final point is critical and merits further elaboration. Various authors have noted that from early in life, many gay men share in common the need to 'pass' in 'straight,' dominant culture in order to hide their social stigma (Sullivan 1995; Troiden 1989, 1987; Goffman 1963). Before 'coming out of the closet,' gay men and lesbians must hide and deny a socially condemned sexual orientation and methodically construct a social identity or personae which is sharply at odds with their most deeply felt personal and sexual self-knowledge. Thus, it is not surprising that many gays and lesbians may develop well-developed appreciation and understanding of artifice and appearances in general (see Sullivan 1995). In many social situations, a gay man or lesbian must carefully present a facade to a potentially hostile audience. This *dasein* or mode of experiencing one's own social and cultural world leads often to a sensitivity or appreciation of the ironies and inversions contained within camp experience, art, or products. One might go as far as to claim that a gay man's unique perspective of the world as sexual suspect and outsider is a fertile breeding ground for the production of the sensibility and aesthetic–in short, the style–which humourously, ironically, and sometimes subversively emphasizes artifice as opposed to substance, and appearance over reality.

Camp has emerged as a very etic, cultural construct which appears somewhat removed from its contextualized lived reality. By studying it naturalistically, *in situ*, from the perspective of those who experience it, it is possible to grasp and explore its sophistication, complexity, and cultural richness and understand its 'lived experience' dimension–how it is encountered, perceived, appreciated, and incorporated into the consciousness of the informants' social worlds. Hence, one may ask the following questions: how do individuals experience camp or campy products? What is its importance in their lives? How does an object or commodity acquire 'campy' meanings? Such is the contribution which this paper seeks to provide: a thick description of camp, grounded in data and situated within the overall perspective of an experiential, hedonic, symbolically meaningful consumer behaviour.

METHOD

Camp is an amalgam of deep meanings, often related to possessions and consumption experiences. Such a phenomenon lends itself to humanistic enquiry (Hirschman 1986) within the overall interpretive paradigm (Burrell and Morgan 1979). Thus, in the spirit of ethnographic discovery, qualitative methods including a combination of long interviews (McCracken 1988) and participant observation (Jorgensen 1989) were employed as part of a larger, more comprehensive study of the consumption patterns of gay men within the urban subculture (Kates 1996). In this study, forty-four gay men were interviewed, and the topic of camp was broached; other topics such as coming out stories, personal histories, favourite possessions and consumption experiences, and dining out were also discussed. These participants were selected purposively, using an emergent design. Interviews were semi-structured and lasted between one hour and three and a half hours. All were audiotaped. The tapes were transcribed verbatim.

Moreover, participant observation was employed in order to enrich my own experience of camp products and the gay subculture. For almost one year and a half, I dwelled within the gay subculture in a large, Canadian city. During this period, I lived as an openly gay man within the physical area of the 'gay ghetto,' frequented gay bars, parties, and festivals such as Lesbian and Gay Pride Day, and participated in political actions such as marches. Also, I joined two different groups. One was a gay and lesbian youth group in which I took on the role of respectful, interested researcher. The other was a gay men's professional and social club in which I had been an active member for almost four years previously. Associating myself with these groups provided me with the opportunity of interviewing and interacting with a broad spectrum of gay men from the ages of 16 to 52 of multiple races and diverse cultural, professional, and ethnic backgrounds. Moreover, such a diversity assisted me in finding informants who would both reinforce and challenge preconceptions or interpretations through an overall process of refutation (see Spiggle 1994). I noted my experiences in journals throughout my time studying the groups. The actual demographics of the forty-four men actually interviewed are as follows: the majority (27) were between the ages of 20 to 35; six were between the ages of 15 to 19 and nine were 36 and older. Thirty-five of the informants were from European backgrounds; four were Black, and four were southeast Asian.

Once transcribed, I read over several times and sifted through the data (approximately two thousand types pages) and coded it according to different areas of interest, using a naturalistic orientation (Lincoln and Guba 1987). I categorized the data according to similar topics of interest by comparing informants' experiences, and then searched for patterns which were collapsed into overall, broad themes which described the informants' lived experience of camp, carefully ensuring that the data determined the broad categories as opposed to imposing them myself upon the data. I chose one interview, coded it, and then coded the other interviews according to this coding scheme, adding categories and taking care to cross-categorize data as well. Finally, I interpreted the categories, relating topics of interest, developing a thick description, articulating the relationships between dominant themes and categories in order to extend the individual events to the broader cultural logics as reflected in the data (Spiggle 1994; Wallendorf and Brucks 1993; Geertz 1973). During this process, I attempted first to understand

camp from the informants' perspectives and *then* extend the interpretation by distancing myself from the data in order to relate various overall patterns and cultural codes of meanings.

RESULTS: THE LIVED EXPERIENCE OF CAMP

A number of broad and inter-related themes emerged after coding the data and tacking between it and the literature: 1) camp products, 2) camp people and celebrities and 3) gender subversion. Each of these will be described and fleshed out below, using rich and detailed quotes from the participants themselves.

Camp 'Products'

According to the data, camp is very much a subjectively experienced phenomenon, but it has some shared, cultural characteristics. There exists a significant level of agreement among the informants as to what objects and experiences are camp and what renders them so:

...anything tacky, which is great (laughs). Through the whole era of the fifties, the whole thing is camp or tacky. Um, There's like flat painted ceramics that are worth quite a bit, but you think 'Oh, my God, they're junk!' because the colours are *tacky*. The ceramic itself is not like high quality the way we expect it to be now. (Gay white male, 25; my italics)

There are campy things and there are campy objects, but there's also campy people... Whereas camp is more an idea that sometimes manifests itself in objects. A campy object tends to be a kitschy object as well. But it has specific significance for the gay community. A pink flamingo is a kitschy object. It's also camp for gay people, because there's a whole representation behind pink flamingoes that doesn't quite apply in the straight community. I mean, the straight community may associate pink flamingos with trailer parks and pink fibreglass and stuff like that but for the gay community, pink flamingos were used very often, especially in Florida, in the Miami communities to represent gay people and was often used as a symbol for gay people, and for us there's an added dimension to it...I mean, we'll just look at it and go, 'that's so *tacky*!' It's hilariously funny, *it's so horrible, it's funny!* (Gay Asian male, 23)

Consistent with the prior literature (e.g Babuscio 1993; Ross 1989; Bronski 1984), camp objects or possessions are described as extreme, exaggerated, somewhat ridiculous, and humourous. The data support the previously accepted notion that camp products, objects, or possessions are the meaning constructions which emerge from gay subcultural taste. Yet, the data lends itself to a deeper interpretation. Many of the objects listed above such as pink flamingos and pastel ceramics are appropriated from the heterosexual mainstream culture. The gay men herein are reinterpreting these 'straight' artefacts in a particular manner which mocks them and reveals their absurdity. Our understanding is further enhanced when we take into account that some cultural critics (e.g Ross 1989; Bronski 1984) interpret camp as a form of defence mechanism which gay men employ to protect themselves from the indignities they endure due to the dominant sexual norm. As McCracken (1988a) notes, goods tangibly manifest the dominant categories and ideas of a culture, and one may infer from this statement that material goods are another form of discourse or power structure which maintains the *status quo* (Foucault 1980). Camp sensibility, thus, may be meaningfully interpreted as a significant 'shift in lens' for gay men which may lead to alternative, more inclusive forms of discourse. The data supports these notions. Camp emerged as a lived experience which provides the informants with a new outlook, perceived as largely private and exclusive from the heterosexual mainstream, an alternative way of viewing the relics and experiences of culture.

Camp Celebrities and People

People such as drag queens and certain popular celebrities have also acquired important camp meanings. At the outset of my study, I was very curious as to how it was that gay men appeared to be so fond of various celebrities, particularly female singers and actors. This study has provided some valuable insights in this regard, from an emic, consumer perspective. Consider one informant's view of one of his favourite celebrities, Jackie Kennedy Onassis:

...I mean, coming out and dealing with everything and a lot of us have dealt with various things in our lives, whether it's dealing with a health crisis issue or whether it's dealing with uh, a sexual abuse of some sort or something. *We've had very hard lives! And so when we look at other people like this, by exaggerating their lives, we can make our lives a little bit easier in a sense.* It's like entertainment to us. Bette Midler, for example, tends to be very campy, in a sense. It's not her in itself, but it's rather her act. She tries to go over and above and beyond and just as outrageous as she can get because the more you do that, the more pleasurable experience it's going to be, the more positive and the more funny. Because you're looking at something that, uh, Jackie Onassis, this is the perfect example. She passed away this past weekend...One of the bars, up the street, is having a...our angel in a pillbox festivity, so to speak. So they're going to honour and tribute her, but they're going to do it in a campy way because with the pillbox, they're referring to her hats, of course, not necessarily that she had a drug problem. But the type of artistry that'll be perceived is something...*Sometimes the best way to deal with tears is through laughter*, and that's exactly what the gay community is doing...Judy Garland had led such a tragic life. Therefore, they honour her with laughter, through their campiness. With Jackie Onassis, at the GCDC [Gay Community Dance Committee] dance, actually, um, there was the best costume I've ever seen, a Hallowe'en costume and it was Jackie Onassis, dressed exactly...well, Jackie Kennedy at the time, I should say, exactly as she was, when her husband was murdered. And she was splattered in blood, and she was just..that is very, very campy!!! It's so outrageous. It's horrible! But at the same time, it's real! But it's not real!

SK: How was she dressed at the time?

How was she dressed? She was dressed in the pillhat, she was dressed in the pink outfit, like the business suit, quasi business suit, I should say. Um, she had on the same hairstyle, the same shoes and everything. But then, it was as if...she was splattered...with blood. And there was an incredible, incredible type costume and I...Chris was the person who was wearing it...because she went over and above, and not only was it a costume, but she brought the person...she made the person come alive. And she did the wave...she spoke the way that Jackie did. And in so many ways, she...took an experience that people held as being so horrible, I mean, people can remember exactly where they were that day, and she brought humour in a different perception to people. She brought that double entendre so to speak, in a sense that, yes, it happened in reality, let's take it for face value, we don't ever, ever want to forget

what happened, but at the same time, let's laugh as well. We can't constantly cry. I mean when I think of some of the things um, with the Holocaust, for instance, that is such a horrible, horrible experience, and I don't ever want to ever see anything like that happen again. Yet, at the same time, only so many movies and so many plays and so many stories can hold the serious monotone...the educational type force behind it. That suddenly, the perception gets lost in a sense, we only see it as that's the way it was, and there is no other way we can ever achieve it except on that serious monotone note. Whereas by taking like that Jackie Onassis type character, we can see it for something else. Wait a minute! We can get to that exact same spot other ways and through humour, through other types of stories and all the rest, we can have the same profound meaning, but it's with a double entendre. It's like this did happen. This is so important to history, did you get the point? And that's exactly what camp is all about. There is a message there but you have to find it. (Gay white male, 28)

I think there's a...most of these women are very strong women. Barbra Streisand, Jackie Onassis. They're very strong women, and I think gay men identify with women because women have a lot of obstacles in their way that they have to overcome in order to succeed.
(Gay white male, 23)

Celebrities are another form of camp 'product,' the work of whom many of the gay men in this study experienced. Bette Midler, Bette Davis, Barbra Streisand, Madonna, Marilyn Monroe, and Judy Garland were frequently mentioned as camp female figures. By comparison, few men were named. Generally, the women artists were described in both stereotypically masculine and feminine terms. Jackie Kennedy Onassis 'overcame' great pain and hardship (ie. she 'took it like a man'), but she 'looks great!' in a feminine manner. The conflation of these binary opposite dimensions—masculine/feminine, pain/pleasure, failure/success—as embodied within the lives of the female stars perhaps exemplifies the very essence of camp sensibility. Symbolic inversion, as commonly defined as a reversal or negation of conventional thought or orthodoxy (Babcock 1978), depends quite heavily upon irony and incongruous juxtapositions of various symbols or ideas; it is a form of cultural *bricolage* (e.g. Hebdige 1979). The pain and struggle as contrasted within the achievements of the great 'larger than life' women of Hollywood and popular culture acts as a mirror for gay men's own lives. Yet, the campy mirror is a distorted one. Camp sensibility relies upon a significant shift in perspective in order to render the unbearable bearable and the tragic hilarious: *'We can't constantly cry.'* A humourous, incongruous *style* is introduced to resonate with an often lamentable substance, and it is the former which dominates the overall viewpoint.

Much of camp consumption does revolve around lamentable circumstances—the widowhood of a young woman (Kennedy Onassis), the drug abuse and personal downfall experienced by a greatly admired singer and actor (Garland) or the criticism and ostracism endured by a multi-talented and extremely accomplished entertainer (Streisand). As McCracken (1989) has noted, both the art and the lives of Hollywood artists are 'consumed' within the context of the star system. Yet, the camp consumption perspective mellows and soothes the tragedies by introducing a measure of melodrama and humour. It is as if the tragedy and pain itself is framed as a performance rather than as real life. The tragic circumstances of the 'great women' are, to a significant extent, reflected and experienced within the lives of their primary audience: gay men. The conflation of dramatic pain and pleasure closely parallels the pain and etiolation experienced by these sexual outsiders. Yet, the same camp lens which is focused upon the lives of camp women is also directed toward these gay men's own lives. Camp as a survival or coping mechanism allows them to achieve an ironic, dual stance in relation to their own paradoxical understandings of themselves as insiders (when 'passing') and outsiders and as males who share something significant in common with the denigrated, binary opposite social category–women. The pleasure associated with camp style or perspective ameliorates the pain of another experienced subjectivity.

Gender Subversion

Previous literature has noted that gays radically transform the meanings of products through the fashion system (McCracken 1986) through subverting the socially constructed notion of gender. As noted previously, the gay men here identified with women to a certain extent. The following comments by this informant elaborates on this theme:

Um, I think a political aspect goes back to a little bit to the gender bending, I guess, in a way. Just the way we define gender in the postwar period. Not before. And gender in the postwar period was that, males had certain characteristics. Boom, boom, boom, boom, and when I mean boom, boom, you can just state them all–the breadwinner, the dominant force in the family, and all of the things which we all know are totally fucking false anyhow, but this is what we project, and this is the foundation during the 50's that I say and it never even existed that much before, but yeah, that's what we're dealing with, that's what we're aspiring to today. And the political element in campiness is the allowance for a couple of guys to sit around no matter how macho and to sit there and just laughing their heads off at the most ridiculous experiences which women should only be able to kind of be able to identify with whether it be about crying or laughing or whatever, some aspect of domestic life. Relationships. And all that other kind of thing that aren't quote unquote what we always kind of identified with as now, so in that particular respect, that's what we're opening...allowing ourselves these experiences...So, in that particular respect, uh, I think it does have that type of political element because it challenges that structure that we seem to have built for ourselves. Little boys play with this. Little boys don't change dolls. Well, isn't it a little bit of campiness when little boys playing around with...little boy's setting up his dollhouse and changing so and so and doing the diapers and that stuff? I think there is, a little bit. (Gay White Male, 28)

J: [Barbra Streisand]'s so funny, man! That film is funny. Let's take The Way We Were or something like that. Perfect relationship, fell in love at first sight. *The campiness to me comes out of the fact that as the guy, you don't identify with Robert Redford, you identify with 'Bahbwa,' you know. And that may be stretching what campiness is all about, but for me, that's basically, what a lot of times what happens for...what happens in campiness is that, on whatever level it may be, as a male, you're identifying very strongly with the female character and what the female character is going through,* 'cause she's kind of the one who falls in love, and doesn't like, you know, trying to seek love and all that kind of thing. All the things that, you know, men aren't usually supposed to be doing or something like that. They fall easy and their hearts break easy and that kind of stuff. (Gay white male, 28)

Perhaps Sontag's most controversial and disputed statement in her 1964 essay was to assert the 'apolitical' nature of camp (Bergman 1993; Ross 1989). Recent critics have strongly objected; Bergman, by contrast, claims that camp 'could have a powerful, radical role to play in cultural politics...' (1993; p. 7). The above quote by an informant and other, similar accounts in the data reinforce and elaborate upon Bergman's point of view. Indeed, the politics of camp are 'foregrounded' when one contemplates the notion that gender *inv*ersion generally constitutes a powerful form of gender *sub*version. Drag, one of the most common forms of camp, has been criticized as sexist and degrading to women, as it presents an extreme, gaudy, and somewhat grotesque image of femininity (Babuscio 1993). Yet, it is arguable that this rather simplistic point of view is incomplete and ungrounded in gay men's own experience. True, camp is experienced often by the participants as a parody of conventions or orthodoxy; but it is a parody and satire of common stereotypes of femininity, not of women *per se*. Moreover, in the study, the emergent finding is that the gay men feel a form of kinship or empathy with the problems and experiences of women. This empathic form of identification breaks a social taboo. Not only do these gay men challenge serious societal norms by engaging in sexual relations with other men (and thus assuming women's culturally inferior *sexual* role), but also they exacerbate their offence by attempting to connect emotionally with the other sex, assuming (one of the many) feminine, inferior *social* roles. Camp has the subversive capacity to expose certain societal contradictions and conspire in their ridicule and eventual overthrow. Through it, gay men may develop a form of revolutionary consciousness in order to challenge their collective oppression.

DISCUSSION: THE CULTURAL LOGICS OF CAMP, MEANING TRANSFER, AND CULTURAL (RE)APPROPRIATION

Meaning Transfer, Inversion, and Camp

Overall, inversion has emerged as the key, operative 'meaning creating' mechanism which grants camp its power and depth. Camp depends upon a diverse set of symbolic inversions: reversals of conventional roles, (sometimes dramatic) irony, cross-gender identification, and juxtapositions of disparate elements. The phenomenon of the drag queen, as an excellent example (and particularly well depicted in the film *Paris is Burning*), is a juxtaposition between the male sex and stereotypically feminine gender signifiers. As such, (s)he represents a radical and socially proscribed form of social role reversal. Like much of camp, the drag queen as radical cultural icon represents a combination of exaggeration, humour, wit, tragedy, histrionics, and style.

Both 'ordinary' commodities or products (such as feather boas or pink flamingos) and female celebrities may acquire camp-related meanings through a process resembling that of McCracken's (1986) meaning transfer model. Through the conduits of mass media, word of mouth, and propinquity (elements of the fashion system; moreover, all of which are relevant to small communities such as urban gay 'ghettos'), certain objects and people from the 'straight' or mainstream cultural world become associated with a set of complex, inverted 'gay', meanings which 'stand the world on its head' in a form of mocking parody; these meaningful goods are then consumed experientially for both their utilitarian functions and their sign values (Gottdiener 1995, 1985); consistent with the concept of hedonic consumption, they are appreciated for fun and for their value as 'offbeat' works of art or as entertainment. Gay men (and to a lesser extent, lesbians) learn about and accept camp meanings into their lives and self-concepts through various grooming, possession, exchange, and divestment rituals (McCracken 1986).

'Straight' Camp?!

However, in terms of interpreting the important, cultural logics as contained in the data, it should be noted that something more than simple meaning transfer is occurring here. It is interesting to note that camp meanings do not remain within the cultural context of the gay community. Rather, many are reappropriated by 'straight society.' Some informants noted that while heterosexuals do not usually 'get' camp, they appreciate their own form of camp which also contains significant elements of wit, humour, inversion and excess. There has been considerable evidence of this phenomenon from other studies. 'Glam' rockers such as David Bowie, the New York Dolls, and even Mick Jagger have appeared in public drag; Andy Warhol introduced the world to his own excessive, campy, and artistic vision in the 1960's (Ross 1989). The hugely campy Rocky Horror Picture Show, despite its blatant homoerotic content, remains popular with a largely heterosexual audience. Pop Diva Annie Lennox cross-dressed at the Grammy Awards during the early 1980's.

Yet, there is reason to question whether this 'straight' camp retains the 'substance' of the original subcultural style. Is 'straight' camp but a shadow of its gay progenitor? Given the dramatically differing social situations of gay men versus the heterosexual majority, it is highly likely that the painful, subversive, and political meanings and tensions which give camp its 'edge' are 'stripped' and 'sanitized', leaving humour, wit, and excess–and nothing more. In his study on English punk culture, Hebdige (1979) noted that punk style may be interpreted as a subcultural, rebellious response to English class hegemony. Through processes such as bricolage and homology, the signifiers of English class structure were subverted and parodied. Yet, in a further development, fashion designers and journalists (as agents of the fashion system) respectively reappropriated and popularized punk style into 'To Shock is Chic' fashion, commodifying and depoliticizing punk subcultural style. Furthermore, Schouten and McAlexander (1995) in their ethnographic study of the new urban bikers described the process of reappropriation of original biker culture by wealthy, urban, middle-class professionals. Analogously, the distinct, cultural lens–the window on the world–which camp represents may be lost when objects and experiences are (re)appropriated, (re)absorbed, and (re)diffused into the heterosexual dominant culture.

Further Directions for Research

One important future direction could be a comprehensive exploration of 'straight camp.' Researchers in consumer behaviour or cultural critique could inquire whether there are any deep, painful, or subversive meanings contained within the perspectives of heterosexual audiences of camp. Within the cultural processes of meaning transfer, co-optation, appropriation and recycling, is the camp artefact 'returned' in its original condition or does it carry with it the 'taint' of homosexual meaning? Do other marginalized subcultures (such as African-Americans or Hispanic-Americans) construct their own consumption 'codes' or sensibilities which are native to them and serve similar purposes as camp does for gay men or punk style does for the English underclasses? Is some form of cultural inversion a significant mechanism in their development? Celebrity endorsements and meanings are also a relatively unexplored phenomenon in the consumer behaviour field. As described above, many famous women acquire powerful, subtle, and complex meanings as described by McCracken (1989). Do the camp meanings render Barbra Streisand or Bette Midler any more or less

effective as endorsers? Would they be appropriate as endorsers for companies who target the supposedly lucrative gay market?

Consumer researchers are only now beginning to penetrate the world of deeper meanings of consumers and the world of hedonic, largely experiential consumption, largely (but not exclusively) through qualitative methods. Camp has emerged a system of related, complex, subversive and powerful consumption related meanings. The consumer research field may certainly benefit from its fuller elucidation.

REFERENCES

Arnould, Eric J. and Linda L. Price (1993), "River Magic: Extraordinary Experience and the Extended Service Encounter", *Journal of Consumer Research*, 20, 1, 24-45.

Babuscio, Jack (1993), "Camp and the Gay Sensibility," in *Camp Grounds: Style and Homosexuality*. Ed. David Bergman. Amhert, MA: University of Massachusets Press.

Babcock, Barbara A. (1978), "Introduction," in *The Reversible World: Symbolic Inversion in Art and Society*. ed. Barbara A. Babcock. Ithaca: Cornell University Press.

Belk, Russell, John F. Sherry Jr. and Melanie Wallendorf (1988), "A Naturalistic Inquiry into Buyer and Seller Behaviour at a Swap Meet", *Journal of Consumer Research*, 14, March, 449-470.

Belk, Russell, Melanie Wallendorf, and John F. Sherry Jr. (1989), "The Sacred and the Profane in Consumer Behaviour: Theodicy on the Odyssey", *Journal of Consumer Research*, Vol. 16, June, pp. 1-38.

Bergman, David (1993) , "Introduction," in *Camp Grounds: Style and Homosexuality*. Ed. David Bergman. Amhert, MA: University of Massachusets Press.

Bronski, Michael (1984), *Culture Clash: The Making of a Gay Sensibility*. Boston, MA: South End Press.

Burrell, Gibson and Gareth Morgan (1979), *Sociological Paradigms and Organizational Analysis*. Portsmouth, NH: Heinemann Educational Books.

Celsi, Richard, L., Randall L. Rose, and Thomas W. Leigh (1993), "An Exploration of High Risk Leisure Consumption Through Skydiving", *Journal of Consumer Research*, 20, 1, 1-23.

Foucault, Michel (1980), *The History of Sexuality, Part One*. Harmondsworth: Penguin.

Garber, Marjorie (1992), *Vested Interests: Cross Dressing and Cultural Anxiety*. New York: Routledge.

Geertz, Clifford (1973), *The Interpretation of Cultures*. New York: Basic.

Goffman, E. (1963), *Stigma: Notes on the Management of Spoiled Identity*. Harmondworth: Penguin.

Gottdiener, M. (1995), *Postmodern Semiotics: Material Culture and the Forms of Postmodern Life*. Cambridge, Mass: Blackwell.

Gottdiener, M. (1985), "Hegemony and Mass Culture: A Semiotic Approach," *American Journal of Sociology*, 90, 5, 979-1001.

Hebdige, Dick (1979), *Subculture: The Meaning of Style*. New York: Routledge.

Hirschman, Elizabeth C. (1986), "Humanistic Inquiry in Marketing Research: Philosophy, Method, and Criteria", *Journal of Marketing Research*, XXIII, August, 237-249.

Holbrook, Morris B. and Elizabeth C. Hirschman (1982), "The Experiential Aspects of Consumer Behaviour: Consumer Fantasies, Feelings, and Fun", *Journal of Consumer Research*, 9, 132-140.

Jorgensen, Danny L. (1989), *Participant Observation: A Methodology for Human Studies*. London: Sage Publications.

Kates, Steven (1996), "Closets are for Clothes: "An Ethnographic Exploration of Gay Men's Consumer Behaviour," unpublished doctoral dissertation, York University, North York, Canada.

Kinsman, Gary (1991), "'Homosexuality Historically Reconsidered Challenges Heterosexual Hegemony", *Journal of Historical Sociology*, 4, 2, 91-111.

Kleinberg, S. (1992), "The New Masculinity of Gay Men, and Beyond", in *Men's Lives*, M. Kimmel and M. Messner, eds. Toronto: Maxwell MacMillan Canada.

Lincoln, Yvonna S. and Egon G. Guba (1987), *Naturalistic Inquiry*. Beverly Hills, CA: Sage.

McCracken, Grant (1989), "Who is the Celebrity Endorser? Cultural Foundations of the Endorsement Process", *Journal of Consumer Research*, 16, 310-321.

McCracken, Grant (1988), *The Long Interview*. Newbury Park: Sage Publications.

McCracken, Grant (1988a), *Culture and Consumption: New Approaches to the Symbolic Character of Consumer Goods and Activities*. Indianapolis: Indiana University Press.

McCracken, Grant (1986), "Culture and Consumption: A Theoretical Account of the Structure and Movement of the Cultural Meaning of Consumer Goods", *Journal of Consumer Research*, 13, June, 71-84.

Miller, D.A. (1993), "Sontag's Urbanity," in *The Lesbian and Gay Studies Reader*. Ed. Henry Abelove, Michele Aina Barale, and David M. Halperin.

Newton, Esther (1993), "Role Models," in *Camp Grounds: Style and Homosexuality*. Ed. David Bergman. Amhert, MA: University of Massachusets Press.

Richins, Marsha (1994), Valuing Things: The Public and Private Meanings of Possessions," *Journal of Consumer Research*, 21, 3, 504-521.

———, "Special Possessions and the Expressions of Material Values," *Journal of Consumer Research*, 21, 3, 522-534.

Ross, Andrew (1989), "Uses of Camp," in *No Respect: Intellectuals and Popular Culture*. New York: Routledge.

Schouten, John W. and James H. McAlexander (1995), "Subcultures of Consumption: An Ethnography of the New Bikers", *Journal of Consumer Research*, 22, 1, 43-61.

Sontag, Susan, "Notes on Camp" (1964), in *Against Interpretation*. New York: Farrar, Straus, and Giroux.

Spiggle, Susan (1994), "Analysis and Interpretation of Qualitative Data in Consumer Research," *Journal of Consumer Research*, 21, 3, 491-503.

Sullivan, Andrew (1995), *Virtually Normal: An Argument about Homosexuality*. New York: Alfred A. Knopf.

Troiden, Richard R. (1989), "The Formation of Homosexual Identities," *Journal of Homosexuality*, 5(3), 43-73.

Troiden, Richard R. (1987), "Becoming Homosexual", in Rubington, Earl and Martin S. Weinberg, eds. (1987), *Deviance: The Interactionist Perspective*, 5th ed. New York: Macmillan Publishing Co.

Wallendorf, Melanie and Eric J. Arnould (1991), "'We Gather Together': Consumption Rituals of Thanksgiving Day", *Journal of Consumer Research*, 18, 13-31.

Wallendorf, Melanie and Merrie Brucks (1993), "Introspection in Consumer Research: Implementation and Implications," *Journal of Consumer Research*, 20, 3, 339-359.

Acculturation : Cross Cultural Consumer Perceptions and the Symbolism of Domestic Space

Malcolm Chapman, University of Leeds, U.K.
Ahmad Jamal, University of Bradford, U.K.

INTRODUCTION

This paper discusses some problems arising in cross-cultural perception, in the context of a meeting between an immigrant and host community. It is one of a pair of papers, with a similar theoretical background, but dealing with a different range of empirical material.

Within social anthropology, there has long been a keen interest in what is often called 'classification'–the process through which order is imposed upon the material and conceptual world by a particular society or social group. It is well-established that different societies classify their conceptual and material universe in different and often incongruent ways. By drawing primarily on the social anthropological tradition, we are looking to an intellectual lineage of interest in 'classification' which goes back to Durkheim and Mauss (1963) and Saussure (1955); this lineage then proceeds through Levi-Strauss (1962, 1963), and on into the French, British and North American ethnographic traditions (in Britain, particularly through the work of: Leach, 1961; Needham, 1973 ed.; Douglas, 1966; Ardener, 1971).

Alongside the general anthropological interest in classification, we also draw upon various disciplines that have looked at the consumption experiences of immigrants, and the impact of migration and resettlement on these experiences. Social anthropology, sociology, social psychology and consumer behaviour have all contributed here. Some researchers perceived the situation as one of assimilation, and so examined 'the degree to which a subcultural group becomes similar to the dominant culture in a nation over time' (Gordon 1964 cited in Penaloza 1994, p. 34). They used this framework to make sense of the differences between the consumption practices of immigrants and those of the local host society, and to understand changes in these differences (see for example Reilly and Wallendorf 1987; Wallendorf and Reilly 1983). Alongside the assimilation framework, others worked within the closely related acculturation framework, dealing with those 'phenomena which result when groups of individuals having different cultures come into continuous first hand contact, with subsequent changes in the original culture patterns of either or both groups' (Redfield, Linton, and Herskovits 1936, cited in Berry 1980, p. 9); using this, they attempted to explain differences in consumption patterns (see for example Berry 1980; d' Astous A. and Naoufel Daghfous 1991; Gentry, Jun and Tansuhaj 1995; Padila 1980; Penaloza 1994). Both research traditions have generated useful research and insight, and enhanced our understanding of ethnic consumer behaviour. There is still, however, a need for empirically-based theory concerning the question of why some immigrant communities do not readily assimilate or acculturate, but rather segregate or isolate themselves, attempting to keep the new cultural environment at arm's length; this can continue even when the immigrant population has been established in the new environment for decades. The self-imposed segregation of the immigrants is often mirrored by a discourse of 'otherness' on the part of the host population. The present paper is an attempt to throw light on how the host society perceives the consumption patterns of the immigrants and consequently may also segregate itself from the immigrants.

THE STUDY

The research upon which this paper is based is an ethnographic study of the consumption experiences and practices of an immigrant and host community in an industrial town, Bradford, in the county of West Yorkshire, in the north of England. The study has looked at both Pakistani immigrants (and their Bradford-born children and grandchildren), and the local indigenous population. The authors of this paper share the cultures of the peoples under study. One (the doctoral supervisor) is from the host community, born and bred in Bradford. The other (the doctoral candidate) is a native Pakistani, carrying out consumer research in England.

During the research we have concentrated our attention on domestic life–on the detail of food and household consumption, family life, interaction with neighbours and the neighbourhood, gender issues, and so on. Many of these issues interact, and we have tried to respect this interaction, within the generally holistic research ethic deriving from social anthropology.

The fieldwork started in January 1995 and finished in March 1996. Ten English households agreed to participate in the study; since the start of the fieldwork one of the researchers has visited each English household every fortnight to participate in cooking, eating and discussing issues related to the study. The same researcher has also lived from January 1995 among the Pakistani immigrants, developing a journal of his daily interaction with a group of forty Pakistani immigrants. He, with the help of his wife, has conducted in-depth interviews with twenty five of these Pakistani informants.

Bradford was selected for the study because it is home to a large number of Pakistanis. Immigrants from Pakistan to Bradford began arriving in large numbers in the late 1950s, and many of the older immigrants have been in Bradford for more than thirty years. There is now also a large number of second- (and even third-) generation, British born 'immigrants'; these young people are British nationals, but their primary cultural identification is often with their parents. The population of the city of Bradford is about 300,000, and the immigrant population, as commonly defined, is about 80,000. The immigrant population tends to live near the inner city, in the older suburbs; this adds to the apparent demographic preponderance of the immigrant population. The immigrants are overwhelmingly Muslim in religious affiliation, which has important implications both for how they perceive the members of the local host society (which is nominally Christian), and for how they are perceived by them.

The terminology for ethnic description that is popularly used in Bradford is that which we will use here. In this terminology, immigrants from Pakistan, and all the members of their households, whether immigrant or Bradford-born, are referred to as 'Pakistanis'. Similarly, all the members of the host population are referred to as 'English' or 'white'. The substance of this terminology is broadly accepted within both ethnic communities, both in English and in Punjabi (which is the language of the Pakistani community). All the Pakistanis that we talked to used the word 'Gora' (male singular) or 'Gorey' (plural) to describe 'white Englishmen'. The word 'gora' in Punjabi means someone who is 'white'. The Pakistanis do not, however, use this word to describe a Pakistani who may have fair skin. The word (in the local ethnographic context) is exclusively used to describe English people. The word used by Pakistani informants to designate other Pakistanis is 'apna' (male singular) or 'apney' (plural); this means something like 'our own people'. A boundary is created, by the use of these words, between their own community and the 'outsiders'.

It is noteworthy that the evidence of the ethnic terminology confirms the evidence deriving from social classification–that there are enduring boundaries between the two communities. The many Bradford-born children of immigrant couples remain, in the eyes of themselves, in the eyes of their parents, and in the eyes of the host population, predominantly 'Pakistani'. At best, they are 'between two cultures' (see V. Saifullah Khan 1977). In this sense, the terminologies are lagging behind demographic realities, while expressing important classificatory realities within the communities in question.

In this paper, we try to show how social 'classification' generates and explains perceptual barriers between an immigrant and a host community. It is important to stress that our approach here is resolutely even-handed. It would be easy to perceive immigrant exclusion from the host society as being imposed by the prejudices of the host society, and fought against by the immigrant community. There are areas of social action in our example where this would be a relevant description. We are not, however, concerned here primarily with these. We are, by contrast, interested in a series of misperceptions and category problems, whereby *both* groups construct a series of symbolic boundaries which excludes the other, and which achieve *de facto* self-segregation. In a previous paper (see Chapman and Jamal, 1996) we discussed some examples from food consumption. In that paper we showed how, through the perception and use of food, the immigrant Pakistani community defined itself, and excluded the native English population. The Pakistani community perceived the English population as 'polluted', and as engaged in dirty and undesirable habits in food preparation and food consumption. Because of this, the Pakistani community has been reluctant engage in social intercourse or commensality with the English population, and has voluntarily segregated itself, within household and within neighbourhood. A system of food supply and production has grown up in Bradford which allows the Pakistani community to meet its own requirements, allowing the necessary independence from the existing systems. Within the food example, the Pakistani community finds reason for distancing itself from the host population. In the paper which follows, we discuss a different example, concering domestic space, and private and public space. Within this example, the burden of apparent impropriety lies upon the Pakistani population, and the host community finds reason for distancing itself from the immigrant community. The two papers, discussing food and space, are essentially different illustrations of the same problem, and taken together provide a moral balance that might seem to be missing in either of them alone.

CATEGORY DISTURBANCE

Our general position concerning classification can be summarised through the following quotation, from an author whose work is in the British social anthropological tradition:

"It is in the nature of social classification to produce differences, categories, oppositions and distinctions, which are lived as real by those who are members of the society. Apparent variations in the underlying reality can be overridden and obscured by the demands and requirements of the system; and it is the system which is socially 'real' and which dominates perception" (Chapman, M. 1992, p.156).

On the basis of this, we can attempt to describe, first theoretically and then empirically, what happens when two different category systems meet. In order to illustrate the problem simply, we can imagine two different category systems, in which a single range

of continuous physical variation is divided into meaningful units. The divisions are made differently in the two systems, and the two different systems are different 'cultures'. This is a crude dealing with a subtle problem, and the idea of social reality as 'a single range of continuous physical variation' hardly does justice to the Saussurean ideas which lie behind our thinking. Nevertheless, we could be talking about, for example, a range of vowel sounds, a human limb, a genus or family of animals, a range of relatives; in this example, reality is merely a long black horizontal line. Both 'cultures' divide the line up into meaningful units, where each unit takes its place in contradistinction (or 'opposition', in Saussurean terms) to the others; only they do so differently. Culture A divides it up like this:

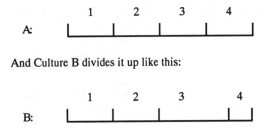

And Culture B divides it up like this:

Each creates four categories, but the boundary between categories 3 and 4 is differently placed. The boundaries between the categories, and the categories themselves, are 'lived as real' by those within the two different societies. What then happens when one society looks at the other? Take the example of society A looking at society B. Society A has a significant boundary between categories 3 and 4. When it looks at society B, it perceives an absence of this boundary where the boundary is expected. Within Society B, category 4 elements seem, in Society A's terms, to mingle with category 3 elements. What is worse, Society A cannot see the boundary that Society B makes between Society B's categories 3 and 4. Society A's own classification dominates its perception, and the category boundary that Society B makes is invisible to it. Accordingly, Society A supposes that Society B makes no distinction at all between categories 3 and 4. The difference between Society A's system and Society B's system may be only slight, a minor shift of category boundary; and yet, Society A can perceive Society B as failing entirely to make an important distinction.

To try to illustrate this in a more concrete manner, and to move towards engagement with relevant empirical material, we can consider that we are dealing with two societies, each of which has a boundary between the places where domestic waste is, and is not, allowed to be deposited. Space (reduced to a horizontal black line) in the two societies looks like this:

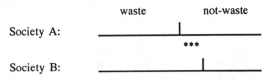

Society A can look at Society B, and perceive that part of Society A's 'not-waste' area is, in Society B, occupied by waste (the area occupied by asterisks). Society A, dominated in its perception by its own category boundaries, cannot see the different boundary that Society B has erected. Society A perceives, instead, a complete absence of boundary–'the floodgates open'. This is a crude attempt to summarise the real ethnographic situation, whose detail is explored below.

The ethnographic record is rich in detail of the moral importance that peoples attach to maintaining the integrity of the systems of classification (see, among many other works: Evans-Pritchard, 1956; Lienhardt, 1961). Systems of classification are an ordering of the world, and a threat to them is often perceived as a threat to order *tout court*. 'In all societies, any tampering with the boundaries of categories does awaken the fear of anomaly–generating pollution beliefs, inversion phenomena, and taboo' (Ardener, 1989, p.11). Mary Douglas, in her classic summary of the problem (1966), showed the close association, in social perception, between correct classification and moral and ritual purity. For Douglas, dirt was 'matter out of place'.

We have seen, in our imaginary example above, that once Society A's boundary is breached, Society A cannot perceive the new and different boundary erected by Society B. As far as Society A is concerned, the entire contents of categories 3 and 4 invade the space of category 3. The phrase 'the floodgates open' was used to describe this classificatory phenomenon by the British social anthropologist Edwin Ardener, whose work is cited in various places in this paper. Ardener used the phrase as a passing metaphor (in conversation with one of the authors in 1975), and never intended it to be used as a theoretical construct; accordingly, we do not wish to seem to give the phrase or the metaphor too much concrete importance. Nevertheless, the metaphor of 'floodgates' captures the sense that once-secure material categories seem to become alarmingly fluid, with an ability to flow unchecked, when a classification is threatened or broken.

Wherever there are differences of classification as between two cultures (or societies, ethnicities, social classes, or whatever), then cross-cultural perceptions of this kind are likely to arise. This is important for any study of acculturation in the realm of consumption experience, as between two different cultural groups. As we have seen, the notion of 'acculturation' as used in consumer research today, implies that a group of immigrants can maintain some aspects of their original cultural values and traditions, even while moving in other respects towards the culture of the host society. We have also seen that 'acculturation' also implies change in any of the two groups that are involved in the cultural encounter (hence we should also look into the changes in the consumption patterns of the host society after such cultural encounters). We believe that the phenomena of category disturbance are important during the 'process' of acculturation, and determine the shifting 'outcomes' of such a cultural encounter.

We move on to a discussion of a particular empirical area, from the Bradford material, the understanding of which is enhanced by the theoretical issues raised so far.

CLEANLINESS AND THE DOMESTIC SPACE

Here we are concerned with the system of boundaries (or classifications) between domestic and public space. In the following section we first explain the perceptions and the classifications used by the host society in the UK about their domestic, public and private spaces. Then we describe the same for the immigrants in their original culture. And finally we see how the host society perceives the immigrants, on the basis of the host society classifications, and in relation to the consumption acts of the immigrants.

In Bradford, the host population has a rapid history of urbanisation, based upon the first industrial revolution, and upon its central industry, the textile industry. In the nineteenth century, and for the first half of the twentieth, Bradford was one of the key towns of the world woollen industry, specialising in fine worsteds. The problems of mass-industrial-urbanisation were fought through for the first time in places like Bradford–housing, sewage, water-supplies, public health, universal education, labour laws, and so on.

From the late nineteenth century onwards, the bulk of the working-class of Bradford lived in streets of terrace houses, one-up and one-down (i.e. one room on the ground floor, one room above), in which two dwellings backed on to one another on the same terrace. These were known as 'back-to-back' houses, or 'back-to-backs'. At the front, they usually gave directly out onto a road, with two terraces facing one another across the road. At the back, they sometimes gave directly out onto another road; more usually, in the Bradford case, there was some kind of back yard (stone paved, with a covered outside privy, and room for hanging washing out to dry; access to this back yard, for the front of the pair of 'back-to-backs', was via a tunnel between each pair of dwellings). After this generation of houses, the subsequent generation were built as through-terraces, in that a single dwelling shared both the front and back of the terrace; this meant that each dwelling was two-up and two-down (at least). This generation of terrace houses tended to have a 'front' garden which was ornamental, outside the 'front' door which led into the 'front' room; the front room was the polite and posh room of the house, usually carefully cleaned and little used. Outside the 'back' door was the yard which was analogous to the yard of the back-to-backs, with the outside privy and space for hanging washing to dry. This new architectural development allowed a spatial realisation, within a single dwelling, of an opposition between 'front' and 'back', which contained or was analogous with other oppositions:

front	back
formal	informal
special	ordinary
garden	yard
ornament	function
flowers	stone-flags
polite	vulgar (the toilet was in the back yard)
front-room	living-room/kitchen
festivals	ordinary life

Most everyday coming and going was through the back door, directly into the room in which most of life was lived, the living-room/kitchen, with its direct link, via the back yard, to the toilet. The front door and the front room were rarely used; they came into their own at Christmas, and at family celebrations of the usual kind– weddings, christenings, funerals.

The front garden (often very small, perhaps only a yard or so in width) was a celebration of ornamental non-functionality, as befitted its opposition to the routine of the back yard and back entrance (and the human corporeal analogy is fully alive in this; remember where the toilet was!). The front garden was a place for fantasies of rockery in quartz, for flowers and shrubs, and for careful display of propriety and cleanliness. The terrace-house tradition of this kind was supplanted in its turn with the construction, from the 1920s onwards, of what became known as 'semi-detached houses', or 'semis'. A 'semi' was a dwelling forming one-half of a built unit, with its mirror image fastened to it forming another 'semi'. Each dwelling was surrounded on three of its sides by land, air, garden. The toilet, by this time, had moved indoors, so that the sense of 'back-yard (containing toilet)' was lost; all the garden was influenced by the proprieties of the 'front' garden; in a sense, the 'front garden' of the older style terrace now spread all around the house. The garden, more or less elaborate, was a showcase for tidiness, display, neatness; flowers and shrubs were grown, lawns carefully tended. The garden, moreover, had sharply defined boundaries, separating the private (outside) domestic space from the public street; the boundaries were often shrub hedges (usually of privet), carefully clipped; sometimes the boundaries were stone or brick walls, or wooden or wrought-iron fences. The car and the garage came along to complicate matters, as the twentieth century rolled by, but the basic pattern is still as described.

One of the authors of this paper grew up in Bradford in the immediate post-war period. At this time, all three kinds of house so-far described (back-to-back, terrace, semi) were common. There existed a minutely detailed, acute, and also gross sense of upward social mobility, involved in the passage from back-to-back, to terrace, to semi. The most manifest symbol of the terrace house (as opposed to the back-to-back) was its garden. The garden was important. The propriety and neatness of the garden was an extension of the propriety and neatness of the house, the housewife, the household, and the family. The garden, for the semi-detached, was equally important, spreading its land-owning allure round the house on three sides. A great deal of social status was attached to being able to walk round at least one side of your own house, from front to back.

Many of the back-to-backs were knocked down, as part of ambitious schemes of urban renewal in the 1970s and 1980s. Those displaced from the back-to-backs, often the poorest in society, were rehoused in the architects' new Utopia of the tower block, the high-rise. This Utopia, built with such optimism, soon showed a strong tendency to become unpleasant and dysfunctional. People lived in 'flats' in 'tower blocks' only because they had to, because they could not afford to live elsewhere. One thing that was conspicuously lacking, in a high-rise flat, was a garden. From the old back-to-back, the vanity and social status of a garden had been an object of longing; with the shift to tower-blocks, the longing remained, *a fortiori.*

This is, again, a crude summary; a wealth of detail and complication could be added. The focus could be narrowed down to the detail of decoration, of paint-colour, of choice of garden flowers. The focus could be opened up, to look at regional or national elements. It is impossible to broach issues of this kind, without remarking the very general pastoral romanticism which is so strong in Britain (and which Britain in a sense gave to the rest of the world in the late eighteenth century); this pastoral romanticism was elaborated by Wordsworth, and seized upon by the tourist industry; it generated the 'Lake District', and subsequently the Alps, the National Trust, and a variety of National Parks, as objects of urban desire; it led to the 'Garden Cities' of the turn of the century; it led on to pastoral tourism, rambling and fell-walking, mountain climbing, and gardening. Gardening, caring for the garden, is one of the prime leisure pursuits of British suburban life. The garden of the semi-detached house has an entire cosmology of urban and industrial life built into its rockeries, an entire historiography of modernity growing out of its flower-beds.

The Pakistani immigrants to Bradford knew little of this. The researchers were told by almost all of the Pakistani informants that they were never exposed to life in the UK before they came to Bradford. Most of the Pakistani immigrants came from a rural background, and belonged to the farming community. Their emigration from Pakistan was provoked by a desire for economic self-betterment. In Pakistan they raised crops and tended animals such as cows, buffaloes and oxen. They lived in small villages or village-like areas in Pakistan. Their houses were made of mud. Since land was relatively cheap, large areas (about three to four thousand square yards) were feasible. The buildings (mostly rectangular in shape) had outer walls of about six feet in height. These outerwalls served to establish the 'domestic space' against the public space. In most cases the house consisted of two or three flat-roofed rooms along one side of the boundary wall (each room measuring about 15 yards by 10 yards in area). The rooms were mainly used for shelter in the event of rain or cold weather. The rooms were also used as storage places. The rest of the 'house'

consisted of the open-air courtyard. There was no concept of front vs. back room (still less of dining room, living room, guest room and the like). In most cases there were trees along one side of the courtyard. In the summer the family could stay in the courtyard during the night and under the shadow of the trees during the day. While one side of the courtyard served as an open-air kitchen for the household, the other side of the courtyard served to keep their cattle. The trees were grown inside the courtyard only for utilitarian purposes (one could enjoy the shade during the summer, and use branches or even the entire tree for cooking fires). Various vegetables were grown (e.g., garlic, coriander, spinach, tomatoes, onions etc.,) along one side of the boundary wall in the courtyard. That particular section of the land within the house (where vegetables were grown) was always perceived as an extension of the fields where crops were grown. Hence the place was only for 'growing' purposes, and not for reflecting oneself through the maintenance, cleanliness and beauty of the place. There was no concept of front or back 'garden' (whether structurally or perceptually) in these houses. Cleaning and maintenance of the house was entirely a woman's job. She took great pains to clean the entire house including the courtyard up to the doorsteps (excluding the space where vegetables were grown). 'You did not need to clean the area where vegetables were grown, because this was a wild space, like the fields, a space 'where dirt became part of the soil and turned itself into fertiliser', as one informant told. There were no sewerage systems in the villages. People used to go 'outside' their homes into open fields to defecate.

Coming from this background, the immigrants found the Bradford 'garden' incomprehensible. The immigrants perceived the frontier between the private domestic space and the public space to be the house-wall itself. The garden was treated as 'outside' the domestic space; the garden hedge, wall or fence, so carefully tended and guarded by the host community, was irrelevant; it was a classificatory boundary that was, in important senses, invisible. In consequence, the immigrants treated the 'garden' as a place to put things that were not desired in the house; this included household waste (food remains, general household rubbish), unwanted furniture, old mattresses, and so on. One of the English informants (who could look over the back garden of her Pakistani neighbour through the window of her back room) described her experience of watching an old Pakistani immigrant lady 'doing her business' (i.e. defecating) in the back garden of her house as 'totally disgusting. How could they do that?' she wondered.

A floodgate opened indeed. The host population, perceiving the gardens of immigrant households to be filled with filth, drew their own conclusions. For the host population, a tidy and clean garden was the outward manifestation of a tidy and clean house and household; the garden was a publicly visible metaphor for the interior of the house. The immigrant boundary between domestic privacy and cleanliness and the outside world, which was the house wall itself, was not visible in this boundary form to the native population. For the host population, what happened in the garden also, in important senses, happened inside the house. If the garden was a pile of dirt, untended and unkempt, then so too, in their perception, was the inside of the house. Social intercourse between the host and immigrant communities was, for various reasons (most of them related to the kinds of issues discussed in this paper), very limited. Even after decades of being immediate neighbours, most members of the host community had never passed the threshold of a Pakistani household. The classificatory imagination had only a very limited empirical check upon its speculations. We have said above that the garden had an entire cosmology built into it; this was the cosmology of the host community, into which the immigrant community seemed to be tipping its dustbin.

For the host population, the outside of the house was, since it was within the domestic boundaries, a part of the domestic space. The external appearance of the house was, just like that of the garden, perceived to be a metaphor for its internal state. The woodwork around windows, the woodwork of doors, gutters, and eaves, were all carefully painted and maintained. The pointing of stone and brickwork was attended to. This, again, seems to have been only dimly perceived by the immigrant population. For them, the inside wall of the house was the boundary between public and private. They did not perceive the outside wall of the house as its private face to the public gaze. No painting was done; no care lavished upon appearance. The effect of this, in the perception of the host community, was just as described in the previous paragraph.

For the host population, the boundary between the garden and the public road (with its pedestrian walkway and traffic) was immensely important. For the immigrant population, the boundary was irrelevant. Fences and walls were left to fall down. Hedges were left to die or grow wild, however they would. High stone walls that had been landmarks throughout living memory were allowed to collapse, while weeds grew on the rubble. Again, there seemed, in host community eyes, to be no attention to propriety left at all; where this could happen, anything could happen.

Another interesting elaboration concerns the growing and eating of garlic by the Pakistani immigrants in the Bradford. Northern Europe has long tended to regard garlic-eating as a habit peculiar to foreigners: the Germans attribute the habit to Turkish immigrants, or to the southern flanks of Europe; the English attribute the habit to the French, and to (inter alia) Pakistani immigrants. The situation has changed over the last decade or so, and today many English people (perhaps particularly young and educated people) eat garlic as a fairly regular part of the their diet. In the 1950s, however, most of England was probably a garlic-free zone. The immigrant Pakistanis brought garlic-eating with them. There is, as anybody familiar with the herb will attest, a noticeable difference between people that have eaten garlic and people that have not. The host community in Bradford put the smell of garlic into their inventory of Pakistani immigrant characteristics. Some Pakistani immigrants in Bradford conceived the idea of using the patch of earth outside their front door as an ideal place to grow garlic (this is because they were used to grow vegetables in their own homes in Pakistan; although the patch of land used for growing vegetables was never conceived as part of domestic space). In native Bradfordian usage, the front garden was never used to grow vegetables: the front garden was for ornament and for flowers; if utilitarian vegetables were to be grown, then this should be either in a separate allotment or in the back garden. By growing garlic (a prime marker of their 'otherness') in the front garden (where vegetables should not be grown), the immigrants were committing a whole series of classificatory errors, in the perception of the host community.

Another interesting feature, related to those already discussed, concerns curtains. Within the host community, windows were draped inside the house with curtains. Often there were two sets of these. The nearest to the window were 'net' curtains, which allowed the person inside to see out, but prevented the person outside from seeing in; these 'net' curtains were always white or cream, and were woven in various open lace-like patterns. They were usually immovable, in the normal routine (although of course they could be taken down for washing, or pulled slightly aside to give a better view on the outside world to the curious eye) (such 'net' curtains have gone a little out of style, although many households still have them). Inside the net curtains, was a more substantial and totally opaque pair of curtains; these were drawn at

night, and opened during the day. The position of the curtains gave, in the native tradition, a very clear message to the outside world about the state of the household. If the curtains were drawn closed during the day, then either somebody was asleep when they should not be (slovenly, lazy), or had forgotten to open the curtains (slovenly, lazy), or was doing something that respectable people did not do during the day (having sex? adultery? prostitute at work?), or was working night-shifts (this was an enforced acknowledgement of working-class status, but at least the neighbours would understand and tolerate).

Once again, the immigrant community had no understanding of these micro-proprieties. For the Pakistanis the windows in their houses in Pakistan were for the purpose of getting fresh air and the sunlight. The windows in their houses always looked into the courtyard, and were neither visible to, nor overlooked by, a more general public than the family. There was no need for putting curtains on them, particularly since this could stop the inflow of fresh air and light into the rooms. In Bradford, however, it became necessary to cover windows to keep out the gaze of strangers. It became common to see, in immigrant households, windows which were veiled, inside, by more-or-less permanent hangings, not necessarily symmetrically hung or matching in colour. To keep the world out, this was effective. As a means of communicating with the host population about the state of the household, it was, in the light of what has already been said, disastrous.

The overall effect of these phenomena was to give the host community a very poor idea of the immigrant community; the immigrant community seemed to be giving out consistent signals that it was lazy, dirty, and contemptuous of propriety and decency. The result was that the members of the host society started to leave the places or areas where immigrants started to live. Consider this example. One of the English informants, pointing towards the 'for sale' sign outside a house in the street he lived said, 'you will be surprised to see so many of these signs in a street. This is not because people really want to sell their houses. The fact is that once a Pakistani family moves in the street, the neighbouring houses (of the English) go up for sale. And then no one except other Pakistani families buy those houses from the English. This is the way the English leave the area and Pakistanis develop clusters of their households.' 'Where do the English move, then?', the researcher asked. 'Well, if you go towards the outskirts of Bradford, you will find many of these English families have moved into that area. You may not find many Pakistani houses there', replied the informant. The view was reinforced by many Pakistani informants who stated that 'these goreys (the English) do not like to stay in the areas where we live because they do not like the way we live.'

We are not talking here about an explosive racial situation, where the two populations routinely hate one another and commit violence upon one another. Bradford is rightly proud of its record in what are often called 'race relations'. Nevertheless, phenomena of the kind described have tended to keep the two populations, immigrant and host, apart, even when they live (as is often the case) next door to one another. The effects of this upon housing patterns are clear: the English do not want to live in the areas dominated by the Pakistani households and tend to move into 'white only' areas; reciprocally, the Pakistanis create enclaves of their own.

SOME RESERVATIONS

Various reservations need to be made concerning the above account. It perhaps needs to be stressed that the household interiors of Pakistani immigrant households are not, as the host community tends to suppose, dirty. On the contrary, great attention is paid to their cleanliness, particularly by women. This attention stops at the inside of the external door, however, and does not extend outside the house. It is precisely the point of this paper, to argue that because of the shift of boundary, totalising conclusions are reached; the shift of boundary is perceived, by the host community, as no boundary at all.

We also need to observe that some of the lack of attention to household exteriors, on the part of immigrant households, can be explained in other ways. The first generation of Pakistani immigrants (males only) to Bradford held firmly to the view that their stay in Bradford was only to be temporary. They lived for the most part in rented accommodation (during their initial years in Britain), for whose upkeep they were not responsible. Their economic and social ambitions were directed towards their lives (their 'future' lives) in Pakistan. Many built themselves houses in Pakistan, in which they were never (yet) to live, and this was a heavy financial commitment for them. However, when the wives and the children of these immigrants started to arrive in the late 1960s and early 1970s, the immigrants started to buy houses in the UK instead of living in rented accommodation. According to the 1991 Census (Owen 1992), 81.7 % of the Pakistani households in the UK are owner-occupied as compared to 66.6 % of the White and 77.1 % of all the south Asian groups in the Britain. Most of our informants in Bradford had more than one house (often living in one of them and renting out the rest). The researcher participated in the purchase and sale of many houses by the informants. The existence of a nice or clean 'garden' was never taken into account in this process. The search was on price (cheap), and the interior size of the house (most of the informants had extended families to house, and size was an important criterion). Hence even though many houses are owned by Pakistanis they do not consider a 'need' to maintain the house exteriors in the same way as the host population. This derives from the classificatory issues already discussed.

The problem can be attributed to poverty as well. It is notable that many houses which are provided by the town council for cheap rental, and which are lived in by the members of the host community, have gardens in a state of neglect (as, too, do many houses rented by groups of university students). On poverty, it is true that the Pakistani immigrants have tended to come in at the bottom of the job market (as perceived by the host population), and are only slowly working their way up, in the classic pattern of social mobility of immigrant groups. However, we have found that the Pakistani informants never felt 'poor', because they consistently compared their standard of living with that of their relatives, both inside the UK and back in Pakistan. They had their own standards of comparison based on their own shared categories. In Pakistan, the state of the interior of a house was a ground for comparison and competition with other households; this remained true in the UK. In the UK, Pakistani informants spent thousands of pounds on carpets, large television sets, the latest VCRs, new sofas, microwaves, computers, new makes of car, even new houses; they rarely, however, spent a few hundred pounds on maintaining the exterior of their houses. The informants, when asked about this, always gave the impression that spending a few hundred pounds on the exterior of their houses was a very 'expensive act'; an act that was useless and wasteful. Interestingly the informants always looked for government grants or insurance claims (again to minimise 'wasteful' expense) for funding improvements to their houses (e.g., for building an extension within the house, for improving the windows, or for repairing the rooves, etc.,), as if maintenance of the house was not their problem.

CONCLUSION

It would be easy to conclude, from a study of host community expression alone, that we were dealing here with simple expressions of 'racial stereotyping', with accusations of impropriety generated on purely theoretical grounds. It will be clear from our study, however, that this is an inadequate approach. Both parties to this cultural meeting have genuine empirical grounds for their perceptions. These perceptions are grounded in their own classifications of the social space, and upon the meeting of two incongruent category systems that derives from the encounter of the immigrant and host communities. These perceptions have profound effects upon the ways in which the two communities interact.

Our primary aim in this paper has been to show that relatively minor classificatory issues (the shift of a boundary from one place to another) can lead to serious perceptual and experiential dislocation, in the relationship between two culturally different communities. As a result, ethnic segregation is generated and maintained. The nature and rate of assimilation and/or acculturation can be profoundly affected by classificatory issues of the kind discussed. This is the central conclusion in the consumer behaviour context–that the two communities remain separate, as consumer groups, at least in many important product areas.

Given the luxury of greater length, we could discuss the fine detail of some of these areas–the consumption of space, housing, home-care products, DIY, gardening equipment, electrical goods, and so on. Detailed examination of these examples will be carried out in future papers.

REFERENCES

Ardener, E. (1971) "Social anthropology and language," in *Social Anthropology and Language* (ed. E. W. Ardener), London, Tavistock.

Ardener, E. (1989) *The Voice of Prophecy and other essays by E. W. Ardener*, Oxford, Blackwell (ed. M. Chapman).

Berry, W. J. (1980), "Acculturation as Varieties of Adaptation," in Amado M. Padilla (ed.) *Acculturation: Theory, Models and Some New Findings*, Boulder, Colorado, Westview Press.

Chapman, M. (1992) *The Celts, the construction of a myth*, London, Macmillan.

Chapman, M. and Jamal, A. (1996) "The floodgates open: category disturbance in inter-ethnic consumer perception", American Marketing Association 1996 Summer Educators' Proceedings, vol. 7, "Enhancing Knowledge Development in Marketing"

d' Astous A.and Naoufel Daghfous (1991), "The Effects of Acculturation and Length of Residency on Consumption-Related Behaviours and Orientations of Arab-Muslim Immigrants," in Proceedings of ASAC Conference, Niagara Falls, Ontario.

Douglas, M. (1966) *Purity and Danger*, Harmondsworth, Penguin.

Durkheim, E. and Mauss, M. (1963) *Primitive Classification* (trans, ed. and intro. R. Needham), London, Cohen and West.

Evans-Pritchard, E. (1956), *Nuer Religion*, Oxford, Clarendon Press.

Gentry W. James, Jun S. and Tansuhaj P. (1995), "Consumer Acculturation Processes and Cultural Conflict: How Generalizeable Is a North American Model for Marketing Globally?," *Journal of Business Research* Vol. 32, pp 129-139.

Leach, E. (1961), *Rethinking Anthropology*, London, Athlone Press.

Lévi-Strauss, C. (1962), *La Pensée sauvage*, Paris, Plon.

Lévi-Strauss, C. (1963), *Totemism (trans. from Le totémisme aujourd'hui)*, 1962, by R. Needham), Boston, Beacon Press.

Lienhardt, R.G. (1961), *Divinity and Experience*, Oxford, Clarendon Press.

Needham, R. (ed.) (1973), *Right and Left: essays on dual symbolic classification*, Chicago, Chicago University Press.

Padilla M. Amado (ed.) (1980), *Acculturation: Theory, Models and Some New Findings*, Boulder, Colorado, Westview Press.

Owen D. (1992), *"Ethnic Minorities in Britain: Housing and Family Characteristics,"* 1991 Statistical Paper 4: Centre for Research in Ethnic Relations, University of Warwick.

Penaloza, Lisa (1994), "Atravesando Fronteras/Border Crossings: A Critical Ethnographic Exploration of the Consumer Acculturation of Mexican Immigrants," *Journal of Consumer Research*, 21 (June), 289-294.

Reilly Michael D. and Melanie Wallendorf (1987), "A Comparison of Group Differences in Food Consumption Using Household Refuse," *Journal of Consumer Research*, 14 (September), 289-294.

Saussure, F. de, 1955 *Cours de Linguistique generale*, Paris, Payot (first edn, 1915).

V. Saifullah Khan (1977), "The Pakistanis: Mirpuri villagers at home and in Bradford," in *Between Two Cultures: migrants and minorities in Britain*, ed. J. L. Watson, Basil Blackwell, Oxford, pp 66-8.

Wallendorf, Melanie and Michael Reilly (1983), "Ethnic Migration, Assimilation, and Consumption," *Journal of Consumer Research*, 10 (December), 292-302.

The Target and Its "Other": Exploring the Social Context and Interaction Of Consumer Segments

Sonya A. Grier, Stanford University

N. Craig Smith, Georgetown University

This session aimed to shed light on target marketing through a focus on the meaning, coexistence, and interaction of consumer segments in their socio-cultural context. Target marketing is an increasingly crucial component of marketing strategy, particularly given the expanding diversity of the nation's population. Socio-economic, demographic, and other trends are driving marketer attention towards consumer groupings not typically included in the more traditional conceptualizations of the US market, such as ethnic minorities, immigrants, gay/lesbian consumers, and disadvantaged consumers (e.g. Peñaloza, 1995). Increases in target marketing have been touted as a response to marketplace diversity (e.g. Berman, 1991) and even praised in conjunction with the development and marketing of programs targeting women and minorities (Ringold, 1995). At the same time, however, societal concerns threaten the social acceptability of target marketing. Increased use of target marketing strategies, such as more ethnic advertising, have been accompanied by growing criticism. This commentary comes not only from the targeted segment, but also from members outside of the target population who are exposed to the marketing efforts.

Prior consumer research has examined consumer behavior in relation to target marketing from a variety of perspectives. A diversity of research has examined how various consumer groups such as older consumers, women, African-Americans, and Hispanics respond to target marketing (e.g. Tepper, 1994; Widgery and McGaugh, 1993; Williams and Qualls, 1989). Research has also explored the way people process targeted ads and socio-contextual factors which influence the effectiveness of targeting (e.g. Aaker, Brumbaugh and Grier, 1995; Deshpande' and Stayman, 1994). Further, consumer and policy-oriented research has also emerged to address criticisms of target marketing efforts and its' perceived social effects, addressing controversies about targeting certain segments, and the ethics of target marketing (e.g. Ringold, 1995; Cooper-Martin and Smith, 1995; Spradley, 1993).

Notwithstanding the diversity of research attention to target marketing, the increasing practice of target marketing and the accompanying social commentary draw attention to our need for a richer understanding of the influence of social context on consumer reactions to targeting. Researchers have noted that segmentation is inherently problematic because it explicitly includes and excludes groups of consumers (Smith and Quelch, 1993). From this perspective, a key consideration is brought to the fore: members of groups outside the targeted segment are also exposed to targeted marketing efforts. This suggests that a target segment must also be considered in relation to the remainder of the marketplace from which it is drawn, those who are not in the target market. Consider that the demographic characteristics of a target market also describes both 1) others with those characteristics, but not the particular product need, and 2) those who don't have the specific characteristics or need, but who are exposed to the targeted efforts (Star, 1989). These "others", i.e. those consumers who are not in a marketers' intended target market, are not only exposed to, but also potentially influenced by, and may respond to, targeted marketing efforts. For example, Coors "Swedish Bikini Team" ads met with resistance from women's groups, not their target market, and were subse-

quently not aired. There will always be some degree of misfit between targeted marketing efforts, the target market, and the actual program audience (Star, 1989), thus it is useful to understand how other audiences may influence consumer response.

Little prior research on targeting has adopted an *explicit* focus on consumers outside the targeted segment who are exposed to, potentially influenced by, and may respond to, targeted marketing efforts. Therefore, this session aimed to bring together research which examined how segmentation and targeting strategies influence, and are influenced by, both the target consumer culture, as well as others in the marketplace who are aware of and/or exposed to targeted marketing efforts. In particular, this session investigated the interaction of consumer segments as manifested in their inclusion or exclusion in target marketing efforts. The session involved three papers which examined "the other" in target marketing from different perspectives, yet all converged to address the role that "other" consumers play in understanding responses to targeted marketing efforts. Further, all three papers used different methodological approaches to consider characteristics of both the target and others outside of the defined target market, the nature of intergroup relations, the significance of the descriptors used to designate consumer segments, and how these segment "meanings" may influence consumer responses toward targeted marketing efforts.

The first presentation was *"The Reproduction and Consumption of the "One" and Its "Others": An Examination of the Constitution and Interdynamics of US Consumer Cultures"*, by Lisa Peñaloza and Sylvia Allegretto. This presentation explored consumer research issues associated with the increasing phenomena of marketplace diversity. It began with a slide presentation of Latino/a and gay/lesbian consumers to the music of Gil Scott-Heron's 1974 recording, "The Revolution Will Not Be Televised." Peñaloza then described the intersections of three consumer cultures-the US mainstream and two of its "others," namely Latinos and gays/lesbians. She discussed the relationship of each groups' social movement activism with marketing practice, specifically market targeting by large multinational firms of Latinos/as and gays/lesbians following their activism for basic civil rights. Discussion emphasized the inherent dialectical relationship between consumer behavior and market practice, and proceeded to explore the paradoxical relationship of White consumer behavior to mainstream and to Latino/a and gay/lesbian consumer cultures. Consumer research implications included: 1) the significance of meanings associated with various descriptors used to designate consumer cultures (e.g. race, gender, ethnicity), 2) the notion of multiple, juxtaposed cultural consumer configurations which consumers continuously navigate and contest, and 3) the role of consumer researchers in constituting and reproducing notions of the mainstream and otherness in the marketplace.

The second presentation was *"Noticing Difference: Ad Meanings Created By The Target And Non-Target Markets"* by Sonya Grier, Anne Brumbaugh and Jennifer Aaker. They discussed a study which examined the type and nature of consumer responses to targeted advertising among both the target and non-target markets. They detailed an analysis of consumers' open-ended responses to ads targeted both to their group, as well as two other groups of which they were not a member. Their qualitative analysis of consumer responses to targeted advertising was conducted at two levels: a) when the consumer was a member of the target market versus non-target market, and b) across particular social categories, namely race, gender and sexual orientation. Consumer responses in their study illustrated that consumers will actively process ads even when they feel the ad is not directed towards them. Further, their analysis found differences in the pattern of responses among groups. In particular they found that White subjects were most likely to respond to advertisements when they were in the non-target market, while Black and lesbian/gay subjects were less vocal about being in the non-target market. Further, they found that Black and gay/lesbian subjects were more vocal about advertisements targeted to them. Further, the nature of the comments differed among the various groups. They interpreted these results as suggesting that responses to targeted advertising by non-target market members may be strongest among the least distinctive (i.e. numerically and/or socially predominant) consumers. Conversely, the most distinctive consumers may be most likely to notice and process advertisements targeted to them. Results of the qualitative analysis suggested that socio-contextual factors influence who notices exclusion, who responds, and the type of attributions created by ads. These results were discussed in light of how responses to targeted advertisements may be influenced by who has typically been targeted by marketers. This latter point reinforced the prior presentation's assertion of the dialectical relationship between market practice and consumer behavior.

The last presentation was *"Consumer Ethical Evaluations Of Target Marketing Strategies"*, by N. Craig Smith and Elizabeth Cooper-Martin. This work investigated how we construct notions of what constitutes "vulnerable" consumer segments, and how this construction influences the ethical evaluation of targeting strategies. They sought to propose explanations for controversy and ethical concern over targeting. Their presentation detailed two experiments which examined how perceptions of target vulnerability and product harm influence ethical evaluations of the targeting strategy, and behavioral intentions such as consumer boycotts. Further, they examined whether consumer ethical evaluations of targeting strategies differed according to whether the consumer was within the target market or not. Results found strong support for public concern about the ethics of certain targeting strategies. This concern was a function of both perceived target vulnerability and perceived product harm. For example, they reported effects for both "sin" (e.g. cigarettes) and "non-sin" (hamburgers) products on evaluations of the targeting strategies. They also identified concern influenced not only by the products involved, but also based on perceived consumer vulnerability. This ethical concern was also found to give rise to disapproving behavioral intentions including boycotts and negative word of mouth. Further, they identified the types of respondents most likely to be concerned about targeting, including women, non-white and older consumers. They also found that the ethical evaluations of respondents "in target" (i.e. those with the same demographic characteristic as the target consumer in the study scenarios) were significantly lower than those of "non-target" respondents (i.e. those outside the target described in the scenario), if the targeting strategy was directed at a more vulnerable consumer. Their presentation reinforced the session theme of the importance of considering consumers outside the targeted segment to gain insight into the intricacies underlying responses to targeted marketing efforts.

The synthesizer for the session, Rohit Deshpandé, conceptualized the "big picture" of the interrelationships of the target and the non-target markets in their social context. He emphasized three

dialectics related to the session presentations. First, is the definition of the target market "etic" or "emic", i.e. who establishes the boundaries of target segments? Are they those intended by the marketer or due to self-ascription by the consumer? Also, he highlighted the significance and influence of the metaphors we implicitly apply to our understanding of social relations, e.g. a "melting pot" (i.e. a longitudinal, linear assimilation model) versus that of a "mosaic" (i.e. non-linear, group-identification resurgence model). Lastly, he addressed our need to consider the dialectic of collective consumer culture versus increasing social (i.e. racial, religious, ethnic) fragmentation. The discussion generated by the synthesizer's comments and the three presentations focused upon understanding the factors which influence response to targeted marketing efforts by "others", including personal relevance, social concern, and the impact of changing market demographics on areas of consumer research inquiry. The papers and discussion also demonstrated how the designation of a consumer segment wields influence on consumer behavior beyond its use as a vehicle for marketing strategy. Further, the discussion implied how considering target segments in the context of "others" provides an additional source of meaning through which we can understand target marketing. The session contributed to understanding target marketing more holistically, and brought some provocative yet unexplored consumer behavior research issues to the fore. Additionally, the session demonstrated how multiple methodological approaches can illuminate the same issue. The session provided a platform for future research to incorporate the influence of contextual factors on consumer researchers' understanding of target marketing. Further, the session's methodological pluralism, fit with prior targeting research and social relevance of the topic also supported the conference goal of *"breaking out of the box"*.

REFERENCES

Aaker, Jennifer (1993) "The Non-Target Market Effect: Associated Feelings of Acceptance, Alienation or Apathy", Presented at the Association for Consumer Research conference, Nashville, TN.

Aaker, Jennifer, Anne Brumbaugh and Sonya Grier (1995) "This Bud is NOT for You", Presented at the Association for Consumer Research conference, Minneapolis, MN.

Berman, G. (1991) "The Hispanic Market: Getting Down to Cases", *Sales and Marketing Management*, (October), 65-74.

Cooper-Martin, Elizabeth and N. Craig Smith (1995), "Target Marketing: Good Marketing or Bad Ethics?" Presentation at the Marketing and Public Policy Conference, Atlanta.

Deshpandé, Rohit and Douglas Stayman (1994) "A Tale of Two Cities: Distinctiveness Theory and Advertising Effectiveness", *Journal of Marketing Research*, 31 (February), 57-64.

Peñaloza, Lisa (1995) "We're Here, We're Queer and We're Going Shopping", *Gays, Lesbians and Consumer Behavior: Theory, Practice and Research in Marketing*, Dan Wardlow, ed., Harrington Press.

Ringold, Debra J. (1995) "Social Criticisms of Target Marketing: Process or Product", *American Behavioral Scientist*, 38:4 (February), 578-592.

Smith, N. Craig and John A. Quelch (1993) "Ethical Issues in Researching and Targeting Consumers", in N. Craig Smith and John A. Quelch, *Ethics in Marketing*, Homewood, IL: Richard D. Irwin, 145-195.

Spradley, Thaddeus H. (1993) "Targeting Vulnerable Segments in Cigarette Advertising: Ethical Criteria and Public Policy Implications", *1993 Proceedings of the Academy of Marketing Science, v.XVI, 446-450.*

Star, Steven H. (1989) "Marketing and Its Discontents", *Harvard Business Review*, (November/December), 148-154.

Tepper, Kelly, (1994) "The Role of Labeling Processes in Elderly Consumers Responses to Age Segmentation Cues", *Journal of Consumer Research*, 20:4, 503-519.

Widgery, Robin and Jack McGaugh (1993) "Vehicle Message Appeals and the New Generation Woman", *Journal of Advertising Research*, (September/October), 36-42.

Williams, Jerome and William Qualls, (1989) "Middle Class Consumers and Intensity of Ethnic Identification", *Psychology and Marketing*, 6 (Winter) 263-286.

Puzzles, Choirs, and Archives: Perspectives on Crossing the Quantitative-Qualitative Methodological Divide

James C. Ward, Arizona State University

The first paper by Fournier, McQuarrie, and Mick emphasized that as consumer researchers "break out of their boxes," the use of multiple methods to examine a single phenomenon or research question will become more popular. They noted, however, that writings on method and the philosophy of science have not necessarily equipped us for this task. In their view, the received view on the use of multiple methods within the same research program tends to be grounded in notions of triangulation and convergent validation: multiple methods simply grant comfort that unbiased translation of a phenomenon has been obtained. However, they point out that very little has been written on the art of negotiating findings across methods to arrive at this larger "truth." They also observed that this shortcoming is confounded by a popular relativist philosophy that seems to imply that different methodological approaches, especially those broadly compared as "qualitative" versus "quantitative," represent different "lenses" that render "pictures of reality" that are fundamentally incommensurate.

The presenters organized their talk into two sections. In the first, the authors proposed *the puzzle* as a metaphor for engaging multiple methods within the context of a single line of inquiry. They went on to elaborate this metaphor by suggesting that various qualitative and quantitative methodologies be viewed as providing *pieces to a bigger puzzle* of interest to the investigators. They argued that in puzzles, each piece (method) is unique, but not incommensurable, because each piece helps form a picture of a larger whole. They emphasized that convergence should not be the researcher's dominant goal. Instead, they encouraged researchers to view divergent methods as puzzle pieces that clarify one another's meaning while retaining their own validity.

The second portion of their talk detailed practical issues that arise in implementing the puzzle metaphor and suggested possible solutions form the authors' experiences. They observed that successful completion of the puzzle requires the researcher to ask what pieces to start with, what pieces to bring in at each stage of completion, and how emergent interpretations influence succeeding efforts to complete the picture by integrating qualitative or quantitative data. They discussed the use of qualitative data to assess and refine rather than generate grounded theory, strategies for negotiating findings across "equally valid" methods, and issues in crafting manuscripts of reasonable length that fit together qualitative findings, quantitative data, and statistical testing. Finally, they shared their experiences in managing multi-method manuscripts through the review process.

In the second presentation, Linda Price and Eric Arnould emphasized that the use of multiple methods associated with disparate paradigms is still surprisingly rare in consumer research. To suggest the theoretical and practical consequences of employing different assumptions about doing multi-method science, the presenters proposed the metaphor of doing research as if conducting a choir. They began by noting that a choir, like a research project employing disparate methods, is made up of multiple voices. Elaborating their metaphor, they observed that rather than being redundant, voices in a choir may sing in harmony, may sing partially overlapping melodic lines, may sing in different octaves, and may carry entirely different themes. Like these voices, they argued, disparate methods cannot be spoken of as better or worse

than another. Instead, they urged us to see how the interplay among methodological voices may be composed by a sensitive researcher to reveal a whole greater than the sum of its parts. They continued the choir metaphor by explaining how the researcher can take advantage of multiple methodological voices by composing polyphonous cross rhythms, echoes, and interplays. They illustrated the theoretical and practical consequences of these efforts using data and conclusions from their research. They explained how multi-method research on consumption satisfaction displayed echoes, interplays, and multiplication of meanings among the multiple "voices" composing their study. They also illustrated how two sets of research, one on preference formation and one on commercial relationships illustrate how new patterns and melodic lines are revealed by the interplay among voices.

The third presentation by Ronald Hill and Beth Hirschman recounted their approach to the use of qualitative and quantitative archival data to understand consumers' experience of the Great Depression in the United States. They began by discussing their effort to reconstruct what consumers experienced during the 1930s using data collected for Harry Hopkins, the director of the Federal Emergency Relief Administration (FERA). They found that Hopkins, besides collecting quantitative data on the impact of the Depression, also commissioned the collection of qualitative data to help him gain a deeper understanding of the tragedy of unemployment, its impact on people's lives, and the potential of federal relief to alleviate suffering. The presenters focused on how to blend quantitative and qualitative archival data to provide a holistic view of historic consumer behavior. Besides presenting a compelling view of the social and emotional impact of the depression, Hill and Hirschman provided many insights about the opportunities, problems, and limitations of blending and interpreting statistics, stories, and photos.

John Sherry followed the presentations with a set of insightful comments that drew together the presenters' observations about the theoretical and practical advantages and problems inherent in conducting multi method research. He stimulated a lively discussion that revealed the audiences' interest in the possibility of using multiple methods in their own research programs.

New Directions in Price Signaling Theory and Research

Joydeep Srivastava, University of California at Berkeley

SESSION OVERVIEW

It has long been recognized that price plays at least two distinctive roles in consumer choice processes: an allocative role and an informative role. While the economic theory of consumer behavior considers the allocative role of price, a considerable body of literature has also treated price as an informational cue. The latter research has however been largely confined to studying the price-quality relationship. In recent years, there has been a growing awareness of the complex role that price and price-related strategies play even as an informational cue (Monroe 1990). Recent behavioral research (Monroe 1990) indicates that there is no simple explanation of how price influences individual purchase decisions and more importantly how consumers derive information from prices. The three papers in this session serve to highlight this complexity associated with buyers' subjective perceptions of price. Each paper in the session examines different roles that price and price-related strategies may play in shaping consumers' subjective perceptions and price expectations. The first paper by Stiving examines the effect of price endings on consumers' quality perceptions. The second paper by Simester identifies conditions under which consumers use either frequency or magnitude cues as indicators of the overall price level of a store. The third paper by Jain and Srivastava shows that price-matching refunds can be used by firms to signal low prices under certain conditions. Despite the differences in the three papers, the common themes underlying the papers are: (1) motivated from an economics of information perspective, (2) game-theoretic framework, and (3) empirical testing of the consumer-side implications of the model. A brief summary of each of the three papers as well as key comments from the discussion are given below.

SUMMARY OF INDIVIDUAL PAPERS

"Price Ending as a Signal of Quality: Theoretical and Empirical Evidence"
Mark Stiving, Ohio State University

The first paper by Stiving addresses the effects of price endings (e.g., 24.95 versus 25.00) on quality perceptions. Many texts provide examples of "psychological pricing" such as odd-even pricing, i.e., prices end in odd number or even number. Despite the apparent acceptance of these "psychological" phenomenon, research justifying odd-even pricing has been largely of an anecdotal nature. Stiving provides both a theoretical as well as an empirical justification for such pricing practices.

Stiving argues that when determining its pricing policy, a firm makes at least two decisions: the approximate price level and the price ending. He subsequently demonstrates that these two decisions are not independent and the relationship between the two is consistent with the signaling theory. Stiving's theoretical model demonstrates that under most circumstances a firm will want to set a price just below a round number, but when using price to signal quality the same firm would prefer to use a price that is both high and round. He shows that consumers can rationally interpret a combination of high price and 00 price ending as a signal of high quality while a round price in combination with a lower price does not signal high quality. Further, Stiving provides empirical support for his theoretical framework by demonstrating that firms appear to be sending the signal and that consumers are able to receive it.

In contrast to previous research (Dodds and Monroe 1985, Quigley and Notarantonio 1992, Schindler and Kibarian 1995), Stiving is able to demonstrate that consumers do perceive round prices as higher quality. He reported the results of an experiment which was designed around a real product offered by a firm that behaves as though they are signaling quality with price endings. The subjects in the experiment were shown a description (taken directly from the Franklin Quest catalog which sells binders for loose leaf calendars) including the price for each of two binders (vinyl and leather) and were then asked for a quality rating for each binder. This between subjects design varied the price ending between 95 and 00 for both binders, covering the possible combinations of round and just below pricing. The results indicate that consumers are able to receive the signal, perceiving high, round prices as signals of high quality relative to high prices alone. In contrast, subjects do not perceive low, round prices as signals of high quality relative to low prices alone.

"The Information Content of Frequency and Magnitude Cues"
Duncan Simester, University of Chicago

Simester's presentation began with a description of a series of experiments reported by Alba, Broniarczyk, Shimp, and Urbany (1994) in which they presented subjects with the prices of selected products at two stores. Although the total price for the products was the same, one store charged a lower price on two-thirds of the products while the other store's price was lower on the rest. The authors then examined subjects' overall price perceptions of the two stores. Despite various manipulations of subjects' prior beliefs, the salience of the selected products and the difficulty of aggregating the price differences, most subjects consistently indicated that they believed that the store with the lower price on most products had lower overall prices. They concluded that when subjects are unable to completely process price data, most rely on the frequency heuristic to help form price judgments.

Simester pointed out that the findings suggest that subjects were sensitive to the number of products for which each store charged a lower price, but do not show that subjects disregarded the magnitude of the price differences. Providing a rationale for the subjects' reliance on the frequency cue, he argues that for a consumer to recognize whether a price of $1.50 for a bottle of ketchup is expensive requires considerable knowledge of relative prices. For this reason, observing a price of $1.50 for ketchup reveals little about a store's attributes. However, when subjects are presented with a price comparison in which one store charges $1.50 and another store charges $1.60 for the same bottle of ketchup, it is reasonable to infer that it is more likely that the store charging the lower price enjoys lower costs on that product. Lack of information also hinders the consumer's ability to evaluate the size of a price difference: does a $0.10 price difference in ketchup represent a greater or smaller cost difference that a $0.20 price difference in cereal? Without an answer to this question, the magnitude of a price difference may reveal no more information about unseen prices than its sign; so reliance on a frequency heuristic can improve price predictions.

He argues that this intuition suggests additional hypotheses. First, if reliance on the frequency heuristic improves the accuracy of price predictions, reliance should continue when data processing is unconstrained. Second, if the information contained in the magnitude of price difference is increased, reliance on the magnitude cue should increase relative to the frequency cue. Thus the information content of the magnitude cue can be raised by reducing the product variance confounding the price differences. In particular, if the price information represents prices for the same product collected in separate months, the size of the price differences should be comparable between months. Subjects presented with monthly price differences for a single product should be expected to place more reliance on the magnitude cue and less reliance on the frequency cue relative to those who observe prices for different products. Simester reported the results of regression analysis of prices collected from various stores which provide support for his contention.

"Price-matching Refunds as a Signal for Low Prices: A Theoretical and Empirical Analysis"

Sanjay Jain, Johannes Gutenberg University of Mainz
Joydeep Srivastava, University of California at Berkeley

Price-matching refund strategies or offers by firms to match the prices of others are very common in both consumer and industrial marketing. The final presentation by Srivastava attempted to answer the question—"why do manufacturers and retailers use such price-matching policies?" Srivastava pointed out that while the previous research has justified the use of price-matching refunds either as a means of reducing competition and maintaining high prices or as a device for price discrimination leading to higher prices, casual evidence suggests that price-matching refunds are associated with lower prices. He also noted that consumers have a favorable opinion of price- matching refunds and do not perceive it as a ploy to reduce competition.

In the paper, the inconsistency between extant theory and common wisdom is resolved by developing a model in which consumers are not fully informed of prices in the market. The authors show that price-matching refunds have a different impact on competition and prices in informationally poor environments, than proposed in the prior literature. In particular, they show that in markets where consumers are not perfectly informed about prices at different stores, a price-matching refund can serve as a credible signal of low prices. Thus, such refunds can lead to more intense price competition with lower prices and higher consumer welfare.

The basic model establishes the conditions under which a price-matching refund strategy can be used by firms to signal low prices. Given that firms differ in their cost structure and that consumers are imperfectly informed about prices, price-matching refunds are credible signals of low prices when the difference in the cost structure among the firms is high. Price-matching refunds can also signal low prices when there is a high proportion of high cost firms in the market relative to low cost firms. In contrast to previous research, they find that such a pricing policy can lead to lower prices and increase consumer welfare. Subsequently, the model is extended in two different ways: (1) only a fraction of the consumers actually avail themselves of the price-matching offer (either due to high transaction costs or because they are unaware of lower priced stores); and (2) consumers have prior knowledge about the price levels at different stores. The results indicate that as the proportion of consumers who claim the price-matching offer decreases, high cost stores have more of an incentive to mimic low cost stores by offering to match prices and use it as a price-discriminatory device. They also find that as the proportion of consumers who have prior knowledge (price expectations) about the general price levels of different firms increases, the incentive for low cost firms to signal lower prices by offering to match prices decreases .

The key implications of the analytical framework are then submitted to empirical testing. In a laboratory experiment, they empirically validate their fundamental assumption by testing whether consumers interpret price-matching refunds as signals of low prices. The results of the experiment also provide strong support for the consumer-side implications of the model.

Synthesizer
Russell Winer, University of California at Berkeley

Winer began with a general discussion of the relevance and importance of signaling models. In particular, he pointed out that while all the three papers in the session were concerned with firm-to-consumer signaling, it is important to examine firm-to-firm, consumer-to-firm, and consumer-to-consumer signaling models as well. He noted that the strength of the three papers in the session lies in the fact that not only do these papers develop game-theoretic models but also test these models empirically. He called for more research on topics which are on the interface of economics and psychology. Winer concluded by commenting that inquiries of consumer behavior from an economics perspective serves to enrich and broaden the domain of consumer research in general.

REFERENCES

Alba, Joseph, Susan Broniarczyk, Terence Shimp, and Joel Urbany (1994), "The Influence of Prior Beliefs, Frequency Cues, and Magnitude Cues on Consumers' Perceptions of Comparative Price Data," *Journal of Consumer Research*, 21(2), 219-235.

Dodds, William B. and Kent B. Monroe (1985), "The Effect of Brand and Price Information on Subjective Product Evaluations" in *Advances in Consumer Research*, Vol. 12, 85-90.

Monroe, Kent B. (1990), *Pricing: Making Profitable Decisions,* Mc-Graw Hill Publishers.

Quigley, Charles J. and Elaine M. Notorantonio (1992), "An Exploratory Investigation of Perceptions of Odd and Even Pricing," working paper, Bryant College.

Schindler, Robert M. and Thomas Kibarian (1995), "Increased Sales of Discounted Items Through the Use of 99-ending Prices," working paper, Rutgers University, Camden.

The *Consumer Reports* Mindset: Who Seeks Value — The Involved or the Knowledgeable?

Lien-Ti Bei, National Chengchi University
Richard Heslin, Purdue University[1]

ABSTRACT

The question of how to assess brand choices that represent best value, and causes of brand choices that deviate from that standard was investigated. The role of product knowledge and involvement in selection of best value brands was then examined. Although knowledge and involvement are usually seen as being positively related, when one examines who chooses the best value brands, these two independent variables can lead in different directions.

Whether shopping at a modern-day mall today or buying a rug from a merchant, most consumers seek what they believe is a "good purchase." As Zeithaml (1988) found, some consumers perceive it to be the lowest price, some the best quality, some the product that fills the present need, and some the best value.

The purpose of this study was to examine an operationalization of the concept, "best value," and to look at some factors that may influence who selects a brand that is describable as the "best value." We examined two factors which should relate to consumers' decision choices: prior knowledge and product involvement.

In order to examine influences on choosing the best value brand, this study had to accomplish two subordinate tasks. The first was to objectively operationalize "a smart purchase decision" in terms of price, quality, and value. The second was to examine the effects of consumers' prior knowledge and product involvement on purchase decisions in ways that had good external validity.

For the first task—to operationalize the best purchase decision—it was decided to use Maynes' (1976) measure which he called the "Perfect Information Frontier (PIF)." The PIF represents the brands with higher quality scores and lower prices. These emphases can also be called the "*Consumer Reports* approach" to brand selection.

LITERATURE REVIEW

Three aspects of the study are explored below. First, the definition of a smart purchase in previous studies and this study is clarified. Then, the concept of Maynes' Perfect Information Frontier is reviewed. Finally, the influences of product involvement on consumers' purchase decision are proposed. The hypotheses for this study are developed in each relevant section.

The Best Purchase Decisions

Zeithaml (1988) conducted a study using focus groups and in-depth consumer interviews to determine subjects' definition of "value." She clustered the responses into four definitions of value: (1) low price, (2) utility, (3) the tradeoff between quality and price, and (4) the ratio of gain to loss[2].

Zeithaml's third definition, the tradeoff between quality and price, was consistent with a proposal by Monroe (1979). Monroe stated that the objective value was equal to "the number of units of quality per dollar expenditure, or

$$Value = \frac{quality}{price} \qquad (p.38)."$$

---

[1]The authors would like to thank three anonymous reviewers for helpful comments on earlier drafts.

[2]The labels of the four categories are retitled by the authors.

Since the best purchase decision is predetermined based on an objective point, it is defined as the best valued choice (or brand) that consumers can achieve. Then, based on Monroe's (1979) definition of value, the best purchase decision is the brand which has the highest ratio of quality to price in the market of this product class.

Perfect Information Frontier (PIF)

Maynes (1976) introduced the concept of the Perfect Information Frontier (PIF) and defined it as "the set of points, and the line segments connecting them, for which a given level of quality may be purchased at the lowest price" (p.535) on a price-quality map. According to this definition, the best purchase decision in this study should locate on the PIF.

The Perfect Information Frontier (PIF) can be a point, a straight line, a concave, a convex curve, or a combination of lines and/or curves (Maynes 1978, 1991; Maynes and Assum 1982). The contribution provided by the PIF is that there can be more than one "best value," depending on how much money the consumer wants to spend.

The PIF implies that rational consumers would purchase only those products lying on the PIF if they were perfectly informed and interested only in the best quality for the money. Maynes (1976) then asserted that the number of observed products lying off of the PIF and their distance above the PIF represented the degree of the imperfection of the market. Kamakura, Ratchford, and Agrawal (1988) later applied the similar idea of multiple best purchase to measure market efficiency and welfare loss.

The concept of "quality" in the PIF is the "true quality" (Maynes 1992) or called "objective quality" (Zeithaml 1988). Zeithaml (1988) defined objective quality as "measurable and verifiable superiority on some predetermined ideal standard or standards" (p.4). In contrast, the term "perceived quality" is defined as "the consumer's judgment about a product's overall excellence or superiority" (Zeithaml 1988, p.3). Perceived quality might help explain consumers' purchase decisions more than "true" quality (Maynes 1992). However, "true" quality is preferable in the present study, since it is utilized to determine a "true" smart purchase or a "true" best buy. Because consumers' perception of a good bargain may not be a "true" good deal, it is not used in the present study.

Prior Product Knowledge

Consumers' product knowledge is believed to be associated with their ability to understand the quality of a product. Most previous studies about brand knowledge focused on the relationship between the amount of product knowledge or experience and the amount of information search. The present study focuses on the linkage between consumers' product knowledge and their ability to select the best brands.

Findings of earlier research suggested that product experience was negatively associated with information search (Newman and Staelin 1972; Swan 1969; see Fiske et al. 1994 for a thorough review of knowledge-search relationship). One of the explanations made for these findings is that experienced or knowledgeable consumers knew enough to make a purchase decision, so they did not have to search for external information (Brucks 1984). It follows, then, that if knowledgeable consumers have enough information to make a better purchase decision, their selections should locate closer to the PIF than those of uninformed consumers.

H1: Compared to those with little product knowledge, consumers who know about a product class choose better value brand (closer to the Perfect Information Frontier).

Product Involvement

Product involvement has been applied in consumer behavior research on information search, brand commitment, and price consciousness. Houston and Rothschild (1978) applied Sherif and his colleagues' (Sherif and Cantril 1947; Sherif, Sherif, and Nebergall 1965) involvement concept to consumer behavior. Houston and Rothschild indicated that perceptions of importance varied across consumers. They labeled this varying product importance "product involvement" (Bloch 1981; Houston and Rothschild 1978; Rothschild 1979). They suggested that high involvement occurred when a product is related to a consumer's important values, needs or self-concept (Houston and Rothschild 1978).

Rothschild (1979) presented two types of involvement: situational involvement and enduring involvement. Situational involvement reflects the degree of involvement evoked by a particular situation, such as a purchase (Bloch and Richins 1983; Rothschild 1979). In Rothschild's (1979) definition, situational involvement is influenced by product attributes, as well as situational variables. Important product attributes are price, length of purchase cycle, similarity of choice, and perceived risk. The examples for the situational variables were a purchase occasion, a special purpose of purchase, or a political election (Rothschild 1979).

Enduring involvement, the second form of product involvement, represents an ongoing interest in a product (Bloch and Richins 1983; Rothschild 1979). Houston and Rothschild (1978) suggested that enduring involvement is based on past experiences with the product and the strength of relevant personal values. This definition of enduring involvement has been accepted and applied in many studies (e.g., Richins and Bloch 1986). Some researchers did not use the term "enduring involvement," but they used the same concept. It was called "perceived product importance" by Bloch and Richins (1983), "product involvement" by Bloch (1981) and Lichtenstein, Bloch, and Black (1988).

Richins and Bloch (1986) employed a longitudinal study to examine the temporal context of involvement. According to their findings, enduring involvement is a stable trait that cannot be manipulated. Situational involvement, on the other hand, declines as the stimulus of a purchase fades over time.

Only enduring involvement is examined in this study and proposed to have effects on consumers' brand preferences. Previous studies have discovered some interesting behavioral outcomes of high enduring involvement, such as, low price consciousness (Beatty, Kahle, and Homer 1988), high brand commitment (Lichtenstein et al. 1988), low interest in incentives, for example, coupons or sales (Heslin and Johnson 1992), and more information search (Lichtenstein et al. 1988). Low price consciousness and high brand commitment are proposed to be related to the central issue of this study—optimizing value in brand selection.

Lichtenstein et al. (1988) examined this idea that involved persons spend more money on a product and found that high product involvement was indeed associated with low price consciousness and high price acceptability level. Thus, it follows logically that highly involved consumers are actually less price conscious and do not pay special attention to the ratio of quality to price. Involved consumers may also be more sensitive to image and reputation of product.

H2: Compared to relatively uninvolved consumers, those who are involved with a product class do not attend to

value (i.e., they prefer brands that are farther from the Perfect Information Frontier).

Thus, we have the paradoxical situation of knowledge about, and involvement with, a product class, two consumer attributes that go together, predicting opposite kinds of behavior in terms of the value of their preferred brands. Based on the previous two propositions, consumers who ignore image and look for value should be disinterested experts. Then, Hypothesis 3 is proposed:

H3: Consumers who have both high knowledge and low involvement with a product class attend to the value of a brand compared to other consumers.

METHODOLOGY

This study applied a 2 (product knowledge: ignorant vs. knowledgeable) × 2 (involvement: high vs. low) factorial design, but the two factors were measured rather than manipulated. The effects of these two variables on subjects' purchase decision were examined on three products: ground coffee, jeans, and loudspeakers, which had been selected from 14 product categories by a panel of 12 experts in consumer behavior.

Subjects and Procedures

A survey was distributed by mail to collect data for this study. Samples of consumers for testing coffee and jeans were randomly selected from a purchased telephone list which contains over 81 million American residents' names and addresses.

Half of the loudspeaker subjects were chosen from the same list, while the other half were recruited from a list of music CD buyers. The reason for this special recruiting process for loudspeakers was to ensure a large enough sample size for this product, since a small pretest (n=17) showed that there were fewer people who had experience with loudspeakers than with the other two products.

A postcard which announced the survey purpose and schedule, as well as asking recipients' willingness to participate, was sent to 2700 subjects in 1995. A total of 225 people returned the postcards and claimed that they did not want to receive the survey. Two weeks after the postcard, 2400 surveys were mailed out, 800 for each product. One month after the major survey, subjects received a reminder and another questionnaire.

Independent Variables and Measurers

The two independent variables in this study are prior product knowledge and product involvement. Both are measured variables.

Product Knowledge. Prior knowledge was measured, rather than manipulated, because measuring expertise was considered to be more realistic. Subjects were assigned as experts or novice consumers based on a median-split of scores in a knowledge test. The operational definition of product knowledge is consumers' knowledge of terminology, attributes, and usage situations (Brucks 1984). Other aspects of product knowledge, such as brand facts and decision making procedures (Brucks 1986) were not included in the knowledge questions because they directly linked to other variables in this study.

Three sets of knowledge questions were generated based on experts' opinions and some consumer guide books (*Consumer Reports* 1994; Gall and Gall 1993). There were eleven, twelve, and twelve knowledge items for ground coffee, jeans, and loudspeakers, respectively. The numbers of correct answers given by respondents constituted their knowledge scores.

FIGURE 1
Price-Quality Map of Regular-Roast Caffeinated Coffee

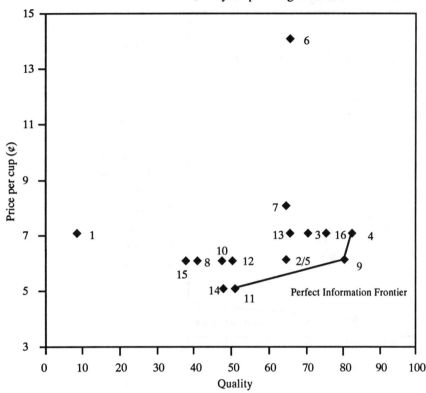

1. Eight O'Clock Roaster's Choice Plus
2. Folgers Aroma Roasted
3. Folgers Gourmet Supreme
4. Folgers Custom Roast
5. Folgers Special Roast
6. Gevalia, Colombia
7. Hills Brothers
8. Hills Brothers High Yield
9. Hills Brothers 100% Colombian
10. Hills Brothers Perfect Balance
11. Maxwell House
12. Maxwell House 1892
13. Maxwell House Colombian Supreme
14. Maxwell House Lite
15. Maxwell House Master
16. Yuban 100% Colombian

Enduring Involvement. Bloch's Involvement Scale (Bloch 1981) seemed to be a good measure for this study because it was primarily designed to measure consumers' long-term interest in a product. His original scale was modified by the author to fit ground coffee, jeans, and loudspeakers. A pretest involved consumers ranging in age from 24 to 74 and showed that these modified involvement scales had Cronbach alpha of .84 (n=38), .92 (n=32), .93 (n=24) for ground coffee, jeans, and loudspeakers, respectively.

Dependent Variables and Measures

The dependent variable of this study was the perpendicular distance of the brand chosen by the respondent from the PIF line. For coffee and jeans, subjects were asked the brand which they usually purchased. For loudspeakers, because relatively fewer consumers had this product experience, the question was formed as "assuming you want to buy loudspeakers now, which brand are you most interested in?"

The PIF was developed for this study using the quality and price information from *Consumer Reports* (1991, 1994)[3]. All brands were located on the price-quality map (Figure 1 to Figure 3). The points of best quality-price ratio were connected to form a line of the PIF[4] that represented the set of brands with the lowest prices at which a given quality might be purchased (Maynes 1993; Maynes and Assum 1982). After forming the PIF for each tested product, the distance from each point to the line of the PIF was calculated. A subject's choice was scored as the perpendicular distance of the chosen brand from the PIF.

Theoretically, these distance scores can range from 0 to infinity. The brands located on the PIF are scored as 0. As the score increases, the brand is farther away from the PIF and the selection is regarded as a poorer value. Ground coffee was separated to caffeinated (Figure 1) and decaffeinated (not shown in the figure) because their price ranges and quality ratings were not comparable.

Because the relationships between dependent and independent variables were not expected to be linear, linear regression models were not suitable. A 2 x 2 ANOVA was employed for the analysis.

RESULTS AND DISCUSSIONS

The average response rate was 23%. There was no significant difference in response rates among the three products. Respondents were mainly white (93.38%) female (63.24%), aged 25 to 54 (69.92%), with some college education or higher (75.80%) and with family annual incomes ranging between $30,000 to $74,999

---

[3]To simplify the available choices of jeans for subjects, the average price and the average quality score of each jeans brand (with multi-models) were used to assign its point on the map. The consideration of esthetics is included in the quality score of jeans. The taste of ground coffee is also evaluated by experts and added into its quality score.

[4]The line connects two point (X1, Y1) and (X2, Y2) is: $aX + bY + c = 0$,
where $a = Y1 - Y2$, $b = X2 - X1$, and $c = Y1 (X1 - X2) - X1 (Y1 - Y2)$.

FIGURE 2
Price-Quality Map of Jeans

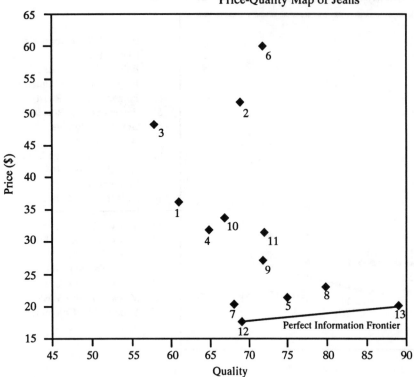

1. Bugle Boy
2. Calvin Klein
3. Chic
4. Gap
5. Gitano
6. Guess
7. J. C. Penney
8. Lands End
9. Lee
10. Levi's
11. L. L. Bean
12. Sears
13. Wrangler

FIGURE 3
Price-Quality Map of Loud Speakers

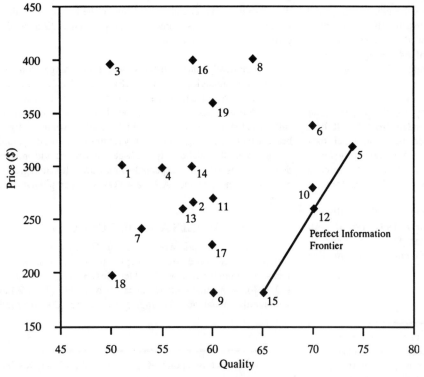

1. Advent Prodigy Tower II
2. Allison AL 110
3. Altec Lansing 96
4. B.I.C. Venturi V620
5. Bose 301 Series III
6. Boston Acoustics HD9
7. Cambridge Soundworks Model Six
8. Celestion 5 MKII
9. Cerwin-Vega L-7-B
10. DCM CX-17
11. Infinity RS 325
12. JBL J2080
13. Optimus STS 1000
14. Pinnacle AC 800
15. Pioneer CS-G303
16. Polk Audio S6
17. Sony SS-U610
18. Technics SB-CX300
19. Yamaha NS-A820A

(56.16%). No significant differences in the demographic characteristics of the respondents to the three product classes were found.

Ground Coffee

The most popular brands are Folgers Aroma Roasted and Maxwell House. The range of respondents' coffee knowledge scores was from 0 to 10, with the mean equal to 5.36 and the median equal to 5. Therefore, subjects with knowledge scores higher than 6 were labeled as experts, while those who had scores lower than 5 were grouped into the novice category. A median-split was also employed on subjects' involvement scores. The range of involvement scores for ground coffee was from 21 to 102. The mean was 54.13 and median was 53. Consequently, subjects who had involvement scores above 54 and below 53 were divided into high and low involvement groups. Subjects with scores of median points were dropped from the hypothesis test. Those respondents who bought only local or private brands were also eliminated. The final sample size of the ground coffee part of the study was 105.

Jeans

Levi's and Lee were the dominating brands with 56.97% of the respondents' market. The range of respondents' knowledge scores was from 0 to 10, with a mean of 4.77 and a median of 5. The range of involvement scores for jeans was from 22 to 104. The mean was 54.22 and the median was 54. The sample size for the jeans' part after median-split was 85.

Loudspeakers

Bose 301 Series III, which was located on the PIF, was the most preferred brand and model (34.33%). Sony SS-U610 was also popular in that 25 respondents said they would choose it if they wanted to buy a pair of loudspeakers.

Respondents' knowledge scores ranged from 0 to 7, with a mean of 2.42 and a median of 2, because few people had knowledge about loudspeakers. Their involvement scores ranged from 34 to 110. The mean score was 67.35 and the median was 66.5. The final sample size of loudspeakers in the hypothesis test was 92.

Correlation between Product Knowledge and Product Involvement

In previous studies, involvement in a product class was found positively related to product knowledge and information search (Bloch et al. 1986; Lichtenstein et al. 1988). If a strong, or even a moderately strong relationship were found in this study, the view of the distinctness of these two independent variables would be questionable.

Product knowledge and involvement were positively correlated at $\alpha<.001$ level in this study, but the Pearson correlation coefficient was only .22, which was smaller than the coefficient of .51 reported by Sujan (1985). Compared with the involvement scale (i.e., Bloch's scale) used in the present study, Sujan's (1985) involvement items were more general. Also, Sujan's knowledge measurement had relatively more items about product usage, whereas the knowledge questions in this study had relatively more items about product materials and technology, (e.g., Ethyl acetate and methylene chloride are two solvents for making (1) instant coffee, (2) roasted coffee, (3) dried coffee, (4) decaffeinated coffee, (5) don't know.) which the involved consumers might not have been interested in knowing. The low correlation coefficient (r=.22) would seen to indicate the absence of a confounding effect between product knowledge and involvement.

This low, but significant correlation between product knowledge and involvement indicated that highly involved consumers may know which brand has the highest prestige level, or where to buy the product, but they may not know the material used in the product or the production process.

Tests of Hypotheses

The final sample size for this study was 282. The three-way ANOVA results showed that there were no product effects. Therefore, the three product classes of coffee, jeans, and loudspeakers were collapsed into one 2 × 2 analysis of variance (Montgomery 1991).

Because the quality scores and price units were different among the three tested products, the original distance scores for brands were not equivalent for combining these three sets. Therefore, the distance score of each brand in the product categories was standardized, with a mean of 50 and a standard deviation of 10, before eliminating subjects with the median points and the merging process.

Hypothesis 1 predicts that, compared to novices, knowledgeable consumers would choose better value brands (small distance from the PIF). The 2 × 2 ANOVA results (Table 1, Figure 4) showed that, as a group, knowledgeable consumers did not choose brands of greater value than novices.

Hypothesis 2 states that, compared to uninvolved consumers, those who are involved with a product class do not attend to value (prefer brands that are farther from the PIF). As can be seen in Table 1 (F=3.86 and p=.05), and Figure 4, the involved, on the average, indeed do not attend to value as much as those who are less involved with the product class (greater distance from the PIF).

Hypothesis 3 states that relatively uninvolved experts would make purchase decisions closer to the PIF than others (Figure 4), and was tested by planned contrast. It was significant at the $\alpha=.05$ level (F=3.76).

Student-Newman-Keuls' post-hoc analysis of the significant interaction showed the highly involved and knowledgeable respondents to differ from low involvement and knowledge respondents (p<.05). Involvement, not knowledge, was driving the preference to ignore or attend to value in selecting brands. Looked at from a different viewpoint, the mean difference in value of product choice between involved and uninvolved experts (52.65 vs. 47.45) was significantly greater than the difference between involved and uninvolved novices (48.96 vs. 49.35) with F value of 5.28 and p value of .02. The involvement effect was stronger on experts than on novices. This joint effect of knowledge and involvement is also illustrated in Figure 4.

Discussion

It first appeared that product knowledge did not relate to respondents' brand preference decisions. However, it was found that relatively uninvolved consumers choose better value brands (closer to the PIF) than involved consumers (i.e., the significance of Hypothesis 2).

The interaction of knowledge and involvement showed that knowledgeable consumers with low involvement select the best value based on *Consumer Reports* information. The effect of product knowledge pulls consumers toward better value products, while the effect of involvement pushes consumers away from the best value purchase. Subsequent analysis showed the mean difference in value of brand chosen by involved experts and novices was significantly larger than the difference between uninvolved experts and novices (with p=.02; shown in Figure 4). Those who selected the best value brands had product knowledge, and did not invest their ego or self-concept in the brand name they used.

TABLE 1
Analysis of Variance for the Purchase Decisions

Source	DF	MS	F
Product Type	2	13.02	0.14
Knowledge	1	44.98	0.47
Involvement	1	371.90	3.86 *
Knowledge × Involvement	1	508.49	5.28 *
Between-Subject Error	276	(96.31)	
Model	5	206.79	2.15 ♦
[$R^2 = 0.04$]			

Note. Values enclosed in parentheses represent the mean square error.
♦ $p < .10$. * $p < .05$.

FIGURE 4
The Joint Effects of Product Knowledge and Product Involvement on Brand Selection

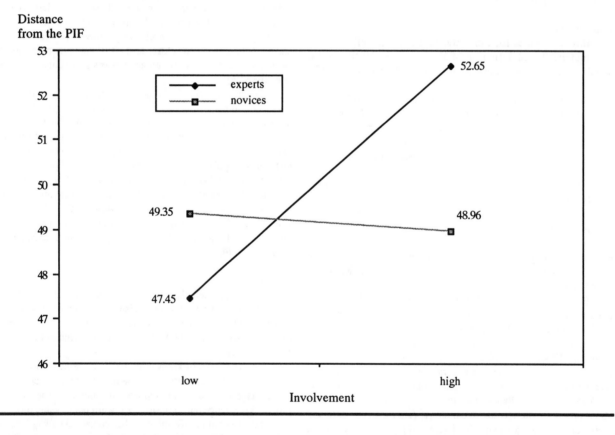

CONCLUSIONS AND IMPLICATIONS

Some consumers buy brands that give more value for the price than do others. According to this study, those value shoppers are knowledgeable about the product class but not have ego involvement with it. They select brands close to the PIF—the better values.

Consumers who select brands farther away from the best choices, are in general highly involved with the product. They involve their personality, ego, value, and interests into the selection of products. For example, they may choose a famous brand because of its prestigious image. To them, the prestigious image is worth the extra cost. Novices also tend to make purchase decisions farther away from the PIF. It is most likely in their case that they are simply not aware of the value-related attributes of each brand (assuming they are aware of which attributes are value-relevant at all). When information becomes costly, some consumers would rather search for less information and remain ignorant. Therefore, providing the ignorant and uninformed with appropriate and inexpensive product information is important.

For marketers and advertisers, it is suggested that when consumers select a product farther away from the PIF, they are purchasing product attributes other than price and objective quality. For a product which is away from the PIF, the add-on value of the brand becomes very important to attract highly involved consumers or the ignorant. For example, marketers may emphasize the prestigious image of a brand to draw the attention of the highly involved consumers. On the other hand, marketers can advertise the overall value of brands to those novices who do not care about, or know how to judge the relevance of product attributes. Those subjective add-on values (such as, brand image and relatively convenient location) become the purchased attributes for those brands located away from the PIF.

This study uses Maynes' Perfect Information Frontier (PIF) as a measure of multiple "best brands." The PIF is a useful tool because it allows multiple "best choices" in a market. This concept is closer to reality than the traditional definition of value that is equal to the ratio of quality to price (Monroe 1979). The best brand may be a high quality product with a high price, or a moderate one for a low price. When a consumer chooses a brand that is different from the "best" price-quality ratio, it is still a good choice if it is the lowest available price at its quality level. The PIF reflects this situation in the real market.

With the help of the PIF, this study effectively surveys real consumers on their purchase decisions of real products and real brands. Most previous studies of consumer behavior and marketing used hypothetical products and brands to create a homogeneous environment and to control the possible confounding factors from the real market. Researchers could use the present study as a framework to investigate consumer behavior in the real market.

Because this study used real products, consumer decisions were influenced by brand images and advertising. These influences were shown where most respondents' answers given about their major reasons of brand selections were "brand names" and "advertising." Unfortunately, the famous and heavily advertised brands for ground coffee and loudspeakers were also the brands located right on the PIF. From the viewpoint of market efficiency, it was a good sign that brand names were also the best choices in the market. So, consumers were less likely to make wrong choices. However, brand image and advertising became viable alternative effects in those cases. It is recommended that for future research, the prestige and image of brands should be explicitly considered when real products and real brands are studied.

REFERENCES

Beatty, S. E., Kahle, L. R. and Homer, P. (1988). "The Involvement-Commitment Model: Theory and Implication," *Journal of Business Research*, 16, 149-167.

Bloch, P. H. (1981). "An Exploration into the Scaling of Consumers' Involvement with a Product Class," *Advances in Consumer Research*, 8, 61-65.

_____ and Richins, M. L. (1983). "A Theoretical Model for the Study of Product Importance Perceptions," *Journal of Marketing*, 47, 69-81.

Brucks, M. (1984). "The Effects of Product Class Knowledge on Information Search Behavior," *Journal of Consumer Research*, 12, 1-15.

Brucks, M. (1986). "A Typology of Consumer Knowledge Content," *Advances in Consumer Research*, 13, 58-63.

Consumer Reports (1991, July). "Blue Jeans," *Consumer Reports*, pp. 456-461.

_____ (1994, March). "Loudspeakers," *Consumer Reports*, pp. 176-179.

_____ (1994, October). "Brewed Coffee," *Consumer Reports*, pp. 640-645.

Fiske, C. A., Luebbehusen, L. A., Miyazaki, A. D. and Urbany, J. E. (1994). "The Relationship between Knowledge and Search: It Depends," *Journal of Consumer Research*, 21, 43-50.

Gall, T. L. and Gall, S. B. (1993). *Consumers' Guide to Product Grades and Terms* (pp. 80-85 & p.99). Detroit: Gale Research Inc.

Heslin, R. E. and Johnson, B. T. (1992). "Prior Involvement and Incentives to Pay Attention to Information," *Psychology and Marketing*, 9, 209-219.

Houston, M. J. and Rothschild, M. L. (1978). "Conceptual and Methodological Perspectives on Involvement," In S. C. Jain (Ed.), *1978 Educators' Proceedings* (pp. 184-187). Chicago: American Marketing Association.

Kamakura, W. A., Ratchford, B. T. and Agrawal, J. (1988). "Measuring Market Efficiency and Welfare Loss," *Journal of Consumer Research*, 15, 289-302.

Lichtenstein, D. R., Bloch, P. H., and Black, W. C. (1988). "Correlates of Price Acceptability," *Journal of Consumer Research*, 15, 243-252.

Maynes, E. S. (1976). "The Concept and Measurement of Product Quality," In N. E. Terleckyj (Ed.), *Household Production and Consumption* (pp. 529-560). New York: National Bureau of Economic Research.

_____ (1978). "Informational Imperfections in Local Consumer Markets," In A. Mitchell (Ed.), *The Effect of Information on Consumer and Market Behavior* (pp. 77-85). Chicago: American Marketing Association.

_____ (1991). "An information Desiderata Evaluation of Sources of Consumer Information," In R. N. Mayer (Ed.), *Enhancing Consumer Choice: Proceedings of the Second International Conference on Research in the Consumer Interest* (pp. 491-509).

_____ (1992). "Salute and Critique: Remarks on Ratchford and Gupta's Analysis of Price-Quality Relations," *Journal of Consumer Policy*, 15, 83-96.

_____ (1993). "Two Challenges: Life and Informationally Imperfect Consumer Markets Reflections of a Consumer Economist," In T. Mauldin (Ed.), *American Council on Consumer Interests: Proceedings of 39th Annual Conference* (pp. 19-28).

_____ and Assum, T. (1982). "Informationally Imperfect Consumer Markets: Empirical Findings and Policy Implications," *Journal of Consumer Affairs*, 16, 62-87.

Montgomery, D. C. (1991). *Design and Analysis of Experiments* (3rd ed., pp. 134-194, pp. 569-587). New York: John Wiley & Sons.

Monroe, K. B. (1979). "Price as an Index of Value," *Pricing: Making Profitable Decisions* (pp. 37-48). New York: McGraw-Hill Book Company.

Newman, J. W. and Staelin, R. (1972) "Prepurchase Information Seeking for New Cars and Major Household Appliances," *Journal of Marketing Research*, 9, 249-257.

Richins, M. L. and Bloch, P. H. (1986). "After the New Wears Off: the Temporal Context of Product Involvement," *Journal of Consumer Research*, 13, 280-285.

Rothschild, M. L. (1979). "Advertising Strategies for High and Low Involvement Situations," In J.C. Maloney and B. Silverman (Eds.), *Attitude Research Plays for High Stakes* (pp. 74-93). Chicago: American Marketing Association.

Sherif, M. and Cantril, H. (1947). *The Psychology of Ego Involvement.* New York: John Wiley.

Sherif, C. W., Sherif, M. and Nebergall, R. E. (1965). *Attitude and Attitude Change: The Social Judgment-Involvement Approach.* Philadelphia: W. B. Saunders.

Sujan, M. (1985). "Consumer Knowledge: Effects on Evaluation Strategies Mediating Consumer Judgments," *Journal of Consumer Research, 12,* 31-46.

Swan, J. E. (1969). "Experimental Analysis of Predecision Information seeking," *Journal of Marketing Research, 6,* 192-197.

Zeithaml, V. A. (1988). "Consumer Perceptions of Price, Quality, and Value: A Means-End Model and Synthesis of Evidence," *Journal of Marketing, 52,* 2-22.

An Investigation of the Relationship Between Perceived Risk and Product Involvement

Utpal M. Dholakia, University of Michigan[1]

ABSTRACT

The constructs of perceived risk and product involvement have been noted to share several similarities in the consumer behavior literature but diversity in the conceptualization and operationalization of these constructs has led to conflicting and confusing findings. Using consistent definitions of the two constructs, this article investigates the relationship between their components. Results support the multi-dimensional and product-specific nature of the perceived risk construct. Additionally, the perceived risk dimensions are found to explain a significant portion of the enduring importance component of product involvement. Suggestions for future research are provided to build on these findings.

INTRODUCTION

The constructs of perceived risk and product involvement have been extensively used as *moderating* or *explanatory* variables in consumer behavior. A significant number of papers have examined the conceptualization, importance and relevance of each construct and its relationship to important consumer behavior phenomena[2]. The level of involvement has been shown to determine the depth, complexity and extensiveness of cognitive and behavioral processes during the customer choice process (Houston & Rothschild, 1978; Laurent & Kapferer, 1985). In the marketing literature, the amount and nature of risk perceived by the customer during purchase has been recognized as important in defining the customer's information needs and in predicting the acquisition, transmission and processing of information during the decision-making process (Gabbott, 1991). These similarities are striking and suggest the need for an investigation of the relationship between the two constructs. An investigation of the relationship has the potential to isolate elements common to the two constructs as well as to explicate the relationship between their components.

Though several researchers have noticed and discussed this relationship (e.g.: Laurent & Kapferer, 1985; Richins, et al., 1992; Venkatraman, 1989), no study has made an explicit distinction between the elements of these constructs and compared them simultaneously for a number of different product classes. The main objective of the present study is to fill this gap in extant literature and investigate the relationship between product involvement and perceived risk. The constructs of perceived risk and product involvement are reviewed and the relationship between particular types of risk and the components of product involvement is investigated. Hypotheses relating to the two constructs are formed and an empirical study is carried out using a recent data-collection advance to test the hypotheses. The paper concludes with a presentation of results of the study along with a discussion of implications from the findings.

PRODUCT INVOLVEMENT

The current view in consumer behavior holds involvement to be a *causal or motivating variable* influencing the consumer's purchase and communication behavior. According to this view, the level of involvement determines the extensiveness of the consumer's purchase decision-making process as well as the nature of processing of communications (Laurent & Kapferer, 1985).

Like other consumer researchers, I view product involvement as a motivating condition, defined as *"the perceived personal relevance of a product to an individual, based on inherent needs, values and interests"* (Antil, 1984; Celsi & Olson, 1988; Richins & Bloch, 1986; Slama & Taschian, 1985; Zaichkowsky, 1985). This definition falls within the domain of *cognitive approaches* to defining involvement (Laaksonnen, 1994), where involvement is treated as a property of an object-related cognitive structure, specifically either an attitude structure or a product-related knowledge structure. The level of involvement is determined by the number of personal needs, goals and values (self-knowledge) engaged by the product, the centrality of this self-knowledge to the individual and the relatedness of the product to this self-knowledge (Celsi & Olson, 1988; Tyebjee; 1979). This kind of product involvement is long-lived, determined by the stable elements of the individual's identity and is therefore labeled *enduring involvement* (Laaksonnen, 1994).

The emphasis of enduring involvement is on the product itself and the value or need satisfaction derived from owning, using and consuming the product (Richins & Bloch, 1986). Each person has a different cognitive structure for different product classes and enduring involvement can be conceptualized as representing the strength or extent of this cognitive structure. Thus in this study, product involvement is conceptualized as specific to a product-class and unique to an individual. However, at the aggregate level, fairly homogeneous perceptions of products are found, especially in relatively homogeneous populations. As a result, it is possible to aggregate perceptions of enduring involvement for a product class for more-or-less homogeneous populations.

Within the extensive marketing literature, two other conceptualizations of involvement can be identified. *Situational involvement* refers to the degree of involvement evoked by a particular purchase situation and is essentially context-dependent and temporary (Houston & Rothschild, 1978). *Response involvement* is concerned with the consequences of the product on the individual in terms of his/her cognitive response and is outcome-oriented (Richins, et al., 1992).

PERCEIVED RISK

Perceived risk is conceptualized as arising from unanticipated and uncertain consequences of an unpleasant nature resulting from the product purchase (Bauer, 1960). In consumer behavior literature, when evaluating risk, the focus is generally on potentially negative outcomes and perceived risk is generally conceptualized in terms of *loss* (Dowling, 1986), in contrast to other disciplines like psychology where both positive and negative outcomes are considered.

Bettman's (1973) distinction between *inherent risk* and *handled risk* identifies perceived risk as a product-class specific construct, i.e. different product classes have different levels of *inherent and handled risk* associated with them. The inherent risk refers to the

---

[1] The author would like to thank Professor Aaron Ahuvia and three anonymous reviewers for valuable comments on an earlier draft of this paper.

[2] For excellent reviews of the involvement construct, see Laaksonnen (1994), Muehling et al. (1993) and Zaichkowsky (1985); for reviews of perceived risk, see Dowling (1986) and Gemunden (1985).

EXHIBIT 1
Categories of loss contributing to perceived risk

Financial loss   Risk associated with losing money because of:(1) functional failure of the product, (2) high repair costs and (3) equivalent or better product available at lower cost.

Performance loss   Risk associated with inadequate and/or unsatisfactory performance of the product.

Physical loss   Risk associated with physical danger because of use of the product.

Psychological loss   Risk associated with the non-congruence between the product and the buyer's self-image or self-concept.

Social loss   Risk associated with the unfavorable opinions of the consumer by others because of the product.

Time loss   Risk associated with age/ inefficient use of time because of the product.

(Adapted from Stone and Gr_nhaug, 1993)

---

aspects of risk in the product class that are temporally stable while the handled risk pertains to the more situational aspects of the product class. In this study, I adhere to this conceptualization of perceived risk as product-class specific and unique to an individual. In other words, each individual perceives each product class to have specific levels of risk associated with it and these levels for a product class are different for different individuals. Perceived risk for a particular product class is defined as *"the subjective expectation of losses"* resulting from the purchase and use of products from the product class. This definition is consistent with definitions used in previous studies (e.g.: Peter & Ryan, 1976).

Perceived risk studies have identified several distinct dimensions within the overall perceived risk for a product-class (Jacoby and Kaplan, 1972; Kaplan et. al., 1974; Roselius, 1971). The risk taxonomy arising from these studies and consisting of six dimensions is widely accepted as relevant to explaining perceived risk and is presented in Exhibit 1.

RELATIONSHIP BETWEEN PERCEIVED RISK AND PRODUCT INVOLVEMENT

A significant similarity between the two constructs is that both perceived risk and product involvement incorporate the notion of "importance" of a product class to a consumer. The notion of perceived risk as the probability and magnitude of loss arising from the purchase and use of a product relates to the anxiety felt by the consumer when dealing with a particular product class and consequently the importance of the product class to the consumer. The importance of the product class is an integral component of the enduring involvement construct from its definition as "the extent of connections of a product class to a person's self-concept, values and motives" (Engel & Light, 1968). The origin of the notion of importance can be traced to the "importance of purchase" construct in the Howard and Sheth (1969) model of buyer behavior. In this model, the "importance of purchase" is defined as the relative intensity of motives that govern the buyer's activities relating to the given product class relative to other product classes. The authors note that the construct has been termed degree of involvement, importance of purchase, importance of the task or seriousness of the consequences. This construct reveals the intimate links between the two constructs.

Another similarity is that high levels of both perceived risk and product involvement are known to result in more extensive information gathering and more elaborate information processing by the consumer (Celsi & Olsen, 1988; Gemunden, 1985). A third similarity is the great diversity and confusion prevailing in both involvement and risk research, prompting one risk researcher to label the construct "fuzzy" (Dowling, 1986). As a result, an explicit definition of the construct is generally specified in a study to clarify and delimit the scope of the study when using either of these constructs. In the present study, conceptualization of both perceived risk and enduring involvement as product-class specific and individual-level constructs facilitates their comparability.

However, there are significant differences between the two constructs. At the broadest level, the distinction between product involvement and perceived risk can be made using the fact that perceived risk considers only the negative consequences arising from the purchase and consumption of the product while the level of product involvement is affected by the positive consequences also. Moreover, involvement also includes characteristics like ego-involvement and commitment (Muehling et al., 1993) which are not related directly to risk associated with the product.

In studying the relationship between the two constructs, the extant literature reveals confusion about whether perceived risk should be treated as an antecedent of involvement (Bloch, 1981), one of its dimensions (Laurent & Kapferer, 1985) or as its consequence. Several studies provide evidence that perceived risk influences situational involvement. Bloch (1981) suggests that situational involvement is experienced by consumers when the stakes associated with a purchase outcome, and consequently the perceived risk is high. This involvement is likely to be temporary and disappear when the purchase is completed. In their development of a standard scale, Laurent and Kapferer (1985) use perceived risk as an antecedent of situational involvement. They find no discrimination between the "perceived importance of a purchase" and the "perceived importance of the negative consequences of a mispurchase" and combine these constructs into a single one. However, they find the subjective probability of a mispurchase to have discriminant validity and conclude that involvement cannot be equated with perceived risk.

Perceived risk has also been used as a dimension of product involvement. Rothschild (1979) advocates the use of perceived risk as an implicit measure of product involvement and points out the usefulness of functional and psychological risk as predictors of product involvement. In their scale development procedure, Chaffee and McLeod (1978) observe that risk perception provides an empirical definition of the general concept of involvement. Bloch and Richins (1983) suggest that instrumental involvement differs from the importance dimension of risk only in that the latter is a "cognitive" state of awareness that the purchase of a product has negative consequences while instrumental involvement also comprises the "motivation" to act on these consequences by avoiding them during purchase.

Interestingly, perceived risk has also been envisioned as a consequence of product involvement. Venkatraman (1989) suggests that since enduring involvement is a long-term product concern while perceived risk is limited to the purchase situation, enduring involvement precedes risk. She finds evidence of low perceived risk for consumers with high enduring involvement and concludes that enduring involvement increases the risk-handling capabilities of consumers. Investigating the applicability of the "availability heuristic," Folkes (1988) finds that the ease of retrieval of product performance experiences from memory (associated with high levels of product involvement) influences consumers' judgments about the likelihood of product failures. Thus, perceptions of risk are found to result from salience of the product to the consumer. This ambivalence about the relationship suggests a need for a systematic study examining the components of the two constructs and the relationship between them.

HYPOTHESES

In the present study, the construct of perceived risk is characterized as multi-dimensional. These dimensions have been considered to be functionally independent at a conceptual level so that for an increase in one category of risk, the other risk categories can increase, decrease or remain unchanged. Support for the multidimensional nature of the perceived risk construct has been well-documented in literature (Jacoby and Kaplan, 1972; Stone and Grönhaug, 1993) and these dimensions have been found to explain a significant portion of the overall risk construct. However, the influence of a particular dimension in contributing to the overall risk is likely to be different for different products. For example, the physical risk associated with a chain saw is likely to be a more significant contributor to the overall risk than the physical risk associated with a CD player. It is therefore essential to determine if the six components of risk together explain a significant portion of the overall perceived risk for different product classes. Previous studies have measured this relationship for multiple products using single measures for each risk category (Jacoby & Kaplan, 1972) or for a single product using multiple measures to measure each category (Stone & Grönhaug, 1993). It is of theoretical importance to extend this relationship using multiple measures across different product classes. If the six dimensions of risk are correctly chosen and measured properly, they must explain a significant portion of the overall perceived risk across product classes. The first hypothesis can therefore be stated as:

H1:   The six dimensions of risk will explain a significant portion of the overall risk across different product classes.

Enduring involvement for a product class arises from the importance of purchase, ownership and use of the product to the consumer. Thus, perceptions of enduring importance result from the product's ability to satisfy the consumer's enduring needs (Bloch & Richins, 1983). The nature of the product plays an important role in determining the product importance perceptions. Thus, though enduring importance for a product is conceptualized as a person-specific variable, I expect that at an aggregate level, different product classes will differ in the level of enduring importance associated with them. Support for this has been found in previous studies. For example, Hupfer and Gardner (1985) found that products differ in the perceived importance to consumers, with cars perceived as more important than facial tissues. As a result, the hypothesis can be stated as:

H2:   At an aggregate level, the enduring importance component of product involvement for different product classes will be different.

The enduring importance construct is a key component of involvement. It is the long-term, cross-situational perception of product importance based on the strength of the product's relationship to the central needs and values of the consumer (Bloch & Richins, 1983) and reflects a cognitive state of awareness about the product (Laaksonnen, 1994). The strength of this tie influences the level of importance and consequently, that of enduring involvement felt by the consumer. The enduring importance for a product class is determined to a large extent by the perceived importance of the consequences resulting from using the product. The "adverse consequences" dimension of perceived risk is concerned with the severity of negative consequences that can occur from the purchase and the use of the product (Dowling, 1986). For products with the possibility of severe adverse consequences, the need for knowledge, awareness and expertise will be greater and consequently enduring involvement for such product classes will be higher. Products with high levels of perceived risk will therefore have high levels of perceived importance associated with them.

I also expect that the risk dimensions will play a different role in explaining enduring importance for different product classes. For example, social risk is likely to be more useful in determining enduring importance for a designer dress while physical risk is likely to be more pertinent for a chain-saw. As a result, the hypothesis can be stated as:

H3:   The six dimensions of perceived risk will explain a significant portion of the enduring importance component of product involvement across different product classes.

These hypotheses summarize essential properties of the two constructs and explain the relationship between their components.

RESEARCH METHODOLOGY

To examine the preceding hypotheses, primary data was collected because of the lack of appropriate secondary data availability. A new method of data collection called *electronic mail* was used, made possible due to recent advances in technology and rapid proliferation of the facility. Electronic mail (e-mail) uses computer text-editing and communication tools to provide a high-speed message service over the Internet. Some important characteristics of e-mail that make it an attractive data-collection device for consumer research are speed of response, reduced costs of sending and receiving surveys, possibility of asynchronous communication between the researcher and the respondent(s) and the absence of intermediaries (Sproull, 1986).

Measurement

Standard scales were used to measure the constructs of perceived risk and product involvement[3]. This gave the assurance of

---

[3]The questionnaire used in the study can be obtained from the author on request.

EXHIBIT 2
The Experimental Design

IMPORTANCE

	High	**Low**
High	Laptop computer	Color Television
COST		
Low	Greeting Card for a Spouse's/ Friend's Birthday	Can of Soup

previously tested validity and reliability and reduced the time for questionnaire construction and pre-testing.

Early studies of perceived risk relied on single measures for each risk dimension. Recent studies, however favor the use of multiple measures for each dimension (Stone & Grönhaug, 1993). For the present study, each risk dimension is measured using multiple items and separate measures are used for the measurement of the overall risk. The scale used is similar to that used by Stone & Grönhaug (1993).

The *Components of Involvement (CI) Scale* (Lastovicka and Gardner, 1979) was used to measure product involvement. Several reasons dictate the choice of the CI scale for the present study. The CI scale was constructed to measure enduring involvement for a product class. It is one of the earliest multi-item scales developed to measure involvement and forms the conceptual basis for subsequent scale development in the field. The CI scale is not product-specific and can be applied across product classes. It is based on the conceptual foundations of involvement (e.g.: Sherif & Cantril, 1947) and not only emphasizes the self-identity/ importance component of involvement but also captures the notion of ego-involvement (Sherif et al., 1965). Previous studies have shown the CI scale to have adequate levels of content, convergent and discriminant validity (Lastovicka & Gardner, 1979; Jensen et al., 1988).

Products

To incorporate heterogeneity of product classes, a 2x2 between-subjects experimental design with two levels of cost (high and low) and two levels of importance (high and low) was used to test the hypotheses. Products were chosen for each of the four cells using criteria of cost, end-use and durability. The four products chosen were: laptop computer, color television, greeting card and can of soup.[4] The diagrammatic representation of the experimental design is presented in exhibit 2.

Data Collection

The data collection was carried out using a three-stage procedure. In the first stage, forty mailing lists were randomly chosen from all the listserv mailing lists.[5] In the second stage, in accordance with "netiquette," letters were sent to list-owners asking permission to post a short solicitation message on the list. Messages requesting list members interested in filling out surveys to respond along with a brief description of the study were sent to the 27 lists whose owners gave permission. Seventy-eight responses were received. In the third stage, entire surveys were sent to these respondents resulting in seventy-two completed surveys. The response rate[6] was 92.3%.

Respondent Characteristics

The respondents were almost equally distributed by gender. Of the 72 respondents, 38 (52.8%) were male and 34 (47.2%) female. The mean family income was $54970 and the mean age was 34.7 years. The respondents belonged to several occupational categories, the major ones being 40 (55.56%) professionals, 17 (23.61%) graduate students and 10 (13.89%) faculty. No claim of representativeness is made for the sample used in the study because of the fairly homogeneous, high socio-economic status of the respondents in the sample. But since the research goal is synonymous to Calder et al.'s (1981) *theory testing*, the sample is appropriate for the present study.

RESULTS

A reliability analysis was carried out to test the reliability of the constructs used in the measurement of dimensions of perceived risk and the components of product involvement. Table 1 reports

---

[4]The products were chosen by carrying out a pre-test. Thirteen subjects (all graduate students) were asked to rate several different products on the dimensions of importance and cost. The four products were chosen on the basis of these evaluations.

[5]Mailing lists are groups of people sharing some common interests and communicating with each other by e-mail. A message sent to the mailing list server is distributed to all subscribed members of the mailing list.

[6]This response rate is not comparable to the conventional response rate reported for mail and telephone surveys, since only people soliciting the questionnaire are considered as potential respondents.

TABLE 1
Reliability analysis for the measured constructs

Construct	Number of Items	Cronbach Alpha
Perceived Risk		
Overall Risk	3	0.8057
Financial Risk	3	0.8715
Social Risk	3	0.8448
Time Risk	3	0.8410
Physical Risk	2	0.8089
Performance Risk	3	0.8355
Psychological Risk	3	0.9074
Product Involvement		
Enduring Importance	11	0.9002

the Cronbach alpha values for each of the measured constructs. All the constructs satisfy the Nunnally Cronbach alpha criterion of 0.7 (Nunnally, 1978).

To determine the relatedness to the dimensions of risk, the correlations were computed.[7] All six risk dimensions had high positive correlations with the criterion overall risk and also had significant positive correlations with each other. To test hypothesis 1, a multiple regression of all the dimensions of perceived risk was carried out with the overall risk as the dependent variable. Table 2 reports the results of the analysis. Time risk and financial risk are found to be significant predictors of the overall risk. For the full model, 84.3% of the total variance in the overall risk is explained using the six dimensions of perceived risk. In general, the six dimensions of risk perform extremely well in predicting overall risk for different product classes.

The generalizability of the predictive power of the six dimensions was tested by carrying out multiple regressions for each individual product class. These results are reported in table 2. Financial risk is found to be significant for laptop computer and color television. This is consistent with the research design where these two products were chosen as high cost products. None of the other predictors are found to be significant for any product class. The adjusted R-square values vary from 0.82 for a greeting card to 0.34 for a can of soup. A reason for the low R-square value for the can of soup could be that the product has very low overall perceived risk associated with it and it is difficult to distinguish that overall risk into distinct types. In general, the six dimensions of perceived risk predict the overall perceived risk across different product classes and hypothesis 1 is supported.

The mean enduring importance values along with standard deviations for the four product classes are presented in table 3. To test hypothesis 2, a one-way ANOVA was carried out and the results are reported in table 4. The results of the F-test indicate that

mean values are different between product classes and the enduring importance depends on the product class under consideration. As a result, hypothesis 2 is supported. Pair-wise comparisons using the Tukey multiple-comparison procedure showed that can of soup has a significantly lower enduring involvement than each of laptop computer, color television and greeting card at the 95% family confidence interval.

To test hypothesis 3, multiple regressions were carried out with the six dimensions of risk as the predictor variables and enduring importance as the dependent variable. Table 5 reports the results of this analysis for all product classes. Almost 43% of the variance in the enduring importance variable is explained by the dimensions of perceived risk for the full model. This indicates support for the hypothesis that the dimensions of perceived risk are useful in predicting importance for a product class. I carried out a separate analysis to test the generalizability of this hypothesis across product classes. Table 5 reports the results of separate multiple regression analyses for different product classes. The R-square values vary from 0.6755 for color television to 0.0235 for a can of soup. These results provide support for the suitability of the perceived risk dimensions in predicting enduring importance.

DISCUSSION

In general, the six dimensions of risk are found to be comprehensive determinants of the overall perceived risk construct. One contribution of this study is the generalizability of this relationship across different products using multiple items of measurement. The perceived risk construct is useful when there is a certain degree of risk in the product. For a product like a can of soup for which the perceived risk is extremely low, there is some doubt of the usefulness of attempting to distinguish the dimensions of risk causing the total amount of risk. Results of the study indicate that the dimensional approach to measurement makes most sense when there is a certain amount of inherent risk present in the product class. Therefore, the conclusion reached is that the conceptualization of perceived risk as a multi-dimensional construct is a sound one and the use of multiple items to measure each of the dimensions is appropriate.

---

[7]Due to space constraints, the correlation matrix is not presented here but can be obtained from the author on request.

TABLE 2
Regression models for perceived risk

Variable	Overall Risk All products	Laptop Computer	Color Television	Greeting Card	Can of Soup
Time Risk	0.1902[a] (2.772)[1]	0.2608[2] (1.62)	-0.0012 (-0.005)	0.0224 (0.06)	0.928 (1.263)
Performance Risk	-0.0565 (-0.843)	0.1359 (0.656)	-0.3132 (-1.389)	-0.0170 (-0.114)	-0.0267 (-0.068)
Physical Risk	-0.0502 (-0.675)	-0.0974 (-0.454)	0.1655 (0.48)	0.8175 (1.658)	0.2278 (0.6)
Finance Risk	0.8673[a] (11.04)	0.9276[b] (4.374)	0.8298[b] (3.841)	-0.1026 (-0.329)	0.2019 (0.585)
Psychological Risk	0.0497 (0.619)	-0.1558 (0.737)	0.6146 (1.623)	-0.0599 (-0.132)	0.9875 (1.653)
Social Risk	-0.0546 (-0.652)	-0.1978 (-0.853)	-0.5025 (-1.296)	0.3182 (1.201)	-1.5984 (-1.668)
R^2	0.8562	0.8099	0.7845	0.8868	0.5371
Adjusted R^2	0.8429	0.6958	0.6592	0.8187	0.3388

[1] Figures in parentheses are t-values.
[2] The values reported are standardized regression coefficients.
[a] p-value< 0.001
[b] p-value< 0.05

TABLE 3
Means of Enduring Importance for products

Product	Mean E. I.[1]	Std. dev
Laptop Computer	4.7187	1.3713
Can of Soup	6.1093	0.5469
Color television	5.0404	1.5390
Greeting card	4.1176	1.1521

[1] Lower values indicate greater enduring importance for the product

It has been noted that one of the earliest and most accepted axioms of consumer behavior theory is that at an aggregate level, consumers consider different products to have different levels of importance (Bloch & Richins, 1983). This study confirms the truth of this axiom *for enduring importance* associated with products. Another important contribution of this study is that it raises and addresses the issue of the temporal nature of the perceived risk construct. There is some ambiguity about the time-variance and the stability of the risk perceived by a consumer for a product class. Most researchers do not make an explicit assertion but implicitly assume perceived risk to be a situational construct, largely determined by the conditions during the purchase occasion.

The dimensions of perceived risk are also ambiguous in making this distinction between the enduring and the situational

TABLE 4
One way ANOVA for enduring importance by product

Source	Sum of squares	df	Mean Square	F	Sig. level
Between Groups	40.2048	3	13.4016	9.5723	0.0000
Within Groups	95.2024	68	1.4000		

TABLE 5
Regression models for enduring importance

Variable	Overall Risk All products	Laptop Computer	Color Television	Greeting Card	Can of Soup
Financial Risk	-0.4552[a] (-3.042)[1]	-0.1980 (0.0932)	-0.2628 (-1.254)	-0.2684 (-0.33)	-0.281 (-0.67)
Performance Risk	0.2527[2] (1.978)	0.2578 (0.793)	0.1569 (0.717)	0.4748 (1.219)	-0.4901 (-1.033)
Physical Risk	0.0814 (0.575)	0.5904 (1.751)	-0.3532 (-1.057)	0.2172 (0.169)	0.7524 (1.63)
Psychological Risk	0.3191[b] (2.087)	0.2067 (0.623)	0.5041 (1.372)	0.0890 (0.075)	-0.3046 (-0.42)
Social Risk	0.3487 (2.185)	-0.0932 (-0.256)	0.4830 (1.284)	0.3503 (0.507)	-0.2812 (-0.241)
Time Risk	0.1704 (1.304)	0.0556 (0.22)	0.386 (1.605)	-0.3005 (-0.305)	0.8134 (0.911)
R^2	0.4780	0.5313	0.7972	0.2361	0.3164
Adjusted R^2	0.4298	0.2501	0.6755	0.2274	0.0235

[1] Figures in parentheses are t-values.
[2] The values reported are standardized regression coefficients.
[a] p-value< 0.001
[b] p-value< 0.05

elements of risk. However, most of the dimensions are related to losses occurring because of product attributes and therefore represent stable perceptions. Also, most of the losses represented by the risk dimension have the same relative importance with respect to each other over time. As an example, for a person interested in fashion clothing, the social and psychological risk associated with the product class "clothing" will be significant, time-invariant and relatively stable. In other words, this consumer will have a high amount of social and psychological risk for the product class, *every time* s/he deals with the product class. The results of this study provide some evidence of the enduring nature of the risk dimensions.

This study also raises the question of the need for a separate conceptualization of the situational perceived risk construct and an examination of the components of this construct. Future studies must address the issues of scale construction and relatedness of this construct to other constructs like instrumental importance (Bloch & Richins, 1983) and situational involvement.

Another important contribution of the study is the success of the perceived risk dimensions in explaining the enduring importance component of product involvement. While this has significance, the result also raises important issues for future research. It is possible that some risk dimensions are antecedents of enduring importance while others are consequences of it. For example, psychological and social risk could result in high enduring importance for champagne for a wine connoisseur, which in turn could result in high performance risk. Future studies should focus on unraveling this causal relationship. The effect of different levels of situational and enduring involvement on perceptions of different types of risk is another promising area for future investigation. Finally, given the high socio-economic status of the subjects in the present study, future replications with different subject pools may also prove to be valuable.

CONCLUSIONS

In this study, a systematic measurement and comparison of perceived risk and enduring product involvement has been made. This study makes several contributions to existing knowledge about the two constructs. First, it extends the generalizability of a multi-item, multi-dimensional approach to the measurement of perceived risk across product classes. Secondly, some support for the enduring nature of the perceived risk construct as characterized by its dimensions is found. Third, the findings from the study suggest the presence of a relationship between the dimensions of perceived risk and the enduring importance component of product involvement. The conclusion drawn is that perceived risk and product involvement though related are distinct constructs and concurs with Laurent and Kapferer (1985) that "involvement cannot be equated with perceived risk."

REFERENCES

Antil, John H. (1984), "Conceptualization and Operationalization of Involvement," in ThomasKinnear (Ed.), *Advances in Consumer Research*, 11, Provo, UT: Association for Consumer Research, 203-209.

Bauer, Raymond A. (1960), "Consumer Behavior as Risk-taking," in R.Hancock (Ed.) *Dynamic Marketing for a changing world: Proceedings of the 43rd Conference of the American Marketing Association*, 389-398.

Bettman, James R. (1973), "Perceived Risk and its Components: A Model and Empirical Test," *Journal of Marketing Research*, 10, May, 184-190.

Bloch, Peter H. (1981), "An Exploration into the Scaling of Consumers' Involvement with a Product Class," in Kent H. Monroe (Ed.), *Advances in Consumer Research*, 8, 61-65, Ann Arbor, MI: Association for Consumer Research.

Bloch, Peter H. and Marsha L. Richins (1983), "A Theoretical Model for the Study of Product Importance Perceptions," *Journal of Marketing*, 47, 69-81.

Calder, Bobby J., Lynn W. Philips and Alice M. Tybout (1981), "Designing Research for Application," *Journal of Consumer Research*, 8, 2, 197-207.

Celsi, Richard and Jerry C. Olson (1988), "The Role of Involvement in Attention and Comprehension Processes," Journal of Consumer Research, 15, September, 210-224.

Chaffee, Stephen H. and J. McLeod (1978), "Consumer decisions and Information Use," in S. Ward and T. Robertson (Eds.) *Consumer Behavior: Theoretical Sources*, 385-415, Englewood Cliffs, NJ: Prentice–Hall, Inc.

Dowling, Grahame R. (1986), "Perceived Risk: The Concept and its Measurement," *Psychology and Marketing*, 3, 193-210.

Engel, James and L. Light (1968), "The Role of Psychological Commitment in Consumer Behavior: An Evaluation of the Theory of Cognitive Dissonance," in F. Bass, L. King and E. Pessemier (Eds.), *Application of the Sciences in Marketing Management*, New York, NY: Wiley & Son, Inc., 179-206.

Folkes, Valarie S. (1988), "The Availability Heuristic and Perceived Risk," *Journal of Consumer Research*, 15, June, 13-23.

Gabbott, Mark (1991), "The Role of Product Cues in Assessing Risk in Second-hand Markets," *European Journal of Marketing*, 25, 9, 38-50.

Gemunden Hans Georg (1985), "Perceived Risk and Information Search: A Systematic Meta-Analysis of the Empirical Evidence," *International Journal of Research in Marketing*, 2, 2, 79-100.

Houston, Michael J. and Michael L. Rothschild (1978), "Conceptual and Methodological Perspectives in Involvement," in S. Jain (Ed.) *Research Frontiers in Marketing: Dialogues and Directions*, 184-187, Chicago, IL: American Marketing Association.

Howard, John A. and Jagdish N. Sheth (1969), *The Theory of Buyer Behavior*, New York, NY: Wiley and Son, Inc.

Hupfer, Nancy T. and David M. Gardner (1971), "Differential Involvement with Products and Issues: An Exploratory Study," in D. Gardner (Ed.), *Proceedings: 2nd Annual Conference of ACR*, College Park, MD: Association of Consumer Research, 262-270.

Jacoby, Jacob and Kaplan Leon B. (1972), "The components of Perceived Risk," in M. Venkatesan (Ed.), *Proceedings of the Third Annual Conference*, Champaign, IL: Association for Consumer Research, 382-393.

Jensen, T., L. Carlsson and C. Tripp (1989), "The Dimensionality of Involvement: An Empirical Test," in M. Wallendorf and P. Anderson (Eds.), *Advances in Consumer Research*, Provo, UT: The Association of Consumer Research, 680-689.

Kaplan, Leon B., G. Szybillo and Jacob Jacoby (1974), "Components of Perceived Risk in Product Purchase: A Cross-Validation," *Journal of Applied Psychology*, 59, 3, 287-291.

Laaksonnen, Pirjo (1994), *Consumer Involvement: Concepts and Research*, London: Routledge.

Lastovicka, John L. and David M. Gardner (1979), "Components of Involvement," in J. Maloney and B. Silverman (Eds.), *Attitude Research Plays for High Stakes*, Chicago, IL: The American Marketing Association, 53-73.

Laurent, Gilles and Jean-Noel Kapferer (1985), "Measuring Consumer Involvement Profiles," *Journal of Marketing Research*, 22, 2, 42-53.

Muehling, Darrel D., Russell N. Laczniak and J. Craig Andrews (1993), "Defining, Operationalizing and Using Involvement in Advertising Research: A Review," *Journal of Current Issues and Research in Advertising*, 15, 1, Spring, 21-57.

Nunnally, Jum C. (1978), *Psychometric Theory*, Second edition, New York, NY: McGraw Hill.

Peter, J. Paul and Michael J. Ryan (1976), "An Investigation of Perceived Risk at the Brand Level," *Journal of Marketing Research*, 13, 5, 184-188.

Richins, Marsha L. and Peter H. Bloch 91986), "After the New Wears Off: The Temporal Context of Product Involvement," *Journal of Consumer Research*, 13, 2, 280-285.

Richins, Marsha L., Peter H. Bloch and Edward F. McQuarrie (1992), "How Enduring and Situational Involvement Combine to Create Involvement Responses," *Journal of Consumer Psychology*, 1, 2, 143-153.

Roselius, T. (1971), "Consumer Ranking of Risk Reduction Methods," *Journal of Marketing*, 35, 1, 56-61.

Rothschild, Michael L. (1979), "Advertising Strategies for High and Low Involvement Situations," in J. Maloney and B. Silverman (Eds.), *Attitude Research Plays for High Stakes*, Chicago, IL: The American Marketing Association, 74-93.

Sherif, Muzafer and Hadley Cantril (1947), *The Psychology of Ego-Involvement*, New York, NY: Wiley and Son, Inc.

Slama, M. and A. Taschian (1985), "Selected Socio-economic and Demographic Characteristics associated with Purchasing Involvement," *Journal of Marketing*, 49, Winter, 72-82.

Sproull, Lee (1986), "Using Electronic Mail for Data Collection in Organizational Research," *Academy of Management Journal*, 29, 1, 159-169.

Stone, Robert N. and Kjell Grönhaug (1993), "Perceived Risk: Further Considerations for the Marketing Discipline," *European Journal of Marketing*, 27, 3, 31-50.

Tyebjee, Tyzoun T. (1979), "Refinement of the Involvement Concept: An Advertising Planning Point of View," in J. Maloney and B. Silverman (Eds.), *Attitude Research Plays for High Stakes*, Chicago, IL: The American Marketing Association, 94-111.

Venkatraman, Meera (1989), "Involvement and Risk," *Psychology and Marketing*, 6, 3, 229-247.

Zaichkowsky, Judith Lynne (1985), "Measuring the Involvement Construct," *Journal of Consumer Research*, 12, December, 341-352.

The Effects of Promotional Bundling on Consumers' Evaluations of Product Quality and Risk of Purchase

Judy Harris, University of Houston

ABSTRACT

This paper presents the results of an experiment designed to assess the effects of promotional bundling on consumers' perceptions of product quality and perceived risk of purchase. The results indicate that for a new product that is *not* a brand extension of an established product, promotional bundling with the established product can *increase* perceptions of product quality and *decrease* perceptions of risk among buyers of the established product. However, for a new product that *is* a brand extension, promotional bundling can *decrease* the perceived quality of the new product and *increase* the perceived risk associated with the purchase. Perceptions of the new product by non-buyers of the established product are not affected by bundling.

Recently, researchers have shown increasing interest in consumer response to bundling (e.g., Mazumdar and Jun 1993; Yadav 1994; Harlam, Krishna, Lehmann and Mela 1995). Bundling generally involves combining of two or more products into a single offering, but there are many forms that a bundle may take. The marketing literature has defined bundling as narrowly as single-product combinations that are physically packaged together, and as broadly as products that are implicitly linked by complementary usage situations (e.g., Mulhern and Leone 1991). Most consumer research, however, has focused on explicit bundles made up of separate products sold for a single price (Simonin and Ruth 1995).

This research concerns *promotional bundling*, one specific type of bundling that has received scant empirical investigation. With this form of bundling, consumers are offered a discount or premium when they buy different products together, such as toothpaste and a toothbrush or cake mix and frosting. As examples, consider the following promotional offers drawn from recent Sunday newspaper FSIs (free standing inserts):

- Save $1.00 on the purchase of new Lay's dip when you buy Baked Lay's Potato Crisps;
- Save $1.50 on Aleve pain reliever with any Vick's product;
- Save 25 cents on the purchase of both Austex Beef Stew and Austex Chili.

Despite a trend toward more widespread use of cooperative sales promotions (Varadarajan 1986), little is known about how consumers respond to offers such as the ones above. Research has demonstrated that evaluations of one product in the bundle are influenced by the quality of the other products in the bundle (Gaeth, Levin, Chakraborty and Levin 1990; Yadav 1994), such that perceptions of a product should be enhanced by associating it with a high quality product. However, it has been argued also that consumers may react negatively to the increased restrictions and lack of flexibility involved with the purchase of a bundle, and will decrease product evaluations accordingly (see Wilson, Weiss and John 1990; Kinberg and Sudit 1979). Moreover, in the case of a promotional bundle, consumers' heuristic beliefs about price discounts and unnecessary promotions might lead to lower evaluations of the quality of the product (e.g., Sawyer and Dickson 1984; Simonson, Carmon and O'Curry 1994).

The purpose of the research reported here is to examine whether consumers' evaluations of a product are, in fact, affected positively or negatively by promotional bundling. We use the

context of a new product introduction and investigate how the promotional bundling of a new product with an established product affects consumers' responses to the new product. First, we review relevant past literature. Second, we report the results of an experiment designed to assess the effect of promotional bundling on evaluations of a new product that either is or is not a brand extension of the bundling partner.

CONCEPTUAL BACKGROUND

Consumers may evaluate the worth of a product differently when it is in a bundle than it is not. Explicitly linking two or more items together is likely to influence the context in which consumers evaluate those items because it will literally force the consumer to evaluate them in the context of one another. Past research has consistently demonstrated that consumers' evaluations of and preferences for a product can be influenced by the context of the choice task, including the set of alternatives considered and the manner in which these alternatives are presented (e.g., Simonson and Tversky 1992). Consistent with this viewpoint, past research in bundling has demonstrated that both the framing of the bundle and the perceived quality of the items in the bundle can influence how consumers evaluate the bundle as a whole and the individual items it contains. This research is reviewed below.

Potential Positive Effects of Bundling on Product Evaluations

Past research has shown that how consumers perceive the quality of one item in the bundle can affect how they perceive the quality of the other items. Gaeth, et al. (1990) found that the perceived quality of a tie-in product offered with a VCR had an influence on subjects' perceptions of the quality of the VCR that far outweighed the monetary contribution of the premium to the bundle as a whole. In addition, Simonin and Ruth (1995) found that attitudes toward the items included in a promotional bundle affect attitudes toward the bundle itself. These findings are consistent with arguments that one potential benefit of joint promotions (whether or not they involve bundling) is a reduction of the perceived risk involved with the purchase of an untried product (Varadarajan 1986). That is, bundling a new product with an established product can serve as an endorsement for the new product. These arguments lead to our first hypothesis:

H1A: Promotional bundling of a new product with an established product will:

a) increase the perceived quality of the new product; and

b) decrease the perceived risk associated with the purchase of the new product

Potential Negative Effects on Evaluations

Although it has been recognized that bundling a product with another product is unwise if the second product is perceived unfavorably by consumers (Gaeth, et al. 1990), scholars have paid much less attention to the potential negative effects that bundling itself may have on product evaluations. Wilson, Weiss and John (1990) and Kinberg and Sudit (1979) argued that some consumers will evaluate the total worth of a bundle less favorably than the sum of the items it contains because of the additional restrictions that the purchase of a bundle entails. Additionally, Diamond and Sanyal (1990) demonstrated that consumers will choose a straight coupon offer over a promotional bundle worth more. They argued that this was because consumers perceived the promotional offer as a reduced loss rather than a gain, but they also suggested that it may have been due to negative reactions toward the loss of freedom associated with the additional requirement of purchasing two products. The logic underlying the latter argument is that a promotional bundle, by offering the consumer a discount and then placing a restriction on it, may evoke psychological reactance and cause the offer to be perceived as less favorable than either a straight promotional offer or no promotional offer would have been (see also Clee and Wicklund 1980). Although these arguments pertain to consumers' evaluations of the bundle itself, rather than evaluations of the individual items in the bundle, negative feelings toward the offering as a whole are likely to color perceptions of the items as well (Simonin and Ruth 1995).

It is also possible that consumers will view the quality of the items in the bundle less favorably when they are bundled. They may attribute the fact that the manufacturer or retailer is offering a promotion to low product quality and a high risk of not being satisfied with the purchase (see Sawyer and Dickson 1984), or react negatively to a promotion that seems unnecessary (Simonson, Carmon and O'Curry 1994). Although this argument applies to straight promotional offers (e.g., a cents-off coupon or a premium offer) as well as promotional bundling, it is possible that a promotional bundle may be more suspect either because it is, in a sense, two promotions in one, or because it is more unusual and may attract more attention than a traditional discount offer. These arguments lead to a hypothesis that is offered as an alternative to H1A.

H1B: Promotional bundling of a new product with an established product will:

a) decrease the perceived quality of the new product; and

b) increase the perceived risk associated with the purchase of the new product.

We offer H1A and H1B as co-equal, alternative hypotheses, because arguments for both effects can be found in the literature. Promotional bundling may have a favorable effect on perceived quality (and therefore perceived risk) of a brand because of the implied endorsement of the bundling partner (H1A). On the other hand, promotional bundling may have an unfavorable effect on perceived quality (and therefore perceived risk) because of psychological reactance caused by additional purchase requirements or suspicion about a relatively unfamiliar type of promotion (H2A). Of course, the relative strength of these opposite effects may be affected by moderating variables. The next section of the paper discusses the likely effects of one potential moderator: the brand name of the product.

Brand Name of the New Product

A brand extension should be more likely to suffer *negative* consequences due to bundling than a new name product. This is because a brand extension does not need the endorsement of the bundling partner to help reduce the perceived risk involved with the purchase. It already has that endorsement by virtue of its name, and therefore will suffer only the negative effects of bundling. On the other hand, a new name product has more to gain by bundling. This argument leads to our second hypothesis:

H2: The effects of promotional bundling of a new product with an established product will:

a) decrease the perceived quality associated with the purchase of the new product when it is a brand extension, but increase it when the product has a new name; and

b) increase the perceived risk associated with the purchase of the new product when it is a brand extension, but decrease it when the product has a new name.

EXPERIMENT

The study used a 2 (promotional bundle or straight discount) x 2 (brand extension versus new name) between-subjects design. The established product was Cheerios cereal and the new product was a round (log-shaped) cereal bar. The bar was either named Cheerios cereal bars or Fruit'n'Oat cereal bars. Additionally, subjects were classified as Cheerios cereal buyers or non-buyers based on whether they had chosen Cheerios out of all cereals available at a local supermarket in a previous task.

Seventy-five cents was chosen as the value of the coupon because an examination of FSI coupons in a local newspaper indicated that it is a common amount for discounts on cereal and cereal bars. Cheerios was chosen as the established product because a pretest (n=75) indicated that it was a popular product with a student sample (25% "market share" when subjects were asked to indicate a choice among all the cereals available in a local supermarket). Cereal bars were chosen as the new product because a second pretest (n= 52) indicated that student subjects purchased cereal bars (86% reported purchasing cereal bars recently). Moreover, the subjects in this pretest thought that the "fit" to Cheerios cereal was relatively high (mean= 6.46 on an 8-point scale ranging from "very poor fit" to "very good fit"). For comparison, the mean rating of "fit" for oatmeal (chosen by Broniarczyk and Alba [1994] as a category that is very relevant to Cheerios) in this pretest was 5.31 on the same 8-point scale. The fit of the product was important given that research on brand extensions has shown that product associations transfer most readily among products with a moderately good fit (Aaker and Keller 1990).

The name Fruit'n'Oat was chosen as the new name because it described the bar and was rated as appropriate by the 18 pretest subjects rating it (the other pretest subjects rated other options). The mean rating for Fruit'n'Oat was 5.82 (on an 8-point scale ranging from "very poor name for a cereal bar" to "very good name for a cereal bar"). The rating of the name "Cheerios Cereal Bars" was 6.28 on the same scale. These means were not significantly different ($t_{1,33}=0.74$, n.s.).

Procedure

One-hundred and fifty three undergraduate marketing students participated in the study. The subjects were randomly assigned to one of the four treatment conditions.

The study was conducted in two parts. First, the subjects were asked to imagine that they were grocery shopping for their household and were given a booklet containing listings of all the brands in several product categories that were available on the shelves of a local supermarket. The brand name, size, flavors and prices of the brands in the categories of soft drinks, cold breakfast cereal, kitchen trash bags and facial tissues were provided. The subjects were asked to indicate which of the brands they would be most likely to purchase given that they were out of the product and the choices listed were what was available on the store's shelves. For each category, the subjects were given the option of not choosing any of the brands listed.

After a distraction task (an unrelated questionnaire), the subjects were given a second booklet containing brands, sizes, flavors and prices of all the brands in several product categories (pasta sauce, cereal/ granola bars, cold breakfast cereal, kitchen trash bags and facial tissue). The list for cereal/granola bars included either the Cheerios or Fruit'n'Oat brand, as well as 10 additional brands of breakfast bars. The price, size and flavor information was based on comparable information for Nutri-Grain cereal bars.

In this task, the subjects again were asked to imagine that they were shopping, but that this time they had the option of using coupons. They were to assume that if they choose a product for which they had a coupon, the shelf price listed in the booklet would be reduced by that amount (with no doubling or tripling). The subjects were instructed that this questionnaire reflected a different shopping trip than the first questionnaire. They could, but did not have to choose the same brands as before. The subjects were then instructed that they should not choose to use the coupons just because they were in the booklet, but rather they should use a particular coupon only if they would be likely to use it in real life.

The coupons were included in advertisements designed to mimic FSI ads, and were bound into the second booklet opposite the appropriate product list. Coupons for Ragu pasta sauce, the appropriate brand of cereal bars (either Fruit'n'Oat or Cheerios) and Glad trash bags were included in the booklet. The coupons for the pasta sauce and trash bags were created from actual FSIs. The coupon for the cereal bars was created using words and pictures from a Cheerios cereal box and Nutri-grain cereal bar box and FSI. The cereal bar FSI contained the picture of the box of cereal bars (which were called Cheerios or Fruit'n'Oat), a picture of the Cheerios cereal box (in the bundled conditions only) and a coupon (good for 75 cents off the purchase of the bar or 75 cents off the purchase of the bar when you also buy Cheerios cereal). After the choice task, the subjects were asked to evaluate several brands, including the appropriate brand of cereal bars.

Dependent Measures

The dependent measures were subjects' evaluations of the quality of the cereal bars and the perceived risk associated with their purchase. The quality of the bars was measured by averaging subjects' ratings of the bars on two seven-points scales ranging from "low quality" to "high quality" and "inferior brand" to "superior brand" (r=0.83). The perceived risk of purchasing the bars was measured by averaging subjects' ratings of the bars on two seven-point scales ranging from "likely to be unsatisfied if purchased" to "likely to be satisfied if purchased" and "risky purchase" to "safe purchase" (r=0.86). Choice of the cereal bar was collected as a potential dependent variable, but was not used because the number of subjects choosing the bar over the other options available was too small (less than 10% in all conditions).

RESULTS AND DISCUSSION

Recall that H1A predicted that promotional bundling would have beneficial effects on perceptions of the cereal bar, H1B predicted detrimental effects, and H2 predicted an interaction between bundling and brand name such that bundling was more beneficial for products with a new name and more detrimental for brand extensions. To test these hypotheses, we conducted separate analyses of variance (ANOVAs) appropriate for unequal sample sizes on perceived quality and perceived risk. The test between H1A and H1B concerned the direction and significance of the main effect for bundling in each analysis, and the test of H2 concerned the significance of the interaction effect between bundling and brand name.

The analyses of the effects of brand name and bundling on perceived quality revealed a significant main effect for brand name ($F_{1,149}$=57.94, p<.0001; with Cheerios bars evaluated more favorably than Fruit'n'Oat bars), a significant main effect for bundling ($F_{1,149}$=6.60, p<.01; with the bundled conditions evaluated *less* favorably than the non-bundled conditions), and a significant interaction effect ($F_{1,149}$=9.50, p<.01). Individual planned contrasts indicated that the Cheerios bars were perceived *less* favorably when they were bundled than when they were not bundled ($F_{1,149}$=56.68, p<.0001), but the Fruit'n'Oat bars were not ($F_{1,149}$= 0.16, n.s.). The presence of a significant main effect for bundling was consistent with Hypothesis 1B, and indicated that promotional bundling had a negative effect on evaluations of quality. The presence of a significant interaction effect was consistent with Hypothesis 2, and indicated that this negative effect occurred for the brand extension, but not for the new name product. Means and standard deviations are given in Table 1.

Similarly, the analysis of the effects of brand name and bundling on perceived risk revealed a significant main effect for brand name ($F_{1,149}$=15.94, p<.0001; with Cheerios bars evaluated as less risky than Fruit'n'Oat bars), and a marginally significant interaction effect ($F_{1,149}$=3.80, p<.06). Individual planned contrasts indicated that the Cheerios bars were perceived as *more* risky when they were bundled than when they were not bundled ($F_{1,149}$=3.81, p<.06), but Fruit'n'Oat bars were not ($F_{1,149}$=0.66, n.s.). These results were consistent with Hypothesis 2, and indicated that promotional bundling of a new product with an established product increases the perceived risk of a new product that is a brand extension, but has no effect for a new product that is not a brand extension. The means and standard deviations are given in Table 2.

From these results, it appears that the promotional bundling of a brand extension with the established product harms evaluations of the extension's quality and risk. The promotional bundling of a new name product with an established product is neither helpful nor harmful to the new name product.

Differences in Evaluations by Cheerios Buyers and Non-buyers

The analyses discussed in the previous section were conducted on the sample as a whole, with no distinction between those subjects who were Cheerios buyers and those who were not. We repeated the analyses of variance on the perceived quality and perceived risk associated with the purchase of the cereal bars, adding whether or not the subject had chosen Cheerios cereal in the first shopping task as a second potential moderator of the effect of bundling (along with brand name). The analyses of the effects of bundling, brand name and previous purchase on the perceived quality of the cereal bar indicated a significant three-way interaction ($F_{1,145}$=6.72, p<.01). Individual planned contrasts revealed that among the non-Cheerios buyers, the pattern was similar to that found in the total population, with bundling significantly *decreasing* evaluations of quality for the brand extension ($F_{1,145}$=4.53, p<.05), but not for the new name product ($F_{1,145}$=0.26, n.s.). However, among Cheerios customers, bundling significantly decreased evaluations of quality for the brand extension ($F_{1,145}$=11.49, p<.001), but marginally *increased* evaluations for the new name product ($F_{1,145}$=3.56, p<.06). In fact, among Cheerios customers, there was no significant difference between the Cheerios brand name and the Fruit'n'Oat brand name within the promotional bundling conditions ($F_{1,145}$=0.43, n.s.). The means and standard deviations are given in Table 1.

TABLE 1

Effects of Brand Name, Promotional Bundling and Prior Purchase on Evaluations of the Quality of the Cereal Bars

Condition	Fruit'n'Oat Bars		Cheerios Bars	
	Not Bundled	Bundled	Not Bundled	Bundled
Non-Cheerios Buyers	3.38 [a]	3.23 [a]	4.87 [b]	4.21 [c]
	(1.27)	(1.26)	(1.35)	(1.00)
	$n = 27$	$n = 30$	$n = 26$	$n = 29$
Cheerios Buyers	3.10 [a]	4.13 [c]	6.20 [d]	4.50 [c]
	(0.94)	(0.64)	(0.70)	(1.22)
	$n = 10$	$n = 8$	$n = 15$	$n = 8$
Entire Sample	3.31 [a]	3.42 [a]	5.35 [b]	4.27 [c]
	(1.19)	(1.21)	(1.32)	(1.05)

Notes: Standard deviations are in parentheses. Within each variable, means with different superscripts are significantly different at the .05 level.

Similar effects were revealed in the analysis on perceived risk. Again, there was a significant three-way interaction ($F_{1,145}=7.78$, p<.001). Individual planned contrasts revealed that among the non-Cheerios buyers, there were no significant differences between the bundled and non-bundled conditions for either the brand extension ($F_{1,145}= 0.21$, n.s.) or the new name product ($F_{1,145}=0.03$, n.s.). However, among the Cheerios buyers, bundling significantly *increased* perceptions of risk for the brand extension ($F_{1,145}=6.31$, p<.05), but significantly *decreased* perceptions of risk for the new name product ($F_{1,145}=5.04$, p<.05). Again, among Cheerios customers, there was no significant difference between the Cheerios brand name and the Fruit'n'Oat brand name within the promotional bundling conditions ($F_{1,145}=0.12$, n.s.). The means and standard deviations are given in Table 2.

Promotional bundling appears to be a bad idea for a product introduced as a brand extension under all of the circumstances examined in this study. However, the results indicate that promotional bundling may be a viable strategy for introducing a new product that is *not* a brand extension. Promotional bundling increased perceptions of quality and decreased perceptions of risk for a new name product among customers of the bundling partner, and had no effect (either positive or negative) among non-customers of the bundling partner.

CONCLUSIONS AND LIMITATIONS

The usual limitations of studies using only student subjects apply to this study. However, pretests were used to ensure that the products used in the sample were relevant to student consumers and the stimulus materials were designed to be as realistic as possible for a pencil and paper choice task.

A second potential limitation is the use of only one of many potential variations on the bundling situation. For example, pretests indicated that the new product and bundling partner "fit" together well, but there are several potential ways that two products may fit (Aaker and Keller 1990; Broniarczyk and Alba 1994). Our product pair had a strong conceptual, or "image" fit, but did not have a high usage fit. Since many promotional bundles involve product complements, future research should examine if promotional bundling is a more viable marketing technique with such a product pair.

Similarly, previous research indicates that the framing of a bundling offer may affect perceptions of value (e.g., Yadav 1995; Harlam, et al. 1995). Our research used only one of many potential frames (i.e., "buy both and save"). Future studies may want to assess the extent to which framing the promotional offer in different ways affects how the offer is perceived.

Despite these limitations, this research has implications for how promotional bundling offers should be used in practice. As indicated by the examples of promotional bundles listed earlier in this paper, many such offers involve brand extensions. The results of this study indicate that this practice is likely to have negative consequences on how consumers perceive the quality of the products and the risk associated with purchasing the product.

Our results also indicate that promotional bundling may be a useful promotional technique for a new product introduced with a new brand name. Although consumers' evaluations and perceptions of risk were most favorable in the condition in which the brand extension was introduced without bundling, there may be situations in which the manufacturer chooses not to use a brand extension. For example, the manufacturer may not want to risk the brand name of the established product on a new product introduction or may not want to forfeit the opportunity to create a new name (Aaker 1990). The results of this study indicate that under such circumstances, bundling may be a way to enhance consumers' perceptions of the new product. Given the risks involved in new product introduction and the large number of new product failures that occur every year (Aaker 1990), this may be a situation in which marketers can use any help they can get.

REFERENCES

Aaker, David (1990), "Brand Extensions: The Good, the Bad, and the Ugly," *Sloan Management Review*, Summer, 47-56.

Aaker, David and Kevin Keller (1990), "Consumer Response to Brand Extensions," *Journal of Marketing*, 54 (January), 27-41.

Broniarczyk, Susan M. and Joseph W. Alba (1994), "The Importance of the Brand in Brand Extension," *Journal of Marketing Research*, 31 (May), 214-228.

TABLE 2
Effects of Brand Name, Promotional Bundling and Prior Purchase on Evaluations of Perceived Risk of the Bars

Condition	Fruit'n'Oat Bars		Cheerios Bars	
	Not Bundled	Bundled	Not Bundled	Bundled
Non-Cheerios Buyers	5.02 [a] (1.32)	5.08 [a] (1.47)	3.46 [b] (1.54)	3.64 [b] (1.34)
Cheerios Buyers	5.15 [a] (0.97)	3.62 [b] (1.35)	2.30 [c] (1.35)	3.87 [b] (1.86)
Entire Sample	5.05 [a] (1.22)	4.78 [a] (1.62)	3.04* (1.56)	3.69* (1.45)

Notes: Standard deviations are in parentheses. Within each variable, means with different superscripts are significantly different at the .05 level (*Significantly different at .06).

Clee, Mona A. and Robert A. Wicklund (1980), "Consumer Behavior and Psychological Reactance," *Journal of Consumer Research*, 6 (March), 389-405.

Diamond, William D. and Abhijit Sanyal (1990), "The Effect of Framing on the Choice of Supermarket Coupons," in *Advances in Consumer Research*, 17, Marvin Goldberg and Gerald Gorn, eds., Provo, UT: Association for Consumer Research, 488-493.

Gaeth, Gary J., Irwin P. Levin, Goutam Chakraborty and Aron M. Levin (1990), "Consumer Evaluations of Multi-Product Bundles: An Information Integration Perspective," *Marketing Letters*, 2 (December), 47-57.

Harlam, Bari A., Aradhna Krishna, Donald R. Lehmann and Carl Mela (1995), "Impact of Bundle Type, Price Framing and Familiarity on Purchase Intention for the Bundle," *Journal of Business Research*, 33, 57-66.

Kinberg, Yoram and Ephraim F. Sudit (1979), "Country/Service Bundling in International Tourism," *Journal of International Business Studies*, 10 (Fall), 51-63.

Mazumdar, Tridib and Sung Youl Jun (1993), "Consumer Evaluations of Multiple versus Single Price Changes," *Journal of Consumer Research*, 20 (December), 441-450.

Mulhern, Francis J. and Robert P. Leone (1991), "Implicit Price Bundling of Retail Products: A Multi-Product Approach to Maximizing Store Profitability," *Journal of Marketing*, 55 (October), 63-76.

Sawyer, Alan G. and Peter R. Dickson (1984), "Psychological Perspectives on Consumer Response to Sales Promotion," in *Research on Sales Promotions: Collected Papers*, Katherine E. Joss, ed. Cambridge, MA, Marketing Science Institute.

Simonin, Bernard L. and Julie A. Ruth (1995), "Bundling as a Strategy for New Product Introduction: Effects on Consumers' Reservation Prices for the Bundle, the New Product, and its Tie-in," *Journal of Business Research*, 33, 219-230.

Simonson, Itamar and Amos Tversky (1992), "Choice in Context: Tradeoff Contrast and Extremeness Aversion," *Journal of Marketing Research*, 29 (Aug), 281-295.

Simonson, Itamar, Ziv Carmon, and Suzanne O'Curry (1994), "Experimental Evidence on the Negative Effect of Product Features and Sales Promotions on Brand Choice," *Marketing Science*, 13 (Winter), 23-40.

Varadarajan, P. Rajan (1986), "Horizontal Cooperative Sales Promotion: A Framework for Classification and Additional Perspectives," *Journal of Marketing*, 50 (April), 61-73.

Wilson, Lynn O., Allen M. Weiss and George John (1990), "Unbundling of Industrial Systems," *Journal of Marketing Research*, 27 (May), 123-138.

Yadav, Manjit S. (1995), "Bundle Evaluation in Different Market Segments: The Effects of Discount Framing and Buyers' Preference Heterogeneity," *Journal of the Academy of Marketing Science*, 23 (3), 206-215.

Yadav, Manjit S. (1994), "How Buyers Evaluate Product Bundles: A Model of Anchoring and Adjustment," *Journal of Consumer Research*, 21 (September), 342-353.

Decision Biases in Evaluating Ambiguous Information

Christina L. Brown, New York University
Alex Chernev, Duke University

I. Introduction

What motivates consumers to hold consistent preferences? One might argue that holding consistent, well-defined preferences serves an important function for consumers, allowing them to understand the preferences underlying their choices and making it easier to choose more accurately among products (West, Brown, and Hoch 1996). On the other hand, products sometimes offer "equivocal" or ambiguous qualities, with the potential for multiple interpretations (Hoch and Ha 1986). In such cases, consumers' attempts to understand their own preferences (thus allowing them to behave in a way consistent with these preferences) can bias their interpretation of subsequent product stimuli. As Hoch and Deighton (1989) suggest:

"Ambiguity emerges as a critical environmental factor enabling the management of experiential learning. When experience is neither vague or open to multiple interpretations, consumers learn fast and the manager has little scope for influencing the result. An ambiguous environment, in contrast, poses both threats and opportunities (p. 10)."

In short, consumers may "theorize in advance of the data," changing their interpretation of ambiguous stimuli in an effort to form consistent preferences, potentially threatening their objectivity. The question of consumer consistency in the face of ambiguity is therefore an important one, since it has powerful implications for marketers' ability to learn the objective relationship between a product's features and consumer preferences.

The objective of this special session was therefore to address the biasing effects of consumers' need for consistency on interpreting ambiguous product information. Specifically, our intention was to contribute to a better understanding of how consumers evaluate ambiguous information, as well as the role of their prior and developing preferences in this process. The session examined these issues from a variety of theoretical, methodological, and analytical perspectives. Russo, Meloy, and Medvec used dissonance research to provide a new perspective on understanding the role of pre-existing and developing preferences in evaluating ambiguous information. Brown and Raghunathan relied on theory and experimental paradigms from the impression-formation literature to address how and why consumers perceive more consistency in ambiguous service encounters than may actually be present. The paper by Chernev investigated consistency biases in consumer choice; specifically, how consumers' motivated reasoning mediates their evaluations of ambiguous product features.

II. "The Distortion of Information During Decisions"

The first paper presented was "The Distortion of Information During Decisions," by J. Edward Russo, Margaret G. Meloy, and Victoria Husted Medvec. Jay Russo was the presenter. This work reported on the presence of predecisional distortion of information. In two studies, participants were asked to choose between two brands (Russo, Medvec & Meloy 1996; Russo, Meloy & Medvec 1996). They received information one attribute at a time (but on both alternatives simultaneously) and stopped whenever they felt confident enough to make a commitment to one alternative. In addition, after announcing their decision, participants were shown the remaining, unrequested attributes of information. This enabled an assessment of the postdecisional distortion driven by dissonance reduction which, in turn, provided a benchmark against which the magnitude of the predecisional distortion could be compared. Each attribute was read and integrated with past information to update the choice process. Then participants were asked choice if all information were available and used. This measure of confidence directly traced the strength of the tentative preference. Finally, participants were asked to rate an attribute's diagnosticity (though not using this term) on a nine-point scale where each end point reflected strong support for one alternative and the midpoint represented neutrality. The difference between a participant's evaluation on this scale and the mean rating on the same scale of a no-choice control group served to measure the distortion of the information.

The main result was the existence of predecisional distortion and its systematic relation to strength of preference. In the absence of any prior information (the two alternatives were identified only by the letters G and Z), distortion occurred from the second attribute on. That is, distortion appeared as soon as there emerged any preference for one brand over the other. Further, the magnitude of the distortion was directly related to the strength of the developing preference. The distortion of an attribute was a linear function of the confidence in the tentative preference after the prior attribute. Thus, the stronger was the developing preference for one brand, the more the next piece of information was distorted to favor that leading alternative.

The magnitude of the observed distortion was substantial. In both studies the predecisional distortion was roughly twice the size of the postdecisional distortion that was due to traditional cognitive dissonance. The phenomenon of predecisional distortion of information has important implications for the nature of decision processes, for theory construction, for decision making in natural environments where such distortion may be costly, and for the validity and value of decision aids.

III. "The Effects of Persuasion Knowledge on Attitude Formation"

Second, "The Effects of Persuasion Knowledge on Attitude Formation," by Christina L. Brown and Raj Raghunathan, was presented by both authors. This work concerned how the resolution of ambiguity surrounding encounters between consumer and marketer depends on the source of the information received.

One way consumers may react to the knowledge that a marketer is trying to persuade them is to activate "persuasion knowledge"—their developed expertise or schema about marketers and the nature of their persuasive efforts (Friestad and Wright 1994). This activation may simply result in a more negative attitude toward the marketer. Alternatively, a consumer may be motivated to develop a more consistent and cohesive attitude or mental model of that marketer, as a way of coping or defending against the persuasive effort. This tendency results in the "disambiguation" of consumers of two sorts: first, as a consumer's attitude towards a particular marketer becomes more internally consistent, marketers will appear more distinct from each other. Secondly, consumer will appear more distinct from each other. Thus, when consumers are consciously aware of a marketer's effort to persuade, they will become more segmented.

The authors tested these assertions in an experiment. The stimuli were sixteen descriptions of consumer experiences in retail clothing stores (descriptions of the store's atmosphere, the personnel, the product assortment, and the service for each of four stores). Subjects rated each description on a series of brand personality scales. The identity of each store was labeled for half the subjects but left unidentified for the other half. Furthermore, the source of information was manipulated: subjects were either told that the descriptions came from friends (the "word-of-mouth" condition), or from an infomercial.

Variance decomposition was used to determine to what extent the variance in store ratings was driven by the store itself, the subject, the particular description, or the interaction between these factors (Park, DeKay, and Kraus 1994). Variance due to "store" represented the extent to which stores were seen as distinct from each other. Variance due to "subject" represented idiosyncratic use of the response scales by different subjects. Of greatest interest, variance due to a "subject-x-store" interaction represented the extent to which each subject viewed a store consistently, yet differently from other subject's reaction to the same store (i.e., the extent to which they were disambiguated).

The authors hypothesized that when the stores were identified, subjects would resolve ambiguity (measured as the variance in behavior across situations) by seeing a store's behavior ass more consistent than in the unidentified case. Secondly, they hypothesized that subjects would resolve this ambiguity in idiosyncratic ways (a subject-x-store interaction). Finally, they expected to show that the source of information exacerbated subjects' tendency to perceive ambiguous descriptions as more consistent than they actually are. The data supported these expectations.

IV. "The Impact of Unfamiliar Product Features on Brand Choice"

Third, Alex Chernev presented his research on *"The Impact of Unfamiliar Product Features on Brand Choice."* This research considered the familiar case in which consumers make choices among brands that share unfamiliar, yet functionally similar features. For example, consider a choice among TV's that have analogous features like PanaBlack screen (Panasonic) and Smart picture (Magnavox) or a choice among two brands of toothpaste that have analogous ingredients such as Fluoristat (Crest) and Triclene (Aquafresh). Unfamiliar with these features, consumers face ambiguity as to how different these features actually are and which of these features is more attractive.

Chernev investigated how consumers evaluate brands that share such analogous unfamiliar features. In particular, his research documents the existence of systematic biases in consumers' evaluations of unfamiliar attributes. Building on the reason-based view of choice (Shafir, Simonson, and Tversky 1988), Chernev's research shows that when consumers have a reason to select a particular brand, they are likely to interpret unfamiliar product features in a way that will result in a consistent and readily justifiable decisions. Thus, when individuals were provided with a reason to choose a particular alternative (e.g., because it is dominant on the most important attribute), adding analogous unfamiliar features to all brands in consumers' consideration set resulted in an increase in the overall evaluations of the brand favored by that reason. In contrast, in the absence of a specific reason to focus on a particular brand (e.g., when brand attributes have similar importance), adding unfamiliar features was found to increase consumers' indifference between choice alternatives.

These data lend support for the preference confirmation view of choice, whereby the evaluation of the available information is often biased by consumers' already established preferences (Hoch and Ha 1986, Hoch and Deighton 1989). More generally, these findings are in agreement with the notion that consumers' reasoning is mediated by their motivation to attain consistent and readily justifiable decisions (Kunda 1990).

V. Discussion

Finally, Steve Hoch made good use of the limited time available as synthesizer. His primary point was that although the three studies purported to be concerned with the reduction of ambiguity, none of them had actually manipulated ambiguity directly. If ambiguity is the driving construct behind the research, it is important to show that reducing ambiguity in the stimuli reduces the reported effects.

REFERENCES

Friestad, Marian and Peter Wright (1994), "The Persuasion Knowledge Model: How People Cope with Persuasion Attempts," *Journal of Consumer Research*, 21 (June), 1-31.

Hoch, Stephen J. and John Deighton (1989), "Managing What Consumers Learn from Experience," *Journal of Marketing*, 53 (April), 1-20.

Hoch, Stephen J. and Young-Won Ha (1986), "Consumer Learning: Advertising and the Ambiguity of Product Experience," *Journal of Consumer Research*, 13 (October), 221-233.

Kunda, Ziva (1990), "The Case for Motivated Reasoning," *Psychological Bulletin*, 108 (3), 480-498.

Park, Bernadette, Michael L. Dekay, and Sue Kraus (1994), "Aggregating Social Behavior Into Person Models: Perceiver-Induced Consistency," *Journal of Personality and Social Psychology*, 66 (3), 437-459.

Russo, J. Edward, Victoria H. Medvec, and Margaret G. Meloy (1996), "The Distortion of Information During Decisions," *Organizational Behavior and Human Decision Processes*, forthcoming.

_____, Margaret G. Meloy, and Victoria H. Medvec (1996), "The Distortion of Product Information During Brand Choice," working paper, Cornell University.

Shafir, Eldar, Itamar Simonson, and Amos Tversky (1993), "Reason-Based Choice," *Cognition*, 49, 11-36.

West, Patricia M., Christina L. Brown, and Stephen J. Hoch (1996), "Consumption Vocabulary and Preference Formation," *Journal of Consumer Research*, 23 (September), 120-135.

Movie Stars and Authors as Brand Names: Measuring Brand Equity in Experiential Products

Aron M. Levin, Washburn University
Irwin P. Levin, University of Iowa
C. Edward Heath, University of Kentucky

ABSTRACT

Using experimental designs analogous to those employed with standard products, brand equity effects were measured for two types of experiential products: movies and novels. Descriptions of the plots of new movies (Experiment 1) and new novels (Experiment 2) were ascribed to well-known or unknown movie stars or authors. Not only were consumer reactions more favorable with well-known movie stars/authors, but interaction effects in each experiment revealed that the effects of critics' comments were attenuated with products ascribed to familiar and trusted stars. However, line extension effects were shown to be negligible for authors associated with unfamiliar genres.

More than a decade ago, Holbrook and Hirschman (1982) urged consumer behavior researchers to break from the traditional information processing paradigm and examine consumer behavior from an *experiential* perspective. In particular, they suggested that marketers interested in consumer search behavior study entertainment, the arts and leisure activities such as musical recordings, novels, paintings, and movies: "Hence, applications of multivariate methods may be more valid with this type of product than with some low-involvement consumer nondurables, such as detergents or canned peas, for which consumers may be unable to make valid perceptual or affective distinctions among more than a few different brands" (Holbrook & Hirschman 1982, p. 134). Since the publication of Holbrook and Hirschman's influential article, a number of studies have examined experiential consumption and consumers' choice of experiential products. Some of the forms of entertainment that have been explored are: comic books (Belk 1987), television programs (Barwise & Ehrenberg 1987; Hirschman 1988), sports and games (Holbrook, Chestnut, Oliva, & Greenleaf 1984), and motion pictures (Holbrook & Grayson 1986).

The purpose of this paper is to describe two experiments that build onto previous research on consumers' choice of experiential products. Specifically, we are interested in whether consumers use "brand names" (in this case well-known actors or authors) for experiential products such as movies and novels in a similar manner to their search for low involvement, tangible products. Our analog of "star" as "brand" is based on the notion that popular movie actors and authors, like popular brands, have name recognition, have developed a certain image, and, furthermore, are associated with particular types of products. Consider, for example, the public images of Clint Eastwood and Stephen King.

In an industry where multi-million dollar films are released to compete with one another head-to-head, the presence of a star acts as a beacon that makes the movie stand out and entices larger audiences. A quote by Gorham Kindem in Wallace, Seigerman, and Holbrook (1993) points out the value of the star:

"... the Hollywood star system is a business strategy designed to generate large audiences and differentiate entertainment programs and products, and has been used for over seventy years to provide increasing returns on production investments (Kindem 1982, p.79)."

Thus, the value of including stars in a movie or promoting novels with big name authors may be analogous to the signaling effect of brands. In other words the presence of a recognizable star signals quality to the prospective consumer much as a trusted brand name implies quality in a product.

From a conceptual standpoint, we are interested in whether "brands" in experiential products are capable of possessing the same type of brand equity that they do in non-experiential products. Our operationalization of brand equity is consistent with Keller's (1993) definition of customer-based brand equity: "*a brand is said to have positive (negative) customer-based brand equity if consumers react more (less) favorably to the product, price, promotion, or distribution of the brand than they do to the same marketing mix element when it is attributed to a fictitiously named or unnamed version of the product or service*". We test the applicability of this definition to movie actors in Experiment 1 and to authors in Experiment 2 by comparing consumers' evaluations of unfamiliar movies or novels when the same descriptions are associated with either popular or fictitious actors/authors. Differences in evaluations between conditions will then represent the effects of "star power".

In our study of brand equity effects possessed by star actors and authors, we not only extend the study of brand equity effects to experiential products, we also examine how brand equity can attenuate the effects of other sources of information, in this case the comments of movie or book critics. Like many other consumer decisions, the decision of which movie to see or novel to read has multiple determinants—what we have read about them, promotional material, what friends have told us, how much we like the stars/authors, and so forth. Specifically, in this study we focus on how consumers' decisions are influenced by the following sources of information: identification of "stars" and critic comments. These factors are manipulated experimentally by using plot descriptions of new movies or novels, identifying them in some cases with well-known actors/authors and in other cases using fictitious names, and creating favorable and unfavorable critic comments. Measured reactions to each product include expected degree of liking of the product and the likelihood of patronage.

Critics' comments are particularly interesting sources of social influence for many experiential products because they provide a vicarious learning experience for the consumer. Critics are credible communicators because of their expertise and lack of vested interest in the product. A viable model for consumer preference for experiential products such as movies, plays and novels must assume a role for critics' comments. (See, for example, the model of Reddy, Swaminathan, and Motley, 1996.) Nevertheless, the exact manner in which this source of information is integrated with others is not well understood.

There is a clear expectation of preference for movies/novels with popular stars/authors and preference for products with favorable critic comments. A more interesting prediction is that these two sources will have configural effects. Just as reliance on a trusted brand name has been shown to reduce the influence of other sources of information on consumer behavior (Aaker & Keller 1990; Jacoby, Chestnut, & Fisher 1978; Payne, Bettman, & Johnson

1988), the influence of critic comments is predicted to be reduced for movies/novels featuring popular stars/authors compared to products with unknown stars/authors. Such a result would have important implications for marketing experiential products contingent on whether they feature familiar or unknown artists.

EXPERIMENT 1

There are both economic and psychological reasons for studying movie consumption. The motion picture industry is a multi-billion dollar industry in the United States and around the world. It has been estimated that over $9 billion per year are spent by Americans going to first run movies and renting videos and that a sizable proportion of Americans go to the movie theater at least 20 times every year.[1] Many more rent or buy videos within a year after a movie is released to the theaters. Underlying these gross figures, of course, are a series of specific decisions made by individual consumers. There has been much research showing the large impact that movies have on individual viewers' attitudes, mood, physiological and affective states, and even their outlook on life (Erber & Tesser 1992; Forgas & Moylan 1987; Hirschman & Holbrook 1982; Isen & Gorgolione 1983; Linz, Fuson, & Donnerstein 1990; Palmgren & Lawrence 1989). The enormous economic and psychological significance of movie-going decisions should lead to increased interest in research on this particular form of consumer choice.

Experiment 1 tests the following hypotheses: 1) If brand equity effects extend to experiential products and if our conceptualization of "star as brand" is correct, then the same movie description will elicit more favorable responses when identified with a popular star than when associated with an unknown (ficti-tious) actor. 2) If "star as brand" is a correct conceptualization and if a trusted brand name serves as a heuristic for reducing reliance on other information, then the effects of critics' comments will be attenuated for movies with popular stars. In addition to testing these hypotheses, this experiment will include a follow-up phase to identify key mediators of brand equity effects attributable to movie stars.

Method

Participants. Participants were 62 undergraduate students in marketing classes at a large southeastern university. They were randomly assigned to a critic comments condition (N=31) and a no comments condition (N=31). In response to questions about their movie-going behavior during the past three months, these groups were found to be comparable on number of movies seen in the theater (means=2.90 and 3.48), number of movies watched on cable TV (means=11.32 and 11.00), and number of video rentals (means=7.68 and 7.10).

Experimental design and material. Each subject received eight movie descriptions. Subjects in the no comments condition were given some descriptions that included the actual well-known stars of the movie (e.g., Billy Crystal, Ted Danson, Tommy Lee Jones) and some descriptions with fictitious actors' names. Critics' comments were added for subjects in the critic comments condition. Both movies with and without familiar star names were assigned either favorable comments (e.g., "A pleasant surprise......Very enjoyable") or unfavorable comments (e.g.,"Boring plot......I barely even let out a chuckle"). Except for the critic

---

[1]These figures were obtained from: "The Study of Media and Markets," (1992), Simmons Market Research Bureau, Inc.; and "Critics' Choice and Studio Briefing," America On-Line, Inc.

comments, movie descriptions and star designations were matched in the two conditions. Actual movie descriptions were obtained approximately one month prior to their release and before informa-tion was available to the public.

Procedure. The study was described as one in which we are interested in how people make decisions about which movies to see. Subjects were told that on each page of their response booklet they would be given a short plot summary of an actual movie that will be released in the next 1-3 months. Subjects in the critic comments condition were also told that they would be shown some comments on the movie from the film critic of a major newspaper who had previewed the movie.

Based on this information, they were asked to indicate their likelihood of: a) Going to see the movie in the theater; b) Waiting to see the movie on cable TV; c) Waiting to rent the video; or d) Deciding not to see the movie at all. Subjects were instructed to assign a value between 0 and 100 to each choice and to make sure that they total to 100. Although we are primarily interested in the decision of whether or not to see a movie, we provided multiple options to make the task more realistic and thus obtain more reliable and valid data. Subjects were also asked to rate on a 5-point scale "How much do you think you would like the movie?", with 1="like a lot" and 5="dislike a lot."

Results

The main data concern the rated likelihood of seeing the movie as a function of type of critic comments (positive, negative or none) and whether or not there are known stars. Data from the category "decide not to see the movie at all" were converted to "likelihood of seeing the movie" by subtracting from 100, which is also equivalent to the sum of the stated likelihoods of seeing the movie by each of the designated options (in the theater, through video rental and on cable TV). Figure 1 shows the likelihood of seeing the movie as a function of critic comments and whether or not a well-known star was identified. There was a wide range of mean values, from an 86% likelihood of seeing a movie with stars and positive critic comments to a 32% likelihood of seeing a movie without stars and with negative critic comments. Figure 1 reveals that movies with stars are more desirable than movies without stars—confirm-ing the brand equity effect—and that positive critic comments make the movie more desirable than negative comments or no comments.

Perhaps the most interesting result seen in Figure 1 is that the lines differ in slope such that critic comments have a much greater effect for movies without stars than for movies with stars. For example, positive critic comments are especially helpful to movies without stars. Specific contrasts between the means displayed in Figure 1 were conducted to provide statistical tests of the hypoth-eses of interest. Because one group of subjects received both positive and negative critic comments and another group received no comments, some of the following are within–subject compari-sons and some are between–subjects, with different degrees of freedom for each. Positive critic comments led to higher likelihood ratings than negative comments, $t(30)=8.46$, $p<.01$; positive com-ments led to higher likelihood ratings than no comments, $t(60)=3.97$, $p<.01$; and negative comments led to lower ratings than no com-ments, $t(60)=1.79$, $p<.10$. Supporting the observation that critic comments had a reduced effect for movies with stars compared to movies without stars, the interaction between comments and stars was statistically significant for comparison between positive and negative comments, $F(1,30)=38.40$, $p<.01$; comparison between positive and no comments, $F(1,60)=5.97$, $p<.05$; and comparison between negative and no comments, $F(1,60)=4.28$, $p<.05$. While movies with stars produced higher likelihood ratings than movies without stars, this effect was statistically significant with negative

FIGURE 1
Likelihood of Seeing the Movie

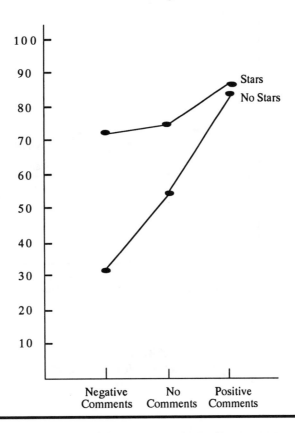

comments, t(30)=7.25, p<.01, and with no comments, t(30)=4.57, p<.05, but was not significant with positive comments, t(30)=.053.

An additional dependent variable of interest was "How much do you think you would like this movie?" Results here, summarized in Figure 2, are very much like those for rated likelihood of seeing the movie (Figure 1), except that the scale is reversed where low numbers represent more favorable ratings. As in Figure 1, the lines systematically converge. (The systematic convergence of lines in both Figures 1 and 2, without a flattening at the top or bottom, rules out ceiling or floor effects as the cause of the observed interaction.) Statistical comparisons were virtually identical for "like" ratings and rated likelihood of seeing the movie.

Discussion

In order to further our understanding of the process of deciding which movies to spend one's money on, we modeled the joint effects of critic comments and "star power." Consistent with our conceptualization of movie stars as possessing brand equity, the same unknown film was more attractive when associated with a well-known star than with a fictitious name. Just as the Intel Pentium microprocessor can transfer its brand equity to an unknown brand of personal computer, the name of Clint Eastwood can enhance our desire to see the new movie he's in.

Our results are consistent with the findings of Wallace, Seigerman, and Holbrook (1993). Specifically, using correlational data, they found that presence of well known stars explained 32% of the variance in film rentals, while controlling for various factors including the film's rating, the cost, the length of the film, etc. The current study builds on the findings of Wallace et. al by uncovering similar effects in a controlled experiment.

Supporting our notion that identification of familiar stars provides movie-goers with heuristic devices for making the decision to see a new movie, the factors "critic comments" and "stars" combined configurally, with the identification of a popular star serving to modify the critic effect. The effects of critic comments on the desire to see a new movie and the expected enjoyment of that movie, while large for movies with unknown stars, were reduced substantially when the movie description included identification of a popular star. Conversely, when a movie receives a "thumbs-up" from the critics, it is less in need of the additional boost provided by a trusted star. These results underscore the need to study such decisions using multi-factor designs rather than assuming that factors can be studied individually as though they had independent effects. The present results support the view that mere identification of a familiar star, like the recognition of a trusted brand name, provides a heuristic for movie-goers to select a new movie without need for much additional information.

A natural question is then: *Why do stars have heuristic value?* To further understand the reasons behind the "star power" heuristic effect, we asked a new group of 70 students to rate their agreement-disagreement with each of a series of statements concerning the influence of stars. Table 1 summarizes the results of this survey. One possibility that we explored was that the movie-going public would enjoy watching their favorite stars no matter what the quality of the movie. This item was generally not endorsed. They did, however, strongly endorse the item "Top stars are usually in good movies." Eighty percent agreed or strongly agreed with this statement, suggesting that movie-goers do indeed make strong assumptions about the quality of a movie based on identification of the movie's star. (Linton & Petrovich, 1988, came to a similar

FIGURE 2
Ratings of How Much Subjects Would Like the Movies

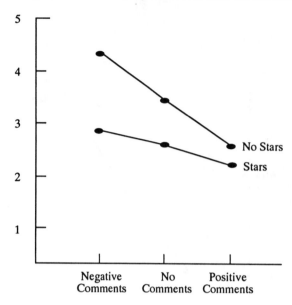

TABLE 1
Why Do Stars Have Heuristic Value?

Item	Mean	SD
When I go to a first-run movie, it is important that the movie has a well-known star.	2.46	.83
Top stars are usually in good movies.	2.11	.75
I enjoy watching the star, regardless of whether it's a good movie.	3.36	.99
Top stars have "sex appeal"	2.20	.73
Top stars more or less portray themselves, so if you like one of their movies, you'll probably like them all.	3.50	.94
Top stars, through their acting talent, can make even a mediocre plot and character seem interesting.	2.51	.83
Familiar stars are like old friends	2.67	.77

<u>Response scale</u>: 1 = strongly agree, 2 = agree, 3 = neither agree or disagree, 4 = disagree, 5 = strongly disagree

conclusion and Bello & Holbrook, in press, concluded that perceived quality is the key mediator of brand equity effects.) Our subjects also endorsed the item "Top stars have 'sex appeal'."

EXPERIMENT 2

Experiment 2 had two major purposes: (1) to extend the findings of Experiment 1 to a different experiential product—novels; and (2) to examine "line extension" effects with experiential products. The first purpose was achieved by comparing reactions to the same plot descriptions provided by known vs. unknown authors and by manipulating the favorability of critics' comments. The second purpose was achieved by including a

condition in which familiar authors were associated with different genres than they're known for.

Method

Participants were 138 students in marketing classes at the same university as in Experiment 1. Participants were assigned at random to three experimental conditions. In the Known Authors, Same Genre condition, participants evaluated four novels each said to be written by a famous author—Michael Crichton, John Grisham, Judith Krantz, and Danielle Steel. Plot descriptions ascribed to each author were constructed to be consistent with that author's usual genre. In the Known Authors, Different Genre condition the same authors and plot descriptions were used but the first two authors were interchanged with the second two authors. In the Unknown Authors condition the same plot descriptions were used but with fictitious author names—two male names to replace Michael Crichton's and John Grisham's assignments in the first condition and two female names to replace Judith Krantz and Danielle Steel.

Plot descriptions were said to be supplied by publicists for the book's publishers and consisted of brief (fictitious) summaries such as "A tribunal conducted aboard a nuclear submarine implicates three generations of a powerful military family in acts of sabotage that go back to the bombing of Pearl Harbor in 1941. The outcome could discredit the first woman candidate for President of the United States."

Critics' comments were said to be supplied by professional book critics and, for a given novel, consisted of three positive statements (e.g., Surprise ending. Suspenseful. Interesting historical background.) or three negative statements (e.g., Inaccurate reconstruction of history. Predictable ending. Slow). Each participant in each condition received two novel descriptions with positive comments and two with negative comments. Within each condition half the participants received positive comments for a given novel and half received negative comments.

After reading the plot description, author's name, and critics' comments for a given novel, the participant was asked to rate (on a scale of 1 to 10) how much he or she thought they would like the novel, the likelihood (from 0 to 100%) that they would read the novel, and the likelihood that they would buy the novel.

As a manipulation check for our designation of familiar vs. unknown authors, at the end of the session participants were asked to indicate which of the authors they had heard of, which they had read before, and how much they liked that author's work.[2]

Results and Discussion

The three dependent variables—expected liking of the novel, likelihood of reading it, and likelihood of buying it—were highly correlated with each other and showed the same statistical results. Figure 3 displays the results for ratings of how much respondents thought they would like the novel.

First compare the Known Authors-Same Genre condition with the Unknown Authors condition. The pattern here is very much like that for movies (Figure 1). Responses were significantly higher for positive comments than for negative comments, t(91)=3.56, p<.01. The difference in the magnitude of the critics' comments effect was less in the Known Authors-Same Genre condition than in the Unknown Authors condition, but this difference was of only marginal statistical significance, t(90)=1.60, p<.06 (one-tailed test). This probably reflects the fact that the authors in Experiment 2 had not attained the same level of star power as the actors in Experiment 1.

Now compare the Known Authors-Different Genre condition to the other two conditions. The pattern of results is almost identical for Known Authors-Different Genre and Unknown Authors. These two conditions were not significantly different from each other although each was different from the Known Authors-Same Genre

condition for negative comments. This demonstrates that the "star power" possessed by our well-known authors did *not* extend to situations in which these authors were associated with a different genre. This is consistent with research with standard products where line extensions may suffer from lack of fit if they don't meet consumers' expectations of the brand (Park, Milberg, & Lawson, 1991; Tauber, 1988).

In summary, Experiment 2 showed that the analog of "star as brand name" with experiential products extends from popular movie actors to popular authors, albeit to a lesser degree. Stephen King, after first publishing a novel under the pseudonym, Richard Bachman, was quoted as saying, "But the fact that *Thinner* did 28,000 copies when Bachman was the author and 280,000 copies when Steve King became the author, might tell you something, huh?"[3] However, Experiment 2 showed that, at least in the case of authors, "line extensions" to a new type of product meet with limited success.

GENERAL DISCUSSION

Following the suggestion of Holbrook and Hirschman (1982) multivariate procedures common to the study of brand equity effects with traditional products were applied to experiential products. The same product descriptions (movies in Experiment 1 and novels in Experiment 2) were ascribed to either well known actors/authors or to fictitious actors/authors. Confirming predictions, brand equity effects were established with experiential products by showing that consumer responses were more favorable in the "star" condition than in the "no star" condition. This held for both popular movie actors and popular authors.

Also consistent with the prediction that both popular actors and popular authors possess "star power", the effects of critics' comments were reduced when the product was ascribed to a popular actor or author. The same form of interaction was found in both experiments but was of lesser magnitude in Experiment 2.[4] In particular, consumers' reactions to negative movie critics' comments were greatly attenuated when the product was ascribed to a popular actor.

Beyond these general findings common to both movies and novels as experiential products, each experiment provided a unique insight. Experiment 1 showed that mediating the effect of "star power" in the movies was a perception that top stars, analogous to trusted brand names, are associated with high quality products. Nevertheless, Experiment 2 suggested that a star of the literary world has limited influence outside of his or her standard domain.

The theoretical significance of these results is that they show that theoretical concepts such as brand equity which have proven useful in the analysis of consumer preferences for standard goods are also useful for analyzing consumer preferences for experiential products. Future studies of experiential products can expand on these notions to examine brand extensions and brand combinations (e.g., the effects of having several popular stars in the same movie) with experiential products.

The primary finding in each experiment of reduced critics' comments effects when stars are identified, has direct marketing implications. When an experiential product such as a movie, play,

---

[2]These manipulation checks confirmed that practically all participants had heard of our "well known" authors, and many had read their work. Female respondents were more apt than males to have read and liked the female authors and vice versa for males. Occasionally, a participant "recognized" the name of our fictitious authors. (In a later survey, we showed that popular movie stars generally have greater familiarity than best-selling authors.)

---

[3]From *The Stephen King Companion*, 1989, by George and Mary Beahm, Andrews and McMeel: Kansas City, MO.
[4]The magnitude of the "star power" effect undoubtedly differs across types of experiential products and constituents. Compare, for example, pop music artists and opera singers and, alas, authors of popular fiction and authors of journal articles.

FIGURE 3
Ratings of How Much Subjects Would Like the Novel

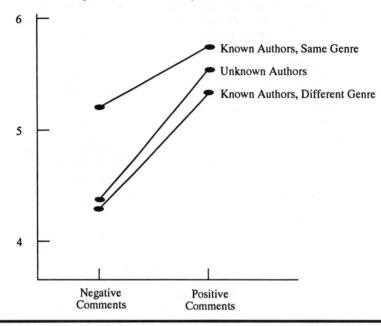

novel or musical composition can be ascribed to an established and trusted star, this feature should be highlighted, especially when the product involves the star's usual genre. When the artist is unknown to the public or is working in an unfamiliar domain (e.g., Clint Eastwood starring in a comedy or musical movie, recording a song, or writing a murder mystery), then additional information such as favorable critics' comments or expanded "previews" is needed.

REFERENCES

Aaker, D. A., & K. L. Keller (1990). Consumer evaluations of brand extensions. *Journal of Marketing*, 54, 27-41.

Barwise, T. Patrick, & Andre S. C. Ehrenberg (1987). The liking and viewing of regular TV series. *Journal of Consumer Research*, 14, 63-70.

Belk, Russel W. (1987). Material values in the comics: A content analysis of comic books featuring themes of wealth. *Journal of Consumer Research*, 14, 26-42.

Bello, David C., & Holbrook, Morris B. (in press). Does an absence of brand equity generalize across product classes? *Journal of Business Research*.

Erber, R., & A. Tesser (1992). Task effort and the regulation of mood: The absorption hypothesis. *Journal of Experimental Social Psychology*, 28, 339-359.

Forgas, J. P., & S. Moylan (1987). After the movies: Transient mood and social judgments. *Personality and Social Psychology Bulletin*, 13, 467-477.

Hirschman, Elizabeth C. (1988). The ideology of consumption: A structural-syntactical analysis of "Dallas" and "Dynasty". *Journal of Consumer Research*, 15, 344-359.

Hirschman, Elizabeth C., & Morris B. Holbrook (1982). Hedonic consumption: Emerging concepts, methods, and propositions. *Journal of Marketing*, 46, 92-101.

Holbrook, Morris B., Robert W. Chestnut, Terence A. Oliva, & Eric A. Greenleaf (1984). Play as a consumption experience: The roles of emotions, performance, and personality in the enjoyment of games. *Journal of Consumer Research*, 11, 728-739.

Holbrook, Morris B., & Mark W. Grayson (1986). The semiology of cinematic consumption: Symbolic consumer behavior in *Out of Africa*. *Journal of Consumer Research*, 13, 374-381.

Holbrook, Morris B., & Elizabeth C. Hirschman (1982). The experiential aspects of consumption: Consumer fantasies, feelings, and fun. *Journal of Consumer Research*, 9, 132-140.

Isen, A. M., & J. M. Gorgoglione (1983). Some specific effects of four affect-induction procedures. *Personality and Social Psychology Bulletin*, 9, 136-143.

Jacoby, J., R. W. Chestnut, & W. A. Fisher (1978). A behavioral process approach to information acquisition in nondurable purchasing. *Journal of Marketing Research*, 15, 532-544.

Keller, Kevin Lane (1993). Conceptualizing, measuring, and managing customer-based brand equity. *Journal of Marketing*, 57, 1-22.

Kindem, Gorham, "Hollywood's Movie Star System: A Historical Overview," in *The American Movie Industry: The Business of Motion Pictures*, ed. Gorham Kindem, Carbondale: Southern Illinois University Press, 1982, pp. 79-94.

Linton, James M., & Joseph A. Petrovich (1988). The application of the consumer information acquisition approach to movie selection: An exploratory study. In Bruce A. Austin (Ed.), *Current Research in Film: Audiences, Economics and Law*, 4, 24-45.

Linz, D., I. K. Fuson, & E. L. Donnerstein (1990). Mitigating the negative effects of sexually violent mass communications through pre-exposure briefings. *Communication Research*, 17, 641-674.

Palmgren, P., & P. Lawrence (1989). Avoidances, gratifications, and consumption of theatrical films: The rest of the story. In B. Austin (Ed.), *Current Research in Film 5*. Norwood, NJ: Ablex.

Park, C. Whan, Sandra Milberg, & Robert Lawson (1991).
Evaluation of brand extensions: The role of product level
similarity and brand concept consistency. *Journal of
Consumer Research*, 18, 185-193.

Payne, John W., James R. Bettman, & Eric J. Johnson (1988).
Adaptive strategy selection in decision making. *Journal of
Experimental Psychology: Learning, Memory, and Cognition*, 14, 534-552.

Reddy, Srinivas K., Vanitha Swaminathan, & Carol M. Motley
(1996). Hits on Broadway: The role of critics' reviews in
the success of an experiential good. Working paper.
University of Georgia, Athens.

Tauber, Edward M. (1988) Brand leverage: Strategy for
growth in a cost-controlled world. *Journal of Advertising
Research*, 28, 26-30.

Wallace, W. Timothy, Alan Seigerman, & Morris B. Holbrook
(1993). The Role of Actors and Actresses in the Success of
Films: How Much is a Movie Star Worth? *Journal of
Cultural Economics*, 17, 1-28.

Values and Attitude Formation Towards Emerging Attitude Objects: From Recycling to General, Waste Minimizing Behavior

John Thøgersen, Aarhus School of Business
Suzanne C. Grunert-Beckmann, Copenhagen Business School & Odense University

ABSTRACT

While a number of studies have dealt with the antecedents of recycling behavior, other waste minimizing behaviors have received much less attention in consumer behavior research. A few studies have tested the so-called values-attitude-behavior hierarchy within the environmental domain, assuming that values are crucial to understand environment-related behaviors but that the importance of values will be underestimated if critical mediating constructs are not assessed. This study follows this tradition while, at the same time, investigating the importance of values for attitude formation towards emerging attitude objects in a Danish setting. The importance of values for attitude formation is confirmed.

RECYCLING VERSUS WASTE MINIMIZATION

The unprecedented growth in economic activity in the post-war period has led to a dramatic increase in the production of waste, making the generation of solid waste a major environmental problem, particularly in the Western hemisphere (Sitarz, 1994). The total amount of waste produced in 1990 in OECD countries has been estimated to 9 billion tons, out of which 420 million tons were municipal waste (OECD, 1991). The quantity of waste paper alone in the OECD countries amounted to 150 million tons in 1990–compressed into bales, it would cover the entire city of Paris to a depth of two and a half meters (Kurth, 1992). Some—especially European—countries incinerate a significant part of their solid waste, but most of this waste is dumped (European Environment Agency, 1995). Waste incineration reduces the volume of the waste and allows to recover some of the resources in the waste as energy, but it leads at the same time to air pollution (Bernes, 1993) and still leaves a large rest product[1] that has to be disposed of.

In the last decade there has been increasing focus on ways to reduce the amount of waste. Two major possibilities exist: (1) recycling of waste products in order to re-use them by other users, for other purposes or as secondary materials (Pieters, 1991), and (2) preventing the origination of waste by, e.g., using fewer primary materials in production processes and designing products that are recyclable or produce less or less harmful waste when disposed of. To be successful, both strategies depend on active consumer involvement and participation.

The past decade has witnessed a marked increase in consumer behavior research focusing on recycling at the household level (for recent, comprehensive reviews of the literature, see Pelton, Strutton, Barnes Jr., & True, 1993; Thøgersen, 1996). However, even though recycling of waste is an indispensable element in solving the waste problem, it is only a second best solution as not all waste materials are recovered and resources are wasted in the transportation and processing of recyclables. Moreover, some consumers may feel that careful source separation of household waste exempt them from changing their buying and consumption patterns in order to prevent waste from arising in the first place. However, as emphasized in the strategy document of the Rio Earth Summit, "a preventive waste management approach which focuses on changes in lifestyles and in production and consumption patterns offers the best chance for reversing [the] current trends [in waste production]" (Sitarz, 1994, p. 222). This is why waste prevention is increasingly emphasized in waste management policy (e.g., European Environment Agency, 1995; Miljø- og Energiministeriet, 1995). Consumers can contribute to waste prevention by demanding products and packaging that are recyclable and/or have a low waste and a high recycling content, and by prolonging the use of products in the household.

We use the notion "waste minimization" to cover activities that a person performs in order to reduce his or her (or his or her household's) contribution to the waste stream. Hence, consumers may perform waste minimization by, e.g., buying beverages in refillable bottles, reuse plastic bags, repair broken household items, or source separating their waste.[2] Consumer behavior research has only very recently begun to investigate general waste minimizing behavior (Taylor & Todd, 1995).

For many consumers in affluent societies, waste prevention is an emerging attitude object. Of course, it is not a newly discovered phenomenon as, e.g., the environmental problems discussed by Stern, Dietz, Kalof and Guagnano (1995). However, it is a "rediscovered" or redefined mode of conduct which breaks with the behavioral pattern of the "buy-and-throw-away" culture, and which has only recently been brought to the attention of a wider public by media coverage and, probably, previous recycling experience.

ANTECEDENTS OF RECYCLING AND WASTE PREVENTION: VALUES AND ATTITUDES

A large body of literature has developed around the hypothesis that individuals hold a relatively stable set of universal values which they use to evaluate objects, events, other people, and themselves, and to select and justify actions (Schwartz, 1992). Because of their stability and centrality in a person's cognitive structure, values are functional in focusing attention to what is important in a situation and thus assisting the person in making more efficient decisions (Dietz & Stern, 1995) which may be especially important when confronted with a new attitude object (Stern et al., 1995). Most scholars view values as fairly distal determinants of behavior working through a number of more proximal determinants, like beliefs about consequences of the behavior and specific attitudes and norms (e.g., Eagly & Chaiken, 1993; Gray, 1985; Grunert & Juhl, 1994; Homer & Kahle, 1988; Rokeach, 1968; Stern et al., 1995; Stern & Oskamp, 1987).

McCarty and Shrum (1993, 1994) have demonstrated the presence of a values-attitude-behavior hierarchy (VAB) regarding recycling in an US-American setting. Not all parts of the value structure are equally relevant for evaluating behaviors in a specific domain. Stern et al. (1995), Grunert (1993), and Grunert and Juhl (1995) report quite consistent findings about which values are most important for decision making within the environmental domain. It

---

[1]The rest products form 39 Danish waste incinerators in 1992 amounted to 20% of the waste burned by weight (Christensen, Paaby, & Holten-Andersen, 1993).

[2]Others have used the term "waste management" to cover this class of consumer activities (Taylor & Todd, 1995a, 1995b). However, we prefer to give this notion the same meaning as it has at the company and municipal level, i.e., covering all activities aimed at disposing of waste whether or not it is recycled.

has been argued that recycling is categorized as altruism by most people in affluent societies (e.g., Hopper & Nielsen, 1991; Smith, Haugtvedt, & Petty, 1994; Thøgersen, 1996). If this is the case, altruistic values should play a crucial role in forming attitudes towards recycling (and presumably towards waste prevention too). Further, research on norm activation (e.g., Schwartz, 1977) suggests that the attitude towards recycling acquires a status as a moral imperative, a sense of personal obligation to act in a certain way (cf. also Dietz & Stern, 1995). Since recycling is now a well ingrained behavior in large segments of the population in the Western world, this literature lets us expect fairly strong influences of values and attitudes on recycling behavior. Additionally, we may expect that the influence of values on recycling is mediated through attitudes.

As already mentioned, waste prevention may be characterized as an emerging attitude object, suggesting that attitudes and beliefs about this type of behavior are less ingrained in the cognitive structure of the average person than are attitudes and beliefs about recycling. The question is, which pattern of relationships between the mentioned construct should we expect in this case? Based on the research of Fazio and others (e.g., Fazio & Zanna, 1981) we may expect weaker associations between attitude-expressing constructs when people are less than when they are more experienced. If values play the role suggested by Stern and his associates (1995; Dietz & Stern, 1995) in guiding attitude formation towards emerging objects, we may expect that in the case of waste prevention a V-A association is established before an A-B association. Hence, we hypothesize (1) that the relationships between values, attitudes and behavior are weaker with regard to waste prevention than with regard to recycling, and (2) that the weakness is more pronounced with regard to the A-B relationship than with regard to the V-A relationship.

STUDYING RECYCLING AND WASTE PREVENTION IN A DANISH SETTING

In summer 1995, a telephone interview survey was conducted with a sample of Danish residents aged 18 years and older (*N*=1002). Households were drawn randomly from a telephone register covering the whole country, and respondents within households were selected using the "next birthday" method. The appropriate individual completed a survey in 53.8% of the households reached. Data were collected concerning values, beliefs about consequences, norms, attitudes, behavior with regard to recycling and waste prevention, and a number of other issues not discussed in this paper. Waste prevention was operationalized as packaging-conscious buying.

The above-mentioned hypotheses were tested using a path analysis approach. Three different models were developed and tested with a series of multiple regression analyses:

(1) values–beliefs about consequences–behavior

(2) values–attitudes/personal norms–behavior

(3) values–beliefs about consequences/attitudes/personal norms–behavior

The following questions from the survey were used to test the models:

- Fourteen items from Schwartz's value indicator SVI[3] (Schwartz, 1992) measured on a 9-point unipolar scale with the end points "not important at all" and "of decisive importance as a guiding principle in my life."

- Eight items covering beliefs about consequences of either recycling or packaging conscious buying (four each) measured on a 5-point bipolar scale with the end points "very unlikely" and "very likely."

- Attitudes towards source-separating glass and bottles, composting appropriate kitchen waste, and buying groceries with excessive packaging,[4] measured on a 5-point bipolar scale with the end points "very negative" and "very positive."

- Feelings of personal obligation (i.e. personal norms) to source separate glass and bottles, to composte appropriate kitchen waste, to avoid groceries with excessive packaging, and to buy beverages in refillable bottles, measured on a 4-point unipolar scale with the end points "no obligation" and "very strong obligation."

- The frequency of source separating glass and bottles, composting appropriate kitchen waste, avoiding groceries with excessive packaging, and buying beverages in refillable bottles, measured as the number of times out of the last five opportunities.

DATA MANIPULATION AND SCALE CONSTRUCTION

As recommended by Maassen (1996), listwise deletion was used in the case of missing values. In order to minimize the detrimental effect of this method on the sample size, we chose to recode missing values in those cases where they could be given a meaningful interpretation. With behavior frequency, we assumed that not giving an answer (which in this case meant choosing the "not relevant" category) is equal to a behavior frequency of 0. Concerning values, we assumed that not being able to answer means that the value in question is unimportant (i.e., MV=1). Regarding attitudes and beliefs about consequences, we assumed that not being able to answer means that the person is undecided (i.e., MV=3). The three following methods were used for scale construction:

(1) The attitude towards packaging conscious buying was represented by one item in the survey only (referring to the buying of groceries with excessive packaging). Hence, this item was used as the scale.

(2) The personal obligation (or norm) and the behavior frequency regarding both of the investigated behaviors and the attitude towards recycling were all represented by two items each in the survey. In these cases, scales were constructed by averaging over the two items. In cases with missing value in one of the two items (questions

---

[3]In the translation of the items to Danish, one item got a slightly different meaning than in the original SVI. "Obedient" in the English version of the SVI became "Pligtopfyldende" in the Danish version. However, the correct English translation of "Pligtopfyldende" is "Conscientious" which is not included in the SVI.

[4]A negative attitude towards *buying* groceries with excessive packaging is interpreted as a positive attitude towards *avoiding* excessive packaging.

about personal norms only), the value on the other item was used. Hence, these scales are based on questions referring to the buying of groceries with excessive packaging and the buying of beverages in refillable bottles in one case, and on questions referring to the source separation of glass and bottles and the composting of appropriate kitchen waste in the other case.

(3) Values and beliefs about consequences of the behavior were based on a sufficient number of items to allow for factor analysis to construct the scales. We used exploratory factor analysis (principal components factor extraction and oblique varimax rotation) in order to increase the comparability of our results with previous research and because of the warnings against using confirmatory factor analysis with value items (which are often quite skewed) voiced in this research (Stern et al., 1995). In choosing the number of factors, we used the standard convention of a minimum eigenvalue of 1.0. However, whereas this resulted in a perfectly intuitive factor structure for perceived consequences, the 5-factor solution produced for values was less intuitive than a forced 4-factor solution. Since other arguments also supported the latter solution (reproducing the factor pattern produced by an unrestricted factor analysis based on the same data, but without missing values being recoded, and the eigenvalue of the fifth factor in the 5-factor solution being only marginally above 1 [1.001]), we chose to use this in the following analyses. Table 1 shows the four resulting factors regarding values.[5]

The pattern found is consistent with the pattern described by Schwartz (1992) and Stern et al. (1995), with two exceptions: (1) a self-enhancement (Schwartz) or egoistic (Stern et al.) value cluster could not be identified (presumably because to few items from this value cluster were included in our measurement instrument), and (2) instead of a unified self-transcendence (Schwartz) or biospheric-altruistic (Stern et al.) value cluster, our factor analysis produced two factors corresponding to the benevolence and universalism motivational types in Schwartz's terminology and to social-altruistic and biospheric values in Stern et al.'s. This latter result is especially interesting because this division was in fact expected by Stern and his associates (1993, 1994, 1995): Based on their review of both theoretical and empirical research, these scholars expect that a separate biospheric value orientation is in the process of emerging in the general population, but at least with the data at hand they were not able to detect it. Our data seems to indicate that the crystallization of a separate biospheric value orientation is more advanced in the general population of Denmark than in that of the USA.[6]

Table 2 shows the two times two resulting factors for beliefs about consequences. Only four items were used to measure beliefs about the consequences of each of the two activities, recycling and

packaging conscious buying (specifically focusing on the avoidance of excessive packaging). As expected, the principal components analysis produced two factors in each case: one that captured personal costs of performing the activity (three of the items in each case) and one that captured the environmental benefits (only one item in each case).

ALTERNATIVE HIERARCHICAL MODELS

As mentioned above, three different models were developed in order to test alternative versions of the values-attitudes-behavior hierarchy hypothesis:

(1) values–beliefs about consequences–behavior

(2) values–attitudes/personal norms–behavior

(3) values–beliefs about consequences/attitudes/personal norms–behavior

Figure 1 illustrates these models and in addition includes possible paths from beliefs about consequences to attitudes and personal norms which will be discussed briefly below. The confirmation of either Model 1 or Model 2 depends on some paths in the illustrated model being non-significant.

Traditionally, in tests of the values-attitudes-behavior hierarchy hypothesis the employed attitude measure has been a composite of beliefs about consequences (e.g., Homer & Kahle, 1988; McCarty & Shrum, 1993, 1994; Stern et al., 1995). However, attitude research indicates that higher explanatory power could be obtained by operationalizing the median level in the hierarchy by means of an instrument that in a more direct way captures the "general feeling of favorableness or unfavorableness" towards the behavior (Ajzen & Fishbein, 1980). In fact, this research predicts that not only the effects of values ("evaluations" in this terminology) on behavior, but also the effects of beliefs about consequences are mediated through attitudes. Since both types of measures were included in our survey instrument, we decided to test which one fares best, our expectation being that a—by the nature of the matter—more narrowly focused beliefs-based measure is inferior to a more inclusive direct measure of the overall attitude towards the behavior. However, considering a recent theory about the function of values in preference formation (Dietz & Stern, 1995), we also suspected that a general favorableness-unfavorableness measure may not be the best way to operationalize attitudes towards the act of recycling or waste prevention.

Dietz and Stern (1995) argue that individuals, both because of their limited mental capacity and because it is often more effective, typically use a classification-and-rule calculus to form attitudes, not the systematic mathematical calculus assumed in subjective expected utility theory: "In most circumstances humans observe a situation, categorize it, and use a simple rule to determine the appropriate behavior for that situation. The choice process relies on processes of classification: for example, 'if this is a situation of type A, then action X is appropriate.' In the most simple circumstances, the situation is classified as one that do not require deliberation: some rule automatically applies, such as habit or moral imperative" (p. 268). This theory predicts that the attitude of an environmentally concerned person towards performing an environmentally friendly activity takes the form of a moral imperative and, hence, becomes identical to what is generally known as a personal norm (Schwartz, 1977; Stern et al., 1995; Fishbein, 1967).

One may argue, as does Fishbein at several occasions (1967, Fishbein & Ajzen, 1975), that the normative beliefs and values that are captured by measures of norms would also be captured by a

---

[5]Some factor analysis literature refer to a standard convention of using a minimum factor loading of 0.4 (e.g., Stern et al., 1995) while others refer to the standard being 0.3 (Kim & Mueller, 1994). Hence, we chose a position in the middle, using a minimum factor loading of 0.35.

[6]Relying on a somewhat different approach, Axelrod (1994) found a separate biospheric value orientation among a sample of Canadien students.

TABLE 1

Factor scales derived from 14 value items

Item	Loading	Motivational type[a]	Schwartz cluster[a]	Stern cluster[b]
VF1: Social-altruistic values				
Responsible	.80	b	ST	–
Helpful	.75	b	ST	SA
Conscientious	.61	–	–	–
Enjoying life	.52	h	O	–
VF2: Biospheric values				
A world of beauty	.80	u	ST	B
Unity with nature	.78	u	ST	B
A world at peace	.35	u	ST	SA
VF3: Openness to change				
Influential	.79	a	SE	E
Independent	.59	sd	O	–
Choosing own goals	.59	sd	O	–
Curious	.42	sd	O	–
VF4: Conservation				
Preserving my public image	.73	p/s	SE/C	–
Respect for tradition	.57	t	C	–
Social order	.50	s	C	–
Curious	-.47	sd	C	–
Conscientious	.46	–	–	–

Scale intercorrelations	Biospheric values	Openness	Conservation
Social-altruistic values	-.24	-.21	-.23
Biospheric		-.17	-.07
Openness			-.08

[a] As defined in Schwartz (1992), b = benevolence, h = hedonism, u = universalism, a = achievement, sd = self-direction, p = power, s = security, t = tradition; ST = self-transcendence, SE = self-enhancement, C = conservation, O = openness to change.

[b] As defined in Stern et al. (1993, 1995), E = egoistic, SA = social-altruistic, B = biospheric.

TABLE 2

Scales of beliefs about consequences

Factors:	Recycling				Packaging conscious buying			
	More re-cycled	Takes time	More effort	Take up space	Less waste	Shorter shelf life	More effort	More ex-pensive
BF1: Costs		.869	.803	.751		.755	.605	.588
BF2: Benefits	.998				.991			

general attitude, if properly measured. However, this idea is based on rather unrealistic assumptions about humans' mental capacity (e.g., Dietz & Stern, 1995). And in practice, Fishbein and a great number of other renowned scholars have taken the consequence of the lack of empirical confirmation of the hypothesis about an allencompassing attitude construct and included normative measures in their models for explaining behavior (e.g., Ajzen, 1991; Fishbein, 1967; Fishbein & Ajzen, 1975; Schwartz & Tessler, 1972; Triandis, 1980).

Hence, in order to test the hypothesis that environmentally concerned consumers are likely to develop a moral stance towards performing the types of activities investigated here, we included two "attitudinal" measures in our analyses: favorableness-unfavorableness towards and felt personal obligation concerning

FIGURE 1
Alternative versions of the values-attitudes-behavior hierarchy

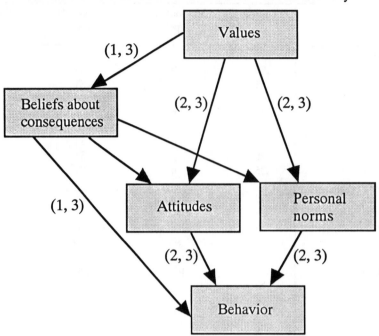

the activity in question. Based on Dietz and Stern's (1995) theory, we expected a stronger correlation between biospheric and also social-altruistic value orientation and the personal norm measure, than between these values and the attitude measure, and also between personal norm and behavior than between attitude and behavior. The results of the tests are shown in Table 3. In order to be able to compare the independent variables' contribution to the explanation of a dependent variable, standardized β weights are reported. The lower half of the table reports the results concerning waste prevention. In each case, the first four rows report multiple regression analyses of the relationships between values and the intermediate variables in the alternative versions of the values-attitude-behavior hierarchy introduced earlier. In the next two rows, beliefs about consequences are added to the equations explaining attitudes and personal norms. In the final step (rows 7 to 10), behavior is regressed on (a) values and beliefs, (b) values, attitudes, and personal norms, (c) values, beliefs, attitudes, and personal norms, and (d) beliefs, attitudes, and personal norms.

As is generally the case in analyses within this line of research, the proportion of variance explained by our analyses (the adjusted R^2) is fairly low. The two most important reasons for this are that a large error variance is difficult to avoid, especially at the more abstract levels (Grunert, 1996) and that a number of variables known to influence behavior in this field (cf., e.g., Pieters, 1991; Thøgersen, 1994) are omitted from the analysis. Moreover, economic and practical constraints have forced us to use simplified measurement instruments which may have aggravated the error variance problem.

Still, beliefs and attitudes concerning both recycling and waste prevention are significantly related to values at the one hand and to behavior at the other. When controlled for the proximal determinants, values add little to the explanation of behavior (cf. the non-significant β-values for values in equation 9), i.e., practically all the influence of values on behavior is mediated through more specific

beliefs and attitudes about the behavior. Surprisingly, conservation values (VF4) turns out to have a significant influence on recycling (equation I.9) when the intermediate variables have been controlled for (note that "Conservation" in Schwartz's terminology refers to conservatism, not to environmental concern.) The factor loadings reported in Table 1 gives a hint to a possible explanation for this relationship. The strongest loading item on this factor is "preserving my public image." Hence, it is possible that individuals scoring high on this factor are more sensitive than others to the social pressure to recycle. Because waste prevention is still in its infancy, it is likely that there is less social pressure to perform this activity. Also, the hypotheses that the associations between values, attitudes and behavior is stronger with regard to recycling than with regard to waste prevention, and that the difference is larger for the A-B than for the V-A relationships, are supported by the data. Only with regard to the equations that relate beliefs about consequences to values (equations 1 and 2) is the adjusted R^2 higher for waste prevention than for recycling

Consistent with the hypothesis that recycling and waste prevention are perceived as altruistic activities, both values and behavior are more strongly correlated with personal norms (felt personal obligation) than with attitudes (favorable/ unfavorable) in both cases (equations 3, 4 and 7-10, except equation I.9). This conclusion is further strengthened by the finding that the attitudinal variables and beliefs about environmental consequences are more strongly correlated with biospheric values than with any other value orientation (equations 1-3). The negative correlations between biospheric and social-altruistic values and beliefs about personal costs with regard to recycling (equation 1) indicate that one of the ways that values guide behavior is by producing selective attention and information processing (Dietz & Stern, 1995; Stern et al., 1995).

Also consistent with our expectations, the attitude and personal norm measures are more strongly related to both values and

TABLE 3
Path analysis of alternative values-attitudes-behavior hierarchy models

Independent Dependent	VF1	VF2	VF3	VF4	BF1	BF2	A	PN	F	adj.R^2	N
I. Recycling											
1. BF1: Costs	-.07*	-.12***	-.01	.01					3.5**	.01	1002
2. BF2: Benefits	.05	.10**	.01	-.08*					4.9***	.02	1002
3. A	.07*	16@	.09**	-.03					7.4@	.03	1002
4. PN	.14@	.27@	.14@	.00					18.4@	.07	969
5. A	.06	.14@	.09**	-.02	-.08*	.13@			8.7@	.04	1002
6. PN	.13***	.25@	.14@	.01	-.09**	.10***			15.7@	.08	969
7. Behavior	.04	.13@	.05	.09**	-.17@	.06			9.9@	.05	1002
8. Behavior	.01	.04	.00	.10**			.24@	.25@	35.9@	.18	969
9. Behavior	-.00	.03	.01	.10**	-.13@	-.00	.24@	.24@	30.0@	.19	969
10. Behavior					-.13@	-.00	.23@	.24@	56.4@	.19	969
II. Prevention											
1. BF1: Costs	.09*	.03	.04	.15@					5.9***	.02	1002
2. BF2: Benefits	.15@	.18@	.04	.03					9.6@	.03	1002
3. A	-.09*	-.10**	-.03	.07*					5.5***	.02	1002
4. PN	.10**	.23@	.18@	-.01					16.0@	.06	977
5. A	-.09*	-.10**	-.03	.06	.06	-.05			4.6***	.02	1002
6. PN	.11**	.22@	.18@	.00	-.07*	.06			12.3@	.07	977
7. Behavior	.04	.10**	.08*	-.06	-.10**	.08*			6.3@	.03	1002
8. Behavior	.00	.03	.01	-.06			-.09**	.34@	28.5@	.15	977
9. Behavior	.00	.02	.01	-.05	-.07*	.06	-.09**	.34@	22.5@	.15	977
10. Behavior					-.07*	.06	-.09**	.34@	44.2@	.15	977

* p < .05   ** p < .01   *** p < .001   @ p < .0001

behavior than the beliefs based measures in all cases except one (equations 1-4). Concerning waste prevention, there is a weaker relationship between values and attitudes than between values and beliefs about environmentally beneficial consequences. As predicted by attitude theory (e.g., Eagly & Shaiken, 1993), values and cognitions (beliefs about consequences) contribute independently to attitude formation, including the formation of a personal norm (equations 5 and 6). In the case of waste prevention, beliefs about consequences only effect personal norms, and this fairly weak.

The attitudinal variables are also related to social-altruistic values (in all cases except one, equation I.5), but generally the relationship is weaker than to biospheric values. These values are traditionally assumed to be the source of morality so this finding strengthen the conclusion about the moral nature of attitudes and

norms concerning recycling and waste prevention. Somewhat unexpectedly we also found a significant correlation between personal norms and the openness to change value orientation. This relationship suggests that both recycling and waste prevention are not only perceived as the morally right thing to do, but also as the "modern" or "progressive" way to behave.

In attitude research it is usually assumed that the effects of beliefs about consequences on behavior are mediated through attitudes (Eagly & Shaiken, 1990). Inconsistent with this assumption, but consistent with Schwartz's (1977) prediction that people are likely to post-rationalize a moral situation to a situation where their moral norms do not apply if the perceived costs of performing the behavior are too high (cf. also Mansbridge, 1990; Thøgersen & Andersen, 1996), beliefs about personal costs contribute significantly to the explanation of behavior when the attitudinal variables have been controlled for (equations 9 and 10). Hence, this result is also consistent with the assumption that many people classify recycling and waste prevention within the "domain of morality" (Schwartz, 1970).

DISCUSSION

In this paper we have analyzed various versions of the values-attitudes-behavior hierarchy model for a class of environmentally friendly, waste minimizing behaviors. Based on a large random sample of Danish consumers, we found that such a hierarchy can indeed be identified with regard to both recycling and waste prevention/packaging conscious buying. Hence, it adds to the number of studies suggesting that values are crucial to understanding environment-related behaviors and that the importance of values is underestimated if critical mediating constructs are not assessed (e.g., Grunert, 1993; McCarty & Shrum, 1993, 1994; Stern et al., 1995). Second, our data confirms a number of hypotheses implying that values are functional in attitude formation towards new or emerging attitude objects and specifically emerging attitude objects within the environmental field. Third, our data supports the hypothesis that a separate biospheric value orientation is crystallizing from what was former a general social-altruistic value orientation. Fourth, biospheric values are found to have the largest (but not the sole) impact on beliefs and attitudinal variables with regard to the analyzed behaviors. Fifth, although both attitudes and personal norms are significantly related to both values and behavior, the personal norm (feeling of a personal obligation) is most strongly related to variables at the other levels of the values-attitudes-behavior hierarchy in both cases. Sixth, although some of the effects of beliefs about consequences on recycling and waste prevention are mediated through attitudes and personal norms, perceived personal costs still have a direct influence on behavior when these variables have been controlled for. The last three findings all point in the same direction, indicating that most people in the analyzed population classify the analyzed activities within the "domain of morality."

These findings contribute to our understanding of antecedents of environmentally responsible behaviors by demonstrating the existence of a values-attitudes-behavior hierarchy and by confirming Stern et al.'s (1995) hypothesis that individuals construct attitudes towards emerging attitude objects by referencing values and beliefs about the consequences of behavior for their values. Moreover, we were able to identify a distinctive biospheric value orientation in the Danish population that in the literature on environmentalism has been mentioned as critical for the willingness to take environmental action–a result which at the same time points at a cultural difference between Denmark and the US.

With regard to policy implications, the findings of this study suggest two strategies: (1) the need to strengthen the salience and importance of biospheric values through educational measures, and (2) the importance of informing citizen-consumers about the environmental consequences of their consumption patterns and their share of responsibility for achieving a sustainable development.

REFERENCES

Ajzen, I. (1991). Theory of planned behavior. *Organizational Behavior and Decision Processes, 50*, 179-211.

Ajzen, I. & Fishbein, M. (1980). *Understanding attitudes and predicting social behavior.* Englewood Cliffs: Prentice-Hall.

Axelrod, L. J. (1994). Balancing personal needs with environmental preservation: Identifying the values that guide decisions in ecological dilemmas. *Journal of Social Issues, 50*(3), 85-104.

Bernes, C. (1993). *Nordens miljø–tilstand, udvikling og trusler.* Nord 1993:10. København: Nordisk Ministerråd.

Christensen, N., Paaby, H. & Holten-Andersen, J. (Ed.) (1993). *Miljø og samfund–en status over udviklingen i miljøtilstanden i Danmark.* Faglig rapport fra DMU. Roskilde: Miljøministeriet, Danmarks Miljøundersøgelser.

Dietz, T. & Stern, P. C. (1995). Toward a theory of choice: Socially embedded preference construction. *Journal of Socio-Economics, 24*, 261-279.

Eagly, A. H. & Chaiken, S. (1993). *The psychology of attitudes.* Fort Worth: Harcourt Brace Jovanovich College Publishers.

European Environment Agency (1995). *Europe's environment.* Copenhagen: European Environment Agency.

Fazio, R. H. & Zanna, M. P. (1981). Direct experience and attitude-behavior consistency. In: Berkowitz, L. (Ed.). *Advances in experimental social psychology*, pp. 161-202. New York: Academic Press.

Fishbein, M. (1967). Attitude and the prediction of behavior. In: Fishbein, M. (Ed.). *Readings in attitude theory and measurement*, pp. 477-492. New York: John Wiley.

Fishbein, M. & Ajzen, I. (1975). *Beliefs, attitudes, intention, and behavior.* Reading, MA: Addison-Wesley.

Gray, D. B. (1985). *Ecological beliefs and behaviors: Assessment and change.* Westport, Connecticut: Greenwood Press.

Grunert, S. C. (1993). Green consumerism in Denmark: Some evidence from the ØKO foods-project. *der markt, 32*(3), 140-151.

Grunert, S. C. (1996). Antecedents of source separation behaviour: A comparison of two Danish municipalities. In: J. Berács, A. Bauer & J. Simon: *Marketing for an expanding Europe. Proceedings of the 25th Annual Conference of the European Marketing Academy*, pp. 525-538. Budapest: Budapest University of Economic Sciences.

Grunert, S. C. & Juhl, H. J. (1995). Values, environmental attitudes, and buying of organic foods. *Journal of Economic Psychology, 16*, 39-62.

Homer, P. M. & Kahle, L. R. (1988). A structural equation test of the value-attitude-behaviour hierarchy. *Journal of Personality and Social Psychology, 54*, 638-646.

Hopper, J. R. & Nielsen, J. M. (1991). Recycling as altruistic behavior. Normative and behavioral strategies to expand participation in a community recycling program. *Environment and Behavior, 23*, 195-220.

Kim, J.-O. & Mueller, C. W. (1994). Factor analysis: Statistical methods and practical issues. In: Lewis-Beck, M. S. (Ed.). *Factor analysis and related techniques.* London: Sage.

Kurth, W. (1992). The mounting pile of waste paper. *The OECD Observer, 174*(February/March), 27-30.

Maassen, G.H. (1996). Handling of missing values in path models for opinions or attitudes. *European Journal of Social Psychology, 26*, 1-13.

Mansbridge, J. J. (1990). On the relation of altruism and self-interest. In: Mansbridge, J. J. (Ed.). *Beyond self-interest.* Chicago: The University of Chicago Press.

McCarty, J. A. & Shrum, L. J. (1993). A structural equation analysis of the relationships of personal values, attitudes and beliefs about recycling, and the recycling of solid waste products. In: McAlister, L. & Rothschild, M. L. (Eds.). *Advances in Consumer Research, Vol. 20*, pp. 641-646. Provo: Association for Consumer Research.

McCarty, J. A. & Shrum, L. J. (1994). The recycling of solid wastes: Personal values, value orientations, and attitudes about recycling as antecedents of recycling behavior. *Journal of Business Research, 30*, 53-62.

Miljø- og Energiministeriet (1995). *Natur- og miljøpolitisk redegørelse 1995*. København: Miljø- og Energiministeriet.

OECD (1991). *Environmental indicators*. Paris: OECD.

Pelton, L. E., Strutton, D., Barnes Jr., J. H. & True, S. L. (1993). The relationship among referents, opportunity, rewards, and punishments in consumer attitudes toward recycling: A structural equation approach. *Journal of Macromarketing*, 13, (Spring), 60-74.

Pieters, R. G. M. (1991). Changing garbage disposal patterns of consumers: Motivation, ability, and performance. *Journal of Public Policy & Marketing, 10*, 59-76.

Rokeach, M. J. (1968). *Beliefs, attitudes, and values*. San Francisco: Jossey Bass.

Schwartz, S. H. (1970). Moral decision making and behavior. In: Macauley, J. & Berkowitz, L. (Eds.). *Altruism and helping behavior*, pp. 127-141. New York: Academic Press.

Schwartz, S. H. (1977). Normative influence on altruism. In: Berkowitz, L. (Ed.), *Advances in experimental social psychology, Vol. 10*, pp. 221-279. New York: Academic Press.

Schwartz, S. H. (1992). Universals in the content and structure of values: Theoretical advances and empirical tests in 20 countries. In: Zanna, M. P. (Ed.). *Advances in Experimental Social Psychology, Vol. 25*, pp. 1-65. San Diego: Academic Press.

Schwartz, S. H. & Tessler, R. C. (1972). A test of a model for reducing measured attitude-behavior discrepancies. *Journal of Personality and Social Psychology, 24*, 225-236.

Sitarz, D. (Ed.) (1994). *Agenda 21: The earth summit strategy to save our planet*. Worldwatch environmental alert series. Boulder: EarthPress.

Smith, S. M., Haugtvedt, C. P. & Petty, R. E. (1994). Attitudes and recycling: Does the measurement of affect enhance behavioral prediction? *Psychology & Marketing, 11*, 359-374.

Stern, P. C. & Dietz, T. (1994). The value basis of environmental concern. *Journal of Social Issues, 50*, 65-84.

Stern, P. C., Dietz, T. & Kalof, L. (1993). Value orientations, gender, and environmental concern. *Environment and Behavior, 25*, 322-348.

Stern, P. C., Dietz, T., Kalof, L. & Guagnano, G. (1995). Values, beliefs, and proenvironmental action: Attitude formation toward emergent attitude objects. *Journal of Applied Social Psychology, 25*, 1611-1636.

Stern, P. C. & Oskamp, S. (1987). Managing scarce environmental resources. In: Stokols, D. & Altman, I. (Ed.). *Handbook of environmental psychology*, pp. 1043-1088. New York: Wiley.

Taylor, S. & Todd, P. (1995a). Understanding household garbage reduction behavior: A test of an integrated model. *Journal of Public Policy & Marketing, 14*, 192-204.

Taylor, S. & Todd, P. (1995b). An integrated model of waste management behavior. A test of household recycling and composting intentions. *Environment and Behavior, 27*, 603-630.

Thøgersen, J. (1994). A model of recycling behaviour. With evidence from Danish source separation programmes. *The International Journal of Research in Marketing, 11*, 145-163.

Thøgersen, J. (1996). Recycling and morality. A critical review of the literature. *Environment and Behavior, 28*, 536-558.

Thøgersen, J. & Andersen, A. K. (1996). Environmentally friendly consumer behavior: The interplay of moral attitudes, private costs, and facilitating conditions. In: R. P. Hill & C. R. Taylor (Eds.). *Marketing and Public Policy Conference proceedings (Vol. 6, 1996)*. Washington, DC. Chicago: American Marketing Association.

Triandis, H. C. (1980). Values, attitudes, and interpersonal behavior. In: Page, M. M. (Ed.). *Nebraska symposium on motivation, 1979*, pp. 195-259. Lincoln: University of Nebraska Press.

Conceptual Issues in the Study of Innovation Adoption Behavior

Mohamed I. Nabih, Tilburg University, the Netherlands
Sjaak G. Bloem, Tilburg University, the Netherlands
Theo B.C. Poiesz, Tilburg University, the Netherlands

ABSTRACT

This paper focuses upon the relationships among the major behavioral concepts associated with different stages in the consumer innovation decision process. Innovation acceptance, adoption, resistance, rejection, postponement, and their conceptual equivalents tend to lack standardized conceptual and operational definitions. On the basis of an analysis of the available literature, a general framework for innovation related consumer responses is presented. The results of a carefully structured qualitative study provide preliminary evidence as to what concepts may be meaningfully identified and related, and suggest theoretical, methodological, and possible managerial implications.

New products and services represent a major source of business growth and profit. Yet, most of these seem to turn into failures before the stage of maturity (see, e.g. Crawford 1977; Cooper 1979; Booz, Allen, and Hamilton 1982). A relevant distinction can be made between new products and innovations (see, e.g. Robertson 1971), innovations being new products that are unrelated to direct or indirect consumer experience. The bottom line of innovation research findings is that if innovations succeed (fail) to meet consumer needs, wants, and preference, they are likely to encounter consumer adoption (resistance) (Ram 1989). However, the fact that many innovations fail to effectively penetrate markets indicates that, apart from the variance due to consumer needs, wants, and preferences, much variance remains to be explained. As a start, this paper will take a closer look at the adequacy of innovation related concepts and operationalizations presented in the literature. More specifically, it attempts to: 1. discuss the chronological development of behavioral concepts in the adoption literature, 2. assess the nature of the relationships between the major concepts, 3. discuss the different measurements of these concepts, 4. propose a conceptual framework as a synthesis of the previous points, and 5. report the results of a carefully structured qualitative study. Finally, implications for the conceptual framework are discussed.

CONCEPTS IN THE ADOPTION LITERATURE

In the innovation literature two general lines of research can be identified. One focuses on innovation adoption, and the other emphasizes consumer resistance to innovation. The first is the traditional and most dominant stream, which assesses how adoption is influenced by product characteristics (e.g. Feder 1982; Fliegel and Kilvin 1966; Zaltman 1973; Rogers 1962; Srivastava, Mahajan, Ramaswami, and Cherian (1985), personal characteristics (e.g. Robertson, Zielinski, and Ward 1984; Bass 1969), and perceived risk (e.g. Ostlund 1974). Researchers in the second line of research explicitly assume that rejection and adoption are two different types of behavior rather than antagonistic forms (Gatignon and Robertson 1991).

In the adoption literature a variety of behavioral concepts is frequently referred to, for example, adoption, rejection, resistance, acceptance, approval, trial, and postponement. Basically, adoption and rejection are the criterion concepts, with a strong emphasis in the literature on the former. Apparently, adoption is the more interesting behavior type to study, even though adoption and rejection are of equal importance from a practical viewpoint: they present each other's complement.

Let us start, therefore, with a critical analysis of the concept of adoption which, in the adoption literature, refers to two different types of behavior. The behavior most commonly referred to in the definition of adoption is 'the acceptance and the continued use' of an innovation (Robertson 1971:56). Alternatively, Rogers (1962) views adoption as 'a decision to continue full-scale use of an innovation' (p.17). Robertson's (1971) definition implies that not every innovation purchase results in adoption. In the case of nondurable innovations, for which continued use would pose an evident problem, Robertson (1971) replaced 'continuous use' by 'repeat purchase decisions', thus indicating that the operationalization of adoption is dependent upon the nature of the product class under consideration. Apparent operational complexities relate to the time frame and the number of repeat purchases to be considered, and to the necessity to allow for product category differences.

Rogers' (1962) definition basically refers to the intention to continue full-scale use of the innovation. There are two problems with this definition, the first being that research has shown that intention is a rather weak determinant of the corresponding behavior (see Howard 1994). The second problem is that the definition seems to address a mere determinant of adoption: innovation acceptance. Thus, there is a risk of confusing the determining concept with the determined concept.

The two different definitions of the same concept illustrate the ease by which conceptual confusion arises in the area of innovative behavior. In order to clarify the definitional issue we will attempt to answer the question whether a distinction between acceptance and adoption is theoretically useful at all. Wilkening (1953) was the first to use the concept of acceptance. However, in his definition, acceptance included both approval and adoption. According to Klonglan and Coward (1970), approval is the affirmative evaluation of a practice whether or not innovation trial has occurred, and adoption refers to the incorporation of the innovation into the behavior pattern. Bohlen (1964) explicitly called for a distinction between acceptance and adoption, considering the time lag between mental acceptance and actual adoption. Beal, Klonglan, and Bohlen (1966), Bohlen (1968), and Rogers (1968) introduced the concept of symbolic adoption, to be defined by Rogers (1968) as the adoption of symbolic ideas without material parallel. Examples of symbolic ideas are migration, occupational choice, and partner choice (Bohlen 1964). Klonglan and Coward (1970) were the first to view symbolic adoption as a part of the adoption process, regardless whether the innovation being adopted is material or immaterial. The underlying assumption is that all innovations include an idea component and that some innovations also include a material component (Rogers 1962; Krampf, Burns and Rayman 1993).

In the adoption literature, the adoption decision process is usually conceived of as a 'hierarchy of effects' model (Gatignon and Robertson 1991). Rogers' (1962) adoption process model, which assumes an awareness-interest-evaluation-trial-adoption sequence, is the most popular. According to Gatignon and Robertson (1991) the model explains the adoption process under conditions of high involvement or cognitive processing. In contrast, under conditions of low cognitive processing, the adoption process may be described in terms of an adapted sequence: awareness-trial-evaluation-adoption. On the basis of the difference between the two sequences, Gatignon and Robertson (1991) state that 'in any conceptualization of the adoption process, it is essential to separate trial and adoption' (p.325). Innovation trial is defined by Rogers and Shoemaker (1971) as applying the new idea by an individual on a small scale in order to determine its utility in his or her own situation. Both under conditions of high and low involvement consumers pass through the psychological stage of innovation acceptance before entering the trial stage. However, under high involvement conditions, relative to low involvement conditions, a more active acceptance develops before trial. Passive acceptance can be attributed to low consumer learning requirements, low innovation costs or switching costs, and low social imitation (Krugman 1965; Ray 1973; Robertson 1976; and Gatignon and Robertson 1985).

As in the case of acceptance, a distinction can be made between active and passive resistance. The concept of innovation resistance has been proposed by Sheth (1981) and Ram (1987). Passive resistance, then, takes place under conditions of low involvement or limited or no cognitive processing: a consumer resists the innovation without considering its potential. On the other hand, active resistance is expected under conditions of high involvement or extensive cognitive processing. Engel, Blackwell, and Miniard (1993) distinguish between active and passive rejection. They refer to active rejection after the innovation is considered (for instance, after trying it), and view passive rejection as taking place if the innovation is never really considered by the consumer. Note that the distinction between active and passive rejection seems to add to the conceptual confusion in the innovation literature. Do the authors mean active and passive rejection or active and passive resistance?

It is difficult to be conclusive with regard to the mutual relationships between the concepts of adoption, acceptance, rejection and resistance. Concepts may differ from each other in terms of their psychological meaning and/or because of their respective positions in the adoption sequence. Should adoption and rejection be viewed as each other's conceptual opposites, or do they reflect different underlying behaviors? Or are they conceptually similar but located at different positions in the adoption process? Are rejection and resistance basically the same, or should they be considered different? How useful is the distinction between active and passive behavior? And what role do trial and postponement play in relation to these concepts? The literature provides no conclusive answers to these questions. Comparisons are reported, but these relate more to individual pairs of concepts than to a systematic overall analysis of conceptual similarities and differences. In the next section we will refer to some of these comparisons.

According to Klonglan and Coward (1970), the two possible outcomes of the evaluation stage in the adoption process are 'mental acceptance' and 'mental rejection', the former possibly leading to trial and eventual continued use. Both acceptance and rejection may be related to other concepts. Innovation acceptance may also be viewed as the obverse of innovation resistance. Then, consumer acceptance and consumer resistance are the same type of behavior, are explained by the same factors, but differ in sign. Sheth (1981) and Ram (1989) attributed innovation resistance to two major sources of resistance factors; perceived risk components and habit or cognitive resistance. However, these resistance factors seem to provide an incomplete explanation of consumer resistance to innovations. If attraction factors leading to innovation acceptance are absent, then a reduction of the resistance factors will not increase the probability of acceptance. Also if repulsion factors are absent, a consumer can still resist the innovation in the absence of attraction

factors. Therefore, the assessment of innovation acceptance and resistance requires the consideration of both repulsion and attraction forces.

Both rejection and resistance refer to the decision not to adopt the innovation. For instance, Gatignon and Robertson (1989) show that the decision to *reject* is not explained by the same factors that explain adoption: '*Rejection* is not the mirror image of adoption but a different type of behavior. Future research could contribute by specifying factors uniquely tied to innovation *resistance*' (p.325, underlining ours). Ram (1987) and Ram and Sheth (1989) define innovation resistance as 'the resistance offered by consumers to an innovation, either because it poses potential changes from a satisfactory status quo or because it conflicts with their belief structure' (p.6). However, it seems that the same terms can be used to define rejection: the definition does allow for a conceptual distinction between the two concepts. If the concepts are not synonymous, their usage in the literature is rather inconsistent. For example, Ram (1989) states that 'two consumers may *resist* the same innovation for different reasons, and these reasons will have effects on the adoption process of each consumer. For example, one consumer may perceive the price of the innovation to be very high and *reject* it.' (p.21).

Summarizing, adoption and rejection relate to the behavioral stage in the adoption decision model, while acceptance and resistance are located at the preceding evaluation and intention level. If this interpretation is correct, resistance is not the obverse of adoption, and acceptance preceeds both adoption and rejection.

The consumer may escape from the dilemma between adoption and rejection by postponing the decision. Postponers are unwilling to commit themselves at a given point in time. They are undecided as to whether they need more information or more information-processing time (Gatignon and Robertson 1991), or are forced to delay adoption by external constraints such as, for example, product availability. There are two types of postponement responses toward innovations: trial postponement and adoption postponement. Trial postponement is a state in which consumers are undecided as to whether or not they should try using the innovation, or they have decided about trial but not about the point in time. Adoption postponement is a state in which consumers are undecided as to whether or not they should continue trial use, or they have decided but external constraints keep them from the purchase. Even though innovation postponement is a major type of consumer response, we know of only one study by Holak, Lehmann and Sultan (1987), that indirectly examined consumer postponement responses to innovations.

THE MEASUREMENT OF INNOVATION RESPONSES

Another possible cause of confusion in the innovation adoption literature is the lack of standardized operationalizations of the dependent variables acceptance, adoption, rejection, resistance, and postponement. This is not surprising, giving the lack of clear and consistent conceptualizations. Many recent adoption studies operationalize adoption in terms of mere purchase behavior, product ownership, or product possession rather than the extensive and prolonged use of the innovation (see, for example, Dickerson and Gentry 1983; Olshavsky 1980). There are two main techniques used by adoption researchers to assess adoption in terms of the continued and extensive use of the innovation. The relatively common technique is to employ subjective recall measures on both the data of purchase and the frequency of use. The other technique is to employ objective measures where researchers depend upon external information for the assessment of adoption behavior. Adoption researchers show a tendency to group the respondents of their studies into two groups: adopters and non-adopters (for instance, see Dickerson and Gentry 1983; Forsythe, Butler, and Kim 1991; Kundu and Bhayana 1992; Strutton and Lumpkin 1992; Shim and Kotsiopulos 1994). Gatignon and Robertson (1989), studying organizational innovation behavior, state that 'some level of information relevant to adoption decision is lost by grouping all nonadopters as a single category. Organizations may still be in the process of evaluating whether or not they should adopt. Therefore it would be erroneous to classify them as having made a decision to *reject* the innovation' (p.42). The same argument applies to consumers: at a particular point in time, nonadopters could be classified as belonging to either resistors, postponers, or rejectors.

It is surprising that in spite of the importance of the differences between these consumer responses to innovations, no standardized measurements of these concepts have been presented in the adoption literature. For the measurement of acceptance and adoption no known scales are available. The only standardized scale to measure consumer resistance to innovation is suggested by Ram (1989). The basic idea of this scale is that resistance can be measured by assessing the psychological antecedents of innovation resistance (in terms of four perceived risk components and two habit resistance components), and the consumer behavioral resistance to try, purchase, and switch to the innovation. We noted earlier that in a complete approach two types of antecedents should be measured: both repulsion and attraction factors. It can be argued, therefore, that an approach which operationalizes consumer resistance in terms of the repulsion (or attraction) factors only is basically incomplete. Ram's (1989) resistance scale only assesses repulsion factors.

The measurement of trial postponement involves the assessment of a type of consumer response to innovations which is located later in the adoption process relative to active acceptance and active resistance. The trial postponement response can be operationalized as the consumer's intention to postpone experiencing a limited application of the innovation to his or her situation after s/he has actively accepted it. The development of scales for the measurement of innovation responses is beyond the scope of the present paper. Conceptual clarity and uniqueness constitute a worthy goal that is to be achieved before specific operationalizations can be presented.

A FRAMEWORK OF INNOVATION RESPONSES

An attempt is made here to summarize the different concepts and their relationships in one overall framework, in which also the adoption sequence is represented. See Figure 1. The conceptual framework may be translated in operational terms (see Figure 2).

THE STUDY

A study was set up to make a preliminary assessment of the relevance and validity of the conceptual framework and its operational translation. The operational goal of the study was to find out how and why consumers proceed in their innovation decision process. No specific hypotheses were formulated, but a qualitative study was carefully designed to assess whether a psychologically meaningful distinction can be made between the various concepts of the proposed framework.

METHOD

Respondents

16 Respondents were recruited by the Product Evaluation Laboratory of the Delft University of Technology. Selection requirements were that the number of men and women should be equal, and that low, medium and high incomes should be approxi-

mately equally represented. Respondents received the equivalent of 8 US$ for their participation.

General set up

The qualitative study was structured according to the conceptual/ operational framework depicted in Figures 1 and 2, respectively. Because subjective newness rather than objective newness is the relevant concept, the procedure was to ensure that each respondent had to be confronted with products subjectively viewed as innovations. For this reason, the interviews were on an individual basis.

Procedure

Respondents had been invited 'to have an interview on new products'. The interviews lasted about 45 minutes. Interviews were videotaped. The interview consisted of two parts. The goal of the first part was to make an inventory of a sufficient number of subjectively relevant innovations. This part was structured as follows:

1. The respondent received an explanation of the word 'innovation';

2. The respondent was asked to give some examples of innovations (unaided);

3. The respondent was asked to select examples of innovations from a predetermined list of categories of new products (aided). Product categories included in the list were food and drinks, personal care products, cleaning products, audio-visual and information technological products, pharmaceutical products, and a rest-category;

4. For each product category, 3 examples of individual products were provided (e.g. CD-interactive, CD-rom, hand-held telephone, pasta snack, Internet, etc.); The respondent had to indicate whether they were aware of these innovations;

5. All innovations of which a respondent was aware (originated from 2, 3 and 4) were rated in terms of perceived newness according to the operationalization employed by Krampf et al., 1993);

The second part of the interview focused on the adoption process itself. This was done for those products that individual respondents had personally identified as innovations in the previous part. To clarify, respondents were first identified as to the stage in the adoption process. This was done with the scheme presented in Figure 3, based upon the operationalizations as presented in Figure 2. Note that respondents did not receive feedback on this identification. Next, they were requested to describe the process from beginning to end in an unstructured interview ('Can you describe how you came to this decision, starting from the moment you were first confronted with the product?'). In this interview, the researcher did not provide any information as to structure of the adoption process.

RESULTS AND DISCUSSION

For the sake of clarity, the results will be reported in the form of individual observations.

– Per respondent, the scheme was applied to 4 products consecutively (these products had been individually iden-

FIGURE 1
Conceptual framework of innovation responses

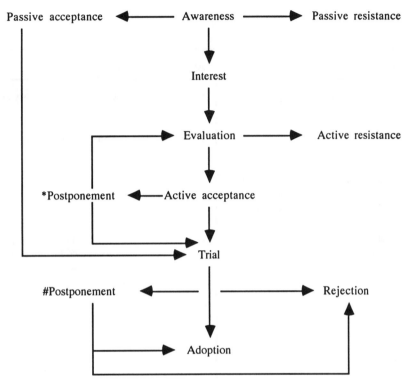

* = Trial postponement; # = Adoption postponement

FIGURE 2
A framework of operationalizations

Concept	Variable
Active or passive acceptance/resistance	Level of perceived newness (Krampf et al., 1993)
	Absence of direct usage experience (*)
	Intention to try (Ram, 1989)
	Intention to purchase (Ram, 1989)
	Intention to switch (Ram, 1989)
Trial postponement	Absence of direct usage exerience (*)
	Intention to postpone trial (*)
Adoption postponement	Presence of direct usage experience (*)
	Intention to postpone purchase (Holak et al., 1987)
	Intention to postpone switching (*)
Adoption	Present innovation usage level (*)
	Perceived level of usage satisfaction
	(Krampf et al., 1993)
Rejection	Presence of direct usage experience (*)
	Intention not to re-use innovation (Robertson, 1971)

(*) (These concepts were proposed by the present authors on the basis of the literature review. Operationalizations were very direct– the questions asked by the interviewer used the same terminology as the concepts themselves).

FIGURE 3
Operational scheme innovation related responses

Do you have direct use experience with the product?

Yes: No:

Presence of direct use experience	Absence of direct use experience

Do you have the intention to (re)buy/(re)use the product?
 	
1. No => **Rejection**
 	
2. If Yes:
 	
    2.1 Postpone (re)buy/(re)use => **Adoption post-ponement**
 	
    2.2 Immediately or continue (re)buy/(re)use => **Adoption**
	Do you have the intention to buy (use/try/switch) the product?
	
	1. No: Did you consider buying (etc.) it?
	
	    1.1 Yes => **Active resistance**
	    1.2 No => **Passive resistance**
	
	2. Yes: To what extent you think you have evaluated the innovation?
	
	    2.1 Low => **Passive acceptance**
	
	    2.2 High => **Active acceptance**
	
	    2.2.1 I will buy (etc.) it soon => **Trial**
	
	    2.2.2 I will postpone buying (etc.) it => **Trial post-ponement**

tified as innovations. A total of 24 products were perceived as innotavations. The nature and combination of these products varied over respondents. In total, the scheme was applied to 64 units of analysis;

— Over respondent-product combinations, a large variety of innovation related responses was observed;

— Respondents reported having no difficulty understanding scheme-related questions;

— With the help of the operational scheme it proved possible to allocate each respondent-product combination to one of the behavior stages. Additional question were not required.

— All innovation related responses in the scheme could be identified. These responses, together with their frequency of observation in parentheses, are: passive resistance (19), adoption (12), adoption postponement (8), rejection (6), active resistance (6), passive acceptance (6), trial postponement (6), active acceptance (5), and trial (1–meaning that one respondent was actually in the stage of trying out one of the products). It should be noted that passive resistance was the behavior most frequently identified;

— For all types of products respondents showed a tendency of proceeding according to a low involvement or 'do-feel-think' process: low initial knowledge, experience (trial),

acquire information. The respondents judged the trial phase very important;

— In the case of actual adoption, it is unclear how often product will be used. This is in line with the concept of adoption as defined by Robertson (1971);

— Respondents spontaneously make a distinction between symbolic and objective qualities innovations (see Klonglan and Coward (1970): accepting the idea or symbolic product qualities versus accepting the actual physical, or objective product qualities. (p.99).

Interpretation of descriptions provided by the respondents was done by two interviewers.

In conclusion, the scheme based upon the conceptual framework could be applied in a meaningful way. Respondents understood the meaning of the concepts and, with the help of the scheme, distinctions between the concepts could be made. If the process is viewed as located on a time-continuum, respondents were capable of locating the different concepts at different points of the continuum. This is important as, to our knowledge, this the first attempt to simultaneously present concepts that show a tendency to be confused in the literature. The results indicate that there is reason to believe that meaning-differences may be identified, although these differences may be small, and may possibly reflect a very small time distance on the continuum representing the adoption process. This study shows also how innovation related behavior may be operationalized. Because all behavior options are included, the likelihood of operational confusion is minimized. The same negative reaction to an innovation may have different psychological meanings, depending upon the stage in the adoption process. This applies, *mutatis mutandis*, to positive reactions as well. The scheme adopted for this study shows how different psychological meanings may be accounted for, even if consumers express them in equal overt behaviors.

A methodological suggestion implied by the results is that in spite of the risks involved in the adoption of innovations, consumers tend to follow a risk reducing strategy in which trial is a critical tactic. If this suggestion is correct, it may imply that existing scales related to adoption behavior are biased toward high involvement behavior.

The framework presented in this paper may be of practical relevance. A marketeer should be able to correctly identify non-purchase as either reflecting active resistance, passive resistance, rejection, trial postponement or adoption postponement. This is only possible if a conceptual and methodological framework is employed in which the competing concepts are simultaneously included. A correct diagnosis of the nature of the undesired behavior may help determine what practical measures need to be taken.

The next step in research will be a quantitative test of the framework and an assessment of associated antecedents. Knowledge of innovation behavior determinants is required to determine whether the adoption continuum referred to earlier should be broken down in different segments reflecting differences in the *nature* of behavior, rather than differences in the *degree* of behavior alone.

REFERENCES

Bass, Frank M. (1969), "A New Product Growth Model for Consumer Durables," *Management Science*, 15 (January), 215-227.

Beal, George M., Gerald E. Klonglan, and Joe M. Bohlen (1966), "Adoption of an abstract idea: psychological adoption of public fallout shelters," Paper presented at *Rural Society meetings*, Miami.

Bohlen, Joe M. (1964), "The adoption and diffusion of ideas in agriculture," in *Our changing Rural Society: Perspectives and Trends*, ed. James H. Copp, Ames: Iowa State University Press, 265-287.

_____ (1968), "Research needed on adoption models," in *Diffusion Research Needs*, Columbia: Missouri Agricultural Experiment Station, North Central Regional Research Bulletin 186, 15-21.

Booz, Allen & Hamilton Inc. (1982), *New Product Management for the 1980's*, Chicago: Booz, Allen & Hamilton.

Cooper, Robert G. (1979), "The dimensions of industrial new product success and failure," *Journal of Marketing*, 43 (3) (summer).

Crawford, Merle C. (1977), "New product failure rates–facts and fallacies," *Research Management*, 22 (September), 9-13.

Dickerson, M. D., and J. W. Gentry (1983), "Characteristics of Adopters and Non-adopters of Home Computers." *Journal of Consumer Research* 10 (3), 225-235.

Engel, James F., Blackwell, Roger D. and Paul W. Miniard (1993), *Consumer behavior*, Orlando, The Dryden Press.

Feder, G. (1982), "Adoption of Interrelated Agricultural Innovations: Complementarity and the Impacts of Risk, Scale, and Credit," *American Journal of Agricultural Economics*, 64, 1, 94-101.

Fliegel, Frederick C., and Joseph E. Kilvin (1966), "Attributes of Innovations as Factors in the Diffusion," *American Journal of Sociology*, 72 (November), 235-248.

Gatignon, Hubert, and Thomas S. Robertson (1985), "A Propositional Inventory for New Diffusion research," *Journal of Consumer Research*, 11, 4 (March), 859-867.

Gatignon, Hubert, and Thomas S. Robertson (1989), "Technology Diffusion: An Empirical Test of Competitive Effects," *Journal of Marketing*, 53, 1 (January), 35-49.

_____ and Thomas S. Robertson (1991). "Innovative Decision Processes," in *Handbook of Consumer Behavior*, eds. T.S. Robertson and H.H. Kassarjian, New Jersey: Prentice-Hall, 316-348.

Holak, Susan L., Lehmann, Donald R., and Sultan, Fareena (1987), "The Role of Expectations in the Adoption of Innovative Consumer Durables: Some Preliminary Evidence," *Journal of Retailing*, 63, 243-259.

Klonglan, G. E., and Coward, E. W. (1970), "The concept of symbolic adoption: A suggested interpretation," *Rural Sociology*, 35, 77-83.

Krampf, Robert F., Burns David J., and Rayman Dale M (1993), "Consumer Decision Making and the Nature of the Product: A Comparison of Husband and Wife Adoption Process Location. *Psychology and Marketing*, Vol. 10 (2) (March/April), 95-109.

Krugman, Herbert E. (1965), "The Impact of Television Advertising: Learning Without Involvement," *Public Opinion Quarterly*, 29 (Fall), 349-356.

Menzel, Herbert, and Elihu Katz (1955), "Social Relations and Innovation in the Medical Profession: The Epidemiology of a New Drug," *Public Opinion Quarterly*, 19, 337-352.

Olshavsky, Richard W. (1980), "Time and the rate of Adoption of Innovations," *Journal of Consumer Research*, 6 (March), 425-428.

Ostlund, Lyman E. (1974), "Perceived Innovation Attributes as Predictors and Innovativeness," *Journal of Consumer Research*, 1 (June), 23-29.

Ram, S. (1987), "A Model of Innovation Resistance," in *Advances in Consumer Research*, eds. Melanie Wallendorf and Paul Anderson, Vol. 14. Provo, UT: Association for Consumer Research.

_____ (1989), "Successful Innovation Using Strategies to Reduce Consumer Resistance: An Empirical Test," *Journal of Product Innovation Management*, 6, 20-34.

_____ and Jagadish N. Sheth (1989), "Consumer Resistance to Innovations: The Marketing Problem and its Solutions," *Journal of Consumer Marketing*, 6, 2, 5-14.

Ray, Michael L. (1973), "Marketing Communication and the Hierarchy of Effects," in *New Models for Mass Communication Research*, ed Peter Clarke, Vol. 2, Beverly Hills, CA: Sage, 147-176.

Robertson, Thomas S. (1971), *Innovative Behavior and Communication*, New York: Holt, Rhinehart & Winston.

_____ (1976), "Low-Commitment Consumer behavior," *Journal of Advertisement Research*, 16 (April), 19-24.

_____ ,Joan Zielinski, and Scott Ward (1984), *Consumer Behavior*, Glenview, IL: Scott Foresman.

Rogers, Everett M. (1962), *Diffusion of Innovations*, New York: The Free Press.

_____ (1968), "A communication research approach to the diffusion of innovations," in *Diffusion Research Needs*, Columbia: Missouri Agricultural Experiment Station, North Central Regional Research Bulletin 186, 27-30

_____ and Floyd F. Shoemaker (1971), *Communication of Innovations: A Cross-Cultural Approach*, New York, The Free Press.

_____ (1983), *The Diffusion of Innovations*, New York: The Free Press.

Srivastava, R.K., V. Mahajan, S.N. Ramaswami, and J. Cherian (1985), "A Multi-attribute Diffusion Model for Adoption of Investment Alternatives for Consumers," *Technological Forecasting and Social Change*," 28 (December), 325-333.

Sheth, Jagdish N., (1981), "Psychology of innovation resistance", *Research in Marketing*, 4, 273-282.

Wilkening, Eugene A. (1953), *Adoption of Improved Farm practices as Related to Family Factors*, Madison: Wisconsin Agricultural Experiment Station, Research Bulletin 183.

Zaltman, G., Duncan, R. and J. Holbek (1973), *Innovations and Organizations*, New York: Wiley.

Suppose You Own the World and No One Knows? Conspicuous Consumption, Materialism and Self

Nancy Y.C. Wong, University of Hawaii

ABSTRACT

Is there a connection between materialism and conspicuous consumption? Materialism has been studied both as a personality trait and a value. Material possessions have also been seen to have both private and public meanings. What is the relationship between materialism and individual characteristics? For example, is there a correspondence between private and public meanings of possessions to private and public selves? What is the effect of societal values such as individualism and collectivism on materialism and conspicuous consumption? A study was conducted to look at the relationships between two existing conceptualizations of materialism and suggest some possible connections between materialism and conspicuous consumption. In addition, the study also tested the moderating effects of individual measures in self-consciousness and individualism-collectivism on materialism.

INTRODUCTION

Conspicuous consumption seems to be making a strong comeback. From New York to New Delhi, sales of luxury brands are experiencing double digit growth.[1] After years of retreat, affluent consumers seems to be coming out of hibernation to indulge their appetites in finer things. America's economic growth recovery over the past years has certainly helped, but it leaves the question of whether there is something more than simply a pure "income" effect to this phenomenon. Is it simply a pendulum's swing back to the free-spending days of the late 80's, after the austere beginning in the 90's? What is behind the "yuppie" culture anyway? What is the relationship between the "public" consumption of luxury products and materialism? Is materialism related to individual achievement and the desire to flaunt one's success?

Why do we study materialism and the consumption of luxuries? Because materialists place a high level of importance on acquiring more possessions (Belk 1985, Fournier & Richins 1991, Richins & Dawson 1992), marketers may wish to learn how to better position their products to appeal to consumers' materialistic desires. The business of catering to customers' materialistic desires are by no means a small one. In a 1991 worldwide study of 14 product categories (*haute couture, pret a porter*, perfume, jewelry, watches, leather goods, shoes, cars, wine, champagne, spirits, tableware, crystals and porcelain), McKinsey & Co. estimated that the luxury goods market was around $60 billion (Dubois and Duquesne, 1993). In addition, since high levels of materialism have been empirically associated with low levels of happiness and life satisfaction (Belk 1984, 1985; Kasser & Ryan 1993; Richins & Dawson 1992), social policy makers may be interested in how to reduce levels of materialism. And because materialism is a central driving force in modern consumer society (Cushman 1990; Looft 1971), academicians studying the nature of marketing and consumption may wish to explore materialism simply because of its theoretical importance.

---

[1]"Luxury steals back", Fortune, pp.112-119, January 1995; "The return of luxury", Fortune, p.18, October 17, 1994; "Luxuriating a bit", Economist , p. 60, July 2, 1994; "Luxury's tide turns", Brandweek, pp. 18-22, March 7, 1994.

RELATIONSHIP BETWEEN MATERIALISM AND CONSPICUOUS CONSUMPTION

Popular notions of materialism

At the lay person's level, there is a general tendency to equate materialism with conspicuous consumption. That is, behaviors most often associated with materialism involve conspicuous consumption, in which product satisfaction is derived from audience reaction rather than utility in use. Not only are materialists viewed as "driven" to consume more, they are also seen to focus on the consumption of "status goods" (Fournier & Richins, 1991; Mason, 1981). Ger and Belk (1994) also found that materialism is commonly related to the competitive display of success and status in a "Veblenesque" fashion in their cross-cultural qualitative research on materialism. The prototypical materialists mentioned as examples are Donald Trump, Imelda Marcos and the self- indulgent Sherman McCoy in the book "Bonfire of the Vanities" (Hirschman 1990).

On the other hand, materialism is seen quite differently in academia. Recent work on materialism has resulted in two different understanding of this phenomenon, materialism as a personality trait and materialism as a value. Neither of these explicitly define materialism as including a predilection for luxury items or conspicuous consumption. But closer examination will reveal that both of them are implicitly consistent with the popular belief that materialist favor showy luxury goods.

Materialism as a personality trait

In his study on the meaning of material possessions, Belk (1984) suggested that our possessions are a major contributor to and reflection of our identities. By ascribing such meaning to possessions, these possessions become the means by which we strive to assert, complete, or attain our "ideal" self. Based on his conceptualization of possessions as "extended self", Belk (1985) sees materialism as akin to personality traits. This includes three original traits of possessiveness, nongenerosity, and envy; and a fourth trait of preservation, which was added in cross-cultural studies of the materialism scale (Ger and Belk, 1993).

Belk sees possessiveness as a concern about loss of possessions and a desire for the greater control of ownership. Since experiences are also potential possessions, there is a tendency to make experiences tangible through souvenirs and photographs. This tendency was later redefined as a new materialistic trait named preservation. Nongenerosity is defined as "an unwillingness to give or share possessions with others", which also includes a reluctance to lend or donate possessions to others and negative attitudes toward charity. Finally, envy is viewed as a desire for other's possessions and the envious person resents those who own the desired possessions. (cf. Belk 1985)

While neither possessiveness, nongenerosity, envy, nor preservation explicitly include conspicuous consumption, materialism and conspicuous consumption are implicitly linked through the personality trait of envy. In the words of Veblen: "In order to gain and hold the esteem of men, it is not sufficient merely to possess wealth or power. The wealth or power must be put in evidence, for esteem is only awarded on evidence" (p.42, Veblen 1899). In other words, expensive items will not serve their other-oriented function unless such possessions are "conspicuous" and in plain view. However, in addition to admiration, such possessions could also be the source of envy. (Such envy could be deadly too, as what have been witnessed in teenage killings for expensive sports jackets and athletic shoes in urban ghettos.) Envy is linked to conspicuous consumption because one only envies the possessions of others when one can not easily obtain comparable possessions. As far as commercially available items are concerned, the primary reason one could not obtain a comparable item is because one couldn't afford it. Therefore, envy is almost always directed at expensive or luxury products. To be an envious person is to place a high value on these expensive products, so envy is inexorably linked to the dynamic of conspicuous consumption.

Materialism as a value

Richins (e.g. Fournier & Richins 1991; Richins 1994a, 1994b; Richins and Dawson 1992) sees materialism as a value (the basic enduring belief that it is important to own material possessions) rather than a behavior or personality variable. This includes beliefs about acquisition centrality, and the role of acquisition in happiness and success. Acquisition centrality refers to the importance materialists attach to acquiring more possessions which allows acquisitiveness to function as a life-goal for them. Materialists also hold strongly to the belief that owning or acquiring the right possessions is a key to happiness and well-being. Finally, Richins also defines materialists as people who believe success can be judged by the things people own.

In principle, none of these three belief domains (acquisition centrality, happiness, or success) is necessarily tied to conspicuous consumption. The devoted beer can collector may have no patience for designer suits and Rolex watches, yet he may be a materialist in all three of these areas; wishing to acquire more beer cans (acquisition centrality), believing that he would be much happier if he succeeds (happiness), and judging his success by the quality of his collection (success). Nonetheless, in mainstream capitalist culture, success is usually defined in financial terms, which is why the term "successful" is often used as a polite euphemism for wealthy. If materialists believe that success can be visibly demonstrated through possessions, it stands to reason that expensive luxury goods would be a natural mechanism for doing so. This inference is confirmed by empirical evidence which showed that in comparison with low materialists, high materialists are more likely to value expensive objects, items that convey prestige, and objects that enhance the owner's appearance (Richins 1994). In sum, we have seen that in both the popular and the academic view materialism and conspicuous consumption are closely linked.

> *H1:* The "success" and "envy" dimensions of materialism
> should be correlated.

CONSPICUOUS CONSUMPTION AND THE SELF

Possessions and meanings

Past research had established the significance of our material possessions to our self identities. McCracken (1988) suggested that possessions may be especially important in cultures where social and cultural categories are diffused and when the environment undergoes constant and rapid change. As a result, given the amorphous and fluid quality of identity, people will "satisfy the freedom and fulfill the responsibility of self-definition....through the systematic appropriation of the meaningful properties of good" (p.80). In his examination of the relationship between possessions and our sense of self, Belk (1988) found that it is a dual process that works in both directions. That is, not only do we inject our self-

identities into our possessions, we also incorporate our possessions into our self-identities, which is reflected in a process that he called "self-extensions".

In her study into the special meaning of possessions, Richins (1994a) found that in comparison to people who are low in materialism, people high in materialism are more likely to value things that signal accomplishment, enhance social status and appearance of the owners. This is also where the question of private versus public meaning of posseisions is raised. According to Richins (1994b), "public meanings are the subjective meanings assigned to an object by outside observers (non-owners) of the object, that is, by members of society at large". Although such assigned meanings often vary by individuals, it is the agreed-upon element of meaning by members of the general population or social subgroups that constitutes an object's shared public meaning. On the other hand, the private meaning of an object is the sum of the subjective meanings it holds for a particular individual. Such meanings could include the object's public meanings as well as the person's personal history or experience with the object. Richins (1994b) further postulated that public and private meanings differ in their sphere of influence. Due to the consensual nature of public meanings, they influence the type of possessions people choose to communicate aspects of themselves to others. Public meanings are also likely to have an important influence in shaping desire, in determining the types of things people hope to acquire. Private meanings, on the other hand, are more important in determining consumers' feelings about the things they already possess.

The self

It has been suggested that all cultures see the self as divided into an inner, private self, consisting of emotions, desires, personal values, memories, impulses, etc., and an outer, public self, based on social roles and the persona presented to others (Lebra 1992, Markus & Cross 1990, Markus & Kitayama 1991). In addition, there are different types of self-esteem that are based on one's ability in reaching such goals. For example, the private self correponds to self-evaluation based on reaching personal goals whereas the public self is based on the evaluations of significant others (Breckler & Greenwald 1986). These different notions of self also have implications for the focus of attention and resources in the consumption of publicly visible possessions. It is postulated here that when purchasing publicly displayed possessions (e.g. a watch), the public self would predominate while in the case of possessions that aren't as publicly visible (e.g. a bed), the private self would predominate. This relates to the current overt conspicuous consumption in several ways. First, people who are more concerned about how they may appear to others are likely to be more concerned with the public meaning of their possessions. This notion is akin to Richin's findings that people high on materialism are more likely to value possessions that convey prestige, enhance appearance and social status. (Implicit in this argument is that the possessions must be "public". Such special meanings would be lost without an audience.) Second, people whose private self are more salient are likely to value the hedonic pleasures, the "being" aspects of their possessions. This is also related to Belk's notion of self-extension in that when one invests one's self-identity in a possession, it is likely to be the private meaning idiosyncratic to the individual's experience/history with the possession.

> *H2:* The public self should be positively correlated with the
> dimensions of materialism.
> *H3:* The private self should be negatively correlated with the
> dimensions of materialism.

H4: *Social anxiety should be positively correlated with the dimensions of materialism.*

Another aspect of self that relates to materialism and conspicuous consumption is the construct of individualism-collectivism (Triandis, 1986; Triandis, Bontempo, Villareal, Asai, & Lucca, 1988; Triandis, McCusker & Hui, 1990). Although this construct is generally used in describing differences between cultures, many of the values associated with individualism and collectivism seem to bear important similarities to the value (i.e. Richins & Dawson's Scale) conceptualization of materialism. In particular, the defining attributes of the construct could bear some significant relationships to materialism. First, individualism has been characterized by emotional detachment from ingroups, primacy of personal goals over ingroup goals, competition and individual achievement. These values correspond to the goal of conspicuous consumption, which is the very "public" nature of luxury consumption as a reflection of one's success and achievement. Second, collectivism has been descibed by the attributes of family integrity, self definition through social roles, hierarchical social structures, and strong ingroup/outgroup distinctions. In a similar vein, these values could correspond to the primacy of personal relationships over "things" and physical possessions. Therefore, people who are highly individualistic are likely to invest more emotions/self-identities in things, be highly competitive, and value their own achievement and success. They may also value their possessions more for their public meaning. On the other hand, people who are collectivistic are likely to value things that enhance their relationships with others within the social ingroups but elevate their social status to members from the outgroups. As a result, they may value a possession due to its private meaning.

H5: *Individualism should be positively correlated with the dimensions of materialism.*

H6: *Collectivism should be negatively correlated with the dimensions of materialism.*

RESEARCH QUESTIONS

Materialism and conspicuous consumption

Based on the earlier discussion, among the dimensions of the trait conceptualization of materialism by Belk (1985), envy could be related to conspicuous consumption because of a person's envy for others' possessions which are better than his/her own. Also, among the values conceptualization of materialism (Richins & Dawson 1991), success could be most easily linked to conspicuous consumption because of a person's desire to flaunt his/her success through material possessions. As a result, one would expect the dimensions of materialism that relate to conspicuous consumption, namely "envy" and "success", to be positively correlated to each other.

Materialism and self

Given that public meaning of possessions are consensual in nature, the type of possessions that people use to communicate their self-identities to others must also relate to their public self. In addition, since such public meanings are also instrumental in shaping people's desires for acquisition, one would expect the existing measures of materialism to be highly correlated with the public self. Conversely, the same argument would also imply that materialism should be negatively correlated with one's private self. Social anxiety is expected to be positively related to the dimensions of materialism for several reasons. First, in addition to the very public or other-directedness of the materialistic desires and motiva-

tion, many of these values or traits such as success and envy could well be anxiety arousing because they could raise doubts about one's social standing and feelings of inadequacies. Second, due to the "image management" aspect of these values and traits, there could well be some amount of anxiety associated with many of them. Similarly, due to the correspondence in values between individualist's emphasis in personal achievement and success orientation, individualist values and measures of materialism should also be highly correlated. Finally, collectivist values should lead to a preference of personal ties and collective identity over individual achievement and therefore, should be negatively related to the dimensions of materialism.

METHODOLOGY

Respondents

Data collection was conducted as part of a larger study in the fall of 1994 in a Midwestern university. Subjects were 200 (110 female) undergraduates from an introductory marketing course who participated in the study to fulfill a course requirement. The object of interest is to look at the relationships between the existing measures of materialism and the two operationalizations of self.

Measures

Materialism. Two different materialism scales were used in this study: Ger and Belk's (1993) revised materialism scale and Richins and Dawson's (1992) materialism scale. In their cross-cultural study on materialism, Ger and Belk (1993) modified and expanded some scale items from Belk's (1985) original materialism scale. The modified scale (Mat_{pers}) includes 4 subscales:

(1) possessiveness–the inclination and tendency to retain control or ownership of one's possessions. This subscale consisted of 4 items, e.g. "I get very upset if something is stolen from me, even if it has little monetary value."

(2) nongenerosity–an unwillingness to give possessions to or share possessions with others. This subscale consisted of 9 items, e.g. "I enjoy donating things for charity" (reverse scored), or "I don't like to lend things, even to good friends."

(3) envy–a displeasure or ill will at the superiority of another person in happiness, success, reputation, or the possession of anything desirable. This subscale consisted of 5 items, e.g. "there are certain people I would like to trade places with."

(4) preservation–the conservation of events, experiences, and memories in material form. This subscale consisted of 3 items, e.g. "when I travel I like to take a lot of photographs."

Richins and Dawson (1992) on the other hand, conceptualized materialism as a set of centrally held beliefs about the importance of possessions in one's life. Their scale (Mat_{vals}) consists of 3 subscales:

(1) Acquisition centrality–the importance materialists attach to possessions which allows acquisitiveness to function as a life-goal. This subscale consists of 7 items, e.g. "I usually buy only the things I need" (reverse scored).

(2) Happiness–the extent to which materialists view possessions as essential to their satisfaction and well-being in life. This subscale consisted of 6 items, e.g. "I have all the things I really need to enjoy life" (reverse scored).

(3) Success–the belief that one's own and others' success can be judged by what they own. This subscale consisted of 5 items, e.g. "Some of the most important achievements in life include acquiring material possessions."

Operationalization of Private vs Public Self: Self-Consciousness Scale. Fenigstein (1975) defined self-consciousness as the "consistent tendency of persons to direct attention inward or outward". Self-consciousness is also conceived as having three dimensions: public self-consciousness; private self-consciousness; and social anxiety.[2] Public self-consciousness involves a general awareness of the self in relation to others and is related to Mead's (1934) analysis of the self as a social object. Private self-consciousness, in contrast, is similar to Jung's (1933) conception of introversion and is concerned with attending to inner thoughts and feelings. Finally, social anxiety is defined by a discomfort in the presence of others. Thus, public and private self-consciousness refer to the process of self-attention, while social anxiety involves a reaction to this process. Research shows that the three dimensions of self-consciousness have an impact on behavior. In particular, people high on private self-consciousness are more attentive and knowledgeable about their own attitudes than are those who score low on this dimension. Markus and Kitayama (1991) showed that people with independent construal of self are more sensitive to self-relevant stimuli and information on self-defining attributes. Therefore, a person with an independent view of self is likely to score higher on private self-consciousness and lower on public self-consciousness, in comparison to a person with an interdependent view of self.[3]

Operationaliztion of Individualist vs Collectivist Self: Individualism-Collectivism Scale. It has been suggested that cultures differ in the extent to which cooperation, competition, or individualism are emphasized (Mead 1967). Although allocentrism and idiocentrism are the psychological equivalents (i.e. at the individual rather than societal level) of the collectivism and individualism construct (Hofstede 1980), the individualism and collectivism measures have always been applied at the individual level and aggregated for the culture as a whole. Therefore, the use of individualism-collectivism scale as a reflection of individual value orientation toward allocentrism and idiocentrism is consistent with past research practices.[3]

RESULTS & DISCUSSION

Materialism and Conspicuous Consumption

First, reliabilities (coefficient α) of the subscale items are computed before composite measures are computed. The results are satisfactory for all measures. Coefficient alphas for the subscale

measures are: .78 for public self-consciousness, .75 for private self-consciousness, .83 for social anxiety, .68 for individualism, .44 for collectivism, .82 for success, .76 for centrality, .77 for happiness, .74 for non-generosity, .55 for possessiveness, .27 for envy, and .74 for preservation. Table 1 below lists the correlations between dimensions of both materialism scales, Self-Consciousness Scale and Individualism-Collectivism Scale.

The results show that success and envy are highly correlated (r=.28, p=.000). Therefore, H1 is supported. As discussed earlier, among the dimensions of the trait conceptualization of materialism by Belk (1985), envy could be related to conspicuous consumption because of a person's envy for others' possessions which are better than his/her own. Similarly, among the values conceptualization of materialism (Richins & Dawson 1991), success could be most easily linked to conspicuous consumption because of a person's desire to flaunt his/her success through material possessions. As a result, one would expect to find these two dimensions to be positively correlated because of the common element of conspicuous consumption. Although it is arguable that these two dimensions of materialism could well be linked as a result of other commonalities, it is at least the first piece of supporting evidence in a nomological network of relationships between materialism and conspicuous consumption.

Materialism and Self

All the dimensions of materialism (both traits and values) are also positively correlated with public self-consciousness and almost all relationships are statistically significant. Correlations between public self-consciousness, centrality, and success are $\rho=.26$ (p=.000) and $\rho=.28$ (p=.000) respectively, which is consistent with the notion that the public self should be more salient in the expression of materialistic values. Or conversely, materialistic values have a highly other-directed and public orientation. As expected, almost all dimensions of materialism are negatively correlated with private self-consciousness. Although there are positive correlations between some dimensions of materialism and private self-consciousness, none is statistically significant. Similarly, social anxiety is also positively correlated with the dimensions of materialism. However, only the correlations between social anxiety and envy ($\rho=.19$, p=.009) as well as nongenerosity ($\rho=.25$, p=.000) reach statistical significance. Therefore, there is support for H2, H3 and H4. Finally, a similar pattern of correlations is also found for the materialism and individualism-collectivism constructs. Again, individualism is positively correlated with all dimensions of materialism while the relationships are negative for collectivism. Both H5 and H6 are therefore supported as well.

Based on the preliminary findings from Table 1, it appears that the individual variables that could be most significant in determining levels of materialism (for both the trait and value conceptualizations) are the constructs of individualism-collectivism. In order to test if materialism levels do differ between individuals who are more individualistic or collectivistic, a dummy variable regression analysis is set up by constructing the dummy variable INDH (for high individualism), which takes on the value of 1 or 0 for individuals who score above or below the median on individualism respectively. The use of dummy variable regression allows the estimation of beta coefficients for both groups (high and low individualism) simultaneously and makes use of the whole sample for testing the significance of the coefficient estimates. Since the relationships are exactly the opposite for collectivism using the dummy variable COLLH (for high collectivism), only one regression analysis is shown here. The sample is split at the median of the individualism measure and beta coefficients are estimated for the following formulations:

---

[2]Fenigstein's (1975) self-consciousness scale consists of 23 items that yield three distinct dimensions: public self-consciousness (7 items), private self-consciousness (10 items), and social anxiety (6 items). Research shows that the scale has high test-reset reliability: .84 for public, .70 for private, and .73 for social anxiety. The 23 items are listed in Appendix A.

[3]The independent self has also been called *individualist, egocentric, separate, autonomous, idiocentric,* and *self-contained,* while the interdependent self is also called *sociocentric, holistic, collective, allocentric, ensembled, constitutive, contextualist, connected,* and *relational.*

[4]See Appendix B for the 21 item individualism-collectivism scale used in the study.

TABLE 1

Trait/ Value Measures	Centrality	Happiness	Success	Public SC	Private SC	Social Anxiety	Individ- ualism	Collect- ivism
Centrality	1.00			.26***	.11	.04	.07	-.17*
Happi- ness	.26***	1.00		.16*	.04	.04	.14*	-.23**
Success	.47***	.40***	1.00	.28***	-.10	.05	.20**	-.24**
Envy	.01	.33***	.28***	.04	-.01	.19**	.26***	-.13
Non- generosity	.13	.25***	.37***	-.01	-.16*	.25***	.39***	-.42***
Possessive -ness	.15*	.07	.16*	.14*	-.00	.05	.08	-.21**
Preserva -tion	.15*	.06	.02	.04	.10	.11	-.04	.01

***p < .001, ** p < .01, * p < .05

TABLE 2

Estimates	Grand mean α_0	INDH α_1	IND β_0	INDH β_1	COLL *IND β_2	INDH* COLL β_3	PU β_4	PR β_5	SA β_6	R^2
Mat$_{pers}$	49.50*** (12.88)	-21.31 (17.28)	.09 (.25)	.47 (.32)	-.77** (.30)	.02 (.40)	.54** (.18)	.01 (.11)	-.05 (.12)	.24
Mat$_{vals}$	47.18*** (10.90)	-1.81 (14.58)	.35 (.21)	.20 (.27)	-.56* (.25)	-.37 (.34)	.08 (.15)	-.04 (.10)	.36*** (.10)	.29

Note: Standard errors are in parenthesis; *** p < .001, ** p < .01, * p < .05

$$Mat_{vals} = \alpha_0 + \alpha_1 \, INDH + \beta_0 \, IND + \beta_1 \, INDH*IND + \beta_2 \, COLL + \beta_3 \, INDH*COLL + \beta_4 \, PU + \beta_5 \, PR + \beta_6 SA + \varepsilon_1$$

$$Mat_{pers} = \alpha_0 + \alpha_1 \, INDH + \beta_0 \, IND + \beta_1 \, INDH*IND + \beta_2 \, COLL + \beta_3 \, INDH*COLL + \beta_4 \, PU + \beta_5 \, PR + \beta_6 SA + \varepsilon_1$$

Where IND = composite score on individualism measure;
COLL = composite score on collectivism measure;
INDH = 0 if composite score below median
= 1 if composite score above median;
INDH*IND = interation term to capture residual effect of individualism on people who are above median in individualism;
INDH*COLL = interaction term to capture residual effect of collectivism on people who are above median in individualism;
PU = composite score on public self-consciousness;
PR = composite score on private self-consciousness;
SA = composite score on social anxiety.

Table 2 shows the results of the dummy variable regression analysis. First, it can be seen that the pattern of relationships are identical across both materialism scales (Mat$_{pers}$ and Mat$_{vals}$). Also, the R-square for both regression analyses are .24 and .29 for Mat$_{pers}$ and Mat$_{vals}$ respectively, indicating significant amount of variance explained for the model. As expected, the main effect of individualism on materialism (β_0's) are positive but are not significant. In addition, for individuals high on individualism, there is a residual positive effect of individualism on materialism (β_1's). In the case of Mat$_{pers}$, this residual effect of individualism is even higher than the main effect on materialism ($\beta_0 < \beta_1$). Collectivism, however, has a negative effect for both groups of individuals but the effect is stronger for people low on individualism than it is for people who are high on individualism ($\beta_2 < \beta_3$). Also, the negative effect of collectivism for people low on individualism are statistically significant. Therefore, it can be concluded that levels of collectivism are significant predictors of materialism (for both Mat$_{pers}$ and Mat$_{vals}$). Although individualism has the expected positive effect on materialism, it seems to exert a weaker influence than collectivism.

CONCLUSION

The above results give some empirical support to a popular criticism of materialists about valuing things over people. The results indicate that levels of individualism bear a direct and positive relationship to materialism as defined in our existing literature (Belk 1985; Richins & Dawson, 1992). To the extent that the individualism-collectivism scale is a measure of people's propensities toward individual achievement, competitiveness, and success or toward community, group goals, and harmony, the results do suggest that high materialists value things and achievement over people and relationships. In addition, the results also support the other-directed orientation of materialism. That is, materialism is far more influenced by our desires for image management, keeping up appearances than what it really means to us personally. Finally, materialists in general do tend to link conspicuous consumption to the desire for display of success and to arouse the envy of others.

The findings from this study are exciting in several ways. First, it might be one of the first studies to look at the relationships between one's value orientation (individualism-collectivism) and materialism, as well as the linkages between private and public meanings of possessions to the self. Secondly, it also brings up a potential linkage between materialism and conspicuous consumption that has not been explored in the past. The relationships between individualism-collectivism and materialism seem contradictory in view of the current surge in luxury consumption in many East Asian countries, which are generally considered to be collectivist societies. This suggest several possibilities for future research: (1) examine applicability of current conceptualizations of materialism in these cultures; (2) re-examine the linkage between materialistic values and their expressions; and continue to (3) look at relationship between conpicuous consumption and achievement motivation.

REFERENCES

Aron, A. & Aron, E.N. (1986). *Love and the Expansion of Self: Understanding Attraction and Satisfaction.* New York: Hemisphere Publishing Corporation.

Aron, A., Aron, E. N., and Smollan, D. (1992). Inclusion of other in the self scale and the structure of interpersonal closeness. *Journal of Personality and Social Psychology, 63,* 596-612.

Aron, A., Aron, E.N., Tudor, M., & Nelson, G. (1991). Close Relationships as Including Other in Self. *Journal of Personality and Social Psychology, 60,* 241-253.

Belk, R. W. (1984). Three scales to measure constructs related to materialism: reliability, validity and relationships to measures of happiness. In *Advances in Consumer Research,* vol.11, (ed.) Thomas Kinnear, Provo, UT: Association for Consumer Research, 291-97.

Belk, R.W. (1988). Possessions and the extended self. *Journal of Consumer Research, 15,* 139-168.

Belk, R.W. (1985). Materialism: Traits aspects of living in the material world. *Journal of Consumer Research, 12,* 265-80.

Blumberg, Paul, (1974). The decline and fall of the status symbol: Some thoughts on status in a post industrial society. *Social Problems, 21,* 490-98.

Breckler, S.J., and Greenwald, A.G. (1986). Motivational facets of the self, in R.M. Sorrentino and E.T. Higgins (Eds.), *Handbook of Motivation and Cognition,* New York: Guilford, pp. 145-164.

Campbell, Colin (1987). *The Consumer Ethic and the Spirit of Modern Hedonism,* London: Basil Blackwell.

Cushman, P. (1990). Why the self is empty: Toward a historically situated psychology. *American Psychologist, 45,* 599-611.

Douglas, M., and Isherwood, B. (1979). *The World of Goods: Toward an Anthropology of Consumption,* New York: W.W. Norton.

Dubois, Bernard, and Patrick Duquesne (1993). The market for luxury goods: Income versus culture, *European Journal of Marketing, 27*(1), 35-45.

Felson, Marcus (1978). Invidious distinction among cars, clothes, and suburbs. *Public Opinion Quarterly, 42,* 49-58.

Fields, G. (1989). *Gucci on the ginza: Japan's new consumer generation,* New York: Kodansha international

Fournier, S. & Richins, M.L. (1991). Some theoretical and popular notions concerning materialism . In *To have possessions: A handbook on ownership and property. Journal of Social Behavior and Personality, 6,* 403-414.

Ger, Guliz, and Belk, R.W. (1993). Cross-cultural differences in materialism. Working paper.

Ger, Guliz, and Belk, R.W. (1994). Global and Local Meanings in Materialism: A Qualitative Study Across Cultures. Working paper.

Hirschman, Elizabeth C. (1990). Secular immortality and the American ideology of affluence, *Journal of Consumer Research, 17,* 31-42.

Ho, D.Y.F. (1977). On the concept of face. *American Journal of Sociology, 81*(4), 72- 78.

Hofstede, Geert, and M.H. Bond (1988). The Confucius Connection: From Cultural Roots to Economic Growth. *Organizational Dynamics, 16*(4), 4-21.

Hsu, F. (1981). *American and Chinese: Passage to differences.* Honolulu, HI: University of Hawaii Press.

Hsu, F.L.K. (1983). *Rugged Individualism Reconsidered.* Knoxville, TN: The University of Tennessee Press.

James, W. (1890). *The Principles of Psychology.* New York: Holt.

Kasser, T. and Ryan, R. M. (1993). A dark side of the American dream: Correlates of financial success as a central life aspiration. *Journal of Personality and Social Psychology, 65,* 410-422.

Lebra, Takie S. (1992). Self in Japanese culture. In N. Rosenberger (ed.), *Japanese Sense of Self,* Cambridge, England: Cambridge University Press.

Lancaster, S. & Foddy, M. (1988). Self-extensions: A conceptualization. *Journal for the Theory of Social Behavior, 18,* 77-94.

Markus, H. and Cross, S. (1990). The interpersonal self. In L.A. Previn (Ed.), *Handbook of Personality: Theory and Research* (pp.576-608). New York: Guilford Press.

Markus, H. R., and Kitayama, S. (1991). Culture and the self: Implications for cognition, emotion, and motivation. *Psychological Review, 98,* 224-53.

Maslow, A.H. (1970). *Motivation and personality* (2nd ed.). New York: Harper & Row.

Mason, Roger (1981). *Conspicuous Consumption: A Study of Exceptional Consumer Behavior,* New York: St. Martin Press.

McCracken, Grant D. (1988). *Culture and consumption,* Bloomington, IN: Indiana University Press.

Richins, M.L. (1994a). Special possessions and the expression of material values. *Journal of Consumer Research,* forthcoming.

Richins, M.L. (1994b). Valuing things: The public and private meanings of possessions. *Journal of Consumer Research,* forthcoming.

Richins, M.L., and Dawson, S . (1992). A consumer values orientation for materialism and its measurement: Scale development and validation. *Journal of Consumer Research,*19, 303-16.

Triandis, H.C., Bontempo, R., Villareal, M.J., Asai, M., and Lucca, N. (1988). Individualism and collectivism: Cross-cultural perspectives on self-ingroup relationships, *Journal of Personality and Social Psychology,* 54(2), 323-338.

Triandis, H.C., McCusker C., and Hui, C.H. (1990). Multimethod probes of individualism and collectivism, *Journal of Personality and Social Psychology,* 59(5), 1006-1020.

Trafimow, D., Triandis, H.C., & Goto S. (1991). Some tests of the distinction between the private self and the collective self. *Journal of Personality and Social Psychology, 60,* 649-655.

Triandis, H.C. (1989). The self and social behavior in differing cultural contexts. *Psychological Review,* 96, 506-20.

Veblen, Thorstein (1899). *The Theory of the Leisure Class,* New York: Mentor Book.

Nationality, Materialism, And Possession Importance

Cynthia Webster, Mississippi State University
Robert C. Beatty, Mississippi State University

ABSTRACT

The research reported in this paper explored the effects of nationality on consumers' level of materialism and possession importance. Specifically, an assessment was made of U.S. and Thai consumers' degree of materialism and the nature of the relationship between U.S. and Thai consumers' public and private selves and possession importance. The results reveal that Thai consumers tend to be more materialistic than U.S. consumers. Although U.S. and Thai consumers place equivalent levels of importance on the centrality and happiness components of the materialism construct, the Thai consumers tend to place more importance on the success component of materialism. Further, U.S. and Thai consumers differ with respect to the relationship between the extent to which possessions reflect the private and public selves and possession importance. More specifically, U.S. consumers place more importance on possessions that reflect the private self and Thai consumers place more importance on possessions that reflect the public self.

INTRODUCTION

Although materialism is one of the most important values of relevance to the study of consumer behavior, little is known about the construct, particularly on a cross-cultural basis. By using samples drawn from the U.S. and Thailand, we explore Western and Eastern levels of materialism. We also examine Western and Eastern self-concepts and how they relate to the importance placed on possessions.

We begin, however, by reviewing the literature on materialism, nationality and materialism, and possession importance. Based on the literature, we develop hypotheses regarding the linkages among the constructs of nationality, materialism, and possession importance. Next, we will describe the methodology used to meet the objectives of the study. The findings and their implications are then presented and discussed.

Materialism

Although materialism has been defined in myriad ways, most researchers agree that it regards placing a relatively high level of importance on material objects (e.g., Belk 1984; Csikszentmihalyi and Rochberg-Halton 1978; Rassuli and Hollander 1986; ; Rochberg-Halton 1986; Ward and Wackman 1971). The construct has been described as a way of being, a mind-set, a focus on acquiring and possessing (Rassuli and Hollander 1986). Thus, materialists are those who view possessions and their acquisition as vital to their lifestyle and sense of self (Richins and Dawson 1992). Materialists revere things and the pursuit of things becomes the focal point from which their lives are structured and the orientation of their behaviors (Bredemeier and Toby 1960). According to Belk (1984), materialists are likely to judge their own and others' success by the quantity and quality of possessions owned (Rassuli and Hollander 1986; Richins and Dawson 1992). Further, materialists tend to value possessions based on cost rather than on satisfactions they yield (Heibroner 1956).

Although several measures of materialism appear in the literature, most are plagued with the lack of commonly accepted standards for scale development (see Richins and Dawson (1992) for a detailed critique). There have been two major approaches to the measurement of materialism. The first type infers materialism from measures of related constructs. For example, materialism has been assessed by the nature of wishes expressed by children and the kinds of jobs they desire when they become adults (Dickins and Ferguson 1957). Some authors have inferred an individual's level of materialism from personality-test batteries (e.g., Belk 1984, 1985, Burdsal 1975). As another relatively indirect measure of materialism, Inglehart 1981) identified postmaterialistic societies in which individuals emphasize such values as belonging and self-expression instead of material possessions.

The second type measures materialism more directly through the use of attitude scales. Richins and Dawson (1992) have done extensive work done in this area. These authors developed a values-oriented materialism scale with three themes. The first theme, *acquisition centrality*, suggests that materialists tend to place possessions and the process of acquiring possessions at the center of their lives. Materialists with acquisition centrality tend to structure their lives and orient their behaviors around either their possessions or the process of obtaining possessions. The second theme, *acquisition as the pursuit of happiness*, states that materialists tend to view their possessions and their acquisition as a means of providing the materialist with some level of personal well-being or satisfaction with their lives. Materialists who acquire as the pursuit of happiness view their possessions or the acquisition of possessions as a way to derive pleasure or self-satisfaction. The final theme, *possession-defined success*, advances that materialists tend to base their own and others' success on the number and quality of possessions. Materialists with possession-defined success attach some level of social status to themselves and others within society according to possession quantity and quality. The validation tests revealed that consumers high in materialism desire a higher level of income, place more emphasis on financial security and less on interpersonal relationships, prefer to spend more on themselves and less on others, and are less satisfied with their lives.

Outside the arena of personality traits and values, very little research effort has been expended on linking consumer characteristics to materialism. One study, however, found that women are more sharing and less materialistic than men (Rudmin 1990). The explanation posed by the authors was that for women, material goods constitute a part of social relations, and for men, material goods are used to aid the establishment of power and competitive relations.

A limited amount of research has examined whether some nationalities are more materialistic than others.

Nationality and Materialism

Although much of the research in the consumer behavior literature views materialism as an individual phenomenon, recent research is beginning to expand the view by including the role materialism plays within and across various cultures. One of these studies compared the degree of materialism in the U.S. to the Netherlands, a country whose prosperity equals that of the U.S. (Dawson and Bamossy 1990). The sample was comprised of middle-class households in both countries. The results indicated that levels of materialism were very similar in each nation across the various scales. However, the sample in the Netherlands revealed slightly higher levels of "possessiveness" toward material goods than the American sample.

Another study compared materialistic values among consumers in Europe, the U.S., and Turkey (Ger and Belk 1990). The

Advances in Consumer Research
Volume 24, © 1997

results revealed that Turkish consumers were simultaneously more materialistic and more generous than American and European consumers. The authors explained that factors unique to the Turkish culture may account for the unexpected findings. Specifically, Turkey has an ancient history of prosperity and perhaps this cultural legacy continues to reveal itself today.

Although there is no published empirical work that compares materialistic values among consumers in Western and Eastern cultures, speculations have been made of Eastern consumers rating higher on materialism than their Western counterparts (Wong and Ahuvia 1995). East Asian consumers, in particular, seem to have an attraction for high image, high status products (i.e., Chanel, Gucci, Louis Vuitton). Indeed, Asia is now the largest market for luxury goods (*Far Eastern Economic Review* 1990). Further, an analysis of advertisements revealed that Japanese advertising stresses status to a much greater extent than U.S. advertising (Belk and Pollay 1985).

Low and high materialists have been found to like the same number of objects but to differ in the kinds of objects they find significant Richins 1994). Compared with low materialists, high materialists are more likely to value expensive objects, items that convey prestige, and objects that enhance the owner's goods looks. Given East Asians preference for precisely these types of items, it seems logical to hypothesize that they are more materialistic than U.S. consumers.

In their cross-cultural study on materialism, Ger and Belk (1993) found an emergence of a "world standard package of goods" such that consumers who do not have the items in this package feel deprived. Such sentiments are particularly acute in the less economically developed nations, leading to higher levels of materialism in these countries. These researchers also found a strong correlation between dynamic changes (i.e., economic) and a rise in materialism. Compared to the U.S., Thailand is a less economically developed nation, and is experiencing rapid economic growth (Textor 1995). These findings and observations lead to the following hypothesis:

H1:   Thai consumers are more materialistic than U.S. consumers.

Perceptions of Self and Possession Importance

The notion of a relationship between one's self and one's possessions has been intuitively appealing for years (e.g., Gardner and Levy 1955). It has even been suggested that this relationship is the most fundamental and influential fact of consumer behavior (Belk 1988).

The importance of a possession is based on the meaning attached to the item by the owner. Possessions have a private meaning in that they are used "...as markers to remind ourselves who we are" (Wallendorf and Arnould 1988, p. 531). They characterize the personal values and beliefs of the owner (Richins and Dawson 1992). Thus, we actually derive our sense of self from our possessions. Possessions also have a public meaning in that they are used to express our sense of self to others. Possessions convey our connection to others and help express who we think we are (e.g., Levy 1981; McCracken 1986). Similarly, the self can be divided into two parts. One's private self is comprised of emotions, desires, personal values, memories, impulses, etc. On the other hand, one's public self is based on social roles, family relationships, national or ethnic affiliations. In other words, the public self is the persona presented to others (e.g., Markus and Kitayama 1991; Wong and Ahuvia 1995). Regardless of any external influence (i.e., culture), it seems logical to expect that a positive relationship will exist between the importance placed on a possession and the meaning (both private and public) attached to the possession. In other words, the more a possession reminds ourselves who we are and conveys who we are to others, the more important and valued that possession becomes. Thus,

H2:   For both U.S. and Thai consumers, there will be a significant positive relationship between the public and private meanings attached to a possession and possession importance.

Because Eastern and Western cultures place different emphases on public and private selves and because of the evidence relating self to possession importance, there is reason to suspect that the nature of the linkage between the types of selves and possession importance will vary according to culture. Hence, we agree with Wong and Ahuvia's (1995) argument that Eastern and Western conceptualizations of self play a significant role in determining the way materialism operates cross-culturally.

Conceptualizations of self have been proposed by Markus and Kitayama (1991) and Triandis (1989). According to Markus and Kitayama, there are two aspects of self: the independent self, which is associated with Western cultures, and the interdependent self, which is commonly found in Eastern cultures. The independent and interdependent selves correspond with Triandis' private and collective selves, respectively. The independent self, also known as separate, autonomous, individualistic, etc., is based on the belief of the inherent separateness of distinct individuals (Wong and Ahuvia 1995). The corresponding private self refers to one's feelings, motivations, and thoughts. Thus, the behavior of the individuals who place emphasis on the independent or private self is guided by their preferences, personal values and convictions, and other internal traits.

The interdependent, collective, or relational self is based on the underlying connectedness of human beings to one another. For those with a dominant interdependent self, one's identity is grounded in one's familial, cultural, and social relationships. The corresponding collective self focuses on how one is viewed by others (i.e., family). It follows, then, that the behavior of individuals who place emphasis on the interdependent or collective self is guided not by self-knowledge, but rather self-in-relation to specific others in particular contexts.

As mentioned previously, material possessions serve the basic function of either reflecting the owner's self-identity or communicating the owner's connection to others. In the case of conspicuous possessions (i.e., jewelry, car, home, clothing, etc.), it seems likely that possession importance would relate more to the private self for those from individualistic cultures and that possession importance would relate more to the public self for those from collectivistic cultures. In other words, U.S and Thai consumers are expected to differ with respect to the relationship between the extent to which possessions reflect the private and public selves and conspicuous possession importance. More specifically,

H3:   The relationship between the private self and conspicuous possession importance will be stronger for U.S. consumers than for Thai consumers.

H4:   The relationship between the public self and conspicuous possession importance will be stronger for Thai consumers than for U.S. consumers.

TABLE 1
Demographic Characteristics of U.S. and Thai Samples

Characteristic	U.S.		Thai		χ^2
	n	Percentage	n	Percentage	
Sex					.24
Female	46	56.1	45	52.9	
Male	36	43.9	40	47.1	
Marital Status					2.12*
Married	55	67.1	72	84.7	
Not married	27	32.9	13	15.3	
Age					.98
22 - 34	9	10.9	11	12.9	
35 - 44	24	29.2	26	30.6	
45 - 54	21	25.6	24	28.2	
55 - 64	17	20.7	14	16.5	
65 and older	11	13.4	10	11.8	
Social Class					.48
Upper	13	15.8	15	17.6	
Middle	50	60.9	49	57.6	
Lower	19	23.2	21	24.7	

*p = .06; all other chi-square values are not significant (p > .10).

METHOD

Possessions

To select the specific product categories, consumers in a pilot study from both the U.S. and Thailand were asked to identify their most "visible" or conspicuous possessions. Although there were one or two individuals who listed possessions such as pets, there was a high level of agreement among the respondents that five types of possessions were most visible: car, house, clothes, jewelry, and furniture.

Sample

The two consumer samples were chosen from major metropolitan areas in the U.S. and Thailand, specifically Dallas and Bangkok. During a one-week time period in the U.S. and another one-week time period in Thailand, trained interviewers selected respondents from two mid-scale shopping malls. The malls were chosen because of their appeal to middle-socioeconomic customers. The selection of the sample was based on the procedures introduced by Sudman (1980). Specifically, the field researchers were stationed in different mall entrances, and their location changed every three hours. Interviews were conducted at different times of day to prevent potential cyclical bias. Special efforts were made to ensure that sample selection was not based on interviewers' judgments. Interviewers were instructed to draw a systematic sample from among the shoppers at the entrance. Specifically, a selection rule was instituted (and supervised) by which individuals were counted as they passed from a specific direction (e.g., left to right) to a certain point in the corridor (about 50 feet from the interviewer), and every nth person was selected. The number of people to be skipped was set according to a predetermined measure of shopping traffic at each location. As Sudman (1980) argued, these procedures cannot ensure "full" protection against interviewer selection bias, but they can help greatly to reduce it.

The interviewers were instructed to intercept individuals until they each had 25 consumers who met the screening requirements (there were 4 interviewers in each country). The screening requirements, which were asked by the researchers, were as follows: (1) the individual had to be a native of the country in which the interview took place, and (2) the individual had to have been the primary decider for the each of their five visible possessions. Those meeting these two screening requirements were asked to participate in the study. Of the 100 consumers who were asked to participate in each country, 82 from the U.S. and 85 from Thailand agreed to complete the survey. Table 1 provides a summary of the sample characteristics. The data in Table 1 indicates that the two national subsamples are comparable with respect to their demographic and socioeconomic characteristics. However, the chi-square value and subsample percentages for marital status suggest that there is a greater proportion of Thais who are married.

Measures

The questionnaire was comprised of measures of four primary constructs: materialism, possession importance, the extent to which the possessions reflect the private self, and the extent to which the possessions reflect the public self.

The materialism scale developed by Richins and Dawson (1992) was used in this study. As described previously, this eighteen-item, values-oriented scale has three components: possession-defined success, acquisition as the pursuit of happiness, and acquisition centrality.

The first step taken to develop measures for the other three constructs was to make an exhaustive list of scale items based on previous research (i.e., Belk 1985; Holbrook; Prentice 1987; Richins and Dawson 1992; Wheeler, Reis, and Bond 1989; Triandris 1994; Wong and Ahuvia 1995). The six-item possession importance scale included elements such as the importance placed on the item, how dear the possession was to the consumer, etc. The scale for measuring the extent to which a possession reflects the private self had 7 items, including those relating to the extent to which the possession expresses who the owner is, symbolizes the owner's personal values, fits with his or her tastes, etc. The public self scale had 10 items, including those which related to the extent to which a possession fits with one's profession, social roles, the image one wants others to have of him or her, etc.

In both countries, each of the three lists was screened by 3 consumer behavior graduate students, 3 marketing faculty, and 6 consumers outside the academic environment for items that were redundant, ambiguous, irrelevant, or omitted. After several screenings, 5 items were retained for the possession importance scale, 6 for the reflection of private self scale, and 6 for the public self scale. A seven-point Likert scale was used for each of the items. Using a time interval of 13 days and a sample of 18 consumers from the U.S. and 20 from Thailand, the test-retest reliability was .91 and .89, respectively. To help prevent social desirability bias that would result from respondents addressing the measures in a manner to make themselves look favorable, the items were mixed together and stated in neutral terms where possible.

To check the dimensionality of the measures, three different factor analyses with a principal component analysis were performed. The results of the factor analysis on the materialism items appear in the top portion of Table 2. Using a scree test, three factors were retained with eigenvalues greater than one. The results show that 15 of the 18 items loaded above .30 on one of the three factors. Although the factor loadings are different, the items generally loaded in the same factors as they did in Richins and Dawson's (1992) study. Both American and Thai materialism scales achieved excellent internal consistency (alphas of .86 and .83, respectively).

The second part of Table 2 reveals the factor analysis results for a possession's reflection of the self. The results show that 10 of the 12 items loaded on two factors: (1) reflection of the private self, and (2) reflection of the public self. Consistent with the research of others (e.g., Belk 1985; Holbrook; Prentice 1987; Richins and Dawson 1992; Wheeler, Reis, and Bond 1989; Triandris 1994; Wong and Ahuvia 1995), a possession reflects the private self when it expresses owners' tastes, preferences, and the way they actually see themselves. On the other hand, the locus of control is external when a possession is perceived as reflecting one's public self. That is, a possession reflects the public self when it expresses owners' familial and social relationships and when an emphasis is placed on the perceptions of others. American and Thai scales achieved adequate internal consistency with alphas of .79 and .68, respectively. Finally, the third part of Table 2 shows that 4 of the 5 possession importance items grouped into one factor with an eigenvalue greater than one. The possession importance scale achieved acceptable reliability in the case of both American (.81) and Thai (.73) samples.

As mentioned previously, information such as sex, marital status, and age was also collected. The occupation and education information for each respondent was collected in a manner that facilitated calculation of the Hollingshead two-factor index of social position (Hollingshead and Redlich 1958).

RESULTS

To determine whether consumers' nationality has a significant effect on their level of materialism, planned comparison tests were performed across nationalities after averaging consumer scores. As can be seen in Table 3, there is a significant difference between U.S. and Thai consumers in their level of materialism. In support of H1, Thai consumers scored higher on overall materialism. Data in Table 3 show that Thai consumers are significantly higher than U.S. consumers on the meaning attributed to success. That is, Thais tend to focus on possessions or material objects when defining success. Consistent with the writing of Wong and Ahuvia (1995), this finding reveals that East Asians tend to place a relatively high degree of importance on other people's perceptions and on the maintenance of their own status. On the other hand, data in Table 3 indicate that U.S. and Thai consumers do not significantly differ on the centrality and happiness components of materialism. This finding suggests that consumers in both cultures place equivalent levels of importance on owning "nice" objects and on acquiring objects.

To investigate the relationship between the extent to which a possession reflects the private or public self and possession importance, several multiple regression analyses were performed. The correlation between the two predictors is low (r=-.09, p=.19); thus, collinearity was not considered a problem. Following other researchers (e.g., Churchill et al. 1976), factor scores were summed to arrive at a consumer's overall possession importance score.

The standardized regression coefficients for thirteen regression models are presented in Table 4. The first part of the table presents the results of regressing private and public selves on general possession importance across all consumers. For the total sample, the two values account for 19 percent of the variance in possession importance. The second part of the table shows that the extent to which possessions reflect the private and public selves has a significant impact on possession importance for both U.S. and Thai consumers, thus supporting H2.

It was hypothesized further that the associations between private self reflection and possession importance will be greater for U.S. consumers than for Thai consumers and that the associations between public self reflection and possession importance will be greater for Thai consumers than for their U.S. counterparts. The difference between the U.S. (.31) and Thai (.15) private self coefficients is significant (t=2.28, p=.05); the same holds true for the difference between U.S. (.17) and Thai(.32) public self coefficients (t=2.05, p=.05). Further, Chow test (Chow 1960) results indicate that the set of coefficients in the regression for U.S. consumers is significantly different from the set of coefficients in the regression for Thai consumers (F=2.89, p<.05). These results provide overwhelming support for H3 and H4.

To understand better the nature of the relationships between private and/or public self reflections and possession importance, the possessions were analyzed separately for both nationalities. As can be seen in the third part of Table 4, the U.S. private self coefficients are particularly strong for consumers' homes, furniture, and jewelry. On the other hand, the Thai public self coefficients are particularly strong for consumers' cars, homes, clothes, and jewelry. These findings are consistent with those of other researchers in that the nature of the self that is "sampled" in consumption behavior must be placed in a cultural context to be adequately understood. Further, these findings suggest that product category moderates the relationships between private and public self reflections and possession importance.

CONCLUSIONS

Although the emphasis placed on materialism and possession importance is noteworthy from a consumer behavior perspective, very little research has examined these constructs cross-culturally. The purpose of the current research was twofold: to explore U.S. and Thai consumers' level of materialism and to determine the nature of the relationship between U.S. and Thai consumers' public and private selves and possession importance.

In general, Thai consumers were found to be more materialistic than U.S. consumers. More specifically, Thai consumers place significantly more importance on the success component of mate-

TABLE 2
Factor Analysis on Materialism, Reflection of Private and Public Selves, and Possession Importance

1. Materialism (from Richins and Dawson 1992)

	Success	Centrality	Happiness
The things I own express how well I'm doing in life	.80		
I notice the material objects other people own	.72		
I like to own things that impress people	.63		
I think material objects are a sign of success	.55		
Acquiring material possessions is an important achievement	.47		
I admire people who own expensive things	.40		
I like a lot of luxury in my life		.73	
I put less emphasis on material things than most people I know		.66	
Buying things gives me a lot of pleasure		.53	
I usually buy only the things I need		.48	
I try to keep my life simple, as far as possessions are concerned		.41	
I would be happier if I owned nicer things			.75
My life would be better if I owned certain things I don't have			.62
I'd be happier if I could afford to buy more things			.53
It bothers me that I can't afford to buy all the things I'd like			.49

2. Private and Public Selves

	Private Self	Public Self
Expresses who I am	.76	
Matches the way I really see myself	.68	
Symbolizes my true personal values	.62	
Fits with my tastes	.55	
Speaks of my self-reliance	.51	
Speaks of others' preferences/expectations of me		.78
Ties in with my desire for social acceptance		.72
Fits my social roles		.64
Speaks of my connectedness to others		.54
Fits with my profession		.43

3. Possession Importance

My ___ is very dear to me	.76
I would be troubled deeply if I lost my ___	.64
My ___ is one of my most prized possessions	.55
I place great importance on my ___	.43

TABLE 3
Mean Factor Scores by Nationality*

	Materialism	Success	Centrality	Happiness
U.S. Consumers	4.84[a]	4.76[a]	4.98[a]	4.81[a]
Thai Consumers	5.09[b]	5.33[b]	5.08[a]	4.92[a]

*Means with the same superscript are not significantly different at p < .05 by Newman-Keuls test.

rialism than their U.S. counterparts. However, nationality appears not to have a significant effect on the other two materialism components, centrality and happiness. While Thais appear to have a greater tendency to use the number and quality of possessions as vehicles to indicate or represent their social status or success, they are similar to U.S. consumers with respect to placing importance on acquiring possessions and to viewing possessions as a means of providing some level of personal well-being. Compared to Thais, U.S. consumers place more importance on possessions that reflect the private self. Conversely, Thais place more importance on possessions that reflect the public self. In sum, the findings were as hypothesized and supported past research on the meaning of self,

TABLE 4
Regression Results

Dependent Variables	Independent Variables		F	R^2
	Private Self	Public Self		
Possession Importance for				
1 All consumers	.24*	.25*	10.29*	.19
2 U.S. consumers	.31*	.17*	10.81*	.17
Thai consumers	.15	.32*	10.31*	.20
3 U.S. consumers				
Auto	.20*	.17*	7.77*	.14
House	.40*	.12	10.92*	.21
Clothes	.22*	.20*	8.82*	.16
Furniture	.41*	.12	11.13*	.22
Jewelry	.36*	.14	10.50*	.19
Thai consumers				
Auto	.13	.36*	10.30*	.18
House	.15	.26*	8.61*	.16
Clothes	.12	.40*	10.92*	.19
Furniture	.19*	.23*	8.80*	.16
Jewelry	.16*	.27*	9.05*	.17

*$p < .05$

the dependent and interdependent selves, and on the individualistic and collectivistic cultures.

Although the results of this study provide some insight into the impact of culture on consumers' level of materialism and possession importance, the results should be viewed with some caution due to two major limitations. First, only one scale—albeit valid and reliable—was used to measure materialism. Thus, future research might use different and/or combined materialism measures. Further, because the East Asian sample used here was selected from Thailand, future research might draw consumers from other East Asian nationalities, such as Japan and Korea. It would be interesting to discover if research relying on alternative materialism scales and samples drawn from different East Asian nationalities would find basically the same kind of relationships among culture, materialism, and possession importance as reported in this study.

REFERENCES

Belk, Russell W. (1984), "Three Scales to Measure Constructs Related to Materialism: Reliability, Validity, and Relationships to Measures of Happiness," in *Advances in Consumer Research*, Vol. 11, ed. Thomas Kinnear, Provo, UT: Association for Consumer Research, 291-297.

_____ (1985), "Materialism: Trait Aspects of Living in the Material World," *Journal of Consumer Research*, 12 (December), 265-280.

_____ and Richard Pollay (1985), "Materialism and Magazine Advertising During the Twentieth Century," in *Advances in Consumer Research*, eds. Elizabeth Hirschman and Morris Holbrook, Provo, UT: Association for Consumer Research, 394-398.

Belk, Russell W. (1988), "Possessions and the Extended Self," *Journal of Consumer Research*, 15 (September), 139-168.

Bredemeier, Harry C. and Jackson Toby (1960), *Social Problems in America: Costs and Casualities in an Acquisitive Society*, New York: Wiley.

Burdsal, Charles, Jr. (1975), "An Examination of Second Order Motivational Factors as Found in Adults," *Journal of Genetic Psychology*, 127 (September), 83-89.

Chow, Gregory C. (1960), "Test of Equality between Sets of Coefficients in Two Linear Regressions," *Econometrika*, 28 (July), 591-605.

Churchill, Gilbert A., Jr., Neil M. Ford, and Orville C. Walker, Jr. (1976), "Organizational Climate and Job Satisfaction in the Salesforce," *Journal of Marketing Research*, 13 (November), 323-332.

Csikszentmihalyi, Mihaly and Eugene Rochberg-Halton (1978), "Reflections on Materialism," *University of Chicago Magazine*, 70 (3), 6-15.

Dawson, Scott and Gary Bamossy (1990), "Isolating the Effect of Non-Economic Factors on the Development of a Consumer Culture: A Comparison of Materialism in the Netherlands and the United States," in *Advances in Consumer Research*, eds. Marvin Goldberg and Gerald Gorn, Provo, UT: Association for Consumer Research, 182-185.

Dickins, Dorothy and Virginia Ferguson (1957), *Practices and Attitudes of Rural White Children and Parents Concerning Money*, Mississippi Agricultural Experiment Station Technical Bulletin 43.

Far Eastern Economic Review (1992), 9 (July).

Gardner, B.B. and Sidney J. Levy (1955), "The Product and the Brand," *Harvard Business Review*, 33 (March-April), 33-39.

Ger, Guliz and Russell W. Belk (1990), "Measuring and Comparing Materialism Cross-Culturally," in *Advances in Consumer Research*, eds. Marvin Goldberg and Gerald Gorn, Provo, UT: Association for Consumer Research, 186-192.

Heilbroner, Robert L. (1956), *The Quest for Wealth: A Study of Acquisitive Man*, New York: Simon & Schuster.

Holbrook, Morris B (1994), "The Nature of Customer Value: An Axiology of Services in the Consumption Experience," in *Service Quality: New Directions in Theory and Practice*, ed. Roland Rust and Richard L. Oliver, Newbury Park, CA: Sage, 21-71.

Hollingshead, A.B. and F.C. Redlich (1958), *Social Class and Mental Illness,* New York: John Wiley and Sons.

Inglehart, Ronald (1981), "Post-materialism in an Environment of Insecurity," *American Political Science Review*, 75 (December), 880-900.

Levy, Sidney J. (1981), "Interpreting Consumer Mythology: S Structural Approach to Consumer Behavior," *Journal of Marketing*, 45 (Summer), 49-61.

Markus, H.R., and Kitayama, S. (1991), "Culture and the Self: Implications For Cognition, Emotion, and Motivation," *Psychological Review*, 98, 224-253.

McCracken, Grant (1986), "Culture and Consumption: A Theoretical Account of the Structure and Movement of the Cultural Meaning of Consumer Goods," *Journal of Consumer Research*, 13 (June), 71-84.

Prentice, Deborah A. (1987), "Psychological Correspondence of Possessions, Attitudes, and Values," *Journal of Personality and Social Psychology*, 53 (December), 993-1003.

Rassuli, Kathleen M. and Stanley C. Hollander (1986), "Desire—Induced, Innate, Insatiable?," *Journal of Macromarketing*, 6 (Fall), 2-24.

Richins, Marsha L. (1994), "Special Possessions and the Expression of Material Values," *Journal of Consumer Research*, 21 (December), 522-533.

_____ and Scott Dawson (1992), "A Consumer Values Orientation for Materialism and Its Measurement: Scale Development and Validation," *Journal of Consumer Research*, 303-316.

Rochberg-Halton, Eugene (1984), "Object Relations, Role Models, and the Cultivation of the Self," *Environment and Behavior*, 16 (May), 335-368.

Rudmin, Floyd W. (1990), "German and Canadian Data on Motivations for Ownership: Was Pythagoras Right?," in *Advances in Consumer Research*, eds. Marvin Goldberg and Gerald Gorn, Provo, UT: Association for Consumer Research, 176-181.

Sudman, Seymour (1980), "Improving the Quality of Shopping Center Sampling," *Journal of Marketing Research*, 17 (November), 423-431.

Textor, Robert B. (1995), "The Ethnographic Futures Research Method: An Application to Thailand," *Futures*, 27 (May), 461-471.

Triandis, H.C. (1989), "The Self and Social Behavior in Differing Cultural Contexts," *Psychological Review*, 96, 506-520.

Wallendorf, Melanie and Arnould, Eric J. (1988), ""My Favorite Things": A Cross-Cultural Inquiry into Object Attachment, Possessiveness, and Social Linkage," *Journal of Consumer Research*, 14 (March), 531-547.

Ward, Scott and Daniel Wackman (1971), "Family and Media Influences on Adolescent Learning," *American Behavioral Scientist*, 14 (January-February), 415-427.

Wheeler, L., H.T. Reis, and M.H. Bond (1989), "Collectivism-Individualism in Everyday Social Life: The Middle Kingdom and the Melting Pot," *Journal of Personality and Social Psychology*, 57 (1), 79-86.

Wong, Nancy and Aaron Ahuvia (1995), "Self-Concepts and Materialism: A Cross Cultural Approach," Winter Educators' Conference, *American Marketing Association*, 112-119.

Failing to Try to Consume: A Reversal of the Usual Consumer Research Perspective

Stephen J. Gould, Baruch College, The City University of New York
Franklin S. Houston, Rutgers University-Camden
JoNel Mundt, University of the Pacific[1]

ABSTRACT

Building on the context of trying to consume, this paper considers what happens when consumers fail to try to consume. Such failure may take two general forms: (1) just not trying (ignoring various consumption solutions) and (2) trying not to try (making an effort not to consume). For each general form there are various reasons or alternatives. Based on this conceptualization, implications are drawn that broaden our view of trying to consume and motivation and that aim at reversing and balancing our usual perspective on consumer research which is skewed toward consumption-seeking and away from failing to try to consume.

INTRODUCTION

Trying to consume which deals with the gap between consumers' reach and their grasp (Bagozzi and Warshaw 1990) has emerged in consumer research as an important theoretical construct. In the main, trying to consume focuses on a goal which a consumer desires but may fail to pursue or achieve because of various expectations in terms of ability to achieve the goal. The Bagozzi and Warshaw model suggests that consumers may try to consume and succeed in achieving their goal, try to consume but fail to achieve their goal, or fail to try altogether. Such variation in possible behavior is consistent with basic psychology which suggests that people approach some things and avoid others (Weiner 1992). This paper focuses on failing to try altogether (avoidance) with the aim of establishing a typological perspective.

Considering the failure to try, we theorize that there are two major categories that emerge: (1) just not trying and (2) trying not to try. Just not trying involves consumers seeing other consumption possibilities but not following up on them. The second type, trying not to try, involves an effort and intention to reduce one's consumption in one or many aspects. Table 1 illustrates the two types and the various reasons/alternatives which are related to them and which will be discussed below.

JUST NOT TRYING

In many consumption situations, consumers may fail to seek new market solutions to their problems or even any market solutions at all. Such behavior may be characterized as "*just not trying*" in that consumers make choices which either ignore or overrule other solutions, even where they may be better in some significant aspect. While just not trying may be a product of varying degrees of ignorance, it also may be also considered in terms of possible alternative behaviors: (1) remaining satisfied with current solutions, (2) engaging in habitual behavior, (3) engaging in inertia or procrastination, (4) allowing impediments to interfere, and (5) being self-reliant.

Remaining Satisfied with Current Solutions

New solutions to old problems are problems in themselves. Finding information regarding alternatives, and then locating the actual (i.e., physical) alternatives requires search effort, and hence search costs, all of which are impacted by a number of personal and situational variables (e.g., Beatty and Smith 1987). Further, adoption of any new solution generally involves transaction costs, start-up costs, and/or switching costs, and frequently superior new solutions are not worth the incremental cost involved in adopting them. Even if the new solution offers a flow of benefits that exceeds the costs involved, an individual must learn of the new solution and how to implement that solution. There is no certainty that this learning will take place.

Engaging in Habitual Behavior

Habits are imbedded attitudes and behaviors that preclude the rational deliberation of alternatives and undercut the prospects for change. Wood (1981) states:

> . . .for the *Gestalt* psychologists our past experiences and the familiar habits and routines to which they give rise are often a block to problem solving and creative thinking–one to be recognized and overcome. However, as Jensen (1960) has argued, there is often value and economy in such habitual routines. When we have available a method of handling a task or classifying objects, we are relatively free to attend elsewhere to the wider context of our activity (p. 534).

Habits can impede new transactions or can preclude the formation of exchange relationships (Bagozzi and Warshaw 1990). Habits vary in strength. In the extreme, the term "habit" has been equated with addiction (Gutherie's usage as described by Sahakian 1976, p. 45). At this level, the behavior will persist even though significant impediments bar the behavior; an example is the smoker who will endure great hardships for a cigarette.

At the other extreme we have learned responses that serve us as decision rules. Included among these are learning that is closely tied to other strongly held values, learning that originates with significant others such as a parent, and learning that is related to important problems in one's life. Examples (respectively) of these can be a person's unwillingness to eat pork, hygiene practices children learn from their parents, and the decisions by persons who experience allergic reactions to avoid sulfites commonly found in wines or at salad bars. Such a conscious decision rule is not to be confused with habitual behavior.

What distinguishes the habit from a simple decision rule is that a habit is "a tendency to respond in a particular way *to a wide variety of circumstances*" (Gutherie, 1938, p. 65, quoted in Sahakian, 1976, p. 45). In the smoking example, the behavior will occur under the most extreme of circumstances. The salad bar example illustrates a behavior that looks habitual but is simply repeat purchase behavior; however, with time the salad bar decision rule could be so ingrained that new information that potentially might influence the behavior is never perceived.

As individuals mature, certain habits are displaced by others. ". . .there are numerous forms of behavior that are considered right and proper during one stage of the life cycle but wrong during another stage" (Whiting and Mowrer, 1943, p. 129). Should the currently proper behavior be impeded, the earlier behavior can surface. The introduction of a disrupter or impediment to the current behavior then can help elicit earlier responses. Alternatively, the sequence of events or sensations that were associated

---

[1] Authors are listed alphabetically. All contributed equally to this paper.

TABLE 1
Aspects of the Failing to Try

Just Not Trying
Satisfaction with current solutions'
Habitual behavior
Inertia or procrastination
Impediments
Self-reliance

Trying Not to Try
Asceticism and self-sacrifice
Deferred gratification
Self-expression
Altruism

---

with the earlier habit might be introduced. Examples of either case can be drawn from individuals who have given up smoking or alcohol.

Inertia or Procrastination

Inertia or procrastination can result from indolence, laziness, or depression, or can function as a coping mechanism in stressful situations. Such maladies may affect potential buyers and/or sellers. For instance, salesforce personnel may be hesitant to cold-call, due to a lack of motivation or due to fear. One can stave off the potential stress through inaction (Lazarus 1993):

One of the psychological mechanisms for controlling emotions is detachment or distancing, and a number of philosophies—including those of the Greek Stoics and the Buddhists—center on renunciation of the standard human goals, which make people vulnerable to emotional distress (p. 28).

Actual stress can be dealt with through *cognitive avoidance coping* and *behavioral avoidance coping.* Cognitive avoidance is denial of the problem; behavioral avoidance coping consists of inactivity on the present problem by turning one's attention to other interests or activities (Moos and Schaefer 1993, p. 243).

Low-involvement decisions can also take on the appearance of inertia (for example, see Assael 1992, p. 101). Thus, we can distinguish between highly involving inertia that exists because of great pressures (e.g., stress) and less involving inertia due to absence of force. For example, the salesperson who cannot make the sales call for fear of rejection is qualitatively different in his highly involving type of inertia than is the peanut butter buyer who is faced with a wide and confusing array of brands at the grocery store.

Allowing Impediments to Interfere

The theories of reasoned behaviors (e.g., Fishbein and Ajzen 1975) rely on two key assumptions: (a) that (buying) action is preceded by deliberate processes culminating in conscious decisions to act, and (b) that, if the individual tries to act, no impediments stand in the way (Bagozzi and Warshaw 1990). Reasoned behaviors, therefore, are conditioned on deliberation and an absence of impediments.

Impediments can exist both to deliberation and to action. Further, an impediment can be a barrier (i.e., something that stops behavior or deliberation) or it can simply be a hurdle (i.e., something that affects the probability of an action or deliberation taking

place). Habitual behavior and the use of some decision rules are examples of impediments to deliberation. Stressful decisions can lead to *premature closure,* "terminating the decisional dilemma without generating all the alternatives and without seeking or appraising the available information about the outcomes to be expected for the limited set of alternatives under consideration" (Janis 1993, p. 57).

Impediments to action can take on many forms. A child may be stopped from seeing a movie because he or she is too young; an adult may be stopped from buying a product because there is a waiting period (e.g., guns) or because its sale is illegal (e.g., illicit drugs) or restricted (e.g., prescription drugs). One important impediment is ignorance or lack of knowledge. One may not know of a problem, be unaware of how to acquire information on potential solutions, or may lack knowledge on how to access the marketplace to acquire the solution itself. Problem solving usually begins with problem recognition. The sick relative who believes he or she doesn't require a physician's services will not seek them out; the salesperson may quit trying if it appears he or she has sufficient sales to make the quota.

Information distortions and other forms of learning deficiencies can lead to misjudgments in the marketplace. Perceptions that a product is limited in its supply can have a promotional effect in some markets with some customer groups. We see this in collectibles markets; examples of such collectibles include coins, stamps, baseball cards and comic books. Similarly, this sometimes bogus theme of limited availability is promoted for musical concerts and popular plays. Yet while this is intended to promote interest in the product offering, it can discourage some potential consumers from attending an event or from seeking a product.

Earlier experience may give invalid expectations regarding the time, effort, or money needed to fulfill a particular need. Some customers frustrated with early models of new products such as PCs and VCRs have been reluctant to tackle new, easier-to-use versions of those products. Further, situations may create misperceptions. For example, a general economic malaise may discourage a company from hiring new workers even though the company continues to be successful.

Personal belief systems and coping mechanisms will bear on perceptions. Individuals seeking dating partners (cf. Hirschman 1987) may have a resource matching strategy (e.g., "I like to dance/ he likes to dance," or "I am wealthy/he is wealthy"), and at the same time attempt to minimize rejection (e.g., if the reader is overweight, he or she may respond only to ads placed by other overweight persons; if the reader feels under-educated, he or she may not respond to ads placed by highly educated individuals). Other related behaviors or reluctance to behave can come from a perceived lack of status.

Being Self-Reliant

When faced with a need, we often first try to internally satisfy that need without entering the marketplace. Such activities, which we call self-reliance, include intra-consumer behaviors such as self-production or "make," or the reorganization of one's resources. Self-production requires a specific set of capital, both human capital and other, and other potency in the form of materials and time. Lusch, Brown, and Brunswick (1992) propose that decisions of internal (i.e., intra-consumer) versus external exchange are a function of capacity (i.e., expertise, resources, and time), rewards and costs (both economic and psychic), and sentiments (e.g., trust and perceived control). However, there is also a continuum of configurations between total self-production and, on the other extreme, total external exchange.

Nonetheless, any of the activities normally identified as self-production still require the consumer to enter the marketplace for supplies or services. The do-it-yourself industry, for example, depends on supplying individuals with materials for self-production. Even the act of baking a pie (whether from scratch or not) in one's own kitchen draws on the marketplace for the ingredients and uses the local utility company for the energy for cooking. Resources can acquire greater value by rethinking their use, and unrealized potency can be extracted through heightened efficiency (Dorfman and Steiner 1954). Attention to reallocation is an important theme today across many industries, and characterizes the Japanese economy in today's economic stagnation. Rather than lay off workers, Japanese managers struggle to rethink how best to use their human and nonhuman capital. Similarly, one focus of Gary Becker's work with the family (1981, 1993) has been on the implications of resource reallocation among family members. In this work, each member is assumed to have his or her own utility function, and Becker models the interrelationships among family members through each's utility function. The Rotten Kid Theorem assumes an altruistic household member who is rewarded through gains in the utility of another family member. Rotten Kids, then, are ". . .induced to act *as though* they are altruistic toward their benefactors because that raises their own selfish welfare. They act this way because otherwise gifts from their benefactors would be reduced enough to make them worse off" (Becker 1993, p. 398). In the context of the organization (e.g., in the Japanese example), the apparently altruistic member would be the owner and/or banker.

"Make" may be an attractive alternative solution to going to the marketplace; one only has to look at the organizational theory literature for extensive discussion of why organizations might elect to rely on "hierarchy" rather than "market" (Williamson 1975). The decision to depend on one's self will depend on a number of factors. Included among these will be the value of a self-made solution relative to a market-supplied solution (Lusch et al. 1992). In addition, the worth of one's resources when put to other uses (i.e., opportunity costs) must be considered. This latter point is discussed by Becker (1981) in his examination of the household's decision to allocate the time resources of individual family members to internal production versus external production.

TRYING NOT TO TRY

We have described a number of reasons why a consumer may fail to draw on the marketplace as a solution to problem solving. A second class of behaviors can be summarized as *the decision by the consumer to try not to try or to engage in self-denial.* Trying not to try, or reducing inner wants and needs by using values to override

inner desires, is an alternative to satisfying needs through exchange. Benett (1913) cites examples such as repression, self-denial, sublimation, abstention, asceticism, austerity programs, celibacy, fasting, penance, mortification, self-denial, humility, silence, solitude, and the "whole train of monkish virtues." Here, we focus on various forms of self-denial, including: (1) asceticism and self-sacrifice, (2) deferred gratification, (3) self-expression, and (4) altruism. Our interest is in consumer-dominated behaviors, although one cannot deny their interdependence to external motivators, such as "demarketing" (Kotler and Levy 1971) or "anti-consuming" (Perloff and Belch 1974) campaigns.

Background: Denial Style and Denial Management

Before continuing with reasons for trying not to try or self-denial, we need to provide a background for how denial style may develop and the role of denial management. A consumer's daily activities can be broken into two broad classes (Reich and Zautra 1983): (a) doing what is necessary to maintain existence, and (b) doing what is really desired. Therefore, denial in this context takes two forms: (a) denial of what is required to maintain an existence, and (b) denial of pleasure.

To the degree that products to be foregone are seen as a part of the extended self (Belk 1988), they must be denied, even as related parts of the identity are denied. For example, in the transition period that the child is separated from its mother, the child may use a transitional object to represent her in her absence (Gulerce 1991). When she returns, the child may be expected to drop the object and therefore engage in the process of its denial. Similarly, in any transition or rite of passage of life, the consumer may be required to forgo or deny aspects of his or her identity, as well as familiar things associated with that identity. The consumer may even deny parts of his or her identity to form new aspects of identity which may be marked by consumer goods. For example, if the consumer feels he or she must look the part of a wealthy individual, he or she may dress the part symbolically to demonstrate and complete this role, while denying other parts of his or her identity.

One can learn *denial management techniques* (Mazur 1986). Whereas one person might attempt to rely on willpower in avoiding a desired object, another might draw upon desire-reducing strategies. For example, substitution of a replacement goal can distract the individual from his or her needs (Hoch and Loewenstein 1991). Denial management techniques can be used to achieve an optimal level of stimulation (Raju 1980). As might be expected, differences in tolerance exist across individuals and across different behaviors for the same individuals (Ashmore 1990; Nataraajan and Goff 1991). Some research has linked these differences to demographic characteristics (cf. Moos and Schaefer 1993).

Asceticism and Self-Sacrifice

For some, a portion of self-denial is centered in morality in which the part of the self related to baser needs is to be sacrificed (White and MacBeath 1923). One extreme form of such self-denial is *asceticism*. Asceticism originally referred to any regular practice directed towards attainment of a special end, and it contained two distinguishable elements: (a) the actual practice of the act in which excellence is desired (e.g., the practice of a music piece); and (b) the observance of rules of living which, by imparting bodily strength and vigor, contribute indirectly to the same result (Benett 1913). Renunciation of ordinary satisfactions is demanded to achieve this highest form of excellence.

Where the ultimate end is excellence of any kind, one's utility function reflects the level of achievement and the process of achievement; this is in addition to what can be done with the output of the production function. Here, we might say that the means justify the ends (see the discussion of product-related goal constraints in Houston 1986). Although one may initially deny himself or herself, with time, the self-imposed habits of restraint are no longer necessary; the behavior to be restrained is abandoned. One example is celibacy among priests, where a person "has been mobilized into a moral base of preexisting moral bases" (Vera 1982, p. 31). This phenomena was described by Vera as "allocation of energy" toward commitment.

Asceticism is more commonly associated with higher pursuits, such as religion and the arts. The focus on a "worldly asceticism" came to Western society with Calvinism beginning in the latter part of the 1500s. This doctrine allowed the practitioner some hope of salvation through diligence and frugality in the conduct of daily living and commerce. This stands in sharp contrast to early church teachings which eschewed interest in commerce (Heilbroner 1972). This doctrine of diligence and frugality was pervasive throughout much of Europe through the eighteenth centuries. Luxury was pilloried everywhere when it manifested itself outside the court and higher nobility, or when not of direct importance to export trade. The objection to self-love was made through scripture as well as through practicality: egocentricity and arrogance are the antithesis of Christian love (Harkness 1957). Further, the basic note in the Christian understanding of material possessions became stewardship, which does not support disparities of wealth and poverty, wasted natural resources, and goods solely for selfish ends (Harkness 1957). Wants are those things which are necessary for the well-being of the body and the mind: "these and nothing beyond" was the dictum (Hopkins 1885). The Christian ideal is often self-realization through self-sacrifice (Harkness 1957).

Deferred Gratification

What is called *deferred or delayed gratification* is an opposite of asceticism. While the concept implies deferral of need satisfaction, it is commonly used to describe a very pragmatic denial of one's needs in the short term to satisfy needs at a later time. Examples of this include individuals and families who deny themselves basics while starting a new business, saving for the down payment on a house, or attending graduate school (Samuelsson 1961). The resulting investment is a function of saving, whether at the micro level or at the macro or societal level.

Self-Expression

Self-denial may be used also as a means of self-expression which can include: (1) expression of personal characteristics (e.g., frugality, restraint, financial prowess), (2) expressions of dissatisfaction with society (e.g., defiance and nontraditionalism), and (3) boycotting of a company and its products as an expression of dissatisfaction with its business practices.

Of the first type, we cite Samuelsson (1981, p. 84), who observed that "many great capitalists have taken pleasure or snobbish pride in a certain personal simplicity, in economy over trivialities." An example of the second type may be the "ascetic" new class (Bourdieu 1984). This consumption pattern may have some basis in morality, as discussed earlier, yet some consumers may also be making statements of anti-materialism or non-materialism (see Elgin 1981; Holt 1995). Such self-expression may be a combination of expressing both personal characteristics and a dissatisfaction with the present world condition, or it might simply be defiance for its own sake.

Boycotting, on the other hand, is "the refusal to conduct marketing transactions with a target" (Garrett 1987) due to dissatisfaction with business practices, often in an attempt to coerce

change, such as is noted by the Reverend Donald E. Wildmon (Winbush and Wildmon 1989):

> Now Pepsi is saying to all the young people of the new generation, 'Here is the person we want you to emulate and imitate.' They can do that. They've got every right to give Madonna $10 million, put it on television every night if they want to. All I'm saying is 'Don't ask me to buy Pepsi if you do. You've got the right to spend your money where you want to; I've got the right to spend my money where I want to. . .' and obviously, evidently, I was somewhat right in that because Pepsi agreed. They canceled their commercial and their world tour.

Altruism

Adam Smith wrote that it was self-interest, not benevolence, that caused the butcher, baker, and brewer to supply our dinner; nonetheless we regularly observe examples of altruistic behavior within the marketing system (Carman 1992, p. 5). Altruism is explained as the individual being willing to sacrifice his or her well-being for the enhancement of another consumer or for the group (see Carman 1992). At the extreme, altruism is defined as "any behavior which promotes the reproductive success of the recipient at a cost to the reproductive success of the altruist" (cf. Badcock 1991, p. 25). Becker, in his *Treatise on the Family*, defines altruism as individual **i**'s utility function being partially a function of **j**'s utility (1981, p. 173). As a result, anticipating altruistic behavior requires knowledge of individual **i**'s utility function and **i**'s perception of **j**'s utility function. It is not enough to know the two functions, nor can one assume the existence of altruistic behavior since, as noted earlier, the Rotten Kid can give the appearance of altruistic behavior without actually being altruistic. However, what is important is that altruism involves a form of self-denial and trying not to try to consume on the part of one person in favor of another.

DISCUSSION AND IMPLICATIONS

This paper has suggested a typology of behavioral alternatives which may cause consumers to fail rather than try to consume and extends the approach of Bagozzi and Warshaw (1990) in which the focus was on trying to consume in terms of expectations of success or failure to achieve a consumption goal. The alternatives fall into two categories: (1) just not trying and (2) trying not to try to consume. Overall, the approach suggested here shifts or broadens the perspective by integrating in the theory of trying reasons and behaviors that are not adequately considered by it. The implications for consumer research are wide-ranging and numerous.

Implications for the Theory of Trying

Researchers might broaden their consideration of trying so that more dimensions of trying are included beyond success and failure. For example, trying might be framed in terms of preconditions of alternatives to trying. Does the consumer even care to try? At a minimum, the perspective considered here suggests that the theory of trying needs to be elaborated or reformulated to include alternatives to trying. For instance, there also may be precursor stages to the trial process not considered in the theory of trying model in which consumers move from habitual behavior or inertia to the state of considering trial (cf. Prochaska and DiClemente 1983).

Broader Implications

Every dimension we have considered in this paper is worthy of further investigation in its own right. Some have already been explored, especially in terms of research on materialism, but not in the present context in which a number of alternative behaviors are considered. Researchers might model the dynamics of such behaviors both in terms of possible interrelationships among them and also in terms of various relevant motivational processes, such as mastery, hedonism, avoidance, and homeostasis (see Weiner 1992 for a review). How do consumers shift from one behavior to another? How does a consumer decide not to try in particular conditions? For example, might time pressure cause one to just not try to consume? Are there individual and/or cultural differences among consumers that should be considered? For instance, more versus less materialistic consumers might be studied in this regard. Finally, are some product types more easily foregone than others?

Another possible dimension for considering both trying and the failure to try involves processes and stages of change such that people may try or not try at various times in relation to a given consumption activity. Various researchers have investigated such processes in terms of change behavior (Prochaska and DiClemente 1983), experimental (trial) product use (Gould 1991), life cycle and age developmental changes (Moschis 1987), and life status changes in terms of facilitating or not engaging in consumption or other behaviors (Andreasen 1984), among others. All these approaches and others might be related to both trying and failing to try.

Research should also be conducted on how consumers integrate and balance all possible ways of trying and not trying to consume. Analogous and perhaps in relation to the optimal level of stimulation (Raju 1980), consumers are likely to seek a balance among all the consumption (as well as other) behaviors they seek, attempt, and engage in (Gould 1991). For instance, they attempt to balance the things which are demanded of them and those which they really desire (Reich and Zautra 1983). All this indicates that consumer researchers need to consider the broad dimensions of consumer behavior across products and services, situations, life-experiences, and individual differences to model the dynamics of what causes consumers to engage or disengage in consumption trying and/or to choose to pursue alternatives that move away from or toward marketplace solutions. Two driving forces in this regard to be investigated are perceived control in one's life, especially as one advances through the life-span (e.g., Heckhausen and Schulz 1995), and values regarding materialism, consumerism and religion.

CONCLUSION

This paper has explored the issue of failing to consume and framed it largely in relation to the concept of trying to consume. The results of our analysis suggest that we need to consider the motivation underlying consumption in broader terms than we have before and to change our usual consumer research perspective so that it reflects both of the two poles of the continuum of possible trying activity, i.e., trying to consume and failing to try to consume, as well as the related constructs of just not trying and trying not to try to consume. Viewing consumer behavior in this way may remove potential biases resulting from favoring the consuming, approach pole and open up consumer research to various avoidance perspectives that may help to account for consumption with greater ecological validity, as well as with deeper experiential insight.

REFERENCES

Andreasen, Alan (1984), "Life Status Changes and Changes in Consumer Preferences and Satisfaction," *Journal of Consumer Research,* 11 (December), 784-794.

Ashmore, Richard D. (1990), "Sex, Gender, and the Individual," in *Handbook of Personality Theory and Research*, ed. L. A. Pevin, New York: Guilford, 486-526.

Assael, Henry (1992), *Consumer Behavior and Marketing Action.* Boston: PWS-Kent Publishing.

Badcock, C. (1991), *Evolution and Individual Behavior*, Oxford, UK: Basil Blackwell.

Bagozzi, Richard. P. and Paul R. Warshaw (1990), "Trying to Consume," *Journal of Consumer Research,* 17 (September), 127-140.

Beatty, Sharon E. and Scott M. Smith (1987), "External Search Effort: An Investigation Across Several Product Categories," *Journal of Consumer Research,* 14 (June), 83-95.

Becker, Gary S. (1981), *A Treatise on the Family,* Cambridge, MA: Harvard University Press.

_____ (1993), "Nobel Lecture: The Economic Way of Looking at Behavior," *Journal of Political Economy,* 101 (3), 385-409.

Belk, Russell W. (1988), "Possessions and the Extended Self," *Journal of Consumer Research,* 14 (September), 139-168.

Benett, W. (1913), *Religion and Free Will*, Oxford: Clarendon Press.

Bourdieu, Pierre (1984), *Distinction*, Cambridge, MA: Harvard University Press.

Carman, James M. (1992), "Theories of Altruism and Behavior Modification Campaigns," *Journal of Macromarketing,* 12 (Spring), 5-18.

Dorfman, R. and P. O. Steiner (1954), "Optimal Advertising and Optimal Quality," *American Economic Review*, 44 (December), 826-36.

Elgin, D. (1981), *Voluntary Simplicity*, New York: Morrow.

Fishbein, Martin and Icek Ajzen (1975), *Belief, Attitude, Intention and Behavior: An Introduction to Theory and Research*, Reading, MA: Addison-Wesley.

Garrett, Dennis E. (1987), "The Effectiveness of Marketing Policy Boycotts: Environmental Opposition to Marketing," *Journal of Marketing*, 51 (April), 46-57.

Gould, Stephen J. (1991), "The Self-Manipulation of My Pervasive, Perceived Vital Energy through Product Use," *Journal of Consumer Research,* 18 (September), 194-207.

Gulerce, Aydan (1991), "Transitional Objects: A Reconsideration of the Phenomenon," *Journal of Social Behavior and Personality*, 6, 187-208.

Harkness, G. (1957), *Christian Ethics,* New York: Abingdon Press.

Heckhausen, Jutta and Richard Schulz (1995), "A Life-Span Theory of Control, " *Psychological Review,* 102 (April), 284-304.

Heilbroner, R. L. (1972), *The Making of Economic Society* (Fourth ed.), Englewood Cliffs, NJ: Prentice-Hall, Inc.

Hirschman, Elizabeth C. (1987), "People as Products: Analysis of a Complex Market Exchange," *Journal of Marketing*, 53 (April), 1-20.

Hoch, Stephen J. and George F. Loewenstein (1991), "Time-inconsistent Preferences and Consumer Self-Control," *Journal of Consumer Research,* 17 (March), 492-507.

Holt, Douglas B. (1995), "How Consumers Consume: A Typology of Consumption Practices," *Journal of Consumer Research,* 22 (June), 1-16.

Hopkins, M. (1885), *The Law of Love and Love as a Law,* New York: Chas. Scribner & Sons.

Houston, Franklin S. (1986), "The Marketing Concept: What It Is and What It Is Not," *Journal of Marketing*, 50 (April), 81-87.

Janis, I. L. (1993), "Decisionmaking Under Stress," in *Handbook of Stress* (2nd ed.), eds. L. Goldberger & S. Breznitz, New York: The Free Press, 556-574.

Kotler, Philip and Sidney Levy (1971), "Demarketing, Yes, Demarketing," *Harvard Business Review,* 49, 74-80.

Lazarus, R. S. (1993), "Why We Should Think of Stress as a Subset of Emotion," in *Handbook of Stress* (2nd ed.), eds. L. Goldberger & S. Breznitz, New York: The Free Press, 21-39.

Lusch, Robert F., Stephen W. Brown and Gary J. Brunswick (1992), "A General Framework for Explaining Internal vs. External Exchange," *Journal for the Academy of Marketing Science,* 20 (Spring), 119-134.

Mazur, J. E. (1986). *Learning and Behavior,* Englewood Cliffs, NJ: Prentice-Hall, Inc.

Moos, R. H. and J. A. Schaefer (1993), "Coping Resources and Processes: Current Concepts and Measures," in *Handbook of Stress* (2nd ed.), eds. L. Goldberger & S. Breznitz, New York: The Free Press, 234-257.

Moschis, George P. (1987), *Consumer Socialization,* Lexington, MA: Lexington Books.

Nataraajan, Rajan and Brent G. Goff (1991), "Compulsive Buying: Toward a Reconceptualization," *Journal of Social Behavior and Personality,* 6 (6), 307-328.

Perloff, R. and M. A. Belch (1974), "Toward an Anti-Consuming Ethic," paper presented at the APA symposium, New Orleans, LA.

Prochaska, James O. and Carlo C. DiClemente (1983), "Stages and Processes of Self-Change of Smoking: Toward An Integrative Model of Change," *Journal of Consulting and Clinical Psychology,* 51 (3), 390-395.

Raju, P. S. (1980), "Optimum Stimulation Level: Its Relationship to Personality, Demographics, and Exploratory Behavior," *Journal of Consumer Research,* 7 (December), 272-282.

Reich, John. W. and Alex. J. Zautra (1983), "Demands and Desires in Daily Life: Some Influences on Well-Being," *American Journal of Community Psychology,* 11 (February), 42-58.

Sahakian, W. S. (1976), *Introduction to the Psychology of Learning*, Chicago: Rand McNally College Publishing Company.

Samuelsson, K. (1961), *Religion and Economic Action,* London: William Heinemann, Ltd.

Vera, H. (1982), *Professionalization and Professionalism of Catholic Priests*, Gainesville, FL: University Presses of Florida.

Weiner, Bernard (1992), *Human Motivation: Metaphors, Theories, and Research*, Newbury Park: Sage.

White, A. K., and A. MacBeath (1923), *The Moral Self,* London: Edward Arnold & Co.

Whiting, John W. M., and O. H. Mowrer (1949), "Habit Progression and Regression: A Laboratory Study of Some Factors Relevant to Human Socialization," *Journal of Comparative Psychology,* 36, 229-53.

Williamson, Oliver E. (1975), *Markets and Hierarchies,* New York: The Free Press.

Winbush, D. and D. E. Wildmon (1989), "Interview: Bringing Satan to Heel," *Time,* June 19, 54.

Wood, D. J. (1981), "Problem Solving and Creativity," in *The Structure of Psychology*, eds. C. I. Howarth & W. E. C. Gillham, London: George Allen & Unwin, 529-550.

Affordability Perceptions in Consumer Research

Arti Sahni Notani, University of San Diego

Consumers commonly desire to own products that they cannot afford to buy. While the impact of affordability on consumers' purchase behavior has aroused considerable interest among marketing practitioners (e.g., Hancock 1993; Serafin and Johnson 1995), this issue has received little attention among consumer researchers. Economic theory recognizes that consumers, when attempting to maximize utility, are limited by their budgets. However, consumer researchers, like psychologists, have tried to predict behavior based solely on preference, neglecting the cost or sacrifice element that entails almost every behavior.

Inspite of it's roots in economics, marketing does not share the economist's wholistic view of consumption. A reason for this is that over time marketing, especially, consumer behavior, has aligned itself more closely with psychology (Leong 1989). This has occurred because the objectives of marketing had more in common with objectives of psychology than that of economics, i.e., explanation and prediction of individual behavior (Mittelstaedt 1990). Microeconomics focuses on aggregates such as price levels, total production and consumption. The differences in the disciplines notwithstanding, greater insight into behavior of consumers can be gained by integrating psychological and economic aspects (van Raaij 1981).

Affordability perceptions are a subjective evaluation of one's economic status, and thus could be considered a psychological manifestation of an economic variable. The purpose of this session is to introduce this new variable into the study of consumer behavior. All three papers in this session examine the role of affordability perceptions in consumer research, albeit from diverse perspectives. The first paper sheds light on the topic by using the framework provided by the discipline of economic psychology. The second paper examines the topic by relating it to frameworks provided by the attitude and price perception literatures. The third paper examines the importance of this topic for the government.

In the first paper, van Raaij elaborated on the theoretical and empirical issues involved in introducing this new variable to consumer research. He described why the concept of affordability can be useful for macro Indices of Consumer Sentiment and Consumer Confidence, well-being, and more micro variables like consumption attitudes, willingness and ability to buy, and the attitude-intention-purchase relationship. The relationship of affordability to individual personality variables like materialism, consumer confidence was also discussed. Further, implications of using a perceptual measure of affordability instead of objective measures (e.g., household income) commonly employed in marketing research were discussed. He extended the affordability concept— mostly thought of as financial costs—to temporal and behavioral (effort) costs as well. His discussion of the various macro, micro and individual variables culminated with an integrative model that showed the interrelationships among these variables by categorizing them as antecendents and consequents.

In the second paper, Notani examined the role of affordability perceptions in the consumer purchase decision process by incorporating it into the attitude and price perception frameworks. The study identified the process by which affordability perceptions interact with price beliefs, attitudes, and perceived value to influence both purchase intent and actual purchase. Second, the study revealed that the relationship of affordability perceptions with the above mentioned variables is dependent upon whether it is purchase intent or actual purchase that is of interest to the researcher. Specifically, the effect of affordability on purchase intent was not mediated by variables like attitude and perceived value. However, when actual purchase instead of purchase intent was examined, attitude and perceived value fully mediated the effect of affordability. Third, affordability perceptions were embedded in the nomological net of the price perception framework to test alternate model configurations. It was found that affordability is best seen as an immediate antecedent of purchase intent. Finally, future research directions were provided. In particular, it was suggested that this topic be explored using the experimental method so that affordability could be manipulated (perhaps by providing credit cards to the experimental group) to isolate cause and effect.

In the third paper, Garner presented results of a research program developed by the Bureau of Labor Statistics, U.S. Department of Labor, that uses respondents' subjective assessments of their incomes and expenditures for use in surveys sponsored by the Federal Government. The qualitative methodology which uses cognitive interviews, concurrent thin-alouds and focus groups was discussed. The results of this methodology were discussed with respect to how respondents: (1) interpret terms used in subjective assessments of income and expenditures, (2) use the various response categories, and (3) are affected by the order in which these questions are asked. Further, she described new research strategies that use subjective assessments of financial need to increase our understanding of policy implications of reduced economic circumstances .

Kent Monroe synthesized the papers and led a skillful discussion on the need, usefulness, and future research possibilities of the topic of affordability. The discussion led to the realization of the broad scope and practical applications of the concept of affordability.

REFERENCES

Hancock, K. E., 1993. Can Pay? Won't Pay? or Economic Principles of 'Affordability'. *Urban Studies* 30 (1), 127.

Leong, Siew Meng (1989), "A Citation Analysis of the Journal of Consumer Research," *Journal of Consumer Research*, 15 (march), 492-497.

Mittelstaedt, Robert A. (1990), "Economics, Psychology, and the Literature of the Subdiscipline of Consumer Behavior," *Journal of the Academy of Marketing Science*, 18, 303-311.

van Raaij, W. Fred (1981), "Economic Psychology," *Journal of Economic Psychology*, 1, 1-24.

Serafin, R. and B. Johnson, 1995. Sticker Shock Relief: Automakers Find Ways to Push Affordability. *Advertising Age* 66 (8), February 20, p. 1.

Special Session Summary
Here's The Beef: Cognitive Evidence for Literary Theory

George S. Babbes, University of California, Berkeley
Nicholas H. Lurie, University of California, Berkeley

SESSION OVERVIEW

The objective of this session was to bring conceptual and empirical rigor to the study of how language (e.g. rhetoric, narrative) influences human thought. Researchers have long speculated that language affects consumer behavior. However, to date, little effort has been made to discuss the underlying cognitive mechanisms and provide evidence for these claims. The session combined work in literary analysis, conceptual metaphor and narrative theory—all of which share a common interest in how cognitive frames are evoked, processed and used—to examine the language of print advertising and service encounters.

SUMMARY OF INDIVIDUAL PAPERS

Figurative Speech in Advertising

Edward F. McQuarrie, Santa Clara University
David Glen Mick, University of Wisconsin, Madison

McQuarrie and Mick presented a theoretical taxonomy that provides a systematic account of how rhetorical figures function in ad contexts. Rhetorical statements, which may be thought of as artful deviations from expectations, capture consumer attention by requiring greater processing than literal ones. For example, the incongruity that defines a complex trope leads to arousal which in turn affects attitude towards the ad.

Rhetorical figures differ in both type and complexity. The degree of deviation varies systematically with the type of figure. Tropes, which use irregular or disordered language, demand more elaboration than schemes, which are characterized by excessive regularity or order. Because tropes require greater depth of processing, they have more attention-getting and pleasure-creating power. These systematic differences between figure types allow the authors to predict differences in consumer response to advertising. In addition to presenting preliminary research that supports the taxonomy, the authors suggested several areas for future research. These include moderating effects of the opportunity to process an ad, individual difference effects, as well as cultural approaches to how figures function in ad texts.

Metaphor and Cognition: Systematic Effects on Consumer Product Evaluation and Mental Representation

George S. Babbes, University of California, Berkeley
Nicholas H. Lurie, University of California, Berkeley
Joydeep Srivastava, University of California, Berkeley

Most marketing research on advertising language has adopted an Aristotelian view towards metaphor. In this view, metaphor effects are seen as primarily emotive; there is no underlying cognitive mechanism. The contemporary theory of metaphor suggests that metaphors create representation through cross-domain mapping. "Metaphors" may be defined as drawing from a source domain to describe a target domain, while "literals" draw only from the target domain. The contemporary theory also suggests that most metaphors are "embodied" and draw their source domains from the world of physical experience. This has implications for consumer choice processes and outcomes.

Babbes, Lurie and Srivastava presented the results of two experiments. The first compared the effects of metaphorical to literal advertising on choice outcomes for more concrete (e.g. motor oil) versus abstract (e.g. financial service) products. Experimental results suggest that metaphorical ads are chosen more often and that this effect is significantly stronger for abstract products. The second experiment examined metaphor effects on choice processes. The authors compared concept maps for metaphorical versus literal ads and found no difference in number of nodes, but did find significant differences in numbers of source domain nodes. This effect is much greater for the abstract products. This suggests that the metaphor effect is one of cross-domain mapping, not elaboration. The results from the concept mapping experiment, and the differences between metaphor effects for concrete and abstract products for both experiments, lead the authors to conclude that for consumers, metaphorical ads are more than "artful deviation"—they affect cognitive representation.

Narrative Frames and Consumer Representations of Experience

Daniel Padgett, University of New Orleans
Jerry C. Olson, Pennsylvania State University

How do consumers understand their consumption experiences? Much of consumer knowledge may be organized in narrative or story form. A narrative representation of a consumption experience has one or more characters, a setting, a plot, and an overall theme. Stories, therefore, are a convenient and efficient form for understanding (and representing) the meanings of a personal experience. Consumers employ interpretive or narrative frames (perspectives or frames of reference) to guide their narrative understanding of consumption experiences. Narrative frames focus consumers attention on certain elements of experience and guide the sense people make of the places, objects, and events in their experiences. Consumers may use multiple frames to create a narrative interpretation (a story) of a consumption experience.

To capture consumers' narrative frames, Padgett and Olson adapted Gamson's (1983, 1989) framework for analyzing political discourse. They collected stories from consumers about their experiences with several ordinary consumer services, and systematically coded the metaphors, exemplars, depictions, justifications, and themes found in these stories. By comparing these elements of meaning (especially themes) across stories and services, Padgett and Olson identified the frames consumers use to interpret and structure their service experiences. They demonstrated this analytical method by showing narrative frames for consumers' health care experiences. In addition, Padgett and Olson suggested several areas for future research. These include developing other coding approaches for identifying narrative frames and determining the stability of frames across situations and time. Other work could look at testing the relationship between personal characteristics and type of narrative frame, identifying the origins of particular frames, and establishing the generality of narrative frames.

Synthesizer

John Deighton, Harvard University

To start the discussion, Deighton quoted a reviewer of the special session who responded to the call for cognitive evidence for literary theory with, "Literary theory doesn't need any validation.

Thank you very much." On the contrary, argued Deighton, theory is never excused the obligation to justify its utility. Since literary theory deals in attributes of the text rather than the psychology of readers, and advertising research tends to do the opposite, this session achieved a long-overdue marriage. Metaphor was an appropriate place to start, being arguably both a feature of text and a method of sense-making. Some of the issues raised in the discussion include: Should sociological and cultural, as well psychological, aspects of language be considered? Are there figures that can be both tropes and schemes? Is there really such a thing as a "literal"? If frames are based in semantic memory and narratives in episodic memory, what is the psychological reality for frames? Are abstractness, knowledge and experience different constructs? These questions demonstrate that there is both substantial interest in, and need for future research on, the relationship between language and cognition.

REFERENCES

Gamson, William A. and Kathryn E. Lasch (1983), "The Political Culture of Social Welfare Policy," in *Evaluating the Welfare State: Social and Political Perspectives*, ed. Shimon E. Spiro and Ephraim Yuchtman-Yaar, New York: Academic Press, 397-415.

_____ and Andre Modigliani (1989), "Media Discourse and Public Opinion on Nuclear Power: A Constructionist Approach," *American Journal of Sociology*, 95 (July), 1–37.

Monetary Promotions vs. Non-Monetary Promotions, Which Is More Effective?

France Leclerc, University of Chicago

SESSION OVERVIEW

Over the past decade, marketers have steadily allocated almost 30% of their marketing budget on consumer promotions, an allocation that was roughly equivalent to advertising expenditures in 1993 (Donnelley 1994). As a marketing tool, the primary objective of consumer promotions is to create an immediate sale by offering consumers an extra incentive to buy the product. This incentive can be monetary (such as price-off, cents-off coupons, rebates) or non-monetary (such as premiums, sweepstakes, sampling) or a combination of both (cents-off coupons with a premium). It is generally believed that 1) monetary incentives are more effective than non-monetary ones; 2) the fewer constraints around the incentives, the better it is from a consumer perspective and 3) non-monetary incentives are more franchise building than monetary incentives. These beliefs, however, haven't been tested empirically. The purpose of this session was 1) to test these premises and; 2) to propose some new theoretical ways to think about what makes a consumer promotion effective.

SUMMARY OF INDIVIDUAL PAPERS

"The Effects of Price vs. Sampling Promotions on Short-Term Sales and Brand Loyalty"
Karen Gedenk, University of Kiel
Scott A. Neslin, Dartmouth College

The question addressed by this research is how price and non-price promotions differ in their short-term effects on sales and their long-term effects on brand loyalty. Economic utility theory predicts a positive short-term effect for both types of promotions, which should be stronger for price than for non-price promotions. The effect of promotion on brand loyalty, however, is not that easy to predict. According to behavioral learning theory (Rothschild, Gaidis 1981) and self-perception theory (Dodson, Tybout, Sternthal 1978) buying on promotion may enhance, detract, or have no effect on brand loyalty compared to non-promotion purchasing. Whatever the direction, however, price promotions should be less favorable than non-price promotions because, in the language of behavioral learning theory, price promotions are more likely to become primary reinforcement, or in the language of self-perception theory, price promotions are more likely to be attributed by the consumers as the reason they buy the brand. In summary then, the authors hypothesize that price promotions are more favorable than non-price promotions in the short term while being less favorable in the long term.

To measure the short and long-term effects of promotions, Gedenk and Neslin use a logit model of brand choice where purchase probability is a function of price, price promotions, non-price promotions and brand loyalty. Brand loyalty is modeled as an exponentially smoothed average of past purchases (Guadagni, Little 1983). The long-term effects of promotions are captured by an augmentation of the Guadagni/Little brand loyalty model in which the build-up and decay of brand loyalty over time depend on the promotion status of a household's purchases. The model is estimated with scanner panel data from the German market for mineral water and the yogurt market in the US. Non-price promotions investigated are features, displays, and in-store sampling.

Results indicate that, in accordance with the hypotheses, price promotions are slightly more effective in the short term than non-price promotions. In the long term, however, price promotions are less favorable. They are associated with lower brand loyalty compared to non-promotion purchases, while non-price promotions have either no effect on brand loyalty or a slightly positive effect. A two-period simulation show that the magnitude of the effects is managerially meaningful.

"A Penny Saved is Not a Penny Earned: Responses to Different Types of Promotions"
Sue O'Curry, DePaul University

Using experiments, O'Curry shows that not all price promotions are equivalent and more importantly that factors other than the magnitude of the deal affect consumer preferences for a type of promotions. From a normative perspective, consumers would be expected to prefer price cuts to all other forms of promotion because the savings are immediate, completely fungible and there are no transaction costs. O'Curry conducted a series of five studies to explore the effects of time delay, transaction costs and fungibility on preference for promotions. One study demonstrated that in some cases, consumers are happier with non-fungible promotional premiums to cash savings, even though cash savings, rebates, and gift certificates were all perceived to be a better deal than premiums.

Three studies examined the impact of time delay, time to realize savings relative to purchase, and constrained fungibility on preferences between promotions, using a forced-choice paradigm. The results indicate that a majority of subjects preferred an in-store coupon to a completely fungible cash rebate at delays of one, three, and six weeks. Similarly, the majority of subjects preferred a gift certificate to a rebate at three weeks. Time to realize savings relative to purchase appeared not to be a significant factor when high transaction costs and absolute time delays were equal. Only when fungibility constraints were explicitly spelled out did a majority of subjects choose a rebate over an in-store coupon. Even with these constraints made explicit, half of subjects preferred a gift certificate to a rebate.

The last study looked at the implied discount rate for rebates by asking subjects to generate amounts that would make price cuts, rebates, and coupons equivalent in value. Discount rates for rebates ranged from 34% to 230,667%, with smaller amounts being discounted at higher rates.

Taken together, the results indicate that consumers are not thinking about money saved with promotions as "real" money.

"The Effect of Economic Appeal in FSIs on Attitudes Toward the Promoted Brand, Propensity to Clip and Coupon Efficiency"
France Leclerc, University of Chicago
John D.C. Little, MIT Sloan School of Management

In this paper, Leclerc and Little investigate whether the short-term effects of price promotions vary as a function of whether a price promotion (cents-off coupons) is reinforced in the print ad component of the coupon (save $0.50 on your next purchase), or combined with some brand-related information (reminder of the brand benefits, suggestions for use, etc..).

In previous work, Leclerc and Little (1996) have shown that advertising executional cues in the print ad component of an FSI can affect attitude toward the promoted brand, and coupon efficiency. Furthermore, they have shown that the effect of executional cues is a function of brand loyalty. More specifically, for brand switchers, an information-oriented ad generated higher attitude toward the promoted brand than an advertisement featuring an attractive picture. Alternatively, for loyal customers, an advertisement featuring an attractive picture generated higher attitude toward the promoted brand than an information-oriented ad. Leclerc and Little have proposed that this differential effect of executional cues was due to the fact that brand switchers are more motivated to process information than loyal customers.

In the current work, the use of an Economic appeal ("Save") was contrasted to the use of a Brand appeal. Based on the work previously reported, it was hypothesized that for loyal customers, an Economic Appeal and a Brand Appeal would have the same impact on attitude toward the promoted brand and coupon clipping. For switchers, on the other hand, given their higher motivation to process information, a Brand appeal should generate higher attitude toward the brand and higher propensity to clip than an Economic Appeal.

In a laboratory experiment, using a real brand, it was found that the effect of these two types of appeals vary as a function of the degree of brand switching as expected. For loyals, the Economic Appeal and the Brand Appeal had the same effect on attitude toward the promoted brand and on propensity to clip. For switchers, however, a Brand Appeal was more effective than an Economic Appeal. Furthermore, in a cross-sectional analysis of coupon events using IRI effectiveness measures, the authors found that when the coupon ad is used primarily to reinforce the price deal (e.g., Save $0.50 by using this coupon), it has a negative effect on incremental sales.

To summarize, if a price promotion is used, providing information about the brand has a more positive impact on switchers than providing a reminder of the money saved by using the coupon.

DISCUSSION SUMMARY
Linda Stone, from University of Minnesota was the discussion leader. After summarizing the main contributions of the session, she suggested the three following directions for future research: 1) The process that underlies price promotions' negative impact on loyalty (self-perception theory, attribution theory, behavioral learning theory) is still unclear. 2) Response to price versus non-price promotion seem to be governed by different mechanisms. What are they and how can managers make use of the information? and 3) Consumers have distinct preferences for different types of promotion. Do these preferences correspond to promotion effectiveness/profitability?

REFERENCES
Dodson, Joe A., Alice M. Tybout and Brian Sternthal (1978): Impact of Deals and Deal Retraction on Brand Switching, *Journal of Marketing Research*, 15 (February), 72–81

Guadagni, Peter M. and John D. C. Little (1983): A Logit Model of Brand Choice Calibrated on Scanner Data, *Marketing Science*, 2 (Summer), 203–38

Leclerc, France and John D.C. Little (1996): Can Advertising Copy Make FSI Coupons More Effective? Working Paper. University of Chicago.

Rothschild, Michael L. and William C. Gaidis (1981): Behavioral Learning Theory: Its Relevance to Marketing and Promotions, *Journal of Marketing*, 45 (Spring), 70-8

The Effects of Negative Information in the Political and Marketing Arenas: Exceptions to the Negativity Effect

Rohini Ahluwalia, University of Kansas
Baba Shiv, University of Iowa

The negativity effect or the greater weighting and subsequently greater impact of negative information as compared to positive information in judgment and decision making, has been well documented in various literatures: decision making (framing effect, Kahneman and Tversky 1979), impression formation (Fiske 1980; Kanouse and Hanson 1972), and persuasion (Meyerowitz and Chaiken 1987). This session questioned the generalizability of the negativity effect to the political and marketing arenas – where information is encountered in the form of "attack" ads and negative publicity releases by consumers/voters who differ in their prior expectations about the brand/candidate.

Baba Shiv and Julie Edell argue that the effectiveness of negatively framed ad claims compared to positively framed ones depends on which cognitions are likely to have a bigger impact on preferences: those related to the claims or those related to the advertising tactics. They propose that when processing is less extensive in nature, message claims are expected to more accessible and hence dominate. This is likely to result in negatively framed claims being more effective than positively framed ones, in line with the negativity effect. When the processing is more elaborate in nature, cognitions related to the advertising tactics are also likely to become accessible. If the tactics are perceived to be unfair, and if they are diagnostic for choice, they are likely to impact preferences resulting in a backlash against the sponsor of a negatively framed ad. Baba Shiv presented results from three experiments that supported their propositions.

A negativity effect has been found in impressions of American presidential candidates: character weaknesses are weighted more heavily in evaluations of candidates than character strengths (Klein 1991; 1996). The second paper dealt with understanding the generalizability of this finding to other countries and cultures. Jill Klein presented the results of data collected with Grzegorz Sedek, Agnes Toth and Gabor Mertz during recent Polish, Hungarian and U.S. Presidential elections. While negativity is consistently found in U. S. presidential elections, negativity did not characterize impressions of candidates in Poland and Hungary. A further study, showing the Poles have a generally negative view of political leaders, while Americans have generally positive views, supports the expectancy-contrast explanation for negativity. Attributes that contrast with expectations receive disproportionate weight in overall judgments.

It has been argued in the literature that negative information is given more weight in overall evaluations because it is perceived to be more diagnostic than positive information (e.g. Skowronski & Carlston 1987). Rohini Ahluwalia, Bob Burnkrant and Rao Unnava, argue that since negative information gets more because of its higher diagnosticity, factors that reduce the perceived diagnosticity of negative information are likely to result in an elimination of the negativity effect. One such factor is the prior commitment of the consumer towards the target brand. Rohini Ahluwalia presented the results of two experiments which examine the effects of negative product information in a publicity context. The researchers find that the prior commitment of the consumer moderates the perceived diagnosticity of negative and positive information. The negativity effect is found only for consumers who were low in commitment towards the target brand. High commitment consumers, on the other hand, demonstrated inferential biases and a reversal effect: they perceived positive information as more diagnostic than negative information.

Dipankar Chakravarti, in synthesizing the session, stated that while a plethora of studies now exist demonstrating the negativity effect and the potential moderators to this effect, little effort has been focused on investigating the role of memory the negativity effect. In other words, is negativity perceptual or representational in nature? He suggests that future research examine whether negativity is moderated by the perceptual salience of information, or alternatively, whether it is moderated by the cognitive and representational processes involved in integrating positive and negative information. He also recommends investigating the way in which context and task factors influence the perceptual and cognitive process involved in attribute weighting.

REFERENCES

Fiske, Susan (1980), "Attention and Weight in Person Perception: The Impact of Negative and Extreme Behavior," *Journal of Personality and Social Psychology*, Vol. 38, 889-906.

Homer, Pamela and Rajeev Batra (1994), "Attitudinal Effects of Character-Based Versus Competence-Based Negative Political Communications," *Journal of Consumer Psychology*, Vol. 3. No. 2, 163-185.

Kahneman, Daniel and Amos Tversky (1979), "Prospect Theory: An Analysis of Decision Under Risk," *Econometrica*, Vol. 47 (March), 263-91.

Kanouse, David E., and Reid L. Hanson Jr. (1972), "Negativity in Evaluations," in *Attribution: Perceiving the Causes of Behavior*, Morristown, NJ: General Learning Press, 47-62.

Klein, Jill G. (1991), "Negativity Effects in Impressions Formation: A Test in the Political Arena", *Personality and Social Psychology Bulletin*, Vol. 17. No.4, 412-418.

Klein, Jill G. (1996), "Negativity in Impressions of Presidential Candidates Revisited: The 1992 Election", *Personality and Social Psychology Bulletin*, Vol. 22. No.3, 289-296.

Meyerowitz, Beth E., and Shelly Chaiken (1987), "The Effects of Message Framing on Breast Self-Examination Attitudes, Intentions, and Behavior", *Journal of Personality and Social Psychology*, Vol. 52, No. 3, 500-10.

Skowronski, J.J., & Carlston, D.E. (1987), "Social Judgment and Social Memory: The Role of Cue Diagnosticity in Negativity, Positivity, and Extremity Biases", *Journal of Personality and Social Psychology*, Vol. 52, 689-699.

Meaningless Differentiation Revisited

Susan M. Broniarczyk, University of Texas at Austin
Andrew D. Gershoff, University of Texas at Austin[1]

ABSTRACT

Recent research by Carpenter, Glazer, and Nakamoto (1994) suggests that brands can gain a competitive advantage with "meaningless" differentiation, even if consumers are aware of its irrelevance. Two experiments are presented that investigate the role that the attribute's label and the decision context play in the consumer inference process associated with meaningless differentiation. Results show that attribute inferences regarding the value of the unique attribute depend on the attractiveness of the differentiated label and its correspondence with the irrelevance disclosure. Additionally, the impact of meaningless differentiation on consumer choice was shown to depend on the degree of meaningful differentiation between the alternatives.

INTRODUCTION

The crux of marketing is to create a niche in the marketplace by differentiating from competitors on an important attribute. A differentiated position increases consumer recall and consideration of the product, resistance to competitive attack, and product preference for market segments that value the distinctive attribute. Recent research by Carpenter, Glazer, and Nakamoto (1994) questions the widely-held assumption that marketers need to differentiate on an attribute that is relevant, meaningful, and valuable. Counter to prevailing marketing strategy (Porter 1985), they find that marketers can benefit even when differentiation is meaningless.

Marketers have long recognized the persuasive powers of advertising. Advertising has been shown to frame consumer decisions such that featuring an attribute in an advertisement increases its importance in consumer product evaluation (Gardner 1983, MacKenzie 1986). Featuring an irrelevant attribute, however, was thought to have long-term negative consequences because consumers would discover during product trial that the attribute did not, in fact, improve product performance. In their review of consumer learning, Hoch and Deighton (1989) questioned this assumption arguing that many product experiences do not provide unambiguous feedback about attribute performance. Furthermore, they asserted that because consumers treat a marketer's claim as a default hypothesis (Hoch and Ha 1986), confirmatory biases in testing would actually lead consumers to perceive the uninformative product experience as verifying the marketer's claim.

This malleability of consumer learning led Hoch and Deigton (1989) to suggest that brands could gain long-term benefits by differentiating on attributes that give the appearance of being valuable, but in fact, are irrelevant to improving product performance. For example, Folger's instant coffee advertises its patented "flaked coffee crystals" although the shape of the coffee crystal is only relevant for ground, not instant coffee.

In two laboratory experiments, Carpenter et al. (1994) (referred to as CGN) found support for meaningless differentiation. Two results are noteworthy. First, consumers valued an irrelevant attribute in the absence of any marketer claim regarding its superiority. Second, CGN found that even after being explicitly informed that the differentiation was meaningless, subjects still positively

valued the differentiated brand. Attribute belief measures confirmed that subjects learned that the attribute was irrelevant (i.e., they reported no value for the unique level of the attribute). Nonetheless, meaningless differentiation had a positive impact.

This latter finding is particularly interesting because it suggests that the uniqueness of a meaninglessly differentiated attribute can result in inferences of alternative superiority apparently without inferences of attribute level superiority. That is, an alternative differentiated by an irrelevant attribute can receive enhanced evaluation without subjects generating positive inferences about the attribute. Given the significance of this finding for marketers and public policy makers, we believe that this study deserves replication and extension in two directions. First, we believe that it is important to examine factors that may impact the likelihood that consumers will draw positive inferences from meaningless differentiation. Experiment 1 examines the moderating effects of the differentiated attribute label's attractiveness and its correspondence with the irrelevance disclosure on meaningless differentiation. Second, we believe it is important to understand the contexts in which meaningless differentiation will affect consumers' decisions relative to other meaningful information. Specifically, a second experiment examines whether an irrelevant attribute can be used to counter a competitive weakness on a relevant attribute.

MEANINGLESS DIFFERENTIATION PROCESS

Several psychological processes may account for meaningless differentiation leading to a meaningful brand advantage. CGN posit that uniqueness may create value because it leads to greater weight in evaluation (Kahneman 1973), prominence in inter-brand comparison (Houston, Sherman, and Baker 1989), and simplification of decision-making (Fiske and Taylor 1984). Although differentiation leads to greater attention directed towards the meaningless attribute level, it is not obvious that the consumer will necessarily infer a positive value. CGN suggest that consumers may believe that the distinctive attribute causes better product performance (McGill 1989) especially if they make pragmatic inferences (Harris and Monaco 1978) that a brand would not offer a unique attribute level unless it added value.

Nonrevelation of Irrelevance

In the CGN study, subjects were not provided with any claims regarding the differentiated attribute's benefits, merely its identifying label and a brief description. Examination of their stimulus materials reveals that meaningless differentiation was achieved by having one brand of jackets described as having "alpine class" down fill whereas the other seven brands in the competitive set were described as having "regular" down fill. Down fill was described as the type of bird feather used with "alpine class" being goose feathers whereas "regular" was a mixture of goose and duck feathers.

Several aspects of the stimuli are worth noting with respect to the likelihood of a positive inference to the meaninglessly differentiated attribute. First, the label "regular" has a baseline connotation suggesting that any differentiation is positive. Second, consumers may prefer a pure to a mixture filling. Third, the attribute labels are nondescript regarding specific attribute performance allowing for multiple interpretations (Hoch and Ha 1986) and a potential likelihood of consumers inferring greater value than warranted given the

[1] Thanks to Joe Urbany and Pat West for their helpful comments on an earlier draft.

descriptive attribute information (Preston 1977). Fourth, consumers may possess prior beliefs that goose feathers are softer than duck feathers. Additionally, they may also use their intuitive beliefs regarding the relationship between "alpine class" and mountains and skiing to generate inferences that compare favorably to the generic "regular" label in the product class of winter jackets (Broniarczyk and Alba 1994).

Thus, consistent with traditional models of consumer evaluation (Fishbein and Azjen 1975), the favorableness of differentiation is expected to be a function of the benefits associated either directly or by inference with the attribute. Therefore, our replication of CGN will include a manipulation of the previously unexamined effect of attribute label attractiveness. Meaningless differentiation is hypothesized to depend on the attractiveness of the differentiated attribute's label relative to the competitive set. Specifically, when the differentiated attribute is described by a more attractive label, it will be positively valued, whereas when it is described by a less favorable label it will be negatively valued. Uniqueness in and of itself is not expected to be sufficient to generate positive value.

Revelation of Irrelevance

The finding that led CGN to ascribe value to uniqueness per se was that subjects positively valued the meaninglessly differentiated alternative, even when pre-warned of the irrelevance of the differentiation. Prior to judging the jackets, one group of subjects was informed that for down fill "the age of a bird matters, the type of bird it comes from does not make a difference." Manipulation checks confirmed the success of the irrelevance instruction with these subjects claiming indifference between alpine and regular down fill yet their product judgments revealed a positive bias towards the alternative with the "alpine class" label. Moreover, CGN still found a positive benefit for meaningless differentiation when analysis was restricted to only subjects who were indifferent or had lower preferences for "alpine class."

This result is counter to a large body of research showing that consumers are discriminating regarding product benefits. In fact, consumers have been found to reduce their likelihood of purchasing products that included unwanted positive features or premiums (Simonson, Carmon, and O'Curry 1994). Notwithstanding the solid evidence of its success, the irrelevance revelation of CGN warrants special consideration because the uniqueness explanation is dependent on subjects believing the differentiation to be meaningless.

Examination of their irrelevance disclosure shows that it corresponded to the attribute description (i.e., goose and duck feathers) but not the attribute label (i.e., alpine and regular). In their principle of correspondence, Ajzen and Fishbein (1977) posited that an equivalent level of specificity in measurement is needed for attitudes to be highly predictive of behavior. Analogously, we propose that an equivalent level of specificity between the irrelevance disclosure and the differentiated attribute's label is necessary for the revelation to be maximally effective in counteracting subjects' inferences.[2] Thus, the irrelevance disclosure of CGN most likely eliminated inferences of "alpine" related to the superiority of goose over duck feathers but not other favorable inferences related to its appropriateness for winter activities.

In related research on deceptive advertising, qualifications of expanded advertising claims have been shown to have partial success in negating some but not all of the positive inferences implied by the expanded claim (Burke et al. 1988). Thus, when the set of positive associations of the attribute label is sufficiently large,

the meaningless differentiation effect may remain robust even when subjects are informed of the irrelevance because discounting is only applicable to those positive associations specifically related to the disclosure.[3] Thus, our second research proposition is that as the correspondence between the the irrelevance disclosure and the label on the differentiated attribute increases, the likelihood of subjects maintaining their inferences decreases, and consequently, the effect of meaningless differentiation decreases.

STUDY ONE: ATTRIBUTE ATTRACTIVENESS AND CORRESPONDENCE WITH REVELATION

Experimental Design

Overview. We had three objectives in Study 1: to replicate CGN, to examine the role that the attractiveness of the unique attribute's label plays in meaningless differentiation, and to examine the role of its correspondence with the irrelevance disclosure. The between-subjects design had three factors: 2 (Attractiveness) X 2 (Correspondence) X 2 (Revelation) and a control condition. Attractiveness was a factor that varied whether the label on the the differentiated attribute was higher or lower in attractiveness relative to the other brands in the choice set. The Correspondence factor compared whether the correspondence between the irrelevance disclosure and the differentiated attribute's label was low or high. Revelation was a factor that varied whether subjects were explicitly informed or not informed that the differentiated attribute was irrelevant.

Pretest. A set of fifty undergraduate subjects participated in a pretest to determine if the down fill attribute levels differed in preference on a 9 point scale ranging from 1=Like to 9=Dislike. As predicted, "alpine" was rated as more preferred than "regular" [M=3.68 versus M=4.92, t(49)=3.42, p<.001] and "goose" was more preferred than "duck" [M=3.88 versus M=5.40, t(49)=3.83, p<.001]. Additionally, there was no preference difference between the high attractiveness labels of "alpine" and "goose" [t<1] nor the low attractiveness labels of "regular" and "duck" [t(49)=1.07, p>.29].

Attribute labels were then selected that varied in correspondence to the irrelevance instruction manipulation. Recall that the irrelevance revelation of CGN was that "the age of a bird matters, the type of bird it comes from does not make a difference." The attribute labels of "goose" and "duck" were deemed to have a high direct correspondence with the irrelevance instruction whereas the labels of "alpine" and "regular" were deemed to have a low direct correspondence.[4]

Procedure. Two hundred and forty undergraduate students from a southwestern university participated for payment of 5 dollars. The procedure and stimuli are replicated from CGN. All subjects evaluated 8 hypothetical down jackets described on 3 binary attributes of fill rating, cover material, and stitching. The description of the fourth binary attribute, down fill, varied between conditions. In the high attractiveness/low correspondence condition, the differentiated brand had a down fill label of "alpine"

---

[2]Thanks to Joe Urbany for suggesting this literature.

[3]We appreciate a reviewer for making this point.

[4]A pretest also confirmed that subjects were likely to have a more diverse set of associations to the labels of "alpine" and "regular" than to "goose" and "duck". Fifty-three different undergraduates rated the specificity of the down fill labels on a 9-point scale (1=Abstract, 9=Concrete). "Goose" (M=7.62) and "duck"(M=6.96) were both viewed as more specific information for down fill than "alpine" (M=4.36) and "regular" (M=6.96).

whereas the 7 other brands were described as having "regular" down fill. This condition is a replication of CGN. In the low attractiveness/low correspondence condition, the reverse scenario was present with the differentiated brand having a down fill label of "regular" whereas the other 7 brands were described as having "alpine". The high correspondence conditions consisted of replacing the ambiguous attribute labels of "alpine" and "regular" with the bird-specific attribute labels of "goose" and "duck", respectively. Thus, the high attractiveness/high correspondence condition compared a brand differentiated by "goose" down fill to 7 other brands described as having "duck" down fill. The low attractiveness/high correspondence condition compared a brand differentiated by "duck" down fill to 7 other brands described as having "goose" down fill.

In the nonrevelation condition, subjects were provided with basic attribute descriptions but no explanations about the preference ordering of the attribute levels. In the revelation condition, subjects were provided with attribute descriptions detailing the preference ordering of the attribute levels and explicitly informed that for the down fill attribute the "age of the bird matters, the type of bird does not." The control condition received no information about the fourth attribute of down fill.

The rating task conformed to CGN's where subjects anchored a blank ten-centimeter rating scale with their least and most preferred jacket. For each of the remaining jackets, they placed a mark on the line corresponding to their relative preference for the jacket. The range of ratings was from 0 (least preferred) to 100 (most preferred) with a ruler used to assign ratings to intermediary markings.

After evaluating the jackets, subjects' preference ratings for the meaningless attribute of down fill were assessed on a 9-point scale where (1) indicates preference for "regular", (5) indicates indifference between alpine and regular, and (9) indicates preference for "alpine." Inadvertently, preference ratings for "goose" relative to "duck" down fill in the high correspondence conditions were not collected.

Results

Manipulation Check. T-tests were performed against the midpoint of the rating scale (5) to see if subjects were indifferent to the attribute level of down fill. Confirming pretest results, when irrelevance was not disclosed, subjects preferred alpine to regular down fill [M=5.85, t(26)=2.26, p<.04]. Consistent with CGN, when irrelevance was disclosed and subjects' choice did not involve the differentiated attribute (i.e., the control condition), the irrelevance revelation was successful with subjects claiming indifference to alpine versus regular [M=5.36, t<1, p>.39]. However, our results show that revelation of irrelevance in the low correspondence conditions was able to reduce but not eliminate the likelihood of inferences [high attractiveness: $M_{revealed}$=5.95, (t(24)=2.47, p<.03) versus $M_{nonrevealed}$=6.75, (t(24)=4.53, p<.01) and low attractiveness: $M_{revealed}$=7.18, (t(27)=6.82, p<.01) versus $M_{nonrevealed}$=7.79, t(24)=10.38, p<.01].

Additionally, these results suggest that the post-choice measure of attribute inference was sensitive to the choice context. For instance, in the low attractiveness condition, the majority of brands possessing "alpine" down fill appeared to convey pragmatic information that was consistent with subjects' intuitive beliefs and thus led to more extreme beliefs about the irrelevant attribute.

Overall Means. The overall mean ratings are presented in Table 1. Comparison of the control conditions revealed differential preference for a nontarget attribute between revelation conditions that was attributable to subjects' unfamiliarity with down jackets. Specifically, our southwestern subjects in the nonrevealed condi-

tion preferred cotton to synthetic cover material whereas subjects in the revealed condition were informed that synthetic was preferred to cotton. Thus, because it was not appropriate to compare differences from the control between revelation conditions, we ran separate analyses for each revelation condition. The data were analyzed using ANOVA with independent variables of attribute attractiveness and attribute correspondence. The dependent variable was the difference in a given subject's rating on the meaninglessly differentiated jacket from the mean rating for that jacket in the control condition.

Replication of CGN. Recall that the high attractiveness/low correspondence condition was identical to the CGN manipulation (1 alpine/ 7 regular). Our findings in this condition replicate the CGN results such that the irrelevant attribute increased brand evaluation regardless of the disclosure of the attribute's irrelevance (nonrevealed: Δ=+38.12, p<.02 and revealed: Δ=+18.25, p<.05). Thus, consistent with CGN, the revelation of irrelevance did not eliminate the benefit of meaningless differentiation. However, unlike CGN, we can not attribute the observed effects to the uniqueness of a meaninglessly differentiated attribute alone. Examination of those 14 of 24 subjects in the revealed condition who reported an equal or lower evaluation of the differentiated level of "alpine" downfill in the manipulation check showed no significant change from the control condition (Δ=+1.53, p>.89).

Attractiveness. The first hypothesis stated that the benefit resulting from meaningless differentiation depended on the attractiveness of the irrelevant attribute's label. As hypothesized, the nonrevealed condition showed a significant main effect of the attractiveness of the differentiated attribute's label [F(1,92)=18.30, p<.0001]. An alternative differentiated by an attribute with an attractive label (Δ=+28.58) was preferred to the control condition whereas it was less preferred when it had an unattractive label (Δ=-3.19).

The revealed condition showed a similar pattern of results for attractiveness [$Δ_{high attractiveness}$=+13.71 vs. $Δ_{low attractiveness}$=-14.44, F(1,92)=14.43, p<.001]. Thus, uniqueness alone is not sufficient to create positive worth and in some cases may decrease product evaluation. These results suggest that the effect of meaningless differentiation is due to subject inferences about the value of the differentiated attribute.

Correspondence. The second hypothesis stated that for the disclosure of irrelevance to neutralize these inferences that there needed to be a high correspondence between the revelation of irrelevance and the label on the differentiated attribute. Analysis is therefore restricted to the revealed condition only. Results showed no main effect for Correspondence (F<1) but the predicted Attractiveness X Correspondence interaction was significant (F(1,92)=5.08, p<.03). As hypothesized, simple effects show that there was a considerable effect of attractiveness at the low correspondence level [$Δ_{high attractiveness}$=+18.25 vs. $Δ_{low attractiveness}$=-21.70, F(1,47)=26.88, p<.001] whereas this effect was reduced, although still significant at the high correspondence level [$Δ_{high attractiveness}$=+9.17 vs. $Δ_{low attractiveness}$=-6.54, F(1,45)=4.40, p<.05].

A stronger picture of correspondence emerges when each cell mean is compared to the control. At low correspondence levels, having an attractive (p<.05) or unattractive (p<.05) label resulted in meaningless differentiation significantly increasing or decreasing alternative evaluation, respectively. However, at the high correspondence level, neither the high (p>.17) nor low (p>.54) atractiveness label resulted in an effect for meaningless differentiation.

TABLE 1
Mean Ratings For Experiment 1

Condition	Nonrevealed		Revealed	
	n	Rating	n	Rating
Control	26	15.42	24	35.54
Low Correspondence				
High Attractiveness	24	53.54*	24	53.79*
Low Attractiveness	24	2.92*	27	15.00*
High Correspondence				
High Attractiveness	24	34.45*	24	44.71
Low Attractiveness	24	21.54	23	29.00

Note: * denotes significant difference from control at p<.05

In summary, uniqueness alone did not lead to a positive valuation. In the high attractiveness/low correspondence condition, we replicated CGN results such that meaningless differentiation had a positive effect on consumer evaluations, but these results were insignificant when analysis was restricted to only those subjects satisfying the manipulation check. Furthermore, our results showed a significant effect for the attractiveness of the irrelevant attribute such that an attractive label led to a favorable effect whereas an unattractive label led to an unfavorable effect for meaningless differentiation. However, a high correspondence between the irrelevant attribute's label and disclosure of its irrelevance nullified the inferences that consumers may have generated regarding the attribute's benefits and hence resulted in no effect for meaningless differentiation.

However, the test used by CGN and replicated here, set a high standard because the eight jackets in Study 1 provided a full factorial representation of the three relevant attributes. The meaninglessly differentiated attribute was included in the description of one of these alternatives and hence the relative rating scale effectively required subjects to value the meaninglessly differentiated attribute over a meaningful one. In Study 2, we contrast the effect of meaningless differentiation in a choice context where products are identical on meaningful attributes to a context where the differentiated alternative is inferior on the meaningful attributes. Additionally, Study 2 was run to further examine the strength and completeness of the revelation of the differentiated attribute's irrelevance and to gain a better understanding of consumer inferences related to the irrelevant attribute.

STUDY 2: CONTEXT EFFECTS AND INFERENCES

Experimental Design

Overview. A robust effect of meaningless differentiation would be evidence that an inferior alternative differentiated by an irrelevant attribute would be preferred over an alternative with a superior level of a meaningful differentiation. However, in this age of parity products, marketers are also concerned about the ability of meaningless differentiation to affect choice for one alternative over another when all other attributes have equal values.

Study 2 was a two-factor between-subjects design: 2 (Choice context) X 2 (Correspondence). The factor of Choice Context

varied whether the meaninglessly differentiated attribute was placed with an alternative that was identical or inferior to its competitor. The Correspondence factor was the same as Study 1 with the bird-specific labels of "goose" and "duck" representing high correspondence and labels of "alpine" and "regular" representing low correspondence. Additionally, detailed process measures were collected to identify the inferences subjects made regarding the irrelevant attribute.

Procedure. Fifty-three subjects participated for course extra credit. Examination was restricted to differentiation of an irrelevant attribute that had high attractiveness and all subjects were informed of the irrelevance of the down fill using the same manipulation as Study 1. In a training phase, subjects evaluated six down jackets all with the common level of "regular" ("duck") down fill. In a subsequent test phase, subjects then choose between Brand X and Y that had identical fill ratings, cover material, hoods, and cleaning requirements. However, Brand X was meaninglessly differentiated with the unique level of "alpine" ("goose") and Brand Y shared the common level "regular" ("duck") with the other six jackets. In the inferior choice context, Brand X also had a lower stitching rating than Brand Y whereas in the identical choice condition, both brands had equal stitching ratings. Note that stitching was chosen because Study 1 revealed it to be the least important of the meaningful attributes. After making their choice, subjects provided open-ended responses describing their choice process and answered close-ended questions regarding the benefits associated with the irrelevant attribute.

Choice Results

Manipulation Check. The same 9-point scale measuring preference for the levels of the down fill attribute was used as in Study 1 where (1) indicates preference for "regular" ("duck"), (5) indicates indifference between "alpine" and "regular" ("goose" and "duck"), and (9) indicates preference for "alpine" ("goose"). Consistent with Study 1, the results show that the manipulation check was affected by the decision context. An ANOVA with independent variables of choice context and attribute correspondence revealed a significant effect of choice context ($F(1,49)=4.02$, p=.05). The manipulation check was successful for both inferior conditions of "goose" (M=5.31, F<1) and "alpine" (M=5.00, F<1) but unsuccessful in the identical condition where choice necessitated that subjects discriminate on the basis of the meaningless differentiated

TABLE 2
Study 2 Attribute Beliefs

| | Low Correspondence | | High Correspondence | |
	Inferior *n=12*	Identical *n=13*	Inferior *n=13*	Identical *n=12*
Softness	3.69^b	4.00^a	3.17	3.46
Quality	3.38	3.67^a	3.16	3.69^b

Note: Attribute beliefs were measured on a 5-point scale.
^{a} denoted difference against scale midpoint at p < .05.
^{b} denoted difference against scale midpoint at p < .10.

attribute [("goose" M=5.93, F=2.14, p=.053) and ("alpine" M=6.23, F=1.92, p<.08)]. Cognitive responses and inference beliefs revealed a similar pattern and will be discussed in more detail later. However, the choice results will show that an irrelevant attribute was not able to overcome a competitor's superiority on a relevant attribute. Thus, it appears that the irrelevance manipulation was sufficient in all cases, but the decision task in the identical context forced some subjects to counteract this disclosure.

Correspondence. Choices were analyzed using a loglinear model with the SAS CATMOD procedure with factors of choice context, attribute correspondence and their interaction. Results show a significant main effect for choice context (χ^2=17.32, p<.01) and no significant effect for correspondence (χ^2<1) nor its interaction with choice context (χ^2<1).

Choice Context. In the inferior condition, 13 out of 14 subjects in the low correspondence condition chose the superior Brand Y mentioning its better stitching and 2 subjects explicitly mentioning the irrelevance of down fill. Of the fourteen subjects in the high correspondence/inferior condition, thirteen also chose the superior Brand Y due to its superior stitching with 6 subjects explicitly mentioning the irrelevance of down fill.

Conversely, in the identical conditions, the majority of subjects chose the alternative differentiated by a meaningless attribute. In the low correspondence/identical condition, 10 out of 14 subjects chose the meaningless differentiated Brand X even though 6 subjects explicitly mentioned that down fill was irrelevant. Similarly, in the high correspondence/identical condition, 9 out of 12 subjects chose the meaningless differentiated Brand X with 2 subjects explicitly mentioning the irrelevance of the down fill. A fairer test in the identical condition is to see if choices differed from chance (proportion=.50). Results showed that choices of the meaningless differentiated alternative in the identical condition were greater than expected by chance (proportion=.73, t(26)=2.60, p<.02).

Thus, the results suggest that even when revealed to subjects that the differentiation of an attribute is meaningless, that subjects will still show preference for the alternative with a irrelevant attribute when there are no other available attributes on which to differentiate the alternatives. However, when subjects can make their choice on the basis of the relevant attributes, a meaninglessly differentiated attribute does not impact their decisions.

Inference Results

Subsequent attribute belief measures confirmed that consumers did infer benefits to the meaninglessly differentiated attribute. Attribute beliefs for the differentiated irrrelevant attribute relative

to its competitors were measured on a 5-point scale. Two inferences suggested from Study 1 were inferences about the attribute performance of softness and quality [Softness:1=Rougher to 5=Softer; Quality: 1=Lower to 5=Higher]. Results are presented in Table 2. These attribute beliefs were collected at the end of the experiment (post revelation and post choice) and thus they represent inferences that the irrelevance disclosure did not eliminate.

Correspondence. Although correspondence had no effect on choice, it did affect the number of inferences consumers retained about the differentiated attribute. Specifically, subjects in the low correspondence condition reported higher softness to the meaninglessly differentiated attribute (M=3.84) than subjects in the high correspondence condition (M=3.32), F(1,46)=4.10, p<.05. The inference of higher softness to "alpine" but not "goose" is especially pertinent because the irrelevance instruction dealt with whether the down fill affected the softness of the jacket. Although the mean levels of inferences about quality were directionally consistent with more inference being made in the low (M=3.52) than high (M=3.44) correspondence condition, this effect was small and nonsignificant, F<1. These findings provide further insight into the results of Experiment 1 because they provide more direct evidence that a high correspondence between the disclosure of irrelevance and the label on the irrelevant attribute is more effective in counteracting inferences related to the attribute. However, these inferences were only utilized in the choice decision if the context required it.

Choice Context. The choice context displayed some effect on inference measures, albeit less, than the choice measure. Specifically, although the mean levels of inferences about softness were directionally consistent with more inferences being made in the identical (M=3.44) than inferior (M=3.72) context, this effect was nonsignificant, F(1,46)=1.14, p>.29. For the quality inference, subjects in the identical context reported significantly higher quality to the meaninglessly differentiated attribute (M=3.68) than subjects in the inferior context (M=3.27), F(1,46)=2.86, p<.10

Note that these inferences were collected after the choice task, so we cannot be certain of the effect of inferences about the meaninglessly differentiated attribute on the choice decision.[5] Thus, subjects may have had an equivalent level of inference making initially but because subjects in the inferior context did not need to utilize the inference to make a decision, they reported lower final levels of attribute beliefs. Alternatively, subjects in the

[5]We appreciate a reviewer for making this point.

identical context may not have formed any spontaneous inferences but later reported making them to justify their choice.

In summary, Study 2 showed that meaningless differentiation only provides "meaningful" differentiation if subjects are forced to choose between two brands that are identical except on the irrelevant attribute. A marketer can not use differentiation on an irrelevant attribute to overcome a competitive deficiency on a relevant attribute if subjects are aware of the attribute's irrelevance.

SUMMARY AND DISCUSSION

Our results show that a meaninglessly differentiated attribute can lead to alternative preference, even if subjects are aware of the differentiation's irrelevance, but only under certain circumstances. CGN claim that positive valuation of meaningless differentiation is primarily driven by uniqueness. We found that attribute inferences regarding the value of the unique attribute depend on the attractiveness of the its label and its correspondence with the irrelevance revelation. There is a limit to the impact of inference-making such that even if consumers make inferences regarding the meaningless differentiated attribute they may not affect choice in the presence of more diagnostic information (Feldman and Lynch 1988).

However, the choice context itself affects the very inferences that consumers draw. Other information about the alternative such as its relative price (CGN), the relative quality of its other attributes, and the relative quality of its competitors are also likely to affect the evaluative inferences regarding meaningless differentiation.

Meaningless differentiation exerted its strongest effect when there was no meaningful differentiation between the alternatives. However, this research only examined high involvement situations where inference-making is more likely to occur (Stayman and Kardes 1992). Future research should examine whether the salience of a unique attribute can overcome meaningful differentiation in low involvement situations. Additionally, uncertainty associated with a meaningful attribute (Brown and Carpenter 1996) may lead to stronger effects for meaningless differentiation.

REFERENCES

Ajzen, Icek and Martin Fishbein (1977), "Attitude-Behavior Relations: A Theoretical Analysis and Review of Empirical Research," *Psychological Bulletin*, 84, 888-918.

Broniarczyk, Susan B. and Joseph W. Alba (1994), "The Role of Consumers' Intuitions in Inference Making," *Journal of Consumer Research*, 21 (December), 393-407.

Brown, Christina L. and Gregory S. Carpenter (1996), " When Are Irrelevant Attributes Relevant? A Strategic Inference Model," working paper, New York University.

Burke, Raymond R., Wayne S. Desarbo, Richard L. Oliver, and Thomas S. Robertson (1988), "Deception by Implication: An Experimental Investigation," *Journal of Consumer Research*, 14 (March), 483-494.

Carpenter, Gregory S., Rashi Glazer, and Kent Nakamoto (1994), "Meaningful Brands From Meaningless Differentiation," *Journal of Marketing Research*, 31 (August), 339-350.

Feldman, Jack M. and John G. Lynch (1988), "Self-Generated Validity and Other Effects of Measurement on Belief, Attitude, Intention, and Behavior," *Journal of Applied Psychology*, 73 (August), 421-435.

Fishbein, Martin and Icek Ajzen (1975), *Belief, Attitude, Intention and Behavior: An Introduction to Theory and Research*, Reading, MA: Addison-Wesley.

Fiske, Susan T. and Shelley E. Taylor (1984), *Social Cognition*, New York: Random House.

Gardner, Meryl Paula (1983), "Advertising Effects on Attributes Recalled and Criteria Used for Brand Evaluations," *Journal of Consumer Research*, 10 (December), 310-318.

Harris, Richard Jackson and G.E. Monaco (1978), "Psychology of Pragmatic Implications: Information Processing Between the Lines," *Journal of Experimental Psychology: General*, 107, 1-27.

Hoch, Stephen J. and John Deighton (1989), "Managing What Consumers Learn From Experience," *Journal of Marketing*, 53 (April), 1-20.

_____ and Young-Wan Ha (1986), "Consumer Learning : Advertising and Ambiguity of Product Experience," *Journal of Consumer Research*, 13, 221-233.

Houston, David A., Steven J. Sherman, and Sara M. Baker (1989), "The Influence of Unique Features and Direction of Comparison on Preferences," *Journal of Experimental Social Psychology*, 25, 121-141.

Kahneman, Daniel (1973), *Attention and Effort*, Englewood Cliffs, NJ: Prentice-Hall, Inc.

MacKenzie, Scott B. (1986), "The Role of Attention in Mediating the Effect of Advertising on Attribute Importance," *Journal of Consumer Research*, 13 (September), 174-195.

McGill, Ann L. (1989), "Context Effects in Judgments of Causation," *Journal of Personality and Social Psychology*, 57, 189-200.

Porter, Michael E. (1985), *Competitive Advantage*, New York: The Free Press.

Preston, Ivan L. (1977), "The FTC's Handling of Puffery and Other Selling Claims Made 'By Implication'," *Journal of Business Research*, 5 (June), 155-181.

Simonson, Itamar, Ziv Carmon, and Suzanne O'Curry (1994), "Experiemental Evidence on the Negative Effect of Product Features and Sales Promotions on Brand Choice," *Marketing Science*, 13 (Winter), 23-40.

Stayman, Douglas M. and Frank R. Kardes (1992), "Spontaneous Inference Processes in Advertising: Effects of Need for Cognition and Self-Monitoring on Inference Generation and Utilization," *Journal of Consumer Psychology*, 1 (2), 125-142.

The Persuasive Impact of Autobiographical Memories in Advertising: Episodic Self-Referencing or Schema-Triggered Affect?

Simani M. Price, Virginia Polytechnic Institute and State University
Danny K. Axsom, Virginia Polytechnic Institute and State University
Eloise Coupey, Virginia Polytechnic Institute and State University

ABSTRACT

Marketers frequently use ads intended to evoke autobiographical memories to influence consumers' evaluations of products. Little empirical evidence exists, however, to explain the processes by which the self-referencing done by consumers during these ads affects persuasion. Moreover, extant studies which build on an episodic, piecemeal view of self-referencing provide inconsistent results on product evaluation.

We propose that autobiographical memories ads are more similar to semantic memory than episodic memory, and that they influence evaluation by invoking schemas that filter self-referencing. A study designed to test the competing explanations supported a schema-based interpretation of the persuasive impact of autobiographical memories in advertising.

Self-referencing has been described as the persuasive mechanism for ads that encourage consumers' retrieval of past autobiographical memories (Sujan, Bettman, & Baumgartner, 1993; Baumgartner, Sujan, & Bettman, 1992). The memory is experienced as the representation of an event at a particular time and location (Brewer & Pani, 1983) and is characterized as having unique cognitive properties of the self (Gergen, 1971). This effect has led researchers to characterize ads which evoke autobiographical memories as representative of episodic rather than semantic memory (Baumgartener et al., 1992). Research has tended to indicate that the presentation of an autobiographical memories ad causes consumers to focus their attention on idiosyncratic experiences associated with a specific past event. This effect leads to an increase in positive affect because people tend to bias their recall in terms of positive memories, and then transfer the positive affect to the product, resulting in a favorable product evaluation (Sujan et al., 1993).

Though this explanation may seem plausible, few studies have actually examined how self-referencing and affect lead to persuasion. Additionally, the studies currently available have found mixed support for the effectiveness of these ads. In one study (Sujan et al., 1993), the researchers found that self-referencing was an effective persuasive technique as it resulted in a higher evaluation of the product compared to a more traditional product focus type of ad. In a different study, the same authors found that the autobiographical memory ad led to a higher evaluation of the ad, but not the product (Baumgartner et al., 1992). In both studies, however, affect levels increased during the presentation of these ads. If self-referencing via autobiographical memories results in a more favorable product evaluation, then one might expect that the more autobiographical memories consumers recall, the more they will like the product. Existing studies, however, have found no link between the proportion of autobiographical memories consumers report and product evaluation. In fact, the results of these two studies suggest that episodic self-referencing of a past event does not occur spontaneously with any great frequency among subjects. Thus, our understanding of the processes which determine the persuasive impact of autobiographical memories ads remains unclear.

In this paper we propose that the persuasive process underlying autobiographical memories ads is more representative of semantic memory or a category-based process rather than episodic memory. Specifically, we use Fiske's schema-triggered affect model to explain how a category-based process might operate and induce persuasion. Further, we hypothesize that retrieving a unique past memory *after* viewing an autobiographical memories can encourage an attribute-based process and reduces persuasion. In the following sections we develop and test hypotheses about the nature of the processes by which autobiographical memories ads may influence persuasion through affect and cognition. To develop our argument for a semantic memory explanation, we briefly review two models that have implications for the reciprocal processes of cognition and affect.

CONCEPTUAL BACKGROUND

Affect in a Category-based versus An Attribute-based Process

The prevailing view in social cognition is that people are cognitive misers, and as such, a category-based rather an attribute-based approach is used initially (Fiske & Taylor, 1991). One model that has direct implications for affect in a category-based process is Fiske's (1982) schema-triggered affect model. Fiske suggests that to the extent that an instance is perceived to fit the schema, it will receive the affect linked to that category. Otherwise, the instance receives a moderate positive affect by default, pending it's categorization as a good example of something else. In this model, affect is stored at the top level of the schematic structure without access to all the category's features and their respective evaluations; affect is linked to the initial act of categorization. Thus, a stimulus that is perceived as a consistent (vs. inconsistent) schema-match will be evaluated as similar to the category label. This matching effect has been demonstrated for a variety of person schemas: old flames, politicians, college majors, occupations (Fiske & Pavelchak, 1986). In a marketing context, the schema-triggered affect model suggests that if a consumer can easily categorize a product initially into a previously learned category label (e.g., Florida spring break package), then knowledge about the category becomes more accessible than any one attribute of the product (e.g., cost). As a result, product evaluation is determined by the category label, rather than by product attributes.

Positive affect can also encourage a category-based process. Isen and Daubman (1984) report that positive affect tends to broaden categories, leading subjects to see items as more similar than do subjects in a neutral mood. In addition, research suggests that people in a positive mood exhibit little systematic processing of information and instead rely on less effortful judgment heuristics (e.g., category-label) (Mackie & Worth, 1991). This finding suggests that consumers with an increase in positive affect would be more likely to engage in a schema-based process in evaluating a product. The preceding discussion suggests that affect should have significant impact in a category-based process, with schema match influencing consumer judgments. Thus, we would expect a favorable category-label to result in a higher product evaluation for a schema-consistent (vs. inconsistent) product.

In contrast to a category-based approach, affect is not as influential or as extreme in judgments using an attribute-based approach (Linville, 1982). Attention to the stimulus has to be increased to encourage an attribute-based approach (Fiske & Neuberg, 1990). One way to encourage attention is to increase the number of dimensions that are considered during judgments. This manipulation attenuates the role of affect and encourages an attribute-based process according to Linville's (1982) self-complexity model. Specifically, Linville proposes that the greater the number of dimensions considered, the greater the likelihood that the affect associated with any given dimension is attenuated during a judgment task. Thus, evaluation is less likely to be extreme (either positively or negatively) under an attribute-based process compared to a category-based process. Complexity or the number of *independent* dimensions underlying a judgment or cognitive structure, can be either manipulated directly (e.g., by instructions to consider x number of factors in a decision) or measured as individual differences. Unlike a category-based judgment, dimensionality is an important component of an attribute-based judgment. For example, a consumer can elaborate extensively on a product category and increase the number of thoughts (i.e., quantity of thoughts) but not the number of dimensions (i.e., quality of thoughts) considered, thus using a schema-based rather than an attribute-based process to evaluate a product. A schema's structure is more intrinsically, coherent, which results in a significant correlation between the schema's dimensions (Tesser, 1978). In an attribute-based process, each dimension independently contributes to the evaluation of the product. Thus, product categorization as schema-consistent or inconsistent and the affect associated with the category-label is *less* influential in determining product evaluation.

Persuasive Effects of Autobiographical Memories

We suggest that persuasive effects from autobiographical memories ads result from a category-based process. Autobiographical memories ads initially encourage attention to the self or self-focus. This focus simultaneously increases positive affect, as people tend to view themselves positively (Bradley, 1978), thus encouraging a category-based process in judgments. An increase in self-focus is a different explanation than episodic memory retrieval. The episodic memory explanation requires that a unique memory has been retrieved (Gergen, 1971). In addition, reduced persuasion may occur if a unique past experience is retrieved *after* viewing an autobiographical memories ad because the ad may serve as a reference point and encourage an attribute-based process. Markus & Sentis (1982) note that information is automatically encoded in a top-down manner in relation to the self until a mismatch occurs. We hypothesize that if people compare their experience to the ad, a mismatch would likely occur. Specific hypotheses designed to compare the schema-based, semantic memory explanation with an episodic memory explanation are detailed in the next section. An overview of the study is provided first to facilitate presentation of the hypotheses.

Study Overview

The goal of this study was to provide a theoretical explanation for the persuasive effects of autobiographical memories ads by juxtaposing our current understanding (i.e., episodic memory) with an alternative explanation (i.e., semantic memory). Fiske's schema-triggered affect model was used to examine the semantic memory explanation. Undergraduate subjects were exposed to a Florida vacation package ad for either Spring (schema-consistent) or Thanksgiving (schema-inconsistent) Break. In addition to Schema-match, Self-referencing was also manipulated where subjects either viewed a product-focus or a self-referencing (i.e., autobiographical memories) ad. The self-referencing manipulation resulted in three different variations (low self-referencing, high self-referencing pre-ad, high self-referencing post-ad). The Low Self-referencing condi-

tion was similar to previous studies examining autobiographical memories ads (Sujan et al., 1993) and was hypothesized to encourage a category-based approach. The two High Self-referencing conditions varied by whether they required subjects to write an essay about a past break experience *before* (high self-referencing pre-ad) or *after* (high self-referencing post-ad) viewing the ad. The High Self-referencing Pre-ad condition was hypothesized to encourage a category-based approach, as subjects could not use the ad as a source of comparison while thinking about their past experience. In contrast, the High Self-referencing Post-ad condition was hypothesized to encourage an attribute-based approach, the ad should serve as a reference point for subjects while thinking about their past experience. The presentation order of two primary dependent measures, the product evaluation measure and a cognitive response measure, was also manipulated to enable assessment of procedural bias. All other dependent variables followed these primary dependent measures.

Hypotheses

In the category-based explanation, the Low Self-referencing and High Self-referencing Pre-ad conditions should encourage self-focus initially and as such, simultaneously increase positive affect and the use of a schema-based process relative to the Product-focus condition. As Fiske's (1982) schema-triggered affect model suggests, the affect associated with the category-label should influence both product evaluation and subsequent ad-induced thoughts. Thus, a consistent schema-match (spring break in Florida) should have a higher product evaluation than an inconsistent schema-match (Thanksgiving break in Florida).

A category-based process may operate more strongly for subjects in the High Self-referencing Pre-ad condition as a result of having a schema primed (writing about a past break experience) *prior* to viewing the ad. The essay for subjects in the High Self-referencing Pre-ad condition should further increase positive affect, as people tend to recall primarily positive memories (Wagenaar, 1986). Because the self-referencing essay was written *prior* to viewing the ad, the ad could not be used as a source of comparison, thus reducing the likelihood of a mismatch occurring between their unique experience and the ad. As participants engage in a category-based process, their idiosyncratic experiences should be assimilated in the schema-consistent condition and contrasted in the schema-inconsistent condition. The preceding rational for a schema-based process is summarized as:

H1: In the Consistent Schema-match, the Low Self-referencing and High Self-referencing Pre-ad conditions should have a *higher* product evaluation than the Product-focus condition.

H2: The Consistent Schema-match should have a *higher* product evaluation than the Inconsistent Schema-match in both the Low Self-referencing and High Self-referencing Pre-ad conditions

An episodic memory explanation, in contrast, would predict that product evaluation should be influenced by the degree of episodic memory retrieval that occurs, *regardless of degree of schema-match*. Therefore, it would simply predict that product evaluations would be higher in the High Self-referencing Pre-ad conditions than the Low Self-referencing and Product-focus conditions in both Schema consistent and inconsistent conditions.

To support our hypothesis that persuasion effects results from a category-based process and not due to the retrieval of a unique self-referenced memory per se, we need to demonstrate reduced persuasive effects during an attribute-based process. Specifically, we need to provide evidence that attention to a past memory under a category-based process leads to a *higher* product evaluation than during an attribute-based process. To encourage attention to a past memory, subjects were asked to write on multiple dimensions of a past break experience either before or after viewing the autobiographical memories ad in this study. As noted earlier, we hypothesize that writing the self-referencing essay *before* viewing the ad would lead to a category-based process for subjects in the High Self-referencing Pre-ad condition. In contrast, we hypothesize that writing about a past break experience *after* viewing the ad, would encourage an attribute-based process for subjects in the High Self-referencing Post-ad condition. The ad presents multiple dimensions of a vacation package (i.e., activities, lodging, etc.) and should serve as a reference point for subjects writing about their own unique experience *after* viewing the ad. Recall that a characteristic of an attribute-based process is dimensionality (i.e., quality of thoughts) (Linville, 1982). Thus, we expect subjects in the High Self-referencing Post-ad condition to discuss more dimensions on the self-referencing essay compared to subjects in the High Self-referencing Pre-ad condition if they are using the ad as a reference point. As subjects in the High Self-referencing Post-ad condition consider multiple dimensions of their past experience, they will likely compare and contrast this with the ad, resulting in a mismatch between the ad and their experience. This should lead subjects to view the ad as *less* representative of their past experience. Further, as subjects engage in an attribute-based process, product category (schema consistent vs. inconsistent) and the affect associated with the category-label should have less influence on product evaluation. This will result in the product being evaluated less extremely (either positively or negatively) regardless of schema-match. The preceding discussion can be summarized as follows:

H3: In the Consistent Schema-match, the High Self-referencing Pre-ad and Low Self-referencing conditions should have a *higher* product evaluation than the High Self-referencing Post-ad condition.

H4: The Consistent Schema-match *should not* differ significantly from the Inconsistent Schema-match in the High Self-referencing Post-ad condition.

The preceding predictions regarding the influence of the self-referencing essay stand in contrast to what might be predicted from an episodic memory perspective. If the underlying persuasive mechanism of autobiographical memories ads is determined primarily by episodic memory, then increasing attention to a unique self-referenced memory should result in the *highest* product evaluation. From this perspective, it is assumed that people generally remember positive experiences from their life, and thus increasing attention to a past event would bias people to consider even more positive experiences associated with a past episode. Thus, from an episodic memory perspective, the two High Self-referencing (Pre-ad and Post-ad) conditions would similarly have the highest product evaluation (irrespective of schema-match) compared to the Low Self-referencing condition. In both of these conditions, attention to a unique past experience is increased by writing the self-referencing essay.

METHOD

Subjects and Procedure

Two hundred and forty undergraduates enrolled in psychology and marketing classes at a southeastern university received extra credit for participation in this study. Stimuli were presented on computers with VGA color monitors. The study used a 4 (Self-

referencing: None (Product), Low, High Pre-ad, High Post-ad) x 2 (Schema Match: Consistent, Inconsistent) x 2 (Response Order: Prod Eval First, Cog Resp First) between-subjects factorial design. Subjects were randomly assigned to one of 16 conditions and completed the study in individual cubicles. See Table 1 for experimental design.

Independent Variables

Self-referencing. Subjects in the Low, High Pre-ad and High Post-ad Self-referencing conditions were presented with an ad that asked them to think back to a past spring (or Thanksgiving) break and provided information on product features. In the two High Self-referencing conditions (Pre-ad, Post-ad), subjects were required to write on multiple dimensions (e.g., social, planning, travel) of a past spring (or Thanksgiving) break experience. Subjects either wrote the essay *before* (High Self-referencing Pre-ad condition) or *after* (High Self-referencing Post-ad condition) viewing the ad. Subjects in the Product-focus condition were also presented with an ad for a Florida spring (or Thanksgiving) break package but were only provided information on product features with no reference to a past break. Subjects in the Low Self-referencing and Product-focus conditions wrote an essay on the multiple uses and dimensions of paper towels (filler task) after viewing the ad. Subjects had five minutes to complete their essays.

Schema-match. Based on the results of pretests, a Florida Spring break was used as the Schema-consistent manipulation and a Florida Thanksgiving break was used as the Schema-inconsistent manipulation in all conditions.

Response Order. Subjects *either* received the *product evaluation questions first* followed by the cognitive response measure *or* received the *cognitive response measure first* followed by the *product evaluation questions.* The other dependent variables (i.e., episodic event rating, schema-match ratings) followed these measures.

Dependent Variables

Cognitive Response Measure. Subjects were provided two minutes to list all the thoughts that went through their minds while viewing the break package ad. Two independent judges coded thoughts into categories and valence. The average interjudge reliability was 95% across all measures. Disagreements were resolved by discussion.

Product Evaluation. Product evaluation was assessed on four 9-point semantic differential scales (i.e., favorable-unfavorable, good-bad, pleasant-unpleasant, positive-negative). The four measures were averaged to form an overall measure of product evaluation (alpha=.82).

Self-referencing Essay. Two independent judges coded thoughts into dimensions (e.g., social, planning, travel). The average interjudge reliability was 90%. Disagreements were resolved by discussion.

Reaction Time. Response latencies were collected for all dependent measures that required ratings on a Likert-type scales. Latencies were rounded to milliseconds.

Manipulation Checks

Schema-Match Ratings. Subjects made ratings on a 9-point scale on whether college students spending spring and Thanksgiving break in Florida was not at all typical (1) or very typical (9).

Episodic Event Rating. Subjects indicated on a 9-point scale whether, while viewing the ad, they thought about a specific spring (or Thanksgiving) break experience from their past (1) or thought of a general idea of what spring (or Thanksgiving) breaks are like for college students (9).

TABLE 1

Experimental Design: Schema-match, Self-referencing and Response Order

	Consistent Schema-match (Spring Break)		Inconsistent Schema-match (Thanksgiving Break)	
Product-focus (No Self-referencing)	Product Evaluation First	Cognitive Response First	Product Evaluation First	Cognitive Response First
Low Self-referencing				
High Self-referencing Pre-ad				
High Self-referencing Post-ad				

Personal and Involving the Self Rating. Subjects indicated on a 9-point bipolar scale whether their thoughts while viewing the ad could be described as (1) impersonal not involving the self or personal involving the self (9) (Sujan et al., 1993).

Related to a Past Break Experience Rating. Subjects indicated on a 9-point bipolar scale whether their thoughts while viewing the ad could be described as (1) not related to past spring (or Thanksgiving) break experience or related to past spring (or Thanksgiving) break experience (9) (Sujan et al., 1993).

RESULTS AND DISCUSSION

Manipulation Checks

Schema-Match Ratings. An ANOVA indicated a main effect for Typicality, F (1, 223)=666.89, p <.001. The Florida spring break was rated as significantly more typical (M=7.2) than the Florida Thanksgiving break (M=2.9).

Episodic Event Rating and Reaction Time. An ANOVA indicated no effects for the episodic event rating (grand mean=5.9). However, an ANOVA on the reaction time for the episodic event rating produced a main effect for Self-Referencing, F (3, 224)=3.58, p<.02. Subjects in the High Self-referencing Post-ad condition displayed significantly quicker response latencies (M=9.7) compared to subjects in both the Low Self-referencing condition (M=11.2), t (118)=1.98, p<.05 and the Product-focus condition (M=11.7), t (118)=2.82, p<.01, but were not significantly different from subjects in the High Self-referencing Pre-ad condition. Response latencies are often used as an indication of accessibility of thought processes (Bargh, 1984). Thus, subjects should respond quicker to items they are already thinking about. These results may indicate that writing about a unique past experience made a specific break experience more accessible for subjects in the two High Self-

referencing conditions compared to other self-referencing conditions.

Related to a past break experience. An ANOVA on "related to a past break experience" rating indicated a marginal main effect for Schema-match, F (1,224)=2.95, p<.09. Subjects in the Schema-consistent condition rated the ad as being more related to a past break experience (M=4.7) compared to subjects in the Schema-inconsistent condition (M=4.1). Post-hoc comparisons between the Schema-consistent and the Schema-inconsistent conditions indicated that the only significant difference occurred in the Product-focus condition. In the Product-focus Prod Eval First condition, subjects with the Consistent Schema-match rated the ad as significantly more "related to a past break experience" (M=6.2) compared to subjects with the Inconsistent Schema-match (M=3.4), t (224), p<.05. Within the other comparable Self-referencing conditions, the Schema-match comparisons did not significantly differ on this rating. These results suggest that the autobiographical memories ads may have encouraged self-focus initially compared to the product focus ads. That is, the autobiographical memories ad may have increased attention to the self *regardless* of schema-match. The increased attention to the self is hypothesized to increase positive affect and as such, encourage the use of a category-based process by participants initially.

Personal and Involving the Self Rating. An ANOVA on the "personal and involving the self" rating indicated a marginal main effect for Self-referencing, F (3, 222)=2.49, p<.06. Post hoc protected t-tests indicated that subjects in the High Self-referencing Post-ad condition rated their thoughts as significantly *more impersonal and not involving the self* while viewing the ad (M=5.6) compared to subjects in the Low Self-referencing condition (M=6.6), p<.05, the High Self-referencing Pre-ad condition (M=6.6), p<.05 and the Product-focus condition (M=6.5), p<.05. These results suggest that a mismatch likely occurred for subjects in the High Self-referencing Post-ad condition, leading them to view the ad as less personal compared to the other Self-referencing conditions. A mismatch was hypothesized to encourage an attribute-based process for this condition.

Product Evaluation

An ANOVA procedure revealed a three-way interaction between Schema-match, Self-referencing, and Response Order, F (3, 221)=4.02, $p<$ .008. Because there were no *a priori* predictions regarding the impact of Response Order on product evaluation, results were examined separately for the different response orders.

When product evaluations were collected *before* cognitive responses, results indicated a 2-way interaction between Schema-match and Self-referencing, F (3,109)=4.70, $p<$.004. Post-hoc protected t-tests provided support for the schema-triggered affect model.

As predicted by hypothesis 1, in the Consistent Schema-match condition, both the Low Self-referencing and High Self-referencing Pre-ad conditions had a significantly higher product evaluation compared to the Product-focus condition (M=6.0), t (221)=2.91, $p<$.01. Additionally, and as predicted by hypothesis 3 in the Consistent Schema-match, both the Low Self-referencing (M=7.5)) and High Self-referencing Pre-ad (M=7.3) conditions had a significantly higher product evaluation compared to the High Self-referencing Post-ad condition (M=6.3), t (221)=2.03, $p<$.05.

Product evaluation comparisons for schema-consistent versus inconsistent cells within each Self-referencing condition also provided some support for the schema-triggered affect model when product evaluations were collected *before* cognitive responses. There was partial support for hypothesis 2. Product evaluation in the Low Self-referencing condition, was significantly *higher* in the Consistent Schema-match (M=7.5) than in the Inconsistent Schema-match (M=6.5), t (221)=2.0, $p<$.05. In the High Self-referencing Pre-ad condition, product evaluation was *directionally higher* in the Consistent Schema-match (M=7.3) than the Inconsistent Schema-match (M=6.7). The difference was only significant, however, in one of the four product evaluation questions (unpleasant–pleasant dimension), where the High Self-referencing Pre-ad Schema-consistent condition was rated as significantly more pleasant (M=8.0) compared to the High Self-referencing Pre-ad Schema-inconsistent condition (M=6.9), t (221)=2.15, $p<$.05.

As predicted in hypothesis 4, product evaluation in the High Self-referencing Post-ad condition, was not significantly different in the Consistent Schema-match (M=6.2) compared to the Inconsistent Schema-match (M=6.8). Interestingly, the results for the Product-focus condition indicated that product evaluation in the Inconsistent Schema-match was significantly *higher* (M=7.4) than the Consistent Schema-match (M=6.0), t (221)=2.69, $p<$.01. One potential explanation for the higher product evaluation in the Product-focus Schema-inconsistent condition is the novelty of a Thanksgiving break package in Florida. Further, because the self was not initially primed in the product-focus-ad as it was in the self-referencing-ads, the package was not viewed as inconsistent with the self in Florida for a Thanksgiving break; it was merely evaluated as a novel product and not inconsistent with a family vacation experience.

When product evaluations were collected *after* cognitive responses, there were no significant differences in the product evaluation across conditions.

Process Measures

Self-referencing and Schema-match Post-hoc Comparisons. The results suggested that the presentation of the cognitive response measure *prior* to the product evaluation measure encouraged all subjects to engage in an attribute-based approach and resulted in similar outcomes across all dependent measures in this study. Further, the schema-triggered affect model was most strongly observed when making self-referencing comparisons in the schema-consistent (vs. inconsistent) conditions. The schema-inconsistent conditions encouraged all participants to engage in an attribute-based process, as a category-label was not readily available. As a result of these factors and for the sake of parsimony, post-hoc comparisons for the Self-referencing conditions are only presented for the Schema-consistent (vs. Schema-inconsistent) conditions all for the product evaluation first condition. Similarly, Schema-match post hoc comparisons are only presented for the product evaluation first condition.

Positive Affect and Product Evaluation Correlation. If subjects in the High Self-referencing Pre-ad and Low Self-referencing conditions were similarly using a schema-based process, then positive affect should strongly influence their judgments. In contrast, the High Self-referencing Post-ad condition subjects were hypothesized to be using an attribute-based process, thus positive affect should be less influential in making judgments. The correlation between positive affect and product evaluation provide empirical support for the two information processing models operating in the different conditions. The following correlations represent the Schema-consistent Prod Eval First condition. The percent of positive thoughts on the cognitive response measure and product evaluation were *significantly* positively correlated in the High Self-referencing Pre-ad (r=.52, $p<$.05) and Low Self-referencing conditions (r=.71, $p<$.01). Subjects in the High Self-referencing Post-ad condition had little correlation between product evaluation and the percent of positive thoughts (r=-.16, $p<$.70). A Fisher's z' transformation indicated that the High Self-referencing Post-ad condition was significantly different from the Low Self-referencing condition (z=2.45, $p<$ .01) and the High Self-referencing Pre-ad condition (z=1.72, $p<$.05).

Percent of Florida Vacation Imagery Thoughts on Cognitive Responses. Florida vacation imagery thoughts represented a general reference to a Florida vacation with no reference to the self (i.e., bikini, beer etc.). Results indicated a main effect for Self-referencing, F (3, 218)=3.15, $p<$.05 in the percent of Florida vacation imagery thoughts mentioned. Post hoc protected t-tests indicated that the High Self-referencing Pre-ad condition (35%) was significantly higher in the percent of Florida vacation imagery thoughts compared to the Low Self-referencing condition (19%), $p<$.05 and directionally higher than the High Self-referencing Post-ad (26%) and Product-focus (25%) conditions. These results appeared perplexing if the Low Self-referencing and High Self-referencing Pre-ad conditions were similarly using a schema-based process as the product evaluation data suggested. To test this hypothesis further, self-referencing comparisons were made in those cells where the likelihood of a schema-based process was strongest (Schema-consistent Prod Eval First conditions). Post-hoc protected t-tests indicated that the percent of Florida vacation imagery thoughts in the High Self-referencing Pre-ad condition (42%) was not significantly different from the Low Self-referencing condition (24%) but was significantly higher than the High Self-referencing Post-ad condition, (18%), t (218)=2.15, $p<$.05 and the Product-focus condition (15%), t (218)=2.15, $p<$ .05. These results suggest that category-related thoughts during the ad in the High Self-referencing Pre-ad and Low Self-referencing conditions were more similar then originally indicated by the main effect. However, the Low Self-referencing condition was not significantly different from any of the self-referencing comparisons. One possible explanation is that a schema-based process was even stronger for subjects in the

High Self-referencing Pre-ad condition compared to the Low Self-referencing condition.

Number of Dimensions Discussed on the Self-referencing Essay. An ANOVA indicated a main effect for Self-Referencing, $F(1, 109)=7.69, p<.007$ in the number of dimensions discussed on the essay. Subjects in the High Self-referencing Post-ad condition discussed significantly more dimensions ($M=4.7$) compared to subjects in the High Self-referencing Pre-ad condition ($M=4.1$). Subjects in the High Self-referencing Post-ad condition appeared to use the ad as reference point, leading them to consider more dimensions of their own past experience. An increase in dimensionality was hypothesized to encourage an attribute-based process for subjects in this condition.

Dimensions Discussed and Product Evaluation Correlation. If subjects in the High Self-referencing Pre-ad condition engaged in a category-based process, their unique experiences may be influenced by the schema-label (consistent vs. inconsistent). In contrast, High Self-referencing Post-ad condition subjects were expected to have engaged in an attribute-based process regardless of schema-match. Correlations between the number of dimensions discussed on the self-referencing essay and product evaluation provide evidence for the two information processing models. The following represent correlations for the Prod Eval First conditions. In the High Self-referencing Pre-ad Schema-consistent condition, the number of dimensions of a past spring break experience ($M=4.2$) was significantly *positively* correlated with product evaluation ($r=.69, p<.01$), suggesting that subjects were more likely to assimilate their idiosyncratic past experiences with the ad. In the High Self-referencing Pre-ad Schema-inconsistent, the number of dimensions of a past Thanksgiving break experience ($M=4.3$) was significantly *negatively* correlated with product evaluation ($r=-.59, p<.02$), suggesting that subjects were more likely to contrast their past experiences with ad. The number of dimensions discussed on essay in the High Self-referencing Post-ad condition had little influence on product evaluation in either the Schema-consistent ($M=4.7, r=.05$) or Schema-inconsistent ($M=4.3, r=.05$) conditions. A comparison of the correlations using Fisher's z' transformation indicated that in the Schema-consistent condition, the High Self-referencing Post-ad condition was significantly different from the High Self-referencing Pre-ad condition ($z=2.20, p<.01$). Similarly, in the Schema-inconsistent condition, the High Self-referencing Post-ad condition was significantly different from the High Self-referencing Pre-ad condition ($z=1.79, p<.05$).

SUMMARY

The pattern of results suggests that a category-based process can be used to explain the underlying persuasive mechanism in autobiographical memories ads, rather than self-referencing based on episodic memory. Autobiographical memories appear to increase self-focus and positive affect, and as such they encourage a schema-based process. When a unique self-experience is retrieved, the ability to assimilate one's idiosyncratic experiences and engage in a category-based process is the critical component in inducing persuasion. If a unique past experience is retrieved *after* viewing the ad, the ad is used as a reference point. This increases the likelihood of a mismatch occurring, thus triggering an attribute-based process which may reduce the ad's effect on persuasion. The results of this study suggest that autobiographical memories ads can be an effective persuasive technique, but that information relating to the self or to a past experience should be kept at a general level so that consumers can assimilate any of their unique experiences with the ad.

REFERENCES

Bargh, J. A. (1984). Automatic and cognitive processing of social information. In R. S. Wyer & T. K. Srull (Eds.), *Handbook of social cognition.* (Vol. 3, pp. 1-43). NJ: Erlbaum.

Baumgartner, H., Sujan, M., & Bettman, J. R. (1992). Autobiographical memories, affect and consumer information processing, *Journal of Consumer Psychology*, 1, 53-82.

Bradley, G. W. (1978). Self-serving biases in the attribution process: A reexamination of the factor fiction question. *Journal of Personality and Social Psychology*, 36, 56-71.

Brewer, W. F. & Pani, J. R. (1983). The structure of human memory. In G. H. Bower (Ed.), *The psychology of learning and motivation: Advances in research and theory* (Vol. 17, pp. 1-38). New York: Academic.

Fiske, S. T. (1982). Schema-triggered affect: Applications to social perception. In M. S. Clark & S. T. Fiske (Eds.), *Affect and cognition: The 17th Annual Carnegie Symposium on Cognition* (pp. 55-78). NJ: Erlbaum.

Fiske, S. T. & Pavelchak, M. A. (1986). Category-based versus piecemeal-based affective responses: Developments in schema-triggered affect. In R. M. Sorrentino & E. T. Higgins (Eds.), *Handbook of motivation and cognition: Foundations of social behavior* (pp. 167-203). New York: Guilford Press.

Fiske, S. T., & Taylor, S. E. (1991). *Social Cognition.* New York, McGraw-Hill, Inc.

Isen, A. M. & Daubman, K. A. (1984). The influence of affect on categorization. *Journal of Personality and Social Psychology*, 47, 1206-1217.

Gergen, K. J. (1971). *The Concept of Self.* New York: Holt, Rinehart & Winston.

Linville, P. W. (1982). Affective consequences of complexity regarding the self and others. In M. S. Clark & S. T. Fiske (Eds.), *Affect and cognition: The 17th Annual Carnegie Symposium on Cognition* (pp. 79-109). Hillsdale, NJ: Erlbaum.

Mackie, D. M. & Worth, L. T. (1991). Feeling good, but not thinking straight: The impact of positive mood on persuasion. In J. Forgas (Ed.), *Emotion and social judgments* (pp. 201-219). Oxford, England: Pergamon Press.

Sujan, M., Bettman, J. R. & Baumgartner, H. (1993). Influencing consumer judgments using autobiographical memories: A self-referencing perspective. *Journal of Marketing Research*, 30, 422-436.

Markus, H. & Sentis, K. (1982). The Self in Social Information Processing. In J. Suls (Ed.), *Psychological Perspectives of the Self* (pp. 41-70). NJ.: LEA.

Tesser, A. (1978). Self-generated attitude change. In L. Berkowitz (Ed.), *Advances in experimental social psychology*, (Vol. 11, 289-338). New York: Academic Press.

Wagenaar, W. A. (1986). My memory: A study of autobiographical memory over six years. *Cognitive Psychology*, 18, 225-252.

Measuring the Hedonic and Utilitarian Dimensions of Attitude: A Generally Applicable Scale

Eric R. Spangenberg, Washington State University
Kevin E. Voss, Washington State University
Ayn E. Crowley, Drake University

ABSTRACT

The first phase of a multi-phase process for developing a generally applicable, reliable, and valid scale for measuring the hedonic and utilitarian (HED-UT) components of attitudes is presented. Six product categories and six brands within those categories were assessed on both HED-UT dimensions. Relationships between the HED-UT scale and involvement, sensation seeking, and need for cognition were examined. Level of involvement was found to have a significant effect on both hedonic and utilitarian dimensions associated with stimuli. The resulting scale should be useful in determining the nature of customer evaluation of products and services and/or related advertising appeals.

Consumer researchers are increasingly looking for a richer understanding of the traditional information processing view of the various dimensions of attitude. Published efforts to establish a reliable and valid scale which measures the hedonic and utilitarian components of attitudes held by consumers regarding products, services, and activities are becoming more common. However, no widely applicable, satisfactory scale has been developed to date. Batra and Ahtola (1990) developed an eight item semantic differential scale using specific products as targets and suggested it be examined in future research. In further research, Crowley, Spangenberg, and Hughes (1992) found the Batra and Ahtola scale severely lacking when applied to product categories as opposed to specific products. Babin, Darden, and Griffin (1994) reported development of a scale based on the hedonic and utilitarian evaluation of shopping as an activity. The resulting scale, due to the focus only on shopping behavior, lacks general applicability to products, services, and other non-shopping activities. This paper reports the first phase of a multi-phase effort to develop a scale (HED/UT) which more closely captures the hedonic and utilitarian components of attitude experienced by consumers across a variety of situations and attitude targets.

BACKGROUND

Investigation of the hedonic and utilitarian components of consumption has been addressed in such various disciplines as sociology, psychology, and economics. One author in the field of economics stated that, "We use goods in two ways. We use goods as symbols of status and simultaneously as instruments to achieve some end-in-view" (Hamilton, 1987, p. 1541). This view clearly combined the hedonic and utilitarian views of consumption, echoing a parallel theoretical development that has occurred in consumer research (Hirschman and Holbrook, 1982).

Interest in the hedonic/utilitarian construct in the discipline of marketing builds on a series of articles by Hirschman and Holbrook. Based on earlier work in motivation research (e.g., Dichter, 1960), Hirschman and Holbrook (1982) developed an experiential view of hedonic consumption centered primarily around aesthetic products such as novels, movies, and art. Their resulting propositions, however, extend to all product classes. Defining hedonic consumption as "those facets of consumer behavior that relate to the multisensory, fantasy, and emotive aspects of one's experience with products" (p. 92), several detailed propositions were developed under the general thesis that hedonically consumed products stimulate internal imagery and emotional arousal based on externally sensed, product related stimuli.

Contrasting the experiential perspective to the more traditional information-processing view, Holbrook and Hirschman (1982) concluded that a synthesis is necessary if the science of marketing is to develop an "enlarged view" of consumer behavior. One aspect of their article was problematic, however, since they apparently viewed attitude as a component of affect. In their discussion of affect they stated that the traditional information processing approach has focused on: "only one aspect of hedonic response — namely, like or dislike of a particular brand (attitude) or its rank relative to other brands (preference). This attitudinal component represents only a tiny subset of the emotions and feelings of interest to the experiential view (Holbrook and Hirschman, 1982, p. 136)."

The aforementioned conception of affect is contrary to the more recent suggestion of Cohen and Areni (1991) that affect is a valenced feeling state. Emotion and mood are examples of these states. On the other hand, attitude, being evaluative in nature, contains a cognitive element and should be distinct from affect. Much work has accumulated regarding the affective and cognitive dimensions of attitude (see e.g., Abelson et al., 1982; Ajzen and Driver, 1992; Bagozzi and Burnkrant, 1979; Breckler and Wiggins, 1989; Fishbein and Ajzen, 1974; and Madden et al., 1988). We offer a competing hypothesis. We suggest that hedonic value is experienced on both affective and cognitive levels while the utilitarian component, which also may include both affective and cognitive dimensions, is dominated by the cognitive element. The affective and cognitive components of hedonic consumption imply that emotional desires compete with utilitarian motives in purchase and consumption decisions. This line of reasoning is linked to the growing body of research concerning compulsive consumption (see e.g., Hirschman, 1992). Compulsive consumers abuse purchasing the same way alcoholics abuse alcohol. They will purchase to achieve emotional arousal without regard to cognitively arrived at conclusions regarding financing, use, impact on others, etc. Short term arousal is sought at the cost of "significant negative consequences" and a disruption of "normal life functioning" (Faber and O'Guinn, 1989, p. 738). It may be possible that compulsive consumers represent the extreme end of a continuum. That is, all consumers may engage in an internal negotiation, motivated by need, to satisfy both hedonic and utilitarian consumption desires.

Hirschman (1983) proposed that some offerings, such as art and ideologies, are almost entirely hedonic. Value for the consumer stems from the subjective response evoked, there being little utility derived from, say, a painting. Establishing a more developed theory, Hirschman (1984) considered all consumption an "experience seeking" phenomenon. Accordingly, Hirschman decomposed experience seeking into three alternatives: 1) Cognition seeking, 2) Sensation seeking and 3) Novelty seeking. Cognitive experience seekers desire to stimulate, or activate, thinking. Sensation seekers desire to experience consumption through one or more of the five senses. Novelty seekers are looking for unique, fresh sources of stimulation through consumption. That is, the perceived uniqueness of a given product, service, or activity may create hedonic value for the consumer. A novel experience realized through consumption, such as finding a new restaurant or "trekking," may

Advances in Consumer Research
Volume 24, © 1997

serve more than one hedonic benefit by acting as a status symbol in the consumer's reference group as well as providing temporal enjoyment. A consumer may realize hedonic value from novel experiences on a cognitive and/or emotional level (Hirschman, 1984). Hirschman seems to have adopted the position that consumers occupy either a high, low, or average posture as a cognition seeker, sensation seeker, or novelty seeker. These postures are hypothesized to be static over time. This position would seem to be contrary to the body of thought on hedonic consumption which implies shifting value orientations dependent on the specific stimulus and the consumer's involvement with that stimulus (see e.g., Holbrook, 1986). Havlena and Holbrook (1986) argued that hedonic and utilitarian components of attitude are situational when they asserted that although "consumption experiences vary in their mix of utilitarian/hedonic, tangible/intangible, or objective/subjective components, the latter, more emotional aspects of consumption experiences occur to a greater or lesser degree in almost all consuming situations (p. 394)."

In the hedonic consumption view, the high interest and involvement generated by aesthetic products is strongly emphasized. Thus, a strong link between involvement and hedonic consumption is implied (Hirschman and Holbrook, 1982; Holbrook and Hirschman, 1982). Stimuli that are highly involving should result in more intense and arousing affective reactions as compared to more peripheral stimuli (Cohen and Areni, 1991). Involvement develops as the consumer experiences intrinsic and extrinsic satisfaction from interaction with the product (Bloch and Bruce, 1984). Stimuli are not inherently involving, consumers possess the capacity to be involved and this involvement will necessarily fluctuate from consumer to consumer and product to product (Traylor and Joseph, 1984). Therefore, high levels of involvement should logically be associated with high levels of hedonic response.

Two additional components, mood and mental imagery, are relevant in any discussion of the hedonic and utilitarian components of attitude. Mood may be a key variable in determining specific hedonic consumption behavior. Mood is generally described as a feeling state of longer duration and lower intensity than emotions. Where emotions are stimuli specific, consumers may experience a mood without being aware of its time of origin, cause, influence, or perhaps even its presence (Cohen and Areni, 1991). It has been suggested that consumers might use consumption as a means to change undesirable moods or achieve highly desired moods (e.g., Babin, Darden, and Griffin, 1994). Further, it has been reported that consumers who experienced negative prior-to-purchase moods, and implemented an information processing approach to purchase behavior, experienced positive post-purchase moods (Gardner and Hill, 1988). It is possible that products judged to be primarily hedonic in consumption value may be an instrument through which consumers manage mood states.

Mental imagery may be stimulated by the hedonic component of the consumption experience. Hirschman and Holbrook (1982) identified two possible forms: 1) historical imagery based on actual events in the subject's life and 2) fantasy (projective) imagery of events that, while perhaps referenced to historical events, have not actually taken place. This aspect would appear especially important in advertising contexts. Advertisers have historically used the power of communication to relate their products to images thought to appeal to consumers. It is, therefore, possible that successful measurement of hedonic consumption may also help to gauge the extent to which such images are adopted by consumers. Among other applications, a reliable and valid HED/UT scale would be useful in evaluating the effectiveness of advertisers in convincing consumers to assign a higher, or perhaps a lower, hedonic value to their offering.

EXISTING MEASURES OF THE HEDONIC/ UTILITARIAN CONSTRUCTS

Batra and Ahtola (1991) reported their development of an eight-item semantic differential scale purportedly measuring the hedonic and utilitarian components of attitude toward products. The scale was developed primarily with specific brands; despite performing acceptably regarding tests of reliability and validity, it suffered inconsistent loadings on stimuli, perhaps due to a concept x scale interaction. The scale also failed to incorporate many of the theoretical concepts (e.g., involvement) outlined by Hirschman and Holbrook (1982) as relevant components of hedonic consumption. Further, as noted earlier, the scale also failed to perform adequately in a subsequent generalization to product categories (Crowley, Spangenberg, and Hughes, 1992).

Crowley, Spangenberg, and Hughes (1992) showed some interesting results mapping product ratings in a two-dimensional space using the eight Batra and Ahtola items. Specifically, almost all of the product categories appeared in the same quadrant indicating relatively high levels of both hedonic and utilitarian value. This may be an artifact of the same concept x scale interaction observed in the original Batra and Ahtola article. Moreover, the eight adjectives chosen may not have adequately reflected the construct since some apparently utilitarian products appeared in very close proximity to items that would seem more hedonic. As an example, kitchen utensils were positioned very close to vacation resorts on the two-dimensional map reported by Crowley, Spangenberg, and Hughes (1992).

More recently, Babin, Darden, and Griffin (1994) reported development of a scale for assessing the hedonic and utilitarian components of shopping behavior (Personal Shopping Value Scale). Their scale is highly specific to retail shopping activity and is not generalizable to products, services, or other activities. Similar to the Batra and Ahtola (1991) work, this study failed to include some of the theoretical constructs (e.g., involvement) proposed by Hirschman and Holbrook (1982). Perhaps more troublesome was the procedure employed to validate the scale within the general population. Students accompanied respondents on a shopping trip to a local mall to observe the respondents shopping behavior and administer the survey. Respondents were informed that students were receiving course credit for the investigation. Upon examination, it appears a strong possibility that this procedure could have introduced demand artifacts into the scale development process. The Personal Shopping Value Scale should be appropriately validated before confidence can be placed in its ability to assess the hedonic and utilitarian value experienced by shoppers.

A generally applicable scale useful for measuring the hedonic and utilitarian components of attitude toward products and services has yet to be developed. This paper reports the first phase in the development of a valid and reliable scale that can fill this void in consumer research.

SCALE DEVELOPMENT

A pool of adjective pairs was generated in two steps. First a thorough review of the literature suggested many possibilities. Then, pretest subjects were asked to describe their attitudes towards products and services. The results of both processes were reviewed and duplicate pairs were dropped. In total, 27 distinct adjective pairs were generated for use in a seven-point semantic differential scale format. Since, as discussed above, there are many factors which may interact in determining the level of hedonic and/or utilitarian attitudes held by consumers, a reliable and valid scale must isolate the hedonic and utilitarian values from possible confounding variables. Accordingly, in addition to the 27 adjective pairs, three additional multiple item scales, to be used for validation checks within a larger nomological network, were jointly administered to the respondents. These scales included a measure of involvement, sensation seeking, and need for cognition.

The notion that product involvement is closely linked to the level of hedonic meaning the consumer associates with the stimuli has strong face validity (Hirschman and Holbrook, 1982). As discussed above, high levels of involvement should lead to stronger hedonic values. It seems reasonable that a scale measuring consumer involvement should be positively associated with a scale seeking to measure hedonic components of attitude. Accordingly, the 10-item reduced form of the Personal Involvement Inventory (PII) (Zaichkowsky, 1990) was administered concurrently with the pool of hedonic and utilitarian semantic differential adjective pairs.

In each of the two existing hedonic and utilitarian scales presented above, positive emotion is characterized strictly as a hedonic value while negative emotions have been attributed to utilitarian value. This is not the meaning ascribed to hedonic consumption by Hirschman and Holbrook (1982), who pointed out that emotions can be positive or negative and still be hedonic; horror movies or stomach turning roller coaster rides, for example, provide little in the way of utilitarian benefits. Both of these activities provide high emotional arousal through what might be considered a negative emotion — fear. Perhaps a more accurate word is one commonly used by bungee jumpers — a "rush". Accordingly, a valid measure of hedonic consumption seeks to identify strong emotional reactions to stimuli, but is sympathetic to the idea that consumers may consume for emotional reactions (sensation seekers) that might not generally be considered pleasant. Therefore, an adaptation of Zuckerman's (1979) 38-item Sensation Seeking Scale (SS) was included to assess subjects' predilection to affective responses.

The evaluative judgment necessary to form attitudes regarding stimuli theoretically contains a strong cognitive component. Emotional reactions to stimuli have been linked to judgments regarding the desirability of the outcome as well as the appeal of the activity (Ortony, Clore, and Collins, 1988). Further, stimuli that match expectations may interact with the consumer's cognitive structure to determine the affective response (Cohen and Areni, 1991). Thus, cognition and affect are intertwined in the evaluative process necessary to develop attitudes about products, services, and activities. Cognitive processing then is potentially present in both hedonic and utilitarian product evaluations. Accordingly, the 18-item short form of the Need for Cognition Scale (NFC) (Cacioppo, Petty, and Kao, 1984) was also administered.

PROCEDURE AND SUBJECTS

Questionnaire booklets including our initial 27 items and the three additional multi-item scales, were prepared for rating the following branded products: IBM Personal Computers, Lay's Potato Chip's, Hilton Vacation Resorts, Wesson Cooking Oil, Dawn Dish Detergent, and Nike Athletic Shoes. Product categories and specific brands were selected in a separate, 2-stage pretest: 1) List products or services purchased predominantly for pleasure/utility, and 2) Within category "x", what brand first comes to mind? The most commonly mentioned brands within each product category were selected to ensure that respondents would be familiar with, and hence able to render judgement on, the target brands. Booklets were also prepared for the product category associated with each brand. Thus, there were a total of twelve versions of the initial combined measures. Subjects in both the pretest and main study were students at Washington State University. In the main study, subjects completed only one of the twelve versions of our instrument in return for course credit in a single lab session. After

removing booklets exhibiting non-response problems, six hundred and eight useable responses were obtained.

RELIABILITY AND ITEM REDUCTION

Principal components exploratory factor analysis using the intial 27 items was conducted separately for both specific branded products and product categories. Rotation and the scree plots indicated that a two-factor solution best explained the data. All of the items loaded, as expected, on the first two factors with the exception of the hedonistic/not hedonistic and utilitarian/not utilitarian adjective pairs which were subsequently dropped (note that these terms may have theoretical meanings different than generally understood meanings) due to low item-to-total correlations and factor loadings. Internal consistency reliability was assessed on both the brand and product category responses. In the case of the brands, the 27 adjective pairs produced a coefficient alpha of .89. For the product categories, alpha was .92. Because we are proposing two dimensions, it is appropriate to compute alpha for each (Churchill, 1979). When used to measure brands both the 13 item hedonic and 14-item utilitarian subscales produced an alpha of .94. For product categories, alpha was .95 and .93 for the hedonic and utilitarian components respectively. Item-to-total correlations were examined separately for each dimension with both the brand and product category data. Deleted adjective pairs with values less than .50 were the hedonistic/not hedonistic and utilitarian/not utilitarian pairs. Recalculation of item-to-total correlations revealed another unsatisfactory value for the convenient/not convenient adjective pair which was also dropped.

Thus, the scale was reduced to 24 adjective pairs with 12 pairs in each of the HED/UT subscales. Dropping the three adjective pairs with low item-to-total correlations did not substantially change coefficient alpha. Thus, initial reliability estimates for the HED/UT scale were encouraging.

CONSTRUCT VALIDITY

Confirmatory factor analysis (CFA) was conducted using EQS (Bentler 1993). For the unidimensional, single-factor, brand name model: $\chi^2=885.0$ ($df=250$, $p<.001$); Bentler-Bonett fit indexes were normed=.86, nonnormed=.88, and CFI=.87. For the single factor model regarding product categories: $\chi^2=940.8$ ($df=250$, $p<.001$); Bentler-Bonett indexes were normed=.84, nonnormed=.86, and CFI=.87. Although the overall the overall χ^2 statistic was significant, it was within the rule of 2.5 to 3 times the number of degrees of freedom, suggested as acceptable by Bollen (1989), a significant improvement over the null model for both brand names and product categories [$\chi^2=6110.2$ (276 df) for brands; 5777.0 (284 df) for product categories]. For both the brand names and product categories, the items loaded, as predicted by the exploratory factor analysis, on two factors providing strong evidence of construct validity (Gerbing and Anderson, 1988). CFA factor loadings and item-to-total correlations are presented in Table 1.[1] Also shown in Table 1 are reliabilities and average variance explained (AVE) calculated according to Fornell and Larcker (1981). In all cases reliability was>.91 and AVE ranged from .47 to .50.

In order to test the relationship between involvement and the HED/UT scale the adjective pairs were separated into their two respective 12-item subscales. We fit the data to ANCOVA models using the summated hedonic subscale and the summated utilitarian

---

[1] EFA results are available upon request from the first author.

TABLE 1
HED/UT Scale Items: Item Identification and Dimensionality Indices

| | Factor Loadings[a] and Item-to-Total Correlations | | | |
| | Brand Names | | Product Categories | |
Items	Factor Loading	Item-to-Total Correlation	Factor Loading	Item-to-Total Correlation
Utilitarian				
Useful/Useless	.77	.73	.79	.73
Practical/Impractical	.76	.75	.79	.75
Necessary/Unnecessary	.78	.73	.80	.75
Functional/Not Functional	.84	.77	.80	.82
Sensible/Not Sensible	.81	.74	.77	.78
Helpful/Unhelpful	.88	.80	.83	.84
Efficient/Inefficient	.81	.74	.77	.78
Effective/Ineffective	.90	.84	.85	.86
Beneficial/Harmful	.81	.75	.80	.76
Handy/Not Handy	.66	.59	.60	.66
Unproductice/Productive	.69	.75	.69	.70
Problem Solving/Not Problem Solving	.67	.57	.58	.66
Hedonic				
Dull/Exciting	.82	.72	.84	.80
Not Delightful/Delightful	.82	.79	.83	.81
Not Sensuous/Sensuous	.71	.68	.71	.70
Not Fun/Fun	.84	.82	.88	.84
Unpleasant/Pleasant	.79	.74	.78	.76
Not Funny/Funny	.60	.60	.65	.65
Not Thrilling/Thrilling	.87	.84	.83	.80
Not Happy/Happy	.85	.83	.80	.80
Not Playful/Playful	.84	.82	.76	.76
Enjoyable/Unenjoyable	.75	.71	.75	.72
Cheerful/Not Cheerful	.76	.75	.76	.76
Amusing/Not Amusing	.65	.64	.71	.71
Explained Variance[b]		60%		59%
Average Variance Explained[c]				
Utilitarian		50%		47%
Hedonic		49%		49%
Reliability[c]				
Utilitarian		.92		.91
Hedonic		.92		.92

[a]From confirmatory factor analysis
[b]From principal components factor analysis.
[c]Calculations described in Fornell and Larcker (1981).

subscales as dependent variables. In addition to the classification variable level of involvement, summated results from the modified Sensation Seeking scale (SS) and the short form of the Need for Cognition scale (NFC) were included as covariates. The hedonic subscale showed a non-significant regression relationship ($F=.14$, $p=.87$). Level of involvement, however, was a significant explanatory variable ($F=63.4$, $p=.0001$). Against the utilitarian subscale, the ANCOVA showed a similar significant result when testing level of involvement ($F=62.5$, $p=.0001$). The regression relationship was, again, not significant ($F=3.3$, $p=.12$). In order to more completely explore the relation between the HED/UT scale and the two covariate scales (SS and NFC), reduced models were tested.

That is, a series of ANCOVA models were fit dropping either the SS or NFC covariate. The only significant covariance relationship was in the model which included the SS scale as a covariate with level of involvement against the utilitarian subscale ($F=4.3$, $p=.04$). Based on the weight of statistical evidence, it was concluded that the SS and NFC scales did not significantly covary with our HED/UT scale. Accordingly, we fit regression lines for each summated subscale with the summated PII scale as the independent variable (Hedonic $R^2=.29$; Utilitarian $R^2=.31$). Figure 1 clearly shows that high scores on the PII led to extreme responses on both dimensions of the HED/UT scale. Low levels of involvement are then associated with lower perceived levels of hedonic and utilitarian attitude

FIGURE 1
Regression of summated Hedonic and Utilitarian subscales on summated PII scale.

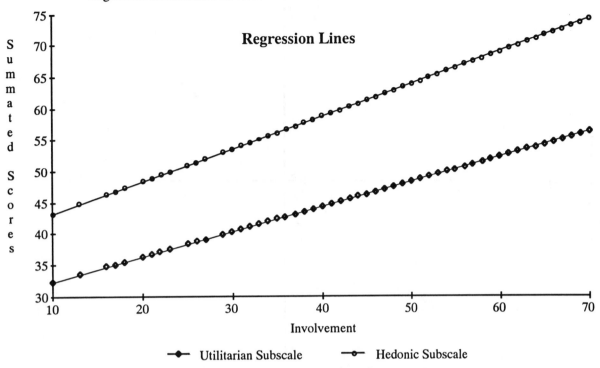

components. Interestingly, personal computers proved to be the most involving to our sample while potato chips and cooking oil were the least involving (dishwashing liquid=4.25; athletic shoes=5.56; cooking Oil=4.02; personal computers=5.73; potato chips=4.03; vacation resorts=5.43).

Our results suggest that level of involvement is positively and significantly related to the level of hedonic and/or utilitarian value. Combining all 24 questions would hide this effect since low utilitarian ratings can offset high hedonic ratings. Specifically, there is a strong positive linear relationship between the summated PII and the hedonic and utilitarian subscales. Although we expected high levels of involvement to lead to high levels of hedonic value, it was interesting to find that high levels of involvement also lead to high levels of utilitarian value. It is worth noting that this effect could be mistaken for standard deviation bias. Standard deviation bias is the tendency for respondents to use either wide or narrow ranges of response intervals (Greenleaf, 1992). In Figure 1 it is clear that respondents with extreme responses on the utilitarian subscale also gave extreme responses on the hedonic subscale (i.e. these respondents used a wide range of response intervals). In the present study however, the PII has provided a surprising explanation for this potential artifact.

The HED/UT scale also discriminates between levels of the construct for branded products and product categories. The two dimensional plot in Figure 2 shows the mean responses for each stimulus for both the brand and product category response data. Some observations become immediately clear. First, both Hilton Vacation Resorts and the product category Vacation Resorts were consistently rated highest on the hedonic adjectives. Also, IBM Personal Computers and the product category Personal Computers were consistently rated the most utilitarian. Finally, Lay's Potato Chips and the product category Potato Chips were seen as the least utilitarian products. Surprisingly, these products were rated ap-

proximately equal to the IBM Personal Computer/Personal Computers in Hedonic value. In general, there were no large differences between ratings of branded products and their respective general product categories.

DISCUSSION

The two-dimensional HED/UT scale developed here appears to be a reliable tool for measuring the attitudes held by consumers with respect to specific products and their related categories. Initial tests of construct validity are consistent with our two-dimensional proposition. As our theoretical background suggests, and our results support, involvement appears to have a strong correlation with level of hedonic response. Somewhat unexpectedly, involvement also shows a strong relationship to the utilitarian component of attitude. Thus, it is suggested that product involvement be measured concurrently with the HED/UT scale in future administrations. This is consistent with Crowley, Spangenberg, and Hughes' (1992) criticism of Batra and Ahtolas' (1991) lack of accounting for involvement in their work.

Affect, as measured by our adaptation of the SS scale, shows mixed results. Our review suggests that affect would strongly influence the hedonic construct. Our results, however, indicate a link to the utilitarian construct. It is possible, as suggested by the negative slope of the regression coefficient in the ANCOVA model, that respondents with a high emotional predisposition evaluate more functional and mundane products in strictly utilitarian terms. That is, they may be willing to judge products which provide arousal along a broad continuum while non-arousing products are judged in a constricted utilitarian space. A less interesting explanation questions the validity of the SS scale.

This study failed to find any relation between cognition, as measured by the NFC scale, and the hedonic or utilitarian components of attitude as measured by our HED/UT scale. It is possible

FIGURE 2

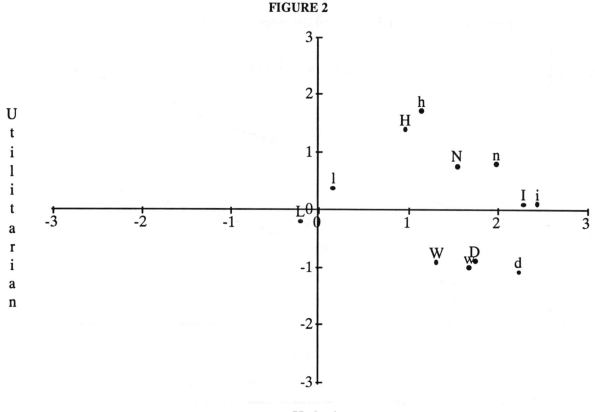

Hedonic

W	Wesson oil	w	cooking oil
I	IBM personal computers	i	personal computers
D	Dawn dish detergent	d	dish detergent
N	Nike athletic shoes	n	athletic shoes
H	Hilton vacation resorts	h	vacation resorts
L	Lay's potato chips	l	potato chips

that since, as we suggested, cognition is involved in both hedonic and utilitarian assessments, the effects were evenly distributed. This, however, is an explanation that our data do not address.

CONCLUSION

We developed a scale to measure both the hedonic and utilitarian dimensions of attitude and showed strong indicators regarding reliability and validity. The scale was internally consistent with a stable factor structure across several product categories and specific brands within those categories; explained variance and average variance extracted was higher than reported for most published scales. The scale had the hypothesized correlation with involvement but did not perform as expected in relation to sensation seeking and need for cognition.

The study was limited in that development was based on student subjects; extension to a non-student population in further tests of validity is desirable. We are conducting further research which incorporates scales measuring imagery, negative emotions, mood, novelty, and compulsive consumption in conjunction with the HED/UT scale. We would expect HED/UT to be highly correlated with the aforementioned constructs indicating further convergent validity.

In addition to further validation efforts, we should like to see future research examine the determinants of the hedonic and utilitarian components of attitude. And, while we see several possibilities for practical application of our scale, the most obvious benefits would accrue to advertisers. If a target market seeks primarily hedonic or utilitarian benefits, appeals could be directed respectively. In fact, marketing researchers may want to investigate whether hedonic- or utilitarian-oriented consumers are more or less responsive to differing methods of sales promotion. Finally, it is possible that our HED/UT scale may measure attitudes that could explain variety seeking behavior (see e.g., Van Trijp, Hoyer, and Inman, 1996).

REFERENCES

Abelson, Robert P., Donald R. Kinder, Mark D. Peters, and Susan T. Fiske (1992), "Affective and Semantic Components in Political Person Perception," *Journal of Personality and Social Psychology*, 42 (4), 619-630.

Ajzen, Icek and B. L. Driver (1992), "Contingent Value Measurement: On the Nature and Meaning of Willingness to Pay," *Journal of Consumer Psychology*, 1 (4), 297-316.

Bagozzi, Richard P. and Robert E. Burnkrant (1979), "Attitude Organization and the Attitude-Behavior Relationship, *Journal of Personal and Social Psychology*, 37 (6) 913-929.

Batra, Rajeev and Olli T. Ahtola (1990), "Measuring the Hedonic and Utilitarian Sources of Consumer Attitudes," *Marketing Letters*, 2(2), 159-170.

Babin, Barry J., William R. Darden, and Mitch Griffin (1994), "Work and/or Fun: Measuring Hedonic and Utilitarian Shopping Value," *Journal of Consumer Research*, 20 (March), 644-656.

Bentler, Peter (1993), *EQS Structural Equations Program, Ver 3.0*. Los Angeles, CA: BMPD Statistical Software, Inc.

Bloch, Peter H. and Grady D. Bruce (1984), "Product Involvement as Leisure Behavior," in Thomas C. Kinnear (ed.), *Advances in Consumer Research, Vol. 11* (pp. 197-202). Ann Arbor, MI: Association for Consumer Research.

Breckler, Steven J. and Elizabeth C. Wiggins (1989), "Affect versus Evaluation in the Structure of Attitudes," *Journal of Experimental Social Psychology*, 25, 253-271.

Bollen, Kenneth A. (1989), *Structural Equations with Latent Variables*. New York: John Wiley, Inc.

Cacioppo, John T., Richard E. Petty, and Feng Chuan Kao (1984), "The Efficient Assessment of Need for Cognition," *Journal of Personality Assessment*, 48 (3), 306-307.

Churchill, Gilbert A. Jr. (1979), "A Paradigm for Developing Better Measures of Marketing Constructs," *Journal of Marketing Research*, 16 (February), 67-73.

Cohen, Joel B. and Charles S. Areni (1991), "Affect and Consumer Behavior," in Thomas S. Robertson and Harold H. Kassarjian (Eds.), *Handbook of Consumer Behavior*. Englewood Cliffs, NJ: Prentice Hall.

Crowley, Ayn E., Eric R. Spangenberg and Kevin R. Hughes (1992), "Measuring the Hedonic and Utilitarian Dimensions of Attitudes toward Product Categories," *Marketing Letters*, 3: (3), 239-249.

Dichter, Ernest (1960), *The Strategy of Desire*. New York, NY: Doubleday.

Faber, Ronald J. and Thomas C. O'Guinn (1989), "Classifying Compulsive Consumers: Advances in the Development of a Diagnostic Tool,' in M. Wallendorf and P. Anderson (Eds.), *Advances in Consumer Research, Vol. 16* (pp. 132-135). Provo, UT: Association for Consumer Research.

Fishbein, Martin and Icek Ajzen (1974), "Attitudes towards Objects as Predictors of Single and Multiple Behavioral Criteria," *Psychological Review*, 81 (1), 59-74.

Fornell, Claes and David F. Larcker (1981), "Evaluating Structural Equation Models with Unobservable Variables and Measurement Error," *Journal of Marketing Research*, 28 (February), 39-50.

Gardner, Meryl P. and Ronald Paul Hill (1988), "Consumer's Mood States: Antecedents and Consequences of Experiential versus Informational Strategies for Brand Choice," *Psychology and Marketing*, 5 (Summer), 169-182.

Gerbing, David W. and James C. Anderson (1988), "An Updated Paradigm for Scale Development Incorporating Unidimensionality and its Assessment," *Journal of Marketing Research*, 25 (May), 186-192.

Greenleaf, Eric A. (1992), "Improving Rating Scale Measures by Detecting and Correcting Bias Components in Some Response Styles," *Journal of Marketing Research*, 29 (May), 176-188.

Hamilton, David B. (1987), "Institutional Economics and Consumption," *Journal of Economic Issues*, 21 (December), 1531-1553.

Havlena, William J. and Morris B. Holbrook (1986), "The Varieties of Consumption Experience: Comparing Two Typologies of Emotion in Consumer Behavior," *Journal of Consumer Research*, 13 (December), 394-404.

Hirschman, Elizabeth C. (1983), "Aesthetics, Ideologies and the Limits of the Marketing Concept," *Journal of Marketing*, 47 (Summer), 45-55.

Hirschman, Elizabeth C. (1984), "Experience Seeking: A Subjectivist Perspective of Consumption," *Journal of Business Research*, 12, 115-136.

Hirschman, Elizabeth C. (1992), "The Consciousness of Addiction: Toward a General Theory of Compulsive Consumption," *Journal of Consumer Research*, 19, 155-179.

Hirschman, Elizabeth C. and Morris B. Holbrook (1982), "Hedonic Consumption: Emerging Concepts, Methods and Propositions," *Journal of Marketing*, 46 (Summer), 92-101.

Holbrook, Morris B. (1986), "Emotion in the Consumption Experience: Toward a New Model of Consumer Behavior," in R. A. Peterson, W.D. Hoyer, and W. R. Wilson (Eds.), *The Role of Affect in Consumer Behavior: Emerging Theories and Applications*. Lexington, MA: Heath.

Holbrook, Morris B. and Elizabeth C. Hirschman (1982), "The Experiential Aspects of Consumption: Consumer Fantasies, Feelings, and Fun," *Journal Of Consumer Research*, 9 (September), 132-140.

Madden, Thomas J., Chris T. Allen, and Jacquelyn L. Twible (1988), "Attitude toward the Ad: An Assessment of Diverse Measurement Indices Under Different Processing 'Sets'," *Journal of Marketing Research*, 25 (August), 242-52.

Ortony, A., G. L. Clore, and A. Collins (1988), *The Cognitive Structure of Emotions*. New York, NY: Cambridge University Press.

Traylor, Mark B. and W. Beanie Joseph (1984), "Measuring Consumer Involvement in Products: Developing a General Scale," *Psychology and Marketing*, 1 (Summer), 65-77.

Van Trijp, Hans C. M., Wayne D. Hoyer, and J. Jeffrey Inman (1996), "Why Switch? Product Category-Level Explanations for True Variety Seeking Behavior," *Journal of Marketing Research*, 33 (August), 281-292.

Zaichkowsy, Judith Lynne (1990), "The Personal Involvement Inventory: Reduction and Application to Advertising," Unpublished manuscript, Burnaby, BC: Simon Fraser University.

Zuckerman, Marvin (1979), *Sensation Seeking: Beyond the Optimal Level of Arousal*. Hillsdale, NJ: Lawrence Erlbaum Associates.

The Intergenerational Flow of Wealth in the Family
Deborah D. Heisley, UCLA

In these three empirical studies, the inter-generational transfer of wealth is studied as a means by which consumption objects are used in an attempt to create shared familial meaning. The flow of wealth (in money, property or goods) among generations within a family is a fundamental aspect of a culture. It is a way in which familial, ethnic, and socioeconomic values are communicated and maintained. All three studies come at this issue from a qualitative data analysis approach primarily using interviews.

The Social Construction of Heirlooms
Deborah D. Heisley, UCLA
Deborah Cours, Cal State University, Northridge
Melanie Wallendorf, University of Arizona

We examine how people define and value heirlooms. Eighteen in-depth interviews were conducted by trained graduate students. Our sample consisted of 12 women and 6 men, representing working class to upper-middle class. Informants ranged from twenty to eighty years old, represented all marital statuses, and were of Judeo-Christian background (including Jewish, Catholic, Protestant). They represented different family structures, including families with adoptions, step-children, various ages of biological children, and childless adults. Sometimes we interviewed multiple informants from the same family. Each interview was transcribed and thickly-coded by at least two of the researchers. For the focus of analysis, we selected the most elaborated and holistically rich coding categories.

We recognized a pattern such that items of high sentimental value but low economic value tend to be called "keepsakes" (e.g. photographs). Items that were relatively low in sentimental value but high in economic value are considered "property" (e.g. cars). Possessions that are called "heirlooms" tend to be high in *both* sentimental and economic value (e.g. wedding rings).

From the etic perspective, the *locus of meaning* (whether the value is inherent in an attribute of the *object* or if the value lies in the representation of *people*) and the *level of shared meaning* (whether the meaning is at a personal (*self*) level, is understood to the *family*, or is *culturally*-based) theoretically differentiated and fully accounted for the valuations of heirlooms by the informants. The six resulting cells of these dimensions are theoretically rich for understanding the use of consumer goods in the construction of meaning inter-generationally.

"You Can't Take It With You:" An Examination of the Disposition Decisions of Older Consumers
Carolyn F. Curasi, University of South Florida
Linda L. Price, University of South Florida
Eric J. Arnould, University of South Florida

Between 1995 and the year 2000, experts predict the largest intergenerational transfer of wealth in American history. As in previous generations, aging confronts consumers with decisions about how to distribute their wealth and the resulting financial culmination of their lives. In this process, decisions related to the disposition of possessions are fraught with tension. This research project is a phenomenological examination of the fundamental problems faced by older consumers when getting rid of possessions they have accumulated over their lifetimes. It is based on depth interviews with 125 consumers between the ages of 65 and 95 who predominantly reside in the Southeastern U.S. The sample includes both men and women in a variety of living arrangements ranging from their own homes of many years to nursing homes. Compared with disposition decisions that have been described in most other consumer behavior research, older consumers' dispositions are often precipitated by growing awareness of their own mortality. The disposition of possessions by older consumers is a process that takes place over an extended period of time. Because of the difficulty of deciding what to do with their most cherished possessions, it is not something that is taken lightly or done quickly. There are many mixed emotions about giving objects away prior to death and many situations may trigger disposition of valued objects. Often, the trigger is a conversation that allows the older consumer to mediate the interpretation of the object and attach one or more life stories to that object. Several important themes emerge from analyses of our data. In our results we can see possessions as the skeletal structure or the materials for telling and retelling of a life story. However, there is always a gap between the object and the narrative it represents. Hence, active mediation is viewed as a key to meaning transfer. A particularly interesting aspect of our informants' comments is that they refer to valued possessions as their own, even though they no longer have them in their possession. It seems they want these sacred possessions to remain symbolically tied to them, even when circulated among other people, in much the same way that Weiner (1995) describes inalienable wealth. Many of the older consumers we talked with explicitly referred to distributing "pieces" of themselves to their children and grandchildren. In contrast to other reports of disposition decisions, our respondents did not seem to feel a loss of self when disposing of possessions that represented who they are and the life they have lived. Rather respondents focused on a type of identity preservation, expansion or immortality. We found older consumers commonly employ a variety of strategies to ensure that meanings are transferred with their possessions. We describe and illustrate many of these strategies including: story telling, visualization, determining the most deserving, meaning matching, giving the gift back to the giver, passing on possessions during a confluence of life transitions, and transferring valued possessions to those most likely to perpetuate their preferred self image.

An Intergenerational Analysis of Ethnic Traditions in Wedding-Gift Giving
Mary Ann McGrath, Loyola University of Chicago
Basil G. Englis, Penn State University

A wedding is an important occasion when consumers select "appropriate" gifts. Guests are faced with the perennial questions: What should be chosen as a gift? How much money should the gift cost? What if it is not enough? What if it is too much? Will the couple understand why the giver thinks this is a good gift? Selecting an appropriate gift is of paramount importance because of the role that gifts can play in strengthening social ties (e.g., Belk 1979; Mauss 1924/1956; Sherry 1983). Yet, these occasions are also fraught with uncertainty (e.g., Sherry, McGrath and Levy 1992; 1993) and risk (e.g., Belk and Coon 1993) associated with giving an inappropriate gift.

In this paper we explore the wedding celebration from the viewpoint of the ritual audience (e.g., Leach 1968; Rook 1985). We emphasize the differing meanings ascribed to the celebration by members of three generations within families of different ethnic orientations, and upon the wedding gifts given by this audience as ritual artifacts (see also Lowrey and Otnes 1993). We consider how the currency of meaning in wedding-gift exchange differs among ethnic subcultures, and how these ethnic traditions of gift selection and presentation are transmitted across generations within a family. Finally, we touch upon reciprocity in wedding-gift exchange.

Thirty-eight undergraduate students were both respondents and associate researchers (see Wallendorf and Arnould 1991). Each was trained in applications of qualitative research methods. Each filled out a five-page questionnaire that related to his or her understanding and experience with weddings and wedding gifts. The students, using identical questionnaires, interviewed a parent or other family member of their parent's generation and a grandparent or other family member of their grandparent's generation. Each also engaged in reflective analysis concerning the effect that their subcultural roots have on their own behaviors and attitudes. The study included Irish-American, Jewish, Asian-American, Italian American, and African-American consumers, as well as consumers with Northern European and Middle Eastern origins.

In order to tap both positive and negative aspects of ethnic wedding traditions and their accompanying gift exchange, which frequently involve extended kinship networks and multiple generations, both structured interviews and projective techniques were employed. The written interviewing protocol tapped both the perceived reality and the fantasy associated with wedding-gift exchanges. The questionnaire consisted of a variety of response formats, including sentence stems (a completion projective method), a story-telling format (a construction projective method), several open-ended questions, dichotomous items, and a series of demographic questions.

Questionnaires were grouped into triads relating to the responses of each extended family. The single largest category of wedding gift was some form of money (e.g., cash, stocks, bonds, etc.), which comprised nearly half of all wedding gifts. However, perceptions of what constitutes an appropriate wedding gift varied considerably between generations within extended families. Moreover, we discovered little reliance upon and much ambivalence toward the use of "formal" wedding registries, and instead found more informal means whereby appropriate gifts (and appropriate monetary levels) were identified. Interpretive analyses revealed a number of themes, which serve to shed light upon the roles of ethnicity and religion in this celebratory consumer context. These analyses are also informative in delineating the "sacred" meanings that are sometimes attached to the seemingly "profane" gift of money.

The Dark and Other Sides of Intergenerational Property Transfers

Dennis W. Rook, University of Southern California

Carolyn Curasi's observation that intergenerational personal property transfers amount to several billion dollars – every year – provides tangible support for my conclusion that the three papers in this session are classically "interesting." They target significant social, psychological and economic phenomena; their findings make you think; they are original and creative, in ways that Melanie Wallendorf elaborated earlier this weekend; and collectively, they represent the pleasantly expanding borders of consumer research. I anticipate that the issues addressed in these papers will continue to attract research interest in the future. My comments are designed to encourage this research stream, and I would like to thank Deb Heisley for inviting me to share my thoughts on several matters.

First, it seems that theory about intergenerational transfers is in the incubation stage, and beginning to emerge from the descriptive analyses we have heard today. While these conceptualizations seems likely to mature into more comprehensive theoretical systems, we might also look to existing theory that directly informs some of the phenomena described today. Because older consumers are typically the donors of heirlooms and other property, Erik Erikson's analysis of the final lifecycle crisis of integrity *versus* despair strikes me as relevant and applicable here. As the Price, Curasi and Arnould paper speculates, innovative services that facilitate intergenerational transfers will materialize as aging populations grow, not only in the U.S., but throughout the world. The Eriksonian perspective encourages an explicit focus on how such marketplace innovations might help consumers successfully negotiate the anxiety and ambivalence that animates these late-in-life exchanges.

Second, I think that other variables could easily provide valuable analytic leverage to this research. Specifically, use of the still-neglected concept of social class helps identify hypotheses about thematic, content, and process variation in intergenerational transfers. Recent comments from an estate attorney friend remind me that behavior involving millions of dollars and teams of lawyers is very different from squabbling over grandma's silver, or her VCR. More explicit consideration of social class and status differences will lead to more nuanced observations about consumers' wealth transfer behaviors and their meanings.

Finally, all three studies in this session imply an intergenerational transfer process that is unidirectional (from an elder to an often younger recipient), and voluntary. This is too restrictive a conceptualization, as an undeniably dark side to this behavior exists. Someone I have known for four decades has been steadily draining his mother's cash reserve. The first $100,000 was transferred in dribbles and drabs over several years; the most recent transfer was swift and dramatic, and depleted this elderly woman of her remaining $150,000. This disturbing case alerted me to the possibility that some intergenerational transfers are less than voluntary. It seems useful to think about this behavior as occurring along a continuum that ranges from voluntary donation to coercive acquisition to outright appropriation. After all, kids may continue to steal from mommy's purse. Recognition of the dark side of wealth transfer illuminates some perhaps unpleasant but important and real ethical and social policy issues.

New Directions in Cultural Psychology: The Effects of Cultural Orientation on Affect and Cognition

Jennifer L. Aaker, UCLA
Durairaj Maheswaran, New York University

SESSION OVERVIEW AND MOTIVATION

The cultural variable, individualism-collectivism, has received an increasing amount of attention in cultural psychology. Briefly, individualism-collectivism refers to the differences in the construal of the self, others and the interdependence of the two (e.g., Cousins 1989; Markus and Kitayama 1991; Triandis 1989). Individualism refers to the view of the self as independent, while collectivism refers to the view of the self as interdependent. Due to these differences in self-construal, members of individualist vs. collectivist cultures tend to exhibit different perceptions of the in-group vs. out-group (e.g., Triandis 1989), patterns of emotions (e.g., Matsumoto 1989), value systems (e.g., Schwartz and Bilsky 1990), and attributional styles (e.g., Morris and Peng 1994).

However, despite the increase in research on individualism-collectivism, limited research has addressed how these cultural differences affect consumer information processing (Aaker and Maheswaran), the structure of emotions (Bagozzi, Wong and Yi) and advertising effectiveness (Shavitt, Nelson and Yuan). In this collaboration, these three areas was examined through three different methodologies. Aaker and Maheswaran focused on an experimental design in which motivation, consensus information, attribute information are manipulated and hypotheses are tested via an ANOVA and regression analysis. Bagozzi, Wong and Yi explored the structure of emotions through survey analysis and test the structure through exploratory and confirmatory factor analysis. Shavitt, Nelson and Yuan examined the differences in cognitive responses to advertisements and test their hypotheses through ANOVA and correlational analysis. Finally, in order to provide a diverse yet synergistic perspective, the three papers explored the effects outlined above in distinct collectivist cultures: Hong Kong (Aaker and Maheswaran), Korea and Chinese (Bagozzi, Wong and Yi) and Taiwan (Shavitt, Nelson and Yuan), while focusing on the United States as an individualist culture.

PRESENTATION SUMMARY

First, Aaker and Maheswaran examined whether cultural differences in persuasive effects are a function of processing differences or perceptual differences in cue diagnosticity. In two experiments, the impact of motivation, congruity of persuasive communication and the diagnosticity of heuristic cues on the processing strategies and product evaluations of members of a collectivist culture were compared with findings documented in past research in individualist cultures. This research supports the view that perceptual differences in cue diagnosticity account for systematic differences in persuasive effects across cultures. It is also suggested that existing theoretical frameworks, specifically the dual process models of persuasion, are robust across cultures and can help predict and explain cultural differences.

Second, Bagozzi, Wong and Yi focused on the similarities and differences in the structure of emotions across cultures. Through measuring the emotions of people from three cultures, Chinese from Beijing (n=210), Koreans from Seoul (n=122) and Americans from Ann Arbor (n=300), the authors found a three-factor affect-positive, affect-negative, and affect-interpersonal attraction struc-

ture. In addition, differences in the intercorrelation and levels of emotions were found. These differences were interpreted from theories on the self-concept and the influence of culture. Other issues addressed included the within-culture structure of emotions, the independence or interdependence of positive and negative affect, and cross-cultural and cross gender similarities and differences in the structure and level of emotions.

Third, Shavitt, Nelson and Yuan examined differences in cognitive response content across two cultures: the United States (individualist culture) and Taiwan (collectivist culture). The types of thoughts that subjects tended to list and the types of thoughts that were the most predictive of brand attitudes varied with cultural orientation. Whereas the U.S. subjects' thoughts focused more on product-related claims in the ads, Taiwanese subjects were more persuaded by their "ad evaluation" thoughts about the appropriateness of the ads than by their product thoughts. These findings suggest that persuasion may be mediated by different cognitive processes across cultures.

In closing, the contribution of this session was to advance cultural research in three substantive domains: persuasion, emotions and advertising effectiveness.

SYNETHSIZING THE RESEARCH

To synthesize the three pieces of research and to highlight areas for future research, Bernd Schmitt commented on where cross-cultural research is progressing in both consumer behavior and psychology.

Exploring Cross-Cultural Differences in Cognitive Responding to Ads

Sharon Shavitt, University of Illinois at Urbana-Champaign
Michelle R. Nelson, University of Illinois at Urbana-Champaign
Rose Mei Len Yuan, University of Illinois at Urbana-Champaign

ABSTRACT

This study explored differences in cognitive response content across two cultures and the role of these responses in predicting advertising effectiveness. In laboratory experiments, subjects from the United States (an individualist culture) and Taiwan (a collectivist culture) listed thoughts toward ads and then evaluated the ads on a series of attitude scales. Thought content was coded into categories reflecting product-oriented or ad-related cognitions. It was found that the types of thoughts that were listed and those that were the most relevant for predicting attitudes varied with cultural orientation. Whereas the U.S. subjects focused more on product-related claims in the ads, Taiwanese subjects were more persuaded by their "ad evaluation" thoughts about the appropriateness of the ads than by their product thoughts. These findings suggest that persuasion may be mediated by different cognitive processes across cultures. In addition, substantial correlations between thoughts and attitudes in both cultures supported the validity of using cognitive response methods cross-culturally.

INTRODUCTION

"...in a time when people consume images, maybe we should... begin figuring out *what people do with advertising*—how they respond to it, how they use it, how they develop relationships with brands based on their experience with it."
(*Advertising Age*, April 18, 1994, Banerjee, p. 23).

This study builds on a program of cognitive response research designed to better predict message effectiveness by understanding what people do with advertising (e.g., Nelson, Shavitt, Schennum and Barkmeier, in press; Shavitt 1990; Shavitt and Brock 1986, 1990). Here, we expand that focus to explore ad processing in cross-cultural contexts that differ in terms of a fundamental value orientation: individualism vs. collectivism (Hofstede, 1980, 1983, 1991; Triandis, 1989, 1990, 1994, 1995). This construct has received increased attention in recent years and offers a valuable theoretical approach to examining cultural differences.

In *individualist* cultures, individuals give priority to personal goals over those of the group and value an independent self, whereas in *collectivist* cultures, individuals focus on the needs of the group and value an interdependent self (Triandis 1994). These differences in cultural orientations hold crucial implications for cognitions and attitudes (Triandis 1989). For example, individualists tend to focus on self-direction and/or on stimulation and hedonism (Schwartz 1994). However, collectivists are more concerned with social appropriateness and building trust within relationships than are individualists (Triandis 1989).

Our research adopts this construct as a theoretical base for understanding differences in ad processing and persuasion between two cultures: the United States and Taiwan. Based on Hofstede's study of individualism across 40 countries (Hofstede 1980), the United States is considered an individualist culture with the highest mean score of 91 and Taiwan is considered a collectivist culture with a mean score of only 17 (note: overall mean for the 40 countries was 51).

Previous advertising research in individualist and collectivist cultures by Han and Shavitt (1994) has shown that collectivists (in this case, Koreans) generally respond more favorably to ads that appeal to collectivist concerns, whereas individualists (Americans) prefer ads that appeal to individualist concerns. This research conforms to the notion that one's underlying cultural values should help to predict one's attitudinal responses. In another study, Miracle, Taylor, and Wilson (1995) compared the effectiveness of television commercials with varying levels of information content in the United States and in Korea. Their results indicated that Korean subjects tend to respond more favorably to low-information advertisements than do United States subjects.

Whereas the extent to which individuals prefer certain types of advertisements is certainly important information for advertising strategists, it is the *process* by which individuals evaluate those ads that may offer important psychological insights for predicting advertising effectiveness. In other words, what are individuals thinking while viewing the ads—and which of those thoughts are most helpful in predicting persuasion?

Consumer Processing of Ads

Although numerous advertising studies in industry (e.g., Leavitt, Waddell, and Wells 1970; McDonald 1993) and academia (e.g., Batra and Ray 1983; Chattopadhyay and Alba 1988; Lutz and MacKenzie 1982; Nelson, et al. in press; Shavitt 1990; Shavitt and Brock 1986, 1990) have examined the persuasion process via cognitive response measures, virtually all of these studies have been conducted with individuals from North America (but see Blackston, Bunten, and Chadwick 1993 for a noteworthy exception). Our research seeks to discern whether cultural differences will affect cognitive responding and how these responses will relate to persuasion.

Indeed, as Miracle (1987) has suggested, information-processing differences may exist between cultures. In his observation of Japanese consumers' responses to television commercials, Miracle questioned the appropriateness of applying the traditional Western-based "learn-feel-do" (cognitive, affective, conative) hierarchy of effects model (Lavidge and Steiner 1961) to all individuals. Instead, he suggested that a "feel-do-learn" sequence (see Vaughn 1980) may operate in some cultural contexts.

The feel-do-learn model of advertising processing contrasts with the learn-feel-do model in that it assumes the first goal is to "make friends with the target audience, prove that you understand their feelings and show that you are nice" rather than to show "how you or your product is different or why your product is best" (Miracle 1987, p. R75), which is the goal assumed by traditional models. For instance, in Japanese advertisements, the name of the particular brand or company is often not known until almost the end of the commercial (Miracle 1987).

In this way, the company seeks first to build trust or create a relationship with the consumer and then to sell them the product. "Japanese consumers...may select a brand when they feel familiar with, or can relate to, the brand or advertiser in a way that assures them that they can *depend* on the brand or advertising" (Miracle 1987, p. R76). This dependency is reflective of the emphasis on ingroup relationships and consensus-seeking prevalent in collectivist cultures such as Japan.

In contrast, consumers from individualist cultures may generally "tend to process information about a product or company and use it to make up their minds..." (Miracle 1987, p. R76). This emphasis helps individualists to make their own independent judgments based on cognitive processing of product attributes.

These proposed processing differences suggest that different types of thoughts might be generated to an ad by members of individualist versus collectivist cultures and that these thoughts might differ in their importance in the persuasion process. For example, thoughts related to the product (e.g., "will this detergent get my clothes brighter?") might be more prevalent and more predictive of attitudes for individualists, whereas thoughts related to elements of the ad itself (e.g., "The spokesperson seems trustworthy") might be more common and more predictive of attitudes for collectivists.

Other researchers have examined cultural differences between individualists and collectivists in the communication process in general. Triandis (1994) suggests that whereas collectivists emphasize process ("what is said, done, and displayed," p. 190), individualists focus on goals ("what we are supposed to get done," p. 190). Similarly, Gudykunst (1983) advises that collectivists pay more attention to context (e.g., emotional expressions and the "whole picture") than individualists do when they communicate (see also Hall, 1976, 1987). These differences are consistent with the proposed emphasis on the advertiser and advertisement itself for collectivist consumers in a feel-do-learn model and the emphasis on the product for individualist consumers in a learn-feel-do processing model.

Our study set out to examine differences in cognitive responses to explore (and compare) the processes by which individuals across cultures respond to persuasive communications. We wanted to discern whether different types of cognitive responses are more or less prevalent and predictive of brand attitudes in different cultures—and whether these differences are consistent with cross-cultural theories.

Cognitive Response Research

Listed-thought measures of cognitive response reflect the by-products of information-processing activity—the reactions that one generates in the course of receiving an ad or other persuasive message, relating it to prior knowledge, and evaluating it (Petty, Ostrom and Brock 1981). The content of these thoughts typically provides a rich source of information about idiosyncratic responses to messages. Hence, listed-thought measures have become a commonly used method for determining individuals' reactions to advertisements (e.g., Batra and Ray 1986; Chattopadhyay and Alba 1988; Leavitt, Waddell, and Wells 1970; Lutz and MacKenzie 1982).

Cognitive response researchers (e.g., Petty, et al. 1981; Shavitt and Brock 1986, 1990) have suggested that the cognitive responses elicited by a persuasive message contribute strongly to message effectiveness because such responses reflect enduring and personally relevant thought processes. Several different content-coding schemes for cognitive responses have been developed to investigate the degree to which different types of thoughts predict attitudes. For example, studies have shown that product-related cognitions (i.e., those that focus on the performance of the product or restate the selling idea) tend to be more persuasive than execution-related thoughts (i.e., those that refer to the ad's layout or creative strategy) (Lutz and MacKenzie 1982; Swasy, Rethans, and Marks 1984). However, studies examining these types of thoughts were conducted only on subjects from the United States.

Based on the cultural differences outlined previously, we might expect that execution-related thoughts might be more prevalent and persuasive for members of collectivist cultures and product-related thoughts might be more prevalent and persuasive for members of individualist cultures.

METHOD

Subjects and Design

Subjects were comprised of university students from Taiwan and the United States. The 107 Taiwanese participants were from Ming Chi Technical Institute and from a Taiwanese orientation session for students planning to attend the University of Illinois. The 150 American participants were from the University of Illinois. American participants received extra credit in an introductory advertising course in exchange for participation and Taiwanese participants were given small gifts. All Taiwanese data were utilized for the analyses; however, 14 of the 150 subjects attending the University of Illinois were not included in the final analyses because they were not Americans.

We chose products relevant to the consumption habits of our student samples (washing powder, coffee, and greeting cards). Subjects in each culture were assigned randomly to one of six groups that differed in terms of target product and ad headline orientation (individualist vs. collectivist). Thus, product and ad orientation were between-subjects factors in the design[1].

Advertising Stimuli

To avoid any effects of prior brand attitudes, the ads employed were for fictitious brands of the products. Ads contained only a headline and simple product visuals, so as to eliminate any bias created by more elaborate executions (i.e., ads did not contain any pictures of people or other elements suggesting a cultural context). This simple arrangement also helped to control and unify the type of advertising content used across products and to ease the back-translation process. Subjects were informed that the ads were considered "roughs" and were not in finished form.

Ad headlines were manipulated to reflect either an individualist (e.g., "Use Brighty, Your Clothes Will Be Bright and Clean") or a collectivist (e.g., "Use Brighty, Your Family's Clothes Will Be Bright and Clean") claim. In most cases, only a single word was changed to vary the claim.

Using the back-translation scheme proposed by Miracle (1988), the headlines were first written in English and then translated into Chinese (the language used in Taiwan) by a bilingual speaker. A second bilingual speaker then independently translated the new Chinese version of the headlines back into English. The two versions were matched to ensure that the middle versions (in Chinese) were equivalent to the source headlines (original English version).

Procedure and Dependent Measures

In both countries, subjects participated in groups of approximately 30 in classroom settings. Subjects were given the experimental materials and were told they were participating in an advertising research study. After viewing the target ad, subjects read standard thought-listing instructions (Cacioppo and Petty 1981) and were given approximately three minutes to list their thoughts on forms on which six boxes were printed. Next, subjects were asked to rate each of those thoughts according to whether the

---

[1]After responding to the first ad, subjects also viewed the second ad for the same product with a contrasting ad orientation and then reported their ad preferences. However, effects of ad order complicated interpretation of these responses, and thus the within-subject analyses are not reported in this paper. All data presented are based only on the first ad subjects saw and their thoughts and attitudes towards it.

TABLE 1
Advertising Headlines

Product	Ad Orientation (I/C)	Headline
Washing powder	I	"Use Brighty, Your Clothes Will Be Bright and Clean"
Washing powder	C	"Use Brighty, Your Family's Clothes Will Be Bright and Clean"
Coffee	I	"Enjoy the Warmth of Aroma Coffee"
Coffee	C	"Share the Warmth of Aroma Coffee With Your Friends"
Greeting cards	I	"Feel the Joy of Sending Sunshine Cards"
Greeting cards	C	"Let the People you Care About Feel the Joy of Receiving Sunshine Cards"

thought was favorable, unfavorable, or neutral toward the product, on a scale from -2 (very unfavorable) to +2 (very favorable). Subjects then rated their attitudes toward the advertised product they had seen using three semantic differential scales anchored by -4 to +4 (good-bad, desirable-undesirable, and satisfactory-unsatisfactory), and completed some additional measures.

Thought Coding

In order to assess the types of thoughts listed by subjects, native-speaking judges read through all of the responses written by members of their culture to look for meaningful distinguishing categories. After examining the thoughts, it became apparent that the majority of the thoughts listed by members of both cultures were concerned with the advertisement itself (e.g., "the wording of the headline seemed enticing") or feelings evoked by the ad. The second most common category of thoughts in both cultures focused on the product or its attributes (e.g., "should possess basic cleaning power"). These thought categories fit well with theoretical assumptions regarding differing persuasion processes in individualist versus collectivist cultures.

Thus, a coding scheme was developed that focused specifically on relevance of the thoughts to the product or to the ad itself. The *product assertion (PA)* category included comments that focused on the product and its desirability, experience of using/ trying/buying, features of products, packaging comments, and ad claims about the product. The *aesthetic experience/evaluation (AE)* category included thoughts about the ad itself and how it looks or what feelings it evokes. These thoughts often concerned evaluation of layout, background, font and ad aesthetics, such as "fun," "boring," and "refined."

For the American subjects, coding was performed independently by two trained judges who were blind to the product and the orientation of the ad. They agreed on 92% of their classifications. Disagreements were resolved by a third judge. For the Taiwanese subjects, coding was performed independently by two trained native Chinese speakers from Taiwan (who also spoke English). Again, they were blind to the experimental condition. They agreed on 96% of their classifications. Disagreements were resolved by discussing and negotiating until they came to a consensus.

RESULTS

Attitude toward the Brand

Cronbach's coefficient alpha levels for the set of three semantic differentials were .94 for the American subjects and .88 for the Taiwanese subjects. Thus, ratings from the three items were averaged to obtain an attitude score for each individual.

To test effects of culture, ad orientation, and product on brand attitudes, a 2 x 2 x 3 ANOVA was performed. No significant effects relevant to the purposes of this study were found.[2] It appeared that, across all subjects, attitudes were somewhat more favorable for products advertised with collectivist appeals (mean=.24) than with individualist appeals (mean=.01), but this difference was not significant ($F(1, 231)=1.11$, n.s.). The same trend emerged to a nonsignificant degree among both the Taiwanese subjects and the American subjects.

Based on previous findings (Han and Shavitt 1994), we expected that attitude ratings for individualist and collectivist ad orientations would reveal cultural differences. However, it appears that *all* subjects generally preferred collectivist headlines. Perhaps this was due to the greater likability of the collectivist headlines used in this study or to the "match" between the collectivist headline and the products selected.

Product Assertions vs. Aesthetic Evaluation Thoughts Listed

Thoughts were coded according to whether they focused on product assertions (PA) or on the aesthetic evaluation of the ad (AE). Overall, across both the Taiwanese and the American subjects, the proportion of listed thoughts that were coded as AE thoughts was much greater (70%) than the proportion of listed thoughts coded as PA (26%).

More importantly, differences emerged when examining the types of thoughts listed in each culture. Arcsine transformations

---

[2]A significant interaction of sample and product emerged ($F(2, 231)=4.02$, $p<.05$), reflecting the fact that Americans' overall attitudes toward each product differed significantly ($F(2,130)=4.79$, $p<.05$), whereas Taiwanese subjects' attitudes did not.

TABLE 2
Correlations of Mean Favorability Ratings of Ad-Evaluation (AE) Thoughts, Product-Assertion (PA) Thoughts, and Overall (OV) Thoughts with Brand Attitude

	Across All Products		
	AE	*PA*	*OV*
Taiwanese	.54* (N=102)#	.37** (N=42)#	.58** (N=107)
Americans	.67* (N=126)	.65** (N=78)	.72** (N=136)
	Individualist Ads (All Products)		
Taiwanese	.69 (N=52)##	.09** (N=24)##	.70 (N=54)
Americans	.66 (N=62)	.60** (N=41)	.70 (N=67)
	Collectivist Ads (All Products)		
Taiwanese	.41** (N=50)	.51* (N=18)	.49** (N=53)
Americans	.69** (N=64)	.73* (N=37)	.74** (N=69)

* Between-culture difference is marginally significant at $p<.1$.
** Between-culture difference is significant at $p<.05$.

\# Within-culture difference is marginally significant at $p=.1$.
\#\# Within-culture difference is significant at $p<.05$.

Note: Thought favorability indices are based upon the people who actually listed thoughts in a given category.

---

were performed on the proportion of listed thoughts coded into each category, and the transformed data were submitted to a 2 x 2 x 3 ANOVA. Results revealed that Americans listed a significantly smaller proportion (68%) of AE thoughts than did the Taiwanese (77%) ($F(1, 242)=8.30$, $p<.01$). Conversely, for PA thoughts, Americans listed a significantly greater proportion (29%) than did the Taiwanese (19%) ($F(1, 242)=6.65$, $p<.05$).

In addition, significant culture X product interactions emerged for both the proportion of AE thoughts listed ($F(2, 242)=4.10$, $p<.05$) and the proportion of PA thoughts listed ($F(2, 242)=3.14$, $p<.05$), reflecting the fact that the overall differences observed as a function of culture were particularly strong for thoughts listed toward the coffee ads[3].

Although the cultural differences we observed are relatively small, they are significant and are consistent with our expectations about processing differences between members of collectivist and individualist cultures. The Taiwanese listed relatively more thoughts about the ad itself than did the Americans and the Americans focused more on the product than did the Taiwanese.

---

[3]Also, there was a significant main effect of product for the proportion of AE thoughts listed ($F(2, 242)=8.30$, $p<.01$) and the proportion of PA thoughts listed ($F(2, 242)=21.12$, $p<.001$), as well as a significant ad orientation X product interaction for the proportion of AE thoughts listed ($F(2, 242)=4.16$, $p<.05$) and the proportion of PA thoughts listed ($F(2, 242)=4.58$, $p<.05$). However, as these effects did not involve cultural differences, they are not relevant to the issues addressed here.

Predictiveness of AE and PA Thoughts

A mean thought favorability index was created for PA thoughts and another for AE thoughts by averaging the self-rated favorability (on the -2 to +2 scale) of each subject's thoughts for that category. These indices and the overall thought favorability index were then correlated with subjects' brand attitudes to determine the degree to which subjects' listed thoughts predicted their attitudes. It should be noted that these analyses included only those subjects who actually listed thoughts in a given category.

Across all subjects, ad evaluation thoughts ($r=.63$) and product assertion thoughts ($r=.58$) proved to be just as predictive of brand attitudes as the overall thought favorability index ($r=.68$) (i.e., the mean favorability of all of an individual's thoughts). It is also interesting to note that, in general, correlations between thoughts and attitudes were substantial across cultures (ranging from .37 to .74, except for PA thoughts for Taiwanese at .09, see Table 2). These results suggest that both the Taiwanese and Americans are adept at listing thoughts that are predictive of their attitudes, supporting the validity of employing cognitive response techniques cross-culturally. Although most cognitive response research has been done on western samples in the past, these data offer some promise for the use of cognitive responses in gauging advertising effectiveness across cultures.

Within the Taiwanese sample, ad evaluation thoughts predicted attitudes somewhat better ($r=.54$) than product assertion thoughts ($r=.37$), $p<.10$. This was particularly the case for individualist ads, where ad evaluation thoughts were significantly more predictive of attitudes ($r=.69$) than were product-assertion thoughts ($r=.09$), $p=.01$.

These findings are consistent with our hypotheses and with the inverted hierarchy of effects (feel-do-learn) model offered by Miracle (1987), which suggests that members of collectivist cultures process ads by first evaluating the aesthetic quality of the ad in order to form a relationship with the advertiser before (trying the product or) considering the product's attributes. In the present study, Taiwanese subjects were more focused on listing thoughts about the ad itself or discussing the feelings evoked from the ad—and these thoughts turned out to be better predictors of their attitudes.

It should also be noted that the superior predictiveness of AE thoughts in the Taiwanese sample seemed to depend on the ad type (individualist vs. collectivist); differences were significant only for individualist ads. Perhaps this is because members of this collectivist culture did not relate well to the individualist claims and therefore did not process the ads past the "feel" stage. However, when viewing collectivist ads, they may have felt a greater personal connection ("feel") and went on to process the ads by considering product trial ("do") or the product's attributes ("learn").

Within the American sample, there were few differences emerging for the predictiveness of these types of thoughts. The AE and the PA thoughts appeared equally predictive of attitudes. These findings hold true for both individualist and collectivist ad types.

When examining predictiveness of thoughts for attitudes across samples, we note that Americans' listed thoughts tend to be more predictive of their attitudes (r=.72) than the Taiwaneses' thoughts (r=.58) overall (*p*<.05). However, this tendency was particularly strong for PA thoughts, where Americans' listed thoughts showed correlations of .65 and Taiwanese showed .37 (*p*<.05). It should be noted that this difference was not found for AE thoughts. These findings provide evidence for the tendencies of individuals in individualist cultures to focus on product-related claims and to process ads differently than members of collectivist cultures.

DISCUSSION

This study is perhaps the first attempt to experimentally examine cognitive responses to advertising across cultures. Given the extensive amount of translation work involved in constructing equivalent ads and questionnaires and in coding individuals' thoughts, it is understandable why this is the case. However, with the globalization of the world economy and the increased usage of advertisements across cultures, understanding cross-cultural differences in persuasion processes is becoming increasingly important.

Results from this study suggested that the types of thoughts that were listed in response to test ads and those that were most predictive of persuasion (attitude ratings) showed some variation with cultural orientation. U.S. subjects listed relatively more thoughts related to the product than did the Taiwanese and these thoughts were more predictive of attitudes for U.S. than for Taiwanese subjects. Conversely, Taiwanese subjects listed relatively more thoughts related to the aesthetic qualities of the advertisements and were somewhat more persuaded by these thoughts than by their product thoughts. Although these differences in proportion of thoughts listed or predictive ability of thought types were not dramatic, they are largely consistent with expectations derived from cross-cultural theory and are suggestive of general differences in ad processing.

Our findings fit well with Miracle's (1987) assertions regarding a feel-do-learn processing model for Eastern cultures. The results are also consistent with cross-cultural differences in communication suggested by Gudykunst (1983) and Triandis (1984), who have argued that members of collectivist cultures pay more attention to contextual cues and to the *process* of communication. Whereas Americans focused more on product-related thoughts than did the Taiwanese, the Taiwanese seemed more concerned with the aesthetic nature of the ads than were the Americans.

These findings hold significance for advertising creatives designing messages in individualist and collectivist cultures. Advertising practitioners need to understand how cultural differences may influence the way individuals process ads and form attitudes. For example, if individuals process ads in a manner congruent with feel-do-learn models of persuasion, more emphasis should be placed upon the aesthetic qualities of the ads in order to "win over" the audience before making a sales pitch. However, if individuals process ads in a manner congruent with a learn-feel-do model, greater attention should be placed upon conveying product information in the message. Our research offers preliminary evidence for how culture might affect such processing styles.

REFERENCES

Batra, R. and M.L. Ray (1983), "Operationalizing Involvement as Depth and Quality of Cognitive Response," in *Advances in Consumer Research*, Vol. 10, eds. R.P. Bagozzi and A.M. Tybout, Ann Arbor, MI: Association for Consumer Research, 309-313.

Banerjee, A. (1994), "Global Campaigns Don't Work; Multinationals Do," *Advertising Age*, April 18, 1994, 23.

Blackston, M., N. Bunten and S. Chadwick (1993), "Cognitive Response Analysis After Circumnavigating the World," in *Proceedings of the Society for Consumer Psychology*, eds. K. Finlay, A. A. Mitchell, and F.C. Cummins, Clemson, SC: CtC Press, 48-54.

Cacioppo, J.T. and R.E. Petty (1981), "Social-psychological Procedures for Cognitive Response Assessment: The Thought Listing Technique," in *Cognitive Assessment*, eds. T.V. Merluzzi, C.R. Glass and M. Genest, New York: Guilford Press, 114-138.

Chattopadhyay, A. and J.W. Alba (1988), "The Situational Importance of Recall and Inference in Consumer Decision Making," *Journal of Consumer Research*, 15 (1), 1-12.

Gudykunst, W.B. (Ed.), (1983), *Intercultural Communication Theory*, Beverly Hills, CA: Sage.

Hall, E.T. (1976), *Beyond Culture*, Garden City, NY: Anchor Press/Doubleday.

Hall, E.T. (1987), *Hidden Differences*, New York: Doubleday.

Han, S., and S. Shavitt (1994), "Persuasion and Culture: Advertising Appeals in Individualistic and Collectivistic Societies," *Journal of Experimental Social Psychology*, 30, 326-350.

Hofstede, G. (1980), *Culture's Consequences: International Differences in Work-related Values*, Beverly Hills, CA: Sage.

Hofstede, G. (1983), "Dimensions of National Cultures in Fifty Countries and Three Regions, in *Explications in Cross-cultural Psychology*, ed. J. Deregowski et al., Lisse, The Netherlands: Swets and Zeitlinger.

Hofstede, G. (1991), *Cultures and Organizations: Software of the Mind*, London: McGraw-Hill.

Lavidge, R.C. and G.A. Steiner (1961), "A Model for Predictive Measurements of Advertising Effectiveness," *Journal of Marketing*, 25(4), October: 59-62.

Leavitt, C., C. Waddell, and W. Wells (1970), "Improving Day-after Recall Techniques," *Journal of Advertising Research*, 10, 13-17.

Lutz, R.J. and S.B. MacKenzie (1982), "Construction of a Diagnostic Cognitive Response Model for Use in Commercial Pretesting," in *Straight Talk About Attitude Research*, eds. M.J. Maples and J.S. Chasin, Chicago: American Marketing Association, 145-156.

McDonald, C. (1993), "Point of View: The Key is to Understand Consumer Response," *Journal of Advertising Research*, September/October, 63-69.

Miracle, G. E. (1987), "Feel-Do-Learn: An Alternative Sequence Underlying Japanese Consumer Response to Television Commercials," in *Proceedings of the LA Conference of the American Academy of Advertising*, ed. F.G. Feasley, Columbia: the University of South Carolina.

Miracle, G. E. (1988), "An Empirical Study of the Usefulness of the Back-translation Technique for International Advertising Messages in Print Media," in *Proceedings of the 1988 Conference of the American Academy of Advertising*, ed. John D. Leckenby, Austin, Texas: The University of Texas at Austin, RC51-RC56.

Miracle, G., R. Taylor, and D. Wilson (1995), "The Impact of Information Level on the Effectiveness of U.S. and Korean Television Commercials," working paper, Michigan State University.

Nelson, M.R., S. Shavitt, A. Schennum, and J. Barkmeier (in press), "The Prediction of Long-term Advertising Effectiveness: New Cognitive Response Approaches," in *Measuring Advertising Effectiveness*, eds. W. Wells and T. Jonas, Hillsdale, NJ: Erlbaum.

Petty, R.E., T.M. Ostrom, and T.C. Brock (1981), "Historical Foundations of the Cognitive Response Approach to Attitudes and Persuasion," in *⌐ognitive Responses in Persuasion*, eds. R. Petty, T. C trom, and T. Brock, Hillsdale, NJ: Erlbaum, 5-29.

Schwartz, S. (1994), "Are There Universal Aspects in the Structure and Contents of Human Values," *Journal of Social Issues*, 50(4), 19-45.

Shavitt, S. (1990), "The Role of Attitude Objects in Attitude Functions," *Journal of Experimental Social Psychology*, 26, 124-148.

Shavitt, S. and T.C. Brock (1986), "Self-relevant Responses in Commercial Persuasion: Field and Experimental Tests," in *Advertising and Consumer Psychology*, vol. 3, eds. J. Olson and K. Sentis, New York: Praeger, 149-171.

Shavitt, S. and T.C. Brock (1990), "Delayed Recall of Copytest Responses: The Temporal Stability of Listed Thoughts," *Journal of Advertising*, 19 (4), 6-17.

Swasy, J.L., A.J. Rethans, and L.J. Marks (1984), "Extending Cognitive Response Coding Schemes to Assess Advertising Effects: The Role of Attitude Toward the Ad," in *New Cognitive Response Approaches in Commercial Persuasion*, ed. T.C. Brock (Chair), Symposium presented at the 92nd annual convention of the American Psychological Association, Toronto.

Triandis, H.C. (1995), *Individualism and Collectivism. New Directions in Social Psychology*, Boulder, CO: Westview Press.

Triandis, H.C. (1994), *Culture and Social Behavior*, New York: Mc-Graw Hill Inc.

Triandis, H. C. (1990), "Cross-cultural Study of Individualism and Collectivism," in *Nebraska Symposium on Motivation*, ed. J. Berman, Lincoln: University of Nebraska Press.

Triandis, H. C. (1989), "The Self and Social Behavior in Differing Cultural Contexts," *Psychological Review, 96(3)*, 506-520.

Vaughn, R. (1980), "The Consumer Mind: How to Tailor Ad Strategies," *Advertising Age*, June 9: 45-6.

Beyond Brand Equity: Managing Mature Brands

Cynthia Huffman, University of Pennsylvania

Consumer researchers have developed a substantial body of research that can be applied to the management of mature brands. For example, research on consumer expertise directly acknowledges that over time consumers may form extensive knowledge bases regarding brands and their attributes, etc., and that this knowledge influences how they process information and make decisions. However, research indicating that consumers may have long-lived relationships with brands has often not been explicitly or consistently applied to mature brands. This session was designed to begin this process and to stimulate research addressing the unique concerns and challenges of mature brands.

Recent research in consumer behavior that does have direct implications for the concerns of mature brands has concentrated on leveraging brand equity through brand extensions. This stream has been valuable for managers and has brought to practice much of the promise of categorization research conducted throughout the 1980s. However, marketers and consumer researchers are both beginning to question the wisdom of indiscrimant brand extension and to seek other means of managing a brand franchise. Thus, a second purpose of this session was to stimulate research that moves brand equity beyond its focus on brand extensions.

Two themes underlie the collection of papers in this session. First, mature brands often enjoy opportunities that newer brands do not. For example, consumers' knowledge of mature brands may in some cases facilitate learning new information, and many mature brands enjoy widespread positive attitudes among consumers. Second, mature brands may face different challenges than do new or growth brands, because of consumers' established beliefs about the brand and the necessity of working with those beliefs.

The Role of Brand Quality in Meaningless Differentiation
Susan Broniarczyk, University of Texas
Andrew Gershoff, University of Texas

Susan Broniarczyk and Andrew Gershoff of the University of Texas examined the role that brand names play in the value inferred to a unique, but irrelevant, attribute. Their research extends recent research by Carpenter, Glazer, and Nakamoto (1994) questioning the widely-held assumption that marketers need to differentiate on an attribute that is relevant, meaningful, and valuable. Specifically, Carpenter et al. (1994) found that products can benefit by differentiating on attributes that give the appearance of being valuable, but in fact are irrelevant to improving product performance. Moreover, this benefit occurred even after subjects were explicitly informed that the attribute was meaningless.

Broniarczyk presented two laboratory experiments exploring the mechanisms through which a brand name affects the value inferred to a differentiated, irrelevant attribute. Brand equity suggests that high-tier brands should benefit most from differentiation because consumers confidently infer high performance to the attribute and are more likely to make pragmatic inferences that the brand would not offer the unique attribute unless it positively improved performance. However, the decision-making literature suggests that consumers may have different ambiguity tendencies depending on the quality tier (Einhorn and Hogarth 1985; Kahn and Sarin 1988). In the domain of high-quality brands, people tend to display ambiguity-aversion such that they may prefer to stay with the status quo and avoid the differentiated alternative if they are uncertain of its benefit. Thus, even though consumers may have

high expectations about the performance of a brand's unique attribute, the existing attribute level offered by other high-quality brands is more than acceptable. Conversely, in the domain of low quality brands, people tend to be ambiguity-seeking such that even if there are low expectations about the performance of a unique attribute, consumers may be willing to take a chance saying "what do I have to lose?"

Results from the first experiment supported an ambiguity tendency such that low-quality brands increased their tier market share through use of a meaningless differentiation more than high-quality brands. However, as uncertainty about the irrelevance of the attribute increased, high tier brands also benefited from a meaningless differentiation strategy. The second study found a reversal of context effects such that the leading quality brand in a category was penalized for using a questionable differentiation strategy whereas the middle quality brand was rewarded. The implications of consumers making manipulative inferences to high quality brands using a meaningless differentiation strategy were discussed.

The Impact of Brand Familiarity on Advertising Repetition and Brand Identification
Margaret Campbell, UCLA
Kevin Lane Keller, UCLA

Margaret Campbell and Kevin Lane Keller, of UCLA and the University of North Carolina, respectively, presented a paper examining how the equity of a brand (e.g., the extent to which the brands are well-known or well-liked) influences consumers' responses to alternative advertising tactics. Specifically, they examine the effects of one executional tactic–the timing of brand identification within the ad–and one media tactic–the degree of ad repetition–for high equity versus unfamiliar brands. They propose that brand equity influences the effects of these advertising tactics on consumer evaluations of the ad and brand.

Campbell and Keller argue that the manner in which advertising works may, in fact, be quite different for high equity brands than for brands that are unfamiliar (Machleit, Allen and Madden 1993). For example, recent research suggests that familiar brands have important advantages in terms of consumer recall of advertising information (Kardes 1994; Kent and Allen 1993). Kent and Allen (1994) found that brand familiarity increased ad memorability, produced greater recall of new information, and reduced the negative effects of competitive interference. Such findings suggest the need for a better understanding of differences in the advertising process due to the equity of the advertised brand.

Campbell and Keller reported the results of an experimental study of TV advertisements in which three factors were varied: the equity of the advertised brand (high vs. low), the timing of brand identification (early vs. delayed), and the number of exposures to the ad (one, two, or three). They found the hypothesized differences in evaluative responses to the ad and sponsoring brand, differences that were not equivalent to differences in memory. Specifically, the results indicated that an unfamiliar brand received significantly lower evaluations than a well-known and well-liked brand when advertised with an ad employing late identification or at a high level of concentrated ad repetitions.

Overall, these results suggest that high equity brands can use certain advertising tactics more successfully than can unfamiliar brands. Brand equity provides some greater acceptance of delayed brand identification and postpones the onset of advertising wearout (whereas wearout occurred for the unfamiliar brand, it did not occur for the high equity brand). The research presented substantiates the importance of brand equity and sheds some light on how a familiar, well-liked brand can facilitate advertising effectiveness by influencing consumer reactions to the advertising tactics employed.

The Effectiveness of Composite Branding Strategies
Sung Youl Jun, University of Pittsburgh
Robert Gilbert, University of Pittsburgh
C. Whan Park, University of Pittsburgh

Sung Youl Jun, Robert Gilbert, and C. Whan Park of the University of Pittsburgh presented a paper investigating composite branding as an alternative branding strategy and examining the effectiveness of two different ways that this might be operationalized. Their paper builds on research on brand equity and brand image associations and is based on the idea that composite branding strategies may afford cost efficiency and competitive advantages.

Composite branding involves combining two existing brand names to create a name for a new product (e.g., Eggo Waffle by Special K). Jun et al. based their study on the concept combination literature in psychology which explains the formation process of composite concepts ("apartment dog," "ocean book," etc.). According to this literature, when two different concepts are combined to form a composite concept, the perceived value of an attribute of the composite is determined by the levels of the attribute values of the constituent brands. Specifically, even if an attribute (e.g., nutrition) is strongly associated with one concept (e.g., Special K cereal) but not with the other (e.g., Eggo Waffle), the attribute becomes strongly associated with the composite. Thus, the composite can take on attributes of both of the "sponsoring" brands.

The effectiveness of the composite branding strategy was examined across two combinations of product category membership. In the first context, Jun et al. examined composite branding when both "sponsoring" brands were in the same category as the to-be-introduced product (e.g., Jaguar sedan by Toyota). In the second context, only one sponsoring brand was in the same category as the new product (e.g., Eggo Waffle by Special K). Jun presented results suggesting that when the two sponsoring brands had complementary characteristics, the new product was more favorably perceived than direct extensions of a single brand. For extensions of mature brands into new categories (e.g., suppose Domino's pizza introduces breakfast rolls), the implication was that co-branding with a breakfast food manufacturer facilitated consumer acceptance of the new product. Co-branding effects on the original brands, and the importance of "fit" between the established brands and the new product category, were discussed.

Revitalizing Mature Brands
Cynthia Huffman, University of Pennsylvania
Brian Wansink, University of Pennsylvania

Cynthia Huffman and Brian Wansink presented a framework to guide the choice of revitalization strategies for mature brands. They argued that when management refuses to see the product life cycle as deterministic or product category size as static, numerous options for increasing a brand's sales arise. These options can be categorized based on whether they impact how consumers perceive the brand, the likelihood they will choose the brand, or how they use the brand. Considerations for choosing among the options, based on brand market share and including effects on brand equity, etc., were discussed.

Perceptions were defined as the beliefs and evaluations a consumer holds in memory regarding a brand and its attributes, and their relation to the consumer's goals and the usage situations in which the brand might or might not be appropriate. Based on accessibility research and the goals literature, Huffman and Wansink argued that managers can revitalize a brand by creating or strengthening associations that will bring the brand to salience when new goals are activated. For example, the growing importance of convenience in many consumers' lives suggests that in order for a brand to be considered, it must be associated in memory with the goal of convenience. Similar principles of accessibility apply to usage situations, and accordingly other revitalization tactics focus on influencing perceptions of brand appropriateness for alternative usage situations (e.g., Arm & Hammer being used in multiple ways) and evaluations of using the brand in those situations.

Revitalization can also focus on increasing the likelihood of choice and the quantity purchased on any single purchase occasion. In particular, product availability and favorable comparisons given the product context are especially important. Finally, management can influence usage by focusing on either the frequency of usage or the amount used. Drawing on research on stockpiling and promotional and package size effects, Huffman and Wansink suggested that for many types of products, a marketer can encourage increased usage by keeping the brand salient and by altering the perceived unit price of the brand.

SUMMARY

In sum, the session papers all expressed the theme that brand maturity and consumer familiarity offer both opportunities and challenges. Broniarczyk and Gershoff examined how a mature brand might successfully differentiate itself in a crowded marketplace. Campbell and Keller's paper demonstrated that mature brands enjoy advantages over unfamiliar brands in terms of the advertising executional and media strategies they use. Jun et al.'s work investigated various methods to extend a mature brand into categories and usage situations that are removed, in some sense, from the original equity. Huffman and Wansink presented an overall framework tying the three empirical pieces together.

REFERENCES

Carpenter, Gregory S., Rashi Glazer, and Kent Nakamoto (1994), "Meaningful Brands From Meaningless Differentiation," *Journal of Marketing Research*, 31 (August), 339-350.

Einhorn, Hillel J. and Robin M. Hogarth (1985), "Ambiguity and Uncertainty in Probabilistic Inference," *Psychological Review*, 92 (4), 433-461.

Kahn, Barbara E. and Rakesh K. Sarin (1988), "Modeling Ambiguity in Decisions Under Uncertainty," *Journal of Consumer Research*, 15 (September), 265-272.

Kardes, Frank R. (1994), "Consumer Judgment and Decision Processes," in *Handbook of Social Cognition*, Vol. 2, R. S. Wyer and T. K. Srull (Eds.) Hillsdale, NJ: Lawrence Erlbaum Assoc.

Kent, Robert J. and Chris T. Allen (1993), "Does Competitive Clutter in Television Advertising 'Interfere' with Recall and Recognition of Brand Names and Ad Claims?" *Marketing Letters*, 4 (2), 175-184.

Kent, Robert J. and Chris T. Allen (1994), "Competitive Interference Effects in Consumer Memory for Advertising: The Role of Brand Familiarity," *Journal of Marketing*, 58 (July), 97-105.

Finding Consumers for Consumer Research: A Participatory Perspective on Moving Towards 'Marketing Science'

Terrance G. Gabel, University of Memphis
Mark Ritson, Lancaster University

ABSTRACT

Recent philosophy of science thought suggests that: 1) the usefulness of an academic discipline's theories is one of the key criteria for the attainment of honorific scientific status, and 2) theoretical usefulness is to be judged by the consumers of disciplinary knowledge. This paper contends that if consumer research is to attain long-sought scientific status it must better identify and cater to the needs of its diverse customer constituencies. Most importantly, it develops both theoretical and methodological perspectives by which these objectives may be achieved. Specifically, we first describe a behavioral-based scholarly market segmentation strategy and then advocate the application of participatory research as one method for furthering the scientific aims of consumer research.

One of the lesser explored implications of the postmodern moment (Brown 1995) for marketing in general and consumer research in particular[1] has been a reassessment of the role that universities assume in society. Consumer research has suffered from the postmodern trend of the "decentring of knowledge" and "the loss of intellectual mastery" which have been posited a major influences on contemporary academe (Hebdidge 1988). The resulting "mid-life crisis" (Brady and Davis 1993) which has afflicted marketing has manifested itself explicitly in consumer research in the form of the recent debates on the scientific nature of the discipline. Although some contend that science has been achieved, others, viewing science as socially constructed, hold that a disciplinary bias which favors certain users of consumer research at the expense of other societal groups suggests that this honorific status has yet to be realized.

This paper supports the latter view and contends that attainment of scientific status in marketing and consumer research is predicated on better segmentation of the *total* scholarly market served. It develops a behavioral-based perspective on how the market for marketing and consumer research knowledge may be segmented. Taking a methodological perspective, it then introduces participatory research into consumer research as one means by which the highly differential needs of disciplinary customers may be more effectively met.

CONSUMER RESEARCH AND THE QUEST FOR SCIENCE

A decade ago the traditional conception of marketing was challenged by a new definition of scientific knowledge and the steps marketing had to take in order to achieve that status. That debate, which continues to reverberate around the discipline, centered on the rejection of the theoretical monism derived from the neo-positivistic orientation of marketing. The traditional conception of science based on a positive "point of demarcation" (Anderson 1989, p. 10) stressed that scientific knowledge was "empirically

---

[1]This paper adopts Anderson's (1986, p. 155) point that the discussion of marketing science can be seen to relate to consumer research generally. As a result, although marketing in general forms the basis for many of the points made in this paper, where possible, consumer research is referred to directly.

testable" (Hunt 1983, p. 368-372) and thus separable from the common-sense non-scientific knowledge of the everyday. Inspired by a combined corpus of revisionary philosophers of science (notably Kuhn, Laudan and Feyerabend) a concerted effort was made by a number of marketing and consumer research scholars to reposition the traditional model of marketing science in relation to the edifying role of extant philosophies of science (Sherry 1991). Their most fundamental contribution to the discipline was to posit that science was not a singular (neo-positivistic) field but rather consisted of a number of differing approaches conceptualized in consumer research as "macro-structures" (Anderson 1986, p. 159). Each macro-structure possesses its own internally consistent approach to ontology, epistemology and associated methods and, crucially, each macro-structure has differing criteria for evaluating the value of knowledge claims (Peter 1991, p. 541). Just as neo-positivistic consumer research utilized measures validity, reliability and objectivity (Calder, Phillips and Tybout 1983) other approaches such as interpretive consumer research will apply alternative assessment techniques such as trustworthiness (Wallendorf and Belk 1989) or anti-foundational gestalts (Thompson 1990).

Thus the scientific panorama of consumer research has changed from a uniform to polyform perspective with many different macro-structures applying many different criteria to scientific knowledge. The resulting paradigmatic pluralism in consumer research (Sherry 1991) has complicated the establishment of a general criteria of scientific consumer research. Rather than applying the criterion from one macro-structure (i.e. the "truth value" of knowledge statements [Hunt 1990, p. 12]), the criterion for scientific consumer research became context dependent (Peter and Olson 1983).

In order to answer the question "what is scientific consumer research?", academicians began to look at knowledge from an external rather than internal perspective. Thus, in a move highly consistent with their own discipline, consumer researchers began to view the value of knowledge claims from a market-oriented rather than production-oriented perspective in which the scientific content of knowledge is determined by societal consensus (Anderson 1983; Peter and Olson 1983; Zinkhan and Hirschheim 1992). The paradigmal lesson was clear: If consumer research wanted to be recognized as a science it must first produce knowledge judged "useful" by those using it. This concern for the needs of its customers resulted in an ironic paradigmal twist: The discipline of marketing, which had originally attempted to evolve from its practical, problem solving origins in order to reach the abstraction of science (Arndt 1983 p. 20), had returned to exploring how its theories were used by society in order to attain honorific scientific status.

At this point, having isolated the holy grail of scientific status to be dependent on a societally oriented quest to produce useful knowledge, consumer research encounters a second set of problems. Society is not a singular, homogenized group of individuals with identical uses for consumer research knowledge. Rather it is a complex mass of highly differential individuals with often conflicting conceptions of what constitutes *useful* consumer research. In order to orient consumer research towards these differing uses and needs it is clearly necessary to identify and distinguish between customer segments within the total market for consumer research knowledge.

SEGMENTING THE MARKET FOR CONSUMER RESEARCH

Marketing and consumer research scholars have for decades at least implicitly addressed the differentiated nature of the discipline's customer base. Although a more detailed explication is beyond the scope of this paper, several studies have attempted to identify and describe the various customer segments served by the discipline (e.g., AMA Task Force 1988; Fine 1994; Kotler 1972; Priddle 1994). As depicted in Figure 1 below, review of this work suggests the existence of four general customer segments.

The conflicting interests and needs of the four segments, indicated in Figure 1 by a series of transecting arrows, essentially represent dialectical tensions based on the inherent power relationships that exist between each group. In effect, one man's (sic) empirical meat is another man's disciplinary poison as "useful" consumer research knowledge for one segment serves to undermine the discipline in another.

In a display of disciplinary hypocrisy consumer researchers continue to espouse the segmentation of markets in their theoretical corpus whilst simultaneously failing to apply this approach in practice. At best, the net result of this undifferentiated approach favoring the interests of industry is confusion. At worst, this persistent practice both legitimates and perpetuates the notion that consumer research is exclusively the a tool of profit-minded industry. Thus, the vast majority of those associated with consumer research (i.e., practitioners, teachers, and researchers) are collectively viewed by the public as marketer-oriented individuals (Anderson 1983 p. 27) or "corporate libertarians" (Korten 1995) who staunchly defend the corporate will with little or no regard for the often detrimental impact of industrial "progress." Further, due to the socially constructed nature of science and its relative indifference to the needs of civil society, marketing and consumer research can by no means claim to be "scientific."

In summary, if marketing and consumer research is to be viewed as anything more than a manipulative means of public-to-elite wealth transfer it must first better deploy one of its most basic principles: market segmentation. Although this task can be fruitfully approached from a variety of perspectives, one holding particular promise is behavioral segmentation in which customers "are divided into groups on the basis of their knowledge, attitude, use or response to a product" (Kotler 1984, p. 259).

Behavioral Market Segmentation

Each of the four segments of the total market for consumer research knowledge depicted in Figure 1 utilizes this knowledge in a different way and consequently possesses a different attitude toward the discipline. The critical, developmental uses of the student segment, for example, differ and often conflict with the competitive, eclectic utilization of knowledge by marketing academe (Anderson 1992 p. 9). Similarly the profit oriented, aquisitory focus of industry means that their consequent uses for consumer research often conflict with the educational, non-profit uses which civil society typically applies to consumer research (Andreasen 1991, p. 460).

Consumer researchers have largely chosen to accept the myth that what is good for marketing academe can only be good for its customers (Brown 1995, p. 50). The results of ignoring the differences in the behavioral segments in the market for consumer research are identical to the results of any attempt at undifferentiated positioning in a highly differentiated market: A bias towards the largest segment of the market, the undersatisfaction of smaller segments, and poor marketing results (Kotler 1984, p. 269). As the following segment-by-segment discussion illustrates, consumer research, as a result of its current undifferentiated positioning, has failed to maximize its usefulness in any of the four segments it serves.

POSITIONING CONSUMER RESEARCH

Academe

From the perspective of disciplinary researchers consumer research is viewed as something they do and inform others about as part of what is perceived as a competitive race for tenure and disciplinary acclaim. While this perception is perhaps well founded given the realities of disciplinary reward systems, it detracts greatly from the production of innovative, meaningful disciplinary knowledge. Such a mindset not only invokes an overemphasis on "hot topics" in order to get published, but also leads to a concern for expediency at the cost of relevance (i.e., short duration, "one-shot," research projects). This situation is particularly disturbing in the context of doctoral education in that such practice and thought is often both reinforced and perpetuated (AMA Task Force 1988).

The positioning of consumer research to ourselves as relevant is not, in itself, problematic. The problem occurs with the implicit assumption that what we as academicians do is automatically relevant to other customer segments. A paradoxical consequence of the "publish or perish" reward structure and the mentality that it fosters arises: While individual scholars prosper, the discipline as a whole loses prestige and credibility in the eyes of its external customers.

Students

Students, not only as a distinct customer segment but also as members of civil society and future members of industry, are arguably the most important customers for consumer research. Students need marketing knowledge to help them become productive members of both the business community and civil society. They also need information which will help them become efficient and responsible consumers. Within this multifaceted context part of the educational process involves the setting of reasonable and realistic expectations. It is on these grounds that our knowledge product is at least implicitly positioned.

Unfortunately, viewing and treating students as customers in the sense of their needs being the primary drivers of knowledge creation and dissemination is rare (Stafford 1994). When students are considered as customers to be served they are often viewed almost exclusively from a selling orientation as the targets of promotional recruitment efforts (Conant, Brown, and Mokwa 1985). Further, consistent with Priddle's (1994) discussion of business education as more a form of corporate indoctrination than education, when student needs are addressed what is taught is a narrow, industry-dominated "hyperreality" which fails to sample an adequate range of marketing phenomena of potential importance. Finally, students rarely reap significant benefit when they are *used* as data-gatherers or as subjects in experimental research (Wells 1993).

Although efforts on the part of the discipline to correct the neglect of students as customers are evident (see: Cannon and Sheth 1994; Ramrocki 1994) these individuals are valued far too extensively on the basis of the financial or empirical contributions they make to marketing departments. From a long-term perspective it benefits all parties involved (i.e. students, marketing scholars, industry, and civil society) when students are prepared not only to serve industry but also to critically evaluate its structure and practices from a systemic level. Unfortunately, prevailing reward systems reinforcing the "publish or perish" mindset among educators often render them unwilling and ill-advised to take the risks necessary to facilitate creation of such knowledge.

FIGURE 1
The Market for Consumer Research

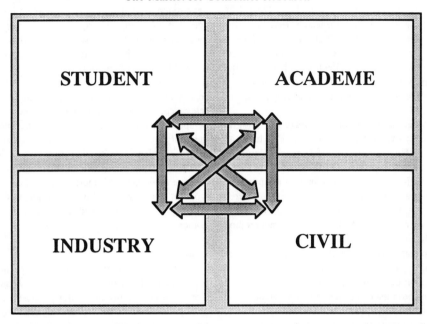

Industry

Knowledge produced for customers in the industrial segment takes at least two basic forms. First, scholars conduct research activities and report results with a view towards application in strategic planning and implementation efforts. In less direct fashion marketing scholars provide human resources (i.e., graduated, well-educated students) to organizations. Marketing knowledge is thus often aggressively positioned to practitioners as: 1) explanatory of relevant marketplace phenomenon or 2) as central to the preparation of productive organizational employees.

Although marketing persists in its differential focus on meeting the needs of industry, evidence suggests that the discipline may not be serving segment members nearly as well as is commonly perceived (Priddle 1994, p. 50). Indeed, a common criticism of marketing's contribution to industrial efforts is its lack of "real significance" (Anderson 1983, p. 28). This lack of significance relates to the fact that for many consumer researchers the "real world" is no such thing. In fact, it is "alien and unrecognizable to many of the executives who actually have to manage marketing for real" (Piercy 1992, p. 15). According to Zinkhan and Hirschheim (1992), reasons for the inability of academe to relate consumer research to the world of industry can be attributed to both a lack of communication and the disciplinary practice of referring to human phenomena in non-human terms (i.e., reification [Berger and Luckman 1967]). In accord with Wells' (1993) contention that a common error on the part of consumer researchers remains the assumption that statistical significance confers real world significance the discipline has relied so heavily on reified conceptualizations (e.g., statistical measures of human behavior and motivations) that these abstract forms have obscured their relative lack of importance for our industrial customers (Arndt 1985).

Civil Society

Civil society has generally been recognized as the most important focus for "useful" consumer research (Peter 1991, p.

543). Despite this focus, disciplinary theories have been so heavily weighted in favor of the industry perspective that many societal market segment members have become alienated and disillusioned with the marketing concept (Kotler 1972). When societal factors are taken into account the narrow emphasis on purchase orientation at the expense of macro-factors continues (Andreasen 1991).

From a segmentation and positioning perspective, civil society has rarely been targeted with knowledge-creation efforts and little effort is put into improving the discipline's position as servient to the will of industry. Positioning, in the minds of civil society at least, is clear but highly negative. To reposition the discipline in a more favorable light marketing knowledge could and should better serve this vital customer segment by creating consumption-related information of greater societal relevance which is more effectively and widely disseminated.

THE ROLE OF PARTICIPATORY RESEARCH

A common denominator in extant disciplinary calls for the creation of more relevant knowledge (e.g., Churchill 1979; Fine 1994; Jacoby 1978; Priddle 1994; Wells 1993) is a focus on better including customer input at an early stage of the knowledge creation process. Despite this consensus, there has been at best limited discussion as to exactly how this is to be achieved. The alternative epistemological and methodological perspective of participatory research is adopted here as one possible solution in that it offers a means by which scholarly activity in consumer research may be made both more relevant and, given the socially constructed context of science, more scientific.

Participatory Research

Based on the independent work of Swantz, Freire, and Hall in the late 1960s and early 1970s (Hall 1992; Park 1992), participatory research (PR) entails a partnership between academic researchers and non-researcher partners (i.e., knowledge customers) in which the latter play an active role at all stages of the research process (i.e., agenda-setting and the collection and analysis of data). Freire, for example, holds that "Authentic education is і. т carried on by 'A' for 'B' or by 'A' about 'B,' but rather by 'A' with 'B'" (1970, p. 82). Furthering this perspective, Stoecker and Bonacich (1992) view PR as an educational process in which all parties involved learn together how best to effect positive social change. In this capacity, PR serves not only as a means of data collection and analysis, but also as a form of teaching non-academic participants in the knowledge creation process the meaning, purpose, and importance of academic research (Lynd 1992).

In common with other interpretive approaches (e.g., ethnography, hermeneutics and existential phenomenology) PR shares an epistemological focus on the naturalistic collection and interpretation of the informant's lived experience. PR extends this focus, however, into the disciplinary structure of a particular approach. Specifically, PR enables a closer link at *all stages* of the research process between the academic researcher and the external customer thus improving "customer relations" and offering a direct method for the increased production of useful knowledge.

The dynamic implications of PR suggest it to be an excellent method for re-evaluating paradigm-centric research agendas and refocusing the production of knowledge back into the realm of society, the final arbiter and consumer of scientific knowledge. The application of PR to consumer research would facilitate several such changes in the disciplinary structure of consumer research. In particular it offers consumer research a chance to reappraise the role it plays in the lives of the different customers it serves. Through its support of disenfranchised, underrepresented minorities, it may serve to level the playing field and remove traditional biases in the orientations of consumer research knowledge. The following four sections detail possible implications of applying PR to the consumer research "marketplace."

Academe

The impact of PR on academe would first limit the degree to which consumer research is produced with no thought to its long-term impact on the discipline. A great deal of emphasis could be removed from personal publication goals and the competitive nature of publication in favor of a more holistic approach to knowledge formation. PR-based consumer research both within the discipline and involving researchers from other disciplines necessitates a long-term, integrative approach much in accord with the founding principles of the Association for Consumer Research. PR in this context implies a continual awareness not only of where the individual researcher stands in the disciplinary hierarchy but, as a result of joint researcher efforts aimed at the creation of meaningful disciplinary-level knowledge, also where the disciplinary hierarchy itself is and where it is headed. As such, consumer researchers are, with the influence of PR, encouraged to reject a production-oriented perspective in favor of a market-oriented approach (i.e., "What can I work on which will develop the field of consumer research?" rather than "What can I do with the work I am doing?"). As with other segments but more particularly the case with internal academic customers our suggestions for the integration of PR into consumer research thought and action share one recurrent theme with the AMA Task Force's (1988) guidelines: A need for the restructuring of disciplinary reward systems to better encourage the taking of risks inherent in the creation of more widely relevant and useful knowledge.

Students

Consumer research *using* students as respondents is exemplary of research done *on*—rather than for or with—student customers. The common practice of *using* students as simple data gatherers is similarly far removed from the ideal of PR. Both practices use students rather than treating them as customers who have much to gain from more extensive involvement in research activities. Although not applicable to every research context, by more actively involving students in every stage of the research program, rather than simply in data collection, they would benefit from a far more critical, in-depth view of the research process (e.g., it's objectives, capabilities, and overall value). Furthermore, research as an activity, whether aiming for industrial or social relevance, would be perceived from a new and perhaps revealing perspective. This approach to education could also be applied more generally to teaching regardless of the students' role in current research projects. Rather than simply resorting to traditional texts which specify the mainstream marketing corpus teaching could become enlivened and interactive through references to on-going work in the field. In this way students could develop a more contemporary, realistic, and critical perspective of marketing phenomena.

Industry

Although marketing and consumer researchers frequently produce knowledge directly for industry-based clients most discussions of what is commonly referred to as "collaborative research" have been of technology-oriented (i.e., R&D) alliances between two or more business organizations (see: Branscomb 1992; Hakanson 1993; Peterson 1993; Werner 1991). Relatively little attention has been given to the joint efforts of industry and academicians and, when it has, it has often taken the perspective of the practitioner, focusing on how to best locate and work with university-based research partners (see: Bloedon and Stokes 1994; Quintas, Wield, and Massey 1992). Relative to PR, such research efforts, as well as the vast majority of consulting projects, exhibit far lower levels of joint knowledge creation: Marketing practitioners typically describe their problems to academic researchers, who, being experts in research methodology and statistical analysis, collect and analyze data on their own. Such research is most commonly conducted either on or for rather than with industry customers. PR affords consumer researchers a unique opportunity to create knowledge *both for and with* industry-segment customers.

Society

While undeniably good-intentioned, insightful, and often actionable, much "societally relevant" consumer research is done for, rather than *for and with*, members of civil society. Far more problematic is research done *on* society which uses disadvantaged and vulnerable individuals as informants and is not guided by real-life problems experienced by these persons but rather by disciplinary interpretation of what these real-life problems must surely be. Joint researcher-societal customer PR offers the potential to move beyond traditional "societally relevant" marketing and consumer research. At the research design stage, such efforts are likely to provide new insight into the consumption-related problems experienced by disadvantaged members of society which all parties, regardless of segment or perspective, *should* want addressed in greater detail. At the stage of data collection, societal customers come to gain a better understanding of the research process while researchers benefit from constant interaction with the consumers of the knowledge being created. This interaction not only assures production of more insightful knowledge but also turns the traditional human experience of consumer research (i.e., questionnaires) into a catharsis or therapeutic exercise for the informant (McCracken 1988). A positive experience of the research process can be seen as a direct method for altering the public's predominantly negative interpretation of consumer research. Finally, in the result-based stage of the research, joint interpretation and reporting entails dissemination of consumer research knowledge via new outlets more accessible and palatable to civil society customers. Obviously, for this to occur, disciplinary reward systems must be modified to reflect the fact that jointly produced, societally relevant knowledge is at least as—if not more—important to the lived experience of most humans as it is to the hierarchy of academic publications. The PR perspective reminds us that we should never compromise ourselves by forgetting that we can serve as mediators of meaningful social change.

DISCUSSION: FROM CONSUMER RESEARCHERS TO CONSUMER SCIENTISTS

Central to this discussion is the assumption that consumer research can attain scientific status only to the extent that disciplinary knowledge is judged as relevant and useful by those persons using it (i.e., disciplinary customers). PR acts as a catalyst for the production of useful knowledge through the elevation of the subject to the role of participant. From this elevated position the consumer is not simply a passive responder to the a priori agendas of consumer researchers but rather an active force ensuring that the future progress of the discipline follows the needs of the market. PR, even if adopted in only a limited sense by a limited number of consumer researchers, forces disciplinary scholars to realize that they do not hold a monopoly on good research ideas. Although a portion of control over the research process is necessarily relinquished, PR creatively applied allows the researcher the unique opportunity to intimately involve in the knowledge creation process those persons possessing the highest level of knowledge of the focal phenomenon. Moreover, it encourages the discipline to differentiate between the various segments its knowledge is created to serve. Perhaps most persuasively of all, PR ensures that consumers for consumer research are given what they want: A relevant corpus of useful knowledge. In the quest which we all share to ensure consumer research's attainment of scientific status such a contribution may well be invaluable.

REFERENCES

AMA Task Force (1988), "Developing, Disseminating, and Utilizing Marketing Knowledge," *Journal of Marketing*, 52 (October), 1-25.

Anderson, Martin (1992), *Impostors in the Temple*, New York: Simon and Schuster.

Anderson, Paul F. (1983), "Marketing, Scientific Progress, and Scientific Method," *Journal of Marketing*, 47 (Fall), 18-31.

_____ (1986), "On Method in Consumer Research: A Critical Relativist Perspective," *Journal of Consumer Research*, 13 (September), 155-173.

_____ (1989), "On Relativism and Interpretivism-With a Prolegomenon to the 'Why' Question," in *Interpretive Consumer Research*, ed. Elizabeth C. Hirschman, Provo, UT: Association for Consumer Research, 10-23.

Andreasen, Alan R. (1991), "Consumer Behavior Research and Social Policy," in *Handbook of Consumer Research*, eds. Thomas S. Robertson and Harold H. Kassarjian. Englewood Cliffs: Prentice Hall, 548-591.

Arndt, Johan (1985), "On Making Marketing More Scientific: Role of Orientations, Paradigms, Metaphors, and Puzzle Solving," *Journal of Marketing*, 49 (Summer), 11-23.

Berger, Peter L. and Thomas Luckman (1967), *The Social Construction of Reality*. London: Allen Lane.

Bloedon, Robert V., and Deborah R. Stokes (1994), "Making University/Industry Collaborative Research Succeed," *Research-Technology Management*, 37 (March-April), 44-48.

Brady, J. and I. Davis (1993), "Marketing's Mid-life Crisis," *McKinsey Quarterly*, 2, 17-28.

Branscomb, Lewis M. (1992), "Does America Need a Technology Policy?," *Harvard Business Review*, 70 (March-April), 24-31.

Brown, Stephen (1995), *Postmodern Marketing*, London: Routledge.

Calder, Bobby J., Lynn W. Phillips and Alice M. Tybout (1983), "Beyond External Validity," *Journal of Consumer Research*, 10 (1), 112-114.

Cannon, Joseph P. and Jagdish N. Sheth (1994), "Developing a Curriculum to Enhance Teaching of Relationship Marketing," *Journal of Marketing Education*, 16 (Summer), 3-14.

Churchill, Gilbert A., Jr. (1979), "A Paradigm for Developing Better Measures of Marketing Constructs," *Journal of Marketing Research*, 16 (February), 64-73.

Conant, Jeffrey S., Jacqueline Johnson Brown, and Michael P. Mokwa (1985), "Students Are Important Consumers: Assessing Satisfaction in a Higher Education Context," *Journal of Marketing Education*, 7 (Summer), 13-20.

Fine, Seymour H. (1994), "Inequitable or Incomplete Social Marketing: The Case of Higher Education," in *Marketing Exchange Relationships, Transactions, and Their Media*, ed. Franklin S. Houston. Westport, CT: Quorum Books, 155-165.

Freire, Paulo (1970), *Pedagogy of the Oppressed*. New York: Herder and Herder.

Hakanson, Lars (1993), "Managing Cooperative Research and Development," *R & D Management*, 23 (October), 273-285.

Hall, Budd L. (1992), "From Margins to Center? The Development and Purpose of Participatory Research," *The American Sociologist*, 23 (Winter), 15-28.

Hebdidge, Dick (1988), *Hiding in the Light: On Images and Things*. London: Routledge.

Hunt, Shelby D. (1983), *Marketing Theory: The Philosophy of Marketing Science*. Homewood, IL: Irwin.

_____ (1990), "Truth in Marketing Theory and Research," *Journal of Marketing*, 54 (July), 1-15.

Jacoby, Jacob (1978), "Consumer Research: A State of the Art Review," *Journal of Marketing*, 42 (April), 87-96.

Korten, David C. (1995), *When Corporations Rule the World*. West Hartford, CT: Kumarian Press, Inc.

Kotler, Philip (1972), "A Generic Concept of Marketing," *Journal of Marketing*, 36 (April), 46-54.

_____ (1984), *Marketing Management: Analysis, Planning and Control*, London: Prentice-Hall International.

Lynd, Mark (1992), "Creating Knowledge Through Theater: A Case Study With Developmentally Disabled Adults," *The American Sociologist*, 23 (Winter), 100-115.

McCracken, Grant David (1988), *The Long Interview*. London: Sage.

Park, Peter (1992), "The Discovery of Participatory Research As A New Scientific Paradigm: Personal and Intellectual Accounts," *The American Sociologist*, 23 (Winter), 29-42.

Peter, J. Paul (1991), "Philosophical Tensions in Consumer Inquiry," in *Handbook of Consumer Research*, eds. Thomas S. Robertson and Harold H. Kassarjian. Englewood Cliffs: Prentice Hall, 533-547.

_____ and Jerry C. Olson (1983), "Is Science Marketing?," *Journal of Marketing*, 47 (Fall), 111-125.

Peterson, John (1993), "Assessing the Performance of European Collaborative R&D Policy: The Case of Eureka," *Research Policy*, 22 (June), 243-264.

Piercy, Nigel (1992), *Market-led Strategic Change*. Oxford: Butterworth-Heinemann.

Priddle, John (1994), "Marketing Ethics, Macromarketing, and the Managerial Perspective Reconsidered," *Journal of Macromarketing*, 14 (Fall), 47-62.

Quintas, Paul, David Wield, and Doreen Massey (1992), "Academic-Industry Links and Innovation: Questioning the Science Park Model," *Technovation*, 12 (April), 161-175.

Ramocki, Stephen P. (1994), "It Is Time to Teach Creativity Throughout the Marketing Curriculum," *Journal of Marketing Education*, 16 (Summer), 15-25.

Sherry, John F. (1991), "Postmodern Alternatives: The Interpretive Turn in Consumer Research," in *Handbook of Consumer Research*, eds. Thomas S. Robertson and Harold H. Kassarjian. Englewood Cliffs: Prentice Hall, 548-591.

Stafford, Thomas F. (1994), "Consumption Values and the Choice of Marketing Electives: Treating Students Like Customers," *Journal of Marketing Education*, 16 (Summer), 6-33.

Stoecker, Randy and Edna Bonacich (1992), "Why Participatory Research? Guest Editor's Introduction," *The American Sociologist*, 23 (Winter), 5-14.

Thompson, Craig J. (1990), "Eureka! and Other Tests of Significance: A New Look at Evaluating Interpretive Research," in *Advances in Consumer Research*, ed. Marvin Goldberg. Provo, UT: Association for Consumer Research, 25-30.

Wallendorf, Melanie and Russell W. Belk (1989), "Assessing Trustworthiness in Naturalistic Consumer Research," in *Interpretive Consumer Research*, ed. Elizabeth Hirschman. Provo, UT: Association for Consumer Research, 64-84.

Wells, William D. (1993), "Discovery-oriented Consumer Research," *Journal of Consumer Research*, 19 (March), 489-504.

Werner, Jerry (1991), "Can Collaborative Research Work?," *Industry Week*, 240 (July 1), 47.

Zinkhan, George M. and Rudy Hirschheim (1992), "Truth in Marketing Theory and Research: An Alternative Perspective," *Journal of Marketing*, 56 (April), 80-88.

Re-assessing the Generalizability from Artificial to Real: Another Look at the Predictive Validity of Conjoint

W. Steven Perkins, M/A/R/C
Daniel R. Toy, California State University at Chico

ABSTRACT

Although several studies have indicated that conjoint models predict holdout samples or first choices of profiles rather well, one subset of studies has found conjoint to be weak in its ability to predict preferences for "real" objects. In this study, involving fast food restaurants, a conjoint model was estimated from preference ratings for profiles of hypothetical, artificial restaurants. A similarly constructed multiattribute model was estimated from ratings for existing, real restaurants. High convergent validity (generalizability) was found between preferences imputed from the conjoint model and observed preferences for real restaurants (R=.78). We demonstrate that discrepancies between affect imputed from the conjoint model and affect predicted from the multiattribute model can provide useful marketing information about the real restaurants, rather than cause for discounting the generalizability of the results.

In their recent review of conjoint analysis, Green and Srinivasan (1990) examine a number of studies involving assessments of model validity. They summarize these studies by saying that "the empirical evidence points to the validity of conjoint analysis as a predictive technique (1990, p. 13)." There are other studies, however, such as Holbrook and Havlena (1988), that have not found a high correspondence between consumer preferences predicted from conjoint methods and preferences for real objects. In what might loosely be described as "generalizability" research models estimated in the domain of artificially manipulated stimuli (i.e., conjoint analysis) have often provided weak predictions of preferences for real products.

The purpose of this project was to re-assess the finding that models of affect for artificial stimuli do not generalize well to affect for real stimuli. (We adopt the terms used by Holbrook and Havlena, with the term "artificial" meaning affect for hypothetical objects designed by the researcher as in conjoint, and the term "real" meaning existing objects experienced by consumers.) First, we demonstrate that a reasonable level of generalization can be achieved. Preference models were estimated from consumers' ratings of conjoint profiles and ratings of existing fast food restaurants, artificial and real stimuli, respectively. Using a hybrid conjoint model and a relatively tangible, familiar product category, a higher level of generalizability from artificial to real was obtained than in many previous studies. Second, we take the perspective that discrepancies between the models estimated from artificial and real stimuli may be seen as useful marketing signals, rather than strictly as a cause for rejecting the generalizability of the models. Contrary to previous research which has expressed concern over the lack of convergence between conjoint and multiattribute models, we argue that this divergence can be exploited. Specifically, preferences calculated from conjoint utilities can serve as a standard of comparison for the preferences for real restaurants. Any difference between the two sets of estimated preferences may reveal the effects of the brand itself.

The paper is organized as follows. First, previous research investigating preference generalizability will be briefly reviewed. Next the models to be estimated will be outlined. Then a study involving preferences for real, existing restaurants and artificial, hypothetical restaurants is described. After examining the results, the implications are discussed.

PREVIOUS RESEARCH ON GENERALIZING FROM ARTIFICIAL TO REAL

A Framework for Assessing Generalizability

Studies addressing generalizability across domains have modeled affect in the domain of artificial objects, denoted Y_a, and affect in the domain of real objects, denoted Y_r. Often conjoint models are estimated in the artificial domain and multiattribute models in the real domain. Each model could then be used to calculate a predicted value, $\hat{Y}$, in its respective calibration domain. Typically, though, the interest is in the ability of the model to capture affect outside of the calibration domain, using the model to calculate an imputed value, Y. In essence, imputing is accomplished by applying the weights estimated in the calibration domain to the corresponding independent variables in the opposite domain.

Table 1 outlines the four values which could be calculated from the models. Correlating observed and predicted values within each domain results in a measure of internal predictive validity: the observed affect for the artificial stimuli, Y_a, with the conjoint predictions, $\hat{Y}_a$, and the observed affect for the real stimuli, Y_r, with the multiattribute predictions, $\hat{Y}_r$. The multiple R for a regression equation represents internal predictive validity. Correlating observed and imputed values across domains provides a measure of external predictive validity: the observed affect for the artificial stimuli, Y_a, with the multiattribute imputations, $\dot{Y}_a$, and the observed affect for the real stimuli, Y_r, with the conjoint imputations, $\dot{Y}_r$. Imputing preferences from the conjoint model is in effect the same process as estimating preferences for new products in the simulation stage of conjoint studies. Research on generalizability typically focuses on external predictive validity, and considers internal predictive validity as simply a standard of comparison.

Relevance and Previous Research Regarding Generalizability

In discussing the relevance of the generalizability of models, Holbrook and Havlena (1988) state that the issue is of critical importance to marketing researchers. For example, the validity of research evaluating new product design using conjoint procedures prior to market launch would be impacted by such findings. If the models are generalizable then marketing managers should have confidence in predictions generated from conjoint analysis of preferences for artificial stimuli. In recent review articles, both Green and Srinivasan (1990) and Wittink and Cattin (1989) state that there has been little published evidence of the predictive validity of conjoint except for cross validation to holdout sets of profiles.

Holbrook, Moore, Dodgen, and Havlena (1985) review the few existing pieces of research directly addressing the issue of generalizing from artificial to real. In addition, Holbrook and Havlena (1988) review the complementary issue, generalizing from real to artificial. Thus, previous research will be only briefly considered, followed by a discussion of unresolved issues. Note that precise comparisons across studies are difficult because they differ greatly in terms of models employed and product categories investigated.

259

TABLE 1
Domains and Models Investigated

	Affect for artificial stimuli	Affect for real stimuli
Predictive models	Y_a	Y_r
Conjoint	$\hat{Y}_a$	$\dot{Y}_r$
Multiattribute	$\dot{Y}_a$	$\hat{Y}_r$

Green, Rao, and DeSarbo (1978) devised the procedures which have been followed in most of these studies. To compare affect across domains, in their 1978 study, 54 students rated seven actual vacation sites (e.g., Disney World) on six attributes, with each attribute at three levels; they then rated 18 profiles of hypothetical vacation sites constructed from those same six attributes and same three levels. Subjects also rank ordered the vacation sites. Individual level conjoint equations were then estimated for the profile ratings. Preferences were imputed to the real vacation sites by multiplying the group level attribute ratings for the sites by the estimated utilities.

Correlating the imputed values with the observed rankings, r $\{Y_r, \dot{Y}_r\}$, resulted in a median Kendall tau of .73. The model predicted significantly better than chance for 74 percent of the subjects. Most subsequent studies have not achieved even this moderate level of correlation.

Following a similar procedure, Moore and Holbrook (1982) found correlations of only r=.55 on average between preferences imputed from conjoint models and observed preferences for real stimuli. In this study, 67 students rated preferences and attributes for real dogs (e.g., beagle) and rated hypothetical dogs presented as conjoint profiles constructed from the same attributes. Interestingly, the conjoint model imputed preferences to a holdout sample of real dogs as accurately as a model which had been calibrated in the real domain.

In a detailed follow up study, Holbrook, Moore, Dodgen, and Havlena (1985) attained an even lower average correlation of r=.52 between preferences imputed with conjoint weights and observed preferences for musical recordings (e.g., Barry Manilow). That is, only about 25 percent of the variance in the observed preferences could be explained with the imputed preferences. The authors concluded that poor generalizability to real products occurred because the 20 subjects weighted the relevant dimensions in the artificial world differently than the same dimensions in the real world. This low level of convergence was particularly disconcerting because the individual level conjoint equations predicted the artificial stimuli well, producing an average R=.81 coefficient of determination. And the multiattribute equations calibrated on real recordings predicted the real stimuli well, averaging R=.82.

In addition, Holbrook and Havlena (1988) re-analyzed the same data used in Holbrook, et al. (1985) to look at the generalizability from real to artificial, specifically r $\{Y_a, \dot{Y}_a\}$. Predicting affect for artificial objects from models developed on real objects was equally unsuccessful, resulting in a group level correlation of r=.56 between observed and predicted affect for profiles.

In contrast, strong external validity between predictions derived from surveys and actual choices has been demonstrated in several studies reviewed by Levin, Louviere, Schepanski and Norman (1983). Choices related to transportation mode, store patronage, and residential location were predicted quite well, with correlations above .90 in some cases. Several of these studies differ from those noted earlier in that the models were calibrated and tested on different respondent samples. Again, the stimuli were relatively tangible, everyday items which may improve the generalizability from artificial to real. They conclude that external validity can be improved by taking greater care in the design of the respondents' task and in the estimation of the model parameters.

In sum, the ability of models estimated from preferences for artificial stimuli to predict preferences for existing objects is crucial to the usefulness of conjoint analysis. Yet there has been little published research on this issue. And the extant research in marketing has produced mixed results about the ability of conjoint models to generalize to the "real" world.

Our study re-examined this apparent lack of generalizability from artificial to real. There were two goals: first, to see if a reasonable level of convergence across domains could be achieved, and second, to study what the gap between artificial and real may have to tell us. The published research which has found lower external predictive validity has dealt with categories not often considered in applied marketing research settings (e.g., dogs and music) as compared to the research finding higher external predictive validity (e.g., vacations and transportation mode). Our study concerns fast food restaurants, a relatively familiar, common category which may improve generalizability. In addition, in contrast to previous research which has regarded the lack of generalizability as a problem, it could in fact offer an opportunity to understand consumers' preferences better. The lack of generalizability may itself be seen as valuable information. This research addresses the possibility of exploiting the information revealed by the gap between artificial and real.

MODELS

Hybrid Conjoint Model of Affect for Artificial Stimuli

One modeling approach which could help bridge the gap between artificial and real stimuli is hybrid conjoint (Green 1984). In hybrid, respondents provide self-explicated desirabilities for the levels of each attribute and self-explicated importance weights for each attribute. Combining these utilities and weights produces a compositional utility for every attribute-level combination. Respondents then rate the desirability of a limited number of conjoint profiles drawn from a larger master design. As in traditional conjoint, consumer preferences are decomposed from their ratings by partitioning out the variance due to the levels of the attributes in the profiles, but in hybrid the self-explicated utility for the profile is also included in the model.

The hybrid conjoint model can be formulated several ways as shown in Green (1984). The notation for the model has been adapted from Moore and Semenik (1988). First, the expected affect for hypothetical, "artificial" products, is calculated from the self-explicated data for an individual as follows:

$$\tilde{Y}_a = \sum_{j=1}^{J} w_j \sum_{k=1}^{K_j} u_{jk} \, x_{ajk} \qquad [1]$$

where

$\tilde{Y}_a$ = expected utility for artificial stimulus a, calculated from self-explicated data

w_j = self-explicated importance of attribute j

u_{jk} = self-explicated desirability of level k of attribute j

x_{ajk} = dummy variable indicating whether stimulus a possesses the k th level of the j th attribute

The self-explicated utility value is then included as one term in the model representing affect for the conjoint profiles:

$$Y_{ia} = \hat{\alpha} + \hat{\gamma} \tilde{Y}_{ia} + \sum_{j=1}^{J} \sum_{k=1}^{K_j-1} \hat{\beta}_{jk} \, x_{ajk} + \varepsilon_{ia} \qquad [2]$$

where

Y_{ia} = i th respondent's observed affect for artificial stimulus a

$\tilde{Y}_{ia}$ = expected utility for stimulus a, calculated from self-explicated data for the i th respondent

$\hat{\alpha}$ = estimated intercept term

$\hat{\gamma}$ = estimated coefficient for self-explicated utility

$\hat{\beta}_{ia}$ = estimated coefficient for level k of attribute j

ε_{ia} = error in predicting respondent i's affect for stimulus a

The weights are estimated by one OLS regression run across all respondents.

Multiattribute Model of Affect for Real Stimuli

Affect for "real" products can be represented with an identically formulated multiattribute model:

$$Y_{ir} = \overset{*}{\alpha} + \overset{*}{\gamma} \tilde{Y}_{ir} + \sum_{j=1}^{J} \sum_{k=1}^{K_j-1} \overset{*}{\beta}_{jk} \, x_{rj} + \varepsilon_{ir} \qquad [3]$$

where all terms are as defined before and

Y_{ir} = i th respondent's affect for real stimulus r

$\tilde{Y}_{ir}$ = expected utility for real stimulus r, calculated from self-explicated data for the ith respondent

The x_{rjk} represent the respondents' judgment that stimulus r has level k on attribute j. These ratings of the attributes can be expressed as dummy variables, making the model parallel to hybrid conjoint (see Green, Rao, and DeSarbo 1978 for a similar method).

Use of the Models to Generalize Affect Across Domains

All of the values in Table 1 could then be calculated after estimating equation [2] and equation [3]. Assessing the generalizability from artificial to real has typically focused on the correlation between observed affect for real products and affect imputed from the conjoint model, r $\{Y_r, \dot{Y}_r\}$. The relationship between these two sets of preferences can be defined more clearly by examining the mathematical models used to represent them. Specifically, equation [3] expresses observed preferences; the imputed preferences come from estimating equation [2] and then applying the weights to the independent variables in [3]. Observed and imputed affect for the real objects differ according to:

$$Y_{ir} - \dot{Y}_{ir} = (\alpha - \hat{\alpha}) + (\overset{*}{\gamma} - \hat{\gamma}) \tilde{Y}_{ir} + \left(\sum_{j=1}^{J} \sum_{k=1}^{K_j-1} \overset{*}{\beta}_{jk} - \hat{\beta}_{jk} \right) x_{rjk} + \varepsilon_{ir} \qquad [4]$$

Differences between observed and imputed can be stated in terms of the weights estimated from the conjoint model, the weights which would be estimated for the multiattribute model, and the error in the multiattribute model.

An additional point to consider in assessing the ability of a model calibrated in the artificial domain to generalize to the real domain is the relationship between affect imputed from the conjoint model and affect predicted from the multiattribute model. The multiattribute model must predict preferences for real stimuli at least as well as the conjoint model imputes those preferences. Therefore, the conjoint model could be assessed relative to the multiattribute model. In other words, how does r $\{Y_r, \dot{Y}_r\}$ compare to r $\{Y_r, \hat{Y}_r\}$? The difference between predicted and imputed results can be seen by substituting $Y_{ir} - \hat{Y}_{ir}$ for ε_{ir} in equation [4], resulting in:

$$\hat{Y}_{ir} - \dot{Y}_{ir} = (\alpha - \hat{\alpha}) + (\overset{*}{\gamma} - \hat{\gamma}) \tilde{Y}_{ir} + \left(\sum_{j=1}^{J} \sum_{k=1}^{K_j-1} \overset{*}{\beta}_{jk} - \hat{\beta}_{jk} \right) x_{rjk} \qquad [5]$$

This model says that any difference between affect imputed from the conjoint model, $\dot{Y}_r$, and affect predicted from the multiattribute model, $\hat{Y}_{ir}$, is due to discrepancies in the two sets of regression weights. Regressing $\hat{Y}_{ir}$ on Y_r brings out more clearly the discrepancies between the predicted and imputed results. The regression equation itself will simply remove the scale effects between predicted and imputed, but its residuals capture the total effect of the differences in the estimated weights. As the differences in the weights estimated in the two domains increase, the amount of unexplained variance $(1 - R^2)$ increases. This unexplained variance might be seen as a useful indication of the differences between consumers' utilities for artificial and real stimuli.

RESEARCH DESIGN AND DATA COLLECTION

This study assessed the ability of models of affect calibrated on artificial stimuli to impute affect to real stimuli. For the study, the product category of fast food restaurants was selected because a) it entailed the evaluation of relatively tangible, objective, simple attributes and b) it was familiar and meaningful to the (student)

TABLE 2
Fast Food Attributes and Levels

Atmosphere	Price	Food quality
below average	inexpensive	below average
average	moderate	average
better than average	expensive	better than average
Cleanliness	Service speed	Variety of food
below average	slow	very limited
average	moderate	moderate
better than average	fast	extensive

Calibration restaurants		Holdout restaurants
Burger King		Hoss's Arby's
Denny's	Roy Rogers	McDonald's
Hardee's	Wendy's	Ponderosa

subjects. This product category may enhance the likelihood of generalizing between artificial and real domains.

Stimuli

Restaurant attributes and their levels, as well as the "real" stimuli, were derived from focus groups conducted with students, a report on fast food restaurants in *Consumer Reports* and the corporate management of one fast food chain. The final list of six attributes, each at three levels, appears in Table 2. In addition, the nine fast food restaurants which were selected also appear in Table 2.

Subjects

For this study, 150 undergraduate marketing students completed the tasks during class. (Because the conjoint design requires an equal number of respondents per subset of profiles, six randomly chosen subjects were dropped to produce three balanced blocks of 48 subjects each.) Out of the nine restaurants, most of the 144 remaining students had eaten at all nine. The median number was eight. Every respondent ate at least one meal a month at one of these restaurants, with an average of at least once a week.

Design of the Respondents' Tasks

First, subjects completed the self-explicated utility tasks following the steps outlined in HYCON (Green and Toy 1985). For the three levels on each attribute, they rated whether the level was best, acceptable, or unacceptable; ratings were later coded as 1.0, .5, and 0, respectively. These serve as the u_{jk} in equation [1]. Subjects then rank ordered the six attributes by importance; the reflected rankings were normalized by dividing each one by the sum of the ranks. These serve as the w_j in equation [1].

For the second task, a fractional factorial design of 18 full profile conjoint combinations was selected from an orthogonal main effects only design (Hahn and Shapiro 1966, Plan 6). Restaurant brand name was not included in the profile. The x_{ajk} in equations [1] and [2] represent the dummy coded variables from these profiles. Three subsets of profiles were developed such that every subject responded to only six profiles, with one-third of the subjects receiving each subset. All subjects also responded to the same three holdout profiles. Respondents rated their preference for each profile on a 7 point equal-interval scale from very undesirable up to very desirable.

In the third task, each real restaurant was presented to the respondent with scales for the same six attributes at the same three levels used in the conjoint profiles. Respondents circled the one level which matched their perception of that restaurant on each attribute. Respondents rated, for example, their perception of McDonald's on cleanliness. These ratings become the x_{rjk} in equation [3]. Then they rated the desirability of each restaurant on a seven point scale, exactly as in the conjoint task.

Model Fitting and Analysis

Determining which real restaurants to include in the model estimation and which to include in the holdout sample occurred after gathering the data. The three holdout restaurants were chosen to match the preference ordering of the three holdout profiles compared to the other profiles. That is, one holdout profile ranked near the bottom of all the profiles, one above the middle, and one near the top. In the same relative positions were Arby's, McDonald's, and Ponderosa which became the holdout sample for testing the predictive validity of the model estimated on the other six restaurants.

Two models were run: equation [2] estimated the preference structure in the artificial domain and equation [3] estimated the preference structure in the real domain. In both cases, one OLS regression was run across the 144 respondents and their six ratings. In addition, the self-explicated utility was calculated for each profile and restaurant using equation [1].

After estimating the two models, predicted and imputed affect values were calculated, then correlated with the observed ratings at a total group level, to match the entries in Table 1. Then, following equation [5], the predicted affect for the real restaurants was regressed on the imputed affect to investigate the consequences of the differences in the estimated weights across domains.

RESULTS

Model Estimation

Table 3 presents the parameters for the two estimated models. Both capture the majority of the variance, but the multiattribute

TABLE 3
Parameter Estimates

Variables	Levels	Models	
		Conjoint	Multiattribute
Food Quality	Better	1.459	1.958
	Average	.978	1.165
Atmosphere	Pleasant	.498	1.335
	Average	.609	.819
Cleanliness	Better	.868	.864
	Average	.766	.572
Service Speed	Fast	.281	.359
	Moderate	.303	.244
Price	Expensive	-.624	-.280
	Moderate	-.418	-.216
Variety of Food	Extensive	-.008 n.s.	.325
	Moderate	-.115 n.s.	.126 n.s.
Self-explicated utility		2.579	.379 n.s.
Intercept		.529	1.402
multiple R		.733	.829
F (13,850)		75.968	143.729

all coefficients significant at $p<.01$,
unless otherwise noted as not significant (n.s.),

model produces a higher multiple R value of .83 compared to .73 for the conjoint model. In the conjoint model, the self-explicated utility was significant while in the multiattribute case it was not. Rank ordering the attributes by the magnitude of the coefficients, the food quality attribute had the largest impact on preference and the variety of food the least significant impact in both domains. Compared to the coefficients based on the real restaurants, subjects appear to be more price sensitive, but less influenced by atmosphere in rating the profiles.

Group Level Correlations

To examine the generalizability of the models across domains, the predicted and imputed ratings were correlated with the observed ratings as presented in Table 4. Reading across the first row in the table, the group level conjoint model attained a .73 correlation between the predicted and observed ratings for the artificial stimuli. Imputed and observed ratings for the real stimuli correlated at the .78 level. Surprisingly, the conjoint model produced a somewhat higher external validity score, $r\{\dot{Y}_r, Y_r\}$, than internal validity score, $r\{\dot{Y}_a, Y_a\}$. The same pattern occurs with the holdout profiles and holdout restaurants, though as might be expected the correlations are lower.

In the second row, the group level multiattribute model yields a .67 correlation between the observed preferences for the profiles and those imputed by the model. This compares to a correlation of .83 between the observed preferences for the real restaurants and the model predictions. The multiattribute model was very successful at the internal prediction of the restaurants, $r\{\dot{Y}_r, Y_r\}$, but it dropped off considerably when predicting the profiles, $r\{\dot{Y}_a, Y_a\}$. The same pattern is seen in predicting the holdouts, again at a lower level of correlation.

For comparison, the self-explicated results appear in the third row. The conjoint and multiattribute models out perform the self-explicated model in every case, except when the multiattribute model is used to predict the holdout conjoint profiles. In both models, there was a significant increase in the variance explained by adding the dummy variables (i.e., Equations 2 and 3) compared to simply including the self-explicated utility (Equation 1). For artificial stimuli, the amount of variance explained improved from .64 to .73 (F (12,850)=18.05, p=.01) but it improved even more for real stimuli from .69 to .83 (F (12,850)=48.19, p=.01).

Generalizing from Artificial to Real

These results indicate that generalizing from the hybrid conjoint model to real affect is relatively reliable—imputed and observed ratings correlated .78. As expressed in equation [5], differences between the preference structure (captured by regression weights) estimated in the domain of real objects and that estimated

TABLE 4
Predictive Validity of Group Level Models

Predicted by		Observed rating for calibration sample		Observed rating for holdout sample	
		Artificial stimuli n=864	Real stimuli n=864	Artificial stimuli n=432	Real stimuli n=432
Conjoint	r	.73	.78	.63	.69
Multiattribute	r	.67	.83	.51	.74
Self-explicated	r	.64	.69	.57	.61

r = correlation between rating calculated from model and observed

in the domain of artificial objects can be modeled through $\hat{Y}_r$ and $\dot{Y}_r$. Regressing affect predicted from the multiattribute model on the affect imputed from the conjoint model, results in the following equation (only the six restaurants in the original estimation of the multiattribute model are included):

$$\hat{Y}_r = .644 + .970 \, \dot{Y}_r$$

With an R^2 of .87, the equation leaves 13 percent of the variance unexplained. Applying the above equation to each of the predicted and imputed values for the nine restaurants, the residuals were computed, and tested against the expected residual of 0 for each restaurant. These results appear in Table 5. An alternative approach would be to regress the observed ratings for the real restaurants on the imputed ratings. While this would also allow us to detect differences by restaurants, it would not focus on the differences due to the estimated weights as shown in equation [5].

Arby's, Burger King, Hardee's, and McDonald's received significantly lower predicted values from the multiattribute model than might be expected. In other words, if we ignore the intercept of .644, then for these restaurants the preference value predicted from the multiattribute model was less than the preference inputted from conjoint, $\hat{Y}_r < \dot{Y}_r$. The negative residual for Hardee's, for example, means that a conjoint profile with the characteristics of a Hardee's would have received (on average) a higher rating than it did in the "real" world. Conversely, Hoss's received higher than expected multiattribute predictions, $\hat{Y}_r > \dot{Y}_r$. The positive residual for Hoss's implies that a conjoint profile that "looked like" a Hoss's would have received a lower rating. For the remaining four restaurants, the residuals did not differ significantly from 0.

One explanation for these results could be that the residuals of the multiattribute model itself differ by restaurant, possibly due to positive or negative halo. Following the same steps, the residuals of equation [3] were calculated and tested against the expected residual of 0 by restaurant. None of the six restaurants in the calibration set differed from 0, even at a $p<.10$ level. Thus, the multiattribute model captured the preferences equally well for each real restaurant.

DISCUSSION AND CONCLUSIONS

There are two important findings from our research on the generalizability from artificial to real. First, preferences imputed from the hybrid conjoint model, $\dot{Y}_r$, converged well with the observed preferences, Y_r, for the real, existing restaurants. Almost two-thirds of the variability (R=.78) in the restaurant preferences was captured by the conjoint model which had been calibrated in the artificial, hypothetical domain. This level of generalizability from artificial to real is higher than that found in most previous research in this area. Our results suggest that models based upon artificially manipulated stimuli can provide reasonable predictions of behavior in the world of real products. Interestingly, the hybrid model performed as well in the domain of real restaurants as it did in the domain of artificial stimuli. Moore and Holbrook (1982) also found that a conjoint model predicted well on holdouts in both domains.

This study begins to address the lack of research on the ability of conjoint models to predict actual preferences, choices, sales, or market shares. In recent review articles, both Green and Srinivasan (1990) and Wittink and Cattin (1989) state that there has been little published evidence of the predictive validity of conjoint except for cross-validation to holdout sets of profiles. In our study, cross-validation resulted in a total group level correlation of .63 between predictions from the hybrid model and holdout profiles. But the more interesting result was the .78 correlation between predictions from the hybrid model and preferences for the real restaurants. These results provide some confidence in the predictive validity of conjoint models relative to real stimuli as well as relative to holdout profiles.

The second finding of this research is that the differences between preference structures estimated in the two domains may provide useful marketing information. The effects of the differences in the estimated weights of the conjoint and multiattribute models were brought out more clearly by regressing predicted preferences, $\hat{Y}_r$, for real restaurants on imputed preferences, $\dot{Y}_r$. Examining the regression residuals provides a measure of how well each restaurant would fare according to the conjoint equation compared to the multiattribute equation. Applying the conjoint weights to the real attribute ratings finds that consumers would be expected to prefer McDonald's, for instance, to a greater extent than that which was predicted from the multiattribute model. The

TABLE 5
Testing Residuals of Predicted Affect Regressed on Imputed Affect

Restaurant	Mean residual	t
Arbys (h)	-.143	-4.50 **
Burger King	-.093	-2.86 *
Denny's	+.048	1.52 n.s.
Hardee's	-.209	-7.99 **
Hoss's	+.133	4.06 **
McDonald's (h)	-.205	-6.78 **
Ponderosa (h)	+.074	2.15 n.s.
Roy Rogers	+.044	1.55 n.s.
Wendy's	+.077	2.31 n.s.

* $p<.05$, Bonferroni familywise t=2.77,
** $p<.01$, Bonferroni familywise t=3.26,
(h) = holdout from the calibration of the multiattribute model

imputed preferences represent a benchmark, "objective" level of preference which the product "should" be able to command, ceteris paribus. As measured in the conjoint task, consumers say they would like a restaurant with the characteristics of a McDonald's. But when rating McDonald's in the multiattribute task, consumers could draw upon their experience of actually going there (all 144 subjects had eaten at McDonald's). Thus the discrepancies between the preference structures estimated in the two domains point out the value of the image of the real restaurant itself. In this instance, the effect of being "McDonald's" appears to lower the preference compared to an identical but unnamed restaurant profile.

These residuals could also be thought of as a measure of brand equity. As defined in Farquhar (1989), brand equity is the "added value with which a given brand endows a product" (p. 24). One approach to measuring brand equity has been to ask consumers' their preferences for branded and unbranded versions of the same product, such as colas or cereals. Any difference in the two sets of preferences is the effect of the brand name, the brand's equity (Chay 1991). This "residual analysis" approach is quite similar to our analysis of the differences between imputed and predicted preferences for real restaurants. We do not use a direct measure of preference as that obtained from a taste test, but infer preferences through the estimated models. As a result there is the possibility that the residuals we examine are correlated with omitted variables. The apparent negative equity for McDonald's could be due to a poor location for instance. (In this study, the residual amounts were not related to demographic or usage variables.)

Future research could map out the boundary conditions for generalizing from artificial to real. Holbrook, et al (1985) may have identified a lower bound where the estimated models predict well within their respective domains, but predict poorly across domains. In fact the series of studies from Holbrook (1981) to Holbrook and Havlena (1988) serve as a warning that consumers' preferences cannot always be validly predicted from conjoint alone. Is there

also an upper limit to how well conjoint models can predict preferences for real products? We have speculated that one factor affecting generalizability is the product category itself. When preferences for real products are determined by relatively tangible, simple attributes, a conjoint model based upon those attributes might be expected to predict well across domains. Although it may seem ironic, a real brand that is predicted well with conjoint in effect has no brand equity, following the logic of residual analysis as applied in this paper. Such a brand is nothing more than the sum of its attribute parts. On the other hand, in product categories where brand name has a larger influence on preferences, we would expect generalizability from artificial to real to decrease.

REFERENCES

Chay, Richard F. (1991), "How Marketing Researchers Can Harness the Power of Brand Equity," *Marketing Research*, 3 (June), 30-37.
Farquhar, Peter H. (1989), "Managing Brand Equity," *Marketing Research*, 1 (September), 24-33.
Green, Paul E. (1984), "Hybrid Models for Conjoint Analysis: An Expository Review," *Journal of Marketing Research*, 21 (May), 155-169.
_____, Vithala R. Rao, and Wayne S. DeSarbo (1978), "Incorporating Group-Level Similarity Judgments in Conjoint Analysis," *Journal of Consumer Research*, 5 (December), 187-193.
_____, and V. Srinivasan (1990), "Conjoint Analysis in Marketing: New Developments with Implications for Research and Practice," *Journal of Marketing*, 54 (October), 3-19.
_____, and Daniel R. Toy (1985), *HYCON: Conjoint Analysis and Buyer Choice Simulation.* Palo Alto, CA: The Scientific Press.

Hahn, G.J. and S.S. Shapiro (1966), "A Catalog and Computer Program for the Design and Analysis of Symmetric and Asymmetric Fractional Factorial Experiments," Technical Report No. 66-C-165, General Electric Research and Development Center, Schenectady, NY.

Holbrook, Morris B. (1981), "Integrating Compositional and Decompositional Analyses to Represent the Intervening Role of Perceptions in Evaluative Judgments," *Journal of Marketing Research*, 18 (February), 13-28.

_____, and William J. Havlena (1988), "Assessing the Real-to-Artificial Generalizability of Multiattribute Attitude Models in Tests of New Product Designs," *Journal of Marketing Research*, 25 (February), 25-35.

_____, William L. Moore, Gary N. Dodgen, and William J. Havlena (1985), "Nonisomorphism, Shadow Features and Imputed Preferences," *Marketing Science*, 4 (3), 215-233.

Levin, Irwin P., Jordan J. Louviere, Albert A. Schepanski, and Kent L. Norman (1983), "External Validity Tests of Laboratory Studies of Information Integration," *Organizational Behavior and Human Performance*, 31, 173-193.

Moore, William L. and Morris B. Holbrook (1982), "On the Predictive Validity of Joint-Space Models in Consumer Evaluations of New Concepts," *Journal of Consumer Research*, 9 (September), 206-210.

_____, and Richard J. Semenik (1988), "Measuring Preferences with Hybrid Conjoint Analysis: The Impact of a Different Number of Attributes in the Master Design," *Journal ofBusiness Research*, 16, 261-274.

Wittink, Dick R. and Philippe Cattin (1989), "Commercial Use of Conjoint Analysis: An Update," *Journal of Marketing*, 53 (July), 91-96.

Repositioning Demand Artifacts in Consumer Research

Jean Perrien, University of Québec, Montréal[1]

ABSTRACT

This paper investigates the current status of demand artifacts in consumer research and suggests a new definition of demand artifacts. It is argued that demand artifacts are far from being a major concern in consumer research although they may potentially damage a theoretical relationship. Futhermore, this paper suggests linking demand artifacts to the identification of experimental manipulations, not hypothesis guessing. This new definition of demand artifacts reduces the subjective assessment of the presence or absence of demand biased responses when demand artifacts depends solely on hypothesis guessing.

In their quest for objective knowledge,(scientific) consumer researchers are eager to control as many sources of error as possible. Even if the pursuit of objectivity looks like the" quest for Holy Greil", it remains a legitimate goal (Hunt 1993). Among the myriad of sources of error consumer researchers face within an experiment, the very nature of experimental units–human beings, with feelings, emotions and biases- constitutes a real challenge. Human beings may react to experimental manipulations in a way that is not expected by researchers, depending on the role they adopt during the experiment. This unexpected experimental behavior creates some demand artifacts (Sawyer 1975). When, in an experiment the plausibility of demand artifacts may not be discarded, it offers a rival explanation that challenges theoretical construction, and therefore objectivity, in consumer research.

Five years ago, in a provocative, albeit stimulating article, Shimp Hyatt and Snyder (1991), challenged most of our understanding on demand artifacts. Among other things, they argued that demand artifacts were often accentuated as a source of error, they must be viewed as a random source of error (up until their analysis, demand artifacts were defined as a systematic source of error).

This paper follows in Shimp, Hyatt and Snyder's footsteps by exploring the current and actual status of demand artifacts in consumer behavior experiments and proposes a new -and less subjective- definition of demand artifacts.

DEMAND ARTIFACTS: A FRAMEWORK

Most of the available literature makes demand artifacts dependent on the ability of experimental units to identify the research hypothesis (Orne 1962, Rosenberg 1969, Rosnow and Aiken 1973, Sawyer 1975). When the experimental unit identifies the research hypothesis and that she/he adopts a role resulting from this guessing (experimental units may act as good, negative, apprehensive or faithful subjects, see Berkowitz and Donnerstein 1982), it is most likely that experimental results will be "demand biased". Consequently, it follows that observations on dependent measures will include an additional term of error.

Shimp, Hyatt and Snyder (1991, p. 274; thereafter identified as SHS) agree with this view of demand artifact. They formalize the probability of demand biased responses for an experimental unit i as follows:

$$Pr(Bi)=Pr(Ei) \times Pr(Di/Ei) \times Pr(Ai/Di) \qquad (eq.1)$$

where:

Pr(Bi)=probability that the i subject is demand biased; Pr(Ei) probability of encoding a demand cue; Pr(Di/Ei)=conditional probability of discerning the true experimental hypothesis or a correlated hypothesis; Pr(Ai/Di)=conditional probability of acting on the hypothesis.

This probabilistic formulation depicts the common understanding of demand artifacts. For SHS a demand cue is "a basis for discerning the experimental hypothesis." This definition has been widely accepted in the literature and stresses the key role of hypothesis guessing as the source of demand biased responses. Hence, role adoption derived from hypothesis guessing is at the origin of demand artifacts.

Recently, Darley and Lim (1993) question some of SHS's assumptions. They argue that due to the underreporting of the hypothesis in postexperimental inquiries, the conditional probability of discerning the experimental hypothesis or a correlated hypothesis should be decomposed into two components (detecting and reporting the hypothesis versus detecting but not reporting the hypothesis). According to Darley and Lim (1993, p. 490): "... the existence of underreporting may hide the true nature and seriousness of demand artifacts." Furthermore, they challenge SHS's third condition for demand biased responses (acting on the hypothesis by adopting a role) on the premises that "there is growing evidence to suggest that subjects will be affected directly or indirectly in their behaviors or responses if conditions one and two hold true, regardless of the presence or absence of condition three." SHS (1993) question these arguments in a reply which emphasizes the lack of empirical support of Darley and Lim's statements.

In this paper we will evaluate consumer behavior research practices in relation to demand artifacts and propose a new definition of demand artifacts that we perceive as being less ambiguous that the casual understanding of demand artifacts we just presented.

DEMAND ARTIFACTS IN CONSUMER RESEARCH: CURRENT PRACTICES

SHS stress the fact that in the publication process, gatekeepers (i.e. reviewers) tend to over-emphasize demand artifacts as an alternative explanation for experimental observations. In order to assess to what extent demand artifacts are a real concern in experimental research on consumer behavior, a descriptive analysis of experimental research published between 1990 and 1993 (inclusive) was conducted by one judge. Articles investigating consumer behavior using an experimental methodology, published in the International Journal of Research in Marketing, the Journal of the Academy of Marketing Science, the Journal of Consumer Research, the Journal of Marketing as well as the Journal of Marketing Research were content analyzed. These journals are considered as major academic publications in the consumer behavior area and the official outlets of the four prominent associations in the field (ACR, AMA, AMS, EMAC). Moreover, articles published in these journals suffer less from length constraints than association proceedings. Hence, information on demand artifacts should be more exhaustive than anywhere else.

Out of all the published material, 259 articles referred to experimental manipulations conducted on consumers and were consequently subject to potential demand artifacts (IJRM: 2,7%, JCR: 54%, JMR: 31,3 %, JAMS: 6.2 %, JM: 5,8%). Demand artifacts may be a concern either in the design of an experiment (such as, for instance, the use of a disguise) or in the analysis of

---

[1]The preliminary draft of this paper was written when the author was a visiting professor at ESSEC (France).

experimental results (e.g. removing observations from respondents who, in a post experimental inquiry, guessed the research hypothesis) or both. Hence, demand artifacts will be assessed either *a priori* (in the design of the experiment) or *a posteriori* (in the analysis of experimental results). Albeit, let us mention that such a content analysis does not intend to provide a perfect indicator of the academic attention toward demand artifacts.

From the beginning, it has to be recognized that a demand artifacts controversy may occur "behind the scenes" (i.e. during the reviewing process). However, if reviewers consider the information on demand artifacts assessment not worth including in the final paper (although through the reviewing process, it had been discussed as a potential rival explanation to experimental results), one may really question the statement according to which reviewers overemphasize demand artifacts. Moreover, enhancing knowledge is possible, from a sociological point of view, when the community, and not only reviewers, may not suspect the results of a research to be demand biased. In a sense, by focusing on explicit consideration for demand artifacts, this paper adopt a conservative approach that will have to be considered when interpreting results.

Only 43 articles (16.6 %) formally refer to demand artifacts *a priori* and 41 published experimentations (15.8%) indicate an *a posteriori* concern for this source of error. It must be pointed out that 65.1 % of articles which indicate a concern for demand artifacts in the design of the experiment (*a priori*) never refer to this source of potential error in the analysis of results (*a posteriori*). All in all, 183 articles (70.6 %) never mention any kind of concern for demand artifacts.

In his seminal work on demand artifacts, Sawyer (1975) points out potential procedures to reduce or to control demand artifacts. In this analysis of major experimental research conducted on consumer research we intend to assess to what extent researchers availed themselves of these procedures. Bearing in mind the rather low percentage of articles referring to demand artifacts, the results are not surprising: only 6 experiments (2.3 %) explicitly selected a research design which minimizes demand artifacts, 4 of them (1.5 %) specifically mentioned training the experimenters in view of reducing the occurrence of demand artifacts. Non-experimentation, a methodological solution to detect some demand bias, was reported in only one experiment, and hetero-method was never explicitly mentioned in any article. Let us mention that Darley and Lim (1993, p. 493) suggest relying on both the non-experimentation and hetero-method in the assessment of demand artifacts. Obviously, this is not yet the case. Nonetheless, 34 (13.1 %) published experiments indicated they relied on postexperimental inquiries (PEI) to assess respondents' guessing of the research hypothesis. Although, the most intriguing result concerned the use of deception.

The essence of deception (disguise, cover story...) is to reduce demand artifacts by introducing a distance between the declared and the actual research objectives (i.e. hypothesis). Actually, this is the sole methodological role of deception, the consequences of which have been documented as ambiguous (Christensen 1977, Silverman 1977). Among the *crème de la crème*, 109 articles (42.1 %) explicitly incorporated deception in the design of their experiment, which means that more articles are referring to deception than to demand artifacts... although the latter is the sole justification for the former. The explanation is straightforward: deception is becoming part of the experimental process, despite the fact that it should be contingent to a high probability of demand biased responses. It may be argued that during "behind the scenes negotiations" between authors and reviewers deception was defined as a way to reduce the probability of demand biased responses. Once more, if this is the case, there is a risk of inconsistency between the information provided to reviewers and to the academic

community. Dealing with articles published in the most prominent journals should dismiss such an inconsistency.

Finally, the type of design as well as the nature of respondents have been evidenced as potential sources of demand artifacts (Sawyer 1975). It has been documented that the usage of within subject designs as well as when relying on students, increases the probability of demand biased responses. Please note that the aforementioned does not mean that within subject designs and/or relying on students as experimental units will automatically result in demand biased responses! Once again, it simply implies a greater amount of risk. In addition, there is still some controversy on the plausibility of demand effects due to the selection of students as experimental units. According to Orne (1962), students may inflate theory supportive conclusions by adopting a positive role. Gordon, Slade and Schmitt (1986) while reviewing 32 studies in which students and non-students participated, as subjects, in identical experiments, conclude: " After examining the statistical evidence, it is clear that problems exist in replicating with non-students subjects behavioral phenomena observed in student sample" (Gordon, Slade and Schmitt 1986, p. 200). In the following paragraph we will look at these two issues (the type of design and nature of experimental units).

Our analysis reveals that 20 experiments (7.7 %) relied on within-subject designs and 185 (74.3%) of the published research used students as experimental units. Out of the 20 within subject experiments, only 2 formally cared about demand artifacts *a priori* and 1 *a posteriori*. Out of the 185 experiments which used students as consumer proxy, 38 (20.5 %) showed an *a priori* and 36 (19.4%) an *a posteriori* concern for demand artifacts. These two percentages were slightly higher than what was observed at the general population level (16.6 % and 15.8 % respectively).

Prior to drawing any conclusions, let us stress once again that our observations are derived from an explicit consideration of demand artifacts. Therefore, it may be possible that a researcher, while conducting an investigation, took demand artifacts into consideration but failed to refer to them in the body of the article. This also means that the gatekeepers (reviewers) did not request formal information on demand artifacts to be published. Secondly, our observations only come from published experimentations in the four aforementioned leading academic journals, no information on rejected papers is available. Once more, one might suspect that a large portion of rejections was due to weaknesses in the control of demand artifacts. Nobody will challenge the fact that reviewers accepting and refusing papers are the same people and that there do not exist reviewers specializing in either the acceptance or the rejection of submitted paper. Hence, it is questionable to assume that reviewers overestimate demand artifacts when rejecting a paper and underestimate them when accepting it. Indeed, our results prove that the formal concern with demand artifacts is limited, even in the case of potentially high demand bias. With the previously mentioned limits in mind, we have to acknowledge that demand artifacts do not appear as a crucial concern in published experiments. Finally, if someone still believes that demand artifacts are a prevalent concern in the reviewing processes, our results suggest that gatekeepers should definitely ask authors to provide some basic information on the control of demand artifacts (only a couple of sentences), in order to avoid the academic community of suspecting demand biased effects.

Sawyer (1975) stressed the need to rely on post experimental inquiries (PEI's) to assess demand artifacts. Although we agree with SHS that such a measurement of hypothesis guessing may be "tricky and potentially invalid" (SHS, page 280) and subject to demand biased responses, PEI's are the only method of demand artifact measurement which is actually used. Other methods for demand artifact control are highly marginal, which, once more tends to corroborate that demand artifacts are not a major methodological concern in consumer behavior research.

As far as deception is concerned, as stated earlier, we question how and why they are included in an experiment: deception only aims at reducing demand biased responses by masking the true research objective. Consequently, it must not be considered as a casual component in the design of an experiment. If, and only if, the probability of demand artifacts is high, deception should be used, such as, for instance, in experiments where socially desirable measures are involved.

One possible explanation to this situation is that both the definition and measurement of demand artifacts rest on a loose and subjective ground. Up to now, demand artifacts are perceived as a rival explanation to experimental results when units refer to the so-called research hypothesis in a Post Experimental Inquiry (the only method actually used as was pointed out previously). In the following paragraph we will propose a more restrictive, but less ambiguous, definition of demand artifacts. The objective is not to increase the methodological burden but to clarify when, in an experiment, there is a significant probability of demand-biased responses.

DEMAND ARTIFACTS AND HYPOTHESIS GUESSING: TOWARD A NEW DEFINITION OF DEMAND ARTIFACTS

Hypothesis guessing is considered the sole cause of demand artifacts. A consensus seems to exist on this issue, from Orne (1962) to SHS, the ability of experimental units to identify the research hypothesis potentially induces demand biased responses. Coming back to SHS, hypothesis guessing is included in the three conditional probabilities for observing some demand biased responses (see equation 1 above). Of course, adoption of a role by an experimental unit remains a prerequisite to demand biased responses.

Linking demand artifacts to hypothesis guessing is either too restrictive or vague. Indeed, most, if not all, articles referring to the guessing of the hypothesis define the former as "the experiment purpose", in other words, the research question (SHS, p. 275). Such a definition systematically underestimates potential contamination by demand artifacts: whether the research question involves sophisticated constructs or a multi-factor experiment, guessing the research purpose becomes an impossible task, although it does not mean that respondents will not react in a biased manner to experimental manipulations. A consumer may adopt a role which will induce some biased responses without guessing the research hypothesis (see Farber (1963)). *Our contention is straightforward: experimental manipulations may induce demand-biased responses, whereas linking demand artifacts to the guessing of the "experimental purpose" is ambiguous and subject to some fluctuating interpretations by researchers.*

To understand the relevance of connecting demand artifacts to manipulations, in the following paragraphs we will explore the same two experiments on classical conditioning that SHS used to build up their arguments on demand artifacts. When reproducing Gorn's research on classical conditioning (Gorn 1982), Kellaris and Cox (1989) found, in a post-experimental inquiry, that only one subject guessed the experimental hypothesis (i.e. the research question: the effects of classical conditioning on consumer preferences). Thus, SHS (p. 277) conclude that "The fact that fewer than one percent of the subjects discerned the research hypothesis is proof positive that demand artifacts could not have influenced findings obtained in this initial experiment." This is a casual but drastic view of demand artifacts which, to a certain extent, bypasses

the problem of demand biased responses. Because of a sophisticated research purpose, demand biased responses no longer depend on experimental units (skills, attitudes, inferences on manipulations...) and on experimental design, but on the level of formal sophistication of a research question and the ability of experimental unit to identify and formalize the research purpose in an experimental inquiry (which may itself be demand biased). Indeed, it reduces the occurrence of demand biased responses to what SHS qualify as simplistic experiments and transparent procedures (p. 275). Examples of experimental research which bypass the demand artifact problem simply because of a sophisticated research question, instead of respondents behavior and experimental design are numerous.

For instance, in an experiment similar to Gorn's research, Nelson, Duncan and Frontczak (1985) investigated " the effects of distraction in a radio commercial on cognitive responses and message acceptance" (sic). To empirically test the causal relationship between distraction and their two dependent variables, they formalized a set of propositions (i.e. hypotheses) such as: "When controlling for message discrepancy, counterargumentation will show a negative relation with attitude change as advocated by the message." To check for some kind of demand biased responses "at the conclusion of the experiment, selected subjects were debriefed to determine whether they had guessed the purpose of the research." Guess what ?... "Results of the debriefing indicated that subjects did not guess the purpose of the study." Actually, only the experimenters could have guessed the purpose of the research. But, if in the postexperimental inquiry a respondent indicated that the purpose of this research was "to see the impact of the music on my ideas", does that mean there is no risk of demand artifacts?

Furthermore, by reducing demand biased responses to guessing the purpose of the research, one could easily conclude that experiments on sophisticated fields of investigation such as the effects of distraction on conditioning and attitude formation are systematically free of demand artifacts.

Bearing these examples in mind, defining hypothesis guessing as the core for demand biased responses is highly dangerous and conceals what demand artifacts really are: *a source of error in measurements resulting from role adoption by consumers involved in an experiment and induced by subject's reactions to an experimental manipulation, not on the level of sophistication in the formalization of the research purpose.* Of course an experimental manipulation is the outcome of a research purpose; it is a necessary but non-sufficient condition for solving the research question. For instance, in research where two factors are manipulated, the purpose of the investigation may be formalized as follows:

$$PI = F1 + F2 + [F1 \times F2] \qquad (eq.2)$$

Within a strict application of the definition of demand artifacts as resulting from the guessing of the research purpose (PI), this means that to be demand biased, a consumer has to identify both factors 1 and 2 (F1 and F2) as well as the interaction between them (F1 X F2). On the other hand, if demand artifacts are connected to the identification of manipulations, as stated in our revised definition, it means that a consumer having identified either F1 or F2 may be suspected of being demand biased. The rationale for supporting this extended definition of demand artifacts is analytically straightforward: when the consumer adopts a role (consciously or unconsciously) derived from the identification of a manipulated factor, it is most likely (depending on the role) that the observed variance in dependent variables resulting from the manipulation of this factor will be demand biased. This is also true for interaction terms involving this factor. Which, consequently, will damage conclusions about the purpose of the investigation. From an analytical point of view, contrasting respondents who identified a manipulated factor from those who did not allows to check for significant differences in observed results. One must keep in mind that demand artifacts are a sticky issue when they introduce some error variance in observations, not only when a respondent identified either a manipulation or the research hypothesis (our new definition vs. the conventional one). Furthermore, measuring the identification of manipulations instead of the experimental purpose is much more straightforward and far less demand induced than asking experimental units to guess the experimental purpose (see Sawyer 1975 for PEI questions).

If we expect that some researchers, while assessing demand artifacts through, let us say, a post-experimental inquiry, decided to extend identification of potentially demand biased respondents to manipulation discerning, then it is all the more certain that several experimentations did not consider factor identification as a potential source of error. For instance, in one of the Kellaris and Cox experiments duplicating Gorn's pioneering work, it would be very surprising if, in the post experimental inquiry, only one student (out of 299) reported either music influence or pen choice as the purpose of the exercise, taking into account that these variables were not only manipulated but were also subject to some obtrusive measures as far music was concerned (appeal of the music heard was measured on a seven-point scale), and, as stated by the authors, with respect to the choice of pen color (yellow pens wrote in blue and white pens in black)... "it is possible that some subjects may have noticed this difference after they began writing..." (Kellaris and Cox 1989, p. 114). By restricting demand artifacts to hypothesis guessing, researchers adopt a highly conservative approach to error assessment as well as creating some confusion about what hypothesis guessing really means ("guessing the guessing"). We argue that a *manipulation identification* may initiate a role that will result in demand biased responses. Finally, manipulations in behavioral research are twofold: the experimenter may manipulate either instructions (e.g. research on consumption situation) or events (e.g. the content of a message) (Kerlinger 1988). Special attention should be given to both the control and the assessment of demand biased responses in the case of instruction manipulation as it provides subjects with explicit cues on the nature of the experimental factors and requires experimental units to formally play a role.

CONCLUSION

Our content analysis of the formal concern with demand artifacts in published consumer behavior research proves that it tends to be underreported, even if the selected experimental design increases the probability of demand biased responses (e.g. within subject designs).

Our results shed some light on deception. It should be stressed that deception should only aim at reducing the occurrence of demand biased responses. By no means should it be viewed as a casual experimental practice. Bearing in mind the well-documented literature on risks associated with deception, consumer behavior researchers should question the relevance of deception. The key question becomes: does it really reduce the probability of demand biased responses?

Secondly, we argue that manipulation identification should be considered as the source of potential demand artifacts, not hypothesis guessing. Restricting demand artifacts to hypothesis guessing leaves room for a subjective assessment of the presence or absence of potential demand artifacts, based on the researcher's decision about when the research purpose was actually identified. This new definition of demand artifacts may be perceived as very restrictive,

although it reduces the current ambiguity surrounding detection of demand biased responses.

We expect that this new definition of demand artifacts will by-pass such an ambiguity. Yet, as was mentioned earlier, demand artifacts are a threat to theory construction as long as it provides a rival explanation to experimental findings. Hence, we must not restrict demand artifacts to the identification of either a research purpose or a manipulation, for we must also investigate effects of such an identification on dependent variables (through various techniques such as covariance analysis or partitioning of results). We believe that our approach to demand artifact identification will simplify this task and will remove the inherent subjectiveness in the interpretation of the research pupose by experimental units. We cannot search for objectivity by relying on subjective processes of error identification.

REFERENCES

Berkowitz, Leonard and Edward Donnerstein (1982), "External Validity Is More Than Skin Deep: Some Answers to Criticisms of Laboratory Experiments", *American Psychologist*, 37 (March), 245-257.

Christensen, Larry (1980), *Experimental Methodology*, 2nd edition, Boston Mass: Allynand Bacon.

Darley, William K. and Jeen-Su Lim. (1993), "Assessing Demand Artifacts in Consumer Research: An Alternative Perspective" *Journal of Consumer Research* vol. 30 (December) 489-501.

Farber, I.E. (1963), "The Things People Say to Themselves", *American Psychologist*, 18, 185-197.

Fiske, Donald W. (1982), "Convergent-Discriminant Validation in Measurement and Research Strategies" in *New Directions for Methodology of Social and Behavioral Science: Forms of Validity Research*, D. Brindberg and L. Kidder eds. San Francisco: Jossey-Bass Published, 72-92.

Gordon, Michael E., L. Allen Slade and Neal Scmitt (1986), "The "Science of the Sophomore" Revisited: from Conjecture to Empiricism", *Academy of Management Review*, Vol. 11, No 1, 191-207.

Gorn, Gerald J. (1982), "The Effects of Music in Advertising on Choice Behavior: A Classical Conditioning Approach", *Journal of Marketing*, 46 (winter), 94-101.

Hunt Shelby D. (1993), "Objectivity in Marketing Theory and Research", *Journal of Marketing*, 57 (April), 76-91.

Kellaris, James J. and Anthony D. Cox (1989), "The Effects of Background Music in Advertising: A Reassessment", *Journal of Consumer Research*, 16 (June), 113-118.

Kerlinger, Fred (1988), *Foundations of Behavioral Research*, 3rd edition, New York: Holt, Rinehart and Winston.

Kruglanski, Ani W. (1975), "The Human Subject in the Psychology Experiment: Fact and Artifact", in *Advances in Experimental Social Psychology*, vol. 8, ed. L. Berkowitz, Orlando, FL: Academic Press, 101-147.

Nelson, James, J. Calvin, P. Duncan and Nancy T. Frontczak (1985), "The Distraction Hypothesis and Radio Advertising", *Journal of Marketing*, vol. 49 (winter), 60-71.

Orne, Martin M. (1962), "On the Social Psychology of the Psychological Experiment: With Particular Reference to Demand Characteristics and Their Implications", *American Psychologist*, 17 (November), 776-783.

Rosenberg, M. (1969), "The Conditions and Consequences of Evaluation Apprehension", in *Artifact in Behavioral Research*, eds. R. Rosenthal and R. L. Rosnow, New York: Academic Press, 280-350.

Rosnow, Ralph L. and Leona S. Aiken (1973), "Mediation of Artifacts in Behavioral Research", *Journal of Experimental Social Psychology*, 9 (May), 181-201.

Sawyer, Alan (1975), "Demand Artifacts in Laboratory Experiments in Consumer Research", *Journal of Consumer Research*, 1 (March), 20-30.

Shimp, Terence A., Eva M. Hyatt and David J. Snyder (1991), "A Critical Appraisal of Demand Artifacts in Consumer Research", *Journal of Consumer Research*, vol. 18 (December), 273-283.

Shimp Terence A., Eva M. Hyatt and David J. Snyder (1993), "A Critique of Darley and Lim's "Alternative Perspective" *gournal of Consumer Research*, vol. 30 (December), 496-501.

Silverman I.. (1971), *The Human Subject in the Psychological Laboratory*, New-York: Pergamon.

Psychological Correlates of Deal Proneness and Deal-Responsive Behavior

Donald R. Lichtenstein, University of Colorado

Much of the empirical research within the sales promotion domain has relied exclusively on behavioral-based scanner data. While this research is valuable in providing estimates of response elasticities to various promotional vehicles, this research is perhaps less equipped to address the psychological motivations and tendencies affecting consumer decision-making. This session brought together several academics who have been active in conducting research designed to provide insights into the psychological mechanisms associated with deal proneness and deal-responsive behavior. The goal of this special session was be to explore the issue of "why consumers respond to deals as they do." Research in this stream attempts to balance perspectives and provide insight into the findings from the scanner-based sales promotion research stream. As such, the goal of all three presentations in this session concerned generating insights into why consumers respond to deals.

"Psychological Correlates of a Proneness to Deals: A Domain-Specific Analysis"

Donald R. Lichtenstein, University of Colorado at Boulder
Scot Burton, University of Arkansas
Richard G. Netemeyer, Louisiana State University

In the first presentation, Lichtenstein noted that in recent years, packaged goods manufacturers have allocated increasing amounts of their promotional budgets towards consumer sales promotions. Consistent with this trend, and aided by the availability of scanner data, academic researchers have paid increased attention to the effects of sales promotions on consumer shopping behavior. Many of these studies have investigated the impact of observable variables such as deal type, frequency, duration, depth, and retraction on deal-responsive behavior.

Lichtenstein stated that while these studies are very valuable in providing estimates of response elasticities to these promotional mix variables, they are limited in at least a few respects. First, because these studies typically only measure overt consumer behaviors, they do not investigate psychological variables which may underlie deal-responsive behavior. Second, researchers conducting these studies often inference from deal-responsive behavior to deal proneness with no independent measurement of the deal proneness construct. As behavior is usually (if not always) multiply-motivated, deal-responsive behavior will have other antecedents (e.g., price consciousness) in addition to deal proneness. Thus, equating deal proneness with deal-responsive behavior results in a confounding of antecedent constructs. Third, much previous research has treated deal proneness as a generalized, rather than domain-specific, construct. This practice does not allow for the possibility that consumer proneness to deals may depend on the type of deal and that proneness to alternative types of deals may have differing psychological correlates.

Lichtenstein presented findings from two studies which assessed theoretically-based hypotheses for the relationship between several *latent* domain-specific deal proneness constructs (e.g., display proneness, sale proneness, coupon proneness, rebate proneness) and several psychological variables with consumer behavior implications (e.g., brand loyalty, impulsiveness, need for cognition, price-quality perceptions). As such, the studies reported in this presentation complemented and represented a direct extension of the work of Lichtenstein, Netemeyer, and Burton (1995, December,

Journal of Consumer Research). These researchers employed direct measures of a proneness to respond to deals in each of eight domains and related the measures to deal-responsive behaviors assessed unobtrusively in a natural field setting. Lichtenstein et al. (1995) found evidence that the domain-specific deal proneness measures explained differential amounts of variance across deal-responsive behavioral domains in a manner consistent with a domain-specific conceptualization of deal proneness. However, no insights were provided regarding the psychological variables or processes which might differentiate one type of deal proneness from another. To the degree that deal proneness is indeed domain-specific, proneness to alternative types of deals would be expected to have, to some degree, differing psychological correlates. Thus, the purpose of this presentation was to report findings across two studies of grocery shoppers collected from different geographic regions of the country which address this issue. Findings supported the notion that the domain-specific deal prone constructs do have differing psychological correlates.

"Framing the Deal: The Role of Restrictions in Accentuating Deal Value"

J. Jeffrey Inman, University of Wisconsin
Priya Raghubir, Hong Kong University of Science and Technology
Anil C. Peter, University of Southern California

Advertisers and retailers often promote their products using restrictions. For instance, a recent weekly flyer by a prominent retailer limited purchase on *fifty percent* of the specials advertised on their front page. Academics acknowledge the widespread use of scarcity tactics such as restrictions for gaining compliance. However, there is little research in the trade and consumer promotion literature about the effect of these tactics. While the general role of scarcity has been examined in some depth in psychology, most of the empirical work in this area has either been undertaken with little consideration for how a scarcity tactic would affect choice behavior or has been tested under extreme conditions (e.g., a total ban) that leave unclear the applicability of scarcity theory in the context of promotions for commonly known brands.

While offering the basis for predicting a general positive effect on restrictions on choice probability, commodity theory provides little guidance for understanding the contingencies under which restrictions' effect may vary. For example, if restrictions serve as a signal of transaction value, the size of this effect should increase as consumers' ability and/or motivation to independently assess the worth of a transaction using additional information reduces. In attempting to understand the manner in which restrictions work, in the second presentation Inman examineed contextual and individual factors that moderate the effect of restrictions on consumers' response to sales promotions. Further, the possibility of a mediating effect of an attitude change was examined. Commodity theory does not predict whether this attitude change will be due to an increased evaluation of the deal per se, an increased evaluation of the restricted brand, or both.

Inman presented a theoretical framework to examine how restrictions affect consumer purchase behavior, positing that consumers use them as a source of information while making a purchase judgment. Inman and his colleagues constructed this framework through a series of studies that flesh out the framework and test its robustness along the way. A sales restriction was defined as *a tactic that curtails a consumer's freedom to purchase a market offering.* Consumers' freedom may be curtailed through limiting the quantity which a consumer can purchase (e.g., "limit ___ per customer"), which Inman and his colleagues refered to as a *purchase quantity limit*; limiting the duration during which a consumer can avail herself or himself of an offer, such as "Offer expires on ___," commonly referred to as a *time limit*; or instituting a precondition for a consumer to purchase (e.g., "Only available with purchase of ___"), which they referred to as the *purchase precondition.* They examined the nature of the information contained in a restriction and explored conditions that foster or inhibit its use as a source of information for a purchase-related decision. A restriction may be viewed as a signal containing information about the worth of the transaction, the brand, or other aspects of the market context.

They presented findings from four studies using different methods (i.e., grocery sales data, a simulated grocery store experiment and a survey), samples (i.e., West Coast, Midwest, and Hong Kong) and operationalizations of restrictions (i.e., purchase quantity limit, minimum store purchase, and time limit) consistently demonstrating that imposing a purchase restriction on a promoted brand can *increase* the restricted brand's probability of choice. This effect is a function of contextual variables (e.g., price cut) and psychographic and behavioral individual difference variables (e.g., need for cognition, brand usage, and deal proneness). Taken together, they established the nomological validity of the theory that restrictions are a source of information which consumers use to disambiguate deal value, the use of which depends on the availability and diagnosticity of alternative sources of information.

"When Consumers Space-Out at Point-of-Purchase"

Stephen J. Hoch, University of Pennsylvania
Brian Wansink, University of Pennsylvania
Robert Kent, University of Delaware

Most everyday consumption behavior is incredibly mundane. The stakes are low and characterized by flat optima — little gained through making the optimal decision; little lost by making even the worst decision; but plenty to be gained by being expedient and getting on with the rest of life. The basic thesis of the third presentation is that once inside the store, there is a segment of consumers who are readily open to reasonable suggestion prompted by promotional deals. In the context of grocery shopping, a suggestion qualifies as reasonable if: (a) the deal prompting the suggestion looks good at first glance and does not appear to increase the effort consumers must expend in moving toward their meta-goal of purchasing all that is needed to make it through each week; and (b) the promotion does not highlight the self-serving, opportunistic goals of the marketer. Hoch presented: (a) the preconditions (internal psychological and external situational) that lead consumers to "space-out" whereby they relinquish attentional control to the marketer and essentially go on automatic pilot; and (b) a series of experiments focusing on operationally exploiting consumer "spacey-ness."

Specifically, Hoch discussed six experiments that examined the viability of increasing multi-unit purchases through supplanting the default internal anchor of "quantity 1" with innocuous looking higher external "anchors." The external anchors appeared at point-of-purchase through: quantity limits (with findings that could not be explained by product scarcity), size of shipping cartons, "x for $1," etc.... Hoch then discussed the viability of using consumer "spacey-ness" (and the related concept of consumer expertise) as a

variable on which to effectively price discriminate. Hoch discussed the implications of his findings for the domains of credit cards and rebates, where the potential for "spacing out" is even greater due to the temporal separation between initial purchase and eventual payment or redemption. Hoch talked about the opportunity to price discriminate toward those consumers who "space out."

Comments of Terence A. Shimp, Session Synthesizer

With respect to the first presentation, Shimp noted that the evidence presented is consistent with mounting evidence elsewhere that the term "deal" is very general and that all deals are not equivalent. He agreed with the conclusion of the presentation that theorizing needs to be done at a deal-specific level rather than referring to "deals" in general. However, on the premise that the psychological correlates were more likely to be antecedent states to the domain-specific deal proneness variables, he suggested that it may be more appropriate to use them as the independent variables in the regression analysis and the domain-specific deal proneness variables as the dependent variables, rather that visa-versa as done by the authors.

In commenting on the presentation of Inman et al., Shimp noted that the evidence suggested that purchase quantity restrictions do increase purchase behavior and that, once again, the importance of the variable "need for cognition" seems to affect this relationship. However, as a segue into the third presentation of Hoch, Shimp questioned whether either scarcity theory or anchoring and adjustment could account for this phenomenon. There was much discussion of the implications of these theories for the findings of Inman et al. (and subsequently for the findings of Hoch's findings in the third presentation). There was debate as to whether these two theoretical accounts were competing or not in the context of these two studies in their ability to account for the effects obtained.

With specific respect to the third presentation, Shimp noted evidence supporting the phenomenon that marketers can encourage larger purchase quanitities by supplying a larger anchor. However, Shimp noted some inconsistency with the second presentation in that a lower quanity limit (implying scarcity) encouraged larger purchases.

Shimp then noted that if larger purchase anchors were effective, why is it the case that not all marketers are using them. Hoch responded, noting that the market was dynamic and further, some marketers "never get the message." After some discussion where members of the audience recognized that, like consumers, marketers can sometimes not pay careful attention to market factors, the session concluded.

Psychological Correlates of a Proneness to Deals: A Domain-Specific Analysis

Donald R. Lichtenstein, University of Colorado
Scot Burton, University of Arkansas
Richard G. Netemeyer, Louisiana State University

ABSTRACT

Hypotheses are offered for differential relationships between six constructs with implications for consumer behavior (e.g., brand loyalty, impulsiveness, need for cognition) and eight domain-specific deal proneness constructs (e.g., display proneness, sale proneness, coupon proneness). Different from much sales promotion research which relies on scanner data, deal proneness is treated as a latent construct rather than as a behavior. The premise of the paper is that the individual proneness constructs have differential relationships with the aforementioned psychological constructs. Findings from two studies conducted in different geographic regions using samples of grocery shoppers provide support for this premise. Findings highlight the importance of treating deal proneness as a latent, domain-specific construct for theory-based research.

In recent years, packaged goods manufacturers have allocated increasing amounts of their promotional budgets towards consumer sales promotions. Concommitant with this trend, academic researchers have paid increased attention to the effects of sales promotions on consumer shopping behavior (see Blattberg and Neslin (1990) and Blattberg, Briesch, and Fox (1995) for reviews). Many of these studies have relied on scanner data to investigate the impact of observable variables such as deal type, frequency, duration, depth, and retraction on deal-responsive behavior. While these studies are very valuable in providing estimates of response elasticities to these promotional mix variables, they are less valuable in providing insights into the psychological variables/processes which may underly deal proneness. Related to this, these studies have also typically treated deal proneness as isomorphic with deal-responsive behavior, i.e, those who respond to deals are deal prone. Thus, no differentiation is made between the latent deal proneness construct and manifestations of the construct.

Lichtenstein, Netemeyer, and Burton (1990, p. 56) have defined deal proneness as an "increased propensity to respond to a purchase offer because the *form* of the purchase offer positively affects purchase evaluations." Following this definition, deal-responsive behavior may be a manifestation of many variables (e.g., price consciousness, value consciousness) in addition to, or instead of, factors relating to the *form* of the deal (i.e., deal proneness). Adopting this approach suggests that equating deal proneness with deal-responsive behavior is inappropriate and may result in a confounding of deal proneness with other psychological variables (cf. Lichtenstein et al. 1990).

The purpose of this paper is to offer and assess theoretically-based hypotheses for the relationship between several psychological variables (e.g., impulsiveness, need for cognition) and several *latent* domain-specific deal proneness constructs (e.g., coupon proneness, rebate proneness). As such, this paper complements and represents a direct extension of the work of Lichtenstein, Netemeyer, and Burton (1995). These researchers conducted two studies in which they employed scaled measures of a proneness to respond to deals in each of eight domains (coupons, sales, cents-off labels, buy-one-get-one-free, rebates, displays, free-gift-with-purchase, and contest/sweepstakes) and related these scales to deal-responsive behaviors assessed unobtrusively in natural field settings. Lichtenstein et al. found evidence that the domain-specific deal proneness measures explained differential amounts of variance across deal-responsive behavioral domains in a manner consistent with a domain-specific conceptualization of deal proneness. For example, coupon proneness was more related to actual coupon-redemption behavior (than were the remaining 7 domain-specific deal proneness constructs), sale proneness was more related to sale-responsive behavior, display proneness was more related to display-responsive behavior, and so on. However, no insights were provided regarding the psychological variables or processes which might differentiate one type of deal proneness from another. To the degree that deal proneness is indeed domain-specific, pronenesses to alternative types of deals would be expected to have, to some degree, differing psychological correlates. Thus, the purpose of this paper is to investigate this issue. Using data gathered across two studies, this paper assesses hypotheses regarding relationships between pronenesses to alternative deal types and other psychological variables. (A portion of the data reported in the present paper is empirically related to a portion of the data reported in Lichtenstein et al. (1995). Specifically, Study 1 data in the present paper represents a subset of the data that was gathered (but not reported) as part of Study 2 in Lichtenstein et al. (1995); Study 2 in the present paper is an extension which does not relate to any data collection reported in Lichtenstein et al. (1995).)

Insights into psychological variables which may differentiate pronenesses to alternative deal types have important theoretical implications. For example, to the degree that differing psychological correlates are found across alternative deal types, evidence would be provided that theories used to explain deal proneness (e.g., object-perception principles of attribution theory (cf. Blattberg and Neslin 1990), economic utility theory (cf. Dodson, Tybout, and Sternthal (1978)) may be differentially applicable across deal types (e.g., coupons, sales, rebates).

While there is a paucity of research which measures psychological variables and links them to deal proneness, there have been some psychological-based explanations for postulated and/or obtained differences in deal-responsive behaviors. Drawing from this literature, in the following section of this paper hypotheses are offered for differential relationships between domain-specific deal proneness variables and various psychological constructs. Then, two studies are described which empirically assess these hypotheses. Finally, results and implications for theory are discussed.

HYPOTHESES

Economic utility theory suggests that consumers behave to maximize the return on their time and effort. Because rebates, contests, sales, and coupons are promotions located toward the "higher end" of the time/effort continuum, a proneness to these types of promotions implies the belief that the benefits of acting on promotions *of all types* (i.e., including ones requiring less time/effort) outweigh the time and effort required to do so. However, because response to cents-off, buy-one-get-one-free, free-gift-with-purchase, and display promotions represent more passive instore behaviors, they require less effort. Thus, a proneness to these types of promotions does not necessarily imply a general belief that the time and effort it takes to act on promotions, *in general*, are outweighed by the costs of doing so. This rationale is consistent with Schneider and Currim's (1991) finding that consumers who are likely to act on "active-oriented" promotions (i.e., those requiring more effort outside of the store) are more likely to also act on lower effort "passive-oriented" promotions that require no out-of-store effort than vice-versa. Consequently, the following hypothesis is offered:

H1:   Rebate, contest, sale, and coupon proneness are positively and differentially related to expected return on time and effort in responding to promotions in general.

It has often been postulated that deal proneness is negatively related to brand loyalty (e.g., Blattberg and Neslin 1990; Dodson et al. 1978). One rationale for this relationship is that deal prone consumers are simply more likely to respond to deals rather than brands. Hence, when brands go on and off deal, deal prone consumers follow the deal rather than the brand. Dodson et al. (1978) offered a more refined explanation for this effect by investigating if this relationship varied by deal type. They used self-perception theory as a framework for investigating the effect of promotions that varied in terms of financial benefit and effort required on brand switching behavior (taken as a measure of brand loyalty) . They found that when the effort required to act on a promotion was low and the benefit was high, consumers were more likely to switch brands upon deal retraction than when the promotion required a higher level of effort and/or a lower level of financial benefit. The theoretical explanation offered for this effect is that when consumers buy on deals providing relatively large benefits and requiring little effort, a plausible external reason for why the brand was purchased is present. In such instances, consumers are more likely to make purchase attributions to the deal (external attribution) rather than to their own preference for the brand (internal attribution). However, because deals offering less benefit and/or requiring more effort offer a less plausible reason for purchase, consumers are more likely to make internal purchase attributions (e.g., "I bought the brand because I like it."). When the deal is removed, the probability of repurchase is higher than if the benefit/cost ratio had been higher.

Applying this rationale to the domain-specific deal proneness, pronenesses associated with higher benefit/costs ratios should be those most negatively related to brand loyalty, while pronenesses associated with lower benefit/costs ratios should be those most positively related to brand loyalty. While it is difficult to order all eight deal types on a benefit/cost continuum, it does appear plausible to suggest sale proneness as the high endpoint. That is, grocery stores put many items on sale every week and the cumulative benefit to consumers can be very large (far exceeding benefits from less frequently offered promotions (e.g., free-gift deals). Moreover, while sale-responsive behavior often requires some out-of-store search behavior and/or some low-level monitoring of sale items once inside the store, there are no coupons to clip, contests to enter, or rebate forms to mail. Consequently, the following hypothesis are offered:

H2:   Sale proneness is negatively and differentially related to brand loyalty.

"Impulse goods" generally require high visibility locations because they are often bought "on impulse" as unplanned purchases. Treating "impulse" as a trait (rather than as a product characteristic), Blattberg and Neslin (1990) suggest that impulsiveness may underlie purchasing from displays. Applying this rationale more broadly, impulsiveness may also be related to other deal-responsive behaviors associated with instore decision-making. Thus, H3 is offered:

H3:   Cents-off, buy-one-get-one-free, free-gift-with-purchase, and display proneness are positively and differentially related to impulsiveness.

Sales often dramatically increase when a brand is put on display. Inman et al. (1990) suggest that this phenomenon may be due to consumers assuming displays are a signal of a price cut. They further postulated and found support for their hypothesis that the use of a special display as a signal for a price cut was related to the consumer's "need for cognition" (Cacioppo, Petty, and Kao 1984). Consumers who have a higher need for cognition are less likely to assume that promotions are signals of price cuts than consumers with a lower need for cognition. The rationale underlying this phenomenon is that consumers who have a lower need for cognition are more likely to process promotional information peripherally, thereby increasing the likelihood that the promotion is not analyzed for its true meaning and value. However, consumers with a higher need for cognition are more likely to process information centrally—a diligent and active processing of the information. Hence, H4 is offered:

H4:   Display proneness is negatively and differentially related to need for cognition.

Based on this same rationale, because some deals are more likely to be processed via a central route, some types of deal proneness may be positively related to a need for cognition. For example, a contest is "where consumers apply their analytical or creative thinking to try to win a prize" (Berkowitz et al. 1994, p. 511). Thus, H5 is offered:

H5:   Contest proneness is positively and differentially related to need for cognition.

There is also competing rationale suggesting both a positive and a negative relationship between coupon proneness and need for cognition. Schneider and Currim (1991) classify the redemptions of coupons as manifesting "active" deal proneness, requiring purposeful decision-making outside the store. They suggest that such active deal proneness may be positively related to need for cognition. Similarly, Henderson (1985) models the decision to redeem coupons as being very cognitively-driven, also suggesting a positive relationship between coupon proneness and need for cognition. On the other hand, because coupons are offered with such high frequency, Blattberg and Neslin (1990) suggest that coupon use may follow a script such that there is a "mindless" element to the act of redeeming coupons. That is, consumers may follow a script whereby they cut, collect, and redeem coupons, with limited cognitive effort. Consequently, based on these opposing rationales, we offer H6A-H6B:

H6A: Coupon proneness is positively and differentially related to need for cognition.

H6B: Coupon proneness is negatively and differentially related to need for cognition.

Some promotions result in a reduced purchase price. Thus, a proneness to these types of promotions should be positively related to price consciousness. Also, several researchers have suggested that price-quality beliefs may be negatively related to response to price promotions (cf. Blattberg and Neslin 1990). The rationale is that consumers who believe that "higher price means higher quality" are also more likely to make product-related attributions for promotional price discounts ("e.g., the product isn't good enough to sell at its normal price"). Lichtenstein et al. (1993) found a negative relationship between coupon and sale proneness and price-quality inferences. Similarly, we predict a negative relationship between price-quality inferences and deal pronenesses associated with price reductions.

H7: Cents-off, rebate, sale, and coupon proneness are positively and differentially related to price consciousness.

H8: Cent-off, rebate, sale, and coupon proneness are negatively and differentially related to price-quality perceptions.

STUDY 1

To assess the hypotheses, consumers' proneness to promotions was examined in each of the following domains: coupons, sales, cents-off labels, buy-one-get-one-free, free-gift-with-purchase, end-of-aisle displays, rebates/refunds, and contests/sweepstakes. These eight categories were selected because they appear to be among the most commonly employed promotions and they also represent a diversity of promotions in terms of psychological variables which may be related to them (Blattberg and Neslin 1990). Using scale development procedures similar to those advocated by Churchill (1979), multi-item scales for a proneness to respond were used for each of the eight deal categories. The multi-items scales for the eight proneness variables ranged from 5 to 7 items each. Additionally, an eight-item "generalized deal pronenenss" scale was also developed for use as a covariate in order to remove variance in the psychological variables that could be accounted for by the portion of the general deal proneness domain that the domain-specific constructs shared. Scale items for this generalized measure made no reference to any particular type of deal, but rather, only referred to "deals" or "promotions" in general. (The scale development procedures and psychometric properties for all of the scales are provided in detail in Lichtenstein et al. (1995)). Sample items for rebate and buy-one-get-one-free proneness are: "Beyond the money I save, buying products that offer a rebate gives me a sense of joy" and "When I take advantage of a 'buy-one-get-one-free' offer, I feel good." Items for other constructs have similar wording. A sample item for the generalized deal proneness measure is "I feel like a successful shopper when I purchase products that offer special promotions." (The full list of scale items can be obtained by contacting the first author.)

Data were collected via a mail survey distributed to shoppers at two grocery stores (same chain) in a midwestern SMSA. If the shopper agreed to participate, they were given a take-home survey and a postage-paid return envelope. The survey contained the multi-item measures of the domain-specific and generalized deal proneness constructs as well as measures of various psychological constructs referenced in H1-H8. For these latter psychological constructs, where established measures existed, they were used; where they did not exist, items were developed and pretested prior to Study1. These constructs, reliability estimates, and sample items are shown in Table 1. Of the 896 surveys distributed to respondents, 402 (44.9%) usable surveys were returned. Of those, 77.9% were female and 67.3% were married. The median age category was 35-44 and the median annual household income category was $35,000 to $49,999.

Study 1 Results

Study hypotheses were tested via hierarchical regression analysis. The psychological variable hypothesized to be differentially related to the domain-specific deal proneness variables was employed as the dependent variable. The generalized deal proneness measure was entered in the regression in step 1, followed by entry of the eight domain-specific measures in step 2. Results of this analysis are reported in Table 2. (Ignore Study 2 results for the moment.)

Consistent with H1, rebate, sale, and coupon proneness were significant positive predictors of the perception that responding to promotional offers is worth the required time and effort (and display proneness was negatively related to this variable). In accord with H2, sale proneness was negatively related to the propensity to be brand loyal (and display proneness was positively related to this variable). Consistent with H3, buy-one-get-one-free, free-gift-with-purchase, and display proneness were all positively related to impulsiveness (while rebate and sale proneness were negatively related to this variable). Consistent with H4, display proneness was negatively related to need for cognition; inconsistent with H5, however, contest proneness was not positively correlated to need for cognition, yet free-gift-with-purchase proneness was. In accord with H6B, coupon proneness was negatively related to need for cognition. Consistent with H7, rebate and sale proneness were positively related to price consciousness. Finally, in accord with H8, rebate and sale proneness were negatively related to the propensity to make price-quality inferences (and display proneness was positively related to this variable).

Discussion of Study 1 Results

Of the 19 significant relationships, 13 were explicitly hypothesized and there was only one case in which there was a hypothesis that failed to receive any support (H5), however, the relationship was in the hypothesized direction. And, with one exception (the relationship between free-gift proneness and need for cognition), all of the domain-specific variables that were significant *in a hypothesized* direction comprised a subset of those that were hypothesized. That not all hypothesized proneness variables were significant is not viewed as inconsistent with theory. Rather, it is characteristic of sales promotion models which have correlated predictor variables (cf. Blattberg and Neslin 1990, p. 195).

Regarding the 6 unhypothesized significant effects, at least 3 were not "theoretically-inconsistent" in that they were in the direction *opposite* of hypothesized and found effects. For example, while display proneness was hypothesized and found to be positively related to impulsiveness, rebate and sale proneness, while not specifically hypothesized, were found to be negatively related to impulsiveness. Yet, the same rationale for the hypothesized effect could easily be offered for these effects, i.e., as display proneness should be positively related to impulsiveness, promotions such as sales and rebates requiring more purposeful behavior should be negatively related to impulsiveness. The negative relationship between display proneness and expected return on time and effort can be interpreted similarly.

The unhypothesized finding between display proneness and price-quality beliefs warrants particular attention and may suggest a post-hoc explanation that goes beyond rationale offered in the hypotheses. As display proneness is also negatively related to need for cognition, display proneness may be related to a general propensity to inference. For example, Inman et. al. (1990) found that consumers with a lower need for cognition were more likely to infer that displayed items are also price-reduced. Thus, it appears plausible to suggest display prone consumers may be more likely to make other inferences based on signals, e.g., using price to infer quality.

TABLE 1
Psychological Correlates Examined In Studies 1 and 2

Psychological Correlate	Source of Postulated Relationship	# of Items/ Study 1 Reliability[1]/ Study 2 Reliability	Example Item and Source of Scale Measure
Expected Return on Time and Effort	Dodson et al. 1978; Henderson 1985; Schneider and Currim 1991; Shimp and Kavas 1984	4/.82 (.77)/.80	"The money saved by finding a bargain is usually not worth the time and effort"[2]
Brand Loyalty	Blattberg and Neslin 1990; Dodson et al. 1978; Lichtenstein et al. 1990	5/.92/.92	"Once I get used to a brand, I hate to switch" (Jacoby and Chestnut 1978)
Impulsiveness	Blattberg and Neslin 1990	9/.92 (.83)/.84	"When it comes to making grocery purchases, I usually purchase on impulse" (adapted from Martin, Weun, and Beatty 1994)
Need for Cognition	Inman, McAlister, and Hoyer 1990: Schneider and Currim 1990	18/.90/.91	"I only think as hard as I have to" (Cacioppo, Petty and Kao 1984)
Price Consciousness	Blattberg and Neslin 1990; Lichtenstein et al. 1993;Shimp 1990	5/.86/.88	"I am *not* willing to go to extra effort to find low prices" (Lichtenstein et al. 1993)
Price-Quality Schema	Blattberg and Neslin 1990; Kahn and Louie 1990; Lichtenstein, et al. 1993	4/.85/.84	"The price of a product is a good indicator of its quality" (Lichtenstein et al. 1993)

[1]Reliability estimates are coefficient alpha. For measures developed by the authors for use in Studies 1 and 2, coefficient alphas from the pretest (shown in parentheses) accompany the reliability estimate for study 1.

[2]Scale items developed by the authors for use in studies 1 and 2.

STUDY 2

The second study represented a replication of Study 1. The purpose for this replication was twofold. The first purpose was to assess whether domain-specific variables found to be significant predictors of the psychological variables would again represent a subset of those hypothesized to be. The second purpose of Study 2 was to assess the post-hoc explanation offered for the relationship found in Study 1 between display proneness and price-quality inferences. Consistent with this explanation, we offer the following hypothesis:

H9: Display proneness is positively and differentially related to price-quality perceptions.

Overview of Study 2

Study 2 was conducted using shoppers contacted at a grocery store in a different geographic region of the country. Shoppers were approached and asked if they would complete a take-home survey (similar to that used for Study 1) and mail it back to the local university. Of the 500 surveys distributed over a 3 day period, 163 were returned and usable (response rate=32.6%). Most respondents were female (85.4%) and 82.3% were married. The median age category was 35-44, and the median household income category was $25,000-$34,999.

Study 2 Results

Identical to Study 1 procedures, for each regression, generalized deal proneness was initially entered as the sole predictor, followed by the deal-specific measures. Results are shown in Table 2. Consistent with H1, rebate and sale proneness were positive predictors of the perception that responding to promotional offers, in general, is worth the required time and effort (and buy-one-get-one-free proneness was negatively related to this dependent variable). In accord with H2, sale proneness was negatively related to the propensity to be brand loyal (while buy-one-get-one-free was positively related to this variable). Consistent with H3, display proneness was positively related to impulsiveness (while both rebate and coupon proneness were negatively related to this dependent variable), offering further support for differences across deal types. However, although results for need for cognition were

TABLE 2
Hierarchical Regression Analysis Standardized Beta Coefficients for Relationships Between Deal Proneness Conceptualizations and Psychological Variables for Studies 1 and 2[ab]

Psychological Dependent Variables	Study	Generalized Deal Proneness (8-Item Measure)	Adj R²	Domain-Specific Deal Proneness								
				Cent	Free	Gift	Display	Rebate	Contest	Sale	Coupon	Aj R²
Expected Return on	1	.30 [d]	.09	.05	-.07	.07	-.10[e]	.14[d]	-.02	.24[d]	.22[e]	.22[f]
Time and Effort	2	.19[d]	.03	.03	-.26[d]	.03	-.01	.21[d]	-.04	.26[d]	.11	.14[f]
Brand Loyalty	1	-.09	.00	.02	.09	.02	.10[e]	-.09	.08	-.33[d]	.03	.07[f]
	2	.08	.00	.09	.29[d]	-.12	.00	-.02	-.08	-.35[d]	-.01	.12[f]
Impulsiveness	1	.09[e]	.01	-.11	.22[d]	.18[d]	.22[d]	-.14[d]	.05	-.17[d]	.02	.12[f]
	2	.07	.00	-.01	.05	.13	.25[d]	-.17[e]	.00	-.08	-.18[e]	.07[ef]
Need for Cognition	1	-.07	.00	.01	.02	.16[e]	-.12[e]	-.06	.06	.00	-.18[e]	.05[f]
	2	-.24[d]	.05	-.01	-.03	-.11	-.10	-.03	.08	.10	-.11	.04
Price Consciousness	1	.25[d]	.06	-.04	.04	-.05	.02	.21[e]	.01	.23[d]	.08	.13[f]
	2	.21[d]	.04	-.15	-.05	-.06	-.13	.11	.05	.29[d]	.13	.12[f]
Price-Quality	1	-.01	.00	.03	.11	.02	.18[d]	-.14[d]	-.03	-.14[e]	-.0?	.04[f]
	2	.08	.00	-.13	.14	.19[e]	.34[d]	-.03	-.02	-.11	.04	.07[f]

[a]Sample sizes for studies 1/2 ranged from 348/142 to 351/149.

[b]For each dependent variable, generalized deal proneness was entered into the regression equation at step 1 followed by the entry of the remaining independent variables.

[c]**Cent** = cents-off; **Free** = buy-one-get-one-free; **Gift** = free-gift-with-purchase; **Display** = end-of-aisle-display; **Rebate** = rebate/refund; **Contest** = contests/sweepstakes; **Sales** = sale proneness; **Coupon** = coupon proneness.

[d]$p < .01$

[e]$p < .05$

[f]The full model (i.e., generalized deal proneness and eight deal-type specific measure) explains significantly more variance in the dependent variable than does the reduced model (i.e., generalized deal proneness) at the .05 level or better.

generally in the postulated direction, they did not reach statistical significance and thus did not support hypotheses concerning this variable (H4–H6).

Consistent with H7, sale proneness was positively related to price consciousness, however, inconsistent with H8, none of the price-related deal pronenesses were negatively related to the propensity to make price-quality inferences. In accord with H9, the relationship between display proneness and price-quality beliefs was positive, yet inconsistent with predictions, so was the relationship between free-gift-with-purchase and price-quality beliefs.

Discussion of Study 2 Results

With three exceptions, all of the significant relationships between the psychological and domain-specific variables were either: (1) specifically hypothesized, or (2) unhypothesized but not "theory inconsistent." Moreover, seven of the same specific relationships are significant across both Studies 1 and 2. Six of these relationships were hypothesized, while the seventh is consistent with the hypothesis of differences across deal types. Considering the results of Studies 1 and 2 jointly, there were 23 cases in which the relationship between a particular domain-specific variable and a particular psychological variable was significant in either one or both of the studies. In 21 of these cases, the corresponding coefficient in the other study was in the same direction, providing evidence of stability. In the two cases where the corresponding

effect was in a direction opposite of the significant effect, both were insignificant.

CONCLUSION AND IMPLICATIONS

The purpose of the studies reported in this paper was to assess if alternative types of deal proneness had differing psychological correlates. In both studies, the domain-specific variables related to psychological variables in a manner which suggest that the psychogical processes underlying deal proneness may depend on the particular deal proneness domain. The importance of this finding appears most clear in instances when a psychological construct is *positively* related to one type of deal proneness, yet *negatively* related to another. For example, across two studies, rebate proneness was negatively related to impulsiveness, while display proneness was positively related to this construct. Sale proneness was negatively related to price-quality inferences, while display proneness was positively related to this inference.

These findings suggest that researchers testing theoretical relationships between possible antecedents, correlates, or consequences of deal proneness should carefully consider the type(s) of deals to which their theory relates. It is very likely that alternative theories that might be applied to deal proneness will not be appropriate across all deals types. Consequently, these findings call into question the validity of statements such as "self-perception theory would predict that deal proneness could be negatively related to brand loyalty" (Blattberg and Neslin 1990, p.72). Based on our results, statements such as "deal proneness is positively (or negatively) related to X" are ambiguous and beg the question of "which type of deal proneness?"

Results reported in the present study, interpreted in conjunction with those reported in Lichtenstein et al. (1995), also support arguments advanced at the outset of this paper regarding the problems associated with behavioral measurement of deal proneness. Using a behavioral operationalization of deal proneness, behaviors that would be equated with some particular type of deal proneness may actually be a manifestation of multiple types of deal proneness, as well as other constructs outside of the deal proneness domain. For example, the purchase of unadvertised sale items was used as a dependent variable in Lichtenstein et al.'s (1995) Study 2. As both sale and display proneness were positive predictors of this behavior (and other variables such as price consciousness may also be), it would seem inappropriate to equate sale-responsive behavior with any single construct, including sale proneness. Since unadvertised sale items (as well as advertised sale items) are often put on display, both sale and display proneness may manifest themselves in sale-responsive behavior. Moreover, by looking at differences in relationships between these two proneness constructs and other behaviors (e.g., looking at the weekly sale ad, preparation of shopping list—also reported in Lichtenstein et al. (1995)), and differences in *all six* psychological correlates investigated in Studies 1 and 2 (see Table 2), it becomes apparent that display and sale proneness are quite different constructs that, at times, may have common behavioral manifestations. These findings support the notion that deal proneness should be measured at a psychological level and treated as an antecedent of deal-responsive behavior.

Regarding substantive insights into the domain-specific variables, based on regression analyses with psychological correlates across two studies, an expanded perspective can be offered for four of the domain-specific proneness constructs.

Sale Proneness

In relation to other forms of deal proneness that are associated with price reductions, sale proneness was most strongly related to price consciousness. This may be due to the total integration of a sale with the purchase price. Sale proneness was also negatively related to price-quality perceptions in Study 1, suggesting that when consumers act on their sale proneness, they are unlikely to believe they are sacrificing quality by doing so. The total integration of a sale with purchase price also reduces the burden required of shoppers. For example, while acting on sale proneness may require some out-of-store search behavior, there are no coupons to clip and redeem or rebates to mail. This lack of required effort may be the reason that sale proneness was most positively related to return on the consumer's time and effort across Studies 1 and 2. Yet, it may also be the reason that sale proneness is most negatively related to brand loyalty across both studies (i.e., consumers make attributions to the deal rather than to their liking of the brand).

At a more nomological level, the pattern of relationships between several of the domain-specific variables, expected return on time and effort, and brand loyalty provides support for the attribution-based relationship between benefit/cost ratios and brand loyalty offered by Dodson et al. (1978). Specifically, across Studies 1 and 2, domain-specific variables that related significantly to expected return on time and effort in one direction were typically related to brand loyalty in the opposite direction. These relationships suggest that as the benefit/cost ratio increases, brand loyalty decreases. The nature of these findings differ from those of Dodson et al. (1978) in a very important way. Here, deals were not

manipulated and brand-switching behavior was not measured. Rather, individual difference variables of a proneness to deals and a general propensity to be brand loyal are measured and are related to each other. Reaching a similar conclusion based on a very different type of study provides additional support for the attribution-based rationale of Dodson et al. (1978).

Rebate Proneness

With the exception of brand loyalty, the pattern of relationships between rebate proneness and the psychological variables were largely consistent with those involving sale proneness. However, rebate and sale proneness did differ in a theoretically-consistent manner in their relationship with brand loyalty. As responding to rebates involves a larger amount of effort, rebate proneness appears not to undermine the propensity to be brand loyal.

Coupon Proneness

Coupon proneness appears to be related to the belief that the time and effort required to "get a deal" is worth it, and thus, a willingness to spend more time in the grocery store (see relationship with time spent in grocery store reported in Lichtenstein et al. (1995)). However, consistent with the perspective of Blattberg and Neslin (1990), the activity seems to be pursued somewhat "mindlessly" (as suggested by the negative relationship with need for cognition). Consistent with results found for rebates, the effort associated with coupon proneness apparently serves not to undermine brand loyalty as it seems to do for sale proneness. It is also interesting to note that, while sale proneness was positively related to price consciousness, coupon proneness was not. These differential relationships may be partially due to the fact that sales are integrated into the purchase price and coupons are not.

Display Proneness

The correlates of display proneness differ vastly and systematically from correlates of the other types of deal proneness. Display proneness is more strongly positively related to impulsiveness and negatively related to the use of a shopping list (see Lichtenstein et al. 1995) than are other types of deal proneness. Also, based on the positive correlations with price-quality perceptions and negative correlations with need for cognition, it appears that display proneness may be associated with a stronger propensity to inference in general.

Implications for Future Research

Lichtenstein et. al (1995) provided evidence that deal proneness was a domain-specific construct. The present study extends this work by providing evidence that the different domain-specific constructs have some differing psychological correlates. These results are viewed as important for future theory tests. Specifically, results of the present study suggest that theories which have constructs which may relate to benefit/cost ratios, impulsiveness, brand loyalty, price consciousness, price-quality inferences, and need for cognition may relate differentially to different types of promotions. Additionally, domain-specific deal proneness measures may relate differentially to many other psychological correlates not tested here, but nevertheless, have important implications for theory tests. Therefore, it is recommended that researchers wishing to test theories of sales promotions carefully consider the particular type(s) of sales promotions to which the theory might relate prior to empirically testing those theories.

REFERENCES

Donnelley Marketing (1991), "13th Annual Survey of Promotional Practices," Stamford, CT: Donnelley Marketing.

Berkowitz, Eric N., Roger A. Kerin, Steven W. Hartley, William Rudelius (1994), *Marketing*, Fourth Edition, Richard D. Irwin, Inc., Burr Ridge, Illinois.

Blattberg, Robert C. and Scott A. Neslin (1990), *Sales Promotion: Concepts, Methods, and Strategies*, First Edition, Prentice Hall, Englewood Cliffs, New Jersey.

_____, Richard Briesch, and Edward J. Fox (1995), "How Promotions Work," *Marketing Science*, 14, pp. 122-132.

Cacioppo, John T., Richard E. Petty, and Chaun F. Kao (1984), "The Efficient Assessment of Need for Cognition," *Journal of Personality Assessment*, 48 (June), 306-307.

Churchill, Gilbert A., Jr. (1979), "A Paradigm for Developing Better Measures of Marketing Constructs," *Journal of Marketing Research*, 16 (February), 64-73.

Dodson, Joe A., Alice M. Tybout, and Brian Sternthal (1978), "Impact of Deals and Deal Retraction on Brand Switching," *Journal of Marketing Research*, 15 (February), 72-81.

Henderson, Caroline M. (1985), "Modeling the Coupon Redemption Decision," in *Advances in Consumer Research*, 12, Elizabeth C. Hirschman and Morris B. Holbrook, eds., Provo, UT: Association for Consumer Research, 138-143.

Inman, J. Jeffrey, Leigh McAlister, and Wayne D. Hoyer (1990), "Promotion Signal: Proxy for a Price Cut?" *Journal of Consumer Research*, 17 (June), 74-81.

Jacoby, Jacob and Robert W. Chestnut (1978), *Brand Loyalty: Measurement and Management*, New York: John Wiley & Sons, Inc.

Kahn, Barbara E. and Therese A. Louie (1990), "Effects of Retraction of Price Promotions on Brand Choice Behavior for Variety-Seeking and Last-Purchase Loyal Consumers," *Journal of Marketing Research*, 27 (August), 279-289.

Lichtenstein, Donald R., Richard G. Netemeyer, and Scot Burton (1990), "Distinguishing Coupon Proneness From Value Consciousness: An Acquisition-Transaction Utility Theory Perspective," *Journal of Marketing*, 54 (July), 54-67.

_____, Richard G. Netemeyer, and Scot Burton (1995), "Assesing the Domain-Specificity of Deal Proneness: A Field Study," *Journal of Consumer Research*, 22 (December)

_____, Nancy Ridgway, and Richard G. Netemeyer (1993), "Price Perceptions and Consumer Shopping Behavior: A Field Study," *Journal of Marketing Research*, 30 (May), 234-245.

Martin, Wendy, Seungoog Weun, and Sharon Beatty (1994), "Validation of an Impulse Buying Tendency Scale," working paper, University of Alabama, Tuscaloosa, AL 35486.

Schneider, Linda G. and Imran S. Currim (1991), "Consumer Purchase Behaviors Associated With Active and Passive Deal-Proneness," *International Journal of Research in Marketing*, 8, 205-222.

Shimp, Terrence A. (1990), *Promotion Management and Marketing Communications*, Second Edition, Hinsdale, IL: The Dryden Press.

The Effect of Time Pressure and Task Motivation on Visual Attention to Brands

Rik Pieters, Katholieke Universiteit Brabant
Luk Warlop, Katholieke Universiteit Leuven
Michel Hartog, Katholieke Universiteit Brabant

ABSTRACT

We report a study in which eye-tracking data were gathered to examine the impact of time-pressure and task motivation on the flow of visual attention during choice processing from a naturalistic stimulus-based product display. We find patterns of adaptation of visual attention to time pressure in terms of acceleration, filtration, and strategy shift that have not been reported previously. In addition we find, regardless of condition, strong correlations between visual attention to the brands in the choice set and preference for the brands. Results are discussed in terms of strategic and non-strategic information acquisition during stimulus-based choice, and implications for attention theory are offered.

Consumers make multiple choices under time pressure daily; some important, others trivial. Many choices take place in store environments where several brands compete for consumers' attention and consideration. But despite the enormous amounts of money marketers spend on attracting and guiding consumers' attention to their products (Janiszewski and Bickart 1994), the role of attention in consumer choice has generated relatively little research attention.

Moreover, although todays harried consumers experience time pressure frequently, and "... in spite of its potential importance, relatively little research has focused on how it affects decisions about multi-attribute alternatives" (Payne, Bettman and Johnson 1993, p.38). While time pressure reduces the consumer's opportunity to attend to brands, other factors such as consumer involvement with the choice task increase the motivation to attend (Celsi and Olson 1988). Research has not yet examined whether and to what extent increased levels of motivation may compensate for decreased levels of opportunity to attend to brands. Research examining heterogeneous effects of time pressure on visual attention, as a function of factors such as consumer motivation with the task, is absent. In this study we examine the nature of adaptation of consumers' visual attention patterns to time pressure and task motivation.

Most of what we know about the nature of stimulus-based choice processes comes from studies using verbal protocol or information display board methodologies (Payne, Bettman and Johnson 1993) which, despite their contribution to our knowledge about how consumers adapt to task and context constraints, do not allow a natural flow of attention over the decision alternatives. The most direct way to measure attentional flow is eye tracking, which has long been recognized as a complementary method of gathering data on information acquisition in choice tasks (Russo 1978), but has until now received much less attention than more traditional methods. More specifically, very few data are available on whether and how visual attention patterns adapt to constraints on the decision making process. Ours is the first study to analyze adaptation of visual attention patterns to time pressure and task motivation using eye tracking methodology.

TIME PRESSURE AND TASK MOTIVATION

"Real" choice sets are crowded with salient non-attribute elements which may guide or distract consumer attention. Under such conditions information acquisition is not entirely strategic.

The way in which a consumer visually explores a product display is partially driven by global, culturally determined, scanning routines and by salient elements of the display (Janiszewski 1995; Levy-Schoen 1981). Visual scanning of a naturalistic choice display is a free-flowing activity, and we are not always aware of what our eyes exactly do. It is important to understand how information search through visual scanning occurs. Ultimately, this increased understanding should allow marketers to design product packaging and information displays that better manage the flow of consumers' attention (Janiszewski 1995), and that increase the effectiveness of communication efforts.

One of the dominant findings in process-oriented decision research has been that decision makers tend to adapt strategically to the constraints imposed by the decision making context and to their own cognitive limitations (Payne, Bettman, and Johnson 1993). One such constraint, prevalent in many consumer decisions, is time pressure. Time pressure is the subjective experience of a shortage of cognitive resources in order to perform a task in a preferred or optimal manner (Edland and Svensson 1993). Coping with time pressure therefore assumes some kind of change in the way information is processed. Prior research has found evidence for three main coping strategies, although the evidence for each has been somewhat equivocal. Processing may adapt through *acceleration*, which involves a general speeding up of cognitive activity, without changing the way in which information about the decision alternatives is acquired. Research has also found evidence for *filtration*, which involves the deliberate decision to ignore some—less important—information in the face of time constraints, and only to concentrate on the information that is deemed most important for arriving at a "good" decision. In both cases the overall acquisition strategy does not change. It will either be executed faster, or will ignore some of the relevant information. A third way to adapt is by changing one's information acquisition strategy, i.e., *strategy shift*. In decision making research, strategy shifts from more compensatory (and therefore "within alternative") to more non-compensatory strategies (which is more "between alternative") have been reported (e.g., Payne, Bettman, and Johnson 1988; Svensson, Edland and Slovic 1990; Zakay 1985), although the evidence to date is not very convincing yet (Payne, Bettman and Johnson 1993).

Task motivation on the other hand has been shown to increase the amount of information searched (Celsi and Olson 1988), and to lead to more compensatory processing and a more complete weighing of all the available information, which should result in slowing down the information search. We examine the extent to which strategic adaptations of visual attention patterns are found, and whether useful indicators of acceleration, filtration and strategy shift can be derived from eye tracking data.

Preference in the Eye of the Beholder. Two- or multi-stage models have been formulated in which decision making is regarded as an active process in which one alternative is gradually—or in a step-wise fashion—differentiated from the others until it is finally chosen. As a result of this process, the brands that are finally considered receive much more attention than the brands rejected early in the process. Therefore one should expect a monotonically increasing relationship between the amount of attention devoted to the different alternatives in a choice set and the order in which they

Advances in Consumer Research
Volume 24, © 1997

FIGURE 1
Brand Display

are preferred by the consumer. Of particular interest here is the extent to which the selection process that takes place is dependent on time pressure and task motivation.

EYE TRACKING INDICATORS OF VISUAL SEARCH

Information display board methods can distinguish between acceleration, filtration and strategy shift because the display board specifies all relevant information for the task in an idealized manner such that frequency, duration and order of sampling of each information unit can be assessed separately. Our eye tracking study uses a naturalistic brand display, for which this is not possible. We therefore have to develop measures of visual attention and of adaptation to contextual factors that take into account the more naturalistic and "messy" nature of the data.

In Figure 1 the actual brand display used in the current study is shown.

What eye tracking data have in common with data from information display board research is that they should be treated as measures of information acquisition—although to a lesser extent under strategic control—rather than as a direct reflection of cognitive processes (cf. Russo 1978; Viviani 1990). Consistent with information display board research and with recently published eye tracking research (Russo and Leclerc 1994), we define as the unit of observation each saccade or "jump" from one meaningful area of the brand display to another. We define as relevant areas all the brands in the display, as well as the major areas within each stimulus brand's package (i.e., brand name, textual information, and package illustration / pictorial). Exact definitions follow in the Method section.

This approach allows us to focus on the attention switching patterns between areas, both within and between brands, and we derive several summary measures of information acquisition, which we use to assess the impact of time pressure and motivation.

Acceleration. Our subjects are asked to make a choice from a choice set of six brands of shampoo, and we collect eye tracking data while they acquire information in order to make that choice. We define the time difference between the exposure to the brand display and the first fixation on each brand (or any of its relevant areas) as that brand's "starting time." We expect to observe a decrease in average starting time across brands under conditions that lead to acceleration of information acquisition, and an increase in the average starting time when the context forces the consumer to decelerate. In addition we observe the average number of switches per time unit within a brand and between brands. When information acquisition accelerates, the average number of switches per time unit should increase for both measures. When it decelerates, both should decrease.

Filtration. Adaptation through filtration implies that the decision maker ignores some relevant information while acquiring information in order to make a choice. First, because we define three relevant areas within each of the six brands, we can observe the total number of within-brand areas that are skipped as a global measure of filtering. Second, to the extent that each within-brand area contains some decision-relevant information, we can use the number of brands that are entirely scanned, i.e., for which each of the three key areas are fixated, as a measure of *absence* of filtration. We will examine for both these indicators the extent to which they adapt to contextual constraints. Highly motivated decision makers should filter less, while time constrained decision makers should filter more. Third, we can also measure the proportion of skipped areas that contain, respectively brand names, ingredient information and package pictorials. We expect highly motivated decision makers to concentrate on the verbal information on the packages, while decision makers under time pressure will tend to ignore the verbal information.

Strategy Shift. Decision-making research reports that compensatory processing increases when decision makers are highly motivated, and decreases when they work under time pressure. The proportion of within-brand switches relative to the total number of switches observed during information acquisition serves as a measure of within-brand processing. Only when this proportion is high it is reasonable to assume that the decision maker engages in a compensatory decision strategy. If visual attention patterns reflect strategic and adaptive information acquisition the proportion of switches that are within-brand should increase with high motivation and decrease with high time pressure.

Scanning-Preference Relationship. We examine the extent to which emerging preferences are reflected in the way information about the brands is acquired under the different contextual constraints. We measure the relative frequency of fixations and the relative gaze duration as generalized indices of the amount of attention given to each brand (Friedman 1979). If there is a monotonic relationship between preference and attention, rank-order correlations between the preference ranking of the brands and both measures of attention should be high.

METHOD

Subjects. Fifty-two female and twelve male subjects ranging in age from twenty to forty-nine years were invited to participate in the study by a marketing research company. A study session lasted approximately 30 minutes and subjects were paid the equivalent of 15 US$ for their participation.

Design and Stimuli. The stimuli were four color slides each showing a choice set consisting of pictures of six unfamiliar brands in four product categories: rice, shampoo, canned soup, and salad dressing. All brands used in the study were Belgian brands, unknown to the Dutch subjects. All four choice sets were depicted similarly to the way choice sets are typically located on store shelves. Three of the four sets were displayed as two rows of three brands. The salad dressing bottles, due to their height, were displayed as one row of six brands. All packages were clearly visible, and large enough such that all verbal information on the packages was clearly readable. The target slide was the one with the shampoo bottles, shown in black and white in Figure 1.

The experiment was run as a 2 x 2 (Time Pressure x Task Motivation) between-subjects design. In the Low Time Pressure condition, each slide was presented for 20 seconds. A pilot study had shown that this was sufficient to inspect all brands on a slide in detail. The instructions in the Low Time Pressure condition emphasized that subjects would have enough time to inspect the slide at their own pace. In the High Time Pressure condition, each slide was presented for 7 seconds. The instructions mentioned that the subjects would not have much time to inspect the slides.

Motivation was manipulated in two ways. Before being exposed to the first slide, subjects in the High Motivation condition read that the purpose of the study was to test a number of brands that were about to be introduced on the local market, and that their evaluation of the brands was valued highly. Analogous to the procedure used by Petty, Cacciopo, and Schuman (1983) subjects were told that as a reward for their participation they could choose among a number of brands of shampoo. Subjects in the Low Motivation condition were told that the study was part of the

development of a test for new products. Low motivation subjects were not promised an extrinsic reward.

Procedure. Subjects participated individually. Upon entering the experimental room, they read a booklet containing the instructions. They were explained that a camera would record their eye movements while they were exposed to a number of brands from various product categories. An explanation of the study's objectives followed, including the manipulation of motivation. Then the subjects were seated in front of the screen on which the stimulus slides would be projected from behind. They were instructed to place their chin on a small chin rest. Eye movements were recorded by an infrared camera located at the subjects' left side, in order not to interfere with normal viewing behavior. The camera was calibrated on the subject's right eye. During measurement the position of the fovea was recorded fifty times per second.

The onset of each slide was announced through head phones. Each time, subjects were exposed to a slide with the six brands from one of the four conditions. The critical slide (shampoo) was always in second position. When the choice set had disappeared from the screen, subjects saw a slide with six boxes, labeled A through F, whose locations corresponded to those of the brands in the set seen previously. They were asked to indicate their preference by naming the letter of the box that corresponded to the brand they had chosen. Subjects pressed a button when they were done, in order to see the next slide.

After making their final choice, subjects received a questionnaire. First, memory for the brands and products on the slides was assessed. Then subjects answered manipulation check questions about experienced time pressure and task motivation, including six items from Kapferer and Laurent's (1985) involvement scale. Then they saw the slide with the six shampoo brands again, and were asked to rank the brands in order of preference. The most preferred brand corresponded to the brand chosen earlier for all subjects.

At the end of the questionnaire subjects were asked to describe in their own words what they thought the purpose of the study was. None of the subjects guessed the true purpose, nor showed any insight in the motivation manipulation.

RESULTS

Manipulation Checks. As expected, the motivation manipulation has a significant effect on the motivation to form a good judgment about the brands (F $(1,63)$=4.01, p<.05), and on the felt involvement of subjects (F $(1,63)$=4.97, p<.05). The time pressure manipulation had a significant impact on the experience of having sufficient time to make a good judgment about the brands (F $(1,63)$=15.65, p<.005), with subjects in the 7 seconds condition experiencing significantly less time to evaluate as compared to subjects in the 20 seconds condition. None of the interactions is significant. Consistent with these results, subjects in the Low Time Pressure condition remembered significantly more elements from the shampoo slide (X=1.54) as compared to subjects in the High Time Pressure conditions (X=1.03) (F $(1,63)$=3.84, p=.06).

Analysis of eye tracking data. As shown in Figure 2 each shampoo bottle was defined as a separate "major" area of the screen (areas A through F in Figure 2). Within each of these "major" areas three sub-areas were defined, each corresponding to a salient element of the package: the brand name (areas I, L, O, P, T, and X in Figure 2), the pictorial (areas G, K, N, Q, S, and V in Figure 2), and ingredient information (areas H, J, M, R, U, and W in Figure 2). The number of observations on each area and sub-area was counted and utilized to form indicators of visual attention, and of adaptation to contextual factors.

FIGURE 2
Designated Areas on the Brand Display

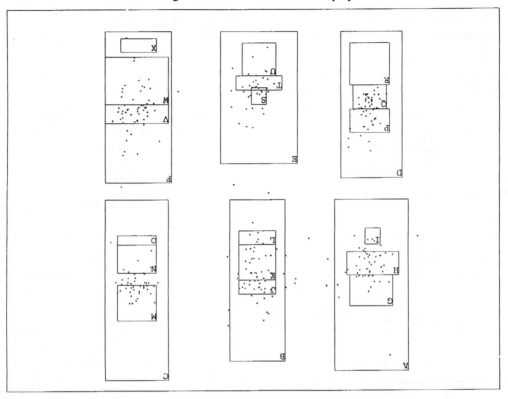

To assess acceleration, the "average starting time" (see Table 1) was determined. First, the time between exposure to the brand display and the first fixation on each of the six brands was determined. Next, the average of these six "starting times" was calculated. Decreasing average starting time indicates acceleration of processing.

To assess filtration, several measures of skipping were created. First, the total number of areas skipped, that is, that received no fixation at all was determined. Next, we determined the proportion of skipped areas that contained the brand name, pictorial and ingredient information respectively. These measures indicate the extent and locus of filtration; they allow us to examine which information is filtered out by a subject in order to cope with the task constraints. Finally, for each subject it was determined how many brands were scanned entirely, that is, the number of brands for which none of the relevant areas was skipped. The more brands that were scanned entirely, the less filtration took place.

To assess strategy shifts in information acquisition, three measures based on saccades were constructed. First, the number of switches, saccades, *within* the six brands per second was determined for each subject. This indicates the extent of processing-by-brand that subjects are engaged in. Second, the number of switches *between* the six brands per second was determined. This indicates the extent of processing-by-attribute. Third, the ratio of the number of switches within brands to the total number of switches made per second was determined. This indicates the extent to which processing-by-brand dominates over processing-by-attribute. Higher values of the first and third measure, and lower values of the second, indicate simplifying information acquisition strategies.

In Table 1, the average starting times, the number and proportions of areas skipped, and the average number and proportion of switches in the four conditions of the experimental design are presented.

Acceleration. When motivation is high, the average starting time of the first fixation on the brands, is significantly *later* than the starting time under low motivation (F $(1,52)$=10.75, p<.005). When time pressure is high, the average starting times decrease (F $(1,52)$=17.80, p<.005). The interaction between time pressure and motivation is not significant (F $(1,52)$=.34, ns.)

Filtration. Filtration appears to be influenced mainly by time pressure. The total number of within-brand areas skipped (F $(1,63)$=18.60, p<.005) was higher under high time pressure than under low time pressure. In addition, subjects under high time pressure were more likely to skip ingredient information (F $(1,63)$=13.25, p<.005), and even entire brands (F $(1,63)$=61.64, p<.005), but less likely to skip the package illustrations (F $(1,63)$=9.10, p<.005) than subjects under low time pressure. These results are clearly indicative of smaller consideration sets (brands that are not looked at can not be chosen) and a more superficial information search within the brands that *are* scanned. Motivation has qualitatively different effects: Highly motivated subjects are less likely to skip brand names and ingredient information than subjects with a low motivation. Higher motivation does not merely increase overall attention; it also directs the eye to information that "promises" to be more diagnostic for brand choice (cf. Easterbrook 1959).

Strategy Shift. Under conditions of high motivation the number of between-brand switches per second decreases (F

TABLE 1
Effect of Motivation and Time Pressure on Visual Attention

Measures	Low Motivation Time Pressure		High Motivation Time Pressure	
	Low	High	Low	High
Average starting time	2.53	1.45	3.76	2.31
Total number of areas skipped	6.62	10.37	5.38	10.74
Proportion Brand Name	.40	.38	.31	.33
Proportion Ingredient Information	.15	.27	.15	.26
Proportion Pictorial	.45	.35	.54	.41
Number of brands entirely scanned	1.85	.26	2.23	.16
Within-brand switches per second	1.46	1.30	1.36	1.46
Between-brand switches per second	.77	1.35	.70	.99
Ratio of within-to-total switches	.66	.49	.66	.60

$(1,63)$=10.70, p<.005), and the ratio of within-to-total switches increases (F $(1,63)$=9.61, p<.005). Under high time pressure, the number of between-brand switches per second increases (F $(1,63)$=34.59, p<.005), and the ratio of within-to-total switches decreases (F $(1,63)$=28.10, p<.005). These significant main effects are indicative of a relative decrease in processing within-brand under conditions of high time pressure and low motivation, and a relative increase in processing between-brands under conditions of low time pressure and high motivation. The results indicate that free-flowing visual attention patterns adapt strategically and very quickly to the constraints imposed by the situation.

The significant interaction between motivation and time pressure for the ratio of within-to-total switches (F $(1,63)$=4.95, p<.05), and the marginally significant interaction for the number of between-brand switches per second (F $(1,63)$=3.83, p=.055) support this interpretation. Table 1 indicates for instance that the lowest extent of processing-within-brands occurs under high time pressure and low motivation (ratio of within-to-total switches is .49).

Brand Preferences. As expected, motivation and time pressure and their interaction had no overall effects on the preference orders of the shampoo brands. Hence, the manipulations did not render any particular brand more salient or attractive. We hypothesized that subjects' preference scores for the brands would be significantly correlated with their gaze durations and fixation frequencies to the brands. Table 2 presents for each of the six brands separately, Spearman rho correlation coefficients between the preference rank order of the brands (1 to 6, from most to least preferred) and respectively the relative gaze duration and relative fixation frequency. Inspection of Table 2 shows that in 11 out of 12 cases, the correlation is statistically significant. In addition, we calculated the relative gaze duration for each position in the preference order (from 1 to 6) across brands. The proportion of total scanning time spent on the most preferred brand was 27.7%. The second most preferred brand receives 16.5% only, the third receives 14.7%. the fourth, the fifth and the sixth preferred brands receive 14.7%, 13.1%, and 12.5% respectively.

A 2 x 2 (x 6) MANOVA, with motivation and time pressure as between-subjects factors, and the relative gaze duration for each of the six preference positions (1 to 6) as the within-subjects factor, revealed no significant interactions, but the effect of preference position was highly significant (F $(5,315)$=23.44, p<.001). In other words, the drop in relative gaze duration is homogenous across the two experimental factors in the design. As the brands were completely unfamiliar to the subjects, preference could only develop during scanning of the choice display. Even under those conditions we find a surprisingly strong relationship between attention and preference.

DISCUSSION

To our knowledge the present study is the first to examine contextual constraints on information acquisition using eye tracking and a naturalistic choice display. Our results reveal that to a surprising extent free-floating visual attention adapts to the constraints imposed by the nature of the choice task. We found clear evidence for acceleration, filtration and strategy shifts in visual attention under time pressure and also under low motivation. For instance, under time pressure, consumers scan the brand display faster, indicating acceleration, they skip more areas of the brand display, and even complete brands, indicating filtration, and they shift more to information acquisition between-brands as compared to information acquisition within-brands, indicating strategy shift.

The results support the generalizability of findings from the contingent processing framework (Payne, Bettman and Johnson 1993) to information acquisition processes, and they go beyond them. While behavior in the contingent processing framework is largely strategic, the speed with which information acquisition was performed in our study suggests that consumers' visual attention adapted largely non-strategically to the contextual factors. In addition, our results suggest that, at least in the present context, high motivation compensates in part for high time pressure, since the overall impact of the two factors on patterns of visual attention were very similar, but reversed.

Our results diverge from the finding in eye movement research that scan patterns are only loosely controlled, and that instead they are driven by global overlearned scanning routines (e.g., top-bottom, left-right), and by salient elements in the display. It may be

TABLE 2
Rank Order Correlation of Brand Preference with Relative Gaze Duration and Fixation Frequency

Brands	Average preference position	Spearman rho [1] Relative gaze duration	Spearman rho Relative fixation frequency
A	3.77	-0.216 [a]	-0.328 [c]
B	2.89	-0.523 [c]	-0.572 [c]
C	3.59	-0.355 [c]	-0.158
D	4.30	-0.377 [c]	-0.361 [c]
E	3.25	-0.506 [c]	-0.558 [c]
F	3.20	-0.358 [c]	-0.326 [c]

[1] Significance levels, a = p < .05, b = p < .01, c = p < .005.

that scanning-for-search induces a higher level of control of eye movements than scanning in service of other cognitive tasks. In addition, we examined visual attention patterns at higher levels of aggregation than is frequently done in eye tracking research. It may well be possible that visual attention patterns are strategically controlled at higher levels ("What do I look at next?") while individual fixations and saccades are more heavily determined by salient display elements and global scanning routines. Finally it could be that the "adaptive behavior" we observed is not strategic adaptation in strict sense, but that consumers over time have learned several scanning routines in response to environmental conditions, and that this "procedural knowledge" is automatically called for when those conditions repeat themselves. We currently paln research in which detailed analyses of scan patterns are combined with other process measures of information acquisition in order to investigate these possibilities.

Another interesting finding is the high correlation between preference and amount of attention devoted to the brands. This would not be surprising in choice situations where the brands vary in familiarity, as familiarity is probably a causal factor in both attention attraction and in preference. This explanation is unlikely to hold for our results because all brands were equally unfamiliar and the choice proportions show that none of the brands was particularly more attractive than any other. It seems that even emerging preferences at first contact are closely related to visual attention, so that preference is, in a way, indeed in the eye of the beholder. Several mechanisms may account for the obtained attention-preference relationship. If consumers engage in a sequential selection process in which brands are dropped until a single brand, the most preferred one, remains, or in which an early preferred brand is compared with the other brands, a significant relationship between preference order and attention results. Then, a significant attention-preference relationship is a concomittant or epiphenomenon of higher order cognitive choice processes. However, if consumers tend to devote more attention to preferred stimuli than to non-prefered stimuli, for hedonic reasons, because it is more enjoyable to "consume" attractive or pleasurable than unattractive or unpleasurable stimuli, a significant attention-preference relationship is obtained as well. Then, the relationship is the outcome of motivated search for positive affect. While research supporting the first explanation comes from research on adaptive decision making and consideration set formation (e.g., Payne, Bettman and Johnson 1993), some research in developmental and social psychology supports the second explanation. For instance, children

and adults tend to gaze longer at attractive as compared to unattractive faces (e.g., Dion 1977), and even two month old infants already prefer attractive over unattractive faces (Langlois et al. 1987).

Unfortunately, only information about starting times, eye fixations and switches aggregated across time was available in the present study. Hence, we cannot determine whether and how eye fixations and saccades change in the course of time, and we cannot distinguish more cognitive from more hedonic explanations of the attention-preference relationship. Future research is needed to provide more insight in the mechanisms underlying attention-preference relationships.

REFERENCES
Easterbrook, J. A. (1959), "The Effect of Emotion on Cue Utilization and the Organization of Behavior", *Psychological Review*, 66, 183-201.

Celsi, Richard L. and Jerry C. Olson (1988), "The Role of Involvement in Attention and Comprehension Processes", *Journal of Consumer Research*, 15, 210-224.

Dion, K.K. (1977), "The Incentive Value of Physical Attractiveness for Younger Children," *Personality and Social Psychology Bulletin*, 3, 67-70.

Edland, Anne and Ola Svensson (1993), "Judgment and Decision Making under Time Pressure: Studies and Findings," in *Time Pressure and Stress in Human Judgment and Decision Making*, eds. Ola Svensson and A. John Maule, New York: Plenum Press.

Friedman, Alinda (1979), "Framing Pictures: The Role of Knowledge in Automatized Encoding and Memory for Gist," *Journal of Experimental Psychology: General*, 108, 316-355.

Janiszewski, Chris (1995), "The Influence of Page Layout on Directing and Sustaining Attention." Working Paper, University of Florida.

Janiszewski, Chris and Barbara Bickart (1994), "Managing Attention," in *Advances in Consumer Research*, 21, 329.

Kapferer, Jean-Noel and Gilles Laurent (1985), "Consumer Involvement Profiles: A New Practical Approach to Customer Involvement," *Journal of Advertising Research*, 25, 48-56.

Langlois, J.H., L.A. Roggeman, R.J. Casey, J.M. Ritter, A. Rieser-Danner and V.Y. Jenkins (1987), "Infant Preferences for Attractive Faces: Rudiments of a Stereotype?" *Developmental Psychology*, 23, 363-369.

Levy-Schoen, A. (1981), "Flexible and/or Rigid Control of Oculomotor Scanning Behavior," in *Eye Movements: Cognition and Visual Perception*, eds. Dennis F. Ficher, Richard A. Monty, and John W. Senders, Hillsdale, NJ: Lawrence Erlbaum.

Payne, John W., James R. Bettman, and Eric J. Johnson (1988), "Adaptive Strategy Selection in Decision Making," *Journal of Experimental Psychology: Learning, Memory, and Cognition*, 14 (3), 534-552.

Payne, John W., James R. Bettman, and Eric J. Johnson (1993), *"The Adaptive Decision Maker,"* Cambridge, NY: Cambridge University Press.

Petty, Richard E., John T. Cacciopo and David Schuman (1983), "Central and Peripheral Routes to Advertising Effectiveness: The Moderating Role of Involvement," *Journal of Consumer Research*, 10, 135-146.

Russo, J. Edward (1978), "Eye Fixations Can Save the World: Critical Evaluation and Comparison between Eye-Fixations and Other Information Processing Methodologies," *Advances in Consumer Research*, 5, 561-570.

Russo, J. Edward and France Leclerc (1994), "An Eye-Fixation Analysis of Choice Processes for Consumer Nondurables," *Journal of Consumer Research*, 21, 274-290.

Svensson, Ola, Anne Edland, and Paul Slovic (1990), "Choices and Judgments of Incompletely Described Decision Alternatives under Time Pressure," *Acta Psychologica*, 75, 153-169.

Viviani, Paolo (1990), "Eye Movements in Visual Search: Cognitive, Perceptual and Motor Control Aspects," in *Eye Movements and their Role in Visual and Cognitive Processes*, ed. Edith Kowler. Amsterdam: Elsevier Science Publishers.

Wright, Peter (1974), "The Harassed Decision Maker: Time Pressures, Distractions and the Use of Evidence," *Journal of Applied Psychology*, 59, 555-561.

Zakay, Dan (1985), "Post-Decisonal Confidence and Conflict Experienced in a Choice Process," *Acta Psychologica*, 58, 75-80.

Effects of Brand Name Exposure on Brand Choices: An Implicit Memory Perspective

Seh-Woong Chung, University of Toronto
Katrin Szymanski, University of Toronto

ABSTRACT

Drawing on the implicit memory framework, this study examines how exposures to brand names affect subsequent brand choices under different involvement conditions. Experimental results show that exposure modality (i.e., visual vs. auditory) affects brand choices more under low involvement than under high involvement. Subjects are more likely to choose the brand when the prior exposure to the brand is visual than when it is auditory. However, the study finds that processing mode (conceptual vs. perceptual) has no effect on brand choice. Theoretical and practical implications are discussed along with suggestions for future research.

INTRODUCTION

Choices in consumer research have typically been categorized into stimulus-based choices and memory-based choices (e.g., Lynch and Srull, 1982; Lynch, Marmorstein, and Weigold, 1988; Alba, Marmorstein, and Chattopadhyay, 1992). In stimulus-based choices, all the alternatives, along with their attributes, are physically present at the time of decision making, and the brand choices are assumed to be based on a rational scrutiny of this information. The multiattribute matrix approach exemplifies this type of choice.

It has been suggested, however, that in most real-life settings, consumers rarely have such information available about the alternatives. Consequently, consumer researchers have become interested in memory-based choices, where the alternatives and relevant information about them must be recalled from memory (e.g., Alba, Marmorstein, and Chattopadhyay, 1992; Lynch and Srull, 1982). In memory-based choices, the consumer consciously retrieves information from memory, and the decision is made on the basis of the information that is accessible and diagnostic (Lynch, Marmorstein, and Weigold, 1988). The information which forms the basis of the choice may consist of product attributes, or the product evaluation formerly formed and stored in memory.

Consumer decisions, however, may be made under mixed choice conditions, where some alternatives are physically available while others must be retrieved from memory. Most real-life purchases are made in these circumstances, as when one looks at several brands at one store, and later makes a purchase at another store (Lynch, Marmorstein, and Weigold, 1988).

Further, consumer decision making often takes place in situations where the consumer expends little cognitive effort in making the decision. Consider the consumer who hurries into a store to buy a grocery item, say, spaghetti noodle. Further suppose that the purchase has to be very quick since, for example, the consumer has his/her car illegally parked on the street outside the store. He/she has limited knowledge in spaghetti noodle, and does not have a preferred brand. Without much knowledge, nor much time to think about it, the consumer runs to the spaghetti section, barely scans the shelf, and quickly grabs a brand that somehow catches his eyes.

The conventional approach outlined above leaves unaddressed this kind of choice. His/her decision is typically labeled as a 'low-involvement' choice. With these types of choices, consumers rely more on peripheral cues than on attribute information (e.g., Petty, Cacioppo, and Schumann, 1983), expend minimal time and effort in making purchase decisions (e.g., Dickson and Sawyer, 1990), and the intensity of information search is reduced (Park and Hastak, 1994). The consumer is not likely to actively engage in the conscious retrieval of information from memory when making

choices, but may instead make choices based on brand familiarity or perceptual fluency (Lee, 1995).

The current study aims to investigate how an incidental exposure to brand names can affect subsequent brand choices even when the consumer is not aware of the effect of the prior exposure. For this purpose, we utilize a framework recently developed in cognitive psychology, often referred to as 'implicit memory' perspective, and demonstrate how this framework can offer an insight for examining brand choices made under different levels of involvement.

CONCEPTUAL BACKGROUND

Companies allocate an increasing amount of money each year to expose consumers to their brand names, and make substantial expenditures placing their products and brand names in movies, television shows, sports arenas, and outdoor billboards (Pracejus, 1995). A few studies have examined the effectiveness of brand name exposures on brand name recall (e.g., Nebenzahl and Hornik, 1985) or recognition (e.g., Pham, 1992). However, the ultimate effectiveness of this strategy should be gauged by whether the exposure increases the likelihood that these brands are chosen in subsequent purchase occasions.

Conventionally, memory tests, such as recall or recognition tests, consist of explicitly asking subjects to retrieve information from memory. Recent developments in cognitive psychology, however, suggest that prior experience can have implicit, as well as explicit, effects on memory and behavior. It has, in fact, been recognized in cognitive psychology that people can be "unconscious of why they behave the way they do" (Bowers, 1984; p. 245), and that some information can affect behavior even when individuals are unaware of being exposed to it (e.g., Jacoby and Kelley, 1987). The unconscious, or implicit, influence of past exposure to stimuli is perhaps best revealed in a class of memory tests called implicit memory tests. Unlike the conventional, explicit memory tests that direct the subjects to consciously recollect past experience, implicit memory tests do not require reference to a prior study episode (Roediger, 1990; Roediger and McDermott, 1993; Schacter, 1987). Subjects participating in implicit memory tests are simply told to perform tasks that presumably do not require conscious, or intentional, recollection of the past episode. The implicit role of memory is revealed in these tests by a change in the performance that is demonstrably attributable to the encoding of information in a prior study episode (Schacter, 1987). This exposure-induced change in the performance unaccompanied by awareness is called 'priming' (Tulving and Schacter, 1990).

Numerous tests have been used to measure implicit memory, which can be broadly classified into two categories: perceptual implicit tests and conceptual implicit tests (Blaxton, 1989; Jacoby, 1983; Tulving and Schacter 1990). The distinction between these two types of tests is important mainly because of the functional dissociations observed between these tests; that is, a number of variables (e.g., modality of presentation, levels of processing, typography) have been found to affect one type of implicit memory tests, while having no effect or the opposite effect on the other type of tests (for a review of the distinction between perceptual and conceptual priming, see Roediger and McDermott, 1993).

Perceptual implicit tests, also referred to as data-driven tests (Blaxton, 1989), are tests which require a reliance on the physical features of the test items. In perceptual implicit tests, stimuli presented for study (e.g., the word 'ELEPHANT') later occur in a perceptually degraded form at test. Examples of perceptual implicit tests include word stem completion (e.g., EL___), word fragment completion (e.g., -L--H---), and perceptual identification (identifying the word 'ELEPHANT' presented very briefly). These tests have been shown to be sensitive to changes in the physical features of the stimuli between study and test, such as picture/word manipulation (e.g., Srinivas and Roediger, 1990), modality of presentation (Blaxton, 1989: Experiment 2), and typography manipulation (Blaxton, 1989: Experiment 3).

In contrast, conceptual implicit tests, also known as conceptually driven tests, reflect conceptual processes (Schacter, 1987). In conceptual implicit tests, the stimuli presented at study are only conceptually related to the cues provided at test, and bear no resemblance to the stimuli (Blaxton, 1989; Lee, 1995; Roediger, 1990). For example, the subject may be presented with the word 'ELEPHANT' for study and later be given a general knowledge question (e.g., what is the largest mammal?), a word fragment completion (e.g., --M--L)[1], or a category exemplar generation (e.g., generate exemplars for the category 'MAMMALS'). These tests require conceptual elaboration of the stimuli at study, and are affected by variables that are also known to influence explicit memory tests, such as levels of processing (Blaxton, 1989) and attentional manipulations (Gardiner and Parkin, 1990; Parkin and Russo, 1990).

Recently, a number of researchers in cognitive psychology have proposed and found evidence for the Transfer-Appropriate Processing model (Blaxton, 1989; Morris, Bransford, and Franks, 1977; Roediger and Blaxton, 1987; Roediger, Weldon, and Challis, 1989; Weldon, 1991) to explain individuals' performance on these different types of tests. Analogous to the encoding-specificity principle, which states that explicit memory performance is determined by the extent of match between the study conditions and retrieval conditions (Tulving, 1985), the Transfer-Appropriate Processing model posits that the performance on implicit memory tests is enhanced to the extent that the types of mental operations performed at study overlap with those required at test.

For example, reading words at study leads to better performance on perceptual implicit tests than generating them from a conceptual cue at study (e.g., Jacoby, 1983), since reading (vs. generating) involves perceptual processing of the stimuli, the same type of processing required in perceptual implicit tests. In a related study, Weldon and Roediger (1987, Experiment 4) had subjects study a list of stimuli in either pictures (e.g., the picture of elephant) or in words (e.g., the word 'ELEPHANT') and later presented them with one of two implicit memory test: the word-fragment completion test and the picture-fragment naming test (i.e., naming the referent of the picture presented in a perceptually degraded form). They found that seeing the words at study produced better performance on word-fragment completion test than did seeing the pictures, whereas the opposite pattern occurred for the picture-fragment naming test. Both of these examples illustrate the basic notion of the Transfer-Appropriate Processing model that the

match in mental operations performed at study (e.g., seeing pictures) and at test (e.g., naming pictures) influences the performance on implicit memory tests. The Transfer-Appropriate-Processing model has been shown to well explain individuals' performance on different types of implicit memory tests, and to account for the dissociations in the effects of various experimental manipulations on the performance on implicit memory tests (e.g., Roediger, 1989; Roediger and McDermott, 1993; Schacter, 1987; Weldon, 1991).

The current study views brand choice as an implicit memory test in the sense that brand choice may be implicitly affected by earlier exposure to brand names even when the consumer is not aware of the fact that his/her choice is being influenced by the previous exposure. This is in line with Roediger and McDermott's (1993) definition of implicit memory tests that "...[E]very sort of judgment or test that is (a) affected by past experience, and (b) given under conditions in which subjects are not explicitly instructed to remember earlier events, would qualify (p.69)" as an implicit memory test.

HYPOTHESES

Viewing brand choice from the implicit memory perspective allows us to develop and test a number of interesting hypotheses. In the current study, we focus on the choice situation in which the consumer is visually presented with the brand names, and is required to make a choice under either high or low involvement. Under low involvement, the consumer expends minimal time and effort in making a choice (Lee, 1995; Park and Hastak, 1994). In these situations, the consumer is least likely to resort to a systematic processing of brand information. Rather, the consumer may make a choice using a simple heuristic, such as perceptual fluency, or increased ease of perceptually processing the stimulus due to prior exposure (Jacoby, 1983), and choose the brand that 'catches the eye', or that somehow 'feels familiar' (see Jacoby, 1983). In other words, the consumer, under low involvement situation, may base the choice on the perceptual features of the brand names, and choose the brand that visually 'pops out' among the alternatives (e.g., Garber, 1995). Thus, brand choices under these circumstances closely resemble perceptual implicit tests in the sense that these choices are based on the physical features of the brand names.

The Transfer-Appropriate Processing model outlined above implies, then, that conceptual processing of the brand names during prior exposure is neither necessary nor efficient when the choice is made under low involvement. Rather, the model suggests that the choice made under low involvement would be sensitive to the modality of exposure (visual vs. auditory), the variable which has been found to affect perceptual implicit memory tests. As aforementioned, when choices are made among a number of *visually* available alternatives, and are made under low involvement conditions, they are likely to be based on the *visual* aspects of the products (Garber, 1995), and therefore, require *visual processing* of the alternatives. Thus, companies would benefit only from *visually (vs. auditorily)* exposing consumers to their brand names if the purchase of their products typically involves a choice among visually available alternatives and is likely to be made in low involvement situations, such as in most grocery shopping occasions. This strategy of visual exposure insures the maximal match between mental operations during the exposure and subsequent choices, which, according to the Transfer-Appropriate-Processing model, enhances the performance on implicit memory tests.

H1: When brand choice is made under low involvement conditions, visual exposure to a brand name will increase the likelihood that the brand is subsequently

---

[1]One may note that the word fragment completion test can be used as both a perceptual implicit test and a conceptual implicit test. When it is used as a conceptual implicit test, it bears no physical resemblance to the study item. Yet the subject is more likely to complete the fragment '—M—L' with 'MAMMAL' due to the exposure to the word 'ELEPHANT' during the study session.

chosen. Auditory exposure to a brand name will not affect the likelihood that the brand is subsequently chosen.

In contrast, when brand choice is made in high involvement situations, the consumer is more likely to engage in an active processing of the available information, is more inclined to expend time and effort to make an accurate decision, and is less prone to be affected by perceptual fluency (Lee, 1995; Park and Hastak, 1994). In other words, brand choice in high involvement situations is likely to be more conceptually based (versus perceptually based). For instance, when highly involved in the purchase decision, the consumer may rely on his/her knowledge about the brand names and the product categories, which in nature is a conceptually-based decision making. Thus, under these circumstances, prior conceptual processing would match the processing requirement of choice, and therefore, exposure to a brand name is expected to affect brand choice only when the consumer conceptually processed the brand name during the exposure.[2]

H2: When brand choice is made under high involvement conditions, conceptual processing of a brand name during exposure will increase the likelihood that the brand is subsequently chosen. In contrast, perceptual encoding will not affect the likelihood that the brand is subsequently chosen.

EXPERIMENT

To test the above hypotheses, we manipulated both the condition at exposure and at choice. High and low involvement conditions at choice were manipulated by varying the amount of the time allowed for choice. Conditions at exposure were manipulated by varying the modality of the presented stimuli (visual versus auditory) and the type of processing induced (conceptual versus perceptual). Conceptual processing was induced by having the subjects judge when during the day each brand was most likely to be used. This instruction forces subjects to elaborate on their knowledge about the brand names and product categories. Perceptual processing was induced by having the subjects count the number of vowels or syllables in the brand names. This task directs subjects to focus on the perceptual features of the brand names while preventing them from elaborating on the concept.

Method

Subjects. One hundred and twenty eight undergraduate business students from a large North American University participated in the experiment in exchange for course credit. In addition,

a separate group of 58 students in a management course volunteered to take parts in the pretest.

Stimuli. Five brands (e.g., Dentyne) from each of fifteen product categories (e.g., chewing gum) were used as targets. The brands selected were based on a pretest, where participants were asked to list all the brands they would consider buying in each of the categories. For each product category, brands named with approximately comparable frequencies were chosen for the experiment, while the brands listed with frequencies distinctly lower or higher than other brands were dropped.

Brands from another set of five product categories were used for practice trials, and also to eliminate primacy effects. Brands from an additional ten product categories were used to eliminate recency effects. These additional brands also served as fillers, thereby increasing the number of brand names and product categories, which makes it more difficult for the subjects to remember which brands were presented during the exposure stage.

In both the exposure session and the subsequent choice session, the order of presentation of the target product categories was randomized across the subjects. Further, to remove an item effect, the brand being presented in the exposure session was randomly selected among the five brands in each product category. Thus, each subject was presented with a randomly selected brand in a given category, which later served as his/her own target brand in that category. In addition, the position of the target brand within each product category was randomized across subjects in the brand choice stage.

Design. The experiment comprised a 2 (Exposure Modality: Visual vs. Auditory) × 2 (Processing Mode: Perceptual vs. Conceptual) × 2 (Involvement: High vs. Low) between-subject factorial design.

Procedure. The different stages of the experimental procedure are shown in Figure 1. As a rule, the subjects participated in groups of two to four individuals, and were randomly assigned to one of the 2 × 2 × 2 cells. On arrival, the subjects were seated in front of IBM PS/2 Ultimedia personal computers, which were used to present the stimuli. They were then told that they would be subjects in three short unrelated studies. Each of the three sessions had separate cover stories which were designed to conceal the relationship between exposure to particular brands and subsequent choices.

As indicated in Figure 1, the experiment comprised of an exposure session, an unrelated filler task, and a choice task. For the exposure session, subjects were told that the researchers were interested in how consumers would process various brand names. For the subjects in the 'visual exposure' condition, a brand name from each product category was presented on the computer screen one at a time. For those in the 'auditory exposure' group, the brand names were auditorily presented one at a time by a cassette-tape player. Half the subjects in the 'visual exposure' group were instructed to count the number of vowels in each brand name while the other half in the same group were told to judge when during the day each brand was most likely to be used (e.g., Morning, Afternoon, Evening, Night). Similarly, half the subjects in the 'auditory exposure' group were directed to count the number of syllables in each brand name while the other half were instructed to judge when during the day each brand was most likely to be used.

Following the exposure session, subjects engaged in an unrelated task that lasted for approximately five minutes. The purpose of this task was to erase short-term memory and to blur the connection between the exposure session and the choice session. For this task, the subjects read the cover story which stated that certain companies were interested in understanding consumer profiles, and were asked a number of questions about some demo-

---

[2]The conceptual/perceptual distinction employed in this study should be distinguished from the central/peripheral processing framework proposed in Elaboration Likelihood Model (Petty and Cacioppo, 1984). Though these two frameworks bear resemblance in the sense that they are both concerned with processing under low/high involvement situations, the latter framework pertains to message relevant/irrelevant processing that lead to differential routes to persuasion. The present study, however, focuses on situations in which the consumer is only exposed to brand names in the absence of any brand information, or advertising message (e.g., brand-name-only billboards). Thus, in the context of the current study, the distinction between conceptual/perceptual processing seems more appropriate than that between central/peripheral processing.

FIGURE 1
Experimental Procedure

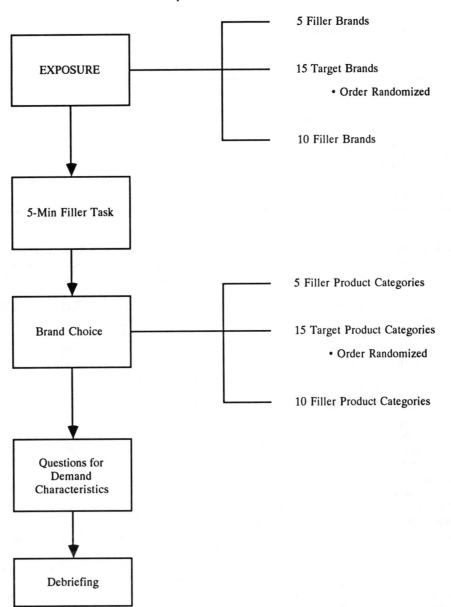

graphic information (e.g., age, gender) and personal life-style (e.g., hobbies).

Finally, the subjects were given the choice task. In this task, the subjects were first presented with the five filler product categories, then with the fifteen target product categories, and finally with the ten filler product categories. The filler and target product categories remained the same as the ones used in the exposure session. The product categories appeared on the computer screen one at a time. A set of five brands from each of the thirty product categories was shown at one time, and the subjects' task was to choose which brand they would purchase from this set of five brands. Of the five brands in each product category, one was presented in the prior exposure session.

For the subjects in high involvement group, the choice set for each category stayed on the computer screen for 10 seconds, and the subjects were told to take as much time as they would like to make each choice. In contrast, for those in the low involvement group,

each choice set remained on the computer screen for 3 seconds only, and the subjects were instructed to make each choice as quickly as possible.[3]

---

[3]Although, in theory, involvement is viewed as an individual difference variable (Laurent and Kapferer, 1988), it is often conceptualized as a multi-faceted construct, which is determined by many situational factors (Batra and Ray, 1983). Thus, involvement is not merely motivational, but is also affected by situational opportunity and ability (Celci and Olson, 1988). We manipulated (vis-à-vis measured) one such factor (i.e., opportunity) by varying the time pressure across the two involvement conditions. This is in line with the suggestion that factors theoretically predicted to influence involvement (e.g., motivation, ability, or opportunity) should be manipulated (Andrews, 1988).

TABLE 1

Mean number of matches between the primed and chosen brands

| | Visual | | Auditory | | |
	Perceptual Processing	Conceptual Processing	Perceptual Processing	Conceptual Processing	
Low involvement	4.13 * (n=16)	4.31 * (n=16)	3.00 (n=16)	2.63 (n=16)	3.52 (n=64)
High involvement	3.31 (n=16)	3.56 (n=16)	2.87 (n=15)	2.81 (n=16)	3.14 (n=63)
	3.72	3.94	2.94	2.72	3.33 (n=127)

*; above chance level ($p < 0.05$).

To measure demand characteristics, the subjects were asked at the end of the experiment to write down what they thought the purposes of the experiment were. Upon completing this, they were debriefed and dismissed.

Dependent Measure. The dependent measure was the number of times one of the primed brands was chosen. If there is no effect of exposure on the subsequent brand choice, the primed brands would be chosen three out of fifteen times, or one fifth of the time, since there were five brands per product category.

RESULTS

The subjects' responses to the demand characteristics question asked at the end of the experiment indicated that the attempt at concealing the relationship between exposure to particular brands and subsequent choices was successful. Only one subject indicated an awareness of this relationship. Data for this subject were dropped in the statistical analyses.

Table 1 shows the mean number of times subjects chose the brand names to which they were previously exposed during the study phase. Overall, a three-way ANOVA on the dependent variable with exposure modality, processing mode, and involvement revealed a significant main effect for exposure modality ($F=15.26$, $p=.000$), such that subjects in the visual exposure condition had a significantly higher likelihood of subsequently selecting the preexposed brands than those in the auditory exposure condition ($M_{visual}=3.83$ versus $M_{auditory}=2.83$). The main effects for processing mode and for involvement were not significant. The modality by involvement interaction approached marginal significance, however, all the other two- and three-way interactions were not significant.

To determine whether choice of the pre-exposed brands was above chance levels (i.e., 3.0) in the different cells, a series of one-sample t-tests were performed. These tests revealed that choice of the pre-exposed brands was significantly above chance for the two cells in the 'Visual exposure/ Low involvement' condition ($M_{visual, perceptual, low involvement}=4.13$, $t=2.52$, $p=0.02$; $M_{visual, conceptual, low involvement}=4.31$, $t=2.78$, $p=0.01$). None of the other cells was significantly above chance ($p>0.05$).

H_1 predicted that modality of exposure would affect brand choice under low involvement, but not under high involvement. Planned comparisons revealed that the probability of choosing the previously exposed brands was higher for the visual exposure group than for the auditory exposure group, when the involvement at choice was low ($M_{visual, low involvement}=4.22$ versus $M_{auditory,}$ low involvement$=2.81$; $F=14.21$; $p=.00$). In contrast, visual exposure group and auditory exposure group differed only marginally when the involvement at choice was high ($M_{visual, high involvement}=3.44$ versus $M_{auditory, high involvement}=2.84$; $F=3.06$, $p=.09$). Thus, support for H_1 was found in the sense that the modality of exposure had a greater impact on brand choice when the involvement at choice was low than when it was high.

Inconsistent with H_2, which predicted that the conceptual processing of brand names during exposure would increase the likelihood of the pre-exposed brands being chosen under high involvement at choice, no effect of processing mode (i.e., conceptual versus perceptual processing) was found in either involvement condition. That is, under both high and low involvement conditions, subjects who conceptually processed the brand names during the exposure did not subsequently choose the pre-exposed brands more frequently than those who perceptually processed them.

DISCUSSION

The results indicate that the modality of exposure (visual versus auditory) affected which brands subjects chose in the subsequent choice occasion, especially under low involvement condition. It appears that consumers rely on perceptual features of the alternatives and select the brand that 'pops out', or that seems 'perceptually familiar', especially if they do not have the adequate opportunity, or are not highly motivated, to make a 'reasoned' choice (e.g., due to time pressure). It is interesting to note that conceptual processing during exposure was not necessary to induce the subjects to choose the pre-exposed brands under these circumstances.

Conforming to the Transfer-Appropriate Processing framework, these findings suggest that brands, especially, frequently purchased packaged goods, with which consumers are not highly involved, would benefit from a visually simple ad which emphasizes the brand name. For these products, it would not be beneficial to clutter the ad with complex design and intricate information. The package for these products would also have to highlight the brand name and be simple in design such that the visual features are maximally matched between the ad and the package.

The results also have implications for advertising media selection. If the product is likely to be purchased in a low-involvement situation, visual media such as print or television ads would be more efficient than audio ads. In addition, use of logos, brand-name-only posters, and outdoor billboards is also justified by the results of this study.

The results pertaining to H_2 were surprising. Contrary to H_2, conceptual processing (versus perceptual processing) of the brand names during exposure did not induce the subjects to choose the brands to which they were exposed even when the subjects were highly involved during choice task. Although we could not address the exact mechanism leading to these results, one possibility may be due to the fact the choice situation in the current study was such that the choices were made in the physical presence of the alternatives. As suggested by Lee (1995), conceptual processing may be more effective than perceptual processing in memory-based choices in which the choice decisions are made in the absence of the alternatives, and therefore, the consumer has to generate the set of alternatives from memory. In memory-based choices, the absence of visual cues would preclude the use of perceptual heuristics. Prior conceptual processing under these circumstances would, for instance, increase the likelihood that the pre-exposed brands are included in the consideration set, and are ultimately chosen. In contrast, it appears that when the alternatives were physically presented to the consumer, modality of exposure was more important than processing mode such that subjects still relied on perceptual cues even when their involvement was high and they had an ample opportunity to expend deliberation in making the choice. Another, related possibility may be found in the fact that we restricted our study to frequently purchased packaged goods with which consumers are not likely to be highly motivated to devote excessive deliberation when making choices.

FUTURE RESEARCH

The current study focused on how various modes of exposures to brand names affected subsequent brand choices in the context in which all the alternatives were physically present whey the subjects were making choices. Future studies may investigate the implicit effect of preexposure on choices in other contexts. For example, it is well-known that the effect of memory differs depending on whether the choice is stimulus-based or memory-based. (Lynch and Srull, 1982; Lynch, Marmorstein, and Weigold, 1988; Alba, Marmorstein, and Chattopadhyay, 1992). Further, the role of involvement, exposure modality, and elaboration mode may also depend on whether the choice is stimulus-based or memory-based.

Examining the effect of multiple (versus single) preexposures on brand choice would also be interesting. Studying this issue would help to determine what the exact nature of the relationship between exposure frequencies and brand choice (e.g., inverted U-shape) is, and whether there is a threshold in the effect of multiple exposures. Similarly, one could introduce various lengths of delays between exposures, and between exposures and brand choice to determine whether the effect observed in the present study is short-lived or relatively long lasting.

Investigating the characteristics of brand names would also provide valuable insight. For example, one might study the effect of exposure on unfamiliar (versus familiar) brands, or examine whether there is a differential effect on meaningful brand names (e.g., Cascade, Mother's) compared to meaningless brand names (e.g., Javex, Unico).

The present study focused on frequently purchased packaged goods, with which consumers are generally not highly involved when making choices. A similar study with high-involvement products (e.g., automobile, personal computer) would reveal whether the preexposure effect observed in the current study can be generalized to these products, and/or whether different factors are responsible for producing the effects when choices are made for high-involvement products.

REFERENCES

Alba, Joseph W., Howard Marmorstein, and Amitava Chattopadhyay (1992), "Transitions in Preference Over Time: The Effects of Memory on Message Persuasiveness," *Journal of Marketing Research*, 29 (November), 406-416.

Andrews, J. Craig (1988), "Motivation, Ability, and Opportunity to Process Information: Conceptual and Experimental Manipulation Issues", in *Advances in Consumer Research*, Vol. 15, ed. M.J. Houston, Provo, UT: Association for Consumer Research, 219-224.

Batra, Rajeev and Michael L. Ray (1983), "Operationalizing Involvement as Depth and Quality of Cognitive Response", in *Advances in Consumer Research*, Vol. 10, eds. R. Bagozzi and A. Tybout, Ann Arbor, MI: Association for Consumer Research, 309-313.

Blaxton, Teresa A. (1989), "Investigating Dissociations Among Memory Measures: Support for a Transfer Appropriate Processing Framework," *Journal of Experimental Psychology: Learning, Memory, and Cognition*, 15, 657-668.

Bowers, Kenneth S. (1984), "On Being Unconsciously Influenced and Informed," in *The Unconscious Reconsidered*, eds. Kenneth S. Bowers and Donald Meichenbaum, New York, NY: John Wiley & Sons, 227-272.

Celci, Richard L. and Jerry C. Olson (1988), "The Role of Involvement in Attention and Comprehension Processes", *Journal of Consumer Research*, Vol. 15, 210-224.

Garber, Lawrence L. Jr. (1995), "The Package Appearance in Choice," in *Advances in Consumer Research*, Vol. 22, eds. Frank R. Kardes and Mita Sujan, Provo, UT: Association for Consumer Research, 319-322.

Gardiner, J. M. and Parkin, A. J. (1990), "Attention and Recollective Experience in Recognition Memory," *Memory & Cognition*, 18, 579-583.

Jacoby, Larry L. (1983), "Remembering the Data: Analyzing Interactive Processes in Reading," *Journal of Verbal Learning and Verbal Behavior*, 22, 485-508.

Jacoby, Larry L. and Colleen M. Kelley (1987), "Unconscious Influences of Memory for a Prior Event," *Personality and Social Psychology Bulletin*, Vol. 13 (September), 314-336.

Laurent, G. and J. Kapferer (1985), "Measuring Consumer Involvement Profiles", *Journal of Marketing Research*, Vol. XXII (February), 41-53.

Lee, Angela Yuk-Kei (1995), "Effects of Stimulus Exposure on Information Processing: An Implicit Memory Perspective", Unpublished Doctoral Dissertation.

Lynch, John G., Jr., and Thomas K. Srull (1982), "Memory and Attentional Factors in Consumer Choice: Concepts and Research Methods," *Journal of Consumer Research*, 9 (June), 18-37.

Lynch, John G., Jr., Howard Marmorstein, and Michael F. Weigold (1988), "Choices from Sets Including Remembered Brands: Use of Recalled Attributes and Prior Overall Evaluations," *Journal of Consumer Research*, 15 (September), 169-184.

Morris, C. D., J. D. Bransford, and J. J. Franks (1977), "Levels of Processing versus Transfer Appropriate Processing", *Journal of Verbal Learning and Verbal Behavior*, 16, 519-533.

Nebenzahl, I. and J. Hornik (1985), "An Experimental Study of the Effectiveness of Commercial Billboards in Televised Sports Arenas", *International Journal of Advertising*, 4, 27-36.

Park, Jong-Won, and Manoj Hastak (1994), "Memory-based Product Judgments: Effects of Involvement at Encoding and Retrieval", *Journal of Consumer Research*, 21 (December), 534-547.

Parkin, A. J. and R. Russo (1990), "Implicit and Explicit Memory and the Automatic Effortful Distinction," *European Journal of Cognitive Psychology*, 2, 71-80.

Petty, R. E. and J. T. Cacioppo (1984), "The Effects of Involvement on Responses to Argument Quantity and Quality: Central and Peripheral Routes to Persuasion", *Journal of Personality and Social Psychology*, 46, 69-91.

Pham, M. Tuan (1992), "Effects of Involvement, Arousal, and Pleasure on the Recognition of Sponsorship Stimuli," in *Advances in Consumer Research*, Vol. 19, eds. John F. Sherry, Jr. and Brian Sternthal, Provo, UT: Association for Consumer Research, 85-93.

Pracejus, John W. (1995), "Is More Exposure Always Better? Effects of Incidental Exposure to a Brand Name on Subsequent Processing of Advertising", in *Advances in Consumer Research*, Vol. 22, eds. Frank R. Kardes and Mita Sujan, Provo, UT: Association for Consumer Research, 319-322.

Roediger, Henry L., III (1990), "Implicit Memory: Retention Without Remembering", *American Psychologist*, 45, 1043-1056.

_____ and Kathleen B. McDermott (1993), "Implicit Memory in Normal Human Subjects," in *Handbook of Neuropsychology*, ed. F. Bollerand J. Grafman, Amsterdam: Elsevier, 8, 63-131.

_____, Mary S. Weldon, and Bradford H. Challis (1989), "Explaining Dissociations between Implicit and Explicit Measures of Retention: A Processing Account," in *Varieties of Memory and Consciousness: Essays in Honour of Endel Tulving*, ed. H.L. Roediger and F.I.M. Craik, Hillsdale, NJ: Erlbaum, 3-41.

Schacter, Daniel L. (1987), "Implicit Memory: History and Current Status," *Journal of Experimental Psychology*, 13, 501-518.

Srinivas, Kavitha and Henry L. Roediger III (1990), "Classifying Implicit Memory Tests: Category Association and Anagram Solution," *Journal of Memory and Language*, 29, 389-412.

Tulving, Endel (1983). *Elements of Episodic Memory*. New York: OxfordUniversity Press.

_____ and Daniel Schacter (1990), "Priming and Human Memory Systems", *Science*, 247, 301-306.

Weldon, Mary S. (1991), "Mechanisms Underlying Priming on Perceptual Tests," *Journal of Experimental Psychology: Learning, Memory, and Cognition*, 17, 526-541.

Consumer Experience and Consideration Sets for Brands and Product Categories

Michael D. Johnson, University of Michigan
Donald R. Lehmann, Columbia University

ABSTRACT

A study examining the effects of experience on consumers' consideration sets at the brand and category levels is reported. The results indicate that, as experience grows, consideration sets increase in size at both the brand and category levels. However, these larger consideration sets contain more atypical alternatives in the case of categories but not in the case of brands. This result is consistent with the argument that experts consider a more homogeneous set of alternatives when the need is more specific and a more heterogeneous set when the need is more general.

INTRODUCTION

Consumer choice research provides a rich understanding of information processing strategies. Yet choice alternatives are often taken for granted. These choice alternatives include both primary demand, or choice among product categories themselves, and secondary demand, or choice among brands within a category (Wärneryd 1988). As the particular array of considered alternatives affects both choice processes and outcomes (Glazer et al. 1991; Simonson 1989), understanding the nature of consumers' consideration sets is an important research question for both levels of choice. Understanding how consideration sets are determined is both theoretically important (Nedungadi 1990) and critical to improving the predictive ability of consumer choice models (Hauser and Wernerfelt 1990). Yet the research that has been conducted has focused on brands. Product categories, as choice sets, have been relatively ignored.

The goal of this study is to examine how consideration sets grow with consumer experience for both brand- and category-level choices. Past research shows that these different levels of choice evoke very different types of perceptions, judgments, and choice processes (Bettman and Sujan 1987; Block and Johnson 1995; Corfman 1991; Johnson 1984, 1988, 1989; Johnson and Fornell 1987; Johnson et al. 1992; Loken and Ward 1990; Park and Smith 1989). Consideration sets should also vary systematically between levels of choice as consumer experience grows. A major difference between brand- and category-level choices centers on the specificity of consumer needs. While these needs are relatively specific or concrete and pertain to particular consumption contexts in the case of brands, needs are more general or abstract and span multiple consumption contexts in the case of categories (Howard 1977). At the brand level, for example, a consumer deciding among an array of soft drinks has a relatively concrete goal in mind. In contrast, a consumer buying beverages during a weekly shopping trip for a family has more general choice criteria in mind, such as purchasing beverages that are healthy and may be used in a variety of contexts (breakfast, kid's lunches, snack time, etc.). This suggests that, as experience grows, consideration sets may grow in very different ways at the different levels of choice.

BRANDS AND CATEGORIES

Past research reveals a number of important processing differences between brand- and category-level choices. Compared to brands, categories are perceived and judged using more abstract attributes (Corfman 1991; Johnson 1984; Johnson and Fornell 1987; Johnson et al. 1992), processed in a more hierarchical or top-down fashion (Johnson 1989; Park and Smith 1989), and involve more alternative-based as opposed to attribute-based comparisons (Johnson 1984 1988; Park and Smith 1989). Of particular interest here is how consumers' needs vary as a function of the level of choice, and how these needs interact with consumer experience to produce a consideration set. Following Alba and Hutchinson (1987), we define experience or familiarity as "the number of product-related experiences that have been accumulated by the consumer" (p. 411). We adopt Hauser and Wernerfelt's (1990) definition of consideration sets as "those brands that the consumer considers seriously when making a purchase and/or consumption decision" (p. 393). The concept of a consideration set rests on the observation that consumers do not seriously consider all available options.

Overall we expect that as experience increases, consideration sets increase. As experience grows, consumers become aware of, try, and subsequently consider an increasing number of options (Howard 1977). This prediction presumes some underlying level of risk aversion, whereby consumers start with an empty consideration set that is "built up" with experience. Whether it is brands of wine, or types of alcoholic beverages, experience should increase the number of considered options. The first hypothesis states that this growth prediction holds for brand- and product category-level choice alternatives alike:

H1: The number of alternatives in a consumer's consideration set increases with experience for both brand-level and category-level choice alternatives.

Alternatively, consumers may begin with an all inclusive consideration set that is pared down with experience. This relative risk seeking view of consideration set formation suggests an opposite prediction whereby consideration sets decrease in size with experience.

Alba and Hutchinson (1987) describe another important effect that experience may have on consideration sets. Consumers use category structures, learned through experience, to organize and differentiate the products in their environment. These category structures vary from subordinate categories that contain highly similar or homogeneous alternatives (e.g., soft drinks) to more basic and superordinate categories that contain more dissimilar or heterogeneous alternatives (e.g., beverages). What differentiates alternatives from one another within a subordinate category is their ability to meet a relatively specific set of needs (e.g., calories, flavor) in relatively specific consumption situations. In contrast, more superordinate category alternatives vary in their ability to meet a more abstract set of basic needs (e.g., nutritional value, life style) across a variety of consumption situations. This led Alba and Hutchinson to predict that: "When the need is specific, experts consider a more homogeneous set of alternatives than do novices; when the need is general, experts consider a more heterogeneous set of alternatives than do novices" (1987, p. 418).

Howard (1977) hypothesized a similar effect as a way of differentiating between brand- and category-level choices. Following earlier work by Rokeach (1973), Howard hypothesized a hierarchy of abstract-to-concrete choice criteria or needs that corresponds to consumers' hierarchies of superordinate-to-subordinate product categories. The more abstract categories should be described and evaluated on the basis of more abstract criteria while the more concrete, subcategory options should be described and evaluated on the basis of more concrete criteria. This led Howard to predict that as consumers move hierarchically from a heterogeneous, category level of choice to a homogeneous, brand level of choice, there should be a corresponding increase in the level of specificity of consumers' choice criteria. For consumers with experience in the product domain, a category-level choice should invoke a more abstract, general set of needs or values while a brand-level choice should invoke a more concrete, specific set of needs or values.

This difference in need specificity should affect the graded structure or *prototypicality* of considered options. According to the prototypicality concept, some members of a category are reliably rated as more typical of the category or considered better exemplars (Cantor and Mischel 1979; Mervis and Rosch 1981; Medin and Smith 1984; Smith and Medin 1981). In the US, for example, popcorn and potato chips are considered more prototypical of snack foods than are olives and tomatoes (Ward and Loken 1986). A body of research suggests that more prototypical members of a category are learned first while less prototypical members and the graded structure of the category are learned with accumulated experience (Loken and Ward 1990; Mervis and Rosch 1981; Rosch 1975, 1977; Sujan 1985; Ward and Loken 1986, 1988). This led Alba and Hutchinson (1987) to further predict that experts and novices vary in their inclusion of atypical products in a consideration set: "it is likely that novice consumers will know about prototypical brands, but not atypical ones (while) expert consumers will be familiar with both types" (p. 416). As experience grows, consumers encounter use occasions or ad hoc contexts in which atypical category members may be more appropriate than prototypes (Barsalou 1983, 1985).

However, this prediction must be considered in light of the specificity of needs and the homogeneity of alternatives. Consider first the case of product category-level choice alternatives and associated general choice criteria. As experience grows, there is a large, heterogeneous set of options available to meet one's general choice criteria. Thus the average prototypicality of alternatives in a consideration set should decrease with experience. Now consider the case of brand-level choice. While experts may become aware of both typical and atypical brands, they are unlikely to include the more atypical options in their choice set. It conflicts with the notion that they are trying to fulfill a specific, well-defined, concrete need. In the case of brands, therefore, we expect experience to have little or no effect on the prototypicality of considered alternatives. Put differently, the predicted effect of experience on prototypicality presumes a relatively heterogeneous set of possible alternatives and related consumption contexts. This leads to our second hypothesis:

H2: Consideration sets decrease in prototypicality with experience at the product category level but not at the level of brands.

To summarize, we predict that consideration sets should increase with experience for both brand- and category-level choice alternatives, but only the product category sets should grow to include a broader range of typical to atypical options. These predictions were tested using data collected though not analyzed as part of a larger study of consumer perceptions of brand- and category-level stimuli (Johnson et al. 1992). It is important to note that the prediction in hypothesis two regarding brand-level consideration sets is meant to be general and may not hold in certain categories or contexts. For example, in categories where "being different" is important to consumers, more atypical alternatives may actually become more preferred with experience, whether it is drinking a unique brand of wine or coffee or wearing a unique brand of jeans (Ward and Loken 1988). Our argument regarding cat-

egory-level choice is likewise meant to be general and not necessarily describe every choice situation. Consumers may face category-level choices involving very specific alternatives (Johnson 1984).

EMPIRICAL STUDY

In our empirical study, consumers were asked to indicate which alternatives, from among a given set of either brands or categories, they would seriously consider buying or consuming. This task follows directly from Hauser and Wernerfelt's (1990) definition of consideration sets. Five sets of alternatives were used to operationalize the brand- and category-level stimuli. Each set contained twelve alternatives and each subject responded to questions regarding one of the five sets. Two sets (soft drinks and candy bars) are very concrete and represent brands from the same product categories. Three sets (beverages, snacks, and lunch products) represent more abstract, product category alternatives that cross salient (basic) category boundaries. The brand-level stimuli included the twelve market share leaders in each category at the time of the study while the category-level stimuli included mostly common with some less common category options. The specific stimuli within each of these five stimulus sets are presented in Table 1. Overall 123 subjects participated in the study, 24, 24, 24, 24, and 27 subjects respectively for the soft drink, candy bar, beverage, snack, and lunch product stimuli.

The data was collected using a two part questionnaire. In part one, subjects provided four measures of experience for each product in their stimulus set. These included the subject's recency of consumption, frequency of consumption, recency of purchase, and frequency of purchase for each product, all rated on five-point scales (past day, past week, past month, past year, and year or more for the recency of purchase and consumption questions; every day, every week, every month, every year, and never for the frequency of purchase and consumption questions). Given the high degree of reliability among these measures (principle component measurement loadings ranging from .865 to .998), we combined them into an equally weighted experience index for our analyses.

Near the end of part one, subjects were also asked to indicate which of the twelve products were in their consideration set. Subjects responded yes or no as to whether they would consider purchasing or consuming each option in the set. They were also asked to list any dietary or health considerations that may be driving their responses.

In part two of the questionnaire, the subjects rated the similarity of each possible pair of sixty-six products in the set. The pairs were rated on a scale from 0 (Very Dissimilar) to 10 (Very Similar). The stimuli were rated in one random order by half the subjects and in the reverse order by the remaining subjects throughout the study. There is general agreement that more prototypical category members are more similar, on average, to other category members than are less typical members (Barsalou 1983; Nosofsky 1988). Therefore, the average similarity judgments are used here to measure the typicality of each alternative within each stimulus set.

In a completely separate study conducted by one of the authors, 46 subjects provided both pair-wise similarity ratings and simple judgments of typicality for beverage products (brands of beer). The typicality measure computed from the similarity judgments and the direct prototypicality ratings were very highly correlated (r=.841), supporting the use of the similarity-based measure here. As a further step, we standardized this typicality measure within each stimulus set. This allows observed increases or decreases in prototypicality with experience to reflect differences beyond any base-line differences in prototypicality across the five stimulus sets.

TABLE 1
Stimulus Sets

Brand-Level Stimuli

Soft Drinks	Candy Bars
Sprite	Three Musketeers
Seven Up	Mars Bar
Diet Sprite	Milky Way
Diet Seven Up	Snickers
Orange Crush	M&M Plain
Diet Orange Crush	M&M Peanut
Coke Classic	Hershey's Plain
New Coke	Hershey's Almond
Pepsi	Nestle's Crunch
Cherry Coke	Reece's Peanut Butter Cups
Diet Coke	Twix Caramel
Diet Pepsi	Kit Kat

Category-Level Stimuli

Beverages	Snacks	Lunch Products
Ice Cream Soda	Popcorn	Carrot
Milk Shake	Nacho Chips	Apple
Chocolate Milk	Crackers	Fruit Juice
Milk	Potato Chips	Yogurt
Fruit Juice	Cheese	Milk
Lemonade	Grapes	Ice Cream
Soft Drink	Apple	Cookie
Diet Soft Drink	Yogurt	Candy Bar
Club Soda	Ice Cream	Soft Drink
Iced Tea	Cookie	Pizza
Bottled Water	Candy Bar	Chicken Sandwich
Iced Coffee	Brownie	Hamburger

Analyses

Two types of analyses were conducted in order to test hypotheses one and two. We first used regression models in which the dependent variables of interest were the size of each subject's consideration set and its average prototypicality. The independent variables of interest were the continuous experience index and the categorical level of the choice. As experience also varies with the level of choice (consumers have more experience with product category options than with brands), we conducted a second set of analyses. For each level of choice, k-means clustering was used to categorize the consumers into a group of relative experts and a group of relative novices. This assures that the groups differ maximally in experience. The hypotheses were then tested using ANOVA models involving an experience factor (experts versus novices) and a "level of choice" factor (brands versus categories). This analysis retains much of the experience-related information while limiting any confound between experience and choice level. According to the k-means clustering, there are 9 relative experts compared to 39 relative novices at the brand level ($F(1,46)=57.412$, $p<.001$) and 46 relative experts compared to 29 relative novices at the category level ($F(1,73)=129.459$, $p<.001$).

RESULTS

Effects of Experience on Consideration Set Size

The regression analysis demonstrates a significant overall increase in the size of the subjects' consideration sets with experience ($r=.639, p<.001$). Separate analysis of the brands and categories reveals an increase in set size with experience in both cases ($r=.265, p<.05$ for brand-level stimuli; $r=.588, p<.001$ for category-level stimuli). Further analysis within each of the five stimulus sets also reveals a relatively high level of consistency ($r=.531, p<.001$ for soft drinks; $r=.218$, not significant for candy bars; $r=.436, p<.05$ for beverages; $r=.333$, $p<.10$ for snacks; $r=.399$, $p<.05$ for lunch products).

The ANOVA results also reveal a general increase in consideration set size with experience ($F(1,119)=7.229$, $p<.01$). There was a significant increase in consideration set size with choice level ($F(1,119)=27.609$, $p<.001$), which is consistent with the increase in experience from brands to categories described earlier. There was no significant interaction between experience and level on set size. Overall these results support hypothesis one.

FIGURE 1
Effects of Experience on the Prototypicality of Consideration Sets for Brands Versus Categories

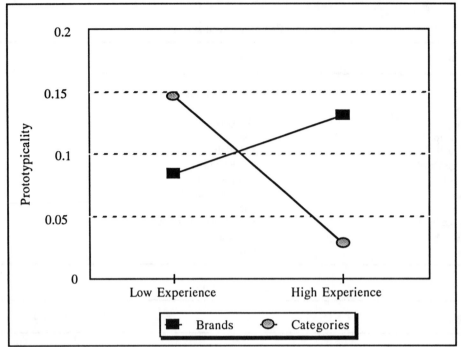

Effects of Experience on the Prototypicality of Alternatives

We now address whether the larger consideration sets for the more experienced consumers contained less prototypical alternatives. As expected, across conditions, consideration set membership tended to be more typical than atypical. Regression analysis was first used to examine the effects of the experience index, the two levels of choice (brands versus categories), and the interaction between experience and choice level on the average prototypicality of considered options. This model explained a significant degree of variance in prototypicality (r=.327, p<.01). There was a main effect of experience on prototypicality (t=2.239, p<.05) and no main effect for level. There was also a significant interaction between experience and choice level on prototypicality (t=-2.887, p<.01). Separate regressions reveal that the interaction is driven by a significant decrease in prototypicality with experience for the category-level stimuli (r=-.551; p<.001) with no corresponding effect for brands (r=.138, not significant). Analyses within each stimulus set also reveal no effect for the brands (r=.060, not significant for soft drinks; r=.007, not significant for candy bars) and negative effects for categories (r=-.031, not significant for beverages; r= -.287, p<.10 for snacks; r=-.326, p<.05 for lunch products).

A similar pattern of results emerges from the ANOVA model. There was no main effect for either brands versus categories or novices versus experts on prototypicality. The level by experience interaction was, however, significant (F(1,119)=6.093; p<.05). This interaction, depicted in Figure 1, shows a clear decrease in prototypicality with experience for the category-level stimuli (from .146 to .029; F(1,73)=27.487, p<.001). In contrast, there is a slight, though nonsignificant, increase in prototypicality with experience for the brands (from .084 to .131). This pattern of results supports hypothesis two. Increases in consumer experience result in a wider range of typical to atypical alternatives being considered, but only at the product category level.

Table 2 summarizes the results for consideration set size and average prototypicality of the consideration sets. Also included is the average number of products in the subjects' consideration sets that were relatively atypical (i.e., below zero on the standardized prototypicality measure). As the table clearly shows, consideration set size increases with experience for both brands and categories. For the brands, average prototypicality increases as the number of atypical members in a consideration set decreases from approximately three to two. For the categories, average prototypicality decreases as the number of atypical members in a set increases from approximately four to six.

When the number of atypical members is used as the dependent variable in the ANOVA model, the pattern of results is unchanged. The interaction involving level and experience is significant as is the increase in atypical alternatives considered for the categories from low experience (novice) to high experience (expert) consumers.

DISCUSSION

In their review of the dimensions of consumer expertise, Alba and Hutchinson (1987) proposed that consideration sets grow in a systematic fashion as consumers gain experience in a product domain. When needs are more general, experienced consumers consider a more heterogeneous or superordinate array of alternatives. When needs are more specific, experienced consumers consider a more homogeneous or subordinate array of alternatives. They also suggest that experts are more aware of atypical or ad hoc category alternatives and more likely to include these in their consideration set. Our discussion suggests that the prototypicality argument presumes a relatively general need and heterogeneous alternatives. While experience should increase the size of consideration sets for brand and categories alike, only the category-level sets should include an increasing proportion of atypical or ad hoc options. We report the results of an empirical study of consumer

TABLE 2
Consideration Set Size, Average Prototypicality, and Average Number of Atypical Alternatives Across Conditions

			Experience	
			Low Experience	High Experience
Stimulus Level	Brands	Set Size	8.538	9.333
		Prototypicality	0.084	0.131
		Atypical Alternatives	3.333	2.444
	Categories	Set Size	10.276	11.457
		Prototypicality	0.146	0.029
		Atypical Alternatives	4.345	6.304

non-durable food and beverage products which supports these predictions.

The study adds to a recent though growing body of literature which demonstrates systematic differences between brand- and category-level choice. It highlights the need to include both types of choices in any comprehensive study of consumer judgment and choice. The study also suggests that different choice models may be appropriate at the different choice levels because these models require identification of the size and composition of consumers' consideration sets (Hauser and Wernerfelt 1990). Naturally, our results may be limited to the types of products and procedures used. Our subjects chose from an externally provided lists of alternatives; the alternatives were not generated or evoked from memory. While our experience measures reflect the subjects' interactions with the products, they may not accurately reflect subject "expertise" or "awareness." Finally, it will be important to replicate the results in the context of more complex consumer durables and/or services.

At the same time, the study demonstrates that consideration sets behave differently at the brand and category levels and represent an important dimension of consumer judgment and choice. Alba and Hutchinson's (1987) prediction that expert consumers are more likely to be familiar with and consider relatively atypical options was not generally supported. As Table 2 shows, this prediction holds for category-level stimuli where both the average typicality of the consideration sets decreased and the number of atypical alternatives in the sets increased from novices to experts. This was not the case for brands where there is actually a slight increase in prototypicality and a corresponding decrease in the number of atypical alternatives considered from novices to experts.

REFERENCES

Alba, Joseph W. and J. Wesley Hutchinson (1987), "Dimensions of Consumer Expertise," *Journal of Consumer Research*, 13 (March), 411-454.

Barsalou, Lawrence W. (1983), "Ad Hoc Categories," *Memory & Cognition*, 11 (2), 211-227.

_____ (1985), "Ideals, Central Tendency, and Frequency of Instantiation as Determinants of Graded Structure," *Journal of Experimental Psychology: Learning, Memory, and Cognition*, 11 (October), 629-654.

Bettman, James R. and Mita Sujan (1987), "Effects of Framing on Evaluation of Comparable and Non-Comparable Alternatives by Expert and Novice Consumers," *Journal of Consumer Research*, 14 (September), 141-154.

Block, Lauren Goldberg and Michael D. Johnson (1995), "The Locus of Context Effects on Product Proximity Judgments," *International Journal of Research in Marketing*, 12 (1), 121-135.

Cantor, Nancy and Walter Mischel (1979), "Prototypes in Person Perception," in *Advances in Experimental Social Psychology*, Vol. 12, ed. L. Berkowitz, New York: Academic Press, 3-52.

Corfman, Kim P. (1991), "Comparability and Comparison Levels Used in Choices Among Consumer Products," *Journal of Marketing Research*, 28 (August), 368-374.

Glazer, Rashi, Barbara E. Kahn, and William L. Moore (1991), "The Influence of External Constraints on Brand Choice: The Lone-Alternative Effect," *Journal of Consumer Research*, 18 (June), 119-127.

Hauser, John R. and Birger Wernerfelt (1990), "An Evaluation Cost Model of Consideration Sets," *Journal of Consumer Research*, 16 (March), 393-408.

Howard, John A. (1977), *Consumer Behavior: Application of Theory*, New York: McGraw-Hill.

Johnson, Michael D. (1984), "Consumer Choice Strategies for Comparing Noncomparable Alternatives," *Journal of Consumer Research*, 11 (December), 741-753.

_____ (1988), "Comparability and Hierarchical Processing in Multialternative Choice," *Journal of Consumer Research*, 15 (December), 303-314.

_____ (1989), "The Differential Processing of Product Category and Noncomparable Choice Alternatives," *Journal of Consumer Research*, 16 (December), 300-309.

_____ and Claes Fornell (1987), "The Nature and Methodological Implications of the Cognitive Representation of Products," *Journal of Consumer Research*, 14 (September), 214-228.

_____, Donald R. Lehmann, Claes Fornell, and Daniel R. Horne (1992), "Attribute Abstraction, Feature-Dimensionality, and the Scaling of Product Similarities," *International Journal of Research in Marketing*, 9 (1), 131-147.

Loken, Barbara and James Ward (1990), "Alternative Approaches to Understanding the Determinants of Typicality," *Journal of Consumer Research*, 17 (September), 111-126.

Medin, Douglas L. and Edward E. Smith (1984), "Concepts and Concept Formation," *Annual Review of Psychology*, Vol. 35, 113-138.

Mervis, Carolyn B. and Eleanor Rosch (1981), "Categorization of Natural Objects," *Annual Review of Psychology*, Vol. 32, 89-115.

Nedungadi, Prakash (1990), "Recall and Consumer Consideration Sets: Influencing Choice without Altering Brand Evaluations," *Journal of Consumer Research*, 17 (December), 263-276.

Nosofsky, Richard M. (1988), "Similarity, Frequency, and Category Representations," *Journal of Experimental Psychology: Learning, Memory, and Cognition*, 14 (1), 54-65.

Park, C. Whan and Daniel C. Smith (1989), "Product-Level Choice: A Top-Down or Bottom-Up Process?," *Journal of Consumer Research*, 16 (December), 289-299.

Rokeach, Milton (1973), *The Nature of Human Values*, New York, NY: The Free Press.

Rosch, Eleanor (1975), "Cognitive Representations of Semantic Categories," *Journal of Experimental Psychology: General*, 104 192-233.

_____ (1977), "Human Categorization," in *Studies in Cross-Cultural Psychology*, Vol. 1, ed. N. Warren, London: Academic Press.

Simonson, Itamar (1989), "Choice Based on Reasons: The Case of Attraction and Compromise Effects," *Journal of Consumer Research*, 16 (September), 158-174.

Smith, Edward E. and Douglas L. Medin (1981), *Categories and Concepts*, Cambridge, MA: Harvard University Press.

Sujan, Mita (1985), "Consumer Knowledge: Effects on Evaluation Strategies Mediating Consumer Judgments," *Journal of Consumer Research*, 12 (June), 31-46.

Ward, James and Barbara Loken (1986), "The Quintessential Snack Food: Measurement of Product Prototypes," in *Advances in Consumer Research*, Vol. 13, ed. R. Lutz, Provo, UT: Association for Consumer Research, 126-131.

_____ and _____ (1988), "The Generality of Typicality Effects on Preference and Comparison: An Exploratory Test," in *Advances in Consumer Research*, Vol. 15, ed. M. J. Houston, Provo, UT: Association for Consumer Research, 55-61.

Wärneryd, Karl-Eric (1988), "Economic Psychology as a Field of Study," in *Handbook of Economic Psychology*, ed. W. F. van Raaij, G. M. van Veldhoven, and K.-E. Wärneryd, Dordrecht: Kluwer, 2-41.

Music, Meaning, and Magic: Revisiting Music Research
Wanda T. Wallace, Duke University

OVERVIEW

Music is regularly touted by advertisers as a way to achieve vitality, memorability, and excitement in an ad campaign, and it is commonly used in television advertising. Despite much enthusiasm about music research over the past several years, we have yet to develop consistent data and overall frameworks to guide research. The purpose of this session was to look again at music with the hope of stimulating new thought and beginning to resolve conflicting perspectives.

"Effect of Background Music on Visual Meaning and Memory"
Annabel J. Cohen, University of Prince Edward Island

Music plays an integral part in the experience of film but exactly how it contributes has been little explored or explained (Cohen, 1990, 1993, 1994). Anecdotal evidence suggests that music impacts upon the interpretation, memory, and sense of reality of the film. Through psychology experiments it is possible to specifically demonstrate some of these effects. A Congruence-Associationist framework for such explorations is proposed to encompass music and film stimuli that are often extremely complex (Marshall & Cohen, 1988; Bolivar, Cohen & Fentress, 1994). The framework considers separately two aspects of film and music: the formal or structural components and the meaning or associationist aspects. These aspects reflect both bottom-up (gestalt/structural) and top-down (higher-level, cognitive, associationist) processes respectively. The basic idea is that when music and film are structurally congruent (e.g., accent patterns are aligned), the associations or meanings of the music have greater impact overall; moreover, it is specifically proposed that the musical associations are directed to that part of the visual display that is in formal congruence with the music. Results from several experiments examining meaning and memory are considered in this context. It is maintained that the framework is useful for organizing the diverse data in this area and in generating new research. It is also suggested that this framework might be relevant to explaining the effects of music on attention and memory in television advertising.

"The Magic of Music: Affective Responses to Television Advertisements"
Wanda T. Wallace, Duke University
Julie A. Edell, Duke University
Marian C. Moore, Duke University

We examine how the presence of music and the presence of various musical structures affect consumers feelings about the ad, attitude toward the ad, and attitude toward the brand for 46 television advertisements. When music is present within an ad, warm feelings increase and uneasy feelings decrease. When music is prominently presented in the ad, upbeat feelings increase and disinterested feelings decrease. Musical structures such as major key, complex harmony, staccato rhythm, volume and tempo, familiarity of the music, and whether the brand name is sung significantly affect whether warm, upbeat, or uneasy feelings will be experienced. Not all structures act in the same manner. For example, a staccato rhythm diminishes warm feelings but increases upbeat feelings; however, the presence of familiar music increases both

warm and upbeat feelings. In addition, features such as music's prominence within the ad, changes in volume and tempo, dancing, and melodic repetition enhance the effects of the musical structures listed above on feeling responses, while music carrying the primary message suppresses the effects of the musical structures. Finally, musical structures significantly affect attitudes toward the ad and brand, in addition to the influence these structures exert on feelings.

"The Role of Music in Advertising: Does It Transform the Audience Experience"
Susan E. Heckler, University of Arizona
Dudley Blossom, University of Arizona

Drawing primarily from the work of Wallace (Wallace, 1994; Wallace, Edell and Moore, 1995; Wallace and Schulkind, 1996), Scott (1990), and work in Music Theory, three operational roles of music in television advertisements were proposed. These three roles are defined as follows: a) background in which music creates a feeling about the ad but not the product or brand; b) context in which music provides a frame of reference which helps the listener understand the advertised product or enhances product characteristics; and c) information in which music conveys specific product information or further defines product characteristics.

An exploratory study was conducted using two existing scales: the transformational scale (Puto & Wells, 1984; Puto, 1986; Puto and Hoyer, 1990; Puto, Julnes and Wooten, 1995) and the involvement scale (Zaichkowsky, 1985). Undergraduate marketing students viewed television advertisements selected by judges for their musical role and the appropriateness of the music for the Ss. Ss responded to the transformation and involvement scale items and to a series of open ended questions designed to support the ad selection and record the emotional response to the ad and music. Based on the findings, it appears that different operational roles of music in television advertisements result in altered levels transformation and involvement in the ads. Additional research is required, however, to ascertain the level of statistical significance of these findings.

"Framing the Complexity of Music"
Wanda T. Wallace, Duke University

Although there has been much interest in music's impact on marketing, research has not presented a consistent and coherent perspective. Using views from music theory and music cognition and perception, musical structures are grouped into the types of processes they evoke. These processes include creating positive/ negative reactions, adding energy, setting expectations, organizing and repeating at encoding, and encouraging elaboration and association. From the combination of these processes, four effects can be produced—emotional, memory, cognitive, and somatic effects. These effects are not independent of each other, and each is needed in order to understand how music influences consumers. Thus, we can observe that music can both increase recallability of lyrics but decrease cognitive processing of the lyrical message. Furthermore, as emotional responses to music increase, cognitive and memory processes may diminish. Therefore, in order to understand the effects that music exerts on consumers we need to examine a full range of effects and consider how these effects interact.

Discussant Comments
Morris Holbrook, Columbia University
Linda Scott, University of Illinois

First, in keeping with the theme of the conference, the audience was encouraged to think out of the box about music and to consider other aspects of music. Surprise is often a very effective persuasive device. In order to extend out knowledge of music, the audience was encouraged to consider music as more than a means to an end or an operational tool by examining aspects such as music as the product, the consumer's aesthetic responses, the perception, evaluation and emotion of music, the intrinsic value of music, and the experience of listening to music.

Second, the audience was reminded that music is not independent of its context. Furthermore, the structures and aspects of music as well as the responses to music should vary by culture. Thus, what one culture considers structure may not be important in another culture.

REFERENCES

Bolivar, V., Cohen, A. J. & Fentress, J. (1994), "Semantic and Formal Congruence and Effects of Film Music," *Psychomusicology*, 13, 28-59.

Cohen, A. J. (1994), "Introduction to the Special Issue on the Psychology of Film Music," *Psychomusicology*, 13, 2-8.

Cohen, A.J. (1993), "An Associationist Framework for Musical Soundtrack Phenomena," *Contemporary Music Review*, 9, 163-178.

Cohen, A. J. (1990), "Understanding Musical Soundtracks," *Empirical Studies of the Arts*, 111-124.

Marshall, S., & Cohen, A. J. (1988), "Effects of Musical Soundtracks on Attitudes Toward Animated Geometric Figures," *Music Perception*, 6, 95-112.

Puto, Christopher P. (1986), "Transformational Advertising: Just Another Name for Emotional Advertising or a New Approach?" *Consumer Psychology*, 4-6.

Puto, Christopher P., George Julnes and David Wooten (1995), "The Transformation Process in Psychology: Implications for Advertising," Work In Process.

Puto, Christopher P. and Robert Hoyer (1990), "Transformational Advertising: Current State of the Art," *Emotions in Advertising: Theoretical and Practical Explorations*, S. Agres, J. Edell, and T. Dubitsky (Eds.), New York: Greenwood Press, 69-80.

Puto, Christopher P. and William D. Wells (1984), "Informational and Transformational Advertising: the Differential Effects of Time," *Advances in Consumer Research*, 11, 638-643.

Scott, Linda M. (1990), "Understanding Jingles and Needledrop: A Rhetorical Approach to Music in Advertising," *Journal of Consumer Research*, 17 (September), 223-236.

Wallace, Wanda T. and Matthew Schulkind (1996), "Song Processing: Evidence from Indirect and Direct Memory Measures," Work in Process, Duke University.

Wallace, Wanda T. (1994), "Memory for Music: Effect of Melody on Recall of Text," *Journal of Experimental Psychology*, 20, 5, 1471-1485.

Wallace, Wanda T., Julie Edell and Marian Chapman Moore (1995), "The Magic of Music: Affective Responses to Music in Television Advertisements," Work in Process, Duke University.

Zaichkowsky, Judith Lynne (1985), "Measuring the Involvement Construct," *Journal of Consumer Research*, 12, 341-352.

Consumer Behavior and Public Health

Anthony D. Cox, Indiana University

Dena Cox, Indiana University

OVERVIEW

The health care system in the United States has profound problems. To begin with, it is enormously expensive, costing Americans about $1 trillion a year, or about $4,000 per capita, the highest rate in the world. These costs place an increasingly heavy financial burden on families, businesses and government. An uninsured family can rapidly be bankrupted by a serious medical problem (e.g. a coronary bypass operation can easily cost $50,000); the exploding costs of Medicaid (the federally-mandated health insurance for the poor, that is largely funded by the states) has thrown dozens of states in severe budget crises.

However, despite these enormous expenditures, the health of the American public lags behind that of many other countries. For example, Americans spend about 40% more per capita on health care than do Canadians, but Canadians live longer (U.S. Industrial Outlook 1994). Similarly, the infant mortality rate in the United States is higher than that of many other industrialized countries.

Why do such health problems persist despite these enormous health care expenditures? In many cases, the underlying cause is problematic consumer behavior. For example, the relatively high rate of infant mortality in the United States is largely traceable to counter-productive consumer behavior: Many new American mothers (particularly if they are young and poor) continue to consume alcohol and tobacco during and after pregnancy, feed both themselves and their children inadequate diets, and fail to get their young children immunized, even when immunizations are available for free. Similarly, the spread of AIDS occurs mainly through problematic consumer behaviors, such the failure to use condoms and the sharing of hypodermic needles among drug users.

Policy makers cannot effectively address these health problems unless they can change the underlying patterns of consumer behavior that contribute to them. This is where consumer researchers can make a crucial contribution. Each of the presentations in this special session explores ways in which consumer research can provide guidance to policy makers trying to solve these important public health problems.

Presentation 1:
Stage Models in Consumer Research: Lessons from Social Marketing

Alan R. Andreasen, Georgetown University

There is substantial evidence in the research literature that consumers do not undertake high involvement behavior changes in single steps. They go through a series of stages from indifference and ignorance through to action and commitment to the new behavior. Marketing scholars have referred to stage models in the past. However, their focus has been either on the "hierarchy of effects" of advertising and similar communications (e.g. Lavidge and Steiner 1961) or on the stages of adoption of new ideas (Rogers 1962, 1983).

In recent years, a number of researchers have developed generalized stage models to look at how people voluntarily change problematic behaviors such as smoking, using drugs, or overeating (e.g. Prochaska and DiClemente 1983). This work has established that (a) stages exist; (b) they can be identified by rather simple measurements, and (c) interventions tailored to particular stages will be more effective than interventions that do not make this distinction. Recently, Maibach (1995) and Andreasen (1995) have employed stage models as basic building blocks to their general approaches to social marketing.

The potential for using stage models to ground research in other areas of consumer behavior has been largely ignored. Yet, stage models can be extremely useful in understanding how consumers come to adopt new eating patterns, take up hobbies or other leisure pursuits, or settle into new patterns when they move to new communities.

This paper outlines the major characteristics of stage models. It summarizes some of the central findings in social marketing and then sets forth a generalized approach that can be used in a wide variety of consumer settings. A number of propositions for field and experimental research are set forth as means of testing these models in more conventional contexts. The paper concludes with recommendations for both researchers and consumer marketers.

Presentation 2:
Perceived Risk of Breast Cancer and Intention to Seek Mammograms

Anthony D. Cox, Indiana University

Dena Cox, Indiana University

In recent years business and political leaders have searched for ways to improve public health while controlling health care costs. Almost every proposal has called for an increased emphasis in the health care system on the prevention and early detection of disease. This shift makes great sense, both economically and medically. Many of the major killers in an industrialized society (e.g. high blood pressure, diabetes, and some cancers) can be detected through relatively inexpensive medical tests, and can be treated much more effectively and cheaply if they are detected early. However the successful implementation of a prevention/detection healthcare strategy represents a major marketing challenge: Persuading consumers who are feeling fine to expend money, time and effort on medical services (e.g., Pap smears, prostate exams) which may appear to offer no immediate benefits.

A good illustration of this challenge is the low rate of adoption of annual screening mammograms. Breast cancer is one of the leading causes of death among women (Miller and Champion 1993), and research indicates that screening mammography can greatly reduce the mortality rate of this disease (Reynolds and Jackson 1991). Yet most women either do not have mammograms at all, or have them less often than recommended by the National Cancer Institute (Lehrman et al. 1990). Why is this so? One possible explanation may be consumers' misperception of their own health risks: Women who shun screening mammograms may tend to underestimate their personal risk of contracting breast cancer (Stein et al. 1992; Lehrman et al. 1990; Vernon et al. 1990) and may tend to have a poor understanding of the risk factors for the disease. For example, there is evidence that as the age of women increases, their **perceived** susceptibility to breast cancer **decreases**, while in fact their **actual** risk **increases** dramatically (Vernon et al. 1993). This is consistent with psychological research indicating that consumers tend to have distorted (usually over-optimistic) perceptions of their own medical and other risks (Plous 1993, pp. 131-144).

This presentation discusses some survey findings regarding the determinants of older women's perceived risk of getting breast cancer, and how these risk perceptions affect their intentions to obtain a mammogram. The data yield some surprising results. Most notably, preliminary analysis suggest that women who perceive themselves as likely to get breast cancer are no more likely to intend to get a screening mammogram. Several interpretations for this finding are discussed, including the possibility that early detection of cancer may be perceived as (at best) a mixed blessing by consumers who perceive themselves to be at high risk.

Presentation 3:
Welfare Reform and Health Care for the Poor: Implications for Social Marketing
Ronald Paul Hill, University of Portland
Debra Lynn Stephens, University of Michigan

Following their defeat of the Democrats in the November 1994 elections, the House Republicans put forth 10 draft bills that make up their "Contract With America." One aspect of this proposed legislation, the Personal Responsibility Act (PRA), would reduce significantly the number of poor Americans on the welfare rolls as well as those currently receiving health insurance through the Medicaid program. However, research demonstrates that the relationship between welfare (Aid to Families with Dependent Children—AFDC) payments and receipt of Medicaid is more complex than policy makers realize.

Schneider (1993) found that the association between these two programs was asymmetrical, meaning that Medicaid spending has an impact on AFDC payments rather than the reverse. Others (see Hill and Macan 1996) have interpreted these results to suggest that poor women who value medical insurance are likely to seek and attempt to maintain AFDC eligibility in order to ensure health coverage. Further, Moffitt and Wolfe (1992) found that an extension of health insurance coverage to the poor would lead to a 25 percent reduction in AFDC caseloads.

This presentation examines research involving welfare mothers and their consumer survival strategies within the current and proposed welfare systems. Further, we will examine this ongoing debate from a historical perspective and submit evidence that demonstrates the failure of proposed reform measures to eliminate/reduce poverty, solve health care dilemmas faced by the poor, or control government spending. The close will advance social marketing implications that may help resolve these failures. Specifically, we will advance the development of outreach programs that encourage the poor to apply for health insurance coverage while simultaneously allowing them to seek employment.

DISCUSSION

As the presentations in this session illustrate, consumer researchers can make significant contributions to understanding serious public health problems. However, consumer researchers wishing to investigate these issues may need to adopt some unaccustomed ways of thinking about consumers and consumer behavior. First, while much traditional consumer research focuses on selective demand (e.g. brand choice, store patronage) public health issues are more likely to relate to primary consumer demand; e.g., consumption of tobacco products, or alcohol, or firearms, or (on the positive side) use of mammograms or immunizations. Second, while traditional marketing strategies tend to focus on research attention on the most *receptive* consumers (i.e., "the best prospects" for one's product), those in public health often must try to reach the most *resistant* consumers, e.g. the "hard core" 25% of the adult population that continues to smoke. Finally, while affluent con-

sumers generally receive the most attention from marketing researchers (and indeed, some definitions of a "market" includes the ability to spend money to satisfy one's needs), those in public health are often most interested in reaching consumers with the *least* income and education, among whom many high risk consumer behaviors are most prevalent. Thus while consumer researchers have many skills that can be useful in addressing public health problems, doing so will involve changing many of the perspectives traditional consumer research.

REFERENCES

Andreasen, Alan (1995), *Marketing Social Change: Changing Behavior to Promote Health, Social Development and the Environment*, San Francisco: Jossey-Bass.

Hill, Ronald Paul and Sandi Macan (1996), "Consumer Survival on Welfare With an Emphasis on Medicaid and the Food Stamp Program," *Journal of Public Policy & Marketing*, 15 (Spring), forthcoming.

Lavidge, R. and G. Steiner (1961), "A Model for Predictive Measurements of Advertising Effectiveness," *Journal of Marketing*, 25 (Oct.), 59-62.

Lehrman, C., B. Reimer, B. Troch, A. Balshem, P. Engstrom (1990), "Factors Associated With Repeat Adherence to Breast Cancer Screening," *Preventive Medicine*, 19, 279-290.

Maibach, E. and R. Parrott (1995), *Designing Health Messages: Approaches from Communication Theory and Public Health Practice*, Thousand Oaks, CA: Sage Publications.

Miller, A. and V. Champion (1993), "Mammography in Women 50 Years of Age," *Cancer Nursing*, 16(4), 260-269.

Moffitt, Robert and Barbara L. Wolfe (1992), "The Effect of the Medicaid Program on Welfare Participation and Labor Supply," *Review of Economics and Statistics*, 74 (4), 615-626.

Plous, S., (1993), *The Psychology of Judgment and Decision Making*. Philadelphia, PA: Temple University Press.

Prochaska, J.O. and C.C. DiClemente (1983), "Stages and Processes of Self-Change of Smoking: Toward an Integrative Model of Change," *Journal of Consulting and Clinical Psychology*, 51 (3), 390-5.

Reynolds, H. and V. Jackson (1991), "Self-Referred Mammography Patients: Analysis of Patients' Characteristics," *American Journal of Radiology*, 157, 481-484.

Rogers, E. (1962, 1983), *Diffusion of Innovations*, New York: Free Press.

Schneider, Saundra K. (1993), "Examining the Relationship Between Public Policies: AFDC and Medicaid," *Public Administration Review*, 53 (July/August), 368-380.

Stein, J., S. Fox, P. Murata, D. Morisky (1992), "Mammography Usage and the Health Belief Model," *Health Education Quarterly*, 19(4), 447-462.

Vernon, S., E. LaVille, G. Jackson (1990), "Participation in Breast Cancer Screening Programs: A Review," *Social Science and Medicine*, 30(10), 1107-1118.

Welfare Reform and Health Care for the Poor: Implications for Social Marketing

Ronald Paul Hill, University of Portland
Debra Lynn Stephens, University of Michigan

ABSTRACT

This paper examines consumer survival on welfare within the context of a history of modern welfare policy that demonstrates its cyclical nature. An analysis of poor families' consumer needs is delineated with special attention paid to health as it is impacted by the largest government program in this area, Medicaid. We close with consumer-based policy implications designed to meet the requirements of financially-disadvantaged families. The reader is directed to Hill and Macan (1996) for a more extensive discussion of this topic.

HISTORY OF MODERN WELFARE POLICY

Historically, welfare policies in the United States were rooted in the English Poor Laws of 1601 (Cunningham 1993). Value judgments that categorized the poor as either "deserving" or "undeserving" emerged from these early laws, and assistance was set at a level below the lowest attainable income an "able-bodied" person could earn. Further, assistance typically was provided through almshouses, and, in several states, the indenture, apprenticing, or placement in orphanages of children living in poverty was sanctioned (Turner 1993).

Such policies became noticeably inadequate as the economy collapsed and social conditions deteriorated during the Great Depression of the 1930s. The segment of the population living in poverty changed dramatically to include many members of the working class, causing a shift in focus away from the worthy versus unworthy debate to a perceived need for protection from the uncontrollable negative events of life (Turner 1993). On June 8, 1934, in an effort to address this national crisis, President Franklin D. Roosevelt articulated a new social agenda for the federal government that included basic "consumer" security.

> This security for the individual and for the family concerns itself with three factors. People want decent homes to live in; they want to locate them where they can engage in productive work; and they want some safeguard against misfortunes which cannot be wholly eliminated in this manmade world of ours. (Cohen 1985, pp. 136-138).

In order to flesh out the details of this agenda, FDR created the Committee on Economic Security on June 29, 1934. The Committee's report, which was sent to the President on January 15, 1935, recommended that the federal government safeguard the citizenry against "the major hazards and vicissitudes of life," including unemployment, old age, poor health, loss of the family breadwinner, industrial accidents, and lack of training (National Conference on Social Welfare 1985). Further, the Committee believed that measures designed to support this goal would reduce the total costs to society of poverty without generating unnecessary dependence.

Using the Committee's recommendations as a basis, FDR forwarded the Social Security Act to Congress, which was quickly passed into law on August 14, 1935. This Act established a two-tier system of support (Bonnar 1985). The first tier is the now familiar contributory insurance program that provides old-age annuities and unemployment insurance. The second tier, conceived of as an extension of the historic means-tested approach to helping the poor, is a residual program designed to support those who meet eligibility requirements for need but are not covered by the first-tier program.

Title IV of the Social Security Act, "Grants to States for Aid to Dependent Children" (ADC), was the predecessor of the current AFDC program. Section 406 specified that ADC was designed to provide monetary payments to:

> ...a child under the age of sixteen who has been deprived of parental support or care by reason of the death, continued absence from home, or physical or mental incapacity of a parent, and who is living with the father, mother, grandfather, grandmother, brother, sister, stepfather, stepmother, stepbrother, stepsister, uncle, or aunt, in a place of residence maintained by one or more of such relatives as his or their own home.

As is true today, this portion of the Act was implemented by extending grants for aid to the individual states so that they could continue to give support through programs currently in place. Each state was allowed to establish criteria for eligibility and payment amounts, resulting in significant differences in both throughout the nation.

For the most part, the principle of less eligibility discussed earlier was used as the guiding tenet in aid provision, especially in the southern states where discrimination against African-Americans was common (Turner 1993). In a study of the average costs for families with two children living simply, the Work Progress Administration (WPA) determined that $1347 a year was a maintenance annual income level and $930 was the bare minimum for survival during the mid-1930s. However, welfare payments per family averaged only $381 during this same period. Additionally, many states established qualifying standards that resulted in the approval for aid of only "deserving" widows who maintained a "suitable" home that fostered religious values in their children.

By the end of the Great Depression, the federal government concentrated its attention on the war effort and, once the war was over, on stimulating a healthy post-war economy (U.S. Department of Health and Human Services 1985). The resulting prosperity and conservative political environment, combined with a shift in the ADC population from widows and orphans to persons of color and out-of-wedlock births, caused negative reactions among members of the rising middle class (Bell 1965; Cunningham 1993). Public support for the provision of welfare waned, and, in August, 1950, the Social Security Act was amended, in part, to reflect changing middle-class attitudes. For example, the amendment required states to notify law enforcement officials of fathers who deserted their families so that they could be prosecuted. If the recipient refused to give permission for this notification, benefits could be terminated.

The social protests and civil rights movement of the 1960s resulted in a renewed emphasis on the poverty population (Turner 1993). Social activists, such as members of the National Welfare Rights Organization (NWRO), rose up in support of welfare recipients and focussed on reducing the stigma associated with relief payments. Consistent with these views, the Kennedy administration laid the foundation for a new welfare system based on the provision of more extensive services and rehabilitation leading to self-sufficiency (Burgess and Price 1963). In 1962, Title IV of the Social Security Act was renamed "Aid to Families with Dependent

Children" (AFDC), and it was amended to allow for assistance to a second adult in the home, the provision of support services such as day care, and earned income that would not reduce benefits in order to encourage employment.

After Kennedy's assassination, Johnson launched the "War on Poverty." The Civil Rights Act subsequently was passed into law on July 3, 1964, followed by the establishment of the Economic Opportunity Act, insurance programs such as Medicare and Medicaid, and the Food Stamp Program. With this renewed interest in serving the poor, the number of families receiving welfare doubled between 1965 and 1970 (U.S. Dept. of Health and Human Services 1985). Nonetheless, the average annual AFDC payments per family were $1643 and $2285 in 1965 and 1970 respectively, far below the established poverty levels of $3223 and $3968 for the same years.

By 1977 the AFDC rolls doubled again, reaching 3,523,000. Approximately 80 percent of recipients lived in urban areas, and the majority of families were headed by single females, many of whom were women of color. When the Republicans captured the presidency and the senate in 1980, their conservative agenda included a plan to lessen federal involvement in welfare programs and to reduce the absolute number of recipients (Glazer 1984; Gilder 1981; Kristol 1985; Murray 1984). The 1990s have been an extension of this downward trend, with a focus on budgetary savings through reduced dependency (Greenstein 1992). In 1991 alone, 40 different states froze or reduced AFDC benefits, and 12 states trimmed special needs payments such as emergency assistance for homeless families. These efforts have reduced payments to the point where AFDC and food stamp disbursements combined are below the 1960 level for welfare relief in constant dollars.

HEATH CARE AMONG THE POOR

Most of the research in the area of welfare reform and health has focussed on the Medicaid Program, which was established in 1965 as Title XIX of the Social Security Act (Gurny, Baugh, and Davis 1992). This entitlement program is a cooperative venture of the federal and state governments, and all AFDC recipients are eligible for its health insurance coverage. The resulting relationship between AFDC and Medicaid expenditures has been controversial, but research indicates that the association is asymmetrical. Thus, Medicaid spending has a significant impact on AFDC spending, but the reverse is not true (Schneider 1993, p.375).

These finding suggest that poor women who value medical insurance are likely to seek and attempt to maintain AFDC eligibility in order to ensure health coverage (Blank 1989). Therefore, the lack of health insurance in many low-paying jobs combined with the mental and physical health problems associated with poverty decrease the likelihood that the head of household will work and increase the likelihood that s/he will be on AFDC (Moffitt and Wolfe 1992; 1993). Such dire circumstances are exacerbated when one or more of the children are disabled, further limiting the parent's ability to work and increasing the need for health insurance (Wolfe and Hill 1995). The unfortunate result is chronic unemployment, low self-esteem, and a cycle of poverty.

Changing regulations brought on by welfare reform designed to reduce expenditures rather than serve the poor often resulted in confusion concerning eligibility. Many people living in poverty frequently were reluctant to confront the bureaucratic maze of procedures and paper work to determine their status. Furthermore, like AFDC, Medicaid has become stigmatized and many among the poor believe that they often receive less than high-quality care. A review of the literature by Rosenbach (1993) revealed that some health care providers are reluctant to extend services to Medicaid

participants because of concerns over malpractice and low reimbursement rates.

This problem particularly is acute for the poor when they need to access medical specialists for problems that are beyond the expertise of primary care physicians or their assistants (Colle and Grossman 1978). However, while low-income children average 2.7 doctor visits per year compared with 3.3 for the non-poor, those children on Medicaid average 2.9 visits compared with the non-insured's mean of 1.8 (Rosenbach 1993). Thus, although poor children are at greater risk for severe illnesses that end in hospitalization and/or death, those on Medicaid have the opportunity to utilize medical services/preventative checkups that reduce their susceptibility to more acute health problems.

CONSUMER-BASED IMPLICATIONS

To end the cycle of poverty that has captured the lives of millions of poor Americans, policy makers must move beyond judgmental rhetoric to action-oriented solutions that are truly consumer-based. These solutions must consider the situational realities of welfare recipients from *their* perspective rather than through the clouded lens of middle-class mores. Only then will legislation be designed and implemented that provides people in poverty with the ability to acquire the basic consumer products that are necessary to ensure physical and mental health.

According to a 1992 study, 31 million Americans are without any form of health insurance, and most of these people are members of the lowest income groups in our society (Mills and Blank 1992). For these individuals as well as for society, their lack of insurance may have serious consequences. For example, many among the uninsured fail to get treatment for illnesses or injuries until their problems have progressed into serious or life-threatening conditions, leading to higher medical costs which must be absorbed by the health-care system (see Hill 1991 for a specific illustration).

A system needs to be developed to provide health insurance to welfare recipients *and* the working poor in order to reduce the ultimate cost of care and improve the quality of their lives. Since research shows that the more employable AFDC recipients have fewer health care needs, the most cost effective policy may be simply to provide Medicaid coverage to all poor citizens (Rofuth and Weiss 1991). Moffitt and Wolfe (1992) found that an extension of health insurance coverage would lead to a 25 percent reduction in AFDC caseloads.

Nonetheless, this reform has significant difficulties from an implementation perspective. Currently, the Medicaid program varies from state to state since individual states have the discretion to set eligibility levels, to determine what services are available, and to define reimbursement policies. Such variability and complexity often lead to confusion regarding eligibility and benefits, particularly among those with lower levels of education and literacy. Further, there is little physician interest in treating Medicaid patients due to reimbursement levels of only 56 percent of the average national charge (Mills and Blank 1992). As a result, many of these areas do not have enough health care professionals to service the clients who are on Medicaid (see Scammon et al. 1995 for more on problems involving the supply of providers).

Thus, reform to the Medicaid system must make the poor *eligible* for health insurance coverage as well as make *utilization* of this insurance easier. One tactic would involve the development of outreach programs in poverty communities (e.g., through churches, schools, community centers) to encourage the poor to apply for coverage. An additional way of improving access includes developing/expanding federal programs to place health care professionals in needy communities. For example, the National Health

Service Corp provides financial assistance for medical students, who repay these loans by working in depressed areas in need of medical personnel (Scammon et al. 1995).

REFERENCES

Bell, W. (1965), *Contemporary Social Welfare*, New York: Maximillian Publishing Co., Inc.

Blank, Rebecca M. (1989), "The Effect of Medicaid Need and Medicaid on AFDC Participation," *Journal of Human Resources*, 24 (Winter), 54-87.

Bonnar, D.E. (1984), *When the Bough Breaks: A Feminist Analysis of Income Maintenance Strategies for Female Based Households*, Boston: Brandeis University Press.

Burgess, E.M. and D.O. Price (1963), *An American Dependency Challenge*, Chicago: American Public Welfare Association.

Cohen, W. (1985), "The Social Security Act of 1935: Reflections Fifty Years Later," *The Report of the Committee on Economic Security*, Washington D.C.: National Conference on Social Welfare.

Colle, A. D. and M. Grossman (1978), "Determinants of Pediatric Care Utilization," *Journal of Human Resources*, 13, 115-158.

Cunningham, Patrick M. (1993), *Welfare Reform: A Response to Unemployed Two-Parent Families*, New York: Garland Publishing, Inc.

Glazer, N. (1984), "Social Policy of the Reagan Administration: A Review," *Public Interest*, 75, 76-98.

Gilder, G. (1981), *Wealth and Poverty*, New York: Basic Books.

Greenstein, Robert (1992), "Cutting Benefits vs. Changing Behavior," *Public Welfare*, Spring, 22-23.
22-23.

Gurny, Paul, David K. Baugh, and Feather Ann Davis (1992), "Chapter 10: A Description of Medicaid Eligibility," *Health Care Financing Review/1992 Annual Supplement*, 207-225.

Hill, Ronald Paul (1991), "Health Care and the Homeless: A Marketing-Oriented Approach," *Journal of Health Care Marketing*, 11 (June), 14-23.

Hill, Ronald Paul and Sandi Macan (1996), "Consumer Survival on Welfare With an Emphasis on Medicaid and the Food Stamp Program," *Journal of Public Policy & Marketing*, 15 (Spring), 118-127.

Kristol, I. (1985) "Skepticism, Meliorism and Public Interest," *Public Interest*, 81, 31-40.

Mills, Miriam K. and Robert H. Blank (1992), *Health Insurance and Public Policy: Risk, Allocation, and Equity*, Westport, CT: Greenwood Press.

Moffitt, Robert and Barbara L. Wolfe (1992), "The Effect of the Medicaid Program on Welfare Participation and Labor Supply," *Review of Economics and Statistics*, 74 (4), 615-626.

Moffitt, Robert and Barbara L. Wolfe (1993), "Medicaid, Welfare Dependency, and Work: Is There a Casual Link?" *Health Care Financing Review*, 15 (Fall), 123-133.

Murray, C. (1984), *Losing Ground*, New York: Basic Books.

National Conference on Social Welfare (1985), *The Report of the Committee on Economic Security of 1935*, Washington D.C.

Rofuth, Todd W. and Henry Weiss (1991), "Extending Health Care to AFDC Recipients Who Obtain Jobs: Results of a Demonstration," *Health and Social Work*, 16 (August), 162-169.

Rosenbach, Margo L. (1993), *The Use of Physicians' Services by Low-Income Children*, New York: Garland Publishers Inc.

Scammon, Debra L., Lawrence B. Li, and Scott D. Williams (1995), "Increasing the Supply of Providers for the Medically Underserved: Marketing and Public Policy Issues," *Journal of Public Policy & Marketing*, 14 (Spring), 35-47.

Schneider, Saundra K. (1993), "Examining the Relationship Between Public Policies: AFDC and Medicaid," *Public Administration Review*, 53 (July/August), 368-380.

Turner, Bobbie Green (1993), *Federal/State Aid to Dependent Children Program and Its Benefits to Black Children in America 1935-1985*, New York: Garland Publishing, Inc.

U.S. Department of Health and Human Services (1985), "Social Security Partnership with Tomorrow–50th Anniversary," *Social Security Bulletin*, 48(8), 461-380: 2002, Washington DC: U.S. Government Printing Office.

Wolfe, Barbara L. and Steven C. Hill (1995), "The Effect of Health on the Work Effort of Single Mothers," *Journal of Human Resources*, 30 (Winter), 42-62.

Consumers and Brand Meaning: Brands, the Self and Others
Albert M. Muniz, Jr., University of Illinois, Urbana-Champaign

OVERVIEW OF SESSION

This session was strongly integrated around the theme of brand meaning. Brands are complex social entities. Yet little is understood about the social processes surrounding the creation of brand meaning. The papers presented in this session examined the important and pervasive role that brands have in the social fabric of consumers' lives, as well as the processes surrounding the development of brand meaning, influences on this meaning development and consumer uses of brand meaning. Drawing from multiple theoretical perspectives (self-concept, symbolic interaction, community) and methodological orientations (informant narratives, depth interviews, participant observation, artifactual analysis, photo-elicitation/autodriving) the authors provided empirical evidence of the multiple ways in which consumers ascribe meaning to brands. These processes include: the symbolic interpretation of brand-related information, community-based negotiation of brand-related information, and the construction of personal narratives based on experiences with the brand.

What a Brand Means: A Symbolic Interactionist Perspective
Jennifer E. Chang

A consumer's preference for a certain brand often depends on what it "means" to that consumer (e.g., Levy 1959; Reynolds and Gutman 1984). While seemingly straightforward, the actual process of developing a brand's meaning is complex and dynamic due to the multitude of brand-related symbols with which a consumer interacts over time. While the nuances of this process have been discussed conceptually (Levy 1959; 1978), they have remained largely unexplored empirically. Moreover, with a few exceptions (e.g., Richins 1994; Solomon 1983), studies to date have focused on the impact of a single influence on brand/product meaning or image (e.g., Kotler 1973-74 on store atmospherics impacting brand image; Olsen 1995 on kinship relations impacting brand meaning). This paper, using qualitative methodology, empirically examined the multiple symbols and intricate processes by which brand meanings are developed. In particular, it was demonstrated that symbols from both public and private influences interact and ultimately impact the consumer's development of brand meaning.

This research draws from sociological and social psychological theories of symbolic interactionism. These theories suggest that an individual is always surrounded by an environment of interpretable symbols. Interactions with such symbols continually define and redefine the meaning of objects over time (Blumer 1969; Mead 1934). Translated into the marketing context, the consumer formulates the meaning of a brand through a rich negotiative process of symbolic interpretation. For instance, packaging symbolizes the brand through shape, size, and color, just as the kinds of consumption experiences (e.g., outdoors, among certain people) characterize other dimensions of the brand's meaning. The integration of such symbols provides a more complete picture of the meaning than considering symbols in isolation.

To understand empirically how consumers give brands meanings, participant-observation, artifactual analysis, and photo elicitation techniques were used within the dinner context. The understanding of a consumer's symbolic encounters in both real time (e.g., actual brand usage) and through reflection (using photos to elicit information) help define a framework with the richness and depth that can account for the process of meaning development. The data thus far have helped define an emerging framework. For example, in understanding Snapple's meaning to particular consumers, both marketer-driven public sources of meaning and idiosyncratic private sources of meaning are evident. The former include advertisements (e.g., "Made from the best stuff on earth"), product placements (e.g., "Seinfeld cast gossiping and swigging), earthy packaging and store atmospherics. Such sources of meaning are symbols of the brand, as are their constituents (e.g., props, actors, color). The latter include kinship relations (e.g., brand as a family totem), and phases of the consumption experience (e.g., displaying Snapple bottles on kitchen shelves). As suggested, the interplay between the symbols adds dimensions to the brand's meaning. Over time, new symbols (e.g., changes in social groups) reinforce or alter the meaning(s) established. The framework and theories also afford subsequent investigations of when public versus private are more salient in defining "what a brand means".

Brand Community and the Negotiation of Brand Meaning
Albert M. Muniz, Jr.

Brands attach meaning to a good. This may be the most important function of branding as it allows marketers to differentiate otherwise identical products. However, consumers do not simply accept the brand as presented by marketers in toto. Consumers, in social groupings, play an important role in the creation of brand meaning. While the field has recognized this, little attention has been paid to the processes surrounding this meaning creation. This paper presented results from an ethnographic study that examined how consumers, as members of brand communities, negotiate the meaning of brands. Data from personal interviews and World Wide Web "home pages" revealed four processes by which members of brand communities socially negotiate brand meaning: recognizing the community aspect of the brand, sharing personal experiences with the brand, emphasizing aspects of brand meaning, and rejecting aspects of brand meaning.

Sociologists have long recognized the role that others play in the creation of knowledge (Berger and Luckman 1966) and meaning (Anderson and Meyer 1988). Consumers, in social groupings, and through social processes regularly create, maintain and "reinvent" brands, just as they do any piece of information. Moreover, specific groups of consumers adhere to certain, fixed, interpretive strategies. These strategies guide the interpretation of any piece of information (Iser 1980; Fish 1980; Radway 1984). Muniz and O'Guinn (1995) suggested that communities coalesce around certain brands. These "brand communities" share many characteristics with communities as they have traditionally been defined by sociologists (Gussfield 1975; Tonnies 1957) and, subsequently, may influence the construction of brand meaning.

Ethnographic fieldwork was conducted to examine the processes by which members of brand communities create meaning for brands. This fieldwork was conducted in two distinct settings. First, members of households from two neighborhoods in a medium-sized Midwestern town were interviewed and observed regarding their experiences with brands and other consumers over a six-month period. This approach provided insight into the ways that brand communities are manifest in the "everyday" lives of consumers. Second, the content of consumer-created home pages devoted to several brands were downloaded and analyzed. The World Wide Web was chosen as this medium allows consumers the ability to form cohesive communities that transcend geographic limitations. Analysis of this data demonstrates the important role that groups play in the creation of brand meaning. Four processes by which members of brand communities socially construct brand meaning were encountered: recognizing the community aspect of the brand, sharing personal experiences with the brand, emphasizing aspects of the brand's meaning and rejecting aspects of the brand's meaning. The pervasiveness of these phenomena suggest that what the consumer does with the brand is at least as important as the variables manipulated by marketers in the production of brand meaning.

Meaningful Self-Brand Connections and Consumer Product Experience Stories
Jennifer Edson Escalas

Consumers value products and brands for different reasons. One reason may be for a product's instrumental features or attributes, which provide tangible benefits (e.g., cars provide transportation and salt adds flavor to food). A second major reason is that sometimes consumers form a special, meaningful connection with products or brands, so that these products come to signify more than just the sum of their features. These brands may take on symbolic meaning, represent who one is or wants to be, communicate some aspect of self to others, and become significantly related to consumers' mental representations of self (e.g., Belk 1988; Belk, Wallendorf, and Sherry 1989; McCracken 1986; Ball and Tasaki 1992; Richins 1994; Kleine, Kleine, and Allen 1995). Meaningful self-brand connections are conceptualized to represent this type of bond between consumers and brands. In order to measure meaningful connections, a ten item scale was developed. The steps taken to create this scale were presented, along with experimental evidence of its reliability, convergent validity, and nomological validity.

While the meaningful self-brand connection scale attempts to measure brands that are symbolically significant to consumers' self-concepts, little is known about the processes by which brands become meaningful in the first place. On a broader scale, people make sense of their lives via narrative thought (e.g., Bruner 1986, 1990; Gergen & Gergen 1988; Polkinghorne 1991). Through the structure of narrative thought, specifically spatio-temporal dimensionality and causal inferences, people organize their experiences, understand others, and create their own identities. In the realm of consumer behavior, consumers construct narratives involving brands. These narratives create meaning and build a connection between the brand and the consumer's self-concept. These stories may arise spontaneously in response to a product usage situation, or may be encouraged and influenced by marketing communications, such as through the use of drama ads that tell a story.

Given that consumers create meaning through narratives, 122 consumer stories about product experiences over a range of meaningful self-brand connection scores were gathered and analyzed, to obtain qualitative support for the meaningful self-brand connection scale. The results are encouraging. Consumers with strong, positive meaningful self-brand connections wrote stories that included themes of the brand having a congruent image with their own self-concept, connections to important people in their lives, and expressed affection towards the brand. Consumers with strong, negative meaningful self-brand connections wrote stories that included themes of the brand representing an aspect of themselves that they didn't want to be a part of them (for example, who they were at an earlier stage in their lives; unwanted gifts; and rejection of the type of person who was the prototypical user of the brand).

Consumers lacking in meaningful connections with the brands wrote about positive and negative product features and wrote shorter, less well-developed stories. Furthermore, these stories make reference to advertising campaigns and brand spokespeople, providing some indication of how marketing communications influence personal brand experiences and meaning.

Synthesis of Session
John F. Sherry, Jr.

The need for consumer-centered understandings of brand image cannot be overstated. Many believe that business schools have become experts at producing MBAs–Murderers of Brand Associations. Business students and academic researchers need to pay more attention to what consumers do with brands. Frequently, the actions of consumers are just as important as those of marketers in determining a brand's image. The papers presented in this session represent the first steps in increasing our understandings of these consumer-generated processes.

Community and Canon: A Foundation for Mature Interpretive Research

Val Larsen, Truman State University
Newell D. Wright, James Madison University

ABSTRACT

This article argues that though its achievements are obvious, interpretive research is built upon an unstable epistemological foundation, the "method of authority." It suggests that interpretive research can be fully credible only if it is grounded in the evolving consensus of an informed interpretive community. And this informed consensus can develop only if an essential element of research infrastructure is established—a canon of texts that can be interpreted and reinterpreted by the research community. The article models the kind of reinterpretation it urges by taking a second look at Mr. Ed's Elephant Museum and Roadside Attraction.

In recent years, interpretive research has so enriched our understanding of consumer behavior that, in our view, the value of thick descriptions of consumer behavior is firmly established. But its achievements notwithstanding, interpretive research is built, we believe, upon an unstable epistemological foundation—what C.S. Pierce (1934) has called the "method of authority." In this paper we argue that interpretive research can be fully credible only if it is grounded in the evolving consensus of an informed interpretive community. And this informed consensus can develop only if an essential element of research infrastructure is established—a canon of texts that can be interpreted and reinterpreted by the research community.

CRITIQUE OF CURRENT FOUNDATIONS OF INTERPRETIVISM

The major weaknesses of the current approach to interpretive research are apparent in the pioneering articles that helped make naturalistic inquiry (Lincoln and Guba 1985) possible in consumer research, e.g., Hirschman (1986), Wallendorf and Belk (1989). We focus our critique on Wallendorf and Belk's "Assessing Trustworthiness in Naturalistic Consumer Research," but what we say generally applies to other founding documents as well. The problems begin with the central metaphor of these papers: the researcher as instrument. If we take this metaphor seriously, then the credibility of each interpretivist study hangs entirely upon the trustworthiness of the researcher. If the researcher-instrument is not a reliable and valid measure, then the study has little value. The authority of the researcher thus becomes the paramount epistemological problem of interpretive research—in our view, an insoluble problem.

Building upon Lincoln and Guba (1985), Wallendorf and Belk (1989) attempt to address this problem by prescribing a methodological fix—a set of procedures that may help establish the trustworthiness of the researcher. Some of these procedures are designed to ensure that the researcher adequately immerses him or herself in the data. These include injunctions to triangulate across informants, to analyze negative cases, and to engage informants over a prolonged period of time. Other procedures—internal team audits, external peer audits, and member checks—are designed to intersubjectively certify the trustworthiness of the researcher. These procedures permit the researcher to say, in effect, "you should trust my interpretation because other team members, an external peer, and my informants say that it is trustworthy." In other words, the authority of a small group supplants that of the individual re-searcher. The epistemological foundation remains the same, however: Pierce's dubious "method of authority."

Wallendorf and Belk are too sophisticated and experienced to suppose that procedures such as the ones they prescribe can ensure the overall quality of interpretive research. Apparently somewhat uncomfortable with their methodological solution, they state at the beginning of their paper that no set of prescriptions can guarantee novel and interesting insights. Indeed, they say that "a list of 'How-to' steps is likely to negate the spontaneity and serendipity that guide good research. It is our personal experience that such ideas are much more likely to emerge from playfulness and openness than from mechanistic procedures" (p. 69). And yet, after conceding, finally, that "merely following the procedures we outline here would likely produce a rather boring output," they devote the bulk of their paper to developing the list of how-to steps that would produce that boring output, steps that have since become, in some measure, standard practice.

Why did this happen? Why did Wallendorf and Belk focus on the relatively unimportant how-to list rather than on the openness and play that they consider more important? For two reasons, we believe. First, they were boxed in by the unfortunate researcher-instrument metaphor. If the researcher must mediate our encounter with the data, then the issue of researcher trustworthiness (reliability) must be addressed. Second, and more importantly, they were compelled by the rhetorical context at the time—by the dominance of positivism and the skepticism of positivistic researchers—to develop a methodology that might warrant interpretive findings as the experimental method warrants positivistic findings. The new interpretivist paradigm had to be sold in a language and mode of thought that had positivistic analogs—and that meant an emphasis on method (Holt 1991). If Hirschman (1986), Wallendorf and Belk (1989), and others had not been persuasive, if subsequent interpretivist research had not proven to be deeply insightful, there would have been no occasion to write this paper.

Let us restate, then, our assessment of our current problem. The researcher-instrument metaphor was probably a rhetorical necessity early on. But it makes the validity of interpretivist research depend upon the personal authority of the researcher. It thus grounds interpretivist research in the dubious method of authority. (Holt [1991] has persuasively argued that the methods Wallendorf and Belk propose do nothing to change this.) It also builds upon a category error, for a researcher is almost infinitely more complex than a thermometer, a Likert scale, or even a particle accelerator. Unlike, say, a tape recorder, a researcher can never be a trustworthy instrument that reliably mediates between a complex data set and other researchers. So if we take this metaphor seriously, the validity of interpretive research will always be in question, and interpretive research will always be perceived as being second rate (Holt 1991). Fortunately, interpretive research has been accepted in some measure by the positivistically inclined ACR/JCR community, so it may now be possible to move beyond the initial spade work and establish this research tradition upon its proper foundation.

PROPOSED NEW FOUNDATIONS FOR INTERPRETIVISM

Our thesis, once again, is that interpretivist research can be fully credible only if it is grounded in the evolving consensus of an interpretive community, an evolving consensus that is possible only if the discipline has a canon. Thus, in our view two elements, among others, are essential in a mature interpretivism, and one is notably neither essential nor desirable.

The first essential element is an informed and critical interpretive community (Fish 1980; Wittgenstein 1969), a group of researchers who are acquainted with the data and who share a sufficient number of assumptions that they can agree on which interpretations are valid, which invalid. In a proper interpretive community of this kind, as group members evaluate and criticize each other's interpretations, an evolving consensus emerges that does not rest upon the authority of any one or two members, for all group members read the texts that are being interpreted and judge for themselves whether a proposed interpretation is valid. Each intersubjectively certifies or decertifies a proposed reading. Consequently, if a finding is broadly judged to be valid, it is certified not by one or two or several members of the discipline but rather by the discipline at large. We expand on this point below.

The second essential element is a canon, a body of publicly available texts (interviews, ads, pictures) that the discipline regards as being a suitable object of study. This infrastructural element is essential because it makes possible unmediated access to the data that are being interpreted. If researchers are to judge for themselves how well an interpretation fits the data it purports to explain, they must have access to and be familiar with the data. A canon makes this possible and, thus, makes it possible to dispense with the method of authority. We discuss below what we mean by a canon.

The element that is not essential or even desirable in a mature interpretivism is an emphasis on method (Holt 1991). In a mature interpretive discipline—the humanities, for instance—no one knows or cares how researchers arrive at a given interpretation. The only thing that matters is how well the interpretation fits with and/or accounts for the data that are being interpreted (Thompson 1990). Thus, in humanities courses, students are generally urged to avoid intellectual autobiography—accounts of their discovery process (i.e., method sections)—and simply cut to the chase, the patterns they have discovered in the text. Their interpretation is evaluated on how well it fits the data, not on the procedures or thought processes they went through to produce it. Commenting on this point in *Truth and Method* (1975), a book that would have been more aptly entitled *Truth or Method*, Gadamer argues that method is the enemy of truth, that interpretive truth emerges from openness and play, not from method. In saying this, he basically affirms Wallendorf and Belk's (1989) pregnant aside on research creativity while calling into question their extended methodological bow to positivism. In his view and ours, method is not an appropriate foundation for validity in interpretive research.

Critique and Consensus within an Interpretive Community

In this section we discuss somewhat more extensively why mature interpretive research requires informed criticism within an interpretive community and, thus, requires multiple interpretations of a text. Unlike positivism, which depends upon *multiplicative corroboration*, interpretivism depends upon *structural corroboration* (Pepper 1970), complex judgments about how fact agrees with fact. Since the object of study in interpretive research is usually a multifaceted text, the number of potentially interlocking facts embedded in the text is generally very large. An adequate interpretation is one that accounts for and interrelates all elements in the text that are relevant to a given interpretation. Thus, "interpretation is inescapably descriptive.... If our interpretation is persuasive, it is so because our description enables others to see the aspects [of the text that] we are pointing out" and that they otherwise would not have seen (Dasenbrock 1986, p. 1035).

The potentially infinite complexity of a text notwithstanding, interpretivist researchers are often certain, both as individuals and as a group, that they have grasped the essential meaning or importance of a text. Building upon insights of Wittgenstein, Dasenbrock (1986) has persuasively argued that researchers attain and progressively deepen their certitude because shared assumptions create a conceptual space within which the range of possible meanings is limited. Within those conceptual limits, the aspect density, the descriptive power of various interpretations of the text can be compared.

For our purposes, the crucial point is that detail-oriented criticism from colleagues is the engine that leads to deeper levels of individual and group confidence in an interpretation. When presenting at a conference an interpretation of a publicly available text, "the speaker ... is always aware (or else is soon made aware) that his paper has slighted some aspects of the work under discussion." The speaker and others develop new levels of insight and depths of certitude in their reading by dealing with these objections. "Most of us" Dasenbrock (1986, p. 1033) says "emerge most of the time from such a discussion or from reading criticism about a work with a more complex perspective on it than we had before [and] an impression of coming to a deeper understanding of the work." The proper warrant of the value of interpretive research is this deep and shared confidence that we have grasped the meaning of the text, confidence grounded in a thorough engagement with textual details that is driven by the close critical scrutiny of other informed readers.

Dasenbrock tells us how certitude about and consensus on the meaning of a text are achieved in fully mature interpretive disciplines such as literary studies. Is similar certitude and consensus possible for us in consumer research? Not at present, because we lack the infrastructure that is necessary if our interpretations are to be intersubjectively ratified by and deepened through the criticism of other researchers. At our conferences, the person making a presentation is often the only one in the room who has read the interviews that are being interpreted. This researcher often provides proof-text quotations that support his or her interpretation. But no one else is in a position to challenge and deepen the interpretation by citing other passages that call the interpretation into question or otherwise compel a more careful and nuanced reading. We will now discuss the infrastructure that would make this kind of critique and deeper insight possible.

Canons and Canon Formation

Let us return to what we earlier said was the second essential element of a mature interpretivism, a canon, for it is a canon that can make possible unmediated access to data and the informed criticism that leads to validated interpretive research findings. For our purposes, the term *canon* has two relevant meanings. Defined broadly, a canon is the complete body of publicly available texts that a discipline regards as appropriate objects of study (Fowler 1982). In this broad sense, the literary canon includes both the classic novels of Jane Austen and the latest novels of obscure science fiction writers. This sense of the term is logically prior but theoretically less interesting than a second meaning. Defined more narrowly, a canon is the subset of texts in this larger collection that have been judged by a discipline to be of special interest and worth. Texts enter this more restricted canon on the nomination of researchers whose interpretations reveal in them important dimensions of meaning. As the interests of researchers change over time, the membership of this more restricted canon changes as well, though certain particularly rich texts tend to be retained (Smith 1984). In this narrower sense, the literary canon includes Jane Austen's work but not the latest science fiction potboilers.

At present, consumer research has no canon in either the broad or the narrow sense of the term. We lack a canon in the broad sense not because there are no texts that are appropriate objects of study for consumer researchers. Over the past decade, researchers have collected thousands of pages of interviews with consumers on a wide range of important topics. We lack a canon because we have not established conventions that encourage and infrastructure that facilitates public availability of the important texts that already exist. Thus, if we want to become a mature interpretive discipline and put the method of authority behind us, our lack of data sharing conventions must be our first concern. And for the moment, resistance to data sharing seems to be firmly entrenched. Over the past year, we have contacted several researchers and asked for access to interviews that were the basis of JCR articles. Though the researchers we contacted are as genial and generous as the average consumer behaviorist, they denied access to the interviews. The conventions of our discipline do not encourage them to share their data. So for various reasons, none of them compelling if our conventions should change, they didn't share them. And yet, data sharing has already proven beneficial to the discipline (Stern 1995).

If we can change our data sharing conventions, our second concern would be to establish the infrastructure that would make canonical texts publicly available. This should be relatively easy, given the growth of the World Wide Web, on which interviews, photographs, video and audio recordings can be stored and accessed electronically at very little cost. The Association for Consumer Research might be the organization best positioned to provide and maintain a web site that archives various canonical texts.

If changes in conventions and infrastructure led to the creation of a canon in the broader sense, a canon in the more important narrow sense would soon follow as certain texts were identified as being especially meaningful and important. The groundwork for the emergence of this subset has already been done. Previously published articles based on interview data implicitly nominate their source interviews for inclusion in this more selective consumer behavior canon (Frye 1971). If some of these interviews were selected for a second interpretation and then still other reinterpretations, they would eventually become standard texts, widely read and deeply understood on account of the various articles devoted to explicating them.

Virtual Canon in Consumer Research

While consumer research has no proper canon, published interpretive research has been grounded to varying degrees in a kind of virtual canon, for it has focused to a greater or lesser degree on phenomena that are familiar to other consumer researchers. Thus, various studies can be plotted on a continuum that reflects the degree to which the object of study is, in this limited sense, canonical. At the canonical end of this continuum, one might place Holbrook and Grayson's (1986) article on the semiology of cinematic consumption. This study interprets a text, *Out of Africa*, that is delimited, tangible, and readily available to other researchers who may wish to assess the quality of the interpretation. Only slightly less available are texts Hirschman (1990) cites in her article on secular immortality: *Connoisseur* and *Avenue*, magazines targeted at the wealthy; *Trump: The Art of the Deal*, an autobiography; and Tom Wolfe's novel *The Bonfire of the Vanities*. Also at the canonical end of the continuum is Belk, Wallendorf, and Sherry's (1989) paper on sacred and profane consumption. This study also treats texts—interviews, photos, videos and audio recordings—that are available, though not readily available, to other researchers. In his article on celebrity endorsers, McCracken (1989) explains why character actors may be more effective endors-

ers than actors who play a wider range of roles. This study interprets ads that are not available except, perhaps, in memory, but virtually all researchers can assess the validity of McCracken's claims based on their daily experience of other ads, so in this respect, the analysis is rooted in a canon. Further toward the noncanonical end of the continuum would be Rook's (1987) "The Buying Impulse." Other researchers may not know any compulsive consumers, and they have no access to the interviews on which this article was based. (Proof texts included in the article naturally don't facilitate critique.) One might anchor the non-canonical end of the continuum with Hill and Stamey's (1990) article on the homeless in America. Researchers have no access to the interviews on which this article was based (again, proof texts have little critical utility) and, in most cases, no firsthand knowledge of the plight of the homeless. They are, therefore, poorly positioned to judge the quality of the interpretations offered in this article.

In plotting these articles on our virtual canon continuum, we do not mean to suggest that articles on the non-canonical end of the continuum offer less valid interpretations than those at the canonical end. We assert only that researchers are ill equipped both individually and collectively to evaluate the quality of interpretations in the more non-canonical articles. And we have a vague sense that reviewers may be somewhat inhospitable to interpretive analyses of phenomena that fall outside their experience since they are not equipped to assess the value of these studies. This is unfortunate since compulsive consumption and consumption among the homeless are legitimate topics for consumer research. Presumably, a canon would open up more opportunities for studying abnormal consumer behaviors such as these because it would make data on these behaviors more widely available and would facilitate informed assessment of articles treating these phenomena.

THEORETICAL AND PRACTICAL BENEFITS OF A CANON

We have already suggested reasons why a consumer behavior canon would enhance the credibility and validity of interpretive consumer research and might facilitate research on abnormal behaviors. We discuss, now, other theoretical and practical benefits that a consumer behavior canon might generate.

Deeper Insights from Close Readings

In their critical review of a set of interpretive studies, Calder and Tybout (1989) offer, among others that we find unpersuasive, one compelling criticism: they suggest that the findings of interpretive researchers often fit the data so loosely that they do not deliver the promised richness of the qualitative approach. They mention as an example the findings that place is important for a retail store, a finding that tells us nothing we don't already know? Though interpretive research has generated some insights much deeper than this one, our broad sense is that it has not delivered in consumer research the kind of aspect-rich descriptions that it routinely produces in more mature interpretive disciplines such as the humanities. For comparison purposes, see Janice Radaway's (1984) wonderfully nuanced analysis of the function of romance novels in the lives of the women who buy them, a paper that could have been published in a consumer behavior journal but was actually published in *Daedalus*, a journal in the humanities.

We attribute the dearth of compelling close readings in consumer research to our discipline lacking the two essential elements of mature interpretive research: a canon and a tradition of critically reinterpreting texts. The lack of a canon is important because researchers cannot engage a phenomenon in detail if they cannot assume their readers will be familiar with the textual details. Our loose, virtual canon does not provide the familiarity that is requisite if we are to have close readings, the kind of readings that most fully illuminate texts and disclose the patterned complexity of the phenomena reflected in them.

The lack of a tradition of critical reinterpretation also leads to comparatively shallow readings. The finest readings of cultural texts usually emerge over time through a process of critical point and counterpoint. Our one-shot tradition provides no opportunity for Holbrook and Grayson's (1986) analysis of consumption in *Out of Africa* to be deepened by subsequent critical responses that challenge and modify the initial interpretation, and it provides even less for Hill and Stamey's (1990) findings to be modified by a reinterpretation of their interviews with homeless people.

Expanded Data Availability, Lower Data Costs

A canon would permit us to expand the availability of data while lowering its cost and increasing our understanding of it. Interpretive research typically uses rich data. It is, therefore, wasteful to spend a great deal of time gathering the data, then subject it to only a single interpretation. Most any set of well conducted interviews can be profitably interpreted from multiple perspectives. But because we lack a canon in which data are shared, single interpretations are normal practice. A colleague of ours recently spend a great deal of time interviewing informants on their collecting hobbies even though she knew other researchers who already had a large set of interviews on this topic. It did not occur to her to use the existing data set or to those who had the data to make it available to her. And yet a critical reinterpretation that responded both to the existing data and to the previous interpretation of that data would probably have yielded deeper insights into collecting behaviors than another, one-shot interpretation of new data. While new data are always welcome, our discipline would certainly benefit if much more time were spent interpreting and reinterpreting the rich data we already have, much less laboriously gathering new data. Though reading the canon takes time, one can carefully read a number of existing interviews in the time it takes to set up, conduct, and transcribe one new one. Provided that the discipline is prepared to accept and publish reinterpretations, carefully reading the canon should prove to be a productive use of researcher time.

It is certain that consumer research should be open to novel reinterpretations of existing data. Judging from the history of literary criticism, we need not suppose that the person who gathers the data and is most deeply immersed in it is best positioned to interpret it. Plato long ago pointed out in the *Ion* that poets are very often poor interpreters of their own poetry. The same may well be true of researchers who collect data. Time spent reading theory will sometimes lead to deeper insights into the meaning of a set of interviews than time spent living with or otherwise immersing oneself in the lives of the informants. But the researchers best equipped to interpret a given data set may not be best positioned to gather it, either because they are not proximate to the informants or because they are not skilled interviewers. A canon permits a division of labor and, thus, a more efficient use of various researchers, whether their skills most lie in data collection or data interpretation. Of course, the discipline must arrange to reward those who collect as well as those who interpret good data.

Broader Perspectives, Larger Samples

Paradoxically, a canon makes possible not only a deeper immersion in the details of consumer behavior (and, thus, closer readings) but also a much broader exploration of changes and continuities in consumer behavior across expanses of space and time. A researcher with access to a consumer behavior canon will likely be much better positioned to study the ways in which self-gift giving differs from the Midwest to California to New Zealand to Singapore than any researcher could be who must draw only upon self-generated data. And a sample drawn from a canon is certain to be larger than any self-generated sample since the existing data could be added to any new data, and the new data, would, in turn, expand the scope of the canon.

As for time, next to its epistemological benefits, perhaps the most important benefit of a canon would be the development of a new degree of historical consciousness in consumer behavior research. Fully mature interpretive disciplines such as those in the humanities have a deep understanding and appreciation of the importance of history, an understanding that the natural sciences have traditionally lacked for reasons Kuhn (1969) has laid out. Perhaps owing to the influence of positivism, consumer researchers have paid relatively little attention to historical developments that have undoubtedly had very important effects upon consumer behavior and that business practitioners, an important constituency, must deal with every day (Smith and Lux 1993). Interpretivist researchers have no reason to ignore history, but in the absence of a canon, they will have little opportunity to study changes in consumption across time since they will lack access to historical data. Such longitudinal interpretivist research as has been done confirms the importance of institutions that preserve data and make it publicly available. Belk and Pollay (1985), for instance, used data preserved in archives to produce a longitudinal study of advertising.

While regional and historical influences would probably receive much attention were a consumer behavior canon to be formed, the range of possible perspectives that could organize the canon and guide research extend well beyond time and space. Judging from other disciplines, a multiplicity of perspectives distributed up and down the ladder of abstraction could and would be used to select relevant data from a consumer behavior canon. These perspectives would likely include but not be limited to product classes (automobiles, shampoo, travel services), demographic groups (women, Hispanics), classes of behavior (binge eating, charitable giving), and conceptual frameworks (structuralism, hermeneutics). A canon would provide a data set rich enough to sustain well grounded work from all of these and many other perspectives.

A BRIEF EXAMPLE

We conclude with an example of the kind of textual reinterpretation that we have been urging. Our focus is Mr. Ed's Elephant Museum and Roadside Attraction, the business in Gettysburg, Pennsylvania, that is profiled in the Marketing Science Institute video "Deep Meaning in Possessions." Offering a "teleological," trusting interpretation that is consistent with Mr. Ed's own view, Belk, Wallendorf, and Sherry (1989) note that this business has two sides, the *sacred* Elephant Museum (from which items are never sold) and the *profane* Roadside Attraction (where Mr. Ed earns his living selling elephant paraphernalia and other souvenirs). We offer a suspicious, unmasking interpretation of this same business, what Ricoeur (1974) calls an "archaeological" hermeneutic, an interpretation that Mr. Ed would probably reject.

Derrida (1973) has pointed out that putatively balanced dichotomies such as rich/poor, mind/body, man/woman, good/bad are actually unbalanced, the first term being preferred or valorized. Thus, in the sacred/profane video and article, the sacred receives much more attention than the profane, for it is the more deeply meaningful and important of the two domains in the minds of those who have created this distinction. Derrida also suggests that by inverting the valorization, one deconstructs a reading and discloses new dimensions of meaning.

Our deconstructive reading builds upon the Marxist distinction between base and superstructure (Marx 1988), a dichotomy that quite neatly inverts the sacred/profane distinction. For Marx, the drive to acquire material wealth is fundamental; meaning making, including concepts of the sacred, subserve that fundamental drive. In this Marxist frame, the more important part of Mr. Ed's business is the Roadside Attraction, the side that produces wealth. The Elephant Museum merely supports this base, perhaps by linking the business to Lincoln, a founder of the Republican party, certainly by attracting customers, indoctrinating them in the sacredness of souvenirs, and modeling for them behaviors that will help sustain the Roadside Attraction. It encourages consumers to prominently display, talk about, and never sell the souvenirs they have purchased. In other words, it fosters word-of-mouth promotion and erects an ideological barrier to competition, all the while lending dignity to an establishment that might otherwise be viewed as tourist trap full of kitsch junk.

Neither our skeptical, perhaps even mean-spirited discussion of this business, nor the more charitable sacred/profane analysis fully encompasses this phenomenon. But in offering a second interpretation, we have presumably thickened the description and increased the aspect density of our understanding, in other words, have produced a more adequate composite interpretation.

REFERENCES

Belk Russell W. and Richard W. Pollay (1985) "Images of Ourselves: The Good Life in Twentieth Century Advertising" *Journal of Consumer Research*, 11 (March), 887-897.

———, Melanie Wallendorf, and John F. Sherry (1989), "The Sacred and Profane in Consumer Behavior: Theodicy on the Odyssey," *Journal of Consumer Research*, 16 (June), 1-38.

Calder, Bobby J. and Alice M. Tybout (1989), "Interpretive, Qualitative, and Traditional Scientific Empirical Consumer Behavior Research," *Interpretive Consumer Research*, ed. Elizabeth C. Hirschman, Provo, UT: Association for Consumer Research, 199-208.

Dasenbrock, Reed Way (1986), "Accounting for the Changing Certainties of Interpretive Communities," *Modern Language Notes*, 101 (5), 1022-1041.

Derrida, Jacques (1973), *Speech and Phenomena*, Evanston, IL: Northwestern University Press.

Fish, Stanley (1980), *Is There A Text In This Class?"* Cambridge: Harvard University Press.

Fowler, Alastair (1982), *Kinds of Literature: An Introduction to the Theory of Genres and Modes*, Cambridge: Harvard University Press.

Frye, Northrop (1971), *The Anatomy of Criticism*, Princeton: Princeton University Press.

Gadamer, Hans-Georg (1975), *Truth and Method*, New York: The Seabury Press.

Hill, Ronald Paul and Mark Stamey (1990), "The Homeless in America: An Examination of Possessions and Consumption Behaviors," *Journal of Consumer Research*, 17 (December), 303-321

Hirschman, Elizabeth C. (1986), "Humanistic Inquiry in Marketing Research: Philosophy, Method, and Criteria," *Journal of Marketing Research*, 23 (August), 237-249.

——— (1990), "Secular Immortality and the American Ideology of Influence," *Journal of Consumer Research*, 17 (June), 31-42.

Holbrook, Morris B. and Mark W. Grayson (1986), "The Semiology of Cinematic Consumption: Symbolic Consumer Behavior in *Out of Africa*," *Journal of Consumer Research*, 13 (December), 374-381.

Holt, Douglas B. (1991), "Rashomon Visits Consumer Behavior: An Interpretive Critique of Naturalistic Inquiry," *Advances in Consumer Research*, eds. Rebecca H. Holman and Michael R. Solomon, 18, 57-62.

Lincoln, Yvonna S. and Egon G. Guba (1985), *Naturalistic Inquiry*, Beverly Hills, CA: Sage Publications.

Marx, Karl (1988), *Selected Writings*, ed. David McLellan, Oxford: Oxford University Press.

McCracken, Grant (1989), "Who is the Celebrity Endorser? Cultural Foundations of the Endorsement Process," *Journal of Consumer Research*, 16 (December), 310-321.

Pierce, Charles Sanders (1934/1965), "The Fixation of Belief," in *The Collected Papers of Charles Sanders Peirce*, Cambridge: Harvard University Press, 5, 223-247.

Pepper, Stephen C. (1970), *World Hypotheses: A Study in Evidence*, Berkeley: University of California Press.

Rook, Dennis W. (1987), "The Buying Impulse," *Journal of Consumer Research*, 14 (September), 189-199.

Smith, Barbara Herrnstein (1984), "Contingencies of Value," in *Canons*, ed. Robert von Hallberg, Chicago: University of Chicago Press.

Smith, Ruth Ann and David S. Lux (1993), "Historical Method in Consumer Research: Developing Causal Explanations of Change," *Journal of Consumer Research*, 19 (March), 595-610.

Stern, Barbara B. (1995), "Consumer Myths: Frye's Taxonomy and the Structural Analysis of Consumption Texts," *Journal of Consumer Research*, 22 (September), 165-185.

Thompson, Craig J. (1990), "Eureka! And Other Tests of Significance: A New Look at Evaluating Interpretive Research," in *Advances in Consumer Research*, eds. Marvin E. Goldberg, Gerald Gorn, and Richard W. Pollay, Provo, UT: Association for Consumer Research, 25-30.

Wallendorf, Melanie and Russell W. Belk (1989), "Assessing Trustworthiness in Naturalistic Consumer Research," in *Interpretive Consumer Research*, Provo, UT: Association for Consumer Research, 69-84.

Wittgenstein, Ludwig (1969), *On Certainty*, New York: Harper & Row.

Social Conventions of a Fast Food Restaurant: An Ethnomethodological Analysis

Hope J. Schau, University of California–Irvine
Mary C. Gilly, University of California-Irvine

"Culture is ordinary: that is where we must start."
(Williams 1993, p. 5)
"By 'culture' I mean the ideas and activities with which we
construe and construct our world."
(McCracken 1988, p. XI)

INTRODUCTION

As reported in a Los Angeles Times article, approximately 96% of people living in metropolitan areas eat fast food at least once per month; American consumers spent $94.5 billion on fast food products in 1993 (Granelli 1994). Further, fast food is quickly becoming a global phenomenon as the culture of fast food is expanded around the world (Caglar 1995; Leidner 1993; Hume 1990). While consumer behavior and service marketing textbooks contain many fast food examples (Bitner and Zeithaml 1995; Solomon 1992; Mahatoo 1985; Peter 1987), there is a paucity of academic research on fast food as a cultural milieu in which individuals work and consume.

While consumers tend to refer to Taco Bell and similar operations such as McDonald's as "fast food," inside the industry it is known as "Quick Service Restaurants" or QSR. The organizational focus is thus on quickly serving customers. Consumers, however, may have a broader definition of "fast" which includes the consumption process. Central to the fast food industry are the notions of routinization and standardization (Leidner 1993). Customers expect that their encounters with the fast food service personnel are routine and that the food is standardized. The maintenance of high uniformity in the encounter and product is a challenging task considering that both the employee and consumer must be familiar with the conventions of the fast food culture (Shelton 1993; Leidner 1993). Cultural participants must maneuver through the physical surroundings, performing the socially agreed upon behaviors or roles (Goffman 1959; Berreman 1962; Grove and Fisk 1983). Physical surroundings impact the local social order of customers and employees and ultimately influence the service encounter outcome (Bitner 1990, 1992; Baker 1987). This research represents an exploratory examination of the culture of fast food using ethnomethodological techniques. This inquiry is designed to examine the process of fast food service and social order found in the culture of fast food. Specifically, it will elaborate on four emergent themes: visible employee hierarchy, routinization through scripting and production parameters, queue formation and the counter as boundary region. The paper begins with a discussion of the study and method employed, followed by a brief description of the cultural participants, articulation of the emergent themes involved in the local social order and concluding remarks.

THE STUDY

Similar to recent research on consumer culture in consumption venues (Sherry 1990; Belk 1991; Belk, Sherry, Wallendorf 1988; Sherry, McGrath 1989), the primary site of investigation is a Taco Bell restaurant in Southern California. It is located in an industrial complex on a heavily trafficked street that leads to three major freeways. There is an industrial plant, a bank and several office towers within walking distance of the restaurant. The attached parking lot accommodates 25 cars, but is bordered by the industrial parking lots, which combined have a parking capacity in the thousands.

Methods

The central task of this project is to describe and understand the social conventions operating at this specific Taco Bell restaurant in Southern California. The knowledge gained from examining locally produced social order is not expected to be generalizable, but rather transferable to other foci of inquiry (Burrell and Morgan 1979).

Ethnomethodology is an interpretive method similar to phenomenology that problematizes everyday life (Heritage 1984):

"ethnomethodology is the empirical investigation ("-ology") of the methods ("method-") people ("ethno-") use to make sense of and at the same time accomplish communication, decision making, reasonableness and action in everyday life." (Rogers 1983)

Ethnomethodology differs from traditional sociological methods in its efforts to articulate the production of social order. Social order is assumed to be locally produced (Livingston 1987). Although social structure is imposed on the local participants, it is their interpretation and performance of the social structure that is examined (Burrell and Morgan 1979). Talk or informants' statements are treated as social acts, or behavioral manifestations of ordinary practice (Benson and Hughes 1983).

For this study, four weekday lunch peaks, five weekday dinner peaks and three off peak periods were observed, recording ethnomethodological data on the manner in which cultural participants performed their "ordinary" behavior (Garfinkel 1967). Customer behaviors of arrival, queuing, ordering, waiting, seat selection, eating and exit were plotted. Employee behavior in order taking, order filling, food preparation and orchestrating of functions were recorded. Behaviors were categorized in an emic perspective and issues to pursue in cultural participants "talk" were identified (Wierder 1974). Queuing, encounters and informal employee gatherings were observed. Seven informants familiar with the fast food service industry were interviewed, six of which were part of the local production cohort of the Taco Bell restaurant. The conversations were phenomenological in nature to access personalized accounts of lived experience in the culture (Kvale 1983). A management trainee meeting was observed and audio taped focus group sessions were reviewed to gain insights into the service philosophy of Taco Bell. A video taped interview with John Martin, CEO of Taco Bell, was accessed to contextualize the examination of the local Taco Bell culture. The resulting analysis is an ethomethodological study of a specific fast food venue augmented by insights into the corporate philosophy.

Informants: "Maria" is a current employee of the Taco Bell restaurant in Southern California. She is a Latina from Central America who entered the US when she was 10 years old. She is now in her early twenties, and has worked for Taco Bell for two years. Maria is usually assigned to the counter, but sometimes rotates to order filler or cleaning duties. Her primary language is Spanish, but her comments about the local production cohort were in English. "Ben" is a manager of a Taco Bell restaurant, Maria's boss, and the coordinator of the day time activities of the restaurant. "Steve" is a management trainee. He is a corporate employee learning the operation from the restaurant level to the corporate. "Phil" is an executive with Taco Bell. He understands the corporation as a whole and is familiar with the intimate details of restaurants as well. "Dave" is a consumer and former Taco Bell employee. He was born and raised in Southern California. "Mike" is a consumer. He grew up in Southern California and is currently a graduate student at UC Irvine.

CULTURAL PARTICIPANTS

The Employee Domain

Order Takers are the front-line employees of this service organization. There are two main types of order takers: counter personnel and "drive-thru" personnel. Counter personnel stand behind the counter on the employee side. Their main tasks are: soliciting orders, recording orders on a computerized cash register, relaying orders to order fillers or filling the orders themselves, relaying special orders to the food preparation crew, handling cash, and instructing consumers on the wait procedure and the use of the beverage bar. Drive-thru personnel are order takers that serve the car queue. They wear headsets to listen to the car orders and perform order taking functions for the car consumers. Outside drive-thru order taking is an adjunct task used in peak times to facilitate efficiency. The outside drive-thru employee wears a cash belt, carries an electronic order pad and performs the order taking function to the car queue, bypassing the mechanical order board and touch pad. Embedded in the tasks of all order takers is the expectation of courteous, consumer oriented behavior.

Order Fillers are employees who manage the space between the order takers and the food preparation crew. Order fillers are responsible for gathering ordered items from the food preparation team and bundling them for distribution. The function is not always present in the service delivery chain. Typically, order fillers are used during peak times to facilitate efficient service.

Food Preparers are personnel who work in the employee realm to assemble Taco Bell entrees to fill consumer orders. All meat, chicken and beans are initially cooked off-site in centralized facilities to ensure standardized food products and are transported to individual restaurant locations for "assembly to order" preparation. The food preparers are responsible for assembling the cooked meats and beans, shredded cheese and cut vegetables according to specific corporate parameters of ingredient ratios, warming the entrees to corporately defined temperatures and wrapping the items for distribution.

The Local Manager is responsible for the daily operations of the restaurant. The manager organizes work teams, supervises employees and rotates human resources as needed throughout the day. The manager moves between the employee and consumer domain performing needed functions, and also fills in for underrepresented tasks, cleans and surveys customer satisfaction.

The Management Trainee is a corporate employee assigned to a local restaurant to become acquainted with the daily operations of the service sites. The trainee is rotated through every function in the service chain and taught to perform each function optimally.

The Consumer Domain

White-collar Employees: The predominant consumers during the lunch rush appear to be from the neighboring industrial office sites. Most of them walk in across the adjoining parking lots and are wearing office, or business, attire. They usually come in sets, not alone. Most often they speak throughout their queue, order wait and eating time. It is not always obvious if they are speaking socially or professionally; however, they appear to be friendly and cordial within and among sets.

Adults and Children: Also common during lunch peak are adult-child groupings. The children in these groups are very young,

e.g., infants, toddlers, and preschoolers. The adults are generally female and appear to be the mothers of the small children. The adult-child groups arrive exclusively by vehicle.

Workers: Some consumers appear to be blue collar workers on lunch break. They wear jeans, T-shirts or flannel shirts and tennis shoes or boots. A few consumers have considerable amounts of dirt and dust on their clothing which indicates that they may be on construction crews. The workers usually arrive by vehicle in sets of two or more.

Students: These consumers carry backpacks, books and notebooks. They lunch alone or in groups. Students range in age from teens to young adults (thirtyish). They wear casual clothing. When in groups they tend to speak together in an animated manner. When alone they tend to read or write. All student consumers arrive by vehicle.

Consumer Interactions

Consumers enter the restaurant either alone or in groups. They usually enter the queue in the same social configuration in which they arrive. Often they carry on conversations in the queue that are unrelated to lunch activities. For most, the service encounter is a momentary, functional pause in their day. It is a behavior they engage in to facilitate the lunching process and not one that they spend considerable time contemplating or performing. Their behavior in this venue is indeed part of their everyday life that is taken for granted. One consumer states, "When I walk up to the counter it should be easy. I tell my order and I move on." One dimension of a successful fast food encounter is ease. The script should allow the consumer to quickly and accurately convey their order. (See section entitled, "Scripting")

When consumers choose seats in the dining area, they often sit with the group they entered with. Even in the case when spaces are limited, most consumers will wait rather than sit with other consumers. An exception to this practice are the white collar workers who enter the restaurant in groups, but do not always sit in those configurations. Among familiar sets, e.g., people who work together, people will negotiate space to accommodate the most consumers, breaking up initial groupings if necessary.

EMERGENT THEMES

Visible Hierarchy

Taco Bell's corporate policy includes the use of employee teams designed to redistribute power within the local restaurants. Teams of employees are purportedly assigned managerial functions like opening and closing the restaurant, scheduling and job rotation. The team concept attempts to empower individual employees and alleviate the monotony of the highly structured employee tasks. According to team policy, one would expect a relatively flat local organizational structure and dilution of the local manager's power.

The hierarchy operating at the Southern California site is apparent to consumers and observers of the venue. It is manifested in the uniforms and in the behavior of the employees and members of management. Employees in the rank and file wear uniforms, while management personnel wear business attire. The predominant employee uniforms of this site are dark blue pants, a blue cotton crew neck T-shirt and a blue baseball style hat with the Taco Bell logo. Members of management wear dark dress pants and a button down dress shirt with a tie.[1] The distinction is further delineated by

---

[1]During our observations, we did not encounter any female management personnel. The management attire is most likely different for females.

the name tag. Employees wear tags that feature the Taco Bell logo and their first name. Members of management wear tags with the Taco Bell logo that identify them by full name and job title, e.g., John Doe, Manager. The clothing and name tags indicate the hierarchy of the social system. Management is afforded a higher degree of formality that in the larger society is indicative of power and authority. An employee commented, "If someone talks to me it's like, they say 'Hey,' or 'Maria, did you get that?' When they wanna talk to my manager they say, 'Where is *the* manager?' or 'Is *Mr.* Smith in?' Even when *we* talk to him *we* don't say, 'Hey, Ben, can I trade shifts with Juan?' We're all supposed to be on this team, right? But it's not like nobody notices I got a T-shirt on and he's wearing a tie." For the employees, the institutionalized distinction between them and management is unambiguous. As demonstrated in the quote, the consumers also practice a degree of deference toward the management by title reference and identification of mangers by their last name. Consumers are not aware of employee teams and the effort to create teams within the local employee group rings false in the face of the obvious visual distinctions.

The order takers, order fillers, food preparers and drive-thru personnel do not socialize with consumers or each other, but rather focus on preparing for, serving and cleaning up from the lunch crowd. The only words they exchange are either task related exchanges with consumers, or to each other regarding the ordered menu items. The manager speaks most often, moving among the employees and dispensing what appears to be advice or instructions, as well as speaking with the consumers as necessary to facilitate the encounters. One informant describes the manager-employee relationship as, "He is like a dictator and we are all his to order about." Employees are under continuous managerial scrutiny and do not feel empowered to consider issues beyond their immediate, structured tasks. An informant comments, "I wasn't paid to think, just to do." The employees appear to accept the hierarchy as a part of fast food service delivery, despite the contradiction with the team emphasis.

Routinization

Routinization is the process put in place to ensure that the encounter does not deviate across time or space. Routinization refers to the issue of standardized product and expectations. Scripting is a strategy to achieve routinization. It is a manner of routinizing the encounter between employee and consumer, similar to product specifications that attempt to achieve standardized product in every location. At the management trainee meetings, the trainees discuss the specifics regarding how much the items should weigh and the exact proportion of ingredients that compose the item weight. A trainee half jokingly said, "Always order the bean burrito. It's the best value if you look at weight per cent spent." The goal of routinization is to achieve the highest degree of conformity for customers across locations. As with all services, the delivery of the service is difficult for consumers to separate from the end product in their overall evaluation. A former employee, and current consumer, justifies the emphasis on routine in the following manner: "People like to come in, order and eat what they asked for. They don't want to have to think or worry about things. Fast food should be easy. God knows the food's not great." For fast food in general and Taco Bell in particular, quality is a sum of the comfort of the encounter and the accuracy of the order. John Martin, CEO of Taco Bell, stressed the corporate priorities (based on consumer preferences) of restaurant cleanliness, encounter speed, order accuracy and appropriate temperature of food items.

Although the appearance of the food is not stated as a corporate priority, the images on the menu board act as a sort of promise to the consumer of what his/her item should be. It is a means to set consumer expectations. An employee comments, "Sometimes people get pissed off that the order doesn't look like the picture." In an audio taped focus group session, one crew member confessed that when consumers complained about food items not matching the menu board picture, she was inclined to overportion to achieve visual congruence. Although overportioning is against Taco Bell policy, it is used as an employee strategy to meet consumer expectations. Accuracy incorporates a visual dimension.

Scripting is a specific term which refers to the role performances of the parties involved in the encounter and more particularly the dialogue (Solomon, Surprenant, Czepiel and Gutman 1985). Scripting is taught in training to employees. In Taco Bell the employees are taught exactly what to say in what order to effectively and efficiently carry out their duty as employees in the encounter. The scripts are memorized and become almost a rote behavior. The sequence of order taking, taking cash, making change and dispensing food items is carefully defined for the employees. A corporate executive describes the process; "We leave nothing to chance. Employees know what to say and when to say it. They know when to ask for money and when to relinquish the ordered items." A front-line employee says that in training "they told me exactly what I should say. 'May I take your order?' Repeat the order back. 'Will that be all?' Take their money. Make change. Hand them the stuff." Later she added, "They like you to smile, but they can't make you." She feels that the exact wording of the counter personnel is very important and asserts that employees who deviate from the expectations are corrected by the manager. A former employee describes his encounter experience as "mechanical" and confessed that he was often "bored."

Scripting is taught in advertisements to consumers and is cued by the menu board. The ads expose consumers to appropriate terminology, e.g., Meximelt and "deals." Customers are given brief written descriptions of the food products matched with the name each product has within the local culture, e.g., a Meximelt is paired with its description and offered as a piece of the consumer script. Usually, the product is depicted by an image. The image is an encoding device for the consumer, who can peruse the menu board and determine what items are in the consideration set and encode them by name and/or picture and/or description. To be faithful to the script, consumers should order by menu title. Departing from the script can cause anxiety for the other party in the dyad. An order taker comments that some people do not order from the menu board and "describe" their order instead. She found this practice disconcerting and said it hindered her ability to quickly and accurately serve the consumer. When a consumer orders by description, the order taker must translate the description into the local terms. As with any translation, there is an increased chance for error as compared to people communicating in a common language system. Similarly, special requests cause confusion for front-line employees. An order taker states, "Sometimes a consumer tells me how the burrito *should* be made. I have to repeat this to the food preparer. I usually do that [special orders] in Spanish to Juan." Translation issues occur on many levels; Taco Bell vernacular and English to Spanish.

To complicate matters, some food options are not listed on the menu. New items are added and old ones are deleted every six months. Taco Bell serves entrees that are not currently listed on the menu board, e.g., the Enchirito. People aware of this practice may choose an unlisted item which the order taker must somehow indicate and charge the consumer for. In ethnomethodology, deviations of this sort are referred to as *breaching exercises* which lead cultural participants to falter in the performance of their ordinary behavior (Garfinkel 1986). The cash registers used at the Taco Bell restaurant are menu based and pose a serious challenge to order takers when faced with non-menu choices. Order takers must also hand relay the instructions to the preparers (similar to the special request scenarios) who are not able to decipher what to make from the register printout or computer screen. The management trainee asserts, "Some dead items live on at various locations, but the registers are standard. It's a tricky practice. Since I started here I've seen it happen a couple of times. When I get into corporate I'm gonna see what I can do about forcing a more standardized menu to relieve this problem." Of course, consumer satisfaction will suffer if old favorites are banished.

The ideal encounter is highly routinized and contains little if any ambiguity. It is a phenomenon that the employees are trained to produce and that the consumers are taught to expect. An ideal encounter occurs if the encounter is tightly scripted, highly routinized and results in an accurate end product. In practice, few encounters are ideal, but many fall within acceptable parameters of success.

Queue formation

In ethnomethodological terms, queues have "particular-queue queue-specific properties" (Livingston 1987).

> In a formatted queue the queue members have come together, organized themselves, managed and monitored their actions and the actions of others so as to produce, as their achievement, this immortal yet transient object. The members of a queue position themselves, enter the queue at its exhibited end, witnessably inspect the order of the queue, distance themselves from each other, advance in observably regular ways, and orient their bodies therein to show, and showing, who is after whom, where the queue is going, where the end of the line is, who is in the queue, who is not, and who may just be visiting. In the case of the formatted queue, the order of service–and all of its associated dependent, observable and observed properties– are produced in and as the way its production cohort has positioned itself so as to exhibit that order of service. (Livingston 1987)

In this local culture, all queues are formed from right to left (if facing the counter). Except for the drive-thru which depends on the driver aligning with the drive-thru window, there is no inherent advantage to the right to left queue formation. It appears to be a convention of the site, which is recognized by those who are familiar with the culture.

The Main Entrance: The layout of the restaurant is depicted in Exhibit 1. The main entrance opens into the dining room, but there is no obvious path toward the queue area. The counter is located directly in front of the incoming consumers. A menu board extends over and in back of the entire counter area, not overtly cueing consumers to join the line from the right. A booth island obstructs movement straight forward to the counter. Customers are faced with a Y path structure, with access to the queue and counter area from both paths. Near the side door on the consumers' right side are a set of red metal bars indicating queue formation. These red bars are not always readily apparent from the main entrance and are visually obstructed from the left path by the booth island. Perpendicular to the counter and to the consumers' left is the beverage bar. As people enter the facility from the main entrance, they either immediately veer right to the queue area, or begin to go left and alter course at, or near, the beverage bar. The beverage bar functions as a visual cue to consumers in the process of line formation. For those who enter the restaurant and initially veer left, the beverage bar is a physical heuristic at which they conspicuously contemplate their behavior and backtrack to proceed right. At times

during lunch peak, there is a large queue that extends into the dining area, but the consumers do not routinely utilize the red bar structure constructed for queue management. Even when the line overflows into the dining room, some consumers still veer left, stop at the beverage bar and backtrack to the right to join the line. No consumers enter the queue from the left.

From the layout and consumer behaviors described above, it appears that those who enter and veer right are more familiar with the local Taco Bell culture and possibly more familiar with fast food culture overall. Furthermore, the consumers who immediately veer right exhibit more confidence about the entire encounter than their left swerving counterparts. Those who immediately veer right demonstrate less hesitation in stepping up to the next open port and less indecision when ordering as compared to those who veer left and then change course to the right. A frequent fast food consumer and customer of the local restaurant offers the following rationale to the local queuing phenomenon: "No one walks past the drinks to order. It's a known sequence: order, money, *then* food." From this statement, it is evident that within the general fast food culture and this specific venue, there are conventions that govern consumer behavior. Describing this phenomenon to Mike, another explanation emerged: No one wants to be accused of stealing from the beverage bar. One thing is clear, a socially accepted sequence exists and must be adhered to. In this case, entering the queue via the beverage bar would seriously and conspicuously disrupt the sequence, resulting in negative consequences to the individual disrupting the socially constructed order, e.g., labeled socially inept, or a thief.

The Side Entrance is rarely utilized because foot traffic from the street is minimal and to enter form the side requires the consumer to cross the drive-thru queue, a potentially dangerous act.

The Counter as Boundary Region

Boundary constructions and the practical order they create become important for cultural participants (Hall 1995; Peñaloza 1994). Cultural participants must perform roles according to their presence in physical and social space (Goffman 1959; Berreman 1962; Grove and Fisk 1983). For this specific focus of inquiry, the counter becomes just such a symbolic border.

The Internal Counter: The counter separates the employee realm from the dining room. It serves as the window from one domain to the other. The counter is the primary site of financial exchange and food distribution. Associated with the boundary region of the counter are instructions in the form of a menu board to cue consumers to the appropriate manner to make their requests.

Although the counter represents the border between employee and consumer, employees can cross the boundary, while consumers are forbidden to do so. A sign indicates that entrance to the employee realm is for employees only. The door is perpendicular to the counter toward the right, side entrance. Furthermore, as the section on hierarchy demonstrates, some employees are less bound by the division between employee and consumer. The manager often crosses the border to clean the facility, direct employees and survey consumer satisfaction. Less often, order takers leave their posts to attend to the housekeeping chores in the consumer domain. Rarely are food preparers able to leave their posts to perform duties in the consumer realm.

The counter serves as a buffer between the realms. Society's hygiene rules and the nature of the employee's primary activities influence employee movement between realms. Food preparers are not seen cleaning the dining room, but may clean items in the employee area, for example, food preparation stations, floors, etc. Order takers and order fillers, who do not directly handle unwrapped food, are more often seen to move between realms as

EXHIBIT 1

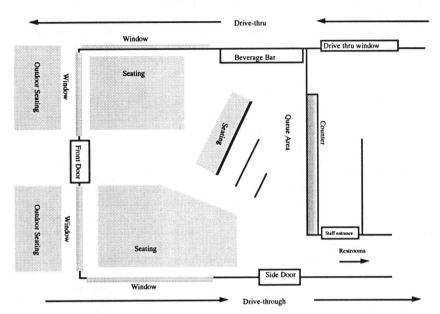

* Note: Customer path to queue from front door is <u>not</u> obvious

compared to those who directly handle food. Those who directly handle food are relegated to the employee realm and a higher degree of cleanliness and sterility. The trainee states, "Food preparers are supposed to wear gloves, but I have seen this is not consistently enforced." An employee comments, "Sometimes order takers do switch to food prep and I see them take money one minute and make food the next without washing their hands. This is not good. Money has many germs." For this employee, the above is not merely an infraction of policy, but is morally repugnant. Germs are a part of the consumer realm that must not be transferred to the food preparation area located well within the confines of the employee domain.

The presence of an order filler further demonstrates the distancing of the two realms. The front-line employees are not always in direct contact with the food preparing employees located in the inner sanctum of the employee domain. Often there is a barrier between the front-line, order takers and the preparers, that is, the warming trays.

The border is an artifact of the cultural divide between the employee in-groups and the consumer out-groups. The consumers are visitors in the fast food culture. They have the ability to contaminate, or dirty. This symbolic construction is similar to that found in research by Belk, Wallendorf and Sherry (1989). For the local culture, what ultimately is seen as unclean is "matter out of place." (Douglas 1966). Phil confirmed Taco Bell's commitment to cleanliness, "All Taco Bell restaurants have a high standard for cleanliness. Part of the Taco Bell brand image is based on healthy, clean alternatives to fat laden products, such as burgers and fries. ... Taco Bell is quality Mexican food *sterilized* for an American market."

The External Counter: For consumers participating in the external car queue, known in the local culture as the "drive-thru," the order board and window act as the border between the consumer and employee realms. The window is literally a window from one region to the other. The foot queue and face-to-face interaction between employee and consumer are modified to include a me-

chanical device and often a blind initial interaction. The consumer in the drive-thru does not initially see the employee with whom she/he is interacting. The voice encountered at the order board may not necessarily belong to the same person who takes the money through the window. While a camera often projects the image of the cars in the queue inside to the drive-thru attendant, employees do not have a clear image of the consumers phenotypes, nor time to study the projected image. The local manager suggests, "The video of the cars ordering and in line is just to give the attendant an idea of the situation outside. It helps them assess the number of incoming orders and get a feel for what's coming next. It is also a security measure."

In extremely busy times, termed "peaks"[2] by the members of the local culture, an order taker goes outside with an electronic order pad, change belt and head phones to relay car requests to the inside personnel who prepare the food items, gather and bundle orders and hand them to a window attendant who dispenses the order. The order pad, belt and headphones act as a counter surrogate. It enables the car consumers to participate in a more personal form of the counter interaction than afforded to those who order by external order board, either by touch pad, or voice communication. When the employee goes outside to take orders, she/he bypasses the electronic mediating device that often distorts the verbal message. Intuitively this suggests fewer communication errors, more accurate orders and increased satisfaction on the part of both actors in the dyad.

Although drive-thru window attendants are front-line employees, they are not in as much direct contact with the consumers and

[2]Peaks vary from restaurant to restaurant. For this location, the largest weekday peak is lunch, which is roughly between 11:30 am and 1:30 p.m. The second largest weekday peak is dinner, which is approximately from 5 p.m. to 7 p.m. Breakfast is a relatively new area for Taco Bell and has not yet developed a strong clientele.

are also in more direct contact with the food preparation crew. Often the employee assigned to the drive-thru window will be reassigned to food preparation when the drive-thru traffic subsides. The employee assigned to the window is not deemed as contaminated as the counter personnel, even though they pass food to the cars and handle money without gloves. The local manager remarks, "The drive-thru window employees are not in as much direct contact with the consumers, especially if an outside attendant is taking money. In that case, I can rotate him through as if he were clean."

Break Behavior: Ironically, despite the careful attention to the manner in which employee tasks are rotated, all employees break in the consumer domain. Order takers, order fillers, managers, trainees and food preparers alike spend their scheduled breaks in the consumer domain eating meals, sipping drinks and/or chatting with each other or consumers. The strict rules of contamination are magically suspended during break time when employees are not officially performing their roles as Taco Bell employees.

All employees are required to wash their hands before they begin their functional roles. This policy enables the employees to ritually shed the outside contaminants. A similar policy mandating that all employees wash their hands prior to role switching, e.g., housekeeping to food preparation, would mitigate the physical possibility of germ spreading, but may not address the symbolic issue of clean and dirty. For Taco Bell management and employees, the employee realm is afforded the delicate status of clean and the consumer domain is relegated to that of the dirty.

CONCLUSION

In the analysis of the locally produced social order found in the specific Taco Bell restaurant, members know the local conventions across roles. The four aspects of practical action in the society visible hierarchy, routinization, queue formation and the symbolic counter, are apparent to all cultural participants. The finer nuances associated with the employees' ordinary behaviors, i.e., order taking, order filling, and task rotation, are not of interest to the consumer members of the culture. The consumers are most interested in the service outcome as measured by the accuracy of the order and the ease of interaction with the employees. This difference in priorities and attention to the details of the fast food encounter are physically signified by the counter across which the encounter takes place. The relationship between consumer and employee is not antagonistic in nature as the expectations are not opposing, but rather are not identical. Employees have more dimensions on which to rate the encounter and more responsibility for the success or failure of each encounter. Possibly to cope with the inequity of responsibility among cultural participants, the counter has become an important boundary region physically separating the employee and consumer domains.

REFERENCES

Baker, Julie (1987), "The Role of Environment in Marketing Service: The Consumer Perspective," in *The Service Challenge: Integrating for Competitive Advantage*, ed. John A. Czepiel, Carol Congram and James Shanahan, Chicago: American Marketing Association.

Belk, Russell W. (Ed.) (1991) *Highways and Buyways: Naturalistic Research from the Consumer Behavior Odyssey*, Provo, UT: Association for Consumer Research.

_____, Melanie Wallendorf and John F. Sherry, Jr. (1989), "The Sacred and Profane in Consumer Behavior: Theodicy on the Odyssey," *Journal of Consumer Research*, vol. 16 (1).

Benson, Douglas and John A. Hughes (1983), *The Perspective of Ethnomethodology*, New York: Longman Group Limited.

Berreman, G.D. (1962), *Behind Many Masks: Ethnography and Impression Management in a Himalayan Village (Monograph no.4)*, Ithaca, NY: Society for Applied Anthropology.

Bitner, Mary Jo (1990), "Evaluating Service Encounters: The Effects of Physical Surroundings and Employee Responses, " *Journal of Marketing*, vol. 54 (April).

Bitner, Mary Jo (1992), "Servicescapes: The Impact of Physical Surroundings on Consumers and Employees, " *Journal of Marketing*, vol. 56 (April).

Burrell, Gibson and Gareth Morgan (1979), *Sociological Paradigms and Organizational Analysis*, London, UK: Heineman.

Caglar, Ayse S. (1995), "McDöner: Döner Kebap and the Social Positioning Struggle of German Turks," in *Marketing in a Multicultural World*, ed. Janeen Arnold Costa and Gary J. Bamossy, Thousand Oaks: Sage Publications.

Douglas, Mary (1966) *Purity and Danger: An Analysis of Concepts of Pollution and Taboo.* New York: Routledge & Kegan Paul.

Garfinkel, Harold (1967) *Studies in Ethnomethodology.* Englewood Cliffs, N.J.: Prentice-Hall.

Goffman, E. (1959), *The Presentation of Self in Everyday Life*, New York: Doubleday.

Granelli, James (1994), "Gauging Consumer's Tastes: Firm Conducts Surveys to Track Diners' Changing Habits," *Los Angeles Times*, October 3, p. D-1.

Grove, Stephen and Raymond P. Fisk (1983), "The Dramaturgy of Services Exchange: An Analytical Framework for Services Marketing," in *Emerging Perspectives on Services Marketing*, ed. L.L. Berry, G.L. Shostack and G.D. Upah, Chicago, IL: American Marketing Association.

Hall, Edward (1995), *West of the Thirties, Discovery Among the Navaho and Hopi*, New York: Doubleday.

Hume, S. (1990), "How Big Mac made it to Moscow," *Advertising Age*, vol. 16 (January 22).

Kvale, S. (1983), "The Qualitative Research Interview," *Journal of Phenomenological Psychology*, vol. 10.

Leidner, Robin (1993), *Fast Food, Fast Talk: Service Work and the Routinization of Everyday Life*, Berkely: University of California Press.

Livingston, Eric (1987), *Making Sense of Ethnomethodology*, New York: Routledge & Kegan Paul.

Mahatoo, Winston H. (1985), *The Dynamics of Consumer Behavior*, New York: John Wiley & Sons.

McCracken, Grant (1988), *Culture and Consumption: New Approaches to the Symbolic Character of Consumer Goods and Activities*, Bloomington, Indiana: Indiana University Press.

McGrath, M. A., J.F. Sherry Jr., and D. Hersley (1993), "An Ethnographic Study of an Urban Periodic Marketplace: Lessons from the Midville Farmers Market," *Journal of Retailing*, vol. 69.

Peñaloza, Lisa (1994), "*Atrevasando Fronteras*/Border Crossings: A Critical Ethnographic Exploration of the Consumer Acculturation of Mexican Immigrants," *Journal of Consumer Research*, vol. 21 (June).

Peter, J. Paul and Jerry C. Olson (1987), *Consumer Behavior Marketing Strategy Perspectives*, Homewood, IL: Irwin.

Rogers, Mary F. (1983), *Sociology, Ethnomethodology and Experience*, Cambridge, UK: Cambridge University Press.

Shelton, A. (1993), "Writing McDonald's, Eating the Past: McDonald's as a Postmodern Space," *Studies in Symbolic Interaction*, vol. 15.

Sherry, John F. Jr. (1990), "A Sociocultural Analysis of a Midwestern Flea Market," *Journal of Consumer Research*, vol. 17 (1).

_____ and M. McGrath (1989), "Unpacking the Holiday Presence: A Comparative Ethnography of Two Midwestern American Gift Stores," in *Interpretive Consumer Behavior*, ed. E. Hirschman, Provo, UT: Association of Consumer Research.

Solomon, Michael R., Carol Surprenant, John A. Czepiel and Evelyn G. Gutman (1985), "A Role Theory Perspective on Dyadic Interactions: The Service Encounter," *Journal of Marketing*, vol. 49 (Winter).

Solomon, Michael R. (1992), *Consumer Behavior*, Allyn & Bacon: Needham Heights, MA.

Weider, D. Lawrence (1974), "Telling the Code," in *Ethnomethodology*, ed. Roy Turner, Baltimore, MD: Penguin.

Williams, Raymond (1993), "Culture is Ordinary," in, *Studying Culture,* ed. Ann Gray and Jim McGuigan, London: Edward Arnold.

Zeithaml, Valarie Ann and Mary Jo Bitner (1996), *Services Marketing*, New York: McGraw-Hill.

A Pluralistic Approach to Visual Communication: Reviewing Rhetoric and Representation in World War I Posters

Maureen Hupfer, University of Alberta[1]

ABSTRACT

A pluralistic research approach that blends historical and art historical methods of inquiry is proposed for the analysis of visual advertising images. Although individually these disciplines fail to provide satisfactory accounts of the meaning(s) that viewers construct in response to advertising visuals, interpretation is enhanced by blending the two methods of inquiry. This pluralistic approach is applied to British World War I posters targeted toward women to encourage their wartime participation. Choosing a historical context that is seemingly remote from our contemporary advertising research concerns assists in the development of a theory of visual rhetoric because it allows researchers to *look directly at*, rather than simply *view through or with,* the ingrained beliefs about visual representation that flaw current research practice.

INTRODUCTION

During the past ten years, an increasingly diverse range of methodologies has been applied to the investigation of consumer behavior (Hirschman 1986; Holbrook 1987). Certain researchers have argued that the interpretive traditions of the humanities may lend greater insight into "the meanings embedded in consumer behavior" than can be achieved within our familiar social science paradigms (Holbrook and O'Shaughnessy 1988). Observing that much of advertising research has been flawed by misconceptions regarding the visual conventions underlying advertisement construction and consumption, Scott has called for a theory of visual rhetoric to improve our understanding of advertising images (1994). Accordingly, she has proposed a pluralistic research program including historical analyses that consider social and cultural context as well as advertising objectives and visual conventions.

This analytical task demands an interdisciplinary approach in which historical and art historical methods of inquiry are blended. Individually, these disciplines fail to provide satisfactory accounts of the social effects of persuasive campaigns. Each, however, has particular strengths: art history's knowledge of visual conventions (Fernie 1995), and history's attention to socially and culturally situated individuals and groups (Green 1993; Shafer 1980). In this paper I argue that by moving back and forth between historical and art historical method, researchers can achieve a synthesis that advances our understanding of how viewers respond to visual advertising images and construct meaning. For illustrative purposes, I have selected three posters from campaigns aimed at British women to encourage their participation in the World War I effort. Corresponding to the primary categories in which female involvement was required throughout the war, these three examples are also representative of the realist aesthetic strategy employed by recruiting organizations. Historical sources provide a social context, and interpretation is enhanced by a close reading informed by art historical understanding of visual conventions.

Selection of an advertising campaign seemingly so remote from our contemporary advertising research concerns offers an important advantage in that it facilitates the understanding that visual images are "re-presentations" rather than simple reflections of observed reality (Mitchell 1986). The belief that pictures copy or mimic real world reality is a thoroughly ingrained and naturalized cultural assumption, and functions as a pictorial schemata or lens through which visual information is processed (Solso 1994). However, Western world pictorial realism is only one of many possible visual conventions available for image production. By examining a context in which social and visual conventions differ from our own experience, we are better able to *look directly at* these learned pictorial conventions rather than simply *view through or with* the copy theory lens that obscures our analysis of contemporary advertisements (Scott 1994). When we return to our contemporary context, we can better identify entrenched beliefs regarding the nature of visual language, rather than view uncritically with these assumptions unquestioned and intact. We recognize that pictures need not be rooted in observable reality when we refer to imagery that is readily perceived as dated, and begin to appreciate that the photographs favored in current print advertising practice are no less constructed and no more "truthful" or "objective" than those painted or drawn (Tagg 1988). As such, we move toward building a theory of visual rhetoric and improving our understanding of the processes by which socially and historically situated audiences respond to advertising images.

METHODOLOGICAL FRAMEWORK

Historical theory is derived through both inductive and deductive processes; relevant primary and secondary data are collected, organized and interpreted to form one or more working hypotheses that guide subsequent evaluation and data collection (Green 1993). Analysis and synthesis merge and overlap as the historian moves toward a final account of an historical phenomenon (Shafer 1980). In their analysis of British World War I poster campaigns, historians treat these images as simple visual evidence of female access to previously male-dominated occupations. As such, the posters are situated within a nineteenth century emancipatory process that culminated with partial enfranchisement in 1918 (Marwick 1977). Rather than considering their active contribution to wartime role construction, historians have cast these posters as artifacts that passively reflect their social and historical context. More recent work acknowledges that these persuasive campaigns did not, and indeed could not, represent the gruelling or dangerous aspects of female wartime labor (Woollacott 1994). Nevertheless, the expectation that pictures *should* represent reality belies the historian's reliance on copy theory.

The tendency among historians to overlook the meaning that pictorial convention lends to the visual image (Robertson 1988) is a shortcoming that can be addressed by the art historian. Art historical investigation proceeds similarly via induction and deduction, but pays particular attention to the object itself. Methods include stylistic analysis, consideration of pictorial traditions, and an examination of social context including conditions of production and reception (Fernie 1995).

Despite the ability of art historians to augment research undertaken by historians, they also treat the war poster in a summary fashion, albeit for different reasons. In general, the poster falls beneath the art historical purview, unless the work can be raised to

---

[1]The author thanks Adam Finn and three anonymous reviewers for their helpful comments in preparation of this paper, and acknowledges the support of the Social Sciences and Humanities Research Council of Canada.

the level of fine art. This brand of art historical redemption is most frequently applied to posters by artists who are well established within the modernist High Art canon, and to work that is avant-garde in style. The British war poster is doomed to obscurity on both counts. Most of these designs were created by anonymous artists in printing house art departments (Darracott 1974, p. ix). More seriously, they featured the narrative realist style made popular by Victorian academic painters and preferred by commercial advertisers who believed that advertisements were less effective when they were "too artistic" (Lay Figure 1917, p. 52). Pejorative judgments attached to these realist images were instituted in early poster studies (Hardie and Sabin 1920) and persist in more recent writing (Ades 1984).

Neither historical nor art historical discussion of the British illustrated war poster provides a satisfactory account of the manner in which an aesthetic strategy of realism was exploited by advertisers to communicate war imperatives. Nor has previous analysis attempted to explain the British public's response to these advertising campaigns or the social impact of these posters in constructing the female wartime role. A reevaluation that addresses these problematic omissions must consider the visual conventions inherent in these images as well as the social and historical context within which they operated.

THE ILLUSTRATED POSTER CAMPAIGNS OF WORLD WAR I BRITAIN

Britain in 1914

Edwardian Britain's social system was one in which the inherited Victorian ideology of separate spheres for the sexes acted as a formidable force in opposition to the fledgling feminist movement. Despite agitation for female emancipation throughout the late nineteenth century, Britain was still steeped in a social construction of gender that assigned passivity, emotion, moral virtue, and responsibility for children to the female domestic sphere. Conversely, men were expected to be active, rational, intellectual, and to provide for their families through their conduct in the economic sphere. Because of its bipolar nature, Victorian gender ideology was a delicate balancing act in which changes in one gender role implied a corresponding adjustment for the other (Poovey 1988).

The Illustrated Poster in British Advertising Practice

Nineteenth century developments in lithography had allowed economic quantity production of visual images with tonal and color gradation, and advertisers were quick to exploit the poster's advantages (Rickards 1970, p. 12). Regarded as a highly effective form of commercial persuasion, the poster had eye-catching appeal that was believed to capture even the uninterested viewer's attention (Lay Figure 1917, p. 52). In addition to its commercial use, the poster had been exploited by suffrage campaigners (Tickner 1988, p. 48-49), and by politicians during the 1910 election. The poster could also offer the government communicative prominence. Because wartime economizing and rising paper prices had curtailed commercial image production, those produced by the government experienced less visual competition than normally would have been the case (Nevett 1982, p. 139). Given these factors, it would have been surprising had the government failed to utilize the visual image for its own campaigns of persuasion.

Poster Production in the Early Stages of WWI

The Parliamentary Recruiting Committee (PRC) was responsible for most of the initial poster production (Crawford 1979). These government recruiting posters typically featured the well-accepted Victorian narrative and illustrative art style that prompted viewers to decipher the story behind the image. As either fine art or commercial image, the Victorian realist picture was a highly familiar visual convention for Edwardian viewers. This style was firmly associated with Britain's nineteenth century Imperial strength, and by extension, an economic and social system structured by separate spheres for the sexes. A well-accepted style and a democratized art form were important considerations in a mass appeal that sought to evoke a glorious past with a rhetoric of sacrifice, moral duty and patriotic fervor. Artists and critics would describe these images as an insult to public taste (Hardie and Sabin 1920, p. 9), but the British public felt otherwise. With Victorian "healthy naturalism" preferred to modernist "heavy eccentricity" (Rickards 1970, p.12), the government was wise to avoid the avant-garde in their promotion of the war effort.

During the early stages of World War I, women were encouraged to persuade their men to enlist. *Women of Britain Say — "GO!"* (Figure 1) was tailored specifically to appeal to the young wives whose husbands were not enlisting in adequate numbers. Historical accounts of this image simply describe this illustration: an ideal British wife and mother, in an attractive state of deshabille on the "morning after the night before", bravely watches the soldiers march away for war (Adam 1975, p.43). Fashionable wrapper gaping open, her hair hastily twisted and pinned, this woman would draw the viewer's eye just as an appealing female posed with a product did for commercial advertisers.

The art historian would go on to address the visual functions of the open window, which demarcates the separate spheres for the sexes and provides justification for the woman's attire. A parallel may be drawn between Romantic art's open window as symbol of longing for adventure and the romantic manner in which the war was first perceived. The lovely countryside view also suggests the female-nature/male-culture dichotomy — it was often said that soldiers were at war to defend Britain's culture. In conjunction with the woman's clothing, the natural setting further signifies middle-class social status. Far from London east end poverty, this family is fortunate to reside in this idyllic locale at a time when the city-based proletariat was estimated at 80% of the population (Marwick 1974, p. 21).

Viewers were thus offered a sentimental appeal that encouraged romantic construal of a husband's departure for the front. A recruitment poster could not be expected to depict women and children subjected to hardship, but the comfortable situation enjoyed by this family was not typical of experience on the home front. Within a few days of the war's outbreak, nearly 40% of women employed in luxury trades lost their jobs as businesses anticipated drastic cuts in luxury purchases (Marwick 1974, p. 60). Working-class families were left badly off, with meagre separation payments that arrived late or never at all (Pankhurst 1932, p. 12).

Additional situational factors reiterated the message of the recruiting posters and encouraged similar response. For example, Admiral Penrose Fitzgerald's campaign had women present white feathers of cowardice to healthy young men who had not yet enlisted (Adam 1975, p. 41-42), while Baroness Orczy's Active Service League attracted over 20,000 female volunteers who pressured men to enlist (Martin 1974, p. 40). Newspapers and women's magazines such as *Home Notes* praised women who had urged their husbands and sweethearts to join the cause (Adam 1975, p. 42).

How would male viewers have responded to these messages? Conscientious objectors could not have regarded them with much enthusiasm. Working-class men also must have viewed them with dismay, knowing that to enlist would leave their families in desperate straits. Some must have resented the government's persuasion tactics and the motives of women who urged them to enlist. "If I

FIGURE 1
Women of Britain Say - "GO!"
E.V. Kealey, 1914 (London: Imperial War Museum)

enlist it will be for my own reasons and not for your own safety, not to protect you against an invasion..." (Adam 1975, p. 42-43).

Wartime strong-arm tactics were also criticized by *Punch*, the journal directed toward the middle to upper-class London professional establishment. In August 1915, *Punch* described the "universal eruption of posters" as the new art of "Government by advertisement." "It may be necessary, but the method is not dignified" (Punch 1919, p. 50). Dignified or not, by 1916 the PRC had printed and distributed nearly 12.5 million copies of some 164 different posters (Sanders and Taylor 1982, p. 104). Both the narrative realism and the rhetoric of sacrifice and duty established by the PRC would set the tone for future war posters.

Poster Campaigns After Conscription in 1916

During the war's first year, the female role was still conceived in traditional Victorian terms. This would soon change. In 1916, the government introduced conscription. War casualties had reached alarmingly high proportions, many more men were needed at the front, and women would have to join the labor force in order to maintain levels of production and service (International Labor Office 1946, p. 1-3).

In *Learn to Make Munitions* (Figure 2), the text "These women are doing their bit," suggests that this woman is making a necessary but temporary sacrifice by producing munitions for men at the front. Woollacott has observed that the visual balance between the woman's cheery wave and the soldier's salute equate her duty with his (1994, p. 112c). However, the woman's placement within the factory and the soldier's position at the open door ensures that the spheres remain separate. The woman's winsome face lends visual appeal, and provides the necessary reassurance that her labor need not entail loss of femininity. One foot extends beyond the poster border, joining her space with the viewer's to encourage identification or self-referencing. The eye-catching gold and purple combination, associated with luxury and royalty, was often used by advertisers to

create favorable impressions, and here may have referred to the praise extended to munitions workers by the King.

Just as the PRC recruitment posters could not suggest hardship at home or danger at the front, neither could these munitions posters have made reference to highly explosive chemicals or the toxic jaundice suffered by armaments workers (Woollacott 1994, p. 112e). Persuasive strategies aside, the long-standing tradition of female beauty as an appropriate subject of high art (Nead 1988) would have prohibited the depiction of a woman's skin yellowed with chemical poisoning.

It is doubtful that the appeal to duty held much interest for the working-class women who flocked to the factories by the hundreds of thousands (Braybon 1981, p. 47). Attracted by high wages and a better standard of living, many women left low-paying domestic positions to work in munitions, creating significant shortages in the domestic labor pool (Martin 1974, p. 58). Certainly the pre-war match factory laborers who had endured the bone deterioration caused by phosphorus poisoning would not have been deterred by hazardous working conditions and long hours. However, a persuasive message that construed this female employment as wartime duty would have encouraged middle and upper-class viewers to respond to the controversial issues of enhanced earning power among lower-class women and domestic labor shortages by equating the horrors of the munitions factories with those at the front. Reports of munitions workers' wartime extravagance occasionally reached the press, but more commonly, the British media reiterated the message of sacrifice by describing their gallantry during tragedies such as the Silvertown explosion of 1917 (Martin 1974, p. 58).

The Voluntary Aid Detachment (VAD) was one program that did attract middle and upper-class women. Paid employment outside the home was inappropriate for young ladies, but voluntarism connoted traditions of charitable acts and noblesse oblige. Once war casualties soared, VAD nurses were posted at hospitals in all the major war theatres, and capably carried out arduous work under

FIGURE 2
Learn to Make Munitions
Septimus Scott, c. 1916 (London: Imperial War Museum)

gruesome conditions. One recruitment poster, captioned *VAD's Urgently Needed*, featured three nurses with snowy white aprons in an updated version of Faith, Hope and Charity. Few could have failed to respond by associating these angels in white with their eminent predecessor, Florence Nightingale. The close identification of nursing with feminine nurture and maternal sacrifice was probably a factor in attracting the middle and upper-class women who were more tightly bound by social constraint than their working-class sisters. As *Punch* observed, there was "nothing new in the function of ministering angel" (Punch 1919, p. 95-96).

The women's war effort reached a new peak when women joined the auxiliary corps of the Armed Services to free men from non-combatant duties. Between 1917 and the war's end, approximately 100,000 British women replaced male soldiers as motorcyclists, drivers, cooks, clerks, storekeepers and typists (Mitchell 1966, p. 221-222). However, the civilian designation meant that an auxiliary corps woman would always be "the girl behind the man behind the gun" rather than an active partner in the war effort.

Art historical analysis of the auxiliary corps posters reveals that these recruiters continued to follow the advertising strategy established by the PRC. Whenever possible, the novel and dangerous aspects of female involvement were glossed over while the more traditional aspects of the female role were emphasized. Such was the case with the example (Figure 3) that urged women to join the Women's Royal Air Force (WRAF). An idealized female figure is posed with a gesture used by Edwardian advertisers to draw attention to a product being promoted. In this case the product is the woman herself and her position as a WRAF, identified or branded by the circular Royal Air Force Insignia. The supportive nature of her role is implied by her placement at an air base out of harm's reach, while overhead the men fly off to fight for their country. The most traditional aspects of the female role are emphasized through the use of larger-scale typography, while the shock value of the request for "experienced motor-cyclists" is softened by the use of

smaller lettering and its placement at the end of a list that advertises for Clerks, Waitresses and Cooks.

RESEARCH SUMMARY

Historians frequently cite the high level of female wartime employment as evidence of a successful British feminist movement that culminated in partial enfranchisement in 1918. In these discussions, war poster images are frequently invoked as a visual validation of this gradual process of female emancipation. However, analyses such as these ignore the prescriptive power of the wartime advertising campaigns in maintaining traditional gender roles.

As a body of persuasive images designed to solicit female involvement in the war effort, the posters produced by government and semi-official bodies played a key role in the formation of attitudes regarding appropriate feminine behavior and occupations in wartime Britain. The unusual demands of war necessitated the widespread employment of women in many previously male-dominated and even hazardous occupations, and this expansion of the female sphere was facilitated by the corresponding new requirements of the male sphere. The poster campaigns contributed to this ideological negotiation by conveying visual information which reassured the British public that expansion of the female role was never intended as anything more than a wartime phenomenon. These patriotic appeals to duty and sacrifice employed a narrative, realistic format and consistently emphasized the supportive and temporary nature of every field of endeavor that women would enter during the war. Whenever possible, recruiters highlighted the most traditional aspects of these new female occupations through appropriate typography, idealized female figures and idyllic settings. Mr. Punch certainly managed this role expansion with great aplomb. Despite their "foibles", he never supposed that British women would be anything but "keen and ready when the hour of need struck" (Punch 1919, p. 96).

FIGURE 3
British Women! — the Royal Air Force needs your help
Anonymous, c. 1917

Even though individual attitudes regarding female capabilities may have changed, the social system relaxed back into its Edwardian balanced state once the war was over. Woman's place, as before, was in the home. Most female factory workers lost their jobs to returning soldiers, with the exception of those employed in sectors that had traditionally exploited female labor. New levels of bureaucracy offered employment for some women, but the majority returned to domestic and family responsibilities. During the 1920s, female labor statistics dropped back to pre-war levels. The ideological expansion necessitated by the war shrank as quickly as it had grown, and not until 1939 would similar expansion occur.

CONCLUSION

I have argued that researchers can enhance their analysis of persuasive imagery by adopting an approach that blends the methods of history and art history, and have demonstrated how application of this interdisciplinary strategy to the British World War I poster achieves greater insight than is offered by either of these disciplines in isolation. Although researchers should value the study of image production and consumption in the past for the counterpoint provided with the present, this methodological framework is also appropriate for investigation of contemporary advertising images. Where contemporary advertisements are concerned, a thorough analysis using historical and art historical methods can assist in the development of an empirically testable hypothesis. One might, for example, test the hypothesis that the depiction of conventionally pretty women in contemporary armed forces recruitment campaigns is an effective means of persuading viewers that women in the armed forces have not sacrificed their "femininity" for their military careers.

Once equipped with the insight that all visual images depend on established conventions for their creation and reception, researchers may also begin to document and explain the shift from illustrated to photographic imagery in advertising, continue to explore relationships between the visual conventions of fine and commercial art, and work toward a more complete understanding of the manner in which consumers read the visual language of advertising. From the investigation of questions such as these, the foundation for a theory of visual rhetoric will be constructed.

REFERENCES

Adam, Ruth (1975), *A Woman's Place: 1910-1975,* London: Chatto and Windus.

Ades, Dawn (1984), *The 20th-century Poster,* New York: Abbeville.

Braybon, Gail (1981), *Women Workers in the First World War: The British Experience,* London: Croom Helm.

Crawford, Anthony R. (1979), *Posters of World War I and World War II in the George C. Marshall Research Foundation,* Charlottesville: University Press of Virginia.

Darracott, Joseph (1974), *The First World War in Posters,* New York: Dover.

Fernie, Eric, ed. (1995), *Art History and Its Methods: A Critical Anthology,* London: Phaidon.

Green, William A. (1993), *History, Historians, and the Dynamics of Change,* Westport: Praeger.

Hardie, Martin and Arthur K. Sabin (1920), *War Posters Issued by Belligerent and Neutral Nations 1914-1919,* London: A & C Black.

Hirschman, Elizabeth C. (1986), "Humanistic Inquiry in Marketing Research: Philosophy, Method and Criteria," *Journal of Marketing Research,* 23 (August), 237-249.

Holbrook, Morris B. (1987), "What is Consumer Research?" *Journal of Consumer Research,* 14 (June), 128-132.

Holbrook, Morris B. and John O'Shaughnessy (1988), "On the Scientific Status of Consumer Research and the Need for an Interpretive Approach in Studying Consumer Behavior," *Journal of Consumer Research,* 15 (December), 398-402.

International Labor Office (1946), *The War and Women's Employment: The Experience of the United Kingdom and the United States,* Montreal: International Labor Office.

Lay Figure (1917), "On the Possibilities of the Poster," *The Studio* 69, (15 January), 52.

Martin, Christopher (1974), *English Life in the First World War,* London: Wayland.

Marwick, Arthur (1974), *War and Social Change in the Twentieth Century,* London: Macmillan.

_____ (1977), *Women at War 1914-1918,* London: Imperial War Museum.

Mitchell, David (1966), *Women on the Warpath: The Story of Women of the First World War,* London: Jonathan Cape.

Mitchell, W.J.T. (1986), *Iconology,* Chicago: University of Chicago Press.

Nead, Lynda (1988), *Myths of Sexuality: Representations of Women in Victorian Britain,* Oxford and New York, Basil Blackwell.

Nevett, T.R. (1982), *Advertising in Britain: A History,* London: Heinemann.

Pankhurst, E. Sylvia (1932), *The Home Front: A Mirror to Life in England During the World War,* London: Hutchinson.

Poovey, Mary (1988), *Uneven Developments: The Ideological Work of Gender in Mid- Victorian England,* Chicago: University of Chicago Press.

Punch (1919), *Mr. Punch's History of the Great War,* London, New York, Toronto and Melbourne: Cassell.

Rickards, Maurice (1970), *Posters of Protest and Revolution,* New York: Walker.

Robertson, Peter (1988), "More Than Meets the Eye," in *Clio's Craft: A Primer of Historical Methods*, ed. Terry Crowley, Toronto: Copp Clark Pitman, 65-75.

Sanders, M.L. and Philip M. Taylor (1982), *British Propaganda During the First World War, 1914-1918,* London: Macmillan.

Scott, Linda (1994), "Images in Advertising: The Need for a Theory of Visual Rhetoric," *Journal of Consumer Research,* 21 (September), 252-273.

Shafer, Robert Jones (1980), *A Guide to Historical Method,* 3rd edition, Belmont: Wadsworth Press.

Solso, Robert L. (1994), *Cognition and the Visual Arts,* Cambridge: MIT Press.

Tagg, John (1988), *The Burden of Representation: Essays on Photographies and Histories,* Minneapolis: University of Minneapolis Press.

Tickner, Lisa (1988), *The Spectacle of Women: Imagery of the Suffrage Campaign 1907- 1914,* Chicago: University of Chicago Press.

Woollacott, Angela (1994), *On Her Their Lives Depend: Munitions Workers in the Great War,* Berkeley: University of California Press.

SPECIAL SESSION SUMMARY
New Directions in Reference Price Research
David Bell, UCLA,
Eyal Biyalogorsky, Duke University
Ziv Carmon, Duke University

A remarkably robust finding in consumer behavior is that consumers typically evaluate attributes relative to a standard, rather than in an absolute manner. The influence of deviations from these standards on the assessment of the attributes is commonly called a reference effect. Reference price effects in brand choice have been particularly well documented in both experimental work and in research that uses secondary (e.g., scanner panel) data. Despite this, several key areas for research remain. These include: exploration of the fundamentals of the reference price construct and its interaction with consumer expectations, operationalization and empirical testing of multiple reference price constructs, and the notion that reference effects may be important in many consumer decisions (of which brand choice is just one example). In this note, we summarize findings of recent research that seeks to answer specific questions from each of these new research domains. Specifically: how are reference prices formed, how should they be operationalized, and do they affect the purchase incidence decision?

Reference Price Formation

A considerable stream of research relies on the notion that consumers' price expectations serve as reference values. This research illustrates that reference prices help predict consumers' brand choice decisions. However, little work has attempted to more directly examine how price expectations are utilized in the formation of reference prices. Biyalogorsky and Carmon (1996) look at the reference price as an endogenous construct. In an experimental setting they obtain measures of participants' price knowledge, expectations and choices. Their research develops the following important insight: choice models can have good predictive ability *despite* the fact that these models provide a poor description of consumers stated price expectations. This finding has significant implications for how researchers should conceptualize and operationalize reference values.

Operationalizing Reference Prices

Even though the reference effect phenomenon is well documented, there is controversy regarding the correct way to operationalize important constructs such as reference prices. A key dichotomy concerns whether consumers hold reference prices in memory, or whether they form them at the point of purchase. Some researchers argued that consumers may not recall past prices but can remember the brand chosen on the last purchase occasion, and are therefore likely to use that brand's *current* price as a reference point for price judgments (see e.g. Hardie et al. 1993). However, a majority of researchers have modeled reference prices as a function of past prices with varying carryover weights (Kalyanaram and Little 1987; Raman and Bass 1988; Lattin and Bucklin 1989; Mayhew and Winer 1992; Krishnamurthi et al. 1992). Yet others have operationalized reference price as a function, of not only past prices, but also other contextual factors. Examples include deal proneness of the consumer, how frequently the brand is sold on deal, store characteristics, and price trend (e.g., Winer 1986; Kalwani et al. 1990).

Briesch et al. (1996) seek to develop an exhaustive comparison of these competing ways to operationalize the reference value.

They utilize scanner panel data from several different categories to conduct an empirical assessment of memory-based and point-of-purchase reference prices. Overall, the reference price modeled as the exponentially smoothed history of a brand's own prices appears to provide the best fit to the data. The results are consistent with the notion that consumers retain price information over time and utilize it in current period choices.

Reference Effects in Purchase Incidence

Much of the extant research on reference effects addresses the brand choice decision (an exception is the choice/quantity model of Krishnamurthi, Mazumdar and Raj, 1992). Bell and Bucklin (1996) show that the reference effects are also important in the purchase incidence decision. Furthermore, that the reference effect in purchase incidence arises when consumers make an intertemporal utility maximizing decision: to "buy now" or "buy later." They show that the traditional nested logit model of purchase incidence (that does not consider reference effects) is simply a special case of a more general model that allows for intertemporal effects.

The work also suggests that the tendency to exhibit reference effects varies with other aspects of consumer behavior. For example, consumers who exhibit reference effects in purchase incidence are more likely to be store switchers, and display variability in their purchase timing decisions. One rationale for this finding is that store switchers have more finely calibrated expectations than those shoppers who only see a single store environment, and furthermore that that they are opportunistic with respect to purchase timing.

Conclusion

The purpose of this note was to summarize new findings on reference effects. The notion that reliance on expectations manifests itself in reference effects was made to advance three key research areas: exploring of the multi-faceted nature of reference value formation; empirical testing and validation of alternative reference price constructs; and examination of reference effects in contexts other than brand choice.

REFERENCES

Bell, D. R., and R. E. Bucklin (1995), "Investigating the 'Incidence' of Reference Effects: A Nested Logit Approach with latent Segments," working paper, University of California at L.A., Anderson School of Business, LA, CA 90024.

Biyalogorsky, E., and Z. Carmon (1996), "Consumers' Price Expectations for Frequently Purchased Products," working paper, Fuqua School of Business, Duke University, Durham, NC 27708.

Briesch R. A., L. Krishnamurthi, T. Mazumdar, and S. P. Raj (1996), " A Comparative Analysis of Reference Price Models," working paper, New York University, Stern School of Business, NY, NY 10003.

Kalyanaram, G. and J. D. C. Little (1989), "A Price Response Model Developed from Perceptual Theories," working paper, Sloan School of Management, MIT, Cambridge, MA 02139.

Hardie, B. G. S., E. J. Johnson, and P. S. Fader (1993), "Modeling Loss Aversion and Reference Dependence Effects on Brand Choice," *Marketing Science*, 12 (Fall), 378-394.

Krishnamurthi, L., T. Mazumdar, and S. P.Raj (1992), "Asymmetric Response to Price in Consumer Brand Choice and Purchase Quantity Decisions," *Journal of Consumer Research*, 19 (December), 387-400.

Lattin, J. M., and R. E. Bucklin (1989), "Reference Effects of Price and Promotion on Brand Choice Behavior," *Journal of Marketing Research*, 26 (August), 299-310.

Mayhew, G. E., and R. S. Winer (1992), "An Empirical Analysis of Internal and External Reference Prices Using Scanner Data," *Journal of Consumer Research*, 19 (June), 62-70.

Raman, K. and F. M. Bass (1988), "A General Test of Reference Price Theory in the Presence of Threshold Effects," working paper, University of Texas at Dallas, Richardson, TX 75083.

Winer, R. S. (1986), "A Reference Price Model of Brand Choice", *Journal of Marketing Research*, 13 (September), 250-256.

Measuring Consumption and Consuming Measurement: The Challenge of Studying Consumers from a Federal Perspective

Frederick Conrad, Bureau of Labor Statistics

Vast amounts of information are available to American consumers and businesses that can help them make wiser decisions. Much of this information is provided by the Federal government and is the result of considerable research about consumer behavior. This session presented samples of such research from three domains (1) consumers' use of information on product labels and the implications for labeling policy; (2) accuracy of data collected in national, sample surveys about the public's economic activities and circumstances; and (3) customer satisfaction with government products and services. The session was organized as a first step in fostering more dialogue between consumer researchers working in the public service and those working in the marketing tradition.

Alan Levy reported a study, carried out jointly with Brenda Derby and Brian Roe, to explore how health claims on food labels can affect consumers' evaluations of the labeled product and how this can vary with the length, format, and information content of the health claim. They intercepted grocery shoppers at a mall and presented them with three different food products (cereal, low fat yogurt, and frozen lasagna) whose labels contained health claims about certain ingredients in those products. One food was presented in a control condition (no health claim) and the other two in different experimental conditions. The cereal product was labeled with a health claim about folic acid, the yogurt product included a claim about calcium and the frozen lasagna product carried a health claim about saturated fat and cholesterol. The health claims appeared in either short or long form, either with or without an "authority message" (for example, "The American Heart Association recommends ..."), with or without the seal of the Food and Drug Administration, and with or without an instruction to see the back panel for more information. Because there were more experimental conditions than food products, the assignment of conditions to shoppers was counterbalanced with a Greco-latin square design.

In the control conditions, there were no health claims on the labels. However, in one control condition, the label included a nutrient content claim. This simply mentioned that the food contained the critical ingredient, for example, "low fat." This manipulation made it possible to compare the effect of health claims in general to those of nutrient content alone.

For each food, the shoppers were asked how likely they were to purchase it, how important it would be to a healthy diet, and how universal its health benefits would be. Overall, the presence of labels increased shoppers' rated likelihood of purchasing the food and its healthfulness relative to the control condition. However, the different lengths and formats of the health claim made relatively little difference to shoppers on these measures. In particular, there was no effect of label length. This is significant because the Nutrition Labeling and Education Act of 1990 virtually mandates the use of the longer health claims on labels; yet consumers are deriving no additional relevant information from longer than shorter health claims. Invoking an authority had a negative effect on purchase intentions and perceived healthfulness which the authors interpreted as people's sensitivity to being manipulated. Instructions to see the back panel had a negative effect on purchase intentions and compellingness if the message on the back did not add information; if it did add information, there was no effect on purchase intentions and compellingness.

Like the health claims, the nutrient content claims increased peoples' ratings of purchase intention and healthiness. Moreover, health claims were no more effective in shoppers' ratings than were nutrient content claims. The authors hypothesize this is because the nutrient content claim served as a reminder of dietary information with which the shoppers were already familiar. Consistent with this was the finding that nutrient content claims about folic acid had no effect on shoppers' ratings, and the health effects of this ingredient are not as well known as are the others in the study. They conclude that the way consumers use health and nutrition information depends on their prior knowledge of the food and the health claim for that food.

Frederick Conrad reported two studies conducted collaboratively with Michael Schober to investigate the costs and benefits of standardized versus conversational survey interviewing. Because survey data serve as the basis of major decisions in government, marketing and politics, the quality of the decisions are limited by the quality of the data. Typically, survey questions are read by interviewers, exactly as worded; the interviewers use only "neutral probes" to clarify what they have read. The logic of such standardized interviews is to reduce survey error by controlling the content of the interaction. Unfortunately, respondents do not always interpret the questions as they were intended by the researcher; unlike ordinary conversation, where participants can converse until they believe that they understand each other, standardized interviews prohibit the kind of interaction that would be required to assure mutual understanding. In this sense, standardization may actually increase certain types of error.

In Conrad and Schober's first experiment, professional interviewers asked 43 laboratory participants (who were playing the role of respondents) 12 questions taken from large government surveys. Instead of answering about their own lives, the respondents answered about fictional situations described in a packet of scenarios, diagrams and receipts.

For each question, the authors designed one scenario for which the correct answer was clear and one for which it was ambiguous. The ambiguities could be resolved by referring to official definitions for the particular survey. For example, one receipt leading to an ambiguity was from a furniture store and included a charge for a floor lamp. The respondent was asked if the protagonist had "purchased or had expenses for household furniture." In fact, the survey's definition of furniture specifically excludes floor lamps. The combinations of questions and situations were counterbalanced so that for any one participant, half were clear and half ambiguous.

Half of the interviews were conducted according to standardized procedure, half as conversational or "flexible" interviews. If respondents asked for clarification in the standardized interviews, the interviewers could only repeat the questions or response alternatives; in the flexible interviews, the interviewers could say anything they wanted, including paraphrasing the definitions, to assure that respondents understood the question as intended.

The results showed that the value of either interviewing technique depends on how difficult it is for respondents to interpret the concepts in the questions given the situation about which they are answering. When this is easy, accuracy is high for both standardized (97%) and flexible (98%) interviews. However, when it is difficult, accuracy suffers under standardized interviewing (29%) but is vastly improved in the flexible condition (87%). It is important to consider two practical issues when evaluating these results. First, it is not clear to what extent people's own situations are ambiguous with respect to most survey questions. If this is rare, then standardized wording is justified. Second, flexible interviews take more time than standardized interviews and actual, voluntary respondents may be unwilling to participate in them.

Conrad and Schober carried out a second experiment carried out as a (more) natural telephone survey. Respondents were interviewed twice. The first interview was standardized; the second was standardized in half the cases and flexible in the other half. In each interview, respondents were asked five questions about their housing and five questions about their recent purchases. These questions were all taken from large government surveys. Because the respondents (contacted from a national probability sample) answered questions about their own lives, the experimenters could not validate their responses. As a result, they developed a surrogate measure for accuracy: response change between the first and second interviews. The logic was that if misconceptions were not clarified in the initial standardized interview they could be clarified in a subsequent flexible interview leading to changed responses between interviews. If the second interview was also standardized, the misconception was relatively likely to persist. This prediction was supported by the data even though the authors could not control the complexity of the mappings between questions and respondents' circumstances. When the second interview was standardized, respondents changed their answers between interviews on 11% of the questions. However, when the second interview was flexible, this figure increased to 22%.

Conrad and Schober concluded that practitioners need to be able to demonstrate that complicated mappings are rare enough so that the benefits of standardization outweigh the costs Unless they can do this, data quality may be compromised by standardization techniques.

Tracy Wellens' presentation, based on her collaboration with Elizabeth Martin and Frank Vitrano, concerned the challenges of measuring customer satisfaction with Federal products and services. She reported their experience surveying customers' satisfaction for the products and services of the 14 agencies within the Department of Commerce. The study was a response to an executive order "Setting Customer Service Standards" and the National Performance Review recommendation to "put customers first."

The first issue that Wellens and her collaborators had to confront was how to determine what products and services are provided by the member agencies. These range form Census data tapes to National Weather Service (NWS) weather forecasts, to National Oceanic and Atmospheric Agency (NOAA) fishery inspections, etc. Because the Department of Commerce does not maintain a central list of such services, the authors generated a list and divided it into (1) Information Services and Data Products (e.g. newsletters, catalogues, radio programs and off-the-shelf data products and software), (2) Specialized Services and Products (customized for a particular organization such as data collection, training and disaster relief), and (3) Grants and Regulatory Products and Services (e.g. grants, licenses, inspections and patents).

The survey instrument asked separately asked about each of these three categories, though the types of questions were similar across the three categories. In particular, the questions were concerned with timeliness, quality, documentation, clarity and ease of use, price and competence and responsiveness of agency staff. Most of the questions included a satisfaction rating scale. Each

section included overall questions about how well that category met the respondents' requirements and how much red tape was involved.

The next issue confronted by Wellens and her co-authors was who to survey. They limited their sample to external customers, noting that surveying internal customers is likely to involve different types of questions and formats. However, external customers are not a homogenous group and are not uniformly easy to identify. For example, the customers who most resemble commercial consumers purchase products and services from the government. Agencies are most likely to have records of these customers. The Federal government also serves customers who request and receive products and services free of charge. They are customers because, as tax payers, they have already paid for the product or service, and they may be potential paying customers in the more conventional sense. Agencies are less likely to monitor the identity of these customers. A third class of external customers receives products and services passively or unknowingly. For example, someone listening to a radio broadcast that includes a weather forecast from the NWS or someone eating fish that is safe because of fishery inspections by NOAA are probably not aware that they are the recipient of a Federal service at that time. As it turned out the participating agencies provided customer lists that ranged widely in size and apparent quality.

The initial questionnaire was followed by a non-response follow-up, as recommended by Dillman, and increased response rates from about 30% to 43% on average. This was certainly in the ballpark of response rates in the customer survey literature where 30% rates are viewed as successful. Nonetheless, the rates ranged widely between agencies. The authors intimate that if they could have legally guaranteed confidentiality response rates might have been more uniformly high.

The variation in response rates and quality of customer lists constrained the researchers in the kind of benchmarking activities they could carry out. They identify three such activities: comparing performance on the current survey to results for (1) an ideal organization in the private sector, (2) an average organization, and (3) the Department of Commerce itself surveyed again in the future. Because the samples were not comparable between the 14 agencies, it is virtually impossible to assure comparability with other surveys of other organizations; without this assurance the first two types of benchmarking are not meaningful. Thus comparisons should be made with great caution.

Wellens concluded the presentation with a warning about raising expectations that the quality of products and services will improve as a result of customer satisfaction surveys. If the results are not actually used to make things better, the exercise may increase the cynicism of customers or employees or both.

Norbert Schwarz served as synthesizer and discussion leader. He commented that each presentation represented a different point in a process of developing policy about products which are ultimately consumed (as in the talk by Levy), measuring the consumption of these and other products to create official statistics (as in the talk by Conrad), and measuring the satisfaction of official statistics users as well as consumers of other Federal products and services (as in the talk by Wellens). Schwarz commented that Levy's presentation illustrated the often post hoc nature of consumer research in supporting policies already in place. The more appropriate role of such research is to inform policy as it is developed. He commented that Conrad's talk was in the tradition of work that combines cognitive psychology and survey research and while much of the best work in this area is done in the Federal arena, it is often specific to particular problems on particular surveys. He advocated research in this area can be easily generalized. Finally, he added to the kinds of problems reported by Wellens in identifying customers of Federal products and services: involuntary "customers," such as tax payers filing with the Internal Revenue Service have inherently negative feelings about their experience yet must legitimately be included in the samples for such measurement exercises.

On the Elusive Value of Value: Determinants of Consumers' Value Perceptions

Dan Ariely, Duke University
Ziv Carmon, Duke University

The first paper, presented by Dan Ariely and Ziv Carmon, examines a well documented and systematic discrepancy between value assessments based on a buyer's versus a seller's perspective (WTP vs. WTS estimates, hereafter). This WTP-WTS gap, often termed the endowment effect, has been attributed in the literature to loss aversion. That is, giving up an entity is seen as a loss while forgoing the opportunity to own an item is not. While the traditional notion of loss aversion can account for the direction of this gap, it cannot be used to predict variations in the magnitude of the gap without invoking additional assumptions such as differential loss aversion across individuals and attributes. This paper proposes a parsimonious account for the WTP-WTS-disparity, whereby the two judgments share the underlying task-goal of protecting what one forgoes. As a result, WTP and WTS assessments of exchanges focus on different aspects, each representing what the person may lose in the exchange. Specifically, WTP corresponds more closely with the attitude toward the monetary (expenditure) aspects of the exchange, whereas WTS corresponds more closely with the attitude toward its benefits. Based on this account we made a series of predictions about moderators of the gap and their differential correspondence with WTP and WTS judgments. We found strong support for our hypotheses in four studies that examine value assessments of tickets to NCAA basketball games. Specifically, items related to attitude toward monetary aspects (such as self reported frugality, or reference price) corresponded more closely to WTP judgments than to those of WTS. Measures relating to aspects of the benefits (such as one's level of "fan-ness", the game's perceived importance) corresponded more closely to WTS than to WTP. The paper concludes with a discussion of the implication of the findings and opportunities for further research.

The second paper, presented by George Loewenstein, Drazen Prelec and Catherine Shatto, dealt with cold-to-hot empathy gaps. Hot states refer to periods of elevated drives (e.g., hunger, sexual desire), moods and emotions (e.g., anger, depression), and other somatic states (e.g., pain, fatigue). Cold states represent the times when one is not experiencing those elevated drives or emotions. In day to day life, we must all negotiate through varying levels of hot and cold states. Moreover, we often need to make judgments from one state to another at both a personal and interpersonal level. Interestingly, in spite of the continual need to make such judgments, they argue that most people are systematically inaccurate at predicting their own and others' preferences from one state to another. In support, they report two studies offering a simple demonstration that people who are not currently curious will under predict the force of their own future curiosity. In Study 1, conducted at the Pittsburgh International Airport, participants were shown a sample geography question and asked to complete a quiz that contains similar questions. Half of the participants were asked whether they would prefer a Dove candy bar or the answers as a reward for their participation *before* completing the quiz (cold condition), and half were asked to choose *after* taking the quiz (hot condition). Significantly more participants request the answer key in the hot state after taking the quiz than when they were asked in the cold state before the quiz. In study 2, conducted at Pittsburgh's National Aviary, they replicated the finding in Study 1 and show that current curiosity increases the value of immediate, but not delayed infor-

mation. In this 2x2 design, participants made their candy bar/ answer choice either before or after taking the quiz when the answers were either given immediately or delayed by approximately one hour. As expected, participants who had just taken the quiz and would receive the answers immediately requested the answer significantly more than any of the other three conditions. Finally, the authors discuss insights that cold-to-hot empathy gaps hold for many behaviors thought to be "irrational" with special attention on drug addiction, social influences, spending, and advertising.

In summary, both papers consider the decision maker's underlying goal to be crucial for his or her perception, formulation, and hence the judgment of the task. The first paper examines two perspectives of an exchange (that of sellers and that of buyers). The second paper examines changes in the decision maker's perspective resulting from physical and temporal proximity to the stimulus. In both papers the psychological perspective was shown to be related to the goal of the decision maker. In the first paper the goal was to protect what one stands to lose, and in the second paper it was to reduce the visceral drive of curiosity. The two papers suggest that the utility function partly reflects the underlying goals of the decision maker and his or her perspective. Indeed, the session's synthesizer Drazen Prelec called for a more inclusive formulation of utility that includes such factors as needs and goals of the decision maker.

REFERENCES

Carmon Ziv, and Dan Ariely (1996), "Minding to What They Surrender: A Task-goal View of Why Value Can Appear So Different to Buyers and Sellers," working paper, Fuqua School, Duke University.

Loewenstein, George, Drazen Prelec and Catherine D Shatto (1996), "Cold-to-Hot Empathy Gaps: Predicting Future Curiosity," working paper, Carnegie Mellon University.

Influence Professionals

Harish Sujan, Penn State University

In his presidential address, Peter Wright (1986) suggested that consumers think not only about marketing messages but also the people behind these messages. A useful complement to examining consumers' cognitive and affective responses to persuasive messages would be studying their speculations on the intentions of the creators of the message. A helpful theoretical perspective for this line of inquiry is Robert Cialdini's work on influence. In his work, Cialdini, a psychologist, has identified persuasion strategies and principles that guide influencers' use of persuasion strategies. This special session, aimed at furthering consumer researchers' interest in studying the people who create persuasive communications, comprised of presentations by Peter Wright and Marian Friestad on the thinking of advertising professionals, Robert Cialdini on the ethics of influence professionals, and by Subramanian Sivaramakrishnan (Subbu) and Harish Sujan on consumers' perceptions of salespeople.

Robert Cialdini's Talk

Speaking first, to about 50 ACR participants, Robert Cialdini provided some background on his work on influence and then raised propositions on the consequences to marketing and advertising organizations of employing influence professionals with high rather than low ethical standards. He was given 50 minutes for his presentation.

Robert Cialdini, who had not spoken at ACR earlier said that while his book on influence (1985) had had greater impact than he imagined, in his wildest dreams, the correspondence he received on this book suggested that consumer researchers were affected by it considerably less than advertising researchers and marketing research professionals. Expressing his happiness at being at ACR, he admitted that his hope was that his talk would significantly increase consumer researchers' interest in his work and serve to correct the imbalance. He said that an important motivation he had while writing his book was to help consumers protect themselves better against illegitimate influence attempts: he had observed that influence professionals could successfully persuade even while violating acceptable social norms.

As background for his propositions on the ethics of influence, he explained his earlier work and findings. Over a period of three years he conducted participant-observer investigations of professional influence, infiltrating into training programs and interviewing, in depth, a variety of influence agents. Through this he discovered six basic principles of influence: reciprocity, scarcity, authority, liking/friendship, social validation and commitment/consistency. Each principle, or strategy, could be used ethically or in a manner that was normatively objectionable. He classified people who use these influence principles into bunglers (incompetent use, either ethically or unethically), smugglers (competent but unethical use) and sleuths (competent and ethical use). Illustrating the smuggler, he alluded to an actor who was known primarily for the role he played as a doctor on a popular television serial—this actor used his fame illegitimately by serving as a spokesperson in an advertisement for a medical product.

He proposed that organizations employing sleuths are significantly better off than organizations employing smugglers. Smugglers, he suggested, increase short-term profit relative to sleuths, but harm long-term profit. This is because smugglers damage brand equity while sleuths enhance it. Alluding to Charles O'Reilly's

(1991) work on value-matching, he suggested that smugglers self-select themselves into smuggling organizations, and sleuths into sleuthing organizations. A mis-match, for example a sleuth in a predominantly smuggler organization, fosters low organizational commitment, job dissatisfaction, turnover, absenteeism and stress. Even in homogeneous smuggler organizations, he suggested, because of a real fear of pilferages, kickbacks, and inventory shrinkage, the necessity of sophisticated control systems drive operating costs to be well beyond those for sleuth organizations. Consequently, in the long run, these organizations have greater problems surviving.

Robert Cialdini's propositions suggest two new directions for consumer research: a focus on the influencer rather than the influencee and a shift from the psychology of the individual to organizational psychology. They also suggest that research that helps consumers develop an ability to protect themselves against illegitimate influence attempts is socially valuable.

Subbu's Talk

Following Robert Cialdini, Subramanian Sivaramakrishnan (Subbu) described a study he has conducted with Harish Sujan on consumers' stereotypes of salespeople. Consumers, he pointed out, hold negative stereotypes of many categories of salespeople; their first impressions of salespeople are consequently often negative. Unless they subsequently correct these first impressions, they transfer to their evaluations of the product the salesperson advocates. This mis-judgment has a cost, it leads to opportunity losses for the customer—e.g., wasted time in unnecessary search and purchasing a poorer quality product from a more likable salesperson. So, Subbu argued, it is of importance to understand when consumers' correct their first impressions of salespeople and when they do not.

Following Yacob Trope's (1986) model for person perception, Subbu envisaged that consumers first categorize salespeople, drawing upon their stereotypes, then characterize how they will behave and finally correct for this characterization based on their actual behavior. Reasoning from Dan Gilbert's (1989) work on cognitive busyness he hypothesized that correction, because it unlike categorization and characterization depends on controlled processing, does not always occur. In particular, when consumers are cognitively busy with tasks such as memorizing details of the salesperson's presentation or preparing questions to ask the salesperson, as a result of a reduced capacity to indulge in controlled processing they cannot correct their characterization.

Subbu reported two experiments where he empirically tested this hypothesis. In the first, consumers were exposed to a negatively stereotyped used car salesperson, by means of a written description, and either asked to formulate two questions while reading about the salesperson's behavior during this encounter or to simply observe the behavior. The salesperson's behavior was customer-oriented; i.e., positive. Subjects in the first condition, formulating questions while listening, he found, did not correct their initially negative impression of the salesperson while subjects in the second, non-busy condition did. In both conditions subjects recalled the salesperson's behavior equally well, attesting to the busyness manipulation's being distinct from distraction.

In the second experiment, consumers were exposed to a neutral rather than a negative used car salesperson, by means of an audio-visual description. Again they were either asked to formulate two questions while observing the salesperson's behavior which was customer oriented or to simply observe this behavior. Once again, Subbu showed, the subjects who were thinking of questions were unable to correct their first impressions while subjects who were not busy corrected their initially neutral impressions to more positive evaluations.

In both studies Subbu showed that salesperson evaluations transferred to the product.

He laid out his plan for future research investigations of consumers' perceptions of salespeople; included was identifying how consumers could rectify the ill-effects of cognitive busyness.

Peter Wright's Talk

Marian Friestad and Peter Wright (1995) have investigated consumers' schemas for advertising professionals' influence tactics. Shifting ground they have begun investigating advertising professionals' schemas of the psychology of persuasion. Marian spent six weeks at a major advertising agency interviewing in depth influence professionals there. Included in the interviews were questions aimed at understanding who chooses to become an advertising influence professional and why they believe particular styles of influence are better than others. Complementing this, Marian and Peter are examining popular writings of influence professionals, over the decade, for their views on advertising and sales practices. They are also examining mass media for the tactics used in marketing and political campaigns. They expect this research to complement the work they have done, and continue to do, on lay consumers' views of persuasion tactics used in marketing.

Synthesis

Serving, in addition, as the synthesizer for the session, Peter Wright elicited questions and comments from the audience. Most questions and comments were directed at Robert Cialdini and concerned his propositions. As an example, Chris Puto observed that the propositions he had developed (in keeping with the reactions of different interest groups to his book) were concerned with organizational consequences—propositions relating to consequences to consumers needed to be developed. As another example, Mita Sujan argued that unethical influence methods, even when it was clear the consequences were socially beneficial, were not desirable. Intervening in this debate, Peter Wright suggested, in support of Mita Sujan's position, that the methods used were as important as the consequences, since persuasion methods affected the relationship consumers and the influence professionals developed and since this relationship often is more important than the outcome.

Judging by the fact that most participants stayed till the end, that many asked questions and made comments, and that auidence-presenter discussions caused the session to run over by about ten minutes, interest was high. Hopefully, the session leads to important publications in marketing journals on the relationship between consumers and influence professionals.

REFERENCES

Cialdini, Robert B., *Influence: Science and Practice*, Scott, Foreman & Co.: Clearview, FL.

Friestad, Marian and Peter Wright (1995), "Persuasion Knowledge: Lay People's and Researchers' Beliefs About the Psychology of Advertising," *Journal of Consumer Research*, 22 (June), 62-74.

Gilbert, Daniel T. (1989), "Thinking Lightly About Others: Automatic Components of the Social Inference Process," In *Unintended Thoughts* (J. Uleman & J.A. Bargh, eds.), Guilford Press: New York, 189-211.

O'Reilly, Charles A., Jennifer Chatman and David F. Caldwell (1991), "People and Organizational Culture: A Profile Comparison Approach to Assessing Person-Organization Fit," *Academy of Management Journal*, 34 (September), 487-516.

Trope, Yacob (1986), "Identification and Inferential Processes in Dispositional Attribution," *Psychological Review*, 93 (July), 239-257.

Wright, Peter (1986), "Schemer Schema: Consumers' Intuitive Theories About Marketers' Influence Tactics," In *Advances in Consumer Research* (ed. Richard J. Lutes), 13, 1-3.

What is Consumer Misbehavior?

Ronald A. Fullerton, University of the South Pacific
Girish Punj, University of Connecticut

ABSTRACT

Misbehavior by consumers has been: 1) acknowledged as important; 2) neglected by consumer researchers. This paper aims to encourage wide-ranging research by presenting a broad and flexible definition of the phenomenon which is grounded in several well-established concepts from social science thought—exchange theory, labeling, norms and expectations. The definition fits well with empirical studies and reported accounts of misbehavior by consumers.

Misbehavior by consumers has been little studied despite having been identified as an important yet neglected topic (e.g., Belk 1988, p. 51; McCracken 1988, p. 143n). These calls for attention have produced little response, however, just as did analogous calls during the 1970s (e.g., Wilkes 1978). Recent research exploring compulsive consumption (e.g. Faber et.al 1995) and substance addiction (Hirschman 1993) has focussed attention on the damage that consumers can afflict upon themselves, but perforce not upon the entire consumption setting. The long-established shoplifting literature continues to grow, to be sure, but shoplifting is only one of many variants of consumer misbehavior. Others which are common include vandalism, financial frauds, and physical and verbal abuse of other consumers and of marketer employees. The Exhibit presents illustrative accounts of common consumer misbehavior. There has been little study of these and other forms of misbehavior—or of misbehavior's wider implications for consumer experience and consumer culture. Our overall understanding of consumer misbehavior remains weak.

Consumer misbehavior is in fact a significant phenomenon which affects the experience of all consumers; it is an inseparable part of the consumer experience. It represents the dark, feral side of the consumer. It results in either material loss or psychological damage, or both, to marketers, to marketing institutions, and to other consumers. Those consumers not themselves misbehaving are all inevitably victimized by others' misconduct.

The purpose of this paper is to encourage a broad research agenda by illuminating a key conceptual issue—how to define consumer misbehavior. We draw upon several concepts in social science literature to develop a definition which can encourage thorough and wide-ranging exploration of the scope of consumer misbehavior and its impact upon consumer experience. We then discuss narrower definitional approaches which we do not consider, and indicate promising future research topics.

A DEFINITION OF CONSUMER MISBEHAVIOR

Norms and Expectations in Exchange Settings

The rich literature of the sociology of deviance, ethics, and criminology emphasizes the key roles of norms and expectations. The term "misbehavior" implies that there are norms by which correct, as opposed to incorrect conduct may be judged; norms in turn are tightly linked to behavioral expectations. Consumer misbehavior may thus be defined as behavioral acts by consumers which violate the generally accepted norms of conduct in consumption situations, and disrupt the order expected in such situations. By consumption situations we mean exchange situations, since much of the behavior by consumers is played out within these. We

concentrate on the exchange setting as the basic consumption situation.

Consumer misbehavior acts are externally directed and visible; they are part of people's conduct in their role as consumers. These actions tend to be held in disrepute by marketers and by most consumers, but—and this is essential to comprehending consumer misbehavior—not necessarily with equal conviction or intensity.

Expectations of Behavior in Exchange Settings

The norms regarding conduct in exchange settings are founded upon expectations about behavior. "Successful exchange...relationships," note Houston and Gassenheimer (1987, p. 10), "are made up of well-established sets of expectations about the behaviors of the parties involved." These expectations reflect implicit trust that the conduct of consumers will remain within the bounds of orderliness and respectability (Best & Luckenbill 1982, p.236; Mills 1979, pp.22-23). Usually the trust is what sociologists term "impersonal trust;" that is, faith in people whom one does not and will not know personally. In other words, people expect that consumers will "behave themselves." Misbehavior by consumers disrupts the openness, impersonal trust, and orderliness of the ideal exchange environment (Houston and Gassenheimer 1987).

Networks of Expectations

In an exchange setting, expectations about the ways in which consumers should conduct themselves constitute a network, within which there are three sub-networks: 1) that comprised of the expectations which the marketer has of consumer conduct; 2) that made up of consumers' expectations about other consumers' conduct; and 3) that comprised of the expectations which consumers have of marketer (and marketer employee) conduct.

In a smoothly functioning exchange setting, the norms of the three sub-networks are in consonance with each other, and the behavior of consumers and marketers is in harmony with these norms. Successful exchange relationships are characterized by trust, orderliness, and openness (Houston & Gassenheimer 1987). Almost anyone can enter the exchange settings in which these relationships occur, without fear for his or her security. When in the exchange setting, consumers are implicitly allied with other consumers and with marketers. Steiner, Hadden, Herkomer (1976) posit a "social contract" between the consumer and the marketer; there is also a "social contract" among consumers who are together in an exchange setting.

Acts of consumer misbehavior disrupt the exchange environment by violating one or both of these contracts. They can violate the norms of orderly behavior which marketers apply to consumers, and those which consumers apply to one another. They challenge the trust which marketers have in consumers, and that which consumers have in their peers.

Can Consumer Misbehavior Be Distinguished From Misbehavior at Large?

Acts of consumer misbehavior themselves, of necessity, may also be committed in non-consumption, non-exchange situations. Examples would include acts of vandalism or verbal abuse or theft. But their impacts upon consumer experience will perforce differ. To omit from our definition acts which could also be committed in

Advances in Consumer Research
Volume 24, © 1997

EXHIBIT 1
Experiencing Consumer Misbehavior: Reported Accounts

Credit Card Fraud:	Somebody's got to help me . . . I can't stand for people to think those things about me, that I'm a deadbeat. (Consumer victim, talking about the stigma of debts she did not incur, quoted in Allen 1990).
Exhibitionism:	We had a man expose himself behind the last gondola to two teenagers. (Store manager, exploratory interview).
Abusive Behavior:	"Police have filed assault charges against [a consumer]...The incident occurred at 4 p.m. Wednesday as [the consumer] was waiting in line to pay a utility bill, became impatient with the delay and 'began screaming about why it was taking so long.' [The owner...told him he would have to leave the store if he continued his behavior. [The consumer] then allegedly punched [the owner]...in the chest as he [was being] escorted from the pharmacy, ...got into his car and 'drove at [the owner] at high speed'" ("...Father Charged With Assault" 1993).
Shoplifting:	We had two high-class ladies in here with wallets full of money. They were on a spending spree from Sweden, and they were staying at the Beverly Hilton. They came here and each stole a $1,000 dress. We busted them. These women... didn't care about being caught. They paid the restitution,... pleaded guilty and off they went to San Francisco to rip that city off. (Store security person, quoted in Walter 1988, p. 112).
Price Tag Switching:	I wait until I see a store advertising Buck Owens or something for 47 cents. I'll take the price tag off a couple of them and go over to the rock section (where prices are seldom marked down). After I switch the tags, I look for an old woman clerk who won't know the difference. (Tag switcher, quoted in Bulkeley 1973, p.1).

non-exchange situations would make no sense. In a full-fledged culture of consumption such as characterizes the economically advanced societies, exchange situations are pervasive.

LABELING THEORY AND THE DEFINITION OF CONSUMER MISBEHAVIOR

Labeling theory, which is a well-established element of sociological thought, offers compelling insight into the process by which misbehavers are defined and "labeled." Dotter & Roebuck (1988) critically review this work.

Labeling theory posits an interactive process by which people (in our case, marketers and consumers) interpret or define each other's actions, instead of merely reacting to them. "The imputation of deviance resides not only in the fact of deviance per se; it also depends heavily on the meanings that the audience attach[es] to the behavior and the actor" (Steffensmeier & Terry 1973, p. 425). These meanings are not necessarily uniform. They are shaped by differing perceptions, which in turn sometimes reflect attempts to exercise power—or to reject such efforts. Expectations may thus differ across the players in an exchange setting, and so too may norms; norm and expectation setting is a fluid and dynamic rather than static and immutable process.

Perspectives on Labeling Misbehavior

Correct behavior may be viewed by both consumers and marketers from different perspectives which only partially overlap each other. An ethical perspective demarcates behavior in terms of good and bad: a legal perspective in terms of right and wrong. Still another perspective focuses upon deviance, and perceives some behavior to differ markedly from acceptable standards. Acts labeled deviant arouse strong revulsion in the labeler, yet are not necessarily unethical or illegal; e.g., smoking in one's car while cruising through a Southern California drive-through liquor store.

Labeling/Interactionist theory is borne out in reports of marketers selectively prosecuting apprehended misbehavers according to such factors as age, sex, race, and value stolen (Hindelang 1974; Robin 1963). Consumers too have been shown to label selectively. Steffensmeier & Terry (1973) find that the appearance of a shoplifter plays a major role in whether other shoppers would report him/her or not.

Conflicts in Labeling Misbehaving Consumers

Conflicts can roil the labeling process. Consumers may disagree among themselves. Sheley & Bailey (1985) reveal that a majority of responding consumers has only a mildly condemnatory attitude towards purchasing stolen goods. Guffy, Harris, & Laumer (1979) report distinct segmentation among consumers regarding perceptions about the seriousness of shoplifting. Consumers may also differ with marketers, especially on the seriousness of acts of consumer misbehavior. Wilkes (1978) reports some consumers indifferent to, or even approving of, misbehavior by other consumers.

Does Labeling Define Away Misbehavior?

Labeling illuminates the complexity inherent in defining consumer misbehavior; it suggests an element of moral "relativism" which some would find unsettling. For all the fluidity inherent in the labeling process, however, there is no doubt that when a consumer steals from or otherwise defrauds the marketer, vandalizes the marketer's premises, or psychologically abuses the marketer's employees, his/her acts go against the marketer's expectations and violate the openness and trust which the marketer has invested in the exchange setting. There is similar violation when a consumer is insulted, harassed, or otherwise inconvenienced by fellow consumers; or has to pay higher prices to compensate for their theft, fraud, or other depredations against the marketer.

CRITICAL IMPLICATIONS AND ISSUES OF A LABELING-BASED DEFINITION

Inadequacy of the "Criminality" Demarcation

Labeling challenges assumptions which are based upon absolute and categorical demarcations of legitimate and illegitimate behavior. We began our work by attempting to narrow the definitional spectrum with absolutes, but these efforts floundered badly in light of existing knowledge. Attempts to differentiate between "criminal" and "non criminal" consumer misbehavior, for example, broke down once we penetrated the literature of criminality and sociology of deviance and realized: 1) the inconsistent and arbitrary nature of the reporting of "criminal" acts; 2) the ever-shifting definitions of what exactly constitutes criminal action; and 3) the diverse, often clashing, viewpoints about who has the legitimacy to formulate such definitions. To distinguish between "criminal" and "non-criminal" behavior, would therefore create a misleading impression of precision. It would also blur our intended focus on consumer experience. Acts which may loom large in criminal law; for example, major shoplifting, may be far less unsettling to consumers' experience worlds than actions which may not even be, strictly speaking, illegal; e.g., being cut off by a queue jumper.

Inadequacy of the "Intent" Demarcation

Similarly, "intent" appeared at first to be a useful differentiating element in consumer misbehavior, but proved inadequate because behavioral intent is too often unknowable. It is exceedingly difficult to know when consumer misbehavers are consciously lying about their intention(s), as opposed to deceiving themselves, for example. In some cases the misbehaver may be unconscious of intended outcomes (see Rouke 1957 and Russell 1973). Even when both the victim and the ostensible outcome seem apparent, the intent underlying an act of consumer misbehavior may not be. For example, the intent of an act of vandalism such as attacking a large illuminated sign could be:

▸ To show defiance towards a large, powerful, commercial institution (Baron and Fisher 1984; Smigel 1956); or
▸ To gain revenge for poor treatment from the institution whose sign is damaged (Bedeaud and Coslin 1984); or
▸ To direct attention at the perpetrator or a cause dear to him/her (Garrett 1987); or
▸ To enjoy a thrilling experience (Katz 1988); or
▸ To gain the approval of peers (Sutherland 1947); or
▸ Understandable only in terms of serious mental disturbance such as impulse control disorder, antisocial personality disorder, or dementia (DSM-III-R 1987).

FUTURE RESEARCH

In light of the analysis presented here, five themes are promising for future research:

1. The process by which expectations about consumer deportment originate has not yet been explicitly studied. The process evidently involves cultural values, legal norms, ethical codes, and personal experience; and these are inculcated through a socialization or acculturation process which itself needs to be investigated.

2. Since consumer behavior is linked to cultural values, and since cultural values differ in different places, expectations regarding what is acceptable conduct by consumers are likely to differ somewhat across cultures. As an example, queue jumping infuriates Britons far more than Germans. Cross-cultural differences in the formation of expectations should be investigated; this would include looking at developing as well as developed consumer economies.

3. Similarly, differences and similarities in expectations should be investigated across subcultures and the larger culture of which they are a part. Could for example differences reflect the fact that one or more subcultures do not share the values of the broader culture of consumption, and that they rebel against a value system that is imposed upon them? Recent clashes between Black patrons and Korean store owners in Los Angeles, and earlier in New York, could have been caused by a struggle for power among people with widely differing consumption values.

4. Power is the heart of a related, and extremely important, issue - that of who (if anyone) within a consumer culture has the greatest ability to impose behavioral standards. Defining consumer misbehavior raises issues of power and control. Who has the power to designate others as deviant? Critics of consumer culture assume that marketers have enormous power to manipulate and control consumers (See Leach 1993, p.386); defenders of marketing emphasize consumers' sovereignty and power to influence marketer actions. Most likely the power to define misbehavior is shared—albeit not necessarily equally—between marketers and consumers. The intricacies of this reciprocal power relationship merit serious investigation.

5. Research needs to explore consumers' attitudes towards the full spectrum of types of consumer misbehavior.

CONCLUSION

Our definition of consumer misbehavior is intentionally broad. Does it exaggerate the phenomenon? We think not. Consumer misbehavior has generally been under-reported and subject to widespread denial by both actors and acted upon; it is an unpleasant aspect of a culture which does not like unpleasantness. Misbehavior by consumers challenges some of the very foundations of contemporary consumer society: its implicit norms and role expectations, the legitimacy of marketers to establish boundaries, and the overall capacity of the system to function smoothly. The pervasive underestimation needs to be challenged; the presence of the misbehaving consumer across a wide variety of exchange situations must be acknowledged. Exchange situations are richer and more complex than often assumed. The readiness of consumer researchers during the past several years to explore deviant actions through which consumers damage themselves (e.g., Faber et.al. 1995; Hirschman 1992), and to open up investigation of consumer resistance (Penaloza and Price 1993), leads us to believe that the climate may finally be opportune for sustained investigation of consumer misbehavior.

REFERENCES

Abelson, Elaine (1989), *When Ladies Go A-Thieving: Middle-Class Shoplifters in the Victorian Department Store,* New York and Oxford: Oxford University Press.

Allen, Michael (1990), "Identity Crisis: To Repair Bad Credit, Advisers Give Clients Someone Else's Data," *Wall Street Journal,* 1 August, p. 1.

Baron, R.M., and J.D. Fisher (1984), "The Equity-Control Model of Vandalism: A Refinement," in Claude Lévy-Leboyer, ed., *Vandalism: Behavior and Motivations,* Amsterdam, New York, Oxford: North Holland, 63-76.

Belk, Russell W. (1988), Book Review, Journal of Macromarketing, 8(No. 2), Fall, 47-51.

Best, Joel, and David F. Luckenbill (1982), *Organizing Deviance,* Englewood Cliffs: Prentice Hall.

Bideaud, J., and P.G. Coslin (1984), "Moral Judgement and Attitudes Towards Vandalism," in Claude Lévy-Leboyer, ed., *Vandalism: Behavior and Motivations,* Amsterdam, New York, Oxford: North Holland, 257-268.

Bulkeley, William M. (1973), "Merry Shoppers Find Some Real Bargains—By Switching Tags," *Wall Street Journal,* July 30.

Dotter, Daniel L., and Julian B. Roebuck (1988), "The Labeling Approach Re-examined: Interactionism and the Components of Deviance," *Deviant Behavior,* 9 No. 1, 19-32.

DSM-III-R (Diagnostic and Statistical Manual of Medical Disorders) (1987), 3rd ed. rev. Washington, DC: American Psychiatric Association.

Faber, Ronald J., Gary A. Christenson, Martina de Zwaan, and James Mitchell (1995), "Two Forms of Compulsive Consumption: Comorbidity of Compulsive Buying and Binge Eating" *Journal of Consumer Research,* 22(3), 296-304.

Garrett, Dennis E. (1987), "The Effectiveness of Marketing Policy Boycotts: Environmental Opposition to Marketing," *Journal of Marketing,* 51 No.2 (April), 58-73.

Guffey, H. J., J. R. Harris, and J. F. Laumer (1979), "Shopper Attitudes Toward Shoplifting and Shoplifting Preventative Devices," *Journal of Retailing,* 55 No.3, 75-89.

Hindelang, Michael J. (1974), "Decisions of Shoplifting Victims to Invoke the Criminal Justice Process," *Social Problems,* 21 No. 4, 580-593.

Hirschman, Elizabeth C. (1992), "The Consciousness of Addiction: Toward a General Theory of Compulsive Consumption," *Journal of Consumer Research,* 19(3), 155-179.

Houston, Franklin S., and Jule B. Gassenheimer (1987), "Marketing and Exchange," *Journal of Marketing,* 51 No. 4 (October), 3-18.

Katz, Jack (1988), *Seductions of Crime,* New York: Basic Books.

Leach, William R. (1993), *Land of Desire,* New York: Pantheon.

McCracken, Grant (1988), *Culture and Consumption,* Bloomington: Indiana University Press.

Mills, Michael K. (1979), "A Power-Contextual Analysis of Deviant Consumer Behavior in Retail Stores," unpublished Ph.D. dissertation, University of Pittsburgh.

"Paz" Father Charged With Assault in Cranston" (1993), *Providence Evening Bulletin,* July 30.

Penaloza, Lisa, and Linda Price (1993), "Consumer Resistance: A Conceptual Overview," in Leigh McAlister and Michael L. Rothschild, eds., *Advances in Consumer Research,* 20, 123-128.

Robin, Gerald D. (1963), "Patterns of Department Store Crime," *Crime and Delinquency,* 6 (April), 163-73.

Rouke, Fabian L. (1957), "Shoplifting: Its Symbolic Motivation," *NPPA Journal,* 3, 54-58.

Russell, Donald Hayes (1973), "Emotional Aspects of Shoplifting," *Psychiatric Annals,* 3, 77-86.

Sheley, Joseph F. and Kenneth D. Bailey (1985), "New Directions for Anti-Theft Policy: Reductions in Stolen Goods Buyers," *Journal of Criminal Justice,* 13 No.5, 399-415.

"Shoplifting Dynamics: Who, What, When, Where, and How?" (1985), *Chain Store Age Executive,* 61 No. 9, 79-80.

Smigel, Erwin O. (1956), "Public Attitudes Toward Stealing as Related to the Size of the Victim Organization," *American Sociological Review,* 21, 320-327.

Steffensmeier, Darrell J. and Robert M. Terry (1973), "Deviance and Respectability: An Observational Study of Reactions to Shoplifting," *Social Forces,* 51 (June), 417-26.

Steiner, John M., Stuart C. Hadden, and Len Herkomer (1976), "Price Tag Switching," *International Journal of Criminology and Penology,* 4, 129-143.

Sutherland, Edwin H. (1947), *Principles of Criminology,* 4th ed., Philadelphia: Lippincott.

Terry, Robert M., and Darrell J. Steffensmeier (1988), "Conceptual and Theoretical Issues in the Study of Deviance," *Deviant Behavior,* 9 No. 1, 55-76.

Walter, Joan (1988), "Candid Conversations With People Who Nab Shoplifters," *Orange Coast Magazine* (December), 106-120.

Wilkes, Robert F. (1978), "Fraudulent Behavior by Consumers," *Journal of Marketing,* 42 (October), 67-75.

Can Consumer Misbehavior Be Controlled?
A Critical Analysis of Two Major Control Techniques

Ronald A. Fullerton, University of the South Pacific
Girish Punj, University of Connecticut

ABSTRACT

Misbehavior by consumers has serious financial and social consequences; efforts to control it are an important issue for practitioners and consumers alike. Two major control techniques are deterrence and education; both are based upon considerable theory and empirical study. Given the complexity of reasons which drive consumers to misbehave, however, neither will be effective in all situations.

Consumer misbehavior is defined here as behavior in exchange settings which violates the generally accepted norms of conduct in such situations. Such behavior disrupts the exchange environment. Common forms of consumer misbehavior include vandalism, verbal and physical excuse, shoplifting, and financial frauds involving insurance, credit cards, checks, etc.

Consumer research has traditionally slighted misbehavior by consumers. Recent work on compulsive consumption (Faber et.al. 1995; Hirschman 1992) explores deviance in which consumers wreck harm largely upon themselves. A few other works do acknowledge the wider dimensions and cost of misbehavior (e.g., Cox, Cox, and Moschis 1990; Fullerton and Punj 1993).

Control of consumer misbehavior is an important issue. Such misbehavior inflicts not only financial hardship on many consumers, it can also unsettle the consumption experience. A consumer victimized by credit card fraud lamented: "You feel like you've just walked into your house and there's been an intruder in your home...It leaves you disturbed, frustrated, and anxious about the future" (quoted in Barry and Crombie 1989). Fear of shopping at night, dread of leaving children unattended in exchange settings, helpless rage at being hurt by other consumers—these are common experiences (see Lichter 1994). Financial losses from misbehavior are routinely expressed in billions of U.S. dollars—most of which are recouped by raising prices for all consumers. Automobile insurance fraud in the U.S. is said to cost $10 billion annually (Kerr 1992). Creators of intellectual property have recently become increasingly concerned about theft via the Internet ("Intellectual Property" 1996). News reports of airline passengers going berserk in flight earlier this year, evoked fears that chaos was encroaching upon a once-tranquil consumer experience. The following headlines, most of them from the Wall Street Journal, further illustrate the disruptive potential of consumer behavior:

- "Crime Becomes Occupational Hazard of Deliverers" (7 March 1994)
- "Thefts Hurt Stores in Inner Cities, Suburbs" (28 February 1994)
- "Bad Check Toll Rises as it Becomes Easier to Pull Off Such Fraud" (2 December 1993)
- "Barney-Costumed Woman is Attacked at Store's Opening" (11 April 1994)
- "Cable TV Pirates Become More Brazen, Forcing Industry to Seek New Remedies" (7 May 1992)

Retailing practitioners have long wrestled with the possibility of controlling—if not eradicating—misbehavior by customers (e.g., Abelson 1989; French, Crask, and Mader 1984; Johnson 1987).

They and other marketing practitioners are currently fighting to contain consumer misbehavior with an extensive arsenal of techniques including high technology deterrent devices and bounties. Solutions proposed by academic and other writers have ranged from macro-prescriptions such as ensuring social justice and equality of incomes, to mid-level solutions involving cooperation among marketers of a city or region (Hiew 1981), to micro-level ones such as making the marketing institution less intimidating (Mills 1979), or taking a hard line towards prosecuting misbehavers.

But does any of this work? Most accounts show little if any decline in existing forms of consumer misbehavior and the continual emergence of new ones such as cellular phone fraud. Reports of retailers en masse adopting subliminal messages against shoplifting indicate a certain desperation (McLaughlin 1987). Is it realistic to hope to curtail misconduct? Or is the attitude of passive resignation reported among some retailers by French, Crask, and Mader (1984) the least costly and most realistic alternative?

The aim of this paper is to evaluate critically the methods of control which are most used today—education and deterrence—in light of what is now known about misbehavior by consumers. The effectiveness of these approaches will be assessed from both a general perspective and from one which differentiates consumer misbehavers by their motivations. Both approaches will be contrasted to the "do nothing" passive resignation approach.

CONTROL TECHNIQUES: A GENERAL PERSPECTIVE

Two major avenues to controlling consumer misbehavior have been proposed and are in wide use. One advocates education to change attitudes and (hopefully) behavior; the other emphasizes deterrent measures to make misbehavior difficult.

Education as a Control Technique

The educational approach uses promotional messages to persuade consumers to unlearn patterns of misconduct and to strengthen moral constraints which inhibit misbehavior. Examples include portraying consumer misbehavers as repulsive, sick people (Kallis and Vanier 1985), educating the public that consumer misbehavior is not victimless wrongdoing (Sheley and Bailey 1985), and rehabilitation programs for shoplifters. A rationale for moral education is that since few misbehaving consumers dispute the moral impropriety of consumer misbehavior in general (Hiew 1981; Kallis and Vanier 1985), public education may be able to reinforce consumers' existing sense of moral propriety and thus strengthen moral constraints against misbehavior. Educational campaigns directed at mainstream consumers may be able to shake the indifference with which many of them regard consumer misbehavior; such campaigns should stress the total costs to consumers of misbehavior.

Educational approaches are grounded in Control Theory—the idea that bonding all groups to the values of larger society will reduce deviance. Shaping strongly negative attitudes towards misconduct among the majority of consumers would mean that they would exert more severe informal sanctions against misbehavior by other consumers, which in turn should inhibit misbehavior. One successful community-wide campaign has been reported (Hiew 1981).

Weaknesses of Education

One deficiency in educational appeals is that the messages may actually stimulate misbehavior (Bickman and Green 1977). A bigger hurdle is the well-known difficulty of persuading people to alter their attitudes on highly involving matters. From all reports, misbehaving consumers are highly involved in their actions, as for example this university student interviewed by Katz (1988, p. 71): "The [shoplifting] experience was almost orgasmic for me. There was a build-up of tension as I contemplated the danger of a forbidden act, then a rush of excitement at the moment of committing the crime, and finally a delicious sense of release." Education or not it would be hard to abstain from such a thrill. Strong peer influences (e.g. differential association) among groups of teenage consumers stimulate misconduct: "My best friend and I couldn't walk into a store without getting that familiar grin on our faces," one misbehaver reminisced about high school days (Katz 1988, p. 59). Education would have to counter deeply-held group values. Television ads, radio ads, or posters depicting teenage consumer misbehavers as loathsome losers, as suggested by Kallis and Vanier (1985), will not likely succeed in countering collective values among the targeted groups of teenagers. The same would likely be true of fear appeals.

Deterrence as a Control Technique

Deterrence is the most widely used control strategy today. It emphasizes the use of formal and informal sanctions (Kraut 1976; Mills 1979, pp. 63ff). Deterrence theory (e.g., Tittle 1980) argues that systematic, consistent deterrence policies can effectively block opportunities to misbehave by making the perceived risks too great. The perceived severity of punishment is less important than its perceived certainty and consistence. Typical measures include: human surveillance and electronic security in stores, financial system designs intended to thwart and detect fraud, and vigorous legal prosecution of offenders. The goal is to create formal and informal sanctions which increase the perceived probability that misbehavior by consumers will be both detected and punished. Deterrence meshes well with the influential idea that misconduct is often the outcome of rationally calculated opportunism (Becker 1968): if opportunities are reduced, fewer decisions to misbehave will be made.

Weaknesses of Deterrence

But not all calculations are similar; a major hurdle which deterrence must vault is the differing consumer perceptions of—and reactions to the risks of deterrent sanctions. There is evidence that the misbehavior-prone perceptually downgrade the risk posed by deterrents (Kraut 1976; Piliavin, Thornton, Gartner, and Matsueda 1986). Shoplifters reportedly find laughable such common deterrence techniques as mirrors and electronic article surveillance (EAS) (Kallis and Vanier 1985).

Effective deterrent measures may also have a counterproductive, boomerang effect upon well-behaved consumers if they feel harassed. Retailers have long worried that strong deterrence could alienate honest consumers (Abelson 1989). The sole empirical test (Guffy, Harris, and Laumer 1979) found that 28.9% of sampled consumers were offended by store security, especially surveillance by humans (uniformed guards, floor walkers, dressing room checkers). For over half of the offended, store choice was affected. The finding is telling because human surveillance is considered to be the single most effective deterrent to consumer misbehavior (Kallis and Vanier 1985).

CONTROL STRATEGIES AND REASONS FOR MISBEHAVIOR

Beyond the general strengths and weaknesses just elucidated, a more penetrating analysis of control strategies becomes possible if we realize that the effectiveness of specific control strategies varies with different consumers. Following Moore's (1984) logic, we can differentiate consumer misbehavers based on the dominant reason for their misconduct. This will in turn determine the likelihood that those in each group will be constrained from consumer misbehavior. The reasons for misbehavior used here are based on those advanced in Fullerton and Punj (1993). These reasons need not be mutually exclusive, but one is assumed to predominate in each case of consumer misbehavior. The reasons:

1. Calculating opportunism—Misbehavior as the outcome of a decision-making process based upon conscious and rational calculation of expected benefits and costs as opposed to risks (Becker 1968). Differs from typical consumer decision making only in the absence of ethical constraints. Probably the single most important reason for consumer misbehavior (Moore 1984).

2. The absence of moral constraints—those powerful internal checks against conduct perceived to be wrong; i.e., immoral. A major difference between normal and misbehaving consumers. Absent moral constraints, acts of consumer misbehavior may not be perceived as immoral (Hiew 1981); or acts which are believed immoral in general are not in one's own case (Moore 1984; Kallis & Vanier 1985). A few psychologically troubled consumer misbehavers may lack any sense of moral responsibility (See DSM-III-R 1987, pp. 342-344).

3. The search for thrills—a basic motivation for misconduct (Katz 1988). Misbehavior permits thrilling defiance of legal and moral strictures and of imposing institutions; the risk of being caught only heightens the exquisite tension.

4. The frustration(s) of unfulfilled aspirations as consumers' desires have become overstimulated to the point where few can legitimately afford to realize all of them (Merton 1968). Widely-cited as a major reason for shoplifting (e.g., Cameron 1964).

5. Differential association—deviant behavior learned in intimate groups, especially those made up of teenagers and adult repeat offenders (Sutherland 1934). Misbehavior promotes gang identity and may serve as an initiation ritual; group interaction inculcates the techniques of misbehavior and teaches members how to neutralize attacks on the morality of their conduct.

6. Psychological problems and abnormalities—deeply disturbed, abnormal, psyches may erupt in exhibitionism, brutal treatment of other consumers and marketing employees. Vandalism and shoplifting can be symptoms of psychiatric disorders (DSM-III-R 1987). Unresolved sibling rivalry, sexual frustration and guilt, various compulsions, and the need to be punished can be proximate causes of misbehavior (Kallis and Vanier 1986).

7. Provocative situational factors—crowding, unsettling amounts of heat and noise, enticing displays, seeming

EXHIBIT
Reasons for Consumer Misbehavior and Likelihood of Control

Dominant Reason for Misbehavior	Likelihood of Control via Education	Likelihood of Control via Deterrence
Calculating Opportunism	Moderate for occasional misbehavers (i.e., most consumers); low for repeaters, who tend not to perceive so much immorality in misbehavior.	Moderate to high: effective deterrence shrinks opportunities by making the "costs" of consumer misbehavior high and the "benefits" low.
Absence of Moral Constraints	Low likelihood of re-educating the strongly amoral and strongly self-indulgent. Moderate chance of reaching consumers who are slightly amoral and/or have an unreflective situational ethics outlook.	Moderate to good: strong deterrence provides *ad hoc* behavioral restraints, especially among the opportunistic.
Thrill Seeking	Moderate at best: difficult to counter deeply-felt desires for thrills and entrenched attitudes that misbehavior is rousing	Low to moderate. Deterrence based on human surveillance and administration of sanctions can be moderately effective, though not with hard-core thrill hunters. Technologically-based deterrence; e.g., exploding ink devices on clothing, is likely to be counterproductive.
Unfulfilled Aspirations	Low: the totality of a consumer society fires aspirations in myriad ways. What firm would risk driving its target consumers to substitute products?	Moderate to high: aspiring consumers will resent deterrence as just another barrier to bliss, but should respect it.
Differential Association	Low: group convictions are deeply held, making it improbable that members will yield to another view of appropriate conduct.	Varies from low through moderate to high, depending on how a group perceives and evaluates risks; adult groups are likely to avoid strong deterrence, teenage packs to challenge it.
Psychological Problems and Abnormalities	Low: permissible educational measures far too weak to break through into these troubled psyches.	Low for people who want to be caught and punished. Moderate likelihood that formal sanctions will deter some (Neustatter 1954). Formal barring from premises could work if legally permissible.
Provocative Situational Factors	Low to moderate: educational efforts to explain difficulties and to strengthen self-control hold some promise.	Moderate to high: skilled crowd control could be effective; effective guarding of enticing displays should reduce misconduct by aroused consumers.
Negative Attitudes Towards Exchange Institution	Moderate to high: well-done and thoroughgoing (i.e., not just advertising) promotion could lessen, even reverse, negative attitudes.	Low: deterrent measures likely to reinforce negative beliefs that the institution is distrustful and overbearing.

absence of deterrence may trigger aggressiveness towards other consumers and towards marketers; displays of merchandise may arouse overwhelming urges to shoplift (Moore 1984).

8. Negative attitudes towards exchange institutions—evoked by ownership, physical size, and projected image; perceived impersonality increases the probability of misbehavior by consumers, as does the size of institutions (Kraut 1976; Moore 1984).

The Exhibit shows the likely probability of success of both education—and deterrence—based strategies for the eight different groups.

Calculating opportunists and the impulse-driven should be the easiest to deflect from misconduct, and those driven by psychological problems the hardest. Consumers for whom thrill-seeking and differential association are dominant will be near impervious to education, and fairly difficult to thwart by deterrence. Of the two general avenues to controlling consumer misbehavior, deterrence appears to offer the most promise, particularly in moderating misconduct by calculating opportunists—who are generally believed to constitute the largest pool of potential misbehavers. Strong deterrence lessens opportunities by making the risks—the "costs"—of misbehavior higher than the benefits. It provides ad hoc behavioral impediment among the opportunistic; it supplies restraint where moral constraint may be minimal. Deterrence meshes well with current criminological thought and with the predispositions of many marketing practitioners to take a proactive stance towards consumer misbehavior. However, deterrence will not be effective against consumer misconduct rooted in thrill-seeking or negative attitudes towards an exchange institution; it may not deter misconduct by groups in which these are present. The perception of higher risks may actually spur some misbehavior; thrill-seeking consumers want to be caught and punished (Rouke 1957). Technologically based deterrent apparatus such as exploding ink devices on new clothing, are likely to be counterproductive.

Education could prove superior to deterrence in thwarting consumer misbehavior based on negative attitudes towards some exchange institutions. It will be of little effectiveness, however, in precluding misconduct rooted in unfulfilled aspirations, differential association, psychological problems, and provocative situational factors.

Future Research

The following four areas merit additional research.

1. Further research on the "deterrence boomerang" is urgently needed. At the micro level, the costs of the tradeoffs between controlling consumer misbehavior and offending legitimate consumers should be carefully explored in a variety of exchange settings. At the macro level, the tension between maximizing consumer freedom and control of misbehavior, should be critically analyzed from major social and philosophical perspectives, e.g., the Frankfurt School. Is misbehavior, for example, the result of consumer resistance to an oppressive marketer-dominated culture? Or is it the price of consumer freedom?

2. Efforts to control consumer misbehavior invariably have ethical dimensions. These should be explored. Formally barring the psychologically disturbed from exchange settings, for example, will preclude their misbehaving, but also represents a powerful restraint to their freedom. Some researchers might argue that educational efforts are inherently unprincipled efforts to manipulate consumers.

3. More research is needed to determine how consumers, especially those with a high potential for consumer misbehavior, calculate and relate to risks. Recent research on fear appeals (e.g., Keller and Block 1996) may provide the foundation upon which more effective educational appeals could be designed.

4. A rich agenda exploring the complexities of consumer misbehavior and its control could emerge from the Exhibit, which is based upon conceptual and earlier empirical work.

CONCLUSION

Future research needs to begin with the acceptance that consumer misbehavior is a widespread and potentially ominous phenomenon which can cast a pall over consumer experience. It does need to be controlled, although researchers may disagree among themselves how much control there should be. Passive resignation

to it would be a poor strategy, for that would in effect invite the misbehavior-prone to come in and rampage, creating a sense of loss of control which can be unsettling to employees and consumers. Also, it would result in maximum financial losses—which would have to be made up by other consumers.

It should be clear that the control methods analyzed here will not eliminate misbehavior from consumer experience; nothing will do that. Whatever the method and its context, there will be some consumers whose dominant motivations make them impervious to it, or whom it actually stimulates to misbehave. On the other hand, it is also clear that these two widely-used control techniques can help curb misbehavior Deterrence may be particularly effectual.

REFERENCES

Abelson, Elaine (1989), *When Ladies Go A-Thieving: Middle-Class Shoplifters in the Victorian Department Store,* New York and Oxford: Oxford University Press.

Barry, Dan, and Dave Crombie (1989), "A Slick Credit Card Scheme," *Providence Sunday Journal,* September 17.

Becker, Gary S. (1968), "Crime and Punishment: An Economic Approach," *The Journal of Political Economy,* 76(2), 169-217.

Cameron, Mary O. (1964), *The Booster and the Snitch,* New York: Free Press.

Cox, Dena, Anthony D. Cox, and George P. Moschis (1990), "When Consumer Behavior Goes Bad: An Investigation of Adolescent Shoplifting," *Journal of Consumer Research,* 17(2) (September), 149-159.

DSM-III-R (Diagnostic and Statistical Manual of Medical Disorders) (1987), 3rd ed. rev. Washington, DC: American Psychiatric Association.

Faber, Ronald J., Gary A. Christenson, Martina de Zwaan, and James Mitchell (1995), "Two Forms of Compulsive Consumption: Comorbidity of Compulsive Buying and Binge Eating" *Journal of Consumer Research,* 22(3), 296-304.

French, Warren A., Melvin R. Crask, and Fred H. Mader (1984), "Retailer's Assessment of the Shoplifting Problem," *Journal of Retailing,* 60 (Winter), 108-15.

Fullerton, Ronald A., and Girish Punj (1993), "Choosing to Misbehave: A Structural Model of Aberrant Consumer Behavior," Leigh McAlister & Michael L. Rothschild, eds., *Advances in Consumer Research,* 20, 570-574.

Guffey, H.J., J.R. Harris, and J.F. Laumer (1979), "Shopper Attitudes Toward Shoplifting and Shoplifting Preventative Devices," *Journal of Retailing,* 55(3), 75-89.

Hiew, Chok C. (1981), "Prevention of Shoplifting: A Community Action Approach," *Canadian Journal of Criminology,* 23(1), 57-68.

Hirschman, Elizabeth C. (1992), "The Consciousness of Addiction: Toward a General Theory of Compulsive Consumption,"*Journal of Consumer Research,* 19(3), 155-179.

"Intellectual Property" (1996), *The Economist,* 340 No. 7976 (27 July), pp. 61-63.

Johnson, Elmer H. (1987), "Prevention in Business and Industry," in Elmer H. Johnson (ed.), *Handbook on Crime and Delinquency Prevention,* Westport, CT: Greenwood, 279-301.

Kallis, M.J. and D.J. Vanier (1985), "Consumer Shoplifting: Orientations and Deterrents," *Journal of Criminal Justice,* 13(5), 459-73.

Katz, Jack (1988), *Seductions of Crime,* New York: Basic Books.

Keller, John J. (1992), "Call-Sell Rings Steal Cellular Service," *Wall Street Journal* (March 13).

Keller, Punam Anand, and Lauren Goldberg Block (1996), "Increasing the Effectiveness of Fear Appeals" *Journal of Consumer Research,* 22(1), 448-460.

Kerr, Peter (1992), "A Heavy Toll is Being Paid for Auto Fraud," *Providence Journal Bulletin* (February 13).

Kraut, Robert E. (1976), "Deterrent and Definitional Influences on Shoplifting," *Social Problems,* 23, 358-368.

Lichter, Linda (1994), "Criminal Theft of Time," Wall Street Journal (January 1).

McLaughlin, Mark (1987), "Subliminal Tapes Urge Shoppers to Heed the Warning Sounds of Silence: Don't Steal," *New England Business,* 9 (February 2), 36-37.

Merton, Robert K. (1968), *Social Theory and Social Structure,* New York: Free Press.

Mills, Michael K. (1979), "A Power-Contextual Analysis of Deviant Consumer Behavior in Retail Stores," unpublished Ph.D. dissertation, University of Pittsburgh.

Moore, Richard H. (1984), "Shoplifting in Middle America: Patterns and Motivational Correlates," *International Journal of Offender Therapy and Comparative Criminology,* 28, 53-64.

Neustatter, W. Lindesay (1954), "The Psychology of Shoplifting," *Medico-Legal Journal,* 22, 118-130.

Piliavin, Irving, Craig Thornton, Rosemary Gartner, and Ross L. Matsueda (1986), "Crime, Deterrence, and Rational Choice," *American Sociological Review,* 51, (February) 101 -119.

Rouke, Fabian L. (1957), "Shoplifting: Its Symbolic Motivation," *NPPA Journal,* 3, 5458.

Sheley, Joseph F. and Kenneth D. Bailey (1985), "New Directions for Anti-Theft Policy: Reductions in Stolen Goods Buyers," *Journal of Criminal* Justice, 13 No.5, 399-415.

Sutherland, Edwin H. (1934), *Principles of Criminology,* Philadelphia: Lippincott.

Tittle, Charles R. (1980), *Sanctions and Social Deviance,* New York: Praeger.

Thurber, Steven and Mark Snow (1980), "Signs May Prompt Antisocial Behavior," *Journal of Social Psychology,* 112(2), 309-10.

Use of Negative Cues to Reduce Demand for Counterfeit Products

Goutam Chakraborty, Oklahoma State University
Anthony Allred, Oklahoma State University
Ajay Singh Sukhdial, Oklahoma State University
Terry Bristol, Oklahoma State University

ABSTRACT

The sale of counterfeit products, a $200 billion industry worldwide, represents a serious threat to both the manufacturers of the legitimate products and the welfare of the consumers who purchase counterfeits. Therefore, identifying methods of reducing the counterfeit trade has become a top priority for many businesses and governments. This study examines means of dissuading consumers from knowingly purchasing counterfeit products. Specifically, the findings confirm that cuing negative aspects of consumers' typical beliefs about counterfeits, such as the high failure rate of counterfeits and the country of origin of the counterfeit relative to that of the legitimate product, can reduce their intentions to knowingly purchase counterfeit products.

INTRODUCTION

The sale of counterfeit products represents a serious threat to both the manufacturers of legitimate products and the welfare of the consumers who purchase them. Counterfeit merchandise consists of unauthorized copies sold as legitimate products and accounts for an estimated $200 billion in sales worldwide (Levine and Rotenier 1993). Annual loss estimates for the legitimate manufacturers are considerable across a diverse set of industries, e.g., motor parts ($200 million), Swiss watches ($900 million), perfumes ($70 million), and pharmaceuticals ($50 million) (Matthews 1993). Counterfeit products also present a very real threat to consumer safety. For example, in the auto industry a number of fatal accidents have been traced to the installation and subsequent failure of counterfeit auto parts (Dugan 1984). Other such incidents have occurred with respect to counterfeit pharmaceuticals, medical implants, and airplane parts (Harvey 1988, Ott 1993). Thus, there are numerous instances of counterfeits destroying brand equity and company reputation, increasing the costs of marketing legitimate products, affecting hundreds of thousands of jobs, and threatening consumer health and safety across different industries. Therefore, marketers and public policy makers alike are very interested in identifying ways to reduce and, if possible, eliminate counterfeit products.

Counterfeit activities can be reduced by attacking either of two dimensions—the *supply* of counterfeits or the *demand* for counterfeits. With few exceptions, academic research and actual anti-counterfeiting efforts have focused on how to keep the supply of counterfeits from reaching consumers. Yet the counterfeiting problem continues to grow such that it appears that a generous supply of counterfeits will always exist as long as there is demand for them (Block, Bush, and Campbell 1993). Those few studies that have focused on counterfeit product demand have shown that consumers tend to attribute counterfeits with properties that may be associated with greater risk and that such risk may mediate consumers' evaluations of and feelings toward counterfeit purchases (Bamossy and Scammon 1985; Chakraborty, Allred, and Bristol 1996). Specifically, Bamossy and Scammon (1985) found that consumers believe counterfeits are generally of lower quality and higher in defects and that most counterfeits are manufactured abroad such that U.S. manufacturers are harmed and U.S. jobs are lost because of counterfeit purchases. Thus U.S. consumers appear to be aware of some of the negative outcomes and risks associated

with the typical counterfeit purchase. Chakraborty et al. (1996) showed that for certain groups of consumers such risks are enhanced and affect evaluations of and feelings toward counterfeit purchases.

In our research, we build on these ideas to investigate whether specific information cues can prompt negative beliefs and expectations consumers hold for counterfeits, thereby reducing their demand for such products. Specifically, we conducted a study to investigate the impact of cues such as the failure rate of counterfeits and the country of origin of the original manufacturer of the product on consumers' perceptions of risk of buying counterfeit products. To more closely tie our results to demand for the counterfeits and subsequent future counterfeit sales, we measured the impact of these cues and the mediating effect of perceived risk on actual purchase intentions and post-purchase feelings of guilt, rather than purchase evaluations or attitudes. We expected that increasing perceived risk by using such cues would negatively impact consumers' intentions to purchase counterfeit products. We report the results of this study below and discuss how managers may use our findings to develop strategies to persuade consumers to not knowingly purchase counterfeits.

CONCEPTUAL BACKGROUND

Consumers may purchase counterfeits either knowingly or unknowingly. If at the point of purchase, consumers do not know that they are buying a counterfeit product (i.e., consumers think they have purchased a genuine product when in fact it is a fake) such transactions are called *deceptive counterfeiting* (Grossman and Shapiro 1988). If, however, at the point of purchase, consumers are aware that they are buying a counterfeit based on price, quality, and the type of outlet from which the product is purchased, such transactions are called *nondeceptive counterfeiting*. Grossman and Shapiro (1988) contended that in many cases, the public is well aware of these illegal markets and the availability of bogus products and thus purchase counterfeits knowingly.

From a demand side perspective, there is little (other than educating consumers about how to spot fakes) that can be done to eliminate or reduce deceptive counterfeiting because consumers are unaware that they are purchasing counterfeits. Therefore, to decrease deceptive counterfeiting, marketers typically try to restrict the supply of counterfeits. Proliferation of nondeceptive counterfeiting depends on consumer demand for counterfeits and can thus be decreased by reducing this demand. Because this study deals with issues related to consumer demand for counterfeits, we investigate only nondeceptive counterfeiting.

Consumers' Beliefs About Counterfeit Products

When trying to evaluate new products, consumers classify them based on cues in the purchase environment and apply the beliefs and expectations typical of this knowledge to form an evaluation or choice. We suggest that consumers' knowledge, beliefs, and expectations for counterfeit products form such a category that they may use in judging counterfeit purchase situations. For example, many consumers believe that for commonly counterfeited brands, originals are often manufactured in more developed countries but counterfeits are mostly made in less developed countries (Bamossy and Scammon 1985). American consumers believe that the consequences of buying counterfeits made abroad, given that the country of original manufacture is the U.S., include financial losses to U.S. companies and lost U.S. jobs (Bamossy and Scammon 1985). Additionally, consumers tend to believe that counterfeits rate low on quality and performance and high on defects (Bamossy and Scammon 1985). Consumers also hold positive beliefs and expectations about counterfeits, e.g., that counterfeits are less expensive than the legitimate product (Bamossy and Scammon 1985). Given the high demand for counterfeits, these positive aspects likely are more salient or perhaps outweigh the negative aspects of consumers' knowledge of counterfeits. However, we believe that consumers may be dissuaded from purchasing counterfeit products by cuing, and thus making more salient, the negative aspects of their expectations.

Country of origin of a product is one information cue that may prompt consumers' beliefs about counterfeit products. Chakraborty et al. (1996) suggested that in the context of a nondeceptive counterfeit purchase, there are two countries of origin that are relevant: the country of origin of the legitimate manufacturer (COM) and the country of origin of the counterfeiters (COC). Their study showed that the COM can influence certain consumers' evaluations of and purchase feelings toward counterfeits. Additionally, the influence of the COM on consumers' perceived risk in purchasing counterfeit products appears to mediate those effects.

Another information cue that seems relevant in trying to decrease the demand for counterfeits is the failure rate of such products. Greater failure rates for counterfeit products is consistent with and supportive of an existing belief that might influence consumers' reactions to counterfeit products. We believe that failure rates will cue that negative aspect of consumers' expectations, impacting the perceived risk of the counterfeit purchase and in turn negatively influencing consumers' demand for counterfeit products.

Mediating Role of Perceived Risk

There is some inherent risk in buying a counterfeit instead of the legitimate product since the former may not perform as well as the original. Thus, there may be some risk of loss incurred by purchasing a counterfeit, particularly given the typical beliefs cued by a high failure rate. These risks may take the form of risking wasting money, a low level of performance, safety or well-being should the product fail, and/or time necessary to fix the problem should the product fail. Thus, we expect failure rate cues to impact the risk of such losses, such that the higher the failure rate the greater the perceived risk of loss in purchasing the counterfeit product. Additionally, we expect this greater risk should reduce consumers' intentions to purchase the counterfeit.

There is also risk in purchasing counterfeits because the COM and the COC are typically not the same. Because consumers expect the COC to be a less developed country and the COM to be a more developed country, consumers may also perceive other more psychological or social risks in buying counterfeits, some of which may be derived from the purchase of foreign counterfeits in particular. American consumers believe the COC is foreign, and so they infer that purchasing counterfeits leads to financial losses for U.S. companies and U.S. job loss. In fact, Chakraborty et al. (1996) found that certain consumers tend to perceive higher risk in buying counterfeits made abroad when the original was made in the U.S. This high perceived risk in turn resulted in lower quality evaluations for counterfeits and higher guilt in knowingly buying counterfeits when the original product was made in the U.S. Thus, given the cue that the COM is the U.S. rather than abroad, we expect that nationalistic biases, patriotism, and concerns about U.S. companies

and jobs are likely to mean that American consumers will perceive foreign-made counterfeits as more risky to their self-image or the image portrayed to others. We expect that this greater psychosocial risk should reduce intentions to purchase the counterfeit and increase anticipation of post-purchase feelings of guilt about the purchase.

In summary, we expect that cuing the negative aspects of what consumers believe and expect about counterfeits influences their risk perceptions of such purchases, leading to both decreased demand for the counterfeit and increased anticipation of post-purchase feelings of guilt. We conducted a factorial experiment to empirically examine these ideas, measuring subjects' purchase intentions to gain insight into demand for the counterfeit product. Additionally, since consumers who feel guilty about purchasing would likely be less liable to purchase such products again, we measured subjects' post-purchase feelings of guilt to gauge demand beyond the current purchase.

METHODOLOGY

Subjects were randomly assigned into the cells of a 2 X 2 between-subjects factorial design. Each factor represented a different manipulated information cue. The first factor was the country of manufacturer of the original product (COM), with two levels— U.S. versus foreign. The second factor was the failure rate of counterfeits, with two levels—high (15 percent return rate) and low (1 percent return rate). Across all four cells of this design, the country of origin of the counterfeit manufacturer (COC) was held constant as foreign.

Subjects and Stimulus Product Category

It is difficult to identify a typical consumer of nondeceptive counterfeit products because very little demand-side research related to nondeceptive counterfeiting has been conducted. Because of their low income, college students are likely to be representative of at least one segment of the population that knowingly purchases counterfeits. Therefore, a sample of students was considered appropriate for this study, consisting of 87 undergraduate marketing students (all U.S. nationals) from a large midwestern university. Extra credit was offered as an incentive to the students who participated in the experiment. There were 48 percent males and 52 percent females in the sample.

As mentioned above, a wide variety of products is being counterfeited. Based on the results of informal interviews where we asked students to identify products that they believed were most frequently counterfeited, we chose auto parts for our study. Counterfeit auto parts are also frequently mentioned in the literature. The literature is not clear, however, about which specific counterfeit products are purchased knowingly (nondeceptive counterfeiting). The informal interviews suggested that in the student population, counterfeit auto parts are often purchased knowingly. In fact, 92 percent of our sample owned a car and 42 percent indicated that in the past they had an opportunity to buy counterfeit auto parts.

Procedure

Self-administered questionnaires were distributed and completed in class by the subjects. Participants were asked to read a brief scenario that described a purchase situation where a consumer has a choice of buying a genuine product or a counterfeit at a lower cost. Several pretests were conducted to create scenarios that were realistic and easy to understand. In the scenarios, the COM cue was manipulated by designating the manufacturer of the genuine product as "a U.S. company" or "a foreign company." The failure rate cue was manipulated by describing that the counterfeit had either a "1 percent failure rate" or a "15 percent failure rate." Subjects were

TABLE 1
Psycho-Social Risk in Buying Counterfeits

Country-of-manufacture of the legitimate product (COM)	Low failure rate	High failure rate
U.S.	3.95	5.50
Foreign	4.79	4.76

Note: Scale ranged from 1 (not risky at all) to 9 (very risky).

instructed to imagine that they were in the same purchase situation across conditions before answering any question. After reading the scenario, subjects answered a battery of questions related to perceived risk, purchase intentions, and post-purchase feelings of guilt. The questionnaire took about 15 minutes to complete.

Measures

We were interested in three sets of dependent variables: perceived risk, purchase intentions, and post-purchase feelings of guilt. The risk measures were adopted from Chakraborty et al. (1996) and included eight questions to measure various dimensions of product specific risk associated with tangible losses (financial, investment, performance, safety, time, and opportunity) and risks associated with more psycho-social elements (social and self-image). For instance, the question "What is the risk that the counterfeit will not perform as expected?" was used for measuring performance risk. Subjects responded using a 9-point scale with anchors "not risky at all" and "very risky." Purchase intentions were measured with a single 9-point item question, "Overall, how likely it is that you would buy the counterfeit?" Post-purchase feelings were measured using two questions such as "If you bought the counterfeit, you would feel guilty," with responses indicated on 7-point Likert-type scales.

RESULTS

A factor analysis of the eight questions pertaining to perceived risk confirmed the two orthogonal dimensions as found in the Chakraborty et al. (1996) study. The two dimensions explained 62 percent of the variance. The first dimension, "loss" risk, included the questions pertaining to financial, investment, performance, safety, time, and opportunity and had loadings of 0.63 or more. The second dimension, "psycho-social" risk, included questions pertaining to self-image and what others think of you with loadings of 0.85 or more. In the analysis, we used average scores of the items loading on these two dimensions as measures of loss (Cronbach's alpha=0.89) and psycho-social risk (r=0.80). An index was also formed for post-purchase feelings of guilt by averaging the two items measuring that variable (r=0.89).

To check whether subjects were sensitive to the COM manipulation, at the end of the survey they were asked to indicate the country of manufacture of the genuine product. Eighty-nine percent of the subjects in the experimental conditions where the genuine product was made in the U.S. and 87 percent of the subjects in the conditions where the genuine product was made in a foreign country correctly recalled the country of manufacturer of the genuine product.

We expected the failure rate cue to influence perceived risk (particularly the risk of loss), which in turn would influence consumers' intentions to purchase the counterfeit product and their post-purchase feelings of guilt. We also expected the COM cue to influence perceived risk (especially the psycho-social risk), which

in turn would influence consumers' purchase intentions and post-purchase feelings of guilt.

Effects of Failure Rate and COM Cues on Perceived Risk

We used ANOVA to investigate whether consumers' perceptions of risk in buying counterfeits are influenced by the two information cues: the failure rate of counterfeits and the COM of the original product. The dependent variables are subjects' scores on the loss and psycho-social risk dimensions. As expected, the main effect of failure rate is significant for loss risk ($F(1,83)$=10.47, p=0.01). The means corresponding to the significant main effect of failure rate indicate that subjects perceived higher loss risk in the presence of high failure rate information (means are 5.52 for low failure rate and 6.73 for high failure rate conditions). The main effect of failure rate as well as the interaction effect of COM and failure rate are significant for psycho-social risk ($F(1,86)$=4.47, p=0.04; $F(1,87)$=4.45, p=0.04, respectively). The means for interpreting the interaction effect are reported in Table 1. These means indicate that the knowledge of failure rate about the counterfeit auto part plays no role in influencing psycho-social risk when the original auto part was foreign-made. However, when the original COM is the U.S., the subjects who were told that the counterfeit auto part had a high failure rate perceived significantly more psycho-social risk than the subjects who were told that the counterfeit had a low failure rate.

We did not expect this interaction effect. One explanation for these results is that although failure rate information is useful in making product judgments given a U.S. COM, given a foreign COM the failure rate information is not diagnostic. American consumers, and our subjects in particular, may view foreign manufacturers of auto parts, whether legitimate or counterfeit, in low regard such that the failure rates are not meaningful cues.

Effects of Failure Rate and COM Cues on Purchase Intentions and Post-Purchase Feelings of Guilt

We also used ANOVA to investigate the influence of the failure rate and COM cues on consumers' purchase intentions and post-purchase feelings of guilt. For purchase intentions, the main effect of failure rate as well as the interaction effect of failure rate and COM are significant ($F(1,83)$=5.85, p=0.02; $F(1,83)$=3.84, p=0.05, respectively). The interaction effect of failure rate and COM is also significant for post-purchase feelings of guilt ($F(1,82)$=3.92, p=0.05). The means for interpreting these significant effects are reported in Table 2.

The means corresponding to the significant failure rate main effect on purchase intentions indicate that subjects are less likely to knowingly buy a counterfeit auto part when failure rate is high (mean ratings are 2.78 for high failure rate and 3.94 for low failure rate, with higher numbers indicating more likelihood of buying the counterfeit). However, this main effect is to be judged within the context of the significant interaction effect. The means correspond-

TABLE 2
Mean Purchase Intentions and Post-Purchase Feelings about Buying Counterfeits

COM	Purchase intentions[a]		Post-purchase feelings of guilt[b]	
	Low failure rate	High failure rate	Low failure rate	High failure rate
U.S.	4.57	2.50	1.64	2.79
Foreign	3.28	3.20	1.82	1.64

Note: [a]Scale ranged from 1 (very unlikely) to 9 (very likely).
[b]Scale ranged from 1 (strongly disagree) to 7 (strongly agree) with statements indicating feeling guilty about purchasing the counterfeit.

ing to the interaction effect contained in Table 2 suggest that when the original auto part is made in a foreign country, failure rate has no effect on subjects' intentions to buy counterfeits made abroad. That is, when the original auto part is foreign made, consumers are just as unlikely to knowingly buy counterfeit auto parts whether the failure rate of the counterfeits is high or low. However, for U.S. made auto parts, cuing a high failure rate reduces consumers' likelihood of purchasing counterfeits. This interaction is consistent with the diagnosticity explanation discussed above. Most important to our purpose, demand for the counterfeit product is least given *both* the U.S. COM and high failure rate cues.

For post-purchase feelings of guilt, means reported in Table 2 suggest the following. When the original auto part is made in the U.S., consumers feel more guilty about buying counterfeits when a high failure rate of the counterfeit is cued than when a low failure rate is cued. However, when the original auto part is made in a foreign country, consumers feel equally less guilty in buying counterfeits regardless of the failure rate cued. Again, this interaction is consistent with the diagnosticity explanation discussed above. Critical to our purpose, post-purchase feelings of guilt and thus presumably future demand for the counterfeit product is least given *both* the U.S. COM and high failure rate cues.

Mediating Effects of Perceived Risk

In order to generate some insights about the mediating role of perceived risk on consumers' purchase intentions and post-purchase feelings about counterfeits, we conducted ANCOVA using a technique suggested by Mitchell (1986) and Petty and Cacioppo (1977). First, we used the perceived risk dimensions as the covariates and the consumers' purchase intentions and post-purchase feelings as dependent measures. The results of these analyses indicate that when the effects of perceived risk are controlled for, the failure rate-by-COM interaction effects on consumers' purchase intentions of counterfeits and their post-purchase feelings of guilt are eliminated ($F(1,81)=0.98, p=0.33; F(1,80)=0.50, p=0.48$, respectively). Thus, perceived risk appears necessary to explain the detected differences in purchase intentions and feelings.

Next, to examine the ordering of these effects to determine whether perceived risk precedes and leads to consumers' purchase intentions and feelings (rather than intentions and feelings leading to perceived risk), we analyzed the data using the latter as covariates with the risk dimensions as the dependent variables. The results of these analyses indicate that the failure rate main effect remains significant even after the effects of consumers' purchase intentions and feelings are partialled out of the risk perceptions (loss risk: $F(1,82)=4.24, p=0.04$; psycho-social risk: $F(1,82)=4.85, p=0.03$). This seems to indicate that perceived risk is acting as a mediator between the COM and failure rate and consumers' purchase intentions of counterfeits and their post-purchase feelings of guilt.

Interestingly, the two dimensions of perceived risk have different mediating effects on purchase intention and feelings. In the ANCOVA model for purchase intentions, only the loss risk covariate is significant ($F(1,81)=91.63, p=0.01$). However, in the ANCOVA model of post-purchase feelings of guilt, only the psycho-social risk effect is significant ($F(1,80)=49.96, p=0.01$). These results suggest that loss risk acts as a mediator for purchase intentions and psycho-social risk acts as a mediator for post-purchase feelings of guilt.

DISCUSSION

We started this research attempting to identify strategies for reducing consumer demand for counterfeits. One strategy that we felt might be effective is to cue negative aspects of consumers' knowledge of and expectations for counterfeits, resulting in greater perceptions of risk that would in turn lead to less consumer demand for counterfeit products. The results of this study support our expectations. Specifically, to reduce the demand for counterfeits, companies, trade groups, and/or public policy makers may want to cue or make salient negative aspects of consumers' typical beliefs about counterfeits such as high failure rates and the U.S. as the COM with foreign countries as the COC. In our study, such a strategy appears to lead to higher perceived risk of loss and subsequent lower intentions to purchase the counterfeit product. To reduce future demand for counterfeits beyond the immediate purchase, utilizing the same cues appears to lead to higher perceived psycho-social risk that in turn leads to higher post-purchase feelings of guilt about purchasing such products. Our results suggest that it is critical to use these cues in combination, because the increased risk, reduced purchase intentions, and increased post-purchase feelings of guilt generally only occurred when both cues were made salient.

Our results should be viewed with caution because of the exploratory nature of our study. Specifically, these results are tempered by our choice of measures, cues, subjects, and stimuli. We measured purchase intentions because we were interested in reducing demand for counterfeits and not simply consumers' attitudes toward such products. Future research should examine whether these effects replicate when consumers' actual behavior is measured, e.g., sales. Additionally, future research should examine the impact of consumers' post-purchase feelings of guilt on their future purchases of counterfeits. Our results were limited to two specific cues: failure rate and COM. However, other cues, such as the lack of warranty protection or redress, may also effectively prompt negative expectations, greater perceived risk, and thus reduce demand for counterfeits. Future research should further explore consumers' beliefs about counterfeits and cues that may make these beliefs more salient when consumers consider making counterfeit purchases.

These results were obtained in a single, commonly counterfeited product class— auto parts—with a relatively homogeneous sample of consumers. The information cue effects we detected may diminish somewhat given product classes with attributes that are directly observable or experienced by consumers. Additionally, the likely impact of perceived risk of loss as opposed to psycho-social risk may vary depending on the nature of the product class, e.g., functional versus symbolic. Thus, future research should determine whether these results replicate for other product classes. Additionally, Chakraborty et al. (1996) found that individual differences such as consumer ethnocentrism can moderate some effects of the COM in a counterfeit situation. Thus, different effects may result given consumers varying from our sample in terms of ethnocentrism, expertise, and other factors. Future research should examine whether our results replicate across other samples of consumers.

We offered an explanation of the interaction effects detected that was based on a possible lack of diagnosticity of the failure rate information given a foreign COM. Other explanations are possible. For example, subjects' interpretation of our foreign COM cue (subjects were informed that the COM was simply a "foreign country") may have varied considerably, leading to a wide variance in their responses to that cue. Such variance may have produced the lack of differences we obtained between the high and low failure rate within the foreign COM condition. However, we find that this particular explanation does not hold for our results, because the variance for dependent variables within the foreign COM cells was generally smaller than that within the U.S. COM cells. Regardless, future research should examine whether our explanation holds over other competing ideas.

Finally, the framework used and effects detected in our study may be useful in exploring other, similar purchase contexts. For example, consumers often consider off-brands and "generics" as lower priced and lower quality alternatives to name brand products. Companies marketing name brand products may be interested in further research using our framework to identify techniques for reducing consumer demand for their off-brand competitors.

Limitations notwithstanding, our results provide insights into strategies for reducing consumers' demand for counterfeit products. For managers in the auto parts industry, these findings suggest that anti-counterfeiting strategies should include advertising messages that appeal to consumers in terms of the harmful effects of counterfeits on U.S. companies and American workers' jobs (i.e., appeal to patriotic feelings), as well as messages that emphasize the high risks of inferior quality counterfeit parts breaking down at inopportune times. There is substantial evidence to back up the assertion that counterfeit products are of inferior quality, especially counterfeit auto parts (Bush, Bloch, and Dawson 1989). Advertisements similar to that aired on television by NAPA (National Automobile Parts Association) showing a family stranded at a dangerous neighborhood due to the breakdown of a cheap auto part may prove useful in reducing demand for counterfeit products.

REFERENCES

Bamossy, Gary, and Debra L. Scammon (1985), "Product Counterfeiting: Consumers and Manufacturers Beware," in *Advances in Consumer Research*, Vol. 12, eds. Elizabeth C. Hirschman and Morris B. Holbrook, Provo, Utah: Association for Consumer Research, 334-339.

Bush, Ronald F., Peter H. Bloch, and Scott Dawson (1989), "Remedies for Product Counterfeiting," *Business Horizons*, 32 (January), 59-65.

Bloch, Peter H., Ronald F. Bush, and Leland Campbell (1993), "Consumer (Accomplices) in Product Counterfeiting: A Demand-Side Investigation," *Journal of Consumer Marketing*, 10 (4), 27-36.

Chakraborty, Goutam, Anthony T. Allred, and Terry Bristol (1996), "Exploring Consumers' Evaluations of Counterfeits: The Roles of Country of Origin and Ethnocentrism," in *Advances in Consumer Research*, Vol. 23, eds. Kim P. Corfman and John G. Lynch, Jr., Provo, Utah: Association for Consumer Research, 379-384.

Dugan, T. M. (1984), "Counterfeit!" *Consumers Digest*, 23 (September/October), 21-23 and 72-73.

Grossman, Gene M., and Carl Shapiro (1988), "Foreign Counterfeiting of Status Goods," *Quarterly Journal of Economics*, 103 (February), 79-100.

Harvey, Michael G. (1988), "Industrial Product Counterfeiting: Problems and Proposed Solutions," *Journal of Business and Industrial Marketing*, 2 (Fall), 5-13.

Levin, Joshua, and Nancy Rotenier (1993), "Seller Beware," *Forbes*, 15 (October), 170- 174.

Matthews, Virginia (1993), "Piracy on the High Street," *Marketing Week*, 16 (August), 18.

Mitchell, Andrew A. (1986), "The Effect of Verbal and Visual Components of Advertisements on Brand Attitudes and Attitude Toward the Advertisement," *Journal of Consumer Research*, 13 (June), 12-24.

Ott, James (1993), "U.S. Indicts Broker in Alleged Scam," *Aviation Week & Space Technology*, 138 (April), 36.

Petty, Richard E., and John T. Cacioppo (1977), "Forewarning, Cognitive Responding, and Resistance to Persuasion," *Journal of Personality and Social Psychology*, 35 (4), 645-655.

Meanings and Methods: International Perspectives on the Use of Information Communication Technologies

Mara Alexander, Bilkent University

SESSION OVERVIEW

The meanings of information and communication technologies (ICTs) are defined not by the developers of the technology, but by the consumers who choose to use them, or not. This session explored the meanings of ICTs, including the Internet, to consumers, and how the meanings may aid or hinder adoption and penetration of these technologies. It began by discussing the frustrations with technology encountered by users in a developed society, the United States, moved to a discussion of factors which might potentially influence use of one technology, the Internet, throughout the world, and concluded with a discussion of ICTs by consumers in a developing country, Turkey.

SUMMARIES OF PRESENTATIONS

The first presentation, by David Glen Mick and Susan Fournier, is a refutation of research which claims that technology and its influence in daily life are inconspicuous. Most pertinent to the consumer behavior field, Joerges argues that "'small' everyday technologies" (e.g., appliances, entertainment, and office equipment) are the "peripheral elements' of the "largely out-of-awareness deep structures" that constitute the broad-scaled technization of life. Inconspicuousness, however, does not imply that technoculture is the modern day garden of paradise. Rather, technology reflects the postmodern principle of "double coding" (Jencks 1991) by embodying a variety of existential tensions or paradoxes. For instance, one paradox includes the tension between the tendency of technology to solve problems (or fulfill needs) versus creating others. In sum, it is widely maintained that technology is the singular, overarching manner by which contemporary life is patterned, that the content of this structural orientation reflects a range of existential paradoxes, and that the nature and consequences of consumer technologies in modern life are mostly sunk in deeper recesses of human consciousness. Mick and Fournier presented data from interviews with 16 consumers concerning their technological products. The interviews offer evidence that consumers are aware of the technological enframement of everyday life, and recognize technological paradoxes in common products. The respondents also adopt a variety of acquisition and consumption strategies to cope with these paradoxes.

Thomas Novak reported, in the second presentation, on the research he and Donna Hoffman are doing on Internet demographic and usage differences. The paper deals with 1) methodological and conceptual issues in measuring the number of users of the Internet and World Wide Web, and the behavior of these users, 2) comparison of so-called population projectable surveys based upon random samples and non-population projectable surveys using Web fill-out forms, and 3) a preliminary analysis of cross-national differences in consumer usage of the Internet and the World Wide Web. Wide ranges in the number of users were shown, depending upon the data collection method used and how "usage" is defined. The preliminary results of a cross-national survey of Web usage show a largely linear relationship between number of host computers in a country and number of users. Novak suggests that nonlinearity can be explained in part by geographic location and use of the English language.

The third presentation, by Güliz Ger and Mara Alexander, offered preliminary work on ICT usage by Turkish consumers. ICTs, the skills required to use them, and the information they can be used to communicate are bases of social power in developing societies with immense social inequalities, such as Turkey. As such, they can be used to develop or hinder individual and group identity, and as a means to achieve political power. Ger reported results of qualitative research among affluent and nonaffluent Turks, using comments from focus groups, in-depth interviews, and interviews with experts to illustrate ICTs' capacity for empowerment and creation of identity. Collages from the focus groups were also presented.

SYNTHESIS

Alladi Venkatesh, synthesizer for the session, offered the view that while much research on technology is about the way in which technology shapes people's lives, this session instead focused on how *people* influence the shape of technology. With regard to the Mick and Fournier paper, he noted that consumers can construe their home as physical space, technological space, or social space. In this space, is the paradox resolved, or do consumers learn to live with it? With regard to the paper by Novak and Hoffman, he suggested that research on how the Web is used be extended beyond the few, primarily instrumental, uses mentioned to include experiential uses. For the final paper, Venkatesh recommends considering how the Internet is used cross-nationally, using the concept of "flow" raised in the paper by Novak and Hoffman.

Privacy: A Paranoid's View

Daniel R. Horne, Providence College
David A. Horne, California State University–Long Beach

INTRODUCTION

Some perspectives suggest that we are all part of it, pawns in the great scheme to catalog, categorize, analyze, and eventually control every living soul on the planet. From the innocent newborn whose parents are strongly encouraged to complete a social security application, to the individuals who have their purchases scanned at the checkout counter and then pay with their credit cards, to the unwary motorist passing through an automated tollway's transponder tracking device, portions of their behavior can be monitored for future reference. The technology to accomplish these particular observations and billions more is certainly available and the current hodgepodge of federal, state, and municipal statutes seem to offer little solace for those concerned with this present reality.

Many aspects of our financial, educational, vocational, and personal lives have been routinely recorded for centuries. Church documents dutifully recorded births, baptisms, weddings, and eventually deaths of their parishioners. Private and public school systems record every grade, teacher, and even non-academic behavior from elementary through higher education. Every county seat documents property transactions, births, marriages, divorces, and deaths. The collection of data is certainly not new, so what is all the fuss about?

Two principal features about the "old" mechanism for record-keeping provided a great deal of individual security and probably kept general concerns about such matter to a minimum. First, access to such records was not exactly wide open. Though they may have been kept in public or quasi-public places, the mechanics of actually going to a "hall of records" and searching through rustic files was often an onerous and time-consuming task. Second, the likelihood of a complete altering of an individual's records was negligible. There were too many documents in too many inaccessible places to make wholesale changes possible. These old safeguards are now quaint memories in the era of interconnected database management.

Public perception of the intricate web of personal, corporate, and government data ceaselessly churning around the globe is based on a mix of fact and fiction offered up via news accounts (Phelps, Gozenbach and Johnson 1994), and mainstream entertainment. News stories highlight the gathering and use of personal data (e.g., USA Today, 1995). Popular television programs, movies, and books tell stories of the hapless protagonist caught in a surreal existence where they do not exist according to the "records" or if they do exist, every pertinent fact about them has been altered in some detrimental fashion (e.g., THE NET, Columbia Pictures release 1995). The "obvious" widespread vulnerability of the entire, computer-based information collection, storage, and retrieval system has become an area of general agreement across geo-demographic segments (Harris/Equifax 1994).

The point of this rather paranoid introduction is that many commercial activities associated with consumer behavior have the potential to be classified as intrusions into an individual's private affairs. Indeed, ordinary consumers are reporting increasing levels of concern with matters of privacy and control of personal data (Equifax/Harris 1994, 1993, 1991). The 1994 Equifax/Harris survey of consumer privacy found that over half (51%) of those interviewed were "very concerned" about threats to their personal privacy. Only 15% of those studied were "not very concerned" or "not at all concerned." This contrasts sharply with the 1978 study

in which 36% of respondents showed this lack of concern (Harris 1978). However, whether from increased media exposure or dissatisfaction with their own experiences, consumers' concerns about privacy continue to escalate. If, as this increase suggests, consumers begin to collectively seek relief, then marketers need to make adjustments before governments step in and dictate more restrictive policies (Dentino 1994; Schultz 1988). At the extreme, a recently introduced bill in the California legislature proposes that:

"No person or corporation may use or distribute for profit any personal information concerning a person without that person's written consent. Such information includes, but is not limited to, an individual's credit history, finances, medical history, purchases, and travel patterns." (Personal Rights Privacy–California Senate Bill, S.B. 1659).

The possibility of individual action through the use of mail and telephone preference lists is also a concern to the marketers using direct marketing techniques. More worrisome, however, is the threat posed by individual or class action lawsuits such as the case recently filed in Virginia where a man asked to share in the revenue generated when *U. S. News & World Report* sold other firms a list containing his name (Gearan 1996).

To investigate some consumers' reactions to one such familiar activity, direct marketing, an exploratory study was undertaken to investigate attitudes toward this daily interface. A framework to suggest a segmentation basis for this and other privacy concerns will be offered and discussed, and descriptive findings presented. Finally, the implications of the findings and potential future research questions will be presented.

BACKGROUND

Among all of the uproar, the direct marketing industry is growing and more mainstream marketers have begun to borrow extensively the concepts and technologies of direct marketing (Business Week 1994; Perreault and McCarthy 1996). Consequentially, one key group to consider consists of those consumers who utilize the services of direct marketers. Is this group different in their attitudes toward privacy than the population as a whole? If this is the case, then several steps are available to the industry, to both strengthen positive attitudes of the one group and help allay the fears of the other. A second question involves the dimensions or characteristics by which this group differs from other segments.

An ever-increasing number of U.S. households use direct marketing services such as mail order, and there is some evidence of loyalty and continued purchase from these sources (Gordon 1994; Schultz 1992). The distinction between those that use these service and those who do not might be a relevant factor to examine. The degree of familiarity may be an important differentiating characteristic. Those with a higher number of product experiences, whether due to greater numbers of marketer originated communications or actual purchase behavior, have more expertise than those who have had few, if any encounters (Alba and Hutchinson 1987). Clearly, repeat customers are associated with a positive valence towards the product offered. In general, we might reasonably expect that those with a high degree of expertise would be most accurate in their interpretation and evaluation of risks involved in the commerce of their personal information. Accuracy, however,

Advances in Consumer Research
Volume 24, © 1997

may not be a valid term to describe these potential or hypothetical risks. Further, this situation may be complicated by differences between objective and subjective levels of knowledge (Park, Mothersbaugh and Feick 1994). A likely scenario is that those with higher levels of familiarity will feel less threatened by the use of this personal information.

A study by Nowak and Phelps (1992) examined the level of overall concern with privacy, but went further in trying to establish the presence of underlying causes of this concern. Their work makes a distinction between what they term "ignorance-based consumer concerns" and "knowledge-driven" concerns. This may be readily related to the consequences of familiarity discussed above. The former would result from consumers fearing what they do not understand and possibly making inaccurate inferences about likely characteristics or outcomes. The latter group, differences between objective and subjective knowledge aside, would be based on "accurate" assessments of how disparate data can be collected, combined, analyzed, and segmented and its impact. The significant presence of the latter group, with more expertise, would prove to be much more problematic for marketers because of the difficulties in changing more assuredly held beliefs.

One finding presented by Nowak and Phelps (1992) is that age is significantly related to concerns about privacy, with older consumers expressing higher level of concerns. There may be several reasons for this, for example younger people have grown up with increasingly sophisticated levels of technology and are more likely to be comfortable with its benefits. It may also be that younger consumers are simply used to direct marketing having utilized its services more often. Nowak and Phelps collected data on the respondents home shopping behavior, but other than stating overall usage rates for the sample, no analysis was presented on any relationship between prior behavior and age or concerns with privacy.

A study by Wang and Petrison (1993), investigated how varying levels of concern for personal privacy might depend on personal and situational factors. They too found that negative reactions to certain situations, which included privacy issues, increased with age. More importantly, they found that reactions to situations dealing with privacy depended on their familiarity with the firm and their own personal needs.

Given the empirical evidence cited above, it is possible that previous usage might directly impact concern for privacy. Familiarity might underlie Nowak and Phelps' (1992) finding about age differences. Those who are younger may have more often employed the services of direct marketers because they have been available for a larger percentage of their lives and they feel more comfortable about utilizing the phone and the mail to transact business. This is not implausible when we consider that a two generations ago, phones (and especially long distance phone service) were used solely by the well-to-do or for near emergency situations. Only 20 years ago mechanical rotary phones were still the norm. It is also possible to consider whether prior usage led to the results reported by Wang and Petrison (1993). We might easily imply that firms with which the consumer is most familiar are the firms with which the consumer does business. Further, marketing theory would suggest that the firms with which consumers continue to do business are those that best satisfy their needs.

STUDY

A convenience sample of subjects was drawn from the professional, administrative, and clerical staffs at a medium-sized, private college in New England. Potential subjects were approached and recruited individually and in-person by a student assistant who utilized a campus directory to identify prospects. Because of the possibly sensitive nature of part of the experiment, the entire data gathering process was explained to potential subjects before they were asked to participate. As an incentive, respondents were entered in a lottery, conducted at the completion of the project, for three gift certificates to local restaurants. Approximately 90 individuals were approached about the study and 74 subjects agreed to participate. In all, 70 subjects completing both phases of the study as two subjects did not remember to collect the mail everyday and two withdrew for unspecified reasons after Phase 2 began.

Phase 1 of the study involved a questionnaire which the subjects received directly from the research assistant. Subjects were asked to complete the short questionnaire about direct mail usage and attitudes toward direct marketing and privacy. Subjects were given three days to return the questionnaire to the principle investigator. All questionnaires were returned before Phase 2 was begun.

In Phase 2 of the study, subjects were given a heavy plastic bag with a drawstring and instructed to save all the direct mail pieces which they received for a period of one week. To help control for cyclicality in mailings, all subjects collected mail over the same one week period. Subjects were assured that unopened mail would not be opened and that opened mail would not be examined. After the collection period the mail was classified, counted, and weighed. It was then returned to the subjects.

Phase 2 of the study warrants further comment. It is certainly an imperfect measure as there was a likelihood that people would either forget to place mail in the bag, take and use the mail elsewhere (e.g., a catalog taken to work), or consciously not place potentially sensitive mailings in the bag (e.g., only one subject turned in a *Victoria's Secret* catalog). We tried to control the first situation by calling or leaving messages for each subject on the second day of collection and we felt that the second situation would be minimized by the promise of an immediate return of the mail. The third factor was largely out of our control, but it was hoped that it occurred randomly across the individuals and therefore, did not bias the results. Then too, we were not interested in measuring the actual amount of mail received, but rather use this measure as a proxy for the amount of usage/contact these individuals have with direct marketers.

RESULTS

Because this was a pilot study and only a convenience sample was utilized, generalizability of these results might prove problematic. The demographic makeup of the sample was more upscale than the population as a whole. Two out of three subjects had graduated from college with 29% holding post graduate degrees. Income also reflected this in that nearly half the sample had household incomes of over $50,000 and less than a quarter of the sample had incomes under $25,000. Age of respondents showed little representation of those over 65 (3%) or under 25 (8%). Analysis showed that the demographic variables were not significantly related to any of the questions which addressed privacy concerns.

Four measures were taken of subjects' concern for privacy. These included two questions taken directly from the Equifax/ Harris surveys: "How concerned are you about threats to your personal privacy in America today?" (modal response "somewhat concerned") and a question asking if the situation would get better (21%) or worse (64%) by the year 2000. Two Likert-type items utilizing 10-point scales anchored by "strongly disagree" and "strongly agree" were also asked. These were: "Direct marketing is an invasion of my personal privacy." (hereafter, INVASION),

TABLE 1

	Concern	Concern 2000	INVASION	REGULATION
Weight	.014	.103	-.298	-.238
	P=.910	P=.396	P=.014	P=.051

TABLE 2

	Concern	Concern 2000	INVASION	REGULATION
Satisfaction	-.369	-.062	-.334	-.407
	P=.004	P=.644	P=.011	P=.002

and "I think the direct marketing industry should be regulated more stringently." (REGULATION). The means on these questions were 6.1 for INVASION and 7.1 for REGULATION, showing some level of agreement on average.

Three measures were used to evaluate usage. The first was a self-reported measure of how frequently the subjects used or considered the information they received from direct marketers. The categories on the 4-point scale were "Never," "Rarely," "Occasionally," and "Frequently." These classifications had 9%, 30%, 28% and 33% of the responses, respectively. Analysis was performed by classifying the two highest and the two lowest into groupings of "heavy" and "light" users. ANOVA analyses using the privacy measures discussed above as the dependent variables were performed. The level of usage, so measured, accounted for a significant amount of the variance in responses about concern for privacy today (F=3.88, p=.053). That is, people who were classified as heavy users of direct marketing information were less concerned about privacy. On the other hand, no such relationship was found between self-reported usage and predictions about the privacy situation in the year 2000. The relationship here was also significant for INVASION (F=12.06, p=.001) and for REGULATION (F=14.53, p=.000), with the heavier user being less likely to feel that direct marketing is an invasion of privacy or that stronger regulation is necessary.

The second measure of usage dealt with the weight of the mail received by subjects over the collection period. The mean weight for the six days of "junk mail" was 1.5 pounds and the range was from .3 pounds to 6.3 pounds. Because this was an interval variable, correlation analysis was performed by looking at the bi-variate relationship between weight and the privacy questions. The resulting Pearson correlations are presented in Table 1.

The data showed no relationship between the two Harris survey questions and the volume of direct mail received. However, a significant negative correlation was found for INVASION and REGULATION. That is, the more mail that the subject received, the less likely they were to believe that direct marketing is an invasion of privacy and should be more closely regulated. This is not to suggest that if direct marketers send out more mail, then people will be less likely to demand governmental regulation. Here, mail received is a proxy for usage as it is assumed that people receive more mail because of their past usage history and not their utilizing methods, such as the mail preference service, to have their names removed from lists.

The final usage measure was one that dealt with the respondent's overall level of satisfaction with products and services purchased from direct marketers. Work in customer satisfaction theory (cf., Yi 1990) would suggest that highly satisfied customers show increased likelihood of repurchase behavior. Our position here is not to argue causal mechanisms or the antecedents to satisfaction, but rather to simply imply that if customers are happy then their usage will be higher than those who are not. Clearly there are numerous alternatives available for those who are dissatisfied. The general satisfaction level was measured on a 10-point scale and a correlation analysis was performed to examine the relationship between this variable and privacy concerns. The results are shown in Table 2.

This analysis shows general satisfaction with purchases to be related to all privacy questions except that dealing with predictions of the privacy situation in the future. The negative correlations indicate that those expressing higher levels of satisfaction had lower levels of concern for privacy issues.

DISCUSSION

The clear difference between users and non-users bears further consideration. While Alba and Hutchinson (1987) proposed that familiarity would result in better, i.e., more accurate, inferences, our findings based on the present data do not allow us to go so far as to make that assertion. Here, it appears that familiarity leads to differences in the level of felt risk. Following early work by Bauer (1960), we might find one of two explanations for lower levels of concern among this group, neither of which has to do with "accuracy." In the first place, these individuals may rate the probability of some negative outcome as being extremely low. In the second case, they may rate the negative consequences, although plausible or even likely as being of little importance. Whether objectively "accurate" or not, if either or both of these conditions are present, then the outcome will be a lack of concern similar to that found in the data. This might indicate a case of "knowledge-based unconcern."

That "lack of concern" shows a similar pattern of results as those dealing with feelings of invasions of privacy and need for further regulation, is not surprising. However, there are conceptual differences which lead to differing conclusions. The items INVASION and REGULATION deal specifically with the direct marketing industry. Those that actively participate in the use of this industry's products would intuitively be thought to hold more favorable views. Yet, they are also in a position to spot problems and abuses. Actually, an increase in the amount of personal information available to marketers might be seen as a benefit to this group. More information, leading to better segmentation schemes, increases the likelihood of relevant information reaching these users while at the same time decreasing the amount of unwanted or useless communications (Schultz 1994).

This information leads us to believe that privacy issues are quite complex and contain at least two very different dimensions. Under the privacy umbrella are issues dealing with the bother of unsolicited mail, phone, and personal contacts. People who utilize or directly benefit from these factors will be unlikely to cry out vociferously. However, a second privacy issue, that of the collection and transfer of personal data, occurs, if not surreptitiously then with little acknowledgment. It may be this, more Orwellian, invasion of privacy that drives overall levels of concern. Yet, the evidence showing less concern among heavy users may be the result of either lack of knowledge of the use of information by direct marketers or a willingness to accept the trade-off of information for better service. As one subject noted when she agreed to take part in the study, "Sure, why not? I've got nothing to hide." This seems to indicate some knowledge of the potentially sensitive nature of personal information while at the same time agreeing that in the immediate case at least, the probability of negative consequences from knowing this information was small.

LIMITATIONS

Several factors must be noted that do limit the applicability of these findings across wider consumer segments. First, the sample, though real consumers, was quite narrow in both its location and diversity. A broader group of consumers might have different beliefs. Second, in order to maintain respondent cooperation, the questionnaire was brief and did not allow for multiple measures of the important constructs. For instance, privacy appears to be a multidimensional construct. Third, the measures of direct mail material were based on the respondents' households cooperation which may have been uneven.

FUTURE RESEARCH

The purpose of this pilot study was to offer a framework for understanding and segmenting consumer groups on their concern for marketing-driven intrusions into their personal privacy. While we found that the notion of expertise might be one such framework there are issues, such as the veridicality of self-assessed knowledge, which must be addressed in order to confidently stand on that foundation. Further, the idea of including a perceived risk perspective to this topic should be an avenue for subsequent studies.

Our small investigation raised many more questions than it answered. For instance, exactly how is privacy, with its multiple facets and high variability across individuals best measured and assessed. Secondly, different marketing activities might have different impacts. Things like Internet promotions and advertising may be viewed more ominously since they come up live, literally in one's face. Conversely, because promotions on the Internet, at least in their current form, are largely based on personally provided information, less concern may be generated. Finally and in retrospect, one question that could have been fairly easily examined was not. That is, how much of the mail we collected was opened and how much of it was thrown unopened into our bag as though it were just the waste basket under the sink? This is certainly something that those who are spending money on direct mail campaigns would like to know.

BIBLIOGRAPHY

Alba, Joseph W. and J. Wesley Hutchinson (1987), "Dimensions of Consumer Expertise," *Journal of Consumer Research*, 13 (March), 411-454.

Bauer, R.A. (1960), "Consumer behavior as risk taking," in R.S. Hancock (Ed.), *Dynamic marketing for a changing world*, (pp. 389-398), Chicago: American Marketing Association.

Business Week (1994), "Database Marketing," September 5, 56-63.

Dentino, Karl (1994), "Taking Privacy into Our Own Hands," *Direct Marketing*, (September), 38-42.

Gearan, Anne (1996), "Man Sues Over Sales of His Name," Associated Press Release, February 5.

Gordon, Dinny Starr (1994), "Note on the Mail Order Industry," 9-595-014, Boston, Harvard Business School Publishing.

Harris (1978), *Dimensions of Privacy*, Louis Harris and Associates.

Harris-Equifax Consumer Privacy Survey (1991), Atlanta: Equifax.

Harris-Equifax Consumer Privacy Survey (1993), Atlanta: Equifax.

Harris-Equifax Consumer Privacy Survey (1994), Atlanta: Equifax.

Nowak, Glen J. and Joseph Phelps (1992), "Understanding Privacy Concerns," *Journal of Direct Marketing*, 6 (Autumn), 28-39.

Park, C. Whan, David L. Mothersbaugh and Lawrence Feick (1994), "Consumer Knowledge Assessment," *Journal of Consumer Research*, 21 (June), 71-82.

Perreault, William D., Jr. and E. Jerome McCarthy (1996), *Basic Marketing*, 12 edition, Chicago: Irwin.

Phelps, Joseph, William Gozenbach, and Edward Johnson (1994), "Press Coverage and Public Perception of Direct Marketing and Consumer Privacy," *Journal of Direct Marketing*, 8 (Spring), 9-22.

Schultz, Don E., (1988), "On Merging, Purging, and Privacy," *Journal of Direct Marketing*, 2 (Winter), 4-5.

———— (1992), "The Direct/Database Marketing Challenge to Fixed-Location Retailers," in *The Future of U.S. Retailing*, (ed.) Robert A. Peterson, New York: Quorum Books, 165-184.

———— (1994), "Some Comments on the Absolute Value of the Database," *Journal of Direct Marketing*, 8 (Autumn), 4-5.

USA Today (1995), December 19, Sections A & B.

Wang, Paul and Lisa A. Petrison (1993), "Direct marketing activities and personal privacy–A personal survey," *Journal of Direct Marketing*, 7 (Winter), 7-19.

Yi, Youjae (1990), "A Critical Review of Consumer Satisfaction," in *Review of Marketing 1990*, ed. Zeithaml, Chicago: American Marketing Association, 68-123.

Using Promises of Protection and Empowerment to Market Guns to Women: Implications For the Unfairness Doctrine

Elizabeth Blair, Ohio University
Eva M. Hyatt, Appalachian State University

INTRODUCTION

Women are increasingly being targeted by manufacturers of firearms as well as by organizations selling gun-related products and accessories. The National Rifle Association (NRA) estimates that between 12 and 20 million handguns are currently owned by women in the United States (Jones 1993). Anti-gun proponents believe that the targeting of women is largely due to a sales slump in the firearms market and to the fact that the primary market of white males has been saturated (Sugarman and Rand 1994).

As pro-gun forces increase their efforts to recruit women, there has been a corresponding outcry concerning the ethics of targeting this vulnerable population (e.g., Polter 1994; Neuborne 1994). Jones (1994) is particularly cynical about the NRA's efforts to recruit women through its recent "Refuse To Be A Victim" campaign. While cleverly appealing to both women's desire for empowerment and their fear-induced need for self-protection, the NRA seems to have researched its market well. Jones warns that the NRA does not really have women's best interests at heart, but instead is simply trying to increase its numbers due to a saturated male market. She cites as an example a recent campaign for legislation that would authorize police to confisgate guns from men who have assaulted women. Predictably, the NRA did nothing to stand up for women and instead lobbied against this initiative (Jones 1994).

While there is nothing wrong with an organization wanting to increase it's membership, there are several reasons why a concerned woman should be mindful of the organization's purpose. First, the NRA is a non-profit organization, whose mission is to provide educational materials. (The Legislative Action division has a different tax status.) The NRA has tapped into a greatly underserved niche, providing information on self-defense for women. The NRA now has a "Women's Issues and Personal Safety Programs" division, whose purpose is to provide self-defense courses, firearm safety training, outdoor skills training, and to protect the Second Amendment. One criticism is that there is no comparably-powerful anti-gun organization that is aggressively providing information on firearms and self-defense. A second criticism is that all firms, whether for-profit or non-profit, must be held responsible for providing accurate information concerning the health and safety of it's product. Because the NRA would probably lose members if it openly acknowledged the number of innocent people who are killed due to the large number of firearms in the United States, they have a strong motive for trying to keep this information hidden. According to Larson (1994), the NRA is largely responsible for the fact that no federal agency keeps track of the number of nonfatal gunshot wounds each year. The Consumer Product Safety Commission, responsible for monitoring injuries from toy guns and other consumer products, explicitly excluded firearms from it's jurisdiction, because they feared a battle with the National Rifle Association.

The purpose of this paper is to examine the ethics and public policy implications of promoting of guns and gun-related products to women for the purpose of self-protection. We argue that, in light of the current statistics concerning gun accidents, suicides and homocides, the marketing of guns to women using promises of "empowerment" and "protection" violates current FTC guidelines regarding unfair advertising. This is an especially timely investiga-tion, due to the recent appeal by a coalition of organizations led by the Center to Prevent Handgun Violence to the Federal Trade Commission requesting a ban on firearms advertisements promising protection to women ("Petition" 1996).

THE "GUNS EMPOWER WOMEN" ARGUMENT

There is an argument that gun ownership by women is a move toward empowerment and a way to fight victimization. Leading this new wave of "power feminism," Feminist author Naomi Wolf (1993) uses the increase in gun ownership by women as evidence that women are taking the initiative to fight back and refusing to play the victim role. She has, however, received much criticism for taking this position from feminist critics, who argue that an increase in guns means an increase in violence (Jones 1994). Paxton Quigley, consultant for Smith and Wesson, the apparent leader in the marketing of handguns to women with their LadySmith line, says in her book *Armed and Female*, "Guns are the great equalizer. They have been symbolic of man's culture, but why shouldn't I have the best protection, too? Learning how to shoot can empower women" (Jones 1994).

A related argument uses the increase in violence against women as a reason for women to arm themselves. NRA spokesper-son Tonya Metaksa says that, "In the face of violent crime and a criminal justice system run amok, more and more women are seeking to take responsibility for their own personal safety...The NRA is simply fulfilling a need" (*Women and Guns*, January 1994, p. 10). Another female pro-gun activist (Bates 1993) argues, without substantiating evidence, that guns are actually a strong deterrent of crime, and that a gun is more likely to be used to defend against criminal threat than to kill anybody. An earlier study states that known possession of a handgun by a potential victim is a substantial deterrent to crime and possibly forestalls the commis-sion of a substantial number of violent assaults against women. The authors go on to argue that since there is little difference between male and female capacity for self-defense with firearms, it is a "practical matter" for a woman to own a handgun (Silver and Kates 1979).

THE APPEAL TO WOMEN

Perusal through several recent issues of *Women and Guns* magazine (a publication put out by the Second Amendment Foun-dation and targeted at women) indicates that there are at least ten different gun manufacturers targeting women. Most of the ads directed at women are for protective handguns, as opposed to the majority of ads directed at men, which typically feature guns used for hunting or sport shooting. The primary theme in the ads aimed at women is effective, risk-free personal protection and enhanced home security. Many of these ads use a fear appeal approach. In none of the ads is there a warning that the presence of a gun in the home increases the likelihood of death or injury to family members.

The following is a sample of copy from the NRA "Refuse to Be a Victim" 4-page advertisement:

Chances are good you'll need a personal safety strategy. 73% of all women now over age 12 will be victimized at some point in their lives—over a third of them violently raped, robbed or assaulted. America's criminal justice system isn't working to protect you. Almost half of all rape cases are dismissed before trial, and almost half the rapists who are convicted serve less than a year in prison.

Experts agree that the single most important step toward ensuring your personal safety is making the decision to refuse to be a victim. Criminals prefer easy targets.

You stand a better chance of preventing criminal attack if you make yourself difficult to prey upon. That means that you must have an overall personal safety strategy in place before you need it.

This appeal is definitely tapping into and possibly reinforcing the fears expressed by American women (Blair and Hyatt 1995).

In one ad that appeared in *Ladies Home Journal* (southeast regional edition, July 1992) a mother tucks her child into bed. The headline reads "Self-protection is more than your right...it's your responsibility." The ad copy recommends a Colt semi-automatic pistol "for protecting yourself and your loved ones," and compares a gun in the home to a fire extinguisher, stating that "it may be better to have it and not need it, than to need it and not have it." Another ad from Davis industries says "What with all the crime in the streets these days, a woman needs a body guard more than ever." The irony of this statement is that the company's cheap handguns, as well as those produced by its sister company Raven Arms, are among the guns most often implicated in urban crime. In other words, this is a gun that is likely to be used against a woman in an attack (Larson 1994).

The recent Petition (1996) to the FTC by the Center to Prevent Handgun Violence criticizes this and other similar advertising messages for exploiting the public's fear of crime and for attempting to lure "unsuspecting consumers" to buy their guns. The petition goes on to state that "These ads are unfair and deceptive because they suggest to the consumer that the purchase of a handgun is an effective means of providing for self and family protection without warning the consumer that the introduction of a handgun into the home actually places the home's occupants at an increased risk of death and injury by gun. Moreover, many of these ads appear to endorse ownership of a handgun by people with young children, with no acknowledgement of the special dangers such weapons may pose to young children, especially if the gun is not properly stored" (p.4).

UNFAIRNESS DOCTRINE

The unfairness doctrine has a long history of controversy, largely due to the fact that it was kept intentionally vague, in order to incorporate any potential situation that might be deemed by the court to be "unfair." In 1914, the Federal Trade Commission (FTC) was given the authority under Section 5(a) of the Federal Trade Commission Act to prevent unfair methods of commerce. The emphasis at this time was preventing unfair competition and other unfair acts among businesses. This narrow view of the FTC's jurisdictional mandate faded somewhat in *FTC v. R.F. Keppel & Bro., Inc* (1934). In *Keppel*, the FTC had sought to bring to a halt a candy manufacturer's practice of including lottery-type inducements within the candy's packaging as violative of public policy because it encouraged gambling by children. The jurisdictional issue arose because any of the manufacturer's competitors were free to include the same inducement in their packaging, so the practice was not "unfair" in the sense of placing other manufacturers at a competitive disadvantage. Nonetheless, the Supreme Court sustained the FTC action, ruling that the FTC's jurisdiction was not limited to actions likely to have anticompetitive consequences (Harring 1996). The Wheeler-Lea Amendment of 1938 gave the FTC the authority to regulate "unfair or deceptive acts and practices," and was designed to relieve the FTC of the burden of demonstrating competitive harm in unfairness proceedings, as well as to allow the commission to focus more directly on consumer injury than it had previously done. By 1964 the FTC had developed three criteria to consider when probing for consumer unfairness: (1) whether the practice injures consumers, (2) whether the practice violates established public policy, and (3) whether the practice is unethical or unscrupulous. Consumer injury is the most important of the three factors to consider when evaluating a possible unfairness action because a finding of consumer injury can suffice to warrant a finding of unfairness. To bring about an unfairness determination, an injury must be (1) substantial, (2) not outweighed by any countervailing benefits to consumers or competition, and (3) one that consumers themselves could not reasonably have avoided (Harring 1996). In most cases, a substantial injury involves monetary harm, as when sellers coerce consumers into purchasing unwanted goods and services, or when consumers buy defective goods and services on credit, but are unable to assert against the creditor claims or defenses arising from the transaction. Unwarranted health and safety risks may also support a finding of unfairness. Emotional impact and other more subjective types of harm on the other hand, will not ordinarily make a practice unfair. Thus, for example, the Commission will not seek to ban an advertisement merely because it offends the tastes or social beliefs of some viewers.

Another issue that relates to the unfairness doctrine is the "public's right not to be left uninformed." In this sense the doctrine can be seen as a public interest policy which is concerned with the right to be free from untrue or deceptively incomplete advertising claims. This would include advertising that is silent about negative aspects of the product (Summers 1973). The FTC and courts have long held that an ad is deceptive if it has the tendency or capacity to deceive the public. The first task in the enforcement process is for the FTC to determine the meaning that the public will take from the language and implications of the ad, i.e., the general impression given to the less sophisticated public/target audience (Howard and Hulbert 1973). An ad that is perceived by a substantial portion of the target audience to give a false impression about the product is enough to rule it unfair (O'Toole 1985). Unfairness alone is theoretically enough to test for the legality of ads, and facts which a "reasonably prudent advertiser" should have discovered are required to be disclosed in ads. In addition, the FTC in general has sought restitution of damages in cases of substantial loss to the consumer (Howard and Hulbert 1973). This has important implications for the marketing of firearms to women, especially in light of the petition currently before the FTC.

The unfairness doctrine was not extensively used until 1972, when the Supreme Court (in the case of *FTC v. Sperry and Hutchinson*) concluded that the consumer, as well as the merchant and manufacturer, must be protected from unfair trade practice (Cohen 1974). The unfairness doctrine has since been applied primarily in two major areas regarding consumers. The first area concerns advertising substantiation. It is unfair for advertisers to make claims about their products without having a reasonable basis for making those claims. In other words, advertisers are required to have documentation indicating that they have a reasonable basis for making a claim, prior to the dissemination of advertisements. The second area involves advertising to children. Because children are not able to protect themselves as well as adults are, ads directed toward children may be ruled as unfair for being unethical, unscrupulous or inherently dangerous. For example, an ad for Spiderman vitamins was ruled to be unfair because it encouraged children to take excessive amounts of the vitamin (Cohen 1974).

With vulnerable adult populations, the unfairness doctrine has provided little recourse, largely due to its subjective nature. With alcohol and tobacco, a large public outcry has sometimes been enough to make the marketer reconsider and withdraw the product or the advertisement voluntarily. For example, PowerMaster Malt Liquor and Uptown cigarettes, both targeted toward African-American consumers, were withdrawn largely due to public protest. Uptown was cancelled before it reached the market, not because of legal action, but because of a highly effective media campaign, led by prominant clergy, activists, and public health specialists. Marketed by R.J. Reynolds, Uptown would have been one of the company's most potent cigarettes, topped by unfiltered Camels (Koeppel 1990). PowerMaster was a high-alcohol content malt liquor, a product of the G. Heilman Brewing Company. Two Catholic priests from Chicago were largely responsible for unleashing the Bureau of Alcohol, Tobacco, and Firearms (BATF) on an entire $1 billion dollar malt liquor industry. The BATF found PowerMaster guilty of marketing on the basis of alcohol content, objecting to the use of the word "power" as an indicator of alcohol strength (Teinowitz 1991).

Recently, after a 14-year struggle, Congress and the ad industry have agreed on the legal definition of "unfair advertising" (Colford 1994). The advertising industry had hoped that the "unfairness doctrine" would be banned altogether. American Advertising Federation (AAF) President Wally Snyder said "AAF's opposition to the use of 'unfairness' to regulate advertising rests on it being too vague, subjective and, we believe, in many cases of questionable constitutionality" (Colford 1993). The AAF board endorsed a congressional compromise that defines unfair advertising as an "act or practice that causes or is likely to cause substantial injury to consumers which is not necessarily avoidable by consumers themselves and not outweighed by countervailing benefits to consumers or to competition." An additional constraint is that there would have to be "reason to believe that the unfair or deceptive acts or practices which are the subject of the proposed rulemaking are prevalent" before the FTC could initiate any industrywide rule (Colford 1994).

UNFAIRNESS AND THE MARKETING OF GUNS TO WOMEN

Social scientists estimate that over 1.8 million husbands in the United States badly batter their wives, and often threaten to kill them. Battering of women by husbands or boyfriends is now the single leading cause of injury to American women between the ages of 15 and 44 (French 1992). Domestic violence figures in one quarter of all suicide attempts by American women (Jones 1994). Women are now more than twice as likely to be attacked by men they know than by strangers (French 1992). These findings, in combination with evidence that most female gun owners are not prepared to shoot men they know (Blair and Hyatt 1995), indicate that gun ownership may not be the remedy for violence that gun manufacturers suggest.

According to the more recent definition of unfairness, the current advertising of guns toward women for empowerment and protection could possibly qualify. The first part of the definition is that the act or practice "causes or is likely to cause substantial injury to consumers, which is not necessarily avoidable by consumers themselves." There is plenty of evidence that guns cause physical injury to consumers, and some of this is definitely out of the consumer's control. Research by the Centers for Disease Control in Atlanta found that when a gun is used in domestic violence, death

is twelve times more likely. These deaths are overwhelmingly the woman's (Fishman 1993). Joan Sculli, of the Coalition Against Domestic Violence in Hempstead, New York, says that a woman is very likely to have her own gun used against her (Fishman 1993).

In addition to a woman having her own gun turned against her, there is also the possibility that the gun bought to protect the family will be used in a suicide of a family member. Most researchers agree that suicide is the leading cause of death by handgun. Kellermann and Reay (1986), for example, found that for every time a firearm was used for self-protection, there were 1.3 accidental deaths, 4.6 criminal homicides and 37 suicides involving firearms.

The second part of the definition of unfairness is that the act or practice that causes or is likely to cause injury is not outweighed by counterveiling benefits to consumers or competition. There is some limited evidence that gun ownership provides benefits that outweigh the potential injury. The most credible proponent of this point of view is Gary Kleck, a criminologist at Florida State University, who provides scholarly research to support the benefits of gun ownership. Kleck and McElrath (1991) examine data on violent incidents among strangers, taken from the 1979-1985 National Crime Surveys and 1982 Supplementary Homicide Reports. Results indicate that the possession of deadly weapons by a potential victim, including firearms, appears to inhibit attack and, in the case of an attack, to reduce the probability of injury to the victim. However, if a victim is injured in an attack with a gun, their death is more likely to occur than if there were no lethal weapon involved in the attack. Kleck's theory, that guns actually deter attacks to potential victims (called the "deterrent effect"), is seriously questioned by McDowall, Lizotte and Wiersema (1991). While they admit that there is a potential for a deterrent effect, they believe that Kleck's findings are insufficient evidence for demonstrating that such an effect exists. First, it is uncertain whether civilian gun ownership deters crime overall, or simply displaces it from one victim to another. In other words, if an offender believes a potential victim is armed, he or she may simply find a substitute who is perceived as less likely to be armed. Secondly, violent offenses commonly involve an element of surprise, and therefore, the victim's gun is not likely to be ready for use. The total number of offenders successfully killed or wounded by victims is also quite small (Kleck 1988). Finally, even though criminals say that they are deterred when they believe that a potential victim is armed, criminals typically have very limited information about whether a potential victim is armed. Because most citizens keep weapons hidden inside their homes, it is unlikely that criminals will be deterred unless the weapon is conspicuously displayed.

The third critieria for unfairness is that the unfair or deceptive practices must be prevalent. The current petition with the FTC indicates that the practice has become prevalent enough to stimulate political action from a number of anti-gun and health organizations. Also, the fact that women have become a prime target market indicates that there is a substantial amount of business to be gained from women. Many women today are wondering whether they should own a gun for self-protection. Even those women who are not initially interested may become interested through a husband or boyfriend (Blair and Hyatt 1995), and are likely to be exposed to gun materials and advertisements. To date, most gun advertisements targeted toward women have appeared in magazines targeted toward the gun enthusiast, such as *Women and Guns*, *Guns and Ammo*, and *Shooting Times*. One advertisement also ran briefly in the Southeastern Regional edition of the *Ladies Home Journal*. (Most other women's magazines have refused to run these advertisements.)

In conclusion, most evidence indicates that ownership of guns by women and other citizens is more likely to result in serious harm to the citizen, rather than protecting him or her. That is, the chance for substantial injury to the consumer brought on by the ownership of a gun does not appear to be outweighed by the benefits of gun ownership. There is also evidence to indicate that marketing guns and gun-related products to women is a prevalent practice. Therefore, a strong theoretical and practical argument can be made that it is unfair to advertise guns to women for protection.

RECOMMENDATIONS AND CONCLUSION

Several actions would help to ensure that the FTC takes action to see that these ads are stopped, or at least revised. First of all, it would help to increase the visibility of the case through a major publicity campaign. It could involve women's groups, health organizations, anti-gun groups, etc. A large amount of negative publicity may cause the companies to withdraw the ad campaign, just like the effective media campaign that was successful in getting R.J. Reynolds to withdraw Uptown cigarettes. If the companies don't voluntarily withdraw the ads, negative publicity may cause gatekeepers like magazine editors to think twice before running an ad. Effective negative publicity would also stimulate greater attention from regulatory agencies like the FTC or the Bureau of Alcohol, Tobacco and Firearms.

Secondly, petitions to the Federal Trade Commission drawn up with the assistance of lawyers could also stimulate action. The recent Petition (1996) is currently being considered. The FTC could decide to do nothing, or several possible actions might be taken. They might order the companies to discontinue using promises of protection. The FTC might also order that such claims be substantiated with research and statistics. Or, they could order the companies to include a warning label or disclaimer about the possible dangers of owning a gun.

The marketing of guns to women with claims of protection and empowerment definitely meets the criteria established by the FTC to qualify as unfair advertising. However, it is to be determined by the FTC whether or not the ads cause substantial injury, that are not outweighed by countervailing benefits, and are prevalent enough. In the past, the unfairness doctrine has provided little recourse with other vulnerable populations, due to its subjective nature. In some ways, the advertising of guns to women is similar to the marketing of Uptown cigarettes and PowerMaster malt liquor to African-Americans. In both instances, it could be argued that marketers are preying on a vulnerable population; however, the arguments against Uptown and PowerMaster were considered too subjective to warrant an unfairness ruling. Advertisements for guns containing promises of protection and empowerment are likely to be treated similarly by the FTC, unless there is a major change in the current criteria.

REFERENCES

Assael, Shaun (1990), "Why Big Tobacco Woos Minorities," *Adweek's Marketing Week*, January 29, 20-22+.

Bankston, William B., Carol Y. Thompson, Quentin A.L. Jenkins, Craig J. Forsyth (1990) "The Influence of Fear of Crime, Gender, and Southern Culture on Carrying Firearms For Protection," *The Sociological Quarterly*, Vol. 31 (2), 287-305.

Bates, Lyn (1993), "Why is it in Vogue to Fear Guns," *Women and Guns*, January, 12-13.

Blair, M. Elizabeth and Eva M. Hyatt (1995), "The Marketing of Guns to Women: Factors Influencing Gun-Related Attitudes and Gun Ownership by Women," *Journal of Marketing and Public Policy*, 117-127.

Buck, R. (1991), "Powermaster Trips ANA's Dewitt Helm," *Adweek's Marketing Week*, v.32, July 8, 12.

Cohen, Dorothy (1974), "The Concept of Unfairness as it Relates to Advertising Legislation," *Journal of Marketing*, 38 (July), 8-13.

Cohen, Dorothy (1982), "Unfairness in Advertising Revisited," *Journal of Marketing*, 46 (Winter), 73-80.

Colford, Steven W. (1993), "Congress Looks to Define 'Unfair," *Advertising Age*, May 31, 2+.

Colford, Steven W. (1994), "AAF Supports Pact for Fencing in FTC," *Advertising Age*, March 14, 1+.

Fishman, Steve (1993), "Upfront: What you know about guns can kill you," *Vogue*, October, 142-146.

French, Marilyn (1992), *The War Against Women*, New York, N.Y.: Summit Books.

Harrington, John (1996), "Up in Smoke: The FTC's Refusal to Apply the 'Unfairness Doctrine' to Camel Cigarette Advertising," *Federal Communications Law Journal*, www.law.indiana.edu/fclj/v47/no.3/Harring.html (31 July 1996).

Howard, John A. and James Hulbert (1973), *Advertising and the Public Interest: A Staff Report to the FTC*, Chicago, IL:Crain Communications.

Jones, Maggie (1993), "Gunmakers Target Women," *Working Woman*, July, p. 10.

Jones, Ann (1994), "Living With Guns, Playing With Fire," *Ms.*, May/June, 38-44.

Kellerman, Arthur L. (1992), "Suicide in the Home in Relation to Gun Ownership," *New England Journal of Medicine*, v.327, 467-470.

Kellerman, Arthur L. (1993), "Gun Ownership as a Risk Factor for Homocide in the Home," *New England Journal of Medicine*, v..329, 1084-1090.

Kellermann, Arthur L. and Donald T. Reay (1986), "Protection or Peril? An Analysis of Firearms Related Deaths in the Home," *New England Journal of Medicine*, June 12, 1557-1560.

Kleck, Gary (1988), "Crime Control Through the Private Use of Armed Force," *Social Problems*, 35:1-21.

Kleck, Gary and Karen McElralth (1991), "The Effects of Weaponry on Human Violence," *Social Forces*, March 69(3), 669-692.

Koeppel, Dan (1990), "In Philadelphia, R.J. Reynolds Made all the Wrong Moves," *Adweek's Marketing Week*, January 29, 20-22.

Larson, Erik (1994), *Lethal Passage: The Story of a Gun*, New York, N.Y: Vintage Books.

McDowall, David, Alan J. Lizotte, and Brian Wiersema (1991), "General Deterrence Through Civilian Gun Ownership: An Evaluation of the Quasi-Experimental Evidence," *Criminology*, 29(4), 541-559.

Neuborne, Ellen (1994), "Cashing in on Fear," *Ms.*, (May/June), 46-50.

O'Toole, John (1985), *The Trouble with Advertising: A View from the Inside*, New York, NY: Times Books.

"Petition of the Center to Prevent Handgun Violence, American Academy of Pediatrics, American Public Health Association, American Association of Suicidology, American Academy of Child and Adolescent Psychiatry, and National Association of Children's Hospitals and Related Institutions before the Federal Trade Commission," (1996), February 14.

Polter, Julie (1994), "Annie Get Your Gun," *Sojourners*, (February/March), 4-5.

Silver, Carol Ruth and Don B. Kates, Jr. (1979), "Self-Defense, Handgun Ownership, and the Independence of Women in a Violent, Sexist Society," in *Restricting Hand-guns: The Liberal Skeptics Speak Out*, editor Don B. Gates, Jr., North River Press.

Strange, Mary Zeiss (1994), "How the Media Encourages Violence, Yet Discourages Women From Owning Guns," *Women's Self Defense*, March, 39-43.

Summers, John (1973), "The Fairness Doctrine and Counter Advertising," in *Advertising and the Public Interest*, editor S.F. Divita, Chicago, IL: American Marketing Association.

Sugarman, Josh and Kristin Rand (1994), "Ceasefire," *Rolling Stone*, March 10, 30-42.

Wolf, Naomi (1993), *Fire with Fire*, New York, N.Y: Random House.

Studying Consumer Responses to the Changing Information Environment in Health Care: A Research Agenda

Paul N. Bloom, University of North Carolina at Chapel Hill

ABSTRACT

There has been an explosion in the amount of information available to consumers to guide them in making choices about health care. Much of this information has emerged because of public policies that have sought to use information programs to encourage both more competitiveness in health care markets and more protection for consumers. This paper reviews what is known about how well these programs have achieved their objectives. Several propositions are offered about effective program features, and suggestions are made about priorities for future consumer research on the effects of health information.

INTRODUCTION

The health care system in the United States is undergoing enormous changes. The traditional ways that consumers have searched for, selected, received, and paid for health care are steadily fading, and a new environment emphasizing "managed care" and preventive health is rapidly emerging. A key feature of this new environment is the huge amount of information that has become available to consumers to help guide them in their health care decisions and choices. Compared to only a few years ago, consumers are being exposed to or have access to substantially more information in the form of:

- Advertising by health care professionals and providers
- Direct-to-consumer advertising of prescription drugs
- Social marketing campaigns encouraging preventive health behaviors
- "Hot Lines" and other remote communications programs
- Warning and informational labels
- Provider quality and mortality ratings

Much of this cascade of new information can be attributed to conscious efforts by public policy makers to use information provision as a means of stimulating competition, increasing consumer protection, and encouraging preventive health behaviors. Policy makers have often turned to "information remedies" to help markets function more effectively, particularly when they want to limit the use of more intrusive forms of regulatory control (FTC 1979, Beales, Craswell and Salop 1981). Additionally, much of the new information has been introduced in response to consumer demand for guidance. The American public appears to have developed a huge appetite for health information.

All of the new information certainly has the potential for helping the evolving U.S. health care system function more efficiently and effectively for consumers and society. However, there is also the possibility that some forms of information could produce negative consequences, such as creating consumer confusion or raising health care costs. Consumer researchers, with their extensive experience studying how consumers use and respond to information, clearly have a role to play in helping public policy makers, health care administrators, public health officials, and consumer advocates determine what types of information programs should be encouraged in the future. This paper attempts to identify contributions consumer researchers could make.

PREVIOUS THEORIZING AND FINDINGS

The use of information programs and remedies has had much appeal to those concerned with health policy. In general, propo-nents of information provision have argued that a process similar to the one portrayed in Figure 1 takes place when increased information is supplied about health choices. The model suggests that increased information will allow health consumers to make more informed and satisfying choices. They should be able to use the information to help them eat better, exercise more, avoid dangerous products, get more preventive check-ups, reduce search costs, and find more respected and reasonably-priced providers. Health providers should respond to these informed choices—and to the existence of more information about health options—with more vigorous efforts to (1) provide even more information and (2) supply quality health care offerings at competitive prices or fees. The combination of more informed choices by consumers, better quality offerings, and lower prices should produce improved health outcomes. All this can theoretically be done with regulatory actions that are low in intrusiveness and monitoring requirements, unlike what has historically been done, for example, in regulating the drug and transportation industries to achieve better safety. Once put in place, many information programs can help in allowing health markets to regulate themselves, reducing the need for labor-intensive and paperwork-filled oversight programs that involve peer review, cost monitoring, and continuous reporting (Magat and Viscusi 1992, Adler and Pittle 1984).

In addition to the more general effects portrayed in Figure 1, increased information has the potential of producing several other positive effects. These include:

- improving doctor-patient communication, and thereby patient compliance with physicians' recommendations (Masson 1991).
- reducing the adverse selection problem in markets such as that for health insurance, which forces low-risk consumers to pay more (and high-risk consumers less) for coverage than they should (Folland, Goodman, and Stano 1993). Having better information about policies and rates could make it easier for low-risk consumers to locate and demand low-cost coverage.
- reducing the incidence of supplier-induced demand (Kenkel 1990). More informed consumers may be less susceptible to efforts by providers to persuade them to obtain unnecessary tests and procedures.
- reducing the incidence of malpractice suits. More informed consumers may be more likely to find providers who match their needs well, thereby making them more reluctant to sue. The creation of better patient communication and compliance could also help this situation.
- creating more opportunities for poor and disadvantaged consumers to gain access to health care. Providers who are interested in serving these populations may find it easier to attract patients efficiently using advertising, while these patients may simultaneously find themselves better able to insist on and find good care.

Overall, increased information can potentially help consumers navigate successfully through the confusion associated with the emerging managed care environment in health care.

The ability of increased information to set in motion processes in health care markets like those portrayed in Figure 1 has been discussed by many authors. Bloom and Stiff (1980) have discussed

Advances in Consumer Research
Volume 24, © 1997

FIGURE 1
A Conceptual Model of the Effects of Increased Health Information

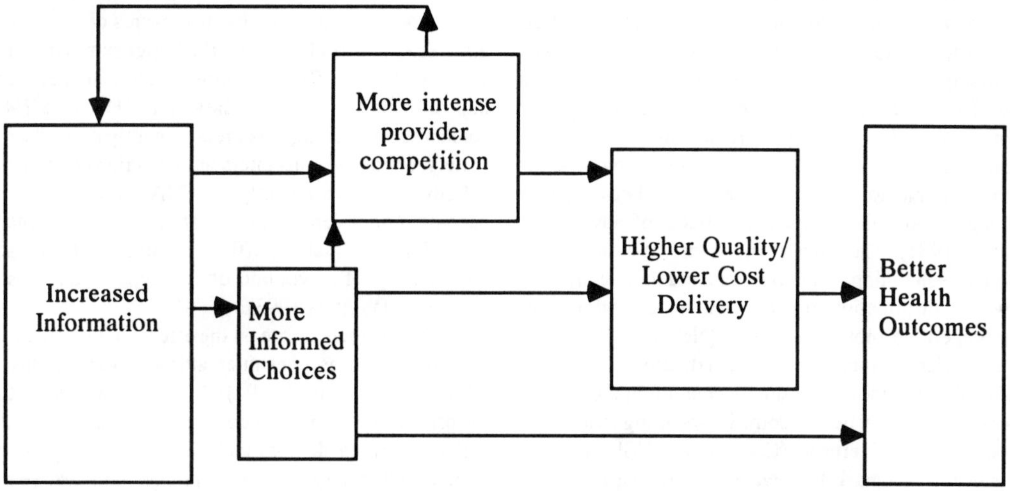

how advertising could help markets for physicians become more competitive, while Masson (1991) and Sheffet and Kopp (1990) have identified the potential benefits of advertising of prescription drugs to consumers. Dorfman and Wallack (1993), Walsh et al. (1993), and Ling et al. (1992) have explored the possibilities of social marketing programs, while Freimuth, Stein, and Kean (1989) have looked at the potential of telephone information services. Bettman, Payne and Staelin (1986) and Stewart and Martin (1994) have discussed how warning labels can reduce poor consumer choices for risky products, while Greenberg (1991) and Sisk et al. (1990) have examined the value of hospital quality and mortality ratings. These authors have drawn from seminal works in the economics of information by Stigler (1961), Arrow (1963), and Nelson (1970, 1974)—as well as fundamental thinking in decision theory, social psychology, sociology, and communications—to shape their views.

Many authors have also recognized the possibility of a negative side to the expansion of information provision in health care markets. One concern is that information can be inaccurate, or it can be literally accurate but incapable of being processed accurately by consumers. Indeed, several authors have expressed concern about the information asymmetry that exists between knowledgeable health providers and inexperienced health consumers who are unable to assess the real utility to them of different options (Folland, Goodman, and Stano 1993). Consumers may, among other things, rely on the faulty recommendations of friends or on certain misleading signals or "sign-posts" of quality such as price (Rizzo and Zeckhauser 1989). The fear is that, whatever the cause, consumers will be mislead into choosing health providers, tests, insurance coverages, therapies, and preventive behaviors that are not a good fit for their personal needs. Regulatory oversight—such as programs to police deceptive advertising—can help to mitigate problems created by misled consumers, but this can potentially make an information-provision program look less like a remedy and more like a new layer of regulation.

Another concern is that information provision can lead to less competitiveness in health care markets by favoring larger providers who are able to advertise more, do more procedures, or otherwise show up better than smaller providers in rating systems. Because of information asymmetry, economies of scale in information

provision, and other factors, the possibility exists that the big and rich will just get bigger and richer, making it difficult for small providers to enter or survive in markets. Ultimately, this could put some providers in positions of exercising monopoly power, leading to higher prices and lower quality service.

Still another concern is that information provision may somehow damage the reputations and public faith held by many health care providers. Advertising could make doctors look too commercial and manipulative, and rating systems could make hospitals or surgeons look too numbers-oriented and calculating.

Finally, there is concern that information provision may prove costly to implement. These costs might actually be passed on to consumers in the form of higher prices or taxes, negating any of the benefits consumers might obtain from the programs (Adler and Pittle 1984).

An effective information program can be viewed as one that produces more competitiveness among health providers and better health outcomes for health consumers without adding a significant regulatory and expense burden to society. To judge effectiveness, the following questions need to be addressed about information programs:

- How much do consumers use the information provided?
- Are consumers misled or confused by the information?
- What impact has the information had on consumer knowledge, attitudes, and behaviors?
- What impact has the information had on the health and financial status of consumers?
- What impact has the program had on how providers supply information, provide services, or price their services?
- What impact has the program had on the functioning and costs of government regulation and oversight activities?

The following sections address what has been learned to date about answers to these questions with respect to different categories of information programs.

Advertising by Health Care Professionals and Providers: A significant amount of research has been done on the effects of advertising by health care professionals and providers. Some of this work was done prior to policy actions that opened up health care markets to more aggressive use of advertising (e.g., the Supreme Court's 1982 ruling against the American Medical Association's advertising ban). In fact, studies done by Benham (1972) on the eyeglasses market and Cady (1976) on the retail prescription drug market—where prices were found to be lower in states that permitted price advertising—were highly influential in persuading policy makers at the FTC and elsewhere to pursue antitrust actions designed to encourage advertising by professionals.

The research on the effects of advertising by health professionals has basically sought to help resolve a debate between two schools of thought about the competitive effects of advertising (Albion and Farris 1981). The "advertising as information" school sees advertising as something that makes demand more elastic by providing low-cost information to consumers about options and encouraging competitive moves by sellers (Nelson 1974). The "advertising as barrier to entry" school sees advertising as something that makes demand more inelastic by creating brand loyalty with consumers that can only be overcome by spending large sums of money on competitive advertising (Comanor and Wilson 1974). The research in health care markets relevant to this debate has found inconsistent results. Advertising has been found to be pro-competitive, lowering prices (and sometimes improving quality) in the markets for eyeglasses (Benham 1972), optometric services (Bond et al. 1980, Haas-Wilson 1986), and prescription drugs (Cady 1976). Advertising has been found to raise prices and (and sometimes hurt quality) in the markets for physician services (Rizzo and Zeckhauser 1992), eye examinations (Parker 1995), and dental services (Kwon, Safranski, and Kim 1993).

Additional research is needed to see if an explanation can be found for the inconsistent results. Previous efforts to explain these results have focused on how advertising tends to produce more pro-competitive outcomes when simpler offerings are being advertised and prices are included in the advertisements (Folland, Goodman, and Stano 1993, Rizzo and Zeckhauser 1992). Another way of looking at this is to say that advertising has more pro-competitive effects when "search" attributes (which can be determined upon inspection, such as price or office hours) are what are most interesting to consumers rather than "credence" attributes (which can never really be understood, such as a doctor's true diagnostic skill).

Consumer researchers have addressed the controversy over advertising's effect on price elasticity, but they have not focused on the health care market. Experimental research—such as the work done by Mitra and Lynch (1995) on the conditions where advertising leads consumers to become more price sensitive—could clearly be done in a health care context. Among other things, comparisons could be made between advertising for search-oriented offerings and credence-oriented offerings. Other experimental studies could extend the work on brand equity by Keller and others (e.g., Keller and Aaker 1992, Campbell and Keller 1996) to understand the power of advertising brand names in health markets. It is conceivable that brand equity is even more powerful in markets that are high in credence qualities (like health markets), since consumers may be forced by information asymmetry to rely on signals of quality such as brand name. Thus, the advertising of strong brand names could have a more deleterious effect on competition in health markets.

Consumer research also could address the conditions under which consumers are easily misled by advertising by doctors, hospitals, and others. Questions that could be addressed include: Are certain types of claims more likely to be misunderstood? And are certain types of people (e.g., the poor) more likely to be deceived?

Advertising Prescription Drugs to Consumers: Little research has been done on the advertising of prescription drugs to consum-

ers. This practice has technically been legal for a long time, but it was discouraged by the FDA for many years—with even a moratorium on its use requested during the early 1980s. The FDA requirement that the lengthy disclosures of contraindications and other scientific findings (i.e., the "brief summary") be included in all ads that make efficacy claims helped to reduce incentives to use this form of advertising (Masson 1991). Late 1980s direct-to-consumer advertising was predominantly of the "see your doctor" variety, exhorting consumers with certain symptoms to seek medical advice. More recently, as FDA views on this practice have become more tolerant, the ads are naming brand names (even on television) and making efficacy claims (with the accompanying disclosures). The volume of this type of advertising is clearly increasing (Winters 1993).

The research to date on the effects of this practice has focused on topics such as consumer attitudes toward this phenomenon (Williams and Hensel 1994). Little has been done to see whether the practice has produced positive results such as better communications between doctors and patients, better patient compliance with drug therapies, and lower prices—or negative results such as doctor-patient conflict, drug abuse, deceptive claims, and higher prices. Consumer researchers could employ a wide range of approaches to address these issues. Survey research of doctors, patients, and others to obtain self-reports on behavior at various stages of advertising campaigns could be revealing. In addition, laboratory experiments could examine whether consumers are confused or deceived by prescription drug advertising. Moreover, field experiments, using test and control markets, could examine effects on visits to doctors, complaints, drug therapy compliance, and other measures. Of course, cooperation in data collection from larger managed care organizations and hospitals would be needed.

Social Marketing Campaigns: Considerable interest has developed in recent years in social marketing approaches to dealing with public health problems. Multi-faceted campaigns, employing marketing tools ranging from advertising to personal selling to publicity to creative branding to unique pricing, have been conducted by numerous government agencies, nonprofit organizations, and private corporations. Campaigns have sought to persuade people to engage in all types of socially-beneficial behaviors, including using condoms, getting a mammogram, wearing seat belts, and drinking responsibly. Large amounts of information are often disseminated in these campaigns.

Several reviews have been done previously of the effects of social marketing campaigns (Adler and Pittle 1984, ICF 1991, Ling et al. 1992, Walsh et al. 1993, and Dorfman and Wallack 1993). These reviews suggest that social marketing campaigns have had a mixed record, with only a few major campaigns that can be considered unqualified successes and many that must be considered disappointments. More evaluations clearly need to be done, even though program managers are frequently reluctant to entertain more than a cursory evaluation out of fear that poor results might get their budgets cut and that good results might raise supporters' expectations to unreasonable levels (Bloom 1980). Consequently, little has been learned about general determinants of effectiveness, other than that it pays to do marketing research first before formulating a campaign and that "tailoring" messages to audience needs and tastes improves communication effectiveness (Rimer and Orleans 1994, Strecher et al. 1994). The value of using certain types of appeals (e.g., stressing personal benefits rather than societal benefits) in certain media (e.g., personal contact) with certain target audiences (e.g., those at the contemplation stage) in field settings needs to be examined more fully, with more emphasis put on understanding the *behavioral* impacts of preventive health messages, not just their attitudinal impacts. The latter have been studied amply in work on fear appeals and persuasive communication done in laboratory settings (e.g., Block and Anand-Keller 1995).

"Hot Line" and Other Remote Communications Programs: Numerous examples exist of hotlines and other information services that consumers can access from remote locations to obtain health information. Often these services are established as components of more comprehensive social marketing programs. Currently, some of these services are moving into providing information through two-way interactive television or through interactive on-line connections. To this point, little has been written on the effectiveness of these initiatives. Freimuth, Stein, and Kean (1989) have done an appraisal of the National Cancer Institute's Cancer Information Service, and Tisdale (1993) and Glasgow et al. (1993) have studied smaller-scale programs. Consumer researchers would seem to be particularly well-suited for doing studies on, for example, how consumers respond to receiving advice from a doctor through a two-way interactive television appointment.

Warning Label and Informational Label Requirements: The effectiveness of labels has been studied extensively. Work has been done on cigarette warning labels (Viscusi 1992), alcohol warning labels (Andrews 1995), chemical warning labels (Magat and Viscusi 1992), nutritional labels (Levy and Derby 1995, Moorman 1990), and other topics. Several comprehensive efforts have already been made to synthesize what has been learned from this research (Stewart and Martin 1994, Bettman, Payne, and Staelin 1986), but more could be done. New types of labels with new types of formats are being tried all the time—such as the new rating system that will be used with television programs—and the effects of these disclosures deserve careful monitoring.

Provider Quality and Mortality Ratings: Considerable data is available that rates the quality and mortality results of hospitals and other providers. Efforts have been made to disseminate these data through guidebooks and the press. For example, the consumer magazine *Consumers' Checkbook* (1992) has published ratings of both hospitals and doctors. Although the theoretical benefits of this type of information provision has been discussed by Greenberg (1991) and Sisk et al. (1990), little empirical work has been done on the effects of these ratings. One study by Wholey et al. (1992) found an association between the competition in HMO markets and the willingness of HMOs to disseminate performance information. Another study by Rudd and Glanz (1991) found that articles about the 1986 HCFA hospital mortality data received moderately high "news play," but it did not examine how patient behavior was affected. Future research could examine the content and format of this information to identify approaches that encourage consumers to use the information to help them make better decisions.

SOME PROPOSITIONS

While it is difficult to draw any general conclusions about the effects of health information programs given the great diversity of these programs and the limited amount of relevant research, a few basic findings or propositions can be offered. The first propositions have to do with which features of a program seem to lead to effectiveness. Most of these ideas come from the work on labeling. The second propositions have to do with features of markets that tend to make them more receptive to information programs. These ideas primarily come from the work on advertising, social marketing, and labeling. All of these propositions are meant to be somewhat general, applying to more than a single type of program but less than all of them.

First, it is proposed that the more effective programs offer information that is:

- easy and low-cost for consumers to access (Bettman, Payne, and Staelin 1986).
- displayed in formats that are easy for consumers to process, with reference points that facilitate comparisons across choices (Moorman 1990, Bettman, Payne, and Staelin 1986).
- credible to consumers (Stewart and Martin 1994), and not unduly alarmist (Viscusi 1993).
- new to consumers rather than old material that they might tune out or discount (Stewart and Martin 1994, Viscusi 1993).
- unambiguous to consumers, presenting accurate probabilities of outcomes and specific guidance on how to avoid negative outcomes (Moorman 1990).
- personally-relevant to consumers (Stewart and Martin 1994), with data "tailored" to their needs and tastes (Rimer and Orleans 1994, Strecher et al. 1994).

Second, possible features of markets that would make them more amenable to the use of information programs can be proposed.: The more effective information programs should appear in markets that have:

- offerings that are relatively high in "search" properties and low in "credence" properties. The amount of information asymmetry that exists between providers and consumers could be low in such markets, thereby allowing consumers to be more capable of using information to locate desired attributes before finalizing purchases (Nelson 1970, 1974, Darby and Karni 1973).
- frequently-purchased offerings (Drumwright and Kane 1988).
- many varied, competing offerings that are confusing and costly to evaluate (Drumwright and Kane 1988).
- low levels of insurance coverage (Pauly 1986). Consumers would have greater incentives to search for better options in such markets.
- offerings that provide consumers with mostly personal benefits rather than mostly benefits for society (Stewart and Martin 1994).
- segments of consumers who respond to increased information very aggressively, perhaps because they possess greater motivation, higher knowledge levels, self-efficacy, or other individual traits.

Examining this last feature would help in gaining an understanding of whether information programs can be effective even if only small segments of a market respond to them, "policing" the market for others (Viscusi 1993, Beales, Craswell, and Salop 1981).

FUTURE PRIORITIES

Given the shift to managed care, it seems that it would be particularly useful for research to be done on how information programs and remedies can be designed to help people make more informed and satisfying choices about (1) which managed care organization to join and (2) how to interact with their chosen managed care system. Research on the effects of advertising by managed care systems would be especially instructive. Questions could be addressed such as:

- Are consumers being deceived by managed care advertising, expecting services and coverages that they cannot obtain?

- Does heavy advertising of brand names (e.g., Kaiser, Harvard) help to create brand equity, making it difficult for lighter advertising providers to compete effectively?
- Has advertising helped to encourage consumers to take advantage of any of the preventive health programs and services of managed care organizations?
- Has advertising helped to create additional mistrust and suspicion about doctors and managed care organizations?

Research might also investigate how to design a label or rating system that could help consumers choose a managed care option that best meets their needs. Additionally, the effectiveness of social marketing and hotline programs conducted by managed care organizations could be evaluated.

Beyond the issues surrounding managed care, there are a host of other important consumer research questions related to health information. Among the most timely topics to investigate are the effects of direct-to-consumer advertising of prescription drugs, the effects on behavior of various types of social marketing appeals (e.g., highly tailored), the effects of new types of remote communications programs (e.g., two-way interactive video), and the effects of new types of warning and informational labels (e.g., the rating system for television programs). In exploring these topics, consideration could be given to testing empirically some of the propositions presented in the previous section.

REFERENCES

Adler, Robert S. and R. David Pittle (1984), "Cajolery or Command: Are Education Campaigns an Adequate Substitute for Regulation?" *Yale Journal of Regulation*, 1 (2), 159-193.

Albion, Mark S. and Paul W. Farris (1981), *The Advertising Controversy*, Boston: Auburn House.

Andrews, J. Craig (1995), "The Effectiveness of Alcohol Warning Labels: A Review and Extension," *American Behavioral Scientist*, 38 (4).

Arrow, Kenneth J. (1963), "Uncertainty and the Welfare Economics of Medical Care," *American Economic Review*, 53 (December), 941-973.

Barton, Hugh M. (1994), "Doc Hollywood Beware: Recent Laws Further Restrict Advertising by Physicians," *Texas Medicine*, 90 (3), 38-40.

Beales, Howard, Richard Craswell, and Stephen Salop (1981), "Information Remedies for Consumer Protection," *American Economic Review*, 71 (May), 410-413.

Benham, Lee (1972), "The Effect of Advertising on the Price of Eyeglasses," *Journal of Law and Economics*, 15 (2), 337-352.

Bettman, James R., John W. Payne, and Richard Staelin (1986), "Cognitive Considerations in Designing Effective Labels for Presenting Risk Information," *Journal of Public Policy & Marketing*, 5, 1-28.

Block, Lauren G. and Punam Anand Keller (1995), "When to Accentuate the Negative: The Effects of Perceived Efficacy and Message Framing on Intentions to Perform a Health-Related Behavior," *Journal of Marketing Research*, 32(May), 192-203.

Bloom, Paul N. (1980), "Evaluating Social Marketing Programs: Problems and Prospects," in Richard Bagozzi, et al., eds., *Marketing in the 1980s: Changes and Challenges*, Chicago: American Marketing Association, 460-463.

Bloom, Paul N. and Ronald Stiff (1980), "Advertising and the Health Care Professions," *Journal of Health Politics, Policy, and Law*, 4 (Winter), 641-656.

Bond, R., J. Kwoka, Jr., J. Phelan, and I. Whitten (1980), *Effects of Restrictions on Advertising and Commercial Practice in the Professions*, Washington, DC: Federal Trade Commission.

Cady, John (1976), "An Estimate of the Price Effects of Restrictions on Drug Price Advertising," *Economic Inquiry*, 14 (4), 493-510.

Campbell, Margaret C. and Kevin Lane Keller (1996), "Familiarity Breeds Content: The Moderating Effect of Brand Familiarity on Advertising Repetition and Brand Identification," working paper, UCLA.

Comanor, William S. And Thomas A. Wilson (1974), *Advertising and Market Power*, Cambridge, MA: Harvard University Press.

Consumers' Checkbook (1992), *Consumers' Guide to Hospitals*, Washington: Consumers' Checkbook.

Darby, M. R. and E. Karni (1973), "Free Competition and the Optimal Amount of Fraud," *Journal of Law and Economics*, 16 (April), 67-88.

Dorfman, L. and L. Wallack (1993), "Advertising Health: The Case for Counter-Ads," *Public Health Reports*, 108 (6), 716-726.

Drumwright, Minette E. and Nancy M. Kane (1988), "Failures of Information in Health Care Marketing," in Michael J. Houston, ed., *Advances in Consumer Research: Volume 15*, Provo, UT: Association for Consumer Research, 249-255.

Federal Trade Commission (1979), *Consumer Information Remedies: Policy Review Session*, Washington, DC: U.S. Government Printing Office.

Folland, Sherman, Allen C. Goodman, and Miron Stano (1993), *The Economics of Health and Health Care*, New York: Macmillan Publishing Company.

Freimuth, Vicki S., Judith A. Stein, and Thomas J. Kean (1989), *Searching for Information: The Cancer Information Service Model*, Philadelphia: University of Pennsylvania Press.

Glasgow, R.E., H. Lando, J. Hollis, S.G. McRae, and P.A. LaChance (1993), "A Stop-Smoking Telephone Help Line that Nobody Called," *American Journal of Public Health*, 83 (2), 252-253.

Greenberg, Warren (1991), *Competition, Regulation, and Rationing in Health Care*, Ann Arbor: Health Administration Press.

Haas-Wilson, Deborah (1986), "The Effect of Commercial Practice Restrictions: The Case of Optometry," *Journal of Law and Economics*, 29 (1), 165-186.

ICF (1991), "Survey of Selected Public Awareness Campaigns," report for the U.S. Environmental Protection Agency, Fairfax, VA: ICF, Incorporated.

Keller, Kevin Lane and David A. Aaker (1992), "The Effects of Sequential Introduction of Brand Extensions," *Journal of Marketing Research*, 29(February), 35-50.

Kenkel, Don (1990), "Consumer Health Information and the Demand for Medical Care," *The Review of Economics and Statistics*, 72 (4), 587-595.

Kwon, I.W., S.R. Safranski, and J.H. Kim (1993), "The Impact of Advertising on Price and Practice Volume: A Case Study of Dental Markets," *Health Services Management Research*, 6(1), 52-60.

Levy, Alan J. and Brenda Derby (1995), "Consumer Use of Food Labels: Impact of the New Food Labeling Regulations," working paper, U.S. Food and Drug Administration.

Ling, Jack C., Barbara A. K. Franklin, Janis F. Lindsleadt, and Susan A. N. Gearon (1992), "Social Marketing: Its Place in Public Health," *Annual Review of Public Health*, 13, 341-365.

Magat, Wesley A. and W. Kip Viscusi (1992), *Informational Approaches to Regulation*, Cambridge, MA: MIT Press.

Masson, Alison (1991), "Direct-to-Consumer Advertising: A Continuing Controversy," in R. Mayer, ed., *Enhancing Consumer Choice*, Columbia, MO: American Council on Consumer Interests, 159-168.

Mitra, Anusree and John G. Lynch (1995), "Toward a Reconciliation of Market Power and Information Theories of Advertising Effects on Price Elasticity," *Journal of Consumer Research*, 21(March), 644-659.

Moorman, Christine (1990), "The Effects of Stimulus and Consumer Characteristics on the Utilization of Nutrition Information," *Journal of Consumer Research*, 17 (3), 362-374.

Nelson, Phillip (1970), "Information and Consumer Behavior," *Journal of Political Economy*, 82 (2), 311-329.

Nelson, Phillip (1974), "Advertising as Information," *Journal of Political Economy*, 82 (4), 729- 754.

Parker, Philip M. (1995), "'Sweet Lemons': Illusory Quality, Self-Deceivers, Advertising, and Price," *Journal of Marketing Research*, 32(August), 291-307.

Pauly, Mark V. (1986), "Taxation, Health Insurance, and Market Failure in the Medical Economy," *Journal of Economic Literature*, 24 (June), 629-675.

Rimer, Barbara K. and C.T. Orleans (1994), "Tailoring Smoking Cessation to Older Adults," *Cancer*, 74 (7 Suppl.), 2051-2054.

Rizzo, John A. and Richard J. Zeckhauser (1992), "Advertising and the Price, Quantity, and Quality of Primary Care Physician Services," *Journal of Human Resources*, 27 (3), 381-421.

Rudd, Joel and Karen Glanz (1991), "Providing Consumers with Quality of Health-Care Information: A Critical Review and Media Content Analysis," in R. Mayer, ed., *Enhancing Consumer Choice*, Columbia, MO: American Council on Consumer Interests.

Sheffet, Mary Jane and Steven W. Kopp (1990), "Advertising Prescription Drugs to the Public: Headache or Relief?" *Journal of Public Policy & Marketing*, 9, 42-61.

Sisk, J. E., D. Dougherty, P. Ehrenhaft, G. Ruby, and B. Mitchner (1990), "Assessing Information for Consumers on the Quality of Medical Care," *Inquiry*, 27 (3), 263-272.

Stewart, David W. and Ingrid M. Martin (1994), "Intended and Unintended Consequences of Warning Messages: A Review and Synthesis of Empirical Research," *Journal of Public Policy & Marketing*, 13 (1), 1-19.

Stigler, George J. (1961), "The Economics of Information," *Journal of Political Economy*, 69, 213-225.

Strecher, V. J., M. Kreuter, D. J. DenBoer, S. Kobrin, H. J. Hospers, and C. S. Skinner (1994), "The Effects of Computer-Tailored Smoking Cessation Messages in Family Practice Settings," *Journal of Family Practice*, 39 (3), 262-270.

Tisdale, G. (1993), "The Results of a Telephone Health Advice and Information Service," *New Zealand Medical Journal*, 107 (975), 128-129.

Viscusi, W. Kip (1993), *Product-Risk Labeling: A Federal Responsibility*, Washington: The AEI Press.

Viscusi, W. Kip (1992), *Smoking: Making the Risky Decision*, New York: Oxford University Press.

Walsh, D. C., R. E. Rudd, B. A. Moeykens, and T. W. Moloney (1993), "Social Marketing for Public Health," *Health Affairs*, 12 (2), 104-119.

Wholey, D. R., J. Christianson, S. Sanchez, R. Feldman, and M. Peterson (1992), "The Voluntary Dissemination of Performance Information by Health Care Organizations," *Advances in Health Economics and Health Services Research*, 13, 1-26.

Williams, James R. And Paul J. Hensel (1994), "Direct-to-Consumer Advertising of Prescription Drugs," *Journal of Health Care Marketing*, 15 (11), 35-41.

Winters, Patricia (1993), "Prescription Drug Ads Up," *Advertising Age*, 64 (3), 10.

Asymmetries in Price and Quality Competition: Experimental Test of Underlying Mechanisms

Timothy B. Heath, University of Pittsburgh
Gangseog Ryu, University of Pittsburgh
Subimal Chatterjee, State University of New York at Stony Brook
Michael S. McCarthy, Miami University[1]

ABSTRACT

Discounting national brands typically attracts consumers from store brands more than discounting store brands attracts consumers from national brands. The current study reviews and tests four mechanisms potentially involved in such asymmetric price competition: (1) differential attribute weights, (2) choice-anchored loss aversion, (3) differential loss aversion to quality and price, and (4) differential distances from indifference. In a choice experiment, price reductions moved subjects from lower to higher quality more than from higher to lower quality, replicating asymmetric price competition. Quality improvements, however, moved subjects from higher to lower quality more than from lower to higher quality. Attribute weights explained much but not all of this variance, whereas differential distances from indifference could not. The results suggest that asymmetric switching arises from differential attribute weights as well as other mechanisms such as loss aversion.

Brands commonly reduce prices to steal consumers from other brands. Recent scanner research shows that the ability to steal consumers is asymmetric across brands differing in relative quality. Consumers of store brands are more likely to switch to a discounted national brand than consumers of national brands are likely to switch to a discounted store brand (Allenby and Rossi 1991; Bemmaor and Mouchoux 1991; Blattberg and Wisniewski 1989; Kamakura and Russell 1989; Sethuraman 1995; Walters 1991). A number of theoretic mechanisms have been proposed to explain this so called asymmetric price competition (for a review of seven mechanisms, see Heath et al. 1996). The current study reviews four such mechanisms and experimentally tests a number of their implications. Since these mechanisms generally apply to attributes other than competition between store and national brands, we focus, when possible, on the broader distinction between higher-quality and lower-quality brands.

POTENTIAL MECHANISMS AND HYPOTHESES

At least four mechanisms have been implicated in asymmetric switching. The first is differential attribute weights. Consumers of lower quality may be more price sensitive than consumers of higher quality (Bronnenberg and Wathieu 1995; Kamakura and Russell 1989). Those consuming lower quality would then naturally react more strongly to price reductions by competitors than would consumers of higher quality.

---

[1]This study was supported by a research grant from the Joseph M. Katz Graduate School of Business, University of Pittsburgh. The first author wishes to extend a very special thanks to Dean Daniel S. Fogel for his strong and continued support of research at the University of Pittsburgh. The authors also wish to thank the following people for their invaluable assistance in data collection: Sandy Milberg, Dave Mothersbaugh, Mike Rich, Jim Patton, Steve Silverman, Krish Krishnan, Lisa Sciulli, Rob Morgan, and Anthony Allred.

H1: Reducing a higher-quality competitor's price will move consumers to higher quality more than reducing a lower-quality competitor's price will move consumers to lower quality (asymmetric price competition).

If differential attribute weights account for asymmetric price competition, it raises the possibility of asymmetric quality competition in the opposite direction. If consumers of higher quality weight quality more than do consumers of lower quality, then quality competition should be asymmetric favoring lower-quality brands.

H2: Improving a lower-quality competitor's quality will move consumers to lower quality more than improving a higher-quality competitor's quality will move consumers to higher quality.

Combined, Hypotheses 1 and 2 predict an interaction between competitor's quality (lower vs. higher) and attribute improved (price vs. quality). Moreover, if the interaction arises from differential attribute weights, then controlling for attribute weights should (1) yield significant attribute-weight effects, and (2) eliminate the interaction between competitor quality and attribute improved.

H3: Greater weight on quality relative to price will reduce switching among choosers of higher quality, whereas greater weight on price relative to quality will reduce switching among choosers of lower quality (regardless of which attribute competitors improve).

H4: Controlling for attribute weights will eliminate asymmetric competition.

The second mechanism is choice-anchored loss aversion. Loss aversion refers to the fact that losses are more unpleasant than equivalent gains are pleasant (Bernoulli 1738; Kahneman and Tversky 1979). This phenomenon is typically represented with value curves that are steeper for losses than for gains from reference states. Loss aversion holds implications for switching behavior if we assume, as has been shown elsewhere, that consumers anchor on the brand they choose initially (Heath et al. 1996; Sen and Johnson 1995). A brand's relative strengths and weaknesses can then be translated into gains and losses, respectively (e.g., a higher-quality brand's quality and price).

Consider the following microwave ovens.

	Price	Quality
Brand A	$319	65
Brand B	$269	55

If you prefer and anchor on B, then switching to A constitutes a gain in quality and a loss in price (lost money). Reducing A's price, therefore, involves reducing a prospective loss for consumers of B, whereas reducing B's price involves increasing a prospective gain for consumers of A. By loss aversion, reducing losses carries more value than increasing gains. Therefore, A benefits more from reducing its loss on price than B benefits from increasing its gain on price. In this context, therefore, loss aversion is strictly a cross-attribute phenomenon (see Heath et al. 1996 for further explanation).

Choice-anchored loss aversion, like differential attribute weights, predicts asymmetric price competition favoring higher-quality brands (Hypothesis 1) and asymmetric quality competition favoring lower-quality brands (Hypothesis 2). Increasing a higher-quality brand's quality improves its relative strength, whereas increasing a lower-quality brand's quality improves its relative weakness. Although both mechanisms yield Hypotheses 1 and 2, they can be disentangled in part statistically. If controlling attribute weights fails to eliminate asymmetric switching (failure to support Hypothesis 4), the data would support some mechanism other than differential attribute weights which, in the current study, we assume to be loss aversion or differential loss aversion discussed next.[2]

The third mechanism is differential loss aversion for quality and price (Hardie, Johnson, and Fader 1993; Tversky and Kahneman 1991). Modeling the effects of price and quality changes within household-level scanner data, Hardie et al. estimated a larger loss-aversion coefficient for quality than for price, where coefficients reflect the differential effects of losses and gains within a particular attribute. Distinguishing choice-anchored loss aversion from differential loss aversion is extremely difficult and is not attempted in the current study.

Blattberg and Wisniewski (1989) proposed the fourth and final mechanism reviewed here: Consumers of higher quality are further from indifference than are consumers of lower quality. We test this mechanism by measuring weights on quality and price and then testing *relative attribute weights* (RAW) which we define for consumers of lower and higher quality in the following way:

$$RAW_{LQ \text{ Consumers}} = Weight_{Price} - Weight_{Quality}$$
$$RAW_{HQ \text{ Consumers}} = Weight_{Quality} - Weight_{Price}$$

Differential distances from indifference suggests that relative attribute weights are larger among consumers of higher than lower quality given the following conditions, all of which held in the current study (see Heath et al. 1996): (1) Perceptions of quality are constant across consumers, (2) trade-offs in price and quality are symmetric across brands (e.g., if going from lower to higher quality involves a 15% increase quality, it also involves a 15% increase in price), and (3) consumers had no sense of what price to pay per unit quality when entering the task (unfamiliar and abstract scales were used to represent quality).[3]

---

[2]The other three mechanisms implicated in asymmetric switching are not likely to be involved in the experiment reported here: No differential asymmetric dominance existed within the stimuli, differential income effects were probably not involved because, among other reasons, the savings were minuscule, and differential changes in perceived value were not likely because price and quality improvements did not leave the competitors' levels close to those of brands initially chosen (for a review of these mechanisms see Heath et al. 1996).

[3]The data support this operationalization of distance from indifference since virtually everyone had positive relative preferences (e.g., choosers of higher quality rated quality as more important than price). If price-quality trade-offs had been skewed in one way or another, choices and the simplified expressions of relative preference would not correspond and more complex operationalizations would be required.

H5: Choosers of higher-quality brands will exhibit larger relative attribute weights than choosers of lower-quality brands.

EXPERIMENT

The experiment was designed to test (1) if asymmetric price competition could be replicated with laboratory stimuli (Hypothesis 1) and (2) if asymmetric quality competition could be demonstrated (Hypothesis 2). Importance weights on price and quality were measured to assess the effects of differential attribute weights (Hypotheses 3 and 4) and to calculate relative attribute weights with which to test differential distances from indifference (Hypothesis 5).

Method

Subjects. Two-hundred-ninety-nine undergraduate and graduate business students served as subjects on a voluntary basis during class time.

Design. Three variables were manipulated between subjects: competitor (lower quality, higher quality), attribute improved (price, quality), and product class (orange juice, microwave ovens, light bulbs). Subjects were randomly assigned to the conditions defined by the crossing of attribute improved and product class. Subjects self selected themselves into competitor conditions by first choosing either a higher-quality brand (lower-quality competitor) or a lower-quality brand (higher-quality competitor).

Overview of Stimuli. Table 1 summarizes the stimuli. Although brands were labeled A and B, their attribute levels were taken from the marketplace to enhance realism. For orange juice, quality levels for the lower-quality and higher-quality brands were borrowed from Hardie et al.'s (1993) *Tropicana Regular* and *Minute Maid* brands, respectively. The authors derived these quality levels from *Consumer Reports* ratings reflecting freshness and taste. Orange juice prices were taken from the prices of these brands in local grocery stores. For microwave ovens, prices and power levels were taken from mid-sized microwave ovens in local appliance stores. Prices and expected life for light bulbs were taken from regular and long-life 75W bulbs, respectively, in local grocery stores.

For the quality-related attributes, we chose overall quality in orange juice to mirror the differences in overall quality that exist in the marketplace. Although overall quality ratings are not listed on packages of orange juice, perceptions of differential quality are likely to exist and are supported in Hardie et al.'s data. We chose power levels in microwave ovens and expected life in light bulbs as the quality-related attributes to enhance generalizability beyond quality ratings and because each is a product feature consumers face in the marketplace.

Scaling Changes in Price and Quality. To facilitate comparisons across brands and attributes, changes in attributes must be scaled carefully. A competitor's weakness was improved by splitting the difference between the competitor and the chosen brand on the relevant attribute. Consider microwave ovens:

	Price	Power
Brand A	$220	650W
Brand B	$160	550W

Weaknesses were improved by reducing A's price from $220 to $190 or by improving B's power from 550W to 600W. These values were then used as a basis for proportional improvements in strengths.

For improvements in the higher-quality brand's strength (quality), proportions were used to mitigate contamination from percep-

TABLE 1
Original Choice Sets and Improvements

Orange Juice

	Original Choice Set		Improved Weaknesses		Improved Strengths	
Brand	Price	Quality	Price	Quality	Price	Quality
A	$2.26	0.487	$2.01 att: 11.1% bbd: 49.0%	—	—	0.635 att: 30.4% bbd: 80.4%
B	$1.75	0.303	—	0.395 att: 30.4% bbd: 50.0%	$1.50 att: 14.3% bbd: 49.0%	—

Microwave Ovens

	Original Choice Set		Improved Weaknesses		Improved Strengths	
Brand	Price	Power	Price	Power	Price	Power
A	$220	650W	$190 att: 13.6% bbd: 50.0%	—	—	710W att: 9.2% bbd: 60.4%
B	$160	550W	—	600W att: 8.3% bbd: 50.0%	$130 att: 18.7% bbd: 50.0%	—

Light Bulbs

	Original Choice Set		Improved Weaknesses		Improved Strengths	
Brand	Price	Expected Life (Hours)	Price	Expected Life (Hours)	Price	Expected Life (Hours)
A	$2.39	1,350	$2.19 att: 8.4% bbd: 50.0%	—	—	1,585 att: 17.4% bbd: 67.1%
B	$1.99	1,000	—	1,175 att: 17.5% bbd: 50.0%	$1.79 att: 10.0% bbd: 50.0%	—

NOTE.— att=the percentage change in the attribute relative to the attribute's original level. For example, reducing Orange Juice A's price from $2.26 to $2.01 constitutes a reduction of 11.1%: 0.25/2.26. bbd=the percentage change in the attribute relative to the between-brand difference on that attribute. For example, reducing Orange Juice A's price from $2.26 to $2.01 reduces the between-brand difference in price by 49.0%: 0.25/(2.26–1.75).

tual relativity and diminishing marginal sensitivity. For example, the improvement in Microwave B's power, its weakness, from 550W to 600W constituted an increase of 8.3% (50/550). Since we predicted that improving B's power (weakness) would induce more switching than improving A's power (strength), it was important to reduce any tendencies to see A's power increase as smaller than B's due to A's higher initial power level. To that end, proportional increases in the higher-quality brand's quality-related attribute (strength) were greater than or equal to proportional increases in that attribute in the lower-quality brand (weakness). For example, Microwave B improved from 550W to 600W (8.3%), whereas Microwave A improved from 650W to 710W (9.2%).

For improvements in the lower-quality brand's strength (price), we used the absolute price reduction applied to the higher-quality brand. This means that the proportional reduction in the lower-quality brand's price was always larger than the proportional reduction in the higher-quality brand's price. Since Microwave A reduced its price from $220 to $190 (a 13.6% discount), Microwave B reduced its price from $160 to $130 (an 18.7% discount). In raw (nonproportional) units, improvements to strengths were generally greater than or equal to improvements to weaknesses.

The proportion-based changes discussed thus far speak to comparisons of strengths and weaknesses within attributes across brands (e.g., comparing price reductions across higher-quality and lower-quality brands). To compare changes in strengths and weaknesses across attributes within brands, we face the problem of noncomparable dimensions such as price and wattage. Ideally, two criteria should be met to reduce the possibility that improvements in weaknesses are perceived as larger than improvements in strengths. The first is that the proportional improvement in a brand's strength be greater than or equal to the proportional improvement in its weakness. For example, we might compare the effect of a 15% increase in quality with a 15% reduction in price.

The second criterion is that changes in strengths and weaknesses comprise comparable proportions of between-brand differences on their respective attributes. This is important because consumers commonly evaluate attributes and changes in those attributes with respect to differences in attributes across alternatives (Bronnenberg and Wathieu 1995; Holman 1995). Consider the higher-quality microwave oven (Brand A). To improve its weakness, it reduces its price by $30, or by 50% of the $60 between-brand price difference ($220 vs. $160). To help ensure that the improvement in Brand A's strength (power) is not perceived as smaller, Brand A should improve its power by at least 50% of the 100 watt between-brand difference in power (650W vs. 550W). These criteria were generally met except for a couple of violations of the second criterion which we address in the experiment's discussion.

Procedure. Subjects received a booklet that initially presented one of the original choice sets seen in Table 1. They were asked to imagine being in the market for that product and to make a choice by circling their preferred brand. They then turned to the next page where instructions led them to one of two other pages depending on which brand they chose initially. At the top of the new page, the original choice set was repeated and subjects were asked to repeat their initial choice. They then read that after entering their favorite store, they find that the competitor (non-chosen brand stated as Brand A or Brand B) recently reduced its price or improved its quality-related attribute. The choice set was then re-stated with the one attribute improved, and subjects circled their choice from the revised set. The primary dependent measure was whether subjects switched brands.

Subjects then filled out a brief questionnaire. It contained filler questions to distract subjects from the key measure which was

the importance of the price and the quality-related attribute in the product class from which they chose. Subjects allocated 100 points across the two attributes according to their relative importance. Attribute weights were measured after choices for two reasons. First, the primary dependent measure was switching, the measure most in need of insulation from carryover effects. Second, whereas carryover from attribute weights to choices would take the form of unwanted consistency biases, carryover from choices to attribute weights might also have a positive component (learning). Since consumers are often uncertain about their attribute weights, making choices first might help them discover their true weights (see Simonson 1990).

Results

We test the data with respect to three issues (see Table 2): (1) asymmetric price and asymmetric quality competition, (2) differential attribute weights, and (3) differential distances from indifference.

Asymmetric Price and Asymmetric Quality Competition. Switching data (no, yes) were subjected to a logit (SAS CATMOD) testing the main and interaction effects of competitor (lower quality, higher quality), attribute improved (price, quality), and product class (orange juice, microwave ovens, light bulbs). Hypothesis 1 predicted that price reductions would yield more switching up than down in quality (standard asymmetry), whereas Hypothesis 2 predicted that improvements in quality would yield more switching down than up in quality. As predicted, the competitor by attribute-improved interaction was statistically significant ($\chi^2_{(1)}=13.38$, $p<.001$; see Figure 1). Consistent with reports of asymmetric price competition in the marketplace (Hypothesis 1), price reductions attracted more consumers from lower quality to higher quality (67.1%) than from higher quality to lower quality (39.7%; $\chi^2_{(1)}=11.70$, $p<.001$). Moreover, consistent with Hypothesis 2, improvements in quality benefited lower-quality brands more than higher-quality brands. Improvements in quality moved consumers from higher to lower quality (59.9%) more than to from lower to higher quality (43.4%; $\chi^2_{(1)}=3.21$, $p=.073$). Collapsing across improvements to price and quality, improving a weakness was more persuasive than improving a strength (62.5% vs. 41.2%).

The competitor by attribute-improved by product-class interaction was also significant ($\chi^2_{(2)}=7.41$, $p=.02$; see Figure 2).[4] Separate models were then run per product class. In microwave ovens, the competitor by attribute-improved interaction was sig-

---

[4]Given this three-way interaction, experimental convention suggests it is inappropriate to interpret the competitor by attribute-improved interaction as we did initially. However, we do so because product class is an unusual moderator that can be viewed in either of two ways, the first of which suggests ignoring its effects. First, we can view multiple product classes solely as a vehicle to enhance generalizability to the larger marketplace. Each product class would then be construed as a sampling unit and any effects of product class as error. The competitor by attribute-improved interaction would then be interpreted without regard to any effects of product class (this interaction remains significant if we drop product class and its interactions from the model). Second, we can view multiple product classes as situations across which we expect, or wish to explore, systematic differences. Here, product-class effects are important and we would not interpret the competitor by attribute-improved interaction without considering the moderating role of product class. Since each view has merit, we plot and interpret both the two-way and three-way interactions.

TABLE 2
Switching Probabilities and Relative Attribute Weights

Product Class	Attribute Improved	Lower-Quality Initial Choice (Higher-Quality Competitor)	Higher-Quality Initial Choice (Lower-Quality Competitor)	Δ
Orange Juice	Price	48.00% (n=25)	23.08% (n=26)	24.92%
		26.00 (n=25)	37.15 (n=26)	11.15
	Quality	50.00% (n=12)	54.05% (n=37)	− 4.05%
		−5.83 (n=12)	20.78 (n=37)	26.61
Microwave Ovens	Price	75.86% (n=29)	47.62% (n=21)	28.24%
		40.62 (n=29)	7.14 (n=21)	−33.48
	Quality	21.74% (n=23)	80.77% (n=26)	−59.03%
		32.17 (n=23)	18.85 (n=26)	−13.32
Light Bulbs	Price	78.95% (n=19)	48.39% (n=31)	30.56%
		16.26 (n=19)	15.42 (n=31)	−0.84
	Quality	66.67% (n=18)	46.88% (n=32)	19.79%
		34.17 (n=18)	11.56 (n=32)	−22.61

NOTE.— Percentages refer to switching probabilities whereas numbers represent relative attribute weights (price weight minus quality weight for choosers of lower quality, and quality weight minus price weight for choosers of higher quality). Differences in switching (Δ) reflect the percentage of consumers switching up in quality minus the percentage of consumers switching down in quality. Differences in relative attribute weights reflect relative attribute weights for choosers of higher quality minus those of choosers of lower quality. Differential preference strengths predict positive values for these differences. For subjects initially choosing lower quality (first data column), improving (reducing) the competitor's (higher-quality brand's) price constitutes improving a relative weakness whereas improving the higher-quality brand's quality constitutes improving a relative strength.

nificant and supported Hypotheses 1 and 2 ($\chi^2_{(1)}$=17.74, p=.001). Price reductions moved consumers up in quality (75.9%) more than down (47.6%; $\chi^2_{(1)}$=4.22, p=.04), whereas quality improvements moved consumers down in quality (80.8%) more than up (21.7%; $\chi^2_{(1)}$=17.07, p<.001).

In orange juice, the competitor by attribute-improved interaction did not achieve statistical significance ($\chi^2_{(1)}$=2.02, p=.15). Testing the individual effects of price and quality improvements on theoretic grounds, we find that consistent with Hypothesis 1 and asymmetric price competition, price reductions moved consumers up in quality (48.0%) more than down (23.1%; $\chi^2_{(1)}$=3.47, p=.06). But in contrast to asymmetric competition, quality improvements moved consumers up and down in quality comparably (50.0% vs. 54.0%; $\chi^2_{(1)}$=.06, ns).

The light bulb data supported Hypothesis 1 but not Hypothesis 2. The competitor by attribute-improved interaction was not significant ($\chi^2_{(1)}$=0.39, ns). Consistent with Hypothesis 1, price reductions moved consumers up in quality (78.9%) more than down (48.4%; $\chi^2_{(1)}$=4.58, p=.03), and quality improvements tended to do the same (66.7% vs. 46.9%; $\chi^2_{(1)}$=1.82, p=.18).[5] Thus, while the overall competitor by attribute-improved interaction supported Hypotheses 1 and 2, Hypothesis 1 was supported in all three product classes, whereas Hypothesis 2 was supported in microwave ovens, reversed in light bulbs, and unsupported by a lack of asymmetry in orange juice.

Differential Attribute Weights. According to Hypotheses 3 and 4, the competitor by attribute-improved interaction arises from differential attribute weights rather than mechanisms such as loss aversion. We tested this by adding attribute weights (and their interactions) to the model. The constant-sum-scaled importance ratings were transformed to a single weight variable by taking quality importance minus price importance. Larger values reflect more weight on quality. The weight variable was mean-centered and standardized within product classes to reduce colinearity and enhance comparability across product classes (Jaccard, Turrisi, and Wan 1990). It was then entered as a continuous variable.

Hypothesis 3 predicted that greater weight on quality would be associated with (1) less switching among choosers of higher quality, and (2) more switching among choosers of lower quality. Hypothesis 3 was generally supported by the significant competitor by weight interaction ($\chi^2_{(1)}$=20.86, p<.001). Logistic regressions revealed that more weight on quality was associated with less switching among choosers of higher quality ($\chi^2_{(1)}$=22.62, p<.001)

---

[5]The only other significant effects were the main effect of product ($\chi^2_{(2)}$ = 5.86, p = .05) and the product by competitor interaction ($\chi^2_{(2)}$ = 8.18, p = .02). There was generally less switching within orange juice (44.0%) than within microwave ovens (58.6%) and light bulbs (57.0%). The interaction arose because there was more switching to higher-quality than lower-quality brands within orange juice and light bulbs (48.6% vs. 41.2% in orange juice, and 73.0% vs. 47.6% in light bulbs), whereas the opposite held in microwave ovens (51.9% vs. 66.0%).

FIGURE 1
Competitor by Attribute-Improved Interaction

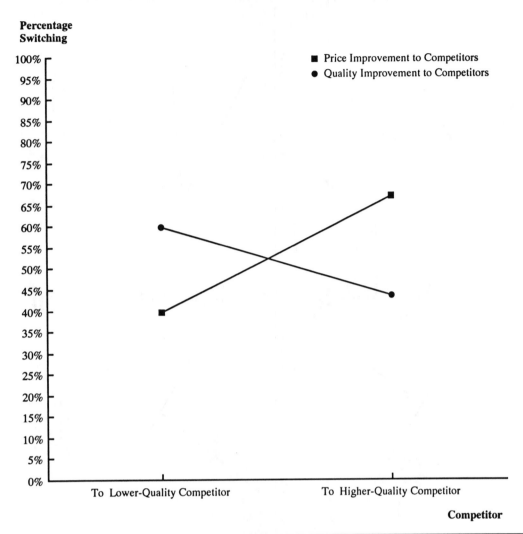

and more switching among choosers of lower quality, although this latter effect did not achieve statistical significance ($\chi^2_{(1)}$=2.10, p=.15).

Hypothesis 4 predicted that adding attribute weights to the model would eliminate the competitor by attribute-improved interaction. The competitor by attribute-improved interaction was, in fact, reduced to nonsignificance overall ($\chi^2_{(1)}$=2.57, p=.11), as was the product-class by competitor by attribute-improved interaction ($\chi^2_{(2)}$=4.53, p=.10). However, a four-way interaction involving product class, competitor, attribute improved, and attribute weights emerged ($\chi^2_{(2)}$=5.62, p=.06). Separate models with attribute weights included were then run per product class.

In all three product classes, the competitor by weight interaction supported attribute-weight effects (Hypothesis 3): microwave ovens ($\chi^2_{(1)}$=6.44, p=.01), orange juice ($\chi^2_{(1)}$=4.38, p=.036), and light bulbs ($\chi^2_{(1)}$=10.16, p=.001). In microwave ovens, the significant competitor by attribute-improved interaction remained significant after adding attribute weights and, therefore, was not consistent with Hypothesis 4's prediction that attribute weights alone drive asymmetric switching ($\chi^2_{(1)}$=8.14, p=.004). In fact, adding attribute weights moved the competitor by attribute-improved interaction in orange juice from nonsignificance to significance ($\chi^2_{(1)}$=4.35, p=.037). We explicate this change in a moment. In

light bulbs, the interaction remained nonsignificant ($\chi^2_{(1)}$=0.61, *ns*), although adding attribute weights failed to eliminate the standard asymmetry (the main effect of competitor; $\chi^2_{(1)}$=5.92, p=.015).[6]

---

[6]The four-way interaction among product class, competitor, attribute improved, and attribute weights is largely inexplicable and occurred because within orange juice there was a significant three-way interaction among competitor, attribute improved, and attribute weights ($\chi^2_{(1)}$ = 4.21, p = .04). When the competitor improved quality, more weight on quality was associated less switching among choosers of the higher-quality orange juice ($\chi^2_{(1)}$ = 5.30, p = .021) and with more switching among choosers of the lower-quality orange juice ($\chi^2_{(1)}$ = 2.31, p = .128). However, when price was improved, more weight on quality was not related to switching regardless of whether consumers chose higher or lower quality ($\chi^2_{(1)}$'s = 0.00 and 0.02, respectively, *ns*). Another way to look at the three-way interaction within orange juice is to test the competitor by attribute-improved interaction at each level of the attribute weights. To do so requires performing a median split on the weight variable which, unfortunately, renders cell sizes too small to obtain reliable tests (e.g., n = 2 in two cases).

FIGURE 2
Competitor by Attribute-Improved by Product-Class Interaction

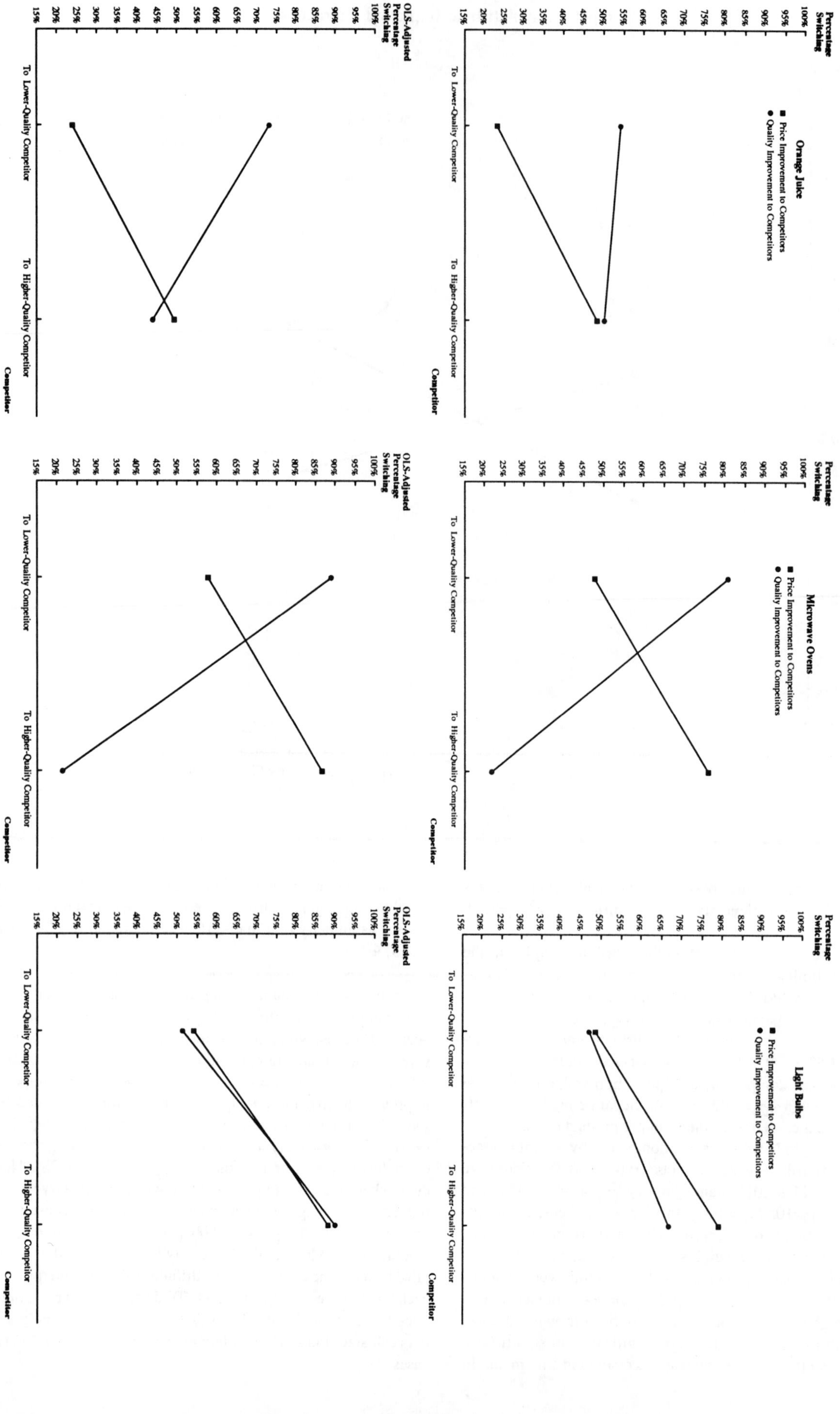

The competitor by attribute-improved interaction was significant in microwave ovens and orange juice after taking into account the effects of attribute weights. However, the possibility remains that the nature of the interaction was altered by the weights. Although we cannot easily adjust switching rates for weight effects using logit's MLE, we do so using adjusted means from OLS. OLS is generally avoided with dichotomous dependent measures because extreme proportions violate its underlying assumptions. However, when proportions remain within the 25% to 75% range, the relationship between probabilities and log-odds should be relatively linear and OLS should yield results comparable to MLE (e.g., Cleary and Angel 1984). The proportions in our results generally complied with this constraint (see Table 2) and OLS does, in fact, yield findings comparable to those from MLE.[7]

For OLS, we coded a switch as 1 and a non-switch as 0 such that means represent proportions of switchers. Figure 2 includes OLS-based switching rates adjusted for weight effects. After factoring in weights, the standard asymmetry remains in tact within all three product categories. Asymmetric quality competition also remains in tact within microwave ovens, becomes slightly more pronounced in orange juice, and is not indicated at all in light bulbs. Although significant weight effects implicate differential attribute weights as a mechanism involved in asymmetric switching, the failure of these effects to eliminate asymmetries implicates other mechanisms as well.

Differential Distances from Indifference. Differential preference strengths predict that choosers of higher quality will be more committed to their brands than will choosers of lower quality. We subjected relative attribute weights to an ANOVA using the brand chosen, product class, and attribute improved as predictors (see Table 2). Hypothesis 5 predicted that relative attribute weights would be larger among choosers of higher quality than among choosers of lower quality. In contrast, the main effect of brand chosen was not significant ($F_{(1,287)}=1.96$, $p=.16$).

The product-class by brand-chosen ($F_{(2,287)}=10.34$, $p<.001$), product-class by attribute-improved ($F_{(2,287)}=5.91$, $p=.003$), and product-class by brand-chosen by attribute-improved interactions were all significant ($F_{(2,287)}=2.99$, $p=.052$). In contrast to Hypothesis 5, relative attribute weights were *smaller* among choosers of higher quality than among choosers of lower quality within microwave ovens and light bulbs, and, therefore, cannot account for the standard asymmetries in those product classes. In orange juice, relative attribute weights were larger for choosers of higher quality ($M=27.54$) than lower quality ($M=15.68$; $F_{(1,287)}=7.35$, $p=.007$). While this is consistent with the standard asymmetry in switching in response to price reductions, it is not consistent with the asymmetric quality competition in response to quality improvements (once weight effects were included). Based on both the relative-attribute-weight and switching data, it is unlikely that differential distances from indifference account for the asymmetric switching found in this experiment.

DISCUSSION

We begin with two problems in the orange juice stimuli which may have played a role in the results (see Table 1). First, the proportional improvement in the lower-quality brand's weakness

(quality) was larger than the improvement in its strength (price; 30.4% vs. 14.3%). This poses an alternative explanation for why improving the lower-quality brand's quality was more effective than improving its price. Second, the improvement to the higher-quality brand's weakness (price) reduced the between-brand difference on price by 49%, whereas the improvement to its strength (quality) increased the between-brand difference on quality by 80.4%. This may have undermined the improvement in the weakness such that the improvement in the weakness and in the strength yielded comparable rates of switching (48.0% vs. 50.0%). Therefore, in the orange juice stimuli, one scaling problem potentially inflated support for our hypotheses while another potentially reduced it.[8]

The experiment generally supports the hypotheses that improving a weakness is more persuasive than improving a strength. Asymmetric price competition favoring higher-quality brands emerged in all product classes, and asymmetric quality competition favoring lower-quality brands emerged in microwave ovens, in orange juice when taking into account attribute weights, but not in light bulbs. These findings suggest that asymmetries in both price and quality competition can be replicated/demonstrated in laboratory settings. It appears that competition can be asymmetric on dimensions other than price, and that asymmetric competition sometimes favors lower-quality rather than higher-quality brands.

Attribute weights had large effects but failed to eliminate asymmetric switching. This pattern implicates differential attribute weights as one, but not the only, mechanism involved in asymmetric switching. Other mechanisms potentially involved include loss aversion and differential loss aversion. The data do not support, however, the hypothesis that choosers of higher quality are further from indifference than are choosers of lower quality.

The experiment holds implications for both theory and practice. For theory, it suggests that standard value functions may apply to dynamic, multi-attribute environments, although the competitor's relative strengths and weaknesses may have to be translated into prospective gains and losses, respectively. For practice, the experiment suggests that marketers of lower-quality brands have recourse for stealing considerable share from higher-quality competitors by improving perceptions of quality or quality-related attributes.

The study suffers from various limitations. First, if subjects viewed 650 watts as sufficient power for microwave ovens, improving the higher-quality microwave's wattage from 650 to 710 may have seemed unimportant despite our use of proportions to mitigate confounding from diminishing marginal sensitivity. This problem can be overcome in future research by using different attribute levels or by replacing specific attributes with overall quality ratings. Second, attribute weights could be measured better by using, for example, revealed preference techniques rather than the current study's self-explicated scales. Third, richer stimuli

---

[7]OLS yields a similar pattern of effects, although the *p* values it generates are generally lower than those produced by MLE. For example, adding attribute weights reduces the overall competitor by attribute-improved interaction to nonsignificance with MLE ($\chi^2_{(1)} = 2.57$, $p = .11$) but not with OLS ($F_{(1,275)} = 12.95$, $p < .001$).

[8]The stimuli in our experiment violated the preferred pattern of proportional relationships in two other instances, although neither is likely to have altered the data. First, in microwave ovens, the single violation was small enough as to pose little threat to internal validity. The proportional improvement in the higher-quality brand's price was slightly larger than the proportional improvement in its quality (13.6% vs. 9.2%). In light bulbs, the proportional improvement in the lower-quality brand's quality was somewhat larger than that in its price (17.5% vs. 10.0%). However, this pattern cannot account for the findings since, in contrast to our hypotheses, the 10% price reduction induced more switching than the 17.5% quality increase.

might be used in the future, although replicating asymmetric price competition with our relatively austere stimuli suggests that people trade off price and quality in fairly standard fashion regardless of the stimuli's richness. Fourth, the study could be enriched by data on process and traits (Simonson 1989). Finally, future research may want to address the anomalous finding in the light bulb data for which we have no immediate explanation: In contrast to microwaves and orange juice, quality improvements benefited the higher-quality light bulb more than the lower-quality light bulb.

REFERENCES

Allenby, Greg M. and Peter E. Rossi (1991), "Quality Perceptions and Asymmetric Switching between Brands," *Marketing Science*, 10 (Summer), 185-204.

Bemmaor, Albert C. and Dominique Mouchoux (1991), "Measuring the Short-Term Effect of In-Store Promotion and Retail Advertising on Brand Sales: A Factorial Experiment," *Journal of Marketing Research*, 28 (May), 202-214.

Bernoulli, Daniel (1738), "Specimen Theoriae Novae de Mensura Sortis," *Commentarii Academiae Scientiarum Imperialis Petropolitanae*, Tomas 5, 175-192. [translated in *Econometrica*, 1954, 22 (January), 23-36.]

Blattberg, Robert C. and Kenneth Wisniewski (1989), "Price-Induced Patterns of Competition," *Marketing Science*, 8 (Fall), 291-309.

Bronnenberg, Bart J. and Luc Wathieu (1995), "Asymmetric Promotion Effects and Brand Positioning," Working Paper, University of Texas, Austin, Texas.

Cleary, Paul D. and Ronald Angel (1984), "The Analysis of Relationships Involving Dichotomous Dependent Variables," *Journal of Health and Social Behavior*, 25 (September), 334-348.

Hardie, Bruce G. S., Eric J. Johnson, and Peter S. Fader (1993), "Modeling Loss Aversion and Reference Dependence Effects on Brand Choice," *Marketing Science*, 12 (Fall), 378-394.

Heath, Timothy B., Gangseog Ryu, Subimal Chatterjee, and Michael S. McCarthy (1996), "Asymmetric Competition and the Elimination of Competitive Disadvantages: Theories and Experimental Tests," Working Paper, University of Pittsburgh, Pittsburgh PA, 15260.

Holman, Frances Galliano (1995), "Relative Value Theory: An Analytic and Predictive Model of Contextual Preference Formation and Choice Behavior," *Marketing Science Conference*, Sydney, Australia, July 2-5.

Jaccard, James, Robert Turrisi, and Choi K. Wan (1990), *Interaction Effects in Multiple Regression*, Newbury Park: Sage.

Kahneman, Daniel and Amos Tversky, (1979), "Prospect Theory: An Analysis of Decision Under Risk," *Econometrica*, 47 (March), 263-291.

Kamakura, Wagner A. and Gary J. Russell (1989), "A Probabilistic Choice Model for Market Segmentation and Elasticity Structures," *Journal of Marketing Research*, 26 (November), 379-390.

Sen, Sankar and Eric J. Johnson (1995), "Now that I have It Do I Want It? Ownership Effects in Consumer Choice," Working Paper, Temple University, Philadelphia, PA, 19103.

Sethuraman, Raj (1995), "A Meta-Analysis of National Brand and Store Brand Cross-Promotional Price Elasticities," *Marketing Letters*, 6 (October), 275-286.

Simonson, Itamar (1989), "Choice Based on Reasons: The Case of Attraction and Compromise Effects," *Journal of Consumer Research*, 16 (September), 158-174.

Simonson, Itamar (1990), "The Effect of Buying Decisions on Consumers' Assessment of Their Tastes," *Marketing Letters*, 2 (January), 5-14.

Tversky, Amos and Daniel Kahneman (1991), "Loss Aversion in Riskless Choice: A Reference Dependent Model," *Quarterly Journal of Economics*, 106 (November), 1040-1061.

Walters, Rockney G. (1991), "Assessing the Impact of Retail Price Promotions on Product Substitution, Complementary Purchase, and Interstore Sales Displacement," *Journal of Marketing*, 55 (April), 17-28.

Log Linear Models for Consumer Brand Switching Behavior: What a Manager Can Learn from Studying Standardized Residuals

Dawn Iacobucci, Northwestern University
Geraldine Henderson, Duke University

We demonstrate the managerial utility of applying log linear models to brand switching data. We examine the overall structure of the French 1989 automobile marketplace, and we adjust for loyalty effects via a model of quasi-independence. We study the resultant standardized residuals and consider several managerial interpretations of the results, including comparative structure between competitors, and the study of customer attraction and retention within a manufacturer. The observed asymmetric trading is also examined in greater detail. The results are enlightening to managers and the methods provide clear instruction to MBA students.

INTRODUCTION

Loyalty and brand-switching are of interest to marketing managers and researchers alike (Carpenter and Lehmann 1985; Deighton, Henderson, and Neslin 1994; Grover and Srinivasan 1992; Novak 1993; Stephan and Tannenholz 1994). In this paper we hope to demonstrate a clear, illustrative example of the potential of log linear models applied to brand switching data. The methods are somewhat underutilized in analyzing brand switching data, perhaps in part because academic treatments of the topic can be somewhat cryptic and technical, or perhaps do not show the richness of the possible managerial implications. We hope to demonstrate in this paper that the insights from these methods are rich. We consider issues of market share and loyalty, and we illustrate the use of studying standardized residuals to examine comparative competitor structure, customer attraction and retention patterns, and asymmetric trading partners. Finally, we present these methods in a straightforward manner and we offer an appendix with instructions for fitting these models, to further enhance ease of adoption. We have found this treatment of these methods to be taught easily in the MBA classroom, and therefore we might expect the methods to be carried more readily into future industry research studies.

THE DATA

The brand switching data we model in this paper represent the automobile manufacturing industry (Colombo, Ehrenberg, and Sabavala 1994). There exists a two-way classification of car purchases wherein the rows of the data matrix describe the owners' previous car makes, and the columns of the matrix describe the makes of the currently owned automobiles, a standard format for brand switching contingency tables. Each cell entry is the number of consumers who had owned the row-brand car and who now own the column-brand car. These data exist for four consecutive years, 1986 through 1989, for two countries, France and Great Britain; as an example, the matrix for the French 1989 market is found in Table 1.[1]

Row and column percentages are also found in Table 1, and these represent basic market share information (for times *t* and *t+1*, respectively). These marginal indices afford an opportunity to make some initial observations on these data. The market contains

a small number of highly active players (the three largest players are ordered: Renault, Peugeot, Citroen), suggesting national loyalty or distribution availability. At the other extreme, the market also contains several players who capture only nominal markets (1-2% market share, including: Alfa Romeo, BMW, Lada, Mercedes, Rover, Seat, Volvo). The remaining manufacturers serve approximately 5% shares (including: Fiat, Ford, GM, VW/Audi).[2]

Marginal information, by definition, does not represent the associations internal to the body of a contingency table. For example, several automobile manufacturers in both markets have large row margins (e.g., Peugeot), suggesting the loss of many customers, but their respective column margins are also large, indicating that the customers are being replaced in nearly equal quantities. These large share competitors simply see much incoming and outgoing action. One might hypothesize that the action of the Citroen, Peugeot, and Renault brands is reciprocal—that the French purchase primarily French cars, so former owners of Citroen will next buy Peugeot, for example. When we examine the associations within the body of the table, shortly, we shall see that this exchange hypothesis is somewhat too simple to describe the transactions.

We also know that the differential margins must be considered before examining the data for indicators of loyalty or brand-switching. There is no single agreed upon definition of loyalty (e.g., 100% brand purchases, majority of household brand purchases, sequences of similar brand purchases, etc.), but one naive view would be to examine the diagonal elements in the matrix in Table 1 because these values represent the number of consumers who purchased the same car at time *t+1* as they had previously owned at time *t*. However, we have seen the variability across manufacturers in the margins, and we must tease apart market size information from market repeat or change behavior. It is nearly a truism that manufacturers that capture larger portions of markets also do tend to attract greater loyalty, but the phenomena are confounded in the raw frequencies, as in Table 1. The models of independence and quasi-independence described in the next section will statistically control for the heterogeneity in the margins, and proceed to reflect cleanly the associations internal to the body of the table.

LOG LINEAR MODELS OF INDEPENDENCE AND QUASI-INDEPENDENCE

The fundamental statistic an analyst examines in a two-way cross-tabulation is the Pearson X^2 of fit for the model of independence. In order to facilitate later generalization, we refer to this model as the log linear model:

---

[1] The analyses for the remaining markets (French 1986, 1987, 1988, and U.K. 1986-1989) are available from the authors.

[2] These relative market share patterns are robust in that they are highly consistent across all four time periods, whether examining row (t) or column (t+1) indices (for both the French and UK markets). The mean Pearson product-moment correlation among the four years' row percentages is .99, as is the mean correlation among the four years' column percentages, and for the row to column comparisons within respective years. However, this apparent stability does not mean there are no interesting dynamic phenomena in these data (as we shall show).

Advances in Consumer Research
Volume 24, © 1997

TABLE 1
Frequencies of Consumers Who Had Owned Row Cars and Now Own Column Cars*

French Market 1989

	AL	BMW	CI	FI	FO	GM	LA	ME	PE	RE	RO	SE	VW	VO	ROW%
AL	97	5	19	19	14	7	0	3	27	35	5	6	17	4	1.18
BMW	4	163	20	9	14	6	0	19	39	40	6	4	29	4	1.63
CI	6	13	1811	136	98	67	21	15	464	477	29	28	90	10	14.92
FI	11	5	69	526	50	49	12	3	134	148	27	17	82	5	5.20
FO	4	10	45	53	696	76	8	8	121	146	20	23	60	7	5.84
GM	2	7	20	23	50	362	7	4	68	80	7	12	39	4	3.13
LA	0	0	12	13	11	12	68	0	25	16	4	3	7	0	.78
ME	2	17	3	3	5	2	0	136	4	10	3	1	5	3	.89
PE	13	23	273	164	195	168	34	23	2928	728	47	60	199	20	22.28
RE	22	37	353	334	308	254	40	33	896	4861	78	106	310	24	35.00
RO	2	4	18	25	30	3	6	1	30	45	115	6	40	2	1.49
SE	2	0	13	10	10	11	0	0	10	29	3	36	13	0	.63
VW	6	21	50	51	65	59	2	10	177	115	13	25	772	9	6.29
VO	1	3	11	5	4	6	0	3	9	17	3	4	18	78	.74
COL%		1.79		7.99		6.30		1.50		39.31		1.93		.78	
	1.00		15.83		9.03		1.15		28.74		2.10		9.79		

AL=Alfa Romeo   GM=GM   RO=Rover
BMW=BMW   LA=Lada   SE=Seat
CI=Citroen   ME=Mercedes   VW=VW/Audi
FI=Fiat   PE=Peugeot   VO=Volvo
FO=Ford   RE=Renault

(1) $\ln \{ E(x_{ij}) \} = u + u_{1(i)} + u_{2(j)}$,

terms that represent a grand total effect, a row effect, and a column effect, respectively. Even cursory inspection of the matrices in Table 1 might lead us to suspect that the model of independence will not fit these data. The hypothesis of independence states that consumer purchases are random, and would yield no apparent pattern in the table; that is, knowing what brand a consumer purchased at time *t* would be of no help in predicting what brand the consumer purchases subsequently (time *t+1*). This hypothesis of randomness appears implausible given the apparent structure in the data, but to officially test for randomness, we compute the likelihood ratio test statistic, $G^2 = \Sigma_i \Sigma_j x_{ij} \ln(x_{ij}/E(x)_{ij})$ which is distributed χ^2 on (I-1)(J-1) degrees of freedom for an I by J table X={x_{ij}}, with subscripts i denoting rows (i=1,2,...I) and j denoting columns (j=1,2,...J; I=J).

The fit statistic indicates that the model of independence does not fit; G^2=22043.749, df=169, p=.000. A substantively interesting plausible explanation for the statistically nonrandom purchase behavior may indeed be loyalty; most of the diagonal values are large, and this suggests that consumers are repeat purchasing (thus purchases at time *t+1* are not independent of those at time *t*). As stated previously, the diagonal values in the matrices in Table 1 are not corrected for differential market shares. However, once the model is fit and the row and column parameters estimated (the $u_{1(i)}$'s and $u_{2(j)}$'s in equation 1), the "standardized residuals" can be computed with the result that the data have been essentially corrected for the margins.

The standardized residual is computed as: $z_{ij} = (x_{ij} - E(x)_{ij})/ \mathrm{sqrt}(E(x)_{ij})$, and is distributed as a z-score (Haberman 1973), so any standardized residual exceeding 1.96 in magnitude is significant.[3] So for example, a large positive standardized residual value on the diagonal would indicate far more consumers repeated their purchase of the focal brand than would be predicted by chance (after correcting for apparent share differences).[4]

Each of these diagonal z-scores exceeded 20, clearly indicating strong loyalty, even after correcting for differential market shares. Therefore, we might wish to address the question, "Even though the model of independence does not fit, in large part due to the loyal purchase behavior reflected in the large diagonal values, is the *brand-switching* random, or are there also predictable, structural patterns in the off-diagonal elements in this matrix?"

This question requires that we fit the model of independence to the off-diagonal frequencies temporarily ignoring the diagonal (loyalty) cells. We can do so by fitting the model of "quasi-independence" as described in Fienberg (1980), whereby the model of independence is fit to a contingency table in which one or more cells have been marked with structural zeros (cf. Colombo and

---

[3]This relationship is not difficult to see. A X^2 is the sum of z-scores squared, and the Pearson χ^2 statistic is computed as the sum of terms, $(x_{ij} - E(x)_{ij})^2/(E(x)_{ij})$; i.e., the square of the z_{ij} standardized residual terms.

[4]Similarly, a large negative value on the diagonal would indicate extreme customer dissatisfaction.

TABLE 2
Coded Table of Standardized Residuals from Quasi-Independence Model

KEY: # > 4.00 (very frequent)
+ > 2.58 (frequent)
– < -2.58 (infrequent)
= < -4.00 (very infrequent)

	AL	BM	CI	FI	FO	GM	LA	ME	PE	RE	RO	SE	VW	VO
AlfaRomeo		•	•	•	•	•	•	•	•	•	•	•	•	•
BMW	•		•	•	•	•	•	#	•	•	•	•	+	•
Citroen	•	•		•	–	–	•	•	#	+	•	•	=	•
Fiat	+	•	•		•	•	•	•	•	•	+	•	+	•
Ford	•	•	•	•		#	•	•	•	•	•	•	•	•
GM	•	•	•	•	#		•	•	•	•	•	•	•	•
Lada	•	•	•	•	•	•		•	•	•	•	•	•	•
Mercedes	•	#	•	•	•	•	•		–	•	•	•	•	+
Peugeot	•	•	•	–	•	•	•	•		+	•	•	•	•
Renault	•	•	•	•	•	•	•	•	•		•	•	•	•
Rover	•	•	•	•	+	–	•	•	–	•		•	+	•
Seat	•	•	•	•	•	•	•	•	–	•	•		•	•
VW/Audi	•	#	•	•	•	•	•	•	•	=	•	•		•
Volvo	•	•	•	•	•	•	•	•	•	•	•	•	+	

Morrison 1989).[5] (For instruction in fitting these models, see the Appendix.)

The G^2 for the model of quasi-independence is 640.659 on 155 df[6] (p=.000), indicating it does not fit. Nevertheless, the improvement in fit from the model of independence to quasi-independence is significant (ΔG^2=21403.105, Δdf=14, p<.001). Thus, the ΔG^2 indicates that correcting for loyalty is important and necessary, and the G^2 indicates that we must conclude the consumer brand-

switching purchases are non-random over time, even after adjusting for loyalty.

In the spirit of exploratory data analysis (cf. Tukey 1977; Velleman and Hoaglin 1981, and others), rather than presenting the table of 182 standardized residual values, we present in Table 2 an easier visual summary of the data. To study the structural patterns, we created a "coded table"; coding the standardized residuals cell-by-cell upon fitting the model of quasi-independence to these data: "#" and "+" represent significantly positive residuals ($z\geq4.00$, and $z\geq2.58$, respectively), and "-" and "=" represent significantly negative residuals ($z\leq-2.58$ and $z\leq-4.00$, respectively).[7] Thus, the first two codes represent those elements in the matrix where there are more consumers purchasing the column car after having owned the row car than would be expected if quasi-independence held, and the second two codes indicate very infrequent transactions.

There are many phenomena in this table that give us a sense of the richness of the data, far beyond the previously reported simple row and column percentages. For example, note that BMW and Mercedes do more inter-trading than the model (hypothesizing quasi-randomness) would predict (the BMW-Mercedes and Mercedes-BMW cells contain "#"s). Consumers considering these car makes are also somewhat more likely to be trading-in or trading-to VW/Audi or Volvos. These consideration sets tell the manufac-

---

[5]Structural zeros are distinguished from sampling zeros in that the former are combinations that will not occur in data (e.g., a cell reflecting the number of consumers purchasing a focal car brand in a market where the car is not available), whereas the latter zeros appear due to sampling or baseline rarity but presumably are possible combinations (e.g., number of consumers purchasing some expensive, exotic, tailored-made car). The typical application of quasi-independence is to fit the model of independence while being sensible about constraining cells corresponding to structural zeros to have expected cell counts of zero, since the observed cell count will necessarily equal zero. In the current paper, structural zeros are imputed into the diagonal cells to focus the modeling efforts to the off-diagonals. This use is still relatively novel (e.g., see Colombo and Morrison 1989), but it is defensible to the extent that: a) we have already analyzed and characterized the entire table, and b) we selected the diagonal cells as focal due to substantive theoretical reasons, not arbitrarily, and not even empirically (a la "data-fishing").

[6]The model of quasi-independence is fit on I(=J) fewer degrees of freedom than the model of independence due to our constraining the I(=J) zeros on the diagonal cells where the loyalty behavior is reflected.

---

[7]We used the more conservative cutoffs of 2.58 and an even higher value of 4.00 rather than 1.96 because we are studying the patterns in so many cells (184=196-14) simultaneously, and we wish to control somewhat for chance, particularly because the cells themselves are presumably interdependent, given that the model of independence did not fit.

turers who their most likely competitors are, as a subset of all possible competitors.

Earlier, we had briefly entertained the hypothesis that the cars within the trio of {Citroen-Peugeot-Renault} were somehow interchangeable. There is some tendency for Peugeot owners to continue to purchase French brands (the "+" in the Peugeot row corresponding to the Renault column), but for example, Renault buyers are literally less predictable in their subsequent purchases (the Renault row is comprised entirely of "."'s, meaning few significant departures from random behavior for Renault owners). Citroen buyers show more structural predictability (there are more clear patterns of especially high or low purchase frequency patterns; i.e., more "#+-=" codes in the Citroen row), and national loyalty.

There are very few combinations that are particularly rare (i.e., the "="s, or even "-"s). The French 1989 market shows two (Citroen to VW/Audi, and VW/Audi to Renault); that is, it was highly unusual (less often than chance) for Citroen owners to purchase VW/Audis, and for VW/Audi owners to purchase Renaults. It would be interesting to understand why these purchase patterns are so rare. One might argue that one car in each pair is in a different sort of "market" from the other in the pair, but that could be true of many of the pairs within these markets, and there were no *a priori* expectations that the data would flag these purchases as particularly unusual temporal combinations.

Finally, these structural patterns could be used by any one of the manufacturers' marketing managers to study their brand in the marketplace compared with others. For example, the Citroen row in the matrix has a fair number of marks ("#+-="s), indicating this competitor is more likely (than randomness) to lose consumers to Peugeot and Renault ("#" and "+"), and not likely to lose consumers to Ford, GM, or VW/Audi ("-" and "="). While that list may seem like a good number of competitors with which to contend in managing the loss of consumers to other manufacturers, at least the Citroen manager's picture is clear: Citroen knows the players in the market to whom it is most likely to lose owners.

Contrast Citroen's picture with say that of Alfa Romeo, Lada, or Renault. For these car makes, the rows (if we are still focusing on where lost consumers are going), show no strong indications of pattern (all cells are "."s). Alfa Romeo, Lada and Renault are likely to lose consumers to any other maker with equal likelihood (in proportion to the market shares which have been factored out). Given this observation, their managements are more challenged because they are just as likely to be losing their consumers to all the other manufacturers. Citroen's competitive picture was more crystalized compared with the near-random behavior of say, the Alfa Romeo purchaser (according to the abundance of non-significant residuals—the "."s).

We can do a similar analysis *within* a competitor comparing its row to its column. For example, Citroen has more "codes" in its row compared to its column. Thus, the data on Citroen indicate more clearly where its customers are going than from which competitors its customers have come. Such a market situation actually suggests that Citroen is not executing (or doing so successfully) a *targeted* marketing plan, but rather is attracting consumers from all sorts of previous car makes. Surely a car manufacturer could be happy in such a situation, as long as incoming volumes were high, but should the volume drop off, or should the manager wish to understand the consumers s/he is likely to attract, this information picture is not clear. On the other hand, the outgoing (row) information is more clearly structured, so Citroen would know where to focus to stop the leak of customers (i.e., Peugeuot and Renault, and not Ford, GM, or VW/Audi). That is, Citroen has a clearer means of identifying how to retain customers than how to attract them.

As a final class of observations, we note the asymmetries in the codes in Table 2. There exist two symmetric dyads, in which the behavior from row i to column j resembles that from row j to column i, including BMW-Mercedes, and Ford-GM. The BMW-VW/Audi pair is also nearly symmetric. For these three pairs, the manufacturers involved are essentially switching a portion of their customers back and forth. All the remaining pairs, however, demonstrate asymmetric switching. For example, more consumers switch from Fiat to Alfa Romeos than the reverse. The same is true for Ford or GM to Citroen, Citroen to Peugeot or Renault, Fiat to Peugeot or Rover, Rover to Ford, VW/Audi to Citroen, Renault to VW/Audi, etc.[8]

In the next section of this paper, we explore symmetry systematically. We have pointed to many pairs of car makes with different codes (e.g., one "." and one "="), but we must acknowledge that the majority of pairs in this matrix are symmetric if only because they are insignficant (".",".")'s. Thus, an objective measure of (a)symmetry is sought.

LOG LINEAR MODELS OF SYMMETRY AND QUASI-SYMMETRY

In this section, we explore a means of testing for symmetry and asymmetry in these brand-switching data. We apply the methods of Bishop, Fienberg, and Holland (1975) who present a log linear model for a two-way table with elements x_{ij} in which a three-way table is created:

(2) $x_{ij1} = x_{ij}$ i>j, 0 elsewhere, and
$x_{ij2} = x_{ji}$ i>j, 0 elsewhere.

The first model fit to this three-dimensional array represents symmetry:

(3) $\text{Ln} \{ E(x)_{ijk} \} = u + u_{1(i)} + u_{2(j)} + u_{3(k)} + u_{12(ij)}.$

The partner model is that of "quasi-symmetry" which is like the above, but with a relaxation on the assumption of homogeneous margins (cf. Novak 1993, p.270)[9]:

(4) $\text{Ln} \{ E(x)_{ijk} \} = u + u_{1(i)} + u_{2(j)} + u_{3(k)} + u_{12(ij)} + u_{13(ik)} + u_{23(jk)}.$

The fit statistic for the model of symmetry is large, indicating the data do indeed display sufficient asymmetries that the model does not fit ($G^2 = 845.723$ df=286, p<.001). While the relaxation of the assumption of marginal homogeneity in the quasi-symmetry model improves the fits significantly ($\Delta G^2 = 752.450$, df=26, p<.001), the quasi-symmetry model nevertheless still does not fit the data ($G^2 = 93.273$, df=260, p<.050).

---

[8]One can imagine a walk through a graph theoretic path structure as descriptive of aspirative car purchases; e.g., perhaps the GM owner moves onto purchase a Citroen, and then a Peugeot, and then a Rover, and Ford, etc. Most manufacturers would desire to be a "sink" in a graph; retaining customers fed from other manufacturers, or "sources."

[9]The model of quasi-symmetry shares with the model of quasi-independence a relaxation of certain assumptions, but while the latter involves structural zeros, the former involves allowing margins to not be perfectly equal (if a matrix were symmetric, it would follow that its row and column margins would be exactly equal).

Thus, while it may be the case that some pairs or small groups of car manufacturers symmetrically trade consumers back and forth (e.g., BMW and Mercedes), these results suggest that asymmetry is a property that describes this market better, on average. It is conceivable that these asymmetries are a result of consumer car purchases being hierarchical, if some cars are more desirable to trade-up to than others, for example.

CONCLUSIONS

In this paper, we analyzed brand switching data using methods created for contingency tables. Specifically, we fit the models of independence and quasi-independence to the two-way contingency table describing consumer car purchases at times t and $t+1$. The modeling is straightforward, and the results are rich and telling. The model of independence did not fit, and the first hypothesis was that this result was driven by likely high loyalties. The model of quasi-independence fit significantly better, confirming the importance of controlling for the loyalties, but it also did not fit, indicating that the brand-switching patterns were also nonrandom and structured.

The analyses also suggested asymmetries in the brand-switching behavior that was not obvious by the simple marginal percentages. The asymmetric structure was confirmed via the fitting of models of symmetry and quasi-symmetry.

The results of inspecting the standardized residuals were especially enlightening. Managerial implications were obvious; cross-competitor comparisons were possible, as were within-competitor analyses of customers lost versus customers gained.

The methods presented in this paper are easy to execute, understand, and communicate, and they yield clear insights into competitive structure and manufacturer properties. We encourage their more frequent utilitization.

REFERENCES

Bishop, Yvonne M.M., Stephen E. Fienberg, and Paul W. Holland (1975), *Discrete Multivariate Analysis: Theory and Practice*, Cambridge, MA: The MIT Press.

Carpenter, Gregory S. and Donald R. Lehmann (1985), "A Model of Marketing Mix, Brand Switching, and Competition," *Journal of Marketing Research*, 22(3), 318-329.

Colombo, Richard, Andrew Ehrenberg, and Darius Sabavala (1994) "The Car Challenge: Diversity in Analyzing Brand Switching Tables," Unpublished manuscript.

Colombo, Richard A., and Donald G. Morrison (1989), "A Brand Switching Model with Implications for Marketing Strategies," *Marketing Science*, 8, 89-99.

Deighton, John, Caroline M. Henderson, and Scott A. Neslin (1994), "The Effects of Advertising on Brand Switching and Repeat Purchasing," *Journal of Marketing Research*, 31(1), 28-43.

Fienberg, Stephen E. (1980), *The Analysis of Cross-Classified Categorical Data*, (2nd ed.), Cambridge, MA: The MIT Press.

Grover, Rajiv, and V. Srinivasan (1992), "Evaluating the Multiple Effects of Retail Promotion on Brand Loyal and Brand Switching Segments," *Journal of Marketing Research*, 29(1), 76-89.

Haberman, Shelby J. (1973), "The Analysis of Residuals in Cross-Classified Tables," *Biometrika*, 29, 205-220.

Novak, Thomas P. (1993), "Log-Linear Trees: Models of Market Structure in Brand Switching Data," *Journal of Marketing Research*, 30, 267-287.

Stephan, S. Kent, and Barry L. Tannenholz (1994), "The Real Reason for Brand Switching," *Advertising Age, 65(25)*, 31.

Tukey, John W. (1977), *Exploratory Data Analysis*, Reading, MA: Addison-Wesley.

Velleman, Paul F. and David C. Hoaglin (1981), *Applications, Basics, and Computing of Exploratory Data Analysis*. Boston: Duxbury Press.

APPENDIX
How to Fit the Models (in SPSS).

```
TITLE 'INDEP & QUASI-INDEP ANALYSIS  FRENCH DATA'.
DATA LIST FILE = 'A:FR89.DAT'
/ I J N.
COMMENT The following commands fit the model of independence:
WEIGHT BY N.
HILOGLINEAR I J (1,14)
/PRINT = ASSOCIATION ALL
/DESIGN I J.
COMMENT The following commands fit the model of quasi-independence:
COMMENT quasi-independence:
WEIGHT BY N.
HILOGLINEAR I J (1,14)
/CWEIGHT ( 0 13*(14*1 0))
/PRINT = ASSOCIATION ALL
/DESIGN I J.
WEIGHT BY N.
LOGLINEAR I J (1,14)
/CWEIGHT ( 0 13*(14*1 0))
/PRINT = ESTIM
/DESIGN I J.
```

FR89.DAT resembles:
```
 1   1    97
 1   2     5
 1   3    19
...
14  14    78
```

```
TITLE 'SYMMETRY AND QUASI-SYM ANALYSIS  FRENCH DATA'.
DATA LIST FILE = 'A:FR893.DAT'
/ I J K N.
COMMENT The following commands fit the models of
COMMENT symmetry and quasi-symmetry:
WEIGHT BY N.
HILOGLINEAR I J (1,14) K (1,2)
/PRINT = ASSOCIATION ALL
/DESIGN I*J I*K J*K
/DESIGN I*J K.
```

FR893.DAT resembles:
```
 1    1 1    0
 1    2 1    0
 1    3 1    0
...
 2    1 1    4
 2    2 1    0
 2    3 1    0
...
 3    1 1    6
 3    2 1   13
 3    3 1    0
...
...
 1    1 2    0
 1    2 2    0
 1    3 2    0
...
 2    1 2    5
 2    2 2    0
 2    3 2    0
...
 3    1 2   19
 3    2 2   20
 3    3 2    0
...
...
```

An Investigation of Some Determinants of Brand Commitment

Utpal M. Dholakia, University of Michigan

ABSTRACT

The construct of brand commitment has been extensively examined in the consumer behavior literature but previous research has found conflicting and confusing relationships between perceived risk, enduring importance and brand commitment. Using consistent definitions of these constructs, this article investigates the relationship of brand commitment with perceived risk and enduring importance. An empirical study shows some evidence of a negative relationship between brand commitment and perceived risk, and stronger evidence of a negative relationship between brand commitment and enduring importance, challenging some existing notions. Existing research on consumer expertise and collecting behavior is useful in explaining this result. Some implications for advertising strategy are provided and several avenues for further research are suggested to build on this study.

INTRODUCTION

The concept of *brand commitment* is related to the loyalty of consumers toward a particular brand in a product class and is gaining increasing importance in consumer behavior (Martin & Goodell, 1991). One reason for this increased importance is the recognition that brand commitment includes both a *behavioral dimension* (consistency of purchase) and an *attitudinal dimension*, in contrast to the one-dimensional nature of repeat-purchase behavior which is often used to characterize brand loyalty. A second reason is the current recognition of the beneficial and profitable nature of loyal customers to the firm (Reichheld, 1996).

There are multiple conceptualizations of commitment in the consumer behavior literature. At the brand level, commitment has been thought of as brand loyalty (Martin & Goodell, 1991) and represents one of the most researched areas in consumer behavior (Muncy & Hunt, 1984). Other approaches have defined it as a component of product involvement (Lastovicka & Gardner, 1977). Empirical studies have also examined the antecedents and consequences of brand commitment (e.g., Beatty, Kahle & Homer, 1988) but its relationship with other consumer behavior constructs like product importance and perceived risk is not clear (Jacoby & Chestnut, 1978). The objective of the present study is to add to this body of empirical research and examine the influence of perceived risk and enduring importance on brand commitment. A review of these constructs is presented from extant literature and hypotheses relating perceived risk and enduring importance to brand commitment are derived. An empirical study is carried out using multiple product classes and results are presented. Some explanations based on research on consumer expertise and collecting are provided for the findings.

BRAND COMMITMENT

Early conceptualizations of commitment in marketing equated it with brand loyalty and defined it in terms of the consistency of purchasing a specific brand (Engel & Blackwell, 1982). These conceptualizations followed from sociology where commitment was viewed as a consistent line of behavior by an individual, maintained even when faced with alternative or competing behavior choices (Becker, 1960). Thus brand commitment was viewed as a behavioral phenomenon and commonly defined in empirical studies as *"the proportion of total purchases within a given product category devoted to the most frequently purchased brand"* (Jacoby & Chestnut, 1978, p. 35). However, later on, this was recognized

to be a narrow outlook not considering the reasons underlying the frequency of brand purchase.

As a result, later definitions expanded the scope of commitment by including attitudinal aspects of the construct. For example, in sociology, Johnson (1973) defined commitment as "the extent to which an action is dedicated to the completion of a line of action." In marketing, this attitudinal nature implies that the greater the commitment of an individual to a brand, the more firmly fixed is the brand as the only choice within the product class (Traylor, 1981). Using this perspective, emphasis is placed on both cognitive and affective components of the construct. Measurement is based on purchase intentions and purchase preferences rather than on actual purchases. In the present study, brand commitment is conceptualized as an attitudinal construct and is defined as *"the pledging or binding of an individual to his/her brand choice within a product class"* (Lastovicka & Gardner, 1977). It must be noted therefore that brand commitment though pertaining to brands, is defined as a construct at the level of the product class, i.e., consumers are conceptualized to have different levels of brand commitment for different product classes.

Empirical research has studied the antecedents of brand commitment including personality characteristics like self-confidence (Day, 1969) and susceptibility to reference group influence as well as store loyalty (Carman, 1970) but its connections with other consumer behavior constructs are tenuous.

PERCEIVED RISK

Perceived risk is conceptualized as arising from unanticipated and uncertain consequences of an unpleasant nature resulting from the product purchase (Bauer, 1960). In consumer behavior, risk is conceptualized in terms of *loss* (Dowling, 1986) and thought to arise only from potentially negative outcomes, in contrast to other disciplines like psychology where both positive and negative outcomes are considered.

Bettman's (1973) distinction between *inherent risk* and *handled risk* identifies perceived risk as a product-class specific construct, i.e. different product classes have different levels of *inherent* and *handled risk* associated with them. The inherent risk refers to the aspects of risk in the product class that are temporally stable while the handled risk pertains to the more situational aspects of the product class. In this study, perceived risk is conceptualized as stable, product-class specific and unique to an individual. In other words, an individual perceives each product class to have specific levels of risk associated with it and these levels for a product class are different for different individuals. In this study, perceived risk is defined as *"the subjective expectation of losses"* resulting from the purchase and use of products from the product class. This definition is consistent with definitions used in previous studies (e.g., Peter & Ryan, 1976).

Previous research has identified several distinct dimensions within the overall perceived risk for a product class (Kaplan et. al., 1974; Roselius, 1971). The risk taxonomy arising from these studies and consisting of six dimensions is widely accepted as relevant to explaining perceived risk and is presented in Exhibit 1.

ENDURING IMPORTANCE

The notion of *product importance* is central to consumer behavior and the idea that consumers consider different product classes to be of differing importance is widely accepted in consumer

Advances in Consumer Research
Volume 24, © 1997

EXHIBIT 1
Categories of loss contributing to perceived risk

Financial loss	Risk associated with losing money because of: (1) functional failure of the product, (2) high repair costs and (3) equivalent or better product available at lower cost.
Performance loss	Risk associated with inadequate and/or unsatisfactory performance of the product.
Physical loss	Risk associated with physical danger because of the use of the product.
Psychological loss	Risk associated with the non-congruence between the product and the buyer's self-image or self-concept.
Social loss	Risk associated with the unfavorable opinions of the consumer by others because of the product.
Time loss	Risk associated with age/ inefficient use of time because of the product.

(Adapted from Stone and Grönhaug, 1993)

behavior (Hupfer & Gardner, 1971). This construct is analogous to the well-researched construct of *product involvement* which is defined as "the extent to which a consumer links a product to salient enduring or situation-specific goals" (Laaksonnen, 1994) and has been found to influence consumer decision processes, post-decision processes and response to marketing communications (Bloch & Richins, 1983).

This definition makes a distinction between *situational importance,* which is evoked by a particular purchase situation and *enduring importance* which is related to the emotional and personal aspects of the individual and represents a more stable attitude (Richins et al., 1992). In the present study, the focus is on this type of enduring importance since this is most appropriate when referring to a product class and also facilitates comparability with other constructs. As a result, enduring importance is defined as *"a long-term, cross-situational perception of product importance based on the strength of the product's relationship to central needs and values of the consumer"* (Bloch & Richins, 1983, p. 72). The emphasis of this importance is on the product itself and the value or need satisfaction derived from owning, using and consuming the product (Richins et al., 1992) and is not connected to the temporal and situation-specific process of brand choice. This importance is thus determined by the stable elements of the individual's identity and is therefore stable and long-lasting in nature.

RELATIONSHIP BETWEEN PERCEIVED RISK AND COMMITMENT

Early risk researchers posited a positive relationship between perceived risk and commitment by characterizing brand commitment as a strategy to control or avoid the perceived risk in purchasing an untried or unfamiliar brand (Bauer, 1967). Using this rationale, brand commitment is essentially a *risk-reduction strategy* (Derbaix, 1983). Empirical studies supporting this relationship show that stock-out of favored brands results in the selection of other sizes or varieties of the same brand or delay of purchase when the perceived risk associated with the product class is high (Emmelhainz et al, 1991). A recently formulated product-typology characterizes high-commitment products as those infrequently purchased and having negative consequences of wrong decisions associated with them (Martin & Goodell, 1991), thus favoring a positive relationship between the two constructs.

However, empirical research also shows that the level of perceived risk is commonly cited as an important reason for switching brands by consumers (Cunningham, 1967). Thus, consumers with low perceived risk switch to other brands because of curiosity while high-risk consumers switch in search of better brands. In related work, empirical studies show that increased perceived risk results in increased search for attribute-based information about different brands (Capon & Burke, 1980). Review of extant literature thus reveals conflicting findings about the relationship between perceived risk and brand commitment though there is greater support for a positive relationship.

RELATIONSHIP BETWEEN PRODUCT IMPORTANCE AND COMMITMENT

The close links between product importance and brand commitment can be found in numerous studies relating product involvement to brand commitment. The resulting conclusions from this area are however, often confusing and conflicting. The similarity between the two constructs is highlighted by the use of Krugman's (1965) notion of low-involvement to explain low-commitment consumer-behavior (Robertson, 1976). Other authors have distinguished between the two constructs by defining commitment as referring to a particular position or stance, generally positive, with respect to a brand, and involvement as the general level of interest or concern in a product category without reference to a specific position (Zaltman & Wallendorf, 1983). Yet other authors have identified commitment as one component of product involvement (Lastovicka & Gardner, 1977).

Several consumer researchers have implied that increased product involvement results in brand commitment. Tyebjee (1977) suggests that consumers demonstrate more unstable behavior, characterized by low brand loyalty and greater variety-seeking when dealing with low-involvement products. Lastovicka & Gardner (1977) make the same argument claiming that consumers with low product involvement think of the product class as trivial and have "little bond" to their choice. One empirical study found the level of involvement to determine its relationship to brand commitment (Traylor, 1981). Low-involvement products showed a positive relationship to brand commitment while high-involvement products showed no relationship. Another study found brand commitment to result from purchase involvement (Beatty et al., 1988). A third empirical study however found a strong connection between a consumer's enduring involvement in a product class and the propensity to engage in on-going information gathering about the product class (Bloch et al., 1986). This suggests that the consumer's knowledge about the different brands in the product class is likely to be high in such cases, resulting in lower brand commitment.

Thus, review of earlier work suggests that though the two constructs are closely related, commitment does not necessarily follow from product importance nor can it be accepted as a dimension of the importance construct.

HYPOTHESES

Work in sociology recognizes that consistency of behavior is positively related to the number and strength of the "valuables" or "exit barriers" that an individual has accumulated (Becker, 1960). These valuables are called "side bets." This notion has great relevance in relating the constructs of perceived risk and brand commitment. Perceived risk is generally associated with losses occurring in one or more of the loss categories in Exhibit 1. For a product class with high levels of overall perceived risk, the "valuables" or the "exit barriers" accumulated when the individual interacts with a product class will be high. The person will prefer to purchase the same brand or one of a few acceptable brands within the product class and as a result, the commitment to the product class for the individual will be high.

For example, buying a car is a significant investment and is generally associated with high levels of perceived risk (e.g., physical loss from an accident, social loss from disapproval of friends, performance loss from bad functioning etc.). In such a case, the individual is likely to have high exit barriers and would prefer to buy the same brand (e.g. a Ford) every time or one of a few select brands (e.g., one or more Ford, GM or Toyota). Using this reasoning, the following hypotheses can be stated:

Hypothesis 1:   *Overall perceived risk will be positively related to brand commitment for the product class.*

Hypothesis 2:   *The six categories of risk will be positively related to brand commitment for the product class.*

Enduring importance for a product is felt when the product is related to central needs and values of the individual. In such cases, the importance for the product class arises from the inherent ability of the product to satisfy the consumers' intrinsic needs and while specific purchase and usage goals may increase the importance level still further, temporarily during purchase, these are not essential to the inherent importance of the product class to the consumer (Bloch & Richins, 1983). This perception of enduring importance or personal relevance is likely to translate into strong cognitive and affective associations with one or a few particular brands within the product class. For example, a wine connoisseur with very high enduring importance for wines is likely to favor certain particular brands of wines strongly, particularly those which have favorable past associations for him/her. As a result, he/she is likely to buy and consume the same brands repeatedly. Thus, brand commitment is likely to be high for such individuals for that particular product class.

Alternatively, for products with low enduring importance, few consumers are likely to exhibit loyalty. In cases where there is low situational importance and little differentiation among the brands within the product category (e.g., salt or other commodity-like products), the consumers are likely to have many brands within their evoked set (Martin & Goodell, 1991). Alternatively, for low enduring importance product classes where there is considerable instrumental involvement because of various situational factors, the consumers are likely to search extensively and pick from a large number of brands. Thus, in both cases, brand commitment is likely to be less.

This argument can also be justified within the framework of *social judgment theory* (Sherif & Cantril, 1947). Greater enduring importance is associated with narrower latitudes of acceptance and non-commitment and wider latitudes of rejection in this theory. As a result, assuming that the different brands are randomly located within the whole domain of the consumer's preferences, greater enduring importance is likely to result in fewer acceptable brands and consequently, greater brand commitment. On the basis of this reasoning, the following hypothesis can be stated: commitment[1].

Hypothesis 3:   Enduring importance will be positively related to brand commitment for the product class.

These hypotheses provide a framework for conceptualizing the relationship of brand commitment with both perceived risk and enduring importance at the level of the product class.

RESEARCH METHODOLOGY

To examine the preceding hypotheses, primary data were collected because of the lack of appropriate secondary data availability. The data were collected using electronic-mail, possible due to recent advances in technology and rapid proliferation of this facility. Electronic-mail (e-mail) uses computer text-editing and communication tools to provide high-speed message service over the Internet. Some important characteristics of e-mail which make it an attractive data-collection device for consumer research are speed of response, reduced costs of sending and receiving surveys, possibility of asynchronous communication between the researcher and the respondent(s) and the absence of intermediaries (Sproull, 1986).

Measurement

Standard scales were used to measure the constructs of perceived risk, enduring importance and brand. This gave assurance of previously tested validity and reliability and reduced the time for questionnaire construction and pre-testing. While early studies of perceived risk relied on single measures for each risk dimension, later studies favor the use of multiple measures for each dimension (Stone & Grönhaug, 1993). For the present study, each risk dimension was measured using multiple items and separate measures were used for the measurement of the overall risk. The scale used was similar to that used by Stone & Grönhaug (1993).

Items from the *Components of Involvement (CI) scale* (Lastovicka and Gardner, 1979) were used to measure enduring importance and brand commitment. Items pertaining to using the product for self-expression, attaining an ideal type of life etc. were used to measure enduring importance while brand commitment was measured using items evaluating the adherence to a particular brand under different circumstances. The constructs were measured at the level of the product class and the items chosen could be applied across product classes since the CI scale is not product-specific. Previous work has shown these items to have adequate levels of content, convergent and discriminant validity (Lastovicka & Gardner, 1979, Jensen et al., 1988).

Products

Several different product classes were chosen to incorporate heterogeneity in terms of different levels of felt risk as well as enduring importance. A pre-test was carried out in which thirteen subjects, all graduate students, were asked to rate several different

---

[1]The questionnaire used in the study can be obtained from the author on request.

TABLE 1
Regression models for overall perceived risk

Dependent variable: Brand Commitment

Variable	All products	Laptop Computer	Color Television	Greeting Card	Can of Soup
Overall Risk (Standardized regression coeff.)	- 0.1954	-0.5974	-0.1559	-0.1398	0.2232
t-value and significance of coefficient	-1.666 (0.1001)	-2.885 (0.0113)	-0.6110 (0.5502)	-0.5470 (0.5926)	0.9980 (0.3309)

products on the dimensions of importance and cost. Four products were chosen on the basis of these evaluations, to allow the hypotheses to be tested for different levels of risk and importance. The product classes chosen included laptop computer, color television, greeting card for spouse's or friend's birthday and can of soup.

Data Collection

The data collection was carried out using a three-stage procedure. In the first stage, forty mailing lists were randomly chosen from all the *listserv mailing lists*[2]. In the second stage, in accordance with "netiquette," letters were sent to list-owners asking permission to post a short solicitation message on the list. Messages requesting list members interested in filling out surveys to respond along with a brief description of the study were sent to the 27 lists whose owners gave permission. Seventy-eight responses were received. In the third stage, entire surveys were sent to these respondents resulting in seventy-two completed surveys. The response rate[3] was 92.3%.

Respondent Characteristics

The respondents were almost equally distributed by gender. Of the 72 respondents, 38 (52.8%) were male and 34 (47.2%) female. The mean annual family income was $54,970 and the mean age was 34.7 years. The respondents belonged to several occupational categories, the major ones being 40 (55.56%) professionals, 17 (23.61%) graduate students and 10 (13.89%) faculty. No claim of representativeness is made for the sample used in the study because of the fairly homogeneous, high socio-economic status of the respondents. But since the research goal is synonymous to Calder et al.'s (1981) *theory testing*, the sample is appropriate for the present study.

---

[2]Mailing lists are groups of people sharing some common interests and communicating with each other by e-mail. A message sent to the mailing list server is distributed to all subscribed members of the mailing list.

[3]This response rate is not comparable to the conventional response rate reported for mail or telephone surveys since only people soliciting the questionnaire are considered as potential respondents.

FINDINGS

To test hypothesis 1, regressions were carried out with overall perceived risk as the independent variable. Table 1 lists the standardized regression coefficients for the "all products" model which included all four products as well as for the four individual product classes.

While regression coefficients for all models except the can of soup are negative, the p-values in table 1 indicate that the regression coefficient is significant only for laptop computer at the (=0.05 level of significance. As a result, the analysis indicates that brand commitment decreases as overall perceived risk increases for laptop computer while no relationship is found for other product classes. Thus in general, support is not found for hypothesis 1 and there is some evidence to suggest that an opposite relationship may exist.

Hypothesis 2 was tested by obtaining models with the six dimensions of risk as the independent variables with brand commitment as the dependent variable. Because many coefficients were not significant, a step-wise procedure using a cut-off value of (=0.05 was used to obtain parsimonious models in each case. The results from this step-wise regression procedure for the all-product as well as for the four individual products are provided in table 2.

Social risk is found to be a highly significant predictor of brand commitment for the "all-product" model. Financial risk predicts brand commitment for the product class of laptop computers while psychological risk is important in predicting brand commitment for color televisions. It is interesting to note that different dimensions of perceived risk play a role in predicting the brand commitment for different product classes. In general, brand commitment is found to decrease as the level of the risk component increases, contrary to expectations. Thus, support is not found for hypothesis 2. In general, the conclusion drawn is that the analysis provides some evidence of reduction in brand commitment as the level of perceived risk increases.

To test hypothesis 3, regression models were run with enduring importance as the independent variable. Table 3 presents the models for all products as well as for individual product classes. The enduring importance coefficient is negative for all models and significant for the "all products" model as well as for the laptop computer. In general for all products, brand commitment decreases as the level of enduring importance for the product class increases. This is contrary to the relationship predicted in hypothesis 3. As a result, hypothesis 3 must be rejected. Interaction models including

TABLE 2
Step-wise multiple regressions with six risk dimensions

Dependent variable: Brand Commitment

Variable	All products	Laptop Computer	Color Television	Greeting Card	Can of Soup
Finance Risk	—	-0.5143 (0.0347)	—	—	—
Psychological Risk	—	—	-0.5087 (0.037)	—	—
Social Risk	-0.3327[a] (0.0043)[b]	—	—	—	—
R^2 with significant risk components only	0.1107	0.2645	0.2587	—	—
R^2 with all six components of risk	0.1322	0.3156	0.3796	0.3721	0.2705

[a] - The values given are standardized regression coefficients.
[b] - Figures in parentheses are p-values.

TABLE 3
Regression models for enduring importance

Dependent variable: Brand Commitment

Variable	All products	Laptop Computer	Color Television	Greeting Card	Can of Soup
Enduring Importance (Standardized regression coeff.)	-0.4519	-0.5816	-0.2806	-0.3167	-0.176
t-value and significance of coefficient	-4.238 (0.0001)	-2.769 (0.0143)	-1.132 (0.2753)	-1.293 (0.2156)	-0.779 (0.4453)
R^2	0.2043	0.3383	0.0788	0.1002	0.0319

the overall risk, enduring importance and the interaction term were also run for all five cases. The interaction term was not found to be significant in any of the models, suggesting that overall risk and enduring importance do not impact each other's effect on brand commitment.

DISCUSSION

In general, the results suggest that greater levels of perceived risk and enduring importance result in lower brand commitment. These results challenge some of the existing notions about brand commitment and also suggest the need for additional work. In general, support is not found for the argument of brand commitment as a risk reduction strategy in the face of high levels of perceived risk. On the contrary, the findings suggest that when the product class is perceived as having high overall risk, consumers search for more information and include more brands within their consideration set. This is consistent with Capon and Burke's (1980) finding that greater perceived risk results in greater attribute-based processing about different brands. In contrast, consumers are more likely to be loyal to one or a few brands when the risk associated with the product-class is low. This has significant implications for advertising strategy, suggesting that for high perceived-risk products, companies should focus on providing price reductions, sales and other promotions, and use comparative advertising to emphasize advantages of the company's brand over competitors. This finding therefore provides support to the strategies commonly adopted by furniture retailers, mattress manufacturers etc., of frequent promotions and comparative advertising. In contrast, companies marketing low perceived-risk products should focus on high repetition of the advertising message to reinforce brand efficacy without mention of specific competitors.

While this study has evaluated the overall perceived risk and its dimensions from a "degree of risk" context, the differential impact of the severity of adverse consequences and the probability of adverse consequences on brand commitment is not clear. Future studies must address this issue to better understand the relationship between perceived risk and brand commitment.

Another surprising and non-intuitive finding of the study is that normative or enduring importance for a product class is negatively related to the level of brand commitment felt for the product. In essence, when a product class is intimately linked to a person's goals, values and motives (self-knowledge), he/she is found to be less loyal to one or a few brands within that product class. Conceptual and empirical work on consumer expertise is useful in providing an explanation for this finding. High enduring importance with the product class is generally associated with greater consumer expertise, i.e., "ability to perform product-related tasks successfully" (Alba & Hutchinson, 1987). In their scale-development procedure, Lastovicka & Gardner (1979) find product familiarity to be one dimension of product involvement. Work on cognitive product structures of expert consumers suggests that the category structure is more veridical, complex and less stereotyped for experts than for novices (Adelson, 1984; Murphy & Wright, 1984), allowing more brands to be included within the consumer's evoked set. Experts are aware of both prototypical and atypical brands within the product class in contrast to novice consumers who know only prototypical brands (Nenungadi & Hutchinson, 1985). In a recent empirical study, Johnson and Lehmann (1996) found that as consumer expertise grows, consideration sets become larger through the assimilation of relatively atypical alternatives into a set of more prototypical alternatives. Further, empirical work suggests that experts tend to cluster brands together in memory so that all brands are recalled together when needed (Hutchinson, 1983). These characteristics of experts suggest that consumers with high enduring importance and expertise are likely to have larger consideration and evoked sets and consequently exhibit lower commitment to one or more brands. Thus, conceptualizing high-enduring importance consumers as experts, an explanation is found for the apparently anomalous finding. The natural extension to this research is verifying this conceptual link between high enduring importance and consumer expertise empirically.

Research on collecting behavior of consumers also helps to explain this relationship in certain contexts. While collecting is specialized and limited to some high enduring-importance consumers, it results in gathering objects belonging to a particular product category, where the entire set or collection of objects has an extraordinary meaning and intrinsic value, greater than the sum of the individual objects (Belk, 1982). Diversity and breadth of the objects in the collection is often an important goal for the consumer (Belk et al., 1991). In such cases, the collector is likely to focus on brands or types within the product category that he/she does not possess, resulting in no or even negative brand commitment. An important research topic for the future is the examination of brand attitudes and commitment for collectors in a longitudinal manner.

Another implicit assumption made in this study is that risk perceptions and importance pertaining to a product class are more or less stable. It would be interesting to determine the effect of situational perceived risk as well as instrumental importance perceptions on the level of brand commitment felt during the purchase situation. Knowledge of this relationship is likely to have significant implications for advertising message presentation, in-store display design etc.

CONCLUSIONS

The study provides rich insights into the complexity of the brand commitment phenomenon. There is some evidence of a negative relationship of brand commitment with overall perceived risk and its components while there is stronger evidence of a negative relationship with enduring importance associated with a product class. In general, these findings clarify the relationship between the constructs and challenge some existing notions. Existing research on consumer expertise and collecting behavior is useful in providing an explanation for the findings. Several avenues for future research are suggested with the objective of further understanding the nature and implications of brand commitment.

REFERENCES

Adelson, Beth (1984), "When Novices Surpass Experts: The Difficulty of a Task May Increase with Expertise," *Journal of Experimental Psychology: Learning, Memory and Cognition*, 10, July, 483-495.

Alba, Joseph W. and J. Wesley Hutchinson (1987), "Dimensions of Consumer Expertise," Journal of Consumer Expertise," *Journal of Consumer Research*, 13, 4, 411-454.

Bauer, Raymond (1960), "Consumer Behavior as Risk-taking," in R.Hancock (Ed.) *Dynamic Marketing for a changing world: Proceedings of the 43rd Conference of the American MarketingAssociation*, 389-398.

Beatty, Sharon E., Lynn R. Kahle and Pamela Homer (1988), "The Involvement-Commitment Model: Theory and Implications," *Journal of Business Research*, 16, 2, 149-167.

Becker, Howard S. (1960), "Notes on the Concept of Commitment," *American Journal of Sociology*, 66, 1, July, 32-40.

Belk, Russell W. (1982), "Acquiring, Possessing and Collecting: Fundamental Processes in Consumer Behavior," in Ronald F. Bush and Shelby J. Hunt (Eds.), *Marketing Theory: Philosophy of Science Perspectives*, Chicago, IL: American Marketing Association, 185-190.

Belk, Russell W., Melanie Wallendorf, John F. Sherry Jr., and Morris B. Holbrook (1991), "Collecting in a Consumer Culture," in Russell W. Belk (ed.), *Highways and Buyways: Naturalistic Research from the Consumer Behavior Odyssey*, Provo, UT: Association for Consumer Research, 178-215.

Bettman, James R. (1973), "Perceived Risk and its Components: A Model and Empirical Test," *Journal of Marketing Research*, 10, May, 184-190.

Bloch, Peter H. and Marsha L. Richins (1983), "A Theoretical Model for the Study of Product Importance Perceptions," *Journal of Marketing*, 47, 69-81.

Bloch, Peter H., Daniel L. Sherrell and Nancy M. Ridgway (1986), "Consumer Search: An Extended Framework," *Journal of Consumer Research*, 13, 1, 119-126.

Calder, Bobby J., Lynn W. Philips and Alice M. Tybout (1981), "Designing Research for Application," *Journal of Consumer Research*, 8, 2, 197-207.

Capon, Noel and Marian Burke (1980), "Individual, Product-class and Task-related Factors in Consumer Information Processing, *Journal of Consumer Research*, 7, December, 314-326.

Carman, James M. (1970), "Correlates of Brand Loyalty: Some Positive Results," *Journal of Marketing Research*, 7, February, 67-76.

Cunningham, Scott (1967), "Perceived Risk and Brand Loyalty," in D. Cox (Ed.) *Risk-taking and Information Handling in Consumer Behavior*, Boston, MA: Harvard University Press, 507-523.

Day, George (1969), "A Two-dimensional Concept of Brand Loyalty," *Journal of Advertising Research*, 9, September, 29-35.

Derbaix, C. (1983), "Perceived Risk and Risk Relievers: An Empirical Investigation," *Journal of Economic Psychology*, March, 3, 1, 19-38.

Dowling, Grahame R. (1986), "Perceived Risk: The Concept and its Measurement," *Psychology and Marketing*, 3, 193-210.

Emmelhainz, Margaret A., James R. Stock and Larry M. Emmelhainz (1991), "Consumer Responses to Retail Stock-outs," *Journal of Retailing*, 67, Summer, 138-147.

Engel, James and Roger Blackwell (1982), *Consumer Behavior*, Fourth Edition, Chicago, IL: Dryden Press.

Hupfer, Nancy T. and David M. Gardner (1971), "Differential Involvement with Products and Issues: An Exploratory Study," in D. Gardner (Ed.), *Proceedings: 2nd Annual Conference of ACR*, College Park, MD: Association of Consumer Research, 262-270.

Hutchinson, J. Wesley (1983), "Expertise and the Structure of Free Recall," in *Association for Consumer Research, Volume 11*, Eds. Richard P. Bagozzi and Alice M. Tybout, Ann Arbor, MI: Association for Consumer Research, 585-589.

Jacoby, Jacob and Robert W. Chestnut (1978), *Brand Loyalty: Measurement and Management*, New York, NY: John Wiley & Son.

Jensen, Thomas D., Les Carlsson and Carolyn Tripp (1989), "The Dimensionality of Involvement: An Empirical Test," in M. Wallendorf and P. Anderson (Eds.), *Advances in Consumer Research*, Provo, UT: The Association of Consumer Research, 680-689.

Johnson, Michael D. and Donald R. Lehmann (1996), "Consumer Experience and Consideration Sets for Brands and Product Categories," *1996 ACR Conference*, forthcoming.

Johnson, Michael P. (1973), "Commitment: A Conceptual Structure and Empirical Application," *The Sociological Quarterly*, 14, 3, Summer, 395-406.

Kaplan, Leon B., George Szybillo and Jacob Jacoby (1974), "Components of Perceived Risk in Product Purchase: A Cross-Validation," *Journal of Applied Psychology*, 59, 3, 287-291.

Krugman, Herbert E. (1965), "The Impact of Television Advertising: Learning Without Involvement," *Public Opinion Quarterly*, 29, 349-356.

Laaksonnen, Pirjo (1994), *Consumer Involvement: Concepts and Research*, London: Routledge.

Lastovicka, John L. and David M. Gardner (1979), "Components of Involvement," in J. C. Maloney and B. Silverman (Eds.), *Attitude Research Plays for High Stakes*, Chicago, IL: American Marketing Association, 53-73.

Martin, Charles L. and Phillips N. Goodell (1991), "Historical, Descriptive and Strategic Perspectives on the Construct of Product Commitment," *European Journal of Marketing*, 25, 1, 53-60.

Muncy, James A. and Shelby D. Hunt (1984), "Consumer Involvement: Definitional Issues and Research Directions," in T. Kinnear (Ed.), *Advances in Consumer Research*, Provo, UT: Association for Consumer Research, 11, 193-196.

Murphy, Gregory L. and Jack C. Wright (1984), "Changes in Conceptual Structure with Expertise: Differences Between Real-World Experts and Novices," *Journal of Experimental Psychology: Learning, Memory and Cognition*, 10, January, 144-155.

Nenungadi, Prakash and J. Wesley Hutchinson (1985), "The Prototypicality of Brands: Relationships with Brand Awareness, Preference and Usage," in *Advances in Consumer Research, Vol. 12*, Eds. Elizabeth C. Hirschman and Morris B. Holbrook, Provo, UT: Association for Consumer Research, 498-503.

Peter, J. Paul and Michael J. Ryan (1976), "An Investigation of Perceived Risk at the Brand Level," *Journal of Marketing Research*, 13, 5, 184-188.

Reichheld, Frederick F. (1996), *The Loyalty Effect: The Hidden Force Behind Growth, Profits and Lasting Value*, Boston: Harvard University Press.

Richins, Marsha, Peter H. Bloch and Edward McQuarrie (1992), "How Enduring and Situational Involvement Combine to Create Involvement Responses," *Journal of Consumer Psychology*, 1, 2, 143-153.

Robertson, Thomas (1976), "Low-commitment Consumer Behavior, *Journal of Advertising Research*, 16, April, 19-24.

Roselius, Ted (1971), "Consumer Ranking of Risk Reduction Methods," *Journal of Marketing*, 35, 1, 56-61.

Sherif, Muzafer and Hadley Cantril (1947), *The Psychology of Ego-Involvement*, New York, NY: Wiley and Son, Inc.

Sproull, Lee (1986), "Using Electronic Mail for Data Collection in Organizational Research," *Academy of Management Journal*, 29, 1, 159-169.

Stone, Robert N. and Kjell Gronhaug (1993), "Perceived Risk: Further Considerations for the Marketing Discipline," *European Journal of Marketing*, 27, 3, 31-50.

Traylor, Mark B. (1981), "Product Involvement and Brand Commitment," *Journal of Advertising Research*, 21, 6, December, 51-56.

Tyebjee, Tyzoon T. (1979), "Refinement of the Involvement Concept: An Advertising Planning Point of View," in J. C. Maloney and B. Silverman (Eds.), *Attitude Research Plays for High Stakes*, Chicago, IL: American Marketing Association, 94-111.

Zaltman, Gerald and Melanie Wallendorf (1983), *Consumer Behavior: Basic Findings and Management Implications*, New York, NY: John Wiley & Son.

Noneconomic Motivations for Price Haggling: An Exploratory Study

Michael A. Jones, University of Alabama
Philip J. Trocchia, University of Alabama
David L. Mothersbaugh, University of Alabama

ABSTRACT

It is assumed that consumers' primary motivation to price haggle is to obtain a better dollar value for their purchases. This study, however, explores nonfinancial reasons for consumers to price haggle. From depth interviews, we found that consumers may fulfill three primary needs when haggling over price. These are the needs for achievement, affiliation, and dominance. The paper provides implications for retailers and areas for future study.

Consumers often haggle over price and features in a variety of shopping contexts including appliances, furniture, automobiles, and homes (Evans and Beltramini 1987; Vaccaro and Coward 1993). Attaining better dollar value for their purchases appears to be a primary bargaining motive. However, financial gain may not be sufficient to motivate bargaining behavior in the face of the many costs, both economic and psychological, that accompany the bargaining task (Evans and Beltramini 1987; Pruitt and Carnevale 1993). The importance of noneconomic factors in motivating shopping behaviors has been well-documented (Babin, Darden, and Griffin 1994; Tauber 1972; Westbrook and Black 1985). Noneconomic factors may also be important in motivating consumers to engage in bargaining. Sherry (1990, p. 26), for instance, states that the essence of bargaining "surely transcends...the satisfaction of mere economic gain." Increased awareness of these noneconomic motivations may be an important step for retailers in developing appropriate and effective pricing policies, promotional strategies, and salesforce training programs. Retailers who recognize these motivations may increase customer satisfaction by a) implementing optimal pricing policies for their particular clientele, b) promoting the benefits of negotiated pricing policies, and c) altering salesforce behaviors in order to better address customer motivations. We examined the noneconomic motives for consumer price haggling by conducting a series of in-depth interviews with persons who had recently engaged in the process of price bargaining.

BACKGROUND

Haggling has traditionally been discussed in financial terms. Uchendu (1967, p. 37) defines haggling as a rational system of price formation "which aims at establishing particular prices for specific transactions, acceptable to both buyer and seller within the price range that prevails in the market." More recently, Kassaye (1990, p. 53) defined haggling as "an intricate behavior of give and take engaged by buyer and seller in an attempt to establish a price acceptable to both." Although it is clear from these definitions that people haggle over price, the current study examines the noneconomic motivations for consumers to bargain with salespersons.

Prior research has investigated the manner in which individual needs influence consumers' interpersonal orientations in the bargaining process (e.g., cooperative versus competitive), but has not investigated noneconomic benefits that might motivate consumers to bargain (Chaney and Vinacke 1960; Terhune 1968). For instance, Terhune (1968) designed a study in which subjects dominant in either the need for achievement, affiliation, or power played a series of Prisoner's Dilemma games. They found that these motives influenced subjects' behavior in the games. Individuals high in the need for achievement appeared most likely to cooperate while individuals high in the need for power were most likely to seek exploitation. However, since subjects were *required* to negotiate, the study only measured the bargaining strategies that subjects employed and the financial outcomes that resulted. As such, the subjects' motivations regarding whether or not they should bargain at all were not considered. Furthermore, while Rubin and Brown (1975) suggest that the personal needs for affiliation, achievement, and power influence bargaining behaviors (such as willingness to cooperate) and attitudes (such as interest in maximizing financial gain), the effects of these needs on individuals' motivations to bargain were not addressed. Likewise, neither Pruitt (1981), Pruitt and Carnevale (1993), nor Neale and Bazerman (1985), in their comprehensive reviews of negotiation studies, addressed nonfinancial motives for persons to engage in bargaining behaviors.

METHOD

Depth interviews were chosen as the data collection method. According to Strauss (1990), such qualitative methods are appropriate when (a) attempting to uncover what lies behind any phenomena about which little is known and (b) seeking to provide intricate details of phenomena that are difficult to convey with quantitative methods. Additionally, depth interviews are thought to provide more flexibility than the conventional questionnaire approach (Patton 1990) and have been used in numerous consumer studies seeking to understand motivations (cf., Hirschman 1992; Otnes, Lowery, and Kim 1993). We included multiple stage data collection, which was iterative and guided by an emergent design (Lincoln and Guba 1985). As such, the structure of the interview guide changed based on the results of previous interviews. As the interviews progressed, greater attention was focused on emergent themes.

A purposeful sampling technique was employed. This technique selects information-rich cases whose study will provide a comprehensive understanding of the issues (Patton 1990). In the current study, we interviewed individuals who bargained over a substantial purchase within the last two years. In addition, we sought to interview a subset of individuals who either enjoyed to bargain or considered themselves to be particularly good bargainers. Of 38 interviews conducted, 16 fit into this subset. Confidentiality to all participants was assured in order to aid open and honest discussion on the part of the informants.

DATA GATHERING AND ANALYSIS

Each formal interview lasted between 30 and 90 minutes and was audiotaped. A verbatim transcript of each audiotaped interview was produced. Significant ideas and findings were identified in the margins of each interview transcript. The ideas and findings were categorized by content. These categories developed into themes, because they (a) appeared many times, and/or (b) appeared infrequently but carried important analytical impact (Ely, Anzul, Friedman, Garner, and Steinmertz 1992).

In order to ensure accuracy in the interviews, investigator triangulation was employed. This technique involves the use of multiple researchers to study the same research questions (Denzin and Lincoln 1994). Member checks were also conducted after all interviews were completed (Celsi, Rose and Leigh 1993; Denzin and Lincoln 1994). First, all informants were delivered copies of their interview transcripts. They were asked to state whether any remark had been misquoted, and were encouraged to add any comments they felt would enhance the clarity of their previous thoughts. Second, key informants were asked to respond to a series of written follow-up questions based on information received in subsequent interviews with other participants. Third, emergent themes were presented to several key informants and asked if the quotes attributed to them were taken in the proper context of their earlier statements.

RESULTS AND DISCUSSION

The interviews yielded a rich body of data in which several themes emerged. After identifying these themes, it became apparent that the "trio of needs" theory provides an excellent framework for understanding and discussing consumers' bargaining motives. Psychologists believe that a trio of basic human social needs can be used in explaining the fundamentals of human behavior (Carlson 1990; Schiffman and Kanuk 1994; Terhune 1968). This trio includes the needs for (a) achievement, (b) dominance, and (c) affiliation. It was evident from the results of our interviews that consumer motives for engaging in bargaining behaviors clearly fit into the previously discussed trio of needs; the act of bargaining helps some individuals to satisfy these underlying needs. The following discussion defines these needs and demonstrates their importance in precipitating consumer bargaining behavior.

Need for Achievement

Murray (1938) states that the need for achievement manifests itself when individuals want to accomplish difficult tasks, overcome obstacles, attain high personal standards, and surpass others. Further, individuals who possess a high need for achievement attempt to accomplish difficult tasks as well and as quickly as possible. They also tend to be more self-confident and enjoy taking calculated risks. From our interviews, we uncovered two ways in which the need for achievement manifests itself in bargaining situations: (a) attaining high personal standards and (b) surpassing others.

Attaining High Personal Standards. Some individuals have a need to do everything well. For these people, bargaining behaviors are a manifestation of this need. The feelings that these consumers derive from bargaining are similar to the "smart-shopper feelings" introduced by Schindler (1989). Schindler states that the excitement felt by some consumers when paying a low price is a function of their ego-expressive needs. Similarly, Holbrook, Chestnut, Oliva, and Greenleaf (1984) found that paying a low price on a particular item might lead a consumer to feel proud, smart, or competent. Bargaining can also generate these good feelings. Some consumers generate these feelings by accomplishing the goal of price reduction by using their agent, topic, and persuasion knowledge in a beneficial way (Friestad and Wright 1994). Consistent with these thoughts, Sherry (1990, p. 26) states the following: "...dickering is linked...to feelings of competence and mastery." These feelings are evident in the following example.

Interviewer: So how do you feel about yourself [when you bargain]?
Informant: I feel good about myself for doing it because I'm doing what I've been taught to do. I'm applying my business skills to my personal financial life.

Other consumers attempt to satisfy this need for achievement by working hard for what they believe is right. These individuals, when faced with the feeling that a retailer is trying to take advantage of them, attempt to seek justice by dickering with the merchant. The following response indicates these feelings.

"...kind of the innate sense of what's right-not getting ripped off. It's not so much the $15 that you're going to get on the dress, it's knowing that they don't need to be charging that for that. It's like 'who do you think you're fooling?' This is not worth that. I don't want to pay that."

Surpassing Others. One outlet in which consumers may demonstrate their superiority is through communicating their expert bargaining skills to others. One informant stated that she asked friends how much they paid for their cars in an attempt to "flaunt" the superior deal she received. Another informant provided a similar sentiment.

"Quite a few guys who had [Ford] Probes asked me how I got it for that ...whenever I buy a new car I carefully remove the sticker from my window and I photocopy it and keep it in my folder. So the guys who bought the same thing... they say they paid more than what I paid."

Some people bargain because they enjoy competition and are determined to win. These individuals often view their participation in bargaining transactions as if they were playing a game. One informant, for instance, equated bargaining with playing poker. As such, he stated that automobile salespeople usually ask him to reveal the price that he is willing to pay. He equated this to "showing his hand" in poker. The following quotations indicate the concept of bargaining as a game in which one participant wins at the expense of his opponent. The first informant expresses the feeling of satisfaction that he derives from winning (or surpassing the competition); the second appears disconsolate when describing the act of paying full price. He equates this to losing (or being surpassed).

"Partly the enjoyment of it [bargaining] is winning the game. Part of the enjoyment is the pleasure that it gives...There is the thrill of victory as well as the 'I saved twenty dollars'...In most cases the pleasure is more the motivation [than the price savings]—just for the satisfaction of winning. That is why people with a lot of money still do it."

"It's like a game...It's just that feeling that you lost the game [when you pay full price]. Even if you come away with the product you wanted, and you could afford it, you lost the game."

Another informant indicated her pride in "defeating" the auto dealership from which she recently purchased her car. The informant happily related to us that, due to her tough bargaining stance, the salesperson told her at the conclusion of negotiations, *"We don't want to see you around here anymore."*

Need for Dominance

The need for dominance (also referred to as the need for power) relates to an individual's need or desire to control his or her environment (Murray 1938). According to Schiffman and Kanuk

(1994, p. 116), "Many individuals experience increased self-esteem when they exercise power over objects or people." The notion that some people bargain in order to feel a sense of power was evident in a number of our interviews. For some, victory in bargaining is viewed as a sign of virility. One informant, for instance, regarded the desire to haggle as a "macho" characteristic, reflecting an exhilarating feeling of power or strength. Similarly, others express a need to dominate their environments through the use of war as a metaphor for their bargaining experiences.

War. Some individuals who are seeking to satisfy their need for power consider bargaining as a war against the salesperson or business. Unlike the informants who expressed the act of bargaining in terms of a friendly game, these individuals revealed an open hostility toward their salesperson "adversary." Consider the strong emotions expressed by this informant.

> "*My attitude toward car dealerships is they're out to screw me. I'm not going to go in there and be a jellyfish—a sponge for those people to take advantage of me. They've left a bad taste in my mouth. From now on, I'm going to battle. My attitude toward buying a car is more like a fight...A one price policy would mean I automatically lost the fight.*"

Control. Informants also expressed a need for dominance in terms of a desire to control their environments. Bargaining is one venue in which these individuals can satisfy this need. These informants' high need for control can be seen in the following passages:

> "*I seize control. I turn the tables and seize control. I have the money. He [the salesman] wants the money so I make the offer. I determine what I'm going to offer for it. Now if he is unwilling to do that, then I walk out.*"

> "*I like being able to be in control of things...I would say that it plays into my sense of wanting to control the negotiation—to control the situation in other words. As long as you are in control, I think you live with the outcome a lot better no matter what it is.*"

> "*The other thing, too, is you've got to get to someone who can make a decision [referring to the manager]. You explain what the situation is.*"

Need for Affiliation

Individuals who are seeking to satisfy their need for affiliation attempt to develop friendships and seek acceptance and belonging from others (Murray 1938). The act of bargaining can play an important role in fulfilling consumers' needs for affiliation. Informants expressed a need for affiliation with three types of audiences. These audiences included (1) the individuals with whom they negotiate such as salespeople, (2) invited purchase pals, including friends and family, and (3) significant others who may or may not be physically present during negotiations.

Company Representatives/Salespeople. Many informants expressed concern with what salespeople think of them. These individuals feel as if salespeople expect customers to bargain and will form negative evaluations of them if they fail to bargain. By engaging in negotiations, they believe that they are more likely to find acceptance by sales personnel. This desire for acceptance was evident in the following response.

> "*If I don't bargain, those salespeople will laugh at me when I leave because I paid full price.*"

Purchase Pals. Some individuals bring along friends whom they believe to be effective negotiators in order to assist them in their bargaining. Previous literature has identified such assistants as "purchase pals" (Bell 1967). A number of our informants expressed fond memories of their bargaining experiences with purchase pals. These life experiences produced a sort of "bonding" between friends. The following interview excerpt provides an example.

> "*I had a friend with me who was kind of my guide who came along with me and helped me bargain. It was my first purchase of a car. My friend had purchased cars before and basically knew a little about cars. He'd been through the process. He kind of knew what to look for. He could tell if some cars had been in accidents or had work done. Personally, I didn't know what to look for. He went so they wouldn't take advantage of me. Like he knew what was wrong with the car and he talked the price down...It was nice having him around to help me.*"

Significant Others. Some people engage in bargaining behaviors in order to be viewed more positively by friends and family. They feel that negotiating over price is a socially desirable practice. These informants expressed such concerns.

> "*I was able to play 'Big Man Daddy' in front of my daughters. And they were being impressed. In a way I was putting on a show. And you know daughters, they just think you're wonderful anyway and when they see you telling the dealer you're not going to pay that much money and I can remember telling Barbara, "We'll just let them squirm for a bit."*"

> "*[I bargain because I] want to say that I got a good deal on that car. I want to be thought of as a person that wouldn't throw away her money and doesn't waste money. It's more appealing to be thrifty and to spend money wisely.*"

SUMMARY AND IMPLICATIONS

A plethora of studies have investigated the subject of negotiation. To our knowledge, however, no study has considered the noneconomic motivations that consumers have to engage in retail bargaining. These noneconomic motives can be classified using three basic human social needs: the needs for achievement, dominance, and affiliation. Of those who bargained for noneconomic reasons, some informants seemed motivated to bargain in order to satisfy only one particular need. For other consumers, however, bargaining served to fulfill multiple needs. Clearly, our results indicate that, to some consumers, bargaining is more than just a "necessary evil."

Implications for marketing managers are numerous. Since some consumers receive noneconomic benefits from bargaining, retail managers and manufacturers should carefully consider their decision before implementing and promoting a "no haggle" policy. Some consumers who buy goods and services without the opportunity to negotiate may be less satisfied with their purchase experiences. Salesforce behaviors should therefore be modified to reflect these customer needs. For instance, a salesperson who can recognize and react to his client's need for dominance can alter his sales presentation by yielding on particular issues. From a promotional standpoint, advertising may reflect the need for achievement by promoting consumers' sense of victory that they associate with successful bargaining.

Future research should investigate the characteristics of individuals who derive the greatest satisfaction from bargaining. These characteristics might include demographic, personality, and cultural variables. Future studies should also investigate the importance of each of the trio of needs as they relate to bargaining. For instance, is the need for achievement the primary motive for most consumers to engage in bargaining? If so, does it supersede the other motives? Research should also address the issue of consumer attitudes toward bargaining. How do different types of consumers feel about the bargaining process in general?

We believe that this emergent research stream can provide valuable insights to practitioners who are interested in maximizing their customers' shopping enjoyment. Given the lack of attention in the consumer literature regarding individuals' motivations to bargain, we believe that this exploratory study provides a useful starting point for future academic research.

REFERENCES

Babin, Barry J., William R. Darden, and Mitch Griffin (1994), "Work and/or Fun: Measuring Hedonic and Utilitarian Shopping Value," *Journal of Consumer Research*, 20 (March), 644-656.

Bell, Gerald D. (1967), "Self Confidence and Persuasion in Car Buying," *Journal of Marketing*, 4 (February), 46-52.

Carlson, Neil R. (1990), *Psychology: The Science of Behavior*, Boston: Allyn and Bacon.

Celsi, Richard L., Randall L. Rose, and Thomas W. Leigh (1993), "An Exploration of High Risk Leisure Consumption Through Skydiving," *Journal of Consumer Research*, 20 (June), 1-23.

Chaney, Marilyn V. and W. Edgar Vinacke (1960), "Achievement and Nurturance in Triads Varying in Power Distribution," *Journal of Abnormal and Social Psychology*, 60 (2), 175-181.

Denzin, Norman and Yvonna S. Lincoln (1994), *Handbook of Qualitative Research*, Thousand Oaks, CA: Sage Publications.

Ely, Margot, Margaret Anzul, Teri Friedman, Diane Garner, and Ann McCormack Steinmertz (1992), *Doing Qualitative Research: Circles within Circles*, London: The Falmer Press.

Evans, Kenneth R. and Richard F. Beltramini (1987), "A Theoretical Model of Consumer Negotiated Pricing: An Orientation Perspective," *Journal of Marketing*, 51 (April), 58-73.

Friestad, Marian and Peter Wright (1994), "The Persuasion Knowledge Model: How People Cope with Persuasion Attempts," *Journal of Consumer Research*, 21 (June), 1-31.

Hirschman, Elizabeth C. (1992), "The Consciousness of Addiction; Toward a General Theory of Compulsive Consumption," *Journal of Consumer Research*, 19 (September), 155-179.

Holbrook, Morris B., Robert B. Chestnut, Terence A. Oliva, and Eric A. Greenleaf (1984), "Play as a Consumption Experience: The Role of Emotions, Performance, and Personality in the Enjoyment of Games," *Journal of Consumer Research*, 11 (September), 728-739.

Kassaye, Wossen W. (1990), "The Role of Haggling in Marketing: An Examination of Buyer Behavior," *Journal of Consumer Marketing*, 7 (4), 53-62.

Lincoln, Yvonna S. and Egon Guba (1985), *Naturalistic Inquiry*, Newbury Park, CA: Sage Publications, Inc.

Murray, Henry. A. (1938), *Explorations in Personality*, New York: Oxford University Press.

Neale, Margaret A. and Max H. Bazerman (1985), "Perspectives for Understanding Negotiation," *Journal of Conflict Resolution*, 29 (March), 33-55.

Otnes, Cele, Tina M. Lowery, and Young Chan Kim (1993), "Gift Selection for Easy and Difficult Respondents: A Social Roles Interpretation," *Journal of Consumer Research*, 20 (September) 229-244.

Patton, Michael Q. (1990), *Qualitative Evaluation and Research Methods*, Newbury Park, CA: Sage Publications, Inc.

Pruitt, Dean G. (1981), *Negotiation Behavior*, New York: Academic Press.

_____ and Peter J. Carnevale (1993), *Negotiation in Social Conflict*, Pacific Grove, CA: Brooks/Cole.

Rubin, Jeffrey Z. and Bert R. Brown (1975), *The Social Psychology of Bargaining and Negotiation*, New York: Academic Press.

Schiffman, Leon G. and Leslie Lazar Kanuk (1994), *Consumer Behavior*, Englewood Cliffs, NJ: Prentice Hall.

Schindler, Robert M. (1989), "The Excitement of Getting a Bargain: Some Hypotheses Concerning the Origins and Effects of Smart-Shopper Feelings," in *Advances in Consumer Research*, Vol. 16, ed. Thomas K. Srull, Provo, UT: Association for Consumer Research, 447-453.

Schouten, John W. (1985), "Price Negotiation Among Retail Merchants: Who Dickers and Who Doesn't?," in *Advances in Consumer Research*, Vol. 14, eds. Melanie Wallendorf and Paul F. Anderson, Provo, UT: Association for Consumer Research, 576.

Sherry, John F., Jr. (1990), "A Sociocultural Analysis of a Midwestern Flea Market," *Journal of Consumer Research*, 17 (June), 13-30.

Strauss, Anselm (1990), *Qualitative Analysis for Social Scientist*, New York: Cambridge University Press.

Tauber, Edward M. (1972), "Why Do People Shop?," *Journal of Marketing*, 36 (October), 46-49.

Terhune, Kenneth (1968), "Motives, Situation, and Interpersonal Conflict Within Prisoner's Dilemma," *Journal of Personality and Social Psychology Monograph Supplement*, 8 (March), 1-24.

Uchendu, Victor C. (1967), "Some Principles of Haggling in Peasant Markets," *Journal of Economic Development and Cultural Change*, 16 (1), 37-50.

Vaccaro, Joseph P. and Derek W. F. Coward (1993), "Selling and Sales Management in Action: Managerial and Legal Implications of Price Haggling: A Sales Manager's Dilemma," *Journal of Personal Selling and Sales Management*, 3 (Summer), 79-86.

Westbrook, Robert A. and William C. Black (1985), "A Motivation - Based Shopper Typology," *Journal of Retailing*, 61 (1), 78-103.

Consumer Perceptions of Multi-Dimensional Prices

Hooman Estelami, Fordham University[1]

ABSTRACT

Multi-dimensional prices are prices which consist of multiple components–such as prices quoted in terms of the combination of monthly payments and number of payments–rather than a single lump-sum dollar amount. This paper investigates how consumers form their price perceptions of multi-dimensional prices. Using an information integration approach, results from a laboratory study indicate that under conditions typical of the market place, consumers do not evaluate multi-dimensional prices rationally. Instead they utilize a simplified model, resulting in inaccuracies in their price perceptions. Increasing the dimensionality of price is also found to result in price perception inaccuracies. Moreover, consumers are found to place a larger weight on the monthly payment amount than on the number of payments. These results have implications from both a marketing, and a policy-making point of view.

> "1995 Acura Integra ... $189 a month ... 36 months ... No down payment!"
>
> (Advertisement in the November 11, 1994 edition of the New York Times).

Offers like the one mentioned above are hard to avoid now a days. The drive to finance the ownership of products rather than to pay a single lump-sum payment has caused the media to literally become flooded with complex pricing schemes for products ranging from luxury automobiles to sneakers. For example, the automobile leasing business alone is expected to double in the next five years, and the purchase of 3 out of every 4 new cars sold today is financed (Business Week 1994). What is unique about prices such as the one mentioned above is their multi-dimensional nature–the fact that the price no longer consists of a single dollar amount (e.g., $15,395), but rather consists of multiple dimensions (e.g., monthly payment of $189, 36 monthly payments, and $0 down). As such, we will refer to these kinds of prices as "multi-dimensional prices" (MDP) in the balance of this paper.

One of the fundamental questions brought about by the wide presence of multi-dimensional prices is regarding the consumers' ability to appropriately evaluate them. Consumers are often bombarded with a large number of multi-dimensional prices through newspaper, TV, and radio ads, such as the one shown in Figure 1. For example, each Sunday issue of the New York Times (for the first 12 weeks of 1995) on the average featured over 65 MDP ads. Moreover, multi-dimensional prices communicated through TV and radio ads are typically included in a 15 to 30 second presentation, in conjunction with a large amount of non-price information, and for many product categories–such as household appliances, new automobiles, and telecommunication services–the dominant form of price quotation is MDP. In the case of new automobiles for example, over 70% of the advertised prices are in an MDP format.

Interestingly, the existing research on consumer price perceptions has had limited coverage of MDPs. Little is known about how consumers integrate the various components of an MDP. Meanwhile, MDPs may offer the firm the ability to increase consumer demand without dropping the effective price–for example by re-ducing the magnitude of one price dimension (e.g., monthly payments) and compensating for it in another dimension (e.g., number of months). MDPs are also relevant from a policy-making perspective, as they make inaccurate consumer price perceptions a very likely possibility. In this paper, we investigate how consumer price perceptions of multi-dimensional prices are formed. In specific, using an information integration approach, the paper studies the integration model used by consumers in consolidating the various dimensions of a multi-dimensional price. Findings from a laboratory study indicate that under conditions typical of the market place, consumers do not evaluate MDPs rationally. Instead they use a simplified integration model, resulting in inaccuracies in their price perceptions.

LITERATURE REVIEW

Pricing is perhaps the oldest research area in marketing. Interestingly, a review of three classic pricing books (Nagle and Holden 1995, Monroe 1990, DeVinney 1991), and Rao's (1993) pricing review indicates no specific references relevant to the topic of multi-dimensional pricing. However, what seems to exist in the current literature is evidence on consumer difficulty in evaluating complex prices. This evidence can be found in the works of Greenleaf, Morwitz and Johnson (1994), Gourville (1994) and the unit pricing literature, to be discussed below. Greenleaf, Morwitz and Johnson (1994) have proposed that breaking up the price of a product (for example by charging the tip as a separate item rather than incorporating it into the menu prices of a restaurant) reduces the consumer's price sensitivity. Since the objective value of the price is not affected by its division into different parts, from the perspective of classical economic theory, consumers should be indifferent to divided prices. Using a series of simulated shopping experiments, the authors demonstrated that divided prices are perceived as significantly less expensive, and produce stronger purchase intentions. Gourville (1994) has also found evidence for consumers' inability in dealing with complex prices. Gourville's work has primarily concentrated on the concept of pennies-a-day (PAD) pricing, whereby prices are framed in terms of the much smaller daily amounts rather than a large lump-sum dollar amount (e.g., "Support a starving third world child for *50 cents a day*" vs. "*$183 a year*"). Based on the concept of categorization (Mervis and Rosch 1981) and mental accounts (Thaler 1985), Gourville argues and demonstrates that in spite of objectively large dollar values associated with some transactions (e.g, $183 per year), PAD framing (e.g., 50 cents a day) can significantly reduce consumers' price sensitivity.

Both the works cited above seem to suggest that consumers have difficulty in evaluating prices when the presentation of the price is made more complex. Additional evidence on consumers' difficulty in coping with price complexity can be found in the unit pricing literature. For example, Russo (1977) studied consumers' utilization of unit price information in an actual field setting. He found that unless unit price information is made explicitly available, consumers are unlikely to estimate and utilize unit prices in their purchase decisions, thereby making sub-optimal purchases. Russo therefore concluded that information processing factors can drastically impact consumers' ability to process price information. Capon and Kuhn (1982) have also shown that when a product is offered in various package sizes at different price levels, consumers are highly inaccurate in identifying the "best buy". Moreover, their

[1]The author would like to thank Prof. Donald R. Lehamann for his helpful comments on earlier drafts of this paper.

FIGURE 1
Sample Multi-Dimensional Price Ad

study showed that this inaccuracy is not dependent on the level of education and training of the consumer. Other evidence relating to unit prices can be found in the widely practiced retail strategy of quantity surcharges (Nason and Della Bitta 1983, Widrick 1979). Quantity surcharges occur when a larger package of the same brand is more expensively priced (on a per unit basis) than a smaller package (Agrawal, Grimm and Srinivasan 1993). The frequent occurrence of quantity surcharges across many product categories (Cude and Walker 1984) seems to suggest that consumers are unable to conduct the mental arithmetic required to recognize that they may be paying a higher per-unit price for the larger size packages.

Parallel evidence to the above can be found in the area of bundling, which is primarily concerned with how consumers evaluate a product which itself is made of multiple sub-products. For example, Yadav (1994) has shown that in assessing the quality of a bundle, consumers utilize a process similar to anchoring and adjustment (Tversky and Kahneman 1974). They assess the quality of one component first (anchoring) and adjust their initial assessment based on subsequent assessments of the remaining components (adjustment). As a result of using the anchoring and adjustment heuristic, an additive integration rule best represents how consumers integrate the values of the individual components of a bundle (Gaeth et al. 1990). Therefore, as will be discussed below, similar heuristics and simplification strategies may be used by consumers when encountering multi-dimensional prices.

While the works cited above indicate that consumers have difficulty in dealing with complexity in prices, none of the existing research in pricing has investigated how consumers integrate the individual dimensions of price to form their price perceptions–the primary focus of this paper.

CONSUMER PRICE PERCEPTIONS OF MULTI-DIMENSIONAL PRICES

In this section of the paper, the characteristics of the integration model used by consumers to evaluate multi-dimensional prices is studied. From a rational point of view, certain price dimensions in an MDP need to be configurally (interactively) integrated into the consumers' price perceptions. For example, given a series of multi-dimensional prices made of monthly payments, number of pay-

ments and a down payment, there exists a rational pattern of price perceptions corresponding to the various MDPs. This pattern would have to be based on some mathematical principle which would arrive at the net offered price. In the case of the MDPs mentioned, the rational model, assuming no discounting, would be determined by multiplying the number of payments by the monthly payments and incrementing that by the down payment. What therefore characterizes the rational evaluation models for multi-dimensional prices is that certain price dimensions (e.g., monthly payments and number of payments) need to be configurally integrated into the consumer price perceptions. In other words, combined changes in each price dimension must create large shifts in consumer price perceptions. This configural evaluation of the price dimensions needs to take place either through direct numerical processing of the required arithmetic, or by an interactive utilization of the relevant price dimensions. In what follows, we examine literature which would provide insight on the likelihood of either of these two events taking place. It is argued that in the environments in which multi-dimensional prices are communicated to the consumer (e.g., through newspaper ads such as those shown in Figure 1, or TV and radio ads), the individual dimensions of an MDP are likely to be independently integrated into consumer price perceptions. Moreover, hypotheses on the relative weights of the price dimensions, and the effects of increasing price dimensionality on price perception accuracy are put forward.

Evidence from Cue Utilization Research

In order for a consumer to evaluate a multi-dimensional price, he/she must use the individual dimensions of the MDP as information cues in his/her judgements. Related works on human utilization of information cues seem to suggest that the most commonly used integration rule used to form human judgements is linear (Anderson 1981). Summarizing the results of the early works, Slovic (1972) concluded that when utilizing information, judges tend to use "only the information that is explicitly displayed in the stimulus object ... information that has to be stored in memory, inferred from the explicit display, or transformed tends to be discounted or ignored" (p. 14). Across a large variety of tasks, these studies indicate that the most prevalent form of cue integration by judges is linear. Complex curvilinear or configural (interactive) cue utilization strategies, although at times observed, are typically not undertaken by the majority of judges. Further work by Brehmer et al. (1980; experiments 4 and 5) has shown that linear integration in human judgements may persist even under conditions where the task instructions explicitly require the judges to configurally integrate the cues. As a result of using a linear integration model, information cues which from a normative point of view need to be configurally treated, are often independently integrated into human judgements. The primary reason for linear cue utilization is the limitations on human information processing abilities which force judges to use a simplifying heuristic when evaluating a multi-attribute alternative. Process tracing studies of human judgements have shown that when judging a multi-attribute alternative, judges tend to use a process much like the anchoring and adjustment heuristic of Tversky and Kahneman (1974; e.g., Lopes 1982, Russo and Dosher 1983). In this process, judges initially focus their attention on one particular attribute, and form an initial overall judgement based on the value of that attribute. They then proceed to examine the remaining attributes and adjust their overall judgement accordingly. The serial nature of the process therefore creates primacy in the judgements while also limiting the degree by which configural integration of attribute information can take place. As a result, there is a tendency for the individual attributes to be independently integrated into the overall judgement.

Birnbaum's Subtractive Theory

Additional evidence for independent integration of stimuli dimensions can be found in Birnbaum's (1978) Subtractive Theory of stimuli integration. For many continua, when people are asked to judge "ratios" and "differences" of stimuli, they appear to use only a subtractive operation regardless of the instructions. This phenomenon has been shown to exist for stimuli such as the loudness and pitch of tones (Elmasian and Birnbaum 1984), heaviness of weights (Mellers, Davis, and Birnbaum 1984), and darkness of dot patterns. Birnbaum's works suggests that when instructed to evaluate either the ratio or the difference between stimuli, in both cases subjects evaluate only the algebraic difference (i.e., subtraction) between subjective stimuli values. Therefore, their responses reflect the independent integration of the stimuli scale values into their judgements. The implication of Subtractive Theory on multi-dimensional price perceptions is that in cases where individual price dimensions need to be configurally treated, they may in fact be independently integrated into consumer price perceptions.

Evidence from Studies on Mental Arithmetic

If the consumer decides not to process the individual price dimensions of an MDP as qualitative judgement cues, he/she may instead proceed to numerically process the necessary arithmetics. Studies of human mental arithmetic processes have established that conducting mental arithmetic requires the retrieval of both declarative knowledge (e.g., multiplication tables) and procedural knowledge (e.g., multiplication algorithms) from long term memory (Groen and Parkman 1972). In conducting mental arithmetic, humans break down the original problem into a series of sub-problems, which are then serially solved. The execution of these sub-problems involves a series of steps which requires the temporary storage of the intermediate results, and as a consequence, the capacity for conducting multi-digit mental arithmetic problems required to evaluate most MDPs tends to be severely limited by the capacity to process and store information in short-term memory. Studies focusing specifically on the timing and effort required to conduct mental arithmetic have for example shown that conducting the mental arithmetic needed to evaluate a multi-dimensional price

(e.g., a 3-digit by 2-digit multiplication) is both time consuming and demanding, at times taking subjects well over 120 seconds to complete (Dansereau and Gregg 1966, Hitch 1978). The primary reason for the slow processing speed is the large number of arithmetic operations (e.g., hold, carry, add, etc.) associated with multi-digit arithmetics, which need to take place mentally, using the limited capacity of short-term memory. The timing results of these studies indicate that the length of time required to conduct the mental arithmetic associated with most MDPs may in fact far exceed the limited time period available to consumers (e.g., 15 to 30 seconds) when faced with the large number of MDPs they are bombarded with in the media on a daily basis. Moreover, studies focusing on the physiological effects of mental arithmetic processes have also shown that conducting mental arithmetic is an effective producer of physiological stress (e.g., Linden 1991, Caroll et al. 1986). In fact, in studies where physiological tension manipulations are required, mental arithmetic has been found to be one of the most reliable ways of creating cardiovascular change in subjects, increasing their oxygen consumption and raspatory rate (Turner and Caroll 1985, Seraganian et al. 1985, Levenson 1979). As a result, these studies suggest that conducting the mental arithmetic required to evaluate multi-dimensional prices may be a stressful task, which consumers may seek to avoid in order to avoid the associated physiological stress.

The above indicates that under circumstances typical of the environments in which MDPs are encountered, consumers may fail to numerically carry out the necessary mental arithmetics. Both Dawes et al. (1989) and the findings of Hoffman et al. (1987) indicate that in conducting many judgement tasks, judges tend to use the judgement cues as qualitative rather than quantitative (numerical) attributes. By doing so, judges ignore the necessary mental computations which need to take place. Dawes et al. (1989) believe this phenomenon to be due to the judges' overconfidence in their accuracy. Hammond et al. (1987) on the other hand, attribute judges' reluctance to explicitly use formulas to their fear of making mistakes when carrying out the necessary computations. In fact the later authors show that with increased time pressure and stimuli complexity, reliance on linear integration models increases. Based on the above arguments, it is therefore quite possible that consumers fail to account for the configural relationship between the price dimensions. We therefore hypothesize that:

H_1: Consumer perceptions of MDPs are formed by independently integrating each price dimension into the overall price perception.

Dominance of the Monthly Payments

If the consumers' perceptions of multi-dimensional prices are formed by integrating the price dimensions independently, as suggested by Hypothesis 1, an interesting question is whether consumers place more weight on one price dimension or another. For example, are consumers more sensitive to increases in the number of payments or the monthly payments? A budgetary perspective would suggest that the monthly payment dimension should be more critical than the number of payments in driving consumer perceptions of a multi-dimensional price. The monthly payments will in essence determine the amount of monthly budget that the consumer will have to allocate to the purchase. As a result, the monthly payment would directly impact the consumer's living standards throughout the payment period, and is therefore highly influential in a consumer's perception of an MDP. Thaler (1985), summarizing an unpublished 1982 field study concluded that: "the most relevant time horizon is the month since many regular bills tend to be monthly. Thus the budgeting process, either implicit or explicit, tends to occur on a month-to-month basis" (p. 207). We therefore conclude that:

> H_2: *The monthly payment dimension has a higher weight than the number of payments in driving consumer price perceptions of MDPs.*

Number of Dimensions in an MDP and Consumer Accuracy

One of the key concerns regarding multi-dimensional prices is that the existence of multiple price dimensions may have a negative influence on the 'processability' of the price and the resulting accuracy in consumer price perceptions. It is likely that as the number of price dimensions increase, evaluation of the objective (rational) value of multi-dimensional prices becomes more difficult to make.

Studies of mental arithmetic processes, cited earlier indicate that with increases in the number of dimensions in a multi-dimensional price, the number of arithmetic processes that need to take place mentally (e.g., add, carry, hold) would increase. Such an increase could in turn negatively impact consumers' price perception accuracy. Within the context of consumer decision making, a large body of literature showing the inverse relationship between the number of judgement cues and consumer accuracy also exists. For example, Jacoby (1976) has demonstrates that increasing the amount of information available to the consumer can in fact hinder the consumer's decision quality and force the consumer to make suboptimal choices. The work by Johnson and Payne (1985)–using simulation of choice processes–also concludes that stimuli complexity leads to choice sub-optimality. It is therefore proposed that:

> H_3: *Increasing the number of price dimensions in a multi-dimensional price will reduce the consumers' price perception accuracy.*

METHODOLOGY

In conducting this study, the approach of Anderson's (1981, 1982) information integration theory is adopted. In dozens of studies, Anderson and his colleagues have demonstrated the capability of information integration methods in revealing the underlying integration models used in human judgement tasks. The information integration approach has been used by Bettman, Capon and Lutz (1975) in studying models of product attitude formation and by Gaeth et al. (1991) in studying consumers' integration rule for judging the quality of product bundles, and has demonstrated its ability to detect complex integration models used by subjects (e.g., Stevenson 1986).

In the information integration approach, subjects are exposed to a factorial orientation of the stimuli under study (e.g., price dimensions), and their responses (e.g., price perceptions) to each profile are measured. The pattern of the subjects' responses will enable the researcher to determine the structure of the underlying integration model used to consolidate the individual stimuli dimensions. Typically, studies employing the information integration methodology have two main characteristics: (1) the use of within subject designs where each subject is run through a factorial orientation of the stimuli dimensions, two or more times, and (2) the use of rating scales, most preferably graphic scales with end-anchors (Anderson 1982). Within subject designs are central to the information integration framework, since–unlike between subject designs–within subject designs prevent individual differences from contributing to the error term in the analysis of variance, enabling the study of the integration model at the individual level. They also

are representative of many scenarios in which consumers are exposed to numerous offers in the market place, as in the case of multi-dimensional price ads shown in Figure 1. Graphic scales, although not required, are also commonly utilized for measuring the subjects' external response. Typically, stimuli end-anchors–representing profiles slightly outside the range of the factorial design–are used to define the two ends of the graphic scale, and the experimental administration starts with stimuli representing these two end-anchors.

Once the appropriate measures have been obtained through the method described above, one is able to detect the form of the underlying price perception model by examining the form of interactions among the price dimensions[2]. The sign of independent integration of the price dimensions is that the factorial plot of the subjects' responses (i.e., MDP perceptions) exhibit a pattern of parallelism. The statistical test of parallelism is that the bi-linear interaction between the individual price dimensions must be statistically nonsignificant (Anderson 1982, p. 58). On the other hand, should the price perception model be multiplicative–as the rational model would require–the factorial plot of the consumers' responses must exhibit a linear fan pattern, and the bi-linear interaction between specific price dimensions (e.g. between monthly payments and the number of payments) must be statistically significant. As such, satisfying this condition will imply that the underlying price perception model is multiplicative (Anderson 1982, p. 73).

Stimuli and Design

A within subject design was utilized. The design was intended to represent the real-life scenario where the consumer has to evaluate a series of MDPs in a limited time period. A typical example is when a consumer scans car dealership advertisements in a newspaper. Subjects were told that they were to evaluate the prices offered at different dealerships for a new Hyundai Excel. They were told that the prices vary in the monthly payments and the number of payments to be made, and that the potential buyer would obtain full ownership of the car at the end of the payment period. Multi-dimensional prices consisting of a full factorial combination of monthly payments M at three levels ($189, $229, $279) and number of payments N at three levels (24, 30, 36) were administered to each subject. The order of presentation of the price dimensions was counter-balanced across subjects. The subjects were asked to rate the expensiveness of each MDP profile on a 10 centimeter long graphic scale. The first two profiles corresponded to the end-anchors, representing stimuli slightly outside the range of the factorial design, and were intended to familiarize the subjects with the scale and to establish the scale's end-anchors in their minds. The remaining profiles were the profiles from the factorial design and were randomized for each individual subject. After responding to the first set of profiles, subjects were administered a filler task, after which the same profiles were administered for a second time, but in a different random order. At the end, subjects were asked questions regarding their perception of interest rates, their experience level with financing packages, and also asked an open-ended question on how they evaluate multi-dimensional prices. Half of the subjects responded to MDP profiles with prices

---

[2]Anderson (1981, 1982) has developed two theorems which he terms the *Parallelism* and *Linear Fan* theorems of information integration theory to describe what is to follow. In order to avoid unnecessary terminology, the essence of these two theorems are briefly described instead.

TABLE 1
ANOVA for the MxN Profiles

Source	Degrees of Freedom	Sum of Squares	Mean Square	F Value	Pr > F
Model	27	1,200.01	44.44	38.19	0.0001
Error	332	386.37	1.16		
Total	359	1,586.39			
Monthly	2	640.59	320.30	275.22	0.0001
Number	2	351.39	175.70	150.97	0.0001
Monthly x Number	4	0.59	0.15	0.13	0.9724
Subject	19	207.44	10.92	9.38	0.0001

consisting of monthly payments (at 3 levels) and number of payments (at 3 levels), referred to as the MxN format. The other half of subjects responded to MDP profiles with prices consisting of down payment at 2 levels ($799, $1,199), monthly payments at 2 levels ($159, $239), and number of payments at 2 levels (24, 36), referred to as the DxMxN format. The primary reason for the inclusion of the second MDP format was to enable the study of the effects of increasing price complexity. Moreover, the levels of the individual price dimensions were chosen based on a survey of market prices for this class of cars, thereby providing ecologically valid stimuli for the experiment.

Subjects

The subjects were graduate business students at an east coast educational institution who participated in this study in return for a monetary compensation ($5). Twenty subjects were administered profiles of the MxN format and 20 subjects were administered the profiles of the DxMxN format. Data from 4 additional subjects was obtained but could not be utilized, due to incomplete responses. To ensure the involvement of the subjects, they were told that the consistency of their responses will determine their chances of winning a small prize. Subsequently, 3 prizes valued at about $20 each were distributed to the three subjects which exhibited responses most consistent with the rational model (i.e., highest response correlation). The presence of the monetary rewards helped motivate the subjects to be more attentive and to make an effort to follow the rational model.

RESULTS

Table 1 shows the analysis of variance (ANOVA) table for the MxN profiles across all subjects. The dependent variable is perceived expensiveness, and the independent variables are the price dimensions: monthly payments, and the number of payments. As can be seen from the ANOVA table, the main effects of the monthly payment dimension (M) and the number of payments dimension (N) are both significant. However, the bi-linear MxN interaction is not ($p \leq 0.972$, $\eta^2 = 0.0004$). Figure 2, showing the factorial plot of the response measure, clearly displays a pattern of parallelism, and no signs of a linear fan can be found.

A similar ANOVA was conducted for the MDPs in the DxMxN format and factorial plots were generated. As can be seen in Table 2, the main effects for monthly payment, number of payments, and down-payment are significant. However, as in the MxN case, the bi-linear interaction between monthly payments and number of payments is not statistically significant ($p < 0.737$).

Moreover, the factorial plots in the DxMxN format also exhibit a pattern of parallelism. Based on the parallelism theorem of information integration theory (Anderson 1982, p. 58), the above two indications, namely a non-significant interaction between the price dimensions and the observed parallelism of the factorial plots of the subjects' responses, imply that the underlying integration model is not multiplicative, as the rational model would require. Instead the subjects seem to be forming their MDP price perceptions by independently integrating the monthly payments and the number of payments as suggested by Hypothesis 1.

In order to test Hypothesis 2, the marginal means in the DxMxN format were utilized. The DxMxN format was specifically designed such that the high level for each price dimension reflected a 50% increase over the low level (e.g. monthly payments at high=$239, and at low=$159). Moreover, as discussed earlier, the levels were chosen based on observations in the marketplace, providing for a reasonable level of ecological validity. This therefore enabled us to assess the relative impact of the various price dimensions on the overall price perceptions. As predicted by Hypothesis 2, the main effect for monthly payments, at 2.38 was found to be larger than the main effect for the number of payments, at 1.60 with a significance level of $p < 0.05$. This indicates that the monthly payments have a larger impact on MDP price perceptions than do the number of payments. Additional support is provided by the η^2 measure, which is an index of the amount of variation in the subjects' responses explained by a given price dimension. The η^2 for monthly payments was found to be 0.403, while for the number of payments it was only 0.221–thereby suggesting that the monthly payments explain more of the variance in price perceptions than do the number of payments. The same pattern was also observed in the DxMxN format where the η^2's for M and N were found to be 0.310 and 0.177, respectively, providing additional support for Hypothesis 2.

In order to test Hypothesis 3 regarding the accuracy of price perceptions when increasing the number of price dimensions, the correlation between the subjects' perceptions of the MDPs and the objective values determined by the net present value of the offered MDPs was obtained. To calculate the objective net present values, each subject's self-reported interest rate for consumer loans under $10,000 was elicited and used. The correlation was found to be 77.4% in the simpler MxN format. However, in the more complex DxMxN format, the correlation dropped to 71.5%. This difference, assessed using the Fisher z transformations (Morrison 1990, pp. 104-105), was found to be statistically significant at the $p < 0.01$ level. Therefore Hypothesis 3–stating that increasing the number

FIGURE 2
Plot of Profile Means (MxN Format)

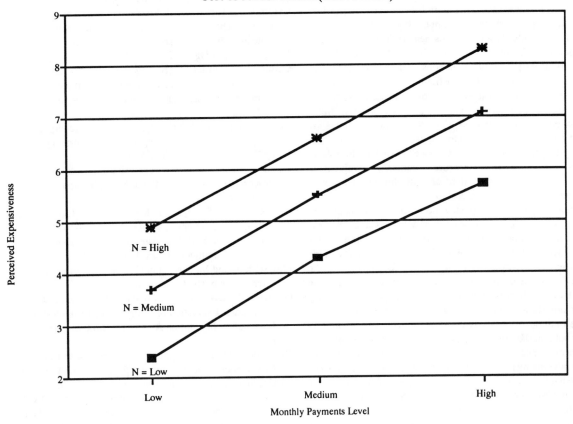

Monthly Payments Level

TABLE 2
ANOVA for the DxMxN Profiles

Source	Degrees of Freedom	Sum of Squares	Mean Square	F Value	Pr > F
Model	26	972.49	37.40	22.21	0.0001
Error	293	493.53	1.68		
Total	319	1,466.02			
Monthly (M)	1	454.10	454.10	269.60	0.0001
Number (N)	1	260.28	260.28	154.53	0.0001
Down Payment (D)	1	139.66	139.66	82.91	0.0001
M x N	1	0.19	0.19	0.11	0.7371
M x D	1	0.28	0.28	0.16	0.6859
N x D	1	1.57	1.57	0.93	0.3354
M x N x D	1	1.01	1.01	0.60	0.4388
Subject	19	115.41	6.07	3.61	0.0001

of price dimensions results in less accurate price perceptions–was supported.

DISCUSSION AND CONCLUSION

The key results of the present study are as follows: (1) consumers form their price perceptions of MDPs by integrating the price dimensions independently, and (2) their price perceptions become less accurate as the number of price dimensions increases. Moreover, (3) they place a larger weight on the monthly payment amount than on the number of payments.

Clearly, the external validity of the above findings is limited by the use of a laboratory setting, and subjects that are not necessarily shoppers in the market for a given product. Therefore, replication of the results in field settings may be required. The design utilized in the study encouraged the subjects to provide their first impression of the price. This in fact is very similar to the common scenario where–as was shown in Figure 1–in the early stages of the decision making process, the consumer is bombarded with many MDP's, for example through various dealership/retailer ads in a newspaper, the TV, or radio. Nevertheless, these initial price perceptions can largely influence the consumer's subsequent search and purchase processes. As such, the findings are not representative of the detailed level of analysis one would expect consumers to undergo toward the final stages of the purchase process. Many questions remain to be answered. For example, do consumers use the same price perception model to evaluate other complex prices (e.g., service prices) in the market place? What is the role of individual differences (e.g, expertise, familiarity, involvement, etc.) in consumer price perceptions of multi-dimensional prices? How is the price/quality relationship affected in a multi-dimensional pricing context? Moreover, a more generalized framework for conceptualizing price dimensions may be possible. For example, each price dimension, in addition to its numerical value may vary in terms of its importance level and its salience in the consumer's mind. These may further be influenced by factors such as the consumer's level of experience and information search costs. The effect of the above factors on the MDP price perceptions model may therefore provide an interesting area for future research.

The findings of the study do however have certain implications for both marketing managers and policy makers. Marketing managers may need to reconsider their MDP communication strategies, by advertising MDPs that yield the lowest perceived level of expensiveness, especially in the early stages of the consumer decision making process. At the same time, policy makers need to pay careful attention such that MDP communication practices do not become deceptive and misleading in nature. As a minimum, it is hoped that this paper will inspire additional research in a relatively unstudied, yet substantive area of behavioral pricing research.

REFERENCES

Agrawal, J., P. Grimm, and N. Srinivasan (1993), "Quantity Surcharge on Groceries", *Journal of Consumer Affairs*, 27, 2, 335-356.

Anderson, N.H (1981), *Foundations of Information Integration Theory*, Academic Press.

Anderson, N.H. (1982), *Methods of Information Integration Theory*, Academic Press.

Bettman, J. (1975), "Issues in Designing Consumer Information Environments," *Journal of Consumer Research*, 2, 169-177.

Bettman, J., N. Capon and H. Lutz (1975), "Cognitive Algebra in Multi-attribute Attitude Models," *Journal of Marketing Research*, v12 n2, May, 151-164.

Birnbaum, M. (1978), "Differences and Ratios in Psychological Measurement", in N. Castellan and F. Restle (eds.), *Cognitive Theory* (vol. 3, pp. 330-374), Hillsdale, NJ: Erlbaum.

Birnbaum, M., and R. Elmasian (1977), "Loudness Ratios and Differences Involve the Same Psychophysical Operation," *Perception and Psychophysics*, 23, 403-408.

Brehmer, B., R. Hagfors, and R. Johansson (1980), "Cognitive Skills in Judgment: Subjects' Ability to Use Information about Weights, Function Forms, and Organizing Principles," *Organizational Behavior and Human Performance*, 26, 373-385.

Business Week (1994), "Leasing Fever," February 7, 1994, 92-96.

Capon, N. and D. Kuhn (1982), "Can Consumers Calculate Best Buys?", *Journal of Consumer Research*, 8, 4, 449-453.

Caroll, D., J. Turner and R. Prassad (1986), "The Effects of Level of Difficulty of Mental Arithmetic Challenge on Heart Rate and Oxygen Consumption," *International Journal of Psychophysiology*, 4, 3, 1670173.

Caroll, D., R. Turner, and S. Rogers (1987), "Heart Rate and Oxygen Consumption During Mental Arithmetic, a Video Game, and Graded Static Exercise," *Psychophysiology*, 24, 1, 112-118.

Cude, B, and R. Walker (1984), "Quantity Surcharges: Are They Important in Choosing a Shopping Strategy?", *Journal of Consumer Affairs*, 18, 2, 287-295.

Dansereau, D.F. and L.W. Gregg (1966), "An Information Processing Analysis of Mental Multiplication," *Psychonomic Science*, 6, 71-72.

Dawes, R.M., D Faust, and P. Meehl (1989), "Clinical Versus Actuarial Judgement," *Science*, 243, 1668-1674.

DeVinney, T. (ed.) (1991), *Issues in Pricing: Theory and Research*, Lexington Books, Lexington, MA.

Elmasian, R. and M. Birnbaum (1984), "A Harmonious Note on Pitch," unpublished manuscript.

Gaeth, G., I. Levin, G. Chakroborty and A. Levin (1991), "Consumer Evaluation of Multi-Product Bundles: An Information Integration Analysis," *Marketing Letters*, v2 n1,47-57.

Gourville, J. (1994), "Pennies-a-Day: Increasing Consumer Compliance through Temporal Re-Framing," Working Paper, Graduate School of Business, University of Chicago.

Greenleaf, E., V. Morwitz, and E. Johnson (1994), "Divide and Prosper: When Breaking Up is Good to Do," Marketing Science Institute working paper, July 15, 1994.

Groen, G., and J. Parkman (1972), "A Chronometric Analysis of Simple Addition," *Psychological Review*, 79, 329-343.

Hitch, G. (1978), "The Role of Short-term Memory in Mental Arithmetic," *Cognitive Psychology*, 10, 302-323.

Jacoby, J. (1976), "Consumer Psychology: An Octennium," *Annual Review of Psychology*, 27, 331-358.

Jacoby, J. and D. Speller (1974), "Brand Choice Behavior as a Function of Information Load–Replication and Extension," *Journal of Consumer Research*, June, 33-41.

Johnson, E., and J. Payne (1985), "Effort and Accuracy in Choice," *Management Science*, v31 n4, 395-414.

Levenson, R. (1979), "Effects of Thematically Relevant and General Stressors on Specificity of Responding in Asthmatic and Nonasthmatic Subjects, " *Psychosomatic Medicine*, 41, 28-39.

Linden, W. (1991), "What do Arithmetic Stree Tests Measure? Protocol Variations and Cardiovascular Responses," *Psychophysiology*, 28, 1, 91-102.

Lopes, L. (1982), "Toward A Procedural Theory of Judgement," *Wisconsin Human Information Processing Program, WHIPP 17*, Department of Psychology, University of Wisconsin, Madison, Wisconsin 53706.

Mellers, B., D. Davis, and M. Birnbaum (1984), "Weight of Evidence Supports One Operation for 'Ratios' and 'Differences' of Heaviness," *Journal of Experimental Psychology*, 10, 2, 216-230.

Mervis, C.B. and E. Rosch (1981), "Categorization of Natural Objects," *Annual Review of Psychology*, 32, 82-115.

Monroe, K. (1990), *Pricing: Making Profitable Decisions*, 2nd Edition, McGraw-Hill.

Morrison, D.F. (1990), *Multivariate Statistical Methods*, 3rd edition, McGraw-Hill Series in Probability and Statistics.

Nagle, T. (1995), *The Strategy and Tactics of Pricing: A Guide to Profitable Decision Making*, Prentice Hall.

Nason, Robert, and Della Bitta, Albert (1983), "The Incidence and Consumer Perceptions of Quantity Surcharges," *Journal of Retailing*, 59, 2, 40-54.

Rao, V.R. (1993),"Pricing Models in Marketing," in J. Eliasberg and G. Lilien (eds): *Marketing*, North Holland.

Russo, E. (1977), "The Value of Unit Price Information," *Journal of Marketing Research*, May, 193-201.

Russo, J. and B. Dosher (1983). "Strategies for Multi-attribute Binary Choice," Journal of Experimental Psychology: Learning, Memory and Cognition, 9, 4, 676-696.

Seraganian P., J. Hanley, B. Hollander, and E. Smilgaet al. (1985), "Exaggerated Psychophysiological Reactivity: Issues in Quantification and Reliability," *Journal of Psychosomatic Research*, "4, 393-405.

Slovic, P. (1972), "From Shakespeare to Simon: Speculations and Some Evidence About Man's Ability to Process Information," *Oregon Research Institute Research Monograph*, v12 n2.

Stevenson, M., "A Discounting Model for Decisions With Delayed Positive and Negative Outcomes," *Journal of Experimental Psychology:General*, 115,2,131-154.

Thaler, R. (1985), "Mental Accounting and Consumer Choice," *Marketing Science*, v4 n3, 199-214.

Turner, J., and D. Caroll (1985), "Heart Rate and Oxygen Consumption During Mental Arithmetic, a Video Game and Graded Exercise: Further Evidence of Metabolically Exaggerated Cardiac Adjustments?," *Psychophysiology*, 22, 261-267.

Tversky, A. and D. Kahneman (1974), "Judgement Under Uncertainty: Heuristics and Biases", *Science*, 185, 1124-1131.

Yadav, M. (1994), "How Buyers Evaluate Product Bundles: A Model of Anchoring and Adjustment," *Journal of Consumer Research*, 21, 2, September, 342-353.

Consumer Reactions to Price-Matching Signals

Subimal Chatterjee, SUNY at Stony Brook
Suman Basu Roy, Rutgers University

ABSTRACT

Price matching or the practice whereby sellers guarantee to match the lowest market price can either raise market prices through price collusion or lower market prices through more competition. Sixty-five undergraduate business students and 41 MBA students served as subjects in an experiment that tested these conflicting theories. Prior to participating in the experiment, the MBA students analyzed a business case that described how price matching by two industrial sellers led to implicit price collusion over a period of time and higher market prices. Yet, when given a choice between stores that advertised to match each other's prices and stores that did not, both MBAs and undergraduates preferred the former and expected that they would get lower prices there. However, when MBA subjects assumed the role of a price-setting seller whose only competitor had announced a price-matching policy, they appeared to understand the collusive possibilities of such arrangements. Implications of such buying-selling asymmetry are discussed.

Firms often publicly commit themselves to match or beat competitors' prices in industrial as well as consumer markets. In industrial contracts, for example, *meeting competition clauses* guarantee customers that firms will meet prices offered by competitors. Similarly, *most favored customer clauses* give customers the right to obtain the lowest price paid by any other customer (see Levy, 1994). In consumer markets, retailers often pledge to match or beat competitors' current prices as shown by the following newspaper insert from Sears Roebuck (*Chicago Tribune*, March 5, 1989)

"Yes, we'll meet or beat the competition's current advertised price on the identical item! Just bring the competition's current ad to any of our retail stores"

and Montgomery Ward's retaliatory announcement on the same day

"We'll match any competitor's current advertised sale price on national brand names 365 days a year! If you see a lower advertised price for the same national brand name item, we'll match that price at the time of purchase or if you find a lower advertised price within 30 days after purchase, just bring in your receipt and we'll gladly refund the difference" (as quoted in Coughlan and Vilcassim, 1989: ps. 19-20).

In fact, supermarkets carry this policy one step further by offering to honor store coupons offered by other supermarkets, thereby effectively matching "coupon prices" (Hess and Gerstner, 1991).

Although price matching has been extensively researched in the industrial economics literature, little attention has been devoted to studying how consumers interpret and respond to such signals. Understanding consumer responses to such signals is important since price matching can facilitate tacit collusion among sellers and result in higher market prices (e.g., Zhang, 1995). Hence, if consumers think that price matching signals lower market prices, then proper decision aids have to be designed to help consumers correctly interpret such signals and make the proper shopping choice. We report an exploratory experiment that investigates how undergraduate and MBA subjects react to price-matching signals.

Prior to participating in the experiment, the MBA subjects analyzed a real-world business case that demonstrated how price matching by two industrial sellers led to tacit price collusion and higher market prices over a period of time. The undergraduates received no such instructions. The experiment we report examines the differences in the reactions of the MBAs and undergraduates to price-matching announcements when they play the role of price-taking consumers as well as price-setting sellers.

THEORY

Several theories have been advanced as to how sellers may use price matching as a strategic tool, and how consumers may use these signals in their search and purchase decisions (see Levy, 1994; Hess and Gerstner, 1991 for reviews). At the simplest level, stores desiring to build market share at the expense of profits may use price matching to convince customers that they will find low prices if they visit the store. Consumers, on the other hand, may be encouraged to search more for the lowest price, thereby lowering market prices. If consumers have to bring proof of competitors' lower advertised prices, then price matching may discriminate between the more knowledgeable and less knowledgeable consumers (e.g., Png and Hirshleifer, 1987). Less knowledgeable consumers, unable or unwilling to search for prices at other stores, may be charged higher prices than their more knowledgeable counterparts.

Sellers may benefit strategically by offering to match prices. For example, if all sellers maintain high prices, and one seller is inclined to reduce prices to gain market share, all others may follow suit, thereby reducing industry profits. Price-matching arrangements, therefore, may serve as deterrents to price cuts, since the seller contemplating the price cut knows that other competitors are likely to retaliate by initiating their own price cuts. Taking this argument one step further, some authors have suggested that price-matching can support a collusive price, encouraging sellers to raise prices to levels that maximize joint profits (Salop, 1986; Sargent 1993; Baye and Kovenock, 1994; Chen, 1995; Zhang, 1995). The little empirical data that exists support this notion. Hess and Gerstner (1991) collected weekly price data for 114 frequently purchased products from five supermarkets in North Carolina between 1984 and 1986. Out of these 114 products, 79 were covered under price-matching guarantees and their prices published in a weekly *Price Finder*. The other 35 products that were not included in the *Price Finder* (due to fluctuations of wholesale prices or legal issues) were not guaranteed to match the lowest market price. The authors found that not only did price matching result in a high degree of price coordination between the supermarkets engaging in the price-matching schemes, but also resulted in greater price coordination among all supermarkets, with or without price-matching policies. Over time, there was a significant increase in prices of the products covered by the price-matching policy relative to the products that were not.

Unlike research on sellers' reactions to price-matching signals, not much research exists on consumers' reactions to such signals. The marketing literature, for example, documents how consumers are affected by unilateral price promotions such as "*x%* off" or "*x dollars off*" regular prices. Unilateral signals, however, are different from competitive signals such as price matching. The latter do not advertise the amount of price cut, but only promise to match a lower price should the customer find one. In this case, the

Advances in Consumer Research
Volume 24, © 1997

TABLE 1
Experimental Stimuli

Township X	Township Y
Township X has two furniture stores, A and B	Township Y has two furniture stores, C and D
Stores A and B guarantee that they will match each other's prices. For example, if Store A advertises a price lower than that of Store B, then Store B will match that price. Similarly, if Store B advertises a price lower than that of Store A, then Store A will match that price	Stores C and D *do not* offer to match each other's prices. For example, if Store C advertises a price lower than that of Store D, Store D *need not* match that price. Similarly if Store D advertises a price lower than that of Store C, then Store C *need not* match that price.

customer does not know whether the current store-price of an item is any different from the original price, i.e., if s/he is getting a deal, and, lowest in the market. The absence of any information about the amount of price reduction and/or competitor prices may make consumers suspicious, more vigilant, and encourage them to search for the lowest available price. Conversely, consumers may (wrongly) assume that stores guaranteeing to match the lowest market price, must have the lowest prices themselves, and hence, use the price-matching signal as a heuristic to simplify the decision of making a store choice (e.g., "choose any store that advertises to match the lowest market price.")

Since price-matching practices can lead to higher market prices, the issue becomes how to make consumers aware of this possibility so that they can make informed decisions. The current experiment attempts to accomplish this in two ways. First, we put subjects in the role of sellers whose task is to set prices in a market where all sellers engage in price matching. Putting subjects in the role of sellers may make them more aware about the collusive potentials of price-matching practices, a notion that has to be tested empirically. Second, and more directly, we make some subjects analyze a real-world business case that explicitly deals with the collusive aspects of price-matching policies. We expect that when subjects are given actual market data about implicit price collusion resulting from price-matching practices, they will be less likely to choose stores making such claims.

The experiment that follows puts 106 subjects in the role of price-taking buyers and price-setting sellers and investigates their responses to price-matching signals. Sixty-five subjects (undergraduate business students) approached the experiment without any formal instructions on price-matching strategies and their consequences, while the remaining 41 subjects (MBAs) were instructed about the anti-competitive aspects of such strategies through the analysis of a business case.

EXPERIMENT

Method

Stimuli and measures. Subjects were asked to imagine that they planned to buy a couch, and had to decide which of the following two townships, X or Y to visit. Both townships were equidistant from where subjects lived, and subjects were told that they had time to visit only one township. Each township had two furniture stores as described in Table 1. Following the descriptions, subjects were given a choice between Township X, Township Y, or remain indifferent. Thereafter, they were asked (1) about their impressions of prices in the two Townships, on a 9 point scale ranging from 1 (*Definitely Lower in Township X*) to 9 (*Definitely Higher in Township X*) with 5 (*About the Same*) as the mid-point,

and (2) the perceived difficulty of the decision, on a 9 point scale ranging from 1 (*Not at all Difficult*) to 9 (*Very Difficult*). On the next page of the stimuli booklet subjects were asked to imagine that they were about to open a new furniture store. Their only competitor had recently announced that it would match the lowest advertised price on comparable items. Subjects indicated whether they, too, would offer a similar price-matching guarantee (Yes / No) or remain indifferent. Once the subjects had made their choice, they were told that the *Better Business Bureau* had prepared a list of suggested prices for furniture retailers. The list was not available to consumers. Subjects rated the price they would set on a 1 to 9 scale, ranging from 1 (*Definitely Lower than the Bureau's Suggested Prices*) to 9 (*Definitely Higher than the Bureau's Suggested Prices*), with 5 (*About the Same*) as the mid-point. The order in which subjects played the role of buyer and seller (buyer first, then seller vs. seller first, then buyer) was counterbalanced across subjects.

Subjects. Sixty-five undergraduate business students enrolled in a business strategy class at a large northeastern university, and 41 MBA students enrolled in a business strategy class at another large northeastern university served as subjects. The undergraduate business students had little or no work experience. For these subjects, the experiment was run during the first week of regular classes, when little material had been covered in class. To the best of our knowledge, these subjects had never been exposed to case or text materials on price-matching. The MBA students, on the other hand, had substantial work experience. For these subjects, the experiment was conducted towards the latter half of the semester. Four weeks prior to the experiment, as part of their course requirements, these students were given to analyze a real world business case dealing with the pricing policies of General Electric and Westinghouse for turbine generators during the mid 1960's (*General Electric Vs. Westinghouse in Large Turbine Generators (A), (B), (C)*, Harvard Business School, 1980, Case nos. 9-380-128, 129, 130). The case describes how General Electric instituted a price protection clause in their contracts that guaranteed customers that "in the event that prices were lowered, General Electric would retroactively reduce prices to any customers who had purchased a turbine generator in the previous six months" (*General Electric vs. Westinghouse in Large Turbine Generators (B)*, Harvard Business School, 1980, 9-380-129). Westinghouse quickly followed with a similar price protection clause, and within months there was a rise in market prices. The Justice Department, after investigating the matter, concluded that the pricing system succeeded in assuring the two companies that the other would not deviate from the published prices, even though the companies did not directly or covertly communicate with each other. One full class period was devoted to the study of the case, at the end of which the students submitted a written report.

TABLE 2

Store Choice Among MBAs and Undergraduates

	Township X	Township Y	Indifferent
MBAs	63.41% (*n*=26)	19.51% (*n*=8)	17.07% (*n*=7)
Undergraduates	64.62% (*n*=42)	16.92% (*n*=11)	18.46% (*n*=12)

TABLE 3

Price Perception Among MBAs and Undergraduates

	Township X	Township Y
MBAs	Δ = 1.31 (*n*=26)	Δ = 1.13 (*n*=8)
Undergraduates	Δ = 1.43 (*n*=42)	Δ = 1.09 (*n*=11)

TABLE 4

Decision Difficulty Among MBAs and Undergraduates

	Township X	Township Y	Indifferent
MBAs	3.28 (*n*=25)	3.75 (*n*=8)	4.71 (*n*=7)
Undergraduates	2.71 (*n*=42)	4.45 (*n*=11)	4.17 (*n*=12)

Analyses and Results

There was no order effect of subject's role (buyer then seller, seller then buyer) in any of the analyses. Hence the data are collapsed across the two conditions.

Store choice as buyers. Sixty four percent of the subjects chose Township X (where the stores advertised price-matching policies) while the remainder chose Township Y (where the stores did not offer to match prices), or were indifferent ($Z=2.91, p<0.005$). The pattern was uniform across MBAs and undergraduates. Even the MBA students who were made aware about the possibilities of price collusion in price-matching schemes preferred Township X to Township Y (see Table 2).

Price expected as buyers. It is reasonable to assume that subjects choosing to visit Township X would expect lower prices at the stores in Township X, whereas subjects choosing Township Y would expect lower prices at the stores in Township Y. Indeed, when subjects' price expectations, ranging from 1 (*Definitely Lower in Township X*) to 9 (*Definitely Higher in Township X*), with 5 (*About the Same*) as the mid point, were subjected to a two-way ANOVA (SAS GLM) with choice of Township (Township X, Township Y, Indifferent) and population (MBAs vs. Undergraduates) serving as predictors, only the main effect of choice was significant ($F_{(2,100)}=30.00, p<0.001$; $M_X=3.62, M_{Indifferent}=4.74$, and $M_Y=6.11$). We conducted follow-up tests that examined the "strength" of their expectations, i.e., how firmly were subjects convinced that they would get lower prices in the township they chose to visit. To do this we transformed subjects ratings around the midpoint of the scale into a variable "Delta" defined as follows:

Delta = 5 - Subject's Rating, for subjects choosing Township X, and

= Subject's Rating - 5, for subjects choosing Township Y.

Subjecting the variable Delta to a two way ANOVA with choice of township, and population as predictors however yielded no significant effects. Subjects choosing Township X and subjects choosing Township Y were equally convinced that they would get lower prices in Townships X and Y respectively ($\Delta_X=1.38, \Delta_Y=1.11$; $F_{(1,83)}<1$). The results were unchanged across MBAs and undergraduates (Interaction $F_{(1,83)}<1$; see Table 3).

Felt decision difficulty as buyers. Consumers can use price-matching signals as a heuristic to simplify their choice of store (e.g., "visit the store that guarantees that it will match the lowest price"). We tested this hypothesis by subjecting decision difficulty ratings to a two-way ANOVA with choice of township and population serving as predictors. The main effect of choice was significant and showed that subjects choosing Township X felt their decision to be easier than those choosing Township Y or those who remained indifferent between the two ($F_{(2,99)}=5.31$, $p<0.01$; $M_X=2.92$, $M_Y=4.16, M_{Indifferent}=4.37$). Contrasts using Dunnett's test showed that, compared to the subjects who were indifferent between the two townships, subjects choosing Township X found the choice significantly easier ($\Delta=1.44, p<0.05$), but not those subjects choosing Township Y ($\Delta=0.21$). Once again the pattern was identical across MBAs and undergraduates (Interaction $F_{(2,99)}<0.84$; see Table 4).

Choice as sellers. When subjects assumed the role of a seller and were asked what they would do if their only competitor announced a price-matching policy, 75% of them (79 out of 106) opted to retaliate with a similar clause ($Z=5.04, p<0.001$). The proportions were similar across MBAs and undergraduates (see Table 5).

TABLE 5
Price Matching Policy Adopted by MBAs and Undergraduates

	Advertise to Match the Lowest Price	Not Advertise to Match the Lowest Price	Indifferent
MBAs	78.05% (*n*=32)	14.63% (*n*=6)	7.32% (*n*=3)
Undergraduates	72.31% (*n*=47)	16.92% (*n*=11)	10.77% (*n*=7)

FIGURE 1
Buying-Selling Asymmetry in Response to Price-Matching Signals

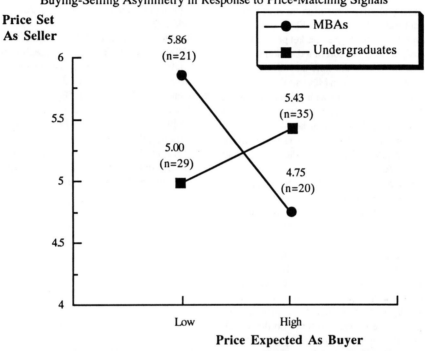

Comparing buying and selling prices. When subjects assumed the role of sellers, they were informed that the *Better Business Bureau* had prepared a list of suggested prices. They were asked how the price they would set compared with the Bureau's prices on a 9 point scale, ranging from 1 (*Definitely Lower than the Bureau's Suggested Prices*) to 9 (*Definitely Higher than the Bureau's Suggested Prices*), with 5 (*Same as the Bureau's Prices*) serving as the mid point. We compared this selling price that subjects set in response to a competitor's price-matching claim to the buying price that subjects expected to find in stores that announced to match their competitors' prices. One prediction is that the price set as a seller will parallel the price expected as a buyer. For example, as a consumer you may believe that price matching implies lower market prices through more competition. You may continue with this line of reasoning when asked to play the role of a seller and set lower prices compared to those who believe that price matching leads to price collusion and higher market prices. Another prediction is that, as a buyer, you may believe that price matching implies more competition and lower market prices, but as a seller you may realize the possibility of price collusion. Hence, the price you set may be just as high as those set by your counterparts who believe that price matching leads to collusion and higher market prices.

We tested these predictions by subjecting the selling price to an ANOVA with the price subjects expected as buyers and population as predictors. Subjects' price expectations as buyers were mean centered to reduce colinearity and entered into the model as a continuous predictor. Only the interaction between population and price-expected was significant ($F_{(1,101)}$=6.98, p<0.01). To explicate the interaction, a median split divided subjects into a "low" and "high" price group with respect to the price they expected as buyers. Among the MBAs, the "low" group (subjects who thought price matching led to lower prices) set higher prices than their counterparts who thought price matching led to higher prices ($t_{(39)}$=2.14; p<0.05; $M_{Expect\ Low\ Price}$=5.86, $M_{Expect\ High\ Price}$=4.75; see Figure 1). Among undergraduates, however, there was no significant difference between the price set by the "low" and the "high" group ($t_{(62)}$<1; $M_{Expect\ Low\ Price}$=5.00, $M_{Expect\ High\ Price}$=5.43).

The pattern of the means in Figure 1 shows that prices undergraduates expected to get as buyers had no influence on the prices they set as sellers. For the MBAs however, those who expected to get lower prices as buyers set significantly higher prices compared to those who expected to get higher prices as buyers. It appears that when they play the role of sellers, those MBA subjects who expected price-matching to lead to more competition and lower market prices, realized the collusive possibilities of such arrangements. The price they set as sellers were, in fact, higher than their counterparts who expected price matching to lead to higher prices. The implication is that informing customers about the possibilities of price collusion in price-matching schemes may not be enough. Rather, they should be encouraged to play the role of sellers if they are to recognize the collusive aspects of price-matching arrangements.

DISCUSSION

Price-matching promotions can send conflicting signals to consumers. On one hand, price matching may signal that sellers are colluding with each other to keep market prices high. On the other hand, price matching may signal stiff competition and lower market prices. In our experiment, subjects were more likely to associate price matching with lower rather than higher market prices. In fact, they may have used the signal as some sort of a decision heuristic to simplify their choice (e.g., "choose the store that advertises that it will match its competitor's price"). Even MBA subjects who had read and analyzed a real life case dealing with price collusion in markets exhibited this bias. However, the latter subjects seemed to have realized the possibilities of collusion when they were put in the role of sellers. A direct implication is that consumers can avoid the trap of false signals and high prices if they asked themselves what they would do if they were the sellers.

Our experiment takes the first step toward understanding a very complex issue. Hence, we may have risked oversimplifying the environment when designing the stimuli. First, we examined price matching in the context of a durable product purchase, whereas empirical evidence is limited to frequently purchased grocery items. Since durables are purchased infrequently and typically entail high expenditure, consumers may rely on the price-matching signal to shorten search and simplify choice. Second, we gave no information other than the absence or presence of price-matching policies, setting up a rather artificial experimental environment. This may have forced subjects to focus on the signal, when in real life such signals may be superseded by other factors such as quality of the product, or image of the store. Third, our method of instructing subjects may not have been relevant to a consumer-goods buying context. Subjects analyzed a case that dealt with price matching in industrial markets (turbine generators) where price matching took the form of a contractual price-protection clause. Subjects may not have seen connection between industrial sellers in the case and their role as consumers. However, when put into the role of sellers, that connection may have become more apparent.

Price-matching signals are unique because unlike straightforward promotion signals, they do not advertise the amount of price cut, and may leave consumers with a false sense of security. Claims like "guaranteed lowest price" or "we won't be undersold" are often misleading because such claims are seldom accompanied by systematic monitoring of competitor prices or lower shelf prices (*Advertising Age*, April 18, 1988, p. 79, 82). They are, however, a common tool of retailers. It is hoped, therefore, that future research will build on our work to gain a better understanding of consumer reactions to the phenomena, and devise methods to aid consumers correctly interpret such signals.

REFERENCES

Baye, Michael R. and Dan Kovenock (1994), " How to Sell a Pickup Truck," *International Journal of Industrial Organization*, 12 (1), 21-33.

Chen, Zhiqi (1995), "How Low is a Guaranteed Lowest Price?," *Canadian Journal of Economics*, 28 (August), 683-701.

Coughlan, Anne and Naufel J. Vilcassim (1989), "Retail Marketing Strategies: An Investigation of Everyday Low Pricing vs. Promotional Pricing Policies, " working paper, Kellogg Graduate School of Business, Northwestern University, Evanston, IL 60208.

Hess, James D. and Eitan Gerstner (1991), "Price-matching Policies: An Empirical Case," *Managerial and Decision Economics*, 12 (August), 305-315.

Levy, David T. (1994), "Guaranteed Pricing in Industrial Purchases," *Industrial Marketing Management*, 23 (October), 307-313.

Png, I. P. L. and D. Hirshleifer (1987), "Price Discrimination Through Offers to Match Price," *Journal of Business*, 60 (3), 365-383.

Salop, Steven C. (1986), "Practices that (Credibly) Facilitate Oligopoly Coordination," in Joseph E. Stiglitz and G. Frank Mathewson (eds.), *New Developments in the Analysis of Market Structure*, Cambridge, MA: MIT Press.

Sargent, Mark T. L. (1993), "Economics Upside-Down: Low Price Guarantees as Mechanisms for Facilitating Tacit Collusion," *University of Pennsylvania Law Review*, 141 (May), 2055-2118.

Zhang, John Z. (1995), "Price-matching Policy and the Principle of Minimum Differentiation, " *Journal of Industrial Economics*, 43 (September), 287-299.

Framing Effects with Differential Impact: The Role of Attribute Salience

Kathryn A. Braun, University of Iowa
Gary J. Gaeth, University of Iowa
Irwin P. Levin, University of Iowa

ABSTRACT

The purpose of this research is to investigate attribute framing effects in an information complex environment where consumers view the frame via a realistic product package and experience a taste test. The framed attribute (content of chocolate expressed as "20% fat" or "80% fat-free")used in our experiment is differentially meaningful to male and female respondents. Framing effects were limited to female consumers for whom the framed attribute was particularly salient.

INTRODUCTION

"Framing effects" has become a generic term to represent the idea that people respond differently to different representations of equivalent information. This apparent difference has been linked to availability of only one side of the information—the glass half full, half empty phenomenon. We are specifically interested in studying attribute frame effects—verbal labels that describe objectively equivalent product attributes in different ways. This paper's purpose is to better understand the processes that underlie framing effects by bringing attribute framing into a realistic consumer choice environment involving direct experience with a chocolate bar. In this environment, it is predicted that attribute salience will moderate the frame effects.

We begin by briefly describing prior effort to make framing studies more realistic. We introduce our perceiver need/salience explanation to describe how framing effects may operate in a more information complex environment. We then look at frame effects from a hierarchy of evaluative responses.

BACKGROUND

Much of the research on framing effects has been confined to either risky choice paradigms or environments which become hard to generalize to the consumer environment. Levin and Gaeth (1988) made framing studies more consumer-oriented by adding a direct product experience to the frame paradigm. Levin and Gaeth (1988) found when ground beef was described as "75% lean" respondents rated their actual taste experience more favorably than when it was described as "25% fat." Though the experience diminished the frame effect, it did not negate it. They suggest that an averaging model may be used to describe the information integration process—as more information is made available to consumers, each piece of information will have less weight on the decision. Therefore, we see diminished effects of the framing of a single attribute in a more complex environment.

This study extends that work by adding to the direct experience a viewing of the framed information within the realistic context of information provided on a product package. The significance of this addition is that individual consumers may differentially attend to this information (fat content of a chocolate bar) depending upon its personal relevance to them. In our study we manipulate the frame's salience by choosing an attribute that has differential relevance to males and females.

PERCEIVER NEEDS/SALIENCE OF FRAME

We know consumers often limit their information search to attributes of direct interest to themselves. Based on the averaging model, we predict under a more complex environment where there is much information competing for the consumers' attention, only consumers for whom the framed attribute is salient will experience the frame effects on the end choice behavior. The salience of the framed information will depend on consumers' perceived relevance of the fat information. We build on the perceiver and communication interaction model proposed by Taylor and Thompson (1980) in order to account for differences in use of vivid information to explain the magnitude of the framing effects.

Salience refers to the phenomenon when one's attention is differentially directed to one portion of the environment rather than to others. The information contained in that portion will receive disproportionate weighting in subsequent judgments (Taylor and Thompson 1980). According to the Taylor and Thompson model, whether vivid information becomes salient to the consumer depends on how relevant the information is to their needs. In our study we make the framed fat attribute vivid on the target chocolate bar by displaying the information in a bright yellow box. Salience is measured indirectly in this study by having consumers freely list the attributes which were important when making their decision. It is directly manipulated through the choice of the gender-relevant attribute, fat content and the product, chocolate bar. Several manufacturers have begun to offer products geared toward females' need for a low-fat indulgence, e.g. Snackwell's line of fat-free cookies which use highly excited women who chase the Snackwell "cookie man" as the focal point in their advertising messages.

In our study we expect gender differences in perceived relevance of the framed information, where females find the fat information to be more relevant, and subsequently weight it higher in their decision making.[1] Rothman, Salovey, Antone, Keough and Martin (1993) have found that gender differences in level of involvement with a health issue led to differences in their message framing study. This difference has not yet been shown in the attribute framing domain. In addition, research on nutritional labeling has found that individual difference variables, such as nutritional motivation, may affect consumers' perception, processing, and evaluation of specific claims and nutrient information offered on product packages (Moorman 1990). In our study, psychographic variables related to the need to use the fat information are measured as manipulation checks in order to verify that it was the perceiver's need which led to the attribute's salience.

HIERARCHY OF FRAME EFFECTS

We propose that in representing a complex consumer environment the framed attribute has to go through several stages before it has an impact on end-behavior, a response hierarchy of effects, similar to what we study in advertising, a learn-feel-do sequence, beginning with 1) cognitive recognition of the frame, 2) moving toward a higher level of affective feelings, to 3) overall evaluation, then finally 4) the choice decision. Previous framing researchers have looked at parts of this process but not the entire chain. In particular, most studies of attribute framing use rating measures of

---

[1] In a pilot study we found females were more likely to notice the framed fat information, recalled it better, and said it influenced their decision more than males.

overall evaluation and cognitive ratings; most studies on attribute frame effects do not measure cognitive and affective dimensions of judgment nor choice.

Below we discuss each stage of this hierarchical frame effect process. We believe attribute salience to moderate this process: that is, if the attribute is salient to an individual, it will be noticed more and receive more attention in processing; it will lead to greater impact on feelings toward the product; both the cognitive and affect components will influence overall evaluation; and that will lead to a choice decision. We expect that for many females, because of their perceived need and interest in the framed information, they will experience frame effects throughout this process. Maheswaran and Meyers-Levy (1990) have suggested that level of processing may be related to findings of frame effects in the message framing domain. This has not yet been investigated in attribute framing studies. (Levin, Schneider, Gaeth and Conlon 1996)

Cognition. For the framed information to have impact it first has to be perceived and processed. We will test for this processing of the framed information using a recognition test. To check for frame effects on cognition we use our evaluative measures where consumers rate the chocolate on various attribute dimensions. We expect that only attributes closely related to the frame will be impacted.

Affect. Earlier work done by Levin and Gaeth (1988) posits that a positive frame invokes positive associations whereas a negative frame causes disagreeable associations, suggesting the frame might have also have an effect on feelings toward the product. In risky choice framing studies (Frisch 1993) and message framing studies (Rothman et al 1993, Homer and Yoon 1992, Maheswaran and Meyers-Levy 1990, Meyerwitz and Chaiken 1987), research begun to look at the frame's impact on feelings. Frisch used an interesting within-subject design where consumers saw both positive and negative sides of the same risky choice scenario but still were more likely to pick the positive frame because of the regret associated with the negative frame. She suggests that this feeling should be included in the assessment of "value" in certain gambles. In studies of the effects of advertising, the affective component of evaluation has been shown to be more important in explaining attitude toward the ad than the cognitive component (Homer and Yoon 1992). In the current study we look at the framed attribute's effect on consumers' feelings towards the chocolate bar overall and towards the fat attribute in particular. We also look to see if earlier work on the frame's cognitive effects, where the frame has shown to only affect the rating of attributes closely associated with the frame, replicates in this study. We are interested in seeing whether the frame has that same focused effect on the affect dimension, or if the frame transfers an overall positive or negative feeling to the chocolate bar. We expect that females, who are processing the framed information more deeply, would experience greater effects on the affect dimension.

Overall Evaluations. Overall evaluations incorporate both consumers' cognitive reactions to the product and their feelings toward the product. In our study we have a comprehensive measure of product evaluation. We again expect that only consumers for whom the framed information is salient (females) would experience frame effects on evaluation.

Choice. We thought it would be interesting to see whether the "valence consistent" shift (where a product with a positive attribute frame is rated more favorably than under the negative attribute frame) observed in earlier studies would carry over to a real choice decision. Choice has rarely been studied in attribute frame research (Levin et al 1996). For reasons discussed above, we expected that only females would experience an effect on choice.

METHOD

Participants

56 students (30 females and 26 males) from an undergraduate Introduction to Marketing class participated in this experiment for course credit. They were randomly assigned to the positive or negative frame condition.

Stimulus

The stimulus chosen was a milk chocolate bar. We chose to frame the fat attribute as either "80% fat-free" for our positive frame and "20% fat" for our negative frame. We designed the package to be realistic. Along with the fat attribute information, the wrapper contained additional information—e.g. weight, brand name (Suisse, a fictitious name), country of origin, logo, ingredients, type of chocolate, and help line number.

Description of Experimental Procedure

Consumers were told that they would be evaluating a new chocolate bar and would be asked questions as to whether or not it might succeed. They first had the opportunity to observe the candy bar in its wrapper. They each got a square inch sample of the chocolate bar served in white paper doily containers. After the taste test they filled out five overall evaluation measures which were later pooled to form our evaluation index. This index will be discussed in more detail later. In addition, one overall *feeling toward the product* measure was asked. They were then given the choice between a candy bar or 50 cents, and were asked to write down why they made that choice and what attributes were important to them.

Consumers then proceeded to answer a collection of individual attribute questions—evaluation of the candy bar on certain attributes and rating the importance of each attribute in their product evaluation, which comprised the cognitive task. Two attributes of interest were embedded in this list—health benefits and fat content. Consumers were given a distraction task where they rated their own general usage of information. This was given because we wanted to assess recall later and did not want them thinking about the chocolate bar prior to that test. Following that task, they were asked to freely recall attributes from the chocolate bar and again asked to describe what factors influenced their decision to choose or not choose the chocolate bar. A recognition test for the wrapper information was then given. The respondents then filled out two feeling/affect measures. Next consumers filled out several product involvement scales. Lastly, the respondents filled out demographic measures—gender, health consciousness, and past diet experience.

INDEPENDENT VARIABLES

Frame

There were two sides of the frame—80% fat-free as the positive side, 20% fat as the negative side.

Salience

Gender was treated as the surrogate for attribute salience because of the expected difference in perceiver need/relevance of the framed attribute. We had several checks for attribute salience: if the fat attribute was reported as a reason for choice, importance rating of fat attribute in their decision, correct free recall of the fat attribute and freely stating during recall that fat was part of their decision to choose or not choose the chocolate bar.

Perceiver Relevance of the Frame Check

We asked psychographic information we thought to be related to perceivers' needing/finding the fat attribute to be important.

TABLE 1

Fat Salience in Decision

	Fat— reason for choice t1*	Fat— recalled as reason for choice t2*	Fat Recall*
Female	50%	23%	90%
Male	15%	0%	73%

*Significantly different between gender.

These included past diet history, a self-reported measure of health consciousness, and a self-reported measure of likelihood of buying low-fat products. Zaichowsky's (1994) new 10 item PII scale was used to measure involvement in chocolate and fat. The new scale has been used to break down cognitive and affective components of involvement.

DEPENDENT VARIABLES

Cognitive/ratings of Chocolate bar's Attributes

The attribute rating measures contained both taste experience —such as creaminess of the chocolate bar—and marketing characteristics —like quality of the brand name. This was deemed the "cognitive" task because it involved rating the chocolate on specific attributes, not supplying feelings or attitudes about those ratings. The complete list of attributes is given later in Table 4. They were measured on the following scale:

Rate the quality of the chocolate's _____

Poor   Excellent

and for importance:

How important was the chocolate's _____ to your overall evaluation of the chocolate?

Very little   Very much

Negatively worded items were recoded so that higher scores always reflected higher construct values.

Affect

We had several measures of affect (operationalized as feelings). We measured both feelings toward the fat attribute and overall feelings toward the chocolate bar. The same 85 mm scale was used to score the overall feelings (with the score of 85 reflecting highest impact on feelings).

Overall Affect: We had three measures of overall affect. The following scale appeared early in the questionnaire:

What are your overall feelings toward the Suisse chocolate bar?

Not very favorable   Very favorable

We adapted two additional measures from Hausknecht (1990) to capture the affect differences using "smilie face" and "feeling thermometer" scales. The smilie faces ranged from full smiles to deep frowns. Consumers were asked to circle the face which best fits their feeling toward the fat, and toward the chocolate bar

overall. We later converted those faces into values from 1 to 7, with 7 being the most favorable. The feeling thermometer had consumers put a degree of warmth or coldness toward the fat and the overall chocolate bar, measured in degrees from 0 to 100, with 100 being the most favorable.

Overall Evaluation

Our overall evaluation measure was an attempt to integrate both cognitive and affective responses about the chocolate bar. The participants were asked to rate the chocolate bar on the following five dimensions using continuous line mark scales (85 mm):

(1) "Overall how would you rate the specific sample of the chocolate bar?" (anchored by 'poor' and 'excellent');

(2) "Overall how would you rate the chocolate bar?" (anchored by 'poor' and 'excellent');

(3) "How much would you like to finish the rest of the candy bar?" (anchored by 'very little' and 'very much');

(4) "Compared to your favorite chocolate bar, how would you rate this one?" (anchored by 'poor' and 'excellent');

(5) "Would you recommend this brand of chocolate to your family or friends?" (anchored by 'definitely no' and 'definitely yes').

Choice

Our main dependent variable of interest was choice. It was measured early in the experiment. After consumers had seen the wrapper, tasted the chocolate, and filled our evaluation measures, they were given the choice between a chocolate bar or a cash payment of 50 cents. These two values were pretested to yield about a 50/50 preference split.

RESULTS

Salience Manipulation Check

We found that gender was an effective surrogate for attribute salience. Females were more likely to state openly (without cueing) that the fat attribute affected their decision to choose or not choose the chocolate bar. Table 1 summarizes those results. This gender difference is apparent as they stated reasons just after they made their choice, and after some time, in their recall for their decision (χ^2(1, 56)=5.6, p=.02) for time 1, χ^2(1, 56)=7.44, p=01) at time 2. Many consumers, male or female, recalled the fat attribute, the gender difference was significant χ^2(1, 56)=2.7, p=.099).

Perceiver Need Check. We believed that the framed attribute was salient to females due to the relevance of the fat attribute to this group. Table 2 contains those results. Females were significantly

TABLE 2
Characteristics Associated with the Framed Fat Attribute

	Health consciousness*	More likely to buy low fat products*	Been on a diet*
Female	62.9	69.7	70%
Male	53.2	51	38%

*Significantly different between gender. Measured on a 85 point scale.

TABLE 3
Involvement Measures
(rated on a 7 point scale, where higher means more involved)

	/ Chocolate			/ Fat		
	Overall	Cognitive	Affect	Overall*	Cognitive*	Affect
Female	4.25	3.97	4.48	5.79	6.35	5.24
Male	3.76	3.54	3.98	5.05	5.4	4.7

*Significantly different between gender.

TABLE 4
Attribute Ratings
Measured on a 85 point scale, where the higher rating means more positive evaluation

Attribute	Overall		Female		Male	
	Positive	Negative	Positive	Negative	Positive	Negative
Fat Rating* (reverse scaled)	61	30	57	23	66	38
Health benefits*	44	27	46	21	42	33
Freshness	63	67	61	66	65	67
Greasiness	26	20	23	17	29	23
Brand	53	46	53	43	53	51
Package	34	31	31	21	37	44
Nut flavor	29	26	26	21	32	33
Color	61	64	60	65	63	63
Smell	50	55	49	61	51	48
Texture	60	64	66	67	54	60
Country of Origin	64	65	60	66	69	64
Ingredients	53	55	52	57	54	57
Aftertaste	56	53	58	48	54	59

*There was a main effect of frame for both these attributes at ($F(1,52)$= 31.47 for fat, p=.0001) and ($F(1,54)$=9.95, p=.002) for health benefits.[3]

more health conscious ($F(1, 52)$=6.35, p=.01). Females were also more likely to say they buy products because they are low in fat ($F(1,52)$=16.25, p=.002). And, for our behavioral measure, females were also more likely to have been on a diet at some point in their lives $\chi^2(1, 56)$=6.06, p=.02).

We expected that females might also be more involved with the product or with the framed fat attribute. Table 3 contains those results. We used Zaichowsky's new 10 item PII to separate the different components of involvement.[2]

We compared the means for each product/attribute across gender. We found that chocolate involvement did not differ by gender. We did find differences between the level of involvement in the framed attribute, however. Females were both overall more

[2]The factor analysis did not reveal the two distinct factors for affect and cognition as described by Zaichowsky— interest and involvement loaded highly on both the cognitive (factor 1) and affect (factor 2).

[3]There was only one attribute where there was a significant frame*gender interaction and that was for smell— females seem to think the chocolate smelled much better with the negative frame ($F(1,51)$=6.00, p=.0178), there was no such difference for males.

TABLE 5

Affect Ratings

(Measured on a 100 point scale)

	Fat affect		Overall affect	
Gender	Positive	Negative	Positive	Negative
Female*	83	41	82	65
Male**	70	57	72	75

*Females are significantly different between frames on both affect dimensions.
**Males are significantly different between frame for only the fat attribute.

TABLE 6

Correlations Between Cognitive and Affective Measures

	Cognitive Measures					
	Health rating			Fat rating		
Affect Measures	All	Female	Male	All	Female	Male
Smilie-fat affect	0.62	**0.72**	**0.4**	0.62	**0.7**	**0.43**
Therm-fat affect	0.63	**0.75**	**0.37**	0.68	**0.78**	**0.49**
Overall feeling/affect	0.27	**0.52**	**-0.08**	0.19	0.35	-0.03
Smile-overall affect	0.15	0.26	-0.01	0.04	0.09	0.03
Therm-overall affect	0.15	0.14	0.19	0.05	-0.01	0.24

Correlations in bold face are significantly different between gender.

involved with the fat attribute ($t(53)=2.19$, p=.03) and specifically on the cognitive dimensions of involvement ($t(53)=2.75$, p=.008).

Because we did find the expected differences in perceiver needs by gender, which resulted in the framed attribute's greater salience in evaluation, for the following dependent measures we use gender (as a proxy for attribute salience) and frame as the independent variables in our model.

HIERARCHY OF EFFECTS

Cognitive Effects of Frame

Our recognition test showed that most consumers processed the framed information; 100% recognition for females, 92% for males. As expected, the frame effect on ratings was focused on beliefs toward the framed attribute, fat, and a closely related attribute, health benefits, demonstrating that the cognitive effects of frame exist for all consumers and are narrow in their focus. The other attributes were not affected. (See Table 4)

Affect

Affect Response Indices. We separated the affect dimension into two areas: feelings specific to the fat attribute and overall feelings toward the chocolate bar. We combined our two fat feeling attribute measures (the smilie face scale and the feeling thermometer) which were correlated at .92. We combined our three measures of overall feelings toward the chocolate bar (the verbal measure, and the smilie face and thermometer scales) which had an alpha of .96.).[4]

Specific Fat Affect. There was a main effect for frame ($F(1,51)=19.88$, p=.0001) for feelings toward the specific fat at-

tribute and a gender by frame interaction ($F(1,51)=5.6$, p=.02). Females reported more extreme positive feelings under the positive frame, and more negative feelings under the negative frame, than did males.

Overall Affect Toward the Chocolate Bar. We found a significant gender by frame interaction for feelings toward the overall chocolate bar ($F(1,52)=6.02$, p=.018) where only females showed the frame effects on the overall affect dimension.

Overall Evaluation

By using factor and coefficient alpha analyses we found that the five dependent evaluation measures loaded on one factor and

[4]We looked at the correlations between our affect measures and cognitive attribute ratings to show that we were indeed measuring different constructs. Table 6 shows those correlations. As a group these correlations are rather low. The gender differences on the correlations were interesting—the correlations between the males' affect and cognitive ratings toward the health and fat attributes were low, but this was not the case for females. Females appeared to be more consistent in their affect and cognitive ratings toward the fat attribute. For health ratings both feelings toward the fat attribute scales were significantly different between gender, for smilie face (($F(2,25=12.68$, p=.001), and the feeling thermometer (($F(2, 52)=13.05$, p=.0001) and also the verbal overall feelings toward the chocolate bar scale ($F(2, 52)=2.78$, p=.07). For fat ratings there are significant differences just for the fat feeling scales, for the smilie face ($F(2, 52)=17.48$, p=.0001), and for the feeling thermometer ($F(2, 52)=24.01$, p=.0001).

TABLE7

Overall Evaluation of the Chocolate Bar

(measured on a 85 point scale)

	Positive Frame	Negative Frame
Female	60	49
Male	54	56

TABLE 8

Choice Percentages

Gender	Positive Frame	Negative Frame
Female	100%	53.3%
Male	61.5%	83.3%

TABLE 9

Evaluative Measures Correlated with Choice*

	Overall	Female	Male
Overall evaluation	.92	.96	.85
Overall affect	.26	.39	.05
Fat & health evaluation (cognitive)	.74	.87	.49
Fat affect	.58	.67	.39

*Pearson's product moment correlation was used.

yielded a coefficient alpha of .90. Therefore, a chocolate evaluation index was created by averaging these five dependent measures. That index was then used in the following analysis.

Evaluation Findings

There was a significant gender by frame interaction ($F(1,51)=7.71$, p=.0076). Follow up tests using the Bonferronni technique found females to be significantly different between frame conditions, M=60 in the positive frame versus M=49 in the negative frame, (t(28)=3.55, p=.02) with no such difference for males, M=54 for the positive frame, M=56 for the negative frame (t(23)=.50). This interaction is consistent with our choice results where only females experience the frame effects.

Choice

Table 8 contains the percentages of choice of the chocolate bar in each framing condition for males and females. There was no overall significant frame effect, M=82% for the positive frame and M=66% for the negative frame, but there was a significant difference between frames for females, M=100% for the positive frame versus 53.3% for the negative frame $\chi^2(1, 30)=9.13$, p=.003), showing the expected frame effects. Males were not significantly different across frames, and even went in the opposite direction, 61.5% for the positive frame, 83.3% for the negative frame $\chi^2(1, 25)=1.470$, p=.225)

Correlations between Overall Evaluation, Affect, Cognitive Rating and Choice

For further illustration of the hierarchy of effects, we looked at the correlations between our evaluative dimensions and choice. We expected that dimensions closer in the hierarchy to choice would show higher correlations. We also suspected that the relationship between other dimensions and choice would be particularly strong for females. We grouped the two cognitive ratings of health and fat together for this analysis. As Table 9 shows, the overall evaluation measure, closest to choice in the hierarchy, was the most correlated to choice—probably because it incorporates both affective and cognitive evaluations. Both the cognitive and affective measures are more closely related to females' rather than males' choices; however, the affect measures in particular seem to relate only to females' choices.

DISCUSSION

One female in our positive 80% fat-free condition noted: "The 80% fat-free jumped out at me" while a female in our 20% fat condition said "The packaging was poor...you could not read the name. In fact, you might have thought it was called 20% FAT!" By contrast, male respondents seemed to focus their comments on the taste of the bar: "Very tasty and I would like to eat more. Taste was most important to me. I assume most types have the same nutritional value." These seem to mirror our results in this study:

females' attention was drawn to the framed attribute and it was an important part of their decision, even with a direct taste experience. Males, in contrast, focused on other attributes in their decision making. In this paper we investigated three new issues in attribute framing: first, the importance of attribute salience based on perceiver needs, the effect on the affect dimension of evaluation, and its impact on consumer choice.

First, framing effects have typically been viewed as a generic bias in evaluation. In this study we show that a more information complex environment can lead to differential frame effects—the more salient the attribute being framed, the greater the frame effects. The hierarchy of frame effects explains how as consumers move up the ladder of depth in processing, the greater the influence of perceiver need and salience of the frame. In our study it was clear that females used the framed information more in their decision; it seemed to be a central cue. There is no product involvement difference between genders that might account for the difference. We think that the high correlation between the evaluation components for females further suggests that the framed fat information was guiding their decision on both affective and cognitive levels. This is consistent with past research done by Shavitt and Fazio (1991) who found greater consistency between attitudes based on a salient attribute and subsequent behavior.

Second, researchers are becoming more interested in the role of affect in decision making. The affective component of evaluation was particularly important in this study because it seemed to be the breakpoint in the hierarchy, the step that differentiated well between those affected and those not affected by the frame. Males showed differences between the frames for feelings toward the fat attribute, but not to the same extent as females. We believe that females' transference of overall positive or negative feelings toward the chocolate bar because of the frame demonstrates higher processing of the framed information. For females, the frame seems to conjure up good/bad feelings about the chocolate bar. For males, no such overall feeling seems to be activated.

Lastly, we have shown that the valence consistent bias observed in past research on evaluation can translate to actual consumer choice. This choice difference is particularly relevant to managers because while evaluation measures may offer some meaningful information, product choice is what ultimately determines market impact. The fact that our overall evaluation measure was highly correlated with choice should make researchers more confident in generalizing prior attribute framing findings into a choice environment.

Limitations and Applications of this Research

We acknowledge that our three primary findings may not be entirely generalizable to all framing situations. This experiment intentionally included an attribute that was differentially meaningful to respondents. Also, chocolate may be viewed as a hedonic product where guilt and affect may have greater influence. (We note the recent growth of Snackwell's indulgent fat-free cookie line targeted to females.) One female consumer said in their explanation of their decision not to choose the candy bar: "It would be good, but I'd regret it later." In addition, there could be a curvilinear relationship between perceived need and frame effect—perhaps as we increase importance of the framed attribute even higher to some individuals, they might be able to "see through" the frame. We had several females in this study who could be classified in that manner. One said "The label said 20% fat...it should say 80% non fat or something in a positive way." We hope that this research has brought some new perspectives in which to study framing effects in the consumer domain.

REFERENCES

Frisch, Deborah (1993), "Reasons for framing effects," *Organizational Behavior and Human Decision Processes*, 54, 399-429.

Hausknecht, Douglas R. (1990), "Measurement scales in consumer satisfaction/dissatisfaction," *Consumer Satisfaction/Dissatisfaction & Complaining Behavior*, 3, 1-5.

Homer, Pamela and Sun-Gil Yoon (1992), "Message framing and the interrelationships among ad-based feelings, affect and cognition," *Journal of Advertising Research*, 21, 19-23.

Levin, Irwin P. and Gary J. Gaeth (1988), "How consumers are affected by the framing of attribute information before and after consuming the product," *Journal of Consumer Research*, 15, 374-378.

Levin, Irwin P., Sandra L. Schneider, Gary J. Gaeth, and Amy B. Conlon (1996), "All frames are not created equal: A typology of differences in framing effects," working paper.

Maheswaran, Durairaj, and Joan Meyers-Levy (1990), "The influence of message framing and issue involvement," *Journal of Marketing Research*, 27, 361-367.

Meyerowitz, Beth E. and Shelly Chaiken (1987), "The effect of message framing on breast self-examination attitudes, intentions, and behavior," *Journal of Personality and Social Psychology*, 52, 500-510.

Moorman, Christine (1990), "The effects of stimulus and consumer characteristics on the utilization of nutrition information," *Journal of Consumer Research*, 17, 362-374.

Nisbett, Richard E. and Lee Ross (1980), *Human inference: Strategies and shortcomings of social judgment.* Englewood Cliffs, N.J.: Prentice Hall.

Rothman, Alexander J., Peter Salovey, Carol Antone, Kelli Keough, and Chloe Drake Martin (1993), "The influence of message framing on intentions to perform health behaviors," *Journal of Experimental Social Psychology*, 29, 408-433.

Shavitt, Sharon and Russell H. Fazio (1991), "Effects of attribute salience on the consistency between attitudes and behavior predictions," *Personality and Social Psychology Bulletin*, 17, 507-516.

Taylor, Shelley E. and Suzanne C. Thompson (1980), "Stalking the elusive 'vividness' effect," *Psychological Review*, 89, 155-181.

Zaichowsky, Judith Lynne (1994), "The personal involvement inventory: reduction, revision, and application to advertising," *Journal of Advertising*, 23, 59-69

'5' Calories or 'Low' Calories? What Do We Know About Using Numbers or Words to Describe Products and Where Do We Go From Here?

Madhubalan Viswanathan, University of Illinois, Urbana-Chamapign
Terry L. Childers, University of Minnesota

ABSTRACT

Marketing information about products is often conveyed by providing numerical or verbal information along specific attributes. Such information is the basic input to consumer decision making that is utilized to make higher-level decisions. This paper reviews empirical work on numerical and verbal information with the aim of synthesizing past research in terms of what we know and where we go from here. In keeping with this goal, the review of empirical research is organized in terms of different elements of decision making, specifically, information search, comparisons, memory, and evaluations. Details on the empirical design of each study reviewed here are provided to enable comparisons across studies. Insights drawn from each area are synthesized in a discussion of theoretical implications and future research directions in terms of dimensions along which numerical and verbal information differ and the impact of ability and motivation to process information.

This paper reviews empirical work on numerical and verbal information with the aim of synthesizing past research in terms of what we know and where we go from here. The review of empirical research is organized in terms of different elements of decision making, specifically, information search, comparisons, memory, and evaluations, in order to isolate factors that affect one or more elements of the decision making process and provide insight into different elements of consumer decision making. Insights drawn from each area are synthesized in a discussion of theoretical implications and future research directions. This review is selective in nature and does not include several studies in consumer behavior that have not directly compared numerical versus verbal information such as research on nutrition information (cf., Levy et al., 1985), pricing (Mazumdar and Monroe, 1990), and alpha-numeric brand names (Pavia and Costa, 1993).

INFORMATION SEARCH

Several studies have examined differences in the information search process for numerical versus verbal information. Stone and Schkade (1991) argued that it is easier to perform certain operations such as computing differences on numerical labels (i.e., numbers on a rating scale) when compared to verbal labels (e.g., the meaning of the subtraction between one verbal label and another such as 'good' and 'very good' is not clear). Therefore, a greater degree of attribute-based processing (i.e., search across brands within an attribute) as well as less processing time was predicted for numerical information. The authors used a task where subjects were required to choose the best information system from a set of alternatives described along four attributes (Table). Five levels of a rating scale either in numerical (i.e., 2, 4, 6, 8, and 10) or in verbal (i.e., very poor to excellent) modes were used to describe product attributes and subjects were instructed about the correspondence between numerical and verbal labels. Moreover, the study manipulated the mode of information between tasks in that the same subjects participated in two sessions scheduled six days apart, one involving numerical information and the other, verbal information. Task complexity (i.e., 2, 4, or 8 alternatives) as well as similarity of alternatives (high versus low levels of similarity) were manipulated within subjects. The study was administered using computers with subjects being able to access a piece of information from a matrix.

Concurrent protocols were collected for several sessions. The authors found a greater degree of attribute-based search for numerical when compared to verbal information as well as directionally less processing time for numerical information and directionally fewer pieces of information examined for numerical information (Table). These results were consistent with the rationale that less effort is required to process numerical information.

Huber (1980) used a task where subjects chose the best candidate for a post using a design where the mode of information (i.e., numbers on a rating scale from 1 to 9 or verbal labels such as bad and optimal), the number of alternatives, and the number of dimensions were manipulated. Subjects completed several tasks in random order with each of the factors mentioned above being manipulated across these multiple tasks. Concurrent protocols were collected. Comparisons such as calculating differences or finding the maximum value within attributes were performed more frequently on numerical information while evaluations were made more frequently on verbal information.

Viswanathan and Narayanan (1992) argued that the conclusions drawn from the Stone and Schkade (1991) paper may not generalizable to the kind of numerical information often used in marketing, i.e., unit-specific numerical information (e.g., 200 calories). They argued that, unit-specific numerical information unlike numerical ratings on a scale, do not necessarily convey equal intervals at a psychological level. Therefore, the computation of differences may not be as meaningful an operation to perform on such information. Moreover, unlike ratings on a scale, unit-specific numerical information has meaningful reference points that consumers can relate to in order to interpret numerical values (e.g., interpreting "200 calories" by using a meaningful reference point rather than comparing across brands). The authors used a design where task (i.e., choice versus learning) was manipulated between subjects and information mode (numerical versus verbal; e.g., display width of '12 digits' versus 'wide') was manipulated within subjects. Information was presented on four fictitious brands of calculators along four attributes using a matrix display on a computer. The sample consisted of undergraduate students who were likely to be knowledgeable about the product category. In contrast to the Stone and Schkade study, neither a greater degree of attribute-based processing nor less processing time was found for unit-specific numerical information when compared to verbal information (Table).

Research on information search brings out the importance of the distinction between numerical information on specific units of measurement and artificial or preprocessed numerical information (Figure). This research also suggests the importance of consumers' knowledge in assessing numerical labels (Figure). When consumers are knowledgeable about product attributes, they may be able to interpret numerical labels without engaging in attribute-based search (i.e, Viswanathan and Narayanan's (1992) sample). However, lower levels of knowledge may necessitate attribute-based processing for unit-specific numerical information as well.

COMPARISONS

The comparative judgment task from research in psychology (Banks, 1977) requires subjects to compare stimuli on a dimension and make judgments based on the magnitudes of the stimuli along

Advances in Consumer Research
Volume 24, © 1997

TABLE
Selective Summary of Empirical Studies

Study	Task	Sample	Manipulation of information mode	Stimuli Numerical	Verbal	Key findings for numerical versus verbal information
Information search						
Stone & Schkade (1990)	Choosing an information system	Graduate business students	Between tasks	2-10 on a rating scale	very poor to excellent	More attribute-based search & less processing time for numerical info.
Viswanathan & Narayanan (1992)	Learning vs. choice for calculators	Under-graduate business students	Within subjects	No. of functions = 38	No. of functions = High	No difference in attribute-based search & processing time
Comparisons						
Jaffe-Katz et al. (1989)	Choosing higher/lower probabilities	Native English speakers aged 21-30	Same as above	20%	Unlikely	Faster comparisons for numerical labels; distance effect for all conditions
Viswanathan & Narayanan (1994)	Choosing higher/lower labels for calculators	Under-graduate business students	Same as above	12 digit display width	Wide display width	Faster comparisons for numerical labels; no distance effect for numerical info.
Memory						
Childers et al. (1992)	Learning for calculators	Same as above	Same as above	400 hours battery life	Long battery life	Faster recognition of numerical info.
Viswanathan & Childers (1995)	Learning vs. choice for calculators	Same as above	Same as above	12 digit display width	Wide display width	Higher recall/recognition & lower processing time for numerical information; some boundary conditions for effect
Viswanathan (1994, 1995)	Judging cereals	Same as above	Between & within subjects	125 calories	High calories	Higher recall & recognition of verbal info.
Evaluation/Usage						
Yalch & Yalch (1984)	Viewing commercials for tellers	Members of social organizations	Between subjects	"95% of their banking at .. teller"	"Virtually all their banking at teller"	Source expertise increased favorability of attitudes only for quantitative message
Artz & Tybout (1991)	Read product claims	MBA students	Same as above	"60% reduc-tion in .. delays"	"significant reduction in ..delays"	Same as above & effect of source trustworthiness on attitude for verbal message
Scammon (1977)	Viewing ads for butter	Californians	Same as above	Niacin 20% of RDA	Niacin 'Good'	More accurate identifica-tion of nutritious brand for verbal info.
Viswanathan (1994, 1995)	Judging cereals	Undergraduate buss. students	Between & within subjects	125 calories	High calories	Greater weight for verbal info. in judgments

that dimension. Several robust findings from research on compari-sons in cognitive psychology across a range of dimensions include the distance effect (i.e., faster and more accurate comparisons with increasing distance between pairs of stimuli being compared).

In a study which directly compared numerical versus verbal labels, Jaffe-Katz et al. (1989) examined comparisons of pairs of numerical labels, pairs of verbal labels, and pairs of numerical/verbal labels. Subjects were asked to choose the higher (or lower) of a pair of labels. Faster comparisons were observed for pairs of numerical when compared to verbal probability expressions (Table). Such a finding was argued to occur due to the the relatively precise

nature of numerical expressions which leads to lesser overlap between a pair of numerical expressions. Several robust findings from research on comparisons in cognitive psychology were also found such as the occurrence of the distance effect. The authors explain their findings in terms of a modified version of the reference point model (Holyoak, 1978) which suggests that comparative judgments of a pair of stimuli are based on the ratio of the distance of each stimulus from a reference point. The distance effect occurs due to multiple comparisons of distances of a pair of stimuli from a reference point being made until a decision is reached, with the instructions for choosing higher or lower stimuli leading to the high

FIGURE
Summary of Proposed Rationale for Findings

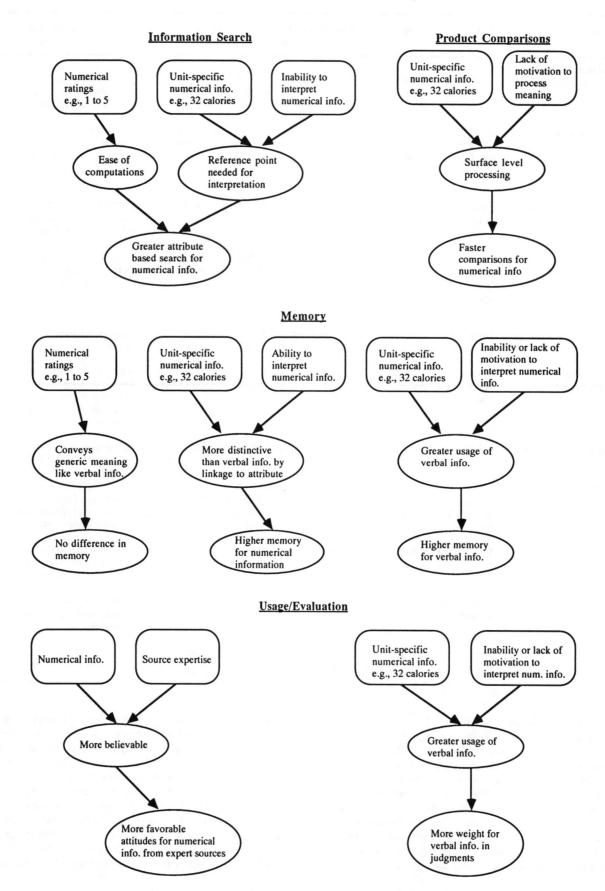

or low ends of the continuum serving as reference points, respectively. As the distance between a pair of stimuli increases, fewer comparisons will be required to reach a decision.

Viswanathan and Narayanan (1994) examined labels describing product attributes using product information about attributes of calculators (e.g., display width of '12 digits' versus 'wide'). Subjects (undergraduate students) compared pairs of labels describing calculators along specific attributes, a product category that they were likely to be knowledgeable about. Similar to the Jaffe-Katz study, the authors found that comparisons of pairs of numerical labels take less time than comparisons of pairs of verbal labels or numerical/verbal label-pairs. However, unlike the Jaffe-Katz study as well as past research in cognitive psychology (cf., Banks, 1977), several robust effects from past research were not found for comparisons of numerical labels. For example, the distance effect occurred consistently only for verbal labels, and not for numerical labels (Table). On the basis of this difference, the authors argue that the results for comparisons of numerical labels cannot be explained in terms of the reference point model (Holyoak, 1978). Rather, they argue that numerical labels may have been compared based on the sizes of numbers involved without attention to the distances from the labels to the reference point implied in the instruction.

These findings suggest that even though subjects were knowledgeable about the product category and had the ability to interpret the numerical labels, they may have engaged in surface level processing (Figure) in contrast to studies on comparative judgments in psychology. Viswanathan and Narayanan (1994) suggest that product dimensions may be distinct from other dimensions used in psychology such as magnitudes of digits and probability expressions in that numerical labels describing product attributes are generally bounded by a narrow context (i.e., the product category in question) rather than being relevant across a broad range of situations as may be the case for the dimensions used in psychology. Consequently, consumers may have less experience with and less knowledge of labels describing product attributes than with dimensions such as digits and probability expressions though they may have high knowledge about a product category in a relative sense. Therefore, the effect of product knowledge may be moderated in consumer settings by motivation to expend effort required to interpret a label's meaning.

MEMORY

Some research has examined memory differences between numerical and verbal information. Childers et al. (1992) used a design where subjects learned fictitious brand information about calculators with numerical versus verbal information being manipulated within subjects. Subjects then performed a speeded recognition task where the mode of information was again manipulated to be either numerical or verbal. Numerical information was recognized faster than verbal information when both types of information were presented in the same mode at recognition as well as in a different mode at recognition (Table).

Viswanathan and Childers (1995) argued that numerical information, such as 32 mpg., is a number in the context of a unit of measurement and consequently more specifically linked to an attribute through its unit of measurement (e.g., mpg. for mileage). Verbal information, such as 'high mileage', is a generic descriptor that readily conveys meaning (i.e., degree of highness on mileage). Consequently, numerical information was argued to be easier to distinguish, i.e., less likely to be confused with similar information on another attribute, and, therefore, easier to encode and/or retrieve than verbal information. They used a design where task (i.e., learning versus choice or judgment) was manipulated between

subjects and information mode (numerical versus verbal information) was manipulated within subjects. Four fictitious brands of calculators were described along four attributes, with equal proportions of numerical versus verbal information along each attribute. Information was presented to subjects sequentially in a brand-based format using computers. Numerical information was found to require less time to process than verbal information during a learning task, and was subsequently recognized faster and more accurately, and recalled more accurately than verbal information. Several of these differences persisted for a choice and a judgment task. Additional experiments showed that differences between numerical and verbal information during learning were decreased or eliminated if information along an attribute was presented either numerically or verbally for all brands (i.e., because such a presentation clearly linked a particular verbal anchor (e.g., narrow-wide) to a specific attribute (e.g., display width)) or by presenting numerical information in a more generic form that is similar to verbal information (i.e., numbers on a rating scale) (Table).

Viswanathan (1994) assessed the influence of summary information (e.g., the mean of all brands along an attribute) in facilitating the usage of numerical nutrition information by consumers. The design involved four groups of subjects assigned to the following conditions; numerical nutrition information, numerical nutrition information with the mean as summary information, numerical nutrition information with the range as summary information, and verbal nutrition information. Information on fictitious brands of cereal along three attributes was presented using computers. Following exposure to information on each brand in one experiment and following exposure to information on all brands in another experiment, subjects completed scales relating to evaluations of each brand. Subjects then completed a free recall task and a recognition task. The provision of summary information along with numerical nutrition information led to greater accuracy of recall, as well as greater recall of numerical information in a verbal form. Verbal presentation of information also led to greater recall accuracy than numerical presentation (Table). Verbal presentation of information also led to greater recognition accuracy than numerical presentation with or without summary information. These results represent a reversal of the advantages for numerical information reported by Viswanathan and Childers (1995).

Viswanathan (1995) used a within subjects design where subjects were shown information on four fictitious brands of cereal along four attributes, two of which were presented numerically and two verbally, and asked to provide judgments. Therefore, numerical versus verbal information were in direct competition. Following exposure to information on each brand, subjects completed scales relating to evaluations of each brand. Subsequently, subjects completed an attribute rating task where they rated each fictitious brand along each attribute, and then a free recall task. Three groups of subjects were assigned to different conditions where the information on numerically presented attributes was presented without summary information, with the mean, or with the range of all brands as summary information. Accuracy of ratings of brands based on attribute information, and accuracy of recall of brand information were higher for the attributes presented verbally rather than numerically (Table). These advantages appeared to persist even when numerical information is presented with summary information to facilitate its interpretation.

Several differences and similarities in these studies on memory are noteworthy. Comparing the Viswanathan and Childers (1995) experiments where verbal information involved the use of unique anchors for each attribute (e.g., narrow-wide for display width, long-short for battery life, etc.) to the nutrition studies (Viswanathan

1994; 1995), it is possible that the description of all information on an attribute verbally in the nutrition studies may have contributed to the reversal of effects. However, the use of non-specific verbal labels across all attributes in the nutrition studies suggests that the effect of this factor may have been minimal.

The nutrition studies involved instructions to perform a judgment task similar to some experiments reported by Viswanathan and Childers (1995) where the advantages for numerical information persisted for a judgment task as well. Moreover, the reversal of effects in the nutrition studies were found when judgment ratings were collected after exposure to each brand, as well as after exposure to all brands as in the Viswanathan and Childers (1995) experiments. Therefore, task instructions and sequencing of evaluations may not have contributed to the reversal of effects.

A key difference between the studies that may explain the results is the subjects' level of prior knowledge about cereals versus calculators and their consequent ability to interpret numerical information (Figure). Because subjects (undergraduate students) are likely to know about and own a calculator, they may have been able to interpret the numerical information provided to them on attributes when compared to subjects in the nutrition studies and their ability to interpret numerical labels describing, say, fiber content, of cereals. Consequently, they may have used numerical information to a lesser degree than when it was provided with summary information or when nutrition information was presented verbally leading to lesser subsequent recall and recognition for numerical information.

Motivation to process numerical information appears to be an important factor in understanding memory for numerical versus verbal information (Figure). As with the studies on comparisons, even with the availability of summary information to interpret numerical information, verbal presentation led to better memory suggesting that consumers were more likely to use verbal information rather than expend the effort to interpret numerical labels and extract meaning from it.

USAGE AND EVALUATION

Several researchers have examined the impact of numerical versus verbal information on product evaluations. Beltramini and Evans (1985) compared quantitative versus qualitative information on believability. A national sample of auto registrants completed a questionnaire containing print ads for a car with quantitative (e.g., "60 out of 100 consumers prefer ...") versus qualitative (e.g., "most consumers prefer ...") information. Unexpectedly, qualitative information was found to be significantly more believable than quantitative information. Yalch and Yalch (1984) argued that, because a quantitative message is more complex than a qualitative message, it may reduce consumers' motivation to process the message and increase the likelihood of processing based on peripheral cues (see also Witt, 1976). They examined the effect of source expertise on attitudes for numerical versus verbal information by using a design that manipulated source expertise at two levels (expert versus non-expert) and the degree of message quantitativeness at two levels. Subjects viewed commercials inserted within a program which discussed the advantages of the automatic teller at a local bank with message quantitativeness being manipulated by the amount of numerical data (quantitative–"...many people do 95% of their banking..." versus qualitative–"...many persons do virtually all their banking...."). Subjects completed scales relating to their attitudes toward the message. An interaction between source expertise and quantitativeness was found, with no difference in attitudes for expert versus non-expert sources for qualitative messages and a significantly more favorable attitude toward the

message for expert when compared to non-expert sources for quantitative messages (Table).

Artz and Tybout (1991) argued that numerical versus verbal information may require different source characteristics in order to be believable. Because numerical information is precise in nature, source expertise is likely to enhance believability. Because verbal information is evaluative, trustworthiness of source is likely to enhance believability. The authors used a between subjects design where information mode (numerical–"...60% reduction in the computer delays..." versus verbal–"...significant reduction in the computing delays..."), source expertise (expert/non-expert), and source trustworthiness (trustworthy/untrustworthy) were manipulated. Subjects read a brief introduction to a micro-computer utility and then indicated their attitude toward the product. Consistent with the predictions, expertise had a significant effect on attitudes only for numerical information as in the Yalch and Yalch (1984) study and trustworthiness had a significant effect on attitudes only for verbal information (Table).

Scammon (1977) compared adjectival versus percentage of Recommended Daily Allowance presentations of nutrition information using a between subjects design. Subjects viewed 30 second commercials for two brands of peanut butter with nutritional labels from packages being superimposed on the last 6 seconds of each commercial, and then completed a questionnaire about the information they saw. Scammon (1977) found that adjectival rather than percentage descriptors of nutritional information led to more accurate identification of most nutritious brands (Table). Greater decision satisfaction and less need for information were found with the use of percentage information. The author points out that percentage versus adjective information differ in the extent to which percentage information is unprocessed and adjective information is preprocessed.

Viswanathan (1994; 1995) compared verbal versus numerical presentations in facilitating the usage of nutrition information. The valence of numerical versus verbal information was manipulated for each brand such that it was positive for attributes presented verbally and negative for attributes presented numerically or vice versa. Differences between brands on overall ratings were used to assess the weight given to numerical versus verbal information. Results of several experiments suggested that verbal information may be given greater weight in judgments of healthiness. These advantages persisted even when numerical information was presented with summary information to facilitate its interpretation (Table).

Svenson and Karlsson (1986) examined attractiveness of student apartments using a design where subjects were shown information along three attributes with the assignment of numerical versus verbal information to attributes manipulated between subjects. They found weak support for more weight being given to numerical information in overall judgments, with this effect being obtained for poor alternatives.

In summary, past research suggests that the believability of numerical versus verbal information may be moderated by source characteristics (Figure). Moreover, verbal information which directly conveys meaning may enhance the accuracy of overall judgments. More weight may also be given to verbal information in overall judgments. These results appear to hold when consumers' knowledge about a product category is not high. Consumers who lack the ability to interpret numerical information in terms of its meaning may be motivated to process verbal information which is preprocessed (Scammon 1977), when compared to numerical information.

THEORETICAL IMPLICATIONS AND FUTURE RESEARCH

Two categories of factors are noteworthy in examining the research across different elements of decision making; differences in numerical and verbal information along certain dimensions, and ability and motivation to process numerical information in terms of its meaning. Research on information search brings out the distinction between unit-specific numerical information and numerical ratings along the dimension of ease of computations (Figure) as well as the importance of knowledge about a product category and the consequent ability in assessing numerical magnitudes along attributes. Research on comparisons of product labels suggested that the effect of product knowledge may be moderated by motivation to expend effort required to interpret a label's meaning.

Research on memory suggests additional dimensions that distinguish between numerical and verbal information; the degree to which a magnitude is linked to a specific attribute and the degree to which a magnitude readily conveys meaning (Figure). Consumers' ability to interpret numerical labels appears to be central to the different results found across the studies. Advantages for numerical information may occur when consumers' have the ability to interpret numerical labels and may be reversed when consumers do not have such ability. Even with ability, motivation to process numerical information in terms of its meaning is an important factor. Hence, advantages for verbal information were found even when numerical information was presented with summary information to facilitate its interpretation. Research on evaluations suggests that more weight may also be given to verbal information in overall judgments when consumers' ability to interpret numerical labels is low (Figure).

Numerical and verbal information appear to differ on some important dimensions that influence their processing including the degree to which a magnitude is linked to a specific attribute, and the degree to which a magnitude readily conveys meaning. Numerical information along a unit of measurement versus generic verbal descriptors represent extremes along these dimensions. Numerical ratings are like generic verbal descriptors, whereas percentage information, such as % of USDA, are similar to numerical information along a unit of measurement in not conveying meaning directly, and similar to generic verbal descriptors in not being specific to an attribute. Certain verbal magnitudes may be relatively more specifically linked to an attribute to the extent that they are exclusively associated with it (e.g., "roomy" interior for an automobile, on the attribute, interior space). Certain numerical magnitudes along a unit of measurement may convey meaning more directly (e.g., the "1 calorie" cola which directly conveys very low calorie content). Ease of computations is another factor on which verbal information may represent one extreme and numerical ratings the other with unit-specific numerical information and % of USDA being in between. Believability is another dimension on which numerical and verbal information may differ that is contingent on factors such as source characteristics.

Ability to process numerical information as well as motivation appear to be central to understanding the studies reviewed here. Central to the processing of numerical information is the ability to derive meaning from it using prior knowledge or external reference information. Lacking this ability as well as the motivation to acquire and/or use reference information, consumers may depend more on verbal information. Consumers may also process numerical information at a surface level in terms of the sizes of numbers involved. On the other hand, with a high level of ability to interpret numerical labels almost effortlessly using prior knowledge, consumers may depend more on numerical information. With intermediate levels of prior knowledge where some effort is required in comparing numerical information to reference information available in memory, motivation may play a role in determining whether numerical information is processed in terms of its meaning. A similar scenario may occur when reference information is provided to consumers with low levels of ability to enable them to interpret numerical information. Such interpretation may require effort and consequently lead to greater dependence on verbal information if motivation is low.

A parallel can be drawn to the Elaboration-Likelihood Model (Petty and Cacioppo, 1981) wherein processing numerical information in terms of its meaning roughly overlaps with central processing and surface level processing or lack of processing of numerical information roughly overlaps with peripheral processing. The role of ability can be distinguished in terms of consumers' prior knowledge versus the provision of external information that enables central (i.e., meaning level) processing, with the latter perhaps requiring greater effort. The role of motivation to engage in central (i.e., meaning level) processing in light of task characteristics are noteworthy. When the task can be accomplished without meaning level processing, consumers may not be motivated to do so even when they have the ability. For example, consumers may compare two brands of cereal with fiber content of 1 and 2 grams per serving and choose the one with 2 grams in the belief that it has "high" fiber content when it is below average on fiber content for cereals. Such "peripheral" processing may be particularly likely for consumers who lack ability and may persist even when external information is available to interpret numerical information. It may also occur when consumers have ability based on prior knowledge but need to expend some effort to interpret numerical information, i.e., engage in "central" processing.

Key avenues of future research include an examination of different types of numerical and verbal product information. Key characteristics of magnitude information suggested here should be considered in examining the processing of numerical versus verbal information. Numerical information ranging from ratings on a scale to unit-specific numerical information and percentage information should be examined as should descriptive verbal information (such as "high" calories), evaluative verbal labels (such as "good" on calories), and the use of unique versus generic verbal anchors to describe attributes. Whereas past research has focused on only one or a few elements of consumer decision making, all elements should be studied in future research. Research should also examine the impact of information load (i.e., the number of attributes and brands).

Future research should also examine two key aspects of processing; ability and motivation to process numerical information. A host of issues relating to different elements of consumer decision making need to be examined while manipulating the level of product knowledge and the consequent ability to interpret numerical information along an attribute (i.e., the availability of a reference point). The effects of providing reference information to consumers with low knowledge need to be examined in terms of consumers' motivation to interpret numerical information versus using simpler verbal information. Motivation also appears to be an issue with knowledgeable consumers who may still engage in more superficial processing rather than expend effort depending on the nature of the task.

Research should continue to uncover empirical effects that provide a basis for theorizing about numerical and verbal information. Boundary conditions as well as reversals of effects need to be identified for all elements of consumer decision making. If the research reviewed here is an indication, this area of research offers several interesting empirical findings that may be moderated by various factors. In conclusion, research on numerical and verbal information offers important insight into consumer decision making and interesting avenues for future consumer research.

REFERENCES

Artz, Nancy, and Alice Tybout (1991), "Numeric and Verbal Information and Source Credibility," *Working Paper*.

Banks, W.P. (1977), "Encoding and Processing of Symbolic Information in Comparative Judgments," In G.H. Bower (ed.), *The Psychology of Learning and Motivation, 11*, 101-159, New York: Academic Press.

Beltramini, Richard F., and Kenneth R. Evans (1985), "Perceived Believability of Research Results Information in Advertising," *Journal of Advertising*, 14 (3), 18-31.

Childers, Terry, Esra Gencturk, and Janette Shimanski (1992), *Issues in the Organization and Representation of Consumer Information in Memory*, Unpublished Manuscript.

Holyoak, K. J. (1978), "Comparative judgments with numerical reference points," *Cognitive Psychology, 10*, 203-243.

Huber, Oswald (1980), "The Influence of some Task Variables on Cognitive Operations in an Information Processing Decision Model," *Acta Psychologica*, 45 , 187-96.

Jaffe-Katz, A., D. Budescu, and T. S. Wallsten (1989), "Timed magnitude comparisons of numerical and nonnumerical expressions of uncertainty," *Memory and Cognition, 17* (3), 249-264.

Levy, Alan S., Odonna Mathews, Marilyn Stephenson, Janet E. Tenney, and Raymond E. Schucker (1985), "The Impact of a Nutrition Information Program on Food Purchases," *Journal of Public Policy and Marketing*, 4, 1-13.

Mazumdar, Tridib, and Kent B. Monroe (1990), "The Effects of Buyers' Intentions to Learn Price Information on Price Encoding," *Journal of Retailing*, 66 (1), 15-32.

Pavio, Teresa M., and Janeen Arnold Costa (1993), "The Winning Number: Consumer Perceptions of Alpha-Numeric Brand Names," *Journal of Marketing*, 57, 85-98.

Petty, R. E., and T. J. Cacioppo (1981), *Attitudes and persuasion: Classic and contemporary approaches*, Dubuque, IA: Brown.

Scammon, Debra L. (1977), "'Information Load' and Consumers," *Journal of Consumer Research*, 4 (December), 148-155.

Stone, Dan, and David Schkade (1991), "Numeric and Linguistic Information Representation in Multiattribute Choice," *Organizational Behavior and Human DecisionProcesses*, 49, 42-59.

Svenson, Ola, and Gunnar Karlsson (1986), "Attractiveness of decision alternatives characterized by numerical and non-numerical information," *Scandinavian Journal of Psychology*, 27, 74-84.

Viswanathan, Madhubalan (1994), "The Influence of Summary Information on the Usage of Nutrition Information," *Journal of Public Policy and Marketing,* 13 (1), 48-60.

Viswanathan, Madhubalan (1995), "A Comparison of the Usage of Numerical Versus Verbal Nutrition Information by Consumers," *Advances in Consumer Research,* Vol. 23, Kim Corfman and John Lynch eds., Provo, UT: Association for Consumer Research, p. 277-81.

Viswanathan, Madhubalan, and Terry Childers (1995), "Processing of Numerical and Verbal Product Information," *Working Paper*, University of Illinois.

Viswanathan, Madhubalan, and Sunder Narayanan (1992), "Processing Numerical Versus Verbal Attribute Information: A Study Using Information Acquisition Patterns," *Marketing Letters*, 3 (2), 201-208.

Viswanathan, Madhubalan, and Sunder Narayanan (1994), "Comparative Judgments of Numerical and Verbal Attribute Labels," *Journal of Consumer Psychology*, 3 (1), 79-101.

Witt, William (1976), "Effects of Quantification in Scientific Writing," *Journal of Communication*, 26, 67-69.

Yalch, Richard F., and Rebecca Elmore Yalch (1984), "The Effect of Numbers on the Route to Persuasion," *Journal of Consumer Research*, 11, 522-527.

Metaphors in Marketing: Review and Implications for Marketers

Kristine Bremer, University of Colorado at Denver
Moonkyu Lee, Yonsei University

ABSTRACT

Metaphors are used extensively in marketing, yet little research exists in the consumer behavior and marketing literature on how consumers react to them. This paper reviews selected research in the psychology and linguistic literature on metaphor comprehension and processing, and suggests several implications for marketers. The paper also discusses future research directions in the area.

INTRODUCTION

Marketers use metaphors extensively in their persuasive communications to consumers. These metaphors make implicit or explicit statements or suggestions that a product, service, brand, or company is some unique idea or concept. Marketing metaphors can have linguistic, visual, and/or symbolic components. Some examples include (1) slogans such as *"Budweiser*, the king of beers," *"Chevrolet*, the heartbeat of America," and *"Pioneer*, the art of entertainment," (2) brand names like *Safari* (a perfume), *Tide* (a laundry detergent), and *Fiesta* (a car), and (3) visual or symbolic metaphors such as the image of the young, nude female in the advertisement for *Obsession for Men* (a cologne).

Marketers use metaphors to achieve many objectives; i.e., to gain consumer attention, evoke imagery, provoke comparisons, suggest similarity between a product and a concept, explain a complex or technical product, or influence consumer beliefs and attitudes. Marketers spend considerable time and money developing metaphors to achieve their marketing objectives. Then it seems likely that marketers would benefit from knowing how consumers process metaphors, how metaphors are stored in memory, whether or not metaphors used in marketing are understood by consumers, when they are more or less effective, or what effects metaphors have on consumer affect or preferences.

Metaphor research in the psychology and linguistic literature is extensive (Bartel 1983; Black 1962; Gildea and Glucksberg 1983; Glucksberg et al. 1982; Johnson and Malgady 1980; Katz 1989; Lakoff and Johnson 1980; McCabe 1983; Ortony et al. 1978; Shinjo and Myers 1987; Sternberg and Nigro 1983; Tourangeau and Sternberg 1983; Trick and Katz 1986; Verbrugge and McCarrell 1977). However, very little research is found in the consumer behavior and marketing literature on the nature of metaphors in marketing (Ward and Gaidis 1990). Therefore, the purpose of this article is to review the relevant literature on metaphor and discuss several implications for marketers who use metaphors.

THE MEANING OF METAPHOR

Metaphor is a form of figurative or nonliteral language. Figurative language expresses one thing in terms normally denoting another with which it may be regarded as analogous. We reason analogically when we make the inference that if two or more things agree with one another in some respects they will probably agree in others. Metaphor is linguistically distinguished from simile, which is less bold, asserting a relation of similarity by using a comparative term such as "like" or "as" (e.g., the freeway is like a snake). In metaphor, the comparative term is omitted (e.g., love is a rose).

Aristotle defined metaphor as "the application of an alien name by transference either from genus to species, or from species to genus, or from species to species, or by analogy." The application of an "alien" name means taking a word that usually denotes one thing and using it to describe another that it literally does not denote

(Billow 1977). The "thing" can be an object, abstract idea, or feeling.

A metaphor has two parts: topic and vehicle (Richards 1936). The topic, also called the tenor, is the subject of the metaphor, the "general drift" or underlying idea which the metaphor expresses. The vehicle is the basic analogy which is used to embody or carry the tenor. For example, in the advertising slogan, *"Budweiser*, the king of beers," the brand name *Budweiser* is the topic, and "the king of beers" is the vehicle, or concept with which the topic is compared. The tenor and vehicle interact, and their "transaction" generates the meaning of the metaphor (Hawkes 1972). The resemblance between the domains of the tenor and vehicle is called the ground, or ground concept. The ground relates the vehicle and topic. Since the ground is usually implicit, the receiver must discern the resemblance on his/her own. In the above example, the product (or brand) and the referent, i.e., *Budweiser* beer and the king, have no prior intrinsic relationship but are paired together arbitrarily and metaphorically by marketers.

Wheelright (1962) describes two general types of metaphor: ephiphor and diaphor. Ephiphors *express* a similarity between something well known or concretely known (the vehicle) and something which is less well known or more obscure (the tenor). The use of an ephiphor presupposes a notion that can readily be understood when indicated by a suitable word or phrase (MacCormac 1985). The success of an ephiphor depends on our ability to recognize features of similarity between the referents. Some ephiphors are so successful that they lose their semantic anomaly and fade into ordinary language, becoming "dead" metaphors. Usage leads to our acceptance, and one (or both) of the referents is given additional new meaning. Diaphors have a suggestive function. Rather than expressing similarities between referents, diaphors *suggest* new possible meanings by emphasizing the dissimilarities between them. In the example, "toasted Susie is my ice cream," a new meaning is underscored by the distinction between warm ("toasted") and cold ("ice cream"). All metaphors have ephiphoric and diaphoric aspects. Some tend to be more expressive (ephiphoric), others more suggestive (diaphoric), and some equally both.

Many researchers suggest that what is termed "metaphor" is a cognitive operation of analogical reasoning in which new meaning is created (see e.g., Richards 1936; Ortony 1979; MacCormac 1985; Haskell 1987). Allegories, similes, idioms, and proverbs are understood in this same way. Richards (1936), seen by many as one of the most important contributor to our understanding of metaphor, holds that metaphor is the "omnipresent principle" of all language. He asserts that language contains deeply embedded metaphorical structures which influence meaning and meaning creation. For example, language cannot be cleared of metaphor without using a metaphor in the verb, "clear." Metaphor is the way language works (Hawkes 1972). MacCormac (1985) theorizes that metaphor results from the human mind operating hierarchically to juxtapose widely disparate semantic concepts which produce metaphors that can be comprehended. This process identifies similar attributes of the referents of the metaphor to form an analogy and identifies dissimilar attributes to create semantic anomaly, or disanalogy.

For purposes of this paper, metaphor is defined as a method of description, using language or symbols, which likens one thing to another thing or concept by referring to it as if it were the other one. In marketing metaphors, words and/or pictures frequently

Advances in Consumer Research
Volume 24, © 1997

implicitly or explicitly suggest that a product, service, brand, or company is some other concept. In the previous example, the slogan, *"Budweiser,* the king of beers," suggests rather explicitly that the *Budweiser* brand beer *is* king of, or ruler over, all beers on the market. One of the implications flowing from the metaphor research is that marketers might achieve greater persuasion if they carefully consider what their metaphors express to the target audience. Measures of perceived meaning and similarity of domains of popular marketing metaphors may shed new light on whether or not they communicate effectively to the audience. In addition, selection of type of metaphor used may have an impact on comprehension and effectiveness. For example, the advertising slogan *"Revlon,* Revolutionary" expresses similarity between the well known brand of cosmetic products and less known term, revolutionary. A perceived similarity between the two may be the shared first three letters, *R-E-V.* Further, the mere juxtaposition of the two words implies a relation, perhaps that the *Revlon* brand creates a radical change in the user of the product and does so quickly. Whatever the intended meaning, the success of this metaphor may be defined in terms of the target's ability to comprehend the meaning quickly and recognize features of similarity between the two referents.

LITERATURE REVIEW

General Findings. Tourangeau and Sternberg (1982) describe three main views of metaphor comprehension: anomaly, comparison (or similarity), and interactionist. The anomaly view emphasizes the dissimilarity of the semantic features of the metaphor topic (subject) and vehicle. In linguistic theory, "selection restrictions" are violated when the vehicle does not fall into the exclusive category ranges determined by the message recipient. This results in sentences being perceived as anomalous, or deviant (Katz 1964), which in turn creates tension. The comparison view contends that the message recipient comprehends a metaphor of the form A is B by finding the set of similarities between A and B. The meaning of the metaphor is the set of similarities between the concepts (Johnson and Malgady 1979). The interactionist view emphasizes both similarity and dissimilarity of the topic and vehicle but denies the simple positive or negative relationship between semantic relatedness and metaphor attributes. This view holds that the process of metaphor comprehension is a more complex process that involves relationships between relatedness, metaphor "goodness" (one that lends itself to a single interpretation), degree of metaphoricity, and ease of interpretation (or comprehensibility). Other views emphasize the importance of perception (Verbrugge and McCarrell 1977), verbal processes (Koen 1965), imaginal processes (Paivio 1971) or perceptual processes analogous to Gestalt principles (Malgady and Johnson 1976).

The domains-interaction approach to metaphor processing, originally proposed by Tourangeau and Sternberg (1982), is viewed by many metaphor theorists as the most complete explanation of how metaphor is comprehended. The process uses the same component processes that analogy processing involves (Trick and Katz 1986), and the steps are proposed to be executed sequentially (Sternberg and Nigro 1983; Tourangeau and Sternberg 1982):

(1) Tenor and vehicle are encoded.

(2) Domains (categories) of the tenor and vehicle are inferred.

(3) Structures to be seen as parallel are inferred.

(4) The correspondence between the structures is mapped between domains of the tenor and vehicle.

(5) The tenor and vehicle of the metaphor are compared and the match is evaluated.

(6) A response is generated.

In the example, "the engine is the life of your car," the tenor ("engine") and the vehicle ("life of your car") are encoded. Then, the relevant domains are found: the "engine" in the domain of mechanically powered objects and "life" in the domain of organic existence. The characteristics or attributes of the tenor and vehicle that are likely to be relevant are chosen next. This process involves restricting the possible characteristics that the tenor and vehicle could share to those that would give a sense of their relative positions within their respective domains. If the characteristics of the tenor (or vehicle) are not known, the message recipient will use dimensions that give a sense of the relative position of the vehicle (or tenor) within its domain (Sternberg 1982). If possible, a potential within-domain factor is found. Next, the relative standing of the vehicle compared to its domain on this factor is "mapped" onto the domain of mechanically powered objects. The relative positions of the "engine" and "life of the car" are compared with respect to the dimension "aggression." If the two domains were superimposed, points for the engine and life would lie very close to each other (would be strongly similar). Lastly, this correspondence between the tenor and vehicle is evaluated, and a response is generated.

Gildea and Glucksberg (1983) show that some types of simple metaphors are understood automatically and that processing is initiated by appropriate linguistic and semantic inputs without our control. The message recipient derives a literal meaning of the metaphor first. If this meaning does not work, that is, makes no sense in the context it is presented in, then s/he proceeds to do the additional work of finding a nonliteral meaning that does work.

Research shows that the similarity and dissimilarity between the topic and vehicle of a metaphor play a fundamental role in their appreciation (Ortony 1979; Tourangeau and Sternberg 1981, 1982). In the metaphor, "the sky is a mirror," "sky" and "mirror" are categorically dissimilar; i.e., sky is in a natural object category and mirror in an artifact category. However, they are perceptually or affectively similar in that they share some features or attributes (e.g., bright, clear, etc.). Kusumi (1987) shows that high categorical dissimilarity of topic to vehicle increases message recipients' interest in the sentence.

There appears to be general agreement in the metaphor literature that metaphor is both a linguistic construct as well as a cognitive process involving analogic reasoning in which new meaning is created. However, there is general disagreement as to *how* that meaning is created. The anomaly, comparison and interactionist perspectives on metaphor comprehension suggest that marketers may also, upon further investigation of marketing metaphors, find themselves divided on the issues. Possible emphases may be metaphor structure, perception processes, imagery and/or pictorial interactions with metaphors. Any empirical research conducted by marketers on how consumer process metaphors could contribute to the existing literature in each of the disciplines and help resolve some of the many unanswered questions.

Marketing Implications. The research suggests that marketers studying metaphor have a complicated set of issues to examine including such concepts as comprehensibility, relatedness, and metaphoricity. These concepts need to be examined in light of the information processing paradigm, as well as automaticity, similarity, and other concepts found in the psychology and consumer behavior literature. Further, the information processing approach to metaphor comprehension described above suggests that, to have any impact on marketing metaphor comprehension, the marketer must develop apt metaphors with clear, structured domains (categories) so that the message recipient is led to infer the intended categories early in the comprehension process. Though the research is not conclusive, it also suggests that, to increase consumer interest in marketing metaphors, marketers may want to use those with higher dissimilarity between topic and vehicle.

Comprehensibility and Aptness of Metaphor

Research Findings. Comprehensibility refers to whether or not the receiver understands the intended meaning of the metaphor. A metaphor is thought to be comprehensible if the receiver understands its intended meaning. An apt metaphor is one which is "good, pleasing, and appropriate" (Katz et al. 1985). A metaphor must at least be comprehensible to be apt.

Tourganeau and Sternberg's (1982) domains-interaction model describes the most apt metaphors as those having a close point-by-point correspondence between the two domains, and suggests that a metaphor's comprehensibility should increase to the extent that within-domain similarity increases. The model emphasizes two types of correspondence: between-domain and within-domain correspondence. In the former, a metaphor is perceived as more apt, but less comprehensible, to the degree that the tenor and vehicle are from dissimilar categories. In the latter, correspondence is based on the degree to which the beliefs about the tenor are perceived as corresponding to beliefs about the vehicle. For example, *Calvin Klein*'s cologne is metaphorically named *Obsession*. Cologne is a distinctively different category than mental states including haunting preoccupation, yet the company has created the name and promoted the product to have attributes similar to an obsession. According to the model, the metaphor's comprehensibility should increase to the extent that within-domain similarity increases, that is, the degree to which we believe *Obsession*, a cologne, is like a mental state of preoccupation. If the tenor and vehicle are from similar categories, the metaphor will seem less apt because the comparison is too easy or obvious. Kusumi (1987) found that high affective similarity increases comprehensibility and novelty, and comprehensibility and interest have positive effects on metaphor aptness. Quality (or goodness) and clarity of interaction between tenor and vehicle can increase comprehensibility and aptness (Sternberg and Nigro 1983).

Marketing Implications. The research on comprehensibility and aptness suggests several issues of concern for marketers. First, consumers must understand the intended meaning of the metaphor (frequently the marketing message) in order for comprehension to occur. If the consumer does not understand the meaning, use of the metaphor does not achieve the marketer's objectives. Second, the perceived degree of correspondence between the domains of the metaphor is dependent on consumer beliefs. This suggests that marketers should examine the target segment's beliefs about the product and message to determine what metaphors will work better than others. Third, to increase comprehensibility and novelty, marketers should design metaphors that have high perceived similarity between domains. To increase aptness, the metaphor used should be comprehensible and interesting to the target. Another way to increase aptness is to create metaphors that involve strong dissimilarity between referents, e.g., cologne and mental states. Lastly, high quality metaphors, ones that are apt and lend themselves to a single interpretation, may increase comprehensibility and aptness.

Contextual Influence on Metaphor Comprehension

Research Findings. Context has an impact on metaphor comprehension, affecting the message recipient's understanding of its intended meaning (Harwood and Verbrugge 1977; Tversky 1977). Also, people need contextual information to identify and understand metaphors. Context can facilitate metaphor comprehension by making a specific and relevant concept available and accessible at the time of processing. In the psychology and linguistic literature, context refers to the primes (e.g., words, sentences, or paragraphs) which set the stage for metaphor interpretation, helping the message recipient understand the intended meaning. The context can be minimal, one that provides nothing more than the relevant dimension of an implicit comparison. If a communicator does not provide a context that is minimally informative, the message recipient will not understand the metaphor rapidly (Ortony et al. 1978).

Two contexts are defined in the literature: social and linguistic. The social context refers to the circumstances or facts surrounding the message recipient's exposure to the metaphor. The linguistic, or semantic, context of the metaphor refers to the language preceding or following the metaphor.

Gildea and Glucksberg (1983) find that both literal and figurative priming contexts facilitate metaphor comprehension. Figurative primes are abstract, metaphorical words or sentences. Literal primes are factual words or sentences holding the primary meaning of the metaphor vehicle. Figurative primes are more likely to facilitate metaphor comprehension than literal primes. This is because a figurative prime uses the same sense of the critical word as the metaphor target does. If the literal and figurative senses of a word are psychologically distinct from one another (i.e., if they are stored as separate entries in memory), a figurative prime should be more effective with a figurative target than a literal prime.

Gildea and Glucksberg also find that it takes longer to reject a figuratively primed metaphor than it does to reject a figuratively primed scrambled metaphor. In unprimed and literally primed contexts, subjects took less time to accept or reject the metaphor. The researchers show that metaphors appearing in the immediate context of stimuli (in sentences) that activate relevant ground concepts are understood more rapidly than those same metaphors appearing in unrelated immediate contexts. They conclude that the literal sense of a word can activate the figurative sense of a related word concept and this in turn facilitates comprehension of a simple nominative metaphor (one that juxtaposes nouns, as opposed to verbs).

Marketing Implications. Several implications flow from the research on the role of context in metaphor comprehension. First, Tversky and Kahneman's (1974) concepts of availability and accessibility are directly relevant to metaphor context and comprehension. Studies of the relationships among these concepts and metaphor comprehension would be valuable to marketers designing marketing metaphors. Second, the contextual prime in linguistics is analogous to the verbal and visual stimuli (external imagery) researched in advertising (Lutz and Lutz 1977; MacInnis and Price 1987). Marketers could enhance their understanding of consumers' metaphor comprehension by applying some of the imagery research and methods to marketing metaphors. Third, adequate and appropriate primes should be used with marketing metaphors if consumers are to comprehend them. Marketers should use figurative primes (as opposed to literal primes) to facilitate metaphor comprehension. Lastly, they should develop metaphors that appear in the immediate context of sentences that activate the relevant ground concept rather than metaphors that appear in unrelated contexts.

Automatic Processing and the Metaphor Interference Effect

Research Findings. Shiffrin and Schneider (1977) show that metaphor processing is initiated by appropriate linguistic and semantic inputs, and the message recipient normally has no control over whether a metaphor is understood or not. Stroop (1935) also shows that fluent readers cannot inhibit reading words that are shown to them. Gildea and Glucksberg (1983) demonstrate that fluent speakers of a language cannot inhibit understanding the metaphorical meanings of some types of sentences. They show a "metaphor interference effect" which serves as a sensitivity index of how quickly and automatically metaphorical meanings are comprehended. In their experiment, subjects made literal true-false decisions on four types of test sentences. The simple metaphor "all jobs are jails" was literally false, and subjects had no difficulty deciding that the statement was false. But they had available a true nonliteral interpretation, that people can feel trapped in their jobs. This nonliteral interpretation interfered with their literal-false decision. When a metaphorical interpretation of a literally false sentence was available, subjects took significantly longer to decide that the sentences were literally false. Glucksberg et al. concluded that the subjects had comprehended the "true" metaphorical meanings automatically, or non-optionally, and that they did this quickly enough so as to interfere with a seemingly straightforward literal-false decision.

Gildea and Glucksberg contend that with poor metaphors, such as "all marriages are iceboxes," people have no trouble deciding that the metaphor is literally false and that the metaphor does not work. Ortony (1979) asserts that if the ground concept is available and accessible when the metaphor is being processed by the message recipient, then the metaphor should be understood automatically and rapidly. Their research suggests that making a relevant dimension of comparison implicit in a nominative metaphor will significantly facilitate metaphor comprehension.

Marketing Implications. Several marketing issues arise out of the discussion on automatic processing of metaphors. First, the consumer's lack of control of processing of some metaphors suggests that marketers may want to use metaphors that have this characteristic. Marketing messages could then be more rapidly understood. Second, consumers may have little trouble determining whether a metaphor works (or is apt) or not, and marketing metaphors currently in use may simply be discounted by consumers, diminishing the effects of the marketer's intended message. Third, marketers may have little control over metaphor comprehension when their marketing metaphor is imbued with cultural meaning. Finally, to facilitate nominative metaphor comprehension, marketers should make the ground concept implicit.

Heuristics and Metaphor Comprehension

Research Findings. People use strategies for understanding metaphors which cause metaphor comprehension to be automatic (Gildea and Glucksberg 1983). These strategies, or heuristics, are used in everyday discourse and are so pervasive and well-practiced that they are no longer under conscious control. One is Grice's (1975) cooperative principle which asserts that when trying to understand a statement like "X is a Y," we assume the statement is informative. Another is Clark and Haviland's (1977) rules for marking given and new information. If given "X is a Y," we conform to a protocol in our mind, and then look for new information in Y that would be informative about X. Next, those properties of Y that are salient (normally activated in the mental representation of Y) are applied to X. If those properties are applicable to and informative about X, this provides a ready interpretation of the statement. Properties, or attributes, of the vehicle (Y) that are uninformative about the metaphor topic (X) rarely provide suitable grounds for interpretation. People ignore these attributes unless they are explicitly pointed out or are used in a context where they are informative.

Marketing Implications. The literature on metaphor comprehension strategies is not well developed, but provides some insight and future research directions for marketers. First, the unconscious use of the cooperative principle and conventions for marking given and new information suggests that marketers may have very limited control over the consumer's processing of metaphors. Second, these strategies could be empirically tested with marketing metaphors to add to the literature on metaphor comprehension. In the process, new or undiscovered consumer processing strategies may be revealed.

Metaphors and Imagery

Research Findings. It is suggested that the priming context in the metaphor literature operates much like pictures and symbols do in advertising message comprehension. Pictures can facilitate comprehension of the intended meaning of the advertising message and elicit internal imagery. To elicit imagery, marketers use visual or pictorial stimuli, concrete verbal stimuli, and imagery instructions. Pictures are best remembered because they elicit imagery; words alone are less likely to evoke imagery (Lutz and Lutz 1978).

External imagery effects on learning have been researched within the paired-associate learning paradigm. Subjects shown an interactive image relating two items have higher recall scores than those not presented with an interactive image (Davidson 1964). A necessary condition for a facilitative effect on learning is the interactive feature of the mediating message. The image integrates the two items in some mutual way (Bower 1972).

The concreteness of a stimulus attribute is found to be positively correlated with the learnability of the material presented, and mental imagery aids recall (Bower 1972). Subjects prefer concrete over more abstract vehicles in metaphor completion tasks (Katz 1989). Paivio (1979) suggests that vehicle imagery should be more important than topic imagery in the interpretation of metaphors. He says that the vehicle serves as an "efficient conceptual peg" for metaphor comprehension such that it promotes the retrieval of images and verbal information from memory that combines with the information elicited by the topic. Verbal information increases the probability of finding a connection between the topic and vehicle of the metaphor and keeps the search process "on track" (Marschark et al. 1983).

Marketing Implications. The research on external and internal imagery holds several implications for marketers who use metaphors. First, the concept with which a brand or product is metaphorically compared should be carefully crafted by the marketer to enhance retrieval of the desired imagery and increase the probability of message comprehension. The image used should be interactive with the verbal message to facilitate metaphor comprehension. Second, the literature suggests that vehicle imagery is more important than topic imagery in the interpretation of metaphors. However, marketers are advised to strive for strong pairing of vehicle with topic imagery because placing an uneven emphasis on vehicle imagery can create a situation where the audience remembers the metaphor but forgets the brand. Lastly, they should include verbal information in their advertising to increase the probability of comprehension of visual metaphors.

Other Research Findings

Other concepts and findings in the literature lead to several additional questions about metaphor comprehension and effectiveness. Briefly, Hill and Mazis (1986) demonstrate that emotional ads produce more affective comments from subjects. This finding yields the question: Do metaphors with strong emotional content have greater impact on consumer affect than those with non-emotional content? Childers and Houston (1984) show that pictorial ads do better than verbal-only ads on both immediate and delayed recall when processing focused on appearance features of the ads (see Miniard et al. 1991 for the moderating role of involvement). With semantic processing instructions, verbal-only stimuli did as well on immediate recall but worse on delayed recall. Recall was superior when brand name, attributes, and visual components were integrated pictorially but the copy conveyed discrepant information. Elaborative processing may be heightened by discrepant pictures and words. These findings prompt the questions: When is metaphoric language more or less effective? What types of metaphors have stronger recall? Is there a relationship between the findings on elaborative processing of discrepant pictures and words, and dissimilarity between metaphor domains? These questions should be dealt with by future research in the area.

SUMMARY

This article reviewed selected psychology, linguistic and marketing literature on metaphor comprehension and provided several implications for marketers who use metaphors in their persuasive communications to consumers. The review unveiled the following: (1) a preliminary assessment of consumer perception of metaphoric meanings should be made prior to use to enhance comprehensibility, (2) consumer beliefs about the parts of the metaphor impact comprehensibility and should be considered in marketing metaphor development, (3) the availability and accessibility of the metaphor's ground concept affects the consumer's ability to comprehend the metaphor, (4) to be more rapidly understood, metaphors should appear in the immediate context of sentences that activate a relevant ground, and (5) consumers use heuristics to comprehend metaphors. This article contributes to the marketing literature by analyzing the metaphor literature, extending several of the concepts found therein to marketing metaphors, and providing implications for marketers who use metaphors in their persuasive communications to consumers.

REFERENCES

Bartel, Roland (1983), *Metaphors and Symbols: Forays into Language*, Urbana, IL: National Council of Teachers of English.

Billow, Richard M. (1977), "Metaphor: A Review of the Psychological Literature," *Psychological Bulletin*, Vol. 54 (1), 81-92.

Black, Max (1962), *Models and Metaphors*, Ithaca, NY: Cornell University Press.

Bower, Gordon (1972), "Mental Imagery and Associative Learning," in *Cognition in Learning and Memory*, ed. Lee Gregg, New York: John Wiley.

Childers, Terry L. and Michael Houston (1984), "Conditions for a Picture Superiority Effect on Consumer Memory," *Journal of Consumer Research*, 11 (September), 643-655.

Clark, Herbert H., and S. E. Haviland (1977), "Comprehension and the Given-New Contract," in *Discourse Production and Comprehension*, ed. R. O. Freedle, Norwood, NJ: Ablex Publishing.

Davidson, R. E. (1964), "Mediation and Ability in Paired-associate Learning," *Journal of Educational Psychology*, 55, 352-356.

Gildea, P. and S. Glucksberg (1983), "On Understanding Metaphor: The Role of Context," *Journal of Verbal Learning and Verbal Behavior*, 22, 577-590.

Glucksberg, S., P. Gildea, and H. Bookin (1982), "On Understanding Nonliteral Speech: Can People Ignore Metaphors?" *Journal of Verbal Learning and Verbal Behavior*, 21, 85-98.

Grice, H. P. (1975), "Logic and Conversation," in *Syntax and Semantics: Speech Acts*, Vol. 3, ed. P. Cole and J. L. Morgan, New York: Academic Press.

Haskell, Robert E. (1987), *Cognition and Symbolic Structures: The Psychology of Metaphoric Transformation*, Norwood, NJ: Ablex Publishing.

Harwood, D. L. and R. R. Verbrugge (1977), "Metaphor and the Asymmetry of Similarity," paper presented at the annual meeting of the American Psychological Association, San Francisco.

Hawkes, Terence (1972), *Metaphor*, London: Methuen and Co.

Hill, Ronald P. and Michael B. Mazis (1986), "Measuring Emotional Responses to Advertising," in *Advances in Consumer Research*, Vol. 13, ed. Richard J. Lutz, Provo, UT: Association for Consumer Research, 164-169.

Johnson, M. E., and R. Malgady (1979), "Some Cognitive Aspects of Figurative Language: Association and Metaphor," *Journal of Psycholinguistic Research*, 8, 253-265.

_____, and R. Malgady (1980), "Toward a Perceptual Theory of Metaphoric Comprehension," in *Cognition and Figurative Language*, ed. R. Honeck and R. Hoffman, Hillsdale, NJ: Erlbaum.

Katz, A. (1964), "Semi-sentences," in *The Structure of Language*, ed. J. Fodor and J. Katz, Englewood Cliffs, NJ: Prentice-Hall.

_____ (1989), "On Choosing the Vehicle of Metaphors: Referential Concreteness, Semantic Distance, and Individual Differences," *Journal of Memory and Language*, 28, 486-499.

_____, A. Paivio, and M. Marschark (1985), "Poetic Comparisons: Psychological Dimensions of Metaphoric Processing," *Journal of Psycholinguistic Research*, 14 (4), 365-383.

Koen, F. (1965), "An Intra-verbal Explication of the Nature of Metaphor," *Journal of Verbal Learning and Verbal Behavior*, 4, 129-133.

Kusumi, Takashi (1987), "Effects of Categorical Dissimilarity and Affective Similarity Between Constituent Words on Metaphor Appreciation," *Journal of Psycholinguistic Research*, Vol. 16, 6, 577-595.

Lakoff, G. and M. Johnson (1980), *Metaphors We Live By*, Chicago: University of Chicago Press.

Lutz, Kathy A., and Richard J. Lutz (1977), "Effects of Interactive Imagery on Learning: Application to Advertising," *Journal of Applied Psychology*, Vol. 62, 4, 493-498.

_____ and Richard J. Lutz (1978), "Imagery-eliciting Strategies: Review and Implications of Research," in *Advances in Consumer Research*, Vol. 5, ed. H. Keith Hunt, Ann Arbor, MI: Association for Consumer Research, 611-620.

MacCormac, Earl R. (1985), *A Cognitive Theory of Metaphor*, Cambridge, MA: Bradford Books, MIT Press.

MacInnis, D. and L. Price (1987), "The Role of Imagery in Information Processing: Review and Extensions," *Journal of Consumer Research*, Vol. 13, March, 473-492.

Malgady, R. G. and M. G. Johnson (1976), "Modifiers in Metaphors: Effects of Constituent Phrase Similarity on the Interpretation of Figurative Sentences," *Journal of Psycholinguistic Research*, 5, 43-52.

Marschark, M., A. Katz, and A. Paivio (1983), "Dimensions of Metaphor," *Journal of Psycholinguistic Research*, 12, 17-40.

McCabe, Allyssa (1983), "Conceptual Similarity and the Quality of Metaphor in Isolated Sentences Versus Extended Contexts," *Journal of Psycholinguistic Research*, Vol. 12, 1, 41-63.

Miniard, Paul W., Sunil Bhatla, Kenneth R. Lord, Peter R. Dickson, and H. Rao Unnava (1991), "Picture-based Persuasion Processes and the Moderating Role of Involvement," *Journal of Consumer Research*, 18 (June), 92-107.

Ortony, Andrew (1979), "Beyond Literal Similarity," *Psychological Review*, 86, 161-180.

_____ D. L. Schallert, R. E. Reynolds, and S. J. Antos (1978), "Interpreting Metaphors and Idioms: Some Effects of Context on Comprehension," *Journal of Verbal Learning and Verbal Behavior*, 17, 465-477.

Paivio, Allan (1971), *Imagery and Verbal Processes*, New York: Holt Rinehart andWinston, Inc.

Reeves, Lauretta M., and R. W. Weisberg (1994), "The Role of Content and Abstract Information in Analogical Transfer," *Psychological Bulletin*, 115, 3, 381-400.

Richards, I. A. (1936), *The Philosophy of Rhetoric*, London: Oxford University Press.

Shiffrin, R. M. and W. Schneider (1977), "Controlled and Automatic Human Information Processing: II. Perceptual Learning, Automatic Attending, and a General Theory," *Psychological Review*, 84, 127-190.

Shimp, Terence A. (1993), *Promotion Management and Marketing Communications*, 3rd Edition, New York: The Dryden Press.

Shinjo, Makiko, and J. I. Myers (1987), "The Role of Context in Metaphor Comprehension," *Journal of Memory and Language*, 26, 226-241.

Sternberg, R. J. (1982), "Understanding and Appreciating Metaphors," *Cognition*, 11, 203-244.

Sternberg, R. J., and G. Nigro (1983), "Interaction and Analogy in the Comprehension and Appreciation of Metaphor," *Quarterly Journal of Experimental Psychology*, 35 (A), 17-38.

Stroop, J. R. (1935), "Studies of Interference in Serial Verbal Reactions," *Journal of Experimental Psychology*, 18, 643-662.

Tourangeau, R., and R. J. Sternberg (1982), "Understanding and Appreciating Metaphors," *Cognition*, 11, 203-244.

Trick, Lana, and A. N. Katz (1986), "The Domain Interaction Approach to Metaphor Processing: Relating Individual Differences and Metaphor Characteristics," *Metaphor and Symbolic Activity*, 1 (3), 185-213.

Tversky, Amos (1977), "Features of Similarity," *Psychological Review*, 84, 327-352.

_____, and Daniel Kahneman (1974), "Judgment under Uncertainty: Heuristics and Biases," *Science*, 185, 1124-1131.

Verbrugge, Robert R., and N. S. McCarrell (1977), "Metaphoric Comprehension: Studies in Reminding and Resembling," *Cognitive Psychology*, 9, 494-533.

Ward, James, and W. Gaidis (1990), "Metaphor in Promotional Communication: A Review of Research on Metaphor Comprehension and Quality," in *Advances in Consumer Research*, Vol. 17, ed. Marvin E. Goldberg, Gerald Gorn, and Richard Pollay, Provo, UT: Association for Consumer Research, 636-642.

Wheelright, P. (1962), *Metaphor and Reality*, Bloomington, Indiana, Indiana University Press.

Upgrading by Association: An Experimental Investigation of a New Format of Comparative Advertising

Ali Kara, Pennsylvania State University–York
Erdener Kaynak, Pennsylvania State University–Harrisburg
Donghoon Lee, Oricom Inc.

ABSTRACT

In recent years, a new type (associational claims against their own products) of comparative advertising is being used by the practitioners. In order to develop more effective comparative advertisements, advertisers started making associational claims against their own better performing brands. The purpose of this research is to develop and test a conceptual framework regarding the effectiveness of associative brand comparisons against the company's own brand. We use the hierarchy-of-effects model as a framework for examining the relative effectiveness of NewCA in comparison with traditional comparative advertising (CA) and noncomparative advertising (NoCA).

INTRODUCTION

A review of advertising and marketing literature makes it quite evident that a considerable amount of research has been conducted on the topic of comparative advertising since the FTC's encouragement of the comparative advertising in 1971. In their seminal article, Wilkie and Farris (1975) proposed that comparative advertisements will be more effective than their noncomparative counterparts. Accordingly, much of the research effort in the area has been directed at trying to determine whether comparative advertisements are more or less effective in influencing and shaping consumer responses than noncomparative advertisements. However, research concerning the effectiveness of comparative advertising has produced inconclusive or mixed results at best. For instance, a number of studies showed that comparative advertising can exert more positive effects than noncomparative ads (Pechmann and Stewart 1990; Jain, Hackleman 1978; Gorn and Weinberg 1983; Rogers and Williams 1989; Murphy and Amundsen 1981; Goodwin and Etgar 1980; Alba and Chattopadhyay 1986; Droge and Darmon 1987), while other studies provided little or no evidence to comparative advertising's superiority over noncomparative ads (Ash and Wee 1983; Belch 1981; Droge 1989; Gorn and Weinberg 1984; Grossbart, Muehling, and Kangun 1986; Sujan and Dekleva 1987; Swinyard 1981; Muehling and Kangun 1985; Shimp and Dyer 1978; Wilson and Muderrisoglu 1980). Finally, Rogers and Williams (1989) summarized the positive, neutral and negative effectiveness of comparative advertising.

Results of surveys indicate that executives view comparative advertising as important for their strategic planning purposes and it is often used as a creative approach in advertising by many industries today (Rogers and Williams 1989). As a result, many practitioners have developed different variations of comparative advertising to achieve their advertising objectives. For instance, many consumer goods manufacturers compared non-comparable products or brands to capture audiences' attention and also they used two-sided comparative advertisements to increase believability of the claims made. In the literature, it is argued that the use of two-sided ads is one way of increasing the effectiveness of comparative advertising. However, recently a new type (associational claims against their own products) of comparative advertising is being used by the practitioners. To develop more effective comparative advertising, advertisers started making associational claims against their own better performing brands. In other words, they wanted to upgrade the low performer or inferior product by associating it to the high performer brand of the same company. In this format of comparative advertisement, advertiser makes associational comparison to its high performing/high market share brand to upgrade the low performing product. For instance, Accura's advertisement for its Integra makes association with its Legend with a comparison slogan of "...feels like Legend, drives like Legend." Also, in the video that was mailed to prospective customer by Toyota when its Avalon model was introduced, they used significant amount of associative comparisons to their Lexus model.

A taxonomy for comparative advertising research is given by Lamb, Pride, and Pletcher (1978) which includes associative comparative advertisements, but previous research on associative comparative advertising has been limited. To the best of our knowledge, no research has been done to determine the effectiveness of this new format of comparative advertisement (NewCA). Therefore, the purpose of this research is to develop and test a conceptual framework regarding the effectiveness of associative brand comparisons against the company's own brand. In the NewCA, associative comparisons are made to the company's own better performing brand for the purposes of upgrading the low-performing brand. The notion of the NewCA is based on the idea that the comparison brand is not a directly competing brand against the advertised brand. We use the hierarchy-of-effects model as a framework for examining the relative effectiveness of NewCA in comparison with traditional comparative advertising (CA) and noncomparative advertising (NoCA).

CONCEPTUAL FRAMEWORK AND RESEARCH PROPOSITIONS

According to Wilkie and Farris (1975), comparative advertising "...compares two or more specifically named or recognizably presented brands of the same generic product or service class or type and makes a comparison in terms of one or more specific product or service attribute." Some researchers on the other hand, argued that this definition was too restrictive and therefore took a broader perspective by incorporating advertising forms which implied a competitive superiority on any dimension (McDougall 1978). The current study falls within the first classification which uses the concept of direct comparative ads in which the sponsor makes verbal or visual references to a clearly identified brand. However, the comparisons made to stress brand similarities rather than brand differences for the purposes of upgrading the low performing product or brand.

In their review, Ash and Wee (1983) summarized the measures used to understand the effectiveness of comparative advertising. Almost all of the studies which have attempted to measure the effectiveness of CA used hierarchy-of-effects model or the situational effects model. Recent research (Barry 1987; Barry and Howard 1990) suggested that the hierarchy-of-effects model (Lavidge and Steiner 1961; Preston 1982) provides an effective and efficient framing reference for CA research. The hierarchy-of-effects model, which is used in the study as a framework of measuring the effectiveness of NewCA, include three components, namely; cognitive, affective and conative. The research hypotheses

Advances in Consumer Research
Volume 24, © 1997

with regards to each components of the hierarchy-of-effects model is developed separately for each component of the model which is illustrated below.

Cognitive Component

The cognitive component of the hierarchy-of-effects model involve awareness (i.e., attention, recall and retention) and perceptual evaluations (i.e., believability, comprehension) of the advertisements. It is generally accepted that consumer awareness of the advertised brand is a necessary condition for subsequent intention to buy and actual purchase behavior. Therefore, one measure of an ad's effectiveness in increasing brand awareness is its ability to capture the attention of the target audience. To do that, advertisers use a variety of CA format to capture audiences' attention. For instance, in a recent TV commercial, Subaru's subcompact car was compared with German sports car Porche. In another commercial, IBM airs TV commercials in different languages. Similarly, Energizer's "... still going" bunny can be examples of attention getting ads. Although these could be criticized as "laughable," whether or not they "worked" is an empirical question to investigate.

In summary, in terms of the effects of CA on the cognitive component, current literature has been inconclusive and mainly reported negative effects. In this study, it is hypothesized that most of the negative effects of CA mentioned in the current literature are to be eliminated by the use of NewCA where the comparisons (associations) are made against the same company's own brand. There are several justifications behind this assertation. First, CA was criticized in the advertising literature because it gave unnecessary exposure to the competing brand(s). This might be eliminated in the NewCA because there will not be any competitors' brand mentioned in the advertisement. Second, it is unlikely that traditional CA format will be continued to be perceived as "novel" or "new" following nearly twenty-five years of use. However, the new format of CA could provoke more consumer interest simply because it is something different and novel. Using the same arguments that Wilkie and Farris put forward in 1975 about the comparative advertisements, the NewCA may be viewed as something very original and new which is expected to increase audience's attention. It is known in the current consumer behavior literature that, consumers quite often seek novel stimuli (Bettman 1975; Lynch and Srull 1982). Such behaviors are considered as personality characteristics possessed by everyone to a degree (Hirschman 1980; Midgeley and Dowling 1978). Therefore, the NewCA, which compares the two products from the same company, is a new and novel way of CA. Finally, CA found to be less believable and credible due to the several factors such as counter arguments and source derogation (Belch 1981; Swinyard 1981; Wilson and Muderrisoglu 1980). Attribution theory suggests that a message lacking in credibility will be discounted and will not be very persuasive (Kelly 1967). According to the attribution theory, an audience who sees a comparative advertisement's claim, tries to decide why these claims were made. One might argue that the advertiser of a comparative advertisement for one brand might not be viewed as a highly credible source of information about competing brands because of the likelihood of manipulative intent. Research has identified that source credibility is comprised of expertise and trustworthiness (Dholakia and Sternthal 1977). In this case, audience decides whether the source is a knowledgeable person and/or is biased. However, since both products (advertised and compared) belong to the same advertiser (source) in the NewCA, believability of the claims and the credibility of the source are expected to be higher. Hence, it is argued in this study that the new format of the comparative advertising will create higher source credibility and message believability. Finally, the results of recall studies are also mixed in the literature. Several studies failed to demonstrate superior recall for comparative formats (Murphy and Amundsen 1981; Shimp and Dyer 1978; Earl and Pride 1980) while others found greater recall for the comparative advertising (Muehling, Stoltman, and Grossbart 1990; Jain and Hackleman 1978). Earlier, it was hypothesized that the new format of comparative advertising would create greater level of awareness and several studies in the literature have established that there is a strong positive correlation between awareness and the subjects' recall of brands (Alba and Chattopadhyay 1986). Therefore, the high awareness level that the NewCA is expected to create might effect the message involvement which will consequently contribute to a greater recall. This expectation is consistent with psychological research. Based on these discussions the following hypotheses were formulated.

H1: *The new comparative advertising (NewCA) will result in higher consumer attention than comparative advertising (CA) and noncomparative advertising (NonCA).*

H2: *Consumers' perception of advertising believability will be significantly higher for those who are exposed to the NewCA than those who are exposed to CA and NonCA.*

H3: *The NewCA will result in less misidentification of the sponsoring brands than the CA and NonCA.*

H4: *The NewCA will generate more message recall than a CA and NonCA.*

Affective Component

The affective component of the hierarchy-of-effects model relates to the intensity and direction of the consumer's feelings and tendencies toward the "totality of components" contained in the comparative advertisement (Ash and Wee 1983). In other words, affect deals with audiences' predispositions or attitudes toward brands and specific advertisements or commercials. These attitudes act as predispositions toward brands which may lead to specific brand purchase behavior at a later stage.

Muehling (1987) found that CA formats used in this study did not influence attitude toward the sponsor's brand. However, Kangun, Muehling, and Grossbart (1984) found that CA elicited less recall than any of the other forms of illustration. Shimp & Dyer (1978) found that CA were viewed to be more offensive and sponsoring companies of CA were viewed as less trustworthy. Also, Goodwin and Etgar (1980) found that CA did not improve respondents' attitudes toward the advertised brand. Thus, there is considerable evidence that CA might be risky with respect to generating favorable attitudes toward the advertisement. Also, heavy brand loyal consumers are likely to resist comparative messages which downgrades their brands and thus this information can be perceived as threatening to them. In short, there is little evidence to suggest that comparative advertising is a superior format in terms of generating positive or favorable attitudes towards brands and advertising itself.

The new format of comparative advertising, however, is expected to have higher ability to generate more favorable attitudes than its noncomparative and comparative counterparts. Consumer reactions to a particular advertisement are dependent on the strength of the advocated position, source credibility, attribute saliency, cognitive response, and message credibility (Wright 1973; Wilkie and Farris 1975). Also, consumers might think favorably since a relatively credible source (advertiser) made the comparisons. It is indicated in the advertising literature that there is a positive relationship between the cognitive responses and the evaluation of the ads or attitudes toward ads (Belch 1981). Therefore, a relatively more favorable evaluation of the ad, product, and sponsoring corporation should be obtained in the NewCA compared to the CA and NoCA. Based on these discussions the following hypothesis was formulated.

> H5: *Subjects' evaluations of advertising, product, and the sponsoring corporation will be more favorable for NewCA than CA and NoCA.*

Conative Component

The ultimate persuasiveness of advertising is to move brands through points of final consumption or purchase. Therefore, the final stage of the hierarchy-of-effects model is to determine if the new format of comparative advertising is more effective than comparative advertising and noncomparative advertising. Ash and Wee (1983) indicated that three dimensions of measurement of conative component namely buying intentions, brand preference, and purchase behavior have been studied. There have been, however, a few studies investigating the effectiveness of comparative advertising and noncomparative advertising to elicit behavior. Similar to other components of the hierarchy-of-effects model, mixed results were obtained and there is no conclusive evidence on the effectiveness of comparative advertising on conation (Shimp and Dyer 1978; Belch 1981; Holmes and Holley 1986; Kangun, Muehling and Grossbart 1984; Swinyard 1981). The conation hypotheses in this study were based on the assumption that holding other factors constant, the new format of comparative advertising is more likely to enhance purchase intention to the extent that it attracts attention, promotes favorable brand perceptions and attitudes, and reduces sponsor misidentification. Hence, it is hypothesized that:

> H6: *Consumers are most likely to be persuaded to purchase if they were exposed to NewCA than consumers who were exposed to CA or NoCA.*

METHODOLOGY

Overview of Experimental Design

To test these hypotheses the experiment manipulated three variables namely type of advertisement, product performance/quality, and product involvement. Involvement is included for exploratory purposes. There were no prior hypothesis about the effects of the involvement on the results. Thus, the study employed a 3 (new comparative, comparative, noncomparative ads) X 2 (high vs. low performance/quality product) X 2 (high vs. low involvement products) factorial design.

A preliminary questionnaire was administered to 57 undergraduate students to determine the product categories for high and low involvement products and high and low performance brands within the product categories. Cars, beers, computers, soaps, and detergents were included in the questionnaire to select the product categories for high and low involvement products. The objective here was to select two products that represented high and low involvement products for that target consumer group. Also, to represent high and low performance/quality brands within each product category, several real brand names under each product category were included in the questionnaire. Subjects evaluated different product categories and brand names within each category in terms of involvement, familiarity, brand preference, attitudes toward brands, and product performance/quality. Based on the preliminary survey results, cars were selected to represent the high involvement product category and detergents were selected to represent the low involvement product category. Under the high

involvement products—cars, Honda and Hyundai were selected to represent the two groups of high-low performance/quality brands in that category. Also, Honda Civic and Hyundai Excel were selected as the advertised brands. On the other hand, for the low involvement products—detergents, Procter & Gamble's Tide and Lever Brothers' Whisk were selected to represent the high and low performance/quality brands in the detergents category. Similarly, Cheer and Surf were selected as the advertised brands in the detergents category. There were also questions to determine the salient attributes for each of the product categories selected. These were open ended questions and they were content analyzed for internal validity by the authors.

Three different black and white print ads (new comparative, comparative, and noncomparative) were developed for detergents and cars which yielded 12 different ads. A completely randomized design was used for the data collection and each subject was exposed to one type of ad only. Thus, the effects of repetition was eliminated.

Subjects

The subjects in this study were 400 undergraduate students attending in business administration classes in a large southeastern university in the U.S. The use of student subjects as a convenience sample requires the researchers to be careful in their research design (Etgar and Goodwin 1977). A problem occurs if students are used in studies of advertised products primarily used and/or purchased by consumers in advanced life-cycle stages. Yet the student sample may be entirely acceptable and consistent with improved external validity if the product classes advertised are salient to them. Therefore, use of student samples in this study is considered appropriate for cars and detergents as both products are utilized by most of the students in the U.S.A. The participation was rewarded as extra credit in that course. Subjects were randomly assigned to each experimental conditions.

Stimulus Ads

The ads promoted two brands of cars and two brands of detergents. Using the experimental conditions in the study, twelve full-page black and white print ads were constructed. The same layout was used for all of the ads to minimize confounds.

The headline of the ad took two lines and it was almost the same for the twelve different ads. If the ad was a new comparative ad, for the cars, the headline read, *"Think of it as a baby [comparison brand], not hungry for gas. Introducing all new 1994 [advertised brand]."* The comparison brand for Honda was *Honda Accord* and it was *Hyundai Sonata* for Hyundai. For the detergent ads, the headline stated, *"The New [advertised brand] from [sponsoring company] will grow up to the level of [comparison brand]."* The comparison brand for Procter and Gamble was *Tide* while it was *Whisk* for Lever Brothers. If the ad was a comparative ad, for the cars, the headline stated, *"The New 1994 [advertised brand] provides the best gas mileage in its class of cars."* For the detergent ads, the headline read, *"The New [advertised brand] gets out the toughest dirt and odors like no other brands can do."* Finally, if the ad was a noncomparative ad, for the cars, the headline stated, *"Introducing the All New 1994 [advertised brand] which provides a very good gas mileage."* For the detergent ads, the headline stated, *"The New [advertised brand] gets out your toughest dirt and odors."*

After the headline, approximately a 3" by 5" picture depicting the advertised brand was placed. The pictures were actual product pictures and were adapted from the actual advertisements. Picture combined with the headline took approximately half of the page. All ads contained relevant information about attributes, determined in a pretest to be salient. Therefore, the second half of the page contained approximately 150 words of text describing the advertised brands as follows: Cheer and Surf as "tough on dirt and odors," "powerful cleaning system," "effective with smaller scoop," and "more affordable," and Honda Civic and Hyundai Excel as "more gas mileage," "more safety features," "modern design," and "more affordable."

For the new comparative ads, the advertised brands were associated with the compared brands (the high performance brand of the same company) on the attributes mentioned above. Therefore, for cars category, comparisons between Honda Accord (comparison brand) and Honda Civic (advertised brand) were made for Honda while Hyundai Excel (advertised brand) was compared to Hyundai Sonata (comparison brand) for Hyundai. On the other hand, for the detergents category, comparisons between Tide (comparison brand) and Cheer (advertised brand) were made for Procter & Gamble while comparisons between Whisk (comparison brand) and Surf (advertised brand) were made for Lever Brothers. For the comparative ads, comparisons to other products (no mention of the brand name) were made on the same dimensions explained above. And finally, for the no comparison ads the advertised brands were described using the same dimensions.

Constructs and Measures

Following exposure to the print ads (approximately 15 minutes later), subjects completed a questionnaire that asked about attention to the ads; sponsor identification; purchase intentions; recall; attitudes toward ad, product and sponsor; and believability.

Attention was measured with a three item-scale used by Muehling, Stoltman and Grossbart (1990). Subjects were asked (1) How much attention did you pay to the written message in the ad? (2) How much did you notice the written message in the ad? and (3) How much did you concentrate on the written message in the ad? A reliability test indicated that all three items measured the same construct (Cronbach's $\alpha = .87$).

Recall was measured with three different measures of recall—brand recall, claim recall and attribute recall. Brand recall responses were dichotimized into "recall" and "no recall," depending upon whether or not the correct name was remembered. Claim recall was measured using an open ended question which asked respondents to summarize the main message in the ad. Responses to this question were content analyzed and scored on the basis of extent of reproduction of the major and secondary claims contained in the advertisement. Also, they were asked to identify the direction of the comparisons made in the ad (comparisons against it own brand, comparisons against competing brands and no comparison). Finally, attribute recall was measured by the number of correctly identified product attributes mentioned in the ad.

Sponsor identification was measured with an open ended question that asked "Which brand did the ad promote or advertise?" In other words, subjects were simply asked to write down the name of the brand which sponsored the ad. A similar question was also used by Pechmann and Stewart (1990).

Purchase intention was measured on three semantic differential scales, likely-unlikely, probable-improbable, and possible-impossible (Cronbach's $\alpha = .94$). The purchase intention measure used in the analyses was calculated by averaging the three scales.

Attitudes toward ad, product, and sponsoring corporation was measured by several likert-type statements (strongly agree-strongly disagree, very negative-very positive, and very favorable-very unfavorable) using 7-point scales. Items used were internally consistent and thus a summative index was used for assessing attitudes toward ad, product, and sponsoring corporation.

Believability was measured by using several statements. First, subjects were asked to indicate their perceptions of advertiser objectivity and credibility using six semantic differential scales (bias, truthfulness, honesty, believability, and sincerity). Second, they were asked to indicate the extent of certainty that the advertiser's ability to deliver the benefits claimed in the ad using a likert-type scale. Finally, they were asked to indicate whether they would feel comfortable enough to base their purchase decision solely on the ad or whether or not they would acquire more information from other sources.

Involvement levels of products were measured using a 20-item involvement scale developed by Zaichkowsky (1985). Finally, questionnaire included several other questions regarding the familiarity, involvement, product similarity, product performance/quality and category exemplar product. Also, some demographic and socio-economic data were collected.

ANALYSIS AND RESULTS

Separate analyses of variance (ANOVA) were performed for the dependent variables with ad format (comparative, new comparative, and no comparison) and involvement levels (high involvement and low involvement).

Table 1 shows that the NewCA for high involvement products generated more attention than the other two types of advertisements used while no significant differences were found for the low involvement product. Hence, the NewCA were successful in getting attentions of the respondents at least for the high involvement products. An important point needs to be explained here. In the preliminary study, less number of respondents correctly identified the two detergents compared were actually manufactured by the same company. Although, the manufacturer's name was printed at the bottom corner of the advertisement, it is possible that the manufacturer's name was not noticed. On the other hand, for the car advertisements, the manufacturer's name (Honda or Hyundai) was incorporated in the advertisements.

Contrary to our predictions, the results for brand recall and sponsor identification for the NewCA were significantly poorer than the other types where the compared product's name was not mentioned. A significant portion of the respondents could not clearly identify the advertised brand and were confused between advertised brand and the associated brand. Amongst the three types of advertisements used in the study, no comparison advertisements had the highest brand recall rate. Results were also similar in terms of the claim recall. However, there were no significant differences in terms of the attribute recall.

Believability hypothesis is partially supported. There were some statistically significant differences in terms of credibility of the advertiser and the advertisers' ability to deliver the claimed product benefits. In terms of the amount of information needed to make decision, NewCA results were significantly different than the other types. In other words, more respondents indicated that they could base their decision solely on the advertisements and need very little extra information to make a purchase decision. Finally, results show that NewCA generated more favorable attitudes than the other two types of the advertisements used. Similarly, NewCA yielded relatively higher purchase intentions than the other types of ads used in the study.

CONCLUSIONS

The study tested the proposition that associative comparative ads with the same company's best performing brand are more effective than noncomparative and comparative ads. In this context, the study examined the perceptual and processing differences

TABLE 1
The ANOVA Results

| | High Involvement | | | | | | Low Involvement | | | | | |
| | High Performance | | | Low Performance | | | High Performance | | | Low Performance | | |
	NoC	Comp	NewCA	NoC	Comp	NewCA	NoC	Comp	NewCA	NoC	Comp	NewCA
ATTENTION[1]	3.11	3.77	4.95*	2.59	3.97	4.55*	3.50	3.21	3.48	3.08	3.62	3.19
RECALL												
Brand[2]	86.9	83.3	57.6	91.6	85.7	68.4	95.4	91.3	66.7	91.3	87.5	52.2
Claim[3]	5.91	6.03*	3.09	5.23	6.51*	3.10	6.55*	5.26	4.73	6.56*	5.04	4.13
Attribute[4]	3.17	3.48	3.21	3.01	3.40	3.25	2.89	3.11	2.95	2.78	2.56	2.73
BELIEVABILITY												
Credibility[5]	2.81	2.83	2.25	2.94	2.89	2.25	3.01	2.48	1.98*	3.04	2.81	2.66*
Ability to deliver[6]	3.77	4.11	3.24	4.05	4.37	3.00*	3.73	3.70	3.28	4.57	4.17	3.47*
More info. needed[7]	4.00	1.38	1.26*	3.27	1.47	1.54*	3.83	3.32	2.09*	3.68	3.54	1.58*
SPONSOR IDENTIFICATION[8]	86.9	83.3	57.6	91.6	85.7	68.4	95.4	91.3	66.7	91.3	87.3	52.2
ATTITUDES[9]	2.93	3.67	2.52*	3.45	3.42	2.67	3.21	3.05	2.21*	3.86	3.58	3.09*
PURCHASE INTENTION[10]	4.10	4.71	5.01*	4.41	4.82	5.03	3.36	4.04	4.93*	4.41	4.42	4.71

* Significant at p<.05; [1]A 7-point scale was used where 1=none, not at all and 7=very much; [2]Percent of respondents recalled brand name correctly; [3]A 7-point scoring was used where 1=very good and 7=very poor; [4]Average number of attributes recalled correctly; [5]A 7-point scale was used where 1=strongly agree and 7=strongly disagree; [6]A 7-point scale was used where 1=absolutely certain and 7=absolutely uncertain; [7]A 7-point scale was used where 1=very little and 7=very much; [8]Percent of respondents identified the brand which sponsored the ad; [9]A 7-point scale was used where 1=very favorable and 7=very unfavorable; [10]A 7-point scale was used where 1=unlikely and 7=likely;

using hierarchy-of-effects model and alternative measures of ad effectiveness.

The study findings indicated that "New Comparative Ad" resulted more attention than the other types of ads examined in the study. Consumers quite often seek novel stimuli in the advertisements which NewCA might have provided. This effect was not very evident for the low involvement products (detergents). This does not mean, however, that the NewCA may not generate more attention for the low involvement products, but rather, we think that in order to NewCA be effective in terms of getting the consumers' attentions, consumers should have the strong prior knowledge that the associated brands were manufactured by the same company. Otherwise, it is almost no different than the regular comparative ads. Hence, the firms that plan to use this format of advertisement should makes this point as explicitly as possible. This can be done by clearly mentioning it or in some other creative ways, or if the products have a family brand, then advertisers' job is much easier.

However, contrary to predictions, NewCA did poorly in terms of the brand recall and sponsor identification. A higher proportions of subjects exposed to the NewCA ads misidentified the sponsors of the brands. Consumers were confused about the advertised brand. Since both products belong to the company, this confusion may not be as harmful as regular comparative ads which mention the competitor's brand name. In other words, NewCA reduces the unnecessary exposure of the competitor's brand name. As, predicted, the study findings indicated that NewCA resulted more favorable attitudes and better purchase intentions than the other types of ads studied.

In sum, our findings suggest that ads making associative claims to the same company's better performing brand are more effective at getting more attention when the consumers can easily identify that the two brands belong to the same company. NewCA is also more effective at enhancing purchase intentions and creating favorable attitudes. On the other hand, our results indicate that noncomparative ads are more effective in terms of brand and claim recall.

REFERENCES

Alba, Joseph and Amitava Chattopadhyay (1986), "Salience Effects in Brand Recall," *Journal of Marketing Research*, 23 (November), 363-369.

Ash, Stephen B. and Chow-Hou Wee (1983), "Comparative Advertising: A Review with Implications for Future Research," in *Advances in Consumer Research*, Vol.10, Richard P. Bagozzi and Alice M. Tybout, eds., Ann Arbor, MI: Association of Consumer Research, 370-376.

Barry, Thomas E. and Roger L. Tremblay (1975), "Comparative Advertising: Perspectives and Issues," *Journal of Advertising*, 4(4), 15-20.

Barry, Thomas E. and Daniel J. Howard (1990), "A Review and Critique of the Hierarchy of Effects in Advertising," *International Journal of Advertising*, 9(2), 121-135.

Barry, Thomas E. (1987), "The Development of Hierarchy of Effects: An Historical Perspective," in *Current Issues and Research in Advertising*, James H. Leigh and Claude R. Martin, Jr., eds., Ann Arbor, MI: The University of Michigan.

Belch, George E. (1981), "An Examination of Comparative and Noncomparative Television Commercials: The Effect of Claim Variation and Repetition on Cognitive Response and Message Acceptance," *Journal of Marketing Research*, 18 (August), 333-349.

Bettman, James R. (1975), "Issues in Designing Consumer information Environments," *Journal of Consumer research*, 2(3), 169-177.

Dholakia, Ruby Roy and Brian Sternthal (1977), "Highly Credible Sources: Persuasive Facilitator or Persuasive Liabilities?" *Journal of Consumer Research*, 3 (March), 223-232.

Droge, Cornelia and Rene Y. Darmon (1987), "Associative Positioning Strategies through Comparative Advertising: Attribute versus Overall Similarity Approaches," *Journal of Marketing Research*, 24 (November), 377-388.

Droge, Cornelia (1989), "Shaping the Route to Attitude Change: Central versus Peripheral Processing through Comparative versus Noncomparative Advertising," *Journal of Marketing Research*, 26 (May), 193-204.

Earl, Ronald L. and William M. Pride (1980), "The Effects of Advertisement Structure, Message Sidedness, and Performance Test Results on Print Advertisement Informativeness," *Journal of Advertising*, 9(3), 36-45.

Goodwin, Stephen, and Michael Etgar (1980), "An Experimental Investigation of Comparative Advertising: Impact of Message Appeal, Information Load, and Utility of Product Class," *Journal of Marketing Research*, 17(2), 187-202.

Gorn, Gerald J. and Charles B. Weinberg (1984), "The Impact of Comparative Advertising on Perception and Attitude: Some Positive Findings," *Journal of Consumer Research*, 11 (September), 719-727.

Grossbart, Sanford, Darrel D. Muehling, and Norman Kangun (1986), "Verbal and Visual References to Competition in Comparative Advertising," *Journal of Advertising*, 15(1), 10-23.

Hirschman, Elizabeth (1980), "Innovativeness, Novelty Seeking and Consumer Creativity," *Journal of Consumer research*, 7(3), 283-295.

Jain, Subhash C., and Edwin C. Hackleman (1978), "How Effective is Comparative Advertising for Stimulating Brand Recall?" *Journal of Advertising*, 7(3), 20-25.

Kangun, Norman, Darrel D. Muehling, and Sanford L. Grossbart (1984), "An Investigation of the Cognitive Effects of Alternative References to Competition in Comparative Advertising: Implications for the F.T.C.,"in *Proceedings of the AMA Educators' Conference*, 50, 314-318.

Kelly, Harold H. (1967), "Attribution theory in Social Psychology," in *Nebraska Symposium on Motivation*, David Levine, ed., Lincoln, NE: University of Nebraska Press.

Lamb, Charles, William M. Pride, and Barbara A. Pletcher (1978), "A Taxonomy for Comparative Advertising Research," *Journal of Advertising*, 7 (4), 43-47.

Lavidge, Robert J. and Gary A. Steiner (1961), "Model for Predictive Measurements of Advertising Effectiveness," *Journal of Marketing*, 25 (4), 59-62.

Lynch, John G. and Thomas K. Srull (1982), "Memory and Attentional Factors in Consumer Choice: Concepts and Research Methods," *Journal of Consumer Research*, 9(1), 18-37.

McDougall, Gordon H. G. (1978), "Comparative Advertising: The Effect of Claim Type and Brand Loyalty," in *Current Issues and Research in Advertising*, James Leigh and Claude R. Martin, eds., Ann Arbor: University of Michigan Press, 39-52.

Midgeley, David F. and Grahame R. Dowling (1978), "Innovativeness: The Concept and Measurement," *Journal of Consumer Research*, 4(4), 229-242.

Muehling, Darrel D., Jeffrey J. Stoltman and Sanford Grossbart (1990), "The Impact of Comparative Advertising on Levels of Message Involvement," *Journal of Advertising*, 19(4), 41-50.

Muehling, Darrel D. and Norman Kangun (1985), "The Multi-Dimensionality of Comparative Advertising: Implications for the Federal trade Commission," *Journal of Public Policy and Marketing*, 4, 112-128.

Muehling, Darrel D. (1987). "Comparative Advertising: the Influence of Attitude-Toward-the-Ad on Brand Evaluation," *Journal of Advertising*, 16(4), 43-49.

Murphy, John H. and Marry S. Amundsen (1981), "The Communications-Effectiveness of Comparative Advertising for a New Brand," *Journal of Advertising*, 10 (1), 14-20.

Pechmann, Cornelia and David W. Stewart (1990). "The Effects of Comparative Advertising on Attention, Memory, and Purchase Intentions," *Journal of Consumer Research*, 17(2), 180-191.

Preston, Ivan L. (1982), "The Association Model of the Advertising Communication Process," *Journal of Advertising*, 11(2), 3-15.

Pride, William M., Charles W. Lamb and Barbara A. Pletcher (1977), "The Informativeness of Comparative Advertisements: An Empirical investigation," *Journal of Advertising*, 8(2), 29-35, 48.

Rogers, John C. and Terrel G. Williams (1989). "Comparative Advertising Effectiveness: Practitioners' Perceptions versus Academic Research Findings." *Journal of Advertising Research*, 29(5), 22-37.

Shimp, Terrence A. and David C. Dyer (1978), "The Effects of Comparative Advertising Mediated by Market Position of Sponsoring Brand," *Journal of Advertising*, 7 (Summer), 13-19.

Sujan, Mita and Cristine Dekleva (1987), "Product Categorization and Inference Making: Some Implications for Comparative Advertising, *Journal of Consumer Research*, 14 (December), 372-378.

Swinyard, William R. (1981), "The Interaction Between Comparative Advertising and Copy Claim Variation," *Journal of Marketing Research*, 18 (May), 175-186.

Wilkie, William L. and Paul W. Farris (1975), "Comparison Advertising: Problems and Potential," *Journal of Marketing*, 39 (October), 7-15.

Wilson, Dale and Aydin Muderrisoglu (1980), "An Analysis of Cognitive Responses To Comparative Advertising," *Advances in Consumer Research*, 7, Jerry Olson, ed., Ann Arbor: Association for Consumer Research, 566-571.

Wilson, R. Dale (1980), "An Analysis of Cognitive Responses to comparative Advertising," in *Advances in Consumer Research*, 1, Jerry C. Olson, ed. Ann Arbor, MI: Association for Consumer Research.

Wright, Peter L. (1973), "The Cognitive Process Mediating Acceptance of Advertising," *Journal of Marketing Research*, 10 (February), 53-67.

Consumer Emotion Space: An Investigation of Semantic Space and Context Effects in Self-Reported Emotion Elicitation

Ross Buck, University of Connecticut
Mats Georgson, University of Connecticut

INTRODUCTION

Consumer research strives to obtain information about how we perceive products and services, and how we make decisions about consumption. One useful source of information is the notion of product involvement. Involvement can be conceptualized as the amount of effort that goes into thinking about something, analytically (how much we analyze it) and emotionally (how much we feel about it). In addition to the above general involvement types, the affective involvement can be studied by addressing specific emotions. For instance, use of a car may be associated with feelings of power, whereas long-distance phone services induce feelings of attachment and loneliness.

Part of the beauty with studying emotions is that they are general responses that occur in a variety of contexts. For a given person, we can use analytic and affective involvement, along with specific subtypes of such involvement, to differentiate and compare product categories or brands (or even products within a brand). Information about affective involvement can be useful in formulating advertising strategies for segmentation and positioning. Unfortunately, the scientific community is still not very successful at pinpointing the relation between affective responses in consumption contexts and subsequent consumption evaluations and behaviors, although we can see that a link exists (Batra and Ray 1986, Holbrook and Batra 1987, Edell and Burke 1987, Swinyard 1993, see also Babin, Darden and Griffin, 1994).

Affective responses have been studied at least as far back as Aristotle. In this century, science has identified a neurological basis of affect (e.g. Buck, 1988). However, most often when we measure affect we rely on self-report measures. In doing so, we inevitably get some analytic thought with the measurement, as you need to use analytic thought to perform introspection and then answer a verbal question. In fact, we use a semantic space, different words covering different parts of an area of meaning, to report what we feel (Osgood, Suci and Tannenbaum 1957). Shaver, Schwartz, Kirson, and O'Connor (1987) conducted a classic study of the semantic space of emotion in general, i.e., emotion unanchored to any specific context. In this paper, Shaver et. al.'s semantic space will be compared to a semantic space derived from data elicited in a consumption context. The question is whether self-report of emotion is a stable measurement device. In other words, is it the case that "emotion is emotion is emotion", regardless of what the context is? Ideally, what we call happiness in normal day usage should be the same happiness when it comes to a consumption context. It should be as different from fear as it is in the normal sense of the word, as close to joy, and so on. On the other hand, if semantic space is different when it comes to the consumption setting, we must reconsider such things as what measurement scales to use and what literature is generalizable to the consumption context. As will be shown in the theory section below, even though it seems like emotions are universal and that there are prototypical emotions, there still might be reason to question whether emotions invoked in a consumer context have the same profiles as emotions in other contexts.

In this study results of two studies, one done by Shaver et. al. (1987) of emotion in a general context and one done by this author concerning emotion in a consumption context will be reported and compared, to determine whether they agree with each other.

EMOTION THEORY

In the long history of studying emotion, approaches vary widely depending on the perspective chosen. It can be useful to start with asking a rhetorical question: why do we have emotions?

MacLean (1990) has proposed the theory of the Triune brain, which one can use to both understand the neurological bases of emotions as well as their functions. The human brain evolved much like an old city, where old buildings are still kept in operation even though more recent, and maybe more sophisticated buildings are added in layers around them. Thus, there is a *reptilian* brain (evolutionary the oldest), primarily the internal capsule and amygdala; surrounded by a *paleomammalian* brain, the limbic system; in turn surrounded by a *neo-mammalian* brain (newest), the neo-cortex. Physiologically, a reptile brain has much in common with the amygdala, while a dog brain is similar to a human brain minus much of the neo-cortex.

The reptilian brain houses what Buck (1988) labels *reptilian* emotions of "raw" sex and aggression; the *paleomammalian* limbic system *individualistic-limbic* emotions such as anger and fear; *prosocial-limbic* emotions of attachment; and *social* emotions like love, pride, guilt, etc. The *neo-mammalian* neo-cortex is associated with *cognitive* emotions such as curiosity and boredom. Again, there are evolutionary rationales for these emotions. Reptiles are typically only concerned with fight-or-flight, territoriality, and reproduction for individual and species preservation. Mammals on the other hand need social emotions to maintain the social structure necessary to protect the young until they can fend for themselves. In humans, the cognitive emotions help utilize analytic capabilities.[1]

There is much confusion in the emotion literature about the definition of emotion. In this work, we are addressing the phenomenon of an internal bodily readout associated with the subjective experience of feelings and desires. This is the introspective awareness of emotional arousal.

The importance of the this distinction is that emotion does typically, but not necessarily, involve a fixed proportion of different readouts. In a dark alley, you might meet a hoodlum who tries to rob you by intimidation. Your heart starts pounding and you start sweating and you feel very scared (and this is what we mean by emotion here) but you do your best not to show the signs of fear. A Samurai warrior in the same situation might show some readout of heartrate increase, show an angry face, but might not be able to introspect any subjective emotional experience (here, no emotion).

DIMENSIONALITY

One school of thought utilizes unidimensional definitions of emotion. These are primarily concerned with evaluation (e.g.

---

[1]Brains are "gas-guzzling" organs: the tissue requires lots of energy for upkeep. Therefore, big brains are only appropriate in beings that can utilize them, and by basic evolutionary rules should not evolve in species that don't need to become "smarter". Scientists are still only speculating why dolphins would need brain sizes that equal ours: we don't understand what interactions of motivation, emotion and cognition might be particularly crucial to them.

FIGURE 1
Shaver map of emotions*

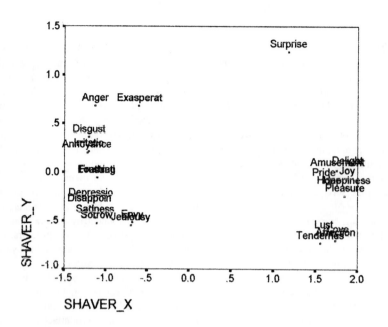

* Note: because of lack of good plotting means, the two data sets are not juxtaposed in this presentation. If clusters are too cluttered, please refer to the coordinates table.

Fishbein and Ajzen 1975). One example of such an affect scale constructed by Holbrook (1981) measures affect in such a general evaluative sense, namely the extent to which the subject perceives some stimulus to be "good". He conceives of arousal as being a separate construct, as well as other special constructs like dominance and pleasure (e.g. Holbrook et. al. 1984).

Multidimensional definitions of emotion typically include at least two dimensions: Evaluation (i.e. good-bad) and Intensity (i.e. how vivid) (Shlosberg, 1952; Shaver et. al. 1987). In a similar fashion, Russell (1979, 1980, 1991), Mano (1991), and Roberts et. al. (1994) call these dimensions Pleasantness and Arousal. Russell (1979, 1980, 1989, 1991) argues that affect is a continuous phenomenon, described by a circumplex model. Emotions would be located on the circumference of a circle, with happiness and sadness opposing each other, and emotions blending over into each other so that a full circle will cover all possible emotions.

Opposing this circumplex view is the theory of primary affects. As early as 1650, Descartes claimed that there are six primary "passions" (Batra and Ray, 1986). Later, Darwin (1872) argued that since facial expressions seem to be inherent in humankind and therefore universal, they should be indicators of corresponding internal emotional states (see also Ekman and Izard 1972). Tomkins (1962, 1963) argues that these affects stem from innate neural structures. This set of biologically based basic emotions does also blend into other, secondary emotions, like mixing primary colors make new colors. This view is supported by approaches where the semantic space of emotion has been mapped; the results show correspondence with proposed primary affects, although the solutions in all fairness also look roughly circumplex.

Thus, the theories are not diametrical to each other, and both can be seen as correct (Buck 1985).

SELF REPORT ISSUES

Self-report measures of emotion have shown convergent validity with physiological measures, such as facial expressions (Westbrook 1987). Still, there are fundamental differences between the measures. What is the correspondence between physiological aspects of emotion and a self-report item, like a Likert scale? When we say that we feel happy, the relation of the word "happy" to the neurological activation of the "happiness" center in the brain is of course a symbolic one, just like the word "tree" has a purely symbolic relation to real trees out in the park. What does this imply?

Given that emotions have a neurological basis, we can draw an analogy to self-reporting emotional states from the study of color perceptions. A human can see light with a wavelength of approximately 0.000035 cm (violet) and above. Thereafter, the light will be perceived as blue, green, yellow, orange and finally red, at a wavelength of 0.000075 cm. But note that the labels of this progression are arbitrary language constructs. There is nothing in the physical quality of light that says exactly where "blue" starts and ends.

There is an African people who only differentiate between dark and light color. The ancient Romans did not differentiate between blue and green color (Eco, 1993). On the other hand, the Mongols of the golden horde reportedly had about 20 terms for different brown hues in horses, as the exact hue of one's mount was an important symbol of status.

A culture will also use the native language to describe the experienced emotion. There is an important difference between colors and emotions though, and that is the concept of prototypicality, mentioned earlier. Prototypical emotions should show up as clusters that go together with space between these clusters. Thereby, we should see the "footprints" of the neurological responses in semantic space.

CONSUMPTION EMOTION

Consumption emotion has been used to refer to the set of emotional responses elicited specifically during product usage or consumption experiences. Consumption emotion has been interpreted as highly accessible affect elements that influenced post-consumption evaluations (Westbrook and Oliver 1991, Cohen and Areni, 1991).

This consumption emotion can be described either by the distinctive categories of emotional experience and expression (e.g. joy, anger, and fear) or by the dimensions underlying emotional categories, such as pleasantness/unpleasantness, etc. (Russell 1979, Westbrook et. al., 1991). These different perspectives correspond roughly to dimensional and prototypical definitions of emotion, respectively (as discussed earlier).

CONTEXT EFFECTS

There are actually two kinds of context effects involved in comparing the dimensionality of two sets of responses. First, there is a general context effect, as reported by Roberts and Wedell (1994). Here "context" refers to the set of stimuli being analyzed for proximity.

In four experiments the aforementioned researchers investigated the effects of giving subsets of emotions for similarity sorting, so that one group might get a general set of emotions, while others might get a set of anger and fear items. Judgments were found to differ. This means that measurement items should represent the full range of emotions for the analysis to be valid.

The other context effect is the nature of emotion in the consumption context. One example is Edell and Burke (1987, 1989) who tested 169 feelings for appropriateness in relation to advertising. Later, 69 items were used for self-reports. Through factor analysis, they ended up with two and three factor solutions, that they labeled Evaluation, Activity, and Gentleness respectively. Mano (1991) compared self-reports of emotion from a lecture (as a neutral context) to self-reports of emotions experienced while watching TV ads (as a consumer context). The responses were analyzed through multidimensional scaling, factor, and cluster analyses for both conditions. Mano was unclear as to exactly how he compared the general and the consumer context MDS solutions; he mentions that the two solutions resemble each other.[2] As Mano points out, one could argue that all emotional states are induced by some external stimulus.[3] Therefore, it is questionable whether a "common everyday event" isn't a mood inducing stimulus, or at least a context. Therefore, the control is not a truly context-free baseline.

METHOD

For investigating differences between the general context and the consumer context, we will use two sets of data, as follows:

The first set of data is derived from an analysis by Shaver et. al. (1987). These researchers approached the issues of prototypicality and/or circumplexity of emotion through mapping emotion using a collection of similarity data. They provided subjects (one hundred students from an introductory psychology course) with a stack of 135 cards, each of which had an emotion term on it, such as "joy" or "anger". The task was to sort these cards into a number of piles,[4] effectively creating an accessible representation of the subjects' cognitive clustering of affect. This similarity data was then used for a hierarchical cluster analysis (which will only be summarily reported here) as well as a multidimensional scaling of emotion space.

The second set of data was collected by the authors as follows. 94 undergraduate students in an introductory communications course were asked to fill out five randomly selected questionnaires, each questionnaire pertaining to a certain product category. Thus, each product was evaluated by an average of 26.7 raters. 17 product categories were chosen for this study to represent a full range of product categories, so that a representational variety of combinations of high and low emotional and analytic involvement would be used. This selection was based on Buck and Chaudhuri (1994). The categories were: Color TV's, Headache Remedies, Candy, Automobiles, Household Cleaners, Long distance phone services, Facial Tissues, Laundry Detergents, Toothpaste, Air Travel, Soft Drinks, Credit Cards, Bath Soap, Insurance Plans, Personal Computers, Greeting Cards, and Canned Beer. Arguably, all of these would have some relevance to the sample. Moreover, the aforementioned study of product categories used a similar sample.

All in all, a total of 455 valid data sheets were properly completed and collected. The questionnaire asked subjects whether usage of a product increased each of 53 emotions listed in the questionnaire. In addition, they were asked if using the product decreased their feelings of 28 of the emotions. (To not completely overwhelm the subjects, all 53 emotions were not duplicated in decrease items, the decrease items were concentrated on the decrease of negative emotion.)

The data thus represents college students' emotional responses to different product categories.

COMPARISON PRINCIPLES

The cluster analysis comparison and the multidimensional scaling comparisons are fundamentally two similar ways of comparing the data sets, both have their respective advantages. Cluster analysis bluntly states what the proposed cluster solution is in terms of cluster memberships, while the MDS allows for visual inspection and analysis of underlying dimensionalities and relations between clusters.

The Shaver data has no emotion eliciting stimulus. If it had, it would automatically have a context. The consumer data, on the other hand, must be elicited by thinking about consumption or it would be context free. Standardizing the measures provided the basis for comparison.

A hierarchical cluster analysis was performed, replicating the cluster analysis by Shaver et. al. The purpose of this cluster analysis is to see whether the clusters around prototypical emotions hold up in the consumer context. Shaver et. al. presented a six-cluster solution: Anger, Sadness, Surprise, Love, Happiness, and Fear.

---

[2]One of the MDS maps must be rotated to match the axes of the other, though. For a formal treatment on this, see the Methods section on MDS comparison. It appears like Mano's matching was more of a face comparison than a formal procedure.

[3]Furthermore: as attribution literature tells us, even if we don't know what induced for instance a general feeling of arousal, we might attribute it to some arbitrary stimulus around us.

---

[4]The actual number of piles was up to the individual subject.

FIGURE 2
Consumer context emotion map*

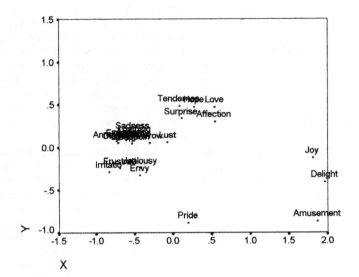

* Note: because of lack of good plotting means, the two data sets are not juxtaposed in this presentation. If clusters are too cluttered, please refer to the coordinates table.

In the consumer context, a six cluster has a pattern of general similarity with two notable differences (as discussed earlier). First, the Anger and Sadness clusters merge into a general "Unpleasant" cluster. Second, Surprise is incorporated into the Love cluster. Instead, we get two new clusters, Pride and Interest. Note, however, that the two new clusters seem to form around emotions that were not included in Shaver's study, namely Pride- and Interest-related emotions.

MULTIDIMENSIONAL SCALING ANALYSIS

The overall measure of fit in Multidimensional Scaling is the stress statistic. The higher the stress, the more variance that is not accounted for by the MDS solution at that dimensionality. The stress for Shaver's solution (with two dimensions) was .10.[5] The consumer context solution held a slightly worse fit, .15. The consumer context solution looks like this (See Figure 2).

Comparison of two multidimensional representations must start with establishing commonality between them. In order to do so, we must fit our map to Shaver's. This can be thought of as juxtaposing our map onto the Shaver representation. A computer program was written explicitly for this purpose (Georgson 1994). To accomplish its task, the computer program works according to the following principles:

Best fit: every operation necessary must be made to minimize errors, Ordinary Least Squares (OLS) error between every corresponding point.

Correspondence: only emotion items that occur in both maps can be used for the fitting procedure, i.e. every item needs a counterpart.

Dimensionality: Shaver et. al. fit their data to two axes, evaluation and intensity. Therefore, let Shaver's map be fixed, and adjust ours to fit it.

Fitting procedure: there are three steps in finding the best fit: *Polar adjustment*: by rotating our map in increments, we will see the optimal polar alignment of our map. This procedure is done by rotating in small increments, calculating the sum of squared error terms, until a full circle has been completed. The best solution found in the entire circle will then be implemented. *Origin matching*: once the rotation is completed, it is necessary to move the center of our map to the center of Shaver's. This is done by first moving along the X-axis and then along the Y-axis, looking for least SS errors. *Stretching/shrinking:* by enlarging or shrinking our map along x and y axes proportionally and simultaneously, we will adjust our map scale to that of Shaver.

The resulting coordinates are shown in figure 5. The first set of coordinates are the Shaver coordinates and describe the location of the emotions in that study, while the Consumer coordinates describe the location of the emotions fit onto that map. The residuals are the differences in the x and y dimensions, respectively. The true residual is the Pythagorean distance between the Shaver

---

[5]The study by Mano (1991) reports Stress values of .11 for both "lecture" and "TV ads" context MDS solutions.

FIGURE 3

MDS comparison (Shaver et. al - this study): Coordinates of evaluation and intensity

Item	Shaver Evaluation	Shaver Intensity	Consumer Evaluation	Consumer Intensity	Change in Evaluation	Change Intensity	Residual
Tenderness	1.56	-0.73	0.08	0.52	1.48	-1.25	1.94
Lust	1.60	-0.62	-0.08	0.10	1.68	-0.72	1.83
Love	1.77	-0.67	0.53	0.51	1.24	-1.18	1.71
Pride	1.60	-0.08	0.19	-0.83	1.42	0.75	1.60
Affection	1.74	-0.70	0.53	0.34	1.21	-1.04	1.60
Hope	1.66	-0.16	0.26	0.51	1.40	-0.67	1.55
Surprise	1.18	1.24	0.11	0.38	1.07	0.86	1.38
Fear	-1.02	0.73	-0.73	-0.54	-0.29	1.27	1.31
Anxiety	-0.84	0.68	-0.76	-0.57	-0.08	1.25	1.25
Nervousness	-0.96	0.70	-0.72	-0.46	-0.24	1.16	1.19
Loneliness	-1.04	-0.57	-0.34	0.25	-0.70	-0.82	1.08
Sorrow	-1.11	-0.53	-0.30	0.10	-0.81	-0.63	1.03
Sadness	-1.12	-0.47	-0.52	0.22	-0.60	-0.69	0.92
Apprehension	-0.77	0.62	-0.57	-0.24	-0.20	0.86	0.88
Amusement	1.75	0.02	1.84	-0.81	-0.09	0.83	0.83
Guilt	-1.10	-0.42	-0.60	0.22	-0.50	-0.64	0.81
Disappoint	-1.19	-0.36	-0.54	0.09	-0.65	-0.45	0.79
Dejection	-1.14	-0.46	-0.64	0.15	-0.50	-0.61	0.78
Depression	-1.17	-0.30	-0.52	0.12	-0.65	-0.42	0.77
Anger	-1.13	0.68	-0.58	0.15	-0.55	0.54	0.77
Shame	-1.16	-0.37	-0.67	0.15	-0.49	-0.52	0.72
Remorse	-1.12	-0.38	-0.63	0.11	-0.50	-0.49	0.70
Humiliation	-1.12	-0.19	-0.60	0.25	-0.52	-0.44	0.68
Worry	-1.13	-0.09	-0.67	-0.59	-0.46	0.50	0.68
Loathing	-1.11	-0.06	-0.49	0.18	-0.62	-0.24	0.68
Happiness	1.87	-0.16	2.27	-0.68	-0.40	0.52	0.66
Regret	-1.10	-0.35	-0.67	0.12	-0.43	-0.47	0.66
Irritation	-1.20	0.21	-0.82	-0.24	-0.38	0.45	0.64
Disgust	-1.20	0.36	-0.71	0.10	-0.50	0.26	0.59
Exasperation	-0.60	0.68	-0.60	0.13	0.00	0.55	0.56
Annoyance	-1.22	0.20	-0.73	0.11	-0.49	0.09	0.55
Jealousy	-0.69	-0.55	-0.42	-0.19	-0.28	-0.36	0.50
Frustration	-1.10	-0.06	-0.69	-0.20	-0.41	0.14	0.45
Delight	1.88	0.04	1.93	-0.36	-0.05	0.40	0.43
Pleasure	1.85	-0.24	2.01	-0.56	-0.16	0.32	0.40
Envy	-0.67	-0.52	-0.43	-0.28	-0.24	-0.24	0.36
Joy	1.88	-0.06	1.78	-0.08	0.10	0.02	0.10

and the consumption position. Correlating coordinates[6] between the two solutions gives us a high correlation of .81 for the Evaluation dimension, but a -.04 on the Intensity dimension. Obviously, evaluation held up well, in fact, and intensity did not.

A univariate regression of Shaver's Evaluation score to the consumer Evaluation score resulted in a b-weight of .58. This regression is significant at p<.001 level, with an $R^2 = .67$.

Looking at the squared residuals bar chart, figure 5, we see that there are seven emotions that stand out as having worse fit than the

others, namely Tenderness, Lust, Love, Pride, Affection, Hope, and Surprise. Quite strikingly, all of these emotions show dramatic decreases in evaluation, which means that they are less positively evaluated. Surprise was also less intense. Note on Figure 1 how Surprise is clearly the most intense emotion in Shaver's representation.

By visual inspection of the MDS solutions, we see clearly how the unpleasantness cluster forms as an undifferentiated mass in the consumer context.

CONCLUSIONS

Overall, there is a very good correspondence between the two studies, considering their large differences in methodology. In the consumer context, certain cluster compositions differed from the general context. Specifically, two new clusters form around pride and interest. Cluster memberships differed the most on negatively evaluated emotions. Specifically, anger and sadness merge into a

[6]Mano (1991), as mentioned before, does not seem to have performed any procedure of optimizing correspondence by juxtaposing the second MDS on the first. Thereby, quantitative results are hard to interpret. The author reports a highly negative correlation of coordinates (x -x : -.77, y to y : -.76) as indicating good fit. If the axes were not perfectly aligned, this would mean underreporting the true correspondence.

general unpleasantness cluster. Emotions can be more or less informative in a consumer context. For instance, negative emotions seem to have little differentiation between them.

A given emotion seems to be evaluated less severely in a consumer context, i.e. there is a limit to how good or bad consumption typically make you feel compared to life in general. Emotion intensity in consumption seems unrelated to emotion intensity in a general context. Intensity therefore seems to be more context/object dependent. Love-related emotions showed the largest difference in semantic space between the two contexts.

DISCUSSION

The findings described here again underscore the complexity of the phenomena of emotion. On one hand, we can not ignore the above indications that there seem to be context effects on the semantic space of emotion. On the other hand, there is also considerable stability present, especially along the evaluative dimension.

It is, however, quite apparent that the overall picture holds up quite well. We have compared two sets of data, collected with different measurements, in response to different tasks, and still arrived at quite similar results. Whether the differences stem from methodological differences or actual context effects is uncertain. We should therefore attempt to explain the differences through substantive interpretation. For example, pride is one of the misfit items. Maybe pride really has to be focused on the self (accomplishments, virtues) to be really positive and intense.

Apart from context effects, we should keep in mind that we have been comparing the emotion patterns of undergraduate students. Therefore, we see the effect of a marketing context in this particular population segment. Now, there is probably no reason to expect differences across population segments on a context-free similarity-sorting task like Shaver's. As long as the subjects vocabulary adheres to normal standards, I could probably get the same results regardless of whether I used airline pilots, nuns, or prison inmates.

On the other hand, if there is context instability, it could imply that language connotations and social norms might intrude on this neutral assessment. If I would get the aforementioned sample of nuns, they might quite honestly indicate very low scores for any consumption emotion. Future research should continue to investigate stability issues. This could be studied across different population segments, different consumer contexts (watching ads, brand experiences, product category experiences, etc.).

Even when progressing on the issue of emotion stability, there is the issue of emotion category fidelity. We notice that the negatively evaluated emotions seem to be perceived as quite similar to one another in the consumer context. Well, the answer seems in hindsight to be quite obvious: there are no markets for products strongly associated with negative emotions. Probably, consumer motivation is concentrated on hedonic emotional experiences. Negative emotions might on the other hand be tapping into to the unidimensional valence of emotion so often used in persuasion studies (e.g. the scale by Holbrook 1981)

On the topic of relevant emotional experiences, Buck et. al. (1994) mentions in discussing the advertising context that a specific ad might be a clear example of a certain emotional type, as exemplified by a Calvin Klein ad (Reptilian) and an AT&T ad (Prosocial-limbic) Therefore, it would be useful to construct more elaborate subscales of a measurement instrument to be used on ads that invoke a first indicator. For instance, if the Calvin Klein ad makes you feel sexually aroused, then a subset of reptilian affect indicators would be used.

Indeed, using standardized measurement scales covering the whole range of human emotion can be highly inappropriate. Consider an ad for charity showing starving children coupled with a response item for sexual desire... Incidentally, focusing on theoretically founded subsets of emotions might provide better consistency across studies. An important function of research on emotion in consumer research is to establish what is useful, as well as appropriate, for different audiences and topics.

In conclusion, it seems like emotion is something that holds up rather well across methods and contexts. Still, taking context differences into account might help create measurements that are more appropriate for the context of interest. If we have market research responses and there seems to be little differentiation between unpleasant emotions, we need not waste measurement items on those affects, instead concentrating efforts where we might find differences.

Emotion is one of the potentially most powerful carriers of information about human motivation. Continuing the efforts to establish valid, reliable, and economical measures of emotions is a good intellectual investment for both social and natural scientists.

REFERENCES

Aaker & Bruzzone (1981). Viewer perceptions of prime-time television advertising. *Journal of Advertising Research*, 21 (5), 15-23.

Aaker, Stayman & Hagerty (1986). Warmth in advertising: Measurement, impact, and sequence effects. *Journal of Consumer Research*, 12 (4), 365-381.

Agres, S. J., Edell, J. A., and T. M. Dubitsky (ed.) (1990). *Emotion and Advertising*. New York: Quorum Books.

Babin, Barry, Darden, William, and Griffin, Mitch. (1994) Work and/or fun: Measuring Hedonic and utilitarian shopping value. *Journal of Consumer Research*, vol. 20, 644-656.

Batra, Rajeev, and Ray, Michael L. (1986) Affective Responses Mediating Acceptance of Advertising. *Journal of Consumer Research*. Vol. 13, September, p. 234-249.

Buck, Ross, and Chaudhuri, Arjun. (1994a). Affect, Reason, and Involvement in Persuasion: The ARI model. In P. Weinberg (ed.), *Konsumentenforschung*. München: Verlag Franz Vahlen.

Buck, Ross, Chaudhuri, Arjun, Georgson, Mats, and Kowta, Srinivas. (1994b) *Conceptualizing and operationalizing affect, reason, and involvement in persuasion: The ARI model and the CASC scale*. Presented at Annual Advances in Consumer Research Conference 1994, Boston, MA.

Buck, Ross. (1984). *The communication of emotion*. New York: Guilford Press.

Buck, Ross. (1988) *Human Motivation and Emotion*. New York: Wiley.

Burke, Marian C., and Edell, Julie A. (1989) The Impact of feelings on ad-based affect and cognitions. *Journal of Marketing Research*, 26, February, 69-83.

Chauduri, Arjun, Buck, Ross. (1994) Are advertisers using brain theory? Introducing the CASC scale. In C. W. Park & D. Smith (eds.), *Marketing Theory and Applications*. Vol. 5. (pp. 193-198). Chicago, IL: American Marketing Association.

Cohen, Joel B., and Areni, Charles S. (1991) Affect and Consumer Behavior. In *Handbook of Consumer Theory and Research*, ed., Thomas S. Robertson and Harold H. Kassarjian, Eaglewood Cliffs, NJ: Prentice Hall, 188-240.

Eco, Umberto. (1993) *Misreadings*. San Diego : Harcourt Brace & Co.

Edell, J. A., and Burke, M. C. (1987) The power of feelings in understanding advertising effects. *Journal of Consumer Research*, 14, 421-433.

Ekman, P., Friesen, W. V., Ellsworth, P. (1972) *Emotion in the human face*. Elmsworth, NY: Pergamon Press.

Fishbein, M., and I. Ajzen (1975). *Belief, attitude, intention, and behavior : an introduction to theory and research*. Reading, Mass. : Addison-Wesley Pub. Co.

Georgson, Mats. (1994). *MDSFIT: A MDS representation comparison program*. Unpublished computer program, University of Connecticut.

Gibson, J. J. (1979). *The ecological approach to visual perception*. Boston: Houghton Miffin.

Gorn, G. J. (1982). The effects on Music in Advertising on Choice Behavior: A Classical Conditioning Approach, *Journal of Marketing*, 46, 94-101.

Haley, R. I., Staffaroni, J., and A. Fox (1994). The missing measures of copy testing. *Journal of Advertising Research*, 34, 46-60.

Hecker, S., and D. W. Stewart (ed.) (1988). *Nonverbal Communication in Advertising*, Lexington, Mass.: Lexington Books.

Holbrook, Morris B. (1981) Integrating compositional and decompositional analyses to represent the intervening role of perceptions in evaluative judgments, *Journal of Marketing Research*, 18, February, 13-28.

Holbrook, Morris B., and Batra, Rajeev. (1987). Assessing the role of emotions as mediators of consumer responses to advertising. *Journal of Consumer Research*, 14, 404-420.

Holbrook, Morris B., Chestnut, Robert W., Oliva, Terence A., and Greenleaf, Eric A. (1984). Play as a consumption experience: the roles of emotions, performance, and personality in the enjoyment of games. *Journal of Consumer Research*, 11, September, 728-739.

Izard, C. E. (1971). *The face of emotion*. Apple-Century-Crofts.

Izard, C. E. (1972). *Patterns of emotions*. Academic Press.

Izard, C. E. (1977). *Human emotions*. New York: Plenum Press.

Kruskal, J. B., Wish, M. (1978). *Multidimensional Scaling*. Sage University Paper Series on Quantitative Applications in the Social Sciences, no. 11. Beverly Hills, CA: Sage Publications, CA.

MacLean, P. D. (1990). *The triune brain in evolution: role in paleocerebral functions*. New York: Plenum press.

Mano, Haim. (1991) The structure and intensity of emotional experiences: Method and context convergence. *Multivariate Behavioral Research*, 26 (3), 389-411.

Microsoft (R) Encarta. *Color*. Copyright (c) 1994 Microsoft Corporation. Copyright (c) 1994 Funk & Wagnall's Corporation.

Osgood, C. E., Suci G. J., and P. H. Tannenbaum (1957). *The measurement of meaning*. Urbana, University of Illinois Press.

Petty, and Cacciopo (1981). *Attitudes and Persuasion: Classic and Contemporary Approaches*, Wm. C. Brown.

Petty, Cacciopo, Sedikides, and Strathman (1988). Affect and persuasion: A contemporary perspective. *American Behavioral Scientist*, 31, p. 355-371.

Petty, Ostrom & Brock (1981). *Cognitive Responses in Persuasion*, Lawrence Erlbaum Associates.

Roberts, James S., Wedell, Douglas H. (1994) Context effects on similarity judgments of stimuli: inferring the structure of emotion space. *Journal of Experimental and Social Psychology*, 30, 1-38.

Rossiter, John R., and Percy, Larry. (1987) *Advertising and Promotion Management*. NY: McGraw Hill.

Russel, J. A. (1980). A circumplex model of affect. *Journal of Personality and Social Psychology*, 39, 1161-1178.

Russell, J. A. (1979). Affective Space Is Bipolar. *Journal of Personality and Social Psychology*, no. 37, 345-356.

Russell, J. A. (1989). Measures of emotion. In R. Plutchik and H. Kellerman (Eds.). *Emotion: Theory, research, and experience* (Vol. 4., 83-111). San Diego: Academic Press.

Russell, J. A. (1991). Culture and the categorization of emotion. *Psychological Bullentin*. 110, 426-450.

Schlosberg, H. (1952). The description of facial expression in terms of two dimensions. *Journal of experimental psychology*, 44, 81-88.

Shaver, P., Schwartz, J., Kirson, D., and O'Connor, C. (1987) Emotion Knowledge: Further Exploration of a prototype approach. *Journal of Personality and Social Psychology*, vol. 52., no. 6, 1061-1086.

Tomkins, S. (1962) *Affect, imagery, and consciousness: The positive affects*, Vol. 1. New York: Springer.

Tomkins, S. (1963) *Affect, imagery, and consciousness: The negative affects*, Vol. 2. New York: Springer.

Tucker (1981). Lateral brain function, emotion, and conceptualization. *Psychological bulletin*, 89, 19-46.

Tversky, A. (1977). Features of similarity. *Psychological Review*, 76, 31-48.

Westbrook, Robert A. (1987). Product/Consumption-based Affective Resonses and Postpurchase processes. *Journal of Marketing Research*, 24, 258-270.

Westbrook, Robert A., and Richard D. Oliver (1991). The Dimensionality of Consumption Emotion Patterns and Consumer Satisfaction. *Journal of Consumer Research*, vol. 18, June, 84-91.

Woodruff, Robert B., Cadotte, Ernest R., and Jenkins, Roger L. (1983) Modeling Consumer Satisfaction Processes Using Experience-based Norms. *Journal of Marketing Research*, no. 20, 296-304.

Thinking and/or Feeling: An Examination of Interaction Between Processing Styles

Jane Z. Sojka, Ohio University
Joan L. Giese, Washington State University[1]

ABSTRACT

The purpose of this research is to examine the relationship between affective and cognitive processing styles. Using a combination of situation-invariant affect and cognition measures, evidence suggests that individuals differ in their propensity to rely on affective, cognitive, or both systems to process information. Rather than viewing affect and cognition as a dichotomy on a continuum, an independent but interactive relationship between affect and cognition is conceptualized and supported.

Marketing researchers have long been intrigued by the relationship between affect and cognition as well as the roles they play in preference formation and decision processing. According to traditional approaches, affect in preferences is an outcome of cognitive representations of the object; i.e., before you can say you like something, you must know what it is. Zajonc (1980) and Zajonc and Markus (1982), however, refuted the traditional approach. They suggested that the cognitive and affective processes may proceed independently, as well as work together. For understanding the consumer decision process, it is more useful to emphasize the interaction between the affective and cognitive systems than to debate about which system is more important or dominant (Peter and Olson 1996).

Recent studies on preference formation and attitude change have focused on how cognition and affect work together. Building on Zajonc's research, both Edwards (1990) and Millar and Millar (1990) investigated affect-based attitudes: intentional responses based on affect. Edwards' (1990) findings that affect-based attitudes were more susceptible to affective means of persuasion directly conflict with Millar and Millar's (1990) findings that affective-based attitudes were more susceptible to rational arguments. Yet, perhaps Edwards' (1990) newly formed attitudes were susceptible to affective persuasion because cognitions had not yet formed. In contrast, the attitudes studied in Millar and Millars' (1990) research had been sufficiently questioned to produce cognitions about the product. Hence, seemingly conflicting results actually support the Zajonc and Markus (1982) views of situational dependency—and possibly individual processing tendencies—of affective or cognitive preference formation.

As a result, Edwards (1990) concluded that individuals most likely use a combination of affective and cognitive processing. Furthermore, that lack of an either/or, affect/cognition dichotomy suggests the two constructs may interact but remain separate. The purpose of this research is to explore the possibility that individuals may process information based on three modes: processing cognitions, processing affective responses, or using both cognition and affect in independent but interactive processing systems.

Cognitive and Affective Processing

Conceptual Relationship. Whereas other means of exploring cognition and affect, such as the Briggs and Meyers Personality Inventory (1984), view these constructs as negatively correlated (as points along a continuum), our distinction between affective and cognitive processing is not a dichotomy; it is unlikely that individuals rely solely on cognitions or affect for all decision processing.

Rather, the relationship between affect and cognition is conceptualized as a biaxial grouping of four quadrants as depicted in Figure 1.

Individuals in the lower right quadrant are high cognitive processors and low affective processors. These individuals, Thinking Processors, generally prefer to think rationally and rely heavily on cognitive information. In terms of consumer purchases, they would likely be oriented towards tangible, quantifiable product attributes such as price or length of warranty. At the other end of the spectrum are people in the upper left quadrant. These are the Feeling Processors who rely on affect; they like the product and it feels good. The cues used to arrive at a decision are affective in nature such as "like" the product or the "feeling" it evokes (Booth-Butterfield and Booth-Butterfield 1990). Although they are not exclusively high on affect intensity, their propensity to use an affective processing style would suggest they experience more affective highs and lows than a cognitive processor (Larsen, Cropanzano, and Diener 1987).

People in the upper right quadrant, Combination Processors, are high on both affect and cognition. Similar to sociological interpretations of androgyny (Bem 1974), these people are comfortable using either processing style. This quadrant is consistent with research on promotion where both cognitive and affective responses were found to be intertwined (Burke and Edell 1989; Kahn and Isen 1993; Munch, Boller and Swasy 1993). Finally, the lower left quadrant exists where individuals are low on both affective and cognitive processing. The type of processing used by these individuals, Passive Processors, is unclear.

Conceptual Definitions. While cognition has been clearly distinguished from affect, researchers have been less than specific in defining affect and distinguishing it from the closely related, although not identical, concepts of attitude and emotion. Eagly and Chaiken (1993) define affect as experiential feelings directed toward attitude objects. Yet, emotions are unique from affect in that they are valenced and can therefore be classified as positive or negative (Abeele and MacLachlan 1994); they are spontaneous, temporary states (Murry, Lastovicka, and Singh 1992); and they can be classified by individuals according to a number of directions or orientations (Oliver 1992) such as happy, sad, angry, or mad. Raman, Chattopadhyay and Hoyer (1995) further distinguish emotions from moods. They conceptualize emotions as longer affective states than moods which are more general and less intensive (Gardner 1985).

In contrast, attitude is defined as an individual's general affective, cognitive, and intentional responses toward a given object, issue, or person. Attitude includes a behavioral and cognitive component not present in the conceptual definition of emotion (Fishbein and Ajzen 1975). Affect—as used in this research—contains the feeling element present in both the emotion and attitude constructs but is viewed as a processing mechanism (Oliver 1993; Peter and Olson 1996). Hence, in this paper, affect is conceptualized and defined as a processing mechanism for feelings.

Cognitive processing, as defined by Engel and Blackwell (1982), involves "interpreting present perceptions in light of past information to reason our way through unfamiliar problems" (p. 237). The key feature in this definition which distinguishes it from affect is the emphasis on reason or logic: feelings or emotions are not included in cognitive processing. Consequently, thinking is to cognitive processing as feeling is to affective processing.

[1]The authors wish to thank Joseph A. Cote and Ayn Crowley for their helpful comments.

Advances in Consumer Research
Volume 24, © 1997

FIGURE 1

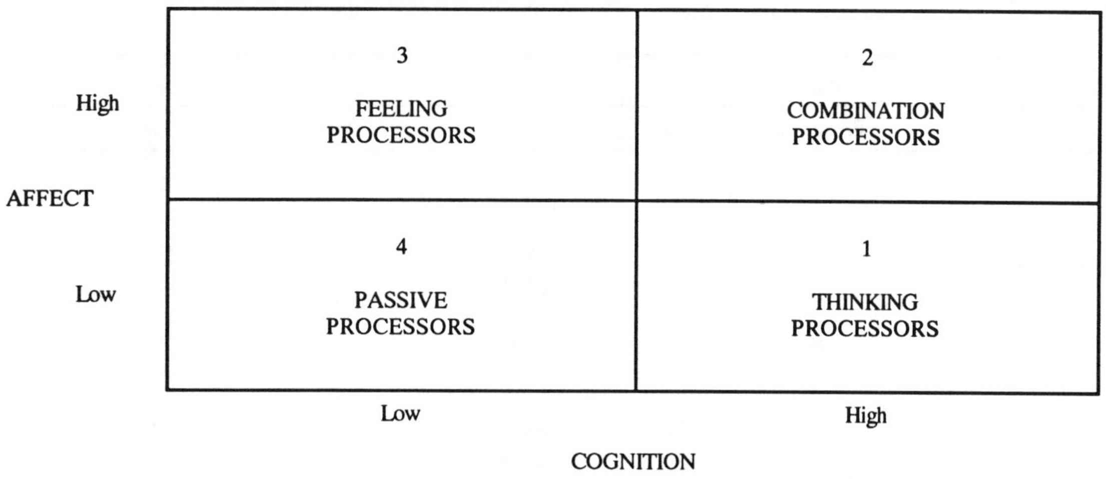

Affect and Cognition Scales. There are several scales designed to measure affect. Both the Leigh (1984) and Obermiller (1985) scales measure affect as a valenced construct suggesting that the scales are not measuring affect but emotion according to the distinctions suggested previously in this paper.

The Feeling Belief Measure (Haddock and Zanna 1993) is designed to assess individual differences in preferences toward using affect or cognition to process environmental stimuli. This scale examines the affect processing preference within context-specific situations and is most appropriate for measuring situations which are likely to evoke affective processing.

The Need for Emotion Scale (Raman, Chattopadhyay and Hoyer 1995) measures individuals' needs to seek out emotional stimuli and is intended to be analogous to the Need for Cognition scale (Cacioppo, Petty and Kao 1984). The scale items, however, are situationally bound suggesting that, like the Feeling-Belief Measure, affect processing is a function of the situation as opposed to an individual processing trait which is relatively stable with respect to situations.

The Affective Orientation Scale (Booth-Butterfield and Booth-Butterfield 1990) attempts to measure awareness and use of emotional cues. While they too conceptualize affect as information in an information processing model, the focus is on the effect of affect processing on communication and message retention.

The Need for Cognition scale (Cacioppo, Petty and Kao 1984) is an 18-item scale which measures the extent to which individuals seek out and use cognitive information when making decisions. The Need for Cognition scale is used to measure cognitive processing across all situations. In contrast, published affect scales were typically situation bound.

METHOD

Measures

A situation-invariant affective processing scale analagous to the cognitive processing scale (Need for Cognition) was developed for the purpose of this research. The steps involved in developing the proposed scale were based on those suggested by Churchill (1979) and Gerbing and Anderson (1988). Using the conceptual domain of affect, as outlined in previous research, and comments generated by a focus group, 108 sample items were generated. The

large number of items represented the breadth of the affect domain as well as the special attention accorded to the wording of statements (Dillman 1978). For example, one item may be reworded four different ways using the terms "vibes," "intuitions," "feelings," or "gut feel" interchangeably.

A panel of nine experts familiar with affect research reviewed the list of sample items and eliminated inappropriate statements. As a result, a total of 62 items remained. These 62 items were randomly interspersed with the 18 items from the Need for Cognition scale (Cacioppo, Petty, and Kao 1984). The Need for Cognition scale, complete with response categories, was reproduced verbatim as a nine-point Likert scale. Scale endpoints were "very strong disagreement" (-4) to "very strong agreement" (+4). The same type of scale and endpoints were used for the affect scale.

Exploratory and confirmatory factor analysis supported the retention of 17 items. Using exploratory factor analysis, all 17 items loaded on the first factor. Of those 17 items, 13 exhibited loadings of .4 or greater and were retained. The four items discarded due to factor loadings of less than .2 shared one quality in common: they were all situationally bound (e.g. Sometimes it feels good to cry during a sad movie.). Confirmatory factor analysis using the 13 items from the exploratory analysis resulted in a good fit for a one-factor model (χ^2=127.809; df=65; CFI=.910). (The scale items and respective standardized parameter estimates appear in the appendix.)

Samples

Using the Need for Cognition scale to measure cognitive processing and the Preference for Affect scale to measure affective processing, two samples were used to examine the relationship between the processing styles. In an effort to avoid extensive cognitive processing of statements, respondents were encouraged to answer each question carefully but were told not to deliberate over any one particular question.

The first sample consisted of 194 students from four undergraduate business and anthropology classes at a large northwestern university. After analyzing responses for inconsistencies and missing data, 176 surveys were usable. The second sample consisted of 191 students from different undergraduate business, communication, and engineering classes at the same university. One hundred sixty-seven surveys were usable.

TABLE 1
Descriptive Statistics for Affect / Cognition Quadrants

	Sample 1:			Sample 2:		
	Frequency	%	Means	Frequency	%	Means
Thinking Processors	42	23.6	63.6[a] 120.7[c]	43	25.7	66.7[a] 124.0[c]
Combination Processors	49	27.5	95.4[a] 120.5[c]	42	25.1	93.1[a] 126.7[c]
Feeling Processors	44	24.7	96.1[a] 94.3[c]	49	29.3	93.6[a] 93.9[c]
Passive Processors	43	24.2	68.5[a] 88.4[c]	33	19.8	71.3[a] 93.1[c]
	178			167		

Note: The four categories are based on a median split of the actual scale data.

a = Preference for Affect (PFA) Scale
c = Need for Cognition (NFC) Scale

(Sample 1: PFA Scale Median = 85; theoretical range = 13 - 117. NFC Scale Median = 107; theoretical range = 18-162.)
(Sample 2: PFA Scale Median = 82; NFC Scale Median = 110.)

RESULTS

Sample 1

Coefficient alpha for the Need for Cognition scale and the newly developed Preference for Affect scale were .8453 and .9136 respectively. There was no significant correlation between the scales (r=-.0267; p=.723). Using a median split of the actual data, results indicated that respondents could be categorized as high on cognition but low on affect (thinking processors); high on both the affect and cognition scales (combination processors); low on cognition but high on affect (feeling processors); or low on both the affect and cognition scales (passive processors). (See Table 1).

Sample 2

As a verification of the results from Sample 1, data were analyzed from another sample. Coefficient alpha for the scales were .8591 (Need for Cognition) and .8721 (Preference for Affect). Again, there was no significant correlation between the scales (r=-.0836; p=.283). (See Table 1.)

DISCUSSION AND FUTURE RESEARCH

These results suggest that affective and cognitive processing systems are independent, yet can operate interactively. Individuals, unbounded by a specific situation, demonstrate a propensity to process information using affect (feeling processors), cognitions (thinking processors), or both (combination processors). Furthermore, some individuals indicate a propensity to not rely on either processing style (passive processors).

Previous research indicates similar results pertinent to combination processors. Booth-Butterfield and Booth-Butterfield (1990) found that individuals high on the need for cognition were as likely to process feelings as they were statistical data suggesting that an affective orientation is not the polar opposite of need for cognition. In addition, Ramon, Chattopadhyay and Hoyer (1995) found a moderate correlation between the Need for Cognition and Need for Emotion scales causing them to conclude that the affective and cognitive systems were interacting.

If, in fact, affect and cognition are simultaneous processes operating at different levels in different situations, several interesting issues for further research should be considered. First of all, much of previous affect/cognition research has assumed a causal order of the two constructs. The critical issue may not be which comes first—affect or cognition—but rather under what situations, or with which personality types, is a combination, affective, or cognitive processing style likely to dominate. It is conceivable that situational variables, such as product involvement, risk level, or spousal processing style, may impact an individual's processing style. For example, purchasing an automobile is most likely more emotionally laden than purchasing paper towels. Likewise, in a family situation, one spouse may take a cognitive approach to purchasing an automobile while the other spouse utilizes an affective process; the sum of which results in two different processes used to arrive at a particular decision. Additional research is needed to examine situational effects on individuals' processing styles and the interaction of affective and cognitive processing styles in specific decision making or choice situations. With dependent decision variables, the influence of processing style and the causal sequence of that influence could be examined.

This simultaneous approach to affect/cognition also raises the issue of information overload. Research in decision processing suggests that in cases of information overload, respondents are likely to either switch heuristics or resort to an affect-referral strategy (Wright 1975). If the affective and cognitive systems respond to cues in a similar fashion, then perhaps affect overload would result in a cognitive processing approach.

In addition, future research should focus on the passive processors, i.e., those who are low on both the cognition and affect scales.

APPENDIX

Scale Item	Standardized Solution
I'm good at empathizing with other people's problems.	.510
I make decisions with my heart.	.576
I often get too emotionally involved.	.628
I appreciate opportunities to discover my true feelings.	.624
I like being around sensitive people.	.625
My feelings reflect who I am.	.579
I am a feeling person.	.679
I'm more of a "feeler" than a "thinker."	.535
When I recall a situation, I usually recall the emotional aspects of the situation.	.606
I prefer a task that is emotional and important to a task that is intellectual and important.	.597
Feeling comes naturally to me.	.676
I enjoy trying to explain my feelings—even if it's only to myself.	.544
Emotion excites me.	.599

Note: Respondents were instructed to indicate the degree of agreement or disagreement with each of the statements listed above. Ratings were made using a -4 to +4 Likert-type scale.

LIMITATIONS

This research was conducted using traditional undergraduate students. Previous research suggests that affective decisions may be more prominent in early years and will decrease as the individual grows older (Larsen and Diener 1987). In addition, the use of student samples may result in an upward bias of results (Brown and Stayman 1992), as well as inhibiting the scale's external validity (Lynch 1982). While some researchers argue that student samples are appropriate particularly when testing theory (Calder, Phillips and Tybout 1981), additional testing with a more diverse population is needed to enhance the generalizability of the results.

The nonverbal nature of affect coupled with research on hemisphere lateralization suggests that it might be difficult to capture affective processes via cognitive methods. Note that there are no reverse-coded items in the final scale. The lack of reverse-coded items, however, is somewhat theoretically consistent since a reverse-coded item requires more cognitive processing to accurately interpret the question. Furthermore, research has shown that scale dimensionality is not compromised in scales lacking reverse-coded items (Obermiller and Spangenberg 1996).

CONCLUSION

Preliminary evidence suggests an interaction between affective and cognitive processing styles in which both processes may operate simultaneously yet separately. While additional research is needed to offer conclusive empirical evidence supporting this conceptualization, the concept is intuitively appealing and is potentially able to accommodate previous research in the field. Clearly, the relationship between affect and cognition holds great promise for future research.

REFERENCES

Bem, D. (1974), "The Measurement of Psychological Androgyny," *Journal of Counseling and Clinical Psychology*, 42, 155-162.

Booth-Butterfield, Melanie and Steve Booth-Butterfield (1990), "Conceptualizing Affect as Information in Communication Production," *Human Communication Research*, 16 (Summer), 451-476.

Brown, Stephen P. and Douglas M. Stayman (1992), "Antecedents and Consequences of Attitude Toward the Ad: A Meta-Analysis," *Journal of Consumer Research*, 19 (June), 34-51.

Burke, Marian Chapman and Julie A. Edell (1989), "The Impact of Feelings on Ad-Based Affect and Cognition," *Journal of Marketing Research*, 26 (February), 69-83.

Cacioppo, John T., Richard E. Petty, and Chaun Feng Kao (1984), "The Efficient Assessment of Need for Cognition," *Journal of Personality Assessment*, 47 (3), 306-307.

Calder, Bobby J., Lynn W. Phillips, and Alice M. Tybout (1981), "Designing Research for Application," *Journal of Consumer Research*, 8 (September), 197-207.

Churchill, Gilbert A., Jr. (1979), "A Paradigm for Developing Better Measures of Marketing Constructs," *Journal of Marketing Research*, 16 (February), 64-73.

Dillman, Don A. (1978), *Mail and Telephone Surveys: The Total Design Method*, New York, NY: John Wiley.

Eagly, Alice H. and Shelly Chaiken (1993), *The Psychology of Attitudes*, Fort Worth, TX: Harcourt Brace Jovanovich College Publishers.

Edwards, Kari (1990), "The Interplay of Affect and Cognition in Attitude Formation and Change," *Journal of Personality and Social Psychology*, 59 (2), 202-216.

Engel, James F. and Roger D. Blackwell (1982), *Consumer Behavior*, New York, NY: The Dryden Press.

Fazio, R. H. and Mark Zanna (1981) "Direct Experience and Attitude-Behavior Consistency," in *Advances in Experimental Social Psychology*, Vol. 14, ed. L. Berkowitz, Orlando, FL: Academic Press, 161-202.

Fishbein, Martin and I. Ajzen (1975), *Beliefs, Attitudes, Intentions, and Behavior*, Reading, Mass: Addison-Welsley.

Gardner, Meryl P. (1985), "Mood States and Consumer Behavior: A Critical Review," *Journal of Consumer Research*, 12 (December), 281-300.

Gerbing, David W. and James C. Anderson (1988), "An Updated Paradigm for Scale Development Incorporating Unidimensionality and Its Assessment," *Journal of Marketing Research*, 25 (May), 186-192.

Haddock, Geoffrey and Mark P. Zanna (1993), "Predicting Prejudicial Attitudes: The Importance of Affect, Cognition, and the Feeling-Belief Dimension," in *Advances in Consumer Research*, Vol. 20, eds. Leigh McAlister and Michael Rothschild, Provo, UT: Association of Consumer Research, 315-318.

Kahn, Barbara E. and Alice M. Isen (1993), "The Influence of Positive Affect on Variety Seeking Among, Safe, Enjoyable Products," *Journal of Consumer Research*, 20 (September), 257-270.

Larsen, Randy J. and Ed Diener (1987), "Affect Intensity as a Individual Characteristic: A Review," *Journal of Research in Personality*, 21, 1-39.

_____, Russell S. Cropanzano, and Ed Diener (1987), "Cognitive Operations Associated with Individual Differences in Affect Intensity," *Journal of Personality and Social Psychology*, 53 (4), 767-774.

Leigh, James H. (1984), "Recall and Recognition Performance for Umbrella Print Advertisements," *Journal of Advertising*, 13 (4), 5-18.

Lynch, John G. Jr., (1982), "On the External Validity of Experiments in Consumer Research," *Journal of Consumer Research*, 9 (December), 225-239.

Millar, Murray G. and Karen U. Millar (1990), "Attitude Change as a Function of Attitude Type and Argument Type," *Journal of Personality and Social Psychology*, 59 (2), 217-228.

Munch, James M., Gregory W. Boller, and John L. Swasy (1993), "The Effects of Argument Structure and Affective Tagging on Product Attitude Formation," *Journal of Consumer Research*, 20 (September), 294-302.

Murry, John P. Jr., John Lastovicka, and Surendra N. Singh (1992), "Feeling and Liking Responses to Television Programs: Examination of Two Explanations for Media-Context Effects," *Journal of Consumer Research*, 18 (March), 441-451.

Obermiller, Carl (1985), "Varieties of Mere Exposure: The Effects of Processing Style and Repetition in Affective Response," *Journal of Consumer Research*, 12 (June), 17-30.

_____ and Eric R. Spangenberg (1996), "Development of a Scale to Measure Consumer Skepticism toward Advertising," Working Paper, Seattle University.

Oliver, Richard (1992), "An Investigation of the Attribute Basis of Emotion and Related Affects in Consumption: Suggestions for a Stage-Specific Satisfaction Framework," in *Advances in Consumer Research*, Vol. 19, eds. John F. Sherry and Brian Sternthal, Provo, UT: Association for Consumer Research, 237-244.

_____ (1993), "Cognitive, Affective and Attribute Bases of the Satisfaction Response," *Journal of Consumer Research*, 20 (December), 418-430.

Peter, J. Paul and Jerry C. Olson (1996), *Consumer Behavior and Marketing Strategy*, Chicago, IL: Richard D. Irwin.

Raman, Niranjan V., Prithviraj Chattopadhyay, Wayne D. Hoyer (1995), "Do Consumers Seek Emotional Situations: The Need for Emotion Scale," in *Advances in Consumer Research*, Vol. 22, eds. Frank R. Kardes and Mita Sujan, Provo, UT: Association for Consumer Research, 537-542.

Wright, Peter(1975), "Consumer Choice Strategies: Simplifying vs. Optimizing," *Journal of Marketing Research*, 12, 60-67.

Zajonc, Robert B. (1980), "Feeling and Thinking: Preferences Need No Inferences," *American Psychologist*, 35 (February), 151-175.

_____ and Hazel Markus (1982), "Affective and Cognitive Factors in Preferences," *Journal of Consumer Research*, 9 (September) 123-131.

Gender Differences In Information Processing Confidence in an Advertising Context: A Preliminary Study

DeAnna S. Kempf, Iowa State University
Kay M. Palan, Iowa State University
Russell N. Laczniak, Iowa State University

ABSTRACT

Previous research suggests that males and females process advertising information differently. However, researchers have yet to explore whether biological sex influences the confidence that receivers have in their ad responses. In addition, prior research has failed to determine the relative influence of biological sex and gender identity on confidence. Results from an experiment featuring a fictitious soft drink brand suggest that males exhibit greater confidence in their attitudes toward the non-claim component of an ad, and suggest that gender identity accounts for variance in several different measures of advertising processing confidence, beyond what was explained by biological sex.

INTRODUCTION

Advertising researchers are becoming increasingly concerned with the impact of gender differences on consumer responses to advertising. Indeed, several studies have reported significant differences between males and females in the processing of advertising information (e.g., Darley and Smith 1995; Meyers-Levy and Maheswaran 1991). What researchers have not yet examined, however, are gender differences with respect to information processing confidence. Specifically, do males and females have different levels of confidence when processing information contained in advertising? Several studies have reported that males and females differ with respect to self-confidence (Lenney 1977; Maccoby and Jacklin 1974; White, DeSanctis, and Crino 1981), suggesting that differences in information processing confidence might also be present in an advertising context. One purpose of this paper is to conduct a preliminary examination of the effect of biological sex, i.e., whether an individual is male or female, on generalized information processing confidence and belief and attitude confidence resulting from an advertising exposure. Further, since there is evidence that gender identity, i.e., an individual's gender self-concept, may explain differences in consumers' responses to advertising (e.g., Coughlin and O'Connor 1985; Jaffe 1991), a secondary purpose is to explore the ability of gender identity to explain differences in information processing confidence and belief and attitude confidence beyond that explained by biological sex alone.

CONFIDENCE CONSTRUCTS IN ADVERTISING RESPONSE

Evaluative confidence, defined as the certainty with which an evaluative judgment is held, is applicable to any consumer evaluation or judgment, but has been studied by marketing and consumer researchers mainly in the form of belief confidence (c_i in Fishbein's expectancy value model of attitudes) and brand attitude confidence (e.g., Bennett and Harrell 1975; Fishbein and Ajzen 1975; Smith and Swinyard 1982; 1983; 1988). Bennett and Harrell (1975) and Smith and Swinyard (1988) found that inclusion of the belief confidence measure as an indication of how certain the consumer feels about his/her belief probability estimate improves the predictive value of the Fishbein and Ajzen model. Researchers have long desired to accurately predict behavior from measured attitudes, and attitude confidence is one variable that has been shown to have significant positive effects on attitude and behavior consistency (Fazio and Zanna 1978; Smith and Swinyard 1983). Therefore, a deeper understanding of the antecedents of confidence would be valuable to both theory and practice in the attitude area. This study makes a first step toward understanding two related antecedents of confidence in a marketing context—biological sex and gender identity.

Although evaluative confidence has been studied in marketing primarily with respect to brand beliefs and brand attitudes, it is also relevant for evaluations of the ad itself (A_{Ad}), including both claim and non-claim components (Miniard, Bhatla, and Rose 1990). In this study, therefore, the effects of biological sex and gender identity on belief confidence, attitude confidence, and attitude-toward-the-ad confidence are investigated.

Marketing researchers have hypothesized numerous effects of confidence, with mixed results. According to Smith and Swinyard (1988), this lack of consistency in empirical findings involving belief and attitude confidence is because most studies including confidence have not specifically manipulated antecedent conditions that should create significant variation in subjects' confidence levels. One exception is the research stream dealing with the effects of product trial, which has shown that attitudes and beliefs formed as a result of a direct trial experience are more confidently held than those formed from advertising or other indirect sources of information (e.g., Fazio and Zanna 1978; Smith and Swinyard 1988; Smith 1993).

Several antecedents of confidence have been proposed including: (1) the quantity of information available for the judgment (e.g., Dover and Olson 1977; Peterson and Pitz 1988), (2) the credibility of the information (Fishbein and Ajzen 1975), and (3) the consistency of the information among sources (Kahneman and Tversky 1973). The current study examines the potential effects of two additional and related variables on confidence constructs: biological sex and gender identity.

While the confidence constructs of belief confidence and attitude confidence discussed above have been studied frequently in the advertising literature, another construct—generalized information processing confidence (GIPC)—has received little attention (Wright 1975). GIPC refers to the degree of certainty or confidence an individual feels in his/her ability to form judgments in response to information exposure. Wright (1975) defined high GIPC more generally as "having quick mental reflexes," although it is important to note that in that study, as well as the current one, GIPC refers to the consumer's *self-perceived* level of ability rather than an objective measure of ability to process information. Again, as with the various forms of evaluative confidence discussed above, the current study investigates the effects of biological sex and gender identity on GIPC.

Although sex and gender identity have not been studied with respect to generalized information processing confidence measures, previous research indicates that both variables are significantly related to another type of person-level confidence—self-confidence. Maccoby and Jacklin (1974) reported that self-confidence is lower for females than for men in almost all achievement situations. In a separate review of the literature, Lenney (1977) concluded that self-confidence among women was lower than among men in only three types of achievement situations: when the specific task being measured is sex-linked, when clear and unambiguous performance feedback is unavailable, and when it is suggested that females' work will be compared to or evaluated by others. More recent studies support Lenney's (1977) contention that differences in self-confidence are situational. For example, Zuckerman (1985) found no differences among female and male students' perceptions of interpersonal self-confidence, but Andrews (1987) found that females had lower self-confidence than males concerning their ability to communicate arguments persuasively. However, Chusmir, Koberg, and Stecher (1992) found no differences in self-confidence among males and females in either the work setting or in social/family situations. In the same study, though, gender identity was significant with respect to self-confidence. Both males and females scoring high on masculine attributes reported greater self-confidence in work than in social situations; the same result also occurred for both males and females scoring high on feminine attributes. Based on these studies, it is reasonable to expect that both biological sex and gender identity will be related to information processing confidence.

GENDER IDENTITY AND BIOLOGICAL SEX IN ADVERTISING RESPONSE

Gender identity represents an individual's self-perceived endorsement of masculine and feminine personality traits, and as such, may or may not be congruent with an individual's biological sex. Therefore, gender identity potentially has effects distinct from those related to biological sex. However, whereas biological sex generally has played a significant explanatory role in consumer research, gender identity has rarely been found to be a significant predictor (Stern 1988), except when used to explain behaviors that are clearly gender-related (Fischer and Arnold 1994). Yet, it is reasonable to expect gender identity to be significant in explaining differences in information processing confidence since Chusmir et al. (1992) found significant relationships between gender identity characteristics and self-confidence. Moreover, biological sex was not significantly related to self-confidence in the same study, suggesting the effects of biological sex and gender identity may be different with respect to information processing confidence.

While several different conceptualizations of gender identity exist, this paper takes the position that gender identity is a multidimensional construct where masculinity and femininity are orthogonal dimensions, coexisting in varying degrees within an individual (Bem 1974, 1975; Spence, Helmreich, and Stapp 1975). Typically, an individual is placed into one of four different categories based on his/her endorsement of both masculine and feminine characteristics: (1) sex-typed, when an individual primarily endorses same-sex traits; (2) cross sex-typed, when an individual primarily endorses opposite-sex traits; (3) androgynous, when an individual endorses both masculine and feminine characteristics to a high degree; and (4) undifferentiated, when an individual endorses both feminine and masculine characteristics to a low degree (Spence et al. 1975). However, some researchers, concerned with the validity of combining sex-typed masculine males and feminine females together, have chosen instead to examine individuals who endorse masculine characteristics to a high degree, relative to feminine characteristics, as masculine schematics and individuals who endorse feminine characteristics to a high degree, relative to masculine characteristics, as feminine schematics (Gentry and Haley 1984; Markus, Crane, Bernstein, and Siladi 1982).

While somewhat limited, advertising research that has used either of these classification schemes for gender identity has pro-

duced interesting results. For example, Gentry and Haley (1984), using three different operationalizations of information processing, found only one significant relationship (out of fifteen possible relationships) between gender identity and ad recall. Coughlin and O'Connor (1985), examining the hypothesis that an individual's reaction to sex-related role portrayals in ads would be consistent with his/her gender identity, found several significant relationships. As expected, androgynous males and females reacted similarly to ads, but, unexpectedly, cross sex-typed males and females responded unfavorably to non-traditional roles. Along these same lines, Jaffe and Berger (1988) and Jaffe (1991) found that cross sex-typed females (i.e., masculine females) and androgynous females prefer modern positioning of females in advertisements, while sex-typed females (i.e., feminine females) and undifferentiated females responded similarly to both traditional and modern positionings.

Biological sex has been shown to be significantly related to several aspects of consumer behavior important to advertising. According to the selectivity model of information processing (Meyers-Levy 1989), males tend to use a selective, heuristic mode of processing information suggesting they tend to base judgments on a single cue. Females, on the other hand, are more likely to use a comprehensive processing mode, basing judgments on all available cues. However, in situations where consumers are motivated to engage in detailed processing, males will drop schema-based processing in favor of detailed processing (Meyers-Levy and Maheswaran 1991). Darley and Smith (1995), using the selectivity model, found significant differences in male and female responses to objective and subjective ad claims. Biological sex has also been found to be significant in response to "gendered ads," i.e., ads specifically designed to appeal to either men or women. For instance, Alreck, Settle, and Belch (1982) found that men were more likely to try and use a masculine brand of soap and women were more likely to try and use a feminine brand of soap, but that masculine gendering was generally more acceptable than feminine gendering to all respondents. Gentry and Doering (1977) found biological sex to be significant in predicting attitudes toward and usage of gendered products.

Importantly, studies that have examined biological sex and gender identity together have generally found that biological sex is a better predictor than is gender identity (Alreck et al. 1982; Gentry and Doering 1977). In our study, both biological sex and gender identity will be examined. Gender identity will be represented in two ways: first, a categorization system for gender identity is used that combines elements from the traditional classification system (Bem 1974; Spence et al. 1975) with Markus et al.'s (1982) classification system, since consumer research has reported better results using the Markus et al. System (Gentry and Haley 1984). Consequently, respondents are organized into one of four gender identity categories—masculine schematic, feminine schematic, androgynous, or undifferentiated. Second, since Spence et al. (1975) showed that identification with masculine characteristics was most strongly related to self confidence (compared to identification or non-identification with feminine characteristics), masculine characteristics are included in the analyses separately by summing the original 5-point scales over the eight masculine items in the PAQ scale, thereby approximating a continuous measure of identification with masculine characteristics.

HYPOTHESES

The previous discussion suggests several hypotheses. First, it is expected that both biological sex and gender identity will have direct effects on generalized information processing confidence

(GIPC). Specifically, since male and female differences exist in information processing and in self-confidence, differences should also be present in GIPC. Further, since high self-confidence is associated with a masculine self-concept (Spence et al. 1975) and masculine traits (Chusmir et al. 1992), it is expected that the GIPC of individuals endorsing a high degree of masculine traits would be higher than for those individuals who do not endorse a high degree of masculine traits.

H1:   Males will score higher on the GIPC relative to females.

H2:   Masculine schematics and androgynous individuals will score higher on the GIPC relative to feminine schematics and individuals who are undifferentiated.

Second, it is expected that both biological sex and gender identity will directly affect several confidence constructs related to subjects' responses to an ad exposure, specifically belief confidence, attitude confidence, $A_{Ad\text{-}claim}$ confidence, and $A_{Ad\text{-}nonclaim}$ confidence. While the hypothesized effects of biological sex are identical across these four dependent variables, since this is a first attempt at studying these effects, they are studied separately in order to highlight any differences in the observed pattern of effects, leading to the following hypotheses.

H3a: Males will report higher belief confidence relative to females.

H3b: Males will report higher attitude confidence relative to females.

H3c: Males will report higher $A_{Ad\text{-}claim}$ confidence relative to females.

H3d: Males will report higher $A_{Ad\text{-}nonclaim}$ confidence relative to females.

Spence et al. (1975) found that it was specifically subjects' level of identification with masculine characteristics that had the highest correlation with self esteem; Chusmir et al. (1992) found a similar relationship between masculine characteristics and self-confidence. By extension, then, stronger identification with masculine characteristics is predicted to produce higher levels of confidence relating to the consumer's advertising responses. Again, the four advertising-response confidence variables are included in separate hypotheses.

H4a: Masculine characteristics will be positively related to higher belief confidence.

H4b: Masculine characteristics will be positively related to higher attitude confidence.

H4c: Masculine characteristics will be positively related to higher $A_{Ad\text{-}claim}$ confidence.

H4d: Masculine characteristics will be positively related to higher $A_{Ad\text{-}nonclaim}$ confidence.

METHOD

Procedure
Subjects for this study were undergraduate and graduate students enrolled in marketing courses at a medium-sized midwestern university. The final sample size was 105 students. The use of a student sample was deemed appropriate, since the use of a homogeneous sampling frame is recommended when a theory application test is being conducted (Calder, Phillips and Tybout 1982). Moreover, since the ad and product used in this study were targeted at college students, a student sample is appropriate.

In classroom settings, subjects were given a portfolio of three professionally developed ads (one test ad and two "filler" ads). The test ad featured a fictitious soft-drink brand (Citrus Springs), and included a picture of a model and superiority claims regarding the taste of the drink (determined to be the most salient attribute in a pretest of subjects similar to those used in the main study). A soft drink was chosen as the advertised product because students constitute a sizeable market for the product, soft drinks are consumed by both males and females, and use of such a product was consistent with the experimental guise utilized in the present study (i.e., subjects would be asked for their opinions of three new brands of products that might be of interest). Fictitious brands of virus protection software and 35mm cameras were featured in the filler ads. The use of unfamiliar brand names was deemed appropriate to ensure that prior brand knowledge and preferences would not influence post-exposure beliefs and attitudes.

Subjects were given two minutes to look through the ad portfolio (determined in a pretest to be sufficient to allow them to thoroughly view all ads). The mean score for a six-item measure of self-perceived advertising message involvement (Andrews and Shimp 1990—alpha=.89) was 4.43 on a seven point likert-type scale (where 1 indicated that subjects would strongly disagree that they were not involved with the test ad's message and 7 indicates they would strongly agree that they were involved). This result indicates that subjects were moderately involved with the test ad's message. Further, results suggested subjects were relatively homogeneous in their self-perceived ad message involvement. Print ads were used to allow subjects an adequate opportunity to elaborate on the test ad's message so that they would be able to formulate beliefs and attitudes which could be confidently held.

After ad portfolios were collected, subjects were presented with questionnaires which gathered their cognitive responses to the test ad, self reports of ad message involvement, and measures of brand beliefs and brand-belief confidence, attitude toward the ad and attitude-toward-the-ad confidence, attitude toward the brand and attitude-toward-the-brand confidence, generalized information-processing confidence and gender identity. As a-priori hypotheses were not developed regarding several of these measures (i.e., cognitive responses, brand beliefs, attitude toward the ad, and attitude toward the brand), our discussion of study measures will focus only on a subset of these measures.

Measures
Brand-Belief Confidence. Belief confidence was measured by asking subjects how certain and confident they were regarding their reported taste beliefs for the advertised brand (Citrus Springs). Seven-point bipolar adjective scales with endpoints, "Not at all certain" and "Very certain" and "Not at all confident" and "Very confident," were used. An average of the six items was computed (for the three belief statements regarding taste) and used as the belief confidence measure (alpha=.85)

Attitude-toward-the-ad Confidence. As the present study views attitude toward the ad in a manner consistent with Miniard, Bhatla and Rose's (1990) contention that attitude toward the ad needs to be decomposed into claims and non-claims components, two measures of attitude-toward-the-ad confidence were gathered. Subjects were asked their degree of certainty and confidence in their attitudes toward the ad's claims (alpha=.98) and attitudes toward

TABLE 1
Mean Levels of GIPC by Gender Identity

Gender Type	n	Mean GIPC Score*
Masculine Schematic	26	6.80
Feminine Schematic	20	5.66
Androgynous	28	7.08
Undifferentiated	30**	5.30

*   All mean differences are significant (p<.05) with the exception of Masculine-Androgynous and Feminine-Undifferentiated using a Scheffe Multiple Comparisons test.

**   One subject in this cell did not complete the full GIPC scale and was therefore omitted from this analysis.

the ad's overall appearance (alpha=.95) on 7-point bipolar adjective scales (with endpoints, "Not at all certain" and "Very certain" and "Not at all confident" and "Very confident").

Attitude-toward-the-brand Confidence. Attitude-toward-the-brand confidence was assessed by asking subjects to rate their degree of certainty and confidence toward their brand attitudes with 7-point bipolar adjective scales with endpoints, "Not at all certain" and "Very certain" and "Not at all confident" and "Very confident." Alpha for this measure was .95.

It is important to note that all the above confidence measures were adapted from a previously published study which investigated effects on advertising on receivers' confidence (Laczniak and Muehling 1993).

Generalized Information Processing Confidence. The generalized-information-processing confidence measure was derived from Wright's (1975) study dealing with individual differences and information processing. This concept was measured with seven nine-point bipolar adjective items (where a response of 1 indicated that subjects felt a statement was "definitely true" and a score of 9 indicated the belief that a statement was "completely false"). Cronbach alpha for this measure was .79. Sample items include: "I often have trouble concentrating" and "I am certainly able to think quickly."

Gender Identity. Gender identity was measured using the Personal Attributes Questionnaire (PAQ) developed by Spence et al. (1975). While the PAQ has been infrequently used in consumer research, there is evidence that it may perform better than the Bem Sex Role Inventory when the moderating role of gender identity is examined (Palan, Areni, and Kiecker 1994). The PAQ contains 24 scale items—8 masculinity items, 8 femininity items, and 8 items that are non-sex specific. Coefficient alphas for the masculine and feminine scales were .83 and .80, respectively. For some of the analyses, these characteristics were summed and treated as continuous measures. For other analyses, median splits of the summed responses for the masculine and feminine scales were used to classify respondents as masculine schematic (high masculine, low feminine), feminine schematic (high feminine, low masculine), androgynous (high masculine and high feminine), or undifferentiated (low masculine and low feminine). This classification system resulted in 11 females and 15 males being categorized as masculine schematic, 10 females and 10 males categorized as feminine schematic, 14 females and 14 males categorized as androgynous, and 16 females and 15 males categorized as undifferentiated.

RESULTS

Effects of Sex and Gender Identity on Generalized Information Processing Confidence

One-way ANOVA results showed that males reported significantly higher levels of GIPC than females ($F_{1,112}=6.87$, p<.01), supporting H1. The mean GIPC score (on a 9-point scale) for males was 6.54, and 5.89 for females. This result, as suspected based on previous research, clearly shows that males tend to possess higher information processing confidence than females.

Next, the effects of gender identity on GIPC were assessed via ANOVA. The results indicated that gender identity had a significant main effect on GIPC ($F_{3,99}=18.70$, p<.0001). The cell means for gender identity are shown in Table 1. Consistent with H2, masculine schematics and androgynous individuals had significantly higher GIPC scores than did feminine schematics and undifferentiated individuals.

To further investigate the effects of gender identity and sex on GIPC, hierarchical regression analysis (Cohen and Cohen 1983) was performed with sex as a dummy variable (F=1, M=0), and the summed scores for masculine and feminine characteristics included separately in the model as continuous variables. For the baseline model including only the sex dummy variable, the R^2=.049. When masculine and feminine traits were added to the model, the R^2 jumped dramatically to .47, a highly significant difference (Partial F test: $F_{2,110}=47.58$, p<.0001). The two gender trait independent variables were statistically significant and positive (masculine traits: ß=.62, t=8.71, p≤.0001; feminine traits: ß=.15, t=2.00, p≤.041). The coefficient of the sex dummy variable was also statistically significant (ß=-.17, t=2.29, p≤.02), indicating that males reported higher GIPC than females. The results of these analyses indicate that gender identity explains variance in GIPC above and beyond that explained by biological sex. And, as was found by Chusmir et al. (1992) with respect to self-confidence, identification with both masculine and feminine traits seems to increase GIPC, with androgynous individuals reporting the highest levels. Thus, H2 is supported, even with the effects of biological sex partialed out.

The second set of hypotheses predicts effects of gender identity and sex on confidence variables more commonly reported in advertising response research: (1) belief confidence, (2) attitude confidence, (3) $A_{Ad\text{-}claim}$ confidence, and (4) $A_{Ad\text{-}nonclaim}$ confidence. For the two-level sex variable, one-tailed t-tests were

TABLE 2

Means of Confidence Variables Across Levels of Sex

Dependent Variable:	Male	Female	Significance Level
Belief Confidence	5.23	5.03	p<.19
Attitude Confidence	5.83	5.67	p<.24
$A_{Ad-claim}$ Confidence	4.89	4.92	p<.45
$A_{Ad-nonclaim}$ Confidence	6.00	5.64	p<.04*

* Significant at p<.05.

TABLE 3

Regression Results for Gender Identity

Dependent Variable:	ß value and Significance Level (p-value)		F value	R^2 Value
	Masculine	*Feminine*		
Belief Confidence	-.02 (p<.85)	.03 (p<.78)	.05 (p<.95)	.001
Attitude Confidence	.19 (p<.02)**	.15 (p<.12)*	3.36 (p<.04)**	.06
$A_{Ad-claim}$ Confidence	.15 (p<.06)*	.11 (p<.27)	1.90 (p<.15)	.04
$A_{Ad-nonclaim}$ Confidence	.21 (p<.02)**	.09 (p<.35)	3.04 (p<.05)**	.06

* Significant at p<.10.
** Significant at p<.05.

performed on the mean differences in these dependent variables. The results are shown in Table 2.

As can be seen in Table 2, although the mean differences are in the hypothesized direction, only the mean differences for $A_{Ad-nonclaim}$ confidence were statistically significant. Thus, H3d was supported, H3a-c were not. Apparently, males have significantly greater confidence than females only with respect to $A_{Ad-nonclaim}$ confidence.

H4a-d were tested via regression analysis, with gender identity included in the model as the summed scores of masculine and feminine characteristics. The standardized regression coefficients and R^2 values are shown in Table 3 below. As the results in Table 3 show, identification with more masculine traits led to higher levels of confidence except for belief confidence.

It is clear from the hypothesis tests that gender identity and biological sex do directly influence GIPC and the other confidence measures. To explore the possibility of a mediating relationship, a regression analysis was performed with the belief confidence, A_B confidence, and A_{Ad} confidence measures regressed on GIPC. None of these relationships were significant, thus precluding a mediating relationship.

DISCUSSION

Importantly, this study presents initial evidence that both biological sex and gender identity are significant antecedents of GIPC. In addition, while biological sex was a significant anteced-

ent of $A_{Ad-nonclaim}$ confidence, gender identity proved to be an antecedent of attitude confidence, $A_{Ad-claim}$ confidence, and $A_{Ad-nonclaim}$ confidence. These results are consistent with previous research that has reported significant differences between males and females in information processing (e.g., Meyers-Levy and Maheswaran 1991), self-confidence (e.g., Maccoby and Jacklin 1974), and self-confidence related to gender identity (Chusmir et al. 1992). This illustrates the relative explanatory power of gender identity as compared to biological sex when studying confidence in an advertising context, a finding contrary to most consumer research that reports biological sex as having more explanatory power than gender identity. These findings suggest that whenever confidence measures are being studied, the effects of both gender identity and biological sex should be considered. At a minimum, these effects should be dealt with as covariates when they are not a central focus of the study.

For advertising practice, these results may indicate that for ads directed toward females, a single ad exposure may not be as successful at creating confidently-held attitudes as it would be for males. To explore this possibility further, future research should examine how additional ad exposures affect males' and females' confidence levels.

Limitations and Suggestions for Future Research

As with any research, several limitations, many of which could be addressed through future research, may have affected the results.

First, the limited sample size may have hampered our ability to find significant results with respect to gender identity; larger sample sizes should be obtained in future studies. Second, our sample was relatively homogeneous in their self-assessments of ad message involvement. Future research may wish to manipulate this concept to determine if sex and gender identity differences noted occur for both more and less involved subjects. Third, because this was a student sample, there should always be caution in generalizing the results to the general population. Fourth, the ad upon which the confidence measures were based included very little copy; future studies should replicate this study using ads with differing levels of central route information to determine the robustness of the results obtained here. Examining the confidence variable more in-depth would also be valuable; for example, it may be that feminine schematics possess greater confidence in their beliefs and attitudes when recalling ads with strong emotional overtones, whereas masculine schematics have greater confidence regarding claims that can be counterargued. Finally, it might also be interesting to replicate the study using gendered ads to determine if an interaction effect would occur between the gendered ads, biological sex, and gender identity.

REFERENCES

Alreck, Pamela L., Robert B. Settle, and Michael A. Belch (1982), "Who Responds to "Gendered" Ads, and How?" *Journal of Advertising Research*, (April/May), 25-32.

Andrews, J. Craig and Terence A. Shimp (1990), "Effects of Involvement, Argument Strength, and Source Characteristics on Central and Peripheral Processing of Advertising," *Psychology and Marketing*, 7(3), 195-214.

Andrews, P. H. (1987), "Gender Differences in Persuasive Communication and Attribution of Success and Failure," *Human Communication Research*, 13, 372-385.

Bem, Sandra L. (1974), "The Measurement of Psychological Androgyny," *Journal of Consulting and Clinical Psychology*, 42 (2), 155-162.

Bem, Sandra L. (1975), "Sex Role Adaptability: One Consequence of Psychological Androgyny," *Journal of Personality and Social Psychology*, 31 (4), 634-643.

Bennett, Peter D., and Gilbert D. Harrell (1975), "The Role of Confidence in Understanding and Predicting Buyers' Attitudes and Purchase Intentions," *Journal of Consumer Research*, 2 (September), 110-117.

Calder, Bobby J., Lynn W. Phillips, and Alice M. Tybout (1982), "The Concept of External Validity," *Journal of Consumer Research*, 9 (December), 240-244.

Chusmir, Leonard H., Christine S. Koberg, and Mary D. Stecher (1992), "Self-Confidence of Managers in Work and Social Situations: A Look at Gender Differences," *Sex Roles*, 26 (11/12), 497-512.

Cohen, Jacob and Patricia Cohen (1983), *Applied Multiple Regression/Correlation Analysis for the Behavioral Sciences*, Hillsdale, NJ: Lawrence Earlbaum Associates.

Coughlin, Maureen, and P. J. O'Connor (1985), "Gender Role Portrayals in Advertising: An Individual Differences Analysis," in *Advances in Consumer Research*, Vol. 12, eds. Elizabeth C. Hirschman and Morris B. Holbrook, Provo, UT: Association for Consumer Research, 238-241.

Darley, William K., and Robert E. Smith (1995), "Gender Differences in Information Processing Strategies: An Empirical Test of the Selectivity Model in Advertising Response," *Journal of Advertising*, 24 (1), 41-56.

Dover, Philip A., and Jerry C. Olson (1977), "Dynamic Changes in an Expectancy-Value Attitude Model as a Function of Multiple Exposures to Product Information," in *Contemporary Marketing Thought*, eds. Barnett A. Greenberg and Danny N. Bellenger, Chicago,IL: American Marketing Association, 455-459.

Fazio, Russell H., and Mark P. Zanna (1978), "On the Predictive Validity of Attitudes: The Roles of Direct Experience and Confidence," *Journal of Personality*, 46 (June), 228-243.

Fazio, Russell H., and Mark P. Zanna (1981), "Direct Experience and Attitude-Behavior Consistency," *Journal of Personality*, 46 (June), 228-243.

Fischer, Eileen, and Stephen J. Arnold (1994), "Sex, Gender Identity, Gender Role Attitudes, and Consumer Behavior," *Psychology & Marketing*, 11 (2), 163-182.

Fishbein, Martin, and Icek Ajzen (1975), *Belief, Attitude, Intention and Behavior: An Introduction to Theory and Research*, Reading, MA: Addison-Wesley.

Gentry, James W., and Mildred Doering (1977), "Masculinity-Femininity Related to Consumer Choice," in *Contemporary Marketing Thought*, eds. Barnett A. Greenberg and Danny N. Bellenger, Chicago:IL American Marketing Association, 423-427.

Gentry, James W., and Debra A. Haley (1984), "Gender Schema Theory as a Predictor of Ad Recall," in *Advances in Consumer Research*, Vol. 11, ed. Thomas C. Kinnear, Provo, UT: Association for Consumer Research, 259-264.

Jaffe, Lynn J. (1991), "Impact of Positioning and Sex-Role Identity on Women's Responses to Advertising," *Journal of Advertising Research*, (June/July), 57-64.

Jaffe, Lynn J., and Paul D. Berger (1988), "Impact on Purchase Intent of Sex-Role Identity and Product Positioning," *Psychology & Marketing*, 5 (3), 259-271.

Kahneman, Daniel, and Amos Tversky (1973), "On the Psychology of Prediction," *Psychological Review*, 80 (4), 237-251.

Koriat, A., S. Lichtenstein, and B. Fischoff (1980), "Reasons for Confidence," *Journal of Experimental Social Psychology: Human Learning and Memory*, 6, 107-118.

Laczniak, Russell N. and Darrel D. Muehling (1993), "Toward a Better Understanding of the Role of Advertising Message Involvement in Ad Processing," *Psychology and Marketing*, 10 (4), 301-319.

Lenney, E. (1977), "Women's Self-Confidence in Achievement Settings," *Psychological Bulletin*, 84, 1-13.

Maccoby, E. E., and C. N. Jacklin (1974), *The Psychology of Sex Differences*, Stanford, CA: Stanford University Press.

Markus, Hazel, Marie Crane, Stan Bernstein, and Michael Siladi (1982), "Self-Schemas and Gender," *Journal of Personality and Social Psychology*, 42 (1), 38-50.

Meyers-Levy, Joan (1989), "Gender Differences in Information Processing: A Selectivity Interpretation," in *Cognitive and Affective Responses to Advertising*, eds. P. Cafferata and Alice Tybout, MA: Lexington Books, 219-260.

Meyers-Levy, Joan, and Durairaj Maheswaran (1991), "Exploring Differences in Males' and Females' Processing Strategies," *Journal of Consumer Research*, 18 (June) 63-70.

Miniard, Paul W., Sunil Bhatla and Randall L. Rose (1990), "On the Formation and Relationship of Ad and Brand Attitudes: An Experimental and Causal Analysis," *Journal of Marketing Research*, 27 (August), 290-303.

Palan, Kay M., Charles S. Areni, and Pamela L. Kiecker (1994), "A Comparison of Gender Identity Scales in a Gift Exchange Context," working paper, Iowa State University.

Peterson, D. K., and G. F. Pitz (1988), "Confidence, Uncertainty, and the Use of Information," *Journal of Experimental Social Psychology: Human Learning and Memory*, 14, 85-92.

Smith, Robert E. (1993), "Integrating Information from Advertising and Trial: Processes and Effects on Consumer Response to Product Information," *Journal of Marketing Research*, 30 (May), 204-19.

Smith, Robert E., and William R. Swinyard (1983), "Attitude-Behavior Consistency: The Impact of Product Trial Versus Advertising," *Journal of Marketing Research*, 20 (August), 257-267.

Smith, Robert E., and William R. Swinyard (1988), "Cognitive Response to Advertising and Trial: Belief Strength, Belief Confidence, and Product Curiosity," *Journal of Advertising*, 17 (3), 3-14.

Spence, Janet T., Robert L. Helmreich, and Joy Stapp (1975), "Ratings of Self and Peers on Sex Role Attributes and Their Relation to Self-Esteem and Conceptions of Masculinity and Femininity," *Journal of Personality and Social Psychology*, 32 (1), 29-39.

Stern, Barbara B. (1988), "Sex-Role Self-Concept Measures and Marketing: A Research Note," *Psychology & Marketing*, 5 (1), 85-99.

White, M. C., G. DeSanctis, and M. D. Crino (1981), "Achievement, Self-Confidence, Personality Traits, and Leadership Ability: A Review of Literature on Sex Differences," *Psychological Reports*, 48, 547-569.

Wright, Peter (1975), "Factors Affecting Cognitive Resistance to Advertising," *Journal of Consumer Research*, 2, (June), 1-9.

Zuckerman, D. M. (1985), "Confidence and Aspirations: Self-Esteem and Self-Concepts as Predictors of Students' Life Goals," *Journal of Personality*, 53, 435-560.

Understanding and Influencing Consumer Complaint Behavior: Improving Organizational Complaint Management

Moshe Davidow, Texas A&M University
Peter A. Dacin, Texas A&M University

ABSTRACT

This article discusses an often overlooked issue in complaint behavior, the interactive exchange between the organization and the consumer. This exchange is at the root of all consumer complaint behavior and determines the ultimate satisfaction or dissatisfaction of the consumer. We review the complaint behavior literature and focus on potential reasons consumers choose not to complain. We then present an updated typology for consumer complaint behavior outcomes and their implications for the organization. Finally, we examine some organizational strategies necessary to encourage non-voicers to complain to the organization allowing effective and efficient complaint management.

INTRODUCTION

A well documented finding in the consumer complaint literature is that a majority of dissatisfied consumers do not voice their complaint to an organization (Best and Andreasen 1977, TARP 1986, Tschol 1994). When consumers do not voice their complaint, an organization loses the opportunity to recognize and redress the problem leaving both the consumer and organization dissatisfied. Consequently, while seemingly paradoxical, it would seem in the best interest of organizations to encourage consumers to complain, and then to react appropriately to the complaint behavior.

With the exception of Fornell and Wernerfelt (1987, 1988), very few researchers argue that it is important to encourage consumers to complain or even investigate appropriate organizational responses to various complaint behavior. In fact, the literature tends to focus on either describing and developing general models of consumer complaint behavior (e.g., Day 1984, Gilly 1987, Singh and Wilkes 1991) or modeling organizational complaint responses (TARP 1986) with few, if any, attempts to integrate these two streams of research.

While Fornell and Wernerfelt make important contributions to understanding some of the appropriate organizational reactions to consumer complaint behavior, their work also opens up avenues for important research. The purpose of this manuscript is to initiate a stream of inquiry that addresses some of these issues. Specifically, we review the complaint literature to identify reasons for why consumers may choose not to voice their complaint, build on an existing framework to illustrate what consumers do when not voicing their complaint, discuss some of the consequences of these behaviors, and present several strategies that an organization can use to shape consumer complaint behavior to their benefit.

The proposed stream of inquiry has important implications for several areas of marketing. First, it contributes to a theoretical understanding of consumer complaint behavior and organizational responses and the integration of these two streams of research. As a number of researchers suggest, it is impossible to detach consumers' responses to dissatisfaction from organizations' responses to complaints (e.g., Garrett, Meyers and Camey 1991, Gilly 1987), yet these two streams remain relatively disparate.

Second, this manuscript extends marketers thinking with respect to consumer complaint behavior. By investigating why consumers do not voice their complaint to an organization (even though they acknowledge having a complaint or basis for dissatisfaction) and demonstrating the consequences of this for the organi-

zation, we believe that we are reinforcing and extending Fornell and Wernerfelt's (1987, 1988) belief of the importance of encouraging consumers to voice their complaints to an organization.

UNDERSTANDING WHY CONSUMERS DO NOT VOICE A COMPLAINT

Existing studies on the topic investigate several variables important for understanding why consumers complain (for reviews, see Andreasen 1989, Robinson 1978, Singh and Howell 1985). These variables include perceived costs (Richins 1980); attributions (Folkes 1984); prior knowledge (Day 1984); probability of complaint success (Day 1984, Richins 1983); significance of the consumption event (Day 1984); attitudes towards complaining (Richins 1982); assertiveness (Richins 1983); product importance (Richins 1985); and demographic and environmental influences (Singh and Wilkes 1991). However, while these researchers attempt to understand why consumers complain, few if any researchers have investigated why some consumers are more inclined not to voice their complaint to an organization.

Perhaps the best known model of the consumer's decision to voice or not voice their complaint to an organization was developed by Day (1984). In this model, the consumer first considers the costs and benefits of complaining, performs an analysis, and then decides whether or not to complain. In addition to the cost/benefit and situational variables, Day also included personality variables as moderators. For example, he proposes that a consumer's attitude towards complaining can moderate the relationship between the results of the cost/benefit analysis and the actual decision of whether to complain.

A second author, Andreasen (1988), suggests three reasons for why dissatisfied consumers do not complain: 1) a cost/benefit analysis shows small benefits or large costs, 2) consumers were discouraged from complaining by others, and 3) an intervening factor caused a delay or the prevention of action (e.g. leaving town, family crisis). Andreasen, however, does not cite personality variables as a reason for not complaining.

Finally, reported analyses of survey responses to questions about complaint behaviors also reveal two main reasons why consumers do not voice their complaint to the organization. First, consumers felt it was not worth the time and effort, and second, consumers didn't think they could get anyone to do anything about it (Day and Ash 1979, TARP 1986). In these studies, there was also no mention of personality variables.

Are personality variables important in the process? We believe they are. As part of a preliminary research project into complaint behavior, we surveyed 154 marketing students in a large University. In the survey we asked respondents to think about a recent situation in which they were very dissatisfied and either complained or did not complain to the organization. Each respondent randomly received only one scenario and completed a questionnaire consisting of open ended questions asking about the major reason why they did or did not complain. We received 267 responses, covering a wide spectrum of reasons. Following Churchill (1979), we then categorized the responses based on the type of reason that respondents gave for their complaint behavior. Unlike content analysis, where the coding categories are predetermined

Advances in Consumer Research
Volume 24, © 1997

(Kassarjian 1977), our purpose was to determine potential categories.

The results of the study suggest four major categories of reasons for complaint behaviors. Of the 267 reasons, personality related variables comprised 48.3 % of the total responses (129). Items included: standing up for their rights, personality, to feel important, to get something for free, higher expectations, nothing better to do-lazy, intimidation and fear of confrontation. The second largest category of reasons consisted of the traditional cost/benefit variables, incorporating 23.2 % of the total responses (62). Items included cost/importance, degree of dissatisfaction, effort and past experience. Next, a situational variables category contained 16.5 % of the total responses (44). Items included social pressure, situation conducive, mood and time. The first two items are external constraints, while the last two items are internal constraints. Finally, a social benefit category contained 12.0 % of the total responses (32). This variable was found to be different from the cost/benefit variable. Cost/benefit variables are internally focused; what do I get out of it, while the social benefit variables are externally focused; can I make a difference that will affect the way this organization does business? Can I change something that benefits everyone?

While we do not claim any scientific basis for our findings, it is interesting to note how many respondents felt that their complaint behavior was motivated by a complaint-related personality variable. Although some researchers suggest that general personality variables may not be a basis for complaint behavior (see for example Zaichkowsky and Liefield 1977) there appear to be consumers who do exhibit complaint-related personality variables in the form of a propensity to complain. Consequently, cost/benefit considerations may not be the only drivers in a consumer's decision of whether to complain. However, cost/benefit considerations may still moderate these consumers' higher propensity to complain.

In summary, while the literature primarily focuses on the role of cost/benefit analyses as driving factors of consumers' decisions to complain, with moderating roles for personality and situational variables, we believe that researchers would gain from positing a more important role for complaint-related personality variables such as propensity to complain. Our literature review and study also indicate that managers must also consider the role of situational and social benefit variables. As we discuss later, these variables become an integral part of our suggestions for how managers can encourage consumers to complain. Prior to our discussion of these suggestions, however, we continue our literature review by discussing the alternative behaviors to the voicing of complaints to an organization.

Non Voice Complaint Behavior

In this manuscript, we suggest that it is important to encourage consumers to voice their complaints to an organization. To understand the basis of this suggestion, it is necessary to understand the alternative behaviors to voicing a complaint to the organization and the consequences to the organization of these alternative behaviors. The most commonly accepted taxonomy of consumer complaint behavior is that of Singh (1988). His taxonomy consists of three categories for classifying consumer complaint behavior—*Voice*, *Private* and *Third-party* responses.

The basis for this taxonomy appears to be the recipient of a consumer's complaint response. The three different responses (Voice, Private, Third-Party) are represented by Singh (1988) on two dimensions: (1) *Social Network*–whether consumers direct their complaints to individuals or organizations that are internal or external to their social circle (i.e., informal relationships), and (2)

Involvement–whether the recipients of the complaints are directly involved in the dissatisfying exchange (e.g., retailer, manufacturer).

Based on the two dimensions, *Voice* represents complaints directed at individuals or organizations external to the consumer's social circle and directly involved in the dissatisfying exchange. *Private* represents complaints directed at individuals or organizations that are internal to the consumer's social circle and not directly involved in the dissatisfying exchange (e.g., self, friends, relatives). *Third-party* represents complaints directed at individuals or organizations that are external to the consumer's social circle and not directly involved in the dissatisfying exchange (Better Business Bureau, legal agencies).

Oddly, in this taxonomy, consumers who do not voice their complaint are classified in the *Voice* category on the basis that "no action" reflects feelings toward the seller who is directly involved in the dissatisfying exchange yet not in the consumer's social circle (Singh 1988). This would be comparable to Hirschman's (1970) "loyalty" construct. In addition, according to Singh (1988), there are no entries in the internal-involved cell.

While, at one level, we believe that the dimensions Singh uses to form his taxonomy are academically useful, we feel that his classification of specific responses may lead to several managerial problems when researchers attempt to assess the potential consequences for an organization of the various complaint behaviors. This is especially true for the private category, where Singh (1988) lumps together both the consumer, and the social network of the consumer. It seems apparent that different types of private responses will have different impacts on the organization. For example, if the consumer limits the response to themselves, deciding to boycott the product or service, then the potential impact on the organization is a loss of one consumer. Alternatively, should the consumer involve others in the response (e.g., word of mouth) then the potential impact on the organization is a loss of several consumers.

As a result of these concerns, we believe that it is necessary to modify Singh's taxonomy to accommodate the differences between private responses in which the consumer decides to act alone and those in which the consumer decides to involve others. We believe that a simple way to accommodate these distinctions is to remove the consumer ("self") from the internal-not involved category (private action, according to Singh), and place it in the internal-involved category (the "empty cell" according to Singh) where it appears most appropriate—the consumer (self) is directly involved in the experience of dissatisfaction. The internal-not involved cell now contains only the consumer's informal social net which is impacted by the consumer's word of mouth. The internal-involved cell, rather than containing no entry, now contains the consumer's own actions, including the relative inaction inherent in consumer loyalty, that is, a consumer deciding to give a reprieve to an organization based on its previous track record. Please note, however, that loyalty does not mean total dismissal of the consumer's dissatisfaction. Instead, it should be looked upon as a form of probation. If the organization lapses again, the consumer may seek retribution for both instances, if possible. The revised taxonomy appears in Table 1.

From a managerial perspective, our minor revisions have important implications. They highlight the complaint behavior possibilities that a consumer faces, from the perspective of the organization, thus allowing managers the option of potentially controlling those behaviors. This option was not viable before our revisions since managers could not differentiate between private action by a consumer and private action by the social network.

TABLE 1
Complaint Behavior Outcomes

Involvement With the Dissatisfaction

		Involved	Not Involved
Involvement of	Internal	Exit or Boycott	Consumer's Social Net (Word of Mouth)
Social Network	External	Organization (Redress or Complaint)	Third Party

TABLE 2
Complaint Behavior and Organization Costs

Behavior Type	*Potential Market Cost*	*Potential Information Gain*
Exit or Boycott	loss of a consumer	a drop in sales statistics
Word of Mouth	loss of several consumers	a drop in sales statistics
Voice Complaint to the Organization	cost of remedy to retain the consumer	know what caused the problem, and how to fix it
Complain to Third Party	cost of handling, loss of consumer	know what caused the problem

In light of this revised taxonomy, we can now investigate the consequences to the organization of the various behaviors of a dissatisfied consumer. Based on our revised taxonomy, Table 2 summarizes the various consequences an organization may expect from each of the types of complaint behaviors.

In Table 2, it appears that the worst possible consumer complaint behaviors for the organization are those that do not involve external sources. Failure to complain to external sources prevents the consumer from obtaining redress, thus increasing the likelihood for continued or increased dissatisfaction. More importantly, the organization risks losing these dissatisfied consumers without understanding the reason for the dissatisfaction, or having the opportunity to correct the problem (Strahle et al. 1992, TARP 1986).

Consumer exit or boycott causes the organization the loss of revenue from a consumer, without providing the organization with an opportunity to redeem itself. In addition, exit does not supply the organization with any marketing information on which to plan for the future. Although it materializes as a decline in the sales statistics, there is no guarantee that the organization will detect or even perceive it correctly. In the worst case scenario, the drop in sales may be offset by a rise elsewhere, and the organization does not perceive the problem.

While consumer exit is bad for the organization, the effects of negative word of mouth are potentially much worse since it can influence many more people (TARP 1986). As with exit, the organization may not realize that it has a problem, and may not understand the reason for a drop in their sales statistics. Again, the organization obtains no long term market information.

On the other hand, complaint behaviors that involve external sources have more positive consequences for the organization. For example, in a third party complaint, the nature of the dissatisfaction eventually comes to the attention of the organization. As a result, the organization realizes that a problem exists, the nature of the problem, and then has the opportunity to correct it. This brings with it the potential for eliminating future dissatisfaction from this source. Unfortunately, however, many third party complaints follow unsuccessful consumer attempts to contact or obtain a remedy from the organization. Consequently, while gaining valuable information, the organization may still lose the consumer as well as incur the added expense of handling a third party complaint.

Given the consequences of these complaint behaviors, we support the contention of the few others (Fornell and Wernerfelt 1987, TARP 1986) who suggest that the best approach for an organization is to encourage complaints to the organization. In addition to the consumer's benefit, the organization also gains from a voiced complaint. At the very least, when a consumer uses an external source to complain about a product or service, the organization becomes aware of the dissatisfaction. Consequently, this is an opportunity for the organization to both solve the consumer's problem and receive valuable information about problems that might impact future consumer satisfaction. By voicing a complaint, the consumer is signaling the need for the organization to address a dissatisfaction. Research has also shown that consumers who complain are more organization loyal than consumers who never voice a complaint to the organization, regardless of whether the complaint was handled satisfactorily (TARP 1986).

However, we believe that just encouraging complaints is not enough—the organization must handle the complaints in an appropriate manner. A key construct in most complaint management situations is the communication between the consumer and the organization (Garrett, Meyers and Camey 1991). The perceived potential for resolution also influences complaint behavior. Consequently, it is important that the organization understand why consumers choose specific complaint behaviors, particularly those that do not involve the direct voicing of a complaint to the organization. A research agenda based on our revision of the Singh typology, would provide the organization with this information. Based on this information, the organization can then begin to carefully manage consumer complaint behavior and their own complaint responses, resulting in higher consumer satisfaction. In the next section, we use the conclusions of our literature review to demonstrate how understanding the nature of the various types of complaint behaviors can be used by managers to encourage more consumers to voice their complaints directly to the organization.

ORGANIZATIONAL RESPONSES

Typical complaint management programs focus on the minority of dissatisfied consumers who complain directly to the organization. While these programs have some benefit, they are missing a substantial audience—dissatisfied consumers who do not voice their complaint. Almost one-third of American households experience product dissatisfaction every year (TARP 1986), with 1 out of every four purchases resulting in some type of problem (Best and Andreasen 1977), yet between 60% (Andreasen 1988) and 70% (TARP 1986) of all dissatisfied consumers take no action. An A. C. Nelson study found that in general only 2% of dissatisfied consumers actually voice their complaint to the organization (this number was 10% in the service sector, see Tschol 1994). For any organization serious about handling complaint recovery, the immediate implication is that they are missing at least two-thirds of their target market. This may explain why the expected increase in consumer complaints due to the increased usage of toll free lines for consumer service departments never materialized. These lines simply targeted complainers, those who would have complained anyway, thus missing most of their dissatisfied consumers.

Suggestions for addressing this problem may lie in defensive marketing (Fornell and Wernerfelt 1987). The implementation of defensive marketing to complaint management entails three main facets. First, an organization identifies dissatisfied consumers, then it tries to understand the complaint behavior from an organizational perspective, and finally it handles their complaint in such a way as to persuade the consumers to remain loyal.

In order to employ defensive marketing, organizations must first be able to reach consumers who do not directly voice their complaint to the organization and convince them to complain. In light of our previous discussions, the organization must in many cases overcome a consumer's negative propensity to complain. Consequently, for an organization's complaint management pro-

gram to be successful with non-voicers, it must focus on the four categories of reasons for not complaining discussed previously: complaint-related personality variables, cost/benefit variables, situational variables, and social benefit variables. However, it is not enough just to understand how these variables influence complaint behavior. Organizations must also develop strategies for influencing these variables and complaint behavior. Following, we discuss some of these strategies.

Complaint-related Personality Variables: Some of the negative attitudes that prevent people from complaining are personality related (i.e., propensity to complain, low expectations, fear of confrontation, and intimidation, etc.). These can be addressed through increasing consumer knowledge by way of consumer education programs (TARP 1983). One way in which the organization can educate the consumer is by raising consumer expectations levels, letting them know that the inferior service that they have experienced will not be tolerated at this organization. Hart (1988) talked of the power of unconditional guarantees, and the conditions that must be met before implementing them. An excellent example of this is Texize who successfully gained market share by guaranteeing to replace any garment from which they could not remove a stain (Kendall and Russ 1975).

Another way an organization can educate the consumer is by focusing on the complaint process, in order to remove the fear of confrontation (Coyle 1994), and the intimidation factor. One way to accomplish this is by focusing on the user friendliness of the process. Burger King's ad campaign of "a suggestion box in every home" is a good example of this technique. Sometimes, it may just be a case of letting consumers know how to get in touch with the organization (Strahle et al. 1992). Through these actions, the organization has the chance to dramatically impact the consumer tendency to complain directly to the organization, instead of elsewhere, especially if the consumer is aware that the complaint will be handled (Richins 1983). Programs designed to show the consumer that the organization will work with them to solve problems should appeal to those consumers who are interested in feeling important and/or in standing up for their rights.

Cost/Benefit Variables: TARP (1986) found that over 55% of the non-voicers thought it was not worth the time or effort to complain. Given this, we believe that organizations can undertake several strategies to lower the cost or increase the benefit of complaining, without "giving away the store."

First, it is important to increase consumer awareness of the complaint handling process. When consumers are ignorant of complaint management departments, policies, or when they are unable to contact the organization, they often perceive a higher cost for complaining. For example, the Coca Cola organization found that a generic booklet distributed to consumers about how to effectively get in touch with organizations increased consumer confidence, positive word of mouth, and the purchase intentions of the consumers toward Coca Cola (TARP 1983). Programs such as these signal a significant commitment by the organization to the consumer and consequently, lower the cost or increase the benefits consumers typically associate with complaining.

Second, organizations can also influence consumers' causal attributions to their advantage. Too often, consumers do not complain because they feel the problem is their fault. Yet, organizations may successfully encourage complaints by adopting strategies that shift the blame away from consumers. For example, Pearl Vision was very successful in letting consumers know that their eyeglasses would be replaced free, if they broke, even if the problem was the consumer's fault (Goodman and Stampfl 1983). The organization was explicitly saying that they would handle any problem. The end result was instrumental in differentiating Pearl Vision from its competitors, as well as lowering the perceived cost of complaining to the consumer.

Finally, managing each "moment of truth" (Carlzon 1987) by making the personal interaction as pleasant as possible is another important way of reducing perceptions of cost. Making the complaint process as easy and as visible as possible, focuses the consumer on the external outlet of complaining, making it more situation conducive to complain.

Social Benefit Variables: An organization may be able to impact consumer complaint intentions by letting the consumer know that it will attempt to act on all complaints (Fornell and Wernerfelt 1987). While it is important to solicit complaints and suggestions, the process should not stop there. Once those comments and complaints have been received, and handled on a single consumer basis, the information should then be compiled for an organization wide analysis. This should allow the organization to spot consumer trends early enough in the cycle to adapt to them quickly (Davidow 1995). It also gives the organization the ability to spot defective machinery, problems on the product line, and problems downstream with the distributors. Following this, organizations need to showcase changes in procedures or products as a result of consumer communications by advertising the changes made in the products due to consumer feedback, thus convincing people that they can make a difference (Lewis 1983).

Situational Variables: Organizations can influence the social pressure brought to bear on consumers by demonstrating organizational social responsibility. The earlier Pearl Vision example and the response of Johnson and Johnson to the Tylenol tampering incident both emphasize the importance of organizational backing of a product. If an organization has a positively perceived image, there should be more of a tendency to encourage complaints. Handling complaints well can add to that image. Malafi (1991) found that social influence, whether through obtaining information from others on how to deal with a situation or by socio-emotional support, has a major influence on complaint behavior. In another study (Malafi et al., 1993), she found that those advised to complain typically do, while those advised not to complain typically do not. An organization must therefore maintain a positive image to influence this social pressure.

In order to follow through on this strategy, an organization must communicate effectively to consumers, and hire complaint handling personnel who are competent communicators and who can interact effectively with complaining consumers (Garrett, Meyers and Camey 1991). Because marketing's success is built on communication with the consumer, if something goes wrong, an organization should be interested in finding out where and how the communication failed to produce a satisfied consumer.

Currently, many organizations are following some of these suggestions. For example, most organizations today have toll free lines to facilitate consumer's communication. Yet, as mentioned previously, this has failed to increase consumer complaints and, in turn satisfaction levels. Until now, organizations have looked at some of these strategies as a grab bag of tools, using them haphazardly. We believe that this is a major misuse of resources. By trying to be everything to everyone, an organization may not be anything to anybody. The key is in understanding why your consumers are not complaining, and then choosing the proper approach in response.

Accessing general consumer surveys done among the public, and integrating this information with information collected by the organization, can let organizations know how many dissatisfied consumers they may potentially have, what percentage of these consumers actually complained, and why the non complainers did not complain. This is critical information for organizations, allowing them to pinpoint crucial areas for improvement, and estimate the market impact of these problems.

The approach we are suggesting is a proactive one which involves looking for problems, and constantly striving to improve. It is the difference between asking a restaurant patron if the meal was satisfactory (the almost automatic response is yes), and asking what can we do to better serve you. Periodic consumer surveys, and proper defections management (Davidow 1995) should allow an organization to uncover a myriad of problems or opportunities within the organization/consumer relationship that would not ordinarily emerge. In turn, these actions should allow the organization to address problems while they are still brewing, thus increasing consumers' satisfaction levels, and preventing future complaints.

SUMMARY AND FUTURE DIRECTIONS

This manuscript attempted to demonstrate the benefits of examining complaint behavior from a variety of perspectives. By initially focusing on the reasons consumers don't complain, we make a case for investigating certain variables in depth. Based on this, we were able to suggest how complaint managers could have a direct and proactive effect on complaint behavior.

This paper makes several contributions to the current complaint literature. First, by synthesizing the consumer and organizational views of complaint behavior, we believe that it presents a more meaningful complaint behavior taxonomy. Second, by focusing on the reasons why consumers don't voice their complaints to the organization, this paper proposes a set of interacting variables to improve the predictability of consumer complaint behavior. Finally, from a managerial perspective this paper posits suggestions to increase the likelihood that consumers directly voice their complaint to the organization.

We believe that an important direction for future research is to continue the focus on the complaint-related personality variables in consumer complaint behavior. For example, we need answers to questions such as: how does a consumer's attitude influence their propensity to complain; what are the interactions among the various variables, for instance does the desire to feel important influence the drive to get something for free; and how much influence does a consumer's social net have in the context of a disappointing experience? Accordingly, it is also important to identify the key variables driving these variables, and understand the ways in which they too can be influenced.

Finally, another fruitful area of investigation should concentrate on the effectiveness of organizational responses on the variables driving consumer complaint behavior. Is the same organizational response equally effective on all the drivers, or are certain responses more effective on some drivers than others. We hope that the issues raised in this manuscript prove to be springboards for future research in the field of consumer complaint management.

It is obvious that organizations cannot respond to a complaint until the consumer complains. Still, organizational actions to encourage consumers to complain have not always been effective, because they have not focused on the proper variables influencing complaint behavior and non-voice complaining. Focusing on the relevant variables to encourage complaints should allow the organization to proactively target specific areas for change which helps the organization prepare a more effective and efficient consumer complaint handling program. However, a program can only be effective if it reaches its intended target audience, the quality of the program alone will not determine it's success and ultimate value to the organization.

REFERENCES

Andreasen, Alan R. (1988), "Consumer Complaints and Redress: What We Know and What We Don't Know," in *The Frontier of Research in the Consumer Interest*, in eds. E. Scott Maynes et al., Columbia, MO: American Council on Consumer Interests, 675-722.

Best, Arthur and Alan Andreasen (1977), "Consumer Response to Unsatisfactory Purchases: A Survey of Perceiving Defects, Voicing Complaints and Obtaining Redress," *Law and Society Review*, Vol. 11 (4), 701-42.

Carlzon, Jan (1987), *Moments of Truth*, Cambridge, MA: Ballinger Books

Churchill, Gilbert A., Jr. (1979) "A Paradigm for Developing Better Measures of Marketing Constructs," *Journal of Marketing Research*, Vol. 16, (February), 64-73.

Coyle, Michael B. (1994), "Quality Interpersonal Communication-Resolving Conflicts Successfully," *Manage*, Vol. 45 (January), 4-5.

Davidow, Moshe (1995), "Organizational Response to Consumer Complaints," in E*nhancing Knowledge Development in Marketing: Proceedings of the 1996 AMA Summer Educators' Conference*, eds. Barbara B. Stern and George M. Zinkham, Chicago, IL: AMA.

Day, Ralph L. (1984) "Modeling Choices Among Alternative Responses to Dissatisfaction," in *Advances in Consumer Research*, ed. Thomas Kinnear Vol. 11, Provo, UT: ACR 469-71.

_____ and Stephen B. Ash (1979), "Comparisons of Patterns of Satisfaction/ Dissatisfaction and Complaining Behavior for Durables, NonDurables and Services," in *New Dimensions of Consumer Satisfaction and Complaining Behavior*, eds. R.L. Day and H.K. Hunt, Bloomington, IN: Division of Business Research, 190-95.

Folkes, Valerie S. (1984), "Consumer Reactions to Product Failure: An Attributional Approach," *Journal of Consumer Research*, Vol. 10 (March), 398-409.

_____ and Birger Wernerfelt (1987), "Defensive Marketing Strategy by Customer Complaint Management: A Theoretical Analysis," *Journal of Marketing Research*, Vol. 24, (November), 337-46.

_____ and _____ (1988), "A Model For Customer Complaint Management," *Marketing Science*, Vol. 7 No. 3, (Summer), 287-98.

Garrett, Dennis E., Renee A. Meyers and John Camey (1991), "Interactive Complaint Communication: A Theoretical Framework and Research Agenda," *Journal of Consumer Satisfaction, Dissatisfaction and Complaining Behavior*, Vol. 4, 62-79.

Gilly, Mary C. (1987), "Postcomplaint Processes: From Organizational Response to Repurchase Behavior," *Journal of Consumer Affairs*, Vol.21, No.2, 293-313.

Goodman, John A. and Ronald W. Stampfl (1983), "The Consumer Affairs Department in Business: Expanding Its Functions and Identifying It's Bottom Line Contributions," Wisconsin Working Paper, 10-83-19, School of Business, University of Wisconsin-Madison.

Hart, Christopher W.L. (1988), "The Power of Unconditional Service Guarantees," *Harvard Business Review*, 66 (July/August), 54-62.

Hirschman, Albert O. (1970) *Exit, Voice and Loyalty: Responses to Decline in Firms, Organizations and States*, Cambridge, MA: Harvard University Press.

Kassarjian, Harold H. (1977) "Content Analysis in Consumer Research," *Journal of Consumer Research*, Vol.4, June, 8-18.

Kendall, C.L. and Frederick Russ (1975), Warranty and Complaint Policies: An Opportunity for Marketing Management," Journal of Marketing, Vol. 39 (April), 36-43.

Lewis, Robert C. (1983), "Consumers Complain-What Happens When Business Responds?" in *International Fare in Consumer Satisfaction and Complaining*, eds. Ralph L. Day and H. Keith Hunt, Bloomington, IN: Bureau of Business Research, 88-94.

Malafi, Teresa (1991), "The Impact of Social Influence on Consumer Complaint Behavior," *Journal of Consumer Satisfaction, Dissatisfaction and Complaining Behavior*, Vol. 6, 81-89.

_____, Marie Cini, Sarah Taub and Jennifer Bertomali (1993), "Social Influence and the decision to Complain: Investigations On the Role of Advice," *Journal of Consumer Satisfaction, Dissatisfaction and Complaining Behavior*, Vol. 4, 144-50.

Richins, Marsha L. (1980), "Consumer Perceptions of Costs and Benefits Associated with Complaining," in *Refining Concepts and Measures of Consumer Satisfaction and Complaining Behavior*, eds. H. Keith Hunt and Ralph L. Day, Bloomington, IN: BBR, 50-53.

_____ (1982), An Investigation of Consumer Attitudes Toward Complaining," in *Advances in Consumer Research*, Vol. 9, ed. Andrew Mitchell, Ann Arbor, MI: Association for Consumer Research, 502-6.

_____ (1983), Word of Mouth as an Expression of Product Dissatisfaction" in *International Fare in Consumer Satisfaction and Complaining*, Ralph L. Day and H. Keith Hunt (eds.), Bloomington, IN: Bureau of Business Research, 100-4.

_____ (1985), "Factors Affecting the Level of Consumer Initiated Complaints to Marketing Organizations," in *Consumer Satisfaction, Dissatisfaction and Complaining Behavior*, eds. H. Keith Hunt and Ralph L. Day, Bloomington, IN: BBR, 82-5.

Robinson, Larry M. (1979), "Consumer Complaint Behavior: A Review with Implications for Further Research," in *New Dimensions of Consumer Satisfaction and Complaining Behavior*, eds. Ralph L. Day and H. Keith Hunt, Bloomington, IN: BBR, 41-50.

Singh, Jagdip (1988), "Consumer Complaint Intentions and Behavior: Definitional and Taxonomical Issues," *Journal of Marketing*, Vol.52 (January), 93-107.

_____ and Roy D. Howell (1985), "Consumer Complaining Behavior: A Review and Prospectus," in *Consumer Satisfaction, Dissatisfaction and Complaining Behavior*, eds. H. Keith Hunt and Ralph L. Day, Bloomington, IN: Bureau of Business Research, 41-9.

_____ and Robert E. Wilkes (1991), "A Theoretical Framework for Modeling Consumer's Response to Marketplace Dissatisfaction," *Journal of Consumer Satisfaction, Dissatisfaction and Complaining Behavior*, Vol. 4, 1-12.

Strahle, William M., Sigfredo A. Hernandez, Hector L. Garcia and Robert C. Sorensen (1992), "A Study of Consumer Complaining Behavior: VCR Owners in Puerto Rico," *Journal of Consumer Satisfaction, Dissatisfaction and Complaining Behavior*, Vol. 5, 179-191.

TARP (1983), *The Bottom Line Benefits of Consumer Education*, Atlanta, GA: Coca Cola. Inc.

_____ (1986), *Consumer Complaint Handling in America: An Update Study*, Technical Assistance Research Programs, 706 Seventh Ave., S.E. Washington, D.C.

Tschol, John (1994), "Do Yourself A Favor: Gripe About Bad Service," *The American Salesman*, Vol. 39 (June), 3-5.

Zaichkowsky, Judy and John Liefield (1977), "Personality Profiles of Consumer Complaint Letter Writers," in *Consumer Satisfaction, Dissatisfaction and Complaining Behavior*, ed. Ralph L. Day, Bloomington, IN: Indiana University Marketing Department, 124-129.

The Impact of Perceived Justice on Customer Satisfaction and Intention to Complain in a Service Recovery

Mary Ann Hocutt, Oklahoma State University
Goutam Chakraborty, Oklahoma State University
John C. Mowen, Oklahoma State University

ABSTRACT

This study investigates how service recovery efforts influence the level of dissatisfaction and intention to complain following a service failure. Results from an experiment show that consumers' satisfaction (intention to complain) are influenced by cause of failure and by perceived distributive and interactional justice in the recovery attempt. Interestingly, when the customer causes the service failure, satisfaction (complaint) levels are higher (lower) after service recovery efforts than in situations where no service failure occurs. Thus a prompt, courteous service recovery effort can have a significant impact on how a customer feels toward a service provider even after a service failure.

Firms that provide higher levels of service gain higher levels of profits than those that do not. In the case of service organizations, consumer satisfaction and loyalty may be determined by the quality of a single service encounter (Solomon, Surprenant, Czepiel, and Gutman 1985). One negative service encounter, or service failure, can result in consumers' becoming dissatisfied. While many researchers have looked at consumer complaint behavior that results from dissatisfaction due to service failures, very little research has explored the impact that service recovery efforts may have on the level of dissatisfaction felt by consumers as a result of service failures (Hart, Heskett, and Sasser 1990).

A service encounter consists of the period of time during which the customer interacts with the employees of the service organization (Czepiel, Solomon, and Surprenant 1985). Most of the dimensions of service quality and/or satisfaction with services identified by Parasuraman, Zeithaml, and Berry (1988) relate directly to the human interaction element of service quality. From a consumer's point of view, the interaction with service employees defines the service encounter. Therefore, it is important for service employees to be trained and empowered to relate to customers in ways that ensure effective service (Bitner, Booms, and Tetreault 1990; Bitner, Booms, and Mohr 1994).

A service failure is said to occur when the service experience falls short of our expectations (Bell and Zemke 1987). It has been suggested that a service failure is profoundly different from the failure of a tangible product (Albrecht 1988). A service usually provides a psychological and largely personal outcome, whereas a tangible product failure is usually impersonal in its impact on the customer. The notion that service failures have greater consequences than product failures was supported by a survey conducted by Andreasen and Best (1977). After surveying 2,400 metropolitan households, service industries were found to yield the lowest levels of satisfaction. Less than half of the consumers who experienced dissatisfaction complained; and of those who did complain, one-third resulted in resolutions that were unsatisfactory. An impressive stream of research concerning complaint behavior has attempted to look at the ways consumers respond to service failures. It is apparent that many service organizations have developed reactive service failure strategies that focus on complaint management rather than service recovery issues.

Service recovery consists of all the actions people may take to move a customer from a state of dissatisfaction to a state of satisfaction. Zemke (1993, p. 463) defined planned service recovery as:

> *. . . a thought-out, preplanned process for returning aggrieved customers to a state of satisfaction with the company or institution after a service . . . has failed to live up to expectations or promised performance.*

Few service firms take a proactive approach in service recovery with respect to consumer satisfaction (Albrecht 1988). In addition, many companies are not prepared to recover from service failures because service employees have not been trained in how to handle disgruntled customers during a service encounter (Berry and Parasuraman 1992).

In the case of a service failure and subsequent recovery, a consumer assesses satisfaction with the outcome of resolution efforts and then reevaluates the overall consumption experience in light of the degree of success or failure in obtaining redress (Andreasen 1977). Thus, the consequences of a service provider's failure to resolve service delivery problems can be severe. Bitner et al. (1990) found that from the customer's point of view, the largest percentage (42.9%) of dissatisfactory outcomes in service encounters was due to the employee's response to service delivery system failures. Bitner et al. (1994) also found that from the service employee's point of view, the vast majority (51.7%) of dissatisfying service encounters were the result of inadequate responses to service failures. Inadequate response to service failures also increases the likelihood that these disgruntled customers will complain about the incident. TARP (1986) research findings suggest that the average customer who has had a problem with an organization tells 8 to 10 people about it, and 90 percent say they will never do business with that company again.

The present study investigates both the level of satisfaction and the likelihood of complaint behavior that may result after a service recovery effort is undertaken in response to a service failure. Specifically, the empirical results of our research would enhance managerial understanding of the impact of three factors on the effectiveness of service recovery efforts: (1) the cause of the failure, (2) the outcome resolution resulting from the recovery attempt, and (3) the manner in which the recovery effort is executed.

THEORETICAL DEVELOPMENT AND HYPOTHESES

According to the disconfirmation paradigm, consumer satisfaction is the result of an evaluative process whereby a consumer compares his/her expectations of how the service should be performed with the actual performance of the service (Oliver 1980). Confirmation (leaving the consumer in a neutral state) occurs when the service is performed as expected. Negative disconfirmation (dissatisfaction) occurs when the service performance does not live up to prior expectations. During service encounters, consumers expect "zero-defects" in service delivery. Despite the service provider's attempts to offer consistent, high-quality service to consumers, service failures may still occur because service delivery is heterogeneous across service encounters due to the variability in situational factors and individual differences between consumers and service employees (Singh 1991). Therefore, based on the disconfirmation paradigm, the following hypothesis is proposed:

H1: The level of consumer satisfaction (likelihood of complaint behavior) with a service encounter will be lower (higher) in the case of a service failure than in the case of no service failure.

Attribution theory provides a basis for understanding how consumers respond to service failures (Folkes 1984). Attribution theory predicts that the perceived reason for a service failure influences the level of consumer satisfaction. The service failure itself is not the only factor influencing the level of satisfaction; consumers try to determine why the failure occurred. The three causal dimensions of attribution theory include: stability (i.e., is the service failure likely to occur very often?), controllability (i.e., could the service failure have been avoided?), and locus (i.e., is the service failure the fault of the consumer or the service provider?). If a customer realizes that a service failure is due to his/her own fault, he/she would be less upset than if the service provider is to blame for the service failure. Therefore, based on the locus dimension of attribution theory, we would expect the locus of causality (other versus self) to influence the level of consumer satisfaction and intention to complain in the following way:

H2: After a service failure, the level of consumer satisfaction (likelihood of complaint behavior) will be higher (lower) if the consumer perceives the locus of causality for the failure to be self versus the service provider.

Researchers have found a relationship between equity and consumer satisfaction (Oliver and Swan 1989) and complaint behavior (Brown and Beltramini 1984). Building on the foundations of equity theory, researchers have suggested three dimensions of equity, which are based on perceptions of justice (Greenberg 1996). Two of these three dimensions are explored in the present study: (1) distributive justice that focuses on the perceived fairness of the outcome of the service encounter (Homans 1961), and (2) interactional justice that focuses on the perceived fairness of the manner in which the customer is treated throughout the service encounter (Bies and Moag 1986). We will not manipulate the third dimension of equity, procedural justice (the perceived fairness of the process used to rectify the service failure) since this dimension has been found to be difficult to manipulate in an experimental situation (Goodwin and Ross 1992).

According to Blodgett, Granbois, and Walters (1993), distributive justice refers to the perceived fairness of the redress offered by the service provider (i.e., whether the customer is offered an exchange, monetary refund, etc.). In the case of a service failure, consumers would expect the service provider to compensate them for any tangible loss they suffered as a result of that service failure. Customers may expect different levels of compensation depending on how severely the service failure affects them. An annoyed customer would expect a "fair fix" for the problem, while a consumer who feels "victimized" as a result of the service failure may expect some value-added atonement (Bell and Ridge 1992).

A distinction needs to be drawn between the actual service recovery outcome and the process of service recovery, which relates to *how* the service recovery is attempted. According to Berry (1986, p. 49),

Service firms that are great at problem resolution—that are accessible and respond with quickness . . . are far more likely to repair the damage done to their quality reputations than are the firms that take a casual . . . attitude.

It has also been shown that prompt complaint resolutions have resulted in more consumers continuing to do business with the organization (Albrecht and Zemke 1985). In addition to prompt service recovery, Goodwin and Ross (1992) found that one aspect of interactional fairness, an apology, seems particularly relevant to complaint resolution.

Therefore, based on the distributive and interactional justice dimensions of equity theory, one would expect that both the tangible outcome and the manner in which the problem was resolved would impact how satisfied customers would be and the likelihood that they would complain about the incident. Consequently, we believe that the level of distributive and interactional justice would impact consumers' satisfaction and intention to complain in the following manner:

H3: After a service failure, levels of satisfaction (likelihood of complaint behavior) will be higher (lower) if consumers perceive high rather than low distributive justice in the service recovery attempt.

H4: After a service failure, levels of satisfaction (likelihood of complaint behavior) will be higher (lower) if consumers perceive high rather than low interactional justice in the service recovery attempt.

RESEARCH METHODOLOGY

Subjects

A convenience sample of 251 undergraduate marketing students (54% women and 46% men) from a large midwestern university participated in this study. Care was taken to choose a service encounter that would be relevant to a student sample. Specifically, we used a service failure in a Mexican restaurant for developing the stimuli in this study. Earlier research has shown that dissatisfying service encounters are particularly prevalent in restaurant settings (Bitner et al. 1990).

Experimental Design

The study used a 2 X 2 X 2 between-subjects factorial design. The factors are cause of failure (customer or restaurant), distributive justice (high or low), and interactional justice (high or low).

Procedure

Subjects were randomly assigned to one of the eight experimental conditions. In addition, there was a control condition that described the same restaurant experience as the other scenarios, but did not include a service failure situation. The subjects were asked to read one of the nine (eight plus one control) versions of a scenario describing a dining experience at a Mexican restaurant. The context of the core service failure described a situation in which a bowl of salsa was spilled onto the customer's table and some of the salsa was also spilled onto the sleeve of the customer's new jacket. The scenarios were pretested for believability, and the mean believability was 5.6 on a 7-point scale (1=not at all believable, 7=highly believable).

Independent Variable Manipulations

Locus of causality attribution, distributive justice, and interactive justice manipulations were pretested. The manipulations were achieved by changing the scenario descriptions as follows:

TABLE 1
MANOVA with Satisfaction and Complaint Behavior as the Dependent Variables

	Df	Sum Sq.	F-Stat	p-value
Satisfaction				
Locus of Causality	1	31.60	24.46	0.0001
Distributive Justice	1	123.31	18.05	0.0001
Interactional Justice	1	62.59	48.46	0.0001
Locus x Distributive	1	0.05	0.04	0.8511
Locus x Interactional	1	5.54	4.29	0.0392
Dist. x Inter.	1	3.10	2.40	0.1231
Locus x Dist. x Inter.	1	0.72	0.56	0.4549
Error	189	244.14		
Total	196	369.08		
Complaint Behavior				
Locus of Causality	1	33.13	27.89	0.0001
Distributive Justice	1	5.20	4.37	0.0378
Interactional Justice	1	15.97	13.44	0.0003
Locus x Distributive	1	0.19	0.16	0.6906
Locus x Interactional	1	6.32	5.32	0.0222
Dist. x Inter.	1	1.51	1.27	0.2604
Locus x Dist. x Inter.	1	0.51	0.43	0.5152
Error	189	224.56		
Total	196	286.76		

Customer's fault: "In your rush to try the extra-hot salsa, you accidentally drop the bowl on the table. Unfortunately, most of the salsa is spilled onto your table."
Restaurant's fault: "As the waiter hands you the bowl, you seem to notice a crack in the handle of the bowl. Sure enough, as you are taking the bowl, the handle suddenly breaks off and most of the extra-hot salsa is spilled onto your table."

High distributive justice: "... the waiter brings a new bowl of extra-hot salsa."
Low distributive justice: "... the waiter is unable to bring you more extra-hot salsa because that was their last bowl."

High interactional justice: "... the waiter shows empathy and takes steps to help you immediately."
Low interactional justice: an irritated waiter must call the manager (which causes a delay in response) instead of helping you immediately.

Dependent Variable Measurements

The two dependent variables, satisfaction and intention to complain, were assessed using multiple measures to increase reliability. Eight Likert-type (strongly disagree=1, strongly agree=7) satisfaction scales were adapted from Oliver (1980) and Bitner (1990). Seven measures assessing intention to com plain were adapted from Singh (1991) and Blodgett et al. (1993). The multiitem satisfaction and intention to complain scale reliabilities (Cronbach's alpha) were 0.93 and 0.87, respectively. Indices for satisfaction and complaint behavior were formed by averaging the respective multi-item measures.

RESULTS

Manipulation Checks

Checks of the perception of attribution for the service failure and the interactional and distributive justice questions revealed that subjects perceived these independent variables as intended. All manipulations were assessed on 7-point semantic differential scales. Results showed statistically significant differences (all with $p < 0.001$) in the expected direction between group means on questions about perceptions of cause of failure (restaurant=4.85, customer=2.17), interactional justice (high=5.88, low=4.34), and distributive justice (high=5.50, low=4.07).

MANOVA

Results from MANOVA indicate that all three main effects are statistically significant at the multivariate as well as the univariate levels. In addition, the two-way interaction effect between the locus of causality and interactional justice are significant at the multivariate and the univariate levels. The relevant F-statistics and p-values for these effects from the univariate analysis are reported in Table 1. In Table 2, we report the means corresponding to the statistically significant main effects.

Hypothesis 1 states that the level of consumer satisfaction (likelihood of complaint behavior) with a service encounter will be lower (higher) in the case of no service failure than in the case of service failure. This hypothesis is partially supported. Results show that satisfaction is significantly higher (F=16.12, p<0.001) and the intention to complain is significantly lower (F=16.18, p<0.001) when there is no service failure versus when the service failure is the fault of the restaurant. However, there are no

TABLE 2
Main Effect Means

	Satisfaction	Intention to Complain
No Failure Condition	5.18	2.68
Restaurant's Fault	4.24	3.47
Customer's Fault	5.04	2.64
High Distributive Justice	4.96	2.92
Low Distributive Justice	4.29	3.23
High Interactional Justice	5.18	2.80
Low Interactional Justice	4.07	3.35

significant differences in levels of satisfaction or levels of intention to complain between the "no failure" condition and the situation where the service failure is the customer's fault (satisfaction: $F=0.26$, $p<0.610$; intention to complain: $F=0.09$, $p<0.768$).

Hypothesis 2 states that after a service failure, consumers would be less satisfied if the service failure is the fault of the restaurant rather than their own fault. Likewise, consumers would be more likely to complain if the service failure is the fault of the restaurant. The means reported in Table 2 are in the predicted direction for both satisfaction and intention to complain. The main effects of the locus of causality for comparing these means are statistically significant for both dependent variables. Predictions from hypothesis 2 are supported.

Hypothesis 3 states that after a service failure, levels of satisfaction (likelihood of complaint behavior) will be higher (lower) if consumers perceived high distributive justice. The means reported in Table 2 are in the predicted direction for both satisfaction and intention to complain. The main effects of distributive justice for comparing these means are statistically significant for both dependent variables. Thus, predictions from hypothesis 3 are supported.

Hypothesis 4 states that after a service failure, levels of satisfaction (likelihood of complaint behavior) will be higher (lower) if consumers perceived high interactional justice. The means reported in Table 2 are in the predicted direction for both satisfaction and intention to complain. The main effects of interactional justice for comparing these means are statistically significant for both dependent variables. Thus, predictions from hypothesis 4 are also supported.

Locus of Causality and Interactional Justice Interaction: While we did not predict any interaction between locus of causality, distributive justice, and interactional justice for either satisfaction or intention to complain, results in Table 1 indicate that the interaction between locus of causality and interactional justice is statistically significant for both dependent variables. The means for interpreting this interaction effect are shown in Figure 1.

The interaction plot shows that regardless of who is to blame for the service failure, there are statistically significant differences in the mean levels of satisfaction between subjects in the low and high interactional justice conditions (customer's fault: $F=38.91$, $p<0.001$; restaurant's fault: $F=12.48$, $p<0.001$). However, the difference between low and high interactional justice conditions is higher when the failure is due to customer's fault rather than restaurant's fault. Intention to complain varies depending on whether the restaurant or the customer is at fault for the service

failure. When the service failure is the restaurant's fault, there is no significant difference between average intention to complain between subjects in the low and high interactional justice conditions ($F=1.17$, $p<0.280$). However, when the service failure is the customer's fault, the average intention to complain is significantly lower for subjects in the high interactional justice condition ($F=18.71$, $p<0.001$).

To aid in interpreting the results in Figure 1, we have also plotted the average satisfaction and intention to complain for the subjects in the control (no failure) group. In Table 3 below, we report the statistical tests for difference in means between the control condition and the four experimental conditions shown in Figure 1. The results of the comparison of means show that all four conditions are statistically significantly different from the control condition. The directionality of these differences suggests that if the failure is the fault of the service provider, in spite of high perceived interactional justice, the average satisfaction of consumers is still lower than the average satisfaction of those who do not experience a failure. However, if the failure is the customer's fault and if customers perceive high interactional justice, their average satisfaction will be higher than the average satisfaction of those who do not experience a failure. The conclusions for intention to complain are similar to the conclusions for average satisfaction.

In summary, we find that after a service recovery attempt is made following a service failure, consumers' perceived interactional and distributive justice have significant positive (negative) effects on satisfaction (intention to complain). Also as expected, we find that consumers are less satisfied (more likely to complain) if the service failure is the provider's fault rather than their own. Interestingly, when failure occurs due to the customers' fault, the average satisfaction (intention to complain) is the same as when there is no failure. Another interesting finding relates to the interaction effect of the locus of causality by perceived interactional justice. The pattern of this interaction suggests that providers can enhance (reduce) customer satisfaction (intention to complain) by simply treating them nicely during the service recovery attempt.

DISCUSSION

Not only does the disconfirmation paradigm predict, but it also seems intuitively obvious, that we would be less satisfied after we experience a service failure than if there had been no failure at all. However, the aggregate results in Table 2 indicate that when the customer blames him/herself for the service failure, there is no difference between the levels of satisfaction or likelihood of complaint behavior between the failure and the no-failure condition.

FIGURE 1
Locus of Causality and Interactional Justice Interaction Plots

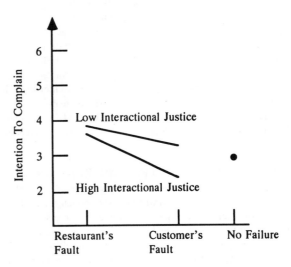

TABLE 3
Differences in Means between Locus of Causality X Interactional Justice and Control Condition

Dependent variable	Customer's Fault: Low Int. Justice vs. Control F-stat(p-value)	Customer's Fault: High Int. Justice vs. Control F-stat(p-value)	Restaur.'s Fault: Low Int. Justice vs. Control F-stat(p-value)	Restaur.'s Fault: High Int. Justice vs. Control F-stat(p-value)
Satisfaction	12.44(0.001)	6.91(0.009)	31.63(0.001)	4.84(0.029)
Complaint Int.	3.80(0.052)	5.19(0.024)	15.47(0.001)	8.72(0.003)

The reason for this apparent discrepancy could be explained by the fact that these means in the failure conditions are also influenced by the service recovery efforts.

It is no surprise that our results suggest that consumers will be less satisfied and more likely to complain when the restaurant is at fault rather than the consumer. It is possible that this impact could be reduced by the front-line service employee, however. In this research, we only looked at one dimension of attribution theory—locus of causality. The two other dimensions of attribution theory, controllability and stability, could provide means for managing the negative effects felt by the customer as a result of a service failure. Customers may be more understanding and/or forgiving if the service employee, after offering a sincere apology to the customer, would also add a comment such as "this sort of thing rarely happens here" (stability) or "I had no idea the bowl was defective" (controllability). These conjectures could be investigated in future research.

Results shown in Tables 1 and 2 confirmed our prediction that there is a difference in the level of satisfaction and the likelihood of complaint behavior depending on whether consumers perceive the outcome to be fair (i.e., high versus low level of distributive justice). The high level of distributive justice in our study was operationalized as just putting the customer back to his/her original state. Instead

of being worse off than before the accident (low distributive justice), the service recovery effort replaced the customer's loss (in this case a bowl of extra-hot salsa). Although most people appear to be content to receive what seems to be fair, i.e., just return them to their original state, other levels of distributive justice (e.g., offer them something extra) could be investigated in future research.

There are also relatively large differences in satisfaction in the high versus low interactional justice conditions. As mentioned earlier, this suggests how important prompt, courteous service may be to customers. An important implication of this finding is that front-line employees should be empowered by the service organization to handle most routine service failures. Both the customer and employee are frustrated when the simplest transactions have to be monitored or approved by supervisors. Not only does the customer have to wait, but the employee is made to feel inferior. An employee who is otherwise qualified for the job of serving customers should be trained and trusted to use discretion in dealing with routine service failure situations. Empowerment may give employees the best avenue to succeed in transforming a potentially unhappy customer into a delighted consumer.

Abrams and Pease (1993) conjectured that it is possible that after a service failure has been successfully resolved, consumers may feel a stronger commitment to the service provider than if no failure had occurred in the first place. We find evidence of this effect under a very specific condition—when service failure occurs due to customers' fault and when customers perceive high interactional justice in the service recovery attempt by the provider. Heskett, Sasser, and Hart (1990) contend that it is necessary for a service firm to attempt a service recovery to create a satisfied customer, irrespective of the cause of the problem or the location of blame. A major implication of this finding is that prompt, courteous service recovery actions on the part of the service provider when the customer has caused a service failure may increase levels of customer satisfaction and decrease the likelihood of complaint behavior above and beyond the levels that would have been reached without any failure.

CONCLUSIONS AND FUTURE RESEARCH

The way in which the service recovery is handled is likely to have an important influence on whether the customer returns to the service firm. There is no reason why service encounters that begin with a service failure can not end as a service recovery success. The inability to respond to a service failure "adds insult to injury"—customers are disappointed twice, first when the service breakdown occurs and later when there is a lack of effort on the part of the service provider to recover from the service failure.

Our research in "the art of service recovery" suggests that the "means" (process or interactional justice) may be more important than the "ends" (outcome or distributive justice) when it comes to service recovery. However, this conclusion is dependent on the particular manipulations of distributive and interactional justice used in this study. Further research with different types of service encounters and different manipulations of means and outcomes related to service recovery are needed to generalize these results. Conditions of an experiment describing a recovery from a core service failure rather than a delivery system failure could be manipulated. Core service failures have been reported most often as being dissatisfactory (Bitner et al. 1990) and as the reason consumers switch service firms (Keaveney 1995).

Future research is needed for other types of service encounters that occur in long-term rather than discrete exchange relationships, such as those experienced for professional services. It would also be interesting to look at a service failure from the employee's point of view. Bitner et al. (1994) suggest that service employees and consumers see service failures in much the same way. It is quite possible that empowering employees to respond appropriately to service failures will result in a win-win-win situation: the customer, the employee, and ultimately the service firm itself will benefit.

REFERENCES

Abrams, M. and M. Pease (1993), "Wining and Dining the Whiners," *Sales and Marketing Management* (February), 73-75.

Albrecht, K. (1988), *At America's Service*, Homewood, IL: Dow Jones-Irwin.

_____ and R. Zemke (1985), *Service America!*, Homewood, IL: Dow Jones-Irwin.

Andreasen, A.R. (1977), "A Taxonomy of Consumer Satisfaction/Dissatisfaction Measures," *The Journal of Consumer Affairs*, 11(Winter), 11-24.

_____ and A. Best (1977), "Consumers Complain—Does Business Respond?" *Harvard Business Review* (July-August), 93-101.

Bell, C.R. and K. Ridge (1992), "Service Recovery for Trainers," *Training and Development* (May), 58-63.

Bell, C.R. and R.E. Zemke (1987), "Service Breakdown: The Road to Recovery," *Management Review* (October), 32-35.

Berry, L. (1986), "Big Ideas in Services Marketing," *Journal of Consumer Marketing*, 3 (Spring), 47-51.

_____ and A. Parasuraman (1992), "Prescriptions for a Service Quality Revolution in America," *Organizational Dynamics*, 20 (Spring), 5-15.

Bies, R.J. and J.S. Moag (1986), "Interactional Communication Criteria of Fairness," *Research in Org. Behavior*, Greenwich, CT: JAI Press.

Bitner, M.J. (1990), "Evaluating Service Encounters: The Effects of Physical Surroundings and Employee Responses," *Journal of Marketing*, 54 (April), 69-82.

_____, B.H. Booms, and L.A. Mohr (1994), "Critical Service Encounters: The Employee's Viewpoint," *Journal of Marketing*, 58 (October), 95-106.

_____, _____, and M.S. Tetreault (1990), "The Service Encounter: Diagnosing Favorable and Unfavorable Incidents," *Journal of Marketing*, 54 (January), 71-84.

Blodgett, J.G., D.H. Granbois, and R.G. Walters (1993), "The Effects of Perceived Justice on Complainants' Negative Word-of-Mouth Behavior and Repatronage Intentions," *Journal of Retailing*, 69 (Winter), 399-428.

Brown, S.P. and R.F. Beltramini (1984), "Consumer Complaining and Word of Mouth Activities: Field Evidence," *Adv. in Consumer Research*, 16,9-16.

Czepiel, J., M.R. Solomon, and C.F. Surprenant (1985), *The Service Encounter*, New York: Lexington Books.

Folkes, V.S. (1984), "Consumer Reactions to Product Failure: An Attributional Approach," *Journal of Consumer Research*, 10 (March), 398-409.

Goodwin, C. and I. Ross (1992), "Consumer Responses to Service Failures: Influence of Procedural and Interactional Fairness Perceptions," *Journal of Business Research*, 25, 149-163.

Greenberg, J. (1996), *The Quest for Justice on the Job: Essays and Experiments*, Thousand Oaks, CA: Sage Publications.

Hart, C.W.L., J.L. Heskett, and W.E. Sasser,Jr.(1990),"The Profitable Art of Service Recovery," *Harvard Business Review* (July-August), 148-156.

Heskett, J.L., W.E. Sasser, Jr., and C.W.L. Hart (1990), *Service Breakthroughs: Changing the Rules of the Game*, New York: Free Press.

Homans, G.C. (1961), *Social Behavior: Its Elementary Forms*, New York: Harcourt, Brace and World.

Keaveney, S.M. (1995), "Customer Switching Behavior in Service Industries: An Exploratory Study," *Journal of Marketing*, 59(April), 71-82.

Oliver, R.L. (1980), "Theoretical Bases of Consumer Satisfaction Research: Review, Critique, and Future Direction," *Theoretical Developments in Marketing*, Chicago: American Marketing Assoc., 206-210.

_____ and J.E. Swan (1989), "Consumer Perceptions of Interpersonal Equity and Satisfaction in Transactions: A Field Survey Approach," *Journal of Marketing*, 53(April), 21-35.

Parasuraman, A., V.A. Zeithaml, and L.L. Berry (1988), "SERVQUAL: A Multiple-Item Scale for Measuring Consumer Perceptions of Service Quality," *Journal of Retailing*, 64(Spring), 12-40.

Singh, J. (1991), "Understanding the Structure of Consumers' Satisfaction Evaluations of Service Delivery," *Journal of the Academy of Marketing Science*, 19, 223-244.

Solomon, M.R., C. Surprenant, J.A. Czepiel, and E.G. Gutman (1985), "A Role Theory Perspective on Dyadic Interactions: The Service Encounter," *Journal of Marketing*, 49(Winter), 99-111.

TARP (1986), Technical Assistance Research Program, *Consumer Complaint Handling in America: An Update Study*.

Zemke, R. (1993), "The Art of Service Recovery: Fixing Broken Customers And Keeping Them on Your Side," *The Service Quality Handbook*, New York: American Management Association, 463-476.

Motivation, Capacity and Opportunity to Complain: Towards a Comprehensive Model of Consumer Complaint Behavior

Kaj P.N. Morel, Delft University of Technology, the Netherlands
Theo B.C. Poiesz, Tilburg University, the Netherlands
Henk A.M. Wilke, Leiden University, the Netherlands

ABSTRACT

In this paper, highlights of the consumer complaint behavior literature are reviewed and implications for a general theoretical framework are assessed. Inspired by models proposed in the area of consumer information processing, a relatively simple overall model is proposed. The main determinants specified by this model are motivation, capacity, and opportunity to complain. A study is reported in which the model is operationalized and assessed. The results provide some support for the hypothesis that complaint behavior is a positive function of the mathematical product of the three determinants. Potential functions of the model are briefly discussed.

Why and how do consumers complain? In the past two decades many researchers have addressed this question, leading to an improved understanding of consumer complaint behavior (CCB). However, it seems that some of the issues raised in the early CCB studies remain unresolved. For example, in 1975, Day and Landon concluded that "a comprehensive theory of consumer complaining behavior remains to be formulated and tested" (p. 263) and "efforts to develop a useful theory of consumer complaining behavior should also go forward" (p. 268). Several years later, Krishnan and Valle (1979) state that "a systematic application of theoretical constructs is necessary for a better understanding of consumer complaint behavior" (p. 445). More recently others have come to similar conclusions: "The need has been cited for a comprehensive, integrated model that can predict complaining behavior" (Kolodinsky and Aleong 1990, p. 61). Maute and Forrester (1993) stated that "as studies of [consumer complaint behavior] emerge, unresolved definitional and taxonomic questions have resulted in a body of research that is largely atheoretical and non-empirical." (p. 219).

These various observations raise the question of what twenty years of research on CCB have yielded. Singh (1988) concluded that research has led to significant agreement on the concept of CCB. In the first place, complaint behavior is assumed to be triggered by feelings of dissatisfaction with a product or service. Secondly, CCB responses are considered to be either behavioral or non-behavioral, behavioral responses being those actions a consumer takes to express some form of dissatisfaction. "CCB, then, is conceptualized as a set of multiple (behavioral and non-behavioral) responses, some or all of which are triggered by perceived dissatisfaction with a purchase episode" (Singh 1988, p. 94). Notwithstanding the agreement, CCB research is characterized by considerable conceptual and methodological variation and differentiation. In spite of the academic efforts made so far, as of 1996 a comprehensive model of CCB is still needed. We will attempt to assess whether theoretical and empirical arguments for such a model can be proposed. First however, we will briefly review the available CCB literature.

REVIEW OF THE COMPLAINT LITERATURE

The literature on CCB research can be divided into three categories of studies: (1) descriptive studies, (2) heuristic studies, and (3) predictive studies. Each category will be briefly summarized below, and for each category, an example in the form of a frequently cited study will be provided.

Descriptive studies do not, by themselves, produce any new theoretical or conceptual ideas; they tend to report the results of large-scale surveys on actual consumer complaint actions. For example, in a sample of 600 respondents, Day and Ash (1979) collected data on the level of consumer satisfaction, sources of consumer satisfaction, and post-dissatisfaction responses for several categories of durable consumer products. Several authors have presented conceptual models of CCB, not with the intention of subjecting them to empirical testing, but to offer a framework for the classification of the results of large-scale surveys. Building on suggestions offered by Day and Bodur (1977) and Day and Landon (1977), Day and Bodur (1978) used the 'no action–private action–public action' scheme for classifying complaint behavior as a basis for formulating questions for a 600 household survey on frequency of dissatisfaction, reasons for dissatisfaction, and post-dissatisfaction responses for a variety of consumer services.

Heuristic studies differ from purely descriptive studies in their emphasis on theoretical progress. These studies review the relevant literature on CCB, present some kind of conceptual model of CCB, and offer suggestions for future research. Some of these studies yield new empirical data. Studies which provide no new data use secondary analyses to support or clarify their respective arguments. A model of complaining behavior is presented by Day and Landon (1977); this model not only describes the behavioral alternatives dissatisfied consumers have (no action, private action, public action), but also proposes factors that influence choices among these alternative actions (marketing factors, consumer factors, circumstantial factors). Other heuristic studies have been reported by Day (1980), Day et al. (1981), and Jacoby and Jaccard (1981). Day and Landon (1975) distinguished four major factors underlying complaining behavior: (1) propensity to complain, (2) opportunities to become dissatisfied, (3) opportunities to complain, and (4) disparity in consumer knowledge. They mention these factors to support their argument that traditional complaint data (i.e. complaints received by third party complaint agencies) are biased and inaccurate because of consumer differences on each of the determinants.

Finally, predictive studies present a theoretical framework for predicting future CCB which is subsequently tested. In several experiments Kolodinsky (1992, 1993, 1995) and Kolodinsky and Aleong (1990) used an operational model based on economic theory to predict CCB for services. According to this model a consumer is assumed to maximize some kind of short-term utility. The level of utility determines whether a consumer will undertake a particular complaint action. On the basis of previous research and economic theory, predictors were selected and incorporated in several logistic models, with dependent variables ranging from various complaint actions (no action, public action, private action) to number of complaints, degree of complaint resolution, and intention to repeat purchase. The logistic models predicted CCB quite well, the percentage of correct predictions ranging from 8% to 100%, with an average of about 80%. The authors observed that, although predictions based on a combination of predictors were quite accurate, very few of the isolated predictors were significant. Another predictive study was reported by Maute and Forrester (1993). Here a different economic model, the investment model, provided the conceptual framework. In this case the predictors were magnitude of the dissatisfaction problem, exit barriers, and attractiveness of alternatives. Consumer complaint actions were predicted using Hirschmann's (1970) three-dimensional classification scheme: exit, voice, and loyalty. The results showed that the three predictors were all significantly associated with the three types of complaint action.

Our review of the literature supports the conclusion that CCB research has led to many interesting and valuable insights. First, extensive survey research has resulted in a large body of data on consumer dissatisfaction and real complaints for a vast array of products and services. In the second place, the structure of consumer complaint actions has been studied intensively, resulting in two accepted taxonomies of post-dissatisfaction behavior: Hirschmann's (1970) voice-exit-loyalty taxonomy, and Day and Landon's (1977) no action–private action–public action classification scheme, both of which seem valid and useful. Third, many factors that influence CCB have been examined, which has shed considerable light on the conceptual structure of the consumer complaining process. Finally, promising results have been reached in predicting CCB using econometric logistic models (Kolodinsky 1992, 1993, 1995; Kolodinsky and Aleong 1990). Consequently, Kolodinsky and Aleong (1990) conclude that "It is possible to build on previous research to develop an integrated model of consumer complaining behavior [based on a theory of complaining behavior] that can be empirically estimated to explain variation in, and predict when complaints are most (or least) likely to occur" (p. 62). With regard to Kolodinsky and Aleong's conclusion, however, it may be argued that an integrated model of consumer complaint behavior is not (yet) available, and that the research reported in the literature is still too fragmented. Determinants of CCB have been studied in isolation or in relatively small groups. More recent experiments have addressed several factors at the same time (Kolodinsky 1992, 1993, 1995; Kolodinsky and Aleong 1990), but the combination of variables employed to predict complaint behavior seems quite arbitrary and incomplete. For example, Kolodinsky (1995) used 15 predictors, divided over four categories intended to cover the whole array of CCB determinants mentioned in the literature. Closer inspection of these variables reveals that none of these variables represent motivational aspects of complaint behavior, which suggests that the selection of behavioral determinants is not based upon an underlying theory of complaint behavior. Lack of a solid theoretical foundation tends to be accompanied by lack of conceptual clarity, resulting in CCB researchers examining "the effect of haphazardly chosen predictors on dissatisfaction responses" (Maute and Forrester 1993, p. 224). The problem that may arise is illustrated in the research of Kolodinsky (1992, 1993, 1995) and Kolodinsky and Aleong (1990), which indicated that few of the isolated predictors were significant, while the combined variables in the overall model significantly predicted CCB. Apparently, it is not clear which variables contribute to the prediction of CCB and which ones do not. There also arises the question of whether the observed significance is simply due to the large number of predictors incorporated in the model.

In view of the preceding arguments, we propose an approach that may contribute to an improved understanding of the complaint behavior of consumers. This approach is intended to provide a useful alternative, or a supplement, to the approaches that have been employed so far. In the next section the approach–referred to as the Triad model–will be introduced. The results of an experimental test of this model will be presented and discussed.

THE TRIAD MODEL

The basic idea of the model was inspired by theoretical developments in an area that is essentially unrelated to consumer complaint behavior: advertising processing. In the latter field, several authors proposed that the problem of fragmentation be solved by using simplifying models focusing on a very limited set of explanatory factors. Petty and Cacioppo (e.g. 1986) proposed motivation and ability to process as the central determinants of processing; Andrews (1988), Batra and Ray (1986), MacInnis, Moorman, and Jaworski (1991), and Poiesz and Robben (1996) focussed on motivation, capacity or ability, and opportunity as the critical factors for explaining the behavior under consideration. The use of such general factors decreases the richness of detail but increases the likelihood that the general determinants of the criterion behavior will be taken into account. In the area of information processing this general approach proved to stimulate theoretical integration (e.g. in the form of the Elaboration Likelihood Model, Petty and Cacioppo 1986). As it was concluded in the previous section that CCB research is fragmented, a simplified heuristic approach will be pursued in the present study. It is for this reason that we propose a model in which consumer complaint behavior is explained by three general factors: motivation, capacity, and opportunity to complain. With this model an attempt is made to avoid an approach that is incomplete, considers isolated variables, or employs an arbitrary combination of variables (these being the shortcomings of existing approaches). We will refer to the model as the 'Triad' model, thereby emphasizing the need to consider the three factors simultaneously when attempting to explain complaint behavior. The Triad model is based on several assumptions:

1. The main assumption of the Triad model is that all determinants of behavior can be 'captured' by three variables: motivation, capacity, and opportunity. People will engage in a specific behavior when their motivation, perceived capacity, and perceived opportunity to execute this behavior are sufficiently high, that is, above some critical subjective minimum level. Motivation refers to the need, interest, or desire to engage in a particular behavior. Capacity is defined as the person's capability, instrumentality, and skill to engage in a certain behavior and to achieve the stated goal. Opportunity concerns the extent to which external circumstances–in the broadest meaning of the word–stimulate or inhibit a particular behavior (viz. complaint behavior).

2. The three determinants are exhaustive concepts. All (potentially) relevant behavior determinants can be represented in terms of these general concepts.

3. The three determinants constitute necessary, but not sufficient factors. For a particular behavior to take place all three Triad factors have to reach some minimum level simultaneously. In other words: the Triad model assumes a multiplicative relationship among the three determinants.

4. A person's subjective assessments of the Triad factors determine whether he or she will engage in a particular behavior. Subjective assessments and objective constraints (objective capacity and opportunity levels) together determine whether the behavior does actually take place and to what extent.

The Triad model is proposed as a framework for CCB research, because the model (a) is based on existing theory; (b) can be applied to all possible complaint actions; (c) includes all possible behavioral antecedents; and (d) can be operationalized and empirically tested.

Goal and hypothesis

The present study constitutes an initial attempt to assess how well complaint behavior may be predicted by the three general determinants of the Triad model. More concretely, it is hypothesized that the subjective probability of complaint behavior can be predicted by the mathematical product of a person's perceived motivation, perceived capacity and perceived opportunity to perform a specific complaint behavior.

METHOD

Subjects and design

The sample of respondents was drawn from the population of a mid-size town in the Netherlands. In view of the critical behavior that was investigated in the present study–" complaining during a dinner in a foreign restaurant"–subjects who could be expected to have some experience with dining in foreign restaurants were recruited. For this reason inhabitants of three neighborhoods with more than average income and educational levels were invited to participate. An analysis of actual income and education levels revealed that (1) all respondents had at least completed secondary school, and 72% also had a higher vocational education or university degree; (2) 88% of the respondents had at least an average income (more than the Dutch equivalent of $25,000) of whom 46% earned an above average income (more than the Dutch equivalent of $50,000). The design was a 2x2x2 factorial design with two levels ('high' and 'low') for each of the three between-subjects factors motivation, capacity and opportunity. A total of 235 respondents received the questionnaire; 210 were dropped off and picked up at their home; another 25 subjects received and returned the questionnaire by mail. Of the returned questionnaires a total of 106 were filled in and could be used for analysis. Subjects were randomly assigned to one of the eight experimental conditions. To control for possible order-of-question effects in each condition, two differently ordered questionnaires were constructed for each condition, resulting in a total of sixteen different questionnaires.

Stimulus material

Considering the fact that written descriptions of scenarios were presented to respondents, several operational and validity issues had to be considered. First, the operationalization of each of the three determinants had to be feasible, in the sense that both a high and a low level condition could be created. Second, both the object of the complaint and the situation had to be selected in such a way that the complaint was perceived by subjects as an actual behavior option. The third consideration was that the scenario had to be as realistic as possible: respondents had to be able to imagine themselves in the circumstances described. Finally, the complaint action had to be relevant behavior for the respondents. They had to have the impression that the complaint action actually would matter. Respondents were told to imagine themselves having dinner with friends in a restaurant in Paris, and that they were disappointed with the wine that was served.

Independent variables

The high and low motivation, capacity, and opportunity conditions were operationalized in the scenarios using positively or negatively formulated motivation, capacity, and opportunity related aspects (see Table 1). The operationalization of the different aspects was subject to several considerations. Most importantly, every aspect had to operationalize the corresponding determinant

as specifically as possible. After all, the three independent variables had to be operationalized independently. Also, the manipulations had to be equally strong: none of the three independent variables should be a priori dominant over the others. Results of a pilot study showed that the manipulations of motivation and opportunity resulted in two significantly different response patterns; the manipulation of capacity did not. The scenarios were subsequently adjusted by situating the restaurant in a foreign country (in this case France)–the original scenarios were not situated abroad–so that the typical capacity-related aspect 'knowledge of culture and language' could be used.

Dependent variables

The main dependent variable was the subjective probability of engaging in a specific complaint action, described as follows: '*You don't accept the wine. You tell the restaurant personnel that the wine does not meet your expectations and you ask them if something can be done about it, for example getting another wine instead.*' The dependent measure was subjects' probability of complaining (scale 0% to 100%).

Procedure

The questionnaire consisted of an introduction, a scenario, and 28 questions. The introduction told the respondents what they were expected to do. The instructions emphasized that subjects were to imagine themselves in the specific situation described by the scenario. The scenarios covered two pages: the actual description and a summary of the most important issues in this description. The respondents were urged to use the summary to remind them of the situation. The majority of the questions in the questionnaire was aimed at measuring the respondentss subjectively perceived motivation, capacity, and opportunity. Perceived motivation, for example, was determined by asking the respondent to indicate on a 9-point scale to which extent he or she would *want* to do something about his or her dissatisfaction. Participation took about 45 minutes.

RESULTS

Outliers

Two respondents showed very deviant response patterns. There was strong, but not conclusive, evidence that these deviations were caused by misinterpretation of the response scales (reversal of the scale end-points). These two respondents were excluded from all analyses.

Manipulation checks

Three 2x2x2 ANOVAs were carried out with the independent variables Motivation (high, low), Capacity (high, low), and Opportunity (high, low), and the dependent variables Perceived Motivation, Perceived Capacity and Perceived Opportunity. One case was missing for each dependent variable, so $N=103$.

Perceived Motivation. Main effects of Motivation ($F(1,95)=73.60$, $p<.001$) and Capacity ($F(1,95)=14.85$, $p<.001$) and interaction effects of Motivation x Capacity ($F(1,95)=7.28$, $p<.01$) and Motivation x Opportunity ($F(1,95)=8.33$, $p<.01$) were found. With regard to the interaction effects, it was observed that when motivation was high, perceived motivation hardly differed for high ($M=8.64$) versus low ($M=8.23$) capacity. However, when motivation was low, there was a significant difference, perceived motivation being higher for high capacity ($M=6.54$) than for low capacity ($M=4.19$). The same held for the Motivation x Opportunity interaction. In a high-motivation condition perceived motivation was almost equal for high ($M=8.19$) and low ($M=8.68$) oppor-

TABLE 1
Aspects used to create the different scenarios

Aspect	Positive	Negative
Motivation-related aspects		
Importance of the situation	- Dinner to thank friends - Very stylish restaurant - Expensive food - Expensive wine	- Dinner with friends - Plain restaurant - Cheap food - Cheap wine
Quality of the wine	- Excellent, famous wine	- Plain, unknown wine
Capacity-related aspects		
Previous experience	- Previous visit to Paris and the restaurant	- Never visited Paris before
Knowledge of wine Knowledge of and experience with French language and customs	- Much knowledge - Familiar with French customs - Fluency in speaking French	- Little knowledge - Unfamiliar with French customs - No fluency at all in speaking French
Opportunity-related aspects		
Circumstances in the restaurant	- No person at the table started to eat yet - Very quiet, always a waiter available	- Each person at the table started to eat - Very crowded, hardly any waiter available
Time available	- Time enough, not in any hurry	- Little time, in a hurry

tunity, but in the low-motivation condition a significant difference in perceived motivation was observed between the high- and low-opportunity conditions (M_{high}=6.15, M_{low}=4.58).

Perceived Capacity. For Capacity only a main effect was found ($F(1,95)$=27.13, p<.001). High capacity resulted in a higher perceived capacity (M=7.43) than did low capacity (M=5.17).

Perceived Opportunity. Two main effects were ascertained, Capacity ($F(1,95)$=22.23, p<.001) and Opportunity ($F(1,95)$=16.64, p<.001). Perceived opportunity was higher under high-capacity conditions (M=6.88) than under low-capacity conditions (M=5.00). Also, high opportunity resulted in higher perceived opportunity (M=6.75) than did low opportunity (M=5.10).

Two conclusions can be drawn from these results. The experimental manipulations did produce differing levels ('high', 'low') of each of the Triad components. However, respondents in the low conditions scored unexpectedly high, their average score lying around the mid-point of the scale (5.00). Apparently, the manipulations did not result in conditions experienced as 'low' in an absolute sense. Secondly, the effects found other than the intended main effects seem to suggest that the manipulations of the Triad variables were not independent. However, interdependence of the experimental manipulations is just one possible explanation for the observed results. These results can also be explained by assuming that the Triad variables influence each other. For example, higher capacity can evoke higher motivation (someone who is good at doing something might be more motivated to do it), and lower opportunity (someone who is good at doing something will need less time to do it).

Probability of complaint behavior

Experimental model. The probability of complaint behavior was examined using ANCOVA with Motivation (high, low), Capacity (high, low) and Opportunity (high, low) as independent variables, and (non-manipulated) prior familiarity with the French language and customs as a covariate ($F(1,93)$=8.05, p<.01). Two cases were missing, so N=102.

Probability of Complaint Behavior was significantly associated with Motivation ($F(1,93)$=45.46, p<.001), Capacity ($F(1,93)$=58.78, p<.001), Opportunity ($F(1,93)$=5.36, p<.05), and Motivation x Opportunity ($F(1,93)$=4.60, p<.05). In Table 2 the means for the Motivation x Opportunity interaction are presented. As predicted, respondents in the high-capacity condition were more likely to complain than respondents in the low-capacity condition (M_{high}=84.00, M_{low}=44.52). The same was true for motivation: respondents scoring high on motivation were more likely to complain than respondents scoring low on motivation. This prediction held independent of the level of opportunity, but in the case of low opportunity the probability was lower (M_{high}=58.08, M_{low}=33.80). For opportunity the effect was more variegated. The probability of complaining was higher for high opportunity than for low opportunity (M_{high}=58.08, M_{low}=33.80), but only when motivation was low. When motivation was high, there was no significant difference between the high-opportunity and low-opportunity conditions (M_{high}=81.73, M_{low}=81.40).

To get an impression of the goodness of fit of the experimental model, the percentage of variance in complaint behavior explained by the model was computed. The total percentage of variance

TABLE 2

Means for the Motivation x Opportunity interaction effect for complaint behavior probability

	High motivation	Low motivation
High opportunity	81.73	58.08
Low opportunity	81.40	33.80

explained ($R^2=SS_{Explained} / SS_{Total}$) was 58.1, motivation explaining 20.5%, capacity 26.5%, opportunity 2.4%, Motivation x Opportunity 2.1%, and the remaining effects 6.6%. Capacity is the Triad variable that contributed most to the prediction of the subjective probability of complaint behavior, motivation being a good second and opportunity playing only a minor role.

Logistic model. There are two reasons justifying use of another statistical model to analyze the data from this experiment. The first reason is the conceptual complexity of the elements in the Triad model. The manipulation checks showed that the operationalizations of the Triad variables may not have been independent. The observed intercorrelations may have been caused by interaction or dynamic effects, but it is equally possible that the correlations between the Triad variables are the result of inaccurate operationalizations. If the latter is the case, the operationalizations of motivation, capacity, and opportunity were not accurate realizations of the subjectively perceived Triad factors they were intended to induce. From this perspective it might be preferable to predict complaint behavior on the basis of the subjectively perceived instead of the induced Triad variables. The second reason to employ a model based on perceived variables is theoretical in nature. The Triad model emphasizes that motivation, capacity, and opportunity as they are perceived by the person who is about to engage in a given behavior may be more important than their objective counterparts for the prediction of behavior initiation.

The relation between perceived Triad variables and the probability of complaint behavior was examined using SPSS-X Logistic Regression Analysis. Logistic regression analysis was used instead of standard multiple regression analysis because the dependent variable, viz. probability of complaint behavior, (1) was not normally divided; (2) showed no linear relation with the independent variables motivation, capacity, and opportunity; and (3) was heteroscedastic. Several models could be analysed, depending on the factors selected a priori for inclusion in the model. On theoretical grounds a multiplicative model was selected, the Triad Product being the predictive variable and the dichotomous variable Probability of Complaint Behavior (high, low) being the dependent variable. After all, the Triad model assumes that behavior is predicted by the mathematical product of a person's subjective motivation, capacity, and opportunity, which we will call the Triad Product. The regression equation was as follows:

$$\text{Subjective probability of Complaint Behavior} = \frac{1}{1 + e^{-z}}$$

in which Z=constant + β Triad Product=-2.311 + 0.015 Triad Product. The Chi-square statistic was found to be significant (χ^2 (1)=69.03, $p<.001$), indicating that at least one of the regression coefficients (in this case there is only one coefficient) was significantly different from zero. The Wald statistic showed that both the constant (Wald(1)=17.60, $p<.001$) and the Triad Product coeffi-

cient β (Wald(1)=20.92, $p<.001$) were significant. So, the Triad product was a significant predictor of the probability of complaint behavior. The positive sign of the regression coefficient indicated that an increase in the Triad product was associated with an increase in the probability of complaint behavior, confirming the hypothesis. It should be noted, however, that the power of the Triad product in predicting complaint behavior was limited, R=.38 (The squared R-value does not indicate variance accounted for like the squared R-value in regression analysis. This value does, however, give an indication of the explanatory power of the model parameters; the closer this value is to 1 the higher the explanatory power.)

Discussion

The goal of the present study was to assess whether an approach using general explanatory variables may prove useful for the study of consumer complaint behavior. In this study, the 'Triad model' was put forward as a possible relevant approach. This model proposes three critical variables (motivation, capacity, and opportunity) as simultaneous determinants of complaint behavior. Before assessing to what extent this goal was achieved we will first consider some methodological issues.

In this study scenario descriptions were used to generate high and low levels of motivation, capacity, and opportunity. Although much care was taken to ensure that the manipulations were effective, the scenario approach is an indirect approach at best. Subjects were asked to imagine themselves in a particular situation. The obvious risk is that mental constructions may be less effective in inducing the required effect than real life experiences. Although the manipulations were successful in generating differences between conditions for each main variable, the absolute levels of the manipulations were not as intended. Respondents in the 'low' conditions in fact experienced 'medium' conditions. A possible reason for this is that it is more difficult for subjects to imagine themselves being in low motivation, capacity, and opportunity conditions than in high motivation, capacity, and opportunity conditions. Here we should note that most of the subjects were likely to have had the experience of having dinner in a Paris restaurant, Paris being merely five hours by car or train from the city in which the study took place.

The results found using an experimental (ANCOVA) model are not entirely in line with the assumed multiplicative prediction of the Triad model. Instead of a third order interaction of the three factors, a main effect of capacity and an interaction effect of motivation x opportunity were found. This somewhat disappointing result may be attributed to the conceptual ambiguity of the relationship between the three general factors motivation, capacity and opportunity, and the consequences of this ambiguity for experimental manipulations of these variables. For this reason we have argued that a model based on subjective perceptions of the Triad factors may be more appropriate for the purposes of explaining complaint behavior variance. The multiplicative prediction was indeed supported when the perceived Triad variables were taken as predictors in a logistic model with the probability of complaint behavior as the criterion variable.

Despite the restrictions associated with our manipulations, the study suggests potential benefits of the approach adopted here. Even though the variance explained by the logistic model is limited, the results are in the expected direction. It should be noted that our study was probably the first attempt ever to apply a three factor model of this general nature to complaint behavior. Obviously, manipulations and operationalizations should be improved in future studies aimed at assessing the model's true explanatory power. The potential advantage of the present approach is two-fold. First, it may be useful as an explanatory model as such. For some theoretical and practical consumer complaint issues it may suffice to know to what extent behavior variance is due to motivation, capacity, or opportunity, or a combination of these. A second possible function of the model is that it may serve as a complementary approach in studies where more isolated and more specific variables are the primary focus of interest. The addition of motivation, perceived capacity and perceived opportunity as research factors would not only facilitate the interpretation of the effect of the manipulation (if any), but would also stimulate interstudy comparisons. It is for these theoretical and meta-theoretical reasons that future research in this direction is warranted.

REFERENCES

Andrews, J. Craig (1988), "Motivation, Ability, and Opportunity to Process Information: Conceptual and Experimental Manipulation Issues," *Advances in Consumer Research*, Vol. 15, 219-225.

Batra, Rajeev and Michael L. Ray (1986), "Situational Effects of Advertising Repetition: The Moderating Influence of Motivation, Ability, and Opportunity to Respond," *Journal of Consumer Research*, Vol. 12, 432-445.

Day, Ralph L. (1980), "Research Perspectives on Consumer Complaining Behavior," in *Theoretical Developments in Marketing*, eds. Charles W. Lamb, Jr. and Patrick M. Dunne, Chicago, IL: American Marketing Association, 211-215.

_____ and Stephen B. Ash (1979), "Consumer Response to Dissatisfaction with Durable Products," *Advances in Consumer Research*, Vol. 6, 438-440.

_____ and Muzaffer Bodur (1977), "A Comprehensive Study of Satisfaction with Consumer Services, " in *Consumer Satisfaction, Dissatisfaction and Complaining Behavior*, ed. Ralph L. Day, Indiana University School of Business, 64-74.

_____ and Muzaffer Bodur (1978), "Consumer Response to Dissatisfaction with Services and Intangibles," *Advances in Consumer Research*, Vol. 5, 263-272.

_____ and E. Laird Landon, Jr. (1975), "Collecting Comprehensive Consumer Complaint Data by Survey Research", *Advances in Consumer Research*, Vol. 3, 263-268.

_____ and E. Laird Landon, Jr. (1977), "Toward a Theory of Consumer Complaining Behavior," in *Consumer and Industrial Buying Behavior*, eds. Arch G. Woodside, J. N. Sheth and P. D. Bennett, New York, NY: North-Holland, 425-437.

_____, Klaus Grabicke, Thomas Schaetzle, and Fritz Staubach (1981), "The Hidden Agenda of Consumer Complaining," *Journal of Retailing*, Vol. 57 (3), 87-106.

Hirschmann, Albert O. (1970), *Exit, Voice and Loyalty: Responses to Decline in Firms, Organizations and States*, Cambridge, MA: Harvard University Press.

Jacoby, Jacob, and James J. Jaccard (1981), "The Sources, Meaning, and Validity of Consumer Complaint Behavior: A Psychological Analysis," *Journal of Retailing*, Vol. 57 (3), 5-24.

Kolodinsky, Jane (1992), "A System for Estimating Complaints, Complaint Resolution andSubsequent Purchases of Professional and Personal Services," *Journal of Consumer Satisfaction, Dissatisfaction and Complaining Behavior*, Vol. 5, 36-44.

_____ (1993), "Complaints, Redress, and Subsequent Purchases of Medical Services by Dissatisfied Consumers," *Journal of Consumer Policy*, Vol. 16, 193-214.

_____ (1995), "Usefulness of Economics in Explaining Consumer Complaints," *Journal of Consumer Affairs*, Vol. 29 (1), 29-54.

_____ and John Aleong (1990), "An Integrated Model of Consumer Complaint Action Applied to Services: A Pilot Study," *Journal of Consumer Satisfaction, Dissatisfaction, and Complaining Behavior*, Vol. 3, 61-67.

Krishnan, S. and Valerie A. Valle (1979), "Dissatisfaction Attributions and Consumer Complaint Behavior," *Advances in Consumer Research*, Vol. 6, 445-449.

MacInnis, Deborah J., Christine Moorman, and Bernard J. Jaworski (1991), "Enhancing and Measuring Consumers' Motivation, Opportunity, and Ability to Process Brand Information from Ads," *Journal of Marketing*, Vol. 55, 32-53.

Maute, Manfred F. and William R. Forrester, Jr. (1993), "The Structure and Determinants of Consumer Complaint Intentions and Behavior," *Journal of Economic Psychology*, Vol. 14, 219-247.

Petty, Richard E. and John T. Cacioppo (1986), *Central and Peripheral Routes to Attitude Change*, New York, NY: Springer-Verlag.

Poiesz, Th. B. C. and Robben, H. S. J., "Motivation, Capacity, and Opportunity to Process Commercial Communication," in Advances in Consumer Research, Vol. 23, ed. Corfman, MI: Association for Consumer Research. (accepted for publication)

Singh, Jagdip (1988), "Consumer Complaint Intentions and Behavior: Definitional and Taxonomical Issues," *Journal of Marketing*, Vol. 52, 93-107.

"I Want To Believe": A Netnography of The X-Philes' Subculture of Consumption

Robert V. Kozinets, Queens University

Mulder: "Hey Scully, do you believe in the afterlife?"
Scully: "I'd settle for a life in this one."
"Shadows"

On 10 September 1993, a daring new television drama debuted on the Fox television network. Created by Chris Carter, *The X-Files* television series features the bizarre exploits of FBI agents Fox Mulder and Dana Scully. These two agents work on the "X-files," cases that have unexplainable elements and often involve the paranormal.

The X-Files features a nearly inseparable juxtaposition of truth and fiction drawn from popular conspiracy theories and belief in supernatural powers. Three canonical maxims summarize the show's guiding philosophy: "Trust No One," "I Want to Believe" and "The Truth Is Out There." Despite these individualist mottoes, *The X-Files* has inspired a large and growing fan culture.

Fans of *The X-Files* wasted no time in coining their own nickname: 'X-Philes,' the 'phile' derived from the Greek word *philos*, meaning 'to love'.... few shows have prompted the sort of emphatic viewer response as *The X-Files* has in such a relatively short time period. Indeed, as with any cultural phenomenon, fan reaction to the series has become as much a part of *The X-Files* story as the show itself, from the conventions that have sprung up around the country to the hours of chat about the series whipping around each week on the Internet." (Lowry 1995: 239).

X-Philes are characterized by their enthusiastic devotion to the series, as well as their sophisticated connoisseurship of all things relating to it. X-Philes are a subset of all viewers of the television series, a "small percentage" of the more than 14 million regular viewers who tune in to the series on an average week (Lowry 1995: 242). Typical viewers of the series are young, urban and educated (Lowry 1995: 22).[1]

The existence of fans is an important cultural phenomenon that has been a part of our social reality since mass media were first developed. The Lisa Lewis edited (1992) volume *The Adoring Audience* considers this history in its examination of the multifaceted relationship between fans, stars, media texts and the media industry. Through a range of contexts ranging from Beatlemania to Elvis worship to science fiction conventions, the contributors to this volume argue that fan behavior has been dismissed by scholars as deviant or trivial. However, they suggest that fandom is a complex, contradictory and fascinating arena that affects a wide range of social behaviors, including consumer behavior, and is therefore worthy of serious academic attention.

Recently, Schouten and McAlexander (1995: 43) defined a "subculture of consumption" as "a distinct subgroup of society that self-selects on the basis of a shared commitment to a particular product class, brand, or consumption activity." The "X-Philes subculture of consumption" (abbreviated to XPSC) thus may represent a transferable site (Lincoln and Guba 1985, Wallendorf and Belk 1989) for studying the consumption of entertainment by

subcultures and these subculture's impact on the consumption of related artifacts and services.

Studying fan cultures such as the X-Philes as subcultures of consumption allows researchers insights into contemporary consumer behavior by (1) exploring the relationship between mass media programming and consumption (see Hirschman 1988, Holbrook and Hirschman 1993), (2) adding to our understanding of the ways in which social values and attitudes are created, expressed and maintained through subcultures of consumption, and mediated by popular culture, and (3) understanding how these cultures are created and maintained, particularly using new communications technologies such as the Internet. Because of its focus on consumption-related meanings, the focal research question of this investigation is "What are the key characteristics of X-Philes consumption practices and how do they extend and inform our knowledge of contemporary consumer behavior?"

METHOD

Data Collection

This ethnography of X-Philes culture was undertaken as part of a larger consumer behavior research project investigating mass media culture and a major fan movement within that culture. However, the investigation possesses sufficient depth and scope to be considered a separate endeavor in its own right. The ability to construct a "thick description" (Geertz 1973, Arnould and Wallendorf 1994) may, however, be constrained by the necessarily limited size of the text.

Data collection by the sole author took place in three venues over a seven-month period that began in August 1995. A form of site triangulation (Wallendorf and Belk 1989) was employed through the use of multiple sites for sampling X-Philes culture. The sampling sites consisted of three areas of highly visible X-Phile activity: at two three-day media fan-related conventions (one which featured Chris Carter as guest of honor), at a media fan club, and on several *X-Files* related sections of the Internet,[2] particularly The Official X-Files Fan Forum on the Official X-Files Web Site (at http://www.thex-files.com) and the Usenet group<alt.tv.x-files>.

The term *netnography*[3] refers to the textual output of Internet-related field work. This paper defines a *netnography* as *a written account of on-line cyberculture, informed by the methods of cultural anthropology*. Cyberculture refers to culture that is mediated by contemporary computerized communications technology (i.e., "the Internet"). Researchers in marketing are beginning to explore consumption and cultural activities on the Internet (e.g., Fischer, Bristor and Gainer 1995).

Netnography as a type of research inquiry is quite new, and hence has few guidelines. The validity of netnographic data may be subject to many of the same validity concerns and evaluations as other types of qualitative data (for guidelines and discussion see Denzin and Lincoln 1994: 479-480; Lincoln and Guba 1985; Wallendorf and Belk 1989). The Internet audience combines computer literacy with other types of technological literacy —in

---

[1] It might be interesting to note that this same group is often the source of recruits for religious and other "cults" requiring high levels of personal devotion (see Cushman 1984).

[2] The entire arena of discussion of *The X-Files* on the Internet is termed "the X-Net" by X-Philes.

[3] I am indebted to an anonymous reviewer for suggested this revised term.

this case television literacy. It thus presents consumer researchers with an interesting site of intersection between the private and public spheres, where the audiencing consumption of television programming overlaps with the interactive cyberculture of Internet use.[4] The XPSC is an excellent site to study this cultural negotiation, because it apparently is the most Internet-active community of fans of any current television show (Lowry 1995: 240-2).

Jenkins and a research assistant[5] (Tulloch and Jenkins 1995: 281-2) "closely monitored the interactions of two computer discussion groups" related to another media fan culture. Jenkins described the reasons he found Internet observation important to his ethnographic project:

> monitoring the nets allowed us to observe the regular interactions of community members within a context that is neither created nor directed by the researcher; that can be legitimately observed without any invasion of privacy or interference with its activity; that offers a dense cluster of information about the group's interpretive categories=and discursive resources.

Due to the richness of this method, this investigation focuses mainly on the analysis of netnographic data. All direct quotations are from Internet sources. However, the mainly observational stance of the researcher in the netnographic component of this work is balanced by *observation of participation* (Tedlock 1991) in the other sampled sites. In observation of participation the researcher actively participates in the studied culture. Participation in several panels and discussions at conventions, at fan club meetings, during informal interviews with media fans, combined with X-Phile fan activities such as viewing and reviewing the show and reading *X-Files* related materials constitutes a prolonged engagement of approximately 350 hours in duration. This prolonged engagement was utilized as a form of triangulation of analysis (Wallendorf and Belk 1989). It also provided indirect quotes, personal involvement in the X-Philes culture, and enhanced cultural fluency.

Ethical Issues

It might be helpful if ethical issues pertaining to this research were briefly addressed, particularly because it involves a new type of research. Although all the Internet areas used are unrestricted publicly accessible forums, to meet ethical research standards, all names of participants were changed in this ethnography so as to ensure confidentiality. In the interest of ensuring informed consent, contact by e-mail was established with all persons whose direct quotations have been used to attempt to gain an extra level of consent. Most of the XPSC members contacted said that they were "flattered" or "honored" to be quoted in this research. Of the fifteen persons contacted, only one asked that their quotation —related to their UFO sighting—not be used. That persons who posted messages to a public forum would still deny the right to quote them in research testifies to the necessity of contacting them and receiving their informed consent. In this ethnography, only persons who provided their informed consent were quoted.

XPSC members contacted through the fan club and through conventions were guaranteed anonymity, and were apprised that the researcher is performing cultural research, thus again establishing informed consent and confidentiality. The use of member checks to solicit comments provided another measure of informed consent to X-Philes members.

Data Analysis

Data was recorded on paper notes, in written and word-processed journal entries, in saved computer files, and in photographs of fans. Archival material such as fan literature and brochures was also collected. A holographic sampling frame (Denzin and Lincoln 1994: 202) was utilized, whereby specific sites are analyzed for their insights into universal phenomena.

The data collected totaled 83,150 words, contained on 606 double-spaced pages. This data was read approximately 9 times, and analyzed using the constant comparative method, categorization, abstraction, and the holistic search for unifying themes (Spiggle 1994). Contacts with fan club members, and with X-Net participants were established and this contact was utilized to perform "member checks" that proved helpful in the revision of the text (Lincoln and Guba 1985, Wallendorf and Belk 1989). Nine interested X-Philes were provided with a complete copy of the text, that had not been rewritten for lay readers. Six XPSC members returned comments. The comments were favorable, and supported the contention that the ethnography was an "accurate and fair" portrayal of X-Philes culture. Among additional comments were some which noted the presence of different subgroups or "subsubcultures" within the XPSC community, Chris Carter's assurances to minimize "overmerchandising," and enforcement of group standards by the e-mail practice of "flaming"[6]. Other comments noted the attraction of the relationship between the show's two protagonists and the series' high production values. The member checks led to the alteration of the text by including these elements.

THEMES

The X-Philes culture is diverse, constituting people from many locations, many age and demographic groups, and many ethnic backgrounds (Lowry 1995: 240). This investigation focuses on three foundational themes that unite this diverse group of people into an X-Philes culture. The culture is based on shared aesthetic tastes, shared experience of awe and mystery, and a shared drive to consume the symbols related to *The X-Files*. The motivations underlying these themes might be termed *"The Meaning Is Out There," "I Want To Believe,"* and *"Trust This One."* These themes are explicitly integrated into the single theme of an individualistic and faith-driven quest to uncover a deeply hidden "Truth," a covert "mystery" theme that also often pervades religious and other sacred cultural beliefs (Belk, Wallendorf and Sherry 1989). Chris Carter, *The X-Files'* creator, says that he thinks the show is "all about religion, really. Not necessarily Christian religion, but it's about beliefs —and meaning and truth" (Stegall 1996: 24).

Finding the "true" interpretation of the television show is obvious in the first theme, the theme of *Negotiating Aesthetic Consumption Standards*, in which fans gather to discuss the consumption of the shows and to collectively build categories for judging their quality. The second unifying theme, *Consuming Beliefs About Mysterious Experiences*, refers to The X-Philes attraction to mysterious paranormal narratives, such as those regarding UFOs, religious manifestations, and psychic abilities. The XPSC's *Connection Through Consumption of Artifacts and Services* is the third theme. These consumption goods and services offer tangible manifestations of the mysterious. They also offer

---

[4] I am also indebted to an anonymous reviewer for this interesting point.

[5] The assistant was not the co-author of the volume, John Tulloch, but presumably a hired student researcher.

[6] Flaming is the practice of sending embarrassing and insulting e-mail messages to a person's mailbox or in response to their public Usenet posting.

opportunities for building communitas both in person and over the Internet. The three themes will be explored in turn.

"The Meaning Is Out There": Negotiating Aesthetic Consumption Standards

A significant amount of activity in the X-Philes cultures can be conceptualized as the socialization of evaluative standards. Consuming media entertainment is an important part of XPSC members' lives, and they create evaluative standards that are well-considered, consistent, and articulated in great depth. Fans negotiate and teach each other these standards regarding *The X-Files* episodes, plots, characters, images, and products. As McCracken (1990: 34) notes, social groups such as subcultures seek to distinguish themselves through cultivating "certain kinds of knowledge." This knowledge can include aesthetic categorization schemes denoting "good taste" regarding their interests. As Bourdieu (1984) notes, "taste classifies, and classifies the classifier." This construction of tastes is a key activity of consumption subcultures, defining the boundaries of their shared interpretations of social reality.

The reception of "Teso Dos Bichos," an episode of *The X-Files* that first aired on 8 March 1996, provides an example of the manner in which episodes are used to teach this "classifying taste." Among members of the XPSC, a clear consensus appeared that the show was "a letdown" and "disappointing," sentiments explained in the following posting by "Matthew": 7

> Man, this thing was all over the place. I appreciate it when they try and put a little bit of a curveball in there, but I also appreciate it when at some future point it becomes coherent. Instead, this just spun out of control. . . . Okay. So it's a jaguar spirit, but it's also a feral-cat spirit?. . . . If the thing can be a jaguar to off the guy in the parking lot, why couldn't it have been a jaguar down in the steam tunnels? Answer: Because if Scully saw it, she wouldn't have been able to come up with her scientific explanation.

In this posting, Matthew not only points out what was wrong with the episode, he notes why it was wrong, and which aesthetic standard was being violated. These comments articulate a "coherency" evaluative criterion. The show, although it is recognizably fiction, must work to maintain the suspension of disbelief necessary for viewers to fully enjoy its consumption as a possible real-world experience. The show must be internally consistent, carefully maintaining the rules of its own universe. As Matthew states, contradictions such as jaguar-feral cat can not simply be left unresolved. Otherwise, the intentions of the writers become transparent and thus reduce the enjoyment of the show. Even the extraordinary must believably conform to physical limitations. "Leanne" noted "What's up with these killer kitties? A cat cannot kill a human! Even if it is possessed by some spiritual dude."

As well, the show must conform to standards of tastefulness in the wider social community, and not excessively "gross-out" its core audience. Sam, another fan, reinforces Matthew's' later comments about the high "gross-out-visual factor" of "rats in toilets." Sam adds, "What's with the glistening entrails-thing anyway? This is two eps in a row we've been treated to human viscera and small furry animals eating the same."

Aesthetic standards extend to shared assessments of actor's physical characteristics. The "David Duchovny Estrogen Brigade" is a homepage, an e-mail list, and a public forum for several dozen women who highly admire "the work" of the actor who plays Agent Fox Mulder. Many of these brigade members also share stories (some of them erotic in nature) featuring the character of Mulder. This XPSC subgroup focuses on an actor. Its members negotiate standards that might enhance the hedonic pleasure (Holbrook and Hirschman 1982) of audiovisually experiencing —and fantasizing about— the actors' televisual and romantic presence.

It is important to note the parallels of these empirical findings with Scott's (1994) and Stern's (1989) use of reader-response theory. As individual viewers of the show, XPSC members "read" meanings from the text of the television shows. They act as skeptical, knowledgeable, imaginative and even resistant readers (Scott 1994). This reading experience is initially idiosyncratic for isolated viewers, but then becomes *collective* subsequent to contact with the fan culture on the Internet. Meanings initially garnered as individuals are then negotiated as a group. For instance, "Martina" originally interpreted the feral cats in "Teso Dos Bichos" as nonphysical manifestations. However, after prompting and explanations from other X-Philes, she changed her interpretation to accord with that of other XPSC members.

> OK, I've thought better of it—the feral cats probably *were* real. . . . I just assumed they were illusions because they vanished at the end of the ep. Could be...doesn't have to be. I'll go with it.

This alteration of taste confirms Scott's (1994: 463) contention that reading is not "completely idiosyncratic," and is "based on collective conventions" allowing for "shared responses." In member checks, some XPSC members pointed out that a lack of conformance to aesthetic standards was often enforced through the persuasive threat of communal "flaming." The relative anonymity of e-mail and postings may contribute to greater license being taken in flaming than would be taken in issuing insults in person. As a positive incentive, throwing off one's idiosyncratic meanings in favor of shared meanings may also contribute to a long-term sense of communitas, defined as the "transcending camaraderie of status equality" and communion with others (Belk, Wallendorf and Sherry 1999: 7). These observations portray the learning, enforcement and reinforcement of these collective conventions in action in the XPSC.

"I Want To Believe": Consuming Beliefs About Mysterious Experiences

Marshall McLuhan posited that television programming reflects humanity's unconscious mind and is therefore our collective dream. *The X-Files* episodes might reflect humanity's collective nightmares and delusions, exploring frightening, paranoid corners of our modern mental world. TV guide calls *The X-Files* a "whole new kind of dark, subversive program" and notes that Chris Carter says that the show is "very dark" "in its tone, mood and look" (Saddy 1995: 15). Based on this core devotion to the darkly mysterious, XPSC members build communitas based on their shared exploration of this creepy threshold, united in their "want to believe."

X-Philes' core devotion to the show seems to depend on its ability to draw on and ambiguously extend extant paranormal and government conspiracy accounts. Chris Carter claims that he was convinced of *The X-Files'* commercial viability by a Roper Organization poll showing that three percent of the U.S. population "believes they've been abducted by aliens" (Lowry 1995: 11). Several fan club X-Philes noted that the conspiracy theories drawn on by *The X-Files* were particularly interesting to them, and that their belief in UFOs predated the show. Panel members at a

---

7To guarantee anonymity, the names of all culture members have been changed.

convention said that their interest in *The X-Files* originated in the "serious way" in which it treated UFOs and governmental UFO conspiracy or cover-up theories. They pointed to actual government cover-ups —such as "CIA testing of LSD on civilians"— to justify their faith in the show's precepts.

An open forum for discussion of these beliefs is also present on the X-Net. A particularly dramatic and dominant area of interest was personal information regarding UFO sightings. "Cassandra" shares her sighting by posting it on the X-Net:

> A couple of nights ago I was driving with my dad and saw these two bright white lights just hanging in the sky. Or so I thought. Then they started moving, kinda slowly. As the lights moved on, a blinking red light appeared between the two white ones, and further on, another white light came into view, making a perfect triangle with the little red light in the middle.

Many XPSC members seem embarrassed by the act of sharing their UFO experiences, likely because this is stigmatic behavior in "normal" society. Some note that they "feel kind of stupid doing this," or ask others to "please contact me if you believe me because others say that I am crazy". Yet the XPSC remains an open forum for the extended discussion of these experiences, providing a unique sanctuary for their display.

XPSC members also produce communitas by sharing their belief in mysterious government conspiracies. Several fan club members expressed their mistrust of "all governments," and their belief in a "worldwide UFO conspiracy". On the Internet, similar confessions could easily be found. On the Usenet group, "Dudley" enthusiastically shares his belief in UFOs and governments conspiracies:

> Greetings all! I'm [Dudley], a believer! I feel that it is my responsibility to tell the truth! . . . . People think that UFO's, Aliens, etc are just Hollywood fantasies. It's not true! It is not true! . . . . Don't be a fool ! Be a believer!

Other XPSC members share somber assessments of conspiracy theories. "Marcus" notes that "one day the truth will finally be presented, and not suppressed under a government's heavy cloak of darkness". Spiritual beliefs and theories were also evident on the X-Net. Some XPSC members, such as "Ted," see belief in UFOs as part of a larger spiritual process that humanity is currently experiencing:

> For the past few years now, I've noticed a dramatic change in the awareness of the paranormal. But not just the paranormal, more spiritual as well. ... As we enter the next century, and grow as a mass, I believe that we will grow into a very spiritual society that will learn to except that we are not alone in the universe.

X-Philes thus consume mysterious and mystical notions through *The X-Files* show and through their Internet activities and membership in the XPSC. As noted by Belk, Wallendorf and Sherry (1989), mystery is an important element of the sacred. Mystery is "above the ordinary" and derives from "profound experiences and meanings" (p. 7). Consumers are increasingly turning to secular sources —such as television shows, and the subcultures of consumption that spring up based on them— to fulfill their deep-seated need for connection with the sacred. It is also possible that in our faithless, hyper-rational and scientific society, many people crave the excitement and energy that the only the unexplained can inspire. Cushman (1984) notes that many people in our current social era are psycho-

logically characterized by an "empty self" that may seek to be filled up by an all-consuming spiritual or religious "truth," or through mass consumption of material objects, or both (Cushman 1990).

The X-Files draws on profound and extraordinary events, mysteries ranging from UFOs to religious phenomena such as reincarnation and stigmata to psychic abilities. Through repeated pairings, the television show and its many associated symbols become associated with these profound symbols. The sacred meaning is transferred (McCracken 1990) and the show itself, its characters and trademarked symbols, becomes sacred.

"Trust This One": Connection Through Consumption Of Artifacts and Services

The X-Philes subculture is based upon shared aesthetic standards regarding the television show, shared mysteries, and a shared belief in the sacred nature of the show. The embodiment of these notions finds its expression in a variety of artifacts drawn from the television series and services related to the show. In this theme, it is suggested that these goods intensify the spiritually fulfilling experience of *The X-Files*, deepening both the feeling of devotion to the series and the communitas felt towards other XPSC members.

An instance of attempting to bring items and images from the show into subculture members' daily lives is provided by "Simon." Simon asks other X-Philes "Where can I find the poster behind Mulder's desk that says 'I Want To Believe' [and contains a picture of a flying saucer]." Presumably, possessing this poster will intensify the experience of being an X-Phile through its immediate physical presence, symbolically announce Simon's fan status to others, and help to connect Simon to the transcendent world of *The X-Files* through evoking its symbolic vocabulary of UFOs and belief. Beyond this, the poster itself both verbally and pictorially reinforces the themes that attract people to the show: belief in the paranormal, in UFOs and, perhaps, simply belief in *something*.

Subculture members desire to bring other elements of *The X-Files* into their daily lives. One X-Phile admires the "equipment used on the show" and expresses a desire to buy "one of the flashlights they use." Other fans inquire about the availability and content of the upcoming music album based on the series. Fans even conceive of new products such as RPGs (role-playing games) that they would like to see developed. All of these products share an emphasis on intensification of *The X-Files* experience, of bringing symbols from the show more concretely into the lived experiences of the XPSC members.

Members of the XPSC reinforce the value of official products through publicizing their capacity for providing hedonic experiential pleasure (Holbrook and Hirschman 1982). "Constance" shares her enthusiasm for official *X-Files* merchandise in terms that might make many marketers envious:

> I am so excited about the month of March. I must've been born under a lucky star or something. The X-Files videos, X-Files "soundtrack" and 2 new episodes to tickle my fancy

XPSC members collectively negotiate acceptable quality and price standards. "Franklin," a collector of the *Topps X-Files Cards* notes that their "quality control" is poor, since he found missing cards in packages, and the distribution of "premium cards" was inconsistent. Price warnings are also communicated to culture members. "Kathryn" states that, after seeing *The X-Files* videos selling for "$19.95," "I feel like I have been mugged." Another XPSC member replies that fans should take this as a "Rip-Off Alert," because he was able to purchase the same videos for a much lower price. These communications can be interpreted as a resistant reading of product offerings, or even as a form of consumer activism. This type of information exchange builds trust, and further differentiates the longer-term communitas of the X-Philes community from the more time-delimited and self-interested exchanges of strangers.

Exchange of information about products and services promotes social adhesion. Exchange of information and exchange of physical artifacts tie the community together by promoting dyadic interaction. There is a considerable amount of trading, buying and selling activity on the X-Net. Fans seek missing editions of comic books, or trading cards, or they may simply want to determine "what something's worth." Sharing items of common value, and remarking on their worth, is another way X-Philes reinforce the merit of their mutual fascination with *The X-Files*.

For some subculture members, the fascination may become stressfully overwhelming. The member might even feel a need to join the on-line group XPA —"X-Philes Anonymous". As "Kevin," a member of XPA notes, XPA has no pretension of actually "curing you of your obsession for the X-Files. It is more like a support group, where you can talk about your problem." However, Kevin states that he has "NO desire whatsoever to be cured!.... This group is for the people that are a lost cause!!!"

Notwithstanding XPA, the X-Philes subculture of consumption members are not going to relinquish their affection for the show, and the multifaceted cyberculture and fan culture based on its consumption. For, despite any anguish the show might cause, as one member exuberantly expressed it:

I think The X-files is the most amazing show on earth and it should be shown until the end of time!!!!!!!!!!!!

Conclusion

Studying mass media fan cultures such as The X-Philes subculture of consumption holds several important insights into contemporary consumer behavior. First, it should be noted that individual audiencing of television programming is an extremely complex act, one that resembles the interactive view of interpretation related in reader-response theories (Scott 1994, Stern 1989). The television viewer, far from a mere passive receiver of meanings, actively, skeptically, and creatively constructs an interpretation of the meaning of the television show, both by building on prior television series, episodes of the same series, and related information regarding the series gleaned from other sources such as TV viewing guides. This finding underlines the importance of reader response theories to understanding the consumption of entertainment media and other performances (Deighton 1994).

Second, it is important to note that among fans (and perhaps among other less involved consumers) the consumption of mass media messages is subculturally mediated. Interpretation is significantly collective in the XPSC. Mass media meanings no longer reside solely in individuals, but are negotiated, enforced communally and presumably *intensified* —through consumption-related exchanges such as this research found occurring over the Internet. These exchanges focus on the enthusiasm and preference for consumption goods and services, their attributes, and even acts of resistant activism regarding their purchase and consumption. As access to sophisticated communication technology continues to proliferate, and as its use in the lives of individuals mounts, the consumption-negotiation and consumer-activism behavior of the X-Net XPSC members may become more and more commonplace in society at large.

Third, the need to consume the mysterious, and to speculate on the spiritual seems to fulfill a specific heartfelt desire for belief in Truths that extend beyond the ordinary, providing support for a specific aspect of Belk, Wallendorf and Sherry's (1989) theory.

This profound need to fill an achingly empty self with spiritual or sacred faith —and consumption— appears to be manifest in the deep devotion of XPSC members and may be related to that particular brand of anomie that seemingly afflicts the young, urban, and educated of the Western world (Cushman 1984, 1990). However, an important insight of this research is the mass mediated, commoditized nature of the sacred experience of XPSC members. For X-Philes, consumption of the show is a sacred experience, occurring during a sacred time slot, and the act of discussing the show transforms the Internet into a sacred space[8] (Belk, Wallendorf and Sherry 1989). This intimate relationship between entertainment media, spiritual beliefs, mass commodification and consumption is an area that might be transferable to explorations of other consumption behavior and subcultures of consumption, such as those based around sports, music, and "high culture."

Finally, this investigation points to the importance of popular culture in the lived experience of contemporary consumers. Popular culture is not merely a vehicle for advertisements, but is itself an exceedingly potent driver of consumption. The images and symbols of popular culture programs such as *The X-Files* provide a new vocabulary for the construction of culture, community, and meaning.

REFERENCES

Arnould, Eric J. and Melanie Wallendorf (1994), "Market-Oriented Ethnography: Interpretation Building and Marketing Strategy Formulation," *Journal of Marketing Research*, 31 (November), 484-504.

Belk, Russell W., Melanie Wallendorf and John F. Sherry, Jr. (1989), "The Sacred and the Profane: Theodicy on the Odyssey," *Journal of Consumer Research*, 16 (June), 1-38.

Bourdieu, Pierre (1984), *Distinction: A Social Critique of the Judgment of Taste*, Cambridge: Harvard University Press.

Cushman, Philip (1984), "The Politics of Vulnerability: Youth In Religious Cults," *Psychohistory Review*, 12, 5-17.

Cushman, Philip (1990), "Why the Self Is Empty: Toward a Historically Situated Psychology," *American Psychologist*, 45 (May), 599-611.

Deighton, John (1991), "The Consumption of Performance," *Journal of Consumer Research*, 19 (December), 362-372.

Denzin, Norman K. and Yvonna S. Lincoln (1994), *Handbook of Qualitative Research*, Thousand Oaks, CA: Sage.

Fischer, Eileen, Bristor, Julia, and Brenda Gainer (1995), "Creating or Escaping Community? An Exploratory Study of Internet Consumers' Behaviors." Paper presented at the 1995 Association for Consumer Research Annual Conference.

Geertz, Clifford (1973), *The Interpretation of Cultures*, New York: Basic Books.

Hirschman, Elizabeth (1988), "The Ideology of Consumption: A Structural-Syntactical Analysis of 'Dallas' and 'Dynasty,'" *Journal of Consumer Research*, 15 (December), 344-359.

Holbrook, Morris B. and Elizabeth C. Hirschman (1993), The Semiotics of Consumption: Interpreting Symbolic Consumer Behavior in *Popular Culture and Works of Art*, Berlin: de Gruyter.

Holbrook, Morris B. and Elizabeth C. Hirschman (1982), "The Experiential Aspects of Consumption: Consumer Fantasies, Feelings, and Fun," *Journal of Consumer Research*, 9 (September), 132-140.

---

[8]This insight was provided by an anonymous reviewer comment.

Lewis, Lisa (1992), *The Adoring Audience: Fan Culture and Popular Media*, New York: Routledge, Chapman and Hall.

Lincoln, Yvonna and Egon G. Guba (1985), *Naturalistic Inquiry*, Beverly Hills, CA: Sage.

Lowry, Brian (1995), *The Truth Is Out There: The Official Guide To The X-Files*, New York: Harper Collins.

McCracken, Grant (1990), *Culture and Consumption: New Approaches to the Symbolic Character of Consumer Goods and Activities*, Bloomington and Indianapolis: Indiana University Press.

Saddy, Guy (1995), "Entertainer Of The Year: The X-Files Open Up," *TV Guide*, December 30, 1995.

Schouten, John W. and James H. McAlexander (1995), "Subcultures of Consumption: An Ethnography of the New Bikers," *Journal of Consumer Research*, 22 (June), 43-61.

Scott, Linda M. (1994), "The Bridge from Text to Mind: Adapting Reader-Response Theory to Consumer Research," *Journal of Consumer Research*, 21 (December), 461-80.

Spiggle, Susan (1994) "Analysis and Interpretation of Qualitative Data in Consumer Research," *Journal of Consumer Research*, 21 (December), 491-503.

Stegall, Sarah (1996), "It's In His Hands: Interview With Chris Carter," *The X-Files Magazine*, 1, Winter.

Stern, Barbara B. (1989), "Literary Criticism and Consumer Research: Overview and Illustrative Analysis," *Journal of Consumer Research*, 16 (December), 322-334.

Tedlock, Barbara (1991), "From Participant Observation to the Observation of Participation: The Emergence of Narrative Ethnography," *Journal of Anthropological Research*, 47 (1), 69-94.

Tulloch, John and Henry Jenkins (1995), *Science Fiction Audiences,* London and New York: Routledge.

Wallendorf, Melanie and Russell W. Belk (1989), "Assessing Trustworthiness in Naturalistic Consumer Research," *Interpretive Consumer Research*, ed. Elizabeth C. Hirschman, Provo, UT: Association for Consumer Research, 69-84.

Andy Warhol: Consumer Researcher

Jonathan E. Schroeder, University of Rhode Island

ABSTRACT

This paper "breaks out of the box" by discussing the work of the artist Andy Warhol as a form of consumer research. The paper asserts that Warhol's career— successful artist, experimental film-maker, prolific writer and diarist, celebrity—offers insights into consumer culture that reinforces, expands, and illuminates aspects of traditional consumer research. Through illustrations, criticism, and interpretation, five specific areas of consumer research that Warhol's work might contribute to are introduced: brand equity; clothing, fashion and beauty; imagery; packaging; and self-concept. This project joins recent efforts by consumer researchers to include humanities based methods such as literary criticism and semiotics into the consumer researcher's toolbox.

I love America and these are some comments on it. The image is a statement of the symbols of the harsh impersonal products and brash materialistic objects on which America is built today. It is a projection of everything that can be bought and sold, the practical but important symbols that sustain us.
— Warhol 1985, p. 78

Humanities based research has changed the parameters of consumer research. Groundbreaking applications of semiotics (Mick 1986), literary theory (Stern 1988; 1989) postmodernism (Firat and Venkatesh 1995), history (Jones and Monieson 1990), visual studies (Scott 1994)—to name a few—have broadened the consumer researcher's palette, adding useful tools to an interdisciplinary paintbox. Belk proposes that art offers a useful medium to study consumption—citing literature, comics, painting, photography, etc., as valuable records of materialism and non-traditional sources of data for consumer researchers (Belk, 1986). Art and science do differ in their methods, biases, and purposes, Belk insists, but there is much more overlap than is usually thought. He concludes by suggesting that uses of art in research "are attempts to draw on art as data for evidence to validate a point or to provide a thicker, richer description" (Belk, 1986, p. 27).

This paper proposes that Andy Warhol—through his world-wide success as an artist, his choice of subject matter, his public statements, and his marketing techniques—may offer insights into several issues of consumer research as an additional way of learning about consumer behavior (Belk, Wallendorf, and Sherry 1989; Hudson and Ozanne 1988; Sherry 1991). Through a turn to the tools of art criticism and art history, Warhol's "contributions" to our understanding of consumer behavior are placed within the frame of consumer research. Warhol, while not trained in experimental methods, nonetheless offers unique insights into consumer behavior through his success as an artist who focused on the mass produced world of brand names, fame, and consumption.

In his career as a commercial illustrator, artist, filmmaker, and author, Warhol produced a voluminous output of material. After his death in 1987, his estate helped fund an Andy Warhol museum in Pittsburgh (Sozanski 1994); another museum houses his work in his ancestral home of Slovakia (Gruber 1993). His name lives on in the news; his estate auction garnered millions and elevated cookie jars into the realm of valued collectors' items (Bourdon 1989). A protracted battle over the value of his estate also served to generate heated interest in his stature as an artist and cultural icon (Peers 1996). Warhol transcended the rarefied world of fine art and became known simply as Andy Warhol throughout the world. His

obituary in *Advertising Age* remembered Warhol this way: "His work pointed out the similarities between mass produced goods— soup, cleaners, celebrities, news "events"—in a way that made clearer how images are manufactured. In this pop culture, Andy Warhol saw America. Through him, America saw itself." (Skenazy, 1987). Breaking out of the box, this paper sketches Warhol and his work for their relevance to consumer researchers.

To frame Warhol as a consumer researcher, this discussion focuses on four aspects of the Warhol oeuvre: several famous artworks, his own writings, critical discourse, and Warhol himself. The methods, training, and outlook of artists and consumer researchers may be quite different, but the underlying issues they are interested in often overlap considerably. Five content areas were selected to paint a portrait of Warhol as consumer researcher: brand equity; clothing, fashion and beauty; imagery; packaging; and self-concept. Two levels of analysis are offered—one focuses the production of Warhol's art, another considers Warhol himself as the ultimate commodity. Thus, Warhol's artistic output can be scrutinized for insights into consumer behavior as well as his self-generated production of the Warhol "brand." Suggestions for systematic application of art criticism and art history are offered, along with a call for broadening the conceptions of who might contribute to the interdisciplinary field of consumer research.

ART AND CONSUMER RESEARCH

Art Criticism is the humanities discipline that investigates art and its objects as cultural documents—reflecting and shaping the culture that both produces and preserves them. Discourse on art has ancient roots—visual images preceded written language as a means of communication. Closely linked to the related fields of aesthetics, art history, art theory, and archeology, art criticism requires an understanding of the styles and functions of art, the social and cultural contexts in which artists have worked, and the technical factors that affect artistic execution. Issues that art criticism addresses include evaluation, value, classification, identification, comparison, etc. (Stokstad 1995). Commentary on art has its origins in Plato's dialogues, in which he established representation as the main function of art; the field of art history became institutionalized within academia during the nineteenth century (Roskill 1989). Like literary criticism, writing on art is characterized by a myriad of schools employing a variety of approaches to the subject, context, meaning, and production of art (cf. Stern 1989). Because art has physical—as in architecture—as well as cultural functions, the object of study varies considerably, depending on the purpose of the analysis. For example, one writer distinguishes between journalistic criticism, pedagogical criticism, and scholarly criticism (Feldman 1987). The art world of museums, collectors, scholars, and the public has increasingly included 'low' forms of art, for example graffiti, advertising, comics, etc. within the realm of fine art—thus focusing critical attention on a wide range of visual communication (e.g. Stich 1987).

Whereas the field of art criticism conceivably offers consumer researchers an astonishing array of tools with which to interpret and understand images, few studies within consumer research have taken advantage of a art-centered approach. However, many art historians have ventured into issues of consumer behavior. For example, Simon Schama discusses many aspects central to consumer research in his monumental study of Dutch art, such as collecting, demand, luxury goods, etc. (Schama 1988). Other art historians take a consumer research approach to the art market, demonstrating that art is governed by market forces similar to manufactured goods (e.g. Watson 1992; Goldthwaite 1993; Jenson 1994). For example, Goldthwaite (1993) includes a chapter titled "Consumer Behavior" in his thorough analysis of the art market during the Italian Renaissance. While art historians are surveying consumption of art, consumer researchers have been slow to turn to art to analyze consumption—a central feature of the culture that art depicts, packages, comments on, and is sold within. One recent paper recognizes the influence of the art market in corporate strategy, dubbing corporate sponsors of art "the Modern Medicis" (Joy 1993). However, most consumer research from an art centered approach focuses on advertising—an important, but limited, application of the rich tradition of art history (Ball and Smith 1992).

For example, Scott's (1994) exceptional system for analyzing visual rhetoric, which borrows language and systems from art history, focuses on advertising imagery. Stern and Schroeder's (1994) turn to literary and visual theory to analyze a Paco Rabanne cologne advertisement. Promising extensions of the use of art based approaches include Percy's (1993) use of art history to look at brand equity; Heisler and Levy's (1991) photography based research technique, autodriving; and Havlena and Holak's work on nostalgic images (1996). Following Belk's (1986) call for art based research on materialism, Schroeder (1992) investigated the connections between materialism and the Pop Art movement, demonstrating the complex links between a consumer research derived concept and artwork. The draw toward art based criticism prompted this observation: "investigating the Pop Art movement through a consumer research framework can shed light on consumption; Pop Art provides impressive and eloquent content to examine materialism" (Schroeder 1992, p. 13).

Another stream of consumer research has focused on aesthetics—an important branch of art history useful for scholars interested in the phenomenology of consumption (e.g. Holbrook and Zirlin 1985). Aesthetics within the consumer context usually refers to a response to a sensory stimulus produced by media, entertainment, or the arts (Holbrook 1980). What sets artistic responses apart is an appreciation of the stimulus for its own sake. Painting, then, enjoys a esthetic reaction due to its existence as a end in itself, rather than a means to some other end. For example, Holbrook has called for a study of the experience of art and its creation as a basis for understanding aesthetics within artistic organizations (Holbrook & Zirlin, 1985). Aesthetics and our perceptual systems are integral to our understanding and appreciation of art (e.g. Arnheim, 1966). The role of the image is critical in understanding issues central to mainstream consumer research—perception, categorization, brand image, advertising response, for example. Thus, borrowing from art criticism seems a logical choice for a more complete analysis of consumer behavior, with the goals of understanding the historical, cultural, and representational contexts of consumption.

CONSUMPTION INTO ART: ANDY WARHOL AND THE POP ART MOVEMENT

By preempting the celebrity of his subjects–from Campbell's soup and Coca-Cola to Marilyn Monroe and Elvis Presley–[Warhol] parlayed his own name and face into commercial commodities that became recognized—and valued—around the world —Bourdon 1989, p. 9

Pop art utilized subjects "that anybody walking down Broadway could recognize in a split second–comics, picnic tables, men's trousers, celebrities, shower curtains, refrigerators, Coke bottles–all the great modern things" (Stokstad 1995, p. 1130). Pop bor-

rowed from the world of advertising, grocery stores, billboards, television, etc., to an unprecedented degree. Warhol, in particular, focused on the objects he consumed on a daily basis—Campbell's soup, Coca-cola, money, famous people, and newspapers. These are stimulus materials for many consumer behavior studies, and provide an important link between the world of art and the realm of consumer research. Depicting material goods and consumer artifacts was not entirely new to the art world. The history of painting is replete with examples of scenes of wealth, possessions, and display (e.g. Berger, 1972). The Dutch, to illustrate, favored paintings of the abundant goods an affluent society produces (Schama 1988). What set Pop apart is the critical and commercial success of a group of artists, all having a common concern with the problems of the commercial image and popular culture (Mashun, 1987).

The Pop movement was, in part, a reaction to the current dominant form of painting of the day, Abstract Expressionism, which focused on the inner imagination of the artist and the technique of creating art. In contrast, Pop artists drew from the popular culture in achieving an easily recognizable and reproducible art form. Warhol realized that people receive the same message over and over, and often like messages or images sheerly through repetition exposure (see Figure). He claimed to eat the same thing day after day, including—yes, indeed—cans of Campbell's soup and lots of Coca-cola.

Unconcerned with painterly style and brushwork, many Pop artists utilized mass production techniques in their work. Indeed, several influential Pop artists, including Warhol, were trained in commercial art and printing and advertising techniques. Pop Art gained commercial and popular (if not always critical) acceptance in the early 1960s. Along with Andy Warhol, success came rapidly for artists such as James Rosenquist, Tom Wesselmann, Claes Oldenburg, and Roy Lichtenstein. Warhol, however, became an icon for the movement, and was dubbed the Pope of Pop.

Warhol was trained in commercial art at Carnegie Institute of Technology (now part of Carnegie Mellon University) and was a highly successful commercial artist in New York City during the 1950s. His advertising work won him several awards and constant work (Bourdon 1989). Warhol's forays into fine art—producing images not driven by specific commercial jobs—drew its inspiration from comic strips and advertising slogans. His first huge success resulted from the Campbell's Soup can series, which attracted widespread attention and notoriety (e.g. Stuckey, 1989; Swenson, 1963, 1964). Other works of this period include the Coca-Cola series, consisting of repeated images of Coke bottles, Brillo box wood sculptures, reproductions of commercial shipping containers, and celebrity portraits. He produced many self portraits throughout his career, as well as dozens of films, several books, and, after he was famous, continued to do commercial work (Bourdon 1971; Hackett 1989; Warhol 1975, 1983, 1985). The Andy Warhol Museum opened its doors in Pittsburgh in 1994, and is the largest museum in the U.S. devoted to a single artist (Sozanski 1994). Currently, his work commands high prices at auction (Vogel 1993), and the "cult" is alive and well (e.g. Gruber 1993).

WARHOL'S CONTRIBUTION TO UNDERSTANDING CONSUMER BEHAVIOR

An analysis of five areas of consumer behavior in terms of Warhol's work and reactions to it demonstrates the potential of placing art within consumer research. The five areas were chosen for this study to demonstrate the diverse potential of turning to visual artists to understand consumer behavior. As a masterful producer of cultural discourse, Warhol isolated and reified the banal and commonplace objects of consumption. Insight gleaned from this exercise complements and reinforces concepts and ideas developed by consumer researchers. This multi-method approach is capable of offering confirmation of experimental research findings, generating new research ideas, and uncovering hidden aspects of consumer behavior. Material for this analysis is drawn from several sources; the art itself; critical comments; Warhol's own reflections and quips; and scholarly writing about Warhol. Warhol's statements are notoriously unreliable—he constantly misled interviews about his background and intentions (Bourdon 1989). However, for the purposes of this paper, his comments provide interesting findings about an accomplished marketer whose most successful product was himself.

Since the birth of Modernism around the turn of the century, a significant project for artists is the development of an individual style (Jenson 1994). Thus, art history might offer lessons in brand equity—an identifiable trademark, designed for consumption (Percy 1993). Andy Warhol was extremely successful in building his own version of brand equity, interestingly enough by using an imitator strategy of adopting ready made symbols in his art.

BRAND EQUITY

Andy Warhol developed one of the most globally recognizable styles in the history of art, even though his work lacked signature brushwork or technique (Stokstad 1995). Moreover, of course, many of his most famous subjects were originally designed by others—the Brillo box designer sued Warhol for breach of copyright (he lost) (Bourdon 1989). Despite the fact that he did not "create" the original image, Warhol became irrevocably linked to his flat depictions of Campbell's soup cans. In essence, then, he developed a strong brand identity and brand equity. By introducing images that were easily identified and linked with himself as an artist, Warhol achieved his own style—in marketing terms, his own brand: "it is one the many paradoxes of Warhol's career that [his images] should be so inescapably his own" (Rockwell 1991, p 347). He aggressively pursued potential buyers for his art; "his metamorphosis into a Pop persona was calculated and deliberate" (Bourdon 1989, p. 6).

Warhol changed the way we look at products, especially Campbell's soup. The Campbell's brand has meaning apart from that of a heavily advertised consumer product, because of Warhol's art and ensuing fame. Indeed, the Campbell's soup company, initially antagonized by Warhol's use of their trademark, hired him to paint a series of Campbell's dry mix soup cartons in the 1980s (Honnef 1991). Warhol's major work prefigured scholarly attention of brand equity, but he was very aware of the powerful associations found in his Pop images: "Andy always seized on the most familiar and recognizable objects" (Bourdon 1989, p. 90). Popular brands tended to promote equal opportunity for consumers, Warhol stated in a famous quote: "A Coke is a Coke, and no amount of money can get you a better Coke" (Warhol 1975, p. 100). His eye, trained in art, and focused on mainstream success and fame, gave him "an uncanny gift for selecting motifs from the glut of visual information characteristic of a modern industrial society overwhelmed by consumer products, newspapers, magazines, photographs, television, and the cinema" (Livingstone 1990, p. 118). Warhol was a shrewd marketer of both his work, and perhaps more significantly, his image. His background in advertising assisted him in knowing what sells and how to sell it.

Through his international success, Andy Warhol became a major "brand" himself, allowing him to command high prices for his prolific output, and amassed a fortune valued at $400 million after his death (Peers 1996). Andy's persona matched that of his art—detached but friendly, familiar, yet distant. His pursuit of fame was legendary, he became a product endorser through his celebrity, appearing in ads for a variety of products (Pomeroy 1971). In 1986, he came full circle by creating Absolut Warhol, thus inaugurating the artist produced Absolut Vodka series. Warhol was a shrewd marketer, his public image designed for maximum impact and appeal. He was driven a desire to be famous—for anything: "I wish I could invent something like bluejeans. Something to be remembered by. Something mass" (Warhol 1975, p. 13). Warhol assured his immortality through the creation of the richly endowed Andy Warhol Foundation for the Visual Arts, which helped develop the Andy Warhol Museum in Pittsburgh. His success has become its own icon: "Warhol's *Dollar Signs* are brazen, perhaps even insolent reminders that pictures by brand-name artists are metaphors for money, a situation that never troubled him" (Bourdon 1989, p. 384).

Warhol also attempted to create "superstars"—celebrities known for their association with him. He had some success in promoting the careers of the rock group The Velvet Underground, the film personality Edie Sedgwick, and an entourage at his studio, dubbed the Factory. This is an interesting example of brand extensions—new "products" associated with old favorites. Warhol was tremendously invested in his "aura," and one company expressed interest in securing his services to promote their products (Bourdon 1989). Warhol represents a charismatic figure totally concerned with strategically marketing the ultimate commodity, oneself. He was careful not to become confused with other early pop artists, such as Roy Liechtenstein, who worked with comics. His insights and concerns with his identity will be addressed further under "self-concept."

Warhol showed us that a well recognized brand name might succeed in attracting consumers in a different context—brand extension. He demonstrated that consumer's positive feelings about products often lay far outside the product itself—he did not paint Campbell's soup, after all, he painted the branded can. His success was phenomenal evidence that brands are psychological entities, with associations far outside the context of consumption. Moreover, he showed that equity is linked to recognizability. Advertisers may have known this far some time, but Warhol's contribution extends beyond the domain of marketing—for his art has created an extra layer of brand equity to such well-known products as Campbell's soup and Coca-Cola. Cigarette brands like Camel and Marlboro are pursuing this concept by selling clothing and Marlboro gear to consumers. Harley Davidson figured out that they can sell more t-shirts and wallets than motorcycles. Coca-Cola has started selling clothing. Perhaps these are more sophisticated examples of brand value, but Warhol remains an compelling figure in the history of brand equity.

CLOTHING, FASHION AND BEAUTY

Warhol was fascinated with celebrities and was profoundly affected by Marilyn Monroe's suicide in 1962. He began to work on a series of paintings of her, starting with a publicity photograph of her he had purchased. In the next several years, he produced what many art critics consider to be his strongest work, the Marilyn series. In the work, Warhol used a silk-screen technique to highlight Monroe's features with brighter than life colors. In this period he began experimenting with repetition, mass production, and "mistakes"—poorly aligned images and smudges. In a famous image, *Marilyn Monroe Twenty Times*, Warhol experiments with repeated the image of Monroe over and over, creating subtle differences in each repetition, while maintaining the mass produced appearance of a consumer good. Moreover, his work comments on the reproduction of images, art, and originality (see Benjamin 1968).

FIGURE 1
Campbell's Soup Can and Dollar Bills, 1962

Celebrities are like goods, Warhol seemed to be saying, by creating similar works with Coca-cola bottles, S & H Green Stamps, and even U.S. currency. Warhol helps us realize that celebrities have brand equity, consumer awareness, etc. In Warhol's paintings, Monroe gazes coolly out at the viewer behind a publicity smile and heavily applied makeup. Warhol felt these paintings were an homage to Monroe's beauty and fame, but art critics have pointed out the ghoulish nature of reproducing the image of a beauty queen amidst evidence of a tragic life and death (Mamiya 1992). In one example, a single image of Monroe is surrounded by a field of gold, like a Byzantine icon: "By symbolically treating the famous actress as a saint, Warhol shed light on his own fascination with fame" (Livingstone 1991). Warhol shows us the construction of fame and beauty. He was perennially dissatisfied with his looks, undergoing plastic surgery and wearing a wig at all times. His portraits of Liz Taylor and Jackie Kennedy also dealt with issues of fame, beauty, and tragedy. Once again, his choice of material rings true— tragic undertones infuse many great works of art and literature. Warhol returned to Marilyn Monroe several times throughout his career, producing an eerie reverse-color series late in his career. In *Reverse Marilyn*, the image is as recognizable from his earlier work as from Monroe's fame—but it seems fraught with trauma, her face darkened and eyes glowing as if on fire. Warhol was willing to show us how we consume celebrities, while also providing a thoughtful reminder of the discrepancies between public persona and private identity. This theme was tremendously important in his own life, as evidenced by his friends and his written work. Warhol was always on stage, even when writing in his diaries, which were produced for public consumption (Hackett 1989).

IMAGERY

Mr. Warhol was among the first to point out that we are a country united, most of all, by commercialism. He opened our eyes with art. Whether silk-screening soup cans or Marilyn Monroe, he showed us that the things we know best and react to most instinctively are those images brought to us via mass markets, mass media, and mass production.
—Skenazy 1987

Imagery is the area that Warhol made perhaps the most profound contributions to issues of consumer behavior. Warhol injected many images into the cultural discourse. His repeated motifs are classics of twentieth century art. Warhol investigated ideas of originality and the original image through his choice of subject matter, technique, and reproduction (silk-screen, prints, reworking). His success, however, was in becoming an icon himself, the image of a fabulously famous artist. His preeminence as a cultural icon is summarized as follows: "In the postwar era, if an artist wants to do more than merely fuel the art apparatus, the most effective strategies usually involve working with the institutions of culture. The artist who most fully met this challenge and who is the paradigm of the artist-producer is Andy Warhol" (Staniszewski, 1995, p. 262). Another critic concurs: "Warhol's art represented the culmination of dilemmas about the relationship of art, media, and advertising that artists had confronted since the turn of the century" (Bogart 1995, p 300).

Warhol's most successful images are tied into the mainstream cultural symbols–abundance, mass marketed products, images of the good life. His subject matter revolves around high involvement images . His art, and the Warhol phenomenon instructs us in how we consume images and symbols. When his household belongings were auctioned, Sotheby's estimates were far exceeded, commonplace cookie jars sold for $1000. People were eager to own

something that belonged to him—he probably would have been thrilled. His image had been carefully constructed–his wigs became progressively more noticeable and odd, his face often caked with white foundation and make-up. He was an original, yet his art blatantly copied mainstream designs. He reflected the ideal of mass marketing techniques—appealing to uniqueness through consuming mass produced goods: "Buying is much more American than thinking and I'm as American as they come" (Warhol 1975, p. 229).

PACKAGING

Warhol's "boxes" series isolates package design, focusing our attention on the package as an object in its own right. These works are wooden sculptures, made to look exactly like shipping cartons for popular consumer goods–Del Monte canned fruits, Brillo cleaning pads, Campbell's soup. Warhol achieved a great deal of notoriety, scorn, and press from the boxes series, and they remain some of his most successful works. In the Campbell's soup can painting series, Warhol takes a close look at packaging, too. In *Big Torn Soup Can*, for example, he shows us the package behind the label, calling attention to the object of consumption. In this painting, a brand extension, if you will, of his earlier soup can paintings, the Campbell's label is torn, hanging off the can, but still instantly recognizable. The can is exposed, and in some hints of a painterly technique, its steel case reflects light toward the viewer. One is struck by the dual packaging of the image—the label and the can. The can looks plain, uncovered, unlabeled without the Red and White Campbell's. We realize that labels reassure us of safe contents, protecting us from harm. Once again, product designers and market tests might pick up these insights, but Warhol made them available for all. He also fixed his attention on the packaging of Coca-cola, painting the patented bottle over and over.

Warhol's work comments on the packaging of celebrities, as well. Marilyn Monroe and Elvis Presley, two of his major subjects, both lived desperate lives in marked contrast to the media image they enjoyed. By choosing their publicity images, Warhol deliberately pointed out contradictions of the package. However, the image of Marilyn Monroe as a beauty outlived her personal anguish, with Warhol's disturbing portraits of her a vague reminder of her private pain.

SELF-CONCEPT

Writing about Warhol's cultural contributions in 1971, one art critic suggested that one of his most important contributions was to show the evolution of a personal mythology by means of an extremely consistent persona (Josephson 1971). Warhol's self portraits are an interesting study in an expression of the self-concept. He was fascinated in the relationships between image and reality—especially his own: "It must be hard to be a model, because you'd want to look like the photograph of you, and you can't ever look that way" (Warhol 1975 p. 63). He completed many self-portraits throughout his career, eventually adopting his repeated techniques for his own image.

In all of his self portraits, he remains aloof, composed, and very much Andy Warhol. It is his self-portraits that are the most well known images of Warhol as a person. Thus, he controls his image by producing it. Warhol's many self-portraits can be viewed as a great marketing campaign for himself. For a Pop exhibition in Germany, he provided a huge self-portrait—a glorious ad for Andy Warhol (Bourdon 1989). Warhol knew that the best marketing for his art was the creation of celebrity, and his self-portraits were an important component of this strategy. Warhol's public record shows a remarkable consistency throughout his career, stretching back into his college years, that is a hallmark of psychological conceptions of the self-concept. His self-portraits offer evidence of the construction of self-concept; a process we all engage in, albeit with somewhat less intention than Warhol.

CONCLUSIONS

Warhol's impact on art and society was tremendous; this paper offers a highly restricted view of his potential for consumer researchers. By applying some methods of art criticism to his vast body of work, insight was gained in key areas of consumer research: brand equity; clothing, fashion and beauty; imagery; packaging; and self-concept. Art history is equipped with much more theoretically challenging theories and frameworks—this paper gleaned insights from a surface skimming of the treasures of art criticism and art history. Further work is necessary to articulate how art historical techniques might complement literary tools that have earned a place within the consumer researcher's toolbox.

As we move into a postmodern society, dominated by visual images, informed by five hundred cable television channels, and obsessed with global symbols, visual literacy takes on greater importance to both the consumer and marketer. Art criticism seems a useful area to study the central role images play in consumer behavior—joining successful applications of other humanities based approaches. Marketing, in particular, encourages symbolic associations: products to images, images to products. To fully understand consumer behavior requires an appreciation of the long heritage of art scholarship. This project represents a step toward mining the rich ground of art history to extract nuggets of wisdom about consumers and the society they live in.

REFERENCES

Arnheim, Rudolf (1966), *Toward a Psychology of Art*, Berkeley: University of California Press.

Ball, Michael S. and Gregory W. H. Smith (1992), *Analyzing Visual Data*, Newbury Park, CA: Sage.

Belk, Russell W. (1986), "Art versus Science as Ways of Generating Knowledge about Materialism," in *Perspectives on Methodology in Consumer Research*, ed. David Brinberg and Richard J. Lutz, New York: Springer-Verlag, 3-36.

_____, Melanie Wallendorf, and John F. Sherry, Jr. (1989), "The Sacred and the Profane: Theodicy on the Odyssey," *Journal of Consumer Research*, 16 (June), 1-38.

Benjamin, Walter (1968), *Illuminations*, trans. Hannah Arendt, New York: Schocken.

Berger, John (1972), *Ways of Seeing*, London: Penguin/BBC. Press.

Bogart, Michele H. (1995), *Artists, Advertising, and the Borders of Art*, Chicago: University of Chicago Press.

Bourdon, David (1971), "Warhol as Filmmaker," *Art News*, 59 (3), 48-53.

_____ (1989), *Warhol*, New York: Abradale Press.

Feldman, Edward B. (1987), *The Varieties of Visual Experience*, 3rd ed., New York: Prentice Hall/Abrams.

Firat, A. Fuat and Alladi Venkatesh (1995), "Liberatory Postmodernism and the Reenchantment of Consumption," *Journal of Consumer Research*, 22 (December), 239-267.

Goldthwaite, Richard A. (1993), *Wealth and the Demand for Art in Italy 1300-1600*, Baltimore: John Hopkins University Press.

Gruber, Ruth Ellen (1993), "Warhol Pops Up in Carpathia," *New York Times*, February 21, 23.

Hackett, Pat (ed.) (1989), *The Andy Warhol Diaries*, New York: Warner.

Havlena, William J. and Susan L. Holak (1996), "Exploring Nostalgia Imagery Through the Use of Consumer Collages," in *Advances in Consumer Research*, vol. 23, ed. Kim P. Corfman and John G. Lynch, Provo: UT: Association for Consumer Research, 35-42.

Heisley, Deborah A. and Sidney J. Levy (1991), "Autodriving: A Photoelecitation Technique," *Journal of Consumer Research*, 18 (December), 257-273.

Holbrook, Morris B. (1980), "Some Preliminary Notes on Research in Consumer Esthetics," in *Advances in Consumer Research*, vol. 7, ed., Jerry Olson, Provo: Association for Consumer Research, 104-108.

_____, and R. B. Zirlin (1985), "Artistic Creation, Artworks and Aesthetic Appreciation," in *Advances in Nonprofit Marketing*, vol. 1, ed. Russell Belk Greenwich, CT: JAI Press, 1-54.

Honnef, Klaus (1991), *Andy Warhol: Commerce into Art*, Koln, Germany: Benedikt Tachen.

Hudson, Laurel Anderson, and Julie L. Ozanne (1988), "Alternative Ways of Seeking Knowledge in Consumer Research," *Journal of Consumer Research*, 14 (March), 508-521.

Jensen, Robert (1994), *Marketing Modernism in Fin-de-Siècle Europe*, Princeton, NJ: Princeton University Press.

Johnston, Jill (1989), "The Artist in a Coca-Cola World," in *Pop Art: The Critical Dialogue*, ed. Carol A. Mashun, Ann Arbor: UMI Research Press, 41-47.

Jones, Brian D. G., and David D. Monieson (1990), "Historical Research in Marketing: Retrospect and Prospect," *Journal of the Academy of Marketing Science*, 18 (4), 269-278.

Josephson, Mary (1971), "Warhol: The Medium as Cultural Artifact," *Art News*, 59 (May-June), 41-47.

Joy, Annamma (1993), "The Modern Medicis: Corporations as Consumers of Art," in *Research in Consumer Behavior*, vol. 6, ed. Russell W. Belk, New York: JAI Press, 29-54.

Lippard, Lucy R. (1966), *Pop Art*, New York: Thames and Hudson.

Livingstone, Marco (1990), *Pop Art: A Continuing History*, New York: Abrams.

_____ (1991), *Pop Art, An International Perspective*, New York: Rizzoli.

Mahsun, Carol A. (1987), *Pop Art and the Critics*, Ann Arbor: UMI Research Press.

Mamiya, Christin J. (1992), *Pop Art and Consumer Culture*, Austin: University of Texas Press.

Mick, David Glen (1986), "Consumer Research and Semiotics: Exploring the Morphology of Signs, Symbols, and Significance," *Journal of Consumer Research*, 13 (September), 196-213.

Peers, Alexandra (1996), "Court Upholds Value of Warhol's Estate," *Wall Street Journal*, February 9, B2.

Percy, Larry (1993), "Brand Equity, Images, and Culture: Lessons from Art History," in *European Advances in Consumer Research*, vol. 1, eds. W. Fred van Raaij and Gary Bamossy, Provo, UT: Association for Consumer Research, 569-573.

Pomeroy, Ralph (1971), "The Importance of Being Andy Andy Andy Andy Andy," *Arts & Artists*, (February), 14-19.

Rockwell, John (1991), *The Meanings of Modern Art*, rev. ed., New York: Museum of Modern Art/HarperCollins.

Roskill, Mark (1989), *What is Art History?* Amherst: University of Massachusetts Press.

Runyon, William M. (1981), "Why Did Van Gogh Cut Off His Ear? The Problem of Alternative Explanations in Psychobiography," *Journal of Personality and Social Psychology*, 40, 1070-1077.

Schama, Simon (1988), *The Embarrassment of Riches: An Interpretation of Dutch Culture in the Golden Age*, Berkeley: University of California Press.

Schroeder, Jonathan E. (1992), "Materialism and Modern Art," in *Meaning, Measure, and Morality of Materialism*, ed. Floyd Rudmin and Marsha Richins, Provo, UT: Association for Consumer Research, 10-14.

Scott, Linda A. (1994), "Images of Advertising; The Need for a Theory of Visual Rhetoric," *Journal of Consumer Research*, 21 (September), 252-273.

Sherry, John F. Jr. (1991), "Postmodern Alternatives: The Interpretive Turn in Consumer Research," in *Handbook of Consumer Behavior*, ed. Thomas S. Robertson and Harold H. Kassarjian, Englewood Cliffs, NJ: Prentice-Hall, 548-591.

Skenazy, Lenore (1987), "Andy Warhol, R.I.P.," *Advertising Age*, March 2, 72.

Smith, Ruth Ann, and David S. Lux (1993), "Historical Method in Consumer Research: Developing Causal Explanations of Change," *Journal of Consumer Research*, 19 (March), 595-610.

Sozanski, Edward J. (1994), "Andy Warhol goes Home," *Chicago Tribune*, June 19, 13:18-20.

Staniszewski, Mary Anne (1995), *Believing is Seeing: Creating the Culture of Art*, New York: Penguin.

Stern, Barbara B. (1988), "Medieval Allegory: Roots of Advertising Strategy for the Mass Market," *Journal of Marketing*, 52 (July), 84-94.

_____ (1989), "Literary Criticism and Consumer Research: Overview and Illustrative Analysis," *Journal of Consumer Research*, 16 (December), 322-334.

_____ and Jonathan E. Schroeder (1994), "Interpretive Methodology from Art and Literary Criticism: A Humanistic Approach to Advertising Imagery," *European Journal of Marketing*, 28 (September), 114-132.

Stich, Sidra (1987), *Made in U.S.A.: An Americanization in Modern Art, the '50s and '60s*, Berkeley: University of California Press.

Stokstad, Marilyn (1995), *Art History*, New York: Abrams.

Stuckey, C. F. (1989). Warhol in Context, in *The Work of Andy Warhol*, ed. G. Garrels, Seattle: Bay Press, 3-33.

Swenson, G. (1963), "What is Pop Art? Part 1," *Artnews*, 62, 25-27, 61, 62.

_____ (1964), "What is Pop Art? Part 2," *Artnews*, 62, 40-43, 62-67.

Vogel, Carol (1993), "A Sotheby's Sale offers the Tops in Pop," *New York Times*, April 9, C23.

Warhol, Andy, (1975), *The Philosophy of Andy Warhol*, San Diego: Harvest/HBJ.

_____ (1983), *Popism: The Warhol Sixties*, New York: Harper & Row.

_____ (1985), *America*, New York: Harper.

Watson, Peter (1992), *From Manet to Manhattan: The Rise of the Modern Art Market*, New York: Random House.

Wilson, Simon (1974), *Pop*, London: Thames & Hudson.

Yenawine, Philip (1991), *How to Look at Modern Art*, New York: Abrams.

The Impact of Cultural Symbols on Advertising Effectiveness: A Theory of Intercultural Accommodation

Jonna L. Holland, University of Nebraska–Omaha
James W. Gentry, University of Nebraska–Lincoln

ABSTRACT

In a country experiencing increasing cultural diversity, the use of target marketing toward ethnic groups can generate strong emotions and controversy on occasion. We introduce a Theory of Intercultural Accommodation to explain differential reactions within an ethnic group to the use of cultural symbols in advertisements. We report the results of an exploratory study which provides partial support for key aspects of the theory.

As the world becomes more diverse and intercultural interactions expand, marketers are increasingly aware of the need to improve communication with groups from varying cultural backgrounds. How can marketers enhance communication by using the target group's language, symbols, and cultural markers as a common backdrop without being patronizing or manipulative? This paper begins the process of providing empirical support for a framework which addresses this issue, the Theory of Intercultural Accommodation. It is based on Socio-linguistic Accommodation Theory, but is broader in scope. Similarity-Attractiveness research serves as a common underpinning to both. The purpose of the current work is to (1) outline briefly the key components of the theory, and (2) provide empirical support for a critical portion of the overall model.

First, what is meant by "Intercultural Accommodation"? In this research, the term is used to indicate those efforts on the part of communicators to make themselves more similar to members of another cultural group in order to improve communication. In marketing, Intercultural Accommodation could be manifested at various strategic levels. For example, in marketing communications, the domain of accommodation behaviors would include such things as using spokespersons of similar ethnic background in advertisements, hiring ethnic salespeople, or using language, music, art, national flags or other cultural symbols as part of the brand or promotion. From a distribution perspective, accommodation behaviors might entail locating a retail outlet in the ethnic community, or franchising to ethnic proprietors. Intercultural Accommodation could also take place at the organizational level in areas such as minority hiring practices, or support of ethnic community causes or scholarships.

The term Intercultural is used to convey the idea that this communication is occurring across at least two cultures. In the United States, typically the organizational communication is originating in the dominant Anglo culture, and is targeted at one or more ethnic cultures, African-American, Hispanic-American, Korean-American, etc. Intercultural Accommodation involves communicators of one group borrowing cultural symbols from another group in order to appear more similar, enhance communication, and gain approval.

How does the presence of cultural symbols in an ad impact its effectiveness? What happens when customers react negatively to accommodation attempts, and what happens when they react favorably? The goal of this paper is to answer these questions and increase our understanding of Intercultural Accommodation. A critical portion of the model will be tested in the context of print advertising targeted to African Americans. First, a brief review of the existing literature on marketing to ethnic groups will demonstrate that these questions have not been addressed in research to date. Next, the Intercultural Accommodation model will be presented as a potential framework for filling these gaps. The hypotheses for one portion of the model will be developed and tested, followed by a discussion of the results of the experiment. And finally, the conclusion will provide directions for future research on this phenomenon.

PREVIOUS RESEARCH ON MARKETING TO ETHNIC GROUPS

A brief overview of previous research in North America on marketing to ethnic groups will serve as a frame for the current study. In general, work in this area can be divided into three eras. First, prior to the 1960s, ethnic groups were largely ignored. Ethnic groups were not considered to be viable market segments and there was no effort to target them or conduct research in this area (Kassarjian 1969). The second era began roughly in the mid-1960s and continued until about 1980. During this period, societal changes caused a reevaluation of the role of previously ignored consumer groups. As far as ethnic groups were concerned, marketers and researchers focused almost exclusively on African-Americans. Blacks began to appear more frequently and in higher status positions in advertisements (Kassarjian 1969). Research during this period was characterized by descriptive analyses of the differences between Black and White consumers in their consumption patterns, media habits, and reactions to advertising (Sturdivant 1973). Little attention was paid to other ethnic groups or to more fundamental questions such as why differences in consumption may exist, or what values may influence ethnic consumer's reaction to marketing stimuli (Hirschman 1981a).

The third era of research on marketing to ethnic groups began in the 1980s and continues today. This stream of work has been concerned more with a variety of ethnic groups and examines ethnicity from an emic, rather than etic, perspective. The more recent studies tend to examine the unique nature and situation of ethnic groups to form hypotheses a priori about why ethnicity may impact consumption behavior. These studies also focus on a wider variety of issues such as Acculturation (O'Guinn and Faber 1985; Penaloza 1994; Reilly and Wallendorf 1987), Situational Ethnicity (Stayman and Deshpande 1989), and the Strength of Ethnic Identification (Deshpande, et al. 1986; Hirschman 1981a; O'Guinn and Meyer 1983; Whittler, Calantone, and Young 1991).

These studies move beyond the descriptive and begin to reveal significant differences in consumption patterns and values between Anglo and ethnic consumers. For example, Stroman and Becker (1987) found differences in media usage between Black and White consumers, even after controlling for SES. Hirschman provided evidence for differences in hedonic consumption (1982), and novelty seeking, information transfer, and divergent processing ability (1981b) among a variety of ethnic groups. Webster (1992) demonstrated differences between high and low Hispanic identifiers in the relative influence of various advertising vehicles, word-of-mouth, and point of purchase displays. While most of these studies found differences between Anglos and the particular ethnic group of interest, many also found differences within the ethnic group, between strong and weak identifiers.

If there are differences in consumption patterns, response to promotional efforts, media habits, and even consumption values between Anglo and ethnic consumers, then a customized marketing mix appears justified. As mentioned earlier, ethnic target marketing is increasing, spurred by the growth in minority media and minority advertising agencies (Campanelli 1991; Delener and Neelankavil 1990), as well as by the realization that these consumption differences exist.

However, the primary gap in our understanding is the consumer's response to targeting attempts. How does the consumer feel about marketers accommodating their culture? Ethnic target marketing has not been examined from the consumer's point of view. We have no theory, models, or evidence to explain or predict how the consumer may respond to a targeted effort. It is generally assumed that the ethnic consumer will react favorably to a message targeted to his/her specific cultural group. Do we have evidence to support this assumption? This research seeks to address these issues, and contribute to our understanding of ethnic target marketing.

At this point in the analysis, what is needed is a theoretical foundation that will help us understand how the consumer may receive and react to targeted messages. We looked to socio-linguistics for research on communication between two cultures. The following section will review relevant literature to provide a theoretical foundation for the proposed model and hypotheses.

SPEECH ACCOMMODATION THEORY

Speech Accommodation Theory (SAT) emerged in the early seventies (Giles, Coupland, and Coupland 1991), and was grounded primarily in Similarity-Attractiveness research (Byrne 1961; Simons, Berkowitz, and Moyer 1970). Studies showed that as A becomes more similar to B, the likelihood is increased that B will favorably evaluate A. Developers of SAT focused on behaviors limited to the socio-linguistic domain (verbal and non-verbal behaviors) such as speech rate (Webb 1970), accent (Giles 1973), and length of utterance (Matarazzo, et al. 1968). When people were motivated to seek approval or improve communication, their speech patterns would converge, or become more similar to the other party's. When a communicator wished to distance him/herself from the other, a pattern of divergence would emerge. This pattern of convergence and divergence is the basis of SAT.

SAT has been applied to settings as varied as health care, court rooms, and bi-lingual education (Giles, Coupland, and Coupland 1991). Bell (1991) applied these concepts to the mass media and found that, although separated by place and often by time, communicators and audience members nonetheless participate in accommodation. Mass communicators obviously have the twin motives of winning the approval of their audience, and of communication effectiveness to justify their use of media. They accommodate their audience by using communication patterns that match those of the intended receiver.

SAT has frequently been used to understand communication patterns across cultures (Bourhis and Giles 1977; Giles, Taylor, and Bourhis 1973). This stream of research found support for the basic tenants of Speech Accommodation Theory; that is, when people want to enhance communication, they make an effort to adopt the language or speech patterns of the other party. When people want to discontinue communication, a pattern of divergence develops.

Extension of SAT to Promotion

In the context of intercultural communication, companies attempt to accommodate their targeted audience by adapting their messages to the receivers' culture. They often go beyond merely matching their target's speech or language styles, however, and use many aspects of cultural symbols to become more similar to and gain the approval of their audience. Despite the apparent applicability to target marketing, the only study in the marketing literature to draw on SAT research is Koslow, Shamdasani, and Touchstone (1994). The authors examined Hispanic consumers' reactions to the use of Spanish in advertisements. They hypothesized that "for accommodation to occur, Hispanics must perceive the choice and use of Spanish in the advertisement as an indicator of the advertiser's respect for the Hispanic Culture and desire to break down cultural barriers through reduction of linguistic dissimilarities" (Koslow, et al. 1994, p. 576). They measured ethnic identification, attitude toward Spanish, attitude toward English, perception of the advertiser's awareness of Hispanic needs and respect for Hispanic consumers, and affective response to the ad. Their findings supported the usefulness of both SAT and Attribution Theories in understanding consumer response to advertising targeted to Hispanics. The use of Spanish language in advertising increased perceptions of the advertiser's sensitivity to Hispanic culture, and this perception was positively associated with affect toward the advertisements.

Although the Koslow, et al. (1994) study makes a valuable contribution to the marketing literature by introducing Sociolinguistic Accommodation Theory to research on advertising effects, there are several areas unaddressed. The Koslow, et al. study examines the response of Hispanic consumers, and may not be generalizable to other ethnic groups. The aspect of accommodation under investigation is language use (English only, Spanish only, or a combination of English and Spanish); therefore, this study remains within the traditional linguistic domain of SAT. It does not examine other aspects of accommodation available in an advertisement, such as using cultural symbols or ethnic spokespersons. Koslow, et al. (1994) investigate both the affective consequences of the accommodation attempt, and the receiver's attributions about the accommodation attempt. Although previous SAT research also found enhanced communication effectiveness and reciprocal behavioral responses as consequences of accommodation, Koslow, et al. (1994) do not measure these.

THE INTERCULTURAL ACCOMMODATION MODEL

The previous work in SAT and the work of Koslow, et al. (1994) provide support for the usefulness of Socio-linguistic Accommodation Theory in aiding our understanding of consumer response to targeted advertising; however, there remain several gaps to be addressed. What is needed is an expanded theory that not only addresses the consumer's affective and cognitive responses to accommodation, but also provides insight to the factors that influence the strength and type of reaction, as well as the consequences of that reaction. The following sections will provide the theoretical background for this expanded theory.

Accommodation Response

The central issue in this model is the consumer's Response to an Intercultural Accommodation attempt. As indicated by the work of Holland and Ball (1995) and Koslow, et al. (1994), it is likely that consumers make attributions about the communicators' motives for using cultural symbols in advertising. Recipients of such accommodation attempts may think that the use of ethnic actors or music in marketing communication is either a sign of respect, or an attempt to manipulate. However, it is also likely that the consumer's attributions may lead to an affective response as well (Koslow, et al. 1994; Simard, et al. 1976; Weiner 1985). Therefore, the central concept in the model, the Consumer's Response, is represented by two constructs; the cognitive component, Attributions, and the affective component, Affect.

Strength of Ethnic Identification as an Antecedent

A variety of antecedents may affect the intensity and the direction of the consumer's reaction to the accommodation effort; however, the consumer's strength of identification with his/her ethnic background is one of the most important. Many studies have documented variation in strength of ethnic identification among ethnic group members (Deshpande, Hoyer, and Donthu 1986; O'Guinn and Meyer 1983; Whittler, Calantone, and Young 1991). If people do not identify strongly with their ethnic group, it is unlikely that ethnic group membership will be a predictor of their behavior or response to an advertisement.

Ethnic group members who identify strongly with their heritage are likely to have a stronger emotional response to the use of their cultural symbols in marketing communications than those who identify less with their heritage. However, this response may be either positive or negative. Previous research has provided evidence that consumers do notice and respond to the use of ethnic cultural symbols in advertisements (Holland and Ball 1995; Koslow, et al. 1994). The following hypothesis seeks to test the link between the strength of ethnic identification and the affective response to such use of cultural symbols.

H1: People who identify strongly with their ethnic group will have stronger affective responses to the use of cultural symbols in advertisements.

Consequences

The proposed consequences of the consumer's response to Intercultural Accommodation attempts are similar to those found in studies of Socio-linguistic Accommodation. Successful accommodation should result in more favorable evaluations of the communicator (Byrne 1969; Koslow, et al. 1994; Simons, Berkowitz, and Moyer 1970), improved communication (Matarazzo et al. 1968), and reciprocal accommodative behaviors (Simard, et al. 1976). Positive evaluative response from the consumer can be operationally defined as attitude toward the Ad and Attitude toward the Brand. Improved communication can be operationally defined as enhanced Message Recall.

Affect and Attitude toward the Ad. From the early 1970s, researchers have emphasized the importance of the consumer's global evaluation of the advertisement as an indication of its effectiveness (Holbrook 1978; Mitchell and Olson 1981; Shimp 1981). The consumer's feelings about the ad are often the primary determination of their attitude toward the advertisement. Brown and Stayman (1992) conducted a meta-analysis of 47 independent samples involving the Attitude toward the Ad construct published from 1981 to 1991. In the 17 studies (representing 1,882 observations) that focused on these two constructs, the corrected mean correlation between feelings and ad attitude was .54. Thus, under a variety of conditions and study types, the relationship between affective response and Attitude toward the Ad proved to be quite robust.

H2: Ad evaluations will be significantly correlated with affect.

Affect and Attitude toward the Brand. Brown and Stayman's (1992) meta-analysis provided support for a strong direct, as well as an indirect, influence of Ad Attitude on Brand Attitude. Given the strong correlation between affect and Attitude toward the Ad, it is fairly safe to predict a relationship between affective response to an ad and Attitude toward the Brand.

In the context of ethnically targeted advertising, in fact, this correlation was found. Pitts et al. (1989) studied the relationship between actor's race and viewer's responses to an advertisement in the context of positive portrayals. The authors reported a positive correspondence between brand evaluations and affect when the actor was of the same race as the viewer. For positive affect resulting from the use of cultural symbols in the ad, similar results are expected in this study.

H3: When consumers experience a positive affective response to the use of cultural symbols in an advertisement, the direct correlation between Affect and Attitude toward the Brand will be stronger than for those who have a negative affective response or those who see advertisements with no cultural symbols.

Affect and Message Recall. The consumer's affective responses to advertisements are likely to impact the cognitive processing of the ad's message. Sujan, Bettman, and Baumgartner (1993) provided evidence that affective responses can interfere with cognitive processing of feature information. In their study, positive affect associated with autobiographical memories inhibited recall of product features presented in the message. The authors attribute this to the richness of autobiographical memories which act as a distracter to processing feature information. In the case of negative affect evoked by the use of cultural symbols in an ad, this is likely to hold as well. Negative affect, either due to negative attributions about the advertiser's motives or as a direct reaction to the cultural imagery in the ad, will most likely generate strong emotions and inhibit cognitive processing of ad content.

H4: Negative affect resulting from the use of cultural symbols in advertisements will impede the effectiveness of advertisements as measured by feature recall.

However, in this context, based on Accommodation Theory, positive affect in response to the advertiser's use of cultural symbols should enhance communication effectiveness and lead the viewer to reciprocal accommodative behaviors, such as paying more attention to the ad information. Therefore positive affect in response to the use of cultural symbols should improve cognitive processing of feature information in an ad. Some studies have found that positive affect may enhance recall. Contrary to the rationale provided by Sujan et al. (1993) discussed above, Whittler (1989) proposed that high identification Blacks would pay *more* attention to the Black spokesperson than to the product information presented in the ad copy. However, his study failed to support this hypothesis. Further, Schlinger and Plummer (1972), and Szybillo and Jacoby (1974) found that positive affect enhanced recall. In these studies, Blacks showed better recall of ad content and had more positive affect toward the ad when Black actors were included in advertisements. We expect similar results to hold.

H5: Positive affect resulting from the use of cultural symbols in advertisements will enhance the effectiveness of ads as measured by feature recall.

In summary, Intercultural Accommodation, in the context of target marketing, is likely to evoke both affective and cognitive responses from the consumer. The intensity and direction of those responses are likely to be influenced by the consumer's Strength of Ethnic Identification. The outcomes of the consumer's response

FIGURE 1
A Partial Model of Intercultural Accommodation

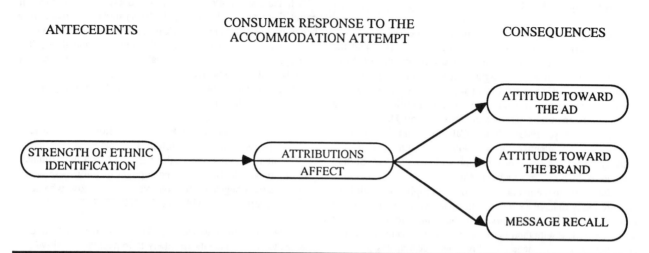

are likely to be affective, cognitive, and behavioral. The nature and intensity of the consumer's response to the accommodation effort will affect his/her Evaluation of the company and its products, the effectiveness of the communication, and the consumer's reciprocal accommodative behaviors. The preliminary model is depicted in Figure 1 below.

METHODOLOGY

An exploratory study was undertaken to test the validity of key aspects of the model. If the relationships among the constructs appear to hold in the limited domain, then further study can be justified. In the context of this study, Intercultural Accommodation was operationalized as print advertisements depicting symbols of African-American culture.

A between-subject, one-factor experimental design was used to test the hypotheses. Positive, negative, and control versions of an ad were developed to manipulate the affective responses to cultural symbols used in print ads. The dependent measure was the number of product features accurately listed in a free recall exercise.

Pretests

Three sets of ads were created, each with a positive, negative, and control version of themes developed to introduce a fictitious brand of portable CD player. The portable stereo was chosen as the advertised product based on the following research goals:

(1) The product category must be somewhat involving to increase the interest in the ad and copy.

(2) The product category must have numerous tangible features to prevent "guessing" on the feature recall measure.

(3) The product category must be applicable and affordable to all socio-economic groups.

Pretests were conducted with 26 African-American subjects from businesses and community groups similar to those used for the main data collection. Subjects were randomly assigned to only one ad from the pretest pool of six cultural symbol ads. All ads contain the same product shot and feature information. The ad theme with the highest separation of positive and negative affective responses

was used. The chosen theme used two African-American male models depicted as jazz musicians in two types of clothing. The positive version was in typical "night-club" attire with a coat and tie, the negative version was in traditional tribal attire, no shirt, kente cloth, and headband.

Subjects and Procedure

One hundred-one African American subjects were recruited from community and business organizations. Two subjects, one in the control group, and one in the negative condition refused to complete the survey instrument. For the effective sample of 99, the average age was 36, ranging from 17 to 71. A wide range of socio-economic backgrounds was also represented with a mean income in the range of $15-20,000. Only 24% of the sample were students, and of the total, 49% were male, 51% female. Subjects were randomly assigned to each of three cells: cultural symbols positive (n=38), cultural symbols negative (n=32) and a control group with no cultural symbols (n=29).

Measures

Subjects first were asked to respond to four seven-point semantic differential scales to measure Attitude toward the Brand (low quality, high quality; not useful, useful; etc.) and a two-item scale to measure product category familiarity. These were followed by five semantic differential scales measuring Attitude toward the Ad (uninteresting, interesting; annoying, pleasant; etc.) and five measuring Affective response to the Ad (cold, warm; angry, contented; etc.).

At this point, subjects were asked to return the ad to the researcher so that it could not be referred to for the remaining measures. A four-item, seven-point Likert scale designed to measure attitude toward advertising in general (based on Boush, Friestad, and Rose 1994) was completed next. This was followed by an open-ended ethnic identification item, and five Likert scale items to measure strength of Ethnic Identification (Holland and Ball 1995). After providing demographic information, the respondents were presented with a surprise unaided feature recall listing exercise. The number of features of the stereo system correctly recalled served as the operationalization of ad effectiveness. Subjects were then debriefed and thanked for their participation.

TABLE 1
Cronbach's Alpha

Construct	Number of Items	Cronbach's Alpha
Attitude toward the Brand	4	.89
Attitude toward the Ad	5	.99
Attitude toward Advertising	4	.60
Affective Response	5	.94
Familiarity	2	.73
Strength of Ethnic Identification	3	.83

ANALYSIS AND RESULTS

The first step of the analysis was to calculate Cronbach's alpha for the Likert scales to assess the quality of the measures. Table 1 presents the alpha coefficients for each scale. Two scales had low alphas: Strength of Ethnic Identification and Attitude toward Advertising. By deleting two items in the Ethnic Identification scale, alpha was improved from .65 to .81. The lowest alpha was for the Attitude toward Advertising scale, and could not be improved significantly through item purification. These internal reliability results are similar to those reported by Boush, Friestad, and Rose (1994), which indicate that the measure still contains an unacceptable level of error. In all other cases, the scales were fairly sound in their internal consistency reliability, therefore the next step was to test the manipulation of affect and the hypotheses.

Manipulation Check

A one-way ANOVA was conducted to test the effects of the use of cultural symbols on brand evaluations, evaluations of the advertisement, and feature recall. The affect measure was used as a manipulation check to verify that the two versions of use of cultural symbols did, in fact, differ in the type of affect evoked, as intended. The results of the manipulation check are provided in Table 2. As can be seen, the manipulation of Affect was successful. The significant omnibus F value was investigated by inspecting the results of the planned comparisons. These revealed that the mean affective response for the positive condition was significantly higher than the negative condition, but neither differed significantly from the control ad.

Hypotheses Tests

H1 states that respondents with stronger ethnic identification will have stronger affective responses to the use of cultural symbols in ads as compared to weaker ethnic identifiers. The measure of the intensity of Affect was represented by how far the Affect ratings differed from neutral (a rating of four). This intensity measure was obtained by summing the responses to the five Affect items and subtracting the sum of all neutral responses (20). The absolute value of the summed Affect measure was expected to be correlated with Strength of Ethnic Identification, indicating that stronger ethnic identifiers also had stronger reactions to the ads. Affect and Strength of Ethnic Identification were significantly correlated at .17, providing support for H1.

H2 states that Attitude toward the Ad will be significantly correlated with affective response across all treatment conditions. For the control group, the correlation was .68. For the positive affect condition, the correlation was .83. And for the negative affect condition, the correlation was .78. These results provide strong support for H2.

H3 predicts that Affect and Attitude toward the Brand will be more highly correlated in the positive affect condition than in the control or negative affect condition. The correlations are .57 (positive), .55 (control), and .45 (negative). The correlations are not significantly different (p.>.05), but the direction is as expected, lending partial support for H3, with affect and brand evaluation being highly correlated in all conditions, and both positive and control conditions having higher correlations than the negative affect advertisement.

Hypotheses 4 and 5 predict differential impacts of Affect on ad effectiveness as measured by feature recall. Results of the one-factor ANOVA (Table 2) demonstrate that these hypotheses were not supported. This can most likely be explained by the low number of features recalled in any condition. Forty-three percent of the sample could not remember a single feature from the ad. This will be explored further in the discussion section.

Although no specific hypotheses were made, Attitude toward the Ad and Attitude toward the Brand were significantly impacted by the treatment conditions. These could be taken as substitute measures of the advertisement's effectiveness. From these results, it can be seen that the negative portrayal resulted in significantly lower brand and ad evaluations than the positive condition, indicating that negative affect resulting from the use of cultural symbols in an ad reduce the consumer's rating of that ad and the brand.

DISCUSSION

In general this study provided mixed results. The central measure of advertising effectiveness, recall, was disappointingly weak. This could be for a variety of reasons. First, it may be that people did not read the advertising copy. Perhaps this is an indication of the ineffectiveness of print messages in communicating feature information. If this is true, it should not be expected that use of cultural symbols in advertisements should have any impact on feature recall.

On the other hand, the weak performance of the recall measure could have been a result of its placement in the questionnaire. The unexpected recall measure was the last question on a 33-question survey. It was placed at the end for the purpose of allowing some time and distance between examining the ad for the Affect, Ad and Brand evaluation measures, and the feature listing exercise. Measures of Attitude toward Advertising and Strength of Ethnic Identification, as well as demographic questions, intervened. However, respondent fatigue may have been accentuated by the difficulty of a recall exercise. This may have led many respondents to give up rather than devote the cognitive effort required for recall. Future research should look at placing this measure earlier in the questionnaire, or should consider the use of an aided recall measure.

The findings that evaluations of the advertisement and of the brand were significantly affected by the use of cultural symbols in the advertisement are important. It is reasonable to propose that the differential impact of positive and negative uses of cultural symbols in an advertisement on ad and brand evaluations is an indication of

TABLE 2
Mean Affective Response, Recall,
Attitude toward the Ad and Attitude toward the Brand and Results of Planned Comparisons

	Control	Positive	Negative	Planned Comparisons	Signif
Affect	4.1	4.5	3.5	C vs P	.22
				C vs N	.06
				P vs N	.01
Recall	2.3	1.7	1.4	not significant	
AttAd	4.1	4.5	3.5	C vs P	.29
				C vs N	.07
				P vs N	.01
AttBrand	4.3	4.6	3.6	C vs P	.34
				C vs N	.07
				P vs N	.01

the impact on ad effectiveness. Cultural images that evoke negative affect can result in lowered brand evaluations. Ads with cultural images that evoke positive affect can significantly improve brand evaluations. Although these results are intuitively obvious, they reinforce the importance of cultural symbols as a determinant of consumer response. Further research should follow these findings with measures of intentions to buy, or preferably, measures of actual purchase behavior.

The correlations between Affect and Ad evaluations, and Affect and Brand evaluations found in this study add to the existing research in this area. Supporting hypotheses 2 and 3, these results extend our knowledge into the domain of affective response to cultural symbols, an area where the impact of affect on ad and brand evaluations had not been tested. The support for H1 is an indication of the importance of segmenting cultural groups by strength of ethnic identification. When attempting to accommodate another group's culture, care must be taken to understand the variations in strength of ethnic identity and its impact on the receiver's response. In this study, group members who identified strongly with their culture had more extreme affective responses (both positive and negative) than their counterparts who identified less with their culture. The practical implication is that marketers may need to segment within ethnic groups; a message designed to appeal to ethnic roots may only reach a portion of the total group.

CONCLUSION

This study has contributed to our understanding of how ethnic consumers respond to targeted marketing communications. The findings add to the growing body of research on ethnic cultures and consumption. But more importantly, these results provide preliminary support for the validity and usefulness of Intercultural Accommodation Theory. The framework presented provides insight into how ethnic consumers respond to target marketing and the potential consequences of this response. This study attempted to validate a small but critical part of the overall model. Other aspects of the overall framework should be developed and validated to test the usefulness and predictive validity of the theory. The current results are limited to the domain of print advertising targeted to African Americans. Future research should test these constructs with other aspects of accommodation behavior and other ethnic groups.

As the demographics of the North American market continue to change, and as international marketing becomes increasingly vital to every business, expertise in communicating with groups of various cultures is becoming an essential marketing skill. Intercultural Accommodation Theory may provide a framework for analyzing and understanding the processes underlying the consumer's response to these communication efforts.

BIBLIOGRAPHY

Bell, Allan (1991), "Audience Accommodation in the Mass Media,: in *Contexts of Accommodation: Developments in Applied Sociolinguistics*, ed. Howard Giles et al., Cambridge: Cambridge University Press, 690-102.

Bourhis, R.Y., and Howard Giles (1977), "The Language of Intergroup Distinctiveness," in *Language, Ethnicity and Intergroup Relations*, ed. H. Giles, London: Academic Press, 119-135.

Boush, David M., Marian Friestad, and Gregory M. Rose (1994), "Adolescent Skepticism toward TV Advertising and Knowledge of Advertiser Tactics," *Journal of Consumer Research*, 21 (June), 165-175.

Brown, Steven P. and Douglas M. Stayman (1992), "Antecedents and Consequences of Attitude toward the Ad: A Meta-analysis," *Journal of Consumer Research*, 19 (June), 34-51.

Byrne, D., (1961), "Interpersonal Attraction and Attitude Similarity," *Journal of Abnormal and Social Psychology*, 62, 713-715.

Campanelli, Melissa (1991), "The African-American Market: Community, Growth, and Change," *Sales & Marketing Management*, 143 (May) 75-81.

Delener, Nejdet and James P. Neelankavil (1990), "Informational Sources and Media Usage: A Comparison Between Asian and Hispanic Subcultures," *Journal of Consumer Research*, 13 (September), 214-220.

Deshpande, Rohit, Wayne D. Hoyer, and Naveen Donthu (1986), "The Intensity of Ethnic Affiliation: A Study of the Sociology of Hispanic Consumption," *Journal of Consumer Research*, 13 (September), 214-220.

Giles, Howard (1973), "Accent Mobility: A Model and Some Data," *Anthropological Linguistics*, 15, 87.

_____, Nikolas Coupland, and Justine Coupland (1991), "Accommodation Theory: Communication, Context, and Consequences," in *Contexts of Accommodation: Developments in Applied Sociolinguistics*, ed. Howard Giles et al., Cambridge: Cambridge University Press. 1-68.

_____, D.M. Taylor, and R.Y. Bourhis (1973), "Towards a Theory of Interpersonal Accommodation through Language: Some Canadian Data," *Language in Society*, 2, 177-192.

Hirschman, Elizabeth C. (1981a), "American Jewish Ethnicity: Its Relationship to Some Selected Aspects of Consumer Behavior," *Journal of Marketing*, 45 (Summer), 102-110.

_____ (1981b), "Religious Differences in Cognitions Regarding Novelty Seeking and Information Transfer," *Advances in Consumer Research*, Association for Consumer Research: Volume 9, 228-223.

_____ (1982), "Ethnic Variation in Hedonic Consumption," *The Journal of Social Psychology*, 118, 225-234.

Holbrook, Morris B. (1978), "Beyond Attitude Structure: Toward the Information Determinants of Attitude," *Journal of Marketing Research*, 15 (November), 545-556.

Holland, Jonna L. and Dwayne Ball, (1995) "Accommodation Attributions: Construct and Measurement Validation," in *Enhancing Knowledge Development in Marketing Vol. .6*, eds. Barbara B. Stern and George M. Zinkhan, Chicago: American Marketing Association, 161-169.

Kassarjian, Harold H. (1969), "The Negro and American Advertising, 1946-1965," *Journal of Marketing Research*, 6 (February), 29-39.

Koslow, Scott, Prem N. Shamdasani, and Ellen E. Touchstone, (1994), "Exploring Language Effects in Ethnic Advertising: A Sociolinguistic Perspective," *Journal of Consumer Research*, 20 (March), 561-574.

Matarazzo, J.D., A.N. Weins, R. G. Matarazzo, and G. Saslow, (1968), "Speech and Silence Behavior in Clinical Psychotherapy and its Laboratory Correlates," in *Research in Psychotherapy Vol. 3*, ed. J. Schlier, H. Hunt, J.D. Matarazzo and C. Savage. Washington, D.C.

Mitchell, Andrew A. and Jerry C. Olson (1981), "Are Product Attribute Beliefs the Only Mediator of Advertising Effects on Brand Attitudes?" *Journal of Marketing Research*, 18 (August), 318-322

O'Guinn, Thomas C. and Ronald J. Faber (1985), "New Perspectives on Acculturation: The Relationship of General and Role Specific Acculturation with Hispanics' Consumer Attitudes," in *Advances in Consumer Research*, Vol. 12, eds. Elizabeth C. Hirschman and Morris B. Holbrook, Provo, UT Association for Consumer Research, 113-117.

_____ and Thomas P. Meyer (1983), "Segmenting the Hispanic Market: The Use of Spanish Language Radio," *Journal of Advertising Research*, 23 (6), 9-16.

Penaloza, Lisa (1994), "Atravesando Fronteras/Border Crossings: A Critical Ethnographic Exploration of the Consumer Acculturation of Mexican Immigrants," *Journal of Consumer Research*, 21 (June), 32-54.

Pitts, Robert E., D. Joel Whalen, Robert O'Keefe, and Vernon Murray, "Black and White Response to Culturally Targeted Television Commercials: A Values-Based Approach, " *Psychology and Marketing*, 6 (Winter), 311-328.

Reilly, Michael D. and Melanie Wallendorf (1987), "A Comparison of Group Differences in Food Consumption Using Household Refuse," *Journal of Consumer Research*, 14 (September), 289-294.

Schlinger, M.J. and J.T. Plummer (1992), "Advertising in Black and White," *Journal of Marketing Research*, 9, 149-153.

Shimp, Terence A. (1981), "Attitude toward the Ad as a Mediator of Consumer Brand Choice," *Journal of Advertising*, 10 (2), 9-15.

Simard, L., D.M. Taylor, and H. Giles (1976), "Attribution Processes and Interpersonal Accommodation in a Bilingual Setting," *Language and Speech*, 19 (October-December), 374-387.

Simons, H.W., N. N. Berkowitz, and R.J. Moyer (1970), "Similarity, Credibility and Attitude Change: A Review and a Theory," *Psychological Bulletin*, 73, 1.

Stayman, Douglas M. and Rohit Deshpande (1989), "Situational Ethnicity and Consumer Behavior," *Journal of Consumer Research*, 16 (December), 361-371.

Stroman, Carolyn A. and Lee B. Becker (1987), "Racial Differences in Gratifications", *Journalism Quarterly*, 55 (Winter), 767-771.

Sturdivant, Frederick D. (1973), "Subculture Theory: Poverty, Minorities, and Marketing," in *Consumer Behavior: Theoretical Sources*, eds. Scott Ward and Thomas S. Robertson, Englewood Cliffs, New Jersey: Prentice-Hall, Inc., 469-521.

Sujan, Mita, James R. Bettman, and Hans Baumgartner (1993), "Influencing Consumer Judgments Using Autobiographical Memories: A Self-Referencing Perspective," *Journal of Marketing Research*, 30 (November), 422-436.

Szybillo, G.J. and Jacob Jacoby (1974), "Effects of Different Levels of Advertising on Integration Preference and Intention to Purchase," *Journal of Applied Psychology*, 59, 274-280.

Webb, J.T. (1970), "Interview Synchrony: An Investigation of Two Speech Rate Measures in the Automated Standardized Interview, " in *Studies in Dyadic Communication: Proceedings of a Research Conference on the Interview*, ed. A.W. Siegman and B. Pope, Elmsford, New York.

Webster, Cynthia (1992), "The Effects of Hispanic Subcultural Identification on Information Search Behavior," *Journal of Advertising Research*, (September/October), 54-62.

Weiner, Bernard (1985), "An Attributional Theory of Achievement Motivation and Emotion," *Psychological Review*, 92 (4), 548-573.

Whittler, Tommy E. (1989), "Viewers' Processing of Actor's Race and Message Claims in Advertising Stimuli," *Psychology and Marketing*, 6 (Winter), 287-309.

_____, Roger J. Calantone, and Mark R. Young (1991), "Strength of Ethnic Affiliation: Examining Black Identification With Black Culture," *The Journal of Social Psychology*, 131 (August), 461-467.

Overload, Pressure, and Convenience: Testing a Conceptual Model of Factors Influencing Women's Attitudes Toward, and Use of, Shopping Channels

Jill K. Maher, Kent State University
Lawrence J. Marks, Kent State University
Pamela E. Grimm, Kent State University

ABSTRACT

This study investigates the influence of role overload, feelings of time pressure, the importance of convenience, and shopping enjoyment on women's attitudes toward and use of traditional and nontraditional shopping channels (specifically, retail store and catalog vs. television and computer shopping). A series of propositions are developed and tested and used to create and test a structural equations model. Results indicate that these factors may be useful in understanding traditional channels, while other variables may be more influential in the use of nontraditional channels.

INTRODUCTION

Prior research has examined factors that influence women's selection of and attitudes toward shopping channels (e.g., Gillett 1976; Bellizzi and Hite 1986; Blakney and Sekely 1994). These studies have analyzed the effects of numerous influences on channel selection, ranging from working status to shopping enjoyment. However, because these studies typically have investigated a very limited set of factors, indeed often only a single factor, they do not present a very complete conceptual picture of the total relationships involved in channel selection. In addition, alternative shopping channels have increased as the demographics of our society have changed. These societal changes include an increased number of working women and increased desire for simplicity and convenience in shopping. Existing studies have rarely considered these new shopping channel alternatives (for an exception, see Blakney and Sekely 1994).

The purposes of this study are to develop and test propositions relating to several important influences which may affect women's attitudes toward both traditional and nontraditional shopping channels, and to develop and test a causal model of these relationships, which has not been attempted before. In the context of the current study, traditional shopping channels are defined as in-store retail shopping and catalog shopping while nontraditional channels are represented by television home shopping and on-line computer shopping. This categorization is based solely on the length of time that each of these shopping channels has been available to the consumer in the marketplace. The choice of channels is important because past research has examined retail, catalog, direct mail, and telephone shopping (Cox and Rich 1964; Reynolds 1974), but has not thoroughly examined television or computer shopping, retail channels which simply did not exist in the 60's and early 70's. This study contributes to the understanding of women's selection of shopping channels by updating the literature to include the newest shopping channels (e.g., on-line computer shopping) and examining women's attitudes toward each channel at the individual channel level.

This paper begins with a review of previous studies conducted in this area, followed by the methodology used in this study, the results, and a discussion of the significance of these results. The final section presents suggestions for future research on channel choice.

BACKGROUND

Women's shopping channel choices are of more interest than men because statistics show that when examining the household tasks of men and women, women shop approximately 3.6 hours per week compared to 1.4 hours for men (Statistical Handbook on the American Family 1992). Therefore, by studying women, we are able to assess the channel selection of the "shopper" in most families. Theoretically, the antecedent variables being examined in this study (i.e., role overload, time pressure, and convenience) are most applicable to women as the majority of role overload studies (for example see Reilly 1982; Gray 1983; and Stephens et. al. 1994) have examined women as their defined population. Additionally, convenience and time pressure studies such as Reilly (1982) and Strober and Weinberg (1980) have concentrated on women.

Of the many influences on women's shopping channel selection, Role Overload, Time Pressure, Importance of Convenience, and Shopping Enjoyment seem to be especially important for today's working wife and mother. Therefore, these factors, discussed below, are the focus of the current investigation.

Role Overload and Time Pressure

While several studies suggest that women employed outside the home receive higher satisfaction in life because of their participation in the work force (Ferree 1984; Hall and Gordon 1973), other research has demonstrated that work force participation increases susceptibility to Role Overload and time stress (Gray 1983). Working women today are often pressured because they are trying to manage time in their multiple roles. Reilly (1982) discusses Role Overload as conflict that occurs when the amount of behavior demanded by the roles in which one is engaged exceeds available time and energy. Such conflict is experienced by many working women who maintain the roles of wife and mother because these roles, along with their household responsibilities, add to the portion of time they actually spend "working" (Berry 1979). In addition, qualitative assessments of time diaries kept by women found that the responsibility for the household and the family was more than simply time spent on household chores. This responsibility includes such qualitative activities as thinking, planning, nurturance, and emotional care of family members (Shaw 1991).

From this information, it seems reasonable that the working woman is constrained by the time involved in her roles as wife, mother, employee and housekeeper. This constraint forces the working woman to allocate time between her various roles and for herself. For instance, if 80% of a woman's time is spent at work or conducting work activities, she must reduce the amount of time with her children, her spouse, and in keeping house, as well as time spent on herself.

Reilly (1982) found that the degree of women's Role Overload influences their consumption of convenience goods and services. From this finding, it is expected that role overloaded women will place greater importance on convenience in shopping channel selection. The above discussion suggests the following propositions:

P1: The degree of Role Overload is positively related to feelings of Time Pressure.

P2: The degree of Role Overload is positively related to Importance of Convenience in shopping channel selection.

Time Pressure and Importance of Convenience

Women, who have traditionally been the shoppers for the family and household, are presented with new shopping channel choices in the mid 1990s. One important reason for the development of nonstore retail shopping channels is women's desires to simplify their hectic lifestyles. The combination of labor force participation and household responsibilities has contributed to the increased consumption of convenience goods and services, as well as to women's decreased amount of participation in leisure activities (Lavin 1993b; Witt and Goodale 1981). Clearly, a woman's leisure time is severely constrained by her commitments to both family and work. Therefore, today's working wife and mother may have intensified feelings of time pressure.

In the past, retail shopping, one traditional shopping channel, was a means for housewives to socialize and interact with the outside world. However, with the increased number of housewives seeking additional employment outside the home, the number of hours available for shopping has decreased. These women have found that their workforce participation provides them with the opportunity to socialize during working hours, therefore they often see shopping as a chore and merely time spent away from home. This feeling stems from the fact that, given their increased involvement in work outside the home, women are now more aware and conscious of the cost of time associated with shopping. Costs such as travel time, parking, purchase time, and interstore travel time (Jacoby, Szybillo, and Berning 1976) may have been less important issues to housewives in the past, but they now affect working women's desire to shop because of the time pressure created by the demands of family and work. Hawes, Gronmo, and Arndt (1977) found that the hours spent shopping per week among American women decreased when the women were employed full-time, as well as when their household size was greater than five. From this information, it seems reasonable that working wives, especially those with young children, would feel time pressure. This feeling may drive them to seek convenience in their choice of shopping channel. This is consistent with a study that found nonstore retailing to attract individuals who possess a strong convenience orientation (Eastlick 1994). More specifically, Cox (1964) found telephone shoppers were more often women who had a great need for convenience in their shopping. His study also found that women under the age of 40, who had children living in their home, were three times more likely to utilize telephone shopping than women under the age of 40 without children.

Some studies have not found support for these relationships (Reynolds 1974; Bellizzi and Hite 1986; Lavin 1993b). The limitation of these studies is their focus on single explanatory factors (e.g., Time Pressure, Role Overload, etc.). In taking such a narrow perspective, it seems possible that several important factors have been overlooked. For the purposes of guiding the current study, the following propositions are made:

P3: Women's perceived Time Pressure is positively related to the Importance of Convenience in shopping channel.

P4: Importance of Convenience is positively related to Attitude toward nontraditional shopping channels and negatively related to Attitude toward traditional retail channels.

Shopping Enjoyment

Because Lavin (1993a) found Time Pressure affected the enjoyment women experience from traditional shopping channels, an examination of the effect of Time Pressure and Shopping Enjoyment on nontraditional channels will be included in this study. Bellenger and Korgaonkar (1980) describe the concept of the recreational shopper as one who enjoys shopping as a leisure activity. In their study, 69% of the adult respondents surveyed enjoyed shopping as a leisure time activity and an overwhelming percentage of these leisure shoppers were women (i.e., 80%). It seems reasonable to believe that women who enjoy shopping will have a greater propensity to utilize a traditional retail channel in order to experience some form of shopping gratification. This belief was confirmed in a recent study conducted by Blakney and Sekely (1994). These researchers examined the level of Shopping Enjoyment experienced by four different segments of shoppers. One of these segments was in-home shoppers who prefer nontraditional shopping modes (i.e., telephone, mail, computer). These in-home shoppers were found to enjoy traditional retail shopping the least. The above discussion suggests the following propositions:

P5: Feelings of Time Pressure are negatively related to Shopping Enjoyment.

P6: Shopping Enjoyment is negatively related to the Attitude toward nontraditional shopping channels and positively related to Attitude toward traditional channels.

Attitude-Behavior Relationship

While a great deal of research has investigated the consistency between attitude and behavior in a variety of contexts, this relationship has seldom been investigated in the context of shopping channel selection. For simplicity in the current study, it was assumed that women's attitudes about shopping channels would be accessible and there would be strong consistency between her attitude and her use of that channel (for attitude-behavior consistency see, Fazio, Powell, and Williams 1989). The above discussion suggests the following proposition:

P7: Attitude toward the channel is positively related to channel use.

A Structural Model of the Relationships

Based on the relationships implied in the propositions, a structural equations model was created. As seen in Figure 1, consistent with the propositions, it was assumed that Role Overload would have a positive influence on Feelings of Time Pressure and Importance of Convenience. Additionally, it was hypothesized that Time Pressure would directly influence Importance of Convenience and negatively influence Shopping Enjoyment. Finally, the model indicates that Attitude Toward the Channel would be directly influenced by Shopping Enjoyment and Importance of Convenience, and that this attitude would directly influence Use of Channel.

METHODOLOGY

Procedure

A survey questionnaire was developed and used to test the proposed relationships. Students from a mid western university's "Principles of Marketing" class were used as administrators. These students received extra credit in the class for administering the questionnaire to working adults with children. Thus, the study utilizes a convenience sample.

Scales

Unless otherwise stated, all items were measured as five-point Likert-type scales, with responses labeled as, "strongly disagree," "disagree," "neutral," "agree," and "strongly agree." In some cases

FIGURE 1
Original Model

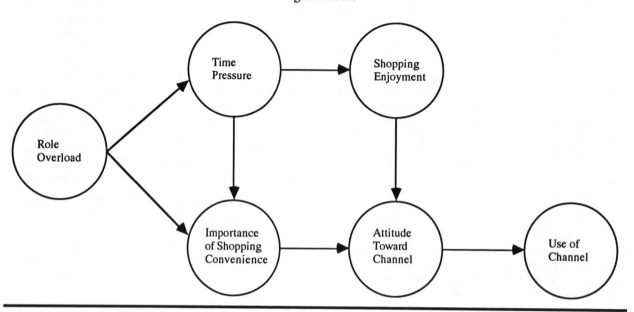

(noted below) this represented a change from six-point scales. Because the questionnaire was rather lengthy and complex, this was deemed necessary to reduce respondent confusion by having consistency across response measures.

Role Overload scale: Role Overload was measured by Reilly's (1982) Role Overload scale. This scale is a 13-item scale that measures the pressure that a woman experiences due to the roles she plays. In the present study, Role Overload has a reliability of .87 which is comparable to the reliability of .88 reported by Reilly (1982).

Time pressure scale: The time pressure scale used for this study was developed by Lumpkin (1985) as a six-item, six-point scale (reported reliability of .69) that measures a person's lack of free time for him/herself in a given day. In the present study, a five-point scale was used which produced a stronger reliability coefficient of .84.

Importance of Convenience scale: Lumpkin and Hunt (1989) developed a six-item scale, with a reported reliability of .62, that measures the convenience of traveling to and ordering from a retail store. Although the present study produced a higher reliability of .75, this scale was not selected for use in the model, because it measures convenience of shopping in a very specific context, that is, the importance of convenience when shopping at a retail outlet. With this in mind, a second measure of the importance of convenience was created for the study. This single item, face valid measure asked respondents for their level of agreement with the statement, "When it comes to shopping, convenience is the most important thing to me."

Shopping Enjoyment scale: The shopping enjoyment scale was developed by O'Guinn and Faber (1989). This three-item scale has a reported reliability of .89 that measures the enjoyment that a consumer experiences from shopping. To assure that all respondents in the current study were thinking of the same type of shopping experience, they were instructed to consider "shopping in general," for products such as clothes, household items, gifts, and accessories, regardless of shopping channel. In the current study, a comparable reliability of .86 was produced.

Attitude toward shopping channel: Attitude toward each shopping channel was a global measurement using three common five-point semantic differential scales reported in Bruner and Hensel (1992). These items were bad/good, dislike very much/like very much, and undesirable/desirable. Respondents were asked to rate each channel alternative when shopping for clothes for themselves. In the current study, reliabilities for attitude toward each channel were adequate, including retail outlet (Att Retail; alpha=.90), catalog (Att Catalog; alpha=.95), television (Att TV; alph=.95), and computer (Att Computer; alpha=.97).

Channel Use: In measuring actual channel use, respondents were asked to rate their use of each shopping channel (Retail Use, Catalog Use, TV Use, Computer Use) from 1 to 5 (1=never, 5=always) when shopping for clothes for themselves.

RESULTS

The Sample

The survey yielded 226 valid questionnaires. Thirty percent of the respondents were male and 70% female. The focus of this study is on the 155 female respondents with children living at home. Over half of these 155 women were 36 years of age or older, 59% worked full-time outside the home and 35% worked part-time, with over 50% working 40 or more hours per week outside the home. Seventy one percent of the women had two or more children and 53% had one or more children under the age of 6. Seventy-three percent were married, 15% were separated or divorced, and 11% reported themselves as single (with children living at home). Based on the assumptions of the study, this group of predominantly working, married women with children should include many who have strong feelings of role overload and who feel under substantial time pressure.

The Measurement Model

Table 1 presents the mean scores and standard deviations for the measures and for revised measures which were developed after testing the initial measurement model. PRELIS was used to create

TABLE 1
Descriptive Statistics for Measures

Original Measures

	Mean	S.D.	Variance	Alpha Coeff.	1-alpha	set error
Role Overload	3.25	0.65	0.4225	0.8728	0.1272	0.0537
Time Pressure	3.63	0.76	0.5776	0.8339	0.1661	0.0959
Shopping Enjoyment (S.E.)	3.08	1.02	1.0404	0.8581	0.1419	0.1476
Importance of Conv. (I.C.)	3.21	0.97	0.9409	0.8225	0.1775	0.1670
Attitude Retail Shopping	3.98	0.82	0.6724	0.9038	0.0962	0.0647
Retail Use	4.23	0.93	0.8649	0.8688	0.1313	0.1135
Attitude Catalog Shopping	3.2	1.06	1.1236	0.9548	0.0452	0.0508
Catalog Use	2.83	0.99	0.9801	0.8688	0.1313	0.1286
Attitude T.V. Shopping	2.09	0.99	0.9801	0.9507	0.0493	0.0483
T.V. Use	1.36	0.76	0.5776	0.8688	0.1313	0.0758
Attitude Computer Shopping	2.13	1.02	1.0404	0.9721	0.0279	0.0290
Computer Use	1.09	0.33	0.1089	0.8688	0.1313	0.0143
Revised Measures						
Rev. Role Overload (R.O.)	3.49	0.81	0.6561	0.8765	0.1235	0.0810
Rev. Time Pressure (T.P.)	3.42	1.04	1.0816	0.9179	0.0821	0.1476

a covariance input matrix for LISREL 7, which was used to test the measurement properties of the scales via confirmatory factor analysis. The items for each scale were run in individual analyses.

The various fit indices indicated the measurement models provided a relatively poor fit to the data for Role Overload and Time Pressure. The scales were improved by examining the squared multiple correlations for each item and dropping those with the poorest fit. Through an iterative process, items were eliminated until the fit measures were deemed acceptable. In order to conserve space, only the measurement model based on the revised scales are reported in Table 2. Descriptive statistics for the two new scales are reported at the bottom of Table 1.

The Structural Equations Model

To simplify the analysis, the structural equations models were tested by creating a series of single-item indicators for each construct, using the mean of the construct, and setting the error equal to 1-alpha times the variance (see Table 1). The error term for the concepts which had only a single item measure (i.e., Importance of Convenience and the Channel Use measures) were set at .86 by taking an average of the alpha for several of the other measures. As before, PRELIS was used to create covariance matrices for input into LISREL 7.

Examination of the path parameters and t-values (Table 3) provides strong support for P1, P5, and P7 across all shopping channels. P6 received only partial support in that Shopping Enjoyment (S.E.) was positively and significantly related to Attitude for the traditional shopping channels (Retail and Catalog), however it was not significantly related to Attitude for the nontraditional channels. None of the propositions that involved Importance of Convenience were supported (i.e., there was not support for P2, P3, or P4).

When considering the proposed model as a whole, the Chi Square and goodness of fit measures provided mixed results for the

different channels (see Table 3). The best fit was for the Retail (C^2=12.8, df=8, p=.144) and Catalog (C^2=15.39, df=8, p=.052) channels and the poorest fit was for the Television and Computer shopping channels. Given the preliminary nature of the proposed model, the results were examined to determine appropriate alternative models which could be theoretical justified.

This analysis suggested two plausible alternative models. Alternative Model One is based on the modification indices provided from the LISREL run. In this model, Importance of Convenience is made an exogenous variable influencing Shopping Enjoyment (see Figure 2). For the second alternative model, Importance of Convenience was dropped entirely, because none of the a prior causal paths involving the construct were found to be significant in the initial analyses (see Figure 3).

As can be seen from the fit values in Table 4, Alternative Model One provides a satisfactory fit for retail, catalog, and computer shopping, and a "marginal" fit for television shopping. The coefficient of determination for the structural equations shows an improvement over that seen for the proposed model (from around 17% to around 24%). However, the t-values do not show support for the path from Shopping Enjoyment to Attitude Toward the Channel for either Television Shopping or Computer Shopping (all other path t-values are significant).

Table 5 presents the standardized path coefficients for Alternative Model Two. While the results are the same as for Model One in terms of goodness of fit measures (support for all but Television) and t-values the coefficient of determination for the structural equations shows no improvement over the proposed model and is weaker than for Alternative Model One.

DISCUSSION

This study has brought together a variety of constructs thought to be important in women's choice of shopping channel and examined them in the context of traditional and nontraditional

TABLE 2
Measurement Model

	Parameter Estimates	t-values	Squared Mult. Corr.	Chi Square	df	prob.	GFI	AGFI	RMSR
Role Overload									
Many Things	.632	9.010	.400						
Demands	.908	14.175	.685						
Need Hours	1.000	0	.797						
Caught Up	.744	9.739	.445						
Self Time	.778	10.372	.481						
Few Hours	.681	9.781	.446						
Overextend	.670	8.879	.393	19.26	14	.155	.966	.932	.051
Time Pressure									
Leisure Time	.894	14.428	.666						
Things for me	.933	16.982	.785						
Self Time	1.00	0.000	.880	1.03	1	.310	.996	.973	.100
Shopping Enjoyment									
Makes Happy	0.956	12.469	0.644						
Is Fun	1	0	0.789						
Gives "high"	0.987	12.709	0.662	0.42	1	0.516	0.998	0.989	0.063
Retail Attitude									
Good	0.836	15.594	0.717						
Like	1	0	0.928						
Undesirable	0.827	15.055	0.693	3.88	1	0.049	0.983	0.900	0.159
CatalogAttitude									
Good	0.933	22.768	0.838						
Like	1	0	0.92						
Undesirable	0.972	26.349	0.898	2.29	1	0.13	0.99	0.941	0.149
T.V. ShopAttitude									
Good	0.872	20.714	0.782						
Like	1	0	0.953						
Undesirable	0.98	34.124	0.948	3.44	1	0.977	0.985	0.908	0.18
ComputerAttitude									
Good	0.967	37.941	0.93						
Like	1	0	0.988						
Undesirable	0.925	28.812	0.871	2.96	1	0.085	0.986	0.918	0.176

channels. The results indicate support for several propositions suggested by the literature. Additionally, a structural equations model was proposed, tested, and a modified model received support for the "more traditional" shopping channels (i.e., retail and catalog as opposed to television and computer shopping).

It is interesting to contemplate the failure of the proposed model to find a significant linkage between the Importance of Convenience in shopping and either Role Overload or Feelings of Time Pressure. It may be that Importance of Shopping Convenience is more strongly influenced by an individual trait variable (e.g., a personal trait) than it is by the measures considered in this study. Alternatively, despite the strong face validity of the measure used (i.e., "When it comes to shopping, convenience is the most important thing to me."), it may be that this single item does not capture the underlying construct adequately.

On the positive side, there is strong support in Alternative Model One for one of the originally proposed paths for Retail and Catalog Shopping. Specifically, and as predicted, for retail and catalog shopping, there are significant relationships along the path linking Role Overload and Time Pressure (positive), Time Pressure and Shopping Enjoyment (negative), Shopping Enjoyment and Attitude toward the Channel (positive), and Attitude and Channel Use (positive). Additionally, though not expected, a significant negative relationship between Importance of Convenience and Shopping Enjoyment is plausible. Likewise, it is quite reasonable that the influence of Importance of Convenience on Attitude may be very strongly mediated by Shopping Enjoyment. Clearly, these relationships must be carefully examined in future studies.

Alternative Model One provided a good fit in capturing the relationships for retail and catalog shopping, but not for either

TABLE 3
Parameter Estimates for Proposed Model

Path	Retail Shopping Standard Estimate	t Value	Catalog Shopping Standard Estimate	t Value	Television Shopping Standard Estimate	t Value	Computer Shopping Standard Estimate	t Value
T.P to I. C.	0.001	0.014	0.004	0.036	-0.010	-0.096	-0.021	-0.196
T.P to S.E.	-0.262	-2.965	-0.272	-3.082	-0.273	-3.054	-0.273	-2.983
I.C. to Att.	-0.101	-1.113	-0.030	-0.335	0.154	1.672	0.095	1.032
S.E. to Att.	0.241	2.699	0.258	2.966	0.103	1.147	0.137	1.517
Att. To Use	0.339	3.907	0.625	8.530	0.460	5.612	0.397	4.715
RO to T.P.	0.414	4.944	0.414	4.925	0.400	4.662	0.394	4.491
RO to I.C.	0.099	0.929	0.096	0.898	0.129	1.199	0.118	1.083
Psi T.P.	0.829	7.708	0.828	7.683	0.840	7.658	0.845	7.472
Psi I.C.	0.990	7.187	0.991	7.174	0.984	7.027	0.988	6.920
Psi S.E.	0.931	7.411	0.926	7.368	0.925	7.262	0.926	7.131
Psi Attitude	0.931	7.779	0.933	8.230	0.966	8.117	0.972	8.173
Psi Use	0.885	7.411	0.609	6.970	0.788	7.153	0.843	7.243
Coeff. Det.	0.178		0.178		0.171		0.165	
CHI-SQ	12.18		15.39		23.92		17.22	
df	8		8		8		8	
prob.	0.144		0.052		0.002		0.028	
GFI	0.975		0.968		0.949		0.962	
AGFI	0.935		0.917		0.866		0.899	
RMSR	0.058		0.063		0.071		0.063	

FIGURE 2
Alternative Model One

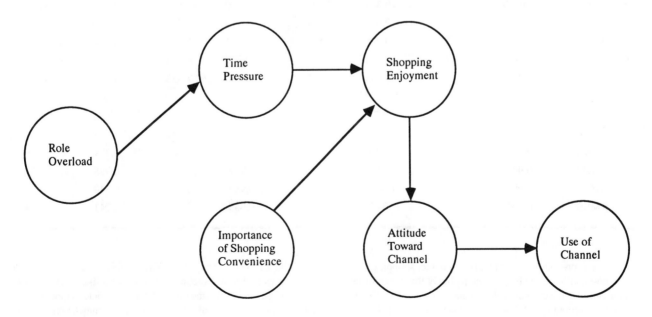

FIGURE 3
Alternative Model Two

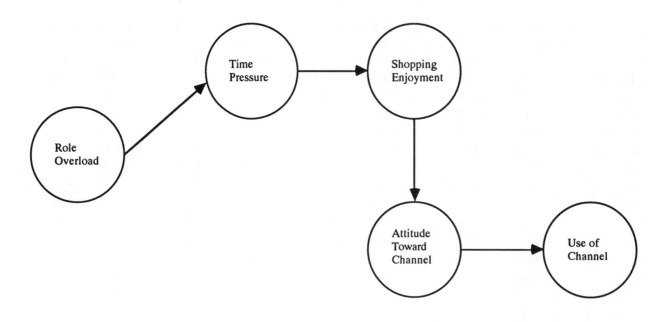

TABLE 4
Parameter Estimates for Alternative Model One (Importance is Exogenous)

	Retail Shopping		Catalog Shopping		Television Shopping		Computer Shopping	
	Standard Estimate	t Value	Standard Estimate	t Value	Standard Estimate	t Value	Standard Estimate	t Value
T.P to S.E.	-0.249	-2.914	-0.260	-3.044	-0.260	-2.983	-0.264	-2.973
S.E. to Att.	0.269	3.022	0.266	3.066	0.058	0.645	0.111	1.225
Att. to Use	0.341	3.935	0.626	8.545	0.459	5.592	0.396	4.702
RO to T.P.	0.413	4.936	0.414	4.917	0.400	4.654	0.393	4.481
I.C. to S.E.	-0.300	-3.331	-0.301	-3.329	-0.290	-3.142	-0.279	-2.964
Psi T.P.	0.829	7.709	0.829	7.684	0.840	7.587	0.846	7.473
Psi S.E.	0.842	7.160	0.835	7.114	0.841	7.025	0.846	6.920
Psi Attitude	0.928	7.784	0.929	8.227	0.997	8.178	0.988	8.201
Psi Use	0.884	7.410	0.608	6.797	0.789	7.153	0.843	7.243
Coeff. Det.	0.251		0.252		0.237		0.225	
CHI-SQ	2.67		4.72		16.88		9.66	
df	9		9		9		9	
prob.	0.976		0.858		0.051		0.379	
GFI	0.994		0.99		0.964		0.978	
AGFI	0.987		0.976		0.915		0.949	
RMSR	0.024		0.03		0.055		0.041	

television (non-significant t-value) or computer shopping (poor fit and non-significant t-value). It seems likely that other variables, unmeasured in the current study, account for women's selection of these two nontraditional shopping channels. Selection of computer shopping may well be related to innovativeness or a person's degree of knowledge about computers. That is, regardless of how much one enjoys traditional shopping, people who like to experiment with computers may be the ones who use computer shopping. On the other hand, the use of television shopping may be less related to Role Overload and Time Pressure than to issues related to

TABLE 5
Parameter Estimates for Alternative Model Two (Dropping Importance)

	Retail Shopping		Catalog Shopping		Television Shopping		Computer Shopping	
	Standard Estimate	t Value	Standard Estimate	t Value	Standard Estimate	t Value	Standard Estimate	t Value
T.P to S.E.	-0.261	-2.959	-0.272	-3.080	-0.273	-3.046	-0.272	-2.981
S.E. to Att.	0.265	2.974	0.265	3.052	0.065	0.714	0.115	1.264
Att. to Use	0.341	3.936	0.626	8.545	0.459	5.592	0.396	4.702
RO to T.P.	0.414	4.944	0.414	4.925	0.401	4.665	0.394	4.491
Psi T.P.	0.829	7.708	0.828	7.683	0.839	7.586	0.845	7.472
Psi S.E.	0.932	7.411	0.926	7.369	0.925	7.257	0.926	7.131
Psi Attitude	0.930	7.787	0.930	8.227	0.996	8.176	0.987	8.199
Psi Use	0.883	7.410	0.608	6.797	0.789	7.153	0.843	7.243
Coeff. Det.	0.171		0.172		0.161		0.155	
CHI-SQ	1.39		4.41		15.14		9.26	
df	6		6		6		6	
prob.	0.966		0.622		0.019		0.159	
GFI	0.996		0.989		0.96		0.974	
AGFI	0.991		0.972		0.9		0.936	
RMSR	0.024		0.034		0.057		0.044	

whether the person perceives this channel as offering low product quality and low status. Future research into the selection of these channels should include measures of such factors. The notion that different factors may determine the evaluation and selection of nontraditional shopping channels is of critical importance in both the modeling of these relationships and to marketers who are interested in influencing people to select a particular channel.

While this study provides some interesting insights into the factors influencing women's attitudes toward and use of traditional and nontraditional shopping channels, there are several limitations which must be acknowledged. First, a convenience sample of women living near a large mid western city were used. Clearly, these women may not be representative of the entire population. Second, the questionnaire had respondents think about "shopping in general," however, it may be that the respondents actually brought to mind retail shopping. Thus, it may be better for future studies to create separate questionnaires for each of the channels being investigated. Third, as mentioned, there are limitations in using the existing data to formulate changes in the structural equations model. Alternative Model One must be tested with another group of people to determine whether the results are robust. Finally, this study provides limited insight into the factors which do influence attitudes toward and use of nontraditional shopping channels. This is an area which may prove interesting for future research.

REFERENCES

Bellenger, Danny N. and Pradeep K. Korgaonkar (1980), "Profiling the Recreational Shopper," *Journal of Retailing*, 56 (Fall), 77-86.

Bellizzi, Joseph A. and Robert E. Hite (1986), "Convenience Consumption and Role Overload Convenience," *Academy of Marketing Science, 14 (Winter)*, 1-9.

Berry, Leonard L. (1979), "The Time-Buying Consumer," *Journal of Retailing*, 55 (Winter), 58-69.

Blakney, Vicki L., and William Sekely (1994), "Retail Attributes: Influence On Shopping Mode Choice Behavior," *Journal of Managerial Issues*, 6 (Spring), 101-117.

Bruner, Gordon C. II and Paul J, Hensel (1992), "Marketing Scales Handbook: A Compilation of Multi-Item Measures, Chicago: American Marketing Association.

Cox, Donald F. and Stuart U. Rich (1964), "Perceived Risk and Consumer Decision-Making–The Case of Telephone Shopping," *Journal of Marketing Research*, 1 (November), 32-39.

Eastlick, Mary Ann and Richard A. Feinberg (1994), "Gender Differences in Mail-Catalog Patronage Motives," *Journal of Direct Marketing*, 8 (Spring), 37-44.

Fazio, Russell H., Martha C. Powell, and Carol J. Williams (1989), "The Role of Attitude Accessibility in the Attitude-to-Behavior Process," *Journal of Consumer Research*, 16 (December), 280-288.

Ferree, Myra Marx (1984), "Class, Housework and Happiness: Women's Work and Life Satisfaction," *Sex Roles*, 11, 1057-1074.

Gillett, Peter L. (1976), "In-Home Shoppers-An Overview," *Journal of Marketing*, 40 (October), 81-88.

Gray, Janet Dreyfus (1983), "The Married Professional Woman: An Exploration of Her Role Conflicts and Coping Strategies," *Psychology of Women Quarterly*, 7 (Spring), 235-243.

Hall, Douglas T. and Francine E. Gordon (1973), "Career Choices of Married Women: Effects of Role Conflict, Role Behavior and Satisfaction," *Journal of Applied Psychology*, 58, 42-48.

Hawes, Douglas K. and Sigmund Gronmo and Johan Arndt (1977), "Shopping Time and Leisure Time: Some Preliminary Cross-Cultural Comparisons of Time-Budget Expenditures," In *Advances in Consumer Research*, Ed. H.Keith Hunt, 5, 151-159.

Jacoby, Jacob and George J. Szybillo and Carol Kohn Berning (1976), "Time and Consumer Behavior: An Interdisciplinary Overview," *Journal of Consumer Research*, 2 (March), 320-339.

Lavin, Marilyn, "Husband-dominant, Wife-dominant, Joint (1993a)," *Journal of Consumer Marketing*, 10, 33-42.

_____(1993b), "Wives' Employment, Time Pressure, and Mail/Phone Order Shopping," *Journal of Direct Marketing*, 7 (Winter), 42-49.

Lumpkin, James R. (1985), "Shopping Orientation Segmentation of the Elderly Consumer," *Journal of the Academy of Marketing Science*, 13 (Spring), 271-289.

_____ and James B. Hunt (1989), "Mobility as an Influence on Retail Patronage Behavior of the Elderly: Testing Conventional Wisdom, *Journal of the Academy of Marketing Science*, 17(Winter), 1-12.

O'Guinn, Thomas C. and Ronald J. Faber (1989), "Compulsive Buying: A Phenomenological Exploration," *Journal of Consumer Research,* 16 (Sept.), 147-157.

Reilly, Michael D. (1982), "Working Wives and Convenience Consumption," *Journal of Consumer Research*, 8 (March), 407-418.

Reynolds, Fred D. (1974), "An Analysis of Catalog Buying Behavior," *Journal of Marketing,* 38 (July), 47-51.

Shaw, Susan M. (1991), "Research note: Women's Leisure Time–Using Time Budget Data To Examine Current Trends and Future Predictions," *Leisure Studies*, 10 (May), 171-181.

Statistical Handbook on the American Family (1992), eds. Bruce Chadwick and Tim Heaton, Phoenix, AZ: Oryx Press.

Stephens, Mary Ann Parris, Melissa M. Franks, and Aloen L. Townsend (1994), "Stress and Rewards in Women's Multiple Roles: The Case of Women in the Middle," *Psychology and Aging,* 9(1), 45-52.

Strober, Myra H. and Charles B. Weinberg (1980), "Strategies Used by Working and Nonworking Wives to Reduce Time Pressures," *Journal of Consumer Research*, 6 (March), 338-348.

Witt, P. and T. Goodale (1981), "The Relationship Between Barriers to Leisure Enjoyment and Family Stages," *Leisure Sciences*, 4, 29-49.

Buy Now, Pay Later: Does a Future Temporal Orientation Affect Credit Overuse?

Norma A. Mendoza, University of Florida

John W. Pracejus, University of Florida

INTRODUCTION

Why do some people overuse credit and acquire debt beyond their means? Why do consumers fail to recognize they have too much debt, and what might affect this lack of insight? Although credit has become a common way by which consumers acquire goods, for some, managing credit can be problematic. Credit problems arise when consumers obtain credit beyond what they can afford to pay back and accumulate debt that exceeds their annual income.

Consumers can accumulate debt from credit via personal loans, revolving credit on credit cards (bank or store-issued), or installment credit. Of these, credit cards are one of the primary vehicles of consumer debt (Chicago Tribune, July 11, 1994). Consider the following statistics: in 1995, 376 million VISAs and MasterCards were in circulation, an increase of 80% over the previous five years. Consumers owe $360 billion on their credit cards, a debt load comprising a third of all consumer loans (Gullo and Marino, 1996). Credit cards have become such a common mode of payment because they are easily obtained and can help consumers cushion the effects of unexpected expenses and hard economic times. However, excessive use of credit cards may result in unmanageable debt and could lead to a tainted credit record. Accompanying the increase in consumer debt, for instance, has been an increase in personal bankruptcies. In mid-1995, 832,415 consumers declared themselves insolvent, up 6% from the previous year (Gullo and Marino, 1996).

In addition to the serious financial consequences, there is a social stigma associated with excessive debt. Debtors are perceived to be reckless, overindulgent, impatient and irresponsible individuals (Livingstone & Lunt, 1992). Given such lasting and negative consequences of credit overuse, the importance of investigating its antecedents cannot be overemphasized. Although attempts have been made to identify sociodemographic and personality variables that profile consumer types likely to get into problematic financial situations (e.g., Dessart and Kuylen, 1986; Livingstone and Lunt, 1992), few studies have focused directly on the antecedents of credit card overuse. Specifically, there may be dispositional characteristics that lead consumers to accumulate excessive credit card debt. Credit cards are more easily accessible than many other forms of credit, and their convenience of use may contribute to the their *overuse* by impulsive (Rook, 1987) or compulsive shoppers (Faber and O'Guinn, 1988).

Consumers' tendency to focus on a specific temporal "region" may also contribute to their indebtedness. Both impulsive and compulsive shoppers exhibit a general tendency to focus on the present, and a lack of insight into the long-term consequences of current spending patterns, both of which can lead to problematic debt situations (Rook, 1987; O'Guinn and Faber, 1989; Hoch and Loewenstein, 1991). The relationship between problematic debt and temporal orientation, however, has not been empirically documented. The objective of this paper is to explore the relationship between consumers' temporal orientation (i.e., present versus future) and overuse of credit cards.

LITERATURE REVIEW

Credit card users and usage

The study of credit cards has focused on profiling users versus nonusers on demographic (Matthews and Slocum, 1969; Adcock, Hirschman, and Goldstucker, 1977; Hirschman and Goldstucker, 1978; Lindley, Rudolph, and Selby, 1989; Martell and Fitts, 1981; Kinsey, 1981), life style (Plummer, 1971), and psychographic variables (Wiley and Richard, 1975). The general profile that emerges from this research describes credit card users as educated, socially active and mobile individuals from upper income brackets. Moreover, heavy credit card users are described as younger (25-34), married, college graduates, with professional or managerial occupations (Wiley and Richard, 1975).

An additional research stream has focused on credit card usage and its effects on spending patterns. For instance, Hirschman (1979) finds that the total amount of expenditures is higher when consumers use credit cards (bank or store-issued) than when they use cash in a real spending situation. Feinberg (1986) offers an explanation for the increased spending observed when consumers use credit cards, suggesting that credit cards serve as conditioning stimuli for spending. Specifically, Feinberg finds that the probability of spending, speed of decision to spend, and amount of spending are facilitated by credit card cues. Deshpande and Krishnan (1980), however, find that consumers who use credit cards do not necessarily spend more, but instead use credit cards when purchasing more expensive items. These researchers also find that, contrary to popular beliefs, credit card possession is unrelated to impulse buying. In sum, the literature links credit cards to increased spending (Hirschman, 1979), and as a conditioning stimuli, credit card cues are proposed as contributors to credit overuse (Feinberg, 1986).

Consumer psychology of debt and savings

While the literature does not address the characteristics of consumers with a potential to accumulate excessive debt from credit cards, several studies have profiled consumers with problematic debt in general. Dessart and Kuylen (1986), for instance, conclude that those families more likely to have excessive debt are renters, have children between 7 and 18, and have a number of outstanding balances with different companies, especially mail order firms. They further suggest that factors contributing to problem debt include (a) a lack of understanding of the consequences of financial dealings, (b) easily accessible credit, and (c) a lack of money-management skills.

Livingstone and Lunt (1992) also identify characteristics of consumers in debt as well as demographic and economic factors that discriminate debtors from non debtors. Specifically, they find that social class has a negative relationship with debt, while disposable income is positively related to debt. They also note that the absolute number of debts one has is positively related to the overall level of indebtedness. While stereotyped conceptions of savers and borrowers suggest that their behaviors have different motivations and consequences, Livingstone and Lunt (1993) report that their financial strategies are not necessarily mutually exclusive. In fact, these researchers find a considerable number of respondents who simultaneously possess both debt and savings.

In addition to sociodemographic and economic variables, individual difference variables and attitude measures have been used to identify problem debtors. Awh and Waters (1974) find, for example, that consumer's attitudes towards bank charge cards are related to the activity of their cards. Livingstone and Lunt (1992) also suggest that debtors tend to hold somewhat favorable attitudes towards credit and debt, especially because credit cards allow immediate purchases which would otherwise need to be postponed. One individual difference variable found to impact excessive debt is locus of control (Dessart and Kuylen, 1986; Lunt and Livingstone, 1991; Livingstone and Lunt, 1992). Dessart and Kuylen (1986) explain that "the more borrowers feel that they can control their lives and the things around them (internal control), the less likely they are to get into financial difficulties" (p.320).

The psychological profile of those in problem debt has also been studied from the perspective of addiction theory (Tokunaga, 1993). Tokunaga (1993) hypothesizes that consumers with credit-related problems have a psychologically similar profile to that of addicts. He finds, for instance, that external locus of control and lower self-efficacy are among the characteristics of credit overusers. According to Tokunaga, these consumers see money as a source of power and prestige, and are less likely to take appropriate steps to retain their money. However, contrary to Tokunaga's expectations, consumers with credit problems do not exhibit higher levels of risk-taking or sensation-seeking, as would be predicted by an addiction model.

Temporal Orientation

One unexplored individual difference variable with the potential to contribute to a better understanding of problem debt is temporal orientation, or an individual's tendency to focus on one temporal region. An individual's future orientation, for instance, may be exhibited by his/her tendency to set goals and chart plans to meet them, while a present orientation may be exemplified by a tendency to behave spontaneously (Jones, 1994). Jones (1994) developed the *Temporal Orientation Scale* to measure individual differences in this construct. Simple correlations with several other personality variables support the face validity of this scale. Specifically, impulsivity/sensation seeking is negatively related to a future orientation (r=-.45), while neuroticism/anxiety is negatively related to a present orientation (r=-.12).

Individual differences in perceptions of the present-future dichotomy have been studied across cultures (e.g., Jones, 1988), and investigated in relation to scholastic achievement of college students (e.g., Jones, 1994). However, research addressing the effects of temporal orientation on consumer behavior in general, and on credit overuse in particular, are somewhat limited (e.g., Walsh, 1994; Walsh and Spiggle, 1993; Bergadaa, 1990).

Bergadaa (1990), for example, posits that differences in temporal orientation lead to different consumption patterns and product preferences. She bases such argument on the fact that future oriented consumers do not believe in fate and judge themselves to be responsible for their own future, while present oriented individuals are more reactive to their environment and consider themselves to be more subject to fate. In addition, present oriented consumers' primary concern is with improvement of their current situation, while future oriented individuals look forward to changes, and try to remain flexible in order to take advantage of upcoming opportunities.

Walsh (1994), on the other hand, argues that temporal orientation affects consumers' higher-order choices (i.e., choices which precede all purchase decisions) such as savings and spending. Walsh (1994) reports that present-oriented consumers give minimal thought to saving and spend freely in the present. Future-oriented respondents, however, exhibit a pattern of higher order choices suggesting anticipation of future responsibilities and potential restrictions. Walsh (1994) concludes that "future oriented individuals recognize trade-offs between present and future higher order choices while present oriented individuals do not" (p.316).

Temporal Orientation and Credit Card Overuse

It is important to recognize that consumers' concept of time and their focus toward a specific temporal region may not only influence higher order choices, but more specific consumption actions as well. Specifically, when using credit cards, temporal orientation may influence consumers' decisions to: (a) charge purchases, (b) carry a balance and pay finance charges or (c) pay the full balance every month. Each of these decisions hinges upon a specific conceptualization of time.

First, consumers who overuse credit fall into what Matthews and Slocum (1969) refer to as the "installment segment". That is, unlike the "convenience segment," who uses credit cards for convenience and pays off the balance at the end of each month, the "installment segment" relies upon credit cards as a high-interest source of financing. Today, the installment segment appears to be quite large. Over 50% of all purchases charged by consumers are still owed to card issuers a year later, and the average balance of a typical credit card user is in excess of $3,000 (*Chicago Tribune*, July 11, 1994).

A consumer's decision to use installment credit has to be made after considering his/her future ability to pay. This entails thinking about how long it will take to pay off the debt (i.e., how many installments?, over how many months?), as well as consideration of the finance charges that will be accumulated while paying off the debt. For instance, it has been reported that on a balance of $1,800 at 18 percent interest, it would take a consumer 22 years and 4 months to pay off the debt when only the required minimum payment is made. After such a time, the interest paid would amount to $3,797, making the total debt $5,597 (Gullo and Marino, 1996). We propose that a present as opposed to a future temporal orientation may hinder such reasoning, contributing in turn to an overuse of credit.

Second, since present oriented consumers are not concerned with planning for the future and prefer to live in the now (Bergadaa, 1990; Jones, 1994), they may be less likely to consider the long-term consequences of overuse of credit cards. These consumers may be more likely to have a revolving credit, to make only the minimum payment on their cards, and to resort to additional cards as they "max-out" their credit limits. Thus, these consumers may have an above average number of credit cards. The current study empirically investigates the relationship between temporal orientation and credit overuse, with our hypothesis being that consumers who possess a present versus a future temporal orientation are more likely to overuse credit.

STUDY

Method

Overview To explore the relationship between temporal orientation and credit card overuse, the temporal orientation scale (Jones, 1994) was administered. Subjects were also queried about the number of credit cards they possessed (a surrogate for abuse potential) and whether or not they were employed (a covariate found to be relevant in previous research (e.g., Martell and Fitts, 1981). The nature of the dependent measure (number of credit cards) required a loglinear modeling approach to analysis.

Subjects Eighty-eight University of Florida students in an Introduction to Marketing course completed the survey in exchange for course extra credit. The data from one subject who refused to respond to the dependent measure had to be dropped from the analysis, leaving eighty-seven usable subjects.

Dependent Measures The desire to study credit card overuse presented us with several logical dependent measures. These

TABLE 1
Parameter estimates for the loglinear model

Parameter	df	Estimate	Std Error	Chi-Square	Pr>Chi-Square
Intercept	1	-0.1363	0.5625	0.0587	0.8085
Employment	1	0.3479	0.1363	6.5156	0.0107
Temporal Orientation	1	0.0095	0.0048	3.8692	0.0492

included total amount of credit card debt, average monthly payments, debt to income ratio, and the number of cards held. Unfortunately, all but the last measure were obtainable from our sample. Many of the subjects flatly refused to answer questions about balances and income. Lea, Webley, & Levine (1993) note that the sensitive nature of this topic has at times prevented an accurate and complete description of the causes and consequences of excessive debt and credit overuse.

In addition to a refusal to give sensitive information, inconsistencies found in the replies of those who responded suggested to us that this sensitive data was unreliable (e.g., a subject states that he never carries a balance, but reports currently having one). There also seems to have been a great deal of confusion about credit terminology. By examining the responses, it was clear that many subjects were reporting their "minimum monthly payment" as their "total balance". The combination of outright refusal to give information and clear confusion about credit terms made the data for most measures in the survey uninterpretable and unusable.

These problems were, however, almost completely absent from the "number of cards held" measure (87 of 88 responded). Apparently, subjects in our sample did not find responding to this question inappropriate, and the question format appears to have made it much more easily understood. While this measure is perhaps a less than ideal dependent measure, it is so because of its relative insensitivity. It is a discrete variable with a somewhat limited potential range. Therefore, it should be rather difficult to show a statistically significant impact of a personality characteristic upon such a rough surrogate, making it a statistically conservative dependent measure.

Materials The temporal orientation scale (Jones, 1994) is a 22-item measure of a person's general present vs. future orientation (a trait). To prevent socially desirable responding the scale was embedded in a series of unrelated measures. Questions about credit usage, including balance amount, monthly minimum payment, and number of credit cards held were asked. Demographic questions about age, gender, employment, class and major were also included.

Procedure The survey was administered to subjects in small groups. Upon arrival, subjects were told that the purpose of the study was to collect general information about college students which would be of interest to marketers. They were then handed the packet and instructed to answer at their own pace. After finishing, subjects received proof of participation, were thanked and dismissed.

Results

Demographic data Results from frequency analyses of these data reflect the typical profile of a college undergraduate. Median age 20 (43.2%), with a range of 19 to 45. Most were female(67%), and unemployed (72.7%).

Credit card use in the sample As discussed earlier, the proportion of those who use credit cards has continued to increase since their introduction. The current group of subjects reflected this trend, with only 6.9% indicating that they do not use credit cards. Since we were interested in overuse, only subjects with credit cards were included in the analysis

Due to violations of normality in the distribution of the number of cards held, an ANOVA approach is clearly inappropriate. Not only is it impossible for this measure to take on negative values, but the measure is discrete, and an examination of the raw data indicates strong skew. Therefore, a loglinear model is the correct method of analysis.

The model consisted of the temporal orientation score (independent variable) the number of credit cards currently held (dependent variable), and whether or not the subject was employed (a covariate). The model was a simple Poisson regression with a log link (see table 1). As previous research had shown (Martell and Fitts, 1981), employment was positively related to number of credit cards held. Employed subjects held an average of 3.6 cards, while unemployed subjects held only 2.5 (ChiSquare=6.52, p<.02) As predicted, temporal orientation was also found to have a significant impact upon the number of credit cards held (ChiSquare=3.87, p<.05). This significant impact, however, was in the opposite direction to that which was predicted. Having a future temporal orientation was associated with holding *more* credit cards. These results are contrary to the argument that a present temporal orientation leads to credit card overuse. Higher values on the temporal orientation scale denote a future orientation. In this sample, subjects who scored higher also tended to have more credit cards.

Discussion

Several explanations can be posited to account for the observed, counterintuitive results. One is that college students do not fully grasp the nature of debt. We reject this explanation for several reasons. Specifically, there is evidence to suggest that college-aged students with some debt are quite good at calculating loan repayment schedules in their heads (Lewis and Venrooij, 1995). Thus, college students are capable of understanding the consequences of debt. In order to explain why those with a future temporal orientation should choose to hold more cards we may need to examine the origins of our initial hypothesis.

It was assumed that those who looked forward would be less likely to acquire the means to get into excessive debt. This was perhaps based upon the simplistic idea that "saving is good and debt is bad." The preeminence of this notion in western cultures can be traced back to the middle ages (see Warneryd, 1989 for an interesting discussion). If, however, one takes a life-cycle approach to debt and savings (see Modigliani, 1985 for a review) the results of this study seem to make more sense.

College students may have higher expectations than the rest of the population as to their ability to repay debt. They may feel confident in their ability to get a good job upon graduation, and thus may feel justified in their current use of credit cards (e.g., Dominitz and Manski, 1996). If that is the case, the results are not totally incompatible with a temporal orientation explanation, given that these subjects' decision to spend now could be driven by their plans and expectations regarding their future financial outlook. It may be the case that "buying now and paying later" is logically enhanced by "living in the future" when that future is perceived to involve drastically improved earnings.

Further investigations should attempt to document the plausibility of this explanation. Extensions of this research may point to yet another example of how "college sophomores in the laboratory" represent a unique subset of the population (Sears, 1986).

Limitations and Future Research

"Buy now, pay later" has been the prevalent message to consumers from credit card companies. They have made immediate gratification a reality. In a society driven by consumption, being in debt has become a way of life (Lea et al., 1993). We have demonstrated one aspect of credit consumption (number of credit cards held) which is affected by temporal orientation. While researchers have used number of credit cards as an indicator of problematic debt (e.g., O'Guinn and Faber, 1989; d'Astous, 1990), we recognize that it is a less-than-ideal dependent variable, and suggest that future research incorporate more sensitive measures of credit overuse (e.g., income to debt ratio).

The current finding may be unique to college students, so replication with non-student samples is imperative. Equally important is a better understanding of developmental influences on the acquisition of money-management skills and specific consumption patterns. Specifically, the process by which children are enculturated into a modern market economy where debt and savings play an important role, must be investigated (e.g., Webley, Levine, and Lewis, 1991). Similarly, the impact of early consumption experiences on dysfunctional buying behavior should be examined. d'Astous (1990) reports, for instance, that patterns of compulsive buying begin to emerge in adolescence. Finally, by college-age, consumers have acquired some financial responsibility and make a variety of independent consumption decisions. Understanding the forces that shape such decisions can help explain much of these consumers' adult behavior, including the decision to save and to acquire debt.

Future research should also explore other consumption behavior which can be potentially affected by an individual's temporal orientation. For instance, Livingstone and Lunt (1992) argue that "savings provide present resources drawn from past income and borrowing provides present resources drawn from future income" (p. 116). Studies of saving behavior might benefit from an understanding of consumers' temporal orientation as it explains likelihood of planning, and general feelings of optimism as reinforced by general economic circumstances (Katona, 1975; Walsh, 1994). Similarly, impulse buying could be affected by temporal orientation. This consumption phenomenon specifically relates to a present orientation and the need for immediate gratification. As Rook (1987) points out, "marketing innovations such as credit cards, cash machines, 'instant credit,' 24-hour retailing, home shopping networks, and telemarketing now make it easier than ever before for consumers to purchase things on impulse, " (p.189). Whether people with different temporal orientations are more or less likely to plan purchases or buy on impulse should be investigated. Finally, the potential interrelationship between credit over-

use, propensity to save, and impulse buying could be investigated in the context of temporal orientation.

Policy Implications

The main goal of consumer protection efforts that focus on problem debt should be to empower consumers through education (Hill, 1994). Whether information is provided by government agencies, credit counseling entities, or the credit card industry, it is important to address the temporal perspective that colors consumers' perceptions of their spending, borrowing and savings behavior. Consumer education programs may be more effective in preventing problematic debt if, for example, they frame specific purchases in terms of the amount of time it will take to repay them and the interest accumulated in such time. Also, consumers may re-think the way they use their credit cards if repayment is framed in terms of the number of work hours needed to repay specific purchases. In sum, consumers may be able to make better financial decisions once they are aware of the impact of the present-future dichotomy on their behavior.

REFERENCES

Adcock, William O., Elizabeth C. Hirschman, and Jac L. Goldstucker (1977). "Bank Card Users: An Updated Profile," in *Advances in Consumer Research, Vol. 4*, ed. William D. Perrault, Jr., Atlanta: Association for Consumer Research, 236-241.

Awh, R. V., and D. Waters, (1974). "A Discriminant Analysis of Economic, Demographic, and Attitudinal Characteristics of Bank Charge-Card Holders: A Case Study," *Journal of Finance, 29*, 973-980.

Bergadaa, Michelle M. (1990). "The Role of Time in the Action of the Consumer," *Journal of Consumer Research, 17*, 289-302.

d'Astous, Alain (1990). "An Inquiry into the Compulsive Side of 'Normal' Consumers," *Journal of Consumer Policy, 13*, 15-31.

Deshpande, Rohit, and S. Krishnan (1980). "Consumer Impulse Purchase and Credit Card Usage: An Empirical Examination Using the Log Linear Model," in *Advances in Consumer Research, Vol. 2*, ed. Mary Jane Schlinger, Provo, UT: Association for Consumer Research, 792-795.

Dessart, W. C. A., and A. A. A. Kuylen (1986). "The Nature, Extent, Causes, and Consequences of Problematic Debt Situations," *Journal of Consumer Policy, 9*, 311-334.

Dominitz, Jeff and Charles F. Manski (1996). "Eliciting Student Expectations of the Returns to Schooling," *Journal of Human Resources, 31*.

Faber, Ronald J. and Thomas C. O'Guinn (1988). "Compulsive Consumption and Credit Abuse," *Journal of Consumer Policy, 11*, 97-109.

Feinberg, Richard A. (1986). "Credit Cards as Spending Facilitating Stimuli: A Conditioning Interpretation," *Journal of Consumer Research, 13*, 348-356.

Gullo, Karen and Vivian Marino (1996). "Rise in Credit Card Spending Causes a Black Hole of Debt; Consumer Debt has Surged 39 percent in 5 years, Now Totaling Over $1 Trillion," *The Austin American Statesman*, April, D1.

Hill, Ronald Paul (1994). "Bill Collectors and Consumers: A Troublesome Exchange Relationship," *Journal of Public Policy and Marketing, 13*, 20-35.

Hirschman, Elizabeth C. (1979). "Differences in Consumer Purchase Behavior by Credit Card Payment System," *Journal of Consumer Research, 6*, 58-66.

_____, and Jac L. Goldstucker (1978). "Bank Credit Card Usage in Department Stores: An Empirical Investigation," *Journal of Retailing, 54*, 3-12.

Hoch, Stephen J. and George F. Loewenstein (1991). "Time-inconsistent Preferences and Consumer Self-Control," *Journal of Consumer Research, 17*, 492-507.

Jones, James M. (1988). "Cultural Differences in Temporal Orientation," in *Toward a Social Psychology of Time: New Perspectives*, ed. J. McGrath, Beverly Hills, CA: Sage.

_____ (1994). "An Exploration of Temporality in Human Behavior," in *Beliefs, Reasoning, and Decision Making: Psycho-logic in Honor of Bob Abelson*," ed. Roger C. Schank, Ellen Langer, New Jersey: Lawrence Erlbaum Associates, Inc., 389-411.

Katona, George (1975). *Psychological Economics*, New York: Elsevier Scientific.

Kinsey, Jean (1981). "Determinants of Credit Card Accounts: An Application of Tobit Analysis," *Journal of Consumer Research, 8*, 172-182.

Lea, Stephen E. G., Paul Webley, and R. Mark Levine (1993). "The Economic Psychology of Consumer Debt," *Journal of Economic Psychology, 14*, 85-119.

Lewis, Alan and Marlies van Venrooij (1995). "A Note on the Perceptions of Loan Duration and Repayment" *Journal of Economic Psychology, 16*, 161-168.

Lindley, James T., Patricia Rudolph, and Edward B. Selby (1989). "Credit Card Possession and Use: Changes Over Time," *Journal of Economics and Business, 41*, 127-142.

Livingstone, Sonja M., and Peter K. Lunt (1992). "Predicting Personal Debt and Debt repayment: Psychological, Social and Economic Determinants," *Journal of Economic Psychology, 13*, 111-134.

_____ and _____ (1993). "Savers and Borrowers: Strategies of Personal Financial Management," *Human Relations, 46*, 963-985.

Lunt, Peter K. and Sonja Livingstone (1991). "Psychological, Social, and Economic Determinants of Savings: Comparing Recurrent and Total Savings," *Journal of Economic Psychology, 12*, 621-641.

Martell, Terrence F. and Robert L. Fitts (1981). "A Quadratic Discriminant Analysis of Bank Credit Card User Characteristics," *Journal of Economics and Business, 33*, 153-159.

Matthews, H. Lee, and John W. Slocum, (1969). "Social Class and Commercial Bank Card Usage," *Journal of Marketing, 33*, 71-78.

Modigliani, F. (1985). "Life Cycle, Individual Thrift and The Wealth Of Nations," Nobel lecture delivered in Stockholm, Sweden, December 9.

O'Guinn, Thomas C., and Ronald J. Faber (1989). "Compulsive Buying: A Phenomenological Exploration," *Journal of Consumer Research, 16*, 147-157.

Plummer, Joseph T. (1971). "Life Style Patterns and Commercial Bank Credit Card Usage," *Journal of Marketing, 35*, 35-41.

Rook, Dennis W. (1987). "The Buying Impulse," *Journal of Consumer Research, 14*, 189-199.

Sears, David O. (1986). "College Sophomores in the Laboratory: Influences of a Narrow Data Base on Social Psychology's View of Human Nature," *Journal of Personality and Social Psychology, 51*, 515-530.

Tokunaga, Howard (1993). "The Use and Abuse of Consumer Credit: Application of Psychology Theory and Research," *Journal of Economic Psychology, 14*, 285-316.

Walsh, Patricia Ann (1994). "The Impact of Temporal Orientation on Higher Order Choices: A Phenomenological Investigation," *Advances in Consumer Research, Vol. 22*, Provo, UT: Association for Consumer Research, 311-317.

_____ and Susan Spiggle (1993). "Consumer Spending Patterns: Dimensions and Dichotomies," *Advances in Consumer Research, Vol. 21*, UT: Association for Consumer Research, 35-40.

Warneryd, Karl-Eric (1989) "On the Psychology of Saving: An Essay on Economic Behavior," *Journal of Economic Psychology, 10*, 515-554.

Wiley, James B., and Lawrence M. Richard (1975). "Applications of Discriminant Analysis in Formulating Promotional Strategy for Bank Credit Cards," in *Advances in Consumer Research, Vol. 2*, Provo, UT: Association for Consumer Research, 535-544.

Webley, Paul, Mark Levine, and Alan Lewin (1991). "A Study in Economic Psychology: Children's Savings in a Play Economy," *Human Relations, 44*, 127-146.

Smart Shopping: The Origins and Consequences of Price Savings

Haim Mano, University of Missouri-St. Louis
Michael T. Elliott, University of Missouri-St. Louis

ABSTRACT

This research focuses on *smart shopping*, defined as a tendency for consumers to invest considerable time and effort in seeking and utilizing promotion-related information to achieve price savings. The study develops a measure of smart shopping and assesses its relationships to other related marketplace traits and behaviors as well as shopping-specific outcomes. The results indicate that smart shopping is a distinct behavioral construct. Furthermore, when individuals attribute price savings to their shopping skills and efforts, smart shopping is positively associated with favorable utilitarian and hedonic evaluations and purchase satisfaction.

Prominent in many shopping experiences is the belief that certain activities such as organizing and redeeming coupons, reading product labels, or knowing where to buy certain products will lead to price savings. These activities are often described in the popular press as "smart-shopping." This concept is associated with transactions involving an effective use of one's marketplace skills and resources that ultimately leads to enhanced economic utility.

In addition to these strictly economic aspects, smart shopping may provide a variety of psychological and social benefits to consumers (Schindler 1989). For example, paying a reduced price for a particular item might lead a consumer to feel proud, excited, or to have a sense of accomplishment (Holbrook et al. 1984), thereby enhancing one's self image. The satisfaction of utilizing one's shopping expertise to "beat the system" or to help others find bargains may also serve self-esteem needs (Feick et al. 1988). It is not clear, however, under what conditions price savings lead to psychological benefits. There is evidence which suggests that the extent of hedonic responses to shopping depends largely on how "responsible" consumers feel for getting a discount (Schindler 1989). If such conditions facilitate positive shopping experiences, then it is important to examine how and when attribution of responsibility may lead to them.

The purpose of this paper is three-fold. First, we conceptualize and measure the smart shopping trait. Second, we explore the construct's links with related marketplace behaviors. Third, we investigate the role of *attribution of responsibility* in moderating utilitarian and hedonic evaluations as well as purchase satisfaction. Though exploratory in nature, this study attempts to establish smart shopping as a unique behavioral construct with respect to other consumer involvement traits.

THE CONCEPT OF SMART SHOPPING

We define smart shopping as *the tendency to invest considerable time and effort in seeking and utilizing promotion-related information in order to achieve price savings.* Our discussion of this construct revolves around three interrelated components: (1) marketplace knowledge, (2) behaviors designed to acquire promotion-related information, and (3) the consequences of taking advantage of price promotions.

Smart Shopping Knowledge

Kassarjian (1981) contends that some individuals may feel it is their obligation to become knowledgeable consumers. An essential element of the hypothesized smart shopping trait is a willingness to invest effort to gather information for specific product purchases. Many shoppers (cf. Furse et al.'s 1982, *preparatory shoppers*) are likely to believe that doing their "homework" is important in taking advantage of sales opportunities, getting the best deal possible, or finding high quality merchandise at discount prices.

Smart shopping is reflected in two forms of marketplace knowledge and skills: (a) sales awareness and (b) ability to effectively evaluate prices. First, smart shoppers exhibit an awareness of sales promotions in the marketplace since they are motivated by the utility of saved financial resources. Therefore, these consumers know when an item is on sale, where to shop for specials, and frequently note sales announcements.

Second, smart shoppers are believed to have general price knowledge and the ability to effectively evaluate prices. Smart shoppers may undertake a number of covert and fairly elaborate *mental price evaluation activities* including price-related memory searches, drawing inferences about the seller's reputation and motives, and sophisticated reasoning to determine whether a price is high or low (Schindler and Bauer 1988). They are also likely to be involved in *overt price evaluation activities* (Schindler 1989) such as examining ads, checking labels, asking salespeople and friends, or monitoring the price accuracy. The utilization of these cognitive skills is a major factor leading the smart shopper to take credit for transactional savings.

Smart Shopping Behaviors

Even though a number of behaviors may be indicative of effective shopping, two types of behaviors reflect critical elements of smart shopping: information search and organizing activities. Finding discounts requires time and effort. Smart shoppers will typically engage in *ongoing information search* in which they monitor both out-of-store and in-store promotional information. They are more likely to pay attention to sales promotions in the media, seek out pricing information in consumer magazines, and engage in store browsing. During in-store purchasing, they tend to exhibit price monitoring behaviors such as searching for store coupons or asking store personnel for information. As a result, they are more likely to locate promotions, find quality merchandise at reduced prices, and engage in more in-store price negotiation than other individuals. Moreover, *organizing activities* such as developing shopping lists, budgeting groceries, and calling to check product availability and prices represent behaviors that lead to finding better prices.

Smart Shopping Evaluations

The third aspect of smart shopping is the evaluative consequences of a shopping experience. Recent research has identified two primary dimensions of consumption-related evaluations: *utilitarian and hedonic* (Hirschman and Holbrook 1982). Previous research has focused on shopping's utilitarian aspects. For example, Stone's (1954) taxonomy identified *economic consumers*, shoppers who regard shopping as "work" and seek shopping efficiency. In the case of smart shopping, this would include the value of the alternative uses of money saved versus the alternative purchases which would be foregone.

Hedonic evaluations reflect shopping's potential for emotional and entertainment worth (Hirschman and Holbrook 1982). Compared to shopping's utilitarian aspects, hedonic values derived from shopping experiences that result in price savings include competence or a sense of accomplishment (Schindler 1989). Clearly, shoppers can experience both utilitarian and hedonic responses to price savings. Consider, for example, a consumer who is accompanied by a "shopping buddy" and finds the product that motivated the shopping trip at the first store visited and at a very low price. This is likely to elicit both types of evaluations. Utilitarian is represented by the ease of acquisition and hedonic because the bargain may be a source of pride and accomplishment which can be shared with another person.

Attribution of Responsibility for Price Savings

A central element in activating smart shopper's utilitarian and hedonic evaluations is whether a consumer feels "responsible" for getting the discount or savings. Schindler (1989) tested the idea that attribution of responsibility affects consumers' satisfaction from a purchase. He found that consumers were more satisfied with having received a discount if they felt responsible for having found that discount than if they received the same discount based on luck or some other external factor (e.g., receiving in-store coupons from a cashier). Given the goal-directed nature of smart shopping, the attribution shoppers make to themselves for finding a shopping bargain is likely to accentuate the positive consequences of their actions.

HYPOTHESES

The nomological net of the smart shopping trait is examined with two sets of hypotheses. First, as proposed, smart shopping should be positively related to a series of marketplace skills and behaviors that include: (1) marketplace knowledge, (2) information monitoring, (3) pre-purchase organization, (4) in-store price evaluations, and (5) couponing behaviors. Operationally, the hypotheses will be tested by (a) the correlation of smart shopping with the relevant behavior and (b) regression analysis, i.e., by the additional contribution of smart shopping on the dependent variable after partialling out the effects of three relevant market-involvement scales—market mavenism, value consciousness, and coupon proneness.

As defined by Feick and Price (1987), market mavenism is a trait that assesses "the degree to which an individual has information about many kinds of products, places to shop, and other facets of markets, and initiates discussions with consumers and responds to requests from consumers for market information." As such, market mavenism is similar to smart shopping in many respects. Market mavens tend to be involved in the planning of preshopping activities such as shopping with ads, budgeting groceries, and using coupons (Price, Feick, and Guskey-Federouch 1988), have been shown to enjoy shopping, and to use the mass media as an information source (Feick and Price 1987).

Coupon proneness is defined as "an increased propensity to respond to a purchase offer because the coupon form of the purchase offer positively affects purchase evaluations" (Lichenstein, Netemeyer, and Burton 1990). Similarly, smart shoppers are posited to exhibit a heightened sensitivity to coupon usage. However, the extent to which consumers view couponing as a means rather than an end to effective shopping may point to the difference between being a smart shopper or simply being coupon prone.

Value consciousness has been conceptualized as reflecting "a concern for price paid relative to quality received" (Lichenstein, Ridgeway, and Netemeyer 1993). The idea that some consumers hold more accurate perceptions of the relationship between price and quality is also central to the concept of a smart shopper. However, value consciousness is a necessary but not a sufficient condition for smart shopping.

Smart Shopping Skills and Characteristic Behaviors

Marketplace knowledge. As with market mavenism, marketplace knowledge is purported to be a cornerstone of smart shopping. Thus,

H_1: After taking into account market mavenism, smart shopping explains a significant amount of variation in marketplace skills and knowledge such as (a) knowledge about products, places, and sales, (b) expertise in product prices, and (c) knowledge regarding which is the best brand to buy.

Monitoring Promotion-Related Information. Similar to market mavenism, smart shopping reflects a general interest in the marketplace and manifests itself through an ongoing search for prepurchase information. Smart shopping is likely to be more goal-oriented and focused on price saving information surrounding a specific purchase situation such as sales announcements, reading consumer magazines, and collecting in-store coupons. Since market mavenism and coupon proneness both lead to these type of searches,

H_2: After taking into account market mavenism and coupon proneness, smart shopping explains a significant amount of variation in behaviors related to the monitoring of promotion-related information such as (a) attending to ads for sales announcements, (b) reading consumer magazines, and (c) searching for in-store coupons.

Prepurchase Organizing Behaviors. As mentioned earlier, an important characteristic of smart shopping is the tendency to collect and organize shopping information. These planning behaviors are also the trademark of value conscious and coupon prone consumers. Hence:

H_3: After taking into account value consciousness and coupon proneness, smart shopping explains a significant amount of variation in prepurchase organization behaviors such as (a) use of shopping lists, (b) budgeting groceries, (c) tracking expiration date on coupons, and (d) planning shopping trips with coupons.

Price Evaluation Behaviors. The term smart shopping connotes that consumers are willing and able to undertake price evaluations that depend on memory search, complex mental computations, and/or physical search activities. This study focuses on the overt search aspects of price evaluation. Thus,

H_4: After taking into account value consciousness, smart shopping explains a significant amount of variation in behaviors related to price evaluation such as (a) comparing "unit prices," (b) watching the checkout scanner, (c) checking prices for low-priced items.

Couponing Behaviors. Smart shoppers' involvement in the marketplace and desire to achieve transaction savings should be manifested in money-saving marketplace behaviors. Since couponing is the most frequently used sales promotion device, we expect smart shopping to provide a unique contribution in explaining this behavior.

H_5: After taking into account coupon proneness, smart shopping explains a significant amount of variation in coupon behaviors such as (a) percentage of coupon usage, (b) number of coupon used, (c) value of coupons redeemed.

The Role of Attribution of Responsibility in the Consequences of Price Saving

We propose that when a shopper feels responsible for taking advantage of a price discount, smart shopping tendencies will be related to positive consequences derived from that shopping trip.

H_6: When consumers feel responsible for price savings, smart shopping is positively related to (a) utilitarian evaluations, (b) hedonic evaluations, and (c) satisfaction from the shopping experience.

METHOD

Subjects

A total of 228 subjects participated in the main study: 192 business undergraduates at a Midwest public university and 36 evening MBA students at a private Midwest university.

Procedure and Instruments

The research materials were enclosed in a booklet entitled, "Shopper Survey," and distributed to subjects prior to a scheduled class meeting. The subjects responded anonymously and at their own pace.

Smart Shopping Items. In the survey's first section, subjects were asked to respond to a set of 39 items designed to measure the smart shopping construct. These items were screened from an initial pool of 52 items generated to reflect our conceptual definition of the smart shopping concept and generated through in-depth interviews and a perusal of newspapers, trade publications, and academic literature using relevant key terms (e.g., "smart shoppers," "savings," "bargain hunters,"). The items were assessed using 5-point Likert scales ranging from strongly disagree (1) to strongly agree (5).

Shopping Behaviors. In section two, subjects were instructed to provide frequency estimates (using 5-point scales, 1=never, .. 5=very often) for several shopping behaviors: using shopping lists, budgeting groceries, planning shopping trips with coupons, reading consumer magazines such as *Consumer Reports*, seeking out the advice of friends regarding which brand to buy, spending time talking with friends about products and brands, paying full price for merchandise, paying attention to TV ads when something is on sale, and going to stores just to browse. They were then asked about the frequency of the following behaviors: number of stores visited in a typical week, percent of shopping trips using coupons, number of coupons used in a typical week, value (savings) of coupons used in a typical week, number of coupons given in a typical month, and number of coupons received in a typical month.

Shopping and Market-Related Traits. In the third section, subjects responded to four scales designed to measure individual shopping and market-related traits. Using a 5-point Likert scale (ranging from strongly disagree "1" to strongly agree "5"), subjects responded to items designed to measure the three shopping-related traits: market mavenism (Feick and Price 1987; six items; alpha=.83), coupon proneness (Lichtenstein, Netemeyer and Burton 1990; eight items; alpha=.88), and value consciousness (Lichtenstein, Netemeyer, and Burton 1990; seven items; alpha=.86).

Attribution of Responsibility for a "Smart Purchase". In the fourth section–entitled A Recent Shopping Experience–subjects were randomly assigned to either a "smart purchase" or a "routine purchase" scenario. This was accomplished through elicitation instructions. Subjects in the "smart purchase" scenario were asked to think about a recent purchase in which they got a bargain and for which they were responsible (i.e., visited several stores, compared prices, or talked to a knowledgeable friend) for the discounted price. Subjects in the routine scenario were asked to consider a recent purchase (without any mention of price savings or responsibility). For both scenarios, participants were asked to list the name of the product or brand they purchased, to estimate its price, and to briefly describe how they collected the information for purchasing it.

Shopping Evaluations: The remainder of the materials were identical for both groups. First, subjects provided utilitarian and hedonic evaluations of the shopping experience using a 25-item seven-point semantic differential (Mano and Oliver 1993). Varimax analysis revealed three factors with eigens greater than one (12.00, 2.83, and 1.48; explained variance=65.3%). The decrease in eigenvalues indicate the predominance of two factors. The constrained-to-two-factors solution revealed a hedonic and a utilitarian factor. Two scales were used in subsequent analyses: hedonic (items: nice, pleasant, exciting, agreeable, interesting, positive, appealing, fascinating, desirable, wanted; alpha=.86), and utilitarian evaluation (valuable, relevant, important, means a lot to me, of concern to me, matters to me, significant, useful, beneficial, needed, essential, vital, and fundamental; alpha=.95).

Purchase Satisfaction: Subjects rated their satisfaction with the purchase with a single 11-point unipolar item ranging from 0% (dissatisfied) to 100% (satisfied). Lastly, subjects provided general demographic and background information.

RESULTS

Smart Shopping Scale Development and Validation

Item Selection and Initial Validation. Factor analysis of the 39 items provided initial validation for the smart shopping measure. Principal components analysis revealed one main factor (eigenvalue=10.1, 26% explained variance) widely separated from the second factor (eigenvalue=2.3). Based on content analysis, factor analyses, and validity checks, seven items were included in the smart shopping scale (see Table 1).

Consistent with our conceptual definition, these items reflect the various aspects of the effort invested in acquiring and using information necessary for attaining price savings. As defined, smart shoppers invest effort in collecting promotion-related information (e.g., gather information before shopping, browse stores just to get information), make it a point to learn about promotions (keep abreast of sales), engage in activities aimed at finding bargains (investing effort in preparing for shopping trips, waiting until an item is on sale, shop for specials), and effectively seek and attain price savings (find top quality products at discounts).

The one factor confirmatory factor analysis of the seven items showed strong improvement in fit over the null model (null model χ^2=494, d.f.=21, p<.0001; one factor model χ^2=60.6, d.f.=14, p<.001; χ^2 difference between models=423.4, d.f.=7, p<.0001; all t-values significant<.0001; Tucker and Lewis index=.86) suggesting unidimensionality. Item-to-total correlations ranged from .61 to .78 and the scale's reliability was high (alpha=.91). The mean of the smart shopping measure on a 5-point scale was 3.04 (s.d.=.69).

Discriminant Validation. To further examine its validity, the seven-item smart shopping scale along with the items from the coupon proneness, value consciousness, and market mavenism scales were subjected to principal components and maximum likelihood factor analyses. As mentioned, the other three scales measure individual traits closely related to the proposed smart shopper construct. The results supported the four-factor solution (null model χ^2=3174, d.f.=378, p<.0001; four factor model χ^2=634, d.f.=270, p<.001; χ^2 difference between models=2904, d.f.=108,

TABLE 1

Factor Loadings of Smart Shopping Items in the Main and Validation Studies

LOADINGS		
Main Study Student Sample (n=228)	Validation Study University Staff Sample (n=225)	SCALE ITEMS
77	84	I keep abreast of when stores have sales.
73	64	I generally wait until an item is on sale before purchasing it.
70	74	I like to gather as much information as possible before going on shopping trips.
69	79	I shop a lot for specials.
67	50	I often find top quality merchandise at reduced prices.
64	71	I spend a considerable amount of time and effort preparing for shopping trips
61	52	At times I browse just to get information for future purchases.

NOTE: Loadings are multiplied by 100 and rounded to the nearest integer.

$p<.0001$; all t-values significant$<.0001$; Tucker and Lewis index=.84). As required for discriminant validity, each scale emerged as a distinct factor whereby each scale's items loaded strongly on one single factor ($>.46$) and weakly ($<.44$) on the other three.

In separate analyses, the fit of correlated two factor models of the smart shopping and each of the other three scales was examined using LISREL. As required for construct validation, in all three cases, the correlation between the construct pairs was significantly less than one and the confidence intervals around these correlations did not include the value of one. Taken together, these results suggest that the smart shopping scale is unidimensional and internally consistent.

Further Scale Validation–University Staff Sample

To further validate the scale, we conducted a separate survey with a more representative sample of university employees. After eliminating 12 of the original 39 items, a one-page questionnaire (accompanied by a cover letter and a self-addressed envelope) containing 27 items and a few background questions was mailed to 468 staff members at a large Midwest university. Of the 468 questionnaires mailed, 225 (48%) were returned. The participants were primarily female (76%), averaged 14 years of formal education and were considerably older than the student sample (42.3 vs. 26.5 years).

Supportive of construct validity, factor analysis of the 27 items revealed one main factor with an eigenvalue of 9.1 (34% of the variance) widely separated from the second factor (eigen=2.6). Moreover, the seven items selected in the initial sample also loaded heavily (and in similar order) in the validation sample (Table 1, column 2). A one-factor model confirmatory factor analysis of the 7 items (χ^2=60.6, df=14, p<.0001) showed very strong improvement over the null model (χ^2=494, df=21, p<.0001; between models χ^2 difference=437, d.f.=7, p<.0001; Tucker-Lewis index=.86). Item-to-total correlations ranged from .60 to .78 and the scale's reliability for the validation sample was .89. The scale mean was 3.08 (s.d.=.70; there were no differences in scale means between the two samples, t=1.2, p>.05).

Hypotheses Testing (H1-H5): Nomological Net

Table 2 shows the simple correlations with smart shopping and the regression analyses (standardized coefficients and R^2) after the relevant scale(s) were jointly used in the predicting the dependent variables. The simple correlations of smart shopping with each

dependent variable were all significant (ranging from .15 to .50), thereby providing initial support for H1-H5. F-tests reveal that all regression equations were significant (p<.05).

The concept of smart shopping explicitly includes possession of general market knowledge. H1 posits that when the effects of market mavenism are taken into account, smart shopping will still have a considerable impact on market knowledge related to products, prices, etc. For each of the three measures of marketplace knowledge, the regression coefficient was significant. In fact, the smart shopping coefficient was higher than the corresponding market maven coefficient for each dependent variable.

H2 states that smart shopping will significantly explain promotion monitoring behaviors. After controlling for market mavenism and coupon proneness, smart shopping was a significant predictor of paying attention to TV ads and searching for coupons in stores. Despite a moderate bivariate relationship (r=.16, p<.05), the regression did not support the effect on reading consumer magazines such as *Consumer Reports* (Beta=.10, p>.05).

H3 predicts that smart shopping explains prepurchase organizing behaviors after controlling for the effects of coupon proneness and value consciousness. Smart shopping was a significant predictor for two coupon-related prepurchase activities, tracking coupon expiration dates (Beta=.13, p<.05) and planning shopping trips with coupons (Beta=.14, p<.05). However, budgeting groceries and use of shopping lists–while positively correlated with smart shopping (p<.05 and p<.01)–failed to reach significance. For these two behaviors, value consciousness appears to make the most contribution. Thus, H3 is partially supported.

There is also support for smart shopping's contribution in explaining price evaluation behaviors (H4). Smart shopping is a significant predictor for watching checkout scanners (Beta=.32, p<.01) and checking prices for low-priced items (Beta=.20, p<.01). Despite the high correlation (r=.35, p<.01), the item "comparing unit prices" failed to reach significance in the regression equation. For this particular behavior, it appears that smart shopping explains little unique variance when value consciousness is taken into account. H4 is therefore partially supported.

The idea of smart shopping suggests that some consumers may rely on consumer promotions to realize price savings. H5 proposes that smart shopping will explain various couponing behaviors after taking into account coupon proneness. For each of the three reported couponing behaviors (percent of time using coupons, number of coupons used/week, and dollar value of coupons re-

TABLE 2
Regression Analysis (Standardized Coefficients) for the Effects of Smart Shopping and Relevant Constructs on Shopping Skills and Behaviors

Dependent Variable	Independent Variables[a]				R^2	Simple r[d]
	Smart Shopping	Market Mavenism	Coupon Proneness	Value Conscious.		
H1: Marketplace Knowledge						
I feel more knowledgeable about products, places, and sales	.35[c]	.30[c]	—	—	.32	.50[c]
I consider myself an expert when it comes to pricing	.44[c]	.24[c]	—	—	.35	.56[c]
I have a lot of knowledge how to select the best brand	.30[c]	.21[c]	—	—	.20	.40[c]
H2: Promotion Monitoring						
Pay attention to TV ads when something on sale	.13[b]	.18[c]	.26[c]	—	.19	.30[c]
Read consumer magazines	.10	.19[b]	-.10	—	.05	.16[b]
Search for coupons in store	.21[c]	-.08	.55[c]	—	.42	.39[c]
H3: Prepurchase Organizing Behaviors						
Use Shopping list	.00	—	.17[b]	.27[c]	.15	.20[c]
Budget Groceries	-.08	—	.00	.47	.19	.15[b]
Tracking Coupon expiration	.13[b]	—	.36[c]	.06	.22	.31[c]
Plan shopp. trip with coupons	.14[b]	—	.51[c]	.10	.42	.42[c]
H4: Price Evaluation Behaviors						
Comparing unit prices	.07	—	—	.53[c]	.33	.35[c]
Watching checkout scanner	.32[c]	—	—	.15[b]	.19	.40[c]
Check prices for small items	.20[c]	—	—	.40[c]	.29	.41[c]
H5: Couponing Behaviors						
% time use coupons	.23[c]	—	.40[c]	—	.30	.41[c]
Number of Coupons used/week	.26[c]	—	.28[c]	—	.22	.39[c]
$ value of redeemed coupons/wk.	.25[c]	—	.35[c]	—	.26	.40[c]

[a] N=228
[b] coefficient significant at $p<.05$;
[c] coefficient significant at $p<.01$
[d] Simple correlation of smart shopping scale with the dependent variable

deemed/week) smart shopping was a significant predictor (all p's<.01), thereby supporting H5.

Hypotheses Testing (H6): Attribution of Responsibility Effects

Manipulation Check. To avoid demand artifacts, a manipulation check was conducted with a separate pretest sample of 85 students randomly assigned to either of the two purchase scenarios. Subjects listed the product/brand they were thinking about, its price, and how they collected information prior to making the purchase. Subjects then rated (on a 5-point Likert scale) the extent to which they "felt like a smart shopper," "felt responsible for finding the bargain," or saved money. Next, subjects provided estimates of the percent savings based on the regular price. Supporting the manipulation check, subjects in the "smart purchase" scenario felt more like smart shoppers (M_{high}=4.19 vs. M_{low}=3.45, t(83)=3.55, p<.0001), felt more responsible for finding the product, (M_{high}=3.91 vs. M_{low}=3.47, t(83)=1.76, p<.05), and saved more

money (M_{high}=3.33 vs. M_{low}=2.19, t(83)=4.51, p<.0001) than those in the "routine purchase" scenario.

Smart Shopping and Consequences of Shopping Experiences. H6 predicts positive relationships between smart shopping and utilitarian, hedonic, and satisfaction evaluations in the "smart purchase" scenario. As seen (Table 3, last column), the simple correlations with smart shopping provide initial support for H6. Conversely, in the "routine purchase" scenario, correlations between smart shopping and shopping outcomes ranged from .04 to .11 (n.s.).

As noted earlier, H6 has two implications. First, that the simple correlations of smart shopping with the positive consequences in the "routine purchase" scenario would not be significant. As seen above, all three correlations were low and not significant. In addition to this directional support, the between-conditions differences between correlations were significant: utilitarian (.30 vs .03, t=2.08, p<.02, one-tailed), hedonic (.43 vs. .07,

TABLE 3

Regression Analyses (Standardized Coefficients) for the Effects Of Smart Shopping (SSH), Market Mavenism (MM), Value Consciousness (VC), Coupon Proneness (CP) on Shopping Outcomes

Outcomes	"Routine" Purchase						"Smart" Purchase					
	SSH	VC	MM	CP	(R^2)	r^a	SSH	VC	MM	CP	(R^2)	r^a
Utilitarian	-.04	.08	.08	-.15	(.04)	.04	.27[b]	.20[b]	.00	-.16	(.13)	.30[c]
Hedonic	.04	.03	.34[c]	-.28[b]	(.13)	.07	.42[c]	.10	-.05	-.04	(.20)	.43[c]
Satisfaction	.06	.15	.10	-.05	(.05)	.11	.27[b]	.08	.05	-.13	(.10)	.32[c]

Note: N=114 in both groups.
[a] Simple correlations of smart shopping with shopping outcomes.
[b] Coefficient significant at p<.05;   [c] Coefficient significant at p<.01

t=2.91, p<.01), and satisfaction (.32 vs .11, t=1.65, p<.05). As indicated by the R^2s, the effects of the four traits were considerably weaker for the "routine" scenario than the "smart purchase" situation.

Second, we proposed that attribution of responsibility is a critical factor in smart shopping: smart shopping should have a positive effect on these consequences after controlling for the other scales in the "smart purchase" scenario. The results supported this contention. For the "smart purchase" scenario, after taking into account the other traits, the coefficients for smart shopping were positive and significant in explaining utilitarian evaluation (Beta=.27, p<.05), hedonic evaluations (Beta=.42, p<.01), and purchase satisfaction (Beta=.27, p<.05). Taken together, these results provide further support for the proposed framework.

SUMMARY

The smart shopping construct was hypothesized to consist of three inter-related concepts: knowledge, behaviors, and post-purchase evaluations. Using a series of methodological approaches, we confirmed the scale's validity and after controlling for relevant market-related traits, we have shown the scale to have a considerable effect in explaining a series of market behaviors.

Responsibility for attaining a discount was a central factor leading to smart shoppers' positive evaluations/reactions (i.e., utilitarian, hedonic, and satisfaction) during shopping trips. When consumers felt responsible for saving money because of their own efforts and/or expertise, smart shopping was positively related to these positive shopping-related outcomes.

With respect to utilitarism, the extra value received from a "smart purchase" may be a major motivational factor that increases smart shoppers' involvement in the marketplace. This view is a departure from studies that focus on consumers who see "shopping as work" or "an errand" and closer to the view which describes utilitarian shopping in terms of success and accomplishment. Smart shoppers may indeed perceive shopping as "work," but take credit for making a smart purchase and value the fruits of their labor.

Lastly, smart shopping was also closely related to hedonic evaluations of shopping when consumers felt responsible for finding bargains. Compared to the functional and goal-directed (e.g., "important", "needed") aspects of utilitarism, hedonic shopping experiences were operationalized as "exciting," "fascinating," and "desirable" and reflect shopping's potential for entertainment and emotional worth (Hirschman and Holbrook 1982).

REFERENCES

Feick, Lawrence F. and Linda L. Price (1987), "The Market Maven: A Diffuser of Marketplace Information," *Journal of Marketing*, 51 (January), 83-97.

Feick, Lawrence F., Linda L. Price, and Audrey G. Federouch (1988), "Coupon Giving: Feeling Good by Getting a Good Deal for Somebody Else," Working paper, Grad. Sch. of Business, University of Pittsburgh, Pittsburgh, PA.

Folkes, Valarie S. (1990), "Conflict in the Marketplace: Explaining Why Products Fail," in *Attribution Theory: Applications to Achievement, Mental Health, and Interpersonal Conflict,"* eds. Sandra Graham and Valerie S. Folkes, Hillsdale, NJ: Erlbaum

Furse, David H., Girish N. Punj, and David W. Stewart (1982), "Individual Search Strategies in New Automobile Purchases," in *Advances in Consumer Research,* Vol. 9, Andrew Mitchell, ed., Ann Arbor, MI: ACR, 379-384.

Hirschman, Elizabeth C. and Morris B. Holbrook (1982), "Hedonic Consumption: Emerging Concepts, Methods and Propositions," *Journal of Marketing*, 46 (Summer), 92-101.

Holbrook, Morris B., Robert B. Chestnut, Eric A. Greenleaf (1984), "Play as a Consumption Experience: The Roles of Emotions, Performance, and Personality in the Enjoyment of Games," *Journal of Consumer Research*, 11 (Sept.), 728-739.

Kassarjian, Harold (1981), "Low Involvement: A Second Look," in *Advances in Consumer Research*, Vol. 15, H.K. Hunt, ed., Ann Arbor, MI: Association for Consumer Research.

Lichtenstein, Donald R., Richard G. Netemeyer, and Scot Burton (1990), Distinguishing Coupon Proneness From Value Consciousness: An Acquisition-Transaction Utility Theory Perspective," *Journal of Marketing,* 54 (July), 54-67.

Lichtenstein, Donald R., Nancy M. Ridgway, and Richard G. Netemeyer (1993), "Assessing Perceptions and Consumer Shopping Behavior: A Field Study," *Journal of Marketing Research*, 30 (May), 234-45.

Mano, Haim and Richard L. Oliver (1993), "Assessing the Dimensionality and Structure of the Consumption Experience: Evaluation, Feeling, and Satisfaction," *Journal of Consumer Research*, 20 (December), 451-466.

Price, Linda L., Lawrence F. Feick, and Audrey Guskey-Federouch (1988), "Couponing Behaviors of the Market Maven: Profile of a Super Couponer," in *Advances in Consumer Research*, Vol. 15, Michael J. Houston, ed. Provo, UT: Association for Consumer Research, 354-359.

Schindler, Robert M. (1989), "The Excitement of Getting a Bargain: Some Hypotheses Concerning the Origins and Effects of Smart-Shopper Feelings," in *Advances in Consumer Research*, Vol. 16, Kent Monroe, ed. Ann Arbor, MI: Association for Consumer Research, 447-453.

Schindler, Robert M. and Diana M. Bauer (1988), "The Uses of Price Information: Implications for Encoding," in *1988 AMA Educators' Proceedings*, eds. Gary Frazier et al., Chicago, IL: AMA, 68-73.

Stone, Geogory P. (1954), "City Shoppers and Urban Identification: Observations on the Social Psychology of City Life," *American Journal of Sociology,* 60 (1), 36-45.

Weiner, Bernard (1982), "The Emotional Consequences of Causal Attributions," in *Affect and Cognition*, eds. Margaret S. Clark and Susan T. Fiske, Hillsdale, NJ: Erlbaum.

A Qualitative Investigation of Web-Browsing Behavior

Niranjan V. Raman, University of Tennessee

INTRODUCTION

More than a decade ago, McQuail (1984) predicted that newer communication technologies would change the nature of the communication process from dissemination of information from one source to mass audiences, to individual search and interaction with the source(s). Interactive media like the Internet appear to fulfilling that prophecy.

The growth of the Internet has been projected at nearly 10 percent every month, with a large part of this growth fueled by the development of the World Wide Web (referred to as the Web), and Web browsing software such as Mosaic and Netscape (Ellsworth and Ellsworth 1995). The Web is a popular Internet service that enables documents, pictures and images to be accessed easily from any computer connected to the Internet, by merely pointing and clicking on hyper-text linked words, phrases or images. Millions of consumers now browse through Web pages and sites that enable them to access articles, pictures, and computer programs on the Internet, and participate in discussion forums in cyberspace. Commerce over the Web is gathering momentum with cybermalls, interactive storefronts, and classified advertising. In short, we have new forms of dissemination and assimilation of information on products, services, and interactions between consumers and marketers that is significantly different from traditional mass communication forms like advertising.

Historically, advertisers were able to use programming to their advantage in an environment where viewers did not have many media choices, and typically had little choice but to watch whatever was on the television set (Draft 1992; Olney, Holbrook and Batra 1991). The main assumption for advertising effectiveness was that audiences could be influenced by repeated exposures to advertising messages. This repeated exposure approach pioneered by Ebbinghaus (1885/1987) in experimental psychology, and extended to applications in advertising with Krugman's work (1962; 1975), has dominated much of advertising research and practice. For example, researchers have shown that repetition moderates ad effectiveness (Grass and Wallace 1969), persuasiveness (Wilson and Miller 1968), attitudes (Batra and Ray 1986; Belch 1982; Cacioppo and Petty 1979), and recall (Cacioppo and Petty 1989; Hornik 1989), at different levels of repetitions.

However, over the last decade, audiences have been increasing their influence on what they wish to view. One example of this is their avoidance of exposure to commercials by zipping and zapping (Heeter and Greenberg 1985; Kaplan 1985; Olney, Holbrook and Batra 1991). Interactive media will afford the consumer even better influence and choice of the material available for viewing (Draft 1992; Rust and Oliver 1994; Shell 1994).[1]

With such choices available to consumers, exposure to commercials can be at the consumer's volition (Raman and Leckenby 1995). Clawson (1993) reports the findings of a survey of 1,912 television viewers and electronic enthusiasts that indicates that consumers desire "control, convenience, and customization." Thus, audience members are being extremely selective over what they watch, when they watch, and how much of the content they watch

---

[1]Control in this context means specification of what a viewer wants to see, and excludes other forms of control such as leaving the room, zapping, zipping, turning off the device, or just not paying attention.

(Stewart 1992). The change in audience behavior, from adopting a passive role to a more active one has been suggested as a premonition that traditional intrusive advertising in interactive media is unlikely to happen (Draft 1992; Rust and Oliver 1994). Unlike *incidental* exposure to advertising in conventional media, exposure to marketing messages and commercial communication in interactive media may have to be voluntarily sought by the consumer, such as clicking on an icon or button, in order for exposure to the ad to occur. Additionally, the consumer also exercises a choice of selecting different levels of an interactive message. In other words, the consumer can be exposed to varying amounts or levels of exposure.

Advertisers will therefore have to find some way of inducing consumer exposure to their messages (Shell 1994), or study the conditions under which such desired exposure is likely to result. Furthermore, interactive media also make it possible for marketers to obtain information on consumers preferences and information use in this medium because selection of material and specific file requests can be logged and recorded. This information can be very useful to marketers in instituting upgrades and improvements in products and service offerings (Raman and Leckenby 1995). Hence, it is very important to examine Web-browsing behavior of consumers.

This study adopted a qualitative approach using a combination of natural observations and short interviews to examine how consumers navigate the Web, what experiences they have in their cybertravels, and the elements of Webpages and browsers that they frequently use to navigate. The methodology adopted to study this behavior is presented in the next section. This is followed by a discussion of the findings punctuated by relevant subject comments, and the interpretations and emergent themes identified from the results. Finally, implications for advertisers and marketers are presented.

METHODOLOGY

Web-surfing is generally a solitary personal activity, more similar to reading of a newspaper or magazine, as compared to viewing television which is more social. Studying the ways in which users navigate the Web is very important because it enables insights into the effectiveness of elements of the browser, the homepage, individual habits, and styles of navigating. Besides, studying the experiences of Web users can yield rich insights of communication processes in this medium that cannot be detected by objective measures like hits. Thus, the objectives of this study were two-fold: (i) to observe the styles and ways of browsing the Web, and (ii) to understand the experiences Web users have in their Web navigation and homepage visits.

A phenomenological perspective was adopted for examining the research issues. Palmer (1969) defines phenomenology as "letting things become manifest as what they are, without forcing our own categories on them." According to this author, a phenomenologist examines lived experience to know more about the object or event. This approach enables enhanced theoretical sensitivity to the findings, a valued component of qualitative research (Strauss and Corbin 1990). Such methods of inquiry are being valued in contemporary consumer behavior research (Belk, Sherry and Wallendorf 1988; Hudson and Ozanne 1988; Thompson, Locander and Pollio 1990) for their deeper insights into individuals' behaviors. For example, Thompson, Locander and

Pollio (1990) used an existential phenomenology approach to study everyday shopping experiences of contemporary married women. Sherry (1990) studied the experiences that consumers had at a contemporary flea market with the help of field observations and long interviews with consumers.

This study used a blend of qualitative methods and consisted of field observations and post-observation interviews. Eight individuals, five men and three women, were the subjects of study as they surfed the Web in a computer lab at a large Southwestern university. The ages of the subjects ranged from 15 to 31. The ethnicity of the subjects varied; there was one black, one Hispanic, one Asian, and the remainder white. In exit interviews, all subjects reported having moderate knowledge of the Web, and spending an average of about 8-16 hours on the Web per week. Although this was a small convenience sample, it must be stressed that the goal was to gain insights into the ways that individuals use the Web, and observe usage styles that would help understand what consumers find useful and appealing on the Web. It was also to trace individuals' reasoning processes through their actions.

An observation period began when a subject occupied the computer station adjacent to the researcher's station in the computer, and began surfing the Web. Field notes were rapidly taken on all actions of the user, especially styles of interaction, topic selection and preferences, navigational button usage, and style of browsing. Since individuals in a computer lab typically are engrossed in their work, it was very easy to observe subjects at adjoining computer stations without the knowledge of the subjects. Observation periods averaged over thirty minutes each.

At the end of an observational period, the researcher introduced himself, informed the subject that his/her actions had been recorded for research purposes, and requested the subject for permission to use the observations. The subjects were assured of confidentiality, and all subjects agreed to use of the observational notes in this research. Exit interviews were conducted to check for consistency with actions, and additionally, to get an understanding of the users' actions. In this interview, the subjects were asked on their style of looking up information and topics on the Web, the amount of time they spent on the Web per week, their method of navigation and interaction, and the Web pages that they liked and disliked. Thus, these interviews also helped to serve as a reliability and validity check as mentioned in qualitative research approaches (Kirk and Miller 1986).

OBSERVATIONAL FINDINGS

Analysis of the observations of the subjects on the Web enabled insights into styles and pattern of interactions that come into play in Web-surfing. Each of these phenomena is discussed below, with instances of specific incidents and description of users' actions.

Reject Unless Interesting Phenomenon

Surfing on the Web relates to the ability of individuals to select choices and topics by pointing and clicking on hypertext links to view or obtain other documents and files running on different computers at different places, on their own computers. Ellsworth and Ellsworth (1995) point out that most Web users are very quick at finding out that clicking on highlighted words, pictures, or parts of pictures can enable them to view another page or image.

The subjects observed were found to start their browsing session by clicking open a link from the browser's homepage, or the default homepage which happened to be the university's homepage. Frequently, the first link would be from a What is New or similar topic list. Subsequent topics were selected using related links on topics that were of interest to the user. In other words, the clicking

seemed to have some purpose to it rather than at random. This was confirmed in the exit interviews:

> I start by clicking on Escapes from the Netscapes Home Page. I do this because it has interesting things, especially on science (Matt)

> I usually start off by clicking on the Netscapes icon to get to the Netscapes home page, and then click on What's New (Viola)

> I usually like to read sports and business news stories because I am a journalist. I usually start by looking at Clarinet News on the UT Web home page, and click to What's New and Good (Gail)

This exploratory behavior was also reflected in the selection of subsequent pages and topics. Usually, subjects scanned the first couple of sentences. If it interested them, they scrolled down and were actively involved in reading the whole page or document. Otherwise, they were observed to quickly move on to other topics and links. For example, Matt, averaged about 20 seconds on the first four pages that he glanced at, hitting the *Next* link on the page to move on to other topics. However, he was observed to concentrate on a story *Sand in his Face* taking nearly twice the time on this page (about 48 seconds). He also spent longer time-periods when viewing photographs of *Iceland*, the *Kennedy Space Center Homepage*, and reading the *Apollo* flight summary. He also spent considerable amount of time on the details of the *Space Shuttle* and the images of *Apollo*.

Similarly, Gail took more time (45 seconds) scrolling down to completely read a news story in *ESPNet's Sportzone*, than other pages that she rapidly skimmed at about 12 seconds on average. Gail's method was very purposeful; she took notes on a writing pad when she was on topics/articles that she appeared to be involved in.

Again, this behavior was confirmed in the exit interviews where all respondents indicated that their strategy was to skim the first few lines to decide whether to read the story in its entirety or not:

> I usually scan the stuff and I'll only read something if it's interesting (Chad)

> I click on whatever catches my eye. Then I usually read the first couple of paragraphs. If it's interesting, I go on, else I go back (Matt)

This apparent "need to move on" phenomenon was also reflected in another behavior exhibited by the subjects. When a document or image took longer than twelve seconds to download, subjects canceled these by moving on to other pages and documents. Many Web publishers are using fancy graphics and icons which lead to longer download times. Although such graphics may add to the aesthetic appeal of a Web page, it is more likely not to be seen at all if the download takes more than a few seconds. Moreover, with home computers that access the Web using phone lines, these download times are likely to be longer, and thus, less likely of being viewed.

Such skimming behavior mirrors related research involving CEOs of organizations in Canada. Auster and Choo (1993) reported that environmental scanning behavior of chief executives increased with source accessibility and source quality. In a test of the information overload theory, Grether and Wilde (1983) found that subjects were able to ignore unnecessary or unwanted information, and only select information relevant to their needs. The "reject unless interesting" phenomenon observed may be a main strategy used by subjects to discriminate between useful and not useful information.

Lead Me To The Holy Grail

Subjects enjoyed the fact that it was so easy to find information on any topic on the Web. The most common method appeared to be using a search engine like *Yahoo* or *Web Crawler* to find specific information. This was the most popular method employed by subjects in an exploratory surfing mode. For example, Tom frequently used *Yahoo* to download many files especially on compact discs, scavenge hunts, and theoretical physics. He appeared to read very little, most of the time, he scanned material and moved on. Viola used *InfoSeek* and typed in keywords to get a list of topics. She then clicked on places of her interest like *Brasenose College, Oxford* map, and the *Brad Pitt* page.

> You use *Web Crawler* or something and type in whatever that I am interested in. I put in Los Angeles which gives a bunch of different sites, you can check out. Or it may have related information and then I usually check out a couple of these (John)

Subjects typed in the Uniform Resource Locator (URLs) only to go to specific sites or Web pages. This was usually the case when the subject wished to go to a personal page of a friend or a fellow student. Zahir, 23, an engineering major, frequently typed in URLs to specific personal pages of individuals. Along similar lines, Tom reported getting e-mail from friends giving URLs that is easier to copy and paste in the Open Location box directly instead of having to type it in. Viola also referred to a magazine that had URLs to sites that were highlighted as cool places on the Web.

No bookmark usage was detected in this study. This finding was not wholly surprising since these users were on lab computers with no assurance that a particular computer (that did not rebuild after logging out) would be available to the same user on subsequent days. Bookmark use is probably more prevalent when individuals use their own computers from home.

Back Up

Of all the elements of the browser, the back button on the tool bar of the browser was used most often. All the subjects used this button extensively in their navigation on the Web.

Typically, subjects would click on links to topics. If this was interesting, they would continue to read scrolling down or clicking on subsequent related links. However, when subjects clicked open a topic and decided not to read it or read related material, they would use the back button to get back to the previous page. Thus the previous page appeared to serve as a reference point for the next phase of exploration. For example, Tom used the page links to go from *Bootleg Lists* to *Yahoo*, where he typed in *Entertainment*, and selected *Music*, followed by *Artists*. He then clicked on the back button of the browser (Netscape) three times quickly to get back to *Yahoo* search. Later, he used the back page button four times in succession to get back to *Theoretical Physics Group* page from the *Time Machine* page.

> I go back by hitting the Back button. I use the Back button a lot because it's the easiest way to get back to the previous page. I never type the URL (Matt)

> I use the Back button all the time. I hardly ever use any of the others (Gail, referring to the other buttons on the toolbar of the browser)

> Sometimes I'll spend nearly ten minutes doing nothing but clicking aimlessly (Jim, in response to clicking on links and buttons)

> I use the Back button and links a lot. Usually, I have the addresses of new places. Or if the heading is interesting, I'll look at it. Otherwise, I'll just go back (Joe)

These observations and comments suggest that the back button is vital for Web users. The back button appears to enable using a previous page as a reference point while exploring. It suggests that when the back button can be incorporated into a Web page itself, and linked to the homepage, then the Web user is more likely to use the homepage as a reference page for clicking on other links. For example, subjects were found to use Next buttons and End buttons built into Web pages that were independent of browser buttons. Matt used the scroller frequently to get to the bottom of each topic page and click the Next button there to access the next story. When he reached the last story, he clicked on the End button in this document.

Three of the subjects were also observed using the Stop button. In all cases, this occurred when downloads of Web pages took more than twelve seconds. Although no subjects were observed using any of the other buttons on the toolbar of the browser, one subject reported using the forward and home buttons infrequently.

Use of buttons enables the user to exercise control over what they wish to see or read. This suggests that marketers may be able to offer this control by incorporating navigational buttons into their homepages. This would enable them to both encourage consumers to use their homepages as a reference mark, as well as gather research on individual users' actions by examining file requests and the time they spend on different topics and pages.

You Name It, You Got It

The plethora of information and convenience of access to information emerged as the most important reason given by subjects for browsing the Web. Gail indicated that the Web really helped her career as a journalist. She said that she usually looked at news concerning sports, finance and stock markets, and international news:

> I like browsing because it helps me as a journalist. At the touch of a button, I can get information. It gives my story depth, substance, and fact, and is very convenient. I can even do my interviews on the Web. It saves time and is really very convenient (Gail)

> I like to use the Web because it's so easy to find information, and it's really easy to use. The information is at my finger-tips and I don't have to search books in libraries (Matt)

> The nice thing about the Web is that you can pretty much find anything you want. One can get a lot of information (Chad)

While information is readily available, subjects also conceded that it was easy to lose track of time and the purpose when browsing. For instance, Chad added that it was easy to get sucked up and end up spending 40 hours per week or so just browsing at different things.

> It's like wandering around a library or theme park—it's easy to get lost in both.

Are You Telling Me The Truth?

While the Web provides ready access to information and facts on virtually anything, little interest was evidenced in finding out information about products and services from commercial sites, electronic storefronts, and marketer developed Web pages. One important reason that emerged was the perceived lack of credibility.

None of the subjects were observed on commercial homepages.[2] Very few of the subjects had visited commercial homepages, and some didn't even know of their existence. The ones that did indicated that they did so because they thought that it would be interesting. Some subjects expressed their concern regarding biased information, or questioned the need for information from marketers:

> I visited the Kodak homepage. This happened because I was looking at something, and Kodak was one of the topics on this page. I recognized the name, clicked on it, and took a look. It had pictures of landscapes and monuments. Then I clicked the Back button and went back (Matt)

> After realizing it was from the mutual fund company, I kind of figured that probably their information is going to be biased, trying to make you buy their products. They talked about the shambles that the retirement, that is, the social security is in, and they encourage you to think about retirement and invest it. I thought they might have exaggerated things because it was an actual company trying to sell you some mutual funds. and you can get more of a reaction if they make it seem like you are not going to have any money. I think that is biased because they are trying to make the investment seem more important for you to buy, by making the present system sound not too stable (John)

> I won't ever look at those pages because the information will be provided on products by marketers, and is likely to be one-sided (Tom)

> I have never seen or visited a marketer site. It'll be like reading a commercial. Why would anyone want to read a commercial? (Joe)

To examine subjects' behavior on commercial homepages, all the subjects were requested to go to specific commercial homepages (e.g. *Sony*, *Coca-Cola*) and subsequently observed. Since, at the time of data collection, not many commercial homepages were in existence, with many were under construction, it was decided to use homepages of organizations that were well-known and complete.

All the subjects clicked on links on these pages at random, adopting the skimming behavior. Gail clicked on a couple of links at random on a commercial site, and then clicked right back to her earlier page (*ESPN Sports Zone*) hitting the back button repeatedly.

Viola was observed on the *Coca-Cola* page. She began by typing in Coca-Cola in the search prompt of one of the popular search engines on the Web, and clicking on one of the links. She scanned the homepage, opened links to *Advertising Coca-Cola*, and *Coca-Cola FAQ*. She was amused to read about older campaigns of *Coke*, and chuckled to herself. Next, she came to the *FAQ* page,

read a couple of paragraphs and commented: "Some of this stuff is seriously boring." She later mentioned that she had also visited the *Budweiser* site because she heard from her friends that it was a cool site. She added:

> I probably wouldn't see information on products on the Web because you want to buy what you see. I will probably look at a product if I'm planning to buy that but I'd rather look at comments from other consumers on the product.

In general, the style of browsing does not vary very much when users browse commercial homepages but they are extremely wary about marketer's messages because of fears that it would not be biased. This finding is in line with previous research examining use of advertising as an information source. Haller's (1974) study on college students reported that 45% of respondents disagreed with the statement that "Advertising is a good information source," with nearly 75% indicating that "More than half of all advertising contains too little information." 79% disagreed with the statement that "Most people don't pay much attention to advertising." Additionally, this sample found magazine and newspaper ads to be more informative and enjoyable than direct mail, outdoor, radio, or television. A similar finding was reported by Bauer and Greyser (1968).

Mittal's (1994) investigation into consumer perceptions of television advertising indicate that consumers generally held a negative attitude toward TV advertising, describing commercials as misleading, irritating, offensive, and boring. Although 33% of the respondents agreed that television commercials were useful sources of market information (e.g. sales, brand attributes, and new products), over 60% of respondents did not feel that such information contributed to their buying confidence.

Along similar lines, Mehta and Purvis (1995) found that 40% of respondents felt that advertised products do not perform as well as claimed in the advertising. However, their study did find that nearly half of the adults surveyed considered advertising to be useful in keeping "up-to-date about products and services." Consequently, it appears that consumers are more likely to read/view commercial homepages only when they found interesting information related to the products, and adopted a non-biased approach in dissemination of this information. It also indicates that clicking open commercial Webpages may also be affected by an individual's attitude toward advertising in general.

DISCUSSION

This investigation adopted a descriptive approach to understand and interpret the actions of individuals surfing the Web. Unlike conventional forms of marketing communication such as advertising, interactive forms enable the consumer to exercise considerable control over receipt of communication. Marketers and advertisers need to understand consumers' styles and manners of browsing the Web in order to create and build effective Web pages as a new form of marketing communication.

The findings of this study suggest that individuals typically rely on the Web links and browser buttons to navigate on the Web. Browsing behavior typically is a "reject unless interesting" activity, suggesting that if the homepage does not capture the visitor's interest in the first few seconds, it is replaced by something else very quickly. Thus it is important to build interest and excitement from the opening page and paragraph onward. Marketers should keep this in mind when developing their unique homepages.

Since a key homepage is used as the point of departure for exploration by consumers, marketers should collaborate amongst suppliers and providers to set up links that help in both access, and

---

[2]The ad banners and buttons found in many Web pages now were not that prevalent when the data for this study was collected. None were observed in this study, and hence, there is no reference to these ads.

cooperative marketing plans. For instance, it may be advantageous for a car dealer to have links to the car brands carried, car tint and accessories specialists, insurance agents and tire retailers, in his homepage. Likewise it would be mutually beneficial for each of these suppliers to have links to the dealer in their individual homepages. Related articles and stories of interest (e.g. characteristics of the electric car, sneak previews of next year's models) could be periodically included in the homepages to maintain the level of interest in selection of the homepage as the reference point.

Emulating the navigational directional buttons onto Web pages can benefit marketers because individuals use the Back button extensively. By enabling individuals to click on Webpage buttons instead of the browser buttons, marketers may be able to track consumer visits to their homepages more accurately. This data can then used in consumer databases to more closely understand the consumer and his/her needs.

Individuals were found to rarely wait for long periods of time for the picture or graphic to unfold, and instead move on to another Webpage. With the growth of the Web and resulting competition from homepages for attention, it would be more appropriate to adopt simpler, yet elegant designs that both appeal and load in a very short time.

A more important concern seems to be consumers' lack of interest in commercial Websites. This was found to stem from the perception of being led astray by marketers. One strategy to counter this could be to facilitate greater control and use of information to consumers by offering links to nonbiased sources of information. Selective exposure may also be overcome by ubiquity. Atkin and Bowen (1973)'s research into televised political ads suggested that the pervasiveness of television commercials helped overcome the selective exposure bias.

Selective exposure may be also driven by consumers' needs and the satisfaction of those needs from information sources, one of the key contemporary assumptions of the uses-and-gratifications perspective (Rubin 1993). As mentioned earlier, consumers are skeptical of advertising, and may consequently, receive less gratification from such sources of information. This contention remains to be tested in subsequent studies.

The optimal stimulation level literature (Steenkamp and Baumgartner 1992) also indicates that individuals' browsing behavior could be a function of their individual stimulation levels. Hence, devising homepages that stimulate curiosity may facilitate exposure to marketers' messages. Future research could address this issue.

Organizational credibility may assume greater importance in ensuring visibility of the organization in cyberspace. Awareness of an organization or a brand, and a positive attitude toward the marketer may be an important determinant of exposure in this medium, and is again left open to future investigations.

Finally, this study has its limitations. First, a small convenience sample of students was used which enables little information on non-student consumers browsing the Web from their work-place or homes. However, the use of a student sample in this study is appropriate because students are frequent computer users, both for work and entertainment, and large universities maintain Websites. Second, the Web is a dynamic place and its features, the Websites, homepages, search programs, advertising and graphics, are changing constantly. Consequently, consumers tend to change their browsing behavior as the Web, and its elements change. This study is a necessary first step in this area, and more extensive testing of the contentions advanced in this discussion via experiments or surveys would enable a better understanding of how consumers use this medium.

REFERENCES

Atkin, Charles K. and Lawrence Bowen (1973), "Quality Versus Quantity in Televised Political Ads," *Public Opinion Quarterly*, 37 (2), 209-224.

Auster, Ethel and Chun-Wei Choo (1993), "Environmental Scanning by CEOs in Two Canadian Industries," *American Society for Information Science Journal*, 44 (4) 194-203.

Batra, Rajeev and Michael L. Ray (1986), "Situational Effects of Advertising Repetition: The Moderating Influence of Motivation, Ability, and Opportunity to Respond," *Journal of Consumer Research*, 12 (March), 432-445.

Bauer, Raymond A. and Stephen A. Greyser (1968). *Advertising in America: The Consumer View*. Boston, MA: Harvard University, Graduate School of Business Administration, Division of Research.

Belch, George E. (1982), "The Effects of Television Commercial Repetition on Cognitive Response and Message Acceptance," *Journal of Consumer Research*, 9 (June), 56-65.

Belk, Russell, John Sherry and Melanie Wallendorf (1988), "A Naturalistic Inquiry into Buyer and Seller Behavior at a Swap Meet," *Journal of Consumer Research*, 14 (March), 449-470.

Cacioppo, John T. and Richard E. Petty (1979), "Effects of Message Repetition and Position on Cognitive Response, Recall and Persuasion," *Journal of Personality and Social Psychology*, 37 (1), 97-109.

_____ and (1989), "Effects of Message Repetition on Argument Processing, Recall and Persuasion," *Basic and Applied Psychology*, 10 (1), 3-12.

Clawson, Pat (1993), "Study: Consumers Want Interactive TV," *Electronic Media*, August 23, 24-25.

Draft, Howard C. (1992), "The Destiny of Direct," *Direct Marketing*, December, 28-32.

Ebbinghaus, Hermann (1987). *Memory: A Contribution to Experimental Psychology*. New York: Dover Publications Inc. (Original work published in German in 1885)

Ellsworth, Jill H. and Matthew V. Ellsworth (1995). *Marketing on the Internet*. New York, NY: John Wiley and Sons.

Grass, Robert C. and Wallace H. Wallace (1969), "Saturation Effects of TV Commercials," *Journal of Advertising Research*, 9 (3), 3-8.

Grether, David M. and Louise L. Wilde (1983), "Consumer Choice and Information: New Experimental Evidence," *Information Economics and Policy*, 1 (2), 115-144.

Haller, Thomas F. (1974), "What Students Think of Advertising," *Journal of Advertising Research*, 14 (1), 33-38.

Heeter, Carrie and Bradley S. Greenberg (1985), "Profiling the Zappers," *Journal of Advertising Research*, 25 (April/May), 15-19.

Hornik, Jacob (1989), "Temporal Instability as a Moderating Factor on Advertising Effectiveness," *Journal of Business Research*, 18 (2), 89-106.

Hudson, Laurel A. and Julie L. Ozanne (1988), "Alternative Ways of Seeking Knowledge in Consumer Research, *Journal of Consumer Research*, 14 (March), 508-521.

Kaplan, Barry M. (1985), "Zapping-the Real Issue Is Communication," *Journal of Advertising Research*, 25 (April/May), 9-13.

Kirk, Jerome and Marc L. Miller (1986). *Reliability and Validity in Qualitative Research*. Beverly Hills, CA: Sage.

Krugman, Herbert E. (1962), "An Application of Learning Theory to TV Copy Testing," *Public Opinion Quarterly*, 26 (4), 626-634.

_____ (1975), "What Makes Advertising Effective," *Harvard Business Review*, 23 (2), 96-103.

McQuail, Denis (1984). *Communication (2nd ed.)*. London: Longman.

Mehta, Abhilasha and Scott C. Purvis (1995), "When Attitudes Toward Advertising in General Influence Advertising Success,"in*Proceedings of the 1995 Conference of the American Academy of Advertising*, Charles S. Madden (Ed.), Waco, TX: American Academy of Advertising, 190-196.

Olney, Thomas J., Morris B. Holbrook and Rajeev Batra (1991), "Consumer Responses to Advertising: The Effects of Ad Content, Emotions, and Attitude toward the Ad on Viewing Time," *Journal of Consumer Research*, 17 (March), 440-453.

Palmer, Richard E. (1969). *Hermeneutics: Interpretation Theory in Schleiermacher, Dilthey, Heidegger, and Godamer*. Evanston, IL: Northwestern University Press.

Raman, Niranjan V. and John D. Leckenby (1995), "Advertising in Interactive Media: Some Issues, Some Suggestions," in *Proceedings of the 1995 Conference of the American Academy of Advertising*, Charles S. Madden (Ed.), Waco, TX: American Academy of Advertising, 247-251.

Rubin, Alan (1993), "Audience Activity and Media Use," *Communication Monographs*, 60 (1), 98-105.

Rust, Roland T. and Richard W. Oliver (1994), "The Death of Advertising," *Journal of Advertising*, 23 (4), 71-78.

Shell, Adam (1994), "A Map of the Information Highway," *Public Relations Journal*, 50 (January), 27.

Sherry, John F. (1990), "A Socio-Cultural Analysis of a Mid-Western American Flea Market," *Journal of Consumer Research*, 17 (June), 13-30.

Steenkamp, Jan-Benedict E. M. and Hans Baumgartner (1992), "The Role of Optimum Stimulation Level in Exploratory Consumer Behavior," *Journal of Consumer Research*, 19 (December), 434-448.

Stewart, David W. (1992), "Speculations on the Future of Advertising Research", *Journal of Advertising,* 21 (3), 1-18.

Strauss, Anselm and Juliet Corbin (1990). *Basics of Qualitative Research*. Newbury Park, CA: Sage Publications

Thompson, Craig, William Locander and Howard Pollio (1990), "The Lived Meaning of Free Choice: An Existential-Phenomenological Description of Everyday Consumer Experiences of Contemporary Married Women," *Journal of Consumer Research*, 17 (December), 346-361.

Wilson, Warner and Howard Miller (1968), "Repetition, Order of Presentation, And Timing of Arguments and Measures as Determinants of Opinion Change," *Journal of Personality and Social Psychology*, 9 (2), 184-188.

Consuming Cyberseniors: Some Personal and Situational Characteristics That Influence Their On-Line Behavior

Charles A. McMellon, Baruch College, CUNY
Leon G. Schiffman, Baruch College, CUNY
Elaine Sherman, Hofstra University

ABSTRACT

Of the many consumer groups allocating time to on-line activities, the elderly appear to be of special interest since they are breaking the stereotypical image of a group not especially receptive to new technology. Our exploratory study of these "Cyberseniors" was designed to examine their sociodemographic and personality characteristics. Interviews were conducted on-line over a six month period. What emerges suggests two different types of cyberseniors: the technology lover—individuals' whose life long fascination with technology has led them to readily adopt computers, and the technology user—a more pragmatic group of individuals, who accept technology and consider computers just another tool. The differences in these two types of on-line consumers are discussed.

Computers and the internet are beginning to play an important role in the lives of millions of elderly consumers (Dickerson 1995). They send e-mail to their grandchildren, communicate with distant friends, search for information and purchase products and services on-line, and perform many other beneficial activities. They are "cyberseniors," consumers over the age of fifty-five who are active on the internet. It appears that computers and the internet are especially relevant to this segment of older consumers, since they make it easier for them to do what they want to do, when they want to do it (Wylde, 1995). The elderly's involvement with the internet is also important to marketers, who for years thought they would not be innovative with respect to new technology, but are now beginning to recognize the importance of this behavioral change in the elderly. Firms like Apple, Intel, and Microsoft have new programs targeting older adults.

The economic importance of the elderly as a consumer subgroup and the internet as a marketing phenomena are well documented and will not be discussed here. Yet from a consumer behavior perspective, examination of these two important trends, as they interact, appears to have been largely overlooked. Although we know something about who cyberseniors are demographically (e.g., The 4th Hermes 1995 Survey reports less older women than men using the internet), we know little of the factors that influence their internet behavior.

The purpose of our study is to examine the personal differences that may influence older consumer's use of the internet. We begin with a discussion of older consumers and their involvement with the internet. We then examine related research and various models of time allocation which may aid our understanding of this phenomena. Next, we discuss our method of data collection on the internet. Little has been written on this subject. Thus, our method of interacting with subjects was developed through past personal experience. Results of our analysis are presented along with limitations and future research direction. What emerges suggests two different types of cyberseniors: the *technology lover*—individual's whose life long fascination with technology has led them to adopt computers, and the *technology user* — a more pragmatic individual, who accepts technology and considers computers as just another tool. If time spent on the internet is time consumed, then knowledge of these consumer segments may aid those interested in a variety of consumer behavior issues and topics.

THE ELDERLY AND THE INTERNET

The cybersenior phenomenon is growing. Nationally, over 20 percent of all older consumers own computers (Stock 1995). The AARP reports over two million computer members among its members, and SeniorNet—a national computer training organization for the elderly— has trained over 30 thousand individuals. These numbers should not surprise marketers. Enders (1995) points out the irony of stereotyping older consumers as afraid of technology. Older consumers have seen their world evolve to laser beam surgery and men walking on the moon. Older consumers— both the young elderly and the older elderly—have adopted many new technologies. Thus, it should not be too surprising that they are adopting computers and the internet as they begin to discover its benefits of increased productivity and quality of life (McMellon, Schiffman, and Sherman 1995).

In addition, the very nature of the elderly may also be changing. The new-age elderly (Schiffman and Sherman 1991) are an emerging subgroup who not only perceive themselves as younger than their chronological age, but are generally more experiential, less materialistic in their life activities, more self-confident, and more in control than the generations that have gone before them. This experiential dimension might be a motivating factor in why more and more elderly are going on-line. Sheehy (1995) sees this phenomenon as a general shift downward of all adulthood stages by about ten years. Many adults in their sixties now think and act like they are in their forties or fifties.

THE ALLOCATION AND CONSUMPTION OF TIME

Although the use of the internet by the older consumers appears in the popular press regularly (e.g., Stock, 1995), little has been written about elderly behavior on-line and any of the factors that might influence such behavior. Thus, we look to related theoretical and empirical research for possible guidance.

Previous research has examined the allocation of travel time (Barff, Mackay, and Olshavsky 1982), time spent watching mass media (Hornik and Schlinger 1981), and shopping time (e.g., Arndt and Gronmo 1980). In these studies, the value a consumer places on their time and its influence on their time allocation decisions are examined in relation to a variety of personal characteristics (e.g., demographics or personality traits) that might influence such behavior. These studies begin to demonstrate that a relationship exists between a consumer's allocation of time and various socioeconomic, demographic, and psychological variables.

Another approach which offers guidance for our exploratory study of time consumed on the internet is the area of time allocation frameworks (e.g., Feldman and Hornik 1981). These frameworks focus on organizing various influential variables that aid in understanding the consumption aspect of products and services as measured by time.

Feldman and Hornik (1981) offer a comprehensive conceptual model for the allocation of time which includes: (1) time structure (i.e., work time and the various components of non-work time), (2) resource availability (i.e., what constraints money, time and space have on allocation), (3) activity availability (i.e., how accessibility to the activity affects allocation), and (4) and personal characteristics (i.e., what demographic and personality differences influence time allocation). Time structure and resource availability define a time domain construct while activity availability and personal characteristics influence the individual's perceived value of the activity. Time value is operationalized as satisfaction in the activity itself and satisfaction based on interaction with others while performing the activity (Kaplan, 1972; Neulinger and Raps, 1972). The time domain and perceived value constructs influence the allocation of time to the activity. In our study, it is the amount of time spent on-line.

While some of the independent variables that are included in these models have been identified (e.g., socioeconomic and situational), personality characteristics, which may also contribute significantly to our understanding of time allocation, have not been identified. It appears identifying them will be a more difficult task since personality characteristics may be specific to each type of leisure activity (Martin and Myrick, 1976).

While researchers have yet to discuss what personality types gravitate toward the internet, some writers offer clues. Rheingold (1993), after ten years of talking with people on the internet, suggested two personality types gravitate towards on-line activities: those whose professional background seems a good fit with the internet method of communication—which is the typing and reading of words or symbols (e.g., computer programmers or librarians), and those individuals who were not afraid of computers and were curious about the internet as some kind of cultural phenomenon.

Researchers studying the elderly's attitudes toward computers also offer some clues. Jay (1989) found a relationship between attitudes toward computers and external locus of control, indirect experience (e.g., past experience with calculators), and intellectual control beliefs. Igbaria and Parasuraman (1989) found a relationship between age, education, external locus of control, and cognitive style (feeling-thinking) and computer attitudes. Specifically, external locus of control and math anxiety had an indirect effect through a measure of computer anxiety. Computer anxiety, in turn, was strongly related to negative attitudes towards computers.

In summary, a general lack of knowledge on what influences the allocation and consumption of time on-line among the elderly suggests exploratory research as a necessary first step. Related literature offer some clues. It appears as if the satisfaction one derives from a behavior may influence the time spent in the activity. Also one's attitude towards computers is important. Last, a number of personal and situational characteristics may be influential and should be examined. They would include personality traits (e.g., need for cognition and locus of control), socioeconomic and demographic factors (e.g, income and education), psychographic (e.g., cognitive age), and situational or lifestyle variables (e.g., money constraints).

METHOD

A semi-structured interview approach using e-mail was chosen based on the lead author's personal on-line experience. The alternate approach of real-time interviewing on the internet was deemed too difficult since it appeared that most respondents would not want to spend the continuous time on-line necessary to complete a single depth interview. Respondents also appeared more comfortable with a more prolonged interchange with time to consider answers.

Depth interviewing can be defined as "...repeated face-to-face encounters between the researcher and informants directed toward understanding informants' perspectives on their lives, experiences, or situations as expressed in their words" (Taylor and Bogdan,

1984, p.77). The most obvious difference with our approach is that on-line interviewing is not a face-to-face interaction but occurs in the realm of cyberspace, a reality that is created between people who communicate on the internet. The following method was developed to communicate in this "cyber-reality."

Insight Development

Potential respondents were identified by browsing special interest group libraries in commercial on-line services (e.g., Compuserve). Fifteen cyberseniors, who had written on-line autobiographies, were chosen as potential subjects since publishing one's life story on-line suggested a willingness to talk. On-line autobiography is a technique commonly used to involve the new user in computing. We recognize that identifying potential respondents in this manner can bias our sample, but as the study was exploratory in nature and with little to guide us in method, we chose those who might facilitate our research by their willingness to communicate. An initial e-mail message was sent to each of them. It contained a favorable comment about their autobiography, a request that they participate in our research project, and a few questions to give them some practice in communicating with us.

How they responded was also of interest so that further communication could be adjusted to their style. We asked if they would like to participate in this research project because internet protocol suggests one does not send unsolicited e-mail such as a survey or an advertisement without the recipient's agreement ahead of time. Researchers risk being flamed (i.e., your e-mail mailbox becomes stuffed with rude, ALL CAPITALIZED, messages) if "netiquette" is breached. Nine of the 15 potential respondents replied within three days. The other six never responded. They may not have been reading their mail or simply were not interested. A few more questions were sent off to the nine who responded. We added an additional question asking them if they would like to continue to participate in a dialog. Six agreed to continue the discussion. These six respondents continued the discussion over a six month period in 1995, as the on-line depth interviews were conducted via e-mail. Individual weekly correspondence was conducted with each of the respondents covering a variety of subjects suggested by our literature review. The lead author is still in weekly communication with these six respondents discussing a wide range of subjects. All on-line responses were captured and stored in ASCII files for later analysis.

Communication Analysis

Our data included the respondent's original autobiographies and their responses to a wide variety of personality related, situational, satisfaction, and computer usage questions suggested by the literature and the authors personal experience on-line.

Analysis of the responses proceeded systematically using iterative processing (Spiggle 1994). At the completion of the response collection period, each respondent's answers and comments were converted into hard copy. An analysis outline was developed which listed each of our discussion areas and the respondent's answers along with a space for the researcher's comments. The responses were analyzed both vertically and horizontally. Vertical analysis examines each respondent independently of the other respondents while horizontal analysis examines each response area of all respondents independently of the other response areas. The vertical and horizontal interpretation procedures were repeated until the diminishing returns of interpretation suggested further analysis was not necessary. The vertical and horizontal analyses and interpretations were then integrated into the following.

ANALYSIS

Our analysis focuses on the understanding of on-line consumer behavior through individual differences of the respondents. We began by examining the respondent's autobiographies. Our sample appeared to be comprised of a relatively varied group of individuals with differences in family life, past careers, and retirement activities. The length of their autobiographies began to tell us something about their differences. The amount of what they wrote suggested some level of need to communicate with the outside world (i.e., the more written, the more the need to communicate). It became apparent later, as familiarity with each of the respondents grew, that a need to communicate was stronger in some individuals than in others. Four of the respondents wrote long, detailed autobiographies while two wrote very short ones. For example, one respondent wrote five pages of text while another wrote a single paragraph. The writer of the short paragraph was very dissatisfied with life, apparently influenced by the death of a spouse and the serious illness of a parent. The four long autobiographies were all written by respondents who were very satisfied with their lives. These respondents tended to be very active in their retirement, with activities that ranged from church volunteering to long distance bike riding. They were also extremely interested in computers and electronic communication. Those with a high interest in computers seemed different. Five respondents embraced, even loved, technology while one respondent was neutral towards technology and "just used it." As Igbaria and Parasuraman (1989) have shown, a continuum of attitudes toward technology exists. Therefore, given the potential for added dimensions in an individual's relationship with technology, we suspect that attitude towards computers may be only one dimension in the segmentation of computer consumers. What emerges from our research are two possible segments of on-line consumers: the *technology lover* and the *technology user*. They appear to behave differently in terms of on-line behavior and to vary in terms of some personal characteristics.

Technology Lovers and Technology Users Emerge as Segments

We asked participants if they "loved" technology. Seven of the original nine respondents answered positively, while one was neutral, and one did not answer. As we discussed technology, it became clear how they felt:

(From the tech-user)
"It (technology) exists and we must make the best of it...I have a PC which I use mainly for word processing....I find technology somewhat less than intuitive."

(From tech-lovers)
"I've always been interested and involved with technology."

"I was fascinated by the concept of computers."

"(A friend)...showed me how to use a doorbell battery and a screwdriver to make a flashlight bulb burn. To my young mind, it was a remarkable feat...the process became so clear, I was astounded!"

As we began to examine the data, it became apparent that loving or using technology might define the segments of our sample. To better understand this notion, we asked the respondents to define the word "technology." Here are a few responses:

"The application of human knowledge. To accomplish practical and useful objectives through the use of physical materials and methods."

"The body of knowledge of particular skills."

"The use of science in everyday life for the improvement of the quality of life."

We also discussed satisfaction. The tech-lovers appear more satisfied with their lives although it was also apparent that certain situational variables modify life satisfaction. Indeed, the most dissatisfied subject is also a tech-lover. In this person's case, both personal and family health problems have made him "a prisoner in his own home." Another tech-lover who did not rate life satisfaction as high as others cites problems with children and grandchildren. Thus, for these respondents, it appears that computers and on-line activities, while highly satisfying activities, are not the dominate contributors to life satisfaction.

In addition, we examined two dimensions of on-line satisfaction. That is, satisfaction with the activity and satisfaction with the people who also do the same activity (Kaplan, 1972; Neulinger and Raps, 1972). The tech-lover appeared to be more satisfied than the tech-user on both satisfaction subdimensions. In addition, we asked a variety of cognitive age questions (i.e., age self-perception with respect to looking, feeling, doing, and thinking). Tech-lovers saw themselves as generally younger than their chronological age, whereas the tech-user did not. These findings are in general agreement with earlier research reported by Sherman, Schiffman, and Dillon (1988) that the younger the cognitive age, the more likely the person is to be satisfied. As to why they felt this way, the tech-user stated, "I feel as though I am in my 60's because I know I am." A tech-lover said, "...I still have a great intellectual curiosity and interest in so many different fields..." Tech-lovers appear to have a youthful enthusiasm and outlook that is absent in the tech-user.

Overall, tech-lovers seem to view the impact of computers and on-line services on their lives more positively. They see it as a tool to expand their horizons, to create new programs, to communicate their ideas, and to meet new people while the tech-user views the impact of computers less positively; that is, with a more inward direction where computers help make tasks easier (e.g., word processing is easier than typing).

Attitudinal and Situational Characteristics

The tech-lover's responses suggest that they are innovators and more in control of their lives. Also they may be a little healthier and happier. There were no differences between tech-lovers and the tech-user in propensity to collect things, amount of travel, and whether or not computers were seen "as magical." Upon finishing the preliminary questioning, we began a dialog on a wide range of subjects with the six respondents who had indicated a willingness to continue. The three respondents that dropped out at this stage appeared to be of the tech-user type and seemed overly concerned over the cost of continuing communication.

We began our dialog by asking the six remaining participants how they became involved with computers. Tech-lovers stated involvement usually began with an early childhood interest in things electronic. The tech-user had little interest in technology and became involved with computers because of the influence of another (i.e., at the prompting of a grandchild). We speculate this may be one of the key differences between these segments. Tech-lovers have been involved with technology from an early age, perhaps due to an internal motivation or early learning from parents. Thus, when computers were developed these participants quickly became involved, while the tech-user needed some outside motivation to adopt computers. (One of the advantages of electronic interviewing is the ability to easily go back and ask another question during the analysis stage. Thus, we asked respondents about childhood or early interest in technology.) Their answers were relatively consistent. Here are two excerpts from tech-lovers:

"As a boy, I was particularly interested in airplanes and the principles of flight. I loved to go to the airport and watch the planes landing and taking off and to climb up into the cockpits of those in the hangers. There was little need of airport security in those days."

"...as a kid I built radios out of razor blades and rusty nails, then with Galina crystals, then graduated to one tube radios. I read Popular Mechanics, Popular Science...My wish when I was a kid was the Edmund Scientific catalog."

The responses of tech-lovers suggests to us a life long involvement and fascination with technology. As for current involvement with computers and on-line services, the tech-lovers, had more equipment and were more computer literate. This determination was made from their ability to communicate with us on-line and from how they described their hardware and software. They also spent more time with their computers, purchased more products on-line, and performed a greater variety of on-line activities (e.g., joined on-line groups, sought out more information, and met more people).

Situational constraints (i.e., amount of free time, money and space available for on-line activities) were also discussed. A variety of answers suggested no clear direction except for their general concern for money (e.g., "..if it were free, I'd do more."). Their answers supported the general assumption that these variables can act as constraints on time spent on consumer behavior (Becker 1965; Feldman and Hornik 1981). Health (either one's own or of others in the household) also emerges from our discussions as a potential constraint on elderly consumer behavior. A comment from one of our respondents supports this notion:

"I am the sole care giver to my mother with advanced Alzheimer's disease, which makes me a prisoner in my own home."

Personality Characteristics

It is generally accepted in marketing that personality traits influence consumer behavior in some manner (Schiffman and Kanuk 1994); while specific traits may influence specific behaviors. We suspect certain traits (e.g., need for cognition and locus of control) are influential in on-line behavior.

Need for cognition is an individual's predisposition to enjoy thinking and do more of it than others (Cacioppo and Petty 1982). We discussed the subject in some detail with respondents. Tech-lovers appear to have a higher need for cognition than tech-users. Tech-lovers like the intellectual challenge of computers and of learning new applications. Here is what two said:

"I do like complex problems, and I enjoy the intellectual pursuit of new and better ways to solve problems."

"I usually prefer a hard thinking job with new technologies and new solutions. I'm not satisfied with only a finished work but I continue to think of improvements even after the task is done. Perhaps I am a perfectionist."

Locus of control is the level of internal (i.e., one's own) or external (i.e., others or fate) control that an individual perceives in their life (Rotter 1966). It is potentially important for older consumers: Lumpkin (1986) has demonstrated that the elderly tend to have a more external locus of control. He hypothesizes that as aging individuals deteriorate in health and lessen in activities, they feel they are losing control of their lives. If this is true, than computer use for the elderly may be an activity that provides an opportunity to regain some of that lost control. Our findings suggest this might be true. Tech-users appeared to be "generally" in control of their lives "as far as any of us are" while tech-lovers told us in no uncertain terms that they were in control of their lives.

"I learned, in the beginning, by hit or miss but I kept on plugging away and slowly made sense out of what I was doing. Now I can usually go on-line and accomplish whatever it was I set out to do."

"Bad luck is usually because I jumped in without taking the time to think out just what it was I wanted to do."

Additional Insights Also Emerge

Some additional insights on the differences between tech-lovers and tech-users emerged from their "response style." The tech-lovers generally responded with more enthusiasm and with more detail than the tech-user. Tech-lovers also responded faster. As mentioned earlier, we felt tech-lovers had a stronger need to communicate (at least over the computer). That is, they appear to have a need to pass on information they have accumulated through their years of experience or to talk with like minded people on subjects that interest them. One respondent, when asked a simple question on how he fared during hurricane Opal, responded with two pages of detail rich text. This type of response stands out in the domain of computer mediated communication since most communication appears much shorter and to the point. Another respondent was more direct in indicating a need to communicate by saying, after a short absence from the net, "I am glad to be back to communicating." Other tech-lovers felt:

"I think we can improve our knowledge by communicating to each other our experiences."

"...all of us around the world need to have a glimpse about what other people feel and think."

This need to communicate does not seem to be driven by loneliness but appears to be related to their need for cognition and may be more a function of a sheer need to communicate with like-minded people or to pass on information to the next generation. This need to communicate may be important to marketers. For example, it may aid in better understanding word-of-mouth, which appears to be quite common among internet users.

Finally, we were interested in the changing nature of the elderly (Schiffman and Sherman 1991; Sheehy 1995). If there was a difference, did it somehow influence their use of computers? We asked respondents how they saw themselves in relation to their parents. Their answers suggest they are different than their parents including the perception of better health, more positive attitudes, and a much higher level of physical activity. We could find nothing to link computer use to these differences. From two tech-lovers:

"When my father was 64 or 65, he could not climb a tree or a ladder. I'm still able to paint a ceiling."

"I think on the whole I am a lot younger at my age than my parents were. They seemed ready for the rocking chair...(while I'm) riding a bike at my age."

CONCLUSIONS

In summary, tech-lovers feel younger and appear very satisfied with their lives. They have a stronger internal locus of control, a higher need for cognition and communication, and are more impressed with computers and what can be done with them (e.g., meet new people). They also appear to be more satisfied with their on-line activities, to spend more time on-line, to search for more information, to join more on-line groups, and buy more products. The tech-user does not feel younger and appears to have a lower need for cognition and communication. They also seem less impressed with computers (e.g., "It helps me type better"). Both tech-lover and tech-user are constrained somewhat by money. The tech-lovers had been involved with computers for many years, thus when on-line services became available, they gravitated to them easily. The tech-user appeared to have had a more reluctant involvement (e.g., through the urging of children). Tech-lovers seem to be going somewhere with computers expanding their lives. Tech-users seem to be coming from somewhere with computers aiding in their current situation.

The respondents in this exploratory study offer new insights into the nature and motivations of the elderly internet user. Situational and personal characteristics, which may shape how the elderly consumer behaves on-line, were examined. Two potential types of on-line consumers emerged: the *technology lover* and the *technology user*. They emerge as distinct segments and behave differently in their consumer behavior on-line. Our findings should be considered preliminary due to the exploratory nature and limitations of our method. Two of these limitations are small sample size and method of sample recruitment which may bias our results. We justify our approach given the newness of on-line research. Limited by the difficulties of on-line recruitment, we chose a small number of respondents who appeared willing to cooperate with us. This method was also a learning process for us. As this is a first step into a new and uncharted area of investigation, we feel the method may be justified.

We have identified and examined a number of situational and personal variables that may have an influence on the older consumer's on-line behavior. More qualitative and quantitative research is needed to better understanding of the differences between tech-lovers, tech-users, and any other segment that might exist.

REFERENCES

Arndt, Johan and Sigmund Gronmo (1980), "The Time Dimension of Shopping behavior: Some Empirical Findings," *Advances in Consumer Research*, Vol. 7, ed. Jerry C. Olson, Ann Arbor, MI: Association for Consumer Research, 230-235.

Barff, Richard, Mackay, David and Richard W. Olshausky (1982), "A Selective Review of Travel-Mode Choice Models," *Journal of Consumer Research*, 8(March), 370-380.

Becker, Gary S. (1965), "A Theory of the Allocation of Time," *The Economic Journal*, 75(September), 493-517.

Cacioppo, John T. and Richard T. Petty (1982). "The Need for Cognition," *Journal of Personality and Social Psychology*, 42(1), 116-131.

Dickerson, John. F. (1995). "Never too old," In *Time Special Issue: Welcome to Cyberspace*, 145(Spring), p. 41.

Enders, Alexandra (1995), " The Role of Technology in the Lives of Older People," *Generations*, 19(Spring), 7-12.

Feldman, Laurence P. and Jacob Hornik (1981), "The Use of Time: An Integrated Model," *Journal of Consumer Research*, 7(March), 407-419.

Hermes@cochrane.bus.umich.edu, (1995), "Results from the 4th GVU/Hermes WWW User Survey are ready!," December 24, 1995,

Hornik, Jacob and Mary Jane Schlinger (1981), "Allocation of Time to the Mass Media," *Journal of Consumer Research*, 7(March), 343-355.

Igbaria, Magid and Parasuraman, Soroj (1989), "A Path Analytic Study of Individual Characteristics, Computer Anxiety and Attitudes toward Microcomputers," *Journal of Management*, 15(3), 373-388.

Jay, Gina Marie (1989), "The Influence of Direct Computer experience on older Adults' Computer Attitudes, Skills, and Continued Use," Doctoral Dissertation, College of Health and Human Development, The Pennsylvania State University, MUI #9018231.

Kaplan, Max (1972), "New Concepts of Leisure Today," *Journal of Health, Physical Education and Recreation*, 43, 43-46.

Lumpkin, James R. (1986), "The Relationship Between Locus of Control and Age: New Evidence," *Journal of Social Behavior and Personality*, 1(2), 245-252.

Martin, Warren S. and Fred L. Myrick (1976), "Personality and Leisure Time Activities," *Research Quarterly*, 47, 246-252.

McMellon, Charles A., Schiffman, Leon G., and Elaine Sherman, (1995), "Cyberseniors: Consuming Behavior On-Line," Paper presented at the *Quality of Life Conference* of the Academy of Marketing Science. Williamsburg, VA.

Neulinger, John and Charles S. Raps (1972), "Leisure Attitudes of an Intellectual Elite," *Journal of Leisure Research*, 4, 196-207.

Rheingold, Howard (1993), *The Virtual Community. Homesteading On the Electronic Frontier*, Reading, PA: Addison-Wesley Publishing.

Rotter, J B. (1966), "Generalized Expectancies for Internal Versus External Control of Reinforcement," *Psychological Monographs*, 80(1), (Whole No. 609).

Schiffman, Leon G. and Leslie L. Kanuk (1994), *Consumer Behavior*, Englewood Cliffs, NJ: Prentice Hall.

———— and Elaine Sherman (1991), "Value Orientations of New-Age Elderly: The Coming of an Ageless Market," *Journal of Business Research*, 22, 187-194.

Sheehy, Gail (1995), *New Passages. Mapping Your Life Across Time*, New York: Random House.

Sherman, Elaine, Schiffman, Leon, G. and William R. Dillon (1988), "Age/Gender Segments and Quality of Life Differences," in *1988 Winter Educator's Conference Proceedings*, Stanley Shapiro, et. al., eds., Chicago: American Marketing Association, 319-320.

Spiggle, Susan (1994), "Analysis and Interpretation of Qualitative Data in Consumer Research," *Journal of Consumer Research*, 21(December), 491-503.

Stock, Robert W. (1995), "Removing Roadblocks to Computer Usage," *The New York Times*, September 14, p. C11.

Taylor, Steven J. and Robert Bogdan (1984), *Introduction to Qualitative Methods. The Search for Meanings*, New York: John Wiley & Sons.

Wolfe, David B. (1994), "Targeting the Mature Mind," *American Demographics*, March, pp. 32-36.

Wylde, Margaret A. (1995), "If You Could See It through My Eyes: Perspectives on Technology for Older People," *Generations*, 19(Spring), 5-6.

New Technologies for the Home–Development of a Theoretical Model of Household Adoption and Use

Alladi Venkatesh, University of California, Irvine
Franco Nicosia, University of California, Berkeley

ABSTRACT

The burgeoning growth in information/communication/multimedia technologies and their possible impact on American consumers and households continue to arouse a great deal of popular and scholarly interest. In particular, the phenomenon of computing in the home has given rise to much debate because of its potential impact on different segments of the society. With the diffusion of these new technologies to the household level, there is a need to understand and develop models of technology adoption and use. In this paper, we present a model that considers two key elements, the *social space* and the *technological space* as building blocks for the development of a theoretical model of household adoption and use of new information technologies.

INTRODUCTION

No technology in recent memory has aroused as much national and global interest as the computing technology (Scientific American 1995). Not since the emergence of television about forty years ago has there been a technology with such possibilities for profound social change. The new digital age, now augmented by the ubiquitous microcomputers, is variously described as "the mode of information" (Poster 1990), or "cyberculture" (Escobar 1994) and the like. The burgeoning growth in information/communication/multimedia technologies and their possible impact on American consumers and households continue to arouse a great deal of popular and scholarly interest (Venkatesh 1996, Hoffman and Novak 1996). In particular, the phenomenon of computing in the home has given rise to much debate because of its potential impact on different segments of the society. With the diffusion of these new technologies to the household level, there are several interesting and important issues relating to and resulting from their adoption and diffusion.

Under the general rubric of computing in the home, researchers have investigated issues such as the profile of innovators (Dickerson and Gentry 1983), symbolic dimensions of the new technology (Turkle 1995), the nature of computer diffusion (Dutton, Rogers and Suk-Ho 1987, Venkatesh, Dholakia and Dholakia 1996), social psychological factors affecting computer use (McQuarrie and Langemeyer 1987), educational use of computers at home by children (Giacquinta, Bauer, and Levin 1993), post-adoption analysis of home computers (Venkatesh and Vitalari 1987), gender differences in use of computers (Ruddell 1993), telecommuting and work at home (Kraut 1989, Venkatesh and Vitalari 1992), and the growing use of internet (Dholakia, Mundorf and Dholakia 1995, Hoffman and Novak 1996, Blattberg, et. al 1994). There are also international perspectives on home computer use (Bakke 1993, Bjerg and Borreby 1994).

This study provides a theoretical basis for the social processes and factors accounting for the greater integration, or "domestication" of the PC and related information technologies into the American household.

CONCEPTUAL FOUNDATION

Based on our previous empirical work, we offer two views that dominate our thinking about computers in the home, or more generally, technology in the home (Nicosia 1983, Venkatesh and Vitalari 1990, Venkatesh and Vitalari 1992).

They might appear obvious, yet they are quite important. They go something like this:

- *Technology shapes people's lives.*

- *People shape the character of technology.*

The question then is, since both statements seem so self-evident, how can we utilize these statements to say anything meaningful, especially about the technology and the users of technology. The first part of the statement, "technology shapes people's lives," implies that if the producers of the technology do understand the technology and its implications, they can see the future a little more clearly than others who may not have such a clear understanding. One requirement to see this with such clarity is to acknowledge the reality of the second statement, that is, "people shape the character of the technology." This does not mean that the users of the technology actually shape the physical characteristics of the technology, for that is still in the hands of the makers of the technology. It only means, that the users determine the shape of the technology by their uses and these specific uses become inputs into the next stage of development.

The second statement also means that the computer (or any other technology for that matter) is socially embedded. Many theories of the human/computer interface that we know of rely on models of cognitive scientific research. The reason why cognitive sciences have played such a key role in our vision or understanding of computers is because of our fascination with the idea of the computer's likeness to human brain (mind?). We have scores of books on the mental models of computers, as well as computer models of the mind. But there is a competing model, or a complementary model, which is the *social model of the computer technology*. Translated into the household context, we are looking at two issues, the *computerization of the household as* well as the *domestication of the computer*. They represent, respectively, the two statements that we made earlier as part of our main thesis. That is, the producers of technology can play a key role in determining how the modern household is computerized. They have the technological prowess to do so—if only the household participates in this enterprise.

When we began to study computers at home, we were interested in what type of computers did households purchase and what they did with them, how they used them and who used them. We were really focused on learning how families adapted to computers. But, after a few years of intense research, we found that something was missing in our research. Our insights were not as profound as we wanted them to be. It took a while, but it dawned on us, that in order to understand what families did with a computer, we needed first to understand what families did with their vacuum cleaners, with their refrigerators, TVs, telephones, family car, their washing machines, dishwashers, and a whole host of technologies that occupied the physical and social space called the home. So, we came up with an epigrammatic statement that the route to the understanding of how people related to computers was through the study of other domestic techniques.

Before long, we realized that we had to go inside people's homes, and see how people behaved with respect to their technologies. We wanted to learn what families did with their household technologies. We had to talk to families at length about their experiences with and impressions of household technologies. We realized that for many families, the computer was only one among many other domestic technologies. Some people told us that the computer was not the most important technology in the home. On the other hand, we learnt that family life would come to a dead stop if the refrigerator did not work, for the refrigerator symbolized food and no family can go without food. Similarly, there would be panic if the family telephone went out of order, for telephone meant communication with loved ones, friends, and emergency contacts. In the same fashion, families cannot go to work, or the grocery store, or take children to school if the family car failed. We found that some technologies in the home could be classified as survival technologies and very central to the functioning of the household. Before long, it dawned on us that there was a *technological space* in which many these technologies were embedded. These technologies are not passive objects in the technological space, they are live, full of meanings for the members of the families who use them. The technological space is also a social space, and more importantly, it is also a symbolic space.

OBJECTIVE OF THE STUDY

The main objective of the study is to develop a theoretical model that gives us the best understanding of the household adoption and use of new information/interactive/multi-media technologies and their diffusion into the various aspects of home life.

TECHNOLOGY AND THE HOUSEHOLD

Some Preliminary Issues

Over the years, a surge of interest in technology and households has been triggered by a multiplicity of factors. The entry of women into the labor force has created the possibility that households might be acquiring a greater number of time-saving devices. Such investigations have been carried out by consumer researchers (Oropesa 1993, Reilly 1982, Strober and Weinberg 1980). Some time-budget research has also been reported in Europe and in the US looking at related issues (Szalai 1972, Michelson 1980, Robinson and Nicosia 1988). The emergence of information and interactive technologies have aroused much popular and scholarly interest (Blattberg, Glazer and Little 1994, Hoffman and Novak 1995, Mick and Fournier 1995). The home of the future seems to be somewhere between fantasy and reality (Berg and Borreby 1994). In addition, there has been much attention paid to the issue of home technologies by feminist sociologists who are rather critical that that of some of the household technologies have in fact perpetuated women's domestic roles instead of liberating them (Cockburn and Ormrod 1993, Cowan 1989, Vanek 1978, Zimmerman 1983). Considering these various developments on home-based technologies, one is forced to recall a quote by Nicosia (1983): "technology is usually associated with production processes and various social science disciplines have researched the effects of technology in work activities...The effect of technology in consumption 'activities' has been largely ignored or taken for granted...By focusing on family as the institutional setting for a great deal of consumer behavior, we should gain a better understanding of the interdependencies between technology and consumers..."

Given that the household is a central social setting for the adoption and use of the new technologies, the question remains as to what appropriate theoretical model is or can be made available for studying this relationship. Such a model will certainly be most useful for consumer researchers as well as practitioners engaged in producing products and services for the households. The purpose

of this study is therefore to develop a "household-technology interaction model" as a conceptual basis for understanding household behavior as it pertains to the adoption and use of household technologies.

A THEORETICAL FRAMEWORK: HOUSEHOLD/ TECHNOLOGY INTERACTION

Background Issues

Although research on household technology is limited in the consumer literature, some key studies have been reported over the past few years (Nickols and Fox 1983; Oropesa 1993; Strober and Weinberg 1980). Typically, these studies have focused on the purchase decisions of families in regard to household technologies (e.g. kitchen appliances) and/or the use of technologies primarily as time saving devices. While these studies provide some important and useful theoretical background for our work, there are three ways in which our approach differs from or extends their work. First, our focus is the actual use of technology, not just the purchase decision or incidence of ownership. Second, we examine how technology fits into the over all consumption context of household behavior and not just on cost or time savings. Finally, we consider the social context of technology adoption and use to be a key element of our theoretical framework.

Once we go beyond consumer research, we find that several researchers have formulated basic theoretical notions about the social, economic, and cultural aspects of technology utilization in various contexts ranging from communities, organizations, households, and across individuals.

We now identify some key issues from previous studies which can be classified into four primary streams.

First, the socio-technical systems theory of technology adoption and use views an organization (in our case the household) as a social system, and technology as an autonomous environmental system that acts on the social system as an external agent (Hedberg and Mumford 1975; Danziger 1979; Danziger and Kraemer 1986). This view is a product of systems theory which was a reigning paradigm in the social sciences during the fifties up until the mid-seventies. This approach has been criticized as being too deterministic and considering technology only as external to the adopting organization, and the organization/technology interface merely as the meeting point of two independent systems. In other words, the socio-technical systems approach fails to recognize that technology is interior to the household environment (although produced physically outside of the home) and not external to it, and that there is a dynamic relationship between the two. As Woodward (1994) has shown, technology is neither neutral nor autonomous but is integral to the social character of the (social) system.

The second approach, which is more common among organizational theorists and social constructivist theorists in Europe, views technologies as socially embedded processes (Cronberg 1994; Kling 1980, 1995). That is, unlike the socio-technical systems approach which views technology as autonomous and outside the social organization, the social-embeddedness theory examines technology as integral to the social organization. The basic position here is that no technology can be examined in isolation but only in the social context of its use and not its physical origin. We take this position in the current study, utilizing the underlying idea and applying it specifically to the household.

The third approach is based on the extensions of the new-home economics (Becker 1976) which' consider technology in the context of household production and consumption (Berk 1980). In this view, technologies are viewed as time (and/or cost) saving devices, and households as optimizers of time/cost-allocations based on household preference functions. This is a valuable framework for understanding household behavior, and more importantly, to assess the task environment within the household.

The fourth stream of research is reflected in the time-budget studies and is closely related to the third stream. Robinson is credited with the main contributions to this area (1977, 1980, 1990). The focus here is on developing a scheme of time allocation by households for various household activities. The approach is more descriptive, analytical, and data rich, but not too theoretical. In other words, time-budget studies allow researchers to draw some conclusions about how household time allocation patterns change temporally and cross-sectionally, but there are no adequate theoretical explanations for these changes.

A synthesis of previous work in these three areas of research (Berk 1980, Hardyment 1988; Morgan et al 1966; Nicosia 1975, 1983; Nickols and Fox 1983; Oropesa 1993; Vanek 1978; Strober and Weinberg 1980) suggests that the household may be viewed as a social system divided into task environment and non-task environment, and technologies as part of the social system. The basic approach here may be described as structural/functional. Typically, households, or members of a household, appropriate technologies to perform a variety of activities within these two environments. One objective of using these technologies is to increase time savings or achieve other efficiencies specific to the situation. This is particularly true of task oriented technologies (washer, dryer, vacuum cleaner etc.,). Household members also use technologies with the purpose of relaxing and experiencing the aesthetic enjoyment associated with watching TV or listening to Stereo music. With the structural/functional perspective of technology-use serving as the springboard, we have expanded our theoretical design into a structural/dynamic model of household-technology interface, which is the focal model for our present study.

Model Development and Specification

Our theoretical framework is motivated by a concern to understand the role technology plays in family life. We conceptualize the household[1] in terms of two main components that are interlinked–the *social space* in which the family behavior occurs and the *technological space* in which the household technologies are embedded. It is the interaction between the social space and the technological space, and the resulting behaviors that are focus of this paper. Figure 1 provides a schematic relationship between the social space and the technological space. Figure 2 is an internal structural representation of the household that incorporates the key elements of Figure 1 in greater detail.

Modified Structural/Functionalist View

The theoretical framework underlying our approach may be labeled the modified structural/functional approach to the study of family behavior.

The theoretical grounding for our study requires that we come up with a framework that integrates some general concepts of

---

[1]For the most part, we use the terms family and household interchangeably. Sometimes, "household" may sound more appropriate as in household technology (rather than family technology) and some times the opposite is true as in the case of family dynamics or family values. The technical distinction between the two terms is that family denotes kinship, that is, a network of people who are related through blood or marriage while household refers to a group of related or unrelated people sharing a common domestic space (Netting, Wilk and Arnould 1984).

family behavior and some specific concepts of behavior oriented toward technology use. Since there is no single theory of family behavior that would meet these needs, we resort to two levels of theoretical integration. First, we propose a theory of family behavior that combines certain key elements from the structural/functional theory of the family, the new-home economic theory of activity-time allocation, the social dynamics approach of family development theories, and the feminist theories which focus on sexual-division of labor in the family. Second, this integrated product is further integrated into another theoretical stream of research that focuses on technology.

Our starting point is the structural/functionalist approach of Parsons (1957) further elaborated in the works of others. According to the structural-functional view, the internal structure of the family is based on generational and gender structure and attendant roles; the domestic social environment in which household activities are performed; the symbolic modes of behavior that contribute to family development and emotional stability; and, finally, the domains of family life that act as links to external environment such as paid-work or employment and education. Generally speaking, the structural-functional configuration of the family constitutes the family as practically but not completely autonomous for it is subject to external influences from the changing technological environment.

While the basic ideas of the structural/functionalist approach are still valid, a significant number of them have been contested. For example, many earlier ideas on sexual-division of labor are now considered outmoded along with the notion of nuclear family as the ideal family type. Several authors (Oakley 1984, for example) have noted that, in recent years, new family forms have emerged giving rise to new theories of family structure and gender relationships. We nevertheless agree with the main tenets of the structural/functionalists that families are not isolated institutions but are differentiated from other institutions in their specific role within the society and the functions they perform.

We recognize the key ideas of the new-home economists that households undertake production and consumption functions and perform various activities associated with these functions, and allocate time across activities according to their needs. However, we are not totally convinced that households engage in rational/utility maximum behaviors to the exclusion of expressive behaviors. Family behavior is much more motivated by social-psychological concerns and is very much embedded in the larger cultural context of rituals, meanings and other practices that are bound by tradition (Sahlins 1976).

Finally, we agree with the family development theorists that psycho-social determinants of family behaviors are very important in understanding those behaviors. But we reject the notion that family behaviors arise primarily out of pathological conditions. The idea that family space is a social space and family dynamics are a special form social dynamics is quite relevant to our study.

Finally, according to the structural-functionalist view (Parsons and Bales 1957; Coser 1964; Goode 1964; Hareven 1982), the family is conceptualized as a social organization which has an external orientation in relation to the larger social order and an internal orientation in relation to its own domestic order. In this study, our main (but not exclusive) concern is with the internal orientation of the family which comprises the social space and the technological space.

Social Space

As shown in Figure 1 [A], the social space is configured in terms of the *family members* [A.1] (i.e. the adopters and users of household technology), the *sub-environments* [A.2] in which the

FIGURE 1
Household Structure and Technology Use

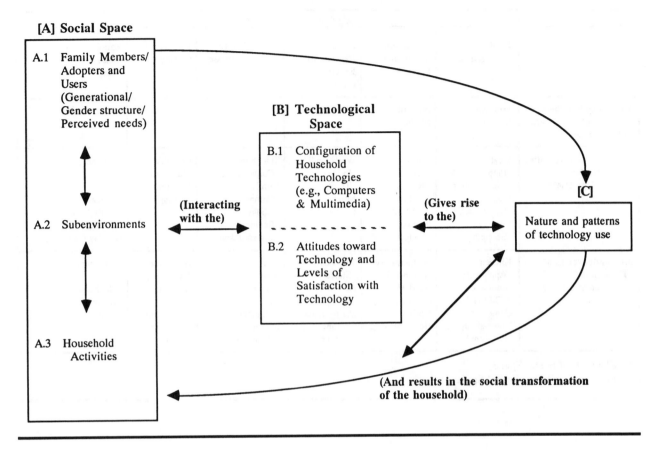

family members conduct their lives, and *household activities* [A.3] which are performed within the sub-environments by the family members. The family membership is structured *generationally* (parent/child) as well as by *gender* (male/female) and the family members are presumed to be motivated by personal and social *needs* in performing household activities.

Figure 2 gives a more derailed picture of the *sub-environments* in which the family life takes place—food management, household management/finance, leisure/recreation/entertainment, social/family communication, work/employment, family development/well being. Similarly, it also identifies *the family members* (who are the adopters and users of technology), and *the household activities* that they perform.

The first component [A.2, Figure 1], the sub-environments corresponds to the categories identified by Robinson (1977) and Robinson et al. (1989) in their time-budget studies. The second component [A.1] suggests that the characteristics of the family members as adopters and users of the technologies are relevant in terms of the nature and patterns of technology use and the particular social roles and responsibilities that they assume within the household. The third component [A.3], which is the set of household activities performed by family members in each sub-environment, suggests that these activities are targeted for technology use. The activities shown in the Figure 2 are illustrative, not exhaustive.

Technological Space

Within this broad structural/functionalist view of the family, we introduce some basic theoretical ideas concerning the technological space. Technology is viewed by some as a system of tools

and tool-using behavior (Escobar 1994). It is premised on the notion that technology is a means to achieving practical ends and therefore tends to be viewed in utilitarian terms. That is, other things being equal and given the specific needs of the users of technology, the users will be interested in the functionality of technology and will always prefer a particular technology that performs better than some other equivalent technology based on the criterion of functionality.

With specific reference to information technology, Moses (1981) notes that the adoption of information technology is more complex than most household technologies, and therefore is mediated by a more in-depth knowledge/understanding of the technology and an evaluation of its applicability to specific user needs. In contrast to this utilitarian approach, Kling (1981) proposes that information technology also needs to be assessed in terms of the social context in which it is embedded—the implication for our study being that since the household is a social organization that gives rise to various social interactions and dynamics, technologies acquire meanings in relation to such family dynamics. The adoption of technologies therefore may be a socially motivated decision rather than a purely utilitarian decision. It is our view that both the utilitarian and social perspectives are relevant, and together they determine the nature of the technological space.

The technological space consists of the *configuration of household technologies* (Figures 1 [B.1]) that are used within each sub-environment and are subject to a variety of *uses* by the family members in the performance of their activities. Technological space also *includes family attitudes [toward] and levels of satisfaction [with]* technology[B.2].

FIGURE 2

A Representation of the Internal Structure of the Household-Technology Interaction

	A.2 Sub-Environments**					
	Food Management	Household Maintenance Finance	Leisure/ Recreation Entertain- ment	Social/Family Communication	Work/Emp- loyment	Family/Develop- ment/Well- being
A.1 Family Members (As Adopters & users of technology)**	Primarily (parents)	Primarily adults	Whole Family	Whole Family	Primarily adults	Children and adults
A.3 Household Activities Targeted for Technology Use**	Meal Preparation & Consumption Washing Dishes etc., Grocery Shopping	Family Shopping Cleaning Tax Pre- paration Family Budget	Watching TV Holiday Travel Movies Games	Telephone Conversations Family Communication Holiday Reunion Correspondence	Job-related Activites Telecom- muting	Children's Education Adult Education Family Fitness Dieting Holiday Gathering
B.1 Configuration of Household Technologies #	Kitchen Appliances Automobile ATM Machine Computer Home-shopping (On-Line)	Washer, Dryer Automobile ATM Machine Computer On-line Home-banking	TV, VCR, Stereo Automobile Computer Multi-media On-Line Services	Telephone Answering Machine Fax Computer/email Internet On-Line Services	Telephone Answering Machine Fax Automobile Computer Internet	Typewriter VCR Telephone Computer Internet

**   Elements of Social Space
\#   Elements of Technological Space

Sub-environments, Activities, and Technologies

Figure 2 exemplifies the fit of a technology into the social organization of the household, as defined by the sub-environments. The notion of the sub-environment is key to our study. The term environment suggests that members of the household occupy a certain social and physical space. These environments are not mutually exclusive but conceptually distinct.

> Food Management
> Household Maintenance/Finance
> Leisure/Recreation/Entertainment
> Work/Employment
> Social/Family Communication
> Family Development/Well-Being

We postulate that a variety of household activities are performed by the members of the family in each sub-environment. These activities are determined by family needs and structural conditions appropriate to each sub-environment. The members of the household who perform the activities are a key component of the model for without them the social and technological spaces have no meaning. While the members of the household collectively occupy the subenvironment space, none has equal participation in them. For example, adults are more likely to be involved in cooking within a household as compared to children, and therefore are considered central actors within that environment. Another component not specifically shown in the model but is certainly implied is the household composition and the demographics of the household. This component is particularly critical if one were to study the changing family structure over its life cycle.

The technologies of the household are the other component of the model and are linked to the sub-environment by their location in the social space, and linked to the set of activities by their functionality. Collectively, the technologies constitute the techno-logical space. Not only is it logical and necessary to put technologies in each sub-environment as part of the structural aspect of the model, but the structure of the sub-environment is such that a given technology may belong to more than one sub-environment. In addition, household technologies may either compete with or complement each other within the same sub-environment or across subenvironments. Thus, computers are shown in more than one sub-environment (family development (children's education), leisure and recreation, work/employment, and household mainte-nance/finance). Similarly, automobiles and telephones can also be embedded in multiple sub-environments.'

So far we have discussed the structural aspects of the model. We shall now turn our attention to the "dynamic" aspects of the model. That is, it is necessary to address the issue of how this model functions in practice and how the components are related to each other.

The model relies on the basic idea that domestic technologies (e.g. computers) must fit the social space of the household and, specifically, they have to fit the perceptual and physical space of the sub-environments in which they are located. This fit is achieved when the members of the household are able to perform the activities within a given sub-environment using the appropriate technologies. The notion of fit is very central to our conceptualization of the household/technology interaction and requires that the fol-lowing four conditions be satisfied in respect to the technology and the sub-environment.

Condition A: The sub-environment must be salient to the household.

Example: In families with children, the Family Development environment will be very salient.

Condition B: The technology must be seen as significant or important for the sub-environment. That is, the technology must be seen as contributing to the performance of an activity within the sub-environment. As a corollary, in the event that a technology is designed to replace an existing technology the replacing technology must be seen as performing at a superior level (or at the very least at an equal level) compared to the existing technology.

Example: The computers must be seen as being useful to children's education.

Condition C: There must be at least one member of the household who uses the technology in a given sub-environment. For our purpose, a member may include hired help.

Example: Households with children are more likely to have children's educational software than families without children.

Condition D: The technology must be easy enough to operate by members of the household who occupy the particular social space.

Example: This condition is critical because the complexity of computing technology might limit or restrict the members' use of it, even if they have a need for it.

It is important to point out that just because a technology belongs to more than one environment, it does not mean it has a stronger position within the social space compared to a technology that belongs to only one sub-environment. For example, in our field work, when asked to name the two most important technologies in the home, a majority of our respondents cited the refrigerator as the most important technology followed by the telephone. When we analyzed our in-depth probings, we found that the meanings of these technologies to the users appeared to be that the refrigerator represents food and, therefore, survival, while the telephone represents communication and, therefore, social interaction. The refrigerator example is particularly interesting because it demonstrates that a technology might belong to only one subenvironment and be most salient for that environment, and, therefore, considered most critical to the household. At the other extreme, a technology might belong to many sub-environments and still have low salience in all of them. Alternatively, another technology might belong to multiple sub-environments and might be salient to a sub-set of these. In the case of computers, we show in Figure 2 that the computer can theoretically fit into all the sub-environments. The question that needs to be answered is how salient is it in each of the sub-environments in which it is located.

In sum, the theoretical framework helps us identify two key building blocks for our proposed model: the *social space and the technological space,* the former constituted by the social structure of the household and the activities performed within the household, and the latter representing the nature of the technological environment within the household.

How does the model help us understand computer use? First, it is based on the perspective of the user, that is, the emic perspective, rather than being imposed from outside.

Second, related to the first, the household-technology model enables us to examine computers not merely from the point of view of the technology but from an understanding of the household behavior. That is, what we have proposed is not a technology-driven model but a user(household)-oriented model.

Third, our household-technology model looks at a whole range of technologies, giving us an opportunity to examine computers in relation to other technologies. During the ethnographic field work, it became very clear that in order to understand the adoption/use issues of computers, one must view the total technological space of the household. Otherwise, very little insights will be gained by looking at computers alone.

Finally, the total fit of the computer into the sub-environment, that is, the ability to satisfy all the conditions (A to D), reveals its use potential.

Let us elaborate some of these issues still further. The model helps us understand two constructs: how computers and new media technologies may be adopted and used, and what the internal dynamics of family life are that determine the successful (or unsuccessful) adoption and use of the technologies, that is, the interaction between the social space and the technological space.

More specifically, our earlier research has shown that computers were once located in the *sub-environment* called "Work/Employment," and did not diffuse into other environments in any significant way. With the emergence of new technologies of multimedia and on-line services and their potential for a greater variety of family applications, coupled with the growing sophistication of the users of technology, the model recognizes this possibility and provides an enabling structure for examining the technological diffusion into other sub-environments. Thus the nature of multimedia diffusion into other sub-environments can be a very important focus of future studies.

Second, there is growing evidence that the *adopter and user* profiles are changing. The modal user in earlier studies was the adult male in the family. Current trends suggest a growing number of users are children as young as four or five years old. In other words, the diffusion of information technology occurs not only across the sub-environments, as stated above, but across and among family members.

Third, in a similar fashion to the changing profile of users and uses, their is some evidence that new household activities are emerging that did not exist before. That is, not only do existing household activities determine the nature of information-technology use but there is a feed back in the opposite direction from technology to household activities. Some recent examples include (but not limited to) the use of electronic mail for communication, developing family archives and medical histories, and home banking and check payment.

Fourth, our model will be useful in examining the claim as to how the new technologies of information are gradually becoming the key technology in the home replacing the telephone and television which currently enjoy this status.

Finally, the model enables us to evaluate the dynamic relationship between the social space (i.e. the sub-environments/the users/the activities) and the technological space (the configuration of the technologies) and make predictions about the social transformation of the household both in terms of its internal environment and external environment.

CONCLUSION

No technology works in a vacuum. The social setting of the household must be clearly understood in order to gain a clear understanding on household adoption and use of technologies. We see two forces acting in this regard. First, the technology itself—up to a point—has the ability to change the way family life is organized. Second, and simultaneously, the household itself can shape the character of the technology by acting upon it. These two forces are, respectively, the computerization of the household and the domestication of the computer. Besides these two forces, there is a third element which states that the new technologies of information/communication/entertainment must be understood in the context of the other technologies in the household.

Our aim in the paper was to develop a conceptual model of the household, its organization within a social space and, second, a conceptualization of the technological space within the household. 'We have labeled this model the "household/technology interaction" model. Using this model, we discussed discuss how domestic technologies (not just the computers) interact with the sub-environments of the household. Hopefully, our model can be improved further and refined as we keep examining the relevant issues with greater care and attention.

SELECTED REFERENCES

(For a complete list of references please contact the first author)

Bakke, John (1993), "A Nordic Approach to Teleworking," in J. Pekola (Ed.) *Telework–A New Vision,* Helsinki, Ministry of Labor.

Bjerg, Kresten and Kim Borreby Eds. (1994), *Home Informatics and Telematics & Automation,* Proceedings of the Home Informatics Conference, Copenhagen, June-July 1994.

Blattberg, Robert C., Rashi Glazer and John D.C. Little (Eds.)(1994), *The Marketing Information Revolution,* Harvard Business School Press.

Dholakia, Ruby Roy, Norbert Mundorf, Nikhilesh Dholakia (Eds.) (1995), *Information Technology in the Home: Demand Side Perspectives,* Lawrence Erlbaum Associates.

Dickerson, M.D. and J.W. Gentry (1983), "Characteristics of Adopters and Non-Adopters of Home Computers," *Journal of Consumer Research,* 10(2) 225-235.

Dutton, William, Everett M. Rogers and Suk-Ho Jun (1987), "The Diffusion and Impacts of Information Technology in Households", in *Oxford Surveys in Information Technology,* Oxford University Press, Vol. 4, 133-193.

Escobar, Arturo (1994), Welcome to Cyberia: Notes on the Anthropology of Cyberculture," *Current Anthropology,* Vol. 35, No. 3, June, 211-231.

Giacquinta, Joseph B., Jo Anne Bauer, Jane E. Levin (1993), *Beyond Technology's Promise: An Examination of Children s Computing at Home,* New York: Cambridge University Press.

Hedberg, B., and E. Mumford (1975), "The design of computer systems: Man's vision of man as an integral part of the systems design process," *Human Choice and Computers,* E. Mumford and H. Sachman, Eds., North-Holland, 31-59.

Hareven, T. (1987), Historical Analysis of the Family, in M. Sussman and S. Steinmetz (eds.) *Handbook of Marriage and Family,* Plenum Press.

Hoffman, Donna L. And Thomas P. Novak (1996), "Marketing in Hypermedia Computer-Mediated Environments: Conceptual Foundations," *Journal of Marketing,* July.

Kling, R. (1980), "Social Analyses of Computing: Theoretical Orientations in Recent Empirical Research," *'Computing Surveys, 12, 61–110.*

Kraut, Robert E. (1989) "Telecommuting: The' Trade-Offs of Homework," *Journal of Communication,* Vol. 39 (3), 14-40.

McQuarrie, E.F. and D. Langmeyer, (1987), "Planned and actual spending among owners of home computers," *Journal of Economic Psychology* 8, 141–159.

Mick, David and Susan Fournier (1995), *"Technological Consumer Products in Everyday life: Ownership-Meaning-Satisfaction,"* Working Paper, Marketing Science Institute.

Nickols, Sharon Y. And Karen D. Fox (1983), "Buying Time and Saving Time: Strategies for Managing Household Production," *Journal of Consumer Research,* V 10, September, 197-208.

Nicosia, Franco M. (1983), Individual and Social Choice, Vol. 1, in F.M. Nicosia et al., *"The Consumer-Technology Interface,"* National R&D Assessment Program", National Science Foundation.

Oropesa, R.S. (1993), "Female Labor Force Participation and Time-Saving Household Technology: A Case Study of the Microwave From 1978 to 1989, *"Journal of Consumer Research,* Vol 19, March, 567-579.

Parsons, T. (1957), "The American Family," in T. Parsons and R. Bales (eds.), *Family Socialization and Interaction,* Glencoe: Free Press.

Poster, Mark (1990), *The Mode of Information: Poststructuralism and Social Context,* Cambridge UK: Polity Press.

Robinson, John (1977), *How Americans Use Time,* Praeger.

Rudell, Frederica (1993), "Gender Differences in Consumer Decision Making for Personal Computers: A Test of Hypotheses," in Janeen A. Costa (Ed.) *Gender and Consumer Behavior: Proceedings of the Second Conference,"* University of Utah, 1-16.

Strober, Myra and Charles B. Weinberg (1980), "Strategies Used by Working and Non-working Wives to Reduce Time Pressures," *Journal of Consumer Research,* Vol. 6, March, 338-348.

Venkatesh, Alladi (1996) "Computer and Interactive Technologies for the Home: Past, Present and the Future," *Communications of the ACM,* December, Vol. 39, No. 12, 47-54.

Venkatesh, Alladi, Ruby R. Dholakia and Nikhilesh Dholakia (1996) "New Visions of Information Technology and Postmodernism: Implications for Advertising and Marketing Communications," in W. Brenner and L. Kolbe (eds.), The *Information Highway and Private Households–Case Studies of Business Impacts,* Germany: Physica/Springer.

Venkatesh, Alladi and Nicholas Vitalari (1992) "Emerging Distributed Work Arrangement: An Investigation of Computer-Based Supplemental Work at Home," *Management Science,* Vol. 38, No 12, December, 1687-1706.

Venkatesh, Alladi and Nicholas Vitalari (1990) "A Longitudinal Analysis of Computing in the Home," University of California, Irvine: National Science Foundation Report.

Venkatesh, Alladi and Nicholas Vitalari (1987)"A Post-adoption Analysis of Computing in the Home, in *Journal of Economic Psychology,* June 1987.

Zimmerman, Jan (ed.) (1983), *The Technological Woman,* New York, Praeger.

Promotion Over Time: Exploring Expectations and Explanations

Carl Mela, University of Notre Dame
Joe Urbany, University of Notre Dame

ABSTRACT

The potential impact of long-term promotional patterns on brand quality perceptions is an important and under-researched question. Most research has focused solely upon the effect of current period's pricing on brand perceptions. We interviewed 18 consumers to explore what, if any, inferences they make about frequently purchased brands in response to different price promotional patterns. Our interviewees participated in a "buying game" (cf. Krishna 1994) which exposed them to a simulated series of 36 monthly prices for three brands with different promotional patterns in a category. Several insights emerged from the analysis which suggest that consumers make inferences in response to a brand's pricing history. Moreover, there is considerable heterogeneity in how respondents make those inferences. For example, some tended to believe that a brand with infrequent, deep discounts (i.e., more significant price variation) were slow movers and, therefore, of inferior quality. However, this inference was less common when price reductions were clearly flagged as sales. Consumer categorization of brands into brand tiers were moderated by respondents' attention to brands' regular prices relative to competitors' prices. Research directions are discussed.

INTRODUCTION

Owing to the managerial relevance of promotions, the attention they have received from innovative modelers, the availability of data, and simulated purchase paradigms studying promotional effects experimentally, the study of price promotions by marketers has been prolific (Blattberg, Briesch, and Fox 1995). Yet, issues relating to the long term effects of promotions remain important and largely unexplored (for exceptions, see Boulding, Lee, and Staelin 1994; Lal and Padmanabhan 1995). Such effects are important because it has repeatedly been suggested that the long term health of a brand (i.e., brand franchise or equity) may be put at risk by a pattern of frequent price promotions (Blattberg and Neslin 1990; Nagle and Holden 1995). In spite of the recent panel-based stream of studies regarding promotions and consumer choice, there currently exists little empirical evidence on consumer interpretation of promotion patterns over time. It is our objective to examine whether and why promotion patterns which vary in frequency and depth (Rao, 1991; Krishna 1992, 1994) affect consumer price expectations and brand evaluations (specifically, perceived quality).

Price Expectations and Explanations

It is well-known that pricing patterns over time influence subsequent consumer price expectations (Jacobson and Obermiller 1990; Krishna 1991, 1992, 1994a,b; Lattin and Bucklin 1989; Winer 1986, 1989). Moreover, the literature on the frequency effect (Alba and Marmorstein 1987; Alba et al. 1994) leads to the prediction that brands with greater frequency of promotion will be perceived as having a lower reference price, although the issue of quality effects remains unexplored. Our point of departure from these studies is to explicitly examine whether and how deals affect brand perceptions in addition to price expectations.

We define consumer explanations to be inferences arising from promotional patterns about products or marketers. We consider the possibility that consumers observing promotion patterns over time may make inferences about why sellers price promote as they do and that the lowering of expected price which likely occurs with frequent promotion could reduce consumer perceptions of brand quality (cf. Blattberg and Neslin 1989) if quality is somewhat ambiguous over time (even with experience; Hoch and Deighton 1989). Since measures of perceived quality and other brand perceptions are not readily available or operationalized in standard scanner data sets, we turn to interviews with consumers to assess whether and what "explanations" consumers form in response to dealing patterns.

The exploratory and hypothesis generating nature of our research mandates the use of in-depth open ended interviews of consumers to assess the presence of promotional attitudes and decision protocols, we report the results of four phases of such interviews. Each wave of interviews was predicated upon what was learned in prior waves. Our method attempted to avoid injecting our research biases by being as general and non-leading as possible.

ANALYSIS

Overview

Eighteen respondents were interviewed in four different phases. In each phase, a standard set of exploratory questions were asked regarding the respondent's shopping routines, products purchased, and response to advertising. They were also asked about their perceptions regarding prices and price promotions in stores and in particular product categories—initially (in the earliest interviews) by having respondents "walk through" recent store features in the newspaper, and later by having them describe a trip through their usual store and the categories they frequently shopped. In the eleven interviews comprising phases 2, 3, and 4 (as discussed below), respondents were additionally presented with a formal "buying game" that simulated category purchases over several periods. Interviews took 30 minutes to an hour. The presentation below focuses on insights obtained from the buying game.

Phase 1

Phase 1 consisted of interviews with seven consumers, the latter four of whom were presented with prices for what were said to be three relatively new brands of cookies currently sold in other markets. Prices for the three brands were presented sequentially on 20 index cards, each card presenting prices for three brands in a given week. The control brand maintained a constant price of 2.49. The other two brands had regular prices of 2.49 and different promotion patterns. Each pattern yielded a total of $2.00 in discounts over the twenty weeks: the frequency brand had 10 price reductions during the 20 weeks to $2.29; while the depth brand was reduced twice to $1.49. We then asked respondents for their "impressions" regarding the brands. Two results emerged consistently across subjects: First, the control brand was thought to be a better or more popular brand because its price was constant (more direct questions are noted, otherwise the quotes below reflect responses to the general question about impressions):

> ... if (the control brand)'s staying at the same price all the time, they probably sell a lot of product at that price. (then in response to a direct inquiry about which of the three might be a national brand:) I think (the control brand) would be the national brand. (Jennie)

529

... (the control brand) would probably be the name brand 'cause they don't fluctuate. (Edie)

... (the company making the control brand) obviously has a good following. (Tom)

Second, the brand with the infrequent, deep discount was put in a lower quality class:

I think A and B are probably more similar, and (the depth brand) is a different quality... for example, if you bought Pop Tarts... (the) Kroger brand is terrible. (The depth brand is like a Kroger Brand). (Peggy)

I would question the quality (of the depth brand). (Tom, written notes)

Another respondent indicated that the depth brand "would be the store brand" in response to a question explicitly asking her to classify the brands.

There was no consistent mention across the four respondents regarding the frequency brand. The frequency brand was alternatively described as "probably the Kroger brand ... because it's lower consistently than the others" (Edie), "the mid-brand" (Jennie), and a "good quality brand" (Tom, written notes).

Phase 2 Procedure

The phase 1 results suggested the possibility that consumers extracted information from price promotion patterns—specifically, that higher, more constant prices reflected better quality and that deep discounts signalled something wrong with the brand. In phase 2, we attempted to replicate these results with a more formal buying game. Three modifications were made. First, we created a game that mimicked the purchase task used by Krishna (1994a, b). The game instructed consumers to choose brands and purchase quantities such that they minimize their overall purchase and inventory costs subject to minimum consumption constraints. To enhance involvement, a $20 reward was offered to the respondent most successful at this task. The task was inserted after a few relatively innocuous questions regarding shopping routines and typical product categories purchased. The economic nature of the task served to discourage consumers from guessing our experimental objective. Moreover, the task encouraged them to attend to the pricing information. Second, we lengthened the number of periods over which the game was carried to 36 to present a longer history of price promotion patterns. Third, we used shampoo instead of cookies, given the precedent in Kahn and Louie (1990) and its longer interpurchase cycle, which allowed us to simulate monthly as opposed to weekly purchase intervals, thereby simulating three years of pricing history.

In the four phase 1 interviews in which prices were presented, the constant price brand had a higher average price than the frequency and depth brands. To provide a more stringent test of the notion that low price variance signals a better product, prices were set across the 36 months such that *all three* brands had an identical average price of $2.39. Our control brand was always $2.39, which was $0.10 lower than the regular price of the other two brands. The other two brands each had "regular" prices of $2.49; the frequency brand offered $0.20 discounts in 18 periods and the depth brand offered $1.20 discounts in three periods.

Based upon respondent open ends in phase 1, we also developed a more complete set of questions that followed the buying game. The questions elicited general reactions to the task, whether subjects made decisions similarly to their normal decision-making,

what they were thinking about as they went through the task, and how they might subsequently choose between the frequency and depth brands if they were both priced at $2.49. We continued to ask for brand impressions. We then solicited specific price estimates: average price of each brand over the 36 periods, number of times each was on sale, the regular and "on sale" prices for each brand, a general categorization question, and a quality rating. The categorization question first asked respondents whether they felt they had enough information to categorize brands as "high-end/premium," "mid-range," or "low-end," and, if so, which brand(s) would go in which category (we emphasized that they could put all in one or each in one if they wanted). The quality rating was a 10 point scale ranging from 1 ("very poor quality") to 10 ("very good quality").

Phase 2 Results

The second phase involved two interviews; Carol and Linda. Carol is in her late 20's and lives with her brother. She lives near the market "super store" called Meijer and shopped there almost exclusively. Linda is in her late 30's/early 40's, is married, with two children at home. Linda is the prototype of a vigilant shopper (cf. Urbany, Dickson, and Key 1991). She carefully reviews the grocery ads which came with the paper every Monday, determines where the best specials are, and develops a detailed shopping list. On Friday afternoon, given this preparation, Linda and her husband spend about three hours traveling to 4-5 stores buying specifically what was dictated by the specials at various stores. In the interview, Linda easily discussed which stores she felt had the best prices on particular items.

Price Expectations and Perceived Quality. Table 1 shows estimates of average prices, sale frequency and brand classification and quality ratings provided by respondents after the 36 period buying game. The frequency effect literature (Alba and Marmorstein 1987; Alba et al. 1994) suggests that the frequency brand would be perceived as having the lowest average price due to its large number of discounts. Carol ordered her average price estimates in a manner consistent with this effect—the frequency brand received the lowest estimate ($2.29) and the depth brand the highest ($2.49) even though both brands actually had identical average prices. Her estimate for the average price for the constant brand was exactly correct, as was Linda's. In contrast, Linda dramatically *underestimated* the average price for the depth brand. As the table indicates, she also substantially underestimated the number of times the frequency brand was on sale (Carol estimated this number correctly). Linda's estimates were unexpected, given (1) her hyperprice sensitivity and vigilance in her actual shopping, and (2) the fact that she participated sincerely and earnestly in the buying game. Consider, however, how Linda described her play in the game:

Well, you just kind of figure when they put on a good sale like that for $1.29, it's going to be a little while before it happens again. So you want to stock up. And until they have another sale like that, I'll have enough to last me....So if you see a good one you go for it.

Once Linda had seen the $1.29 sale price for the depth brand she apparently adapted a heuristic of lying in wait for the next big sale from that brand and buying enough quantity to tide her over to the next $1.29 sale. It is possible that Linda's misperception of the frequency brand's promotion cycle (every sixth month instead of every other month) was due to diminished attention to its price variation induced by increased attention to the depth brand's price.

Note that both Linda and Carol estimated the constant brand to have been price-promoted five times during the 36 months even

TABLE 1
Price and Quality Estimates in Phase 2 Interviews

	Actual	Carol	Linda
AVERAGE PRICE			
frequency brand	2.39	2.29	2.35
depth brand	2.39	2.49	2.00
constant price brand	2.39	2.39	2.40
SALE FREQUENCY			
frequency brand	18 @2.29	18 @2.29	5 @ 2.29
depth brand	3 @ 1.29	8 @ 1.29	6 @ 1.29
constant price brand	0	5 @ 2.29	5 @ 2.39
BRAND CLASSIFICATION /QUALITY RATING[a]			
frequency brand		lower / 7	higher / 6-8
depth brand		lower / 5	lower / 6-8
constant price brand		higher / 9	higher / 6-8

[a] NOTE: The brand classification question asked respondents to indicate first whether they had enough information to classify the brands into categories labelled high-end/premium, mid-range, or low-end and then, if yes, to classify. The quality rating was made on a scale from 1 (very poor quality) to 10 (very good quality).

though it had never been promoted. The result suggests that perception may be induced by a cross brand comparison of the $2.39 constant price to the competing brands' $2.49 depromoted price. In addition, both respondents significantly overestimated the number of sales held for the depth brand (consistent with Krishna's (1991) results).

Price Variance and Brand Quality. Linda stated with fairly strong confidence that she generally did not believe there was a relationship between price and quality (i.e., "[many] private labels [had just as good] quality") and gave the brands all ratings of 6-8 on the quality scale. Carol rated the depth brand lowest on quality (5 on the 10 point scale), attributing its occasional deep discounts to the fact that it apparently did not sell as well as the other brands:

> (The frequency and control brands) stay pretty much level. (The depth brand) doesn't really sell very well. You have to really push its sales and get it going. (Carol)

Further, Carol suggested that "I'd probably put (the control brand) in the upper and the other two in the lower... (The control brand's price stays) pretty much right on track."

Phase 2 Discussion. The phase 2 results added a complication to our consideration of whether promotion patterns produced inferences—the possibility that consumers do not accurately interpret price information presented sequentially. Carol behaved precisely as we initially expected subjects to behave; she estimated the number of sales for the frequency brand accurately across the 36 months and estimated that brand to have a lower average price, noting that its price did not vary much (see quote above). Also in accordance with our expectations, she believed the constant price brand was of better quality than the other two brands, citing its

limited price variance. Linda, on the other hand, was unexpectedly inaccurate. She was an active shopper and attentive respondent, but had not attended to the "sales" held by the frequency brand, even in this simple environment. The significant variation for the depth brand swayed Linda's estimate of its average price and led her to anticipate large price reductions for the depth brand, consequently distracting attention from other prices. Alternatively, she simply may have not interpreted the $.20 price variations for the frequency brand as "sales."

Phase 3 Procedure

Phase 2 results were partially consistent with phase 1 results in showing a link between promotion pattern and quality perceptions. We were interested in phase 3 in seeing if similar results emerged and also in seeing if the inaccuracies in Linda's perception of the promotion patterns were unusual. Further, in making an incremental step toward greater realism, we decided to provide more brand information to respondents to address the potential problems associated with providing only a single cue for quality judgments (Olson 1977).

In the phase 3 interviews, we presented brand attribute information to respondents prior to beginning the buying task. Ratings were provided for the brands on attributes identified via the most recent *Consumer Reports* article on shampoo. The brand by attribute matrix was constructed so that no brand dominated all the remaining alternatives (Ha and Hoch 1986). The five attributes on which ratings were provided were combing, manageability, body, package, and lather (definitions based upon the Consumer Reports article was provided to respondents). While an initial pretest of 9 consumers prior to the interviews indicated no statistically significant difference across subjects regarding mean brand quality rat-

TABLE 2
Price and Quality Estimates in Phase 3 Interviews

	Actual	Marie	Janet	Peggy
AVERAGE PRICE				
frequency brand	2.39	2.49	2.30	2.39
depth brand	2.39	1.75	2.00	2.29
constant price brand	2.39	2.39	2.40	2.49
SALE FREQUENCY				
frequency brand	18 @ 2.29	4-5 @ 2.29	15@2.29	1 @ 2.39
depth brand	3 @ 1.29	3 @ 1.29	6/7@1.79	3 @ 1.29
constant price brand	0	0	15@ 2.29	0
BRAND CLASSIFICATION /QUALITY RATING[a]				
frequency brand		high / 8	middle/7	high /10
depth brand		middle / 8	low/5	low / 6
constant price brand		lower / 6	high end/9	middle / 8.5

[a] NOTE: The brand classification question asked respondents to indicate first whether they had enough information to classify the brands into categories labelled high-end/premium, mid-range, or low-end and then, if yes, to classify. The quality rating was made on a scale from 1 (very poor quality) to 10 (very good quality).

ings (MANOVA, Wilks'=.57, $F\{2,7\}$=2.67, p=.14), subsequent pilot testing indicated that Brand B's attribute set was favored somewhat over A's and C's (A and C had equal ratings). Given that Brand B was always the constant price brand, however, this has little bearing on interpretations of results for the frequency and depth brands, which were rotated between positions A and C.

Phase 3 Results

Marie is in her late 20's, with husband and several children at home and regularly shops Aldi's (for canned goods), Kroger, and Martin's. Peggy is also married with children. Janet is single and in her late twenties.

Price Expectations and Perceived Quality. Table 2 shows estimates of average prices, sale frequency, brand classification and quality ratings for these three respondents, showing that they more closely resemble the responses of Linda (who we first thought was an outlier) than Carol (our model respondent) from Phase 2. Specifically, all three respondents gave the *depth brand* a lower average price than the other brands, two of whom did so by fairly substantial margins. In addition, two of the three dramatically underestimated the number of sales for the frequency brand.

Price Variance and Brand Quality. Counter to our expectations, Marie gave the constant price brand the lowest quality rating. This rating was apparently based upon her careful attention to *relative* price levels—she noted that the constant brand's price was lower than the regular price charged by the promoted brands, suggesting to her that it was more likely a "low-end" brand. Both Marie and Peggy ironically regarded the (incorrectly) perceived lower price variance of the frequency brand to reflect a better selling or better quality brand:

I expect (the frequency brand's price in the next 12 months) to go up. It rarely went on sale, so it must have a good turnover for them not to put it on sale. (Marie)

Actually, I think that when I shop, the better brand's don't tend to go on sale a lot. Actually, the medium shampoos probably do ... (The frequency brand is) probably a premium ... (Peggy H.)

Consistent with the lower evaluations described above, some questions were raised about the depth brand

(The depth brand) was normally $2.49 and on sale for $1.29, which is quite a blast. I kind of wonder why. If I thought the quality was just the same, I would go with the cheaper one. I'm wondering if they have so much in stock that they can't push, so they put them on sale to get rid of it or what. I'm not sure. (Marie)

(The depth brand) probably a low, because it went on sale a lot. (Peggy H.)

Peggy also interpreted the *Consumer Reports* information as indicating that the constant price brand was "a little cheaper," yet she still rated it an 8 or 9 on quality in part because its "price stayed the same." Janet distinguished the frequency and constant price brands by saying that these brands "had the same price," while the depth brand "dropped often." Janet further stated "(the brands) kept going back and forth so much, $0.10, $0.20 constantly". So, even though she believed that the frequency brand had been promoted 15 times, she still concluded that its price had not varied much. She gave her

TABLE 3
Price and Quality Estimates in Phase 4 Interviews

	Actual	Steven	Amy	Jen	Ed	Sue	Lori
AVERAGE PRICE frequency brand	2.39	2.40	2.35	2.39	2.39	2.29	2.40
depth brand	2.39	2.20	2.10	2.29	2.29	2.39	2.36
constant price brand	2.39	2.39	2.39	2.39	2.39	2.39	2.39
SALE FREQUENCY frequency brand	18 @ 2.29	10 @ 2.29	10@2.29	9 @ 2.29	12@2.29	6@2.29	12@2.29
depth brand	3 @ 1.29	3 @ 1.29	3@1.29	3 @ 1.29	3@1.29	5@1.29	3@1.29
constant price brand	0	2 @ 2.39	0	0	0	4@2.29	0
BRAND CLASSIFICATION /QUALITY RATING[a] frequency brand	/6	/6	middle/6	middle/9	middle/8	/7	middle/7
depth brand	/5	/8	high end/8	premium/10	premium/7	/7	store/5
constant price brand	/7	/5	store/5	store/8	middle/8	/6	middle/8

[a] NOTE: The brand classification question asked respondents to indicate first whether they had enough information to classify the brands into categories labelled high-end/premium, mid-range, or low-end and then, if yes, to classify. The quality rating was made on a scale from 1 (very poor quality) to 10 (very good quality).

highest quality ratings to the constant price and frequency brands. Apparently, she relied upon the attribute information rather than the pricing history to make her quality judgments. She primarily purchased the frequency brand and mentioned that the lather and manageability (rather than price) drove her choices. She was therefore a prototypical loyal and her relatively accurate assessment of the number of deals (15 estimated) for the frequency brand may have been driven by her loyalty and involvement with this brand.

Phase 4 Procedure

The surprising failure of respondents to note the number of times the frequency brand went on sale appears to be in part a function of the small increments by which its price was changed and the attention attracted by the relatively large promotions of the depth brand. Past research has shown, however, that the "flagging" of promotions (e.g., shelf tags) can have a powerful impact on promotion response (at least among some consumers; Inman, McAlister, and Hoyer 1990) and, presumably, perception of promotions. To investigate the effect of a promotional announcement, and to determine if the frequency effect would become more obvious when promotions were signaled, in phase 4 we labeled the price changes on the monthly price cards as "sales." Respondents were 6 consumers who were primarily responsible for the grocery shopping in their households. Other experimental manipulations were similar to those previously described.

Phase 4 Results

Price Expectations and Perceived Quality. Table 3 presents the results for our Phase 4 respondents. Our initial expectation was that labeling the price reductions as "sales" would create greater attention to the frequency brand's larger number of promotions and produce more accurate perceptions of the number of sales and potentially lower price expectations for that brand. In fact, the frequency bias did not go away. When sales were not flagged (in phases 2 and 3), the mean perceived number of deals for the frequency brand was 8.8, compared to 9.8 in phase 4 with the sales flagged. However, the phase 4 respondents did perceive the number of promotions for the depth and constant price brands much more accurately. Five of six phase 4 respondents estimated the number of depth brand promotions correctly, while 4 of 6 recognized that the constant brand never promoted. It is possible that the processing and consequent storing of a small number of dichotomous cues such as deals is an easier task than memorizing a distribution of absolute prices. Even though the flags did apparently enhance the accuracy of the depth and constant sales deal frequency perceptions, the depth brand was still most frequently estimated to have the lowest average price.

Brand quality perceptions also changed compared to phase 3. While none of the phase 3 subjects had rated the depth brand as "premium" or "high-end," three of the six phase 4 subjects classified it in the high tier and a fourth (who gave no brand classification) gave it the highest quality rating. One possibility for this reversal is the fact that it is the brand most frequently priced at $2.49 (33 of 36 periods) became clearer when sales were flagged, leading respondents to give the brand a higher evaluation:

> "... I think (the depth brand) was higher priced, it was a high end product, even though its sale price dropped really low. I think it was an incentive to make us buy the product and like it." (Ed)

The quality inferences also furnish insight into the reversal in categorizations for the depth brand.

Price Variance and Brand Quality. It is interesting that none of the phase 4 respondents classified the constant price brand in the high tier; four of six gave it the lowest quality rating and two of them classified it as a store brand. Consider the following explanations:

The store brand doesn't go on sale (Amy).

The (constant price brand) wasn't ever on sale, therefore it would be a store brand. (Jen)

Evidently, some consumers believe (and much store scanner data bears this out) that low-tier brands in many categories do not go on sale very often. By defining price changes as sales in the phase 4, it is possible that we made it clearer that the constant price brand never changed (see also Marie in Table 2). When unflagged, it appeared that the frequency and constant brands were vacillating in relative price. So, while low price variance is consistent with brand popularity (as indicated in our earlier phases), it may signal store brand quality when coupled with a somewhat lower regular price.

SUMMARY

The results suggest some potential biases in consumer interpretation of price promotion frequency over time in a controlled setting, but also suggest some interesting differences in consumer beliefs about the meaning of promotion patterns. Respondents dramatically underestimated the frequency of sales for a brand promoted half the time, possibly because of the difficulty in tallying or remembering large counts in memory and a tendency to rely on some base rate perception of promotion frequency even when sales are flagged. However, flagging price reductions as sales reduced the tendency to overestimate low and zero promotion frequencies, making it clearer to respondents that our constant price brand was never on sale and that the depth brand had a specific "reason" for its price reductions.

There was heterogeneity across our respondents in their explanations regarding the relationship between low price variance and quality. Some felt that lower price variation reflected "better" (or at least more popular) brands. Similarly, our initial interviews suggested that a greater variance in price indicated low sales or something wrong with the brand (e.g., Carol, Marie, Peggy). At the same time, the high variance-low quality heuristic was less evident when price reductions were clearly flagged as sales, possibly because this provided an alternative explanation for the deal (incentive to buy).

These findings, along with the results of a larger follow-up study, suggest some speculative hypotheses. Noticeable swings in price over time may motivate inferencing about the seller and brand quality when quality cannot be judged directly prior to purchase, although such inferencing may be moderated by the presence of an explanation for the price reduction. Stable prices, on the other hand, may be associated with brands that have a clearer positioning in the market (either low-end or high-end). However, what the consumer concludes from stable prices about brand quality may vary significantly, depending upon the regular price levels of the brand and, naturally, brand name. What may be of particular interest is how promotion patterns *within* a tier influence consumer perceptions of relative brand quality.

Limitations and Research Agenda

The most important limitation here is our ability to generalize results from the 11 respondents who participated in the full buying game. At the same time, a small sample was merited in providing insight into individual level perceptions. The research is also limited in that the information environment, while essentially the same as other simulations reported in the literature (e.g., Krishna 1994), is much simpler than the real marketplace and therefore may overestimate consumer attention to price information (e.g., Dickson and Sawyer 1990). However, the open-ended portions of our interviews did suggest that nearly all interviewees knew prices in

their stores for at least two or three products, and that some were very confident in their knowledge of price promotion patterns. The methodology simulates the behavior of at least a portion of the consumer market for a given category, since, for all categories, there is a segment of the market who is knowledgeable about prices. Further, and in spite of the simplicity of the methodology, the key empirical findings—that small promotions may not be noticeable (or memorable) and that brand perceptions may be influenced by variation in prices over time—both make intuitive sense and have important dynamic pricing implications for retailers. While there may be some concern that the structured nature of the task motivated inferences that may not have occurred otherwise, we note Winer's (1986) refutation of a similar concern in the attribution theory literature. It is not clear that a more subtle method would reveal less inferencing among those who attend to price (although it would, by definition, find no inferencing among those who ignored price).

Subsequent research should examine differential promotion pattern effects for brands in low, middle, and high tiers, and more fully examine the price sensitivity implications of these different patterns. For example, there may be greater resistance to purchase off promotion (see Kahn and Louie 1990) for brands with different promotion patterns, yet equivalent average prices. In addition, our early interviews and a subsequent study suggest that the different promotion patterns may produce different perceptions of price fairness, which may influence brand choice. This research is a first step in pursuing a more in-depth understanding of consumer inferencing in light of information regarding brand marketing activity. Not all consumers attend to pricing information, but enough may become aware of such activity that any inferences they make from it will have an impact on a brand's equity over time.

REFERENCES

Alba, Joseph W. and Howard Marmorstein (1987), "The Effects of Frequency Knowledge on Consumer Decision Making," *Journal of Consumer Research*, 14 (June), 14-25.

Alba, Joseph, Susan Broniarczyk, Terence A. Shimp, and Joel E. Urbany (1994), "The Influence of Prior Beliefs and Frequency Cues on Consumer Perceptions of Comparative Price Information," *Journal of Consumer Research*, 21 (September), 219-235.

Blattberg, Robert C., Richard Briesch, and Edward J. Fox (1995), "How Promotions Work," *Marketing Science*, 14 (Summer), G122-G132.

_____, and Scott A. Neslin (1989), "Sales Promotion: The Long and Short of It," *Marketing Letters*, 1 (December), 81-97.

_____, and _____ (1990), *Sales Promotion: Concepts, Methods, and Strategies*, Englewood Cliffs, NJ: Prentice-Hall.

Boulding, William, Eunkyu Lee, and Richard Staelin (1994), "Mastering the Mix: Do Advertising and Promotion and Sales Force Activity Lead to Differentiation?," *Journal of Marketing Research* (May), 201-205.

Dickson, Peter R. and Alan G. Sawyer (1990), "The Price Knowledge and Search of Supermarket Shoppers," *Journal of Marketing*, 54 (July), 42-53.

Hoch, Stephen J., and John Deighton (1989), "Managing What Consumers Learn from Experience," *Journal of Marketing*, 53 (April), 1-20.

Hu, Young-Won, and Stephen J. Hoch (1989), "Ambiguity, Processing Strategy, and Advertising-Evidence Interactions," *Journal of Consumer Research*, 16 (December), 354-360.

Inman, J. Jeffrey, Leigh McAlister, and Wayne D. Hoyer (1990), "Promotion Signal: Proxy for a Price Cut?" *Journal of Consumer Research*, 17 (June), 74-81.

Jacobson, Robert and Carl Obermiller (1990), "The Formation of Expected Future Price: A Reference Price for Forward-Looking Consumers," *Journal of Consumer Research*, 16 (March), 420-432.

Kahn, Barbara E. and Therese A. Louie (1990), "Effects of Retraction of Price Promotions on Brand Choice Behavior for Variety-Seeking and Last-Purchase-Loyal Consumers" *Journal of Marketing Research*, 27 (August), 279-289.

Krishna, Aradhna, (1991), "The Effect of Dealing Patterns on Consumer Perceptions of Deal Frequency and Willingness to Pay," *Journal of Marketing Research*, 28 (November), 441-451.

_____, (1992), "The Normative Impact of Consumer Price Expectations for Multiple Brands on Consumer Purchase Behavior," *Marketing Science*, 11 (Summer), 266-286.

_____ (1994a), "The Impact of Dealing Patterns on Purchase Behavior," *Marketing Science*, 13 (Fall), 351-373.

_____ (1994b), "The Effect of Deal Knowledge on Consumer Purchase Behavior," *Journal of Marketing Research*, 31 (February), 76-91.

Lal, Rajiv, and V. Padmanabhan (1995), "Competitive Response in Equilibria," *Marketing Science*, 14 (Summer), G101-G108.

Lattin, James M., and Randolph E. Bucklin (1989), "Reference Effects of Price and Promotion on Brand Choice Behavior," *Journal of Marketing Research*, 26 (August), 299-310.

Nagle, Thomas T. and Reed K. Holden (1995), *The Strategy and Tactics of Pricing*, 2nd Edition, Englewood Cliffs, NJ: Prentice-Hall.

Olson, Jerry C. (1977), "Price as an Informational Cue: Effects on Product Evaluations," in *Consumer and Industrial Buying Behavior*, eds. ARch G. Woodside, Jagdish N. Sheth, and Peter D. Bennett, New York: American Elsevier, 267-286.

Rao, Ram C. (1991), "Pricing and Promotions in Asymmetric Duopolies," *Marketing Science*, 10 (Spring), 131-144.

Urbany, Joel E., Peter R. Dickson, and Rosemary Key (1990), "Actual and Perceived Consumer Vigilance in the Retail Grocery Industry," *Marketing Letters*, 2:1, 15-25.

Winer, Russell S. (1986), "A Reference Price Model of Brand Choice for Frequently Purchased Products," *Journal of Consumer Research*, 13 (September), 250-256.

_____ (1989), "A Multi-Stage Model of Price Incorporating Reference Prices," *Marketing Letters*, 1, 27-36.

Decisions Past and Decisions Present: Modelling Broader Patterns of Consumer Choice

Margaret K. Hogg, University of Manchester Institute of Science and Technology
Paul C.N. Michell, University of Manchester[1]

ABSTRACT

The creation of meaning via consumption is achieved in different ways and includes positive and negative choices: these are often used to mark inclusion and exclusion. The focus of traditional models and studies of consumer behavior has largely been on positive aspects of choice at the micro level (product or brand level) of decision-making. Examination of choices as a series of often interdependent decisions by consumers contributes to understanding the meanings created by consumption. Broader models of consumption are proposed and the findings from a study of U.K. mail order catalog shoppers indicate that patterns can be found in consumers' stream of consumption choices.

INTRODUCTION

Consumption involves the search for, choice, acquisition, possession and disposal of goods and services. Traditional models of consumer behavior (Nicosia 1966, Howard and Sheth 1969, Bettman 1979, Engel, Blackwell and Miniard 1995) and studies of consumer choice (e.g. Bettman and Zins 1977, Bettman and Park 1980, Brucks 1985) largely concentrate on the earlier stages in the consumption process; and on the positive aspects of consumer choice. We propose the development of broader models of consumer behavior–involving consumption configurations–which include both the positive and negative aspects of consumer choice within the stream of consumer decisions.

We present three Models in which consumption configurations represent the combination of positive (constellations) and negative (anti-constellations) aspects of consumers' choices. We extend existing conceptualizations by developing the construct of 'anti-constellations' to represent negative choices. This allows us to incorporate both positive and negative aspects of consumption choices into our model building. We argue that the positive and negative aspects of consumption choices–over time–can be linked to the creation of meaning and identity.

In the first Model we draw on the symbolic interactionist perspective within social psychology to model the relationship between consumption, social roles and identities. The first Model integrates consumption with identity by relating levels of product and brand choices with levels of roles and identity. The second Model proposes the major internal and external forces which influence patterns of consumption (configurations). The third Model expands on one part of the first, integrative, model to explore how consumer decisions at the product category/brand level can be linked to the creation of consumption configurations. A preliminary study of U.K. consumers is used to examine consumption configurations and to explore combinations of consumption choices within the context of the third Model.

The central argument in this paper is that consumption is more than a series of single, simple and independent decisions; consumption involves serial, complex and interdependent decisions. When the positive and negative aspects of consumer choices are considered over a period of time and as a series of interdependent–rather than a series of independent–decisions, then it is possible to discover patterns in consumption which can be linked to systems of meaning. Our model-building contrasts with earlier models of consumer behavior which concentrate largely on aspects of search, choice and acquisition; which embrace only the positive aspects of decision making; and which are concerned with decisions about individual products.

In this paper we review the literature on self and identity; on product and consumption constellations; and on the factors which influence consumption. We then describe the model building; outline the research design and methodology; and briefly discuss the findings and the limitations of the study and indicate possible areas of future research.

IDENTITY, SELF AND CONSUMPTION

Identity arises from the interdependence of self and society. Following Mead (1934) activities, such as consumption, are behaviors which are 'constituted' into action and have meaning in creating, confirming, maintaining or transforming situated identities. Self, identity and consumption are viewed as socially constituted and linked (Dittmar 1992).

Social positions or roles; Self image and self concept

The social role or position provides the context for decisions made by individual consumers and is: "a behavioral repertoire characteristic of a person or a position". (Biddle and Thomas 1966:11). McCall and Simmons (1982) argued that collections of products and activities were taken by society as defining social roles. Studies have confirmed that characteristics of self-image are congruous with characteristics of brand image (e.g. Dolich 1969; Green et al 1969; Landon 1974; Ross 1971; Sirgy 1982; Snyder and DeBono 1985). Self concept and self image (Sirgy 1982, Lee 1990) are used to model the layers of meaning between self and consumption. Situational self concept "... acknowledges that consumers have many self concepts and that consumption of a brand may be highly congruent with the self image in one situation and not at all congruent in another situation" (Schenk and Holman 1980:612). This reflects the view that consumers have a number of 'me's' (Solomon 1983:321) which are enacted as part of self, and that some are more central to self-definition than others (Stryker 1968).

When individuals have a number of different social identities or 'me's' which derive from their social roles–some of which are partly constituted by their acts as consumers of goods and services–there will not necessarily be congruency across all their consumption choices. However, consumption decisions which can be linked to the enactment of particular roles would be expected to display functional, symbolic or socio-cultural complementarity. Following Rogers (1951) and Alderson (1957) it would be expected that consumers would seek a 'fit' among consumption choices within the context of the relevant role/identity.

CONSUMPTION CONSTELLATIONS

Douglas and Isherwood(1978) argued that the 'exchange of goods...involved shared systems of meaning' which echoed earlier views (Veblen 1899; Alderson 1957) that individuals use *groups of products* to communicate messages about themselves relating to status and social position. A number of studies have explored the association between consumers and groups of products (Boyd and Levy 1963; Alpert and Gatty 1969; Kernan and Sommers 1967; Wells 1968; McCall and Simmons 1982; Kehret-Ward 1988).

[1]The authors would like to acknowledge the generous assistance of BMRB/TGI, Ealing, London with this study.

Kehret-Ward (1988) examined a series of studies on the functional complementarity of products (Holman 1976, 1980; Solomon 1983; Rook 1985; Kehret-Ward, Johnson and Louie 1985; Kehret-Ward 1987). Kehret-Ward (1988) discussed the different labels which had been given to product configurations including: 'consumption system' (Levy 1978); 'product constellation' (Solomon 1986); and 'ritual artifacts' (Rook 1985). Solomon (1986) described 'product constellation' as 'the set of products which support a role' (Kehret-Ward 198:191). However Solomon and Assael extended Alderson's work on the functional complementarity of products to symbolic complementarity of product assortments which they also described as 'product constellations': "clusters of complementary products, specific brands and/or consumption activities" (Solomon and Assael 1987:191). Consumption constellations were seen as "the identification of discriminable clusters of symbolically complementary products, services and/or activities–spanning a range of functionally dissimilar consumption categories" (Solomon and Buchanan 1991:98). Underlying the constructs of both product and consumption constellations is the idea of complementarity in the product and service choices of consumers (Alderson 1957; Green et al 1972; Kehret-Ward 1987). The two terms 'product constellations' and 'consumption constellations' would seem to be used often interchangeably in the literature; although there is a suggestion in the defintions above that product constellations demonstrate 'functional complementarity' whereas consumption constellations demonstrate 'symbolic complementarity'. We would argue for a clarification of existing conceptualizations of product and consumption constellations. We would propose using product constellations to describe goods or services within a product category which can demonstrate some form of complementarity (e.g. functional, symbolic, aesthetic or cultural). An example would be the 'retail constellation' which would represent a constellation at the *product* level and which would involve the series of choices made by a consumer among a series of retail outlets and distribution channels. In contrast, we would reserve *consumption* constellation for multi-category choices which demonstrate some form of complementarity. Consumption constellation would relate more closely to the original notion of the series of choices made by an individual consumer across multi-category products and services.

If consumption constellations can be taken to represent a consumer's set of positive choices across multi-category products, then consumption anti-constellations represent sets of consumers' *negative* choices across multi-category products and services. Anti-constellations can also be understood at two levels: product and consumption. Product anti-constellations would represent the negative aspects of product category choices. Consumption anti-constellations would represent the negative aspects of consumer choices across multiple product categories.

Anti-constellations

Anti-constellations represent the anti-complementarity of negative choices–within and across–categories of goods and services (Hogg and Michell 1996). Anti-constellations involve two aspects of consumers' negative choices: non choice and anti-choice. Non-choice includes goods and services which are simply not chosen, often because they are beyond the means of the consumer. Anti-choice includes goods and services that are positively not chosen (Wilk 1994) because they are seen as incompatible and/or inconsistent with the consumer's other consumption choices and preferences. Anti-constellations relate to Bourdieu's concept (1984) of 'distastes' and to Wilk's studies (1994, 1995) of inclusion and exclusion. Wilk's research demonstrated that distastes are important indicators of socially-linked preferences, notably for food and music. Food and music are two important product categories which

can be linked to the socio-cultural aspects of complementarity.

The reason for the emphasis on negative aspects of choice in this model-building is that consumers use the positive and negative meanings, which can be attached to their consumption choices, to create social and cultural identities (McCracken 1986). Consumers use product, brand and activity choices to mark, and also to understand, inclusion and exclusion in relation to different social groups (Bauman 1990).

FACTORS INFLUENCING CHOICE

Products (Tangible and intangible)

One important influence on consumer choice is the nature of the product or service. The functional-symbolic split in product images is well-established in the literature, although questions have been raised about the tendency to see 'product image' as unproblematic interpretations by individual consumers (Dittmar 1992:99). Consumer goods are viewed as possessing self-referent meanings which serve as symbols for the individual's personal qualities, attitudes and values, and, at the same time, as markers for social affiliation and position (Dittmar 1992).

Personal (physiological/psychological)

Individuals use consumption to meet a variety of needs. Maslow's conceptualization of needs and need deficiencies (1943) has been subjected to a number of criticisms. However, evidence has been found to support the pervasiveness of Maslow's hierarchy and the potency of higher order needs (such as esteem and self-actualization), once the lower order needs (e.g. physiological, safety and social) have been met (Kast and Rosenzweig 1985:291ff). Maslow's hierarchy will be used here to represent the personal factors–physiological and psychological–which influence consumption choices.

Social/situation

The third important moderating factor in consumer choice, highlighted in this Model, is the social and situational context in which consumption takes place. Bearden and Etzel's study (1982) highlighted the distinction between public and private consumption of necessities and luxuries and the implications for the selection of products and brands by consumers.

MODELS

The first Model (Figure 1) proposes that consumers, consumption and consumer goods can be understood via a system of layers of meaning. The Model begins with the micro level of decision making: the product or brand (see Bearden and Etzel 1982 for a discussion of the relevance of product and brand level choices). The Model proposes that a number of linkages exist: firstly between products and brands–and their associated evoked and inert sets–and consumers' self images and self concepts. Secondly, linkages exist among consumption choices and non choices (represented by product constellations and anti-constellations) which relate to social roles and positions. Thirdly, there are linkages between cumulative consumption choices (represented here by consumption constellations and anti-constellations) and social role repertoires.

An important final linkage is proposed between consumption constellations and anti-constellations which together form consumption configurations. Using configurations, consumption can be linked to social identities, or 'me's', and to the creation of self.

Three forces (Figure 2) have been modelled as influencing the 'fit' of consumption choices. Firstly, the force embodied by the product or service, which involves both symbolic and functional

FIGURE 1

Layers of Meaning: Self and Consumption–Consumption configurations and social identities

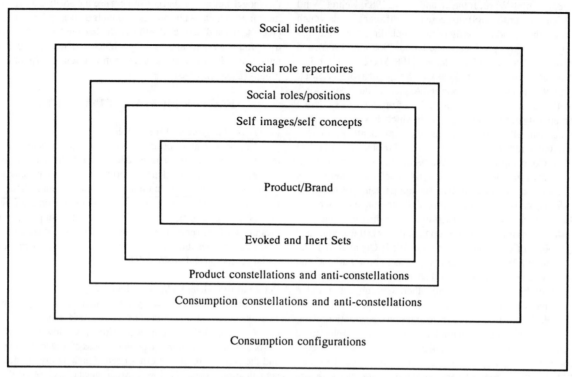

aspects. Secondly, a personal force which involves both physiological and psychological aspects. Thirdly, the social/situational force (involving the public and private aspects of consumption).

The third Model (Figure 3) represents the relationship between the forces which influence consumption (and the respective positive and negative consumption choices) and the different levels of consumption combinations. The focus of the research reported below is an exploratory study to operationalize the third Model in order to elicit consumption configurations. These consumption configurations are then discussed within the context of the second Model.

RESEARCH DESIGN [2]

The primary aim was to identify combinations of consumption choices represented by constellations and anti-constellations. The second aim was to interpret the positive and negative choices within the framework of broader models of consumer behavior. The third aim was to confirm the selection of certain product and service categories for exploring consumption configurations.

Quantitative and qualitative data on shoppers was used from the U.K. in-home catalog shopping industry. For the quantitative data, a two-phase procedure was used to construct and interpret the consumption combinations. The second, qualitative, stage of the research design used interview data to confirm the broader patterns of consumption found in the quantitative analysis.

Earlier studies of cumulative consumption (i.e. consumption of a range of product and service categories over time)(Wells 1968; Alpert and Gatty 1969; Solomon and Buchanan 1991; Fournier, Antes and Beaumier 1992) analyzed large consumer databases. The initial phase of this research design involved the extraction of behavioral data from a large commercial consumer database, across a range of products and services, on the users of eight mail order catalogs.

Catalogs

Users of eight in-home shopping catalog titles (G.U.S., Kays, Littlewoods, Freemans, Grattans, Empire Stores, Next Directory and J.D.Williams) were selected for the study. The first six are mainstream in-home shopping catalogs, generally seen as appealing to the same mass market. J.D.Williams and Next Directory represent niche players: J.D.Williams positioned towards older, larger women; and Next towards a prosperous, younger, fashion-conscious market.

Products

Seventeen product groups were used in the study. Solomon and Assael (1987) had identified three product groups which potentially carried image laden messages, and which had been linked to occupation and social roles: clothing, electronics and automobiles. Other product groups selected were: liquor and tobacco; media; food; personal care products; sports and home equipment; luxury appliances; credit cards; discretionary use of time; and retail outlets. Retail outlets were included as an example of a service. Retail outlets embody both symbolic and functional aspects of consumption decisions and are potentially of significance because of the greater awareness of retail brands among U.K. shoppers.

---

[2]See Hogg (1995) for an extended discussion of the application of correspondence analysis to this data set, and the detailed contingency tables and transition formulae which support the subsequent analysis offered in the next sections.

FIGURE 2
Model of Three Forces Which Impact Consumption Configurations

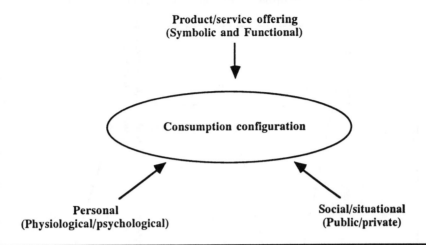

METHODOLOGY

The matrix of behavioral data consisted of eight columns (the users of the mail order catalogs) by over two thousand rows of product category information. Correspondence analysis was used to identify potential groups and sub groups among users of U.K. catalog shopping; and to identify combinations of product and service choices and non choices which could be linked to mail order shoppers.

A two-phase procedure was adopted for constructing and interpreting consumption combinations in the data. Transition formulae tables were used to identify consumption constellations and anti-constellations among the row profiles. The row variables clearly associated with a predominant axis were included as part of the 'set of consumables' which could be linked to catalog users also associated with that dimension or axis.

Anti-constellations had not been operationalized in previous studies; however we wished to identify the potential anti-complementarity of goods and services. Absence was treated both explicitly and implicitly: interpretation of explicit non-consumption was based on 'non-usage' of categories by groups of shoppers, and this information was included in the correspondence analysis of cross-tabulated data. Implicit non-consumption was derived from the absence of specific categories from the constellations.

The second aim was the interpretation of the consumption combinations, found in the quantitative data, within the framework of the model-building. It was expected that consumption constellations and anti-constellations would reflect the differing responses to the forces which influence consumption choices. Where influences were predominantly symbolic-expressive, then constellations would be expected to show a concern with symbolic consumption of goods and services, notably by the use of particular brands (e.g. Harrods store; Levi jeans). Where influences were predominantly functional-instrumental, we expected different consumption configurations would be found with the emphasis on factors such as value for money or shopping convenience. We also predicted that configurations would be influenced by needs (physiological/esteem/self-actualization) reflected in consumer choices. Where the consumption choices were central to self and identity, then the congruence between the series of consumption choices and self image would be important, shown by the selection of particular product and service (including retail) brands.

The second part of the research design involved seven semi-structured interviews with marketing managers from the in-home shopping industry; and one interview with a marketing consultancy firm with expertise in the in-home shopping catalog industry. The objective was to use qualitative data to confirm the broader patterns of consumption found in the quantitative analysis.

FINDINGS [3]

Our findings provided confirmation of the relationship between social roles, social identity and consumption combinations; illustrated the differential impact of consumption forces on consumer choices; and indicated the key product categories in consumption combinations.

Correspondence analysis of the behavioral database showed evidence of constellations and anti-constellations of consumption from which consumption configurations could be derived. The qualitative data, collected during the second stage of the empirical study, confirmed the existence of identifiable and separable groups amongst consumers, in their roles as mail order shoppers: firstly Next Directory shoppers; secondly J.D.Williams shoppers; and thirdly users of the mainstream in-home shopping catalogs: Grattans, GUS, Kays, Littlewoods, Freemans and Empire Stores.

Consumption configurations

The consumption configuration of Next Directory shoppers was influenced primarily by the interaction of symbolic and expressive forces. The consumption constellation was characterised by extensive patronage of restaurants, branded clothing goods such as Levi 501 jeans and L.A. Gear, Reebok and Nike trainers, upmarket foreign automobiles, expensive electronic equipment, particularly cameras, as well as a range of telephonic machinery, and patronage of a range of fashionable retailers. The consumption anti-constellation included non patronage of mass market mail order catalogs as well as non use of package vacation trips, non patronage of food stores such as Gateway, Morrisons and Kwiksave for grocery shopping, non purchase of such women's magazines as *Woman*,

---

[3]In view of space constraints only brief illustrative findings will be given here.

FIGURE 3
Model of the influence of consumption forces on product/service choices to create consumption constellations and anti - constellations from which consumption configurations are formed

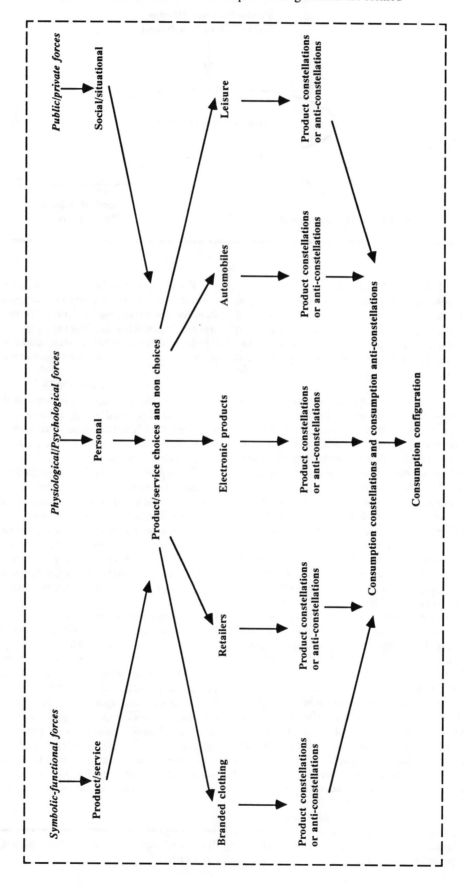

Woman's Own and *Woman's Journal* and non readership of the tabloid press. The emphasis in many of the consumer choices was on meeting such psychological needs as esteem and self-actualization. This was an important influence on the formation of the consumption configuration for Next Directory shoppers.

Product categories

Evidence was found to support the choice of product categories associated with particular roles (and identified by Solomon et al in earlier studies, 1987, 1988, 1991) to explore cumulative consumption including: automobiles, clothing and electronic goods. In this study automobiles had the potential to reflect the different interaction of the forces which influence consumption among groups. Other important product categories included electronic goods, clothing and discretionary use of time (e.g. use of leisure time) and retail patronage. The qualitative data also confirmed the importance of understanding brand choices within the stream of decisions made by the consumer.

DISCUSSION

Evidence was found of broader patterns in the stream of consumers' decisions. The quantitative analysis of the behavioral data demonstrated a number of consumption configurations which could be linked with different groups of in-home catalog shoppers. A set of product categories, which had been successfully linked to social roles in earlier studies, were used to explore the broader patterns of consumption choices and non choices. Discriminators amongst constellations have been found, and these are particularly linked to branded clothing products, electronic products and the discretionary use of time and these can all be related to Solomon's work on intermediate patterns of cumulative consumption. Retail outlets represented a new component within the consumption constellations and exhibited the potential to differentiate amongst the various groups. The other important product constellation was automobiles and this product category tended to overlap a number of profiles, suggesting that automobiles represented 'fuzzy sets'.

LIMITATIONS

No study at this stage of exploratory research into the complex area of consumers' cumulative consumption choices and non choices can offer a comprehensive picture of consumer profiles. There was only limited consideration of some product categories (e.g. branded clothing and electronic goods).

DIRECTIONS FOR FUTURE RESEARCH AND CONCLUSION

The creation of social and cultural meaning by consumption notably in the formation of tastes and distastes to mark inclusion and exclusion; and the creation of identity via material goods–such as branded jeans and trainers–as well as via the consumption of services such as leisure activities (e.g. pubs, discos, rave parties, football) are both areas which would reward further study. An important framework has been proposed within which to explore the broader patterns of consumption and the linkages among consumers' product and service choices, self images and social identities.

REFERENCES

[a full set of references is available on request].
Dittmar, Helga (1992): *The Social Psychology of Material Possessions: To Have Is To Be.* Harvester Wheatsheaf, Hemel Hempstead.

Solomon, Michael R. (1988): "Mapping Product Constellations: A Social Categorization Approach to Consumption Symbolism", *Psychology and Marketing* 5 (3, Fall), 233-258.

Wilk, Richard R. (1994): "'I hate Pizza': Distaste and Dislike in the Consuming Lives of Belizeans," paper read at American Anthropological Association Meeting, November, Atlanta.

Wilk, Richard R. (1995): "Learning Distaste: The Social Importance of Not-Wanting", conference paper read at "Learning to Consume", Lund University, August.

Consumption of Discretionary Time: An Exploratory Study

Wai-Kwan Li, University of Texas–Pan American
Kineta Hung, The Chinese University of Hong Kong

ABSTRACT

Time is a scarce resource. Apart from time spent on work, individuals can decide how to consume their discretionary time. The purpose of this study is to explore the antecedents that may affect time consumed in various categories of activities. Three sets of antecedents were examined, namely, cultural values, personality factors, and demographic variables. Five-hundred and twenty-seven respondents, including Chinese in Hong Kong, Americans in Texas and Michigan, and Canadians, participated in this study. The results suggest that these three sets of antecedents have significant unique explanative power on time consumed in eight categories of activities.

Time is a scarce resource. Each person is limited to 24 hours a day, though some people combine activities simultaneously to produce an output of more than 24 hours (Kaufman, Lane, and Lindquist 1991). However, even though time is *the* scarce resource (Leclerc, Schmitt, and Dubé 1995), it has received little research attention until recently (see Jacoby, Szybillo, and Berning [1976], Gross [1987], Hirschman [1987] for reviews). As an individual's daily discretionary time is essentially fixed, the choice to participate in one activity must necessarily affect the possibility for this person to engage in another. However, the factors that may affect the amount of time that an individual spends on various activities remain unclear. Therefore, the purpose of this study is to identify the factors that explain how people allocate their time among various non-work activities. Specifically, this study examined three sets of antecedents: demographic variables, psychological factors, and cultural values. To capture enough variances for these variables (especially in cultural values), a survey was conducted in four regions/countries, where the respondents may hold different cultural values.

Research On Time Used In Discretionary Activities

To examine time used in various discretionary activities systematically, Holbrook and Lehmann (1981) categorized 50 discretionary activities into seven sets of activities. They are audience, outdoor, games, family and social activities, hobbies, eating activities, and literary activities. Fifteen years have elapsed but a general theory for partitioning discretionary (and/or leisure) activities has not been developed. Moreover, the survey data used by Holbrook and Lehmann (1981) were collected in 1975. Since then, activities that were not popular 21 years ago are now popular among average consumers. These activities include video/computer games, virtual reality games, writing e-mail letters, and "surfing" the World Wide Web. Because of the scant literature in this area of research, it would be premature for us to develop specific hypotheses that postulate the relationships among demographic, psychological, and cultural factors, and the time consumers spend on each set of discretionary activities. Instead, we will employ an exploratory, discovery approach to examine the relationships between the antecedents of time usage and exemplars of sets of discretionary activities.

Antecedents of Time Consumed in Discretionary Activities

Although individuals may not have the luxury to choose how they use their "working" time, people should have the freedom to decide how they spend their "discretionary" time. Due to the finite nature of time, individuals often need to choose among various activities. Jackson-Beeck and Robinson (1981) found that as compared to television-viewers, non-television viewers reported more time spent on work, domestic chores, child rearing, recreation, personal care, education, and social interaction. This finding suggests that there is a tradeoff in time use. While Jackson-Beeck and Robinson (1981) identified the "consequences" of time spent on a specific activity (watching television), it is equally important to identify the "cause" for people to engage in this specific activity instead of another (e.g., education, domestic chore). Based on the existing literature, three sets of factors seemed to be related to individuals' time consumed in different categories of discretionary/leisure activities. These three sets of factors are: demographic variables, personality factors, and cultural values.

Demographic Variables. Traditional gender roles prescribe different responsibilities for men and women: Work is for men; family responsibility and home maintenance is for women (Gutek, Searle, and Klepa 1991). Hersch and Stratton (1994) found that, within households in which both spouses are employed full-time, the husbands spend about seven hours per week on housework, while the wives spend about 17 hours per week on housework. Consistently, Hochschild and Machung (1989) found that women worked approximately 15 hours more per week than did men on housework. In a survey of American psychologists, Gutek et al. (1991) reported that while male and female respondents spent practically identical amount of hours in paid work (male was 41.5 and female was 41.3 hours), women reported a total of 33.7 hours on household chores, child care, shopping and household maintenance, as compared to men's 22.1 hours. These findings consistently suggest that women spend more time on domestic duties than men.

Research findings also indicate women spend more time than men on shopping activities. Polegato and Zaichkowsky (1994) found that 36% of the husbands did none of the family food shopping. Among those husbands who shared the family food shopping role with their wives, they spent 51 minutes in the store, as compared to their wives' 60 minutes. Fischer and Arnold (1990) found that women gave Christmas gifts to 12.5 recipients while men gave to eight; women spent 2.4 hours per recipient while men spent 2.1 hours.

Bryant and Gerner (1981) found that the number of work hours was negatively related to the time spent on watching television. Bivens and Volker (1980) and Nickols and Fox (1983) consistently reported that female employment had a negative impact on the time spent on meal preparation. In fact, Nickols and Fox (1983) concluded that employed wives had less leisure time. These research findings suggest that the number of working hours may be negatively related to the amount of time spent on various leisure activities and domestic chores.

Settle, Alreck, and Glasheen (1978) reported that education level is the best single socioeconomic status determinant of leisure choice. Bryant and Gerner (1981) found that education level is negatively related to television use. Consistently, Hornik and Schlinger (1981) found that as education level goes up, time spent on watching television decreases, while the time spent on reading magazines and newspapers increases.

Furthermore, Hornik and Schlinger (1981) reported that as age increases, the time spent on reading newspapers increases. On the other hand, Bryant and Gerner (1981) found that as age increases, the time spent on watching television decreases. These research results suggest that while age is negatively related to the time spent on watching television, it may be positively related to the time spent on reading (especially newspaper).

Marmorstein, Grewal, and Fishe (1992) found that as wage rate increases, the time spent on price-comparison shopping decreases. Bryant and Gerner (1981) also reported that as income increases, the time spent on watching television decreases. These findings suggest that income level is negatively related to the time spent on shopping and watching television.

To sum up, we expect that demographic variables, including gender, the number of working hours, education level, age, and income would be related to the time consumed in various sets of activities.

Personality Factors. Certain leisure activities may be fun to some people, but boring to others. Graef, Csikszentmihalyi, and Gianinno (1983) suggest that some people may be more prone to perceive leisure to be boring, while others may be more resistant to boredom. Iso-Ahola and Weissinger (1987, 1990) defined *leisure boredom* as "the subjective perception that available leisure experiences are not sufficient to instrumentally satisfy needs for optimal arousal." People who have low level of leisure boredom may have an inner quality that enables them to discover rewards in events that others may find neutral and unrewarding. For example, while bird-watchers can spend a whole day identifying (and appreciating) the differences among various kinds of birds, others may find it boring to watch "similar" birds for hours. Therefore, it is logical to expect that people with high leisure boredom may allocate less time to participate in leisure activities that involve repetitive motions, such as riding exercise bicycles, aerobics, and weight lifting.

While the level of leisure boredom may explain why some people *will not* engage in a certain category of activities, the motivation to maintain a desired *arousal level* may explain why some *will* engage in other activities. Consumers who have a high need of arousal may spend their time in leisure activities that are novel, complex, and risky (Hendrix, Kinnear, and Taylor 1979). For example, individuals who have a relative high arousal seeking tendency may prefer to go to amusement parks rather than museums. Therefore, we expect that a person's arousal seeking tendency is positively related to time consumed in activities that can provide a higher level of excitement. Examples of these activities include participating in football games, going to parties, tasting exotic foods and drinks.

While leisure boredom and arousal seeking tendency may explain why consumers spend their time on various leisure activities, the *need for cognition* (Cohen, Stotland, and Wolfe 1955; Cacioppo and Petty 1982) may shed light on why some consumers spend their time on domestic chores and activities that allow them to think. Cohen, Stotland, and Wolfe (1955, p.291) described the need for cognition as "a need to structure relevant situations in meaningful, integrated ways. It is a need to understand and make reasonable the experiential world." A similar description can be found in Murphy (1947): "thinkers" feel it is fun to think, and to quest for reality. "Thinkers" may feel more comfortable in a well-organized and tidy home rather than a disorganized and untidy home. Consequently, they may use their time in domestic chores, especially those that result in a tidy, organized environment. On the other hand, "non-thinkers" may prefer to engage in activities that will require low mental effort, such as running, jogging, walking, aerobics, and weight lifting.

To sum up, we expect the three personality factors, leisure boredom, arousal seeking tendency, and the need for cognition, to be related to the time consumed in various sets of activities.

Cultural Values. While an activity may be perceived to be fun for some, it may be perceived to be "work" for others. Babin, Darden, and Griffin (1994) found that for people who have high hedonic shopping values, shopping is fun; while to people who have high utilitarian shopping values, shopping is work. In a national survey, Kamakura and Novak (1992) found that human values are related to respondents' engagement in a wide variety of activities. In a cross-national study of leisure activities, Beatty et al. (1994) reported that American students spent more time on sport activities than French, Danish, and New Zealand students because Americans are more competitive in nature. It appears that cultural values may explain some of the underlying motivations for engaging in certain activities.

Among the well-documented cultural value theories (such as Hofstede [1980], Bond [1988], Rokeach [1973]), we feel that Schwartz and Bilsky's (1987, 1990) theory on universal content and structure of human values is most related to the present study. One of the concerns of their cultural value theory is to understand the *value priorities* in different cultures. For example, in one culture, achievement may be of top priority, but in another culture, hedonism may be the most important value. In the context of allocating the finite amount of time among many discretionary activities, the *priority* of values seems to be useful in predicting which activities consumers would be most likely to participate in.

Schwartz (1992) identified ten universal value domains exist among the 20 countries studied. These value domains include power, achievement, hedonism, stimulation, self-direction, universalism,[1] benevolence, tradition, conformity, and security. While some of these value domains may have strong relationship with the time that consumers spend on discretionary activities, others may not be relevant. For example, consumers who believe that hedonism (which is defined as pleasure, enjoying life) is the most important values are more likely to engage in activities that will allow them to enjoy life, such as eating, drinking, or taking a nap. On the other hand, they may be less likely to engage in domestic chores, such as cleaning the home, or doing laundry. Consumers who believe that achievement (which is defined as successful, capable) is the most important goal in their lives are more likely to engage in activities that can offer them a sense of achievement, such as body building (when muscles develop) or gardening (when flowers bloom).

Unfortunately, no published research has reported the relationships between specific cultural domains and participation in leisure activities. Therefore, we have adopted a discovery approach to provide directions for developing hypotheses for future research.

METHOD

Samples

A survey was conducted in four regions/countries, namely, Texas, Michigan, Ontario(Canada), and Hong Kong. A total of 527 junior/senior business majors and MBA students (244 from Texas[2],

---

[1]According to Schwartz (1992), universalism refers to an understanding, appreciation, tolerance, and protection for the welfare of all people and for nature. Benevolence refers to the preservation and enhancement of the welfare of people with whom one is in frequent personal contact. That is, while universalism embraces a broader scope of prosocial values, benevolence is limited to a narrower scope of prosocial value.

[2]Eighty-two percent of the Texas students were Mexican-Americans.

145 from Hong Kong, 60 from Michigan, and 78 from Ontario) participated in this study. Respondents were rewarded extra credits upon the completion of the questionnaire.

The major advantage of using student samples is the homogeneity of demographics and lifestyles. Moreover, the respondents had similar academic requirements from their respective schools. This homogeneity of "job" responsibilities minimized the undesirable effects caused by different job responsibilities as found in business executive or adult consumer samples. It should also be noted that data were collected in the middle of the fall and spring semesters in all four regions, which were suitable for both indoor and outdoor activities.

Questionnaire

An English questionnaire was prepared, since English is the native language for students in the United States and Canada. Students in Hong Kong are Chinese-English bilingual, and virtually all of them are fluent in English. Therefore, no translation was necessary. The questionnaire consists of four sections. The first section measured the time the students spent on various discretionary activities. The second section was composed of the three psychological factors discussed above. The third section measured the respondents' cultural values, and the fourth section recorded the respondents' demographic information.

By integrating the lists of activities reported in Holbrook and Lehmann (1981), Philipp (1992), Floyd and Gramann (1993), Spring (1993), and the authors' experiences with these four (sub)cultures,[3] a list of 103 activities was composed. To capture all possible types of discretionary activities, three "other (please specify)" activities were also listed. Respondents were asked to recall[4] the amount of time they spent on each of the 106 activities in the past seven days.

After that, respondents were asked to respond to a short version of Mehrabian's (1978) Arousal Seeking Tendency Scale (AST-II), which contains 12 items (see Baumgartner and Steenkamp [1994] for item reduction). Then, respondents were asked to respond to the short version of the Need For Cognition (NFC) Scale, which contains 18 items (Cacioppo and Petty 1982; Cacioppo, Petty, and Kao 1984). Next, respondents were asked to respond to 16 items of the Leisure Boredom (LB) Scale (Iso-Ahola and Weissinger 1990). All of these items were measured on seven-point scales that ranged from strongly disagree to strongly agree. The Cronbach alphas for the AST-II scale ranged from .72 to .78 across the four samples. The Cronbach alphas for the NFC scales ranged from .79 to .88 across the four samples, and that for the LB scale ranged from .83 to .87 across the four samples.

A 36-item version of Schwartz and Bilsky's (1987, 1990) value scale was used to reveal the impact of cultural values on the time spent on discretionary activities. Similar to Schwartz (1992), respondents were asked to rate each value "as a guiding principle in my life," using the following nine-point scale: opposed to my

values (-1), not important (0), (unlabeled; 1, 2), important (3), (unlabeled; 4,5), very important (6), of supreme importance (7).

Finally, the respondents' gender, age, education level, number of children, number of working hours per week, nationality, marital status, annual income, and race were recorded. In addition, the amount of thinking activities required by the respondents' occupation was measured on a 7-point scale, ranging from "not at all" to "a lot". It should be noted that the measurements of income and racial background were modified to match each sample's local currency and racial composition.

RESULTS

Analysis Procedures

An Overview. First, two factor analyses were performed to identify the discretionary activity structure and the cultural value structure. Next, regression analyses were conducted to identify the relationships between the antecedent variables and the time spent on each set of discretionary activities. Since no a priori theory was available to guide the entry order of each set of antecedents, stepwise regression procedures were performed. To reduce the potential misleading effects of multicolinearity, three sets of hierarchical regression analyses were performed to examine the unique explanatory power of each set of antecedent variables.

Discretionary Activity Structure. First, the frequency distribution of each of the 106 activities (including the three "others" activities) were examined. Activities that were participated by less than 10% of the respondents were screened out. As a result, only 42 activities were retained. A principal component factor analysis, with oblique rotation, was performed to identify the structure of these discretionary activities. By examining the slope of the scree plot, and the eigenvalues (>1.00), an eight-factor solution was retained (see Exhibit 1). All factor loadings of this eight-factor structure were larger than .30, and 42% of the variance was explained.

Cultural Value Structure. A principal component factor analysis, with oblique rotation, was performed to identify the structure of the 36 cultural values. After examining the slope of the scree plot and eigenvalues (>1.00), a nine-factor solution was retained (see Exhibit 2). All factor loadings of this nine-factor structure were larger than .30, and 61% of the variance was explained.

Antecedents of Time Consumed in Discretionary Activities

Eating and Social Activities. The stepwise regression results suggest that four demographic variables (gender, education level, number of children, and occupation nature) and one psychological factor (arousal seeking tendency) were significantly related to the amount of time spent on eating and social activities (see Table 1). The non-standardized beta coefficients suggest that females, respondents who had higher education level, whose job requires more thinking activities, and people who had higher arousal seeking tendency, spent more time on eating and social activities. On the other hand, respondents who have more children spent less time on this category of activities. These five demographic and psychological factors explained 12.0% of the variance[5] in this set of activities. The results of hierarchical regression analyses show that while

---

[3]Both authors were born and raised in Hong Kong. While the first author was educated in the Mid-West and is living in Texas, the second author was educated in Canada, and is living in Hong Kong.

[4]Bishop, Jeanrenaud, and Lawson (1975) have provided evidence for good convergent validity between recall- based and diary-based activity measures of duration (r=.78) and frequency (r=.88). Therefore, although the recall-based measurement used in this study may not be the best measurement method, it is considered as reliable.

[5]In a study about time allocated to mass media, Hornik and Schlinger (1981) reported that the demographic and lifestyle variables explained 5-21% of variance of time spent on different types of mass media. Therefore, the regression results reported in this study should be evaluated against this benchmark.

EXHIBIT 1
The Eight Sets of Discretionary Activities

Sets (number of activities)	Activities
Eating and social activities (6)	Dining out, eating, social events, phone conversation, writing letters, shopping (excluding grocery).
Routines/habitual activities (4)	Shopping (grocery), reading news, religious activities, bodybuilding.
Hedonic entertainments(6)	Going to a bar, drinking alcoholic beverage, billiards/pool, taking a nap, watching video/laser disc, playing cards/games
Sports (6)	Running/jogging, aerobics, attending a sport event, dancing, team sports, weight lifting.
Hobbies (6)	Driving (for pleasure), watching movies, gardening/lawn caring, smoking cigarette/tobacco, working on computers (for pleasure), visiting friends/relatives.
Family/personal maintenance (5)	Cleaning the home (laundry, dishes), cooking and baking, caring of/playing with animals, drinking non-alcoholic beverage, walking (for pleasure).
Music and family activities (5)	Singing, listening to the radio, listening to music, going to parties, family organizations.
Reading and Television (4)	Reading magazines, reading books, watching television, video games.

EXHIBIT 2
The Nine Domains of Cultural Values

Domains (number of items)	Values
Achievement (3)	Ambitiousness, independence, success.
Hedonism (4)	Enjoyment of life, friendship, pleasure, freedom.
Power (3)	Social power, wealth, authority.
Wisdom (3)	Wisdom, competence, broadmindedness.
Universalism (6)	Protection of the environment, a world of peace, a world of beauty, national security, social justice, helpfulness.
Stimulation (4)	A varied life, being daring, creativity, an exciting life.
Spirituality (4)	A spiritual life, devoutness, meaning of life, family security.
Restriction to conformity (4)	Forgiveness, humility, politeness, self-discipline.
Conform to tradition (5)	Respect for tradition, honor of parents and elders, social order, honesty, obedience.

demographic variables and psychographic factors had significant unique explanative power on this set of activities (8.3% and 2.2%, respectively), cultural values domains had no unique explanative power (see Table 2). This pattern of results is consistent with that suggested by the stepwise regression results. (See Figure 1)

Routines/habitual activities. The stepwise regression results suggest that three cultural domains (achievement, restriction to conformity, and hedonism) were significantly related to the amount of time spent on routines and habitual activities (see Table 1). The non-standardized beta coefficients suggest that individuals who placed high priority for achievement and hedonism spent less time on routines and habitual activities, such as grocery shopping and reading newspaper. On the other hand, respondents who believed that restriction to conformity was highly important spent more time

TABLE 1
Stepwise Regression Results

Sets of Activities	Regressors	Beta	Change of R^2	Total R^2
Eating and Social Activities	Gender**	6.82	.046	
	Arousal seeking tendency**	3.14	.030	
	Education**	1.52	.019	
	# of children**	-2.86	.012	
	Thinking required by job*	.80	.008	.120
Routines/habitual activities	Achievement**	-1.30	.025	
	Restriction to conformity**	1.35	.025	
	Hedonism**	-0.92	.012	.052
Hedonic entertainment	Arousal seeking tendency**	2.55	.088	
	Universalism**	-1.06	.007	
	Conform to tradition**	1.05	.021	.117
Sports	Achievement**	1.46	.064	
	Arousal seeking tendency**	1.22	.031	
	Wisdom**	-1.14	.026	
	Leisure boredom**	-1.17	.022	
	Hours of work**	-0.02	.017	
	Restriction to conformity**	0.60	.011	
	Need for cognition**	-0.75	.009	.181
Hobbies	Conform to tradition**	1.73	.037	
	Arousal seeking tendency**	1.21	.011	
	Universalism**	-1.04	.009	
	Achievement**	1.01	.009	.067
Family/personal maintenance	Gender**	5.95	.067	
	Need for cognition**	2.43	.044	
	Leisure Boredom**	1.34	.012	.123
Music and family activities	Arousal seeking tendency**	3.42	.041	
	Leisure boredom**	-2.83	.034	
	Gender**	4.37	.017	
	Achievement**	1.72	.013	.106
Reading and TV	Income**	-0.85	.025	
	Achievement**	-1.72	.012	
	Hedonism**	1.48	.014	
	Thinking required by job**	0.76	.011	
	Leisure boredom*	1.29	.009	.071

Note: ** $p < .05$; * $p < .10$.

on routines and habitual activities. The three value domains explained 5.2% of the variance in this set of activities. The hierarchical regression results reported in Table 2 show that only cultural value domains had significant unique explanative power on the amount of time spent on routines and habitual activities, R^2=.065. Again, this finding is consistent with that performed by stepwise regression analysis (See Figure 1).

Hedonic Entertainment. The stepwise regression results reported in Table 1 suggest that one psychological factor (arousal seeking tendency) and two cultural domains (universalism and restriction to conformity) were significantly related to the amount of time spent on hedonic entertainment. The non-standardized beta

coefficients suggest that individuals who had high arousal seeking tendency, and those who believed that conforming to tradition was important, spent more time in these hedonic activities, such as going to a bar, or drinking alcoholic beverage. On the other hand, respondents who valued universalism spent less time on hedonic activities. These three variables explained 11.7% of the variance in this set of activities. The hierarchical regression analyses suggest that only psychological factors have significant unique explanative power on the time spent on hedonic entertainment, R^2=.056 (see Table 2). After partialling out the explanative power of these psychological and demographic variables, the unique explanative power of cultural value domains was not significant. These find-

TABLE 2
Unique Explanative Power# of Each Type of Antecedents

Sets of Activities	Demographic Variables	Psychological Factors	Cultural Domains
Eating and social activities	.083**	.022**	.029
Routines/habitual activities	.014	.019*	.065**
Hedonic entertainment	.014	.056**	.025
Sports	.022	.055**	.085**
Hobbies	.031	.007	.028
Family/personal maintenance	.089**	.039**	.019
Music and family activities	.034	.048**	.025
Reading and TV	.052**	.011	.040*

Note: # Hierarchical regression analyses were performed to evaluate the unique explanative power of each set of antecedents. Specifically, to evaluate the unique explanative power of demographic variables, the three psychological factors and nine cultural value domains were first regressed on the time used in a set of activities. After that, all demographic variables were entered simultaneously. Similarly, to evaluate the unique explanative power of psychological factors (or cultural value domains), the other two sets of antecedents were first entered into the regression model.

** $p < .05$; * $p < .10$.

ings suggest that the explanative power of universalism and conformity to tradition were not reliable. (See Figure 1.)

Sports. The stepwise regression results indicate that all three types of antecedent variables were related to the time spent on various sport activities (see Table 1). Specifically, the non-standardized beta coefficients suggest that individuals who valued achievement, who believed that restrictions to conformity was important, and who have a high arousal seeking tendency allocated more time to sports activities, such as jogging, aerobics, or attending sports events. On the other hand, individuals who valued wisdom, those who had low resistance to leisure boredom, and who had to work for long hours, spent less time on these activities. These seven variables explained 18.1% of the variance in this set of activities. The results of hierarchical regression analyses suggest that only psychological factors and cultural value domains had significant unique explanative power on time spent on sports activities, $R^2 = .055$ and .085, respectively (see Table 2). However, after removing the explanative power of these two sets of antecedents, the unique explanative power of demographic variables was not significant. This finding suggests that the explanative power of the number of working hours was not reliable. (See Figure 1.)

Hobbies. The stepwise regression results indicate that three cultural value domains and a psychological factor were related to the amount of time spent on hobbies. Specifically, the non-standardized beta coefficients suggest that individuals who believed that conforming to tradition was important, who valued achievement, and who have a high arousal seeking tendency, allocated more time to hobbies such as driving for pleasure and watching movies. On the other hand, individuals who valued universalism spent less time on hobbies. These four variables explained 6.7% of the variance in this set of activities. The results of hierarchical regression analyses show that none of the three sets of antecedents have significant unique explanative power on the time spent on hobbies (see Table 2). This finding suggests that the stepwise regression results reported above may not be reliable.

Family/Personal Maintenance. The stepwise regression results indicate that gender and two psychological factors were related to the time spent on family and personal maintenance (see Table 1). Specifically, the non-standardized beta coefficients

suggest that, female respondents, respondents who had high need for cognition, and who felt leisure activities were boring, spent more time on family and personal maintenance such as cleaning the home, cooking, and taking care of pets. These three variables explained 12.3% of the variance in this set of activities. The hierarchical regression results suggest that both demographic and psychological factors had significant unique explanative power on time spent on family and personal maintenance (see Table 2). This finding is consistent with the results produced by stepwise regression reported above. (See Figure 1.)

Music and Family Activities. The stepwise regression results indicate that all three types of antecedents were related to the time spent on music and family activities (Table 1). Specifically, the non-standardized beta coefficients suggest that respondents who had high arousal seeking tendency, female respondents, and respondents who valued achievement, spent more time listening to the radio and attending family organizations. On the other hand, the respondents who felt that leisure activities were boring spent less time on these activities. These four variables explained 10.6% of the variance in this set of activities. The results of the hierarchical regression analyses suggest that only psychological factors had significant unique explanative power on the time spent on music and family activities (Table 2). This finding suggests that gender and achievement values were not reliable in predicting the time respondents spent on music and family activities. (See Figure 1.)

Reading and Television. The stepwise regression results indicate that all three types of antecedents were related to the time spent on reading books and magazines, and watching television (Table 1). Specifically, respondents who believed that hedonistic lifestyle was important, and respondents whose jobs require more thinking activities, and respondents who felt leisure activities were boring, spent more time reading books and magazines, and watching television. On the other hand, respondents who had higher incomes, and respondents who believed that achievement was important, spent less time watching television or reading books and magazines. These five variables explained 7.1% of the variance in this set of activities. The hierarchical regression analyses results suggest that only demographic factors had significant unique explanative power on the time spent on reading and watching televi-

FIGURE 1
Antecedents of Time Consumed in Eight Categories of Activities

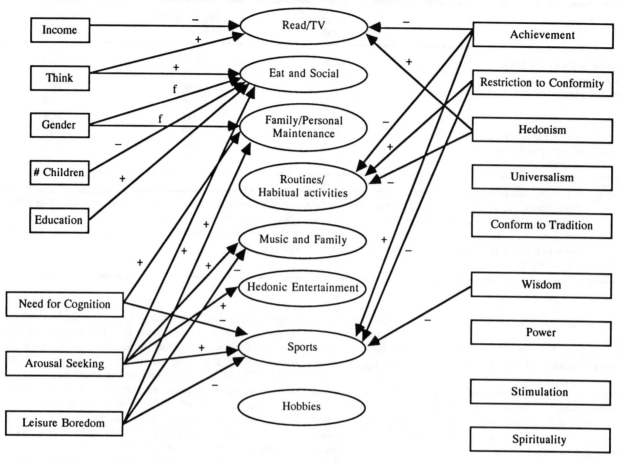

Note: Paths with "+" ("–") stands for positive (negative) relationships between the variables;
Paths with "f" indicate females were more likely to engage in these activities.

sion (see Table 2). This finding suggests that achievement, hedonism, and leisure boredom were not reliable in predicting the time respondent spent on reading and watching television.

CONCLUSION AND DIRECTIONS FOR FUTURE RESEARCH

The purpose of this study was to identify the antecedents of time spent on various non-work activities. As summarized in Figure 1, the specific relationships between the three sets of antecedents (demographic, psychological, cultural factors) and time spent on eight categories of discretionary/leisure activities were identified.

The Impact of Demographic Characteristics on Time Consumption

As a category, demographic variables were found to be most strongly related to family and personal maintenance, eating and social activities, and reading and watching television (see Table 2 and Figure 1). Of special interest are family and personal maintenance: They are necessities for virtually every *household,* but not necessarily necessities for each *individual.* For instance, in a traditional household, the wife/mother usually assumes the duties of doing laundry, cooking, grocery shopping, etc. Consequently, the *role(s)* taken by each household member pressed them to

allocate time to their role-related activities. In this study, only 11.7% to 12.3% of the variances in time spent on these three sets of activities were explained. By incorporating family role(s) as a predictor for time spent on these activities, future research should be able to achieve a better predictive power. In addition, to extend the validity of the present findings, future research should employ a non-student sample.

The Impact of Psychological Characteristics on Time Consumption

As expected, consumers with high arousal seeking tendency are more likely to dine out, consume various hedonic entertainments, and listen to music/radio. With little surprise, people who perceive leisure as boring, spend less time on sports and music, but spend more time on family and personal maintenance. It seems that these people would rather spend their time working than to having fun. On the other hand, there is a significant relationship between need for cognition and family and personal maintenance. This finding suggest that "thinkers," who prefer to structure their minds in meaningful ways also prefer to structure their environment in an organized manner. As a group, these three psychological factors were found to be related to six out of eight sets of discretionary activities. This finding suggests that need for cognition, arousal seeking tendency, and leisure boredom are useful in understanding consumers' time spent on various activities. Future study should identify additional psychological factors, which may enhance our understanding of the consumption of discretionary time.

The Impact of Cultural Values on Time Consumption

As expected, people who prefer hedonic lifestyle spend less time on routines and habitual activities (such as grocery shopping and religious activities), but spend more time on reading and watching television. On the other hand, people who value achievements spend less time reading and watching television, and, routines and habitual activities, which can be considered unproductive activities. From the perspective of motivation theory, "achievers" choose to engage in various sports activities because these activities may help them to obtain a sense of achievement. Interesting enough, people who value wisdom, spend less time on sport activities. Finally, people who are more restricting to conformity spend more time on routines and habitual activities, but less time on sports activities. Despite these significant findings, only four out of nine cultural value domains contribute to our understanding of the time consumers spend on discretionary activities. One explanation is that some mediating variables are involved. They may help establish the paths between cultural values and time spent on various activities. Future study should explore variables that may mediate the relationships between cultural values and time spent on various activities.

REFERENCES

Babin, Barry J., William R. Darden, and Mitch Griffin (1994), "Work and/or Fun: Measuring Hedonic and Utilitarian Shopping Value," *Journal of Consumer Research*, 20(March), 644-656.

Baumgartner, Hans and Jan-Benedict E. M. Steenkamp (1994), "An Investigation Into The Construct Validity of the Arousal Seeking Tendency Scale, Version II," *Educational and Psychological Measurement*, 54(4), 993-1001.

Beatty, Sharon E., Jung-OK Jeon, Gerald Albaum, and Brian Murphy, (1994), "A Cross-National Study of Leisure Activities," *Journal of Cross-Cultural Psychology*, 25(3), 409-422.

Bishop, Doyle W., Claudine Jeanrenaud, and Kenneth Lawson (1975), "Comparison of a Time Diary and Recall Question-naire for Surveying Leisure Activities," *Journal of Leisure Research*, 7, 73-80.

Bivens, Gordon E. and Carol B. Volker (1986), "A Value-Added Approach to Household Production: The Special Case of Meal Preparation," *Journal of Consumer Research*, 13(September), 272-279.

Bond, Michael (1988), "Finding Universal Dimensions of Individual Variation in Multicultural Studies of Values: The Rokeach and Chinese Value Surveys," *Journal of Personality and Social Psychology*, 55, 1009-1015.

Bryant, W. Keith and Jennifer L. Gerner (1981), "Television Use by Adult and Children: A Multivariate Analysis," *Journal of Consumer Research*, 8(September), 154-161.

Cacioppo, John T. and Richard E. Petty (1982), "The Need For Cognition," *Journal of Personality and Social Psychology*, 42(1), 116-131.

Cacioppo, John T., Richard E. Petty, and Chuan Feng Kao (1984), "The Efficient Assessment of Need For Cognition," *Journal of Personality Assessment*, 48(3), 306-307.

Cohen, A., R. Stotland, and D. M. Wolfe (1955), "An Experimental Investigation of Need For Cognition," *Journal of Abnormal and Social Psychology*, 51, 291-294.

Fischer, Eileen and Stephen J. Arnold (1990), "More than a Labor of Love: Gender Roles and Christmas Gift Shopping," *Journal of Consumer Research*, 17(December), 333-345.

Floyd, Myron and James H. Gramann (1993), "Effects of Acculturation and Structural Assimilation in Resource-Based Recreation: The Case of Mexican Americans," *Journal of Leisure Research*, 25(1), 6-21.

Graef, R., M. Csikszentmihalyi, and S. Gianinno (1983), "Measuring Intrinsic Motivation in Daily Life," *Leisure Studies*, 2, 155-168.

Gross, Barbara L. (1987), "Time Scarcity: Interdisciplinary Perspectives and Implications for Consumer Behavior," in *Research in Consumer Behavior*, Vol.2, ed. Jagdish Sheth and Elizabeth Hirschman, Greenwich, CT:JAI, 1-54.

Gutek, Barbarba A., Sabrina Searle, and Lilian Klepa (1991), "Rational Versus Gender Role Explanations for Work-Family Conflict," *Journal of Applied Psychology*, 76(4), 560-568.

Hendrix, Philip, Thomas Kinnear, and James Taylor (1979), "The Allocation of Time by Consumers," in *Advances in Consumer Research*, Vol.5, William Wilkie, ed. Ann Arbor: MI:ACR, 38-44.

Hersch, Joni and Leslie S. Stratton (1994), "Housework, Wages, and the Division of Housework Time for Employed Spouses," *American Economic Review*, 84(May), 120-125.

Hirschman, Elizabeth C. (1987), "Theoretical Perspectives of Time Use: Implications for Consumer Behavior Research," in *Research in Consumer Behavior*, Vol.2, ed. Jagdish Sheth and Elizabeth Hirschman, Greenwich, CT:JAI, 55-81.

Hochschild, Arlie and Anne Machung (1989), *The Second Shift: Working Parents and the Revolution at Home*. New York: Viking.

Hofstede, Greet (1980), *Culture's Consequences: International differences in work-related values.*" Beverly Hills, CA: Sage.

Holbrook, Morris B. and Donald R. Lehmann (1981), "Allocating Discretionary Time: Complementarity Among Activities," *Journal of Consumer Research*, 7(March), 395-406.

Hornik, Jacob and Mary Jane Schlinger (1981), "Allocation of Time to the Mass Media," *Journal of Consumer Research*, 7(March), 343-355.

Iso-Ahola, Seppo E. and Ellen Weissinger (1987), "Leisure and Boredom," *Journal of Social and Clinical Psychology*, 5, 356-364.

Iso-Ahola, Seppo E. and Ellen Weissinger (1990), "Perceptions of Boredom in Leisure: Conceptualization, Reliability and Validity of the Leisure Boredom Scale," *Journal of Leisure Research*, 22(1), 1-17.

Jackson-Beeck, Marilyn and John P. Robinson (1981), "Television Nonviewers: An Endangered Species?" *Journal of Consumer Research*, 7(March), 356-359.

Jacoby, Jacob, George J. Szybillo, and Carol Kohn Berning (1976), "Time and Consumer Behavior: An Interdisciplinary Overview," *Journal of Consumer Research*, 2(March), 320-339.

Kamakura, Wagner A. And Thomas P. Novak (1992), "Value-System Segmentation: Exploring the Meaning of LOV," *Journal of Consumer Research*, 19(June), 119-132.

Kuafman, Carol J., Paul M. Lane, and Jay D. Lindquist (1991), "Exploring More than 24 Hours a Day: A Preliminary Investigation of Polychronic Time Use," *Journal of Consumer Research*, 18(December), 392-401.

Leclerc, France, Bernd H. Schmitt, and Laurette Dubé (1995), "Waiting Time and Decision Making: Is Time Like Money?" *Journal of Consumer Research*, 22(June), 110-119.

Marmorstein, Howard, Dhruv Grewal, and Raymond P. H. Fishe (1992), "The Value of Time Spent in Price-Comparison Shopping: Survey and Experimental Evidence," *Journal of Consumer Research*, 19(June), 52-61.

Mehrabian, Albert (1978), "Characteristics Individual Reactions to Preferred and Unpreferred Environments," *Journal of Personality*, 46, 717-731.

Murphy, G. (1947), *Personality: A Biosocial Approach to Origins and Structure*, New York: Harper.

Nickols, Sharon Y. and Karen D. Fox (1983), "Buying Time and Saving Time: Strategies for Managing Household Production," *Journal of Consumer Research*, 10 (September), 197-208.

Philipp, Steven (1992), "Time Orientation and Participation in Leisure Activities," *Perceptual and Motor Skills*, 75, 659-664.

Polegato, Rosemary and Judith L. Zaichkowsky (1994), "Family Food Shopping: Strategies Used by Husband and Wives," *The Journal of Consumer Affairs*, 28(Winter), 278-299.

Rokeach, Milton (1973), *The Nature of Human Values*, New York: Free Press.

Settle, Robert B., Pamela L. Alrek, and John W. Glasheen (1978), "Individual Time Orientation and Consumer Life Style," in *Advances in Consumer Behavior*, Vol.5, ed. Keith H. Hunt, Ann Arbor, MI: Association for Consumer Research, 315-9.

Schwartz, Shalom H. and Wolfgang Bilsky (1987), "Toward A Universal Psychological Structure of Human Values," *Journal of Personality and Social Psychology*, 53(3), 550-562.

Schwartz, Shalom H. and Wolfgang Bilsky (1990), "Toward A Theory of the Universal Content and Structure of Values: Extensions and Cross-Cultural Replications," *Journal of Personality and Social Psychology*, 58(5), 878-891.

Schwartz, Shalom H. (1992), "Universals in the Content and Structure of Values: Theoretical Advances and Empirical Tests in 20 Countries," *Advances in Experimental Social Psychology*, 25, 1-65.

Spring, Jim (1993), "Seven Days of Play," *American Demographics*, 50(March), 50-53.

Constellations, Configurations and Consumption: Exploring Patterns of Consumer Behaviour Amongst U.K. Shoppers

Margaret K. Hogg, Manchester School of Management, UMIST, UK
Paul C.N.Michell, Manchester Business School, UK[1]

ABSTRACT

This paper extends existing U.S. work on product and consumption constellations and examines the formation of these intermediate patterns of joint consumption amongst U.K. consumers within the framework of symbolic interactionist approaches to understanding self. Following the conceptualization of the forces which influence the formation of consumption constellations and anti constellations, consumption configurations are proposed and a series of models are developed and tested via the application of correspondence analysis to data on shoppers drawn from a large U.K. commercial database. It is argued that retail outlets represent an important service category and that retail constellations can be used alongside other major product constellations such as cars, clothing and electronic goods (identified in earlier research) in exploring intermediate patterns of joint consumption.

BACKGROUND

In examining intermediate levels of joint consumption this research lies between studies of consumer behaviour which concentrate on micro issues (i.e. decision making at the product or brand level) and those studies which concentrate on macro issues (such as the factors which influence societal patterns of consumption, Firat 1978). The important argument for this study is that shopping channels, as well as products, are used by consumers to create and interpret cultural meaning; and that patronage choices are inherently part of the process by which consumers construct and constitute their world.

The aggregation of choices across products and services amongst consumers has been explored in a series of U.S. studies (Levy 1964, Kernan and Sommers 1967, Wells 1968, Green, Wind and Jain 1972, Solomon 1983, Solomon and Assael 1987, Kehret-Ward 1987, Solomon 1988, Solomon and Buchanan (1991)). Solomon and Assael (1987) and Solomon (1988) developed role-related consumption constellations: "a cluster of complementary products, specific brands, and/or consumption activities associated with a social role" (Solomon and Assael 1987:191) in examining patterns of joint consumption. This study will argue that constellations and anti constellations together can be taken to constitute consumption configurations which represent a series of joint consumer choices and non choices amongst products and services which can be associated with different groups of U.K. shoppers. Underlying the model building is the assumption that product and consumption constellations and anti constellations can be linked with the creation, maintenance and enhancement of social identities.

LITERATURE REVIEW

The framework for the model building of the forces which influence intermediate patterns of joint consumption was the social psychological perspective of symbolic interactionism (Cooley 1902,

Mead 1934, Solomon 1983) which was used to establish the link between consumption, identity and social roles. Symbolic interactionism proposes that individuals make sense of their world in terms of the social realities from which they derive their identities; and that actions and behaviours constitute ways of enacting their social reality and identities. Consumption is seen as one of the means by which individuals create their identities and this is linked with McCracken's approach to culturally constituted meaning systems:

"They [consumers] use the meaning of consumer goods to express cultural categories and principles, cultivate ideas and sustain lifestyles, construct notions of self, and create (and survive) social change... " (McCracken 1990:xi).

Biddle and Thomas' (1966:11) definition of social role as: "a behavioral repertoire characteristic of a person or a position .. a set of standards, descriptions, norms or concepts held (by anyone) for the behaviours of a person or a position ... a position" has been adopted for exploring the associations between groups of consumers as shoppers and consumption configurations. McCall and Simmons (1982) argued that collections of products and activities are taken by society as defining social roles. Schenk and Holman (1980) and McCracken (1986) argue that roles are culturally constituted:

"Social role performance are learned behaviors that are culturally determined. An individual's actual role performance cannot be studied by assessing only the requirements of his/her social position since the individual combines the broad culturally defined demands of his/her position with individually-defined goals". (Schenk and Holman 1980:611)

The interdependence between the cultural context and the individual context can be seen when examining the role of parents, mothers and fathers as consumers and shoppers. Their social role performance involves learned behaviours which are culturally determined, and yet these demands are mediated by individually-defined goals.

Self image and self concepts are also central to this examination of the relationship between self and consumption. Rogers' (1951) theory of individual self-enhancement has been used to propose that as the self concept was of value to the individual then behaviour would be directed towards the protection and enhancement of an individual's self concept (Grubb and Grathwohl 1967). Despite some concerns about the use of the self concept construct in the consumer behaviour research literature (Sirgy 1982, Lee 1990), situational self concept (Schenk and Holman 1980) will be used here because of the recognition of the central role of the situation or context in determining consumer decision-making, and the emphasis again on the interdependency between the consumer and the cultural context. Studies have confirmed that characteristics of self-image are congruous with characteristics of brand image (Dolich 1969; Green et al 1969; Landon 1974; Ross 1971; Sirgy 1982; Snyder and de Bono 1985). However the idea that a single product or brand can be seen as representative of a consumer's self

[1]The authors would like to acknowledge the generous support of the British Market Research Bureau/Target Group Index, Ealing, London, for this study.

FIGURE 1
Configurations–The Formation of Intermediate Patterns of Joint Consumption

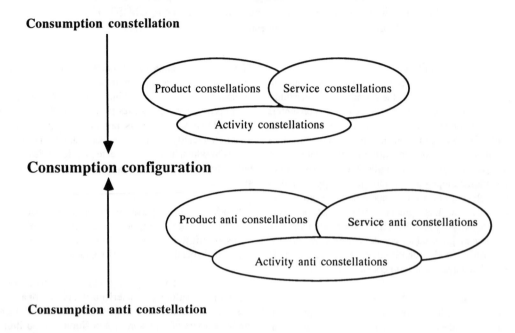

concept has been challenged (Douglas and Isherwood 1979, Solomon and Assael 1988). It is proposed here that configurations (Figure 1) consist of consumption constellations and anti constellations, which in turn represent the complementarities and anti complementarities amongst the goods and services used by consumers.

This paper reports constellations which can be associated with groups of U.K. shoppers. Marchand's ensembles (1985) and McCracken's Diderot unities (1988) are also linked to the argument (Douglas and Isherwood 1979, Belk 1988) that in order to understand consumption it is necessary to examine the full picture of consumption, and not just the choice of any particular item. Associated with the idea that consumption decisions reflect consumers' statements about themselves, the model building also includes 'anti constellations' which represent non consumption which involves both non choice and anti choice. Non choices can include products and services which are not purchased (possibly because they are outside the means of the consumer). Anti choices involve goods which are positively not chosen (Wilk 1994) and relate to Bourdieu's (1979) concept of the 'refusal of taste'.

It is proposed that there are three forces which can be identified as influencing configurations within consumers' patterns of consumption: a symbolic-functional force, represented by the nature of the product (understood in its widest sense of goods or services); the physiological-esteem-self actualization force which is represented by the nature of the need(s) to be met (covert behaviour); and the instrumental-expressive force which is represented by the nature of the overt behaviour, that is the actions and activities which are involved (Figure 2). Consumption configurations are seen to be the result of the interaction of these three interdependent forces.

RESEARCH OBJECTIVES AND METHODOLOGY

The general research objective proposed that the composition of the intermediate patterns could be established via the quantitative analysis of a large consumer database using correspondence analysis.

Previous studies of joint consumption (Wells 1968, Alpert and Gatty 1969, Solomon and Buchanan 1991) have employed the analysis of large consumer databases in pursuit of evidence of patterns of joint consumption. For this study data was extracted from a large, commercial database: BMRB/TGI which is compiled from an annual consumer survey based on stratified sampling using self completion postal questionnaires which are distributed to 40,000 households to generate 25,000 usable responses.

The BMRB/TGI contingency tables contain aggregated categorical data. Correspondence analysis was chosen as the most appropriate statistical technique for analyzing this type of data, as it is a variant of principal components analysis which operates on categorical rather than continuous data (Greenacre and Hastie 1987) and because its multivariate treatment of data allows it to reveal relationships which would not be detected via a series of pairwise comparisons (Hoffman and Franke 1986:213). Using the 'transition formulae' produced by correspondence analysis it is possible to see not only which features are clustered together, but also to understand why they are clustered together (Underhill and Peisach 1985:41). However, the element of subjectivity in interpretation has also to be acknowledged (Dittmar 1992): "By its flexibility, correspondence analysis can lead to greater insight into the phenomena being studied because it affords several different views of the same data set. Subjectivity of analysis is part of the price of this flexibility" (Hoffman and Franke 1986:225).

PRODUCT CATEGORIES AND THE MODEL BUILDING

The formation of the consumption combinations: constellations, anti constellations and configurations, was seen as determined by the interaction of three forces: symbolic-functional, physiological-esteem-self actualization, and expressive-instrumental. Drawing on earlier research which had identified a series of drivers of consumption combinations (Solomon 1983, Solomon and Assael 1987, Solomon 1988, Solomon and Buchanan 1991) it

FIGURE 2
Model of Three Forces of Consumption

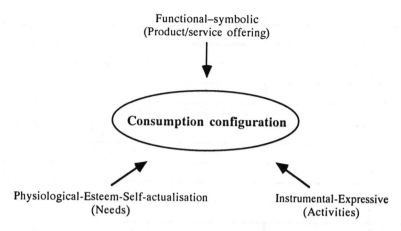

was expected that certain product categories would be found within the different combinations of consumption and that certain commonalities would be found across the different combinations of consumption.

In choosing the components to represent joint consumption in the configurations, the aim was to incorporate categories which had been established by earlier studies as being significantly linked to occupation and social roles in exploring joint consumption (see Table 1). Seventeen categories were included in the model building and this was similar in number to earlier studies (e.g. Solomon and Assael(1987)).

Solomon and Assael (1987) had found that three categories: clothing, electronic equipment and cars, had represented almost half of the product elements elicited when subjects were asked to specify the products which they associated with a particular range of occupations and these product categories were therefore included as components for consumption constellations since they could potentially represent significant differences amongst the consumption constellations. Other categories carried forward for the model building included liquor and tobacco, media, food, personal care products, sports equipment and home products (Solomon and Assael 1987). In order to extend the product categories some components from the later studies (Solomon 1988 and Solomon and Buchanan 1991) were also included such as luxury appliances, credit cards and discretionary use of leisure time. Some additional categories, which complemented existing categories, were also incorporated into this model building and included holidays (which linked to the category: 'discretionary use of time'), and health and diet (which were linked to sports and keep fit equipment). The most important new addition to the product/service components in this model building was represented by the inclusion of retailers as a separate and identifiable category. It was expected that retail constellations would form a significant feature in consumption constellations and anti constellations, and would indicate important differences between the groups of shoppers which could be linked to the forces which influence the formation of consumption configurations.

THE STUDY

Data was extracted from the BMRB/TGI database on users of eight mail order catalogue titles (representing the eight major U.K. mail order companies (G.U.S., Kays, Littlewoods, Freemans, Grattans, Empire Stores, Next Directory and J.D.Williams)) across

a range of categories. The data matrix for the study consisted of over two thousand rows by eight columns. Correspondence analysis was used to identify potential groups and subgroups among the users of U.K. in-home shopping; and to identify combinations of retailers, goods and services which were used and which were not used by the various mail order shoppers.

The relationship between the mail order catalogues (the column profiles) and the dimensions can be seen from Table 2. *Inertia* indicates how well each column or row is represented by a particular dimension. The *inertias* for the seven dimensions produced by correspondence analysis of the BMRB/TGI data are shown in Table 3. Over 60% of the *inertia* is represented by the plot of first two axes.

A two stage procedure was adopted in constructing and interpreting the constellations. The tables of transition formulae were examined to identify constellations amongst the row profiles from which to elicit product constellations and anti constellations. Those row variables which could be clearly associated with one predominant axis were included as part of the 'set of consumables' which were relevant to the users of the catalogue which could be linked to that dimension or axis. One difficulty was deciding what the measure of 'relevance' should be, particularly in the absence of any preceding research using correspondence analysis for identifying combinations in the data set. Table 3 had shown that nearly 61% of the *inertia* in the data had been accounted for on the first two axes, and that the remaining 40% *inertia* had been accounted for by the remaining five dimensions. Within the context of these *inertia* figures it was decided to use *COR* values of over 500 for the shoppers linked to dimension 1; *COR* values of over 400 for shoppers linked to dimension 2; and *COR* values which fell between 300 and 400 for the remaining five dimensions, when identifying the consumption combinations. The other important research objective of the study was to identify the potential anti complementarity of goods and services. Anti constellations have not been operationalized in any of the existing studies of constellations and therefore theory building about this aspect of consumption choices remains largely undeveloped. For the purposes of this study it was decided that absence could be treated either explicitly or implicitly. Interpretation of explicit non consumption could be based on a study of the details of the 'non usage' of categories by groups of shoppers, and some of this information was extracted from the BMRB/TGI database and was included in the correspondence analysis of the cross tabulated data. Implicit non consump-

TABLE 1

Table of categories used to construct product and consumption constellations

Category	S&A 1987	S 1988b	S&B 1991	*MKH
Clothing	*			*
Electronics	*			*
Jewelry/acc	*			
Liquor	*	* beer & wine	* wine	*
Media	*	*	* 'upscale'	*
Food	*		*gourmet icecr	*
Personal care	*	* toiletries		* aftershave
Sports equip	*			*
Luggage	*			
Furniture	*			
Tobacco	*			*
Home Prods	*			*
Records/tapes		*		
Cars	*	*	*	*
Credit cards			*	*
Financial instr.				*
TV progs			*Yuppie	
Lux Appliance			*	*
Discretionary time			* Urban sports	*Leisure, hobbies, sports
Holidays				*
Retailers				*
Health/diet				*
Total	13	5	8	17

Key: S&A 1987 Solomon and Assael 1987; S 1988b Solomon 1988b; S&B 1991 Solomon and Buchanan 1991; MKH M.K.Hogg's extracts from BMRB/TGI database.

TABLE 2

Column contributions for eight mail order catalogues from correspondence analysis

COLUMN CONTRIBUTIONS

L NAME	QLT	MAS	INR	k=1	COR	CTR	k=2	COR	CTR	k=3	COR	CTR	k=4	COR	CTR	k=5	COR	CTR	k=6	COR	CTR	k=7	COR	CTR
1 ES	1000	136	84	-62	148	30	-64	158	70	62	146	95	69	181	189	-14	7	8	-96	349	450	16	10	22
2 FM	1000	160	102	76	217	53	-75	210	112	61	138	108	-82	252	318	-65	159	208	22	18	27	12	5	14
3 GR	1000	119	72	26	26	5	18	12	5	36	50	28	-65	164	147	136	730	677	-21	18	19	-2	0	0
4 GS	1000	111	77	-62	133	25	9	3	1	75	193	115	83	233	223	25	21	20	109	404	477	21	14	29
5 KY	1000	245	97	-54	177	41	-0	0	0	-113	763	570	-5	2	2	-5	2	2	4	1	1	30	55	138
6 LW	1000	151	38	-21	40	4	-14	20	4	-31	91	27	14	18	9	-13	16	8	7	5	3	-93	810	795
7 ND	1000	48	334	514	899	720	152	78	138	-26	2	6	73	18	75	-16	1	4	-20	1	7	10	0	3
8 JW	1000	30	195	-269	263	123	423	653	670	97	34	52	-65	16	38	-89	29	72	-38	5	15	-0	0	0

Source: Correspondence Analysis of BMRB/TGI data

Key: L=Line number: ES=Empire Stores, FM=Freemans, GR=Grattans, GS=GUS, KY=Kays, LW=Littlewoods, ND=Next Directory, JW=J.D.Williams

TABLE 3

Inertias and percentages of inertia for seven dimensions

Dimension	Inertia	Percentage of inertia	
1	0.017580	41.69%	***
2	0.008009	19.00%	**********************
3	0.005482	13.00%	****************
4	0.003404	8.07%	**********
5	0.003277	7.77%	*********
6	0.002761	6.55%	********
7	0.001651	3.92%	*****
	0.042164		

(Source: Correspondence Analysis of BMRB/TGI data)

tion could be constructed from the absence of specific categories from the constellations. There is evidence from earlier studies on the complementarity of goods that certain choices are seen as more feasible than others, e.g. choices made by consumers amongst different menu listings (Green, Wind and Jain 1972).

The second stage of this procedure, the interpretation of the constellations, anti constellations and configurations was undertaken within the framework of the model building of the forces which influence intermediate patterns of joint consumption. It was expected that different product constellations and anti constellations would be found and these consumption combinations would reflect the differing responses amongst consumers to the various forces which influence decisions on consumption. Where the influences were predominantly symbolic and expressive then consumption constellations and configurations would be expected to show a concern with symbolic consumption of goods and services, notably by the use of particular brands (e.g. product brands such as Levis; or retail brands such as Harrods). Where the influences were predominantly functional and instrumental then it would be expected that different consumption configurations would be found, consisting of different constellations of goods and services (with the emphasis on factors such as value for money; and the convenience of shopping). Consumers' configurations of consumption would also be influenced by their needs (physiological-esteem-self actualization) which would be reflected in the consumer choices. Certain product fields could be associated with the consumption combinations and could therefore be taken as proxies of consumer behaviour.

FINDINGS AND DISCUSSION [2]

Correspondence analysis of the behavioural data showed that constellations and anti-constellations of consumption could be identified from which consumption configurations could be derived. These consumption configurations could be linked with three different groups of users of mail order catalogues: two groups were associated with focused catalogue offerings, and one group with the mass market mail order catalogue offering. It was possible to associate combinations of product and service usage and non usage with distinct groups within the mail order shopping popula-

tion. For the purposes of this paper, only the three main groupings will be reported.

The first important consumption constellation could be associated with Next Directory shoppers(an up market niche catalogue). The consumption constellation on the positive axis of the first dimension was characterized by the presence of a range of branded goods (e.g. Levi 501 jeans, L.A.Gear trainers); strong retail brands (e.g. Benetton, Laura Ashley and Harrods); high status foreign cars (e.g. BMW, Saab and Volkswagen Golf); electronic products which were linked both to status items (e.g. cordless telephones) and to goods from the top end of the price range (e.g. expensive cameras); and upmarket branded toiletry products (e.g. Chanel, Paco Rabanne and Yves St. Laurent aftershave). The consumption anti constellation included the absence of the tabloid press; British cars; package holidays; tobacco products; tinned food products; and mainstream mail order catalogues. A concern with health could be seen in the absence of tobacco and tinned food from this configuration. The features of this consumption configuration were indicative of the importance of the symbolic and expressive forces in influencing the formation of this consumption combination.

On the second dimension (positive axis) a significant consumption configuration could be associated with the J.D.Williams catalogue shoppers (mainly larger, older women shoppers using a niche catalogue) and this consumption constellation displayed an emphasis on large, particularly foreign, cars (e.g. Austin Rover, Audi, Mercedes, Mitsubishi); a very detailed food constellation (which was seen by the variety of detail about bread); a strong association with a series of mail order catalogues (e.g. Ambrose Wilson, Fashion Extra, Fashion Plus, Heather Valley, Oxendales, Personal Selection and J.D.Williams); and a rather different combination of leisure activities, relating to watching sports, compared with the dimension discussed above. This consumption configuration included watching bridge, cricket, golf and show jumping in its consumption constellation. The consumption anti constellation included electronic products (as explored in this data set); branded clothing products and also branded toiletries; holiday destinations such as Canada and the U.S.A.; eating out in the evenings (apart from at steak houses); and fashionable high street stores such as Next Retail, Principles, River Island and Wallis Shops. This consumption configuration suggested the importance of the instrumental rather than the expressive force in the choice of retail outlet; and also suggested a concern with needs from the physiological end of the spectrum. The presence of large, often foreign, cars suggested the influence of the symbolic force on this aspect of consumption decisionmaking.

[2]Details of the tables of transition formulae, and most importantly of the *COR* figures for the product categories, are not included in the paper because of lack of space.

TABLE 4

Some of the key product categories within consumption configurations

Product category	Upmarket niche catalogue shoppers	Older, larger female niche catalogue shoppers	Mass market catalogue shoppers.
Clothing	Branded jeans/trainers		Branded jeans/trainers
Electronic	Telephones, cameras		Computer games; cameras
Drink	Wine, beer spirits		Beer, spirits
Media	Numerous titles	Newspapers and magazines rather than TV/radio	Satellite, cable, ILR
Food	Fresh fruit and vegetables, fresh coffee	Bread	Branded foods
Personal care	Aftershave brands		Aftershave brands
Sports equipment	Keep fit equipment		Camping equipment
Tobacco			
Home Products			China/crockery
Cars	Various	Various	Various
Financial instr.	Varied	Premium Bonds; affinity cards	Credit cards
Lux appliances	Video, dishwasher, hobs		
Discretionary time	Restaurants; cultural & sports activities	Cultural and leisure activities; outings;	
Holidays	France, Canary Is, West Indies		Majorca, Minorca, Ibiza, Holiday camps
Retailers	Fashionable + upmarket	Mail order usage	High street chains
Health/diet	Vitamins	Vitamins/dieting	Slimming foods

The consumption configurations on the remaining dimensions could be associated with the six mass market catalogues, and were representative of a series of subgroups within this mass market group of catalogue shoppers. For the purposes of illustration the details for one of the major catalogue in this mass market group, Kays, will be described. On the third dimension (negative axis) the consumption configuration which could be linked to Kays shoppers consisted of small and medium sized cars (e.g. Cavalier, Citroen, Nissan/Datsun Sunny); some electronic products from the medium price range; limited branded clothing products (Champion trainers); and an association with the two largest mainstream mail order catalogues (Kays and Littlewoods). The discretionary use of time included watching cricket, horse racing and bridge. The anti constellation included most notably high street retail brands (e.g. Ravel, Russell and Bromley, Laura Ashley, Jaegar, Richards and Solo). This consumption configuration seemed to have been influenced by instrumental and functional rather than expressive and symbolic forces in the choice of retail brands. The minor presence of branded clothing and electronic products suggested a compromise between symbolic and expressive needs and budgetary pressures in this combination. In Table 4, the main points are summarized for each of the major groups of catalogue shoppers.

Table 5 indicates the presence of the product categories in the various consumption constellations and confirmed earlier research about the importance of clothing, electronic goods and cars as important distinguishing characteristics of consumption combinations. Discretionary time and retailers also emerged as important distinguishing characteristics of consumption choices.

From the consideration of the *COR* figures for the row points it was clear that some of the product category items overlapped the various dimensions (e.g. some of the cars and some of the branding clothing products). This can be understood in terms of 'fuzzy sets';

TABLE 5

Some of the key product categories in the consumption constellations within the configurations
Dimensions +/-

Dimensions +/-

Product category	1 +	1 −	2 +	2 −	3 +	3 −	4 +	4 −	5 +	5 −	6 +	6 −	7 +	7 −
Clothing	x	x		x		x	x	x	x		x		x	
Electronic	x	x		x	x	x	x	x	x	x		x		x
Drink	x													
Media	x	x	x	x	x	x	x	x	x	x	x	x	x	x
Food	x		x						x					
Personal care	x	x		x				x	x	x				
Tobacco									x					
Cars	x	x	x	x	x	x	x	x	x	x	x	x	x	x
Discretionary time	x	x	x	x	x	x	x	x		x	x	x	x	x
Holidays	x	x	x											x
Retailers	x	x	x		x	x	x	x	x		x	x	x	

Key: x indicates the presence of this product category in the consumption constellation

---

especially where certain product categories carry image-laden messages and have symbolic meanings which are pursued by more than one group of consumers.

CONCLUSIONS

The specific objectives of this research were firstly to identify the composition of constellations of products, services and activities from the behavioural data and from which configurations could be derived; secondly to elicit constellations of retailers, as representative of a service category of consumption, hitherto not explored in detail in earlier studies of patterns of joint consumption; thirdly to identify potential anti complementarity constellations; and fourthly to see whether consumption configurations could be formed from consumption constellations and anti constellations, and could be associated with different groups of shoppers. The most important product categories elicited by earlier studies proved to be significant components of consumption constellations in this research and the constellations which emerged were close to those of previous studies (Solomon et al).

These findings contribute to our understanding of the interaction between the patronage and product decisions made by consumers, and would also suggest that shopping is more central to the creation and maintenance of social identity for some consumers than for others. It is important to recognize both the importance of retail patronage decisions for some consumers, and that retail constellations will vary considerably across different dimensions. Retail constellations will contribute to the picture of the enactment and maintenance of social identity; and thus to our understanding of different 'consumption communities' (Solomon 1987:210). However, retail constellations would probably not, by themselves, be sufficient to distinguish amongst all the dimensions. The value of the retail constellations will lie in the contribution which they can make to attempts to refine understanding of the different intermediate patterns of joint consumption.

The relationship between social roles, social identities and consumption constellations has been explored here using quantitative data analysis techniques and these findings confirm that the relationship between social roles, social identities and consumption configurations would reward more detailed study in searching for further understanding of the patterns in the stream of consumer decision making.

REFERENCES

A complete list of references is available on request

Alpert,Lewis and Gatty,Ronald (1969): "Product Positioning by behavioral life styles", *Journal of Marketing* 33 (April), 65-69

Dittmar, Helga (1992): *The Social Psychology of Material Possessions: To Have Is To Be.* Harvester Wheatsheaf, Hemel Hempstead.

Green, Paul E; Wind,Yoram and Jain, Arun K. (1972): "Preference measurement of item collections", *Journal of Marketing Research* 9 (November), 371-377.

Greenacre, M. J. and Hastie, T. J. (1987): "The Geometric Interpretation of Correspondence Analysis", *J. of the Am. Statistical Assoc* 82(June),437-447.

Hoffman, D. L. & Franke, G. R. (1986): "Correspondence Analysis: Graphical Representation of Categorical Data in Marketing Research", *Journal of Marketing Research* (August), 213-227.

Kehret-Ward,Trudy (1987): "Combining Products in Use: How the Syntax of Product Use Affects Marketing Decisions". In: *Marketing and Semiotics: New Directions in the Study of Signs for Sale.* (Ed: Umiker-Sebeok,Jean) Mouton de Gruyter, Berlin, 219-238.

Kernan, Jerome B. and Sommers, Montrose S. (1967): "Meaning, Value and Theory of Promotion", *Journal of Communication*, 17 (2) 109-135

Lee, D. H. (1990): "Symbolic Interactionism: Some Implications for Consumer Self-Concept and Product Symbolism Research", in *Advances in Consumer Research:* Vol. 17. (Eds: Goldberg; Gorn; Pollay) ACR Provo, UT, 386-393.

Levy,Sidney J. (1964): "Symbolism and life style", in: *Towards Scientific Marketing*, Proceedings of the American Marketing Association Conference. (Ed: Greyser,Stephen) American Marketing Association, Chicago, .

McCall,George J. and Simmons J.C.(1982): *Social Psychology: A Sociological Approach*. The Free Press, New York.

McCracken,Grant (1990): *Culture and Consumption*. Indiana University Press, Indianapolis.

Schenk, Carolyn Turner and Holman, Rebecca H. (1980): "A Sociological Approach to Brand Choice: The Concept of Situational Self Image", in: *Advances in Consumer Research*. Vol. VII. (Ed: Olson,Jerry C) ACR, Ann Arbor, 610-614.

Solomon, Michael R. (1983): "The Role of Products as Social Stimuli: A Symbolic Interactionism Perspective", *Journal of Consumer Research* 10(December), 319-329.

Solomon, Michael R. (1988): "Mapping Product Constellations: A Social Categorization Approach to Consumption Symbolism", *Psychology and Marketing* 5(3, Fall), 233-258.

Solomon, Michael R. and Assael, Henry (1987): "The Forest or the Trees? A Gestalt Approach to Symbolic Consumption". In: *Marketing and Semiotics:New Directions in the Study of Signs for Sale*. (Ed: Umiker-Sebeok,Jean) Mouton de Gruyter, Berlin, 189-217.

Solomon, Michael R. and Buchanan, Bruce (1991): "A Role-Theoretic Approach to Product Symbolism: Mapping a Consumption Constellation", *Journal of Business Research* 22, 95-109.

Wells, William D. (1968): "Backward segmentation", in: *Insights into Consumer Behavior*. (Ed: Arndt,Johan) Allyn and Bacon, Boston, 85-100.

Wilk, Richard R. (1994): "'I hate Pizza': Distaste and Dislike ..." American Anthropological Association meeting, Atlanta, November.

AUTHOR INDEX